Less managing. More teaching. Greater learning.

STUDENTS...

Want to get **better grades?** *(Who doesn't?)*

Ready to do **online interactive assignments** that help you apply what you've learned? *(You need to know how to use this stuff in the real world...)*

Need **new ways** to **study** before the big test?
(A little peace of mind is a good thing...)

With **McGraw-Hill's Connect® Management,**

STUDENTS GET:

- **Interactive, engaging** content.

- Interactive Applications – chapter assignments that help you **APPLY** what you've learned in the course.

- **Immediate feedback** on how you're doing. (No more wishing you could call your instructor at 1 a.m.)

- **Quick access** to lectures, practice materials, e-book, and more. (All the material you need to be successful is right at your fingertips.)

- **LearnSmart** – intelligent flash cards that adapt to your specific needs and provide you with 24 x 7 personalized study.

Want an online, **searchable version** of your textbook?

Wish your textbook could be **available online** while you're doing your assignments?

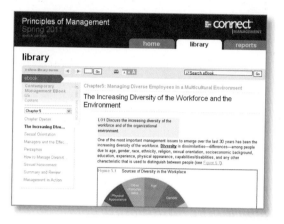

Connect® Plus Management e-book

If you choose to use *Connect® Plus Management*, you have an affordable and searchable online version of your book integrated with your other online tools.

Connect® Plus Management e-book offers features like:

- Topic search
- Direct links from assignments
- Adjustable text size
- Jump to page number
- Print by section

Want to get more **value** from your textbook purchase?

Think learning management should be a bit more **interesting**?

Check out the STUDENT RESOURCES section under the *Connect®* Library tab.

Here you'll find a wealth of resources designed to help you achieve your goals in the course. You'll find things like **quizzes**, **PowerPoints**, and **Internet activities** to help you study. Every student has different needs, so explore the STUDENT RESOURCES to find the materials best suited to you.

management

A PRACTICAL INTRODUCTION

sixth edition

Angelo Kinicki

Arizona State University

Brian K. Williams

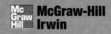
McGraw-Hill
Irwin

**McGraw-Hill
Irwin**

MANAGEMENT: A PRACTICAL INTRODUCTION, SIXTH EDITION

Published by McGraw-Hill/Irwin, a business unit of The McGraw-Hill Companies, Inc., 1221 Avenue of the Americas, New York, NY, 10020. Copyright © 2013 by The McGraw-Hill Companies, Inc. All rights reserved. Printed in the United States of America. Previous editions © 2011, 2009, 2008, 2006, and 2003. No part of this publication may be reproduced or distributed in any form or by any means, or stored in a database or retrieval system, without the prior written consent of The McGraw-Hill Companies, Inc., including, but not limited to, in any network or other electronic storage or transmission, or broadcast for distance learning.

Some ancillaries, including electronic and print components, may not be available to customers outside the United States.

This book is printed on acid-free paper.

5 6 7 8 9 0 DOW/DOW 1 0 9 8 7 6 5 4

ISBN   978-0-07-802954-7
MHID   0-07-802954-6

Senior Vice President, Products & Markets: *Kurt L. Strand*
Vice President, General Manager, Products & Markets: *Brent Gordon*
Vice President, Content Production & Technology Services: *Kimberly Meriwether David*
Managing Director: *Paul Ducham*
Executive Brand Manager: *Michael Ablassmeir*
Executive Director of Development: *Ann Torbert*
Development Editor: *Jane Beck*
Development Editor: *Andrea Heirendt*
Senior Marketing Manager: *Elizabeth Trepkowski*
Director, Content Production: *Sesha Bolisetty*
Lead Project Manager: *Harvey Yep*
Content Project Manager: *Danielle Clement*
Senior Buyer: *Michael R. McCormick*
Cover/Interior Designer: *Pam Verros*
Cover Image: *MCT via Getty Images*
Senior Content Licensing Specialist: *Jeremy Cheshareck*
Photo Researcher: *Judy Mason*
Typeface: *10.5/12 Times New Roman*
Compositor: *Aptara®, Inc.*
Printer: *R. R. Donnelley*

All credits appearing on page or at the end of the book are considered to be an extension of the copyright page.

Library of Congress Cataloging-in-Publication Data

Kinicki, Angelo.
    Management : a practical introduction / Angelo Kinicki, Arizona State University,
Brian K. Williams.—sixth edition.
        pages cm
    Includes index.
    ISBN-13: 978-0-07-802954-7 (alk. paper)
    ISBN-10: 0-07-802954-6 (alk. paper)
    1. Management. I. Williams, Brian K., 1938- II. Title.
HD31.K474 2013
658—dc23

                                                    2012026826

The Internet addresses listed in the text were accurate at the time of publication. The inclusion of a website does not indicate an endorsement by the authors or McGraw-Hill, and McGraw-Hill does not guarantee the accuracy of the information presented at these sites.

brief contents

ABOUT THE
authors

Angelo Kinicki is a professor of management at the W. P. Carey School of Business at Arizona State University. He also was awarded the Weatherup/Overby Chair in Leadership in 2005. He has held his current position since 1982, when he received his doctorate in organizational behavior from Kent State University.

Angelo is recognized for both his teaching and his research. As a teacher, Angelo has been the recipient of six teaching awards, including the John W. Teets Outstanding Graduate Teacher Award (2009–2010); the Outstanding Teaching Award—MBA and Master's Programs (2007–2008); the John W. Teets Outstanding Graduate Teacher Award (2009–2010); Graduate Teaching Excellence Award (1998–1999); Continuing Education Teaching Excellence Award (1991–1992); and Undergraduate Teaching Excellence Award (1987–1988). He also was selected into Wikipedia, Who's Who of American Colleges and Universities, and Beta Gamma Sigma.

Angelo is an active researcher. He has published more than 90 articles in a variety of leading academic and professional journals and has coauthored six college textbooks (27, counting revisions). His textbooks have been used by hundreds of universities around the world. Angelo's experience as a researcher also resulted in his selection to serve on the editorial review boards for *Personnel Psychology*, the *Academy of Management Journal,* the *Journal of Vocational Behavior,* and the *Journal of Management.* He received the "All-Time Best Reviewer Award" from the *Academy of Management Journal* for the period 1996–1999.

Angelo also is an active international consultant who works with top management teams to create organizational change aimed at increasing organizational effectiveness and profitability. He has worked with many Fortune 500 firms as well as numerous entrepreneurial organizations in diverse industries. His expertise includes facilitating strategic-operational planning sessions, diagnosing the causes of organizational and work-unit problems, implementing performance management systems, designing and implementing performance appraisal systems, developing and administering surveys to assess employee attitudes, and leading management/executive education programs. He developed a 360° leadership feedback instrument called the Performance Management Leadership Survey (PMLS) that is used by companies throughout the United States and Europe.

One of Angelo's strengths is his ability to teach students at all levels within a university. He uses an interactive environment to enhance undergraduates' understanding about management and organizational behavior. He focuses MBAs on applying management concepts to solve complex problems; PhD students learn the art and science of conducting scholarly research.

Angelo and his wife, Joyce, have enjoyed living in the beautiful Arizona desert for 28 years but are natives of Cleveland, Ohio. They enjoy traveling, golfing, and hiking with Nala, their golden retriever.

Brian Williams has been managing editor for college textbook publisher Harper & Row/Canfield Press in San Francisco; editor-in-chief for nonfiction trade-book publisher J. P. Tarcher in Los Angeles; publications and communications manager for the University of California, Systemwide Administration, in Berkeley; and an independent writer and book producer based in the San Francisco and Lake Tahoe areas. He has a BA in English and an MA in communication from Stanford University. Repeatedly praised for his ability to write directly and interestingly to students, he has coauthored 21 books (62, counting revisions). This includes the 2013 *Using Information Technology: A Practical Introduction* with his wife, Stacey C. Sawyer, now in its 10th edition with McGraw-Hill. He and Stacey are also coauthors, with Susan Berston, of *Business: A Practical Introduction*. In addition, he has written a number of other information technology books, college success books, and health and social science texts. Brian is a native of Palo Alto, California, and San Francisco, but since 1989 he and Stacey, a native of New York City and Bergen County, New Jersey, have lived at or near Lake Tahoe, currently in Genoa (Nevada's oldest town), with views of the Sierra Nevada. In their spare time, they enjoy foreign travel, different cuisine, museum going, music, hiking, contributing to the community (Brian is past chair of his town board), and warm visits with friends and family.

Management: A Practical Introduction has twice been the recipient of McGraw-Hill/Irwin's Revision of the Year Award, for the third and fifth editions.

dedication

A promise: To make learning management easy, efficient, and effective

The sixth edition of *Management: A Practical Introduction*—a concepts book for the introductory course in management—uses a wealth of instructor feedback to identify which features from prior editions worked best and which should be improved and expanded. By blending Angelo's scholarship, teaching, and management-consulting experience with Brian's writing and publishing background, we have again tried to create a research-based yet highly readable, innovative, and practical text.

Our primary goal is simple to state but hard to execute: to make learning principles of management as easy, effective, and efficient as possible. Accordingly, the book integrates writing, illustration, design, and magazine-like layout in **a program of learning that appeals to the visual sensibilities and respects the time constraints and different learning styles of today's students.** In an approach initially tested in our first edition and fine-tuned in the subsequent editions, **we break topics down into easily grasped portions** and incorporate **frequent use of various kinds of reinforcement techniques.** Our hope, of course, is to make a difference in the lives of our readers: to produce a text that students will enjoy reading and that will provide them with practical benefits.

The text covers the principles that most management instructors have come to expect in an introductory text—planning, organizing, leading, and controlling—plus the issues that today's students need to be aware of to succeed: customer focus, globalism, diversity, ethics, information technology, entrepreneurship, work teams, the service economy, and small business.

Beyond these, our book has **four features that make it unique:**

1. A student-centered approach to learning.

2. Imaginative writing for readability and reinforcement.

3. Emphasis on practicality.

4. Resources that work.

> *"Kinicki/Williams is an effective principles of management textbook that does an excellent job of conveying the excitement of management and leadership to undergraduates. Engaging and practical, it comes with a comprehensive set of support materials that range from the traditional to exciting new uses of technology that supercharge the teaching of critical concepts. We looked at over ten textbooks before we adopted Kinicki, and we're most certainly glad that we did. Publisher support has been excellent."*
>
> **—Gary B. Roberts,**
> *Kennesaw State University*

CHAPTER OPENERS: Designed to help students read with purpose

Each chapter begins with four to eight provocative, motivational **Major Questions,** written to appeal to students' concern about "what's in it for me?" and to help them read with purpose and focus.

Instead of opening with the conventional case, as most texts do, we open with **The Manager's Toolbox,** a motivational device offering practical nuts-and-bolts advice pertaining to the chapter content students are about to read—and allowing for class discussion.

CHAPTER SECTIONS:

Structured into constituent parts for easier learning

Chapters are organized to cover each major question in turn, giving students bite-sized chunks of information. Each section begins with a recap of the **Major Question** and includes **"The Big Picture,"** which presents students with an overview of how the section they are about to read answers the Major Question.

"This style textbook succeeds in presenting management information with a fresh face. Each chapter is filled with current and useful information for students. The chapters begin by asking major questions of the reader. As the student reads, [he or she is] engaged by these questions and by the information that follows. A totally readable text with great illustrations and end-of-chapter exercises!"

—Catherine Ruggieri, St. John's University, New York

Chapter tools help students learn how to learn

In focus groups, symposiums, and reviews, instructors told us that many students do not have the skills needed to succeed in college. To support students in acquiring these skills, we offer the following:

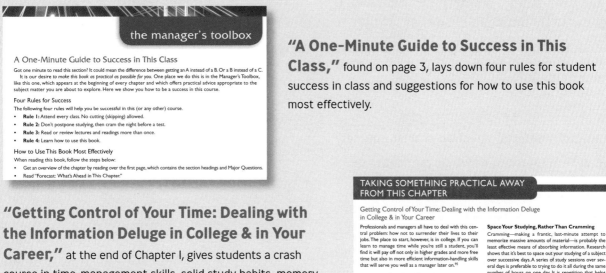

the manager's toolbox

A One-Minute Guide to Success in This Class

Got one minute to read this section? It could mean the difference between getting an A instead of a B. Or a B instead of a C.

It is our desire *to make this book as practical as possible for you.* One place we do this is in the Manager's Toolbox, like this one, which appears at the beginning of every chapter and which offers practical advice appropriate to the subject matter you are about to explore. Here we show you how to be a success in this course.

Four Rules for Success

The following four rules will help you be successful in this (or any other) course.

- **Rule 1:** Attend every class. No cutting (skipping) allowed.
- **Rule 2:** Don't postpone studying, then cram the night before a test.
- **Rule 3:** Read or review lectures and readings more than once.
- **Rule 4:** Learn how to use this book.

How to Use This Book Most Effectively

When reading this book, follow the steps below:

- Get an overview of the chapter by reading over the first page, which contains the section headings and Major Questions.
- Read "Forecast: What's Ahead in This Chapter."

"A One-Minute Guide to Success in This Class," found on page 3, lays down four rules for student success in class and suggestions for how to use this book most effectively.

"Getting Control of Your Time: Dealing with the Information Deluge in College & in Your Career," at the end of Chapter 1, gives students a crash course in time-management skills, solid study habits, memory aids, and learning from lectures.

TAKING SOMETHING PRACTICAL AWAY FROM THIS CHAPTER

Getting Control of Your Time: Dealing with the Information Deluge in College & in Your Career

Professionals and managers all have to deal with this central problem: how not to surrender their lives to their jobs. The place to start, however, is in college. If you can learn to manage time while you're still a student, you'll find it will pay off not only in higher grades and more free time but also in more efficient information-handling skills that will serve you well as a manager later on.[95]

Using Your "Prime Study Time"

Each of us has a different energy cycle.[96] The trick is to use it effectively. That way, your hours of best performance will coincide with your heaviest academic demands. For example, if your energy level is high during the

Space Your Studying, Rather Than Cramming

Cramming—making a frantic, last-minute attempt to memorize massive amounts of material—is probably the least effective means of absorbing information. Research shows that it's best to space out your studying of a subject over successive days. A series of study sessions over several days is preferable to trying to do it all during the same number of hours on one day. It is repetition that helps move information into your long-term memory bank.

Review Information Repeatedly—Even "Overlearn It"

By repeatedly reviewing information—what is known as

The Systems Viewpoint

The 52 bones in the foot. The monarchy of Great Britain. A weather storm front. Each of these is a system. **A *system* is a set of interrelated parts that operate together to achieve a common purpose.** Even though a system may not work very well—as in the inefficient way the Russian government collects taxes, for example—it is nevertheless still a system.

The *systems viewpoint* regards the organization as a system of interrelated parts. By adopting this point of view, you can look at your organization both as (1) a collection of *subsystems*—parts making up the whole system—and (2) a part of the larger environment. A college, for example, is made up of a collection of academic departments, support staffs, students, and the like. But it also exists as a system within the environment of education, having to be responsive to parents, alumni, legislators, nearby townspeople, and so on.

Key terms are highlighted and terms and definitions are in boldface, to help students build their management vocabulary.

Other devices to help students develop understanding:

- Important **scholar names in boldface** so students remember key contributors to the field of management.

- Frequent use of **advance organizers, bulleted lists, and headings** to help students grasp the main ideas.

- **Illustrations positioned close to relevant text discussion** so students can refer to them more easily and avoid flipping pages.

■ A *policy* is a standing plan that outlines the general response to a designated problem or situation. Example: "This workplace does not condone swearing." This policy is a broad statement that gives managers a general idea about what is allowable for employees who use bad language, but gives no specifics.

■ A *procedure* (or *standard operating procedure*) is a standing plan that outlines the response to particular problems or circumstances. Example: White Castle specifies exactly how a hamburger should be dressed, including the order in which the mustard, ketchup, and pickles are applied.

■ A *rule* is a standing plan that designates specific required action. Example: "No smoking is allowed anywhere in the building." This allows no room for interpretation.

"It's hard enough to try to make the class exciting, and the only way is to incorporate up-to-date, relevant, and interesting examples. This text and McGraw-Hill have done just that. [It] makes my life easier, but more importantly, the students are getting the valuable education that they've paid for by having better materials and instruction."

—Laura L. Alderson, *University of Memphis*

Imaginative Writing for Readability

Research shows that textbooks written in **an imaginative, people-oriented style significantly improve students' ability to retain information.** We employ a number of journalistic devices to make the material as engaging as possible for students.

We **use colorful facts, attention-grabbing quotes, biographical sketches, and lively tag lines** to get students' attention as they read.

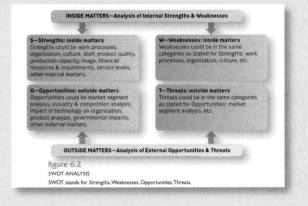

figure 6.2
SWOT ANALYSIS
SWOT stands for Strengths, Weaknesses, Opportunities, Threats.

EXAMPLE

Crisis Leading to the Strategic-Management Process: JetBlue Weathers an Ice Storm

Founded in 1998, JetBlue started out as a low-fare airline, promising fares up to 65% lower than competitors along with, in one description, "creature comforts like assigned seating, leather upholstery, and satellite TV on individual screens in every seat."[36] The formula was an immediate hit, and by 2007 JetBlue had grown from 6 daily flights and 300 employees to 575 daily flights to 52 destinations and 9,300 employees.

Change in Focus. Then in 2005, the founder, David Neeleman, decided to depart from the low-cost model of Southwest Airlines–style carriers and to imitate more traditional airlines. He added different kinds of aircraft, increased routes and airports, and built a $25 million training center in anticipation of expanding the workforce to 30,000 by 2010. "These moves," says one analysis, "increased the airline's costs while drawing it into competition with a greater number of rivals,

which in turn made it harder for JetBlue to raise fares."[37] JetBlue lost $20 million in 2005 and $1 million in 2006.

The Valentine's Day Ice Storm. Then the Valentine's Day crisis happened. On February 14, 2007, an ice storm settled on JetBlue's New York hub at John F. Kennedy International Airport, preventing planes from taking off. Acting on forecasters' predictions that the ice would change to rain, JetBlue continued to load flights and allow them to taxi to the runway. The result: planes couldn't take off, and passengers were stuck in their seats for hours—up to 6 hours, in some cases. In fact, only 17 of the airline's 156 scheduled departures left JFK that day, disrupting the entire system and displacing crews and aircraft. "In subsequent days," says one account, "JetBlue management canceled more and more flights, angering thousands of passengers, until finally, on February 20, normal operations resumed."[38]

Our emphasis on practicality and applications extends to the **Example boxes,** "mini-cases" that use snapshots of real-world institutions to explain text concepts. **"Your Call" invites student critical thinking and class discussion at the end of each example.** Suggestions for how to use the Example boxes are found in the Instructor's Manual.

"The Kinicki/Williams text is attractive and well organized. The writing is engaging, and there is much more than my current text in terms of examples, application, summaries, and cases. The graphical quality of the book is much better than the black and white version[s] [of texts]. Overall, I think this book represents an excellent approach to the subject of management from both an instructor and learner perspective."

—**Jeffrey Anderson,** *Ohio University*

An Emphasis on Practicality

We want this book to be a "keeper" for students, a resource for future courses and for their careers—so we give students **a great deal of practical advice** in addition to covering the fundamental concepts of management. Application points are found not only throughout the text discussion but also in the following specialized features.

PRACTICAL ACTION

How to Achieve Your Important Goals: Don't Keep Every Option Open

We've all been told that "It's important to keep your options open." But should we?

"You don't even know how a camera's burst-mode flash works, but you persuade yourself to pay for the extra feature just in case," writes a journalist about this phenomenon. "You no longer have anything in common with someone who keeps calling you, but you hate to just zap the relationship. Your child is exhausted from after-school soccer, ballet, and Chinese lessons, but you won't let her drop the piano lessons. They could come in handy."[50]

check out the three doors and settle on the one with the highest rewards. But when students stayed out of a room, the door would start shrinking and eventually disappear. Researchers found that most students would waste clicks by rushing back to reopen doors, even though they lost money by doing so—and they continued to frantically keep all their doors open even when they were fined for switching.

Fear of Loss? Were the students just trying to "keep their options open"? Ariely doesn't think so. The real motivation, he suggests, is fear of loss. "Closing a door on an

---

Practical Action boxes, appearing one or more times in each chapter, offer students practical and interesting advice on issues students will face in the workplace. Detailed discussions of how to use these Practical Action boxes appear in the Instructor's Manual.

End-of-Chapter Resources that reinforce applications

Each chapter continues our strategy of repetition for learning reinforcement. We include various unique pedagogical features to help students take away the most significant portions of the chapter's content:

Management in Action cases depict how companies students are familiar with respond to situations or issues featured in the text. Discussion questions are included for ease of use in class, as reflection assignments, or over online discussion boards.

Self-Assessment Exercises enable students to personally apply chapter content. These exercises include objectives for ease in assigning, instructions for use, guidelines for interpreting results, and questions for further reflection. They can also be found on the text website.

Legal/Ethical Challenges present cases—often based on real events—that require students to think through how they would handle the situation, helping prepare them for decision making in their careers.

Resources That Work

No matter the course you teach—on-campus, hybrid, or online courses—we set out to provide you with the most comprehensive set of resources to enhance your Principles of Management course.

Audio Visuals for Your Visual Students We present the richest and most diverse video program on the market to engage your students in the important management concepts covered in this text:

McGraw-Hill's Expanded Management Asset Gallery! McGraw-Hill/Irwin Management is excited to now provide a one-stop shop for our wealth of assets, making it super quick and easy for instructors to locate specific materials to enhance their courses.

All of the following can be accessed within the Management Asset Gallery:

Manager's Hot Seat! This interactive, video-based application puts students in the manager's hot seat and builds critical thinking and decision-making skills and allows students to apply concepts to real managerial challenges. Students watch as 15 real managers apply their years of experience when confronting unscripted issues such as bullying in the workplace, cyber loafing, globalization, inter-generational work conflicts, workplace violence, and leadership versus management.

Self-Assessment Gallery. Unique among publisher-provided self-assessments, our 23 self-assessments provide students with background information to ensure that students understand the purpose of the assessment. Students test their values, beliefs, skills, and interests in a wide variety of areas allowing them to personally apply chapter content to their own lives and careers.

Every self-assessment is supported with PowerPoints and an instructor manual in the Management Asset Gallery, making it easy for the instructor to create an engaging classroom discussion surrounding the assessments.

Test Your Knowledge. To help reinforce students' understanding of key management concepts, Test Your Knowledge activities provide students a review of the conceptual materials followed by application-based questions to work through. Students can choose practice mode, which provides them with detailed feedback after each question, or test mode, which provides feedback after the entire test has been completed. Every Test Your Knowledge activity is supported by instructor notes in the Management Asset Gallery to make it easy for the instructor to create engaging classroom discussions surrounding the materials students have completed.

Management History Timeline. This Web application allows instructors to present and students to learn the history of management in an engaging and interactive way. Management history is presented along an intuitive timeline that can be traveled through sequentially or by selected decade. With the click of a mouse, students learn the important dates, see the people who influenced the field, and understand the general management theories that have molded and shaped management as we know it today.

Principles of Management Video DVDs Volumes I, 2, & 3. Sources from *BusinessWeek* Online, BBC, CBS, FiftyLessons, NBC, PBS, and McGraw-Hill are provided on 2- to 15-minute clips in three DVD sets. These company videos are organized by the four functions of management and feature organizations such as PlayStation, Panera Bread, Patagonia, Mini Cooper, and the Greater Chicago Food Depository. Other subjects are Employer-Subsidized Commuting, Grounded: Are U.S. Airlines Safe?, Using Facebook at Work, Adult Bullies, and Encore Careers. Corresponding video cases and a guide that ties the videos closely to the chapter can be found in the Instructor's Manual and online.

- **Instructors Manual.** Authored by Linda Hoffman of Ivy Tech Community College of Indiana-Fort Wayne, the Instructor's Manual was revised and updated to include thorough coverage of each chapter. It also offers time-saving features such as an outline on incorporating PowerPoint slides, lecture enhancers that supplement the textbook, video cases and video notes, and answers to all end-of-chapter exercises.
- **PowerPoint Slides.** Prepared by Brad Cox of Midlands Technical College, the PowerPoint slides provide comprehensive lecture notes, questions for the class, and company examples not found in the textbook.
- **Test Bank.** Written by Tia Quinlan-Wilder from the University of Denver, the Test Bank includes more than 100 questions per chapter in a variety of formats. The package includes a range of comprehension and application (scenario-based) questions as well as tagged Bloom's Taxonomy levels and AACSB requirements.

EZ Test, McGraw-Hill's flexible and easy-to-use electronic testing program, allows instructors to create tests from book-specific items. It accommodates a wide range of question types, and instructors may add their own questions. Multiple versions of the test can be created, and any test can be exported for use with course management systems such as WebCT or BlackBoard.

EZ Test Online, available at **www.eztestonline .com,** allows you to access the test bank virtually anywhere at any time, without installation, and to administer EZ Test–created exams and quizzes online, providing instant feedback for students.

Online Learning Center. Located at **www.mhhe .com/kw6e,** the Online Learning Center allows students to take chapter quizzes to review concepts and review chapter PowerPoint slides. Students can also easily upgrade to a richer set of Premium Online Resources right on this site.

Assurance of Learning–Ready

Many educational institutions are often focused on the notion of *assurance of learning,* an important element of some accreditation standards. *Management: A Practical Introduction,* 6th ed., is designed specifically to support your assurance of learning initiatives with a simple, yet powerful solution.

Each test bank question maps to a specific chapter learning outcome/objective listed in the text. You can use our test bank software, EZ Test and EZ Test Online, or in *Connect Management* to easily query for learning outcomes objectives that directly relate to the learning objectives for your course. You can use the reporting features of EZ Test to aggregate student results in a similar fashion, making the collection and presentation of assurance of learning data simple and easy.

AACSB Statement

The McGraw-Hill Companies is a proud corporate member of AACSB International. Understanding the importance and value of AACSB accreditation, *Management: A Practical Introduction,* 6th ed., recognizes the curricula guidelines detailed in the AACSB standards for business accreditation by connecting selected questions in the text and/or the test bank to the six general knowledge and skill guidelines in the AACSB standards.

The statements contained in *Management: A Practical Introduction,* 6th ed., are provided only as a guide for the users of this textbook. The AACSB leaves content coverage and assessment within the purview of individual schools, the mission of the school, and the faculty. While *Management: A Practical Introduction,* 6th ed., and the teaching package make no claim of any specific AACSB qualification or evaluation, we have within *Management: A Practical Introduction,* 6th ed., labeled selected questions according to the six general knowledge and skills areas.

McGraw-Hill *Connect Management*

Less managing. . . More teaching. . . Greater learning. . .

McGraw-Hill *Connect Management* is an online assignment and assessment solution that connects students with the tools and resources they need to achieve success. With *Connect Management,* students can engage with their coursework anytime, anywhere, enabling faster learning, more efficient studying, and higher retention of knowledge. It also offers faculty powerful tools that make managing assignments easier, so instructors can spend more time teaching.

Features

I. LearnSmart: Adaptive Self-Study Technology. Students want to make the best use of their study time. Within *Connect Management,* LearnSmart provides students with a combination of practice, assessment, and remediation for every concept in the textbook. LearnSmart's intelligent software adapts to every student response and automatically delivers concepts that advance the student's understanding while reducing time devoted to the concepts already mastered. The result for every student is the fastest path to mastery of the chapter concepts.

LearnSmart . . .

- Applies an intelligent concept engine to identify the relationships between concepts and to serve new concepts to each student only when he or she is ready.
- Adapts automatically to each student, so students spend less time on the topics they understand and practice more those they have yet to master.
- Provides continual reinforcement and remediation but gives only as much guidance as students need.
- Integrates diagnostics as part of the learning experience.
- Enables you to assess which concepts students have efficiently learned on their own, thus freeing class time for more applications and discussion.

2. Online Interactives. These engaging interactive scenarios provide students with immersive, experiential learning opportunities so they can apply key concepts and deepen their knowledge of key course topics. Students receive immediate feedback at intermediate steps throughout each exercise, as well as comprehensive feedback at the end of the assignment. All interactives are automatically scored and entered into the instructor grade book.

3. Interactive Presentations. New and specific to this textbook, the interactive presentations in Connect are engaging, online, professional presentations covering the same learning objectives and concepts directly from the chapters. Interactive Presentations teach students the core learning objectives in a multimedia format, bringing the content of the course to life. The Interactive Presentations in Connect Management are a great prep tool for students—and when students are better prepared, they are more engaged and more participative in class.

4. Student Progress Tracking. *Connect Management* keeps instructors informed about how each student, section, and class is performing, allowing for more productive use of lecture and office hours. The progress-tracking function enables you to . . .

- View scored work immediately and track individual or group performance with assignment and grade reports.
- Access an instant view of student or class performance relative to learning objectives.
- Collect data and generate reports required by many accreditation organizations, such as AACSB.

5. Smart Grading. When it comes to studying, time is precious. *Connect Management* helps students learn more efficiently by providing feedback and practice material when they need it, where they need it. When it comes to teaching, your time also is precious. The grading function enables you to . . .

- Have assignments scored automatically, giving students immediate feedback on their work and side-by-side comparisons with correct answers.
- Access and review each response; manually change grades or leave comments for students to review.
- Reinforce classroom concepts with practice tests and instant quizzes.

6. Simple Assignment Management. With *Connect Management,* creating assignments is easier than ever, so you can spend more time teaching and less time managing. The assignment management function enables you to . . .

- Create and deliver assignments easily with selectable end-of-chapter questions and test bank items.
- Streamline lesson planning, student progress reporting, and assignment grading to make classroom management more efficient than ever.
- Go paperless with the eBook and online submission and grading of student assignments.

7. Instructor Library. The *Connect Management* Instructor Library is your repository for additional resources to improve student engagement in and out of class. You can select and use any asset that enhances your lecture. The *Connect Management* Instructor Library includes . . .

- Instructor's Manual
- Test Bank
- eBook
- PowerPoint files
- Management Asset Gallery

8. Student Study Center. The *Connect Management* Student Study Center is the place for students to access additional resources. The Student Study Center offers students quick access to . . .

- Lectures, practice materials, eBooks, and more.
- Practice material and study questions, easily accessible on the go.
- Self-assessments, video materials, Manager's Hot Seat, and more.

9. Lecture Capture Via Tegrity Campus. *Increase the attention* paid to lecture discussion by decreasing the attention paid to note taking. For an additional charge, Lecture Capture offers new ways for students to focus on the in-class discussion, knowing they can revisit important topics later.

10. McGraw-Hill *Connect Plus Management*. McGraw-Hill reinvents the textbook-learning experience for the modern student with *Connect Plus Management*. A seamless integration of an eBook and *Management, Connect Plus Management* provides all of the *Connect Management* features plus the following:

- An integrated eBook, allowing for anytime, anywhere access to the textbook.
- Dynamic links between the problems or questions you assign to your students and the location in the eBook where that problem or question is covered.
- A powerful search function to pinpoint and connect key concepts in a snap.

In short, *Connect Management* offers you and your students powerful tools and features that optimize your time and energies, enabling you to focus on course content, teaching, and student learning. *Connect Management* also offers a wealth of content resources for both instructors and students. This state-of-the-art, thoroughly tested system supports you in preparing students for the world that awaits.

For more information about *Connect,* go to **www.mcgrawhillconnect.com,** or contact your local McGraw-Hill sales representative.

Tegrity Campus:

Lectures 24/7. Tegrity Campus is a service that makes class time available 24/7 by automatically capturing every lecture in a searchable format for students to review when they  study and complete assignments. With a simple one-click start-and-stop process, you capture all computer screens and corresponding audio. Students can replay any part of any class with easy-to-use browser-based viewing on a PC or Mac.

Educators know that the more students can see, hear, and experience class resources, the better they learn. In fact, studies prove it. With Tegrity Campus, students quickly recall key moments by using Tegrity Campus's unique search feature. This search helps students efficiently find what they need, when they need it, across an entire semester of class recordings. Help turn all your students' study time into learning moments immediately supported by your lecture. Lecture Capture enables you to . . .

- Record and distribute your lecture with a click of button.
- Record and index PowerPoint presentations and anything shown on your computer so it is easily searchable, frame by frame.
- Offer access to lectures anytime and anywhere by computer, iPod, or mobile device.
- Increase intent listening and class participation by easing students' concerns about note taking. Lecture Capture will make it more likely you will see students' faces, not the tops of their heads.

To learn more about Tegrity, watch a two-minute Flash demo at **http://tegritycampus.mhhe.com.**

McGraw-Hill Customer Care Contact Information. At McGraw-Hill, we understand that getting the most from new technology can be challenging. That's why our services don't stop after you purchase our products. You can e-mail our product specialists 24 hours a day to get product training online. Or you can search our knowledge bank of Frequently Asked Questions on our support website. For customer support, call **800-331-5094,** e-mail **hmsupport@mcgraw-hill.com,** or visit **www.mhhe.com/ support.** One of our technical support analysts will be able to assist you in a timely fashion.

eBook Options. McGraw-Hill's eBooks (typically 40% of the bookstore price) enable students to save money. Students may choose between an online and a downloadable CourseSmart eBook. Through *CourseSmart,* students have the flexibility to access an exact replica of their textbook from any computer that has Internet service without plug-ins or special software via the version, or create a library of books on their hard drive via the downloadable version.

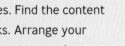

CourseSmart eBooks allow students to . . .

- Highlight, take notes, organize notes, and share the notes with other *CourseSmart* users.
- Search terms across all eBooks in their purchased *CourseSmart* library.
- Print out eBooks five pages at a time.

Access to the CourseSmart eBook(s) is for **I year.** *CourseSmart* allows students to try one chapter of the eBook(s), free of charge, before purchase. Visit **www.coursesmart.com** for more information and to purchase access to our eBook(s).

Create. Craft your teaching resources to match the way you teach! With McGraw-Hill Create, **www.mcgrawhillcreate.com,** you can easily rearrange chapters, combine material from other content sources, and quickly upload content you have written, like your course syllabus or teaching notes. Find the content you need in Create by searching through thousands of leading McGraw-Hill textbooks. Arrange your book to fit your teaching style. Create even allows you to personalize your book's appearance by selecting the cover and adding your name, school, and course information. Order a Create book and you'll receive a complimentary print review copy in three to five business days or a complimentary electronic review copy (eComp) via e-mail in about one hour. Go to **www.mcgrawhillcreate.com** today and register. Experience how McGraw-Hill Create empowers you to teach *your* students *your* way.

McGraw-Hill Higher Education and Blackboard have teamed up. What does this mean for you?

I. **Your life simplified.** Now you and your students can access McGraw-Hill's Connect™ and Create™ right from within your Blackboard course—all with one single sign-on. Say goodbye to the days of logging in to multiple applications.

2. **Deep integration of content and tools.** Not only do you get single sign-on with Connect™ and Create™, you also get deep integration of McGraw-Hill content and content engines right in Blackboard. Whether you're choosing a book for your course or building Connect™ assignments, all the tools you need are right where you want them—inside of Blackboard.

3. **Seamless gradebooks.** Are you tired of keeping multiple gradebooks and manually synchronizing grades into Blackboard? We thought so. When a student completes an integrated Connect™ assignment, the grade for that assignment automatically (and instantly) feeds your Blackboard grade center.

4. **A solution for everyone.** Whether your institution is already using Blackboard or you just want to try Blackboard on your own, we have a solution for you. McGraw-Hill and Blackboard can now offer you easy access to industry-leading technology and content, whether your campus hosts it, or we do. Be sure to ask your local McGraw-Hill representative for details.

Chapter-by-Chapter Changes from the Previous Edition

1. The Exceptional Manager. Yahoo CEO Carol Bartz discussion replaced with IBM CEO Virginia Rometty. Top-earning CEO added: McKesson's John Hammergren. Updates: diversity statistics, e-commerce statistics, top managers' earnings, managers' salaries, white-collar criminals. New Management in Action case: "Target Is Trying to Overcome the Problem of 'Showrooming.'"

2. Management Theory. Cisco Example box updated and repurposed. Theory X/Theory Y updated. Operations research redefined and updated as operations management. **Complexity theory introduced.** Example box content replaced with "Closed Versus Open Systems: When Netflix Didn't Listen." Some material (virtual organization, boundaryless organization, knowledge worker, human capital, social capital) moved to Chapter 9. New Management in Action case: "Boeing Focuses Its Operations & Supply Chain to Improve Productivity & Meet Deadlines." New Legal/Ethical Challenge: "Should the Federal Government Be Allowed to Oust a Drug-Company CEO?"

3. The Manager's Changing Work Environment & Ethical Responsibilities. New Manager's Toolbox: "How Do People Excuse Lying & Cheating?" New chapter lead about California utility PG&E gas explosion killing eight people and questions about who a firm is responsible to. In-text example converted to Example box, "Managing the Media: Johnson & Johnson Succeeds—& Then Fails—in Handling Product Recalls." Updates: economic forces, demographic forces. Material added on Great Recession's impact on today's college freshmen. Section added: "One Type of Social Responsibility: Sustainability, 'Going Green.'" Old section 3.5, "The New Diversified Workforce," moved to Chapter II. **New section added, "Corporate Governance"; includes "The Need for Independent Directors" and "The Need for Trust" and new Example box,** "Corporate Governance: Chesapeake Energy's CEO Gets Some Unusual Breaks from His Board of Directors." New Management in Action case: "Carnival CEO Micky Arison Fails to Provide Interviews After the *Costa Concordia* Sinks." New Legal/Ethical Challenge: "Should Facebook Take a More Proactive Approach in Mentoring the Children's Online Privacy Protection Act?"

4. Global Management. New chapter introduction. Updates: cellphone subscriptions statistics, mergers, multinational corporations. Material added to Example box "Americans Working Overseas," to Practical Action box "Being an Effective Road Warrior," and to Practical Action box "Global Outsourcing: Which Jobs Are Likely to Fall Victim to Offshoring?" Updates and new material: international parts suppliers for Apple iPhone, top 12 exporting countries, U.S. franchises in foreign countries, top 10 nations for U.S. exports, top 10 nations U.S. imports from, tariffs on Chinese solar panels, Europe's embargo of Iran oil, IMF loans to weaker European countries, and statistics regarding NAFTA, EU, and APEC. In section on cultural differences, new material about cultural mistake involving presents in China; different tipping etiquettes worldwide; sections on language, interpersonal space, and communication; and U.S. managers on foreign assignments. Discussion of Hofstede model deleted. New Management in Action case: "Elektrobit Corp. Strives to Make Foreign Assignments a Good Experience." New Legal/Ethical Challenge: "Is Apple Doing Enough to Control Employment Practices in Its Chinese Factories?"

5. Planning. Text updated and converted to Example box, "Thinking Ahead: Ford Plans a Radical Redesign of the Fusion. Example boxes for "Mission Statements" and "Vision Statements" for three different companies revised to cover "Hilton, Amazon, & Patagonia." Statistics added about implementation of clearly articulated strategic direction. Caveat added that strategic planning now done closer to one to two years rather than every five years. New Example box: "Strategic Planning by Top Management: Amazon Manages for the Future, to the Frustration of Short-Term Investors." Section on SMART goals moved to Section 5.3. Example box updated, "Strategic, Tactical, & Operational Goals: Southwest Airlines." In-text examples on programs versus projects expanded. Section heading retitled from "Promoting Goal Setting: Management by Objectives" to "Promoting Goal Setting: SMART Goals & Management by Objectives." Example box expanded, "Setting Objectives: Walmart's CEO Lays Out an Agenda for Change." New Management in

Action case: "Will GM's Strategic Plan Lead to Future Success?" New Legal/Ethical Challenge, "How Do You Think Companies Should Respond to Accusations Made by a Whistle-Blower?"

6. Strategic Management. Material added on how strategy can determine the structure of the organization. Example box updated, "Developing Competitive Advantage: Is Apple's App Store a Model for Ford?" New Example box: "Comparing Strategies: Big-Company 'Make the Consumer a Captive' Versus Small-Firm 'Offer Personal Connections.'" Change of in-text examples for "Growth Strategy," "Stability Strategy," and "Defensive Strategy"—from PepsiCo to IBM, from Best Buy to Alaska Airlines, from Carnival Corp. to Kodak. Example boxes updated: "SWOT Analysis: How Would You Analyze Toyota?" and "Contingency Planning: Southwest Airlines Uses Hedging to Hold Down Price of Aviation Fuel." Use of spreadsheet software added to scenario planning. New Management in Action case: "J. C. Penney Is Changing Its Competitive Strategy." New Legal/Ethical Challenge: "Should Companies Be Pressured to Recruit Females for Boards of Directors?"

7. Individual & Group Decision Making. Example box updated: "Evaluation: The Boeing 787 Dreamliner, a Bet-the-Company Decision." In-text examples added: of Campbell trying to penetrate China's soup market; of entrepreneur's buying I Can Has Cheezburger? silly-cat blog; of Fabulus becoming Fab.com; of Gap closing U.S. stores and expanding in Asia. Example box repurposed as "Use of Analytics: The Oakland A's 'Moneyball' Secret." **New section added "The Uses of 'Big Data'" about data analytics. Practical Action box added, "The Steps in Critical Thinking."** Material on white-collar criminals added to "Making Ethical Decisions." Outdated table deleted, "The Magnificent Seven: General Moral Principles for Managers." Example box replaced. "Confirmation Bias" moved from 2 to 3 on list of biases; "Overconfidence Bias" added as 6, "Hindsight Bias" 7, and "Framing Bias" as 8; "Escalation of Commitment Bias" moved to 9. Example box deleted, "Avoiding Escalation of Commitment." New Management in Action case: "Companies Recognize Mistakes in an Attempt to Increase Creativity & Innovation."

8. Orgnizational Culture, Structure, & Design. Under "Adhocracy Culture" heading, Cisco material deleted. Under "Symbols," "Stories," "Heroes," and "Rites & Rituals," in-text examples replaced—with IKEA, Salesforce.com, and New Belgium Brewery. Under "Leader Reactions to Crises," in-text example replaced by Anne Mulcahy and Xerox. Material added to Practical Action box "Transition Problems on Your Way Up: How to Avoid the Pitfalls." Material added to "Wide Span of Control"; "Accountability" head replaced by "Authority." Section 8.5 introduction replaced with Google decision-making problems. **Introduction and definition of "organizational design," categorized as three types: traditional designs, horizontal designs, and designs that open boundaries between organizations.** Example box replaced with "Horizontal Design: Whole Foods Market." Figure 8.10 "Team-based structure" retitled "Horizontal design." Heading "6. The Network Structure: Connecting a Central Core to Outside Firms by Computer Connections" replaced by "6. Designs That Open Boundaries Between Organizations: Hollow, Modular & Virtual Structures"; term *boundaryless organization* introduced and defined. New heading added entitled "The Hollow Structure: Operating with a Central Core to Outside Firms & Outsourcing Functions to Outside Vendors"; term *hollow structure* introduced and defined. Figure 8.11 "Network structure" retitled "Hollow structure." Example box heading replaced with "EndoStim, a Medical Device Startup Operation, with a Hollow Structure"; material in box edited and compressed. Example box "Modular Structure: Bombardier Builds a Snap-Together Business Jet" deleted and material compressed and pulled into text as in-text example. The terms *virtual organization* and *virtual structure* introduced and defined. **Heading introduced, "The Link Between Strategy & Structure," with two paragraphs of discussion.** New Management in Action case: "Verizon Is Creating a Culture That Focuses on Shareholder Value." New Legal/Ethical Challenge: "What Type of Culture Is Being Created by the New Orleans Saints?"

9. Human Resource Management. Paragraphs resequenced in Manager's Toolbox, "How to Stand Out in a New Job." Some updating of "Best Companies to Work For." The terms *human capital, knowledge workers,* and *social capital* introduced and defined, with discussion. Table 9.1 shortened to one page. Change of term *discrimination* to *workplace discrimination.* Terms *adverse impact* and *disparate treatment* introduced and discussed. Update of EEOC statistics. Heading added, "What Managers Can Do" (about sexual harassment), and paragraph of discussion. **Material added about use of social networks in recruiting.** New discussion about résumés. To Practical Action box "Applying for a Job? Here Are Some Mistakes to Avoid," addition of material warning employers may check students' Facebook pages. Material added about integrity tests, with in-text example. Statistics added about performance reviews, forced ranking, and benefits. **Four pages added of new section, "9.8 Labor-Management Issues," discussing labor unions, with the following subsections: "How Workers Organize," "How Unions & Management Negotiate a Contract," "The Issues Unions & Management Negotiate About" (also covers right-to-work laws, COLA, and givebacks), and "Settling Labor-Management Disputes" (including mediation and arbitration).** New Legal/Ethical Challenge: "You Have Been Offered a Promotion, but You're Pregnant: Should You Say Anything Before Receiving the Formal Offer?"

10. Organizational Change & Innovation. Sequence of chapter sections reorganized: Former "10.4 The Threat of Change: Managing Employee Fear & Resistance" now follows "10.1 The Nature of Change in Organizations" and precedes old "10.2 Organizational Development: What It Is, What It Can Do"; the last section of the chapter is former "10.3 Promoting Innovation Within the Organization." Material about speed as a competitive weapon added to Manager's Toolbox, "Managing for Innovation & Change Takes a Careful Hand." In section "Some Traditional Companies May Not Survive Radically Innovative Change," in-text example of Eastman Kodak replaced with Nokia. Material added about survey of CEOs and incremental change. Under head "Reactive Change," new material added on social media and "pink slime." Example box replaced with "Proactive Change: Redbox's Parent, Coinstar, Gets Out Front on New Vending Machines." **To Figure 10.1, "Forces for Change Outside and Inside the Organization," addition of outside forces "Shareholder & customer demands," "Supplier practices," and "Social & political pressures"; two paragraphs of discussion on these follow in text.** Material added under "Changing Technology" on top innovations of the last 30 years and under "Changing Strategy" on "big four" record labels. Section deleted and replaced with "How Does Failure Impede Innovation," including table, "Factors That Reduce an Organization's Ability to Learn from Failure." Added to the Practical Action box "What Makes a Successful Startup?" is an in-text example about Build-a-Bear Workshop. Under "Unfreezing," "Changing," and "Refreezing," example we added the introduction of wireless handheld computers in hospitals. New Example box added: "Kotter's Steps in Organizational Change: Implementing an Electronic Health Record System." New Management in Action case: "SAP Is Counting on Organizational Change to Boost Revenue Growth." New Legal/Ethical Challenge: "Should People Be Allowed to Polish Their Nails in Flight?"

11. Managing Individual Differences & Behavior. New Example box added, "Self-Monitoring Should Include 'the Good, the Bad, & the Ugly.'" New statistics added to section on values.

Table 11.4 deleted and some of the material pulled into the text. Example box replaced by "How Values & Attitudes Affect Behavior: Thinking Beyond Profit to Create Value for Society." Section 11.4, "Perception & Individual Behavior," moved to Section 11.3. Under head "Four Distortions in Perception," we deleted "1. Selective Perception" and renumbered succeeding subsections. Material on sex-role stereotypes and statistics on race/ethnicity revised. Example box revised: "The Halo Effect: Do Good Looks Make People Richer & Happier?" Section added: "The Recency Effect: 'The Most Recent Impressions Are the Ones That Count,'" with Example box, "The Recency Effect: Can You Use It to Get a Better Performance Review?" Section 11.3, "Work-Related Attitudes & Behaviors Managers Need to Deal With," moved to Section 11.4. Paragraphs on job involvement and under "Work-Related Attitudes" deleted, and material added on employee engagement and on job satisfaction; material deleted on turnover and other material added about onboarding. **New section, "11.5. The New Diversified Workforce" moved here from Section 3.5 in Chapter 3.** Material added on younger workers, older workers, men and women pay differentials, and race and ethnicity, including basketball player Jeremy Lin as an example of ethnocentrism. Section 11.5, "Understanding Stress & Individual Behavior," moved to Section 11.6. Material deleted and statistics added on work stress. New Management in Action case: "Steve Jobs's Personality & Attitudes Drove His Success." New Legal/Ethical Challenge: "Is Smoking a Legitimate Individual Difference to Consider When Hiring People?"

12. Motivating Employees. Text material and Figure 12.1 added on an integrated model of motivation. Some material added under extrinsic rewards. Example box replaced with "Looking for Peak Performance: A Hotel CEO Applies Maslow to Employees, Customers, & Investors." Example box replaced with "Acquired Needs Theory: What Motivates Facebook's COO Sheryl Sandberg?" Material added on equity theory and to Example box on expectancy theory. New table added, "Table 12.2. How Does Goal Setting Work?" Four elements of goal-setting theory revised to "Some Practical Results of Goal-Setting Theory." Material on four types of reinforcement was revised. A heading is added, "Is Money the Best Motivator?" and text material is revised. Material on gainsharing revised. New Management in Action case: "School Officials from Marshall Metro High School Attempt to Motivate Students & Teachers to Achieve Higher

Performance." New Legal/Ethical Challenge: "Should Senior Executives Receive Bonuses for Navigating a Company Through Bankruptcy?"

13. Groups & Teams. "Technical & Organizational Redesign" subsection replaced by "Are Self-Management Teams Effective?", including new table, Table 13.3, "Some Ways to Empower Self-Managed Teams." Three opening paragraphs revised. Resequencing of seven considerations in building an effective team into nine considerations, adding cooperation and trust; additions of sections on cooperation and trust. Addition of new tables: Table 13.4, "How to Build & Maintain Trust with Team Members," and Table 13.5, "How to Enhance Cohesiveness in Teams: Ten Factors That Lead to Success." Deletion of table "Ways to Build Collaborative Teams: Eight Factors That Lead to Success." Example box replaced by "How to Develop Team Norms: Creating a 'Fear-Free Zone' of Trust." Example box replaced by "Groupthink: An Enthusiasm for Brainstorming, a Technique That Often Doesn't Work." Paragraph on managing conflict deleted; new material added on workplace incivility. Example box replaced by "'What We Have Here Is a Failure to Communicate': The Plight of the Tongue-Tied." Material added on cross-cultural conflict and new table, "Table 13.6, Ways to Build Cross-Cultural Relationships." Example box deleted, "Use of the Dialectic Method." New Management in Action case: "Hiring Decisions Influence Teamwork & Performance."

14. Power, Influence, & Leadership. Material added on managers versus leaders, including new table, "Table 14.1, Characteristics of Being a Manager & a Leader." **New subsection added, "Managerial Leadership: Can You Be *Both* a Manager & a Leader?" and introduction of concept of managerial leadership.** Example box replaced by "Set a Goal, Maintain Intensity: The Man Who Built Zynga, a Tightly Wired Machine." New material added on Steve Jobs (replacing Bill Gates and Andy Grove), Kouzes and Posner's research, gender studies, and women executives, and old material deleted, including outdated table on women executives. Material added under "Does the Revised Path–Goal Theory Work?" Apple CEO Tim Cook added as an example of a transactional leader. Material added to Example box, "The Superior Performance of Both a Transactional & Transformational Leader: PepsiCo's CEO Indra Nooyi." Nooyi examples added under "Inspirational Motivation," "Idealized Influence," and "Intellectual Stimulation." "Shared Leadership" discussion deleted. Practical Action box deleted, "Ten Tips on Being an E-Leader." **Material added, "Followers: What Do They Want, How Can They Help?"** along with Practical Action box, "How to Be a Great Follower: Benefiting Your Boss—& Yourself." New Management in Action case: "Lynn Tilton's Leadership Helps Turn Around Failing Companies." New Self-Assessment: "Assessing Your Leader-Member Exchange." New Legal/Ethical Challenge: "Is It Ethical to Use Subversive Approaches to Influence Others?"

15. Interpersonal & Organizational Communication. Manager's Toolbox replaced with "Acing the Interview: Communicating Counts in Landing a Job." New material added: on social media (as "lean medium"), on communication problems in a fast-food drive-through line, on buzzwords, on oversized egos, on nonverbal communication, and on gender-related communication differences. "Linguistic style" introduced and defined. Material reduced on women and communication. Material revised in Practical Action box, "How to Streamline Meetings." Material added on Millennials, telecommunications, and security. **Section added: "Social Media: Pros & Cons."** Introduction of "crowdsourcing"; new Example box, "Crowdsourcing: Using Facebook & Twitter to Develop New Ideas." Material added on "active listening" and "What's Your Listening Style—or Styles?" New tables added: "Using Facebook in Your Professional Life," "Six Keys to Effective Listening," "Five Steps to Better Reading," "Five Rules for Business Writing, Both Online & Offline." Updated statistics on fear of public speaking. New Management in Action case: "Procter & Gamble Company Restricts Use of Internet Sites." New Legal/Ethical Challenge: "Should Companies Be Allowed to Check Personal E-Mail Accounts?"

16. Control Systems & Quality Management. New material on why productivity is important and examples of companies that lost control. Example added on 3M Co. revising system to improve productivity. Example of Ford senior managers added to "Strategic Control by Top Managers." Example added of Google's Innovation Time Off program. Quality control and quality assurance definitions repeated. Example box replaced by "Chrysler Does a Makeover: Initiating a New Quality Strategy." Example box replaced by "Do Social Media Ads Work? The Need for Benchmarking." New Management in Action case: "Control Mechanisms & Quality Processes Save a Steel Mill Plant in Burns Harbor, Michigan." New Legal/Ethical Challenge: "Is Corporate Monitoring of Employee Behavior Going Too Far?"

acknowledgments

We could not have completed this product without the help of a great many people. The first edition was signed by Karen Mellon and developed by Glenn and Meg Turner of Burrston House, to all of whom we are very grateful. Sincere thanks and gratitude also go to our former executive editor John Weimeister and to our present executive brand manager Michael Ablassmeir. Among our first-rate team at McGraw-Hill, we want to acknowledge key contributors: Jane Beck, development; Elizabeth Trepkowski, executive marketing manager; Harvey Yep, lead project manager; senior buyer Michael R. McCormick; designer Pam Verros; senior content licensing specialist Jeremy Cheshareck; and photo researcher Judy Mason. We would also like to thank Linda Hoffmann for her work on the Instructor's Manual; Brad Cox for the PowerPoint slides; and Tia Quinlan-Wilder for the test bank.

Warmest thanks and appreciation go to the individuals who provided valuable input during the developmental stages of this edition, as follows:

Laura L. Alderson,
University of Memphis

William Scott Anchors,
University of Maine at Orono

Jeffrey L. Anderson,
Ohio University

James D. Bell,
Texas State University at San Marcos

Daniel A. Cernas Ortiz,
University of North Texas

Linda D. Clarke,
University of Florida

Dean Cleavenger,
University of Central Florida

Loretta Ferguson Cochran,
Arkansas Tech University

Keith Credo,
McNeese State University

Dan Curtin,
Lakeland Community College

Tom Deckelman,
Owens Community College

E. Gordon DeMeritt,
Shepherd University

John DeSpagna,
Nassau Community College

Linda Durkin,
Delaware County Community College

Jud Faurer,
Metro State College of Denver

Gail E. Fraser,
Kean University

Connie Golden,
Lakeland Community College

Reggie Hall,
Tarleton State University

Samuel Hazen,
Tarleton State University

Evelyn Hendrix,
Lindenwood University

Marvin Karlins,
University of South Florida

Renee N. King,
Eastern Illinois University

Guy Lochiatto,
MassBay Community College

Michael Dane Loflin,
Limestone College

Ivan Lowe,
York Technical College

Margaret Lucero,
Texas A & M-Corpus Christi

Christine I. Mark,
University of Southern Mississippi

Marcia A. Marriott,
Monroe Community College

Christopher P. Neck,
Arizona State University

Thomas J. Norman,
California State University-Dominguez Hills

Fernando Pargas,
James Madison University

H. Lynn Richards,
Johnson County Community College

Gary B. Roberts,
Kennesaw State University

Thomas J. Shaughnessy,
Illinois Central College

Jim Smas,
Kent State University

Barb Stuart,
Daniels College of Business

Marguerite Teubner,
Nassau Community College

Carolyn Waits,
Cincinnati State Technical & Community College

We would also like to thank the following colleagues who served as manuscript reviewers during the development of previous editions:

G. Stoney Alder,
Western Illinois University

Phyllis C. Alderdice,
Jefferson Community College

Laura L. Alderson,
University of Memphis

Scott Anchors,
Maine Business School

Jeffrey Anderson,
Ohio University

John Anstey,
University of Nebraska at Omaha

Maria Aria,
Camden County College

James Bell,
Texas State University-San Marcos

Victor Berardi,
Kent State University

Patricia Bernson,
College County of Morris

David Bess,
University of Hawaii

Stephen Betts,
William Paterson University

Danielle Beu,
Louisiana Tech University

Randy Blass,
Florida State University

Larry Bohleber,
University of Southern Indiana

Melanie Bookout,
Greenville Technical College

Robert S. Boothe,
University of Southern Mississippi

Susan M. Bosco,
Roger Williams University

Roger Brown,
Western Illinois University

Marit Brunsell,
Madison Area Technical College

Neil Burton,
Clemson University

Jon Bryan,
Bridgewater State College

Barbara A. Carlin,
University of Houston

Pamela Carstens,
Coe College

Julie J. Carwile,
John Tyler Community College

Glen Chapuis,
St. Charles Community College

Rod Christian,
Mesa Community College

Mike Cicero,
Highline Community College

Jack Cichy,
Davenport University

Anthony Cioffi,
Lorain County Community College

J. Dana Clark,
Appalachian State University

Deborah Clark,
Santa Fe Community College

Sharon Clinebell,
University of Northern Colorado

Glenda Coleman,
University of South Carolina

Ron Cooley,
South Suburban College

Gary Corona,
Florida Community College

Ajay Das,
Baruch College

Kate Demarest,
Caroll Community College

Kathleen DeNisco,
Erie Community College

Pamela A. Dobies,
University of Missouri— Kansas City

David Dore,
San Francisco City College

Lon Doty,
San Jose State University

Ron Dougherty,
Ivy Tech Community College/ Columbus Campus

Scott Droege,
Western Kentucky University

Ken Dunegan,
University of Cincinnati

Steven Dunphy,
University of Akron

Linda Durkin,
Delaware County Community College

Subhash Durlabhji,
Northwestern State University

Jack Dustman,
Northern Arizona University

Ray Eldridge,
Freed-Hardeman University

Bob Eliason,
James Madison University

Paul Fadil,
University of North Florida

Judy Fitch,
Augusta State University

David Foote,
Middle Tennessee State University

Lucy R. Ford,
Saint Joseph's University

Tony Frontera,
Broome Community College

Michael Garcia,
Liberty University

Evgeniy Gentchev,
Northwood University

James Glasgow,
Villanova University

Kris Gossett,
Ivy Tech State College

Marie Gould,
Peirce University

Kevin S. Groves,
California State University, Los Angeles

Joyce Guillory,
Austin Community College

Stephen F. Hallam,
The University of Akron

Charles T. Harrington,
Pasadena City College

Santhi Harvey,
Central State University

Samuel Hazen,
Tarleton State University

Jack Heinsius,
Modesto Junior College

Kim Hester,
Arkansas State University

Anne Kelly Hoel,
University of Wisconsin-Stout

Mary Hogue,
Kent State University

Edward Johnson,
University of North Florida

Nancy M. Johnson,
Madison Area Technical College

Rusty Juban,
Southeastern Louisiana University

Dmitriy Kalyagin,
Chabot College

Heesam Kang,
Bacone College

Marcella Kelly,
Santa Monica College

Richard Kimbrough,
University of Nebraska-Lincoln

Bobbie Knoblauch,
Wichita State University

Todd Korol,
Monroe Community College

Sal Kukalis,
California State University-Long Beach

Rebecca Legleiter,
Tulsa Community College

David Leonard,
Chabot College

David Levy,
United States Air Force Academy

Chi Lo Lim,
Northwest Missouri State University

Natasha Lindsey,
University of North Alabama

Beverly Little,
Western Carolina University

Guy Lochiatto,
MassBay Community College

Mary Lou Lockerby,
College of DuPage

Paul Londrigan,
Charles Stewart Mott Community College

Tom Loughman,
Columbus State University

James Manicki,
Northwestern College

Brenda McAleer,
University of Maine at Augusta

Daniel W. McAllister,
University of Nevada-Las Vegas

David McArthur,
University of Nevada Las Vegas

Tom McFarland,
Mount San Antonio College

Joe McKenna,
Howard Community College

Zack McNeil,
Longview Community College

Jeanne McNett,
Assumption College

Spencer Mehl,
Coastal Carolina Community College

Mary Meredith,
University of Louisiana

Douglas Micklich,
Illinois State University

Christine Miller,
Tennessee Tech University

Val Miskin,
Washington State University

Gregory Moore,
Middle Tennessee State University

Rob Moorman,
Creighton University

Robert Myers,
University of Louisville

Francine Newth,
Providence College

Jack Partlow,
Northern Virginia Community College

Don A. Paxton,
Pasadena City College

John Paxton,
Wayne State College

Sheila Petcavage,
Cuyahoga Community College-Western Campus

Barbara Petzall,
Maryville University

Anthony Plunkett,
Harrison College

Cynthia Preston,
University of Northwestern Ohio

George Redmond,
Franklin University

Rosemarie Reynolds,
Embry Riddle Aeronautical University

Leah Ritchie,
Salem State College

Gary B. Roberts,
Kennesaw State University

Barbara Rosenthal,
Miami Dade Community College/ Wolfson Campus

Gary Ross,
Barat College of DePaul University

Catherine Ruggieri,
St. John's University-New York

Cindy Ruszkowski,
Illinois State University

William Salyer,
Morris College

Diane R. Scott,
Wichita State University

Marianne Sebok,
Community College of Southern Nevada

Randi Sims,
Nova Southeastern University

Frederick J. Slack,
Indiana University of Pennsylvania

Erika E. Small,
Coastal Carolina University

Gerald F. Smith,
University of Northern Iowa

Mark Smith,
University of Southwest Louisiana

Jeff Stauffer,
Ventura College

Raymond Stoudt,
DeSales University

Robert Scott Taylor,
Moberly Area Community College

Virginia Anne Taylor,
William Patterson University

Wynn Teasley,
University of West Florida

Jerry Thomas,
Arapahoe Community College

Joseph Tomkiewicz,
East Carolina University

Robert Trumble,
Virginia Commonwealth University

Joy Turnheim Smith,
Elizabeth City State University

Isaiah Ugboro,
North Carolina Agricultural & Technical State University

Anthony Uremovic,
Joliet Junior College

Barry Van Hook,
Arizona State University

Susan Verhulst,
Des Moines Area Community College

Annie Viets,
University of Vermont

Tom Voigt, Jr.,
Aurora University

Carolyn Waits,
Cincinnati State Technical & Community College

Bruce C. Walker,
University of Louisiana at Monroe

Tekle O. Wanorie,
Northwest Missouri State University

Charles Warren,
Salem State College

Velvet Weems-Landingham,
Kent State University-Geauga

Allen Weimer,
University of Tampa

David A. Wernick,
Florida International University

James Whelan,
Manhattan College

John Whitelock,
Community College of Baltimore/ Catonsville Campus

Wendy V. Wysocki,
Monroe County Community College

The following professors also participated in an early focus group that helped drive the development of this text. We appreciate their suggestions and participation immensely:

Rusty Brooks,
Houston Baptist University

Kerry Carson,
University of Southwestern Louisiana

Sam Dumbar,
Delgado Community College

Subhash Durlabhji,
Northwestern State University

Robert Mullins,
Delgado Community College

Carl Phillips,
Southeastern Louisiana University

Allayne Pizzolatto,
Nicholls State University

Ellen White,
University of New Orleans

We would also like to thank the following students for participating in a very important focus group to gather feedback from the student reader's point of view:

Marcy Baasch,
Triton College

Diana Broeckel,
Triton College

Lurene Cornejo,
Moraine Valley Community College

Dave Fell,
Elgin Community College

Lydia Hendrix,
Moraine Valley Community College

Kristine Kurpiewski,
Oakton Community College

Michelle Monaco,
Moraine Valley Community College

Shannon Ramey,
Elgin Community College

Arpita Sikand,
Oakton Community College

Finally, we would like to thank our wives, Joyce and Stacey, for being understanding, patient, and encouraging throughout the process of writing this edition. Your love and support helped us endure the trials of completing this text.

We hope you enjoy reading and applying the book. Best wishes for success in your career.

Angelo Kinicki   Brian K. Williams

contents

part 4
Organizing
Chapter Eight

Organizational Culture, Structure, & Design: Building Blocks of the Organization 226

Chapter Nine

Human Resource Management: Getting the Right People for Managerial Success 262

The Manager's Toolbox

Practical Action

Self-Assessments

Example Boxes to Illustrate Important Management Concepts
Bringing current issues & companies into the classroom

Management in Action

Case Studies

Legal/Ethical Challenges

management

A PRACTICAL INTRODUCTION

sixth edition

chapter 1

The Exceptional Manager
What You Do, How You Do It

Major Questions You Should Be Able to Answer

1.1 Management: What It Is, What Its Benefits Are

Major Question: What are the rewards of being an exceptional manager?

1.2 Seven Challenges to Being an Exceptional Manager

Major Question: Challenges can make one feel alive. What are seven challenges I could look forward to as a manager?

1.3 What Managers Do: The Four Principal Functions

Major Question: What would I actually *do*—that is, what would be my four principal functions—as a manager?

1.4 Pyramid Power: Levels & Areas of Management

Major Question: What are the levels and areas of management I need to know to move up, down, and sideways?

1.5 Roles Managers Must Play Successfully

Major Question: To be an exceptional manager, what roles must I play successfully?

1.6 The Entrepreneurial Spirit

Major Question: Do I have what it takes to be an entrepreneur?

1.7 The Skills Exceptional Managers Need

Major Question: To be a terrific manager, what skills should I cultivate?

A One-Minute Guide to Success in This Class

Got one minute to read this section? It could mean the difference between getting an A instead of a B. Or a B instead of a C.

It is our desire *to make this book as practical as possible for you.* One place we do this is in the Manager's Toolbox, like this one, which appears at the beginning of every chapter and which offers practical advice appropriate to the subject matter you are about to explore. Here we show you how to be a success in this course.

Four Rules for Success

The following four rules will help you be successful in this (or any other) course.

- **Rule 1:** Attend every class. No cutting (skipping) allowed.
- **Rule 2:** Don't postpone studying, then cram the night before a test.
- **Rule 3:** Read or review lectures and readings more than once.
- **Rule 4:** Learn how to use this book.

How to Use This Book Most Effectively

When reading this book, follow the steps below:

- Get an overview of the chapter by reading over the first page, which contains the section headings and Major Questions.
- Read "Forecast: What's Ahead in This Chapter."
- Look at the Major Question at the beginning of each section before you read it.
- Read "The Big Picture," which summarizes the section.
- Read the section itself (which is usually only 2–6 pages), *trying silently to answer the Major Question.* This is important!
- After reading all sections, use the Key Terms and Summary at the end of the chapter to see how well you understand the major concepts. Reread any material you're unsure about.

If you follow these steps consistently, you'll probably absorb the material well enough that you won't have to cram before an exam; you'll need only to lightly review it before the test.

For Discussion Do you sometimes (often?) postpone keeping up with coursework, then pull an "all-nighter" of studying to catch up before an exam? What do you think happens to people in business who do this?

forecast What's Ahead in This Chapter

We describe the rewards, benefits, and privileges managers might expect. We also describe the seven challenges to managers in today's world. You'll be introduced to the four principal functions of management—planning, organizing, leading, and controlling—and levels and areas of management. We describe the three roles managers must play. Then we consider the contributions of entrepreneurship. Finally, we describe the three skills required of a manager.

major question?

What are the rewards of being an exceptional manager?

THE BIG PICTURE

Management is defined as the pursuit of organizational goals efficiently and effectively. Organizations, or people who work together to achieve a specific purpose, value managers because of the multiplier effect: Good managers have an influence on the organization far beyond the results that can be achieved by one person acting alone. Managers are well paid, with the chief executive officers (CEOs) and presidents of even small and midsize businesses earning good salaries and many benefits.

The risk taker: IBM CEO Virginia Rometty. The Chicago-area native began her career during the early 1980s, when women began entering corporate America in droves. Although "Big Blue," as IBM is called, made her success possible because of diversity and mentorship programs for women and minorities, her predecessor says that gender did not play a role in the choice of Rometty for the top job. "Ginni got it because she deserved it," he said. One quality that helped her gain the job: risk taking.

When Virginia "Ginni" Rometty was named chief executive officer of Armonk, New York–based International Business Machines (IBM) in late 2011, she became the first female CEO in the company's 100-year history. She was also only the 29th woman to hold the job of chief executive of a Fortune 500 company, one of those 500 largest U.S. companies that appear on the prestigious annual list compiled by *Fortune* magazine. (Other big-time female CEOs: Hewlett-Packard's Meg Whitman, Xerox's Ursula Burns, PepsiCo's Indra Nooyi.)

What kind of a person is Rometty, a 30-year IBM veteran? "She's an engaging woman," said one observer. "She's very high energy," said another. "She has a very deep understanding of the company," said a third.[1] Are these qualities—which a lot of people have—enough to propel one to the top of a great company?

Key to Career Growth: "Doing Things I've Never Done Before"

The oldest of four children, Rometty grew up in a Chicago suburb, graduated from Northwestern with a degree in computer science and electrical engineering, and then, after an internship with General Motors Institute, joined IBM as a systems engineer in

1981. A turning point, she says, came early in her career when she was offered a big job but told the recruiter she did not have enough experience and needed time to think about it. That night her husband asked her, "Do you think a man would have ever answered that question that way?" That taught her that "you have to be very confident, even though you're so self-critical inside about what it is you may or may not know. . . . And that, to me, leads to taking risks."[2] The upshot, Rometty says, is that she has grown the most in her career because "I learned to always take on things I've never done before."[3]

Opportunities for women have improved significantly during Rometty's time, and of course both men as well as women have to deal with uncertainty. But the ability to take risks—to embrace change and to keep going forward despite fears and internal criticism—is important to any manager's survival, regardless of gender. As Rometty says, "Growth and comfort do not coexist."

The Art of Management Defined

Is being an exceptional manager a gift, like a musician having perfect pitch? Not exactly. But in good part it may be an art.[4] Fortunately, it is one that is teachable.

Management, said one pioneer of management ideas, is "the art of getting things done through people."[5]

Getting things done. Through people. Thus, managers are task oriented, achievement oriented, and people oriented. And they operate within an *organization*—a **group of people who work together to achieve some specific purpose.**

More formally, *management* is defined as (1) the pursuit of organizational goals efficiently and effectively by (2) integrating the work of people through (3) planning, organizing, leading, and controlling the organization's resources.

Note the words *efficiently* and *effectively,* which basically mean "doing things right."

- *Efficiency—the means.* Efficiency is the means of attaining the organization's goals. **To be *efficient* means to use resources—people, money, raw materials, and the like—wisely and cost-effectively.**

- *Effectiveness—the ends.* Effectiveness is the organization's ends, the goals. **To be *effective* means to achieve results, to make the right decisions, and to successfully carry them out so that they achieve the organization's goals.**

Good managers are concerned with trying to achieve both qualities. Often, however, organizations will erroneously strive for efficiency without being effective.

EXAMPLE

Efficiency Versus Effectiveness: "Let Me Speak with a Person—*Please!*"

We're all now accustomed to having our calls to companies for information and customer support answered not by people but by automated answering systems. Certainly this arrangement is *efficient* for the companies, since they no longer need as many employees to answer the phones. But it's not *effective* if it leaves us, the customers, fuming and less inclined to continue doing business. "Just give me a person to speak with, *please*," pleads a Nevada resident.[6] Even most online shoppers, 77% in one poll, say they'd prefer to have contact with a real person before they make a purchase.[7] (And more consumers are also grousing about the abundance of phone surveys asking about their satisfaction *after* a purchase.)[8]

Efficiency: Saving Phone Dollars. Still, a lot of companies obviously favor efficiency over effectiveness in their customer service. "The approximate cost of offering a live, American-based customer service agent averages somewhere around $7.50 per phone call," says one researcher. "Outsourcing calls to live agents in another country brings the average cost down to about $2.35 per call. Having customers take care of the problem themselves, through an automated response phone system, averages around 32 cents per call, or contact."[9]

Effectiveness: Retaining Customers and Their Dollars. However, the president of one firm that does

Effective? Is this irate customer dealing with a company customer-support system that is more efficient than effective?

surveys on customer service says that 90% of consumers say they want nothing to do with an automated telephone system. "They just don't like it," he says. The most telling finding is that 50% of those surveyed had become so irritated that they were willing to pay an additional charge for customer service that avoids going through an automated phone system.[10] The head of a firm that evaluates the experiences of call-center customers says that companies "create more value through a dialogue with a live agent. A call is an opportunity to build a relationship, to encourage a customer to stay with the brand. There can be a real return on this investment."[11]

YOUR CALL

The average wait for customer service at Facebook was 60 or more minutes (rated "Horrible" by users); for Amazon.com it was 1 minute ("Excellent"). These and other company wait times and ratings appeared recently on a website called Get Human **(www.gethuman.com)**, started by technology officer Paul English to try to "change the face of customer service." Get Human also publishes the unpublicized codes for reaching a company's human operators and cut-through-automation tips.[12] What recent unpleasant customer experience would you want to post on this website?

Why Organizations Value Managers: The Multiplier Effect

Some great achievements of history, such as scientific discoveries or works of art, were accomplished by individuals working quietly by themselves. But so much more has been achieved by people who were able to leverage their talents and abilities by being managers. For instance, of the top 10 great architectural wonders of the world named by the American Institute of Architects, none was built by just one person. All were triumphs of management, although some reflected the vision of an individual. (The wonders are the Great Wall of China, the Great Pyramid, Machu Picchu, the Acropolis, the Colosseum, the Taj Mahal, the Eiffel Tower, the Brooklyn Bridge, the Empire State Building, and Frank Lloyd Wright's Fallingwater house in Pennsylvania.)

Good managers create value. The reason is that in being a manager you have a *multiplier effect:* Your influence on the organization is multiplied far beyond the results that can be achieved by just one person acting alone. Thus, while a solo operator such as a salesperson might accomplish many things and incidentally make a very good living, his or her boss could accomplish a great deal more—and could well earn two to seven times the income. And the manager will undoubtedly have a lot more influence.

Exceptional managers are in high demand. "The scarcest, most valuable resource in business is no longer financial capital," says a *Fortune* article. "It's talent. If you doubt that, just watch how hard companies are battling for the best people. . . . Talent of every type is in short supply, but the greatest shortage of all is skilled, effective managers."[13] Even in dismal economic times—maybe *especially* in such times—companies reach out for top talent.

The Financial Rewards of Being an Exceptional Manager

How well compensated are managers? According to the U.S. Bureau of Labor Statistics, the median weekly wage in 2011 for American workers of all sorts was $758, or $39,416 a year.[14] Education pays: The median 2011 yearly income for full-time workers with at least a bachelor's degree was $59,904, compared to $33,072 for high-school graduates.

John Hammergren. The CEO of health care giant McKesson earned $145 million in 2010, making him the highest-paid manager in the United States that year. In 2011, the head of a typical public company made $9.6 million, up more than 6% from the previous year. What do you think your chances are of making over $100 million even in your entire lifetime?

The business press frequently reports on the astronomical earnings of top chief executive officers (which jumped a median 36.5% in 2010). The top earner was John Hammergren of health care technologies company McKesson, who led the list that year with $145 million.[15] However, this kind of huge payday isn't common. Median compensation for top-ranked CEOs in North America in 2010, based on a survey of 158 companies (on the Standard & Poor's 500 index companies), was $9 million.[16] The more usual take-home pay is as follows (which does not include bonuses and stock options):

- **Small business CEO.** According to recent research, the beginning median salary for a small business chief executive was $233,500. (A small business was classified as a company with up to 500 full-time employees.)
- **Medium-size business CEO.** The beginning median salary for a CEO with 500 to 5,000 employees was $500,000.[17]
- **Large-size business CEO.** In 2007, CEOs earned a median of $849,375 at companies with more than 5,000 employees.[18]

Managers farther down in the organization usually don't make this much, of course; nevertheless, they do fairly well compared with most workers. At the lower rungs, managers may make between $35,000 and $60,000 a year; in the middle levels, between $45,000 and $120,000.

There are also all kinds of fringe benefits and status rewards that go with being a manager, ranging from health insurance to stock options to large offices. And the higher you ascend in the management hierarchy, the more privileges may come your way: a personal parking space, better furniture, lunch in the executive dining room, on up to—for those on the top rung of big companies—company car and driver, corporate jet, and even executive sabbaticals (months of paid time off to pursue alternative projects).

What Are the Rewards of Studying & Practicing Management?

Are you studying management but have no plans to be a manager? Or are you trying to learn techniques and concepts that will help you be an exceptional management practitioner? Either way there are considerable rewards.

The Rewards of Studying Management   Students sign up for an introductory management course for all kinds of reasons. Many, of course, are planning business careers, but others are taking it to fulfill a requirement or an elective. Some students are in technical fields and never expect to have to supervise people.

Here are just a few of the payoffs of studying management as a discipline:

- **You will understand how to deal with organizations from the outside.** Since we all are in constant interaction with all kinds of organizations, it helps to understand how they work and how the people in them make decisions. Such knowledge may give you some defensive skills that you can use in dealing with organizations from the outside, as a customer or investor, for example.
- **You will understand how to relate to your supervisors.** Since most of us work in organizations and most of us have bosses, studying management will enable you to understand the pressures managers deal with and how they will best respond to you.
- **You will understand how to interact with coworkers.** The kinds of management policies in place can affect how your coworkers behave. Studying management can give you the understanding of teams and teamwork, cultural

differences, conflict and stress, and negotiation and communication skills that will help you get along with fellow employees.

■ **You will understand how to manage yourself in the workplace.** Management courses in general, and this book in particular, give you the opportunity to realize insights about yourself—your personality, emotions, values, perceptions, needs, and goals. We help you build your skills in areas such as self-management, listening, handling change, managing stress, avoiding groupthink, and coping with organizational politics.

The Rewards of Practicing Management   However you become a management practitioner, there are many rewards—apart from those of money and status—to being a manager:

■ **You and your employees can experience a sense of accomplishment.** Every successful goal accomplished provides you not only with personal satisfaction but also with the satisfaction of all those employees you directed who helped you accomplish it.

■ **You can stretch your abilities and magnify your range.** Every promotion up the hierarchy of an organization stretches your abilities, challenges your talents and skills, and magnifies the range of your accomplishments.

■ **You can build a catalog of successful products or services.** Every product or service you provide—the personal Eiffel Tower or Empire State Building you build, as it were—becomes a monument to your accomplishments. Indeed, studying management may well help you in running your own business.

Finally, productivity-improvement expert Odette Pollar of Oakland, California, concludes that "This is an opportunity to counsel, motivate, advise, guide, empower, and influence large groups of people. These important skills can be used in business as well as in personal and volunteer activities. If you truly like people and enjoy mentoring and helping others to grow and thrive, management is a great job."[19] ●

Mentoring. Being a manager is an opportunity "to counsel, motivate, advise, guide, empower, and influence" other people. Does this sense of accomplishment appeal to you?

1.2 SEVEN CHALLENGES TO BEING AN EXCEPTIONAL MANAGER

Challenges can make one feel alive. What are seven challenges I could look forward to as a manager?

major question?

THE BIG PICTURE

Seven challenges face any manager: You need to manage for competitive advantage— to stay ahead of rivals. You need to manage for diversity in race, ethnicity, gender, and so on, because the future won't resemble the past. You need to manage for the effects of globalization and of information technology. You always need to manage to maintain ethical standards. You need to manage for sustainability—to practice sound environmental policies. Finally, you need to manage for the achievement of your own happiness and life goals.

The ideal state that many people seek is an emotional zone somewhere between boredom and anxiety, in the view of psychologist Mihaly Csikzentmihalyi.[20] Boredom, he says, may arise because skills and challenges are mismatched: You are exercising your high level of skill in a job with a low level of challenge, such as licking envelopes. Anxiety arises when one has low levels of skill but a high level of challenge, such as (for many people) suddenly being called upon to give a rousing speech to strangers.

As a manager, could you achieve a balance between these two states—boredom and anxiety, or action and serenity? Certainly managers have enough challenges to keep their lives more than mildly interesting. Let's see what they are.

Challenge #1: Managing for Competitive Advantage—Staying Ahead of Rivals

Competitive advantage **is the ability of an organization to produce goods or services more effectively than competitors do, thereby outperforming them.** This means an organization must stay ahead in four areas: (1) being responsive to customers, (2) innovation, (3) quality, and (4) efficiency.

EXAMPLE

Losing Competitive Advantage: How Did Newspapers Lose Their Way?

American newspapers are more widely read than ever before—105.5 million unique visitors a month in 2011 versus 60 million four years earlier.[21] The problem: Many people aren't paying for news; they're getting it free online. Indeed, newspaper revenues have dropped steadily for 20 years, and in 2011 fewer papers were sold than at any other time since the 1940s. Lower revenues have forced newsroom layoffs and thus less original news gathering. What happened to bring this long-standing industry to this point?[22]

First: Giving Away the Product. At the beginning of the Internet age, newspaper proprietors, seduced by the new technology, decided to promote their product by giving it away for free to various websites. They didn't count on more and more readers (especially younger ones) preferring to get their news online, particularly if it was free.

Second: Relying Too Much on Advertising for Revenue. Even before the Web came along, for decades publishers relied more on advertising for revenues than on readers willing to pay, and so were discounting subscriptions, providing premiums, and giving away copies to boost readership figures to attract advertisers. "The new Internet editions," says a veteran newsman, "were merely the ultimate extension of that trend: free news to the consumer, total reliance on the advertiser."[23] But because of search sites and many other new competitors, online ads produced only a fraction of the revenues of print ads. In addition, classified ads, the lifeblood of newspapers, migrated to Craigslist and eBay.

YOUR CALL

Newspapers are protected by the U.S. Constitution because the free flow of news is considered essential to citizens participating in their government. However, the disciplined function of gathering and verifying original news is expensive, not something most bloggers and other Web opinion makers can do. Some critics suggest it's too late for newspapers to now begin charging readers for online news, but *The Wall Street Journal,* a specialized business paper, has done it for years, and *The New York Times* is also now doing so. Other sites, such as Politico and TMZ, dig for news, but none fulfill the tradi-

Kindle DX. After the success of its book-size Kindle 2, Amazon.com introduced the Kindle DX with a 9.7-inch screen, designed to be used for electronic newspapers and magazines.

tional role of traditional newspapers.[24] Some publishers are refashioning their brands for a tablet world, such as the Kindle DX or the Apple iPad. What do you think newspaper proprietors should do to exploit their competitive advantage—professional news gathering?

1. Being Responsive to Customers The first law of business is *Take care of the customer.* Without customers—buyers, clients, consumers, shoppers, users, patrons, guests, investors, or whatever they're called—sooner or later there will be no organization. Nonprofit organizations are well advised to be responsive to their "customers," too, whether they're called citizens, members, students, patients, voters, rate-payers, or whatever, since they are the justification for the organizations' existence.

2. Innovation **Finding ways to deliver new or better goods or services is called** *innovation.* No organization, for-profit or nonprofit, can allow itself to become complacent—especially when rivals are coming up with creative ideas. "Innovate or die" is an important adage for any manager.

We discuss innovation in Chapter 3.

3. Quality If your organization is the only one of its kind, customers may put up with products or services that are less than stellar (as they have with some airlines whose hub systems give them a near monopoly on flights out of certain cities), but only because they have no choice. But if another organization comes along and offers a better-quality travel experience, TV program, cut of meat, computer software, or whatever, you may find your company falling behind. Making improvements in quality has become an important management idea in recent times, as we shall discuss.

4. Efficiency A generation ago, organizations rewarded employees for their length of service. Today, however, the emphasis is on efficiency: Companies strive to produce goods or services as quickly as possible using as few employees (and raw materials) as possible. Although a strategy that downgrades the value of employees might ultimately backfire—resulting in the loss of essential experience and skills and even customers—an organization that is overstaffed may not be able to compete with leaner, meaner rivals. This is the reason why, for instance, today many companies rely so much on temp (temporary) workers.[25]

Challenge #2: Managing for Diversity— The Future Won't Resemble the Past

Today nearly one in six American workers is foreign-born, the highest proportion since the 1920s.[26] But greater changes are yet to come. By mid-century, the mix of American racial or ethnic groups will change considerably, with the United States becoming half (54%) racial or ethnic minority. Non-Hispanic whites are projected to decrease from 66% of the population in 2008 to 46% in 2050. African Americans will increase from 14% to 15%, Asians and Pacific Islanders from 5.1% to 9.2%, and Hispanics (who may be of any race) from 15% to 30%. In addition, in the coming years there will be a different mix of women, immigrants, and older people in the general population, as well as in the workforce. For instance, in 2030, nearly one in five U.S. residents is expected to be 65 and older. This age group is projected to increase to 88.5 million in 2050, more than doubling the number in 2010 (40.3 million).[27]

Some scholars think that diversity and variety in staffing produce organizational strength, as we consider elsewhere.[28] Clearly, however, the challenge to the manager of the near future is to maximize the contributions of employees diverse in gender, age, race, and ethnicity. We discuss this matter in more detail in Chapter 3.

Challenge #3: Managing for Globalization— The Expanding Management Universe

"In Japan it is considered rude to look directly in the eye for more than a few seconds," says a report about teaching Americans how to behave abroad, "and in Greece the hand-waving gesture commonly used in America for good-bye is considered an insult."[29]

The point: Gestures and symbols don't have the same meaning to everyone throughout the world. Not understanding such differences can affect how well organizations manage globally.

American firms have been going out into the world in a major way, even as the world has been coming to us—leading to what *New York Times* columnist Thomas Friedman has called, in *The World Is Flat,* a phenomenon in which globalization has leveled (made "flat") the competitive playing fields between industrial and emerging-market countries.[30] Managing for globalization will be a complex, ongoing challenge, as we discuss at length in Chapter 4.

Overseas business. This Gap online store in Shanghai, China, is an example of globalization. Gap has set out on a deliberate strategy of international expansion of its stores to make up for weaknesses at home.

Challenge #4: Managing for Information Technology

The challenge of managing for information technology, not to mention other technologies affecting your business, will require your unflagging attention. Most important is the *Internet,* **the global network of independently operating but interconnected computers, linking hundreds of thousands of smaller networks around the world.**

By 2015, consumers worldwide are projected to spend $1.4 trillion online, a rise of 13.5% annually.[31] This kind of *e-commerce,* **or electronic commerce—the buying and selling of goods or services over computer networks**—is reshaping entire industries and revamping the very notion of what a company is. More important than e-commerce, information technology has facilitated *e-business,* **using the Internet to facilitate *every* aspect of running a business.** As one article puts it, "[A]t bottom, the Internet is a tool that dramatically lowers the cost of communication. That means it can radically alter any industry or activity that depends heavily on the flow of information."[32]

Some of the implications of e-business that we will discuss throughout the book are as follows:

- **Far-ranging e-management and e-communication.** Using wired and wireless telephones, fax machines, electronic mail, or *e-mail*—**text messages and documents transmitted over a computer network**—as well as *project management software*—**programs for planning and scheduling the people, costs, and resources to complete a project on time**—21st-century managers will find themselves responsible for creating, motivating, and leading teams of specialists all over the world. This will require them to be masters of organizational communication, able to create concise, powerful e-mail and voice-mail messages.

- **Accelerated decision making, conflict, and stress.** The Internet not only speeds everything up, it also, with its huge, interconnected *databases*—**computerized collections of interrelated files**—can overwhelm us with information, much of it useful, much of it not. For example, studies show that employees lose valuable time and productivity when dealing with excessive and unimportant e-mail volume and increasing amounts of cellphone spam (junk messages).[33] Among the unfortunate by-products are loss of privacy and increased conflict and stress.[34]

- **Changes in organizational structure, jobs, goal setting, and knowledge management.** With computers and telecommunications technology, organizations and teams become "virtual"; they are no longer as bound by time zones and locations. Employees, for instance, may *telecommute,* **or work from home or remote locations using a variety of information technologies.** Meetings may be conducted via *videoconferencing,* **using video and audio links along with computers to let people in different locations see, hear, and talk with one another.** In addition, *collaborative computing,* **using state-of-the-art computer software and hardware, will help people work better together.** Goal setting and feedback will be conducted via Web-based software programs such as eWorkbench, which enables managers to create and track employee goals. All such forms of interaction will require managers and employees to be more flexible, and there will be an increased emphasis on *knowledge management*—**the implementing of systems and practices to increase the sharing of knowledge and information throughout an organization.**

Challenge #5: Managing for Ethical Standards

With the pressure to meet sales, production, and other targets, managers can find themselves confronting ethical dilemmas. What do you do when you learn an employee dropped a gyroscope but put it in the helicopter anyway in order to hold the product's delivery date? How much should you allow your sales reps to knock the competition? How much leeway do you have in giving gifts to prospective clients in a foreign country to try to land a contract? In an era of global warming and rising sea levels, what is your responsibility to "act green"—avoid company policies that are damaging to the environment?

Ethical behavior is not just a nicety; it is a very important part of doing business. This was certainly made clear in December 2008, when financier Bernard Madoff confessed that his investments were all "one big lie"—not investments at all, but rather a $50 billion scheme (*Ponzi scheme*), using cash from newer investors to pay off older ones.[35] A few months later, the perpetrator of the world's biggest fraud, then age 71, was sentenced to 150 years in prison.[36] Madoff joins a long list of famous business scoundrels of the early 21st century: Tyco International CEO Dennis Kozlowski (now serving prison time for grand larceny, securities fraud, and other crimes), WorldCom head Bernard Ebbers (doing 25 years for fraud), Adelphia CEO John Rigas (15 years for conspiracy and bank fraud), former Enron chief Jeffrey Skilling (24 years for similar white-collar crimes), Galleon Group hedge fund head Raj Rajaratnam, and Goldman Sachs director Rajat Gupta (11 years each for insider trading). Not since sociologist Edwin Sutherland invented the term "white-collar crime" in the 1930s have so many top-level executives been hauled into court. We consider ethics in Chapter 3 and elsewhere in the book.

World's biggest fraud. Financier Bernard Madoff, who got away with the world's biggest fraud for years, at age 71 was sentenced to 150 years in prison. If you're tempted to stretch your ethics in order to pass a college course, do you think you'd do the same in business, where the pressures can be even worse?

PRACTICAL ACTION

Lying and Cheating Required to Succeed?

Today's teenagers and young adults are much more likely than their parents "to believe they're great people, destined for maximum success as workers, spouses, and parents," says an article summarizing a study spanning the years 1975 to 2006.[37] In part, this may be because their parents were much more likely to praise them.

Young Cynics. Nothing wrong with self-confidence. But another study suggests a more troubling trend: Teenagers and young adults are more cynical than people over 40 and "are more likely to believe it is necessary to lie or cheat to succeed."[38] The study, by the Los Angeles–based Josephson Institute of Ethics, found that younger generations are more likely to engage in dishonest conduct, including cheating on exams in high school, which meant they were "at least twice as likely to become unethical adults."

Some of the findings include the following:[39]

- Of teenagers 17 and younger in 2008, 64% cheated on an exam, 42% lied to save money, and 30% stole something from a store.

- Teens 17 or under are five times more likely than adults over 50 to believe that lying and cheating are necessary to succeed (51% versus 10%) and four times more likely to deceive their boss (31% versus 8%)

- Young adults (18–24) are more than twice as likely to lie to their boyfriend, girlfriend, spouse, or partner about something significant (48% versus 18%).

Does Belief Lead to Action? Regardless of age, people who believe that lying and cheating are a necessary part of success are more likely, in fact, to lie and cheat. They are three times more likely to misrepresent themselves on a résumé; three times more likely to lie to a customer; more than twice as likely to conceal or distort information to their boss; and much more likely to illegally copy software, videos, or music.

YOUR CALL

The Josephson Institute suggests that parents can take a TEAM (Teach. Enforce. Advocate. Model.) approach to help children learn the importance of honesty. But perhaps companies can also take steps to create ethical employees and customers—building trust by trusting. One New York doughnut shop owner, for example, began letting customers make their own change from coins left out on the counter. The result: faster service, more loyal customers, and a leg up on his competitors. Do you think companies should trust their employees on how much vacation to take and not require management approval of expense reports? Do you think such companies would generally have loyal employees?[40]

Challenge #6: Managing for Sustainability— The Business of Green

An apparently changing climate, bringing increased damage from hurricanes, floods, and fires throughout the United States and the world, has brought the issue of "being green" to increased prominence. Former U.S. Vice President Al Gore's documentary film *An Inconvenient Truth,* along with his book by the same name, further popularized the concepts of global climate change and the idea of sustainability as a business model.[41]

Our economic system has brought prosperity, but it has also led to unsustainable business practices because it has assumed that natural resources are limitless, which they are not. **Sustainability is defined as economic development that meets the needs of the present without compromising the ability of future generations to meet their own needs.**[42] In the United States, the U.S. Chamber of Commerce, which is supposed to represent the views of business, has been resistant to climate change legislation.[43] However, several companies—Levi Strauss, Apple, Tiffany, Exelon, Pacific Gas & Electric, PNM Resources, and Mohawk Fine Papers—resigned from the Chamber in protest.[44] Perhaps, then, business can begin to take the lead. After years of being slow to address climate change, major corporations—including industrial giants that make products ranging from electricity to chemicals to bulldozers—have begun to call for limits on global warming emissions.[45]

Challenge #7: Managing for Your Own Happiness & Life Goals

Ann Garcia had the view that good managers push decision making down, spread the compliments, and take the blame, but after being given a team to manage at her technology company, she gave it up. "I'm just not a big enough person all the time to want to do that," she said. "Many of us realize that we don't want the career path that corporate America has to offer."[46]

Some employment experts counsel that the lesson of today is that you're working for yourself—that employees should identify themselves with the job, not the company.[47] Regardless of how well paid you are, then, you have to consider whether in meeting the organization's challenges you are also meeting the challenge of realizing your own happiness.

Many people simply don't find being a manager fulfilling.[48] They may complain that they have to go to too many meetings, that they can't do enough for their employees, that they are caught in the middle between bosses and subordinates. They may feel, at a time when Dilbert cartoons have created such an unflattering portrayal of managers, that they lack respect. They may decide that, despite the greater income, money cannot buy happiness, as the adage goes. Some feel the Great Recession forced them to miss the economic lifestyle they had hoped for. (But most are happier anyway.)[49]

In the end, however, recall what Odette Pollar said: "If you truly like people and enjoy mentoring and helping others to grow and thrive, management is a great job." And it helps to know, as she points out, that "one's experience in management is greatly affected by the company's culture."[50] Culture, or style, is indeed an important matter, because it affects your happiness within an organization, and we discuss it in detail in Chapter 8.[51] ●

1.3 WHAT MANAGERS DO: THE FOUR PRINCIPAL FUNCTIONS

What would I actually *do*—that is, what would be my four principal functions—as a manager?

major question?

THE BIG PICTURE

Management has four functions: *planning, organizing, leading,* and *controlling.*

What do you as a manager do to "get things done"—that is, achieve the stated goals of the organization you work for? You perform what is known as the *management process,* also called the *four management functions:* **planning, organizing, leading, and controlling.** (The acronym "POLC" may help you to remember them.)

As the diagram illustrates, all these functions affect one another, are ongoing, and are performed simultaneously. *(See Figure 1.1.)*

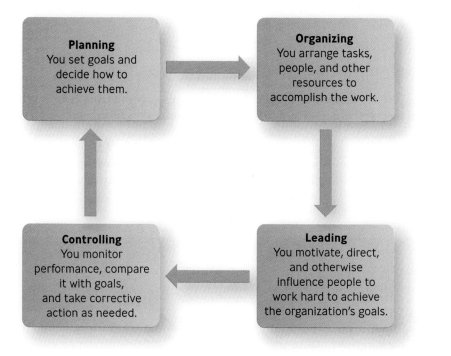

Planning
You set goals and decide how to achieve them.

Organizing
You arrange tasks, people, and other resources to accomplish the work.

Controlling
You monitor performance, compare it with goals, and take corrective action as needed.

Leading
You motivate, direct, and otherwise influence people to work hard to achieve the organization's goals.

figure 1.1
THE MANAGEMENT PROCESS
What you as a manager do to "get things done"—to achieve the stated goals of your organization.

Although the process of management can be quite complex, these four functions represent its essential principles. Indeed, as a glance at our text's table of contents shows, they form four of the part divisions of the book. Let's consider what the four functions are, using the management (or "administration," as it is called in nonprofit organizations) of your college to illustrate them.

Planning: Discussed in Part 3 of This Book

***Planning* is defined as setting goals and deciding how to achieve them.** Your college was established for the purpose of educating students, and its present managers, or administrators, now must decide the best way to accomplish this. Which of several possible degree programs should be offered? Should the college be a residential or a commuter campus? What sort of students should be recruited and admitted? What kind of faculty should be hired? What kind of buildings and equipment are needed?

Organizing: Discussed in Part 4 of This Book

***Organizing* is defined as arranging tasks, people, and other resources to accomplish the work.** College administrators must determine the tasks to be done, by whom, and what the reporting hierarchy is to be. Should the institution be organized into schools with departments, with department chairpersons reporting to deans who in turn report to vice presidents? Should the college hire more full-time instructors than part-time instructors? Should English professors teach just English literature or also composition, developmental English, and "first-year experience" courses?

Leading: Discussed in Part 5 of This Book

***Leading* is defined as motivating, directing, and otherwise influencing people to work hard to achieve the organization's goals.** At your college, leadership begins, of course, with the president (who would be the chief executive officer in a for-profit organization). He or she is the one who must inspire faculty, staff, students, alumni, wealthy donors, and residents of the surrounding community to help realize the college's goals. As you might imagine, these groups often have different needs and wants, so an essential part of leadership is resolving conflicts.

Controlling: Discussed in Part 6 of This Book

***Controlling* is defined as monitoring performance, comparing it with goals, and taking corrective action as needed.** Is the college discovering that fewer students are majoring in nursing than they did five years previously? Is the fault with a change in the job market? with the quality of instruction? with the kinds of courses offered? Are the Nursing Department's student recruitment efforts not going well? Should the department's budget be reduced? Under the management function of controlling, college administrators must deal with these kinds of matters.   ●

Leading. Steve Jobs, the cofounder and CEO of Apple Inc. and Pixar Animation, who passed away in 2011, was famous for being an innovative leader. Do you think you have the ability to take the kind of risks he did?

THE BIG PICTURE

Within an organization, there are managers at three levels: *top, middle,* and *first-line.* Managers may also be *general managers,* or they may be *functional managers,* responsible for just one organizational activity, such as research and development, marketing, finance, production, or human resources. Managers may work for for-profit, nonprofit, or mutual-benefit organizations.

The workplace of the future may resemble a symphony orchestra, famed management theorist Peter Drucker said.[52] Employees, especially so-called knowledge workers—those who have a great deal of technical skills—can be compared to concert musicians. Their managers can be seen as conductors.

In Drucker's analogy, musicians are used for some pieces of music—that is, work projects—and not others, and they are divided into different sections (teams) based on their instruments. The conductor's role is not to play each instrument better than the musicians but to lead them all through the most effective performance of a particular work.

This model differs from the traditional pyramidlike organizational model, where one leader sits at the top, with layers of managers beneath, each of whom must report to and justify his or her work to the manager above (what's called *accountability,* as we discuss in Chapter 8). We therefore need to take a look at the traditional arrangement first.

The Traditional Management Pyramid: Levels & Areas

A new Silicon Valley technology startup company staffed by young people in sandals and shorts may be so small and so loosely organized that only one or two members may be said to be a manager. General Motors or the U.S. Army, in contrast, has thousands of managers doing thousands of different things. Is there a picture we can draw that applies to all the different kinds of organizations and describes them in ways that make sense? Yes: by levels and by areas, as the pyramid on the next page shows. *(See Figure 1.2.)*

Three Levels of Management

Not everyone who works in an organization is a manager, of course, but those who are may be classified into three levels—top, middle, and first-line.

Top Managers: Determining Overall Direction   Their offices may be equipped with expensive leather chairs and have lofty views. Or, as with one Internet company, they may have plastic lawn chairs in the CEO's office and beat-up furniture in the lobby. Whatever their decor, an organization's top managers tend to have titles such as "chief executive officer (CEO)," "chief operating officer (COO)," "president," and "senior vice president."

Some may be the stars in their fields, the men and women whose pictures appear on the covers of business magazines, people such as Facebook founder Mark Zuckerberg or PepsiCo CEO Indra Nooyi, who appeared on the front of *Fortune,* or former eBay (and now Hewlett-Packard) CEO Meg Whitman or AT&T CEO Ed Whitacre,

figure 1.2

THE LEVELS AND AREAS OF MANAGEMENT

Top managers make long-term decisions, middle managers implement those decisions, and first-line managers make short-term decisions.

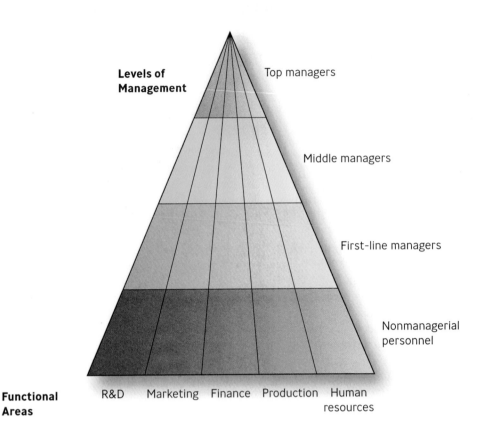

Levels of Management

Top managers

Middle managers

First-line managers

Nonmanagerial personnel

Functional Areas

R&D   Marketing   Finance   Production   Human resources

One kind of top manager. Jeffrey Immelt, chairman and CEO, has worked at General Electric for over 30 years. Known for its consumer appliances, GE also sells aircraft engines, lighting, and medical imaging equipment. Do you see yourself joining a company and staying with it for life, as Immelt did, or is that even possible anymore?

who were on the cover of *Forbes*. As we've seen, the salaries and bonuses can average $233,500 a year for CEOs and presidents of small and midsize companies to pay packages in the millions for top executives in large companies.

Top managers **make long-term decisions about the overall direction of the organization and establish the objectives, policies, and strategies for it.** They need to pay a lot of attention to the environment outside the organization, being alert for long-run opportunities and problems and devising strategies for dealing with them. Thus, executives at this level must be future oriented, dealing with uncertain, highly competitive conditions.

These people stand at the summit of the management pyramid. But the nature of a pyramid is that the farther you climb, the less space remains at the top. Thus, most pyramid climbers never get to the apex. However, that doesn't mean that you shouldn't try. Indeed, you might end up atop a much smaller pyramid of some other organization than the one you started out in—and happier with the result.

Middle Managers: Implementing Policies & Plans *Middle managers* **implement the policies and plans of the top managers above them and supervise and coordinate the activities of the first-line managers below them.** Titles might include "plant manager," "district manager," and "regional manager," among others. In the non-profit world, middle managers may have titles such as "clinic director," "dean of student services," and the like. Their salaries may range from under $45,000 up to $120,000 a year.

Middle managers are critical for organizational success because they implement the strategic plans created by CEOs and top managers. (Strategic planning is discussed in Chapter 6.) In other words, these managers have the type of "high-touch" jobs that can directly affect employees, customers, and suppliers.[53]

First-Line Managers: Directing Daily Tasks The job titles at the bottom of the managerial pyramid tend to be on the order of "department head," "foreman" or "forewoman," "team leader," or "supervisor"—clerical supervisor, production supervisor, research supervisor, and so on. Indeed, *supervisor* is the name often given to first-line managers as a whole. Their salaries may run from $35,000 to $65,000 a year.

Following the plans of middle and top managers, *first-line managers* **make short-term operating decisions, directing the daily tasks of nonmanagerial personnel,** who are, of course, all those people who work directly at their jobs but don't oversee the work of others.

No doubt the job of first-line manager will be the place where you would start your managerial career. This can be a valuable experience because it will be the training and testing ground for your management ideas.

Top manager of another sort. Mark Zuckerberg, shown at the Palo Alto, California, headquarters of Facebook, has become one of today's most watched techno-entrepreneurs. Zuckerberg founded the well-known social networking site in his dorm room at Harvard during a semester break in 2004. Do you think a top manager is always an adventurous type?

Areas of Management: Functional Managers Versus General Managers

We can represent the levels of management by slicing the organizational pyramid horizontally. We can also slice the pyramid vertically to represent the organization's departments or functional areas, as we did in Figure 1.2.

In a for-profit technology company, these might be Research & Development, Marketing, Finance, Production, and Human Resources. In a nonprofit college, these might be Faculty, Student Support Staff, Finance, Maintenance, and Administration. Whatever the names of the departments, the organization is run by two types of managers—functional and general. (These are line managers, with authority to direct employees. Staff managers mainly assist line managers.)

Functional Managers: Responsible for One Activity If your title is Vice President of Production, Director of Finance, or Administrator for Human Resources, you are a functional manager. A *functional manager* **is responsible for just one organizational activity.** Marissa Mayer, who became CEO of Yahoo in 2012, was formerly Google's Vice President of Search Products and User Experience, responsible for overseeing the development of Web search, Google Earth, Google Desktop, and several other products. Leading this specialized sort of research-and-development activity made her a functional manager.

General Managers: Responsible for Several Activities If you are working in a small organization of, say, 100 people and your title is Executive Vice President, you are probably a general manager over several departments, such as Production and Finance and Human Resources. A *general manager* **is responsible for several organizational activities.** At the top of the pyramid, general managers are those who seem to be the subject of news stories in magazines such as *Bloomberg Businessweek, Fortune, Forbes, Inc.,* and *Fast Company.* Examples are big-company CEOs Denise Morrison of Campbell Soup and Jeffrey Immelt of General Electric.. It also includes small-company CEOs such as Gayle Martz, who heads Sherpa's Pet Trading Co., a $4 million New York company with 10 employees that sells travel carriers for dogs and cats. But not all general managers are in for-profit organizations.

Dr. Rick Aubry is president of Rubicon Programs, a San Francisco–area nonprofit formed after California state psychiatric hospitals were closed in 1973. The organization funds training, housing, and employment programs that have helped thousands of former patients and disabled, impoverished, and homeless people reenter society. Rubicon funds its annual budget with $18 million in annual revenues from its rental properties, enterprises, and services, such as the Rubicon Bakery and Rubicon Landscape Services, which also provide job training. Aubrey makes a point of running Rubicon like a business, reflecting the strategic vision of a top-level general manager.[54] Rubicon was a recipient of *Fast Company* magazine's 2008 Social Capitalist awards.[55]

Managers for Three Types of Organizations: For-Profit, Nonprofit, Mutual-Benefit

There are three types of organizations classified according to the three purposes for which they are formed—*for-profit, nonprofit, and mutual-benefit.*[56]

Nonprofit general manager. A general manager is responsible for several organizational activities. Rick Aubry oversees a nonprofit organization serving 4,000 people annually with $18 million annual revenues. Do you think managerial skills are different for nonprofit and for-profit organizations?

1. For-Profit Organizations: For Making Money   For-profit, or business, organizations are formed to make money, or profits, by offering products or services. When most people think of "management," they think of business organizations, ranging from Allstate to Zenith, from Amway to Zagat.

2. Nonprofit Organizations: For Offering Services   Managers in nonprofit organizations are often known as "administrators." Nonprofit organizations may be either in the public sector, such as the University of California, or in the private sector, such as Stanford University. Either way, their purpose is to offer services to some clients, not to make a profit. Examples of such organizations are hospitals, colleges, and social-welfare agencies (the Salvation Army, the Red Cross).

One particular type of nonprofit organization is called the *commonweal organization.* Unlike nonprofit service organizations, which offer services to *some* clients, commonweal organizations offer services to *all* clients within their jurisdictions. Examples are the military services, the U.S. Postal Service, and your local fire and police departments.

3. Mutual-Benefit Organizations: For Aiding Members   Mutual-benefit organizations are voluntary collections of members—political parties, farm cooperatives, labor unions, trade associations, and clubs—whose purpose is to advance members' interests.

Do Managers Manage Differently for Different Types of Organizations?

If you become a manager, would you be doing the same types of things regardless of the type of organization? Generally you would be; that is, you would be performing the four management functions—planning, organizing, leading, and controlling—that we described in Section 1.3.

The single biggest difference, however, is that in a for-profit organization, the measure of its success is how much profit (or loss) it generates. In the other two types of organization, although income and expenditures are very important concerns, the measure of success is usually the effectiveness of the services delivered—how many students were graduated, if you're a college administrator, or how many crimes were prevented or solved, if you're a police chief.   ●

1.5 ROLES MANAGERS MUST PLAY SUCCESSFULLY

To be an exceptional manager, what roles must I play successfully?

major question?

THE BIG PICTURE
Managers tend to work long hours at an intense pace; their work is characterized by fragmentation, brevity, and variety; and they rely more on verbal than on written communication. According to management scholar Henry Mintzberg, managers play three roles—*interpersonal, informational,* and *decisional.* Interpersonal roles include figurehead, leader, and liaison activities. Informational roles are monitor, disseminator, and spokesperson. Decisional roles are entrepreneur, disturbance handler, resource allocator, and negotiator.

Clearly, being a successful manager requires playing several different roles and exercising several different skills. What are they?

The Manager's Roles: Mintzberg's Useful Findings

Maybe, you think, it might be interesting to follow some managers around to see what it is, in fact, they actually do. That's exactly what management scholar Henry Mintzberg did when, in the late 1960s, he shadowed five chief executives for a week and recorded their working lives.[57] And what he found is valuable to know, since it applies not only to top managers but also to managers on all levels.

Consider this portrait of a manager's workweek: "There was no break in the pace of activity during office hours," reported Mintzberg about his subjects. "The mail (average of 36 pieces per day), telephone calls (average of five per day), and meetings (average of eight) accounted for almost every minute from the moment these executives entered their offices in the morning until they departed in the evening."[58]

Only five phone calls per day? And, of course, this was back in an era before e-mail, texting, and Twitter, which now can shower some executives with 100, even 300, messages a day. Indeed, says Ed Reilly, who heads the American Management Association, all the e-mail, cellphone calls, text messaging, and so on can lead people to end up "concentrating on the urgent rather than the important."[59]

Obviously, the top manager's life is extraordinarily busy. Here are three of Mintzberg's findings, important for any prospective manager:

1. A Manager Relies More on Verbal Than on Written Communication
Writing letters, memos, and reports takes time. Most managers in Mintzberg's research tended to get and transmit information through telephone conversations and meetings. No doubt this is still true, although the technologies of e-mail, texting, and Twitter now makes it possible to communicate almost as rapidly in writing as with the spoken word.

2. A Manager Works Long Hours at an Intense Pace
"A true break seldom occurred," wrote Mintzberg about his subjects.

Multitasking. Multiple activities are characteristic of a manager—which is why so many managers carry a smartphone to keep track of their schedules. Most students already use these. Could you get along without one?

A Mintzberg manager. John T. Chambers, CEO of network gear maker Cisco Systems, relies more on verbal than on written communication, works long hours, and experiences an "interrupt-driven day." Interestingly, Chambers is successful despite having had lifelong dyslexia, the common language-related learning disability. He compensates by leaving 40 or 50 voice mails a day, studies summaries in briefing binders, and tapes videos for employees. What kind of personal adversity have you had to overcome?

"Coffee was taken during meetings, and lunchtime was almost always devoted to formal or informal meetings."

Long hours at work are standard, he found, with 50 hours being typical and up to 90 hours not unheard of. A 1999 survey by John P. Kotter of the Harvard Business School found that the general managers he studied worked just under 60 hours per week.[60]

Are such hours really necessary? Three decades following the Mintzberg research, Linda Stroh, Director of Workplace Studies at Loyola University Chicago, did a study that found that people who work more also earn more. "Those managers who worked 61 hours or more per week had earned, on average, about two promotions over the past five years," she reported.[61] Prior to the 2007–2009 Great Recession, researchers at Purdue and McGill universities found that more companies were allowing managers to reduce their working hours and spend more time with their families yet still advance their high-powered careers.[62] However, during economic hard times, top managers may be more apt to see subordinates' work-life flexibility as a luxury they can no longer afford.

3. A Manager's Work Is Characterized by Fragmentation, Brevity, & Variety   Only about a tenth of the managerial activities observed by Mintzberg took more than an hour; about half were completed in under 9 minutes. Phone calls averaged 6 minutes, informal meetings 10 minutes, and desk-work sessions 15 minutes. "When free time appeared," wrote Mintzberg, "ever-present subordinates quickly usurped it."

No wonder the executive's work time has been characterized as "the interrupt-driven day" and that many managers—such as the late Mary Kay Ash, head of the Mary Kay Cosmetics company—get up as early as 5 a.m. so that they will have a quiet period in which to work undisturbed.[63] No wonder that finding balance between work and family lives is an ongoing concern. No wonder that many managers—such as Dawn Lepore, executive vice president of discount broker Charles Schwab & Co.— have become "much less tolerant of activities that aren't a good use of my time" and so have become better delegators.[64]

It is clear from Mintzberg's work that *time and task management* are major challenges for every manager. The Practical Action box, "Executive Functioning: How Good Are You at Focusing Your Thoughts, Controlling Your Impulses, & Avoiding Distractions?" examines this challenge further. The box "Getting Control of Your Time: Dealing with the Information Deluge in College & in Your Career" at the end of this chapter also offers some important suggestions.

Executive Functioning: How Good Are You at Focusing Your Thoughts, Controlling Your Impulses, & Avoiding Distractions?

Managers are executives, of course, and good managers have what psychologists call good "executive functioning." This is a psychological term, rather than a workplace one, and it involves the ability to manage oneself and one's resources in order to achieve a goal. Specifically, this means the ability to focus your thoughts, control your impulses, and avoid distractions.[65]

Gen Z. The 23 million people born from the mid-1990s to the present, known as Generation Z, or the Net Generation, were "practically born with a smartphone in their hand," in one description.[66] How good is their executive functioning? One study found that 8- to 18-year-olds spend more than 7½ hours a day on smartphones, computers, TVs, or other electronic devices. And, because so many of them are multitasking—as in listening to music while surfing the Web—they pack on average nearly 11 hours of media content into those 7½ hours.[67] Today 16- to 18-year-olds multitask by performing seven tasks on average in their free time—such as texting, sending instant messages, watching TV, and checking Facebook—according to psychology researcher Larry Rosen.[68] Add to that the fact that U.S. households consumed a mind-boggling average of 33.8 gigabytes of information and

10,845 trillion words (equivalent to a 7-foot stack of Dan Brown novels) in 2008, and you can see that the challenges to staying focused are considerable.[69]

The Finite Brain. "Life," says Winifred Gallagher, author of *Rapt,* "is the sum of what you focus on."[70] Another writer says, "You can drive yourself crazy trying to multitask and answer every e-mail message instantly. Or you can recognize your brain's finite capacity for processing information."[71] When you read this textbook while listening to music and watching TV, you may think you're simultaneously doing three separate tasks, but you're really not. "It's like playing tennis with three balls," says one expert.[72]

YOUR CALL

Do you procrastinate about getting your work done? Most people do—and in fact the problem has worsened over the years: Today about 26% of Americans think of themselves as chronic procrastinators, up from 5% in 1978. The reason: too many tempting diversions, especially electronic ones.[73] Is this a problem for you? What can you do to improve your "executive functioning"?

Three Types of Managerial Roles

Three Types of Managerial Roles: Interpersonal, Informational, & Decisional From his observations and other research, Mintzberg concluded that managers play three broad types of roles or "organized sets of behavior": *interpersonal, informational,* and *decisional.*

1. Interpersonal Roles—Figurehead, Leader, and Liaison In their *interpersonal roles,* **managers interact with people inside and outside their work units.** The three interpersonal roles include *figurehead, leader,* and *liaison* activities.

2. Informational Roles—Monitor, Disseminator, and Spokesperson The most important part of a manager's job, Mintzberg believed, is information handling, because accurate information is vital for making intelligent decisions. In their three *informational roles—as monitor, disseminator,* and *spokesperson—***managers receive and communicate information** with other people inside and outside the organization.

3. Decisional Roles—Entrepreneur, Disturbance Handler, Resource Allocator, and Negotiator In their *decisional roles,* **managers use information to make decisions to solve problems or take advantage of opportunities. The four decision-making roles are entrepreneur, disturbance handler, resource allocator, and negotiator.**

These roles are summarized in the table on the next page. *(See Table 1.1.)*

table 1.1 THREE TYPES OF MANAGERIAL ROLES: INTERPERSONAL, INFORMATIONAL, AND DECISIONAL

Broad Managerial Roles	Types of Roles	Description
Interpersonal Managerial Roles	Figurehead role	In your *figurehead role,* you show visitors around your company, attend employee birthday parties, and present ethical guidelines to your subordinates. In other words, you perform symbolic tasks that represent your organization.
	Leadership role	In your role of *leader,* you are responsible for the actions of your subordinates, as their successes and failures reflect on you. Your leadership is expressed in your decisions about training, motivating, and disciplining people.
	Liaison role	In your *liaison* role, you must act like a politician, working with other people outside your work unit and organization to develop alliances that will help you achieve your organization's goals.
Informational Managerial Roles	Monitor role	As a *monitor,* you should be constantly alert for useful information, whether gathered from newspaper stories about the competition or gathered from snippets of conversation with subordinates you meet in the hallway.
	Disseminator role	Workers complain they never know what's going on? That probably means their supervisor failed in the role of *disseminator.* Managers need to constantly disseminate important information to employees, as via e-mail and meetings.
	Spokesperson role	You are expected, of course, to be a diplomat, to put the best face on the activities of your work unit or organization to people outside it. This is the informational role of *spokesperson.*
Decisional Managerial Roles	Entrepreneur role	A good manager is expected to be an *entrepreneur,* to initiate and encourage change and innovation.
	Disturbance handler role	Unforeseen problems—from product defects to international currency crises—require you be a *disturbance handler,* fixing problems.
	Resource allocator role	Because you'll never have enough time, money, and so on, you'll need to be a resource *allocator,* setting priorities about use of resources.
	Negotiator role	To be a manager is to be a continual *negotiator,* working with others inside and outside the organization to accomplish your goals.

Did anyone say a manager's job is easy? Certainly it's not for people who want to sit on the sidelines of life. Above all else, managers are *doers.* ●

1.6 THE ENTREPRENEURIAL SPIRIT

Do I have what it takes to be an entrepreneur?

major question?

THE BIG PICTURE
Entrepreneurship, a necessary attribute of business, means taking risks to create a new enterprise. It is expressed through two kinds of innovators, the entrepreneur and the intrapreneur.

Yelp is the 2004 brainchild of Jeremy Stoppelman and Russel Simmons, two engineers in their twenties working for PayPal, the online payments firm in California's Silicon Valley, who wanted to make it easier for consumers to find good businesses and avoid bad ones. "What they created," says one account, "was an online yellow pages with attitude. Yelp lets anyone critique any business and grade it, with ratings from one star to five stars."[74] All kinds of businesses are rated, from restaurants to mechanics to dentists. While the idea of rating businesses is not new, Yelp uses a special algorithm (step-by-step problem-solving procedure) that determines which reviews are deleted, which featured prominently, and which displayed inconspicuously. And the company keeps the algorithm a closely guarded secret.

Starting Up a Startup: The Origins of Yelp

The idea for Yelp came to Stoppelman and Simmons over lunch one fall, when they talked about building a website for people to e-mail friends questions such as "Who knows a good auto mechanic in San Francisco?" and then posting the results online. But, as sometimes happens with new enterprises, the core idea—allowing people to publish reviews without being prompted—was an afterthought. Nevertheless, after lunch the pair went back to the office and successfully pitched their boss (who had made tens of millions on PayPal) to invest $1 million.

With this initial help, the Yelp founders were hoping to build momentum and launch a national company, but the idea failed to catch fire. After a few months, without any additional funding, the two decided they had to stay local. "If we just create a cool city guide to San Francisco and it's worth $10 or $20 million, that would be a win," Stoppelman said.

Entrepreneurs. Jeremy Stoppelman and Russel Simmons founded Yelp in San Francisco in 2004. Most people, even young people, prefer the security of a job with a paycheck rather than the risks of starting a business. Which life would you prefer?

To focus on making Yelp famous locally, they selected a few dozen of the most active reviewers on the site and invited them to an open-bar party; 100 people showed up. Yelp threw more parties for prolific reviewers, which gave casual users a reason to use the site more. By mid-2005, Yelp had 12,000 reviewers. With additional funding, it hired more party planners in New York, Chicago, and Boston. As the Yelp influence grew, bars and restaurants became more willing to host (for free) the parties in the hopes that crowds would come back and write favorable reviews. The company also began setting up call centers to sell advertising to businesses that had been reviewed.

Yelp is not without controversy. By encouraging consumers to be unsparing in their critiques, it helps good businesses to thrive, but it also empowers users to be unnecessarily cruel and to hurt small mom-and-pop businesses already struggling with economic hard times and strong competition. Still, the company seems to have achieved success, earning $27.4 million in the first three months of 2012, reflecting 66% growth from a year earlier.[75]

Entrepreneurship Defined: Taking Risks in Pursuit of Opportunity

Yelp in its early days represents one of the many small outfits in the United States that is one of the primary drivers of the nation's economy. Indeed, according to the Small Business Administration, small outfits create some 75% of all new jobs, represent 99.7% of all employers, and employ 50% of the private workforce.[76] (Note, however: Because many small firms fail, "new businesses are important to job creation primarily because they get founded," says entrepreneurial studies professor Scott Shane, "not because most of them tend to grow.")[77] Today women-owned businesses seem to be becoming America's new job-creation machine. One report projects that female-owned small businesses, which now provide only 16% of total U.S. employment, will be responsible for creating one-third of the jobs by 2018. This could transform the workplace by creating opportunities for other people, creating a positive working environment, and being more customer focused.[78]

Most small businesses originate with people like Stoppelman and Simmons. They are the entrepreneurs, the people with the idea, the risk takers. The most successful entrepreneurs become wealthy and make the covers of business magazines: Oprah Winfrey (Harpo Productions), Fred Smith (Federal Express), Anita Roddick (The Body Shop), Larry Page and Sergey Brin (Google). Failed entrepreneurs may benefit from the experience to live to fight another day—as did Henry Ford, twice bankrupt before achieving success with Ford Motor Co.

What Entrepreneurship Is *Entrepreneurship* **is the process of taking risks to try to create a new enterprise.** There are two types of entrepreneurship:

- **The entrepreneur. An *entrepreneur* is someone who sees a new opportunity for a product or service and launches a business to try to realize it.** Most entrepreneurs run small businesses with fewer than 100 employees.

- **The intrapreneur. An *intrapreneur* is someone who works inside an existing organization who sees an opportunity for a product or service and mobilizes the organization's resources to try to realize it.** This person might be a researcher or a scientist but could also be a manager who sees an opportunity to create a new venture that could be profitable.

An Intrapreneur: Marissa Mayer Develops a Researcher's Little Personal Program into Google News

Some products developed internally are the results of happy accidents. For instance, this was how Post-it Notes came about, the eventual result of an experimental adhesive discovered by 3M employee Art Fry, for which the company at first could find no use.

The Little Program That Could. At Google in 2001, following the terror attacks of 9/11, researcher Krishna Bharat wrote a little program to help him read news better, gathering news from his 15 favorite sources and using artificial intelligence to group them. After using the tool for his personal news reading, he offered it to some colleagues.

"The promise and excitement I felt when I first saw Krishna's tool was immense," says Marissa Mayer, then Google's Vice President of Search Products. "It wasn't impressive in that first form—a plain white page with small groups of five plain blue links per topic and only about 10 topics covered. But I could see immediately how we could make it into a polished online news experience."[79]

The Refinement Process. Eventually the program went through 64 different iterations before it was launched as Google News as a way to facilitate browsing between different sections such as sports, business, and entertainment, tapping into 4,000 news sources.

YOUR CALL

What companies are you aware of that do their own in-house research and development of products?

How Do Entrepreneurs & Managers Differ? While the entrepreneur is not necessarily an inventor, he or she "always searches for change, responds to it, and exploits it as an opportunity," Peter Drucker pointed out.[80] How does this differ from being a manager?

Being an entrepreneur is what it takes to *start* a business; being a manager is what it takes to *grow or maintain* a business. As an entrepreneur/intrapreneur, you initiate new goods or services; as a manager you coordinate the resources to produce the goods or services.

Some of the examples of success we have previously mentioned—Fred Smith and Anita Roddick—are actually *both* entrepreneurs and effective managers. Other people, however, find they like the startup part but hate the management part. For example, Stephen Wozniak, entrepreneurial cofounder with Steve Jobs of Apple Computer, abandoned the computer industry completely and went back to college. Jobs, by contrast, went on to launch another business, Pixar, which, among other things, became the animation factory that made the movies *Toy Story* and *Finding Nemo*.

Entrepreneurial companies have been called "gazelles" for the two attributes that make the African antelope successful: speed and agility. "Gazelles have mastered the art of the quick," says Alan Webber, founding editor of *Fast Company* magazine. "They have internal approaches and fast decision-making approaches that let them move with maximum agility in a fast-changing business environment."[81]

Green entrepreneur. South African–born Elon Musk became a lead investor and later CEO at Tesla Motors in Palo Alto, California, a company incorporated in 2003 to pursue mass production of an electric sports car. The Tesla Model S sedan runs on a lithium-ion battery, has a range of 300 miles on a single charge, and retails for a base price of $50,000. What is your passion that you might turn into a business?

Is this the kind of smart, innovative world you'd like to be a part of? Most people prefer the security of a job and a paycheck. Entrepreneurs do seem to have psychological characteristics that are different from managers, as follows:[82]

- **Characteristic of both—high need for achievement.** Both entrepreneurs and managers have a high need for achievement. However, entrepreneurs certainly seem to be motivated to pursue moderately difficult goals through their own efforts in order to realize their ideas and, they hope, financial rewards. Managers, by contrast, are more motivated by promotions and organizational rewards of power and perks.

- **Also characteristic of both—belief in personal control of destiny.** If you believe "I am the captain of my fate, the master of my soul," you have what is known as *internal locus of control,* **the belief that you control your own destiny,** that external forces will have little influence. (External locus of control means the reverse—you believe you don't control your destiny, that external forces do.) Both entrepreneurs and managers like to think they have personal control over their lives.

- **Characteristic of both, but especially of entrepreneurs—high energy level and action orientation.** Rising to the top in an organization probably requires that a manager put in long hours. For entrepreneurs, however, creating a new enterprise may require an extraordinary investment of time and energy. In addition, while some managers may feel a sense of urgency, entrepreneurs are especially apt to be impatient and to want to get things done as quickly as possible, making them particularly action oriented.

- **Characteristic of both, but especially of entrepreneurs—high tolerance for ambiguity.** Every manager needs to be able to make decisions based on ambiguous—that is, unclear or incomplete—information. However, entrepreneurs must have more tolerance for ambiguity because they are trying to do things they haven't done before.

- **More characteristic of entrepreneurs than managers—self-confidence and tolerance for risk.** Managers must believe in themselves and be willing to make decisions; however, this statement applies even more to entrepreneurs. Precisely because they are willing to take risks in the pursuit of new opportunities—indeed, even risk personal financial failure—entrepreneurs need the confidence to act decisively.

PepsiCo's Indra Nooyi. Are entrepreneurs and managers really two different breeds? India-born Nooyi, CEO of PepsiCo, has taken the lead in attempting to move the company away from fast food and sodas into more healthy foods.

Of course, not all entrepreneurs have this kind of faith in themselves. So-called *necessity* entrepreneurs are people such as laid-off corporate workers, discharged military people, immigrants, and divorced homemakers who suddenly must earn a living and are simply trying to replace lost income and are hoping a job comes along. In the United States, these make up about 28% of entrepreneurs. However, 51% are so-called *opportunity* entrepreneurs—those who start their own business out of a burning desire rather than because they lost a job. Unlike necessity types, they tend to be more ambitious and to start firms that can lead to high-growth businesses.[83]

Which do you think you would be happier doing—being an entrepreneur or being a manager? ●

1.7 THE SKILLS EXCEPTIONAL MANAGERS NEED

To be a terrific manager, what skills should I cultivate?

major question?

THE BIG PICTURE
Good managers need to work on developing three principal skills. The first is *technical,* the ability to perform a specific job. The second is *conceptual,* the ability to think analytically. The third is *human,* the ability to interact well with people.

Lower- and middle-level managers are a varied lot, but what do top managers have in common? A supportive spouse or partner, suggests one study.[84] Regardless of gender, reaching the top demands a person's all-out commitment to work and career, and someone needs to be there to help with children and laundry. Thus, 27 of 29 Fortune 500 female CEOs are married (but only 18 had children), and their husbands have been willing to defer their ambitions to their wives'—just as so many spouses of men have.

IBM CEO Virginia Rometty, who is married but has no children, has been assisted in her rise by her husband, Mark Rometty, who is principally an investor. Although female managers with supportive partners are becoming more common, society is still struggling with what it means for men and women to be peers and whether one's career should come first or both should be developed simultaneously.[85]

Whether or not they have support at home, aspiring managers also need to have other kinds of the "right stuff." In the mid-1970s, researcher **Robert Katz** found that through education and experience managers acquire three principal skills—*technical, conceptual,* and *human.*[86]

1. Technical Skills—The Ability to Perform a Specific Job

Virginia Rometty has a bachelor's degree in computer science and electrical engineering and a well-rounded résumé that includes not only being a systems engineer but also important experience in sales, services, and acquisitions as IBM shifted from selling hardware to selling business solutions. In 2002, she was key in integrating PricewaterhouseCoopers, a global professional services firm, into IBM, the company's largest deal ever at the time, working tirelessly to win over the new firm's consultants, an act deemed instrumental in IBM's transformation.[87] During the Great Recession, she was put in charge of IBM's nearly $100 billion in sales; in 2010, she added marketing and strategy to her responsibilities. She travels thousands of miles a year to attend to customers in China, India, Brazil, and Africa.

Technical skills consist of the job-specific knowledge needed to perform well in a specialized field. Having the requisite technical skills seems to be most important at the lower levels of management—that is, among employees in their first professional job and first-line managers.

2. Conceptual Skills—The Ability to Think Analytically

Conceptual skills are more important as you move up the management ladder. Rometty, for example, has been called a "serious, no-nonsense thinker," with "a very deep understanding of the company, and she's both an operational wiz and a marketing wiz."[88] While she does have a less serious side—she and her husband enjoy scuba diving and Broadway plays—she relishes the opportunity to take on large challenges. "IBM's long-standing mantra is 'Think,'" she told one audience. "What has always made IBM a fascinating and compelling place for me is the passion of the company,

IBM's headquarters. This office complex in Armonk, New York, is headquarters for most of IBM's enterprises, including CEO Virginia Rometty's office. Rometty seems to have the three skills—technical, conceptual, and human—necessary to be a terrific manager for such a complex organization. Which skill do you think you need to work on the most? (Human skills are the most difficult to master.)

and its people, to apply technology and scientific thinking to major societal issues."[89] Her priorities are to continue IBM's current growth initiatives around software that lets companies manage huge amounts of data to make better decisions and to achieve greater focus on emerging markets.[90]

***Conceptual skills* consist of the ability to think analytically, to visualize an organization as a whole and understand how the parts work together.** Conceptual skills are particularly important for top managers, who must deal with problems that are ambiguous but that could have far-reaching consequences.

3. Human Skills—The Ability to Interact Well with People

This may well be the most difficult set of skills to master. ***Human skills* consist of the ability to work well in cooperation with other people to get things done**—especially with people in teams, an important part of today's organizations (as we discuss in Chapter 13). Often these are thought of as "soft skills." These skills—the ability to motivate, to inspire trust, to communicate with others—are necessary for managers of all levels. But because of the range of people, tasks, and problems in an organization, developing your human-interacting skills may turn out to be an ongoing, lifelong effort.

During her three decades at IBM, Rometty has become highly regarded for her ability to expand relationships, to close a sale with companies ranging from State Farm Insurance to Prudential Financial. "She's an engaging woman—great with customers," says one of her former bosses. "Customers just love Ginni."[91] She "combines performance and charisma," says another fan. "She orchestrated a massive charm offensive to bring the PricewaterhouseCoopers people into the fold. That was a trial by fire for her."[92]

The Most Valued Traits in Managers

Clearly, Rometty embodies the qualities sought in star managers, especially top managers. "The style for running a company is different from what it used to be," says a top executive recruiter of CEOs. "Companies don't want dictators, kings, or emperors."[93] Instead of someone who gives orders, they want executives who ask probing questions and force the people beneath them to think and find the right answers.

Among the chief skills companies seek in top managers are the following:

- The ability to motivate and engage others.
- The ability to communicate.
- Work experience outside the United States.
- High energy levels to meet the demands of global travel and a 24/7 world.[94]

Let's see how you can begin to acquire these and other qualities for success. ●

Getting Control of Your Time: Dealing with the Information Deluge in College & in Your Career

Professionals and managers all have to deal with this central problem: how not to surrender their lives to their jobs. The place to start, however, is in college. If you can learn to manage time while you're still a student, you'll find it will pay off not only in higher grades and more free time but also in more efficient information-handling skills that will serve you well as a manager later on.[95]

Using Your "Prime Study Time"

Each of us has a different energy cycle.[96] The trick is to use it effectively. That way, your hours of best performance will coincide with your heaviest academic demands. For example, if your energy level is high during the mornings, you should plan to do your studying then.

To capitalize on your prime study time, you take the following steps: (1) Make a study schedule for the entire term, and indicate the times each day during which you plan to study. (2) Find some good places to study—places where you can avoid distractions. (3) Avoid time wasters, but give yourself frequent rewards for studying, such as a TV show, a favorite piece of music, or a conversation with a friend.

Improving Your Memory Ability

Memorizing is, of course, one of the principal requirements for succeeding in college. And it's a great help for success in life afterward.

Here are some tips on learning to concentrate:[97]

Choose What to Focus On

"People don't realize that attention is a finite resource, like money," one expert says. "Do you want to invest your cognitive cash on endless Twittering or Net surfing or couch potatoing [watching TV]?" She adds, "Where did the idea come from that anyone who wants to contact you can do so at any time? You need to take charge of what you pay attention to instead of responding to the latest stimuli."[98] For example, to block out noise, you can wear earplugs while reading, to create your own "stimulus shelter."

Devote the First 1½ Hours of Your Day to Your Most Important Task

Studying a hard subject? Make it your first task of the day, and concentrate on it for 90 minutes. After that, your brain will probably need a rest, and you can answer text messages, e-mail, and so on. But until that first break, don't do anything else, because it can take the brain 20 minutes to refocus.

Space Your Studying, Rather Than Cramming

Cramming—making a frantic, last-minute attempt to memorize massive amounts of material—is probably the least effective means of absorbing information. Research shows that it's best to space out your studying of a subject over successive days. A series of study sessions over several days is preferable to trying to do it all during the same number of hours on one day. It is repetition that helps move information into your long-term memory bank.

Review Information Repeatedly—Even "Overlearn It"

By repeatedly reviewing information—what is known as "rehearsing"—you can improve both your retention and your understanding of it. Overlearning is continuing to review material even after you appear to have absorbed it.

Use Memorizing Tricks

There are several ways to organize information so that you can retain it better. For example, you can make drawings or diagrams (as of the parts of a computer system). Some methods of establishing associations between items you want to remember are given in the box. (*See Exhibit 1.1.*)

exhibit 1.1 SOME MEMORIZING TRICKS

- **Mental and physical imagery:** Use your visual and other senses to construct a personal image of what you want to remember. Indeed, it helps to make the image humorous, action-filled, sexual, bizarre, or outrageous in order to establish a personal connection. Example: To remember the name of the 21st president of the United States, Chester Arthur, you might visualize an author writing the number "21" on a wooden chest. This mental image helps you associate chest (Chester), author (Arthur), and 21 (21st president).

- **Acronyms and acrostics:** An acronym is a word created from the first letters of items in a list. For instance, Roy G. Biv helps you remember the colors of the rainbow in order: red, orange, yellow, green, blue, indigo, violet. An acrostic is a phrase or sentence created from the first letters of items in a list. Fox example, *Every Good Boy Does Fine* helps you remember that the order of musical notes on the staff is E-G-B-D-F.

- **Location:** Location memory occurs when you associate a concept with a place or imaginary place. For example, you could learn the parts of a computer system by imagining a walk across campus. Each building you pass could be associated with a part of the computer system.
- **Word games:** Jingles and rhymes are devices frequently used by advertisers to get people to remember their products. You may recall the spelling rule "*I before E except after C or when sounded like A as in neighbor or weigh.*" You can also use narrative methods, such as making up a story.

How to Improve Your Reading Ability: The SQ3R Method

SQ3R stands for "survey, question, read, recite, and review."[99] The strategy behind it is to break down a reading assignment into small segments and master each before moving on. The five steps of the SQ3R method are as follows:

1. *Survey the chapter before you read it:* Get an overview of the chapter or other reading assignment before you begin reading it. If you have a sense of what the material is about before you begin reading it, you can predict where it is going. In this text, we offer on the first page of every chapter a list of the main heads and accompanying key questions. At the end of each chapter we offer a summary, which explains what the chapter's terms and concepts mean and why they are important.

2. *Question the segment in the chapter before you read it:* This step is easy to do, and the point, again, is to get you involved in the material. After surveying the entire chapter, go to the first segment—section, subsection, or even paragraph, depending on the level of difficulty and density of information. Look at the topic heading of that segment. In your mind, restate the heading as a question. In this book, following each section head we present a key question. An example in this chapter is "To be a terrific manager, what skills should I cultivate?"

   After you have formulated the question, go to steps 3 and 4 (read and recite). Then proceed to the next segment and restate the heading there as a question.

3. *Read the segment about which you asked the question:* Now read the segment you asked the question about. Read with purpose, to answer the question you formulated. Underline or color-mark sentences that you think are important, if they help you answer the question. Read this portion of the text more than once, if necessary, until you can answer the question. In addition, determine whether the segment covers any other significant questions, and

formulate answers to these, too. After you have read the segment, proceed to step 4. (Perhaps you can see where this is all leading. If you read in terms of questions and answers, you will be better prepared when you see exam questions about the material later.)

4. *Recite the main points of the segment:* Recite means "say aloud." Thus, you should speak out loud (or softly) the answer to the principal question or questions about the segment and any other main points.

5. *Review the entire chapter by repeating questions:* After you have read the chapter, go back through it and review the main points. Then, without looking at the book, test your memory by repeating the questions.

Clearly the SQ3R method takes longer than simply reading with a rapidly moving color marker or underlining pencil. However, the technique is far more effective because it requires your involvement and understanding. This is the key to all effective learning.

Learning from Lectures

Does attending lectures really make a difference? Research shows that students with grades of B or above were more apt to have better class attendance than students with grades of C- or below.[100]

Some tips for getting the most out of lectures:

Take Effective Notes by Listening Actively

Research shows that good test performance is related to good note taking.[101] And good note taking requires that you listen actively—that is, participate in the lecture process. Here are some ways to take good lecture notes:

- *Read ahead and anticipate the lecturer:* Try to anticipate what the instructor is going to say, based on your previous reading. Having background knowledge makes learning more efficient.

- *Listen for signal words:* Instructors use key phrases such as "The most important point is ...," "There are four reasons for ...," "The chief reason ...," "Of special importance ...," "Consequently ..." When you hear such signal phrases, mark your notes with a ! or *.

- *Take notes in your own words:* Instead of just being a stenographer, try to restate the lecturer's thoughts in your own words, which will make you pay attention more.

- *Ask questions:* By asking questions during the lecture, you necessarily participate in it and increase your understanding.

Review Your Notes Regularly

Make it a point to review your notes regularly—perhaps on the afternoon after the lecture, or once or twice a week. We cannot emphasize enough the importance of this kind of reviewing.

Key Terms Used in This Chapter

Summary

1.1 Management: What It Is, What Its Benefits Are

Management is defined as the pursuit of organizational goals *efficiently*, meaning to use resources wisely and cost-effectively, and *effectively*, meaning to achieve results, to make the right decisions, and to successfully carry them out to achieve the organization's goals.

1.2 Seven Challenges to Being an Exceptional Manager

The seven challenges are (1) managing for competitive advantage, which means an organization must stay ahead in four areas—being responsive to customers, innovating new products or services offering better quality, being more efficient; (2) managing for diversity among different genders, ages, races, and ethnicities; (3) managing for globalization, the expanding universe; (4) managing for computers and telecommunications—information technology; (5) managing for right and wrong, or ethical standards; (6) managing for sustainability; and (7) managing for your own happiness and life goals.

1.3 What Managers Do: The Four Principal Functions

The four management functions are represented by the abbreviation *POLC*: (1) *planning*—setting goals and deciding how to achieve them; (2) *organizing*—arranging tasks, people, and other resources to accomplish the work; (3) *leading*—motivating,

directing, and otherwise influencing people to work hard to achieve the organization's goals; and (4) *controlling*—monitoring performance, comparing it with goals, and taking corrective action as needed.

1.4 Pyramid Power: Levels & Areas of Management

Within an organization, there are managers at three levels: (1) *top managers* make long-term decisions about the overall direction of the organization and establish the objectives, policies, and strategies for it; (2) *middle managers* implement the policies and plans of their superiors and supervise and coordinate the activities of the managers below them; and (3) *first-line managers* make short-term operating decisions, directing the daily tasks of nonmanagement personnel. There are three types of organizations: (1) *for-profit*—formed to make money by offering products or services; (2) *nonprofit*—to offer services to some, but not to make a profit; and (3) *mutual-benefit*—voluntary collections of members created to advance members' interests.

1.5 Roles Managers Must Play Successfully

The Mintzberg study shows that, first, a manager relies more on verbal than on written communication; second, managers work long hours at an intense pace; and, third, a manager's work is characterized by fragmentation, brevity, and variety. Mintzberg concluded that managers play three broad roles: (1) *interpersonal*—figurehead, leader, and liaison; (2) *informational*—monitor, disseminator, and spokesperson; and (3) *decisional*—entrepreneur, disturbance handler, resource allocator, and negotiator.

1.6 The Entrepreneurial Spirit

Entrepreneurship, a necessary attribute of business, is the process of taking risks to create a new enterprise. Two types are (1) the *entrepreneur,* who sees a new opportunity for a product or service and launches a business to realize it; and (2) the *intrapreneur,* working inside an existing organization, who sees an opportunity for a product or service and mobilizes the organization's resources to realize it. Entrepreneurs start businesses, managers grow or

maintain them. Both (but especially entrepreneurs) have a high need for achievement, high energy level and action orientation, and tolerance for ambiguity. Entrepreneurs are more self-confident and have higher tolerance for risk.

1.7 The Skills Exceptional Managers Need

The three skills that exceptional managers cultivate are (1) *technical,* consisting of job-specific knowledge needed to perform well in a specialized field; (2) *conceptual,* consisting of the ability to think analytically, to visualize an organization as a whole, and to understand how the parts work together; and (3) *human,* consisting of the ability to work well in cooperation with other people in order to get things done.

Management in Action

Target Is Trying to Overcome the Problem of "Showrooming"

Target Corp. is tired of being used. In one of the starkest signs yet that the chain stores fear a new twist in shopping, Target is asking suppliers for help in thwarting "showrooming"—that is, when shoppers come in to see a product in person, only to buy it from a rival online, frequently at a lower price.

Last week in an urgent letter to vendors, the Minneapolis-based chain suggested that suppliers create special products that would set it apart from competitors and shield it from the price comparisons that have become so easy for shoppers to perform on their computers and smartphones. Where special products aren't possible, Target asked suppliers to help it match rivals' prices. It also said it might create a subscription service that would give shoppers a discount on regularly purchased merchandise.

"What we aren't willing to do is let online-only retailers use our brick and mortar stores as a showroom for their products and undercut our prices without making investments, as we do, to proudly display our brands," according to the letter, which was signed by Target Chief Executive Gregg Steinhafel and Kathee Tesija, Target's executive vice president of merchandising.

Showrooming is an increasing problem for chains ranging from Best Buy Co. to Barnes and Noble Inc., at the same time that it's a boon for Amazon.com Inc.

and other online retailers. This year [2011] store sales overall edged up 4.1% during the holiday shopping season, while online sales jumped 15%. And while online sales represent only 8% of total sales, that is up from 2% in 2000. . . .

Vendors are likely to have little choice but to play ball with Target because of its clout as the second-largest discount chain . . .

Target declined to comment other than to issue a statement saying it "has long prided itself on having truly collaborative vendor partnerships and we continually work with our vendors to remain competitive in the ever-evolving retail environment."

Some analysts said Target's new tactics are unlikely to reverse the showrooming trend, because they fail to address the root problems traditional retailers face. Online-only retailers have significantly lower labor costs and, at least for the time being, don't collect sales tax in most states.

More important, the growing competition from Amazon is based on a different business model entirely; Amazon can sell products so cheaply because it uses its other profitable units—such as cloud data storage and fees it charges others to sell on its website—to subsidize the rest of its business.

"The traditional retailers are still doing business the old way while Amazon has reinvented the model," says Sucharita Mulpuru, retail analyst at Forrester Research.

"Walmart and Target are willing to sell a few things at a loss. Amazon's whole business is a loss leader."

Consumer preferences are also moving to online. "That is where we're heading," said Adrianne Shapira, retail analyst at Goldman Sachs. "You can try and dance around it, but it's a fact."

Retailers like Target and industry giant Walmart Stores, Inc. have a lot of catching up to do, as analysts estimate their websites account for only 1% to 2% of their annual sales. . . .

This fall Target relaunched and upgraded its website, which has been operated by Amazon for the last decade. But the site crashed several times, most notably when shoppers rushed to buy a special line of items made by Italian fashion house Missoni.

Target has a long tradition of getting suppliers to provide exclusive products. It has teamed up for years with fashion designers to offer time-limited discount clothing collections, and it recently announced it will open a series of temporary boutiques featuring clothes, food, and home furnishings from popular regional stores.

FOR DISCUSSION

1. Do you engage in showrooming? If yes, describe why.

2. Which of the six managerial challenges discussed in this chapter is Target facing? Discuss.

3. Using Figure 1.1 as a guide, describe how Target is trying to overcome competition from Internet providers of similar products.

4. To what extent did Target display an entrepreneurial orientation while trying to combat showrooming? Explain.

5. If you were a consultant to Target, what would be your recommendation to overcome showrooming? Discuss.

Source: Excerpted from Ann Zimmerman, "Showdown Over 'Showrooms,'" *The Wall Street Journal*, January 23, 2012, pp. B1, B5. Copyright © 2012 by Dow Jones & Company, Inc. Reproduced with permission of Dow Jones & Company, Inc. via Copyright Clearance Center.

Self-Assessment

To What Extent Do You Possess an Entrepreneurial Spirit?

OBJECTIVES

1. To assess whether or not you have motivations, aptitudes, and attitudes possessed by entrepreneurs.

2. To consider whether or not you would like to start your own company.

INTRODUCTION

Earlier in the chapter we noted that small businesses are creating the majority of new jobs in the United States. We also discussed a variety of personal characteristics that differentiate managers from entrepreneurs. The overall goal of this exercise is for you to take a self-assessment that allows you to compare your motivations, aptitudes, and attitudes to those found in a sample of entrepreneurs from a variety of industries.

INSTRUCTIONS

Take an entrepreneurial self-assessment at **http://www.bdc.ca/EN/advice_centre/benchmarking_tools/Pages/entrepreneurial_self_assessment.aspx.** The quiz enables you to compare your motivation, aptitudes, and attitudes to a group of entrepreneurs.

QUESTIONS FOR DISCUSSION

1. To what extent are your motives, aptitudes, and attitudes similar to entrepreneurs? Explain.

2. Based on your results, where do you have the biggest gaps with entrepreneurs in terms of the individual motives, aptitudes, and attitudes?

3. What do these gaps suggest about your entrepreneurial spirit? Discuss.

4. Do these results encourage or discourage you from thinking about starting your own business? Explain.

To Delay or Not to Delay?

You have been hired by a vice president of a national company to create an employee attitude survey, to administer it to all employees, and to interpret the results. You have known this vice president for more than 10 years and have worked for her on several occasions. She trusts and likes you, and you trust and like her. You have completed your work and now are ready to present the findings and your interpretations to the vice president's management team. The vice president has told you that she wants your honest interpretation of the results, because she is planning to make changes based on the results. Based on this discussion, your report clearly identifies several strengths and weaknesses that need to be addressed. For example, employees feel that they are working too hard and that management does not care about providing good customer service. At the meeting you will be presenting the results and your interpretations to a group of 15 managers. You also have known most of these managers for at least 5 years.

You arrive to for the presentation armed with slides, handouts, and specific recommendations. Your slides are loaded on the computer, and most of the participants have arrived. They are drinking coffee and telling you how enthused they are about hearing your presentation. You also are excited to share your insights. Ten minutes before the presentation is set to begin, however, the vice president takes you out of the meeting room and says she wants to talk with you. The two of you go to another office, and she closes the door. She then tells you that her boss's boss decided to come to the presentation unannounced. She thinks that he is coming to the presentation to look solely for negative information in your report. He does not like the vice president and wants to replace her with one of his friends. If you present your results as planned, it will provide this individual with the information he needs to create serious problems for the vice president. Knowing this, the vice president asks you to find some way to postpone your presentation. You have 10 minutes to decide what to do.

SOLVING THE CHALLENGE

What would you do?

1. Deliver the presentation as planned.
2. Give the presentation but skip over the negative results.
3. Go back to the meeting room and announce that your spouse has had an accident at home and you must leave immediately. You tell the group that you just received this message and that you will contact the vice president to schedule a new meeting.
4. Invent other options. Discuss.

chapter 2

Management Theory
Essential Background for the Successful Manager

Major Questions You Should Be Able to Answer

2.1 Evolving Viewpoints: How We Got to Today's Management Outlook

Major Question: What's the payoff in studying different management perspectives, both yesterday's and today's?

2.2 Classical Viewpoint: Scientific & Administrative Management

Major Question: If the name of the game is to manage work more efficiently, what can the classical viewpoint teach me?

2.3 Behavioral Viewpoint: Behaviorism, Human Relations, & Behavioral Science

Major Question: To understand how people are motivated to achieve, what can I learn from the behavioral viewpoint?

2.4 Quantitative Viewpoints: Management Science & Operations Management

Major Question: If the manager's job is to solve problems, how might the two quantitative approaches help?

2.5 Systems Viewpoint

Major Question: How can the exceptional manager be helped by the systems viewpoint?

2.6 Contingency Viewpoint

Major Question: In the end, is there one best way to manage in all situations?

2.7 Quality-Management Viewpoint

Major Question: Can the quality-management viewpoint offer guidelines for true managerial success?

2.8 The Learning Organization in an Era of Accelerated Change

Major Question: Organizations must learn or perish. How do I build a learning organization?

Evidence-Based Management: An Attitude of Wisdom

"These days, there aren't any hot, new trends, just a lot of repackaged ones from the past," writes *Wall Street Journal* columnist Carol Hymowitz.[1] "Executives have been treated to an overdose of management guides that mostly haven't delivered what they promised. Many bosses have adopted them all, regardless of their company's business model, balance sheet, competition, employee bench strength, or any other unique qualities. They have become copycat managers, trying to find a one-stop, fix-it-all answer to their various problems."

How will you know if the next best-seller "fix-it-all" book is simply a recycling of old ideas? The answer is: You have to have studied history—the subject of this chapter.[2]

Management: Art or Science?

Is the practice of management an art or a science? Certainly it *can* be an art. Lots of top executives have no actual training in management—IBM CEO Virginia Rometty, discussed in Chapter 1, has a BS in computer science and electrical engineering, not business. Great managers, like great painters or actors, have the right mix of intuition, judgment, and experience.

But management is also a science. Rather than being performed in a seat-of-the-pants, make-it-up-as-you-go-along kind of way, management can be approached deliberately, rationally, systematically. That's what the scientific method is, after all—a logical process, embodying four steps: (1) You observe events and gather facts. (2) You pose a possible solution or explanation based on those facts. (3) You make a prediction of future events. (4) You test the prediction under systematic conditions.

Following the Evidence

The process of scientific reasoning underlies what is known as evidence-based management. *Evidence-based management*

means translating principles based on best evidence into organizational practice, bringing rationality to the decision-making process.[3] Evidence-based management embraces what Stanford business scholars Jeffrey Pfeffer and Robert Sutton call *an attitude of wisdom*. This is a mind-set that, first, is willing to set aside belief and conventional wisdom and to act on the facts and, second, has an unrelenting commitment to gathering information necessary to make informed decisions and to keeping pace with new evidence.[4]

"The way a good doctor or a good manager works," Sutton says, "is to act with knowledge while doubting what you know. So if a patient goes to a doctor, you hope the doctor would do two things: first look at the literature and make the best decision given what's available. Then actually track the progress of the treatment and see what unexpected side effects you're having and what things are working."[5]

Three Truths

Evidence-based management is based on three truths:

- **There are few really new ideas:** Most supposedly new ideas are old, wrong, or both.

- **True is better than new:** Effective managers are more interested in what is true than in what is new.

- **Doing well usually dominates:** Organizations that do simple, obvious, and even seemingly trivial things well will dominate competitors who search for "silver bullets and instant magic."

For Discussion Do you think managers are often driven by fads, by what they've read in the latest book or heard in the latest management seminar? Have you ever heard of a manager taking an experimental approach, as in trying out a new idea with an open mind to see what happens? How could you profit by taking an evidence-based approach to the ideas we will discuss in this chapter?

forecast | What's Ahead in This Chapter

This chapter gives you a short overview of the three principal *historical* perspectives or viewpoints on management—*classical, behavioral,* and *quantitative.* It then describes the three principal *contemporary* viewpoints—*systems, contingency,* and *quality-management.* Finally, we consider the concept of *learning organizations.*

What's the payoff in studying different management perspectives, both yesterday's and today's?

THE BIG PICTURE

After studying theory, managers may learn the value of practicing evidence-based management, bringing rationality to the decision-making process. This chapter describes two principal theoretical perspectives—the *historical* and the *contemporary*. Studying management theory provides understanding of the present, a guide to action, a source of new ideas, clues to the meaning of your managers' decisions, and clues to the meaning of outside events.

"The best way to predict the future is to create it," Peter Drucker said. The purpose of this book is, to the extent possible, to give you the tools to create your own future as a manager.

Who is **Peter Drucker**? "He was the creator and inventor of modern management," says management guru Tom Peters (author of *In Search of Excellence*). "In the early 1950s, nobody had a tool kit to manage these incredibly complex organizations that had gone out of control. Drucker was the first person to give us a handbook for that."[6]

An Austrian trained in economics and international law, Drucker came to the United States in 1937, where he worked as a correspondent for British newspapers and later became a college professor. In 1954, he published his famous text, *The Practice of Management,* in which he proposed that management was one of the major social innovations of the 20th century and that it should be treated as a profession, like medicine or law. In this and other books, he introduced several ideas that now underlie the organization and practice of management—that workers should be treated as assets, that the corporation could be considered a human community, that there is "no business without a customer," that institutionalized management practices were preferable to charismatic, cult leaders. Many ideas that you will encounter in this book—decentralization, management by objectives, knowledge workers—are directly traceable to Drucker's pen. "Without his analysis," says one writer, "it's almost impossible to imagine the rise of dispersed, globe-spanning corporations."[7]

Evidence-Based Management: Facing Hard Facts, Rejecting Nonsense

Evidence-based management, described in the Manager's Toolbox, while not invented by Drucker, is very much in the spirit of his rational approach to management. As mentioned, *evidence-based management* **means translating principles based on best evidence into organizational practice, bringing rationality to the decision-making process.**

As its two principal proponents, Stanford business scholars **Jeffrey Pfeffer and Robert Sutton,** put it, evidence-based management is based on the belief that "facing the hard facts about what works and what doesn't, understanding the dangerous half-truths that constitute so much conventional wisdom about management, and rejecting the total nonsense that too often passes for sound advice will help organizations perform better."[8] Learning to make managerial decisions based on evidence is the approach we hope you will learn to take after studying many other approaches—the perspectives described in this chapter.

Two Overarching Perspectives about Management: Historical & Contemporary

In this chapter, we describe two overarching perspectives about management:

- **Historical.** The *historical perspective* includes three viewpoints—*classical, behavioral,* and *quantitative.*
- **Contemporary.** The *contemporary perspective* also includes three viewpoints—*systems, contingency,* and *quality-management.*

Five Practical Reasons for Studying This Chapter

"Theory," say business professors Clayton Christensen and Michael Raynor, "often gets a bum rap among managers because it's associated with the word 'theoretical,' which connotes 'impractical.' But it shouldn't."[9] After all, what could be more practical than studying different approaches to see which work best?

Indeed, there are five good reasons for studying theoretical perspectives:

1. **Understanding of the present.** "Sound theories help us interpret the present, to understand what is happening and why," say Christensen and Raynor.[10] Understanding history will help you understand why some practices are still favored, whether for right or wrong reasons.

2. **Guide to action.** Good theories help you make predictions and enable you to develop a set of principles that will guide your actions.

3. **Source of new ideas.** They can also provide new ideas that may be useful to you when you come up against new situations.

4. **Clues to meaning of your managers' decisions.** They can help you understand your firm's focus, where the top managers are "coming from."

5. **Clues to meaning of outside events.** Finally, they may allow you to understand events outside the organization that could affect it or you. ●

EXAMPLE

Was Cisco's Experiment of 48 Decentralized "Management Councils" the Best Way to Organize a Company?

If Management 1.0 is what we're used to now, with its traditional pyramid hierarchy, what would Management 2.0 look like? What if, as management thinker Gary Hamel suggests, Management 2.0 looked a lot like Web 2.0 as represented in Wikipedia, YouTube, and other online communities?[11] Could the traditional hierarchy of boxes with lines actually become a corporate straitjacket? That's what John Chambers thought.

The Organization of the Future? The CEO of San Jose, California–based Cisco Systems, $36 billion maker of telecommunications gear, Chambers was concerned that large companies begin to slow down when they don't move out of their primary markets fast enough.[12] In order to expand into 30 different markets simultaneously, from flip video cameras to multimillion-dollar data centers, in 2005, Chambers established an unusual system of 48 interlocking management committees, or "councils," so

managers could make decisions without waiting for his approval. The idea was that managers would participate in different committees and make decisions collaboratively.[13]

Doing It Over. In 2011, however, Cisco abandoned the council-based structure. "By requiring employees to petition groups of people for department budgets, the councils slowed decision making," says one report. "It left managers without full control of units."[14] Now Cisco has just three management councils.

YOUR CALL

If the system of 48 management councils added bureaucracy and diluted managerial authority and accountability, what type of organizational arrangement would help Cisco act quicker and more flexibly? Do you think studying management theory could help you answer this question?

If the name of the game is to manage work more efficiently, what can the classical viewpoint teach me?

THE BIG PICTURE

The *three historical management viewpoints* we will describe include (1) the classical, described in this section; (2) the behavioral; and (3) the quantitative. The classical viewpoint, which emphasized ways to manage work more efficiently, had two approaches: (a) scientific management and (b) administrative management. *Scientific management,* pioneered by Frederick W. Taylor and Frank and Lillian Gilbreth, emphasized the scientific study of work methods to improve the productivity of individual workers. *Administrative management,* pioneered by Henri Fayol and Max Weber, was concerned with managing the total organization.

Bet you've never heard of a "therblig," although it may describe some physical motions you perform from time to time—as when you have to wash dishes, say. A made-up word you won't find in most dictionaries, *therblig* was coined by Frank Gilbreth and is, in fact, "Gilbreth" spelled backward, with the "t" and the "h" reversed. It refers to 1 of 17 basic motions. By identifying the therbligs in a job, as in the tasks of a bricklayer (which he had once been), Frank and his wife, Lillian, were able to eliminate motions while simultaneously reducing fatigue.

The Gilbreths were a husband-and-wife team of industrial engineers who were pioneers in one of the classical approaches to management, part of the historical perspective. As we mentioned, there are *three historical management viewpoints* or approaches. *(See Figure 2.1.)* They are

- Classical
- Behavioral
- Quantitative

In this section, we describe the classical perspective of management, which originated during the early 1900s. **The *classical viewpoint,* which emphasized finding ways to manage work more efficiently, had two branches—*scientific* and *administrative*—**each of which is identified with particular pioneering theorists. In general, classical management assumes that *people are rational.* Let's compare the two approaches.

Scientific Management: Pioneered by Taylor & the Gilbreths

The problem for which scientific management emerged as a solution was this: In the expansive days of the early 20th century, labor was in such short supply that managers were hard-pressed to raise the productivity of workers. **Scientific management emphasized the scientific study of work methods to improve the productivity of individual workers.** Two of its chief proponents were **Frederick W. Taylor** and the team of **Frank and Lillian Gilbreth.**

Frederick Taylor & the Four Principles of Scientific Management   No doubt there are some days when you haven't studied, or worked, as efficiently as you

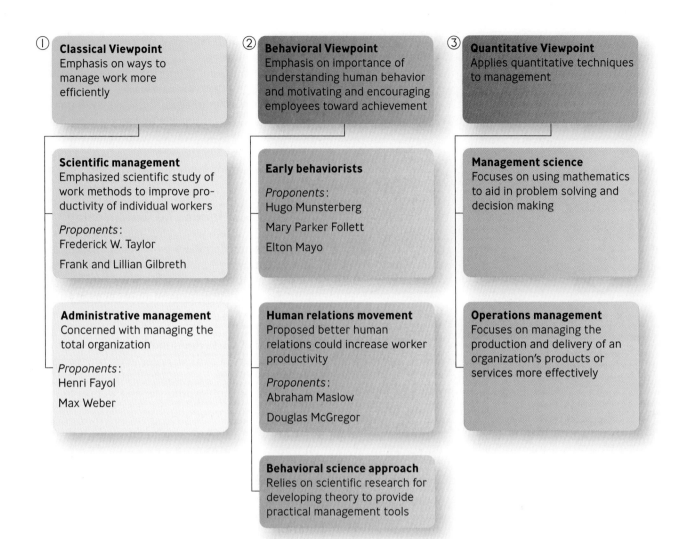

① **Classical Viewpoint**
Emphasis on ways to manage work more efficiently

② **Behavioral Viewpoint**
Emphasis on importance of understanding human behavior and motivating and encouraging employees toward achievement

③ **Quantitative Viewpoint**
Applies quantitative techniques to management

Scientific management
Emphasized scientific study of work methods to improve productivity of individual workers

Proponents:
Frederick W. Taylor

Frank and Lillian Gilbreth

Early behaviorists

Proponents:
Hugo Munsterberg

Mary Parker Follett

Elton Mayo

Management science
Focuses on using mathematics to aid in problem solving and decision making

Administrative management
Concerned with managing the total organization

Proponents:
Henri Fayol

Max Weber

Human relations movement
Proposed better human relations could increase worker productivity

Proponents:
Abraham Maslow

Douglas McGregor

Operations management
Focuses on managing the production and delivery of an organization's products or services more effectively

Behavioral science approach
Relies on scientific research for developing theory to provide practical management tools

figure 2.1 THE HISTORICAL PERSPECTIVE

Three viewpoints are shown. To see a time line, go to www.mhhe.com/kw6e.

Frederick W. Taylor. Called the father of scientific management, Taylor published *The Principles of Scientific Management* in 1911.

could. This could be called "underachieving," or "loafing," or what Taylor called it—*soldiering,* deliberately working at less than full capacity. Known as "the father of scientific management," Taylor was an American engineer from Philadelphia who believed that managers could eliminate soldiering by applying four principles of science:

1. Evaluate a task by scientifically studying each part of the task (not use old rule-of-thumb methods).
2. Carefully select workers with the right abilities for the task.
3. Give workers the training and incentives to do the task with the proper work methods.
4. Use scientific principles to plan the work methods and ease the way for workers to do their jobs.

Taylor based his system on *motion studies,* in which he broke down each worker's job—moving pig iron at a steel company, say—into basic physical motions and then trained workers to use the methods of their best-performing coworkers. In addition, he suggested employers institute a *differential rate system,* in which more efficient workers earned higher wages.

Why Taylor Is Important: Although "Taylorism" met considerable resistance from employees fearing that working harder would lead to lost jobs except for the highly productive few, Taylor believed that by raising production both labor and management could increase profits to the point where they no longer would have to quarrel over them. If used correctly, the principles of scientific management can enhance productivity, and such innovations as motion studies and differential pay are still used today.

Frank & Lillian Gilbreth & Industrial Engineering As mentioned, Frank and Lillian Gilbreth were a husband-and-wife team of industrial engineers who lectured at Purdue University in the early 1900s. Their experiences in raising 12 children—to whom they applied some of their ideas about improving efficiency (such as printing the Morse Code on the back of the bathroom door so that family members could learn it while doing other things)—later were popularized in a book, two movies, and a TV sitcom, *Cheaper by the Dozen.* The Gilbreths expanded on Taylor's motion studies—for instance, by using movie cameras to film workers at work in order to isolate the parts of a job.

Lillian Gilbreth, who received a PhD in psychology, was the first woman to be a major contributor to management science.

Lillian and Frank Gilbreth. These industrial engineers pioneered time and motion studies. If you're an athlete, you can appreciate how small changes can make you efficient.

Administrative Management: Pioneered by Fayol & Weber

Scientific management is concerned with the jobs of individuals. ***Administrative management* is concerned with managing the total organization.** Among the pioneering theorists were **Henri Fayol** and **Max Weber.**

Henri Fayol & the Functions of Management Fayol was not the first to investigate management behavior, but he was the first to systematize it. A French engineer and industrialist, he became known to American business when his most important work, *General and Industrial Management,* was translated into English in 1930.

Why Fayol Is Important: Fayol was the first to identify the major functions of management (p. 15)—planning, organizing, leading, and controlling, as well as coordinating—the first four of which you'll recognize as the functions providing the framework for this and most other management books.

Max Weber & the Rationality of Bureaucracy In our time, the word *bureaucracy* has come to have negative associations: impersonality, inflexibility, red tape, a molasseslike response to problems. But to German sociologist Max Weber, a *bureaucracy* was a rational, efficient, ideal organization based on principles of logic. After all, in Weber's Germany in the late 19th century, many people were in positions of authority (particularly in the government) not because of their abilities but because of their social status. The result, Weber wrote, was that they didn't perform effectively.

A better-performing organization, he indicated, should have five positive bureaucratic features:

1. A well-defined hierarchy of authority.
2. Formal rules and procedures.

3. A clear division of labor, with parts of a complex job being handled by specialists.

4. Impersonality, without reference or connection to a particular person.

5. Careers based on merit.

Why Weber Is Important: Weber's work was not translated into English until 1947, but it came to have an important influence on the structure of large corporations, such as the Coca-Cola Company.

The Problem with the Classical Viewpoint: Too Mechanistic

A flaw in the classical viewpoint is that it is mechanistic: It tends to view humans as cogs within a machine, not taking into account the importance of human needs. Behavioral theory addressed this problem, as we explain next.

Why the Classical Viewpoint Is Important: The essence of the classical viewpoint was that work activity was amenable to a rational approach, that through the application of scientific methods, time and motion studies, and job specialization it was possible to boost productivity. Indeed, these concepts are still in use today, the results visible to you every time you visit McDonald's or Pizza Hut. The classical viewpoint also led to such innovations as management by objectives and goal setting, as we explain elsewhere. ●

Scientific management. Carmakers have broken down automobile manufacturing into its constituent tasks, as shown here for a 2011 Dodge Avenger at a Chrysler assembly plant. This reflects the contributions of the school of scientific management. Is there anything wrong with this approach? How could it be improved?

To understand how people are motivated to achieve, what can I learn from the behavioral viewpoint?

THE BIG PICTURE

The second of the three historical management perspectives was the *behavioral* viewpoint, which emphasized the importance of understanding human behavior and of motivating employees toward achievement. The behavioral viewpoint developed over three phases: (1) *Early behaviorism* was pioneered by Hugo Munsterberg, Mary Parker Follett, and Elton Mayo. (2) The *human relations movement* was pioneered by Abraham Maslow (who proposed a hierarchy of needs) and Douglas McGregor (who proposed a Theory X and Theory Y view to explain managers' attitudes toward workers). (3) The *behavioral science approach* relied on scientific research for developing theories about behavior useful to managers.

The *behavioral viewpoint* **emphasized the importance of understanding human behavior and of motivating employees toward achievement.** The behavioral viewpoint developed over three phases: (1) early behaviorism, (2) the human relations movement, and (3) behavioral science.

Early Behaviorism: Pioneered by Munsterberg, Follett, & Mayo

The three people who pioneered behavioral theory were **Hugo Munsterberg, Mary Parker Follett,** and **Elton Mayo.**

Mary Parker Follett. She proposed that managers and employees should work together cooperatively.

Hugo Munsterberg & the First Application of Psychology to Industry
Called "the father of industrial psychology," German-born Hugo Munsterberg had a PhD in psychology and a medical degree and joined the faculty at Harvard University in 1892. Munsterberg suggested that psychologists could contribute to industry in three ways. They could:

1. Study jobs and determine which people are best suited to specific jobs.
2. Identify the psychological conditions under which employees do their best work.
3. Devise management strategies to influence employees to follow management's interests.

Why Munsterberg Is Important: His ideas led to the field of *industrial psychology,* the study of human behavior in workplaces, which is still taught in colleges today.

Mary Parker Follett & Power Sharing Among Employees & Managers
A Massachusetts social worker and social philosopher, Mary Parker Follett was lauded on her death in 1933 as "one of the most important women America has yet produced in the fields of civics and sociology." Instead of following the usual hierarchical

arrangement of managers as order givers and employees as order takers, Follett thought organizations should become more democratic, with managers and employees working cooperatively.

The following ideas were among her most important:

1. Organizations should be operated as "communities," with managers and subordinates working together in harmony.
2. Conflicts should be resolved by having managers and workers talk over differences and find solutions that would satisfy both parties—a process she called *integration*.
3. The work process should be under the control of workers with the relevant knowledge, rather than of managers, who should act as facilitators.

Why Follett Is Important: With these and other ideas, Follett anticipated some of today's concepts of "self-managed teams," "worker empowerment," and "interdepartmental teams"—that is, members of different departments working together on joint projects.

Elton Mayo & the Supposed "Hawthorne Effect"   Do you think workers would be more productive if they thought they were receiving special attention? This was the conclusion drawn by a Harvard research group in the late 1920s.

Conducted by Elton Mayo and his associates at Western Electric's Hawthorne (Chicago) plant, what came to be called the *Hawthorne studies* began with an investigation into whether workplace lighting level affected worker productivity. (This was the type of study that Taylor or the Gilbreths might have done.) In later experiments, other variables were altered, such as wage levels, rest periods, and length of workday. Worker performance varied but tended to increase over time,

Hawthorne effect. Western Electric's Hawthorne plant, where Elton Mayo and his team conducted their studies in the 1920s. Do you think you'd perform better in a robotlike job if you thought your supervisor cared about you and paid more attention to you?

leading Mayo and his colleagues to hypothesize what came to be known as the *Hawthorne effect*—namely, that employees worked harder if they received added attention, if they thought that managers cared about their welfare, and if supervisors paid special attention to them. However, later investigators found flaws in the studies, such as variations in ventilation and lighting or inadequate follow-through, that were overlooked by the original researchers. Critics also point out that it's doubtful that workers improved their productivity merely on the basis of receiving more attention rather than because of a particular instructional method or social innovation.[15]

Why the Hawthorne Studies Are Important: Ultimately, the Hawthorne studies were faulted for being poorly designed and not having enough empirical data to support the conclusions. Nevertheless, they succeeded in drawing attention to the importance of "social man" (social beings) and how managers using good human relations could improve worker productivity. This in turn led to the so-called human relations movement in the 1950s and 1960s.

The Human Relations Movement: Pioneered by Maslow & McGregor

The two theorists who contributed most to the **human relations movement—which proposed that better human relations could increase worker productivity**—were Abraham Maslow and Douglas McGregor.

Abraham Maslow & the Hierarchy of Needs

What motivates you to perform: Food? Security? Love? Recognition? Self-fulfillment? Probably all of these, Abraham Maslow would say, although some needs must be satisfied before others. The chairman of the psychology department at Brandeis University and one of the earliest researchers to study motivation, in 1943 Maslow proposed his famous *hierarchy of human needs:* physiological, safety, love, esteem, and self-actualization[16] (as we discuss in detail in Chapter 12, where we explain why Maslow is important).

Douglas McGregor & Theory X Versus Theory Y

Having been for a time a college president (at Antioch College in Ohio), Douglas McGregor came to realize that it was not enough for managers to try to be liked; they also needed to be aware of their attitudes toward employees.[17] Basically, McGregor suggested in a 1960 book, these attitudes could be either "X" or "Y."

Theory X represents a pessimistic, negative view of workers. In this view, workers are considered to be irresponsible, to be resistant to change, to lack ambition, to hate work, and to want to be led rather than to lead.

Theory Y represents the outlook of human relations proponents—an optimistic, positive view of workers. In this view, workers are considered to be capable of accepting responsibility, self-direction, and self-control and of being imaginative and creative.

Why Theory X/Theory Y Is Important: The principal contribution offered by the Theory X/Theory Y perspective is that it helps managers understand how their beliefs affect their behavior. For example, Theory X managers are more likely to micromanage, which leads to employee dissatisfaction, because they believe employees are inherently lazy. Managers can be more effective by considering how their behavior is shaped by their expectations about human nature. Underlying both Maslow's and McGregor's theories is the notion that more job satisfaction leads to greater worker performance—an idea that is somewhat controversial, as we'll discuss in Chapter 11.

The Behavioral Science Approach

The human relations movement was a necessary correction to the sterile approach used within scientific management, but its optimism came to be considered too simplistic for practical use. More recently, the human relations view has been superseded by the behavioral science approach to management. ***Behavioral science* relies on scientific research for developing theories about human behavior that can be used to provide practical tools for managers.** The disciplines of behavioral science include psychology, sociology, anthropology, and economics. ●

EXAMPLE

Application of Behavioral Science Approach: Which Is Better— Competition or Cooperation?

A widely held assumption among American managers is that "competition brings out the best in people." From an economic standpoint, business survival depends on staying ahead of the competition. But from an interpersonal standpoint, critics contend, competition has been overemphasized, primarily at the expense of cooperation.[18]

One strong advocate of greater emphasis on cooperation, Alfie Kohn, reviewed the evidence and found two reasons for what he sees as competition's failure:[19]

1. Competition Makes People Hostile. Success, he says, "often depends on sharing resources efficiently, and this is nearly impossible when people have to work against one another." Competition makes people suspicious and hostile toward each other. Cooperation, by contrast, "takes advantage of all the skills represented in a group as well as the mysterious process by which that group becomes more than the sum of its parts."

2. Competition Doesn't Necessarily Promote Excellence. "Trying to do well and trying to beat others simply are two different things," Kohn says. He points out the example of children in class who wave their arms to get the teacher's attention, but when they are finally recognized they then seem befuddled and ask the teacher to repeat the question—because they were more focused on beating their classmates than on addressing the subject matter.

What does the behavioral science research suggest about the question of cooperation versus competition? One team of researchers reviewed 122 studies encompassing a wide variety of subjects and settings and came up with three conclusions: (1) Cooperation is superior to competition in promoting achievement and productivity.

Promoting performance. This open office is designed to encourage spontaneous interaction, cooperation, and teamwork, which foster achievement and productivity among employees. The open layout is particularly favored by younger workers. Why do you think that is?

(2) Cooperation is superior to individualistic efforts in promoting achievement and productivity. (3) Cooperation without intergroup competition promotes higher achievement and productivity than cooperation with intergroup competition.[20]

YOUR CALL

What kind of office would you prefer to have for yourself— a private office, a shared private office, a partitioned cubicle, or a desk in an area scattered with other desks with no partitions? Which would be most comfortable for you personally? Why does the last one (the open office) best promote superior performance?

major question?

If the manager's job is to solve problems, how might the two quantitative approaches help?

THE BIG PICTURE

The third and last category under historical perspectives consists of *quantitative viewpoints,* which emphasize the application to management of quantitative techniques, such as statistics and computer simulations. Two approaches of quantitative management are *management science* and *operations management.*

During the air war known as the Battle of Britain in World War II, a relative few of England's Royal Air Force fighter pilots and planes were able to successfully resist the overwhelming might of the German military machine. How did they do it? Military planners drew on mathematics and statistics to determine how to most effectively allocate use of their limited aircraft.

When the Americans entered the war in 1941, they used the British model to form *operations research (OR)* teams to determine how to deploy troops, submarines, and other military personnel and equipment most effectively. For example, OR techniques were used to establish the optimum pattern that search planes should fly to try to locate enemy ships.

After the war, businesses also began using these techniques. One group of former officers, who came to be called the Whiz Kids, used statistical techniques at Ford Motor Co. to make better management decisions. Later Whiz Kid Robert McNamara, who had become Ford's president, was appointed Secretary of Defense and introduced similar statistical techniques and cost-benefit analyses throughout the Department of Defense. Since then, OR techniques have evolved into **quantitative management, the application to management of quantitative techniques, such as statistics and computer simulations. Two branches of quantitative management are** *management science* **and** *operations management.*

FedEx. What management tools do you use to schedule employees and aircraft to deal with wide variations in package volume—such as December 23 versus December 26?

Management Science: Using Mathematics to Solve Management Problems

How would you go about deciding how to assign utility repair crews during a blackout? Or how many package sorters you needed and at which times for an overnight delivery service such as FedEx or UPS? You would probably use the tools of management science.

Management science is not the same as Taylor's scientific management. **Management science focuses on using mathematics to aid in problem solving and decision making.** Sometimes management science is called *operations research.*

Why Management Science Is Important: Management science stresses the use of rational, science-based techniques and mathematical models to improve decision making and strategic planning. Its use is consistent with the practice of evidence-based management already discussed.

Management Science: Do Calorie Postings in Restaurants Change Eating Habits?

In July 2008, New York City required that restaurant chains post lists of calorie counts for menu items as a way of fighting obesity and diabetes. How well does the approach work?

Researchers tracked customers at several fast-food chains, such as McDonald's, in high-poverty New York City neighborhoods. They collected receipts two weeks before the calorie-posting law took effect and four weeks afterward (paying customers $2 each for their receipts). About half the customers noticed the posted calorie counts, with 28% of those who noticed saying the information influenced their ordering. But when receipts were examined, it was found that orders had a mean of 846 calories after the labeling law took place, compared with only 825 before.[21] Do calories matter? "I'm looking for the cheapest meal I can," said one customer.[22]

YOUR CALL

If, as a restaurant manager, one of your goals is to discourage obesity, do you think the study is useful? Do low-income people not care about calories? Was the study done too soon and failed to capture behavior change that might occur gradually?

Operations Management: Being More Effective

Operations management **focuses on managing the production and delivery of an organization's products or services more effectively.** Operations management is concerned with work scheduling, production planning, facilities location and design, and optimum inventory levels.

Why Operations Management Is Important: Through the rational management of resources and distribution of goods and services, operations management helps ensure that business operations are efficient and effective. ●

Operations Management: Was Toyota's "Lean Management" the Right Approach?

Over the years, Toyota Motor Corp. developed a variety of production techniques that drew in part on operations management.[23] First, it emphasized the smoothest possible *flow of work*. To accomplish this, managers performed *value stream mapping*, identifying the many steps in a production process and eliminating unnecessary ones. They also performed *mistake proofing* or *root-cause analysis*, using teamwork to examine problems and fix them as soon as they appeared. In addition, the carmaker helped pioneer the *just-in-time* approach to obtaining supplies from vendors only as they were needed in the factory. These efficient techniques, which all come under the term *lean management*, enabled Toyota to sell its cars on the basis of their superior quality.[24]

Strategy Change. Then in 1995 the company launched an all-out effort to become the world's largest carmaker. To do so, it opted to use common parts among eight types of cars (Camry, Corolla, Avalon, and others) and to buy them from companies around the globe instead of from its small group of longtime Japanese suppliers. Design engineers may also have cut corners, as by relying on computer simulations rather than building physical prototypes.[25]

Accidents. Suddenly, beginning in 2004, disturbing reports surfaced about Toyota cars running away because of sudden, unintended acceleration.[26] A research firm documented 2,274 similar incidents, including 18 fatalities.[27] In late 2009, thinking the problem was pedals catching on floor mats, Toyota recalled 4.3 million vehicles. Then, in early 2010, suspecting the problem was in the accelerator mechanism itself, it recalled 2.3 million vehicles and completely stopped new production of eight vehicle lines in North America.[28]

YOUR CALL

In Chapter 1, we described the problem of "efficiency versus effectiveness." Which is lean management mostly about? Can a worldwide car company get back to its roots—reclaim bragging rights to "quality"?

How can the exceptional manager be helped by the systems viewpoint?

THE BIG PICTURE

Three contemporary management perspectives are (1) the systems, (2) the contingency, and (3) the quality-management viewpoints. The systems viewpoint sees organizations as a system, either open or closed, with inputs, outputs, transformation processes, and feedback. The systems viewpoint has led to the development of complexity theory, the study of how order and pattern arise from very complicated, apparently chaotic systems. The contingency viewpoint emphasizes that a manager's approach should vary according to the individual and environmental situation. The quality-management viewpoint has two traditional approaches: quality control, the strategy for minimizing errors by managing each stage of production, and quality assurance, which focuses on the performance of workers, urging employees to strive for zero defects. A third quality approach is the movement of total quality management (TQM), a comprehensive approach dedicated to continuous quality improvement, training, and customer satisfaction.

Being of a presumably practical turn of mind, could you run an organization or a department according to the theories you've just learned? Probably not. The reason: People are complicated. To be an exceptional manager, you need to learn to deal with individual differences in a variety of settings.

Thus, to the historical perspective on management (classical, behavioral, and quantitative viewpoints), let us now add the *contemporary perspective,* which consists of three viewpoints. *(See Figure 2.2.)* These consist of:

- Systems
- Contingency
- Quality-management

In this section, we discuss the systems viewpoint.

The Systems Viewpoint	The Contingency Viewpoint	The Quality-Management Viewpoint
Regards the organization as systems of interrelated parts that operate together to achieve a common purpose	Emphasizes that a manager's approach should vary according to—i.e., be contingent on—the individual and environmental situation	Three approaches

Quality control	Quality assurance	Total quality management
Strategy for minimizing errors by managing each state of production	Focuses on the performance of workers, urging employees to strive for "zero defects"	Comprehensive approach dedicated to continuous quality improvement, training, and customer satisfaction
Proponent: Walter Shewart		*Proponents:* W. Edwards Deming, Joseph M. Juran

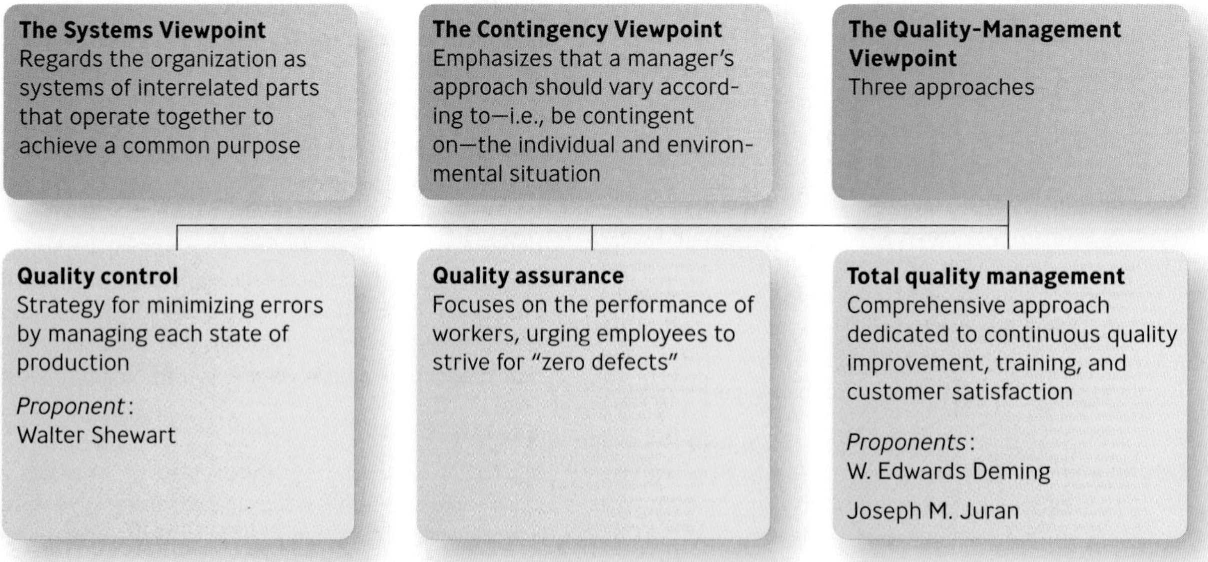

figure 2.2 THE CONTEMPORARY PERSPECTIVE
Three viewpoints.

The Systems Viewpoint

The 52 bones in the foot. The monarchy of Great Britain. A weather storm front. Each of these is a system. **A *system* is a set of interrelated parts that operate together to achieve a common purpose.** Even though a system may not work very well—as in the inefficient way the Russian government collects taxes, for example—it is nevertheless still a system.

The *systems viewpoint* regards the organization as a system of interrelated parts. By adopting this point of view, you can look at your organization both as (1) a collection of *subsystems*—**parts making up the whole system**—and (2) a part of the larger environment. A college, for example, is made up of a collection of academic departments, support staffs, students, and the like. But it also exists as a system within the environment of education, having to be responsive to parents, alumni, legislators, nearby townspeople, and so on.

The Four Parts of a System

The vocabulary of the systems perspective is useful because it gives you a way of understanding many different kinds of organizations. The four parts of a system are defined as follows:

1. ***Inputs* are the people, money, information, equipment, and materials required to produce an organization's goods or services.** Whatever goes into a system is an input.

2. ***Transformation processes* are the organization's capabilities in management, internal processes, and technology that are applied to converting inputs into outputs.** The main activity of the organization is to transform inputs into outputs.

3. ***Outputs* are the products, services, profits, losses, employee satisfaction or discontent, and the like that are produced by the organization.** Whatever comes out of the system is an output.

4. ***Feedback* is information about the reaction of the environment to the outputs that affects the inputs.** Are the customers buying or not buying the product? That information is feedback.

The four parts of a system are illustrated below. *(See Figure 2.3.)*

figure 2.3
THE FOUR PARTS OF A SYSTEM

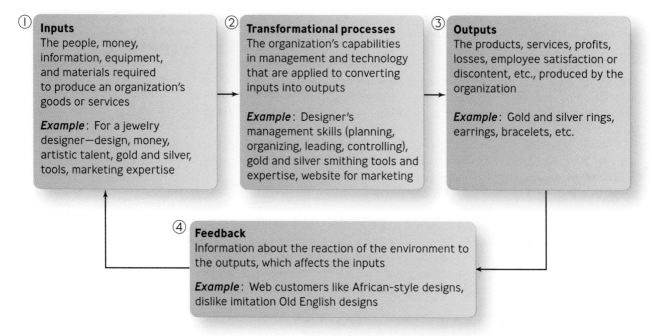

① **Inputs**
The people, money, information, equipment, and materials required to produce an organization's goods or services

Example: For a jewelry designer—design, money, artistic talent, gold and silver, tools, marketing expertise

② **Transformational processes**
The organization's capabilities in management and technology that are applied to converting inputs into outputs

Example: Designer's management skills (planning, organizing, leading, controlling), gold and silver smithing tools and expertise, website for marketing

③ **Outputs**
The products, services, profits, losses, employee satisfaction or discontent, etc., produced by the organization

Example: Gold and silver rings, earrings, bracelets, etc.

④ **Feedback**
Information about the reaction of the environment to the outputs, which affects the inputs

Example: Web customers like African-style designs, dislike imitation Old English designs

Open & Closed Systems   Nearly all organizations are, at least to some degree, open systems rather than closed systems. **An *open system* continually interacts with its environment. A *closed system* has little interaction with its environment;** that is, it receives very little feedback from the outside. The classical management viewpoint often considered an organization a closed system. So does the management science perspective, which simplifies organizations for purposes of analysis. However, any organization that ignores feedback from the environment opens itself up to possibly spectacular failures.

Complexity Theory: The Ultimate Open System   The systems viewpoint has led to the development of *complexity theory,* the **study of how order and pattern arise from very complicated, apparently chaotic systems.** Complexity theory recognizes that all complex systems are networks of many interdependent parts that interact with each other according to certain simple rules. Used in strategic management and organizational studies, the discipline seeks to understand how organizations, considered as relatively simple and partly connected structures, adapt to their environments.

Why the Systems Viewpoint—Particularly the Concept of Open Systems—Is Important: History is full of accounts of products that failed (such as the 1959 Ford Edsel) because they were developed in closed systems and didn't have sufficient feedback. Open systems stress multiple feedback from both inside and outside the organization, resulting in a continuous learning process to try to correct old mistakes and avoid new ones.   ●

EXAMPLE

Closed Versus Open Systems: When Netflix Didn't Listen

Netflix was created in in 1997 in Scotts Valley, California, after one of its founders, Reed Hastings, incurred a six-weeks-late fee of $40 on a videotape of *Apollo 13* that he had rented from a video store. His "better idea" startup was launched with the idea of consumers paying a monthly subscription rate, which entitled them to order DVDs via a website and receive and return them by mail; there were no late fees. Later, Netflix coupled DVDs by mail with unlimited Internet video streaming for $10 per month.

By 2005, the firm's stock was trading in the $11 range. Six years later, having weathered challenges from Blockbuster Video, which went bankrupt, Netflix had 25 million customers, and its stock was up to $304.

Closed System: The Company That Didn't Listen. In July 2011, with no consumer feedback, Netflix announced price increases of as much as 60%, a move intended to force subscribers to drop the DVDs by mail in favor of an $8-per-month streaming plan. Customers responded with outrage, canceling their subscriptions in greater numbers than expected, about a million in total, causing the stock to drop 19%.[29] Then Netflix made them even angrier by announcing it was splitting the company into two distinct units—an online streaming video service

to keep the name Netflix and a new DVD-by-mail rental service to be called Qwikster.[30] Netflix lost 2.76 million DVD customers in the last 3 months of 2011, its market value plunged by 75%, and it abandoned its plans to have DVDs sent by Qwikster.[31]

Open System: The Company That Listened. Still, Netflix was doing something right. All along, it had watched the numbers increase on new streaming subscribers—including a larger than expected 220,000 subscribers in the United States. Worldwide, subscribers also were up, to 26.3 million in early 2012—and Netflix DVD-by-mail rentals, which were offered only in the United States, increased only slightly. "The global opportunity for streaming TV shows and movies becomes more compelling every year with the rise of smart TVs and faster broadband," the company said in a letter to shareholders.[32]

YOUR CALL

"Sometimes you have to destroy your business in order to save it," says financial writer James Surowiecki."[33] Do you agree? Do you think Netflix was actually looking at the right set of data all along in making its decisions—that is, operating as an open system? What should it have done to head off the public relations disaster it experienced?

2.6 CONTINGENCY VIEWPOINT

In the end, is there one best way to manage in all situations? | major question ?

THE BIG PICTURE
The second viewpoint in the contemporary perspective, the contingency viewpoint, emphasizes that a manager's approach should vary according to the individual and environmental situation.

The classical viewpoints advanced by Taylor and Fayol assumed that their approaches had universal applications—that they were "the one best way" to manage organizations. The contingency viewpoint began to develop when managers discovered that under some circumstances better results could be achieved by breaking the one-best-way rule. **The *contingency viewpoint* emphasizes that a manager's approach should vary according to—that is, be contingent on—the individual and the environmental situation.**

A manager subscribing to the Gilbreth approach might try to get workers to be more productive by simplifying the steps. A manager of the Theory X/Theory Y persuasion might try to use motivational techniques. But the manager following the contingency viewpoint would simply ask, "What method is the best to use under these particular circumstances?"

EXAMPLE

The Contingency Viewpoint: What Incentives Work in Lean Times?

Americans of all ages and incomes have grown increasingly unhappy at work, with only 52% of 1,546 adults saying in one recent survey that they felt valued on the job and a third saying they intended to seek work elsewhere within the year.[34] Among the reasons: pay cuts, uninteresting jobs, heavy workloads, and high health insurance costs.[35] So how, in hard economic times, is a manager to motivate nonovertime-earning workers (those remaining after layoffs) to get them to produce more when raises, bonuses, and benefits are frozen?

Quirky Perks. "Pet insurance, at-your-desk meditation services, jewelry discounts, and funeral planning," says one article, "from the quirky to the somber, workplaces are providing a range of unique benefits."[36] Other options: drop-off laundry services, cellphone plan discounts, at-work massages, free theme park tickets, even adoption assistance.

Small Rewards. At Iowa-based aerospace electronics firm Rockwell Collins, manager Jenny Miller persuaded 20 overworked engineers to come in Thanksgiving weekend to meet a deadline to deliver software to a customer. Her lures? Free lunch and $100 gift cards.

At Ford Motor Co., managers use thank-you notes as rewards. At Ohio drug maker Sanofi-Aventis, one manager "e-mails employees to recognize even small accomplishments, and strategically copies higher-ups," says one account.[37]

Another way to increase productivity: screen employees' tasks to remove "discretionary work"—such as internal reports that can be reduced or delayed—in favor of higher priority work. The mix of approaches represents the contingency viewpoint.

YOUR CALL
What other inexpensive ways of improving productivity can you think of? What theories do the approaches just described seem to represent?

Contingency approach. Giving employees more money is not the only way to motivate them to be more productive. Sometimes small rewards, such as a free lunch, are equally effective. Would it make a difference to you if your boss showed appreciation of your efforts even in small ways—as by sending you a thank-you note?

Gary Hamel: Management Ideas Are Not Fixed, They're a Process

Discussion of the contingency viewpoint leads us naturally to the thoughts of **Gary Hamel,** cofounder of the Management Innovation Lab and ranked by *The Wall Street Journal* in 2008 as the most influential business thinker.[38] "Over time," he says, "every great invention, management included, travels a road that leads from birth to maturity, and occasionally to senescence."[39] Hamel holds that much of management theory is dated and doesn't fit the current realities of organizational life and that management innovation is essential to future organizational success. Indeed, he suggests, what we need to do is look at management as a *process,* and then make improvements and innovation ongoing and systematic. After all, if managers now innovate by creating new products or new business strategies, why can't they be equally innovative in how they manage their companies?

How do forward-looking managers get the ball rolling in management innovation, particularly in a traditional, conventional company? Hamel believes that the answer can be found by identifying core beliefs that people have about the organization, especially those that detract from the pursuit of management innovation. He suggests that these beliefs can be rooted out by repeatedly asking the right questions—namely, the following:

1. Is this a belief worth challenging? Is it debilitating? Does it get in the way of an important organizational attribute that we'd like to strengthen?

2. Is this belief universally valid? Are there counterexamples? If so, what do we learn from those cases?

3. How does this belief serve the interests of its adherents? Are there people who draw reassurance or comfort from this belief?

4. Have our choices and assumptions conspired to make this belief self-fulfilling? Is this belief true simply because we have made it true—and, if so, can we imagine alternatives?[40]

Why the Contingency Viewpoint Is Important: The contingency viewpoint would seem to be the most practical of the viewpoints discussed so far because it addresses problems on a case-by-case basis and varies the solution accordingly. ●

PRACTICAL ACTION

Mindfulness over Mindlessness: Learning to Take a Contingency Point of View

"Be flexible." Isn't that what we're told?

Throughout your career, you will have to constantly make choices about how to solve various problems—which tools to apply, including the theories described in this chapter. However, one barrier to being flexible is *mindlessness*. Instead we need to adopt the frame of mind that Harvard psychology professor Ellen Langer has called *mindfulness,* a form of active engagement.[41]

We've all experienced mindlessness. We misplace our keys. We write checks in January with the previous year's date. Mindlessness is characterized by the three following attributes.

Mindlessness #1: Entrapment in Old Categories

An avid tennis player, Langer says that at a tennis camp she, like all other students, was taught *exactly* how to hold her racquet and toss the ball when making a serve. But later, when watching a top tennis championship, she observed that none of the top players served the way she was taught and all served slightly differently.[42]

The significance: There is no one right way of doing things. In a conditional, or mindful, way of teaching, an instructor doesn't say, "This is THE answer," but rather, "This is ONE answer." Thus, all information—even in the hard sciences and mathematics, where it may seem as though there is just one correct answer—should be regarded with open-mindedness, because there may be exceptions. That is, you should act as though the information is true only for certain uses or under certain circumstances.

Mindlessness #2: Automatic Behavior

Langer tells of the time she used a new credit card in a department store. Noticing that Langer hadn't signed the card yet, the cashier returned it to her to sign the back. After passing the credit card through the imprinting machine, the clerk handed her the credit card receipt to sign, which Langer did. Then, says Langer, the cashier "held the form next to the newly signed card to see if the signatures matched."[43]

In automatic behavior, we take in and use limited signals from the world around us without letting other signals penetrate as well. By contrast, mindfulness is being open to new information—including that not specifically assigned to you. Mindfulness requires you to engage more fully in whatever it is you're doing.

Mindlessness #3: Acting from a Single Perspective

Most people, says Langer, typically assume that other peoples' motives and intentions are the same as theirs. For example, she says, "If I am out running and see someone walking briskly, I assume she is trying to exercise and would run if only she could," when actually she may be intending to get her exercise from walking.

For most situations, many interpretations are possible. "Every idea, person, or object is potentially simultaneously many things depending on the perspective from which it is viewed," says Langer.[44] Trying out different perspectives gives you *more choices in how to respond;* a single perspective that produces an automatic reaction reduces your options.

YOUR CALL

Developing mindfulness means consciously adapting: Being open to novelty. Being alert to distinctions. Being sensitive to different contexts. Being aware of multiple perspectives. Being oriented in the present. Picking just one of these characteristics, what would you do to try to become better at it?

Can the quality-management viewpoint offer guidelines for true managerial success?

THE BIG PICTURE

The quality-management viewpoint, the third category under contemporary perspectives, consists of *quality control, quality assurance,* and especially the movement of *total quality management (TQM)*, dedicated to continuous quality improvement, training, and customer satisfaction.

At one time in the 20th century, word got around among buyers of American cars that one shouldn't buy a "Monday car" or a "Friday car"—cars built on the days when absenteeism and hangovers were highest among dissatisfied autoworkers. The reason, supposedly, was that, despite the efforts of quantitative management, the cars produced on those days were the most shoddily made of what were coming to look like generally shoddy products.

The energy crisis of the 1970s showed different possibilities, as Americans began to buy more fuel-efficient cars made in Japan. Consumers found they could not only drive farther on a gallon of gas but that the cars were better made and needed repair less often. Eventually American car manufacturers began to adopt Japanese methods, leading to such slogans as "At Ford, Quality Is Job One." Today the average American car lasts much longer than it used to, and some U.S. cars are equal or superior to the best foreign competitors—for example, the 2011 Cadillac CTS-V Coupe beat the 2011 BMW M3 Coupe, according to one automotive review.[45]

Although not a "theory" as such, the **quality-management viewpoint, which includes quality control, quality assurance, and total quality management,** deserves to be considered because of the impact of this kind of thinking on contemporary management perspectives.

Quality Control & Quality Assurance

Quality refers to the total ability of a product or service to meet customer needs. Quality is seen as one of the most important ways of adding value to products and services, thereby distinguishing them from those of competitors. Two traditional strategies for ensuring quality are *quality control* and *quality assurance.*

Quality Control *Quality control* **is defined as the strategy for minimizing errors by managing each stage of production.** Quality control techniques were developed in the 1930s at Bell Telephone Labs by **Walter Shewart,** who used statistical sampling to locate errors by testing just some (rather than all) of the items in a particular production run.

Quality Assurance Developed in the 1960s, *quality assurance* **focuses on the performance of workers, urging employees to strive for "zero defects."** Quality assurance has been less successful because often employees have no control over the design of the work process.

Total Quality Management: Creating an Organization Dedicated to Continuous Improvement

In the years after World War II, the imprint "Made in Japan" on a product almost guaranteed that it was cheap and flimsy. That began to change with the arrival in Japan of two Americans, **W. Edwards Deming** and **Joseph M. Juran.**

W. Edwards Deming   Desperate to rebuild its war-devastated economy, Japan eagerly received mathematician W. Edwards Deming's lectures on "good management." Deming believed that quality stemmed from "constancy of purpose"—steady focus on an organization's mission—along with statistical measurement and reduction of variations in production processes. He also thought that managers should stress teamwork, be helpful rather than simply give orders, and make employees feel comfortable about asking questions.

In addition, Deming proposed his so-called 85–15 rule—namely, when things go wrong, there is an 85% chance that the system is at fault, only a 15% chance that the individual worker is at fault. (The "system" would include not only machinery and equipment but also management and rules.) Most of the time, he thought, managers erroneously blamed individuals rather than the system.

TQM pioneer. W. Edwards Deming in 1961.

Joseph M. Juran   Another pioneer with Deming in Japan's quality revolution was Joseph M. Juran, who defined quality as "fitness for use." By this he meant that a product or service should satisfy a customer's real needs. Thus, the best way to focus a company's efforts, Juran suggested, was to concentrate on the real needs of customers.

TQM: What It Is   From the work of Deming and Juran has come the strategic commitment to quality known as total quality management. ***Total quality management (TQM) is a comprehensive approach—led by top management and supported throughout the organization—dedicated to continuous quality improvement, training, and customer satisfaction.***
The four components of TQM are as follows:

1. **Make continuous improvement a priority.** TQM companies are never satisfied. They make small, incremental improvements an everyday priority in all areas of the organization. By improving everything a little bit of the time all the time, the company can achieve long-term quality, efficiency, and customer satisfaction.

2. **Get every employee involved.** To build teamwork, trust, and mutual respect, TQM companies see that every employee is involved in the continuous improvement process. This requires that workers must be trained and empowered to find and solve problems.

3. **Listen to and learn from customers and employees.** TQM companies pay attention to their customers, the people who use their products or services. In addition, employees within the companies listen and learn from other employees, those outside their own work areas.

4. **Use accurate standards to identify and eliminate problems.** TQM organizations are always alert to how competitors do things better, then try to improve on them—a process known as *benchmarking*. Using these standards, they apply statistical measurements to their own processes to identify problems.

Why Total Quality Management Is Important: The total quality management viewpoint emphasizes infusing concepts of quality throughout the total organization in a way that will deliver quality products and services to customers. The adoption of TQM helped American companies deal with global competition.

We return to TQM, along with such concepts as benchmarking, reduced cycle time, ISO 9000, and Six Sigma, in Chapter 16. ●

Organizations must learn or perish. How do I build a learning organization?

THE BIG PICTURE

Learning organizations actively create, acquire, and transfer knowledge within themselves and are able to modify their behavior to reflect new knowledge. There are three ways you as a manager can help build a learning organization.

Ultimately, the lesson we need to take from the theories, perspectives, and viewpoints we have described is this: We need to keep on learning. Organizations are the same way: Like people, they must continually learn new things or face obsolescence. A key challenge for managers, therefore, is to establish a culture that will enhance their employees' ability to learn—to build so-called learning organizations.

Learning organizations, says Massachusetts Institute of Technology professor **Peter Senge,** who coined the term, are places "where people continually expand their capacity to create the results they truly desire, where new and expansive patterns of thinking are nurtured, where collective aspiration is set free, and where people are continually learning how to learn together."[46]

The Learning Organization: Handling Knowledge & Modifying Behavior

More formally, a *learning organization* **is an organization that actively creates, acquires, and transfers knowledge within itself and is able to modify its behavior to reflect new knowledge.**[47] Note the three parts:

1. **Creating and acquiring knowledge.** In learning organizations, managers try to actively infuse their organizations with new ideas and information, which are the prerequisites for learning. They acquire such knowledge by constantly scanning their external environments, by not being afraid to hire new talent and expertise when needed, and by devoting significant resources to training and developing their employees.

2. **Transferring knowledge.** Managers actively work at transferring knowledge throughout the organization, reducing barriers to sharing information and ideas among employees. Electronic Data Systems (EDS), for instance, practically invented the information-technology services industry, but by 1996 it was slipping behind competitors—missing the onset of the Internet wave, for

The learning organization. In rigid organizations, employees often keep information to themselves. In learning organizations, workers are encouraged to share information with each other—both inside and outside their department.

example. When a new CEO, Dick Brown, took the reins in 1999, he changed the culture from "fix the problem yourself" to sharing information internally.[48]

3. **Modifying behavior.** Learning organizations are nothing if not results oriented. Thus, managers encourage employees to use the new knowledge obtained to change their behavior to help further the organization's goals.[49]

How to Build a Learning Organization: Three Roles Managers Play

To create a learning organization, managers must perform three key functions or roles: (1) *build a commitment to learning,* (2) *work to generate ideas with impact,* and (3) *work to generalize ideas with impact.*[50]

1. **You can build a commitment to learning.** To instill in your employees an intellectual and emotional commitment to the idea of learning, you as a manager need to lead the way by investing in it, publicly promoting it, creating rewards and symbols of it, and performing other similar activities. For example, Mark Pigott, chairman of PACCAR, Inc., which makes Kenworth and Peterbilt trucks, accomplished this by looking at other kinds of businesses and learning from their success. By focusing intently on how to improve quality, PACCAR can charge up to 10% more than competitors for its trucks.[51]

2. **You can work to generate ideas with impact.** As a manager, you need to try to generate ideas with impact—that is, ideas that add value for customers, employees, and shareholders—by increasing employee competence through training, experimenting with new ideas, and engaging in other leadership activities.

   Soon after Dick Brown became new CEO of EDS, he saw that the company had to be reinvented as a cool brand to make people feel good about working there. His marketing director decided to launch a new campaign at the biggest media event of all: the Super Bowl. EDS ran an ad showing rugged cowboys riding herd on 10,000 cats. The message: "We ride herd on complexity."

3. **You can work to generalize ideas with impact.** Besides generating ideas with impact, you can also generalize them—that is, reduce the barriers to learning among employees and within your organization. You can create a climate that reduces conflict, increases communication, promotes teamwork, rewards risk taking, reduces the fear of failure, and increases cooperation. In other words, you can create a psychologically safe and comforting environment that increases the sharing of successes, failures, and best practices. ●

Key Terms Used in This Chapter

administrative management 44

behavioral science 49

behavioral viewpoint 46

classical viewpoint 42

closed system 54

complexity theory 54

contemporary perspective 41

contingency viewpoint 55

evidence-based management 40

feedback 53

historical perspective 41

human relations movement 48

inputs 53

learning organization 60

management science 50

open system 54

operations management 51

outputs 53

quality 58

quality assurance 58

quality control 58

quality-management viewpoint 58

quantitative management 50

scientific management 42

subsystems 53

system 53

systems viewpoint 53

total quality management (TQM) 59

transformation processes 53

2.1 Evolving Viewpoints: How We Got to Today's Management Outlook

A rational approach to management is evidence-based management, which means translating principles based on best evidence into organizational practice, bringing rationality to the decision-making process. The two overarching perspectives on management are (1) the historical perspective, which includes three viewpoints—classical, behavioral, and quantitative; and (2) the contemporary perspective, which includes three other viewpoints—systems, contingency, and quality-management. There are five practical reasons for studying theoretical perspectives: They provide (1) understanding of the present, (2) a guide to action, (3) a source of new ideas, (4) clues to the meaning of your managers' decisions, and (5) clues to the meaning of outside ideas.

2.2 Classical Viewpoint: Scientific & Administrative Management

The first of the historical perspectives is the classical viewpoint, which emphasized finding ways to manage work more efficiently. It had two branches: (1) Scientific management emphasized the scientific study of work methods to improve productivity by individual workers. It was pioneered by Frederick W. Taylor, who offered four principles of science that could be applied to management, and by Frank and Lillian Gilbreth, who refined motion studies that broke job tasks into physical motions. (2) Administrative management was concerned with managing the total organization. Among its pioneers were Henri Fayol, who identified the major functions of management (planning, organizing, leading, controlling), and Max Weber, who identified five positive bureaucratic features in a well-performing organization. The classical viewpoint showed that work activity was amenable to a rational approach, but it has been criticized as being too mechanistic, viewing humans as cogs in a machine.

2.3 Behavioral Viewpoint: Behaviorism, Human Relations, & Behavioral Science

The second of the historical perspectives, the behavioral viewpoint emphasized the importance of understanding human behavior and of motivating employees toward achievement. It developed over three phases: (1) early behaviorism (2) the human relations movement, and (3) the behavioral science approach. Early behaviorism had three pioneers: (a) Hugo Munsterberg suggested that psychologists could contribute to industry by studying jobs, identifying the psychological conditions for employees to do their best work. (b) Mary Parker Follett thought organizations should be democratic, with employees and managers working together. (c) Elton Mayo hypothesized a so-called Hawthorne effect, suggesting that employees worked harder if they received added attention from managers. The human relations movement suggested that better human relations could increase worker productivity. Among its pioneers were (a) Abraham Maslow, who proposed a hierarchy of human needs, and (b) Douglas McGregor, who proposed a Theory X (where managers have a pessimistic view of workers) and Theory Y (where managers have a positive view of workers). The behavioral science approach relied on scientific research for developing theories about human behavior that can be used to provide practical tools for managers.

2.4 Quantitative Viewpoints: Management Science & Operations Management

The third of the historical perspectives, quantitative viewpoints emphasized the application to management of quantitative techniques. Two approaches are (1) management science, which focuses on using mathematics to aid in problem solving and decision making; and (2) operations management, which focuses on managing the production and delivery of an organization's products or services more effectively.

2.5 Systems Viewpoint

We turn from the study of the historical perspective to the contemporary perspective, which includes three viewpoints: (1) systems, (2) contingency, and (3) quality-management. The systems viewpoint regards the organization as a system of interrelated parts or collection of subsystems that operate together to achieve a common purpose. A system has four parts: inputs, outputs, transformational processes, and feedback. A system can be open, continually interacting with the environment, or closed, having little such interaction. The systems viewpoint has led to the development of complexity theory, the study of how order and pattern arise from very complicated, apparently chaotic systems.

2.6 Contingency Viewpoint

The second viewpoint in the contemporary perspective, the contingency viewpoint emphasizes that a manager's approach should vary according to the individual and the environmental situation.

2.7 Quality-Management Viewpoint

The third category in the contemporary perspective, the quality-management viewpoint is concerned with quality (the total ability of a product or service to meet customer needs) and has three aspects: (1) Quality control is the strategy for minimizing errors by managing each stage of production. (2) Quality assurance focuses on the performance of workers, urging employees to strive for "zero defects." (3) Total quality management (TQM) is a comprehensive approach dedicated to continuous quality improvement, training, and customer satisfaction. TQM has four components: (a) make continuous improvement a priority; (b) get every employee involved; (c) listen to and learn from customers and employees; and (d) use accurate standards to identify and eliminate problems.

2.8 The Learning Organization in an Era of Accelerated Change

A learning organization is one that actively creates, acquires, and transfers knowledge within itself and is able to modify its behavior to reflect new knowledge. Three roles that managers must perform to build a learning organization are to (1) build a commitment to learning, (2) work to generate ideas with impact, and (3) work to generalize ideas with impact.

Management in Action

Boeing Focuses on Its Operations & Supply Chain to Improve Productivity & Meet Deadlines

Boeing Co.'s production struggles with its 787 Dreamliner taught it to regularly stress-test suppliers, a skill that is coming to the forefront as it tackles a mountain of orders for its best-selling 737 jets.

The company's comprehensive reviews are critical to its effort to mount one of its biggest production increases in years. Chicago-based Boeing aims to boost output by about 60% in the next three years—or nearly 300 more jets a year. After winning a series of big contracts, it is sitting on a backlog of 3,500 commercial jets, valued at more than $270 billion.

At Vaupell Holdings Inc., one of about 1,000 suppliers subject to exhaustive reviews of its finances and even tools, Boeing's test regimen prompted the 60-year-old vendor this year to make such changes as replacing shop-floor management software.

Boeing has bolstered its ranks of supplier examiners with about 200 engineers and other supply-chain specialists in the past 18 months. Its teams visit vendors more frequently and conduct evaluations that can take days to complete.

"Boeing has become much more proactive," said Joe Jahn, chief executive of Seattle-based Vaupell. "They've got someone here almost every day." . . .

Looming over the company isn't just its backlog. Its archrival, Airbus, also is aiming for record output, as airlines increasingly demand more fuel-efficient jets and air travel expands in Asia and the Middle East.

Airbus has capitalized on some Boeing production delays. Airlines including Quantas Airways Ltd. and Virgin Atlantic Airways Ltd. decided to buy Airbus 330 jets in recent years because of Boeing's delays in delivering the 787 Dreamliner.

Quality issues are on the rise as suppliers scramble to meet the growing demand for aircraft. Tom Williams, Airbus executive vice president for programs, said: "It's happening fairly frequently that a process that has never given problems is suddenly causing problems." . . .

At Vaupell in Seattle, Mr. Jahn said his company has been working with Boeing to find a replacement for a material used in some Boeing window shades that DuPont Co. has decided to stop manufacturing.

Boeing's intensified reviews are helping Vaupell stay on top of its game, Mr. Jahn said. . . .

Boeing has been conducting roughly four-hour-long monthly and quarterly assessments of Vaupell's ability to speed up production, along with annual reviews that can take two to three days. A Boeing employee is at Vaupell's factory almost daily, compared with about once a week in the past, Mr. Jahn said.

Airplanes are one of the biggest and most complex industrial products. Jets like the Boeing 777 contain several million parts. Problems far down in the supply chain, such as shortages of machines used to mold certain components, can cause delays that ripple across the industry.

Boeing is trying to heed lessons from its past that some executives commonly refer to as "scars" on their backs. In the late 1990s, Boeing had to temporarily shut some of its assembly lines, and took billions of dollars in charges, when bottlenecks and quality issues arose after it tried to expand production too quickly. More recently, in 2008, inadequate training of new mechanics and supply-chain glitches led to quality problems at its 737 plant . . .

Boeing, which relies on more than 1,200 direct suppliers for its commercial jetliners, point to some specific benefits already. For instance, the number of parts shortages at its 737 plant is the lowest in five years, according to company officials.

FOR DISCUSSION

1. To what extent is Boeing using evidence-based management? Are they overdoing it? Explain your rationale.

2. To what extent are the managerial practices being used at Boeing consistent with principles associated with management science and operations management techniques? Discuss.

3. Use Figure 2.3 to analyze the extent to which Boeing is using a systems viewpoint.

4. How are the managerial practices being used at Boeing consistent with both a contingency and quality-management viewpoint? Explain your rationale.

5. To what extent does Boeing represent a learning organization? Discuss.

Source: Excerpted from David Kesmodel, "Boeing Examines Supply Chain for Weak Links," *The Wall Street Journal*, December 30, 2011, p. B3.

Self-Assessment

What Is Your Level of Self-Esteem?

OBJECTIVES

1. To get to know yourself a bit better.
2. To help you assess your self-esteem.

INTRODUCTION

Self-esteem, confidence, self-worth, and self-belief are all important aspects of being a manager in any organizational structure. However, the need for strong self-esteem is especially vital today because organizations demand that a manager manage people not as appendages of machines (as in scientific management) but as individuals who possess skills, knowledge, and self-will. Managers used to operate from a very strong position of centralized power and authority. However, in our modern organizational settings power is shared, and knowledge is to some extent "where you find it." To manage effectively in this situation, managers need strong self-esteem.

INSTRUCTIONS

To assess your self-esteem, answer the following questions. For each item, indicate the extent to which you agree or disagree by using the following scale. Remember, there are no right or wrong answers.

1 = strongly disagree
2 = disagree
3 = neither agree nor disagree
4 = agree
5 = strongly agree

QUESTIONS

1. I generally feel as competent as my peers.	1 2 3 4 5
2. I usually feel I can achieve whatever I want.	1 2 3 4 5
3. Whatever happens to me is mostly in my control.	1 2 3 4 5
4. I rarely worry about how things will work out.	1 2 3 4 5
5. I am confident that I can deal with most situations.	1 2 3 4 5
6. I rarely doubt my ability to solve problems.	1 2 3 4 5
7. I rarely feel guilty for asking others to do things.	1 2 3 4 5
8. I am rarely upset by criticism.	1 2 3 4 5
9. Even when I fail, I still do not doubt my basic ability.	1 2 3 4 5

10. I am very optimistic about my future.	1 2 3 4 5
11. I feel that I have quite a lot to offer an employer.	1 2 3 4 5
12. I rarely dwell for very long on personal setbacks.	1 2 3 4 5
13. I am always comfortable in disagreeing with my boss.	1 2 3 4 5
14. I rarely feel that I would like to be somebody else.	1 2 3 4 5
	TOTAL SCORE _____

ARBITRARY NORMS

High self-esteem = 56–70

Moderate self-esteem = 29–55

Low self-esteem = 14–28

QUESTIONS FOR DISCUSSION

1. Do you agree with the assessment? Why or why not?

2. How might you go about improving your self-esteem?

3. Can you survive today without having relatively strong confidence in yourself?

Legal/Ethical Challenge

Should the Federal Government Be Allowed to Oust a Drug-Company CEO?

The Department of Health and Human Services notified Forest Laboratories Inc. CEO Howard Solomon "that it intends to exclude him from doing business with the federal government. This in turn could prevent Forest from selling its drugs to Medicare, Medicaid, and the Veterans Administration." The government wants the company to relieve Mr. Solomon of his duties if it wants to retain its chances of doing business with the government. Losing this business with the government would seriously jeopardize Forest's future income. Mr. Solomon is 83 years old.

The federal government can legally do this because of a policy contained in the Social Security Act. "This policy allows officials to bar corporate leaders from health-industry companies doing business with the government, if a drug company is guilty of criminal misconduct. The agency said a chief executive or other leader can be banned even if he or she had no knowledge of a company's criminal actions. Retaining a banned executive can trigger a company's exclusion from government business."

The case of Mr. Solomon "has its origins in an investigation into the company's marketing of its big-selling antidepressants Celexa and Lexapro. Last September, Forest made a plea agreement with the government, under which it is paying $313 million in criminal and civil penalties over sales-related misconduct." The company ultimately pleaded guilty to a misdemeanor.

The issue in this case is whether you think it is ethical to force a company to fire an executive even if he or she was unaware of the criminal violations.

SOLVING THE CHALLENGE

Do you think it is fair to force Forest to retire Howard Solomon given that no one has specifically alleged that he did anything illegal?

1. Absolutely not. Individual managers should not be held responsible for the unethical behavior of other people in the organization. After all, Solomon did not personally do anything wrong.

2. Yes. If we don't hold someone accountable for the criminal acts of employees, then companies will be more likely to push the legal limits when marketing their products. After all, Solomon is the CEO.

3. No, but corporations should be held responsible. Individuals can't control the ethical behavior of other employees, but organizations can. The company has already paid $313 million and the issue should be dropped.

4. Invent other options. Discuss.

Source: Material for this case was extracted from Alicia Mundy, "U.S. Effort to Remove Drug CEO Jolts Firms," *The Wall Street Journal*, April 26, 2011, pp. A1, A2.

chapter 3

The Manager's Changing Work Environment & Ethical Responsibilities

Doing the Right Thing

Major Questions You Should Be Able to Answer

3.1 The Community of Stakeholders Inside the Organization

Major Question: Stockholders are only one group of stakeholders. Who are the stakeholders important to me inside the organization?

3.2 The Community of Stakeholders Outside the Organization

Major Question: Who are stakeholders important to me outside the organization?

3.3 The Ethical Responsibilities Required of You as a Manager

Major Question: What does the successful manager need to know about ethics and values?

3.4 The Social Responsibilities Required of You as a Manager

Major Question: Is being socially responsible really necessary?

3.5 Corporate Governance

Major Question: How can I trust a company is doing the right thing?

How Do People Excuse Lying & Cheating?

"Students don't just say 'OK I cheated in school, but now I'm in the workplace and it ends here," says an Arizona ethics professor. "They are forming bad habits that carry over into the market." [1]

The "Holier-Than-Thou" Effect & Motivated Blindness

Have you ever cheated—had unauthorized help on tests? Or plagiarized—misrepresented others' work as your own? Students know it's wrong, so why do they do it?

It's important to understand the psychology here:

- **The "holier-than-thou" effect.** Many of us have an excessively favorable bias about ourselves, a condition known as the *holier-than-thou effect.* "People tend to be overly optimistic about their own abilities and fortunes—to overestimate their standing in class, their discipline, their sincerity," suggests science writer Benedict Carey. "But this self-inflating bias may be even stronger when it comes to moral judgment." [2]

- **Motivated blindness.** In addition, many people are guided by so-called *motivated blindness*—the tendency to overlook information that works against their best interest. "Ample research shows that people who have a vested self-interest, even the most honest among us, have difficulty being objective," say business professors Max Bazerman and Ann Tenbrunsel. "Worse yet, they fail to recognize their lack of objectivity." [3] Motivated blindness enables us to behave unethically while maintaining a positive self-image.

Because of this psychology, cheating and plagiarism have become alarming problems in education, from high school to graduate school—even in graduate business programs. [4] Most students rationalize their behavior by saying, "I don't usually do this, but I really have to do it." They would rather cheat, that is, than show their families they got an F. [5]

The Dynamics Behind Cheating

Habitual cheating, Carey suggests, "begins with small infractions—illegally downloading a few songs, skimming small amounts from the register, lies of omission on taxes—and grows by increments." As success is rewarded, these "small infractions" can burgeon into a way of life that becomes an ongoing deliberate strategy of deception or fraud.

How do people rationalize cheating? The justifications are mainly personal and emotional:

- **Cheating provides useful shortcuts.** We constantly make choices "between short- and long-term gains," suggests Carey, "between the more virtuous choice and the less virtuous one." The brain naturally seeks useful shortcuts and so may view low-level cheating as productive in some situations.

- **Cheating arises out of resentment.** People often justify lying and cheating because they have resentments about a certain rule or a certain abusive boss.

- **Cheating seeks to redress perceived unfairness.** The urge to cheat may arise from a deep sense of unfairness, such as your sense that other people had special advantages.

- **Cheating is to avoid feeling like a chump.** Many people cheat to avoid feeling like a chump—to "not being smart" and "finishing out of the money."

For Discussion How would *you* justify cheating and plagiarism? Is it simply required behavior in order to get through college? ("I'm not going to be a chump.") What do you say to the fact that, as the research shows, students who cheat and thus don't actually do the assigned work are more likely to fail anyway? [6] Do you think you can stop the lying and deception once you're out in the work world?

forecast What's Ahead in This Chapter

This chapter sets the stage for understanding the new world in which managers must operate and the responsibilities they will have. We begin by describing the community of stakeholders that managers have to deal with—first the internal stakeholders (of employees, owners, and directors), then the external stakeholders in two kinds of environments (task and general). We then consider the ethical and social responsibilities required in being a manager, as well as the importance of corporate governance.

THE BIG PICTURE

Managers operate in two organizational environments—internal and external—both made up of stakeholders, the people whose interests are affected by the organization. The first, or internal, environment consists of employees, owners, and the board of directors.

In September 2010, a buried Pacific Gas & Electric natural-gas pipeline in the San Francisco suburb of San Bruno blew up in a spectacular pillar of fire, killing eight people and destroying 38 homes. "The gas-fed flames burned for more than 90 minutes while PG&E scrambled to find a way to shut off the line," reported the *San Francisco Chronicle*.[7] How did this come about?

To Whom Should a Company Be Responsible?

It turned out that PG&E had relied on gas-leak surveys to determine whether transmission pipelines were safe, but the company's incentive system awarded bonuses to supervisors whose crews found fewer leaks and kept repair costs down.[8] Indeed, the company's own internal audit found the incentives actually *encouraged* crews to produce inaccurate surveys.

An independent audit found that over an 11-year period PG&E collected $430 million more from its gas operations than the government had authorized—and it "chose to use the surplus revenues for general corporate purposes" rather than for improved safety.[9] In fact, in the three years prior to the explosion, the company spent $56 million a year on an incentive plan—stock awards, performance shares, and deferred compensation—for its executives and directors, including millions to the

Wall of fire. This 2010 gas explosion in San Bruno, California, which killed eight people, was linked to utility PG&E's low priority given to pipeline safety and high priority to its "focus on financial performance." What group should a company be most responsible to— stockholders, managers, customers, the public?

CEO. Despite this sleazy history—which will probably result in hundreds of millions of dollars in fines—it is unclear, the *Chronicle* concluded, "whether PG&E broke any criminal statutes governing its behavior, unless there was fraud."[10]

The bottom line: Is a company principally responsible only to its stockholders and executives? Or are other groups equal in significance? Further, is it sufficient that a company simply be legal, as PG&E evidently was? Or, isn't it equally important that it be ethical as well?

Internal & External Stakeholders

Perhaps we need a broader term than *stockholders* to indicate all those with a stake in an organization. That term, appropriately, is ***stakeholders*—the people whose interests are affected by an organization's activities.**

Managers operate in two organizational environments, both made up of various stakeholders. *(See Figure 3.1.)* As we describe in the rest of this section, the two environments are these:

- Internal stakeholders
- External stakeholders

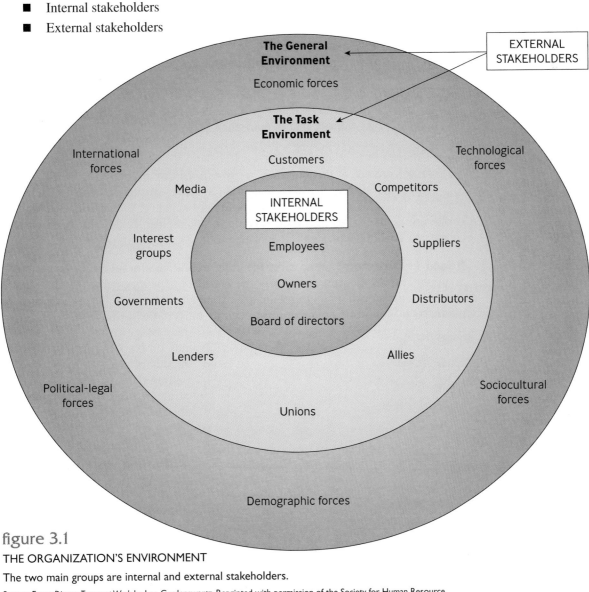

figure 3.1

THE ORGANIZATION'S ENVIRONMENT

The two main groups are internal and external stakeholders.

Source: From *Diverse Teams at Work* by Lee Gardenswartz. Reprinted with permission of the Society for Human Resource Management (www.shrm.org), Alexandra, VA. Copyright © 2003, Society for Human Resource Management.

Internal Stakeholders

Whether small or large, the organization to which you belong has people in it who have an important stake in how it performs. These *internal stakeholders* **consist of employees, owners, and the board of directors, if any.** Let us consider each in turn.

Employees   As a manager, could you run your part of the organization if you and your employees were constantly in conflict? Labor history, of course, is full of accounts of just that. But such conflict may lower the performance of the organization, thereby hurting everyone's stake. In many of today's forward-looking organizations, employees are considered "the talent"—the most important resource.

"My chief assets drive out the gate every day," says Jim Goodnight, CEO of North Carolina–based SAS. "My job is to make sure they come back."[11] SAS is the world's largest privately held software business, No. 1 on *Fortune*'s 2010 and 2011 lists of "100 Best Companies to Work For" and No. 3 on the 2012 list. Even during the recent Great Recession, when there were six unemployed workers for every available U.S. job opening, SAS continued to treat employees exceptionally well, resulting in a turnover rate of only 2% in 2009, compared with a software industry average of 22%.

Owners   The *owners* **of an organization consist of all those who can claim it as their legal property,** such as Walmart's stockholders. In the for-profit world, if you're running a one-person graphic design firm, the owner is just you—you're what is known as a sole proprietorship. If you're in an Internet startup with your brother-in-law, you're both owners—you're a partnership. If you're a member of a family running a car dealership, you're all owners—you're investors in a privately owned company. If you work for a company that is more than half owned by its employees (such as W. L. Gore & Associates, maker of Gore-Tex fabric and No. 38 on *Fortune*'s 2012 "Best Companies to Work For" list, or Lakeland, Florida, Publix Super Markets, No. 78), you are one of the joint owners—you're part of an Employee Stock Ownership Plan (ESOP).[12] And if you've bought a few shares of stock in a company whose shares are listed for sale on the New York Stock Exchange, such as General Motors, you're one of thousands of owners—you're a stockholder. In all these examples, of course, the goal of the owners is to make a profit.

Board of Directors   Who hires the chief executive of a for-profit or nonprofit organization? In a corporation, it is the *board of directors,* whose members are elected by the stockholders to see that the company is being run according to their interests. In nonprofit organizations, such as universities or hospitals, the board may be called the *board of trustees* or *board of regents.* Board members are very important in setting the organization's overall strategic goals and in approving the major decisions and salaries of top management.

Not all firms have a board of directors. A lawyer, for instance, may operate as a sole proprietor, making all her own decisions. A large corporation might have eight or so members on its board of directors. Some of these directors (inside directors) may be top executives of the firm. The rest (outside directors) are elected from outside the firm. ●

Employee ownership. Zachary's Chicago Pizza, based in Oakland, California, uses a device known as an Employee Stock Ownership Plan (ESOP), in which employees buy company stock in order to become owners. Although the idea was conceived over 50 years ago, there are only about 11,500 ESOPs today out of hundreds of thousands of businesses. Why do you suppose more companies aren't owned by their employees?

3.2 THE COMMUNITY OF STAKEHOLDERS OUTSIDE THE ORGANIZATION

major question

Who are stakeholders important to me outside the organization?

THE BIG PICTURE
The external environment of stakeholders consists of the task environment and the general environment. The task environment consists of customers, competitors, suppliers, distributors, strategic allies, employee associations, local communities, financial institutions, government regulators, special-interest groups, and the mass media. The general environment consists of economic, technological, sociocultural, demographic, political-legal, and international forces.

In the first section we described the environment inside the organization. Here let's consider the environment outside it, which consists of *external stakeholders*—**people or groups in the organization's external environment that are affected by it.** This environment consists of:

- The task environment
- The general environment

The Task Environment

The *task environment* consists of 11 groups that present you with daily tasks to handle: customers, competitors, suppliers, distributors, strategic allies, employee organizations, local communities, financial institutions, government regulators, special-interest groups, and mass media.

1. Customers The first law of business (and even nonprofits), we've said, is *take care of the customer. Customers* **are those who pay to use an organization's goods or services.** Many customers value service over price, according to a Forrester Research report, with 54% thinking it would be easy to have a customer service issue resolved in clothing and apparel outlets but only 30% thinking the same in health insurance companies.[13]

2. Competitors Is there any line of work you could enter in which there would *not* be *competitors*—**people or organizations that compete for customers or resources,** such as talented employees or raw materials? Every organization has to be actively aware of its competitors. Florist shops and delicatessens must be aware that customers can buy the same products at Safeway or Kroger.

3. Suppliers A *supplier* **is a person or an organization that provides supplies—that is, raw materials, services, equipment, labor, or energy—to other organizations.** Suppliers in turn have their own suppliers: The publisher of this book buys the paper on which it is printed from a paper merchant, who in turn is supplied by several paper mills, which in turn are supplied wood for wood pulp by logging companies with forests in the United States or Canada.

Take care of the customer. Customers have the most faith in the ability of apparel companies, banks, and hotels to handle complaints, less confidence in Internet service providers, computer companies, and health insurers. Do you think this is partly because a piece of clothing, for example, is less complex than a computer or a health insurance policy?

Taking Care of Customers: Amazon.com Obsesses over "the Customer Experience"

What do Wall Street investors care about? Short-term profits. And profits are what Dell Computer tried to deliver when it scrimped on customer service. So did eBay when it saddled its most dedicated sellers with new costs. "Eventually," says business writer Joe Nocera, "those short-sighted decisions caught up with both companies" and they had to make drastic adjustments.[14]

Drivers of the Customer Experience. By contrast, Amazon.com founder and CEO Jeff Bezos is "obsessed," in his words, with what he calls "the customer experience." Customers "care about having the lowest prices, having vast selection, so they have choice, and getting the products . . . fast," Bezos has said. "And the reason I'm so obsessed with these drivers of the customer experience is that I believe that the success we have had over the past 12 years has been driven exclusively by that customer experience."[15]

Thus, the company has an easy-to-use website, with its online technology ranked as more bug free and user friendly than rivals Walmart.com and Target.com.[16] It also has a money-losing (in Wall Street's view) two-day free shipping policy on all packages for an annual fee of just $79, and a customer-service phone number that you can actually find.

The Extra Effort. In addition, Amazon has a willingness to correct mistakes—even, sometimes, for ones it didn't make. In one instance, it replaced, for free, a $500 PlayStation 3 Christmas present that Nocera had ordered for his son, which disappeared on arriving at his apartment building—and it saw to it that the replacement arrived on Christmas Eve.

YOUR CALL

Spending huge sums of money on "frills" such as free shipping has depressed Amazon's profits from time to time; indeed, in 2011, profits decreased 45%, although revenue increased 41%. The decline in profits resulted from increased costs the company incurred from aggressively expanding its business, Amazon said.[17] Other companies also bend over backward to take care of their customers. Can you name examples?

4. Distributors A *distributor* **is a person or an organization that helps another organization sell its goods and services to customers.** Publishers of magazines, for instance, don't sell directly to newsstands; rather, they go through a distributor, or wholesaler. Tickets to the Black Keys, Foo Fighters, or other artists' performances might be sold to you directly by the concert hall, but they are also sold through such distributors as Ticketmaster, Live Nation, and StubHub.

Distributors can be quite important because in some industries (such as movie theaters and magazine sales) there is not a lot of competition, and the distributor has a lot of power over the ultimate price of the product. However, the popularity of the Internet has allowed manufacturers of cellphones, for example, to cut out the "middleman"— the distributor—and to sell to customers directly.

5. Strategic Allies Companies, and even nonprofit organizations, frequently link up with other organizations (even competing ones) in order to realize strategic advantages. The term *strategic allies* **describes the relationship of two organizations that join forces to achieve advantages neither can perform as well alone.**

With their worldwide reservation systems and slick marketing, big companies— Hilton, Hyatt, Marriott, Starwood, and so on—dominate the high-end business-center hotels. But in many cities, there are still independents—such as The Rittenhouse in Philadelphia, The Hay-Adams in Washington, DC, and The Adolphus in Dallas—that compete with the chains by promoting their prestigious locations, grand architecture, rich history, and personalized service. Recently, however, high-end independents have become affiliated with chains as strategic allies because chains can buy supplies for less and they have more far-reaching sales channels. The 100-year-old U.S. Grant in downtown San Diego, for example, became part of Starwood's Luxury Collection to gain "worldwide exposure," according to a hotel spokesman.[18]

6. Employee Organizations: Unions & Associations   As a rule of thumb, labor unions (such as the United Auto Workers or the Teamsters Union) tend to represent hourly workers; professional associations (such as the National Education Association or the Newspaper Guild) tend to represent salaried workers. Nevertheless, during a labor dispute, salary-earning teachers in the American Federation of Teachers might well picket in sympathy with the wage-earning janitors in the Service Employees International Union.

In recent years, the percentage of the labor force represented by unions has steadily declined (from 35% in the 1950s to 11.8% in 2011).[19] Indeed, most union members are now government employees, and private-sector unionization, mainly because of recession-related job losses in manufacturing and construction, has fallen off.[20] The composition of the membership has also changed, with 45% of the unionized workforce now female and 38% of union members holding a four-year college degree or more.[21]

7. Local Communities   If Boeing, the aircraft manufacturer, moves its operations from Wichita, Kansas—which calls itself the Air Capital of the World—wouldn't that have a major impact? Of course.[22]

Local communities are obviously important stakeholders, as becomes evident not only when a big organization arrives but also when it leaves, sending government officials scrambling to find new industry to replace it. Schools and municipal governments rely on the organization for their tax base. Families and merchants depend on its employee payroll for their livelihoods. In addition, everyone from the United Way to the Little League may rely on it for some financial support.

If a community gives a company tax breaks in return for the promise of new jobs and the firm fails to do so, does the community have the right to institute ***clawbacks—rescinding the tax breaks when firms don't deliver promised jobs?***

EXAMPLE

Local Communities as Stakeholders: What Does a Company Owe Its Community?

Since its founding in 1884 as a cash register company the NCR Corporation, formerly known as National Cash Register and now a maker of automated teller machines and other self-service devices, has been an important company for Dayton, Ohio. But that ended in early 2010 when NCR chief executive Bill Nuti publicly announced the company was relocating its headquarters to Atlanta and posed for photographs with Georgia's governor, whose state had promised a lucrative incentive package.

Galling & Insulting. "The images galled Dayton," reports *The New York Times*, "given Ohio's contention that Mr. Nuti had sidestepped several invitations from its governor since 2007 to discuss NCR's needs and desires."[23] Nuti rejoined that NCR had 22,000 employees around the world, but only 1,200 were in Ohio—fewer than in Georgia. Moreover, he said, Dayton's transportation costs were high, the airport was not easy to connect with, and it was difficult to recruit top talent to live and work in the area. Ohioans found these remarks insulting. In any case, didn't 125 years count for something?

Communities & Clawbacks. As mentioned, many communities offer companies inducements to relocate, often trading tax breaks in return for the promise of jobs. But in cash-strapped times, cities that once bent over backward to lure companies are now resorting to "clawbacks"—asserting their right to rescind the tax breaks when the firms fail to deliver. Target Corp., for instance, got tax abatements from DeKalb, Illinois, city, county, and other taxing bodies after promising at least 500 jobs at a local distribution center. "So when the company came up 66 workers short in 2009," says one report, "Target got word its next tax bill would be jumping almost $600,000— more than half of which goes to the local school district, where teachers and programs have been cut as coffers dried up."[24]

YOUR CALL

Should NCR have given Ohio a chance to match Georgia's incentives? Or is the company's loyalty only to its stockholders? What obligations should a community expect of the companies located there?

Government as stakeholder. Lake Tahoe straddles the state lines of California and Nevada. To help preserve the lake's natural beauty and prevent the clarity of its water from being spoiled by development and pollution, the various counties around the lake agreed to submit to being regulated by a bistate agency, the Tahoe Regional Planning Authority (TRPA). People wishing to build, for example, must submit plans not only to their own county but also to TRPA. In what ways do your local government authorities affect business in your area?

8. Financial Institutions   Want to launch a small company? Although normally reluctant to make loans to startups, financial institutions—banks, savings and loans, and credit unions—may do so if you have a good credit history or can secure the loan with property such as a house. In the recent recession, even good customers found loans hard to get. (Best advice: Get to know some bank loan officers and try to educate them about your business.)[25]

Established companies also often need loans to tide them over when revenues are down or to finance expansion, but they rely for assistance on lenders such as commercial banks, investment banks, and insurance companies.

9. Government Regulators   The preceding groups are external stakeholders in your organization since they are clearly affected by its activities. But why would *government regulators*—**regulatory agencies that establish ground rules under which organizations may operate**—be considered stakeholders?

We are talking here about an alphabet soup of agencies, boards, and commissions that have the legal authority to prescribe or proscribe the conditions under which you may conduct business. To these may be added local and state regulators on the one hand and foreign governments and international agencies (such as the World Trade Organization, which oversees international trade and standardization efforts) on the other.

Such government regulators can be said to be stakeholders because not only do they affect the activities of your organization, they are in turn affected by it. The Federal Aviation Agency (FAA), for example, specifies how far planes must stay apart to prevent midair collisions. But when the airlines want to add more flights on certain routes, the FAA may have to add more flight controllers and radar equipment, since those are the agency's responsibility.

10. Special-Interest Groups   If the fake fur in the clothes you're wearing is actually made out of dog (specifically, the fur of the raccoon dog, found in Asia), would you know it? Federal law requires clothing manufacturers to identify fur on a clothing item only if its value exceeds $150. In 2010, California assemblywoman Fiona Ma introduced a bill in the state legislature requiring apparel makers using fur to label their products accordingly regardless of the clothing's value. The political pressure came from the Humane Society of the United States, which for years had been agitating to close the legal loophole. Similar laws already exist in five other states. "All we are saying is, 'Label it,'" said Ma. "This is about a consumer's right to know as well as about animal rights."[26]

Special interests. Union members demand bank reform to help families keep their homes and expand lending that creates jobs.

Special-interest groups are groups whose members try to influence specific issues, some of which may affect your organization. Examples are Mothers Against Drunk Driving, the National Organization for Women, and the National Rifle Association. Special-interest groups may try to exert political influence, as in contributing funds to lawmakers' election campaigns or in launching letter-writing efforts to officials. Or they may organize picketing and *boycotts*—holding back their patronage—of certain companies, as some public-interest groups did in 2010 of BP gas stations to protest the company's gigantic oil spill in the Gulf of Mexico.[27]

11. Mass Media   No manager can afford to ignore the power of the mass media—print, radio, TV, and the Internet—to rapidly and widely disseminate news both bad and good. Thus, most companies, universities, hospitals, and even government agencies have a public-relations person or department to communicate effectively with the press. In addition, top-level executives often receive special instruction on how to best deal with the media.

EXAMPLE

Managing the Media: Johnson & Johnson Succeeds—& Then Fails—in Handling Product Recalls

What is a company supposed to do when it has a public-relations disaster? The gold standard in brand crisis management is the path followed by health products company Johnson & Johnson in 1982.

Successful Crisis Management. In that year, when several consumers died after taking tainted Tylenol pills, the company responded in a way that has become the preferred strategy taught in business schools, according to one account: "Communicate clearly with the public about a crisis, cooperate with government officials, swiftly begin its own investigation of a problem, and, if necessary, quickly institute a product recall."[28] A big part of the strategy was communicating honestly and frequently through the media.

Unsuccessful Crisis Management. However, a quarter century later, Johnson & Johnson unaccountably abandoned its own model. In early 2010, a J&J division announced the recall—20 months after the initial alarm—of several hundred lots of popular over-the-counter medicines (Benadryl, Rolaids, Tylenol, others) because of customer complaints about temporary digestive problems. The company did not conduct an immediate investigation and did not notify authorities in a timely fashion, resulting in prolonged consumer exposure to the products. The result: a big media black eye for one of the most trusted brands in America, from which it was still recovering nearly two years later.[29]

YOUR CALL

Lots of companies seem to find themselves having a "Tylenol moment"—Toyota in 2010, for instance, when it had to recall cars for sticking accelerators.[30] You may not be able to anticipate what kind of crisis might strike a company you're working for, but can you preplan what the company should do when and if one happens?

The General Environment

Beyond the task environment is the *general environment,* **or** *macroenvironment,* **which includes six forces: economic, technological, sociocultural, demographic, political-legal, and international.**

You may be able to control some forces in the task environment, but you can't control those in the general environment. Nevertheless, they can profoundly affect your organization's task environment without your knowing it, springing nasty surprises on you. Clearly, then, as a manager you need to keep your eye on the far horizon because these forces of the general environment can affect long-term plans and decisions.

1. Economic Forces   *Economic forces* **consist of the general economic conditions and trends—unemployment, inflation, interest rates, economic growth—that may affect an organization's performance.** These are forces in your nation and region and even the world over which you and your organization probably have no control, as happened in the 2007–2009 Great Recession and its aftermath.

Are banks' interest rates going up in the United States? Then it will cost you more to borrow money to open new stores or build new plants. Is your region's unemployment rate rising? Then maybe you'll have more job applicants to hire from, yet you'll also have fewer customers with money to spend. (A record 46 million Americans—18% of families—are presently considered poor, as a result of the recession, the highest rate of poverty since 1993.)[31] Are natural resources getting scarce in an important area of supply? Then your company will need to pay more for them or switch to alternative sources.

One indicator that managers often pay attention to is productivity growth. Rising productivity leads to rising profits, lower inflation, and higher stock prices. In recent times, companies have been using information technology to cut costs, resulting in productivity growing at an annual rate of 2.7% from 2001 to 2007, slumping to 1.2% in the recession year 2008, then roaring back to 3.9% in 2010 and 2.8% in 2011.[32] Aided by technology, U.S. manufacturing has actually surged 40.4% since 2001, although manufacturing jobs have declined.[33]

2. Technological Forces *Technological forces* **are new developments in methods for transforming resources into goods or services.** For example, think what the United States would have been like if the elevator, air-conditioning, the combustion engine, and the airplane had not been invented. No doubt changes in computer and communications technology—especially the influence of the Internet—will continue to be powerful technological forces during your managerial career. But other technological currents may affect you as well.

For example, biotechnology may well turn health and medicine upside down in the coming decades. Researchers can already clone animals, and some reports say they are close to doing the same with humans.

3. Sociocultural Forces Long an American rite of passage, the act of getting a driver's license at age 16 is no longer as popular as it was; it is "on the wane among the digital generation," says one report, "which no longer sees the family car as the end-all of social life."[34] In other words, Facebook, MySpace, Twitter, and other social media are altering long-standing patterns.

Some day, of course, our descendants may well view the craze to have a driver's license as old-fogyish and quaint. That's how it is with sociocultural changes. *Sociocultural forces* **are influences and trends originating in a country's, a society's, or a culture's human relationships and values that may affect an organization.**

Entire industries have been rocked when the culture underwent a lifestyle change that affected their product or service. The interest in health and fitness, for instance,

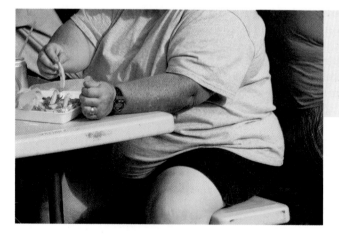

Sociocultural forces. The U.S. obesity rate is one of those sociocultural forces capable of altering entire industries. Which ones do you think would be most affected?

led to a decline in sales of cigarettes, whiskey, red meat, and eggs. And it led to a boost in sales of athletic shoes, spandex clothing, and Nautilus and other exercise machines. Low-carbohydrate, high-protein diets like the Atkins and the South Beach diets triggered a rise in chicken, pork, and beef sales, but then led to an oversupply and consequent dip in prices as consumers turned to a more balanced eating approach.[35] More recently, with more attention focused on the American epidemic of obesity—the rate of obesity among U.S. youths has nearly tripled in some age groups since the 1970s—many restaurants are touting healthier foods.[36]

4. Demographic Forces   *Demographics* derives from the ancient Greek word for "people"—*demos*—and deals with statistics relating to human populations. Age, gender, race, sexual orientation, occupation, income, family size, and the like are known as demographic characteristics when they are used to express measurements of certain groups. ***Demographic forces* are influences on an organization arising from changes in the characteristics of a population, such as age, gender, or ethnic origin.**

Among recent changes: Marriage rates are down, more couples are marrying later, black-white and same-sex marriages are increasing, women are having fewer babies, divorce is declining, secularism (being nonreligious) is up, more households are multigenerational, and the percentage of people living in rural areas is the lowest ever.[37] By 2050, it's predicted, the U.S. population will soar to between 399 million and 458 million (from about 313 million today), and minorities are expected to reach 50% of the population by around 2042.[38]

5. Political-Legal Forces   ***Political-legal forces* are changes in the way politics shape laws and laws shape the opportunities for and threats to an organization.** In the United States, whatever political view tends to be dominant at the moment may be reflected in how the government handles antitrust issues, in which one company tends to monopolize a particular industry. Should Google, for instance, be allowed to dominate the market for Internet search?

As for legal forces, some countries have more fully developed legal systems than others. And some countries have more lawyers per capita. (The United States has an estimated 25% of the world's lawyers, according to University of Wisconsin law professor Marc Galanter—not the 70% figure repeated for years by some conservative political figures.)[39] American companies may be more willing to use the legal system to advance their interests, as in suing competitors to gain competitive advantage. But they must also watch that others don't do the same to them.

6. International Forces   ***International forces* are changes in the economic, political, legal, and technological global system that may affect an organization.**

This category represents a huge grab bag of influences. How does the economic integration of the European Union (EU) create threats and opportunities for American companies? U.S. companies that do significant business in Europe are subject to regulation by the European Union. For instance, in a 3-year antitrust case, the EU ruled that Microsoft Corp. had abusively wielded its Windows and Office software monopoly, fined it the equivalent of $735 million, and ordered it to reduce practices that gave Microsoft an advantage in hooking up its products to Windows, thereby limiting competition.[40] We consider global concerns in Chapter 4.

How well Americans can handle international forces depends a lot on their training. The American Council on Education says there is a "dangerous" shortage of experts in non-European cultures and languages. The council urges that schools teach a wider variety of languages and that instruction begin as early as kindergarten, since waiting until students are in college to begin instruction in more obscure languages hinders their ability to become fluent speakers.[41]   ●

major question? What does the successful manager need to know about ethics and values?

THE BIG PICTURE
Managers need to be aware of what constitutes ethics, values, the four approaches to ethical dilemmas, and how organizations can promote ethics.

"It's a tough issue, choosing between being a law-abiding person and losing your job," says lawyer Gloria Allred, who represented a woman fired for complaining about running her boss's office football pool.[42] Imagine having to choose between *economic performance* and *social performance,* which in business is what most ethical conflicts are about.[43] This is known as an ***ethical dilemma,* a situation in which you have to decide whether to pursue a course of action that may benefit you or your organization but that is unethical or even illegal.**

Defining Ethics & Values

Seventy-three percent of American employees working full time say they have observed ethical misconduct at work, and 36% have been "distracted" by it.[44] Most of us assume we know what "ethics" and "values" mean, but do we? Let's consider them.

Ethics *Ethics* **are the standards of right and wrong that influence behavior.** These standards may vary among countries and among cultures. ***Ethical behavior* is behavior that is accepted as "right" as opposed to "wrong" according to those standards.**

Higher self. If you worked for a drug company, would you think it's acceptable to give a medical society several thousand dollars to use on dinner lectures to inform doctors about high blood pressure and how your company's products can treat the condition? Would your perspective change if you were a patient with high blood pressure?

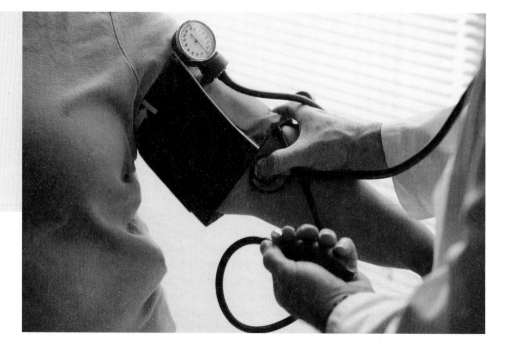

What are the differences among a tip, a gratuity, a gift, a donation, a commission, a consulting fee, a kickback, a bribe? Regardless of the amount of money involved, each one may be intended to reward the recipient for providing you with better service, either anticipated or performed. What should be the expectations of a medical society that accepts $700,000 from three pharmaceutical companies to be used for dinner lectures to brief doctors on the latest news about high blood pressure? What if the main point of these briefings is to expand the concept of high blood pressure, increasing the pool of people taking blood-pressure medications?[45]

Values   Ethical dilemmas often take place because of an organization's *value system,* **the pattern of values within an organization.** *Values* **are the relatively permanent and deeply held underlying beliefs and attitudes that help determine a person's behavior,** such as the belief that "Fairness means hiring according to ability, not family background." Values and value systems are the underpinnings for ethics and ethical behavior.

Organizations may have two important value systems that can conflict: (1) the value system stressing financial performance versus (2) the value system stressing cohesion and solidarity in employee relationships.[46]

Four Approaches to Deciding Ethical Dilemmas

How do alternative values guide people's decisions about ethical behavior? Here are four approaches, which may be taken as guidelines:

1. The Utilitarian Approach: For the Greatest Good   Ethical behavior in the *utilitarian approach* **is guided by what will result in the greatest good for the greatest number of people.** Managers often take the utilitarian approach, using financial performance—such as efficiency and profit—as the best definition of what constitutes "the greatest good for the greatest number."[47]

Thus, a utilitarian "cost-benefit" analysis might show that in the short run the firing of thousands of employees may improve a company's bottom line and provide immediate benefits for the stockholders. The drawback of this approach, however, is that it may result in damage to workforce morale and the loss of employees with experience and skills—actions not so readily measurable in dollars.

2. The Individual Approach: For Your Greatest Self-Interest Long Term, Which Will Help Others   Ethical behavior in the *individual approach* **is guided by what will result in the individual's best *long-term* interests, which ultimately are in everyone's self-interest.** The assumption here is that you will act ethically in the short run to avoid others harming you in the long run.

The flaw here, however, is that one person's short-term self-gain may *not,* in fact, be good for everyone in the long term. After all, the manager of an agribusiness that puts chemical fertilizers on the crops every year will always benefit, but the fishing industries downstream could ultimately suffer if chemical runoff reduces the number of fish. Indeed, this is one reason why Puget Sound Chinook, or king salmon, are now threatened with extinction in the Pacific Northwest.[48]

3. The Moral-Rights Approach: Respecting Fundamental Rights Shared by Everyone   Ethical behavior in the *moral-rights approach* **is guided by respect for the fundamental rights of human beings,** such as those expressed in the U.S. Constitution's Bill of Rights. We would all tend to agree that denying people the right to life, liberty, privacy, health and safety, and due process is unethical. Thus, most of us would have no difficulty condemning the situation of immigrants illegally brought into the United States and then effectively enslaved—as when made to work seven days a week as maids.

The difficulty, however, is when rights are in conflict, such as employer and employee rights. Should employees on the job have a guarantee of privacy? Actually, it is legal for employers to listen to business phone calls and monitor all nonspoken personal communications.[49]

4. The Justice Approach: Respecting Impartial Standards of Fairness Ethical behavior in the *justice approach* **is guided by respect for impartial standards of fairness and equity.** One consideration here is whether an organization's policies—such as those governing promotions or sexual harassment cases—are administered impartially and fairly regardless of gender, age, sexual orientation, and the like.

Fairness can often be a hot issue. For instance, many employees are loudly resentful when a corporation's CEO is paid a salary and bonuses worth hundreds of times more than what they receive—even when the company performs poorly—and when fired is then given a "golden parachute," or extravagant package of separation pay and benefits.

White-Collar Crime, SarbOx, & Ethical Training

At the beginning of the 21st century, U.S. business erupted in an array of scandals represented in such names as Enron, WorldCom, Tyco, and Adelphia, and their chief executives—Jeffrey Skilling, Bernard Ebbers, Dennis Kozlowski, and John Rigas—went to prison on various fraud convictions.[50] Executives' deceits generated a great deal of public outrage, as a result of which Congress passed the Sarbanes–Oxley Act, as we'll describe. Did that stop the raft of business scandals? Not quite.

Next to hit the headlines were cases of *insider trading,* **the illegal trading of a company's stock by people using confidential company information.** In 2004, Sam Waksal, CEO of ImClone, a biotechnology company, sold his shares of stock when he learned—before the news was made public—that the U.S. government was blocking ImClone's new cancer drug. For this act of insider trading, he ultimately was sentenced to 87 months in prison and fined $3 million. (This was the case that affected lifestyle guru Martha Stewart as well.) In 2009, authorities arrested billionaire

Phony financier. Bernard Madoff pleaded guilty to 11 federal crimes connected with his massive Ponzi scheme, which for more than 25 years defrauded investors of between $12 billion and $20 billion. The charges against him included securities fraud, investment advisor fraud, mail fraud, wire fraud, money laundering, false statements, and perjury, among other allegations. Now age 74, his projected release date from federal prison is November 14, 2159.

hedge-fund manager Raj Rajaratnam for trading on tips from persons at companies who slipped him advance word on inside information; he was convicted and sentenced to 11 years in prison.[51]

Also there was the shocking news of financier Bernard Madoff, who confessed to a $50 billion *Ponzi scheme*, **using cash from newer investors to pay off older ones.**[52] He was sentenced to 150 years in prison.[53] Another charged with creating a Ponzi scheme was Texas financier R. Allen Stanford, who built a flashy offshore $7 billion financial empire; he was convicted of 13 counts of fraud in March 2012.[54]

The Sarbanes–Oxley Reform Act   The *Sarbanes–Oxley Act of 2002,* **often shortened to SarbOx or SOX, established requirements for proper financial record keeping for public companies and penalties of as much as 25 years in prison for noncompliance.**[55] Administered by the Securities and Exchange Commission, SarbOx requires a company's chief executive officer and chief financial officer to personally certify the organization's financial reports, prohibits them from taking personal loans or lines of credit, and makes them reimburse the organization for bonuses and stock options when required by restatement of corporate profits. It also requires the company to have established procedures and guidelines for audit committees.[56]

How Do People Learn Ethics? Kohlberg's Theories   American business history is permeated with occasional malfeasance, from railroad tycoons trying to corner the gold market (the 1872 Credit Mobilier scandal) to 25-year-old bank customer service representatives swindling elderly customers out of their finances.[57] Legislation such as SarbOx can't head off all such behavior. No wonder that now many colleges and universities have required more education in ethics.

"Schools bear some responsibility for the behavior of executives," says Fred J. Evans, dean of the College of Business and Economics at California State University at Northridge. "If you're making systematic errors in the [business] world, you have to go back to the schools and ask, 'What are you teaching?'"[58] The good news is that more graduate business schools are changing their curriculums to teach ethics.[59] The bad news, however, is that a recent survey of 50,000 undergraduates found that 26% of business majors admitted to serious cheating on exams, and 54% admitted to cheating on written assignments.[60]

Of course, most students' levels of moral development are established by personalities and upbringing long before they get to college, with some being more advanced than others. One psychologist, **Laurence Kohlberg,** has proposed three levels of personal moral development—preconventional, conventional, and postconventional.[61]

- **Level 1, preconventional—follows rules.** People who have achieved this level tend to follow rules and to obey authority to avoid unpleasant consequences. Managers of the Level 1 sort tend to be autocratic or coercive, expecting employees to be obedient for obedience's sake.

- **Level 2, conventional—follows expectations of others.** People whose moral development has reached this level are conformist but not slavish, generally adhering to the expectations of others in their lives. Level 2 managers lead by encouragement and cooperation and are more group and team oriented. Most managers are at this level.

- **Level 3, postconventional—guided by internal values.** The farthest along in moral development, Level 3 managers are independent souls who follow their own values and standards, focusing on the needs of their employees and trying to lead by empowering those working for them. Only about a fifth of American managers reach this level.

What level of development do you think you've reached?

How Organizations Can Promote Ethics

Ethics needs to be an everyday affair, not a onetime thing. This is why many large U.S. companies now have a chief ethics officer, whose job is to make ethical conduct a priority issue.

There are several ways an organization may promote high ethical standards on the job, as follows.[62]

1. Creating a Strong Ethical Climate An *ethical climate* **represents employees' perceptions about the extent to which work environments support ethical behavior.** It is important for managers to foster ethical climates because they significantly affect the frequency of ethical behavior. Managers can promote ethical climates through the policies, procedures, and practices that are used on a daily basis.

2. Screening Prospective Employees Companies try to screen out dishonest, irresponsible employees by checking applicants' résumés and references. Some firms, for example, run employee applications through E-Verify, a federal program that allows employers to check for illegal immigrants.[63] Some also use personality tests and integrity testing to identify potentially dishonest people.

3. Instituting Ethics Codes & Training Programs A *code of ethics* **consists of a formal written set of ethical standards guiding an organization's actions.** Most codes offer guidance on how to treat customers, suppliers, competitors, and other stakeholders. The purpose is to clearly state top management's expectations for all employees. As you might expect, most codes prohibit bribes, kickbacks, misappropriation of corporate assets, conflicts of interest, and "cooking the books"—making false accounting statements and other records. Other areas frequently covered in ethics codes are political contributions, workforce diversity, and confidentiality of corporate information.[64]

In addition, according to a Society for Human Resource Management Weekly Survey, 32% of human resources professionals indicated that their organizations offered ethics training.[65] The approaches vary, but one way is to use a case approach to present employees with ethical dilemmas. By clarifying expectations, this kind of training may reduce unethical behavior.[66]

4. Rewarding Ethical Behavior: Protecting Whistle-Blowers It's not enough to simply punish bad behavior; managers must also reward good ethical behavior, as in encouraging (or at least not discouraging) whistle-blowers.

A *whistle-blower* **is an employee who reports organizational misconduct to the public,** such as health and safety matters, waste, corruption, or overcharging of customers. For instance, the law that created the Occupational Safety and Health Administration allows workers to report unsafe conditions, such as "exposure to toxic chemicals; the use of dangerous machines, which can crush fingers; the use of contaminated needles, which expose workers to the AIDS virus; and the strain of repetitive hand motion, whether at a computer keyboard or in a meatpacking plant."[67]

In some cases, whistle-blowers may receive a reward; the IRS, for instance, is authorized to pay tipsters rewards as high as 30% in cases involving large amounts of money.[68] Between 1996 and 2005, whistle-blowers helped authorities recover at least $9.3 billion from health care providers who defrauded the government, over $1 billion of which was given to the whistle-blowers themselves.[69] ●

3.4 THE SOCIAL RESPONSIBILITIES REQUIRED OF YOU AS A MANAGER

Is being socially responsible really necessary?

major question?

THE BIG PICTURE
Managers need to be aware of the viewpoints supporting and opposing social responsibility and whether being and doing good pays off financially for the organization.

The Great Recession has had a powerful impact on today's college freshmen, with 85.9% in 2011 declaring that getting "a better job" is the top reason for going to college, their principal goal for the past three years. (The second most cited reason, at 82.9%, was "to learn more about things that interest me," which had held the top spot for the first half of the past decade.)[70] But is money the be-all and end-all in business?

"We tend to categorize value as economic or social," says one observer. "You either work for a nonprofit that creates social value or you work for a for-profit that creates economic value."[71] But what if we did not judge business organizations on profits alone?

If ethical responsibility is about being a good individual citizen, social responsibility is about being a good organizational citizen. More formally, *social responsibility* **is a manager's duty to take actions that will benefit the interests of society as well as of the organization.** When generalized beyond the individual to the organization, social responsibility is called *corporate social responsibility (CSR),* **the notion that corporations are expected to go above and beyond following the law and making a profit.**

EXAMPLE

Corporate Social Responsibility: Office-Furniture Maker Herman Miller Competes on Sustainability

There are all kinds of ways by which corporate social responsibility is expressed, such as fighting poverty, dealing with water scarcity, or stepping up to the problems of climate change. A big challenge for manufacturing companies is sustainability—meeting the needs of the present without compromising the ability of future generations to meet their own needs.[72]

Audacious Goals. Herman Miller, maker of office furniture, wants "to make sure we set our sights on sustainability goals so audacious that they drag us kicking and screaming toward them," says CEO Brian Walker.[73] Herman Miller has vowed not to produce landfill waste, hazardous waste, or manufacturing emissions and to rely

completely on "green energy" by 2020. Thus, they have directed their suppliers on which materials, chemicals, and compounds are and are not allowable.

Customer Expectations. At first customers were willing to pay a premium, but now they expect companies to have a sustainability focus and won't pay a premium for it.

YOUR CALL
Does corporate social responsibility really have benefits beyond the acts of selflessness themselves? Can you think of any highly profitable and legal businesses that *do not* practice any kind of social responsibility?

Is Social Responsibility Worthwhile? Opposing & Supporting Viewpoints

In the old days of cutthroat capitalism, social responsibility was hardly thought of. A company's most important goal was to make money pretty much any way it could, and the consequences be damned. Today, for-profit enterprises generally make a point of "putting something back" into society as well as taking something out.

Not everyone, however, agrees with these new priorities. Let's consider the two viewpoints.

Against Social Responsibility   "Few trends could so thoroughly undermine the very foundations of our free society," argued the late free-market economist Milton Friedman, "as the acceptance by corporate officials of social responsibility other than to make as much money for their stockholders as possible."[74]

Friedman represents the view that, as he said, "The social responsibility of business is to make profits." That is, unless a company focuses on maximizing profits, it will become distracted and fail to provide goods and services, benefit the stockholders, create jobs, and expand economic growth—the real social justification for the firm's existence.

This view would presumably support the efforts of companies to set up headquarters in name only in offshore Caribbean tax havens (while keeping their actual headquarters in the United States) in order to minimize their tax burden.

For Social Responsibility   "A large corporation these days not only may engage in social responsibility," said famed economist Paul Samuelson, who died in 2009, "it had damned well better to try to do so."[75] That is, a company must be concerned for society's welfare as well as for corporate profits.

Beyond the fact of ethical obligation, the rationale for this view is that since businesses create problems (environmental pollution, for example), they should help solve them. Moreover, they often have the resources to solve problems in ways that the nonprofit sector does not. Finally, being socially responsible gives businesses a favorable public image that can help head off government regulation.

Corporate Social Responsibility: The Top of the Pyramid

According to University of Georgia business scholar **Archie B. Carroll,** corporate social responsibility rests at the top of a pyramid of a corporation's obligations, right up there with economic, legal, and ethical obligations. That is, while some people might hold that a company's first duty is to make a profit, Carroll suggests the responsibilities of an organization in the global economy should take the following priorities:[76]

- *Be a good global corporate citizen,* as defined by the host country's expectations.
- *Be ethical in its practices,* taking host-country and global standards into consideration.
- *Obey the law* of host countries as well as international law.
- *Make a profit* consistent with expectations for international business.

These priorities are illustrated in the pyramid opposite. *(See Figure 3.2.)*

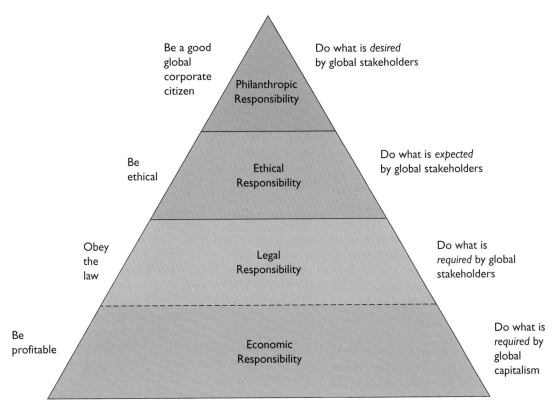

Be a good global corporate citizen

Do what is *desired* by global stakeholders

Philanthropic Responsibility

Be ethical

Do what is *expected* by global stakeholders

Ethical Responsibility

Obey the law

Do what is *required* by global stakeholders

Legal Responsibility

Be profitable

Do what is *required* by global capitalism

Economic Responsibility

figure 3.2
CARROLL'S GLOBAL CORPORATE SOCIAL RESPONSIBILITY PYRAMID

Source: Republished with permission of Academy of Management, from A. Carroll, "Managing Ethically and Global Stakeholders: A Present and Future Challenge," *Academy of Management Executive*, May 2004, p. 116; permission conveyed through Copyright Clearance Center, Inc.

One Type of Social Responsibility: Sustainability, "Going Green"

Sustainability, or "going green," is meeting humanity's needs without harming future generations. *New York Times* columnist Thomas Friedman believes that greening can be used as a competitive advantage to "outgreen" other nations.[77] Carmaker Subaru of Indiana Automotive has proved that adopting environmentally friendly processes does not add to the cost of doing business but actually makes it more efficient (reducing water use by 50%, electricity by 14%, and so on).[78]

Going green has all kinds of payoffs.[79] Insurance companies are offering lower rates for people who drive less, own hybrid cars, or build energy-efficient homes.[80] Office buildings with increased natural light, eco-friendly carpeting, and better ventilation result in employees taking fewer sick days and a rise in their productivity.[81] Hotels that induce guests to reuse towels and skip having carpets vacuumed and bed linens replaced every day save on water and electricity use.[82]

Green power. Many electricity users can run their homes on renewable energy simply by asking their local utility.

Going Green: How Businesses & Individuals Can Fight Global Warming

Global warming is "unequivocal" and will bring "irreversible changes" without immediate action, climate scientists believe, arguing that we can save the planet by investing heavily in alternative energy technology that already exists.[83] A report by energy experts at McKinsey & Company, a consulting firm, says that as much as a 28% reduction in greenhouse gases can be accomplished from steps that would more than pay for themselves in lower energy bills.[84] Small businesses, for instance, report savings of 20%–30% by making energy-saving moves.[85]

Individuals and businesses can do a number of things to attempt to fight global warming, although the problem is complicated and intractable and needs a great deal more research.[86]

Increase Recycling Increasing the recycle rate in the United States from 30% to 60% would save the equivalent of 315 million barrels of oil each year. (See **www .earth911.org** for tips on recycling.) Old computers and other electronics can be recycled or donated. (See **www .eiae.org.**)[87]

Install Energy-Saving Lightbulbs Compact fluorescent bulbs (CFLs) cost more than regular incandescent bulbs, but they last up to 10 times longer, produce 90% less heat, and also produce fewer emissions. They are also cheaper over the long term: Replacing 30 incandescent bulbs with CFLs can save more than $1,000 over the life of the bulbs.[88]

Buy Energy Star Products Energy Star appliances meet strict energy-efficiency guidelines. (See **www .energystar.gov.**) If every home replaced its TVs, DVD players, VCRs, and telephones with these models, it would be the equivalent of taking 3 million cars off the road.[89]

Convert to Green Energy More than half of all retail power customers in the United States can now run their homes on renewable energy—electricity produced by wind, solar, and geothermal power; hydropower; and various plant materials—simply by asking their local utility. The cost is about $5 a month more for a typical residential user.[90] Wind energy, incidentally, now generates more than 1% of U.S. electricity.[91] (See **www.eere.energy.gov/greenpower.**)

Store Documents Digitally Encouraging employees and customers to save documents digitally and not print out millions of paper copies can reduce waste and reduce operating budgets.[92] (See **www.greenbiz.com** and **www.greenerworldmedia.com.**)

Another Type of Social Responsibility: Philanthropy, "Not Dying Rich"

"He who dies rich dies thus disgraced," 19th-century steel magnate Andrew Carnegie is supposed to have said, after he turned his interests from making money to *philanthropy,* **making charitable donations to benefit humankind.** Carnegie became well known as a supporter of free libraries.

More recently, in 2000, Bill Gates of Microsoft, then the richest person in the world, made headlines when he announced that he would step down from day-to-day oversight of the company he cofounded in order to focus on his $29 billion philanthropy, the Bill and Melinda Gates Foundation, which pledged to spend billions on health, education, and overcoming poverty.[93] This news was closely followed by the announcement of the then second-richest man in the world, investor Warren Buffet, chairman of Berkshire Hathaway, that he would channel $31 billion to the Gates Foundation to help in finding cures for the globe's most fatal diseases.[94]

Companies practice philanthropy, too. For example, Google made a pledge to investors when it went public to reserve 1% of its profit and equity to "make the world a better place." Its philanthropic organization benefits groups ranging from those fighting disease to those developing a commercial plug-in, electricity-powered car.[95] But even ordinary individuals can become philanthropists of a sort. Mona Purdy, an Illinois hairdresser, noticed while vacationing in Guatemala that many children coated their feet with tar in order to be able to run in a local race. So she went home and established the nonprofit Share Your Shoes, which collects shoes and sends them around the world. "I always thought I was too busy to help others," she says. "Then I started this and found myself wondering where I'd been all my life."[96]

How Does Being Good Pay Off?

From a hardheaded manager's point of view, does ethical behavior and high social responsibility pay off financially? Here's what some of the research shows.[97]

Effect on Customers   According to one survey, 88% of the respondents said they were more apt to buy from companies that are socially responsible than from companies that are not.[98] Another survey of 2,037 adults found that 72% would prefer to purchase products and services from a company with ethical business practices and higher prices compared with 18% who would prefer to purchase from a company with questionable business practices and lower prices.[99]

Effect on Employees' Work Effort   Workers are more efficient, loyal, and creative when they feel a sense of purpose—when their work has meaning, says Daniel H. Pink.[100] When employers make profits their primary focus, employees develop negative feelings toward the organization. "They tend to perceive the CEO as autocratic and focused on the short term," says one report, "and they report being less willing to sacrifice for the company."[101] When employees observe the CEO balancing the concerns of customers, employees, and the community, plus being watchful of environmental effects, they report being more willing to exert extra effort—and corporate results improve!

Effect on Job Applicants & Employee Retention   Ethics can also affect the quality of people who apply to work in an organization. One online survey of 1,020 people indicated that 83% rated a company's record of business ethics as "very important" when deciding whether to accept a job offer; only 2% rated it as "unimportant."[102] A National Business Ethics Survey found that 79% of employees said their firms' concern for ethics was a key reason they remained.[103]

Effect on Sales Growth   The announcement of a company's conviction for illegal activity has been shown to diminish sales growth for several years.[104] One survey found that 80% of people said they decide to buy a firm's goods or services partly on their perception of its ethics.[105]

Effect on Company Efficiency   One survey found that 71% of employees who saw honesty applied rarely or never in their organization had seen misconduct in the past year, compared with 52% who saw honesty applied only occasionally and 25% who saw it frequently.[106]

Effect on Company Revenue   Unethical behavior in the form of employee fraud costs U.S. organizations around $652 billion a year, according to the Association of Certified Fraud Examiners.[107] Employee fraud, which is twice as common as consumer fraud (such as credit card fraud and identity theft), costs employers about 20% of every dollar earned.[108]

Effect on Stock Price   One survey found that 74% of people polled said their perception of a firm's honesty directly affected their decision about whether to buy its stock.[109] Earlier research found that investments in unethical firms earn abnormally negative returns for long periods of time.[110]

Effect on Profits   Studies suggest that profitability is enhanced by a reputation for honesty and corporate citizenship.[111]

Ethical behavior and social responsibility are more than just admirable ways of operating. They give an organization a clear competitive advantage.   ●

📄 3.5 CORPORATE GOVERNANCE

How can I trust a company is doing the right thing?

THE BIG PICTURE
Corporate governance is the system of governing a company so that the interests of corporate owners and other stakeholders are protected. Company directors should be clearly separated in their authority from the CEO by insisting on strong financial reporting systems and more accountability.

Where, you might ask, were the company boards of directors in recent years when the CEOs of firms such as Enron, WorldCom, Tyco, and Adelphia were doing the things that got them convicted for fraud? Aren't directors supposed to protect the stockholders and other stakeholders by keeping an eye on senior management? Indeed, after the Enron and other scandals, there was a renewed interest in what is known as **_corporate governance_, the system of governing a company so that the interests of corporate owners and other stakeholders are protected.**

The Need for Independent Directors

Perhaps the biggest complaint concerns the independence of the directors. As we mentioned (p. 70), inside directors may be members of the firm, outside directors are supposed to be elected from outside the firm. But in some companies, the outside directors have been handpicked by the CEO—because they are friends, because they have a business relationship with the firm, because they supposedly "know the industry." In such instances, how tough do you think the board of directors is going to be on its CEO when he or she asks for leeway to pursue certain policies?

Now more attention is being paid to strengthening corporate governance so that directors are clearly separated in their authority from the CEO. While, of course, directors are not supposed to get involved with day-to-day management issues, they are now feeling more pressure from stockholders and others to have stronger financial reporting systems and more accountability.[112]

EXAMPLE

Corporate Governance: Chesapeake Energy's CEO Gets Some Unusual Breaks from His Board of Directors

In 2008, CEO Aubrey K. McClendon topped the list of highest-paid chief executives for companies in the Standard & Poor's 500-stock index. His firm, Oklahoma City–based Chesapeake Energy, which he cofounded at age 23, is the second-largest producer of natural gas after Exxon-Mobil, and his personal fortune has been estimated by _Forbes_ as exceeding $1.2 billion. Wrote one interviewer, "He is without doubt the most admired—and feared—man in the U.S. oil patch [the petroleum and natural gas industry]. But he's also the most reckless, . . . with an off-the-charts risk tolerance."[113]

A Little Help from the Company. When aggressive financing practices combined with plunging oil and gas prices in 2008 to lower the value of Chesapeake stock by 80%, it forced McClendon to sell nearly all of his own shares. Strapped for cash, McClendon turned to his hand-picked board of directors, which for 2009 gave him a $100 million pay package plus $75 million over five years to invest in Chesapeake for a 2.5% stake in every well the company drills.

In addition, the company agreed to buy McClendon's personal collection of historical maps of the American

Southwest (which decorated the company's headquarters) for $12.1 million.[114] That amount, the firm pointed out, was McClendon's cost of acquiring the collection over the last six years; however, the company believed it was really worth at least $8 million more. The appraisal, it noted, came from "the dealer who had assisted Mr. McClendon in acquiring this collection."[115]

Shareholders Sue. Besides the above-mentioned perks, the Chesapeake board also voted to give McClendon $600,000 for the private use of the corporate jets, nearly $600,000 for accounting services, and $131,000 for "personal engineering support"—and it agreed to pay $4.6 million to sponsor the NBA's Oklahoma City Thunder, the pro basketball team that is one-fifth owned by McClendon.[116] But when outsiders and stockholders found out about the maps, the story took on a life of its own, prompting several shareholder lawsuits.

Big shareholders like the Louisiana Municipal Police Employees' Retirement System and the New Orleans Employees' Retirement System sued Chesapeake for what they considered an irresponsibly generous 2008 compensation package to McClendon and demanded that the company overhaul its compensation practices.

The map collector. Aubrey McClendon, who earned $112 million in 2008 from natural gas producer Chesapeake Energy, was the highest-paid of CEOs heading the top 500 companies that year. Even so, when plunging gas prices reduced the value of company shares by 80%, he was forced to sell off an antique map collection for $12.1 million. The appraiser: the expert who assembled the collection in the first place. The buyer: Chesapeake Energy. Does this pass the smell test?

In the resulting settlement, McClendon agreed to buy back the 19th-century maps for $12.1 million plus pay a 2.28% interest for the repurchase. In addition, after more than a third of the shareholders refused to endorse the firm's compensation, Chesapeake agreed to install a "more transparent" management pay plan. The company also agreed to some corporate governance reforms, including the hiring of an independent compensation consultant and a majority vote for election of board members and a so-called lead independent director. A final part of the corporate governance reforms was a restriction in which members of senior management, such as McClendon, were prevented from using their stock in the company as collateral to buy more stock in the company, a major cause of Chesapeake's financial strains.[117]

YOUR CALL

What would you say if you learned that, three months after the settlement, Chesapeake Energy was getting involved in new kinds of deals that one analyst said, "The story gets so complex on the company it gets hard to understand the scope of what they have"?[118] Did the corporate governance reforms go far enough? What else is needed?

The Need for Trust

In the end, suggests Fordham professor Robert Hurley, "We do not have a crisis of ethics in business today. We have a crisis of trust."[119] Customers or employees may well think that certain people or companies are ethical—that is, moral, honest, and fair— but that does not mean they should trust them. Trust, says Hurley, "comes from delivering every day on what you promise—as a manager, an employee, and a company. It involves constant teamwork, communication, and collaboration."

Trust comes from asking how likely the people you're dealing with are to serve your interests, how much they have demonstrated concern for others, how well they delivered on their promises, how much they try to keep their word—and how effectively they communicate these skills.

Would you agree? ●

Key Terms Used in This Chapter

clawbacks 73

code of ethics 82

competitors 71

corporate governance 88

corporate social responsibility (CSR) 83

customers 71

demographic forces 77

distributor 72

economic forces 75

ethical behavior 78

ethical climate 82

ethical dilemma 78

ethics 78

external stakeholders 71

general environment 75

government regulators 74

individual approach 79

insider trading 80

internal stakeholders 70

international forces 77

justice approach 80

macroenvironment 75

moral-rights approach 79

owners 70

philanthropy 86

political-legal forces 77

Ponzi scheme 81

Sarbanes–Oxley Act of 2002 81

social responsibility 83

sociocultural forces 76

special-interest groups 74

stakeholders 69

strategic allies 72

supplier 71

task environment 71

technological forces 76

utilitarian approach 79

value system 79

values 79

whistle-blower 82

Summary

3.1 The Community of Stakeholders Inside the Organization

Managers operate in two organizational environments—internal and external—both made up of stakeholders, the people whose interests are affected by the organization's activities. The first, or internal, environment includes employees, owners, and the board of directors.

3.2 The Community of Stakeholders Outside the Organization

The external environment of stakeholders consists of the task environment and the general environment.

The task environment consists of 11 groups that present the manager with daily tasks to deal with. (1) Customers pay to use an organization's goods and services. (2) Competitors compete for customers or resources. (3) Suppliers provide supplies—raw materials, services, equipment, labor, or energy—to other organizations. (4) Distributors help another organization sell its goods and services to customers. (5) Strategic allies join forces to achieve advantages neither organization can perform as well alone. (6) Employee organizations are labor unions and employee associations. (7) Local communities are residents, companies, governments, and nonprofit entities that depend on the organization's taxes, payroll, and charitable contributions. (8) Financial institutions are commercial banks, investment banks, and insurance companies that deal with the organization. (9) Government regulators are regulatory agencies that establish

the ground rules under which the organization operates. (10) Special-interest groups are groups whose members try to influence specific issues that may affect the organization. (11) The mass media are print, radio, TV, and Internet sources that affect the organization's public relations.

The general environment includes six forces. (1) Economic forces consist of general economic conditions and trends—unemployment, inflation, interest rates, economic growth—that may affect an organization's performance. (2) Technological forces are new developments in methods for transforming resources into goods and services. (3) Sociocultural forces are influences and trends originating in a country, society, or culture's human relationships and values that may affect an organization. (4) Demographic forces are influences on an organization arising from changes in the characteristics of a population, such as age, gender, and ethnic origin. (5) Political-legal forces are changes in the way politics shape laws and laws shape the opportunities for and threats to an organization. (6) International forces are changes in the economic, political, legal, and technological global system that may affect an organization.

3.3 The Ethical Responsibilities Required of You as a Manager

Ethics are the standards of right and wrong that influence behavior. Ethical behavior is behavior that is accepted as "right" as opposed to "wrong" according to those standards.

Ethical dilemmas often take place because of an organization's value system. Values are the relatively permanent and deeply held underlying beliefs and attitudes that help determine a person's behavior.

There are four approaches to deciding ethical dilemmas. (1) Utilitarian—ethical behavior is guided by what will result in the greatest good for the greatest number of people. (2) Individual—ethical behavior is guided by what will result in the individual's best long-term interests, which ultimately is in everyone's self-interest. (3) Moral-rights—ethical behavior is guided by respect for the fundamental rights of human beings, such as those expressed in the U.S. Constitution's Bill of Rights. (4) Justice—ethical behavior is guided by respect for the impartial standards of fairness and equity.

Public outrage over white-collar crime (Enron, Tyco) led to the creation of the Sarbanes–Oxley Act of 2002 (SarbOx), which established requirements for proper financial record keeping for public companies and penalties for noncompliance.

Laurence Kohlberg proposed three levels of personal moral development: (1) preconventional level of moral development—people tend to follow rules and to obey authority; (2) conventional level—people are conformist, generally adhering to the expectations of others; and (3) postconventional level—people are guided by internal values.

There are three ways an organization may foster high ethical standards. (1) Top managers must support a strong ethical climate. (2) The organization may have a code of ethics, which consists of a formal written set of ethical standards. (3) An organization must reward ethical behavior, as in not discouraging whistle-blowers, employees who report organizational misconduct to the public.

3.4 The Social Responsibilities Required of You as a Manager

Social responsibility is a manager's duty to take actions that will benefit the interests of society as well as of the organization.

The idea of social responsibility has opposing and supporting viewpoints. The opposing viewpoint is that the social responsibility of business is to make profits. The supporting viewpoint is that since business creates some problems (such as pollution) it should help solve them.

One scholar, Archie Carroll, suggests the responsibilities of an organization in the global economy should take the following priorities: (1) Be a good global corporate citizen; (2) be ethical in its practices; (3) obey the law; and (4) make a profit—in that order.

One type of social responsibility is sustainability, "going green," or meeting humanity's needs without harming future generations. Another type is philanthropy, making charitable donations to benefit humankind.

Positive ethical behavior and social responsibility can pay off in the form of customer goodwill, more efficient and loyal employees, better quality of job applicants and retained employees, enhanced sales growth, less employee misconduct and fraud, better stock price, and enhanced profits.

3.5 Corporate Governance

Corporate governance is the system of governing a company so that the interests of corporate owners and other stakeholders are protected.

One way to further corporate governance is to be sure directors are clearly separated in their authority from the CEO by insisting on stronger financial reporting systems and more accountability.

Management in Action

Carnival CEO Micky Arison Fails to Provide Interviews After the *Costa Concordia* Sinks

Where is Micky Arison?

The chief executive, chairman, and part owner of Carnival Corp. has largely kept himself and Carnival out of the spotlight since one of the company's ships struck rocks off the Italian coast January 13 [2012]. On Sunday, a 13th person was confirmed dead and at least 19 were still missing.

The leaking, submerged *Costa Concordia* represents the stiffest challenge yet for the 62-year-old Mr. Arison, who over more than three decades has

quietly built Carnival into the world's largest cruise-ship company. Today it boasts a stock-market capitalization of $18 billion and annual revenue of $16 billion, more than twice as large by both measures as Royal Caribbean Cruises Ltd., the next-largest company.

Images of the massive shipwreck and transcripts of the chaotic evacuation of more than 3,000 vacationers beamed around the world threaten the reputation of an industry that has enjoyed a reputation for safety and few major accidents. Cruise operators, in the midst of what traditionally is their heaviest booking season, already have been grappling with high fuel prices and Europe's weakening economy.

Mr. Arison is managing the crisis from Carnival's offices a few miles from Miami's port while the crisis continues to unfold in Italy. . . .

Carnival says Mr. Arison has been "in continuous contact" with *Costa*'s Italian executives but that the CEO decided the unit's management is best suited to handle the on-the-ground response. That appears to be in keeping with Mr. Arison's management style, which is less hands-on than many chief executives. He gives great independence to executive teams running each of Carnival Corp.'s 10 cruise lines, which include Holland America, Princess Cruises, Cunard and Carnival Cruise Lines. Most have their headquarters outside of Miami and maintain separate sales, marketing and reservations programs.

"He is a big delegator in that all of his brands operate autonomously," said Joe Hovorka, a cruise-industry analyst at brokerage Raymond James.

By maintaining a low public profile during the *Costa Concordia* crisis, Mr. Arison and Carnival also might limit the focus on the parent company and its other cruise lines. . . .

"He wants to distance Carnival from the disaster," said one longtime acquaintance of Mr. Arison. "If he talks, Carnival is speaking." . . .

Mr. Arison hasn't granted interviews since the accident. Nor has he been seen over the past week and a half at any games of the Miami Heat, the professional basketball team he owns.

Bob Dickinson, a board member and former Carnival executive, said in an interview that management has responded to the catastrophe in "textbook fashion" and praised Mr. Arison for his steadying influence behind the scenes.

"There is a calming reassurance about him," Mr. Dickinson said. "It kind of cuts through the fog of war."

Mr. Arison, who often sleeps aboard a 200-foot yacht in Miami, has a reputation for avoiding the spotlight. But he is a fan of Twitter, and regularly tweets about his team and cruise company. Though he has remained out of public view now, he has expressed condolences to *Costa Concordia*'s victims on Twitter and in company-issued news releases. . . .

Mr. Arison also gave his "personal assurance" Wednesday that Carnival would "take care" of passengers, crew and victims and announced Thursday a comprehensive audit of safety and emergency-response procedures across all of the company's cruise lines. As of Sunday, neither he nor Carnival had made any further public statements.

Some have questioned the wisdom of Mr. Arison not taking a more public role in the wake of the worst cruise-line accident in years. Divers continued over the weekend to search for bodies near the Mediterranean island of Giglio and Italy declared a state of emergency Friday around the *Costa Concordia* shipwreck, with more than 2,000 tons of fuel threatening to escape the vessel's tanks.

"You can't be invisible when the spotlight is shining on you, particularly if you are the CEO," said Richard Torrenzano, head of Torrenzano Group, a crisis-communications consultancy in New York.

Carnival's share price tumbled 14% in the first day of trading in New York after the accident, also wiping hundreds of millions of dollars off the net worth of Mr. Arison, who owns nearly a third of the shares. . . .

Mr. Arison, a university of Miami dropout, has a long history at sea. Ted Arison, his late father, launched Carnival in 1972 with one ship, the *Mardi Gras*, which got stuck on a sandbar near Miami on its maiden voyage. . . .

Today as many as 200,000 guests and 70,000 employees travel aboard Carnival Corp.'s ships on any given day.

Mr. Arison also has won over many investors by overseeing fatter profit margins than rival Royal Caribbean. Even though corporate-governance experts have long criticized his generous pay packages, he kept his father's Formica desk and continues to run the company out of a 10th-floor office with views of Miami's airport and an expressway instead of the ocean.

FOR DISCUSSION

1. Which internal and external stakeholders are positively and negatively affected by Micky Arison's decision to avoid contact with the media?

2. Which of the six general environmental forces influenced Arison's decision to avoid communicating about the sinking of the *Costa Concordia*? Discuss.

3. Use the four approaches to deciding ethical dilemmas to evaluate whether Arison made an ethical decision to avoid communicating about the sinking of the *Costa Concordia*.

4. To what extent did Arison respond to Carnival's internal and external stakeholders in a socially responsible manner? Explain.

5. Do you think Arison is making a good decision to avoid communicating with the media about the sinking of the *Costa Concordia*? What are the pros and cons of his communication strategy?

Source: Excerpted from Mike Esterl and Joann S. Lublin, "Carnival CEO Lies Low After Crash," *The Wall Street Journal*, January 23, 2012, pp. B1, B5. Copyright © 2012 by Dow Jones & Company, Inc. Reproduced with permission of Dow Jones & Company, Inc. via Copyright Clearance Center.

What Is Your Guiding Ethical Principle?

OBJECTIVES

1. To understand your ethical approach.
2. To understand that there are different ways to perceive ethics in the workplace.

INTRODUCTION

Over the centuries people have grappled with defining ethics and behaving ethically. Many different principles have evolved to deal with ethics from different perspectives. None is better or worse than the other—they are simply perspectives. You may choose one to be your guiding principle while your friend follows another. This is also true of companies and their employees. For example, Johnson & Johnson traditionally had a valued reputation for being very ethical and socially responsible, whereas actions by companies such as Ford and Arthur Andersen have placed a large question mark on their ethical conduct and social responsibility.

INSTRUCTIONS

Rank each of the following principles in order from 1 (my most important guiding principle) to 3 (least relevant to my ethical principles).

1. *Utilitarianism:* The greatest good for the greatest number, or any view that holds that actions and policies should be evaluated on the basis of benefits and costs they will impose on society.

    Violation? The Ford Motor Company knew of the problems with its tires 6 years before they became known in the United States. This was information from Europe, and U.S. law did not require that the company report it if it did not happen in this country.

2. *Rights Theory:* A right is an individual's entitlement or claim to something. A person has a right when he or she is entitled to act in a certain way or is entitled to have others act in a certain way toward him or her. It can be a legal right, a moral right, or a human right.

    Violation? Many stockholders at Microsoft want the company to adopt the "U.S. Business Principles for Human Rights of Workers in China," a statement supported by other companies such as Levi Strauss and Reebok. Microsoft management did not agree, arguing that its own principles and code of ethics covered the important points and that the statement principles were too broad and vague. Other companies also thought that American companies should not promote human rights in China because they would be abandoning a position of political neutrality.

3. *Justice as Fairness:* A principle that aims to protect those least able to protect themselves.

    Examples: Companies should establish strong affirmative action plans to redress the wrongs of discrimination. Or, if a company introduces pay cuts, the workers paid the least should receive the smallest pay cut and those who are paid the most should get the largest pay cut.

QUESTIONS FOR DISCUSSION

1. What are the pros and cons of your primary ethical principle in terms of advancing up the corporate ladder? Discuss.

2. Why do you think ethical principles are important in the workplace? Explain.

3. Which of the previous three principles would you want the company that you work for to adopt? Why?

4. In such a competitive world, how ethical can any company really be?

Developed by Anne C. Cowden, PhD, Laura P. Hartman, and Joseph R. DesJardins, *Business Ethics: Decision-Making for Personal Integrity and Social Responsibility* (Burr Ridge, IL: McGraw-Hill, 2008). See Chapter 3 for a detailed discussion for each approach.

Should Facebook Take a More Proactive Approach in Monitoring the Children's Online Privacy Protection Act (COPPA)?

The focus of this challenge involves Facebook's role in monitoring the Children's Online Privacy Protection Act. "The Children's Online Privacy Protection Act generally prohibits website operators from knowingly collecting personally identifiable information from children under 13 without parental consent," according to *The Wall Street Journal.* "It also requires site operators to collect only personal information that is 'reasonably necessary' for an online activity. The law, which was enacted in 1998 and took effect in 2000, says personal information includes a full name, home or e-mail address, telephone number or Social Security number."

"The law was intended to give parents control over the information collected from their children online and how that information is used and shared," the article continues. "Mamie Kresses, a senior attorney at the Federal Trade Commission, which enforces the law, says it grew from concerns in the 1990s about websites that used cartoon characters, prizes, and other techniques to encourage children to submit personal or family information without their parents' knowledge."

A recent survey of 1,007 parents suggests that people are violating COPPA's provisions when registering at Facebook. Results revealed that "36% were aware that their children joined Facebook before age 13 and that a substantial percentage of those parents helped their kids lie about their age in order to join the social networking site," says another *Wall Street Journal* report. More specifically, "55% of parents of 12-year-olds report their child has a Facebook account; 82% of these parents knew when their underage child signed up and 76% assisted in creating the account."

SOLVING THE CHALLENGE

Assume that you are a high-level manager at Facebook. What would you suggest that the company should do in regard to monitoring the requirements of COPPA?

1. Nothing. Parents need to be responsible for the acts of their children. Besides, parents seem to be helping their kids lie during the process of joining Facebook. If parents don't mind lying, so be it.

2. Facebook should be more proactive about ensuring that kids are older than 13. The company could require all people without a valid driver's license to submit proof of age such as a birth certificate.

3. Facebook should lobby against the law. Facebook contains educational and social opportunities and the company should not restrict people under the age of 13 from experiencing these valuable opportunities.

4. Invent other options. Discuss.

Source: Excerpted from Courtney Banks, "Understanding the Children's Online Privacy Protection Act," *The Wall Street Journal.WSJ.com,* September 17, 2010; and Kevin Helliker, "Parents Abet Facebook Use," *The Wall Street Journal,* November 2, 2011, p. B5.

chapter 4

Global Management
Managing Across Borders

Major Questions You Should Be Able to Answer

4.1 Globalization: The Collapse of Time & Distance

Major Question: What three important developments of globalization will probably affect me?

4.2 You & International Management

Major Question: Why learn about international management, and what characterizes the successful international manager?

4.3 Why & How Companies Expand Internationally

Major Question: Why do companies expand internationally, and how do they do it?

4.4 The World of Free Trade: Regional Economic Cooperation

Major Question: What are barriers to free trade, and what major organizations and trading blocs promote trade?

4.5 The Importance of Understanding Cultural Differences

Major Question: What are the principal areas of cultural differences?

Learning to Be a Success Abroad: How Do You Become a World Citizen?

Whether you travel abroad on your own or on a work assignment for your company, there are several ways to make your experience enhance your career success.

Learn How Not to Be an "Ugly American"

Americans "are seen throughout the world as an arrogant people, totally self-absorbed and loud," says Keith Reinhard, former head of advertising conglomerate DDB Worldwide, who is leading an effort to reverse that through a nonprofit group called Business for Diplomatic Action (BDA), from which many suggestions here are drawn.[1] A survey conducted by DDB in more than 100 countries found that respondents repeatedly mentioned "arrogant," "loud," and "uninterested in the world" when asked their perceptions of Americans.[2] Some sample advice for Americans traveling abroad is: Be patient, be quiet, listen at least as much as you talk, don't use slang, and don't talk about wealth and status.[3]

Be Global in Your Focus, but Think Local

Study up on your host country's local customs and try to meet new people who might help you in the future. For example, Bill Roedy, president of MTV Networks International, spent time hanging out with Arab rappers and meeting the mayor of Mecca before trying to sign a contract that would launch MTV Arabia.[4] His efforts helped seal the deal.

Learn What's Appropriate Behavior

Before you go, spend some time learning about patterns of interpersonal communication. In Japan, for instance, it is considered rude to look directly into the eye for more than a few seconds. In Greece the hand-waving gesture commonly used in America is considered an insult. In Afghanistan, a man does not ask another man about his wife.[5]

Learn rituals of respect, including exchange of business cards. Understand that shaking hands is always permissible, but social kissing may not be. Dress professionally. For women, this means no heavy makeup, no flashy jewelry, no short skirts or sleeveless blouses (particularly in Islamic countries). In some countries, casual dressing is a sign of disrespect. Don't use first names and nicknames with fellow employees overseas, especially in countries with strict social strata.[6]

Know Your Field

If you know your field and behave with courtesy and assurance, you will be well received around the world. Indra Nooyi successfully uses this advice in her role as CEO of PepsiCo. She's cosmopolitan and well educated and is respected by people around the globe.[7]

Become at Least Minimally Skilled in the Language

Whatever foreign country you're in, at the very least you should learn a few key phrases, such as "hello," "please," and "thank you," in your host country's language. Successful international managers have learned there is no adequate substitute for knowing the local language.[8]

For Discussion Have you done much traveling? What tricks have you discovered to make it more satisfying?

forecast What's Ahead in This Chapter

This chapter covers the importance of globalization—the rise of the global village, of one big market, of both worldwide megafirms and minifirms. We also describe the characteristics of the successful international manager and why and how companies expand internationally. We describe the barriers to free trade and the major organizations promoting trade. Finally, we discuss some of the cultural differences you may encounter if you become an international manager.

major question

What three important developments of globalization will probably affect me?

THE BIG PICTURE

Globalization, the trend of the world economy toward becoming a more interdependent system, is reflected in three developments: the rise of the "global village" and e-commerce, the trend of the world's becoming one big market, and the rise of both megafirms and Internet-enabled minifirms worldwide.

Is everything for sale in the United States now made outside our borders?

Not quite everything—and Roger Simmermaker, 46, an Orlando, Florida, electronics technician who drives a Michigan-made Lincoln Town Car (1996, 315,000 miles), is seriously focused on buying American-made products. In fact, Simmermaker has authored a book, *How Consumers Can Buy American,* which lists more than 16,000 U.S.-made products.[9] "It's important to understand that workers in China don't pay taxes to America," he says. It's a fallacy, he adds, that most U.S. products cost more.[10]

As it happens, the vast majority of goods and services sold in the United States *are* still produced in this country. However, we might be forgiven for thinking otherwise. With shoes and clothing, for instance, about 36% of U.S. dollars are spent on Chinese-made products, compared with 25% on U.S.-made items.[11]

It's clear that we are living in a world being rapidly changed by *globalization—* **the trend of the world economy toward becoming a more interdependent system.** Time and distance, which have been under assault for 150 years, have now virtually collapsed, as reflected in three important developments we discuss.[12]

1. The rise of the global village and electronic commerce.
2. The world's becoming one market instead of many national ones.
3. The rise of both megafirms and Internet-enabled minifirms worldwide.

The Rise of the Global Village & Electronic Commerce

The hallmark of great civilizations has been their great systems of communications. In the beginning, communications were based on transportation: the Roman Empire had its network of roads, as did other ancient civilizations, such as the Incas. Later the great European powers had their far-flung navies. In the 19th century, the United States and Canada unified North America by building transcontinental railroads. Later the airplane reduced travel time between continents.

From Transportation to Communication Transportation began to yield to the electronic exchange of information. Beginning in 1844, the telegraph ended the short existence of the Pony Express and, beginning in 1876, found itself in competition with the telephone. The amplifying vacuum tube, invented in 1906, led to commercial radio. Television came into being in England in 1925. During the 1950s and 1960s, as television exploded throughout the world, communications philosopher Marshall McLuhan posed the notion of a "global village," where we all share our hopes, dreams, and fears in a "worldpool" of information. **The *global village* refers to the "shrinking" of time and space as air travel and the electronic media have made it easier for the people around the globe to communicate with one another.**

Then the world became even faster and smaller. Fifteen years ago, cellphones, pagers, fax, and voice-mail links barely existed. When AT&T launched the first cellular communications system in 1983, it predicted fewer than a million users by 2000. By the end of 1993, however, there were more than 16 million cellular phone subscribers in the United States.[13] By 2011, there were 5.9 billion mobile-cellular subscriptions, with global penetration reaching 87%.[14]

The Net, the Web, & the World   Then came the Internet, the worldwide computer-linked "network of networks." Today, of the 7 billion people in the world, 35% are Internet users.[15] The Net might have remained the province of academicians had it not been for the contributions of Tim Berners-Lee, who came up with the coding system, linkages, and addressing scheme that debuted in 1991 as the World Wide Web. "He took a powerful communications system [the Internet] that only the elite could use," says one writer, "and turned it into a mass medium."[16]

The arrival of the Web quickly led to *e-commerce,* **or electronic commerce, the buying and selling of products and services through computer networks.** U.S. retail e-commerce sales were estimated at $48.2 billion in the third quarter of 2011.[17]

EXAMPLE

E-Commerce: Resolers to the World

Perhaps the most well-known story of e-commerce companies is that of Amazon.com, which was started in 1994 by Jeffrey Bezos as an online bookstore and later expanded into nonbook areas. Now e-commerce has spread well beyond books, CDs, and electronics to embrace even the most mundane of goods and services—shoe repair, for example.

Global Cobblers. In the 1930s, there were more than 120,000 shoe-repair businesses in the United States. Now there are about 7,000, the result of increased affordability in new shoes. Still, many people (some with special orthopedic needs) want to hang on to favorite footwear. Into the gap vacated by vanished mainstreet cobblers have stepped several online shoe refurbishment and repair services. Some examples are American Heelers, Great Lakes Shoe & Orthopedic Services, NuShoe, Resole America.

Online Service. Reporter Sarah Needleman, trying out these four companies' services, went to the website of American Heelers, launched in 2007 by Ilya Romanov to augment his father's Woodmere, Ohio, repair shop. There Needleman found service descriptions, prices, and instructions on how to request shipping materials. After placing the order online, she received a quote and shoe mailing envelope. Later she received billing and payment information (final cost: $44.99). Sent back within the five to seven days the company promised, the repaired shoes, "were vastly improved," Needleman writes, "with a new set of full heels and soles, plus they'd been shined, cleaned, waterproofed, and conditioned."[18]

YOUR CALL

Can you think of any other specialized medium-sized or small business, domestic or worldwide, that the Internet has made possible? Could you see yourself launching a similar venture? What would it be?

One Big World Market: The Global Economy

"We are seeing the results of things started in 1988 and 1989," said Rosabeth Moss Kantor of the Harvard Business School a decade later.[19] It was in the late 1980s when the Berlin Wall came down, signaling the beginning of the end of communism in Eastern Europe. It was also when Asian countries began to open their economies to foreign investors. Finally, the trend toward governments deregulating their economies began sweeping the globe. These three events set up conditions by which goods, people, and money could move more freely throughout the world—a global economy. **The *global economy* refers to the increasing tendency of the economies of the world to interact with one another as one market instead of many national markets.**

The economies of the world have never been more entangled. As technology writer Kevin Maney wrote, "They're tied together by instantaneous information arriving via everything from currency trading databases to Web sites to CNN broadcasts. Capital—the money used to build businesses—moves globally and moves in a matter of keystrokes."[20]

Positive Effects   Is a global economy really good for the United States? "Ultimately, the medium- to long-term benefits of globalization are positive for everybody,"

"Oh, same old thing." The cellphone represents a boon to less-developed countries because this kind of telephone infrastructure does not entail the costly process of installing miles of telephone poles and landlines.

says the CEO of Infosys Technologies in India. "Let me give you an example. As our industry has increased economic activity in India, it's becoming a bigger market for American exports . . . Today you can't find any soft drinks in India except Coke or Pepsi."[21]

In addition, foreign firms are building plants in the United States, revitalizing parts of industrial America.[22] Indeed, foreign direct investment makes up 15% of the country's gross domestic product (total value of all goods and services). Companies based overseas provide jobs for approximately 10% of the U.S. workforce.[23] When the recession ends, suggests Gregg Easterbrook, author of *Sonic Boom: Globalization at Mach Speed,* worldwide economic growth will pick up, "creating rising prosperity and higher living standards. . . . The world will be far more interconnected, leading to better and more affordable products, as well as ever better communication among nations."[24]

Negative Effects   However, global economic interdependency can also be dangerous. Financial crises throughout the world resulted in vast surplus funds from global investments flowing into the United States and being invested badly in a housing-and-credit bubble that burst (the so-called subprime mortgages meltdown), leading to the 2007–2009 Great Recession that hurt so many people.[25]

Another negative effect is the movement, or outsourcing, of formerly well-paying jobs overseas as companies seek cheaper labor costs, particularly in manufacturing. Soaring new U.S. skyscrapers, for example, are more apt to have windows made in China than in Ohio, a glassmaking state.[26] Some economists fear that many jobs lost through the recession and offshoring may simply never come back.[27]

Indeed, while "the horizon has never been brighter," says Easterbrook, "we may not feel particularly happy about it." The reasons: "Job instability, economic insecurity, a sense of turmoil, the fear that even when things seem good a hammer is about to fall—these are also part of the larger trend. As world economies become ever more linked by computers, job stress will become a 24/7 affair. Frequent shakeups in industries will cause increasing uncertainty."[28] But the global economy isn't going to go away just because we don't like some of its destabilizing aspects.

Cross-Border Business: The Rise of Both Megamergers & Minifirms Worldwide

The global market driven by electronic information "forces things to get bigger and smaller at the same time," suggests technology philosopher Nicholas Negroponte. "And that's so ironic, when things want to do both but not stay in the middle. There will be an increasing absence of things that aren't either very local or very global."[29]

If Negroponte is correct, this means we will see more and more of two opposite kinds of businesses: mergers of huge companies into even larger companies, and small, fast-moving startup companies.

Megamergers Operating Worldwide   Walt Disney + Pixar. Kmart + Sears. Union Pacific + Southern Pacific. Whole Foods + Wild Oats. Bank of America + Merrill Lynch. Chrysler + Fiat. Roche + Genentech. Ticketmaster + Live Nation. Kraft + Cadbury. Comcast + NBC Universal. Mattel (maker of Barbie Doll) + Hit Entertainment (Bob the Builder).

The last 20 years have seen a surge in mergers. Certain industries—oil, telecommunications, automobiles, financial services, and pharmaceuticals, for instance—aren't suited to being midsize, let alone small and local, so companies in these industries are trying to become bigger and cross-border. The means for doing so is to merge with other big companies. In telecommunications, for instance, AT&T targeted T-Mobile and in automobiles Porsche targeted Volkswagen (and then, in turn, VW tried to acquire Porsche), but ultimately both deals fell through.[30] Oil companies, already gigantic from earlier mergers (Exxon + Mobil, Conoco + Phillips), were expected to begin another wave of acquisitions in the near future, and utilities also turned to mergers as power demands slowed (despite the increase in tablet computers, Internet data centers, and electric vehicles).[31]

Minifirms Operating Worldwide   The Internet and the World Wide Web allow almost anyone to be global, which Kevin Maney points out has two important results:

1. **Small companies can get started more easily.** Because anyone can put goods or services on a website and sell worldwide, this wipes out the former competitive advantages of distribution and scope that large companies used to have.

2. **Small companies can maneuver faster.** Little companies can change direction faster, which gives them an advantage in terms of time and distance over large companies. ●

EXAMPLE

Small Companies That Get Started More Easily & Can Maneuver Faster: Bay-Traders

Many small firms have come from nowhere to collapse time and distance. For instance, so-called Bay-traders make a living selling things on eBay, the online auction company. Bay-traders find they get higher prices at Internet auctions than at swap meets or collectibles shows because bidding generates excitement and because the Internet's worldwide reach makes multiple bids more likely.

Mannequin Madness. Judi Henderson-Townsand's Oakland, California, company, Mannequin Madness, began when, while working in marketing for a failing dot-com firm, she saw an online ad from a window dresser offering 50 mannequins. After purchasing the entire inventory, she started renting mannequins and later, after buying more from department stores, started selling them to special-event planners, retail stores, and artists.

Henderson-Townsand claims that the Internet, including eBay, has been by far her greatest marketing resource because it allows the firm to reach customers who could never be reached otherwise.[32]

YOUR CALL

Do you have an idea for some uncommon products you might sell on eBay? What would they be?

major question Why learn about international management, and what characterizes the successful international manager?

THE BIG PICTURE

Studying international management prepares you to work with foreign customers or suppliers, for a foreign firm in the United States or for a U.S. firm overseas. Successful international managers aren't ethnocentric or polycentric but geocentric.

Can you see yourself working overseas? It can definitely be an advantage to your career. "There are fewer borders," says Paul McDonald, executive director of recruitment firm Robert Half Management Resources. "Anyone with international experience will have a leg up, higher salary, and be more marketable."[33] The recent brutal U.S. job market has also spurred more Americans to hunt for jobs overseas (and impelled foreign-born professionals who used to work in the United States to return home).[34]

EXAMPLE

Americans Working Overseas

When Charles Wang, an industrial engineering major, completed his junior year at Georgia Institute of Technology in 2008, he joined United Parcel Service as a project manager. His assignment: Go to Dubai for 10 months and develop a delivery system for the Arab country's first-ever network of streets and addresses. Following graduation, he planned to return to Dubai for a permanent job "because of . . . my inability to find good jobs in the U.S."[35]

Julie Androshick spent two years teaching in Samoa and then worked as a journalist and as an analyst for consulting company McKinsey & Company. Now based in New York, Androshick says working abroad expanded her worldview, gave her the courage to pursue long-shot jobs, and made her a more loyal employee.[36] After graduating from Northwestern University, Nate Linkon found a job in marketing with InfoSys Technologies, the Indian software giant, in Bangalore.[37] Scott Stapleton, formerly of Oakland,

California, also took a marketing job with InfoSys in India. "The job blends practical work experience with life in a developing country," says Stapleton, adding that it's "a rare opportunity to actually witness globalization."[38]

Jacob Schickler, 25, moved to Beijing in 2009 and found a job with a German company working in business development. He hopes the China experience will give him an edge over other young adults in the United States. "Many of my friends are bright, intelligent people with very expensive degrees," he says, "but they have not been able to put them to use yet. I'm getting real work experience."[39]

YOUR CALL

How do you feel about following the paths of these intrepid travelers? How can you begin to prepare yourself for working overseas?

Foreign experience demonstrates independence, resourcefulness, and entrepreneurship, according to management recruiters. "You are interested in that person who can move quickly and is nimble and has an inquiring mind," says one. People who have worked and supported themselves overseas, she says, tend to be adaptive and inquisitive—valuable skills in today's workplace.[40]

Why Learn about International Management?

International management is management that oversees the conduct of operations in or with organizations in foreign countries, whether it's through a multinational corporation or a multinational organization.

Part of the action. If "all of the action in business is international," as one expert says, what role do you think you might play in it? Do you think cultural bias against women in some foreign countries contributes to the low percentage of U.S. female executives working abroad?

Multinational Corporations A *multinational corporation*, or multinational enterprise, is a business firm with operations in several countries. Our publisher, McGraw-Hill, is one such multinational (with a presence in 17 foreign cities). In terms of sales revenue, the largest multinational corporations are the American firms JP Morgan Chase, General Electric, ExxonMobil, Berkshire Hathaway, CitiGroup, Wells Fargo, AT&T, Chevron, and Walmart Stores. The largest foreign companies are HSBC Holdings (major banks, Britain), Royal Dutch/Shell (Netherlands), PetroChina (China), ICBC (major banks, China), and PetroBras Ptr Brasil (Brazil).[41]

Of the world's 500 largest multinational firms, the U.S. economy is home to 139 of them, and they employ about 22 million of the 153 million people in the U.S. workforce. However, since 2000, these firms have shed 2.9 million workers at home while adding 2.4 million workers overseas.[42]

Multinational Organizations A *multinational organization* is a nonprofit organization with operations in several countries. Examples are the World Health Organization, the International Red Cross, and the Church of Latter Day Saints.

Even if in the coming years you never travel to the wider world outside North America—an unlikely proposition, we think—the world will assuredly come to you. That, in a nutshell, is why you need to learn about international management.

PRACTICAL ACTION

Being an Effective Road Warrior

Since business travelers who fly 100,000-plus miles a year are no longer a rare breed, should you prepare for the possibility of joining them?

Business travel can have its rewards. Many people enjoy going to different cities, meeting new people, encountering new cultures. In one survey, people who took business trips of five nights or more said that being on the road provided certain escapes, as from their everyday workplace (35% of those polled), putting out work "fires" (20%), frequent meetings (12%), and coworker distractions (11%).[43]

Business travelers have learned the following three lessons.

Lesson 1: Frequent Travel May Be Needed Because Personal Encounters Are Essential. "There is no substitute for face time," says a *BusinessWeek* article.[44] Yes, technologies such as smartphones, e-mail, and videoconferencing make it easier to connect with others—superficially, at least. "But," says an investment banker, "in a global world you have to get in front of your employees, spend time with your clients, and show commitment when it comes to joint ventures, mergers, and alliances. The key is thoughtful travel—traveling when necessary."[45] Adds another top executive, "If you are going to disagree with somebody, you certainly don't want to do it by e-mail, and if possible you don't even want to do it by phone. You want to do it face to face."[46]

Lesson 2: Travel May Be Global, but Understanding Must Be Local. "In China, we had translators, but we were still used to conducting business American style, where you can get a deal done in two hours and everyone leaves happy," says Ty Morse, whose company develops things like text messaging platforms and mobile payment processing solutions. "But in Asia, every meeting was about 10 hours long and everyone wanted to serve us food. We were so stuffed and jet-lagged, it was ridiculous."[47]

Being a road warrior is all about making bets with one's time, calculating the strategy of where to be when. Thus, world-traveling executives must do their homework to know cultures, organizations, and holders of power.

"Cull information on the individuals and companies you're visiting," says one expert. "Follow the news relating to the region. If possible try to read a few books about the history and culture of the lands you will visit. . . . Learn a few words too."[48] Because in Asia and the Middle East personal relationships are crucial to getting things done, you need to engage in small talk and avoid business talk during after-hours outings. Says Ted Dale, president of international business consulting firm Aperian Global, "You need to spend out-of-office time in social settings." In Asia, the Middle East, and Latin America, it's important to understand organizational hierarchy, as represented by professional titles and age.[49]

Lesson 3: Frequent Travel Requires Frequent Adjustments. How do you cope if you travel all the time? Some people pack their own bags. Others keep complete wardrobes in major cities. Lisa Bergson has a detailed packing list that "comprises everything, from voltage adaptors to herbal teas to foot spray." She has also developed a "day-by-day wardrobe chart for every trip of a week or more, attempting to leverage every item and still look chic."[50] Sales manager Sue Reiss has learned not to carry her identification, cash, and credit cards in the same place (because once her purse was stolen carrying all three things) and she has learned to immediately get on local time to help beat jet lag.[51]

YOUR CALL

As we discussed, managers must be prepared to work for organizations that operate not only countrywide but worldwide. To stay connected with colleagues, employees, clients, and suppliers, you may have to travel a lot. Does this give you cause for concern? What do you think you should do about it?

More specifically, consider yourself in the following situations:

You May Deal with Foreign Customers or Partners While working for a U.S. company you may have to deal with foreign customers. Or you may have to work with a foreign company in some sort of joint venture. The people you're dealing with may be outside the United States or visitors to it. Either way you would hate to blow a deal—and maybe all future deals—because you were ignorant of some cultural aspects you could have known about.

Examples are legion.[52] One American executive inadvertently insulted or embarrassed Thai businessmen by starting gatherings talking about business. "That's a no-no," he says. "I quickly figured out that I was creating problems by talking business before eating lunch and by initiating the talks."

You May Deal with Foreign Employees or Suppliers While working for an American company you may have to purchase important components, raw materials, or services from a foreign supplier. And you never know where foreign practices may diverge from what you're accustomed to.

Many software developer jobs, for instance, have been moved outside the United States—to places such as India, New Zealand, and Eastern Europe. A lot of U.S. software companies—Microsoft, IBM, Oracle, Motorola, Novell, Hewlett-Packard, and Texas Instruments—have opened offices in India to take advantage of high-quality labor. General Electric, Caterpillar, and 3M have spent millions expanding their overseas research labs.[53]

You May Work for a Foreign Firm in the United States You may sometime take a job with a foreign firm doing business in the United States, such as an electronics, pharmaceutical, or car company. And you'll have to deal with managers above and below you whose outlook is different from yours. For instance, Japanese companies, with their emphasis on correctness and face saving, operate in significantly different ways from American companies.

Sometimes it is even hard to know that an ostensibly U.S. company actually has foreign ownership. For example, some American book publishers (though not McGraw-Hill) are British or German owned.

Working for a foreign firm. If you thought you might work for a foreign firm, either at home or overseas, what should you be doing now to prepare for it?

You May Work for an American Firm Outside the United States—or for a Foreign One You might easily find yourself working abroad in the foreign operation of a U.S. company. Most big American corporations have overseas subsidiaries or divisions. On the other hand, you might also well work for a foreign firm in a foreign country, such as a big Indian company in Bangalore or Mumbai.

The Successful International Manager: Geocentric, Not Ethnocentric or Polycentric

Maybe you don't really care that you don't have much understanding of the foreign culture you're dealing with. "What's the point?" you may think. "The main thing is to get the job done." Certainly there are international firms with managers who have this perspective. They are called *ethnocentric,* one of three primary attitudes among international managers, the other two being *polycentric* and *geocentric.*[54]

Ethnocentric Managers—"We Know Best" What do foreign executives fluent in English think when they hear Americans using an endless array of baseball, basketball, and football phrases (such as "out of left field" or "Hail Mary pass")?[55] **Ethnocentric managers believe that their native country, culture, language, and behavior are superior to all others.** Ethnocentric managers tend to believe that they can export the managers and practices of their home countries to anywhere in the world and that they will be more capable and reliable than the native managers. Often the ethnocentric viewpoint is less attributable to prejudice than it is to ignorance, since such managers obviously know more about their home environment than the foreign environment. Ethnocentrism might also be called *parochialism—that is, a narrow view in which people see things solely through their own perspective.*

Is ethnocentrism bad for business? It seems so. A survey of 918 companies with home offices in the United States, Japan, and Europe found that ethnocentric policies were linked to such problems as recruiting difficulties, high turnover rates, and lawsuits over personnel policies.[56]

Polycentric Managers—"They Know Best" *Polycentric managers* **take the view that native managers in the foreign offices best understand native personnel and practices, and so the home office should leave them alone.** Thus, the attitude of polycentric managers is nearly the opposite of that of ethnocentric managers.

Geocentric Managers—"What's Best Is What's Effective, Regardless of Origin" *Geocentric managers* **accept that there are differences and similarities between home and foreign personnel and practices and that they should use whatever techniques are most effective.** Clearly, being an ethno- or polycentric manager takes less work. But the payoff for being a geocentric manager can be far greater. The Manager's Toolbox (page 97) gives some tips on being geocentric. ●

4.3 WHY & HOW COMPANIES EXPAND INTERNATIONALLY

major question? Why do companies expand internationally, and how do they do it?

THE BIG PICTURE

Multinationals expand to take advantage of availability of supplies, new markets, lower labor costs, access to finance capital, or avoidance of tariffs and import quotas. Five ways they do so are by global outsourcing; importing, exporting, and countertrading; licensing and franchising; joint ventures; and wholly owned subsidiaries.

Who makes Apple's iPhone? An estimated 90% of the components are manufactured overseas, by workers in Germany, Singapore, Korea, and elsewhere. The display screens, for instance, come mostly from Asia, especially South Korea and Japan; the phone itself is assembled in China.[57] Who makes the furniture sold by Ethan Allen, that most American of names, evoking Ethan Allen and the Green Mountain Boys of the American Revolution? About half is made overseas, by suppliers in China, the Philippines, Indonesia, and Vietnam.[58] Where is consumer products giant Procter & Gamble going to seek additional consumers? The company operates in developing markets like Africa and parts of Latin America and Asia, which now make up 37% of P&G sales, up from 27% five years ago.[59] (In Mexico, for example, it sells to poor consumers at small, rudimentary markets who will buy a single-use P&G shampoo packet.)[60] There are many reasons why American companies are going global. Let us consider why and how they are expanding beyond U.S. borders.

U.S. export. Popular entertainment is a major U.S. export, as was the 2011 film *Bridesmaids* starring Kristen Wiig and Maya Rudolph, whose Romanian version is advertised here. Are there any negatives to sending American popular culture overseas?

Why Companies Expand Internationally

Many a company has made the deliberate decision to restrict selling its product or service to just its own country. Is anything wrong with that?

The answer is: It depends. It would probably have been a serious mistake for NEC, Sony, or Hitachi to have limited their markets solely to Japan during the 1990s, a time when the country was in an economic slump and Japanese consumers weren't consuming. During that same period, however, some American banks might have been better off not making loans abroad, when the U.S. economy was booming but foreign economies were not. Going international or not going international—it can be risky either way.

Why, then, do companies expand internationally? There are at least five reasons, all of which have to do with making or saving money.

1. Availability of Supplies Antique and art dealers, mining companies, banana growers, sellers of hard woods—all have to go where their basic supplies or raw materials are located. For years oil companies, for example, have expanded their activities outside the United States in seeking cheaper or more plentiful sources of oil.

2. New Markets Sometimes a company will find, as cigarette makers have, that the demand for their product has declined domestically but that they can still make money overseas. Or sometimes a company will steal a march on its competitors by aggressively expanding into foreign markets, as did Coca-Cola over PepsiCo under the leadership of legendary CEO Robert Goizueta. From 2000 to 2010, exports of American goods jumped 66%; the export of services increased even more—84%.[61]

3. Lower Labor Costs The decline in manufacturing jobs in the United States is directly attributable to the fact that American companies have found it cheaper to do their manufacturing outside the States. For example, the rationale for using *maquiladoras*—**manufacturing plants allowed to operate in Mexico with special privileges in return for employing Mexican citizens**—is that they provide less expensive labor for assembling everything from appliances to cars. Even professional or service kinds of jobs, such as computer programming, may be shipped overseas. (However, a countertrend, called "deglobalization," is that some companies are moving production back home, because long supply chains can be easily affected by the whims of geopolitics and energy prices, and the United States remains a manufacturing power for higher value products.)[62]

4. Access to Finance Capital Companies may be enticed into going abroad by the prospects of capital being put up by foreign companies or subsidies from foreign governments. For example, producers of the $100 million movie *Cloud Atlas* (starring Tom Hanks and Halle Berry) received $35 million in financing from investors in China, Korea, Singapore, and beyond.[63]

5. Avoidance of Tariffs & Import Quotas Countries place tariffs (fees) on imported goods or impose import quotas—limitations on the numbers of products allowed in—for the purpose of protecting their own domestic industries. For example, Japan imposes tariffs on agricultural products, such as rice, imported from the United States. To avoid these penalties, a company might create a subsidiary to produce the product in the foreign country. General Electric and Whirlpool, for example, have foreign subsidiaries to produce appliances overseas.

How Companies Expand Internationally

Most companies don't start out to be multinationals. Generally, they edge their way into international business, making minimal investments and taking minimal risks, as shown in the drawing below. *(See Figure 4.1.)*

| Global outsourcing | Importing, exporting, & countertrading | Licensing & franchising | Joint ventures | Wholly-owned subsidiaries |

Lowest risk & investment   ⟷   *Highest risk & investment*

figure 4.1

FIVE WAYS OF EXPANDING INTERNATIONALLY

These range from lowest risk and investment *(left)* to highest risk and investment *(right)*.

Let's consider these five ways.

1. Global Outsourcing A common practice of many companies, *outsourcing* is **defined as using suppliers outside the company to provide goods and services.** For example, airlines farm out a lot of aircraft maintenance to other companies.[64] Management philosopher Peter Drucker believed that in the near future organizations might be outsourcing all work that is "support"—such as information systems—rather than revenue producing.

Global outsourcing extends this technique outside the United States. *Global outsourcing*, or *offshoring*, **is defined as using suppliers outside the United States to provide labor, goods, or services.** The reason may be that the foreign supplier has resources not available in the United States, such as Italian marble. Or the supplier may have special expertise, as do Pakistani weavers. Or—more likely these days—the supplier's labor is cheaper than American labor. As a manager, your first business trip outside the United States might be to inspect the production lines of one of your outsourcing suppliers.

2. Importing, Exporting, & Countertrading When *importing*, **a company buys goods outside the country and resells them domestically.** Nothing might seem to be more American than Caterpillar tractors, but they are made not only in the United States but also in Canada (where, interestingly, workers may be paid higher wage and benefit costs), from which they are imported and made available for sale in the United States.[65] Many of the products we use are imported, ranging from Heineken beer (Netherlands) to Texaco gasoline (Saudi Arabia) to Honda snowblowers (Japan).

PRACTICAL ACTION

Global Outsourcing: Which Jobs Are Likely to Fall Victim to Offshoring?

Will there be any good jobs left for new college graduates?

Americans are rightly concerned about the changing jobs picture, brought about not only by the Great Recession but also earlier in part by offshoring of work to low-wage countries such as China, India, and the Philippines. Few of the millions of factory jobs that have been lost during the last 10 years have been replaced, and today just 10% of American workers are employed in manufacturing (although one report predicted a return in U.S. manufacturing by 2015 because of rising Chinese wages and other factors).[66] This forced many workers—when they were able to work at all—to accept lower paying alternatives, such as jobs in retail and health care, which pay on average 21% less than manufacturing jobs.[67] More recently, the same trend—global outsourcing—has been happening with white-collar jobs. Forrester Research estimates that 3.4 million service jobs will have moved offshore between 2000 and 2015.[68] Among them are jobs in office support, computers, business operations, architecture, legal, sales, and art and design.[69]

How Can You Prepare for an Offshored World? "I believe [companies] should outsource everything for which there is no career track that could lead into senior management," said management philosopher Peter Drucker. An example, he said, is the job of total-quality-control specialist, work that can be done overseas.[70]

"As soon as a job becomes routine enough to describe in a spec sheet, it becomes vulnerable to outsourcing," says another writer. "Jobs like data entry, which are routine by nature, were the first among obvious candidates for outsourcing." But even "design and financial-analysis

skills can, with time, become well-enough understood to be spelled out in a contract and signed away."[71] Says Fred Levy, a Massachusetts Institute of Technology economist, "If you can describe a job precisely, or write rules for doing it, it's unlikely to survive. Either we'll program a computer to do it, or we'll teach a foreigner to do it."[72]

Which Jobs Will Remain in the United States? It is difficult to predict which jobs will remain at home, since even the Bureau of Labor Statistics often can't get it right. However, jobs that endure may share certain traits, listed below, regardless of the industry they serve:[73]

- **Face-to-face.** Some involve *face-to-face contact,* such as being a salesperson with a specific territory or an emergency room doctor.

- **Physical contact.** Other jobs involve *physical contact,* such as those of dentists, nurses, massage therapists, gardeners, and nursing-home aides.

- **Making high-end products.** *High-end products* that require intensive research, precision assembly, and complex technology requiring skilled workers are good candidates for the U.S. labor market, says Eric Spiegel, CEO of the Siemens Corp. Low-end, low-technology products, such as textiles and furniture, will doubtless continue to be offshored.[74]

- **Recognizing complex patterns.** Others involve the human ability to *recognize complex patterns,* which are hard to computerize, such as a physician's ability to diagnose an unusual disease (even if the X-rays are read by a radiologist in India). This also describes such jobs as teaching first grade or selling a mansion to a millionaire or jobs that demand an intimate knowledge of the United States, such as marketing to American teenagers or lobbying Congress.[75]

Survival Rules For you, as a prospective manager, there are perhaps three ideas to take away from all this:

- **Teamwork and creativity.** "Jobs that persist are dynamic and creative and require the ability to team with others," says Jim Spohrer of the IBM Almaden Research Center in San Jose, California, which studies the business operations of IBM's corporate clients. "At its heart, a company is simply a group of teams that come together to create" products and services.[76]

- **Flexibility.** "Jobs used to change very little or not at all over the course of several generations," says Spohrer. "Now, they might change three or four times in a single lifetime." Flexibility—as in being

willing to undergo retraining—thus becomes important. Fortunately, as Drucker pointed out, the United States is "the only country that has a very significant continuing education system. This doesn't exist anywhere else." The United States is also the only country, he said, in which it is easy for younger people to move from one area at work to another.[77]

- **Education.** The more education one has, the more one is apt to prevail during times of economic change. Men and women with four years of college, for instance, earn nearly 45% more on average than those with only a high-school diploma.[78]

YOUR CALL

What kind of job or jobs are you interested in that would seem to provide you with some hopes of prevailing in a fast-changing world?

When *exporting,* **a company produces goods domestically and sells them outside the country.** The United States was ranked the number 3 exporter in the world in 2009, down from number 1 a decade earlier. *(See Table 4.1.)* One of the greatest U.S. exports is American pop culture, in the form of movies, music, and fashion. The United States is also a leader in exporting computers and other information technology.

Rank in 1999	Rank in 2011
1. United States	China
2. Germany	Germany
3. Japan	United States
4. France	Japan
5. Britain	France
6. Canada	South Korea
7. Italy	Italy
8. Netherlands	Netherlands
9. China	Canada
10. Belgium	United Kingdom

table 4.1

TOP 10 EXPORTING COUNTRIES, 1999 AND 2011

Source: F. Norris, "A Shift in the Export Powerhouses," *The New York Times,* February 20, 2010, p. B3; and "Country Comparison: Exports, Top Ten," Index Mundi and CIA Fact Book, www.indexmundi.com/g/r.aspx?t=10&v=85 (accessed January 26, 2012). Exports are measured in U.S. dollars.

Sometimes other countries may wish to import American goods but lack the currency to pay for them. In that case, the exporting U.S. company may resort to *countertrading—that is, bartering goods for goods.* When the Russian ruble plunged in value in 1998, some goods became a better medium of exchange than currency.

3. Licensing & Franchising   Licensing and franchising are two aspects of the same thing, although licensing is used by manufacturing companies and franchising is used more frequently by service companies.

In *licensing,* **a company allows a foreign company to pay it a fee to make or distribute the first company's product or service.** For example, the DuPont chemical company might license a company in Brazil to make Teflon, the nonstick substance that is found on some frying pans. Thus, DuPont, the licensor, can make money without having to invest large sums to conduct business directly in a foreign company. Moreover, the Brazilian firm, the licensee, knows the local market better than DuPont probably would.

Franchising **is a form of licensing in which a company allows a foreign company to pay it a fee and a share of the profit in return for using the first company's brand name and a package of materials and services.** For example, Burger King, Hertz, and Hilton Hotels, which are all well-known brands, might provide the use of their names plus their operating know-how (facility design, equipment, recipes, management systems) to companies in the Philippines in return for an up-front fee plus a percentage of the profits.

By now Americans traveling throughout the world have become accustomed to seeing so-called U.S. stores everywhere. Some recently active companies: Toys R Us opened a store in Poland. Starbucks is looking to do the same in India. Gap is opening an Old Navy store in Japan and a Banana Republic store in Paris. Wendy's is returning to Japan with a burger that features goose-liver pâté and truffles.[79]

Jaguar. A number of formerly British-owned carmakers have gone over to foreign ownership. Jaguar and Land Rover became subsidiaries of Ford Motor Co., but then in 2008 were sold to Tata of India. Do you think the American companies General Motors and Ford could ever wind up under foreign ownership?

4. Joint Ventures   *Strategic allies* (described in Chapter 3) are two organizations that have joined forces to realize strategic advantages that neither would have if operating alone. A U.S. firm may form a *joint venture,* **also known as a** *strategic alliance,* **with a foreign company to share the risks and rewards of starting a new enterprise together in a foreign country.** For instance, General Motors operates a joint venture with Shanghai Automotive Industry Group to build Buicks in China.[80]

Sometimes a joint venture is the only way an American company can have a presence in a certain country, whose laws may forbid foreigners from ownership. Indeed, in China, this is the only way foreign cars may be sold in that country.

5. Wholly Owned Subsidiaries   A *wholly owned subsidiary* **is a foreign subsidiary that is totally owned and controlled by an organization.** The foreign subsidiary may be an existing company that is purchased outright. **A** *greenfield venture* **is a foreign subsidiary that the owning organization has built from scratch.**

General Motors owns majority stakes in Adam Opel AG in Germany and Vauxhall Motor Cars Ltd. in the United Kingdom, both wholly owned GM subsidiaries.   ●

4.4 THE WORLD OF FREE TRADE: REGIONAL ECONOMIC COOPERATION

What are barriers to free trade, and what major organizations and trading blocs promote trade?

major question?

THE BIG PICTURE

Barriers to free trade are tariffs, import quotas, and embargoes. Organizations promoting international trade are the World Trade Organization, the World Bank, and the International Monetary Fund. Major trading blocs are NAFTA, the EU, APEC, ASEAN, Mercosur, and CAFTA.

If you live in the United States, you see foreign products on a daily basis—cars, appliances, clothes, food, beers, wines, and so on. Based on what you see every day, which countries would you think are our most important trading partners? China? Japan? Germany? England? South Korea?

These five countries do indeed appear among the top leading U.S. trading partners. Interestingly, however, our foremost trading partners are our immediate neighbors—Canada and Mexico, whose products may not be quite so visible. *(See Table 4.2.)*

Top 10 Nations for U.S. Exports	Top 10 Nations U.S. Imports From
1. Canada	China
2. Mexico	Canada
3. China	Mexico
4. Japan	Japan
5. United Kingdom	Germany
6. Germany	United Kingdom
7. South Korea	Saudi Arabia
8. Brazil	South Korea
9. Netherlands	Venezuela
10. Hong Kong	France

table 4.2

TOP 10 U.S. TRADING PARTNERS IN GOODS, MARCH 2012

Source: U.S. Census Bureau, "Top Trading Partners for Month of March 2012," May 10, 2012, www .census.gov/foreign-trade/statistics/ highlights/topcurmon.html#exports (accessed June 3, 2012).

Let's begin to consider *free trade,* **the movement of goods and services among nations without political or economic obstruction.**

Barriers to International Trade

Countries often use *trade protectionism*—**the use of government regulations to limit the import of goods and services**—to protect their domestic industries against

Playing by the rules? Four of the five top producers of solar-cell panels are based in China, where the government has subsidized the development of this technology, to the detriment of American and European solar industries. What do you think the United States should do to equalize the situation? Impose tariffs (special taxes) on some Chinese imports? Subsidize our own solar industry?

foreign competition. The justification they often use is that this saves jobs. Actually, protectionism is not considered beneficial, mainly because of what it does to the overall trading atmosphere.

The three devices by which countries try to exert protectionism consist of *tariffs, import quotas,* and *embargoes.*

1. Tariffs   A *tariff* is a trade barrier in the form of a customs duty, or tax, levied mainly on imports. At one time, for instance, to protect the American shoe industry, the United States imposed a tariff on Italian shoes.

There are two types of tariffs: One is designed simply to raise money for the government (revenue tariff). The other, which concerns us more, is to raise the price of imported goods to make the prices of domestic products more competitive (protective tariff). In late 2011, seven U.S. makers of solar panels sought from the U.S. Commerce Department trade tariffs of more than 100% on solar panels made in China, on the grounds that the Chinese manufacturers used billions of dollars in government subsidies to help gain sales in the American market.[81] A couple of months later, four U.S. makers of steel towers for wind turbines also filed a trade complaint against China and Vietnam seeking tariffs of 60% for the same reasons.[82] For its part, China raised tariffs on foreign luxury auto brands, including Cadillac, presumably to protect its own domestic car industry.[83]

2. Import Quotas   An *import quota* is a trade barrier in the form of a limit on the numbers of a product that can be imported. Its intent is to protect domestic industry by restricting the availability of foreign products.

As a condition of being allowed into the World Trade Organization, China agreed, starting in 2005, to cancel car import quotas, which it had used to protect its domestic car manufacturing industry against imported vehicles from the United States, Japan, and Germany.[84] Since then, however, it has decided to stop encouraging growth among foreign auto firms in China, removing preferential tax treatment and streamlined approval processes. Although this is not the reimposition of import quotas, it is "a move that appears to give [Chinese] car companies greater protection from outside rivals," says a *Wall Street Journal* report.[85]

Quotas are designed to prevent *dumping*, the practice of a foreign company's exporting products abroad at a lower price than the price in the home market—or even below the costs of production—in order to drive down the price of the domestic product. In 2009, the U.S. International Trade Commission imposed antidumping duties of 10%–16% more on Chinese government–subsidized steel imported into the United States that damaged the American steel industry.[86]

3. Embargoes   Ever seen a real Cuban cigar? They're difficult for Americans to get, since they're embargoed. **An *embargo* is a complete ban on the import or export of certain products.** It has been years since anyone was allowed to import Cuban cigars and sugar into the United States or for an American firm to do business in Cuba. In early 2012, European countries agreed to embargo—refuse to import—any oil from Iran, amounting to about a fifth of Iran's total exports, if that country did not agree to allow continued sea traffic through the Gulf of Hormuz.[87]

Organizations Promoting International Trade

In the 1920s, the institution of tariff barriers did not so much protect jobs as depress the demand for goods and services, thereby leading to the loss of jobs anyway—and the massive unemployment of the Great Depression of the 1930s.[88] As a result of this lesson, after World War II the advanced nations of the world began to realize that if all countries could freely exchange the products that each could produce most efficiently, this would lead to lower prices all around. Thus began the removal of barriers to free trade.

The three principal organizations designed to facilitate international trade are the *World Trade Organization,* the *World Bank,* and the *International Monetary Fund.*

1. The World Trade Organization Consisting of 153 member countries, the ***World Trade Organization (WTO)* is designed to monitor and enforce trade agreements.** The agreements are based on the *General Agreement on Tariffs and Trade (GATT),* an international accord first signed by 23 nations in 1947, which helped to reduce worldwide tariffs and other barriers. Out of GATT came a series of "rounds," or negotiations, that resulted in the lowering of barriers; for instance, the Uruguay Round, implemented in 1996, cut tariffs by one-third. The current round of negotiations, the Doha Round, which began in Doha, Qatar, is aimed at helping the world's poor by, among other things, reducing trade barriers.

Founded in 1995 and headquartered in Geneva, Switzerland, WTO succeeded GATT as the world forum for trade negotiations and has the formal legal structure for deciding trade disputes. WTO also encompasses areas not previously covered by GATT, such as services and intellectual property rights. A particularly interesting area of responsibility covers telecommunications—cellphones, pagers, data transmission, satellite communications, and the like—with half of the WTO members agreeing in 1998 to open their markets to foreign telecommunications companies.[89]

2. The World Bank The World Bank was founded after World War II to help European countries rebuild. Today the purpose of the ***World Bank* is to provide low-interest loans to developing nations for improving transportation, education, health, and telecommunications.** The bank has 187 member nations, with most contributions coming from Britain, the United States, Japan, and Germany.[90]

In recent years, the World Bank has been the target of demonstrations in Seattle; Washington, DC; Ottawa; and elsewhere. Some protesters believe it finances projects that could damage the ecosystem, such as the Three Gorges Dam on China's Yangtze River. Others complain it supports countries that permit low-paying sweatshops or that suppress religious freedom. Still others think it has dragged its feet on getting affordable AIDS drugs to less-developed countries in Africa. Many of the same protests were leveled against the International Monetary Fund, discussed next. The World Bank has responded by trying to support projects that are not harmful to the environment and that are aimed at helping lift people out of poverty.

3. The International Monetary Fund Founded in 1945 and now affiliated with the United Nations, the International Monetary Fund is the second pillar supporting the international financial community. Consisting of 187 member nations, **the *International Monetary Fund (IMF)* is designed to assist in smoothing the flow of money between nations.** The IMF operates as a last-resort lender that makes short-term loans to countries suffering from unfavorable balance of payments (roughly the difference between money coming into a country and money leaving the country, because of imports, exports, and other matters). In recent times, the IMF has become more high profile because of its role in trying to shore up some weaker European economies, including making loans to Greece, Portugal, and Ireland and considering how to assist Italy and Spain.[91]

Major Trading Blocs: NAFTA, EU, APEC, ASEAN, Mercosur, & CAFTA

A *trading bloc,* also known as an *economic community,* is a group of nations within a geographical region that have agreed to remove trade barriers with one another. The six major trading blocs are the *NAFTA nations,* the *European Union,* the *APEC countries,* the *ASEAN countries,* the *Mercosur,* and *CAFTA.*

1. NAFTA—the Three Countries of the North American Free Trade Agreement

Formed in 1994, the *North American Free Trade Agreement (NAFTA) is a trading bloc consisting of the United States, Canada, and Mexico,* encompassing 435 million people. The agreement is supposed to eliminate 99% of the tariffs and quotas among these countries, allowing for freer flow of goods, services, and capital in North America. Trade with Canada and Mexico now accounts for one-third of the U.S. total, up from one-quarter in 1989.

Is NAFTA a job killer, as some have complained? In Mexico, it has failed to generate substantial job growth and has hurt hundreds of thousands of subsistence farmers, so that illegal immigration to the United States remains a problem. As for the United States, over 682,000 workers lost or were displaced from their jobs because of NAFTA's shifting of jobs south of the border.[92] It also spurred a U.S. trade deficit—$60 billion with Mexico and $31.7 billion with Canada in 2011.[93] However, supporters insist NAFTA ultimately will result in more jobs and a higher standard of living among all trading partners.

2. The EU—the 27 Countries of the European Union

Formed in 1957, **the** *European Union (EU) consists of 27 trading partners in Europe,* covering nearly 500 million consumers. (It will be 28 members in July 2013, with the addition of Croatia.)

Nearly all internal trade barriers have been eliminated (including movement of labor between countries), making the EU a union of borderless neighbors and the world's largest free market, with a gross domestic product of more than $17 trillion, larger than that of the United States.[94]

By 2002, such national symbols as the franc, the mark, the lira, the peseta, and the guilder had been replaced with the EU currency, the euro. There was even speculation

that someday the euro could replace the U.S. dollar as the dominant world currency.[95] However, in 2010–2012, the shaky finances and massive government debts of Portugal, Ireland, Italy, Greece, and Spain (so-called PIIGS) revealed an inherent weakness of the union—that both weak and strong economies were expected to coexist. This affected the euro's *exchange rate—the* **rate at which the currency of one area or country can be exchanged for the currency of another's**—so that the euro began to decline in worth compared to the U.S. dollar. In early 2012, the EU was in full-blown crisis, and it was not clear whether stronger countries such as Germany and the Netherlands would back the rescue of PIIGS or whether some of the latter would actually be expelled from the EU, a path with possibly dire worldwide economic consequences.[96]

3. APEC—21 Countries of the Pacific Rim

Founded in 1989, **the** *Asia-Pacific Economic Cooperation (APEC) is a group of 21 Pacific Rim countries whose purpose is to improve economic and political ties.* Most countries with a coastline on the Pacific Ocean are members of the organization, as highlighted below, although there are

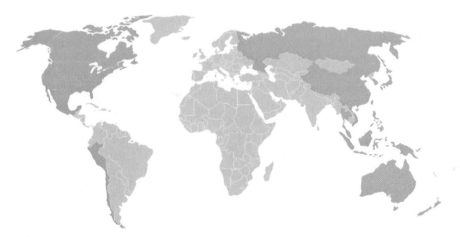

a number of exceptions. APEC members, which include the United States, Canada, and China, work to reduce tariffs and other trade barriers across the Asia-Pacific region.

4. ASEAN—11 Countries of the Association of Southeast Asian Nations

The *Association of Southeast Asian Nations (ASEAN)* **is a trading bloc consisting of 11 countries in Asia:** Brunei, Cambodia, China, Indonesia, Laos, Malaysia, Myanmar (Burma), the Philippines, Singapore, Thailand, and Vietnam. Like other trading blocs, ASEAN is working on reducing trade barriers among member countries. When China was admitted at the beginning of 2010, ASEAN became one of the largest free-trade zones, encompassing 1.9 billion people.[97]

5. Mercosur—10 Countries of Latin America

The *Mercosur* **is the largest trade bloc in Latin America and has four core members—Argentina, Brazil, Paraguay, and Uruguay, with Venezuela scheduled to become a full member upon ratification by the other countries—and five associate members: Bolivia, Chile, Colombia, Ecuador, and Peru.** Besides reducing tariffs by 75%, Mercosur nations are striving for full economic integration, and the alliance is also negotiating trade agreements with NAFTA, the EU, and Japan.

6. CAFTA-DR—Seven Countries of Central America

The *Central America Free Trade Agreement (CAFTA-DR)*, **which involves the United States and Costa Rica, the Dominican Republic, El Salvador, Guatemala, Honduras, and Nicaragua—is intended to reduce tariffs and other barriers to free trade.**[98]

Most Favored Nation Trading Status

Besides joining together in trade blocs, countries will also extend special, "most favored nation" trading privileges to one another. *Most favored nation* **trading status describes a condition in which a country grants other countries favorable trading treatment such as the reduction of import duties.** The purpose is to promote stronger and more stable ties between companies in the two countries. ●

major question ?

What are the principal areas of cultural differences?

THE BIG PICTURE

Managers trying to understand other cultures need to understand the importance of national culture and cultural dimensions and basic cultural perceptions embodied in language, interpersonal space, communication, time orientation, and religion.

Knowing that gifts are often appreciated and even expected in some foreign countries, imagine that you've given four antique clocks wrapped in white paper to a prospective client in China. What you didn't know: the words for *clock* and the number four are similar to the Mandarin word for *death,* and white is a funeral color in many countries. Think you closed the deal?

This story, apparently true, is told by international consultant Dean Foster about an American businessman. "Whether a multinational or a startup business out of a garage, everybody is global these days," he says. "In today's economy, there is no room for failure. Companies have to understand the culture they are working in from Day 1."[99]

In Hong Kong, an American journalist riding in an elevator greeted a Chinese colleague. She responded, "You've gained weight." Three other Chinese coworkers told him the same thing, a remark that in the United States would be regarded as tactless and offensive. "In China, such an intimate observation from a colleague isn't necessarily an insult," the journalist wrote. "It's probably just friendliness."[100]

Such are the kinds of cultural differences American managers are going to have to get used to. In the Arab world, which has historically been segregated by sex, men spend a lot of time together, and so holding hands, kissing cheeks, and long handshakes are meant to express devotion and equality in status. In China, people draw different lines between personal and work spaces, so that, for example, it is permissible for office colleagues to inquire about the size of your apartment and your salary and to give assessments of your wardrobe and your muscle tone.

Tipping point. The culture of tipping in restaurants varies from country to country. Whereas in the United States and Canada 15%–20% of the total bill is considered a standard tip (and 10% insulting), in Japan and China tips are not expected and are even considered inappropriate. In Hong Kong and Singapore, it's up to the diner's discretion (a 10% service charge is already added to the bill). In Europe, hotels and restaurants add a 10% charge and tipping is expected only for exceptional service. In Latin America, a tip of 10% is customary in most restaurants, and you're expected to hand it to the person directly, not just leave it on the table. All clear?

The Importance of National Culture

A nation's **culture** **is the shared set of beliefs, values, knowledge, and patterns of behavior common to a group of people.** We begin learning our culture starting at an early age through everyday interaction with people around us. This is why, from the outside looking in, a nation's culture can seem so intangible and perplexing. As cultural anthropologist Edward T. Hall puts it, "Since much of culture operates outside our awareness, frequently we don't even know what we know. . . . We unconsciously learn what to notice and what not to notice, how to divide time and space, how to walk and talk and use our bodies, how to behave as men or women, how to relate to other people, how to handle responsibility."[101] Indeed, says Hall, what we think of as "mind" is really internalized culture.

And because a culture is made up of so many nuances, this is why visitors to another culture may experience culture shock—discomfort with being in an unfamiliar culture. According to anthropologists, culture shock involves anxiety and doubt caused by an overload of unfamiliar expectations and social cues.[102]

Cultural Dimensions: The GLOBE Project

Misunderstandings and miscommunications often arise in international business relationships because people don't understand the expectations of the other side. A person from North America, Great Britain, Scandinavia, Germany, or Switzerland, for example, comes from a **low-context culture** **in which shared meanings are primarily derived from written and spoken words.** Someone from China, Korea, Japan, Vietnam, Mexico, or many Arab cultures, on the other hand, comes from a **high-context culture** **in which people rely heavily on situational cues for meaning when communicating with others,** relying on nonverbal cues as to another person's official position, status, or family connections.

One way to avoid cultural collisions is to have an understanding of various cultural dimensions, as expressed in the GLOBE project.

The GLOBE Project's Nine Cultural Dimensions   Started in 1993 by University of Pennsylvania professor **Robert J. House, the GLOBE project is a massive and ongoing cross-cultural investigation of nine cultural dimensions involved in leadership and organizational processes.**[103] (GLOBE stands for Global Leadership and Organizational Behavior Effectiveness.) GLOBE has evolved into a network of more than 150 scholars from 62 societies, and most of the researchers are native to the particular cultures they study. The nine cultural dimensions are as follows:

1. **Power distance—how much unequal distribution of power should there be in organizations and society?** *Power distance* expresses the degree to which a society's members expect power to be unequally shared.

2. **Uncertainty avoidance—how much should people rely on social norms and rules to avoid uncertainty?** *Uncertainty avoidance* expresses the extent to which a society relies on social norms and procedures to alleviate the unpredictability of future events.

3. **Institutional collectivism—how much should leaders encourage and reward loyalty to the social unit?** *Institutional collectivism* expresses the extent to which individuals are encouraged and rewarded for loyalty to the group as opposed to pursuing individual goals.

4. **In-group collectivism—how much pride and loyalty should people have for their family or organization?** In contrast to individualism, *in-group collectivism* expresses the extent to which people should take pride in being members of their family, circle of close friends, and their work organization.

5. **Gender egalitarianism—how much should society maximize gender role differences?** *Gender egalitarianism* expresses the extent to which a society should minimize gender discrimination and role inequalities.

6. **Assertiveness—how confrontational and dominant should individuals be in social relationships?** *Assertiveness* represents the extent to which a society expects people to be confrontational and competitive as opposed to tender and modest.

7. **Future orientation—how much should people delay gratification by planning and saving for the future?** *Future orientation* expresses the extent to which a society encourages investment in the future, as by planning and saving.

8. **Performance orientation—how much should individuals be rewarded for improvement and excellence?** *Performance orientation* expresses the extent to which society encourages and rewards its members for performance improvement and excellence.

9. **Humane orientation—how much should society encourage and reward people for being kind, fair, friendly, and generous?** *Humane orientation* represents the degree to which individuals are encouraged to be altruistic, caring, kind, generous, and fair.

Data from 18,000 managers yielded the country profiles below. *(See Table 4.3.)*

table 4.3 COUNTRIES RANKING HIGHEST AND LOWEST ON THE GLOBE CULTURAL DIMENSIONS

Dimension	Highest	Lowest
Power distance	Morocco, Argentina, Thailand, Spain, Russia	Denmark, Netherlands, South Africa (black sample), Israel, Costa Rica
Uncertainty avoidance	Switzerland, Sweden, Germany (former West), Denmark, Austria	Russia, Hungary, Bolivia, Greece, Venezuela
Institutional collectivism	Sweden, South Korea, Japan, Singapore, Denmark	Greece, Hungary, Germany (former East), Argentina, Italy
In-group collectivism	Iran, India, Morocco, China, Egypt	Denmark, Sweden, New Zealand, Netherlands, Finland
Gender egalitarianism	Hungary, Poland, Slovenia, Denmark, Sweden	South Korea, Egypt, Morocco, India, China
Assertiveness	Germany (former East), Austria, Greece, United States, Spain	Sweden, New Zealand, Switzerland, Japan, Kuwait
Future orientation	Singapore, Switzerland, Netherlands, Canada (English speaking), Denmark	Russia, Argentina, Poland, Italy, Kuwait
Performance orientation	Singapore, Hong Kong, New Zealand, Taiwan, United States	Russia, Argentina, Greece, Venezuela, Italy
Human orientation	Philippines, Ireland, Malaysia, Egypt, Indonesia	Germany (former West), Spain, France, Singapore, Brazil

Source: Adapted from M. Javidan and R. J. House, "Cultural Acumen for the Global Manager: Lessons from Project GLOBE," *Organizational Dynamics,* Spring 2001, pp. 289–305.

Recognizing Cultural Tendencies to Gain Competitive Advantage The GLOBE dimensions show a great deal of cultural diversity around the world, but they also show how cultural patterns vary. For example:

- The U.S. managerial sample scored high on assertiveness and performance orientation—which is why Americans are widely perceived as being pushy and hardworking.

- Switzerland's high scores on uncertainty avoidance and future orientation help explain its centuries of political neutrality and its world-renowned banking industry.

- Singapore is known as a great place to do business because it is clean and safe and its people are well educated and hardworking—no surprise, considering the country's high scores on social collectivism, future orientation, and performance orientation.

- By contrast, Russia's low scores on future orientation and performance orientation could foreshadow a slower-than-hoped-for transition from a centrally planned economy to free-enterprise capitalism.

The practical lesson to draw from all this: *Knowing the cultural tendencies of foreign business partners and competitors can give you a strategic competitive advantage.*

GLOBE researchers also set out to find which, if any, attributes of leadership were universally liked or disliked, the results of which are shown in the table on the next page. *(See Table 4.4.)* Throughout the world, visionary and inspirational leaders who are good team builders generally do the best; self-centered leaders seen as loners or face-savers received a poor reception.

Other Cultural Variations: Language, Interpersonal Space, Communication, Time Orientation, & Religion

How do you go about bridging cross-cultural gaps? It begins with understanding. Let's consider variations in five basic culture areas: (1) *language*, (2) *interpersonal space*, (3) *communication*, (4) *time orientation*, and (5) *religion.*

Note, however, that such cultural differences are to be viewed as *tendencies* rather than as absolutes. We all need to be aware that the *individuals* we are dealing with may be exceptions to the cultural rules. After all, there *are* talkative and aggressive Japanese, just as there are quiet and deferential Americans, stereotypes notwithstanding.[104]

1. Language More than 3,000 different languages are spoken throughout the world. However, even if you are operating in the English language, there are nuances between cultures that can lead to misperceptions. For instance, in Asia, a "yes" answer to a question "simply means the question is understood," says one well-traveled writer. "It's the beginning of negotiations."[105]

In communicating across cultures you have four options: (a) You can speak your own language. (The average American believes that about half the world can speak English, when actually it's about 20%.)[106] (b) You can use a translator. (Try to get one who will be loyal to you rather than to your overseas host.) (c) You can try using a translation app, such as Google Translate, that turns a smartphone into an interpreter, although this can be cumbersome.[107] (4) You can learn the local language—by far the best option (as reflected in the *USA Today* headline: "U.S. Firms Becoming Tongue-Tied. Global Trade Requires Foreign Language Skills").[108] Although 93% of U.S. public middle and high schools with language programs offer Spanish, certainly a widely spoken international language, and 46% offer French, unfortunately only 4% offer Chinese (Mandarin), today one of the world's most important languages.[109]

table 4.4

Source: Excerpted and adapted
from P. W. Dorfman, P. J. Hanges,
and F. C. Brodbeck, "Leadership
and Cultural Variation: The
Identification of Culturally
Endorsed Leadership Profiles,"
in R. J. House, P. J. Hanges,
M. Javidan, P. W. Dorfman, and
V. Gupta, eds. *Culture, Leadership,
and Organizations: The GLOBE
Study of 62 Societies,* (Thousand
Oaks, CA: Sage, 2004), Tables 21.2
and 21.3, pp. 677–78.

Universally Positive Leader Attributes		Universally Negative Leader Attributes
Trustworthy	Dependable	Loner
Just	Intelligent	Asocial
Honest	Decisive	Noncooperative
Foresighted	Effective bargainer	Irritable
Plans ahead	Win-win problem solver	Nonexplicit
Encouraging	Administrative skilled	Egocentric
Positive	Communicative	Ruthless
Dynamic	Informed	Dictatorial
Motivational	Coordinator	
Confidence builder	Team builder	
Motivational	Excellence oriented	

2. Interpersonal Space   Men holding hands may raise eyebrows among most Americans, but it is common in the Middle East and does not carry any sexual connotation. "Holding hands is the warmest expression of affection between men," says one Lebanese sociologist. "It's a sign of solidarity and friendship."[110]

People of different cultures have different ideas about what is acceptable interpersonal space—that is, how close or far away one should be when communicating with another person. For instance, the people of North America and northern Europe tend to conduct business conversations at a range of 3–4 feet. For people in Latin American and Asian cultures, the range is about 1 foot. For Arabs, it is even closer.

This can lead to cross-cultural misunderstandings. "Arabs tend to get very close and breathe on you," says anthropologist Hall. "The American on the receiving end can't identify all the sources of his discomfort but feels that the Arab is pushy. The Arab comes close, the American backs up. The Arab follows, because he can only interact at certain distances."[111] However, once the American understands that Arabs handle interpersonal space differently and that "breathing on people is a form of communication," says Hall, the situation can sometimes be redefined so that the American feels more comfortable.

3. Communication   For small companies doing business abroad, "the important thing to remember is that you don't know what you don't know," says the head of a U.S. firm that advises clients on cross-cultural matters.[112] For instance, an American who had lived in Brazil and was fluent in Portuguese was angling to make a deal in São Paulo and thought his pitch was going well. "It was picture-perfect until my client suggested I stay for the weekend to go to a soccer game" and enjoy the local food with him. The American diplomatically declined the invitation, but the next day found the prospective clients not as receptive, saying they liked the program but would need more time to decide. On the plane home, he analyzed what had gone wrong and realized he had given them a "task" reason instead of a "relationship" reason for declining the invitation. "It's a relationship culture, and I could just as easily and more successfully [have said], 'There are people back home who are expecting me to be with them.'" But the reason he gave "sent the message that I was not as Brazilian as they initially thought—and it came out of my profit."[113]

Even single words and sounds can pose difficulties: Promoters of Apple's iPad might encounter difficulties in Ireland, where the sound is indistinguishable from "iPod," or in Japan, where the language doesn't even have a sound for the "a" in iPad.[114]

If you, like a growing number of young Americans, head to China for employment, you need to recall that you were brought up in a commercial environment, but younger Chinese were raised at a time when China was evolving from a government-regulated economy to a more free-market system, and so they may have less understanding of business concepts and client services. "In the West, there is such a premium on getting things done quickly," says an American manager, "but when you come to work in China, you need to work on listening and being more patient and understanding of local ways of doing business."[115] In particular, Americans have to be careful about giving criticism directly, which the Chinese consider rude and inconsiderate.

We consider communication matters in more detail in Chapter 15.

4. Time Orientation   Time orientation is different in many cultures. For example, Americans are accustomed to calling ahead for appointments, but South Koreans believe in spontaneity. Thus, when Seoul erupted in protests over tainted American beef, Korean legislators simply hopped on a plane to the United States, saying they would negotiate with the U.S. government. "But since they failed to inform the Americans ahead of time," says one report, "they were unable to meet with anyone of importance."[116]

Anthropologist Hall makes a useful distinction between monochronic time and polychronic time:

- **Monochronic time.** This kind of time is standard American business practice—at least until recently. That is, *monochronic time* **is a preference for doing one thing at a time.** In this perception, time is viewed as being limited, precisely segmented, and schedule driven. This perception of time prevails, for example, when you schedule a meeting with someone and then give the visitor your undivided attention during the allotted time.[117]

  Indeed, you probably practice monochronic time when you're in a job interview. You work hard at listening to what the interviewer says. You may well take careful notes. You certainly don't answer your cellphone or gaze repeatedly out the window.

- **Polychronic time.** This outlook on time is the kind that prevails in Mediterranean, Latin American, and especially Arab cultures. *Polychronic time* **is a preference for doing more than one thing at a time.** Here time is viewed as being flexible and multidimensional.

  This perception of time prevails when you visit a Latin American client, find yourself sitting in the waiting room for 45 minutes, and then learn in the meeting that the client is dealing with three other people at the same time.

EXAMPLE

Cultural Differences in Time: Peru Strives for Punctuality

Hora peruana, or Peruvian time, which usually means being an hour late, is considered by most citizens of Peru to be an endearing national trait. Students, for instance, are accustomed to professors showing up for class an hour after it has officially begun.

"Time without Delay." However, Peruvian officials believe that constant lateness reflects a negative attitude toward work and hurts national productivity. It's a "horrible, dreadful, harmful custom," President Alan Garcia said in a nationally televised event to kick off *La Hora sin*

Demora—Time without Delay. The campaign, launched in March 2007, aims at asking schools, businesses, and government institutions to stop tolerating tardiness. A technology consultant from London applauded the campaign, saying that "a lot of Latin American countries lose business" owing to lateness. Although the new effort offers no penalties for being late or rewards for compliance, it hopes to shame latecomers into mending their ways.[118]

Varying Tempos. "There is a general tendency toward a different way of timekeeping that dominates in most of Latin America," says Robert Levine, a professor of psychology at California State University in Fresno. The author of *A Geography of Time*, Levine theorizes that different cultures mark time in varying "tempos"—some define events by the clock and others allow events to run their natural courses. Peruvian officials are "taking people who have been living on what we might call 'event time,' and asking them to switch to 'clock time,'" Levine says.[119]

Garcia's campaign did not get off to a good start. An invitation to the 11:00 a.m. kickoff ceremony was delivered by messenger to the Associated Press at 1:30 p.m.—after the event had ended.

YOUR CALL

A poll has found the United States to be an impatient nation, with Americans getting antsy after 5 minutes on hold on the phone and 15 minutes maximum in a Department of Motor Vehicles line.[120] If you were trying to start a manufacturing business in Peru, what would you do to adjust?

5. Religion Trying to get wealthy Muslim investors in Dubai to buy some of your bank's financial products? Then you need to know that any investment vehicle needs to "conform to the spirit of the Koran, which forbids any investments that pay interest," as one writer puts it. "No mortgages. No bonds."[121] Are you a Protestant doing business in a predominantly Catholic country? Or a Muslim in a Buddhist country? How, then, does religion influence the work-related values of the people with whom you're dealing?

A study of 484 international students at a midwestern university uncovered wide variations in the work-related values for different religious affiliations.[122] For example, among Catholics, the primary work-related value was found to be consideration. For Protestants, it was employer effectiveness; for Buddhists, social responsibility; for Muslims, continuity. There was, in fact, virtually *no agreement* among religions as to what is the most important work-related value. This led the researchers to conclude: "Employers might be wise to consider the impact that religious differences (and more broadly, cultural factors) appear to have on the values of employee groups."

Current Followers of the Major World Religions	
Christianity	2.1 billion
Islam	1.5 billion
Hinduism	900 million
Chinese traditional religions	394 million
Buddhism	376 million
Judaism	14 million

Source: Adherents.com, "Major Religions of the World Ranked by Major Adherents," August 7, 2007, www.adherents.com/Religions_By_Adherents.html (accessed February 1, 2012).

U.S. Managers on Foreign Assignments: Why Do They Fail?

According to the State Department, there are about 6.3 million Americans (not including military) who are living outside American borders—a class of people known as *expatriates*—**people living or working in a foreign country.**[123] Many of them, perhaps 300,000, are managers, and supporting them and their families overseas is not cheap. "The tab for sending an executive who earns $160,000 in the U.S., plus a spouse and two children, to India for two years is about $900,000," says one expert.[124] Are the employers getting their money's worth? Probably not.

One study of about 750 companies (U.S., European, and Japanese) asked expatriates and their managers to evaluate their experiences. They found that 10%–20% of all U.S. managers sent abroad returned early because of job dissatisfaction or adjustment difficulties. Of those who stayed for the length of their assignments, about one-third did not perform to their superiors' expectations and one-fourth left the company, often to join a competitor—a turnover rate double that of managers who did not go abroad.[125]

Unfortunately, problems continue when expatriates return home, according to a study by Pricewaterhouse Coopers. Results indicated that 25% of repatriated employees quit their jobs within one year. Organizations can help reduce this turnover by communicating with employees throughout the international assignment and by providing at least six months' notice of when employees will return home.[126]

If you were to go abroad as a manager, what are the survival skills or outlook you will need? Perhaps the bottom line is revealed in a study of 72 human resource managers who were asked to identify the most important success factors in a foreign assignment: Nearly 35% said the secret was *cultural adaptability:* patience, flexibility, and tolerance for others' beliefs.[127] ●

Who made this car? Could you become an American manager in Japan but drive a Japanese car made in the United States? Unlikely, but possible. Still, Japanese carmakers build cars in the United States, such as these Honda Civics, made in Ohio, Indiana, or Alabama, just as Buick builds cars in China. Both automakers' plants are located close to their markets.

Key Terms Used in This Chapter

Asia-Pacific Economic Cooperation (APEC) 114

Association of Southeast Asian Nations (ASEAN) 115

Central America Free Trade Agreement (CAFTA) 115

countertrading 110

culture 117

dumping 112

e-commerce 99

embargo 112

ethnocentric managers 105

European Union (EU) 114

exchange rate 114

expatriates 123

exporting 109

franchising 110

free trade 111

geocentric managers 105

global economy 99

global outsourcing 108

global village 98

globalization 98

GLOBE project 117

greenfield venture 110

high-context culture 117

import quota 112

importing 108

International Monetary Fund (IMF) 113

joint venture 110

licensing 110

low-context culture 117

maquiladoras 107

Mercosur 115

monochronic time 121

most favored nation 115

multinational corporation 103

multinational organization 103

North American Free Trade Agreement (NAFTA) 114

offshoring 108

outsourcing 107

parochialism 105

polycentric managers 105

polychronic time 121

tariff 112

trade protectionism 111

trading bloc 113

wholly owned subsidiary 110

World Bank 113

World Trade Organization (WTO) 113

Summary

4.1 Globalization: The Collapse of Time & Distance

Globalization is the trend of the world economy toward becoming more interdependent. Globalization is reflected in three developments: (1) the rise of the global village and e-commerce; (2) the trend of the world's becoming one big market; and (3) the rise of both megafirms and Internet-enabled minifirms.

The rise of the global village refers to the "shrinking" of time and space as air travel and the electronic media have made global communication easier. The Internet and the Web have led to e-commerce, the buying and selling of products through computer networks.

The global economy is the increasing tendency of the economies of nations to interact with one another as one market.

The rise of cross-border business has led to megamergers, as giant firms have joined forces, and of minifirms, small companies in which managers can use the Internet and other technologies to get enterprises started more easily and to maneuver faster.

4.2 You & International Management

Studying international management prepares you to work with foreign customers or partners, with foreign suppliers, for a foreign firm in the United States, or for a U.S. firm overseas. International management is management that oversees the conduct of operations in or with organizations in foreign countries.

The successful international manager is not ethnocentric or polycentric but geocentric. Ethnocentric managers believe that their native country, culture, language, and behavior are superior to all others. Polycentric managers take the view that native managers in the foreign offices best understand native personnel and practices. Geocentric managers accept that there are differences and similarities between home and foreign personnel and practices, and they should use whatever techniques are most effective.

4.3 Why & How Companies Expand Internationally

Companies expand internationally for at least five reasons. They seek (1) cheaper or more plentiful supplies, (2) new markets, (3) lower labor costs, (4) access to finance capital, and (5) avoidance of tariffs on imported goods or import quotas.

There are five ways in which companies expand internationally. (1) They engage in global outsourcing, using suppliers outside the company and the United States to provide goods and services. (2) They engage in importing, exporting, and countertrading (bartering for goods). (3) They engage in licensing (allowing a foreign company to pay a fee to make or distribute the company's product) and franchising (allowing a foreign company to pay a fee and a share of the profit in return for using the first company's brand name). (4) They engage in joint ventures, a strategic alliance to share the risks and rewards of starting a new enterprise together in a foreign country. (5) They become wholly owned subsidiaries, or foreign subsidiaries that are totally owned and controlled by an organization.

4.4 The World of Free Trade: Regional Economic Cooperation

Free trade is the movement of goods and services among nations without political or economic obstructions.

Countries often use trade protectionism—the use of government regulations to limit the import of goods and services—to protect their domestic industries against foreign competition. Three barriers to free trade are tariffs, import quotas, and embargoes. (1) A tariff is a trade barrier in the form of a customs duty, or tax, levied mainly on imports. (2) An import quota is a trade barrier in the form of a limit on the numbers of a product that can be imported. (3) An embargo is a complete ban on the import or export of certain products.

Three principal organizations exist that are designed to facilitate international trade. (1) The World Trade Organization is designed to monitor and enforce trade agreements. (2) The World Bank is designed to provide low-interest loans to developing nations for improving transportation, education, health, and telecommunications. (3) The International Monetary Fund is designed to assist in smoothing the flow of money between nations.

A trading bloc is a group of nations within a geographical region that have agreed to remove trade barriers. There are six major trading blocs: (1) North American Free Trade Agreement (NAFTA; U.S., Canada, and Mexico); (2) European Union (EU; 25 trading partners in Europe); (3) the Association of Southeast Asian Nations (ASEAN; 11 countries in Asia); (4) Asia-Pacific Economic Cooperation (APEC; 21 Pacific Rim countries); (5) Mercosur (Argentina, Brazil, Paraguay, and Uruguay; and (6) the Central America Free Trade Agreement (CAFTA; the United States and six Central American countries).

Besides joining together in trade blocs, countries also extend special, "most favored nation" trading privileges—that is, grant other countries favorable trading treatment such as the reduction of import duties.

4.5 The Importance of Understanding Cultural Differences

Misunderstandings and miscommunications often arise because one person doesn't understand the expectations of a person from another culture. In low-context cultures, shared meanings are primarily derived from written and spoken words. In high-context cultures, people rely heavily on situational cues for meaning when communicating with others.

Robert House and others created the GLOBE (for Global Leadership and Organizational Behavior Effectiveness) project, a massive and ongoing cross-cultural investigation of nine cultural dimensions involved in leadership and organizational processes: (1) power distance, (2) uncertainty avoidance, (3) institutional collectivism, (4) in-group collectivism, (5) gender egalitarianism, (6) assertiveness, (7) future orientation, (8) performance orientation, and (9) humane orientation.

A nation's culture is the shared set of beliefs, values, knowledge, and patterns of behavior common to a group of people. Visitors to another culture may experience culture shock—feelings of discomfort and disorientation. Managers trying to understand other cultures need to understand four basic cultural perceptions embodied in (1) language, (2) interpersonal space, (3) time orientation, and (4) religion.

Regarding language, when you are trying to communicate across cultures you have three options: Speak your own language (if others can understand you), use a translator, or learn the local language.

Interpersonal space involves how close or far away one should be when communicating with another person, with Americans being comfortable at 3–4 feet but people in other countries often wanting to be closer.

Time orientation of a culture may be either monochronic (preference for doing one thing at a time) or polychronic (preference for doing more than one thing at a time).

Managers need to consider the effect of religious differences. In order of size (population), the major world religions are Christianity, Islam, Hinduism, Buddhism, Chinese traditional religions, and Judaism.

Elektrobit Corp. Strives to Make Foreign Assignments a Good Experience

With all of the communication tools at their disposal, it's easier than ever for executives to direct far-flung operations without globe trotting.

But as more companies become global players or push into new regions abroad, executives are discovering that there are still times when e-mail, conference calls, and Skype aren't enough. Someone has to get on a plane, go to a foreign outpost, and move in for awhile.

The connections established by the "boundary spanners" who take on foreign assignments can replace the competitiveness that often crops up between the home office and a distant outpost with trust, says Professor Andreas Schotter. And that can help a company grow faster, with fewer stumbles along the way.

Elektrobit Corp., a global electronics company based in Finland that develops automotive navigation software and handheld devices, has been shuttling people between offices for more than a decade to improve the business.

A year ago, Damian Barnett, a 13-year veteran of Elektrobit, jumped from his desk in Erlangen, Germany, to the company's office in Novi, Michigan. Barnett, now 40 years old, was given the task of accelerating the Novi office's customer service while expanding its operations.

"What I found was the Novi office was dependent on the Germany office, and a lot of tasks had to wait because they were checking in with Germany," he says. "Over the past year, we have worked to make the office more autonomous. The change has been incredible. Things are more organized, and customers are getting responses in hours instead of days."

Barnett's experience underscores how efficiency spreads more quickly when workers from different regions physically spend time together sharing ideas, says Professor Schotter.

Elektrobit's Erlangen office, which is the headquarters for the company's automotive business, is hosting its own prominent visitor. Manuela Papadopol, who was hired in the United States as Elektrobit's global marketing manager, is in the fifth month of a yearlong assignment at the Erlangen office, where she is building a marketing team. One of the first lessons she learned is that Elektrobit's German workers generally rely on interpersonal communication more than their American counterparts. She used that newfound knowledge to combine the best of both worlds.

"In America we are very fond of technology, and you barely see anybody or pick up the phone to call them," Papadopol says. "In Europe, they like to talk face-to-face, and having conversations at a desk or in the hallway is very important. So we came up with an agreement to continue to have the discussions but to follow up with an e-mail. As a result, actions take place faster, and the content of the discussions is shared with everyone on the team."

Elektrobit moves an average of 10 people a year between its global offices, spending about $10,000 annually for each of them on relocation expenses, housing for the employee, and any family that go along.

Of course, the company makes sure employees have whatever they need to start working efficiently on arrival. But it also tries to help them settle into their everyday lives outside work. As part of that effort, Elektrobit has recent arrivals to an area share their experiences with newcomers, since those two groups have so much in common, says Julie Halfaday, human resources manager at Elektrobit Americas.

Still, there are plenty of ways for an assignment to go wrong, as in any hiring or transfer-personality clashes, family dissatisfaction, or a simple mismatch between the employee and the job, among others. But one of the greatest dangers is misunderstandings about the terms of the assignment.

To avoid that, Elektrobit employees who accept an international assignment have to sign a contract before they leave that spells out their pay, length of stay, and other details of what is expected of them and what kind of help they can expect from the company.

Damian Barnett, who was looking for new challenges after four years in the same assignment in Germany, is now focused on using what he has learned when he returns to the Elektrobit offices there. "My hope, when I return to Germany, is that I can use this experience to grow another team," he says.

FOR DISCUSSION

1. Which of the recommendations listed in the Manager's Toolbox were used by Elektrobit Corp.? Explain.

2. What are the biggest challenges Elektrobit experienced in maintaining offices in multiple countries? Explain why they are important.

3. To what extent did you observe examples of ethnocentric, polycentric, or geocentric attitudes in this case? Provide examples to support your conclusions.

4. Use Table 4.3 to identify cultural differences that are likely to arise between Elektrobit employees working in Germany and the United States. How might these differences affect interpersonal interactions, and what can the company do to reduce any untended conflict from these differences?

5. What are the most important lessons to be learned about global management from this case? Discuss.

Source: Excerpted from Jeff Bennett, "You Had to Be There," *The Wall Street Journal*, October 24, 2011, p. R6. Copyright © 2012 by Dow Jones & Company, Inc. Reproduced with permission of Dow Jones & Company, Inc. via Copyright Clearance Center.

Self-Assessment

How Well Are You Suited to Becoming a Global Manager?

OBJECTIVES

1. To see if you are ready to be a global manager.
2. To help you assess your comfort level with other cultures.

INTRODUCTION

As our business world becomes increasingly globalized, U.S. companies need more managers to work in other countries. This usually means vast adjustments for the manager and her or his family during this job assignment. Flexibility is critical as is the ability to adjust to new ways, new people, new foods, different nonverbal communication, a new language, and a host of other new things.

Before agreeing to such an assignment, you need to know more about yourself and how you function in such situations.

INSTRUCTIONS

Are you prepared to be a global manager? Rate the extent to which you agree with each of the following 14 items by circling your response on the rating scale shown below. If you do not have direct experience with a particular situation (e.g., working with people from other cultures), respond by circling how you *think* you would feel.

1 = Very strongly disagree
2 = Strongly disagree
3 = Disagree
4 = Neither agree nor disagree
5 = Agree
6 = Strongly agree
7 = Very strongly agree

1. When working with people from other cultures, I work hard to understand their perspectives.	1 2 3 4 5 6 7
2. I have a solid understanding of my organization's products and services.	1 2 3 4 5 6 7
3. I am willing to take a stand on issues.	1 2 3 4 5 6 7
4. I have a special talent for dealing with people.	1 2 3 4 5 6 7
5. I can be depended on to tell the truth regardless of circumstances.	1 2 3 4 5 6 7
6. I am good at identifying the most important part of a complex problem or issue.	1 2 3 4 5 6 7
7. I clearly demonstrate commitment to seeing the organization succeed.	1 2 3 4 5 6 7
8. I take personal as well as business risks.	1 2 3 4 5 6 7

9. I have changed as a result of feedback from others.	1 2 3 4 5 6 7
10. I enjoy the challenge of working in countries other than my own.	1 2 3 4 5 6 7
11. I take advantage of opportunities to do new things.	1 2 3 4 5 6 7
12. I find criticism hard to take.	1 2 3 4 5 6 7
13. I seek feedback even when others are reluctant to give it.	1 2 3 4 5 6 7
14. I don't get so invested in things that I cannot change when something doesn't work.	1 2 3 4 5 6 7

INTERPRETATION

This exercise assesses factors associated with being a successful global manager. These factors include general intelligence, business knowledge, interpersonal skills, commitment, courage, cross-cultural competencies, and the ability to learn from experience.

Total your scores, which will fall between 14 and 98. The higher your score, the greater your potential for success as an international manager.

ARBITRARY NORMS

High Potential for Success	70–98
Moderate Potential for Success	40–69
Low Potential for Success	39 and below

QUESTIONS FOR DISCUSSION

1. What do the results suggest about your preparedness to be a global manager? Do you agree with these results?

2. How comfortable would you be going to another country at this time in your life?

3. How have your experiences as a citizen of a very diverse nation helped you to understand the other cultures of the world?

4. How might you improve your preparedness to one day assume an international position? Explain.

Sources: Modified and adapted from G. M. Spreitzer, M. W. McCall Jr., and J. D. Mahoney, "Early Identification of International Executive Potential," *Journal of Applied Psychology*, February 1997, pp. 6–29.

Legal/Ethical Challenge

Is Apple Doing Enough to Control Employment Practices in Its Chinese Factories?

This challenge revolves around a company's responsibility to police and change employment practices used by its suppliers or employees working in operations outside a parent company's country of origin. Consider Apple.

Apple employs about 40,000 people in the United States and 700,000 in China. This is not surprising when you consider the cost of labor in China and the fact that China is the company's fastest-growing region, accumulating over $12 billion in sales. For example, nearly 40,000 people visited Apple's stores in China during parts of 2011.

Apple recently released results of an internal audit of 229 factories in Asia. Results revealed that (1) "62% of suppliers violated Apple's working-hours standards of 60 hours per week," (2) "32% weren't compliant with hazardous-substance management practices," (3) "35% failed to meet Apple's standards to prevent worker injuries," and (4) almost 33% did not follow Apple's standards regarding wages and benefits. On the positive side, Apple indicated that "suppliers have stopped discriminatory screenings for medical conditions or pregnancy" based on its directives.

SOLVING THE CHALLENGE

What do you think Apple should do about results from its internal audit?

1. Nothing. It is not Apple's responsibility to manage the operations of its suppliers.

2. Provide the results to management at the supplier firms and encourage them to follow Apple's standards. Nothing more should be done.

3. Provide the results to management at the supplier firms and mandate that they make efforts to bring their operational policies in line with Apple's standards. Create sanctions for those firms that do not meet the standards.

4. Invent other options.

Source: Materials drawn from Jessica E. Vascellaro and Owen Fletcher, "Apple Navigates China Maze," *The Wall Street Journal,* January 14–15, 2012, pp. B1, B2; and Rich Karlgaard, "In Defense of Apple's China Plants," *The Wall Street Journal.com,* February 2, 2012.

chapter 5

Planning
The Foundation of Successful Management

Major Questions You Should Be Able to Answer

5.1 Planning & Uncertainty
Major Question: How do I tend to deal with uncertainty, and how can planning help?

5.2 Fundamentals of Planning
Major Question: What are mission and vision statements, and what are three types of planning and goals?

5.3 Promoting Goal Setting: SMART Goals & Management by Objectives
Major Question: What are SMART goals and MBO and how can they be implemented?

5.4 The Planning/Control Cycle
Major Question: How does the planning/control cycle help keep a manager's plans headed in the right direction?

Planning Different Career Paths: "It's a Career, Not a Job"

The purpose of planning is to help deal with uncertainty, both for the organization and for your individual career. In this chapter, we discuss planning from an organizational point of view, but of course you also need to do personal planning for a career. Today, experts say, success requires coupling an in-demand degree with expertise in emerging trends, such as mastery of social media.[1]

The three principal career paths, suggested the late management professor Michael J. Driver, are *linear, steady-state,* and *spiral* careers, but there are also others called *transitory* and *portfolio* careers.[2]

The Linear Career: Climbing the Stairs

The *linear career* resembles the traditional view of climbing the stairs in an organization's hierarchy. That is, you move up the organization in a series of jobs—generally in just one functional area, such as finance—each of which entails more responsibility and requires more skills.

Of course, it's possible that a linear career will *plateau*. That is, you'll rise to a certain level and then remain there; there will be no further promotions. Career plateaus actually happen a lot and need not signify disgrace; they happen even to very successful managers.

Another possibility, of course, is the *declining career,* in which a person reaches a certain level and then after a time begins descending back to the lower levels. This could come about, for instance, because technology changes the industry you're in.

The Steady-State Career: Staying Put

The *steady-state career* is almost the opposite of a linear career: You discover early in life that you're comfortable with a certain occupation and you stay with it. Or you accept a promotion for a while, decide you don't like the responsibility, and take a step down.

This kind of career is actually fairly commonplace: Sales representatives, computer programmers, or physicians, for example, may decide they are happy being "hands-on" professionals rather than managers.

The Spiral Career: Holding Different Jobs That Build on One Another

The *spiral career* is, like the linear career, upwardly mobile. However, on this career path, you would have a number of jobs that are fundamentally different yet still build on one another, giving you more general experience and the skills to advance in rank and status.

The Transitory Career Path: Continually Shifting Sideways

It's possible that you might (like some salespeople, actors, chefs, or construction workers) favor the *transitory career* path. That is, you're the kind of person who doesn't want the responsibility that comes with promotion. You're a free spirit who likes the variety of experience that comes with continually shifting sideways from job to job or place to place (or you're afraid of making the commitment to doing any one thing).

Portfolio Careers: Holding Multiple Jobs

Some people put together *portfolio careers,* assembling lists (portfolios) of multiple part-time jobs that, when combined, are equivalent to a full-time position, such as Pilates instructor/art dealer, attorney/minister, teacher/dancer/puppeteer.[3] And some change their professions entirely, perhaps by switching departments within their companies or by going back to school and retraining for something else.[4]

For Discussion What kind of career path do you think you're apt to follow? How are you planning for it?

forecast | What's Ahead in This Chapter

In this chapter, we describe planning, the first of the four management functions. We consider the benefits of planning and how it helps you deal with uncertainty. We deal with the fundamentals of planning, including the mission and vision statements and the three types of planning—strategic, tactical, and operational. We consider goals, action plans, and operating plans; SMART goals and management by objectives; and finally the planning/control cycle.

THE BIG PICTURE

Planning, the first of four functions in the management process, involves setting goals and deciding how to achieve them. Planning helps you check your progress, coordinate activities, think ahead, and cope with uncertainty. Uncertainty is of three types—state, effect, and response. Organizations respond to uncertainty in various ways.

What is known as the *management process,* you'll recall (from Chapter 1, p. 15), involves the four management functions of *planning, organizing, leading,* and *controlling,* which form four of the part divisions of this book. In this and the next two chapters we discuss *planning,* **which we previously defined as setting goals and deciding how to achieve them.** Another definition: *Planning* **is coping with uncertainty by formulating future courses of action to achieve specified results.**[5] When you make a plan, you make a blueprint for action that describes what you need to do to realize your goals.

Planning & Strategic Management

Planning, which we discuss in this chapter, is used in conjunction with strategic management, as we describe in Chapter 6. As we will see, strategic management is a process that involves managers from all parts of the organization—top managers, middle managers, and first-line managers—in the formulation, implementation, and execution of strategies and strategic goals to advance the purposes of the organization. Thus, planning covers not only strategic planning (done by top managers) but also tactical planning (done by middle managers) and operational planning (done by first-line managers). Planning and strategic management derive from an organization's mission and vision about itself, as we describe in the next few pages. (*See Figure 5.1.*)

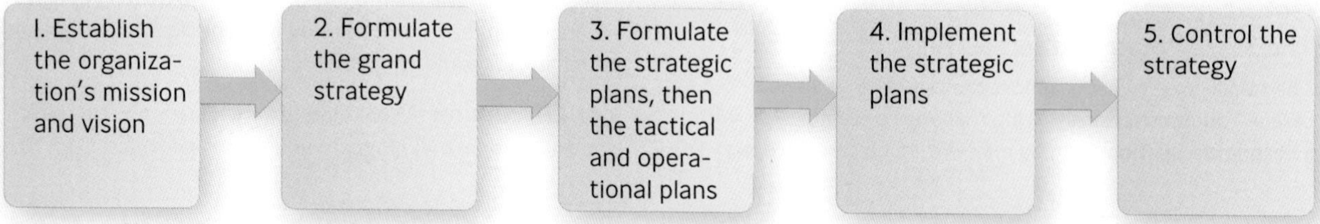

| 1. Establish the organization's mission and vision | 2. Formulate the grand strategy | 3. Formulate the strategic plans, then the tactical and operational plans | 4. Implement the strategic plans | 5. Control the strategy |

figure 5.1

PLANNING AND STRATEGIC MANAGEMENT

The details of planning and strategic management are explained in Chapters 5 and 6.

Why Not Plan?

On the face of it, planning would seem to be a good idea—otherwise we would not be devoting three chapters to the subject. But there are two cautions to be aware of:

1. Planning Requires You to Set Aside the Time to Do It   Time-starved managers may be quite resentful when superiors order them to prepare a multiyear plan for their work unit.

"What?" they may grouse. "They expect me to do that and *still* find time to meet this year's goals?" Somehow, though, that time for planning must be found. Otherwise, managers are mainly just reacting to events.

Planning means that you must involve the subordinates you manage to determine resources, opportunities, and goals. During the process, you may need to go outside the work unit for information about products, competitors, markets, and the like.

2. You May Have to Make Some Decisions without a Lot of Time to Plan In our time of Internet connections and speedy-access computer databases, can't nearly anyone lay hands on facts quickly to make an intelligent decision? Not always. A competitor may quickly enter your market with a highly desirable product. A change in buying habits may occur. A consumer boycott may suddenly surface. An important supplier may let you down. The caliber of employees you need may not be immediately available at the salary level you're willing to pay. And in any one of these you won't have the time to plan a decision based on all the facts.

Nevertheless, a plan need not be perfect to be executable. While you shouldn't shoot from the hip in making decisions, often you may have to "go with what you've got" and make a decision based on a plan that is perhaps only three-quarters complete.

How Planning Helps You: Four Benefits

You can always hope you'll luck out or muddle through the next time a hurricane, earthquake, tornado, or other natural disaster strikes your area. Or you can plan for it by stocking up on flashlight batteries and canned food. Which is better? The same consideration applies when you're a manager. Some day, after you've dealt with some crisis, you will be very happy that you had a plan for handling it. The benefits of planning are fourfold:

1. Planning Helps You Check on Your Progress The preprinted score card that golfers use when playing 18 holes of golf isn't blank. For each hole, the card lists the standard number of strokes ("par"), such as three or five, that a good player should take to hit the ball from the tee to the cup. The score card is the plan for the game, with objectives for each hole. After you play the hole, you write your own score in a blank space. At the end of the 18 holes, you add all your scores to see how you performed compared with the standard for the course.

What's the score? Like a golf score card, planning helps you check on your progress.

How well is your work going in an organization? You won't know unless you have some way of checking your progress. That's why, like a golfer, you need to have some expectations of what you're supposed to do—in other words, a plan.

2. Planning Helps You Coordinate Activities "The right hand doesn't know what the left hand is doing!"

We may hear that expression used, for example, when a crisis occurs and an organization's public relations department, legal department, and CEO's office all give the press separate, contradictory statements. Obviously, such an embarrassment can be avoided if the organization has a plan for dealing with the media during emergencies. A plan defines the responsibilities of various departments and coordinates their activities for the achievement of common goals—such as, at minimum, making an organization not look confused and disorganized.

3. Planning Helps You Think Ahead The service or product with which you're engaged will probably at some point reach maturity, and sales will begin to falter. Thus, you need to look ahead, beyond your present phase of work, to try to be sure you'll be one of the quick rather than one of the dead.

Thinking Ahead: Ford Plans a Radical Design of the Fusion

Alan R. Mulally, CEO of Ford Motor Company, has big plans to restore Ford to its position as a leader in the global auto industry. Those plans are embodied in the Ford Focus, described as "Ford's first truly global car—a single vehicle designed and engineered for customers in every region of the world and sold under one name."[6]

The small, fuel-efficient family sedan is loaded with technology and safety features that Mulally thinks will appeal to consumers in Europe, Asia, and the Americas. A version has also been radically restyled in an attempt to recapture the leadership of the North American midsized car market. It looks, says one report, "more like the ultra-luxury sports car Aston Martin Vantage than the current boxy version."[7] Ford also upgraded its MyFord Touch, which replaces most knobs and buttons for climate, navigation, and entertainment with a touch screen, and announced it is doubling the number of smartphonelike apps available for its Sync in-car infotainment system.[8]

Future Fusion. This version of the Fusion "global car," styled to look like an ultraluxury sports car, is designed to appeal to consumers everywhere—Europe and Asia, as well as the Americas.

YOUR CALL

Mulally's management principles, instilled in the slogan "One Ford . . . One Team . . . One Plan . . . One Goal," have already been demonstrated, first, in Ford's shift away from trucks and sport utility vehicles to cars and, second, in dumping luxury brands (Land Rover, Jaguar, Aston-Martin) that were distracting management. If you were envisioning a car strategy 10 years out from now, what kind of bold plan would you put forward?

4. Above All, Planning Helps You Cope with Uncertainty You don't care for unpleasant surprises? Most people don't. (Pleasant surprises, of course, are invariably welcome.) That's why trying to plan for unpleasant contingencies is necessary (as we'll describe in Chapter 6). Planning helps you deal with uncertainty.

How Organizations Respond to Uncertainty

How do you personally respond to uncertainty? Do you react slowly? conservatively? proactively? Do you watch to see what others do? Organizations act in similar ways.

Four Basic Strategy Types Scholars **Raymond E. Miles** and **Charles C. Snow** suggest that organizations adopt one of four approaches when responding to uncertainty in their environment. They become *Defenders, Prospectors, Analyzers,* or *Reactors.*[9]

Defenders—"Let's Stick with What We Do Best, Avoid Other Involvements" Whenever you hear an organization's leader say that "We're sticking with the basics" or "We're getting back to our core business," that's the hallmark of a Defender organization. *Defenders* **are expert at producing and selling narrowly defined products or services.** Often they are old-line successful enterprises, such as recently bankrupt Kodak, which invented the digital camera but then failed to successfully commercialize it.[10] Or they may be firms like Macy's and J.C. Penney, which in the post-recession era of consumer frugality lost customers to discounters like Walmart.[11] (Penney has now gone to Walmart's everyday-low-pricing strategy.)[12] Defenders do not tend to seek opportunities outside their present markets. They devote most of their attention to making refinements in their existing operations, such as slashing prices.

Prospectors—"Let's Create Our Own Opportunities, Not Wait for Them to Happen" A company described as "aggressive" is often a Prospector organization. ***Prospectors* focus on developing new products or services and in seeking out new markets, rather than waiting for things to happen.** Like 19th-century gold miners, these companies are "prospecting" for new ways of doing things. The continual product and market innovation has a price: Such companies may suffer a loss of efficiency. Nevertheless, their focus on change can put fear in the hearts of competitors. An example of a Prospector company is Gap, which is looking for new sales by expanding abroad.[13] Another such company is Apple.

Red Bull. Austrian energy drink maker Red Bull, which was released into the United States in 1997, believes in making unorthodox marketing moves, such as creating a festival for homemade flying machines and building a half-pipe for Olympic snowboarder Shaun White. In 2010, the company opened a $220 million soccer stadium in Harrison, New Jersey, as home for its recently acquired Major League Soccer team, the New York Red Bulls. What strategy type is being followed here?

Analyzers—"Let Others Take the Risks of Innovating, & We'll Imitate What Works Best" Analyzers take a "me too" response to the world. By and large, you won't find them called "trendsetters." Rather, ***Analyzers* let other organizations take the risks of product development and marketing and then imitate (or perhaps slightly improve on) what seems to work best.** For years, Microsoft has been accused of taking this approach.[14]

Reactors—"Let's Wait Until There's a Crisis, Then We'll React" Whereas the Prospector is aggressive and proactive, the Reactor is the opposite—passive and reactive. ***Reactors* make adjustments only when finally forced to by environmental pressures.** In the worst cases, they are so incapable of responding fast enough that they suffer massive sales losses and are even driven out of business. Kmart, for instance, failed to respond to Walmart's development of its distribution and inventory management competencies, resulting in stalled growth and a significant reduction in market share. Kmart's core business never recovered from this reactive strategy.[15] Now Sears, the shrinking retailer with which Kmart merged, is trying to reconfigure itself in an age of iPhone apps and Twitter.[16]

The Adaptive Cycle Miles and Snow also introduced the idea of the *adaptive cycle,* which portrays businesses as continuously cycling through decisions about three kinds of business problems: (1) *entrepreneurial* (selecting and making adjustments of products and markets), (2) *engineering* (producing and delivering the products), and (3) *administrative* (establishing roles, relationships, and organizational processes).

Thus, a business that makes decisions in the entrepreneurial area that take it in the direction of being a Prospector will in a short time also begin making Prospector-oriented decisions in the engineering area, then the administrative area, and then even more so in the entrepreneurial area, and so on. Thus, as one scholar points out, "With enough cycles and insight, a given business becomes a very good, comprehensively aligned Prospector, Analyzer, or Defender. If a business lacks insight, or if it fails to take advantage of alignment opportunities afforded by the adaptive cycle, it will be an incongruent, poorly performing Reactor."[17] ●

major question?

What are mission and vision statements, and what are three types of planning and goals?

THE BIG PICTURE

Planning consists of translating an organization's mission and vision into objectives. The organization's purpose is expressed as a mission statement, and what it becomes is expressed as a vision statement. From these are derived strategic planning, then tactical planning, then operational planning. The purpose of planning is to set a goal and then an action plan and an operating plan. Types of plans include standing and single-use plans.

"Everyone wants a clear reason to get up in the morning," writes journalist Dick Leider. "As humans we hunger for meaning and purpose in our lives."[18]

And what is that purpose? "Life never lacks purpose," says Leider. "Purpose is innate—but it is up to each of us individually to discover or rediscover it."

An organization has a purpose, too—a mission. And managers must have an idea of where they want the organization to go—a vision. The approach to planning can be summarized in the following diagram, which shows how an organization's mission becomes translated into action plans. (*See Figure 5.2.*)

figure 5.2

MAKING PLANS

An organization's reason for being is expressed in a *mission statement*. What the organization wishes to become is expressed in a *vision statement*. From these are derived *strategic planning*, then *tactical planning*, and finally *operational planning*. The purpose of each kind of planning is to specify *goals* and *action plans* that ultimately pave the way toward achieving an organization's vision.

Mission & Vision Statements

The planning process begins with two attributes: a mission statement (which answers the question "What is our reason for being?") and a vision statement (which answers the question "What do we want to become?").

The Mission Statement—"What Is Our Reason for Being?" An organization's *mission* is its purpose or reason for being. Determining the mission is the responsibility of top management and the board of directors. It is up to them to formulate a *mission statement*, **which expresses the purpose of the organization.**

"Only a clear definition of the mission and purpose of the organization makes possible clear and realistic . . . objectives," said Peter Drucker.[19] Whether the organization is for-profit or nonprofit, the mission statement identifies the goods or services the organization provides and will provide. Sometimes it also gives the reasons for providing them (to make a profit or to achieve humanitarian goals, for example).

EXAMPLE

Mission Statements for Three Different Companies: Hilton, Amazon, & Patagonia

Mission statements answer the question, "What is our reason for being?" or "Why are we here?"

Here are the mission statements for three companies, drawn from their websites. The mission statement for Hilton Hotels, a large company, reads: "To fill the earth with the light and warmth of hospitality."

Amazon's mission statement is "Use the Internet to offer products that educate, inform, and inspire. We decided to build an online store that would be customer friendly and easy to navigate and would offer the broadest possible selection. . . . We believe that a fundamental measure of our success will be the shareholder value we create over the *long term*."

Clothing maker Patagonia's mission statement is to "Build the best product, cause no unnecessary harm, [and] use business to inspire and implement solutions to the environmental crisis."

YOUR CALL

Do you think any of these mission statements could be adapted to different companies offering different products or services? Give an example.

The Vision Statement—"What Do We Want to Become?" A *vision* is a **long-term goal describing "what" an organization wants to become. It is a clear sense of the future and the actions needed to get there.** "[A] vision should describe what's happening to the world you compete in and what you want to do about it," says one *Fortune* article. "It should guide decisions."[20]

After formulating a mission statement, top managers need to develop a **vision statement, which expresses what the organization should become, where it wants to go strategically.**[21]

EXAMPLE

Vision Statements for Three Different Companies: Hilton, Amazon, & Patagonia

Vision statements answer the question, "What do we want to become?" or "Where do we want to go?"

Here is Hilton Hotels' statement: "To be the first choice of the world's travelers, building on the rich heritage and strength of our brands by consistently delighting our customers, investing in our team members, delivering innovative products and services, expanding our family of brands, and continuously improving performance."

Amazon's vision statement: "Our vision is to be earth's most customer-centric company; to build a place where people can come to find and discover anything they might want to buy online."

Patagonia's statement: "We prefer the human scale to the corporate, vagabonding to tourism, and the quirky to the toned-down and flattened out."

YOUR CALL

Do these vision statements work? Do they meet *Fortune*'s criterion of describing "what's happening in the world you compete in and what you want to do about it. It should guide decisions"?

It is one thing to formulate a vision statement, however, and another to find concrete methods to manage and measure the performance that makes the vision a reality. One survey found that 73% of organizations said they had a clearly articulated strategic direction, but only 44% of them said they were able to communicate it well to the employees who must implement it.[22]

Three Types of Planning for Three Levels of Management: Strategic, Tactical, & Operational

Inspiring, clearly stated mission statements and vision statements provide the focal point of the entire planning process. Then three things happen:

■ *Strategic planning by top management.* Using their mission and vision statements, top managers do *strategic planning*—**they determine what the organization's long-term goals should be for the next 1–5 years with the resources they expect to have available.** "Strategic planning requires visionary and directional thinking," says one authority.[23] It should communicate not only general goals about growth and profits but also ways to achieve them. Today, because of the frequency with which world competition and information technology alter marketplace conditions, a company's strategic planning may have to be done closer to every 1 or 2 years than every 5. Still, at a big company like Boeing or Chrysler or Amazon (see Example box below), top executives cannot lose sight of long-range, multiyear planning.

■ *Tactical planning by middle management.* The strategic priorities and policies are then passed down to middle managers, who must do *tactical planning*—**that is, they determine what contributions their departments or similar work units can make with their given resources during the next 6–24 months.**

■ *Operational planning by first-line management.* Middle managers then pass these plans along to first-line managers to do *operational planning*—**that is, they determine how to accomplish specific tasks with available resources within the next 1–52 weeks.**

The kinds of managers are described further in the figure below. *(See Figure 5.3.)*

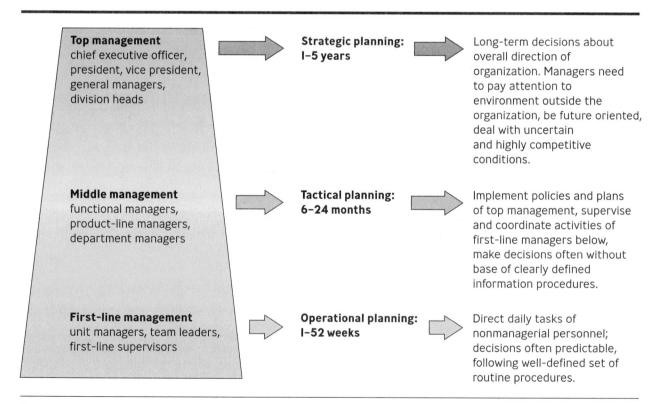

figure 5.3

THREE LEVELS OF MANAGEMENT, THREE TYPES OF PLANNING

Each type of planning has different time horizons, although the times overlap because the plans are somewhat elastic.

Strategic Planning by Top Management: Amazon Manages for the Future, to the Frustration of Short-Term Investors

One thing Amazon CEO Jeff Bezos is famous for is unconventional thinking (or, in that hackneyed expression, "thinking outside the box"). For instance, his early decision to allow customers to post their own book reviews, both negative as well as positive, on the Amazon website puzzled competing booksellers, who thought negative reviews would diminish sales. Bezos's point of view— "We will sell more if we help people make purchasing decisions"—proved correct.[24]

Talking Long Term. Similarly, Bezos has an unconventional opinion about profitability. With most publicly owned companies, which Amazon is (Bezos holds 22% of the stock, worth $16 billion; most of the rest is owned by institutional investors such as Capital World or mutual funds such as American Funds), shareholders constantly pressure management to produce profits that will boost the stock every quarter (3 months) or so.[25] But back in 1997, Bezos warned stockholders that "It's all about the long term. We may make decisions and weigh trade-offs differently than some companies."[26]

Most top managers do strategic planning on a one-to three-year time line. Says Bezos, "If everything you do needs to work on a three-year time horizon, then you're competing against a lot of people. But if you're willing to invest on a seven-year horizon, you're now competing against a fraction of those people, because very few people

are willing to do that." Actually, Bezos is *very* long term, operating on a 10- to 20-year time line.

Ambitions for the Future. The large time window and freedom from having to deliver immediate profits allow Amazon to pursue the powerful long-range strategy it has planned.[27] It is spending money to open 17 new airplane-hangar-size storage and shipping facilities and cutting prices on its merchandise, which will undercut its retail competitors (Borders is gone; Barnes & Noble and Best Buy are struggling).[28] It is realizing Walmart-like economies of scale, achieving enormous savings from buying supplies in huge quantities. It is slashing prices on its Kindle e-book reader and its Fire tablet to get more units into more buyers' hands, developing a future customer base for its e-books, apps, media, and other digital products.

Profits? "Profits will come down the road," says business writer James Stewart, "when Kindle [and Fire] users buy content through Amazon."[29] Says Bezos, "We're willing to plant seeds, let them grow—and we're very stubborn."

YOUR CALL

If Amazon's strategy hurts short-run profits, should your parents or grandparents invest in Amazon? Should you? What if Amazon's strategic plan is wrong?

Goals, Action Plans, & Operating Plans

Whatever its type—strategic, tactical, or operational—the purpose of planning is to set a *goal* and then to formulate an *action plan* and an *operating plan.*

Goals   A *goal*, also known as an *objective*, is a specific commitment to achieve a measurable result within a stated period of time.

As with planning, goals are of the same three types—strategic, tactical, and operational. Also, like planning, goals are arranged in a hierarchy known as a **means-end chain** because in the chain of management (operational, tactical, strategic) the accomplishment of low-level goals is the means leading to the accomplishment of high-level goals or ends.

- *Strategic goals* are set by and for top management and focus on objectives for the organization as a whole.

- *Tactical goals* are set by and for middle managers and focus on the actions needed to achieve strategic goals.

- *Operational goals* are set by and for first-line managers and are concerned with short-term matters associated with realizing tactical goals.

The Action Plan & the Operating Plan   The goal should be followed by an *action plan*, which defines the course of action needed to achieve the stated goal, such as a marketing plan or sales plan. **The *operating plan,* which is typically designed for a 1-year period, defines how you will conduct your business based on the action plan; it identifies clear targets such as revenues, cash flow, and market share.**

EXAMPLE

Strategic, Tactical, & Operational Goals: Southwest Airlines

Although it had a tough time financially during the Great Recession (as did its competitors), Dallas-based Southwest Airlines has continually achieved its strategic goals and as of 2012 had been profitable for 39 consecutive years.[30]

Strategic Goals. The goal of Southwest's top managers is to ensure that the airline is highly profitable, following the general strategy of (a) keeping costs and fares down, (b) offering a superior on-time arrival record, and (c) keeping passengers happy. One of the most important strategic decisions Southwest made was to fly just one type of airplane—Boeing 737s. (The fleet has about 550 jets.) Thus, it is able to hold down training, maintenance, and operating expenses.[31]

Another strategic decision was to create a strong corporate culture that, according to one former CEO, allows people to "feel like they're using their brains, they're using their creativity, they're allowed to be themselves and have a sense of humor, and they understand what the mission of the company is."[32]

Tactical Goals. Cutting costs and keeping fares low is a key tactical goal for Southwest's middle managers. For example, the organization cut costs in its maintenance program by doing more work on a plane when it's in for a check instead of bringing it in three different times. In addition, it gets more use out of its planes every day by limiting the turnaround time between flights to 20 minutes, compared to up to an hour for other airlines.

Southwest also usually flies to less-congested airports, thus saving time and money by avoiding traffic. There is just one class of seating, doing away with the distinction between coach and first class. Even the boarding passes are reusable, being made of plastic. Finally, the airline saves by not feeding passengers: it serves mostly peanuts, no in-flight meals.

How do you make arrival times more reliable? To achieve this second tactical goal, middle managers did away with guaranteed seat reservations before ticketing, so that no-shows won't complicate (and therefore delay) the boarding process. (It changed that policy in 2007 to ensure that passengers paying extra for "business select" fares would be placed at the front of the line.)[33]

In addition, as mentioned, the airline tries to be religious about turning planes around in exactly 20 minutes, so that on-time departures are more apt to produce on-time arrivals. Although the airline is about 83% unionized, turnaround is helped by looser work rules, so that workers can pitch in to do tasks outside their normal jobs. "If you saw something that needed to be done," said one former employee, "and you thought you could do it, you did."[34] Even so, after the airline acquired rival AirTran Airways in May 2011, its on-time record dropped significantly; it scored ninth place in 2011 among major carriers. It also had one of the worst records for lost bags. Both problems are now receiving priority attention.

Still, according to *Consumer Reports,* it is America's favorite airline on quality-of-flight measures.[35] The difference lies in small things: the free peanuts (an emotional subject among travelers), switching of flights without charge, and no charge for checked-in luggage up to two pieces. Charging for bags might have generated an additional $300 million a year, says one report, "but bag fees are so irritating that Southwest decided to go without."[36] However, in mid-2009 it started charging a fee for checking a third bag, as well as fees for flying dogs and cats in the passenger cabin and for children ages 5–11 traveling without an adult.[37]

Operational Goals. Consider how Southwest's first-line managers can enhance productivity in the unloading, refueling, and cleaning of arriving planes. "One example [of productivity] customers mention all the time," said former chairman Herb Kelleher, "is if you look out the window when the airplane is taxiing toward the jetway, you see our ground crews charging before the airplane has even come to rest. Customers tell me that with other airlines nobody moves until the airplane has turned off its engines."[38]

First-line managers also make sure that seat assignments (boarding passes) are not given out until an hour before the plane is due to leave to make sure that the maximum number of passengers will be on hand to fill the seats available.

YOUR CALL

Ranking No. 10 on *Fortune's* 2012 Most Admired Companies list, Southwest has inspired a host of low-fare imitators—big ones like JetBlue and Alaska and small ones like Frontier, Spirit, Virgin America, and Allegiant—which have grown rapidly in the last 10 years compared to mainline carriers such as United, Continental (which merged with United), Delta, American, and US Airways.[39] Do you think by acquiring AirTran Airways, which operates 700 flights a day and consists of a different mix of aircraft (Boeing 717s as well as 737s) and which boosted Southwest's scale by 20%, that Southwest can continue to implement its strategic goals?[40]

Types of Plans: Standing Plans & Single-Use Plans

Plans are of two types—*standing plans* and *single-use plans. (See Table 5.1.)*

Plan	Description
Standing plan	For activities that occur repeatedly over a period of time
• Policy	Outlines general response to a designated problem or situation
• Procedure	Outlines response to particular problems or circumstances
• Rule	Designates specific required action
Single-use plan	For activities not likely to be repeated in the future
• Program	Encompasses a range of projects or activities
• Project	Has less scope and complexity than a program

table 5.1

STANDING PLANS AND SINGLE-USE PLANS

There are three types of standing plans and two types of single-use plans.

Standing Plans: Policies, Procedures, & Rules   **Standing plans are plans developed for activities that occur repeatedly over a period of time.** Standing plans consist of policies, procedures, and rules.

- **A *policy* is a standing plan that outlines the general response to a designated problem or situation.** Example: "This workplace does not condone swearing." This policy is a broad statement that gives managers a general idea about what is allowable for employees who use bad language, but gives no specifics.

- **A *procedure* (or *standard operating procedure*) is a standing plan that outlines the response to particular problems or circumstances.** Example: White Castle specifies exactly how a hamburger should be dressed, including the order in which the mustard, ketchup, and pickles are applied.

- **A *rule* is a standing plan that designates specific required action.** Example: "No smoking is allowed anywhere in the building." This allows no room for interpretation.

Single-Use Plans: Programs & Projects   **Single-use plans are plans developed for activities that are not likely to be repeated in the future.** Such plans can be programs or projects.

- **A *program* is a single-use plan encompassing a range of projects or activities.** Example: The U.S. government space program had several projects, including the *Challenger* project, the Hubble Telescope project, and the space shuttle project.

- **A *project* is a single-use plan of less scope and complexity than a program.** Example: The space shuttle project, one of several projects in the government's space program, consisted of three shuttles: *Discovery, Endeavour,* and *Atlantis.* ●

5.3 PROMOTING GOAL SETTING: SMART GOALS & MANAGEMENT BY OBJECTIVES

major question **?**

What are SMART goals and MBO and how can they be implemented?

THE BIG PICTURE

This section discusses SMART goals—goals that are Specific, Measurable, Attainable, Results-oriented, and have Target dates. It also discusses a technique for setting goals, management by objectives (MBO) is a four-step process for motivating employees.

SMART Goals

Anyone can define goals. But the five characteristics of a good goal are represented by the acronym SMART. **A *SMART goal* is one that is *S*pecific, *M*easurable, *A*ttainable, *R*esults-oriented, and has *T*arget dates.**

Specific   Goals should be stated in *specific* rather than vague terms. The goal "As many planes as possible should arrive on time" is too general. The goal that "Ninety percent of planes should arrive within 15 minutes of the scheduled arrival time" is specific.

Measurable   Whenever possible, goals should be *measurable,* or quantifiable (as in "90% of planes should arrive within 15 minutes . . ."). That is, there should be some way to measure the degree to which a goal has been reached.

Of course, some goals—such as those concerned with improving quality—are not precisely quantifiable. In that case, something on the order of "Improve the quality of customer relations by instituting 10 follow-up telephone calls every week" will do. You can certainly quantify how many follow-up phone calls were made.

Attainable   Goals should be challenging, of course, but above all they should be realistic and *attainable.* It may be best to set goals that are quite ambitious so as to challenge people to meet high standards. Always, however, the goals should be achievable within the scope of the time, equipment, and financial support available. *(See Figure 5.4.)*

If too easy (as in "half the flights should arrive on time"), goals won't impel people to make much effort. If impossible ("all flights must arrive on time, regardless of weather"), employees won't even bother trying. Or they will try and continually fail, which will end up hurting morale.

Results-oriented   Only a few goals should be chosen—say, five for any work unit. And they should be *results-oriented*—they should support the organization's vision.

In writing out the goals, start with the word "To" and follow it with action-oriented verbs—"complete," "acquire," "increase" ("to decrease by 10% the time to get passengers settled in their seats before departure").

Some verbs should not be used in your goal statement because they imply activities—the tactics used to accomplish goals (such as having baggage handlers waiting). For example, you should not use "to develop," "to conduct," "to implement."

Target dates   Goals should specify the *target dates* or deadline dates when they are to be attained. For example, it's unrealistic to expect an airline to improve its on-time arrivals by 10% overnight. However, you could set a target date—3 to 6 months away, say—by which this goal is to be achieved. That allows enough time for lower level managers and employees

figure 5.4

RELATIONSHIP BETWEEN GOAL DIFFICULTY AND PERFORMANCE

Source: Adapted from E. A. Locke and G. P. Latham, *A Theory of Goal Setting and Task Performance* (Englewood Cliffs, NJ: Prentice Hall, 1990).

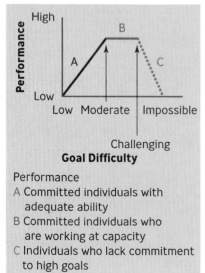

Performance
A Committed individuals with adequate ability
B Committed individuals who are working at capacity
C Individuals who lack commitment to high goals

to revamp their systems and work habits and gives them a clear time frame in which they know what they are expected to do.

Do you perform better when you set goals or when you don't? What about when you set difficult goals rather than easy ones?

Research shows that if goals are made more difficult ("Increase study time 30%"), people may achieve them less often than they would easy goals ("Increase study time 5%"), but they nevertheless perform at a higher level. People also do better when the objectives are specific ("Increase study time 10 hours a week") rather than general ("Do more studying this semester").[41]

These are the kinds of matters addressed in the activity known as *management by objectives*. First suggested by **Peter Drucker** in 1954, MBO has spread largely because of the appeal of its emphasis on converting general objectives into specific ones for all members of an organization.[42]

What Is MBO? The Four-Step Process for Motivating Employees

Management by objectives (MBO) **is a four-step process in which (1) managers and employees jointly set objectives for the employee, (2) managers develop action plans, (3) managers and employees periodically review the employee's performance, and (4) the manager makes a performance appraisal and rewards the employee according to results.** The purpose of MBO is to *motivate* rather than to control subordinates. Let's consider the four steps.

Jointly setting objectives. An important part of MBO is joint manager-subordinate participation in setting objectives. Have you ever held a job that featured this kind of process?

1. Jointly Set Objectives   You sit down with your manager and the two of you jointly set objectives for you to attain. Later you do the same with each of your own subordinates. Joint manager/subordinate participation is important to the program. It's probably best if the objectives aren't simply imposed from above (Don't say, "Here are the objectives I want you to meet"). Managers also should not simply approve the employee's objectives ("Whatever you aim for is okay with me"). It's necessary to have back-and-forth negotiation to make the objectives practicable.

One result of joint participation, research shows, is that it impels people to set more difficult goals—to raise the level of their aspirations—which may have a positive effect on their performance.[43] The objectives should be expressed in writing and should be SMART. There are three types of objectives, shown in the following table. *(See Table 5.2.)*

table 5.2

THREE TYPES OF
OBJECTIVES USED IN MBO

Improvement Objectives
Purpose Express performance to be accomplished in a specific way for a specific area **Examples** "Increase sport utility sales by 10%." "Reduce food spoilage by 15%."
Personal Development Objectives
Purpose Express personal goals to be realized **Examples** "Attend five days of leadership training." "Learn basics of Microsoft Office software by June 1."
Maintenance Objectives
Purpose Express the intention to maintain performance at previously established levels **Examples** "Continue to meet the increased sales goals specified last quarter." "Produce another 60,000 cases of wine this month."

2. Develop Action Plan   Once objectives are set, managers at each level should prepare an action plan for attaining them. Action plans may be prepared for both individuals and for work units, such as departments.

3. Periodically Review Performance   You and your manager should meet reasonably often—either informally as needed or formally every 3 months—to review progress, as should you and your subordinates. Indeed, frequent communication is necessary so that everyone will know how well he or she is doing in meeting the objectives.

During each meeting, managers should give employees feedback, and objectives should be updated or revised as necessary to reflect new realities. If you were managing a painting or landscaping business, for example, changes in the weather, loss of key employees, or a financial downturn affecting customer spending could force you to reconsider your objectives.

4. Give Performance Appraisal & Rewards, If Any   At the end of 6 or 12 months, you and your subordinate should meet to discuss results, comparing performance with initial objectives. *Deal with results,* not personalities, emotional issues, or excuses.

Because the purpose of MBO is to *motivate* employees, performance that meets the objectives should be rewarded—with compliments, raises, bonuses, promotions, or other suitable benefits. Failure can be addressed by redefining the objectives for the next 6- or 12-month period, or even by taking stronger measures, such as demotion. Basically, however, MBO is viewed as being a learning process. After step 4, the MBO cycle begins anew.[44]

Cascading Objectives: MBO from the Top Down

For MBO to be successful, the following three things have to happen.

1. Top Management Must Be Committed "When top-management commitment [to MBO] was high," said one review, "the average gain in productivity was 56%. When commitment was low, the average gain in productivity was only 6%."[45]

2. It Must Be Applied Organizationwide The program has to be put in place throughout the entire organization. That is, it cannot be applied in just some divisions and departments; it has to be done in all of them.

3. Objectives Must "Cascade" MBO works by *cascading* objectives down **through the organization; that is, objectives are structured in a *unified hierarchy*, becoming more specific at lower levels of the organization.** Top managers set general *organizational* objectives, which are translated into *divisional* objectives, which are translated into *departmental* objectives. The hierarchy ends in *individual* objectives set by each employee.

EXAMPLE

Setting Objectives: Walmart's CEO Lays Out an Agenda for Change

Tired of criticism of Walmart's business practices, in a 2008 speech its CEO at the time, H. Lee Scott Jr., laid out new environmental, health, and ethical goals.[46] Besides continuing to promote energy-saving products at low prices in its stores, such as fluorescent lightbulbs, Scott said the company would focus on additional products that use a large amount of energy, such as air conditioners, microwave ovens, and televisions, working with suppliers to make such products 25% more energy efficient within 3 years.

Health Care. On health care, Scott said Walmart would apply its legendary cost-cutting skills to helping other companies deliver health care for their employees. By working with major American employers to help them manage and pay prescription drug claims (an expensive task now handled by companies called pharmacy benefit managers), Walmart hoped to save companies $100 million in that year alone.

Environmental Goals. Scott also said Walmart was committed to creating a more socially and environmentally conscious network of suppliers around the world, pressing suppliers in China, for instance, to comply with that country's environmental regulations. He also urged other major retailers to join a global network of retailers and consumer goods companies that is developing socially conscious manufacturing standards. Later Walmart joined with the Environmental Defense Fund to eliminate 20 million tons of carbon emissions from its global supply chain by 2015.[47]

Better health objectives. Walmart aims to encourage healthier eating by labeling which foods meet their nutritional standards.

By 2012, the company had shot from 15th to 3rd place in the Environmental Protection Agency's rankings of the country's top purchasers of green power (electricity produced by wind, solar, and similar means) for its stores in California and Texas.[48] Perhaps taking a cue from Whole Foods' "Health Starts Here" campaign, Walmart also launched a new health-labeling program for its grocery products that affix "Great for You" labels on foods that meet the company's nutritional criteria.[49]

YOUR CALL

How do the objectives outlined by CEO Scott reflect the criteria for SMART goals?

The Importance of Deadlines

There's no question that college is a pressure cooker for many students. The reason, of course, is the seemingly never-ending deadlines. But consider: Would you do all the course work you're doing—and realize the education you're getting—if you *didn't* have deadlines?

As we saw under the "T" (for "has Target dates") in SMART goals, deadlines are as essential to goal setting in business as they are to your college career. Because the whole purpose of planning and goals is to deliver to a client specified results within a specified period of time, deadlines become a great motivator, both for you and for the people working for you.

It's possible, of course, to let deadlines mislead you into focusing too much on immediate results and thereby ignore overall planning—just as students will focus too much on preparing for a test in one course while neglecting others. In general, however, deadlines can help you keep your eye on the "big picture" while simultaneously paying attention to the details that will help you realize the big picture. Deadlines can help concentrate the mind, so that you make quick decisions rather than put them off.

Deadlines help you ignore extraneous matters (such as cleaning up a messy desk) in favor of focusing on what's important—realizing the goals on time and on budget. Deadlines provide a mechanism for giving ourselves feedback. ●

PRACTICAL ACTION

How to Achieve Your Important Goals: Don't Keep Every Option Open

We've all been told that "It's important to keep your options open." But should we?

"You don't even know how a camera's burst-mode flash works, but you persuade yourself to pay for the extra feature just in case," writes a journalist about this phenomenon. "You no longer have anything in common with someone who keeps calling you, but you hate to just zap the relationship. Your child is exhausted from after-school soccer, ballet, and Chinese lessons, but you won't let her drop the piano lessons. They could come in handy."[50]

Where's the Money? The natural reluctance to close any door is pointed out by Dan Ariely, a behavioral economist at the Massachusetts Institute of Technology and author of *Predictably Irrational: The Hidden Forces That Shape Our Decisions.*[51] In that book, he describes experiments involving hundreds of MIT students who showed that they could not bear to let go of their options—even though it was bad strategy. The experiments involved playing a computer game in which students had 100 mouse clicks to look for money behind three doors on the screen and were paid real cash each time they found it. To earn the most money, a student would quickly find out that the best strategy was to

check out the three doors and settle on the one with the highest rewards. But when students stayed out of a room, the door would start shrinking and eventually disappear. Researchers found that most students would waste clicks by rushing back to reopen doors, even though they lost money by doing so—and they continued to frantically keep all their doors open even when they were fined for switching.

Fear of Loss? Were the students just trying to "keep their options open"? Ariely doesn't think so. The real motivation, he suggests, is fear of loss. "Closing a door on an option is experienced as a loss, and people are willing to pay a price to avoid the emotion of loss," he says.

YOUR CALL

Obviously, this lesson has some practical payoffs for all of us who are overscheduled and overworked and need all the help we can get to stay focused on our important goals. Are you presently considering adding a class, switching majors, or pursuing another career? Are you wondering whether to continue a personal relationship that no longer benefits you? What would be the advantages of— just saying no?

How does the planning/control cycle help keep a manager's plans headed in the right direction?

THE BIG PICTURE
The four-step planning/control cycle helps you keep in control, to make sure you're headed in the right direction.

Once you've made plans, how do you stay in control to make sure you're headed in the right direction? Actually, there is a continuous feedback loop known as the planning/control cycle. (The "organizing" and "leading" steps within the Planning-Organizing-Leading-Controlling sequence are implied here.) **The *planning/control cycle* has two planning steps (1 and 2) and two control steps (3 and 4), as follows: (1) Make the plan. (2) Carry out the plan. (3) Control the direction by comparing results with the plan. (4) Control the direction by taking corrective action in two ways—namely (a) by correcting deviations in the plan being carried out or (b) by improving future plans.** *(See Figure 5.5.)*

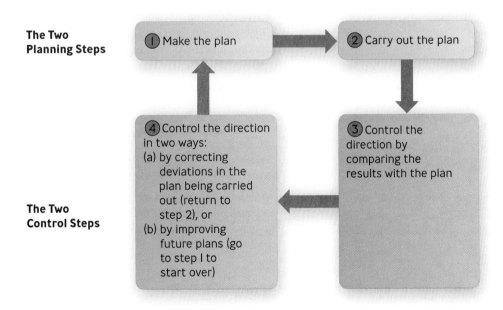

The Two Planning Steps

① Make the plan → ② Carry out the plan

The Two Control Steps

④ Control the direction in two ways:
(a) by correcting deviations in the plan being carried out (return to step 2), or
(b) by improving future plans (go to step 1 to start over)

③ Control the direction by comparing the results with the plan

figure 5.5
THE PLANNING/CONTROL CYCLE

This describes a constant feedback loop designed to ensure plans stay headed in the right direction.

Source: From Robert Kreitner, *Management*, 8th edition, Copyright © 2001 South-Western, a part of Cengage Learning, Inc. Reproduced with permission. www.cengage.com/permissions.

The planning/control cycle loop exists for each level of planning—strategic, tactical, and operational. The corrective action in step 4 of the cycle (a) can get a project back on track before it's too late or (b) if it's too late, it can provide data for improving future plans. ●

The Planning/Control Cycle: Apple Keeps Its Products Secret to Generate Buzz[52]

Most electronics and computer makers talk about their products well in advance of releasing them in order to give big customers and users a chance to prepare for them. Not Apple Inc., maker of the iPhone, iPod Touch, and iPad and *Fortune*'s No. 1 Most Admired Company four years in a row, 2008–2011. In 2008, it was also ranked No. 1 among *Fortune* 500 companies for total return to shareholders over the preceding 10 years.

Secrecy is a big part of the company's marketing strategy. (Even when the late founder and CEO Steve Jobs had cancer surgery, that fact was kept secret.) And the planning/control cycle figures closely in how well it is accomplished.

Step 1: The Plan. About 60% of all personal computers are bought by corporate customers and other big technology purchasers. Because of the hefty investment involved, these customers favor suppliers that let them see major product plans a year in advance. However, Steve Jobs determined that he favored selling technology directly to consumers rather than to corporate buyers and chief technology officers.

By keeping a new product secret, Apple stimulates a great deal of public curiosity. "There's a great deal of mystery and speculation about what it will be," says one seasoned marketing executive. "That's created a marketing aura for them." Such was the plan, for example, when Apple and Hewlett-Packard made a deal to repackage Apple's iPod digital music player and sell it under the H-P label.

Step 2: Carrying Out the Plan. Following its plan to keep new products secret to generate marketing buzz, Apple often didn't tell H-P about new iPod models until the day before they were introduced to the public. It also insisted that H-P work on iPods under tight security, even though Apple's versions were already displayed on store shelves.

The same has been true with other Apple products, with employees being sworn to secrecy for years. When, for example, the company decided to open its own chain of retail stores, an exact replica of a 6,000-square-foot store was built entirely inside a sealed-off warehouse away from Apple's main Cupertino, California, headquarters. When Apple decided to switch to Intel microprocessors, engineers worked on the project for 5 years under hush-hush conditions to adapt the Macintosh operating system to Intel chips.

Step 3: Comparing Results. The use of mystery "helps Apple attract crowds at its retail stores and generally

Secret product. The new version of the iPad was announced in March 2012 after great secrecy. Was Apple's strategy successful at generating buzz?

garner much more visibility than its relatively modest advertising budget would suggest," says a *Wall Street Journal* story. "While new wares from Dell Inc. or H-P rarely get front-page treatment, Mr. Jobs has repeatedly appeared on the covers of *Time, Newsweek,* and *Fortune* showing off a new iPod or Macintosh computer."

The same was true in 2010, when Apple announced its electronic tablet, the iPad.[53] Secrecy was a particular boon to Apple's fast-growing iPod product line. Consumers showed their willingness to abandon their old iPods in favor of newer ones that Apple unveiled with great publicity and fanfare. (On the negative side, Hewlett-Packard decided to terminate its iPod partnership with Apple, in part because of the secrecy issue.)

Step 4: Taking Corrective Action. Leaks have occurred, and Apple has learned that secrecy requires strong measures. Thus, Apple has fired and later sued employees who leaked news about unannounced products. It has even sued websites that have published gossip about Apple products. The company also assigns different departments dissimilar code names for the same product, so it can more easily track where leaks come from. Employees are outfitted with special electronic badges that grant them access only to specific areas within the fortresslike Apple corporate headquarters.

YOUR CALL

Can you think of a more effective way to generate consumer interest in a forthcoming product than just keeping it secret? What kind of planning/control cycle issues would it raise?

Key Terms Used in This Chapter

Summary

5.1 Planning & Uncertainty

Planning is defined as setting goals and deciding how to achieve them. It is also defined as coping with uncertainty by formulating future courses of action to achieve specified results.

Planning has four benefits. It helps you (1) check your progress, (2) coordinate activities, (3) think ahead, and (4) cope with uncertainty.

Organizations respond to uncertainty in one of four ways. (1) Defenders are expert at producing and selling narrowly defined products or services. (2) Prospectors focus on developing new products or services and in seeking out new markets, rather than waiting for things to happen. (3) Analyzers let other organizations take the risks of product development and marketing and then imitate what seems to work best. (4) Reactors make adjustments only when finally forced to by environmental pressures.

5.2 Fundamentals of Planning

An organization's reason for being is expressed in a mission statement. What the organization wishes to become—and the actions needed to get there—are expressed in a vision statement.

From these are derived strategic planning, then tactical planning, then operational planning. In strategic planning, managers determine what the organization's long-term goals should be for the next 1–5 years. In tactical planning, managers determine what contributions their work units can make during the next 6–24 months. In operational planning, they determine how to accomplish specific tasks within the next 1–52 weeks.

Whatever its type, the purpose of planning is to achieve a goal or objective, a specific commitment to achieve a measurable result within a stated period of time.

Strategic goals are set by and for top management and focus on objectives for the organization as a whole. Tactical goals are set by and for middle managers and focus on the actions needed to achieve strategic goals. Operational goals are set by and for first-line managers and are concerned with short-term matters associated with realizing tactical goals.

The goal should be followed by an action plan, which defines the course of action needed to achieve the stated goal. The operating plan, which is typically designed for a 1-year period, defines how you will conduct your business based on the action plan; it identifies clear targets such as revenues, cash flow, and market share.

Plans may be either standing plans, developed for activities that occur repeatedly over a period of time, or single-use plans, developed for activities that are not likely to be repeated in the future. There are three types of standing plans: (1) A policy is a standing plan that outlines the general response to a designated problem or situation. (2) A procedure outlines the response to particular problems or circumstances. (3) A rule designates specific required action. There are two types of single-use plans: (1) A program encompasses a range of projects or activities. (2) A project is a single-use plan of less scope and complexity.

5.3 Promoting Goal Setting: SMART Goals & Management by Objectives

The five characteristics of a good goal are represented by the acronym SMART. A SMART goal is one that is Specific, Measurable, Attainable, Results oriented, and has Target dates.

Management by objectives (MBO) is a four-step process in which (1) managers and employees jointly set objectives for the employee, (2) managers develop action plans, (3) managers and employees periodically review the employee's performance, and (4) the manager makes a performance appraisal and rewards the employee according to results. The purpose of MBO is to motivate rather than to control subordinates.

For MBO to be successful three things have to happen. (1) The commitment of top management is essential. (2) The program must be applied organizationwide. (3) Objectives must cascade—becoming more specific at lower levels of the organization.

Deadlines are essential to planning because they become great motivators both for the manager and for subordinates.

5.4 The Planning/Control Cycle

Once plans are made, managers must stay in control using the planning/control cycle, which has two planning steps (1 and 2) and two control steps (3 and 4), as follows: (1) Make the plan. (2) Carry out the plan. (3) Control the direction by comparing results with the plan. (4) Control the direction by taking corrective action in two ways—namely, (a) by correcting deviations in the plan being carried out or (b) by improving future plans.

Management in Action

Will GM's Strategic Plan Lead to Future Success?

Bailed out by the federal government just three years ago, General Motors Co. has set its sights on a once-unthinkable goal: making more than $10 billion a year.

It already is headed in that direction. On Feb. 16 [2012], GM is likely to report 2011 net income of about $8 billion, its highest ever, according to people who have seen the figures. Behind the gain to nearly twice 2010's $4.7 billion are growth in China and strong profits in North America, where GM has shed billions of dollars of costs and lately has been able to command higher prices.

GM has loftier ambitions still. It aims over the next several years to raise its profit margin—the portion of revenue left after paying expenses—to 10%, Daniel Ammann, chief financial officer, said in an interview. That would be a significant jump from the current margin of about 6% and would be among the highest in the auto industry. . . .

The bailout and restructuring helped GM to shed nearly $40 billion in obligations to become debt-free. It was a contrast with Ford Motor Co., which didn't have a bailout and is still paying off $23 billion it borrowed to survive. GM will pay almost no federal corporate taxes for years as one condition of the bailout. . . .

Now, "we are targeting our best-in-class peers," said GM's Mr. Ammann, referring to South Korea's Hyundai Motor Co. and Germany's BMW AG, both of which are estimated to have had a 10% return on sales for 2011. . . .

Mr. Ammann acknowledged that GM has a ways to go, particularly when it comes to leveraging the company's global scope to generate savings. "We have gaps when it comes to our best-in-class peers, and we are clear that we know where those gaps are," he said.

Adam Jonas, an auto analyst at Morgan Stanley, expressed skepticism that GM can achieve higher margins in their near future because of troubles in Europe and stiffer competition at home, as well as likely lower pickup-truck production. . . .

In South America, where GM's models are outdated, the company is struggling to avoid losses. "Consumers are demanding very good, up-to-date product there and GM is behind," said Brian Johnson, an analyst at Barclays Capital.

In Europe, where GM is weighed down by high labor costs, the company has been losing money for more than a decade. The company still has bloated costs in its engineering and manufacturing operations there. "Clearly we have more work to do," Mr. Ammann said.

GM also faces what promises to be a tougher 2012 in its home market. Toyota and Honda Motor Co. are back to full production after struggling with shortages last year after the Japanese earthquake and tsunami.

Mr. Ammann is setting out to cut billions more in costs while boosting revenue through global sales growth and reduced incentives on some models, he says.

One goal is fewer auto "platforms." GM aims to build vehicles all over the world that are made from the same basic parts and assembled in plants that use the same type of tooling—thus wringing savings out of its massive engineering budget. GM in 2010 had 30 auto platforms. It aims to reduce this total to 24 by 2014 and to 14 by 2018. . . .

Volkswagen and Ford are further down this road. Ford plans to rely on just five common platforms to deliver 75% of sales by the middle of the decade. Globally, Ford made roughly $300 more profit per vehicle sold than GM through September.

"Ford is light years ahead of GM, [which is] just at the beginning," said Morgan Stanley's Mr. Jonas. The process "is expensive and disruptive and will hurt profits for the next couple of years. There is a reason GM had not attacked this before." Though GM's bankruptcy helped it shed debt and excess models, it didn't help the company consolidate vehicle architectures.

Besides cutting costs, GM needs to change its culture. For decades the company focused on selling as many cars as possible, and propping up its U.S. market share, sometimes at the expense of the bottom line.

At the beginning of 2011, GM executives wanted to get sales off to a quick start, and offered plump incentives on Chevrolet trucks, Cadillacs, and GMC sport-utility vehicles. Sales jumped 20%, but soft profit in North America disappointed investors and caused some to fret that GM was back to its old ways.

In December 2011, GM's North American chief, Mark Reuss, huddled with top sales executives to discuss a strategy for the beginning of this year. The group knew it couldn't go heavy on incentives again, but worried that holding the line on them would displease dealers, turn off some customers, and mean a weak monthly sales performance.

"We all had to sit back and think about it and decide how comfortable we were with what was going to happen," recalled sales chief Don Johnson.

In the end, GM chose to cut incentives. On Jan. 30, the night before auto makers would report their January sales totals, Mr. Johnson barely slept, knowing GM would be the only major auto maker to show a decline from a year ago. The next day, Chrysler said its sales had risen 44% in January from the year before, and Ford had a 7.3% rise. GM's sales fell 6%.

"It is so important for the company to guard against focusing on [market] share over profitability,"
said Harry Wilson, who was a member of the Obama administration's automotive task force when it oversaw the restructuring of GM. Losing that focus, he said, would be one of the biggest threats to GM's profitability. . . .

Amid the turnover, GM slimmed down dramatically. It cut its global work force to 208,000 from 263,000 in 2008. The number of union workers in the U.S. fell to 49,000 from 62,000. GM closed 15 plants in the U.S., shed four of its eight brands and trimmed its model line to 49 cars and trucks from 86.

According to GM executives, achieving a healthier margin is becoming the company's main focus. For salaried executives, for example, annual bonuses are based largely on the company's margin.

Recently, when GM released global sales figures showing it had regained from Toyota the title of world's largest auto maker, Mr. Akerson was asked about his feelings on reclaiming the crown.

GM, he replied, needs to focus "on profits and margins and not necessarily try to post numbers on the board."

FOR DISCUSSION

1. Which of the four basic strategy types were used by GM? Explain your rationale.

2. Based on the case, what is GM's vision? Do you think it is realistic? Explain.

3. State two SMART goals for GM based on the case. Are these goals attainable? Discuss.

4. Using Figure 5.5, describe the extent to which GM is using the planning/control cycle.

5. What did you learn about planning based on this case? Explain.

Source: Excerpted from Sharon Terlep, "Target at Post-Bailout GM: Earning $10 Billion a Year," *The Wall Street Journal Europe*, February 7, 2012, pp. 14–15. Copyright © 2012 by Dow Jones & Company, Inc. Reproduced with permission of Dow Jones & Company, Inc. via Copyright Clearance Center.

Self-Assessment

Holland Personality Types & You: Matching Your Personality to the Right Work Environment & Occupation

OBJECTIVES

1. To understand the need to plan for your career.

2. To try to match your personality with an occupation.

INTRODUCTION

What do you want to be when you grow up? Some people seem to know early in life. Others come to a realization in college. Still others may be forced to such awareness by a crisis in later life, such as being dismissed from a job. Of course, most of us make some sort of plans for our careers. But in doing so we may not always be knowledgeable about how to match our personalities with the choices available.

INSTRUCTIONS

There are four parts to this exercise.

First, select a number from the list of six personality types.

Second, match that choice with the personality you think that type would have.

Third, select the work environment you think would be best for that personality type and personality.

Fourth, based on the preceding three choices, select which occupation would fit best. (For example, if you selected number 1, C, and f, the best fit for an occupation would be artist, musical conductor, and other related occupations.)

Try to connect each of the four parts and then check the key to see if your pairings are correct. After that, go through the list again, identifying what you think your personality type is, what your personality is, the work environment you like or think you would like best, and then the occupation that you would like or do like best. See if there is an alignment by using the scoring guidelines and interpretation shown below; if there is such an alignment, this suggests you may be on your way to a successful career.

PERSONALITY TYPE

1. Artistic
2. Conventional
3. Realistic
4. Enterprising
5. Social
6. Investigative

PERSONALITY

A. Prefers to work with things; is present-oriented, athletic, and mechanical.
B. Is analytical, a problem solver, scientific, and original.
C. Relies on feelings and imagination, is expressive, is intuitive, and values esthetics.
D. Sensitive to needs of others, enjoys interpersonal gatherings, and values educational and social issues.
E. Adventurous, has leadership qualities, persuasive, and values political and economic matters.
F. Structured, accurate, detail-oriented, and loyal follower.

WORK ENVIRONMENTS

a. Technical/mechanical and industrial.
b. Traditional and rewards conformity and dependability.
c. Cooperative and rewards personal growth.
d. Managerial role in organizations and rewards monetary gains and achievements.
e. Rewards high academic achievement and uses technical abilities to complete tasks.
f. Unstructured and allows nonconformity and rewards creativity.

OCCUPATIONS

7. Chemist/biological scientist, computer analyst, and emergency medical technician.
8. Lawyer, flight attendant, sales representative, reporter.
9. Accountant, bank teller, medical record technician.
10. Cook, drywall installer, auto mechanic.
11. Artist/commercial artist, musical director, architect, writer/editor.
12. Teacher, clergy, nurse, counselor, librarian.

SCORING GUIDELINES & INTERPRETATION

Scoring is as follows:

1-C-f-11

2-F-b-9

3-A-a-10

4-E-d-8

5-D-c-12

6-B-e-7

The purpose of this type of exercise is to see how personality type, personality, work environment, and occupation can best fit together. When the elements mesh, you will usually feel more competent and more satisfied with your work conditions and occupation. When these elements or factors are mismatched, one can be very frustrated, feel incompetent, or not be good at one's job.

If you wish to know more about career planning, you can avail yourself of a much more in-depth planning process at **www.soicc.state.nc.us/soicc/planning/ jh-types.htm.**

QUESTIONS FOR DISCUSSION

1. Does your assessment suggest that your career choice is best for your personality type? How do you feel about this assessment?

2. What do you think the management challenges are for those who are mismatched in their work? Explain.

3. Can you see and describe yourself more clearly in terms of personality type, personality, work environ-ment, and occupation given the results of your scor-ing? Explain.

Developed by Anne C. Cowden, PhD, based on the information provided by the website **www.soicc.state.nc.us/soicc/planning/jh-types.htm.**

How Do You Think Companies Should Respond to Accusations Made by a Whistle-Blower?

We defined a whistle-blower in Chapter 3 as an em-ployee who reports organizational misconduct to the public. Whistle-blowing is important to organizations for many reasons. One critical one is that the Sarbanes-Oxley law, which was discussed in Chapter 3, man-dates that companies develop processes and procedures for handling whistle-blowing. The Dodd-Frank law further provides financial rewards for employees who implicate security fraud and other types of wrong-doing. Civilians have received millions for exposing wrongdoing in companies that do business with the U.S. government.

This challenge involves consideration of how organizations should plan to respond to claims of misconduct or illegal activity. Consider what happened at Renault SA. An employee at Renault provided an anonymous accusation that a senior manager negotiated a bribe. "After a four-month investigation, Renault in January [2011] dismissed the executive and two other managers. The employees professed their innocence, but the company's chief executive, Carlos Ghosn, said publicly that the com-pany had evidence against them. Over the past two months, however, Renault has uncovered no evidence against the trio." The company's chief operating officer, Patrick Pélata, told *The Wall Street Journal* that "the company may have been 'tricked' into bring-ing the allegations."

SOLVING THE CHALLENGE

What do you think management at Renault should have done about the anonymous accusation about a se-nior official negotiating a bribe?

1. A four-month investigation is enough time to investi-gate the claim of bribery. Renault obviously was "tricked" by the anonymous tipper. I thus would pun-ish the person who made the false claim and hire back the three employees. These employees should also receive pay for the time they were dismissed.

2. Renault obviously did not conduct a thorough inves-tigation prior to firing the three employees. The com-pany needs to develop detailed guidelines for how such matters should be investigated. It also needs to hire back the employees and pay them for the time they were dismissed.

3. Renault should have hired an outside firm to investi-gate the claim, or they should have consulted with an outside law firm to review results from the investiga-tion and render an opinion to senior executives. They also need to hire back the employees and pay them for the time they were dismissed.

4. Invent other options.

Source: Excerpted from Ashby Jones and Joann S. Lublin, "Firms Revisit Whistleblowing," *The Wall Street Journal*, March 14, 2011, p. B5.

chapter 6

Strategic Management
How Exceptional Managers Realize a Grand Design

How Successful Managers Stay Successful: Seeing Beyond the Latest Management Fads

"How can we build organizations that are as nimble as change itself—not only operationally, but strategically?" asks famed management professor Gary Hamel.[1]

Unfortunately, the way many people deal with the uncertainty of change is by succumbing to fads, or short-lived enthusiasms, suggests University of Delaware sociologist Joel Best, author of *Flavor of the Month: Why Smart People Fall for Fads*.[2] A fad, he says, "is seen as the way of the future, a genuine innovation that will help solve a big problem....A lot of the attraction of a fad is that if you embrace it early, then you feel that you're ahead of other people, that you're hipper and maybe smarter than they are."[3]

That the field of management has its fads is evident in the constant production of business books touting the newest cure-all. Still, some ideas that started out as management fads survive. Why? Because they've been found to actually work. And one of those that has been found to work is *strategic planning*, as we describe in this chapter.

Two lessons of successful managers:

Lesson 1—In an Era of Management Fads, Strategic Planning Is Still Tops

Every year since 1993, Bain & Company, a global business consulting firm, prepares a "Management Tools and Trends" survey of the use of and satisfaction with the most popular management tools. The 2011 survey found that the second most widely used management tool in 2010 (after benchmarking, which again took first place and which we describe in Chapter 10) was a familiar tool from 10 and even 12 years earlier—namely, *strategic planning*, favored by about 65% of the senior managers surveyed. The use of *mission* and *vision statements* also continued to be popular, favored by about 63%.[4] Strategic planning is concerned with developing a comprehensive program for long-term success. Mission statements describe the organization's purpose, and vision statements describe its intended long-term goal. Successful managers know how to use all of these.

Lesson 2—Managers Must Be Willing to Make Large, Painful Decisions to Suddenly Alter Strategy

Another lesson is that in a world of rapid and discontinuous change, managers must always be prepared to make large, painful decisions and radically alter their business design—the very basis of how the company makes money. Because of fast-changing world conditions, managers must be able to make difficult decisions: "exiting businesses, firing people, admitting you were wrong (or at least not omniscient)," as writer Geoffrey Colvin puts it. "So the future will demand ever more people with the golden trait, the fortitude to accept and even seek psychic pain."[5]

For Discussion Earlier we described the importance of practicing *evidence-based management*, with managers "seeing the truth as a moving target, always facing the hard facts, avoiding falling prey to half-truths, and being willing to admit when they're wrong and change their ways."[6] Do you think you would have this mind-set when thinking about the overall direction of your organization or work unit?

forecast | What's Ahead in This Chapter

We describe strategic management and strategic planning and why they're important. We go through the five steps in the strategic-management process. Then we consider competitive intelligence and show how grand strategy is developed, using two strategic-planning tools—SWOT analysis and forecasting. Next we show how strategy is formulated, using such techniques as Porter's four competitive strategies and single-product versus diversification strategies. Finally, we show how strategy is carried out and controlled.

Am I really managing if I don't have a strategy?

THE BIG PICTURE

This section distinguishes among strategy, strategic management, and strategic planning. We describe three reasons why strategic management and strategic planning are important and how they may work for both large and small firms.

Sometimes it doesn't take much to start a business. Brian Allman was only 17 years old when he bought a simple vending machine at Sam's Club for $425 and used it to start Bear Snax Vending, stocking the machine and four others he added later with Skittles, M&Ms, and Snickers to serve several small to midsize businesses, such as banks.[7] Allman did this without apparently drawing up a **business plan, a document that outlines a proposed firm's goals, the strategy for achieving them, and the standards for measuring success.** But that's often the case with entrepreneurs, with one study finding that 41% of *Inc.* magazine's 1989 list of fastest-growing private firms didn't have a business plan and 26% had only rudimentary plans, percentages essentially unchanged in 2002.[8]

So, can it be said, as we begin our study of strategic planning, that business plans are unnecessary? Actually, the evidence suggests that firms with formal business plans are the ones that are more apt to survive. For instance, one study of 396 entrepreneurs in Sweden found that a greater number of firms that failed never had a formal business plan.[9]

Business plans embody a firm's strategy. In this section, we do the following:

■ Define strategy and strategic management.

■ Explain why strategic planning is important.

■ Describe the three key principles that underlie strategic positioning.

■ Discuss strategic management in large versus small firms.

Strategy, Strategic Management, & Strategic Planning

Every organization needs to have a "big picture" about where it's going and how to get there. These are matters of strategy, strategic management, and strategic planning.

Strategy   A *strategy* **is a large-scale action plan that sets the direction for an organization.** It represents an "educated guess" about what must be done in the long term for the survival or the prosperity of the organization or its principal parts. We hear the word expressed in terms like "Budweiser's ultimate strategy . . ." or "Visa's overseas strategy . . ." or *financial strategy, marketing strategy,* and *human resource strategy.*

An example of a strategy is "Find out what customers want, then provide it to them as cheaply and quickly as possible" (the strategy of Walmart). However, strategy is not something that can be decided on just once. Because of fast-changing conditions, it needs to be revisited from time to time, probably every year or two.

Strategic Management   In the late 1940s, most large U.S. companies were organized around a single idea or product line. By the 1970s, Fortune 500 companies were operating in more than one industry and had expanded overseas. It became apparent that to stay focused and efficient, companies had to begin taking a strategic-management approach.

Strategic management **is a process that involves managers from all parts of the organization in the formulation and the implementation of strategies and**

strategic goals. This definition doesn't mean that managers at the top dictate ideas to be followed by people lower down. Indeed, precisely because middle managers are the ones who will be asked to understand and implement the strategies, they should also help to formulate them. The steps in this process are covered in Section 6.2.

Strategic Planning   *Strategic planning,* as we stated in Chapter 5, determines not only the organization's long-term goals for the next 1–5 years regarding growth and profits but also the ways the organization should achieve them.

As one consultant put it, "Simply put, strategic planning determines where an organization is going over the next year or more, how it's going to get there and how it'll know if it got there or not."[10]

Why Strategic Management & Strategic Planning Are Important

An organization should adopt strategic management and strategic planning for three reasons: They can (1) *provide direction and momentum,* (2) *encourage new ideas,* and above all (3) *develop a sustainable competitive advantage.*[11] Let's consider these three matters.

1. Providing Direction & Momentum   Some executives are unable even to articulate what their strategy is.[12] Others are so preoccupied with day-to-day pressures that their organizations can lose momentum. But strategic planning can help people focus on the most critical problems, choices, and opportunities. If everyone is involved in the process, that can also help create teamwork, promote learning, and build commitment across the organization. Indeed, as we describe in Chapter 8, strategy can determine the very structure of the organization—for example, a top-down hierarchy with lots of management levels, as might be appropriate for an electricity-and-gas power utility, versus a flat organization with few management levels and flexible roles, as might suit a fast-moving social media startup.

Unless a strategic plan is in place, managers may well focus on just whatever is in front of them, the usual run-of-the-mill problems—until they get an unpleasant jolt when a competitor moves out in front because it has been able to take a long-range view of things and act more quickly. In recent times, this surprise has been happening over and over as companies have been confronted by some digital or Internet trend that emerged as a threat—as Amazon.com was to Barnes & Noble; as digital cameras were to Kodak's film business; as Google News, blogs, and citizen media were to newspapers.[13]

But there are many other instances in which a big company didn't take competitors seriously (as Sears didn't Walmart, IBM didn't Microsoft, and GM didn't Toyota). "We were five years late in recognizing that [microbreweries] were going to take as much market as they did," says August Busch III, CEO of massive brewer Anheuser-Busch, "and five years late in recognizing we should have joined them."[14]

Of course, a poor plan can send an organization in the wrong direction. Bad planning usually results from faulty assumptions about the future, poor assessment of an organization's capabilities, ineffective group dynamics, and information overload.[15]

2. Encouraging New Ideas   Some people object that planning can foster rigidity, that it creates blinders that block out peripheral vision and reduces creative thinking and action. "Setting oneself on a predetermined course in unknown waters," says one critic, "is the perfect way to sail straight into an iceberg."[16]

Strategic planning. In what is known as the "consumer hourglass theory," Procter & Gamble (P&G) and other companies are now focusing their products on the highest-income and lowest-income markets, reflecting the decline of the American middle class (those households earning $50,000 to $140,000 a year) in the wake of the worst recession in 50 years. Thus, P&G now markets premium-priced Tide, Pampers, and Ultra-Soft Charmin for high-end consumers and Cheer, Luvs diapers, and Basic Charmin for low-end buyers. Do you think this could be an enduring strategy?

100 Montaditos. Characterized as a "Spanish Starbucks for sandwiches" or "the dollar store of fast-food franchises," 100 Montaditos is a hugely successful Spanish restaurant chain that has set its sights on the United States. Named for bargain-rate traditional 5-inch sandwiches (such as those stuffed with Serrano ham or duck mousse with crispy onions for only $1), the chain's strategy emphasizes atmosphere combined with low prices. Starting with this Miami restaurant, it aims to open 4,000 American outlets during the next five years—a growth rate that would exceed even that of Starbucks, which took three decades to achieve the same number of U.S. stores. Some business analysts say the Spanish company's plans are too ambitious. Is there anything wrong with a strategy built on bold dreams?

Actually, far from being a straitjacket for new ideas, strategic planning can help encourage them by stressing the importance of innovation in achieving long-range success. Gary Hamel says that companies such as Apple have been successful because they have been able to unleash the spirit of "strategy innovation." Strategy innovation, he says, is the ability to reinvent the basis of competition within existing industries—"bold new business models that put incumbents on the defensive."[17]

Some successful innovators are companies creating new wealth in the grocery business, where Starbucks Coffee, Trader Joe's, Petco, ConAgra, and Walmart, for example, have developed entirely new product categories and retailing concepts. For instance, Starbucks (No. 8 on the 2012 *Fortune* "World's Most Admired Companies"), after going through a period of overambitious growth and an economic meltdown that shut down hundreds of stores, has launched Via as an instant coffee brand that will evolve into "multiple formats and new form factors" for worldwide distribution. It's also the No. 3 consumer brand on Facebook and the top coffee brand on Twitter.[18]

3. Developing a Sustainable Competitive Advantage Strategic management provides a sustainable *competitive advantage,* which, you'll recall (from Chapter 1) is the ability of an organization to produce goods or services more effectively than its competitors, thereby outperforming them. Sustainable competitive advantage occurs when an organization is able to get and stay ahead in four areas: (1) in being responsive to customers, (2) in innovating, (3) in quality, and (4) in effectiveness.

EXAMPLE

Developing Competitive Advantage: Is Apple's App Store a Model for Ford?

"Ford is transforming the car into a powerful smart-phone," reports one writer, "one that lets you carry your digital world along with you and then customizes it."[19] The basis for this is Ford's Sync in-dash communications platform, introduced in partnership with Microsoft in 2007, which allows you "to move seamlessly from the connected world contained in your phone to an equally connected world inside your car—without touching a single button." Currently offered on 14 Ford and 5 Lincoln models, Sync allows you to stream Internet music, access news and podcasts, and send and receive Twitter feeds.[20]

Sync also opens the door for an App Store kind of experience, Apple's spectacularly successful program in which customers can download all kinds of apps (applications) for use on their iPhones and which many companies see as the future model for software distribution.[21] Ford has also introduced voice-activated apps such as one that enables users to verbally activate Pandora, a popular Internet-radio application; one to make phone calls with a verbal command ("Call Paul at home"); or one that responds to you saying "I'm hungry" with some spoken advice about restaurants, along with navigation system directions. "Right now," says an automotive analyst, "Ford has redefined this market, and it has made it very difficult

for anybody to enter the space and compete."[22] In other words, Sync is a distinct competitive advantage for the car company—at least so far. But already General Motors, Mercedes-Benz, and other automakers are striving to catch up.[23]

YOUR CALL

An app store allows a company such as Apple or Ford to tap into ideas from third-party software developers while retaining control over its brand. But in Apple's case, heavy-handed management has irritated developers, causing many to quit building apps for the iPhone, opting instead for "the open, developer-friendly Web," in one description, which allows apps to be run on the iPhone's web browser.[24] Will Ford jeopardize its competitive advantage if it tries too hard to control its third-party app developers for Sync? Could there be safety issues if it opens Sync to all comers? After all, the federal government is already urging carmakers to limit dashboard distractions.[25]

What Is an Effective Strategy? Three Principles

Harvard Business School professor **Michael Porter** "is the single most important strategist working today, and maybe of all time," raved Kevin Coyne of consulting firm McKinsey & Co.[26]

Is this high praise deserved? Certainly Porter's status as a leading authority on competitive strategy is unchallenged. The Strategic Management Society, for instance, voted Porter the most influential living strategist. We will refer to him repeatedly in this chapter.

According to Porter, ***strategic positioning* attempts to achieve sustainable competitive advantage by preserving what is distinctive about a company.** "It means," he says, "performing *different* activities from rivals, or performing *similar* activities in different ways."[27]

Three key principles underlie strategic positioning:[28]

1. Strategy Is the Creation of a Unique & Valuable Position Strategic position emerges from three sources:

- **Few needs, many customers.** Strategic position can be derived from serving the few needs of many customers. Example: Jiffy Lube provides only lubricants, but it provides them to all kinds of people with all kinds of motor vehicles.

- **Broad needs, few customers.** A strategic position may be based on serving the broad needs of just a few customers. Example: Bessemer Trust targets only very high wealth clients.

- **Broad needs, many customers.** Strategy may be oriented toward serving the broad needs of many customers. Example: Carmike Cinemas operates only in cities with populations of fewer than 200,000 people.

2. Strategy Requires Trade-offs in Competing As a glance at the preceding choices shows, some strategies are incompatible. Thus, a company has to choose not only what strategy to follow but what strategy *not* to follow. Example: Neutrogena soap, points out Porter, is positioned more as a medicinal product than as a cleansing agent. In achieving this narrow positioning, the company gives up sales based on deodorizing, gives up large volume, and accordingly gives up some manufacturing efficiencies.

3. Strategy Involves Creating a "Fit" Among Activities   "Fit" has to do with the ways a company's activities interact and reinforce one another. Example: A mutual fund such as Vanguard Group follows a low-cost strategy and aligns all its activities accordingly, distributing funds directly to consumers and minimizing portfolio turnover. However, when Continental Lite tried to match some but not all of Southwest Airlines' activities, it was not successful because it didn't apply Southwest's entire interlocking system.

Does Strategic Management Work for Small as Well as Large Firms?

You would expect that a large organization, with its thousands of employees and even larger realm of "stakeholders," would benefit from strategic management and planning. After all, how can a huge company such as General Motors run without some sort of grand design?

But what about smaller companies, which account for more than half of total employment and the bulk of employment growth in recent years? One analysis of several studies found that strategic planning was appropriate not just for large firms—companies with fewer than 100 employees could benefit as well, although the improvement in financial performance was small. Nevertheless, the researchers concluded, "it may be that the small improvement in performance is not worth the effort involved in strategic planning unless a firm is in a very competitive industry where small differences in performance may affect the firm's survival potential."[29]   ●

EXAMPLE

Comparing Strategies: Big-Company "Make the Consumer a Captive" Versus Small-Firm "Offer Personal Connections"

Big companies—especially big-tech companies such as Amazon, Google, or Apple—"are no longer content simply to enhance part of your life," says one report. "The new strategy is to build a device, sell it to consumers, and then sell them the content to play on it. And maybe some ads too."[30]

Big-Company Ways. That is, the idea is to get consumers tied not just to a brand or device or platform but to make them captive of the company's *ecosystem*—and to get them connected "as tightly as possible so they and their content are locked into one system," says analyst Michael Gartenberg.[31] Thus, Amazon, for example, sells the Kindle e-book readers at a low price so that it can then sell e-books. Apple enables users to easily create book content on its iBook Authors book-creation tool, but authors will only be able to sell the results through Apple. Google has attempted to promote its Google Nexus smartphone as a platform for selling Google Wallet, a cellphone payment system.

Small-Company Ways. "I don't feel they behave in a way that I want to support with my consumer dollars," says Chicago professor Harold Pollack about big Internet retailers like Amazon.[32] So instead, Pollack started buying from small online retailers. Their prices are often higher, but he says he now has a clear conscience.

Whereas the strategy of big e-commerce companies is to try to tightly connect consumers with discounted prices, free shipping, and easy-to-use apps, the strategy of small retailers—like Hello Hello Books in Maine—is to discourage price comparisons (as in creating "buy it where you try it" campaigns or refusing to carry popular items carried by big retailers), offer freebies, and attempt to establish a personal or emotional connection with customers. They also try to exploit the sympathies of shoppers to "support the little guy," as Pollack is doing.

YOUR CALL

Considering the proliferation of price comparison sites (Pricegrabber.com, Bizrate.com, FreePriceAlerts.com) that will usually direct consumers to big e-commerce retailers, do you think low prices will always win in the end? Is there any strategy a small retailer can take to maintain an advantage?[33]

6.2 THE STRATEGIC-MANAGEMENT PROCESS

What's the five-step recipe for the strategic-management process?

major question?

THE BIG PICTURE
The strategic-management process has five steps: Establish the mission and the vision, establish the grand strategy, formulate the strategic plans, carry out those plans, and maintain strategic control. In addition, all the steps may be affected by feedback that enables taking constructive action.

When is a good time to begin the strategic-management process? Often it's touched off by some crisis.

Toyota was compelled to do serious soul searching in 2010, when it encountered severe quality problems involving what seemed to be uncontrollable acceleration in its automobiles (later attributed mostly to driver mistakes). Toyota Motor's president Akio Toyoda concluded that these problems were partly owing to the company's "excessive focus on market share and profits," requiring that the company reorient its strategy toward quality and innovation.[34] For Edward Lampert, who in 2005 merged Kmart and Sears into megaretailer Sears Holdings, the pressure was felt in years of underperforming returns despite cost-cutting and store closures.[35]

EXAMPLE

Crisis Leading to the Strategic-Management Process: JetBlue Weathers an Ice Storm

Founded in 1998, JetBlue started out as a low-fare airline, promising fares up to 65% lower than competitors along with, in one description, "creature comforts like assigned seating, leather upholstery, and satellite TV on individual screens in every seat."[36] The formula was an immediate hit, and by 2007 JetBlue had grown from 6 daily flights and 300 employees to 575 daily flights to 52 destinations and 9,300 employees.

Change in Focus. Then in 2005, the founder, David Neeleman, decided to depart from the low-cost model of Southwest Airlines–style carriers and to imitate more traditional airlines. He added different kinds of aircraft, increased routes and airports, and built a $25 million training center in anticipation of expanding the workforce to 30,000 by 2010. "These moves," says one analysis, "increased the airline's costs while drawing it into competition with a greater number of rivals,

which in turn made it harder for JetBlue to raise fares."[37] JetBlue lost $20 million in 2005 and $1 million in 2006.

The Valentine's Day Ice Storm. Then the Valentine's Day crisis happened. On February 14, 2007, an ice storm settled on JetBlue's New York hub at John F. Kennedy International Airport, preventing planes from taking off. Acting on forecasters' predictions that the ice would change to rain, JetBlue continued to load flights and allow them to taxi to the runway. The result: planes couldn't take off, and passengers were stuck in their seats for hours—up to 6 hours, in some cases. In fact, only 17 of the airline's 156 scheduled departures left JFK that day, disrupting the entire system and displacing crews and aircraft. "In subsequent days," says one account, "JetBlue management canceled more and more flights, angering thousands of passengers, until finally, on February 20, normal operations resumed."[38]

The storm incident cost the carrier around $30 million, according to Neeleman.[39] In addition, he apologized publicly to more than 131,000 customers affected by the cancellations and delays and offered different levels of compensation (such as a full refund and voucher for a free round-trip flight to passengers stuck on a plane for more than 3 hours). He also announced a customer bill of rights, which offered specific kinds of compensation for various types of delays and overbooking that resulted in passengers getting bumped. None of these efforts protected his job, however; Neeleman was replaced as CEO in 2007 and as chairman of the board in 2008.

Lessons from the Crisis. What does the incident teach? Principally that the airline had grown too fast and didn't have enough people to handle all the passengers trying to rebook flights or to schedule crews during the disruptions. For instance, JetBlue's reservations system relied on a dispersed workforce that included many agents working flexible hours from home—"a low-cost solution that works well until thousands of passengers need to rebook at once," points out one author.[40] The company set a goal of doubling the number of agents who could access the company's reservations system. It also created a database to track crew locations and contact information, and initiated cross-training so that 900 employees working near JFK would be available during any future operational crisis.

YOUR CALL

Despite its near collapse after the ice storm, JetBlue bounced back and has been profitable in years when other airlines have not been. Moreover, JetBlue has topped all airlines in J. D. Power's annual customer-service survey for seven years in a row. Do you think the airline will be able to continue to expand and still keep its fares low, its comforts relatively high, and have enough staff and arrangements to avoid another Valentine's Day massacre?

The Five Steps of the Strategic-Management Process

The strategic-management process has five steps, plus a feedback loop, as shown below. *(See Figure 6.1.)* Let's consider these five steps.

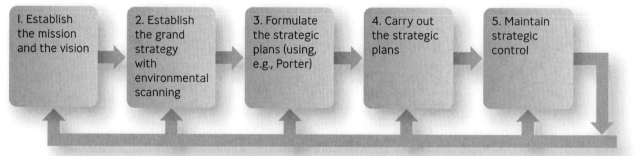

Feedback: Revise actions, if necessary, based on feedback

figure 6.1

THE STRATEGIC-MANAGEMENT PROCESS

The process has five steps.

Step 1: Establish the Mission & the Vision   We discussed mission and vision in Chapter 5. If you were called on to write a mission statement and a vision statement, how would you go about it?

Characteristics of a Good Mission Statement   The *mission,* you'll recall, is the organization's purpose or reason for being, and it is expressed in a *mission statement.* For example, the mission statement of McGraw-Hill, publisher of this book, is as follows:

> *To serve the worldwide need for knowledge at a fair profit by gathering, evaluating, producing, and distributing valuable information in a way that benefits our customers, employees, authors, investors, and our society.*

Family business. Do small, family-owned businesses need a vision statement? If no, why not? How many small-business owners, with firms of, say, five employees or fewer, would you guess have taken the time to compose such a vision?

Characteristics of a Good Vision Statement   An organization's vision, you'll recall, is its long-term goal describing what it wants to become. It is expressed in a *vision statement,* which describes its long-term direction and strategic intent. For example, Walt Disney's original vision for Disneyland went in part like this:

> *Disneyland will be something of a fair, an exhibition, a playground, a community center, a museum of living facts, and a showplace of beauty and magic. It will be filled with the accomplishments, the joys and hopes of the world we live in. And it will remind us and show us how to make those wonders part of our own lives.*[41]

Although a vision statement can be short, it should be positive and inspiring, and it should stretch the organization and its employees to achieve a desired future state that appears beyond its reach. Consider Google, for example. Google's vision is "to organize the world's information and make it universally accessible and useful." Google's former CEO Eric Schmidt estimated that it might take 300 years to achieve the company's vision. Doing so will require Google to have strategic patience and to develop a grand strategy that is broad in focus.[42]

Guidelines for constructing powerful mission statements and vision statements are in the table on the next page. *(See Table 6.1.)* "Visions that have these properties challenge and inspire people in the organization and help align their energies in a common direction," says Burt Nanus of the University of Southern California's School of Business Administration. "They prevent people from being overwhelmed by immediate problems because they help distinguish what is truly important from what is merely interesting."[43]

Step 2: Establish the Grand Strategy   The next step is to translate the broad mission and vision statements into a ***grand strategy*, which, after an assessment of current organizational performance, then explains how the organization's mission is to be accomplished.**[44] Three common grand strategies are *growth, stability,* and *defensive.*

table 6.1 MISSION STATEMENTS AND VISION STATEMENTS

Mission statements: Does your company's mission statement answer these questions?

1. Who are our customers?

2. What are our major products or services?

3. In what geographical areas do we compete?

4. What is our basic technology?

5. What is our commitment to economic objectives?

6. What are our basic beliefs, values, aspirations, and philosophical priorities?

7. What are our major strengths and competitive advantages?

8. What are our public responsibilities, and what image do we wish to project?

9. What is our attitude toward our employees?

Vision statements: Does your company's vision statement answer yes to these questions?

1. Is it appropriate for the organization and for the times?

2. Does it set standards of excellence and reflect high ideals?

3. Does it clarify purpose and direction?

4. Does it inspire enthusiasm and encourage commitment?

5. Is it well articulated and easily understood?

6. Does it reflect the uniqueness of the organization, its distinctive competence, what it stands for, what it's able to achieve?

7. Is it ambitious?

Sources: F. R. David, "How Companies Define Their Mission," *Long Range Planning,* February 1989, pp. 90–97; and B. Nanus, *Visionary Leadership: Creating a Compelling Sense of Direction for Your Organization* (San Francisco: Jossey-Bass, 1992), pp. 28–29.

The first part of the process of developing a grand strategy, then, is to make a rigorous analysis of the organization's present situation to determine *where it is presently headed.* The second part is to determine where it *should be headed in the future.*

Let's consider the three common grand strategies.

1. The Growth Strategy A *growth strategy* is a grand strategy that involves expansion—as in sales revenues, market share, number of employees, or number of customers or (for nonprofits) clients served. Example: IBM under its previous CEO, Samuel J. Palmisano, decided to get out of low-profit businesses that were fading, such as the personal computer business, and shift to services and software, often delivered over the Internet from data centers connecting all kinds of devices—what is today called *cloud computing.*[45]

2. The Stability Strategy A *stability strategy* is a grand strategy that involves little or no significant change. Example: Alaska Airlines, which enjoyed a profitable year in 2011, following a decade in which other carriers went bankrupt, decided to remain a "smallish, specialized, regional airline in a world of global giants," says one report, and to avoid cross-continental alliances and megamergers. Its stability strategy is simply to focus on lowering the cost per available seat mile.[46]

3. The Defensive Strategy A *defensive strategy* or a *retrenchment strategy,* is a grand strategy that involves reduction in the organization's efforts. Example: After Kodak, the iconic film manufacturer, failed to reinvent itself and declared bankruptcy in 2012, it decided to focus on a fresh start on making inkjet printers.[47]

Variations of the three strategies are shown on the next page. (*See Table 6.2.*)

table 6.2

HOW COMPANIES CAN
IMPLEMENT GRAND
STRATEGIES

Growth strategy

- It can improve an existing product or service to attract more buyers.
- It can increase its promotion and marketing efforts to try to expand its market share.
- It can expand its operations, as in taking over distribution or manufacturing previously handled by someone else.
- It can expand into new products or services.
- It can acquire similar or complementary businesses.
- It can merge with another company to form a larger company.

Stability strategy

- It can go for a no-change strategy (if, for example, it has found that too-fast growth leads to foul-ups with orders and customer complaints).
- It can go for a little-change strategy (if, for example, the company has been growing at breakneck speed and believes it needs a period of consolidation).

Defensive strategy

- It can reduce costs, as by freezing hiring or tightening expenses.
- It can sell off (liquidate) assets—land, buildings, inventories, and the like.
- It can gradually phase out product lines or services.
- It can divest part of its business, as in selling off entire divisions or subsidiaries.
- It can declare bankruptcy.
- It can attempt a turnaround—do some retrenching, with a view toward restoring profitability.

How do you establish a grand strategy? Among the strategic-planning tools and techniques used are (1) *SWOT analysis* and (2) *forecasting,* as we describe in Section 6.3.

Step 3: Formulate Strategic Plans The grand strategy must then be translated into more specific *strategic plans,* which determine what the organization's long-term goals should be for the next 1–5 years. These should communicate not only the organization's general goals about growth and profits but also information about how these goals will be achieved. Moreover, like all goals, they should be SMART—Specific, Measurable, Attainable, Results-oriented, and specifying Target dates (Chapter 5).

Strategy formulation **is the process of choosing among different strategies and altering them to best fit the organization's needs.** Because the process is so important, formulating strategic plans is a time-consuming process. Among the techniques used to formulate strategy is *Porter's competitive forces and strategies,* which we describe in Section 6.4.

Step 4: Carry Out the Strategic Plans **Putting strategic plans into effect is** *strategy implementation.* Strategic planning isn't effective, of course, unless it can be translated into lower level plans. This means that top managers need to check on possible roadblocks within the organization's structure and culture and see if the right people and control systems are available to execute the plans.[48]

Often implementation means overcoming resistance by people who feel the plans threaten their influence or livelihood. This is particularly the case when the plans must be implemented rapidly, since delay is the easiest kind of resistance

Wrong strategy? Did PepsiCo CEO Indra Nooyi take her eye off the ball when she decided in 2010 that the snacks-and-cola company ought to triple sales of nutritionally healthy products (yogurt drinks, hummus, oatmeal bars)? Since that time, sales of the sugary Pepsi-Cola have slipped, while Cola-Cola roared ahead. Indeed, on Nooyi's watch, PepsiCo's stock has risen only 2%, compared with 50% for Coke.

there is (all kinds of excuses are usually available to justify delays). Thus, top managers can't just announce the plans; they have to actively sell them to middle and supervisory managers.

Step 5: Maintain Strategic Control: The Feedback Loop *Strategic control* **consists of monitoring the execution of strategy and making adjustments, if necessary.** To keep strategic plans on track, managers need control systems to monitor progress and take corrective action—early and rapidly—when things start to go awry. Corrective action constitutes a feedback loop in which a problem requires that managers return to an earlier step to rethink policies, redo budgets, or revise personnel arrangements. To keep a strategic plan on track, suggests Bryan Barry, you need to do the following:[49]

- **Engage people.** You need to actively engage people in clarifying what your group hopes to accomplish and how you will accomplish it.
- **Keep it simple.** Keep your planning simple, unless there's a good reason to make it more complex.
- **Stay focused.** Stay concentrated on the important things.
- **Keep moving.** Keep moving toward your vision of the future, adjusting your plans as you learn what works.

To see how good you think you'd be, see the Self-Assessment, "Core Skills Required in Strategic Planning," at the end of this chapter.

Now, in Section 6.3, let us consider some of the tools used for Step 2, establishing a grand strategy—competitive intelligence, SWOT, and forecasting. ●

How can competitive intelligence, SWOT, and forecasting help me establish my strategy?

THE BIG PICTURE

To develop a grand strategy, you need to gather data and make projections, using the tools of competitive intelligence, SWOT analysis, and forecasting.

The first part in developing a grand strategy, Step 2 of the five-step strategic-management process, is intelligence gathering—internally and externally. The next part is to make some projections.

Three kinds of strategic-planning tools and techniques are (1) *competitive intelligence*, (2) *SWOT analysis*, and (3) *forecasting*—trend analysis and contingency planning.

Competitive Intelligence

Practicing *competitive intelligence* **means gaining information about one's competitors' activities so that you can anticipate their moves and react appropriately.** If you are a manager, one of your worst nightmares is that a competitor will surprise you with a service or product—as boutique beers did to major brewers and mountain bikes did to major bicycle makers—that will revolutionize the market and force you to try to play catch-up. Successful companies make it a point to conduct competitive intelligence.

Electronics show. Since 1967, the International Consumer Electronics Show (CES) in Las Vegas has traditionally been a place where blockbuster products were introduced and thus a source of competitive intelligence. Recently, however, the hottest gadgets from Apple, Amazon, and Microsoft have been unveiled in other, more exclusive venues. Still, CES remains the world's largest consumer technology convention.

Gaining competitive intelligence isn't always easy, but there are several avenues—and, surprisingly, most of them are public sources—including the following:

- **The public prints and advertising.** A product may be worked on in secret for several years, but at some point it becomes subject to announcement—through a press release, advertising piece, news leak, or the like. Much of this is available free through the Internet or by subscription to certain specialized databases, such as Nexus, which contains hundreds of thousands of news stories.

- **Investor information.** Information about new products and services may also be available through the reports filed with the Securities and Exchange Commission and through corporate annual reports.

- **Informal sources.** People in the consumer electronics industry every year look forward to major trade shows, such as the International Consumer Electronics Show in Las Vegas, when companies roll out their new products.[50] At such times, people also engage in industry-gossip conversation to find out about future directions. Finally, salespeople and marketers, who are out calling on corporate clients, may return with tidbits of information about what competitors are doing.

SWOT Analysis

After competitive intelligence, the next point in establishing a grand strategy is *environmental scanning,* **careful monitoring of an organization's internal and external environments to detect early signs of opportunities and threats that may influence the firm's plans.** The process for doing such scanning is *SWOT analysis*—**also known as *a situational analysis*—which is a search for the Strengths, Weaknesses, Opportunities, and Threats affecting the organization.** A SWOT analysis should provide you with a realistic understanding of your organization in relation to its internal and external environments so you can better formulate strategy in pursuit of its mission. *(See Figure 6.2.)*

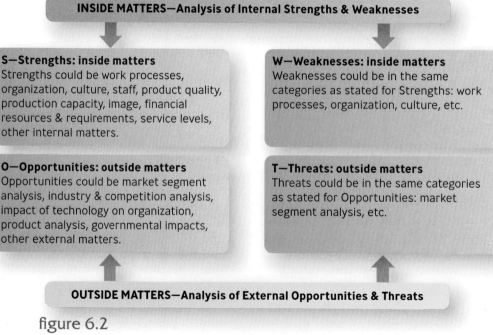

figure 6.2

SWOT ANALYSIS

SWOT stands for Strengths, Weaknesses, Opportunities, Threats.

The SWOT analysis is divided into two parts: inside matters and outside matters—that is, an analysis of *internal strengths and weaknesses* and an analysis of *external opportunities and threats*. The following table gives examples of SWOT characteristics that might apply to a college. *(See Table. 6.3.)*

(See Table. 6.3.)

table 6.3

SWOT CHARACTERISTICS THAT MIGHT APPLY TO A COLLEGE

S—Strengths (internal strengths)	W—Weaknesses (internal weaknesses)
• Faculty teaching and research abilities	• Limited programs in business
• High-ability students	• High teaching loads
• Loyal alumni	• Insufficient racial diversity
• Strong interdisciplinary programs	• Lack of high-technology infrastructure
O—Opportunities (external opportunities)	**T—Threats (external threats)**
• Growth in many local skilled jobs	• Depressed state and national economy
• Many firms give equipment to colleges	• High-school enrollments in decline
• Local minority population increasing	• Increased competition from other colleges
• High-school students take college classes	• Funding from all sources at risk

Inside Matters: Analysis of Internal Strengths & Weaknesses   Does your organization have a skilled workforce? a superior reputation? strong financing? These are examples of *organizational strengths*—**the skills and capabilities that give the organization special competencies and competitive advantages in executing strategies in pursuit of its mission.**

Or does your organization have obsolete technology? outdated facilities? a shaky marketing operation? These are examples of *organizational weaknesses*—**the drawbacks that hinder an organization in executing strategies in pursuit of its mission.**

Outside Matters: Analysis of External Opportunities & Threats   Is your organization fortunate to have weak rivals? emerging markets? a booming economy? These are instances of *organizational opportunities*—**environmental factors that the organization may exploit for competitive advantage.**

Alternatively, is your organization having to deal with new regulations? a shortage of resources? substitute products? These are some possible *organizational threats*—**environmental factors that hinder an organization's achieving a competitive advantage.**

EXAMPLE

SWOT Analysis: How Would You Analyze Toyota?

"I fear the pace at which we have grown may have been too quick," said Akio Toyoda, the grandson of Toyota Motor's founder, in 2010 testimony before a U.S. congressional committee looking into sudden acceleration problems.

"Priorities became confused, and we were not able to stop, think, and make improvements as much as we were able to before."[51] Toyota's U.S. sales fell 9% that month because of safety-related recalls of millions of vehicles, and by late 2010 journalists were writing that the company had lost its edge.[52] By the end of 2011, Toyota Motor, formerly the world's largest automaker, had slipped to third place in production behind General Motors and Volkswagen.

Where does the company stand today? Most significantly, perhaps, its new young president, Akio Toyoda, whose motto is "be fast, be flexible," has energetically taken on the automaker's challenges, traveling to the United States to fire up dealers, personally taking charge of the sagging Lexus brand, and redesigning the firm's reporting system and flattening the management hierarchy.[53] If you were a top Toyota manager, what would be the kinds of things you would identify in a SWOT analysis?

The Internal Strengths. Originally the "Toyota Way," as practiced from assembly line to boardroom, stressed the values of continuous improvement (*kaizen*) and eliminating waste (*muda*). The Toyota Way, says one report, "mandates planning for the long term; highlighting problems instead of hiding them; encouraging teamwork with colleagues and suppliers; and, perhaps most important, instilling a self-critical culture that fosters continuous and unrelenting improvement."[54] Developed in the 1950s, these precepts later became the basis for such concepts as lean manufacturing and just-in-time inventory management (discussed in Chapter 2). "At their core," says one analysis, "was an attention to detail and a noble frugality that shunned waste of every kind."[55] Said its top engineer, "Basically, Toyota's growth has been underpinned by QDR [quality, dependability, reliability] that was very high compared with competitors'."[56]

Because of a perception that Toyota treated its cars like "transportation appliances," falling behind in design leadership, causing buyers to feel less of an emotional connection with Toyota products, it has recently taken initiatives to "improve upon the emotion of cars" with better styling and high-quality interiors. It also has continued to push green technology, as it did with the 2012 plug-in Prius.

The Internal Weaknesses. In the 1990s, Toyota launched an effort to become the world's largest automaker, embarking on aggressive overseas expansion and doubling its plants in North America, Asia, and Europe. During this time, the focus on cost reduction intensified to the point that the virtue became a vice. Suppliers were continually pushed to design parts that were 10% cheaper and 10% lighter. Common parts were used in most Toyota

models, acquired from outside companies instead of trusted traditional suppliers.[57]

From 2000 to 2010, however, driver complaints to the National Highway Traffic and Safety Administration about "vehicle speed control" issues soared, with 11.7% of faulty vehicle components identified as Toyota's.[58] Then came widely publicized problems with sticking accelerators, prompting two huge recalls and suspension of the sales and production of eight models in the American market.[59] Later it developed that the "unintended acceleration" was caused by sticky pedals or floor mats rather than Toyota electronics.[60] By then, however, the damage to Toyota's vaunted reputation for quality was severe. "When your whole deal was quality, every mistake is a big deal," said a manufacturing expert.[61]

A final important internal weakness was that Toyota had succumbed to "big-company disease," becoming ponderous and bureaucratic, with every decision tightly controlled in Japan, to the detriment of its managers in the American market.[62] Today, under the new president's direction, the 1950s-style traditional organization has been modernized, with layers of management removed and with Akio meeting weekly with five top advisors to make on-the-spot decisions.

The External Opportunities. Although slow to awaken to its quality problems in 2009–2010, the company went into full PR battle mode, moving to discredit critics who blamed accelerator problems on faulty electronics and stressing its commitment to its millions of U.S. customers.[63] It joined forces with Ford to jointly develop a gas-electric hybrid fuel system for trucks and sport utility vehicles.[64] It moved to give its cars more exciting designs, including launch of the sporty $375,000 Lexus LFA, a carbon fiber supercar. Finally, despite all the self-inflicted wounds, Toyota continues to lead most other car companies in quality rankings: All three of its 2009 brands appeared in the top 10 J. D. Power 2012 rankings for reliability, with eight Toyota, Lexus, and Scion models winning or tied for first place in their vehicle categories.[65] In early 2012, the company raised its profit forecast, citing faster-than-expected demand and benefits from cost cuts.[66]

The External Threats. For Ford, GM, and Chrysler, Toyota's accelerator-sticking troubles of 2009–2010 presented an unprecedented opportunity to grab their rival's customers.[67] Toyota also faced the worldwide Great Recession, which damaged auto spending. Further, the year 2011 brought the deadly earthquake and tsunami, which devastated plants in the north of Japan and disrupted

the supply of more than 500 parts. In late 2011, severe flooding in Thailand led to new supply difficulties. By the beginning of 2012, Toyota's market share in the United States had fallen from 18.3 to 12.9%.[68] With profits 51% lower than the previous year, Toyota also had to deal with severe currency problems of a strong yen against a weak U.S. dollar, which threatened to further reduce revenues.[69]

YOUR CALL

"Comfortably preoccupied with rooting out internal weakness," says one writer, "the Toyota Way is lost when it comes to contending with outside threats.... If a flaw does get through, the company as a whole is loath to admit that the system broke down."[70] Do you agree? How well do you think Akio Toyoda is dealing with Toyota's threats and opportunities, both internal and external?

Forecasting: Predicting the Future

Once they've analyzed their organization's Strengths, Weaknesses, Opportunities, and Threats, planners need to do forecasting for making long-term strategy. **A *forecast* is a vision or projection of the future.**

Lots of people make predictions, of course—and often they are wrong. In the 1950s, the head of IBM, Thomas J. Watson, estimated that the demand for computers would never exceed more than five for the entire world. In the late 1990s, many computer experts predicted power outages, water problems, transportation disruptions, bank shutdowns, and far worse because of computer glitches (the "Y2K bug") associated with the change from year 1999 to 2000.

Of course, the farther into the future one makes a prediction, the more difficult it is to be accurate, especially in matters of technology. Yet forecasting is a necessary part of planning.

Two types of forecasting are *trend analysis* and *contingency planning*.

Trend Analysis A *trend analysis* **is a hypothetical extension of a past series of events into the future.** The basic assumption is that the picture of the present can be projected into the future. This is not a bad assumption, if you have enough historical data, but it is always subject to surprises. And if your data are unreliable, they will produce erroneous trend projections.

An example of trend analysis is a time-series forecast, which predicts future data based on patterns of historical data. Time-series forecasts are used to predict long-term trends, cyclic patterns (as in the up-and-down nature of the business cycle), and seasonal variations (as in Christmas sales versus summer sales).

Contingency Planning: Predicting Alternative Futures *Contingency planning*—also known as *scenario planning* and *scenario analysis*—**is the creation of alternative hypothetical but equally likely future conditions.** For example, scenarios may be created with spreadsheet software such as Microsoft Excel to present alternative combinations of different factors—different economic pictures, different strategies by competitors, different budgets, and so on.

Fuel proof. Locking in the price of jet fuel with long-term contracts with suppliers, a form of contingency planning, has put low-cost airlines such as Southwest in a competitive position with rivals in controlling costs.

EXAMPLE

Contingency Planning: Southwest Airlines Uses Hedging to Hold Down Price of Aviation Fuel

In early 2008, when the price of crude oil hit all-time highs ($100 a barrel), the cost of jet fuel threatened to take a big bite out of airline profits. Aviation fuel makes up as much as 15% of an airline's operating costs, the second biggest expense after labor.[71]

Locking in Contracts on Future Prices. Most airlines use a technique known as *hedging* to hold down the price of jet fuel, but Southwest Airlines is particularly good at it, having decided to enter fuel hedge transactions "back when oil prices were so low that oil was cheaper than water," as one observer whimsically put it.[72] In this form of contingency planning, airlines hedge the rise of fuel prices in the futures market by locking in contracts that allow them to buy fuel at a fixed price. Compared with traditional carriers, Southwest has been in a better position to buy favorable futures contracts because of its financial strengths: It avoids expensive labor contracts, operates only one type of aircraft, and flies high-traffic routes.[73]

$51-a-Barrel Oil. In the 2008 world of $140-plus-a-barrel oil, for instance, Southwest had 70% of its fuel hedged at $51 a barrel. For 2010, it had 30% of its fuel hedged at $63 a barrel. These prices are way below what other major airlines get. (United Airlines, for instance, had only 15% of its fuel hedged, and at between $91 and $101 per barrel.) By 2011, however, the company had to confront the reality of higher fuel prices as more of its hedging contracts expired, which cost the airline 64% more than the previous year, forcing it to repeatedly raise ticket prices.[74] It also took a loss in the third quarter of 2011 when actual fuel prices fell *below* the locked-in prices of its fuel hedges. However, it finished the year profitable as a result of its hedging impacts and increased passenger revenue.[75]

YOUR CALL

Is hedging like playing poker—like being a riverboat gambler? "You have to have foresight, wisdom, and some courage to hedge," says Tammy Romo, Southwest's treasurer.[76] But if oil consumption will grow by more than 40% over the next quarter century and fuel prices stay high, what do you think airlines will have to do? (*Hint:* increase revenues, decrease costs, consolidate or liquidate assets.)[77]

Because the scenarios try to peer far into the future—perhaps 5 or more years—they are necessarily written in rather general terms. Nevertheless, the great value of contingency planning is that it not only equips an organization to prepare for emergencies and uncertainty, it also gets managers thinking strategically. ●

How can four techniques—Porter's competitive forces, competitive strategies, diversification and synergy, and the BCG matrix—help me formulate strategy?

major question?

THE BIG PICTURE

Strategy formulation makes use of several concepts. Here we discuss Porter's five competitive forces, four competitive strategies, diversification and synergy, and the BCG matrix.

After the grand strategy has been determined (Step 2 in the strategic-management process), it's time to turn to strategy formulation (Step 3). Examples of techniques that can be used to formulate strategy are *Porter's five competitive forces, Porter's four competitive strategies, diversification and synergy,* and the *BCG matrix.*

Porter's Five Competitive Forces

What determines competitiveness within a particular industry? After studying several kinds of businesses, strategic-management expert Michael Porter suggested in his *Porter's model for industry analysis* **that business-level strategies originate in five primary competitive forces in the firm's environment: (1) threats of new entrants, (2) bargaining power of suppliers, (3) bargaining power of buyers, (4) threats of substitute products or services, and (5) rivalry among competitors.**[78]

1. Threats of New Entrants New competitors can affect an industry almost overnight, taking away customers from existing organizations. Example: Kraft Macaroni & Cheese is a venerable, well-known brand but is threatened from the low end by store brands, such as Walmart's brand, and from the high end by Annie's Creamy Macaroni and Cheese with Real Aged Wisconsin Cheddar.[79]

2. Bargaining Power of Suppliers Some companies are readily able to switch suppliers in order to get components or services, but others are not. Example: Clark Foam of Laguna Niguel, California, supplied nearly 90% of the foam cores used domestically to make custom surfboards. When it suddenly closed shop in late 2005, blaming government agencies for trying to shut it down, many independent board shapers and small retailers found they couldn't afford to get foam from outside the country. On the other hand, Surftech in Santa Cruz, California, was one of the few board manufacturers to use resin instead of foam, and so it saw a spike in sales.[80]

3. Bargaining Power of Buyers Customers who buy a lot of products or services from an organization have more bargaining power than those who don't. Customers who use the Internet to shop around are also better able to negotiate a better price. Example: Buying a car used to be pretty much a local activity, but now potential car buyers can use the Internet to scout a range of offerings within a 100-mile or larger radius, giving them the power to force down the asking price of any one particular seller.

4. Threats of Substitute Products or Services Again, particularly because of the Internet, an organization is in a better position to switch to other products or services when circumstances threaten their usual channels. Example: Oil companies might worry that Brazil is close to becoming energy self-sufficient because it is able to meet its growing demand for vehicle fuel by substituting ethanol derived from sugar cane for petroleum.[81]

5. Rivalry Among Competitors   The preceding four forces influence the fifth force, rivalry among competitors. Think of the wild competition among makers and sellers of portable electronics, ranging from cellphones to MP3 audio players to video-game systems. Once again, the Internet has intensified rivalries among all kinds of organizations.

An organization should do a good SWOT analysis that examines these five competitive forces, Porter thought. Then it was in a position to formulate effective strategy, using what he identified as four competitive strategies, as we discuss next.

Porter's Four Competitive Strategies

Porter's four competitive strategies (also called *four generic strategies*) are (1) cost-leadership, (2) differentiation, (3) cost-focus, and (4) focused-differentiation.[82] The first two strategies focus on *wide* markets, the last two on *narrow* markets. *(See Figure 6.3.)* Time Warner, which produces lots of media and publications, serves wide markets around the world. Your neighborhood newspaper serves a narrow market of just local customers.

Strategy	Type of market targeted	
	Wide	Narrow
1. Cost-leadership	✓	
2. Differentiation	✓	
3. Cost-focus		✓
4. Focused-differentiation		✓

figure 6.3

PORTER'S FOUR COMPETITIVE STRATEGIES

Let's look at these four strategies.

1. Cost-Leadership Strategy: Keeping Costs & Prices Low for a Wide Market   The *cost-leadership strategy* is to keep the costs, and hence prices, of a product or service below those of competitors and to target a wide market.

This puts the pressure on R&D managers to develop products or services that can be created cheaply, production managers to reduce production costs, and marketing managers to reach a wide variety of customers as inexpensively as possible.

Firms implementing the cost-leadership strategy include computer maker Dell, watch maker Timex, hardware retailer Home Depot, and pen maker Bic.

2. Differentiation Strategy: Offering Unique & Superior Value for a Wide Market   The *differentiation strategy* is to offer products or services that are of unique and superior value compared with those of competitors but to target a wide market.

Because products are expensive, managers may have to spend more on R&D, marketing, and customer service. This is the strategy followed by Ritz-Carlton hotels and the maker of Lexus automobiles.

Focused differentiation. The world's largest cruise ship, the 1,181-foot-long, 16-deck MS *Allure of the Seas,* features such amenities as four swimming pools, a skating rink, a small golf course, volleyball and basketball courts, a multideck dining room that can seat 3,000, and lavish lodging quarters. Clearly, there's something here for everyone—if you can afford it.

The strategy is also pursued by companies trying to create *brands* to differentiate themselves from competitors. Although Coca-Cola may cost only cents more than a supermarket's own house brand of cola, Coke spends millions on ads.

3. Cost-Focus Strategy: Keeping Costs & Prices Low for a Narrow Market

The *cost-focus strategy* **is to keep the costs, and hence prices, of a product or service below those of competitors and to target a narrow market.**

This is a strategy you often see executed with low-end products sold in discount stores, such as low-cost beer or cigarettes, or with regional gas stations, such as the Terrible Herbst or Rotten Robbie chains in parts of the West.

Needless to say, the pressure on managers to keep costs down is even more intense than it is with those in cost-leadership companies.

4. Focused-Differentiation Strategy: Offering Unique & Superior Value for a Narrow Market

The *focused-differentiation strategy* **is to offer products or services that are of unique and superior value compared to those of competitors and to target a narrow market.**

Some luxury cars are so expensive—Rolls-Royce, Ferrari, Lamborghini—that only a few car buyers can afford them. Other companies following the strategy are jeweler Cartier and shirtmaker Turnbull & Asser. Yet focused-differentiation products need not be expensive. The publisher Chelsea Green has found success with niche books, such as *The Straw Bale House.*

Single-Product Strategy Versus Diversification Strategy

A company also needs to think about whether to have a *single-product strategy* or a *diversification strategy.* After all, if you have only one product to sell, what do you do if that product fails?

The Single-Product Strategy: Focused but Vulnerable In a *single-product strategy,* **a company makes and sells only one product within its market.** This is the kind of strategy you see all the time as you drive past the small retail businesses in a small town: There may be one shop that sells only flowers, one that sells only security systems, and so on.

The single-product strategy has both positives and negatives:

- **The benefit—focus.** Making just one product allows you to focus your manufacturing and marketing efforts just on that product. This means that your company can become savvy about repairing defects, upgrading production lines, scouting the competition, and doing highly focused advertising and sales.

A small-business example: San Francisco's Green Toys makes all its toddler tea sets, toy trucks, and building blocks out of plastic recycled from milk jugs and, in a strategy called "reverse globalization," carries out all its operations in California, a push back against offshoring and outsourcing. (Sales have grown 80% a year since the firm's founding in 2007.)[83] Another example: See's Candies, a chain of 200 stores throughout the West, specializes in making boxed chocolates—something it does so well that when See's was acquired by Berkshire Hathaway, its corporate owner chose not to tamper with success and runs it with a "hands-off" policy.

- **The risk—vulnerability.** The risk, of course, is that if you do *not* focus on all aspects of the business, if a rival gets the jump on you, or if an act of God intervenes (for a florist, roses suffer a blight right before Mother's Day), your entire business may go under.

Example: Small specialty animal farms trying to capitalize on the popularity with consumers of locally grown foods, such as the one in East Montpelier, Vermont, where Erica Zimmerman and her husband produce pasture-raised pigs, have proved vulnerable to a shortage of slaughterhouses, which has led to backlogs and lengthy waits.[84] Another example: Indian Motorcycle Company, once a worthy rival to Harley-Davidson, sold only motorcycles. It went bankrupt twice, the second time because of quality problems, notably an overheating engine. (It was relaunched in 2009 and is presently being manufactured in Spirit Lake, Iowa.)[85]

The Diversification Strategy: Operating Different Businesses to Spread the Risk   The obvious answer to the risks of a single-product strategy is *diversification,* **operating several businesses in order to spread the risk.** You see this at the small retailer level when you drive past a store that sells gas *and* food *and* souvenirs *and* rents DVD movies.

There are two kinds of diversification—*unrelated* and *related.*

Unrelated Diversification: Independent Business Lines   If you operate a small shop that sells flowers on one side and computers on the other, you are exercising a strategy of ***unrelated diversification*—operating several businesses under one ownership that are not related to one another.** This has been a common big-company strategy. General Electric, for instance, which began by making lighting products, diversified into such unrelated areas as plastics, broadcasting, and financial services. Disney, Time Warner, and Sony run different divisions specializing in television, music, publishing, and the like.

Related Diversification: Related Business Lines   In some parts of the world you have to do all your grocery shopping in separate stores—the butcher, the baker, the greengrocer, and so on. In most U.S. grocery stores, all these businesses appear under the same roof, an example of the strategy of ***related diversification,*** **in which an organization under one ownership operates separate businesses that are related to one another.** A big-company example: The famous British raincoat maker Burberry started by making and marketing outerwear clothing but since then has expanded into related business lines, including accessories such as umbrellas, children's clothing, and even fragrances, which it sells in its own stores.

Related diversification has three advantages:

1. **Reduced risk—because more than one product.** If one product is weak, others may take up the slack. Example: When rainwear sales are slow,

Burberry's economic risk is reduced by sales of its other product lines, such as children's clothes.

2. **Management efficiencies—administration spread over several businesses.** Whatever the business, it usually has certain obligatory administrative costs—accounting, legal, taxes, and so on. Example: Burberry need not have separate versions of these for each business line. Rather, it can actually save money by using the same administrative services for all its businesses.

3. **Synergy—the sum is greater than the parts.** When a company has special strengths in one business, it can apply those to its other related businesses. Example: PepsiCo can apply its marketing muscle not only to Pepsi Cola but also to 7-Up and Mountain Dew, which it also owns. This is an example of *synergy*—**the economic value of separate, related businesses under one ownership and management is greater together than the businesses are worth separately.**

An example of a company that went from a single-product strategy to a diversification strategy is Skilled Manufacturing Inc. of Detroit, which used to supply power-train components to the auto industry, but shuttered one of its two Michigan plants in 2005 after one of its automotive clients moved the work to Mexico. Now it has re-opened the factory because it has branched out to other sectors, such as aerospace, in addition to continuing to serve the auto industry.[86]

The BCG Matrix

Developed by the Boston Consulting Group, the **BCG matrix is a means of evaluating strategic business units on the basis of (1) their business growth rates and (2) their share of the market.** Business growth rate is concerned with how fast the entire industry is increasing. Market share is concerned with the business unit's share of the market in relation to competitors.

In general, the BCG matrix suggests that an organization will do better in fast-growing markets in which it has a high market share rather than in slow-growing markets in which it has a low market share. These concepts are illustrated below. *(See Figure 6.4.)* ●

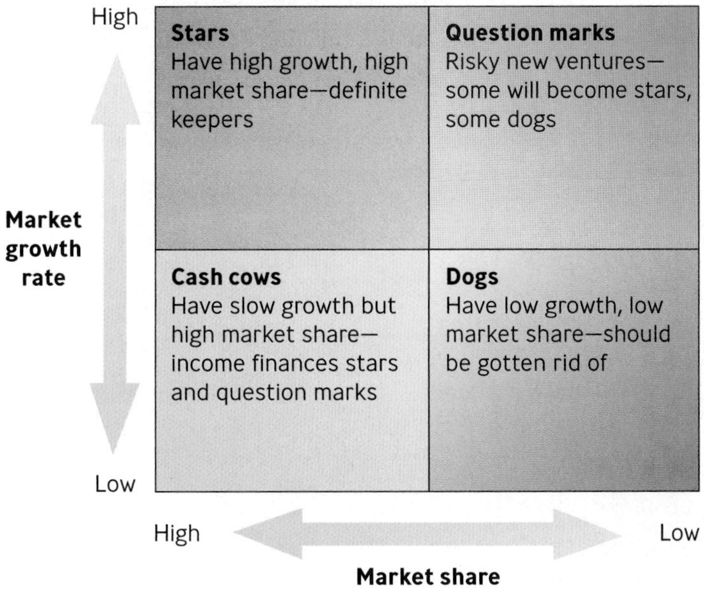

	Stars Have high growth, high market share—definite keepers	**Question marks** Risky new ventures—some will become stars, some dogs
Market growth rate	**Cash cows** Have slow growth but high market share—income finances stars and question marks	**Dogs** Have low growth, low market share—should be gotten rid of

Market share — High ←→ Low

Market share

figure 6.4

THE BCG MATRIX

Market growth is divided into two categories, low and high. Market share is also divided into low and high. Thus, in this matrix, "Stars" are business units that are highly desirable (high-growth, high-market share), compared to "Dogs," which are not so desirable (low-growth, low-market share).

How does effective execution help managers during the strategic-management process?

THE BIG PICTURE

Strategic implementation is closely aligned with strategic control. Execution is a process that helps align these two phases of the strategic-management process.

Stage 1 of the strategic-management process was establishing the mission and the vision. Stage 2 was establishing the grand strategy. Stage 3 was formulating the strategic plans. Now we come to the last two stages—4, strategic implementation, and 5, strategic control.

Execution: Getting Things Done

Larry Bossidy, former CEO of AlliedSignal (later Honeywell), and **Ram Charan,** a business adviser to senior executives, are authors of *Execution: The Discipline of Getting Things Done.*[87] ***Execution,* they say, is not simply tactics, it is a central part of any company's strategy. It consists of using questioning, analysis, and follow-through to mesh strategy with reality, align people with goals, and achieve the results promised.**

How important is execution to organizational success in today's global economy? A survey of 769 global CEOs from 40 countries revealed that "excellence in execution" was their most important concern—more important than "profit growth," "customer loyalty," "stimulating innovation," and "finding qualified employees."[88]

Bossidy and Charan outline how organizations and managers can improve the ability to execute. Effective execution requires managers to build a foundation for execution within three core processes found in any business: people, strategy, and operations.[89]

The Three Core Processes of Business: People, Strategy, & Operations

A company's overall ability to execute is a function of effectively executing according to three processes: *people, strategy,* and *operations.* Because all work ultimately entails

Execution. Occupying a sprawling campus in Cary, North Carolina, software maker SAS was No. 1 on *Fortune's* 2010 and 2011 lists of 100 Best Companies to Work For (and No. 3 in 2012). Its ability to execute effectively has also made it highly profitable and the world's largest privately owned software company.

some human interaction, effort, or involvement, Bossidy and Charan believe that the *people* process is the most important.

The First Core Process—People: "You Need to Consider *Who* Will Benefit You in the Future" "If you don't get the people process right," say Bossidy and Charan, "you will never fulfill the potential of your business." But today most organizations focus on evaluating the jobs people are doing at present, rather than considering which individuals can handle the jobs of the future. An effective leader tries to evaluate talent by linking people to particular strategic milestones, developing future leaders, dealing with nonperformers, and transforming the mission and operations of the human resource department.

The Second Core Process—Strategy: "You Need to Consider *How* Success Will Be Accomplished" In most organizations, the strategies developed fail to consider the "how" of execution. According to the authors, a good strategic plan addresses nine questions. *(See Table 6.4.)* In considering whether the organization can execute the strategy, a leader must take a realistic and critical view of its capabilities and competencies. If it does not have the talent in finance, sales, and manufacturing to accomplish the vision, the chances of success are drastically reduced.

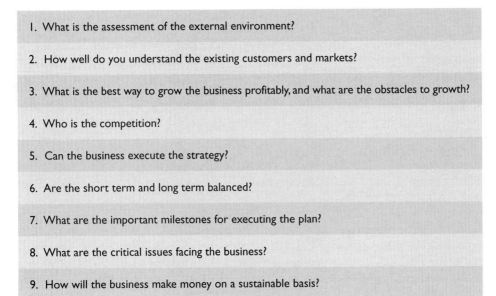

1. What is the assessment of the external environment?

2. How well do you understand the existing customers and markets?

3. What is the best way to grow the business profitably, and what are the obstacles to growth?

4. Who is the competition?

5. Can the business execute the strategy?

6. Are the short term and long term balanced?

7. What are the important milestones for executing the plan?

8. What are the critical issues facing the business?

9. How will the business make money on a sustainable basis?

table 6.4

NECESSARY ANSWERS: WHAT QUESTIONS SHOULD A STRONG STRATEGIC PLAN ADDRESS?

Source: From *Execution* by Larry Bossidy and Ram Charan, Copyright © 2002 by Larry Bossidy and Ram Charan. Used by permission of Crown Business, a division of Random House, Inc.

The Third Core Process—Operations: "You Need to Consider *What Path* Will Be Followed" The strategy process defines where an organization wants to go, and the people process defines who's going to get it done. The third core process, operations, or the operating plan, provides the path for people to follow. The operating plan, as we described in Chapter 5, should address all the major activities in which the company will engage—marketing, production, sales, and so on—and then define short-term objectives for these activities, to provide targets for people to aim at. We also discuss operations management in Chapter 16.

Building a Foundation of Execution

The foundation of execution is based on leadership (as we discuss in Chapter 14) and organizational culture (discussed in Chapter 8). Bossidy and Charan suggest that there are seven essential types of leader behaviors that are needed to fuel the engine of execution. Managers are advised to engage in seven kinds of behaviors, as follows:

Know Your People & Your Business: "Engage Intensely with Your Employees" In companies that don't execute, leaders are usually out of touch with the day-to-day realities. Bossidy and Charan insist leaders must engage intensely and personally with their organization's people and its businesses. They cannot rely on secondhand knowledge through other people's observations, assessments, and recommendations.

Insist on Realism: "Don't Let Others Avoid Reality" Many people want to avoid or shade reality, hiding mistakes or avoiding confrontations. Making realism a priority begins with the leaders being realistic themselves, and making sure realism is the goal of all dialogues in the organization.

Set Clear Priorities: "Focus on a Few Rather Than Many Goals" Leaders who execute focus on a very few clear priorities that everyone can grasp.

Follow Through: "Establish Accountability & Check on Results" Failing to follow through is a major cause of poor execution. "How many meetings have you attended where people left without firm conclusions about who would do what and when?" Bossidy and Charan ask. Accountability and follow-up are important.

Reward the Doers: "Show Top Performers That They Matter" If people are to produce specific results, they must be rewarded accordingly, making sure that top performers are rewarded far better than ordinary performers.

Expand People's Capabilities: "Develop the Talent" Coaching is an important part of the executive's job, providing useful and specific feedback that can improve performance.

Know Yourself: "Do the Hard Work of Understanding Who You Are" Leaders must develop "emotional fortitude" based on honest self-assessments. Four core qualities are authenticity, self-awareness, self-mastery, and humility.

Organizational culture is a system of shared beliefs and values within an organization that guides the behavior of its members. In this context, effective execution will not occur unless the culture supports an emphasis on getting quality work done in a timely manner. Chapter 8 presents 11 ways managers can attempt to create an execution-oriented culture.[90]

How Execution Helps Implement & Control Strategy

Many executives appear to have an aversion to execution, which they associate with boring tactics—with the tedium of doing, as opposed to the excitement of visioning—and which they hand off to subordinates. But, Bossidy and Charan point out, this notion can be a fatal flaw. "There's an enormous difference between leading an organization and presiding over it," they write. "The leader who boasts of her hands-off style or puts her faith in empowerment is not dealing with the issues of the day. . . . Leading for execution is not about micromanaging. . . . Leaders who excel at execution immerse themselves in the substance of execution and even some of the key details. They use their knowledge of the business to constantly probe and question. They bring weaknesses to light and rally their people to correct them."[91]

By linking people, strategy, and operating plans, execution allows executives to direct and control the three core processes that will advance their strategic vision. ●

Mentoring: The New Rules

Who's going to help you learn the ropes in a new organization? Maybe you need a mentor.

If you can find an experienced employee to mentor you—to be your sponsor and help you understand organizational strategy and navigate your way around—it can be a great asset to your career. Indeed, mentoring may be especially useful for female and minority managers, for whom there may be fewer role models within their particular organizations. One survey of 4,561 respondents from 42 countries found that 46% felt that coaching or mentoring had a great impact and 45% a moderate impact on their career success.[92]

What's the best advice about acquiring a mentor? Here are some of the new rules.[93]

Choose Anyone You Can Learn From, Not Just Someone Higher Up. It used to be thought that a mentor should be a seasoned manager higher up in the organization. But a mentor can also be a peer—someone at your own level inside the organization.

Choose More Than One Mentor. It might be nice to have a single mentor who can give you lots of one-on-one attention. But everyone's busy, so look around and see if there are two or three people who might be helpful to you. "Diversify your mentor portfolio," goes one piece of advice.

Pick Your Mentors, Don't Wait to Be Picked. Don't wait for organizational veterans to select you to be their protégé. It's up to you to make the first move, to be assertive in a nice way.

Do a Self-Assessment. Before you begin contacting people to be mentors, assess where you want to go and what skills and knowledge you need to get there, so that you'll know the kind of help you need.

Look for Someone Different from You. It used to be thought the mentor and mentee should have a lot in common, as in personal chemistry or personal style. But someone who is different from you will challenge you and help you be more objective.

Mentoring. Think you could succeed in a new job with a new organization without the help of mentors? Did mentors help you find your way in college?

Investigate Your Prospects. Before approaching prospective mentors, call their administrative assistants, explain your plans, and ask what their bosses are like to work with. Find out the best time to approach them.

Show Your Prospective Mentor How You Can Be Helpful. "Mentoring is a two-way street," says Anne Hayden, senior vice president of Metropolitan Life insurance company. "The person being mentored gets help, advice, and coaching, and the person doing the mentoring generally gets extra effort—someone very committed to working on special projects or on assignments that maybe don't fall within the boxes on the organizational chart."[94]

Agree on How Your Mentoring Relationship Will Work. In your first meeting, set the ground rules for how frequently you will meet and the type of contact, such as whether it will be in the office, over lunch, or at the gym. A minimum of one meeting a month is recommended, and in-between meetings, the two of you should keep in touch by phone and e-mail.

Key Terms Used in This Chapter

Summary

6.1 The Dynamics of Strategic Planning

Every organization needs to have a "big picture" about where it's going and how to get there, which involves strategy, strategic management, and strategic planning. A strategy is a large-scale action plan that sets the direction for an organization. Strategic management involves managers from all parts of the organization in the formulation and implementation of strategies and strategic goals. Strategic planning determines the organization's long-term goals and ways to achieve them.

Three reasons why an organization should adopt strategic management and strategic planning: They can (1) provide direction and momentum, (2) encourage new ideas, and (3) develop a sustainable competitive advantage. Sustainable competitive advantage occurs when an organization is able to get and stay ahead in four areas: (1) in being responsive to customers, (2) in innovating, (3) in quality, and (4) in effectiveness.

Strategic positioning attempts to achieve sustainable competitive advantage by preserving what is distinctive about a company. Three key principles underlie strategic positioning: (1) Strategy is the creation of a unique and valuable position. (2) Strategy requires trade-offs in competing. (3) Strategy involves creating a "fit" among a company's activities.

6.2 The Strategic-Management Process

The strategic-management process has five steps plus a feedback loop.

Step 1 is to establish the mission statement and the vision statement. The mission statement expresses the organization's purpose. The vision statement describes the organization's long-term direction and strategic intent.

Step 2 is to translate the broad mission and vision statements into a grand strategy that explains how the organization's mission is to be accomplished. Three common grand strategies are (1) a growth strategy, which involves expansion— as in sales revenues; (2) a stability strategy, which involves little or no significant change; and (3) a defensive strategy, which involves reduction in the organization's efforts.

Step 3 is strategy formulation, the translation of the grand strategy into more specific strategic plans, choosing among different strategies and altering them to best fit the organization's needs.

Step 4 is strategy implementation—putting strategic plans into effect. Step 5 is strategic control, monitoring the execution of strategy and making adjustments.

Corrective action constitutes a feedback loop in which a problem requires that managers return to an earlier step to rethink policies, budgets, or personnel arrangements.

6.3 Establishing the Grand Strategy

To develop a grand strategy (step 2 above), you need to gather data and make projections. This starts with competitive intelligence, gathering information about one's competitors' activities so that you can anticipate their moves and react appropriately. Three public sources of competitive intelligence are the public prints and advertising, investor information, and informal sources such as trade shows.

The next point in establishing a grand strategy is environmental scanning, careful monitoring of an organization's internal and external environments to detect early signs of opportunities and threats that may influence the firm's plans. The process for doing such scanning is called SWOT analysis, a search for the Strengths, Weaknesses, Opportunities, and Threats affecting the organization. Organizational strengths are the skills and capabilities that give the organization special competencies and competitive advantages. Organizational weaknesses are the drawbacks that hinder an organization in executing strategies. Organizational opportunities are environmental factors that the organization may exploit for competitive advantage. Organizational threats are environmental factors that hinder an organization's achieving a competitive advantage.

Another tool for developing a grand strategy is forecasting—creating a vision or projection of the future. Two types of forecasting are (1) trend analysis, a hypothetical extension of a past series of events into the future; and (2) contingency planning, the creation of alternative hypothetical but equally likely future conditions.

6.4 Formulating Strategy

Strategy formulation (step 3 in the strategic-management process) makes use of several concepts, including (1) Porter's five competitive forces, (2) Porter's four competitive strategies, (3) diversification and synergy, and (4) the BCG matrix.

Porter's model for industry analysis suggests that business-level strategies originate in five primary competitive forces in the firm's environment: (1) threats of new entrants, (2) bargaining power of suppliers, (3) bargaining power of buyers, (4) threats of substitute products or services, and (5) rivalry among competitors.

Porter's four competitive strategies are as follows: (1) The cost-leadership strategy is to keep the costs, and hence the prices, of a product or service below those of competitors and to target a wide market. (2) The differentiation strategy is to offer products or services that are of unique and superior value compared with those of competitors but to target a wide market. (3) The cost-focus strategy is to keep the costs and hence prices of a product or service below those of

competitors and to target a narrow market. (4) The focused-differentiation strategy is to offer products or services that are of unique and superior value compared with those of competitors and to target a narrow market.

Companies needed to choose whether to have a single-product strategy, making and selling only one product within their market, or a diversification strategy, operating several businesses to spread the risk. There are two kinds of diversification: unrelated diversification consists of operating several businesses that are not related to each other; related diversification consists of operating separate businesses that are related to each other, which may reduce risk, produce management efficiencies, and produce synergy or the sum being greater than the parts.

The BCG matrix is a means of evaluating strategic business units on the basis of (1) their business growth rates and (2) their share of the market. In general, organizations do better in fast-growing markets in which they have a high market share rather than slow-growing markets in which they have low market shares.

6.5 Implementing & Controlling Strategy: Execution

The last two stages of the strategic-management process are 4, strategic implementation, and 5, strategic control.

Execution, say Larry Bossidy and Ram Charan, is not simply tactics, it is a central part of any company's strategy; it consists of using questioning, analysis, and follow-through to mesh strategy with reality, align people with goals, and achieve results promised.

Three core processes of execution are people, strategy, and operations. (1) You have to evaluate talent by linking people to particular strategic milestones, developing future leaders, dealing with nonperformers, and transforming the mission and operations of the human resource department. (2) In considering whether the organization can execute the strategy, a leader must take a realistic and critical view of its capabilities and competencies. (3) The third core process, operations, or the operating plan, provides the path for people to follow. The operating plan should address all the major activities in which the company will engage and then define short-term objectives for these activities, to provide targets for people to aim at.

By linking people, strategy, and operating plans, execution allows executives to direct and control the three core processes that will advance their strategic vision.

Management in Action

J. C. Penney Is Changing Its Competitive Strategy

Shortly after taking the top job at J. C. Penney Co. last fall, chief executive Ron Johnson signed up for the company's e-mail alerts. He was shocked by what landed in his inbox.

The former Apple Inc. retail executive was deluged by sales announcements, sometimes two a day. He and his team counted 590 separate sales last year. They didn't bring in shoppers—Mr. Johnson's team found the average customer purchased only four times a year—but they did crush prices. Alarmingly, he learned nearly three-quarters of Penney's products sold at discounts of 50% or more.

"I thought to myself, 'This is desperation,'" Mr. Johnson said.

Now three months into his job, the new chief executive is hoping to turn things around with a far-reaching but risky overhaul of the department store format in an effort to lure consumers back to a chain that's often criticized as dowdy.

Mr. Johnson, who won plaudits for reinventing the retail experience with Apple store's clean lines and empty space, laid out an ambitious plan Wednesday that involves carving stores into a warren of specialty shops, turning the high-traffic center selling space into an entertainment and hang-out area, and eschewing constant "sales" in favor of lower prices every day.

The idea is to make stores more inviting, highlight brand names, and gain more control over pricing.

"Some may call it crazy, but I don't think there is an alternative," Mr. Johnson said in an interview. "In an Internet age where you can have exactly what you want with one keyword, people won't tolerate big stores. You have to break it down for them."

But overhauling the chain's fleet of 1,100 stores will pose costly challenges, and consumers have been reluctant to spend without the incentive of big markdowns.

Penney has been battered in recent years by competition from rivals like Macy's Inc. and Kohl's Corp. Under former chief executive Myron Ullman, Penney shed its catalog business and invested in exclusive brands and partnerships with hot sellers like fast-fashion line MANGO and Sephora cosmetics. But it continued to struggle with lackluster sales and the need to discount heavily to clear merchandise.

At an interview at the Plano, Texas, headquarters last week, Mr. Johnson said he determined that the store's initial prices needed to be realigned with what consumers feel comfortable paying. Beginning in February, Penney will lower the initial price for items by about 40% from where they start now.

He also plans to sharply reduce the number of promotions. Penney will pick a number of in-season items that will be on sale for an entire month. It will have two clearance sales, on the first and third Fridays of the month, called "Best Price Friday's," an idea he picked up while working at Mervyn's, a now defunct regional department store. Prices will be expressed in flat dollar amounts without cents.

Penney plans to spend $80 million a month on the program.

The move is risky, as shoppers have become rabid bargain hunters. But the old strategy wasn't working. Sales at stores open at least a year, a key measure of a retailer's strength, rose a thin 0.7% in the 11 months through December, down from a 2.7% increase the year before and well below Macy's 5.4% gain. . . .

The new CEO also plans to replace the "center core"—the highest traffic middle area where stores typically concentrate cosmetics, accessories and other high-margin impulse buys—with what he calls "Town Square."

The section will be a minimum of 10,000 square feet and rotate monthly attractions and services, such as free back-to-school haircuts or free hot dogs and ice cream in July.

Mr. Johnson equates Town Square with Apple's "Genius Bar," where customers have their products serviced. "Just like in the Apple store, you have to walk through the products to get to the Town Square," he says.

Two things Mr. Johnson isn't interested in are celebrity lines and private-label apparel. Mr. Johnson, a believer in brands, says in-house labels lack distinctiveness and pricing power.

As a result, Penney is slashing the number of private-label lines it has from hundreds to a few strong ones, chief operating officer Mike Kramer said.

The company acknowledges that the changes will require investments, but Mr. Johnson says cost cutting and the elimination of sales have been "engineered to pay for it."

FOR DISCUSSION

1. Using no more than two sentences, describe J.C. Penney's strategy.

2. Based on Michael Porter's discussion of the characteristics of an effective strategy, does J. C. Penney have a good strategy for growth? Explain.

3. To what extent is Penney following the five steps of the strategic-management process?

4. Conduct an environmental scan or SWOT analysis of Penney's current reality and recommend whether the company's current strategy is poised to succeed.

5. Which of Michael Porter's four competitive strategies is Penney trying to follow? Discuss.

6. What is the greatest takeaway from this case in terms of strategic management?

Source: Excerpted from Dana Mattioli, "J. C. Penney Chief Thinks Different," *The Wall Street Journal*, January 26, 2012, pp. B1–B2. Copyright © 2012 by Dow Jones & Company, Inc. Reproduced with permission of Dow Jones & Company, Inc. via Copyright Clearance Center.

Self-Assessment

Core Skills Required in Strategic Planning

OBJECTIVES

1. To assess if you have the skills to be in strategic planning.
2. To see what you think are the important core skill areas in strategic planning.

INTRODUCTION

Strategic planning became important as a method of managing the increasing velocity of change. The business environment no longer evolves at a manageable pace but increasingly through a process Charles Handy calls "discontinuous change"—change that radically alters how we think, work, and often behave. The computer, for instance, has completely changed how we communicate, research, write, and work. To meet this challenge, companies have strategic planners and others knowledgeable about their organizations, culture, and environment to shape strategy. Individuals must develop knowledge about their own abilities so that they formulate their own kind of strategic planning.

INSTRUCTIONS

To see whether you have the required skills needed to be a strategic planner, truthfully and thoughtfully assess your ability level for the following list of 12 skills. Rate each skill by using a five-point scale in which 1 = exceptional, 2 = very high, 3 = high, 4 = low, and 5 = very low.

1. Ability to synthesize	1	2	3	4	5
2. Analytical skills	1	2	3	4	5
3. Computer skills	1	2	3	4	5
4. Decisiveness	1	2	3	4	5
5. Interpersonal skills	1	2	3	4	5
6. Listening skills	1	2	3	4	5
7. Persuasiveness	1	2	3	4	5
8. Problem-solving skills	1	2	3	4	5
9. Research skills	1	2	3	4	5
10. Team skills	1	2	3	4	5
11. Verbal skills	1	2	3	4	5
12. Written skills	1	2	3	4	5

SCORING & INTERPRETATION

According to research conducted at the Ohio State University College of Business, the core required skills for the 12 skills above rate as follows:

Ability to synthesize:	2
Analytical skills:	1
Computer skills:	3
Decisiveness:	3
Interpersonal skills:	1
Listening skills:	2
Persuasiveness:	2
Problem-solving skills:	3
Research skills:	3
Team skills:	2
Verbal skills:	2
Written skills:	3

If you scored mostly 4s and 5s, strategic planning is probably not for you.

If you scored near the "perfect" score, it may be a possible career path.

If you scored all 1s and 2s, you might do extremely well at this type of work and might want to look into it more.

QUESTIONS FOR DISCUSSION

1. Based on your results, do you think you would like to make a career out of strategic planning? Why or why not?

2. What appeals or does not appeal to you about this career? Explain.

3. How might you enhance your strategic skills? Discuss.

Developed by Anne C. Cowden, PhD.

Legal/Ethical Challenge

Should Companies Be Pressured to Recruit Females for Boards of Directors?

A company's board of directors plays a role in the strategic management process. Not only can a board provide input into the planning process, but it ultimately signs off on the intended strategies. Interestingly, a 2011 study by Catalyst, a nonprofit organization, compared financial performance of companies with zero female board members versus those with three or more female members. Results indicated that female representation was associated with (1) 84% higher return on sales, (2) 60% higher return on invested capital, and (3) 46% higher return on equity. This challenge pertains to whether it is appropriate for outside groups to pressure a company to include women on its board of directors.

Small percentages of female board members may be caused by many factors, such as a lack of specific experience (e.g., finance), limited social networks, and negative stereotypes. Regardless of the cause, external groups are sprouting up around the United States that are focused on putting pressure on companies to recruit female directors. One example is a group that calls itself "2020 Women on Boards." This nonprofit group has a goal of mobilizing stakeholders to encourage companies to increase female representation on boards of directors. The group plans to publish a list of the Fortune 1000 companies that have no female directors. Some believe that efforts like this will promote good corporate governance, while others see it as an intrusion into the internal functioning of an organization.

SOLVING THE CHALLENGE

Where do you stand on this issue?

1. It is a great idea to pressure companies to include more females on boards of directors. After all, the Catalyst study showed that female representation was associated with higher financial performance.

2. Companies should be allowed to select people for boards based on their experience, networks, and performance. Gender should not be considered as a relevant criterion for selecting board members. I am not in favor of this type of social pressure because it does not ensure that the most qualified people are placed on boards of directors.

3. I'm middle of the road on this issue. Part of me feels that organizations should be left alone to put whomever they want on a board. At the same time, sometimes organizational leaders need to be nudged to do the right thing, such as putting females on the board. I thus think that social pressure from groups like "2020 Women on Boards" is okay, but organizations should not feel forced to do anything they do not want to do.

4. Invent other options. Discuss.

Source: This case is based on Joann Lublin, "Female Directors: Why So Few?" *The Wall Street Journal,* December 27, 2011, p. B5.

chapter 7

Individual & Group Decision Making
How Managers Make Things Happen

Major Questions You Should Be Able to Answer

7.1 Two Kinds of Decision Making: Rational & Nonrational

Major Question: How do people know when they're being logical or illogical?

7.2 Evidence-Based Decision Making & Analytics

Major Question: How can I improve my decision making using evidence-based management and business analytics?

7.3 Four General Decision-Making Styles

Major Question: How do I decide to decide?

7.4 Making Ethical Decisions

Major Question: What guidelines can I follow to be sure that decisions I make are not just lawful but ethical?

7.5 How to Overcome Barriers to Decision Making

Major Question: Trying to be rational isn't always easy. What are the barriers?

7.6 Group Decision Making: How to Work with Others

Major Question: How do I work with others to make things happen?

How Exceptional Managers Check to See If Their Decisions Might Be Biased

The biggest part of a manager's job is making decisions—and quite often they are wrong. Some questions you might ask next time you're poised to make a decision:

"Am I Too Cocky?" The Overconfidence Bias

If you're making a decision in an area in which you have considerable experience or expertise, you're less likely to be overconfident. Interestingly, however, you're more apt to be overconfident when dealing with questions on subjects you're unfamiliar with or questions with moderate to extreme difficulty.[1] *Recommendation:* When dealing with unfamiliar or difficult matters, think how your impending decision might go wrong. Afterward pay close attention to the consequences of your decision.

"Am I Considering the Actual Evidence, or Am I Wedded to My Prior Beliefs?" The Prior-Hypothesis Bias

Do you tend to have strong beliefs? When confronted with a choice, decision makers with strong prior beliefs tend to make their decision based on their beliefs—even if evidence shows those beliefs are wrong. This is known as the *prior-hypothesis bias*.[2] *Recommendation:* Although it's always more comforting to look for evidence to support your prior beliefs, you need to be tough-minded and weigh the evidence.

"Are Events Really Connected, or Are They Just Chance?" The Ignoring-Randomness Bias

Is a rise in sales in athletic shoes because of your company's advertising campaign or because it's the start of the school year? Many managers don't understand the laws of randomness. *Recommendation:* Don't attribute trends or connections to a single, random event.

"Is There Enough Data on Which to Make a Decision?" The Unrepresentative Sample Bias

If all the secretaries in your office say they prefer dairy creamer to real cream in their coffee, is that enough data on which to launch an ad campaign trumpeting the superiority of dairy creamer? It might if you polled 3,000 secretaries, but 3 or even 30 is too small a sample. *Recommendation:* You need to be attuned to the importance of sample size.

"Looking Back, Did I (or Others) Really Know Enough Then to Have Made a Better Decision?" The 20-20 Hindsight Bias

Once managers know what the consequences of a decision are, they may begin to think they could have predicted it. They may remember the facts as being a lot clearer than they actually were.[3] *Recommendation:* Try to keep in mind that hindsight does not equal foresight.

For Discussion Facing the hard facts about what works and what doesn't, how able do you think you are to make the tough decisions that effective managers have to make? Can you describe an instance in which you were badly wrong about something or someone?

forecast   What's Ahead in This Chapter

We begin by distinguishing between rational and nonrational decision making, and we describe three nonrational models. We then consider evidence-based decision making and the use of analytics. Next we describe general decision-making styles. We then discuss ethical decision making. We follow by considering how individuals respond to decision situations and nine common decision-making biases. We conclude with a discussion of group decision making, including participative management and group problem-solving techniques.

7.1 TWO KINDS OF DECISION MAKING: RATIONAL & NONRATIONAL

major question **?** How do people know when they're being logical or illogical?

THE BIG PICTURE

Decision making, the process of identifying and choosing alternative courses of action, may be rational, but often it is nonrational. Four steps in making a rational decision are (1) identify the problem or opportunity, (2) think up alternative solutions, (3) evaluate alternatives and select a solution, and (4) implement and evaluate the solution chosen. Three examples of nonrational models of decision making are (1) satisficing, (2) incremental, and (3) intuition.

The subject of decisions and decision making is a fascinating subject that is at the heart of what managers do.

A *decision* is a choice made from among available alternatives. *Decision making is the process of identifying and choosing alternative courses of action.*

EXAMPLE

Making a Decision: Which Is Better, Fast or Slow Delivery? Maersk Shipping Line Managers Decide Among Alternatives

Managers of the Danish shipping giant Maersk had a decision to make—a choice between two available alternatives: "Fast is better" versus "Slow is better." That is, in a global marketplace dominated by speed, they could choose to order their container ships to continue to sail as fast as possible from port to port. Or they could halve the ships' speed and greatly reduce fuel-consumption costs.

The focus of the 1990s and early 2000s for Maersk and other shippers had been on speed—"How fast can we get it there?"—because, it was believed, speed was indispensable to serving their clients. Yet the "Need it now" strategy also meant that ships traveled at speeds far above maximum fuel efficiency.

Fuel Efficiency & the Carbon Footprint. Then in 2008, oil prices shot up and there also arose more environmental concerns about carbon emissions—the "CO_2 footprint"—and talk of levying a carbon tax. Between 1985 and 2007, container ship trade grew eightfold, but transport emissions also accelerated.

Maersk found that by halving its ships' top cruising speeds, which reduced drag and friction on the hulls, fuel consumption on major routes was reduced by as much as 30%—and there was an equal cut in the emission of greenhouse gases. Slowing the ships also enabled Maersk to cut prices in an ever more competitive market.

Weighing the Alternatives. Before it could invoke the new policy, Maersk had to "prove that slow speeds would not damage ship engines in order to maintain engine warranties that did not cover such slow travel," reports *The New York Times*.[4] The company also had to reckon on absorbing the higher labor costs of having crews at sea for longer periods and adding two ships on the Germany-to-China run to maintain scheduled deliveries. Finally, Maersk had to determine that customers, especially those involved with time-sensitive products such as fashion apparel and electronics, could factor in extra time for shipping. All such concerns, it turned out, were canceled out by the decreased costs made possible by slow shipping.

YOUR CALL

American drivers on open stretches of interstate highway tend to drive at about 70 miles per hour, regardless of what the legal speed limit is.[5] If you drive a Camry at 55 mph instead of 65, you can reduce carbon dioxide emissions by 20% and you'll get 40 miles to the gallon instead of 35; speeding up to 75 mph will give you only 30 mpg.[6] Do you care? What alternatives are you weighing in deciding whether to drive faster rather than slower?

Decision Making in the Real World

The Maersk example sounds like a model for thoughtful decision making, making rational choices among well-defined alternatives. But that is not always the way it works in the real world.

Two Systems of Decision Making   "Our brains do not contain a single, general-purpose decision-making unit," writes psychologist Christopher Chabris. "Instead, we have two systems: one that is rational, analytical, and slow to act, and another that is emotional, impulsive, and prone to form and follow habits." Thus, for example, politicians "have long known that appeals to emotion are more effective than appeals to logic—not because people are stupid but because the mind is designed to use logic as a tool for supporting our beliefs rather than for changing them." [7]

The "Curse of Knowledge"   Why do some engineers design electronic products (such as DVD remote controls) with so many buttons, devices ultimately useful only to other engineers? Why are some professional investors and bankers prone to taking excess risks? [8] Why are some employees so reluctant to adopt new processes? The answer may be what's known as *the curse of knowledge.* As one writer put it about engineers, for example, "People who design products are experts cursed by their knowledge, and they can't imagine what it's like to be as ignorant as the rest of us." [9] In other words, as our knowledge and expertise grow, we may be less and less able to see things from an outsider's perspective—hence, we are often apt to make irrational decisions.

Let us look at the two approaches managers may take to making decisions: They may follow a *rational model* or various kinds of *nonrational models.*

Rational Decision Making: Managers Should Make Logical & Optimal Decisions

The *rational model of decision making,* **also called the *classical model,* explains how managers *should* make decisions; it assumes managers will make logical decisions that will be the optimum in furthering the organization's best interests.**

Typically there are four stages associated with rational decision making. *(See Figure 7.1.)*

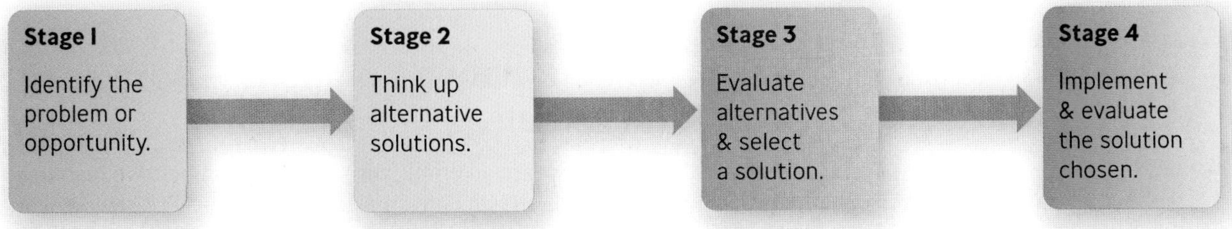

Stage 1	Stage 2	Stage 3	Stage 4
Identify the problem or opportunity.	Think up alternative solutions.	Evaluate alternatives & select a solution.	Implement & evaluate the solution chosen.

figure 7.1

THE FOUR STEPS IN RATIONAL DECISION MAKING

Stage 1: Identify the Problem or Opportunity— Determining the Actual Versus the Desirable

As a manager, you'll probably find no shortage of **problems, or difficulties that inhibit the achievement of goals.** Customer complaints. Supplier breakdowns. Staff turnover. Sales shortfalls. Competitor innovations.

However, you'll also often find **opportunities—situations that present possibilities for exceeding existing goals.** It's the farsighted manager, however, who can look past the steady stream of daily problems and seize the moment to actually do *better* than the goals he or she is expected to achieve. When a competitor's top salesperson unexpectedly quits, that creates an opportunity for your company to hire that person away to promote your product more vigorously in that sales territory.

Whether you're confronted with a problem or an opportunity, the decision you're called on to make is how to make *improvements*—how to change conditions from the present to the desirable. This is a matter of ***diagnosis*—analyzing the underlying causes.**

EXAMPLE

What Do Billionaire Warren Buffett & Female Investors Have in Common? Making a Correct Diagnosis

"Warren Buffett Invests Like a Girl," reads the headline over an article by LouAnn DiCosmo.[10] Is that a good thing? Buffett is the renowned billionaire investor (worth $39 billion in late 2011) known as the "Oracle of Omaha" who heads the financial juggernaut Berkshire Hathaway. His investment decisions are so successful that $1,000 invested with him in 1956 was worth $27.6 million at the end of 2006.[11] So, does he really invest like a girl?

Who's the Frazzled One? As it turns out, Buffett and female investors have something in common: "Women trade much less often than men, do a lot more research, and tend to base their investment decisions on considerations other than just numbers," according to one account.[12] Men, says DiCosmo, tend to be "frazzled, frenetic day traders, with their ties askew, hair on end, and eyes bleary. Patience and good decision making help set women apart here." As a result, according to a study cited by DiCosmo, women's portfolios on average gain 1.4%

more than men's, and single women's portfolios do 2.3% better than single men's.[13]

The Buffet Approach. As for the fabled Buffett, his approach is to use basic arithmetic to analyze several file-cabinet drawers of annual reports and other readily available company financial documents and to look for a record of "high returns on equity capital, low debt, and a consistent, predictable business with sustainable advantages—like Coca-Cola's soft-drink franchise."[14] In other words, Buffett—whose personal fortune gained $10 billion in the recession year 2009—takes pains to make a correct diagnosis before making a decision.[15]

YOUR CALL

When preparing to make decisions—especially financial decisions—do you spend a lot of time trying to make a correct diagnosis, doing deep research (as women investors are said to do), or do you chase "hot" tips and make snap judgments (as men reportedly do)?

Stage 2: Think Up Alternative Solutions—Both the Obvious & the Creative

Employees burning with bright ideas are an employer's greatest competitive resource. "Creativity precedes innovation, which is its physical expression," says *Fortune* magazine writer Alan Farnham. "It's the source of all intellectual property."[16]

After you've identified the problem or opportunity and diagnosed its causes, you need to come up with alternative solutions.

Stage 3: Evaluate Alternatives & Select a Solution—Ethics, Feasibility, & Effectiveness

In this stage, you need to evaluate each alternative not only according to cost and quality but also according to the following questions: (1) Is it *ethical*? (If it isn't, don't give it a second look.) (2) Is it *feasible*? (If time is short, costs are high, technology unavailable, or customers resistant, for example, it is not.) (3) Is it ultimately *effective*? (If the decision is merely "good enough" but not optimal in the long run, you might reconsider.)

Stage 4: Implement & Evaluate the Solution Chosen

With some decisions, implementation is usually straightforward (though not necessarily easy—firing employees who steal may be an obvious decision, but it can still be emotionally draining). With other decisions, implementation can be quite difficult; when one company acquires another, for instance, it may take months to consolidate the departments, accounting systems, inventories, and so on.

Successful Implementation   For implementation to be successful, you need to do two things:

1. **Plan carefully.** Especially if reversing an action will be difficult, you need to make careful plans for implementation. Some decisions may require written plans.

2. **Be sensitive to those affected.** You need to consider how the people affected may feel about the change—inconvenienced, insecure, even fearful, all of which can trigger resistance. This is why it helps to give employees and customers latitude during a changeover in business practices or working arrangements.

EXAMPLE

Faulty Implementation: Customer Service Is Often "Just Talk"

"My claim to fame, the only thing I've ever been really good at, is returning people's phone calls every single day," says Mark Powers. No doubt it is that kind of customer service that is the reason why Excelsior Roofing of San Francisco, founded by Powers's grandfather over 100 years ago, is still in business.[17]

Just Talk. "Executives talk about the importance of responding to customers' needs with top-notch customer service," writes *Wall Street Journal* columnist Carol Hymowitz. "But often it's just talk."[18]

The problem with faulty customer service, however, is that sometimes the company may be the last to hear about it, but a great many other potential customers may hear of it by word of mouth. One study found that only 6% of shoppers who experienced a problem with a retailer contacted the company. However, 31% went on to tell friends, family, and colleagues what had happened. Indeed, if 100 people have a bad experience, a retailer stands to lose between 32 and 36 current or potential customers, according to the study.[19]

In the Shoes of Customers. Consultants working for one large telecommunications company encourage customer service reps at one call center to share their problems and successes with each other and bring in customers to report their positive and negative experi-

ences with the call center. To encourage customer reps to "step inside the shoes of customers," the consultants also presented a weekly award of a pair of baby shoes to the employee who solved the most customer problems.[20]

YOUR CALL

We're all accustomed to pumping our own gas and doing our own banking through ATMs. Now many retailers have moved toward self-service checkout lanes, as is done by some Home Depot stores, and airlines toward self-check-in kiosks.[21]

What do you think the self-serve trend means for customer service?

Evaluation One "law" in economics is the law of unintended consequences—things happen that weren't foreseen. For this reason, you need to follow up and evaluate the results of the decision.

What should you do if the action is not working? Some possibilities:

- **Give it more time.** You need to make sure employees, customers, and so on have had enough time to get used to the new action.

- **Change it slightly.** Maybe the action was correct, but it just needs "tweaking"—a small change of some sort.

- **Try another alternative.** If plan A doesn't seem to be working, maybe you want to scrap it for another alternative.

- **Start over.** If no alternative seems workable, you need to go back to the drawing board—to stage 1 of the decision-making process.

EXAMPLE

Evaluation: The Boeing 787 Dreamliner, a Bet-the-Company Decision

The airline industry is one of the most volatile around, and Boeing Co., the Chicago-headquartered aerospace giant, has been through some rough boom-and-bust cycles. In 1997, for instance, production problems shut down two assembly lines and cost the company $2.5 billion.

A Bold New Strategy for Building Airplanes. Then, at a time when Boeing was losing business to its European rival Airbus, the company was wracked by scandals involving Pentagon contracts, and rising fuel costs were dramatically impacting the commercial airline industry, Boeing management made a bold decision: It would build a new medium-sized commercial jet, the 787 Dreamliner, its first new aircraft in 10 years, that would fly faster than the competition and would consume 20% less fuel than similar-sized planes. To achieve this, the 787 would feature more fuel-efficient engines and the fuselage would be built from plastic composite materials instead of aluminum. This would cut down on structural fatigue and corrosion, thereby reducing the number of inspections necessary and increasing the number of flights possible. "A light, strong plane is the big payoff for the huge technical risk Boeing is taking in crafting parts out of composites," said aerospace reporter Stanley Holmes.[22]

A Bumpy Ride. First planned for a summer 2007 launch, the date was revised for 2008. Then, in mid-2006, the company began

encountering the first of many stories of bad news. The fuselage section had failed in testing, and engineers had discovered worrisome bubbles in its skin. The carbon-fiber wing was too heavy, adding to the plane's overall weight. To hold costs down, Boeing had outsourced about 70% of the production to major suppliers acting as risk-sharing partners and playing a greater role in design and manufacturing. In return for investing more up front and taking on a share of the development costs, suppliers were given major sections of the airplane to build.[23] By late 2007, however, it was apparent that suppliers were struggling to meet the exacting technological demands and deadlines, and their software programs were having trouble communicating with each other. In October, Boeing announced it would no longer meet its May 2008 target date and was postponing its first delivery to late fall of that year.[24]

Changing Dates. In early 2008, the company said the poor quality of outsourced work and the unprecedented amount of coordination among suppliers caused Boeing to shift much of the work back to its Everett, Washington, assembly plant, adding to delays. It said it was working to try to begin deliveries of the 787 to customers not in late 2008 but in the first quarter of 2009.[25] In April, it changed the scheduled delivery date once again—to the third quarter of 2009.[26] Then in 2009, stress testing revealed new flaws around bolts inside the wings.[27]

Decision Making in the Real World

The Maersk example sounds like a model for thoughtful decision making, making rational choices among well-defined alternatives. But that is not always the way it works in the real world.

Two Systems of Decision Making "Our brains do not contain a single, general-purpose decision-making unit," writes psychologist Christopher Chabris. "Instead, we have two systems: one that is rational, analytical, and slow to act, and another that is emotional, impulsive, and prone to form and follow habits." Thus, for example, politicians "have long known that appeals to emotion are more effective than appeals to logic—not because people are stupid but because the mind is designed to use logic as a tool for supporting our beliefs rather than for changing them." [7]

The "Curse of Knowledge" Why do some engineers design electronic products (such as DVD remote controls) with so many buttons, devices ultimately useful only to other engineers? Why are some professional investors and bankers prone to taking excess risks? [8] Why are some employees so reluctant to adopt new processes? The answer may be what's known as *the curse of knowledge.* As one writer put it about engineers, for example, "People who design products are experts cursed by their knowledge, and they can't imagine what it's like to be as ignorant as the rest of us." [9] In other words, as our knowledge and expertise grow, we may be less and less able to see things from an outsider's perspective—hence, we are often apt to make irrational decisions.

Let us look at the two approaches managers may take to making decisions: They may follow a *rational model* or various kinds of *nonrational models.*

Rational Decision Making: Managers Should Make Logical & Optimal Decisions

The *rational model of decision making,* also called the *classical model,* explains how managers *should* make decisions; it assumes managers will make logical decisions that will be the optimum in furthering the organization's best interests.

Typically there are four stages associated with rational decision making. *(See Figure 7.1.)*

Stage 1	**Stage 2**	**Stage 3**	**Stage 4**
Identify the problem or opportunity.	Think up alternative solutions.	Evaluate alternatives & select a solution.	Implement & evaluate the solution chosen.

figure 7.1

THE FOUR STEPS IN RATIONAL DECISION MAKING

Stage 1: Identify the Problem or Opportunity— Determining the Actual Versus the Desirable

As a manager, you'll probably find no shortage of **problems, or difficulties that inhibit the achievement of goals.** Customer complaints. Supplier breakdowns. Staff turnover. Sales shortfalls. Competitor innovations.

However, you'll also often find **opportunities—situations that present possibilities for exceeding existing goals.** It's the farsighted manager, however, who can look past the steady stream of daily problems and seize the moment to actually do *better* than the goals he or she is expected to achieve. When a competitor's top salesperson unexpectedly quits, that creates an opportunity for your company to hire that person away to promote your product more vigorously in that sales territory.

Whether you're confronted with a problem or an opportunity, the decision you're called on to make is how to make *improvements*—how to change conditions from the present to the desirable. This is a matter of ***diagnosis*—analyzing the underlying causes.**

EXAMPLE

What Do Billionaire Warren Buffett & Female Investors Have in Common? Making a Correct Diagnosis

"Warren Buffett Invests Like a Girl," reads the headline over an article by LouAnn DiCosmo.[10] Is that a good thing? Buffett is the renowned billionaire investor (worth $39 billion in late 2011) known as the "Oracle of Omaha" who heads the financial juggernaut Berkshire Hathaway. His investment decisions are so successful that $1,000 invested with him in 1956 was worth $27.6 million at the end of 2006.[11] So, does he really invest like a girl?

Who's the Frazzled One? As it turns out, Buffett and female investors have something in common: "Women trade much less often than men, do a lot more research, and tend to base their investment decisions on considerations other than just numbers," according to one account.[12] Men, says DiCosmo, tend to be "frazzled, frenetic day traders, with their ties askew, hair on end, and eyes bleary. Patience and good decision making help set women apart here." As a result, according to a study cited by DiCosmo, women's portfolios on average gain 1.4%

more than men's, and single women's portfolios do 2.3% better than single men's.[13]

The Buffet Approach. As for the fabled Buffett, his approach is to use basic arithmetic to analyze several file-cabinet drawers of annual reports and other readily available company financial documents and to look for a record of "high returns on equity capital, low debt, and a consistent, predictable business with sustainable advantages—like Coca-Cola's soft-drink franchise."[14] In other words, Buffett—whose personal fortune gained $10 billion in the recession year 2009—takes pains to make a correct diagnosis before making a decision.[15]

YOUR CALL

When preparing to make decisions—especially financial decisions—do you spend a lot of time trying to make a correct diagnosis, doing deep research (as women investors are said to do), or do you chase "hot" tips and make snap judgments (as men reportedly do)?

Stage 2: Think Up Alternative Solutions—Both the Obvious & the Creative

Employees burning with bright ideas are an employer's greatest competitive resource. "Creativity precedes innovation, which is its physical expression," says *Fortune* magazine writer Alan Farnham. "It's the source of all intellectual property."[16]

After you've identified the problem or opportunity and diagnosed its causes, you need to come up with alternative solutions.

Stage 3: Evaluate Alternatives & Select a Solution—Ethics, Feasibility, & Effectiveness

In this stage, you need to evaluate each alternative not only according to cost and quality but also according to the following questions: (1) Is it *ethical*? (If it isn't, don't give it a second look.) (2) Is it *feasible*? (If time is short, costs are high, technology unavailable, or customers resistant, for example, it is not.) (3) Is it ultimately *effective*? (If the decision is merely "good enough" but not optimal in the long run, you might reconsider.)

Finally, after six delays and nearly 10 years of anticipation, the Dreamliner had its first flight, on December 15, 2009.[28] Then, on October 28, 2011, after months of testing and three years behind schedule, the 787 was put into service for the first time, carrying 264 passengers for All Nippon Airways from Tokyo to Hong Kong.[29]

YOUR CALL

While Boeing worked to solve its Dreamliner problems, its European rival, Airbus, was working on a mostly carbon-fiber jet of its own, the A380, with one big advantage—size. The A380 is the world's largest passenger jet. How do you think this will affect Boeing's huge bet on the Dreamliner? As you read this, which plane do you think is receiving more orders, the A380 or the 787?[30] (As of January 2012, Boeing was trailing.) Was Boeing's strategy of reinventing the approach to building airplanes—using carbon composite rather than aluminum and outsourcing so much of the engineering, design, and manufacturing—the right one? How would you evaluate Boeing's decisions?

What's Wrong with the Rational Model?

The rational model is *prescriptive,* describing how managers *ought* to make decisions. It doesn't describe how managers *actually* make decisions. Indeed, the rational model makes some highly desirable assumptions—that managers have complete information, are able to make an unemotional analysis, and are able to make the best decision for the organization. *(See Table 7.1.)* We all know that these assumptions are unrealistic.

• **Complete information, no uncertainty.** You should obtain complete, error-free information about all alternative courses of action and the consequences that would follow from each choice.
• **Logical, unemotional analysis.** Having no prejudices or emotional blind spots, you are able to logically evaluate the alternatives, ranking them from best to worst according to your personal preferences.
• **Best decision for the organization.** Confident of the best future course of action, you coolly choose the alternative that you believe will most benefit the organization.

table 7.1

ASSUMPTIONS OF THE RATIONAL MODEL

Nonrational Decision Making: Managers Find It Difficult to Make Optimal Decisions

Nonrational models of decision making explain how managers make decisions; they assume that decision making is nearly always uncertain and risky, making it difficult for managers to make optimal decisions. The nonrational models are *descriptive* rather than prescriptive: They describe how managers *actually* make decisions rather than how they should. Three nonrational models are (1) *satisficing,* (2) *incremental,* and (3) *intuition.*

1. Bounded Rationality & the Satisficing Model: "Satisfactory Is Good Enough" During the 1950s, economist **Herbert Simon**—who later received the Nobel Prize—began to study how managers actually make decisions. From his research he proposed that managers could not act truly logically because their rationality was bounded by so many restrictions.[31] Called **bounded rationality, the concept suggests that the ability of decision makers to be rational is limited by numerous constraints,** such as complexity, time and money, and their cognitive capacity, values, skills, habits, and unconscious reflexes. *(See Figure 7.2, next page.)*

■ **Complexity:** The problems that need solving are often exceedingly complex, beyond understanding.	■ **Different cognitive capacity, values, skills, habits, and unconscious reflexes:** Managers aren't all built the same way, of course, and all have personal limitations and biases that affect their judgment.	■ **Information overload:** There is too much information for one person to process.
■ **Time and money constraints:** There is not enough time or money to gather all relevant information.		■ **Different priorities:** Some data are considered more important, so certain facts are ignored.
	■ **Imperfect information:** Managers have imperfect, fragmentary information about the alternatives and their consequences.	■ **Conflicting goals:** Other managers, including colleagues, have conflicting goals.

figure 7.2

SOME HINDRANCES TO PERFECTLY RATIONAL DECISION MAKING

Because of such constraints, managers don't make an exhaustive search for the best alternative. Instead, they follow what Simon calls the *satisficing model*—that is, **managers seek alternatives until they find one that is satisfactory, not optimal.** While "satisficing" might seem to be a weakness, it may well outweigh any advantages gained from delaying making a decision until all information is in and all alternatives weighed. However, making snap decisions can also backfire. In the 1990s, for instance, Campbell Soup Co. tried to penetrate China's soup market, where 20 billion servings are consumed a year (versus only 14 billion in the United States). But rather than research Chinese tastes and cooking customs, which would have revealed that most soups are made from scratch, the company simply exported its line of condensed soups—an example of satisficing. Wondering why they should pay for something that could be easily made from scratch and objecting to the canlike tastes of prepared soups, Chinese consumers rejected the Campbell product.[32]

2. The Incremental Model: "The Least That Will Solve the Problem"
Another nonrational decision-making model is the *incremental model,* **in which managers take small, short-term steps to alleviate a problem,** rather than steps that will accomplish a long-term solution. Of course, over time a series of short-term steps

Nonrational decision making? Early in 2012, at the outset of the Chinese Year of the Water Dragon, NorthStar Moving Company of Los Angeles, a city with an ever-expanding Asian population, announced it would offer the services of an expert in feng shui, the Chinese art of creating harmonious surroundings, to assess the external environment of a home or office and make moving in a positive experience. Would you say this idea is a good nonrational decision?

may move toward a long-term solution. However, the temporary steps may also impede a beneficial long-term solution.

3. The Intuition Model: "It Just Feels Right"   Small entrepreneurs often can't afford in-depth marketing research and so they make decisions based on hunches—their subconscious, visceral feelings. For instance, Ben Hugh, 32, decided to buy I Can Has Cheezburger?, a blog devoted to silly cat pictures paired with viewer-submitted quirky captions, when it linked to his own pet blog and caused it to crash from a wave of new visitors. Putting up $10,000 of his own money and acquiring additional investor financing, he bought the site for $2 million from the Hawaiian bloggers who started it. "It was a white-knuckle decision," he said later. But he expanded the Cheezburger blog into an empire that now includes 53 sites.[33]

   "Going with your gut," or **intuition, is making a choice without the use of conscious thought or logical inference.** Intuition that stems from *expertise*—a person's explicit and tacit knowledge about a person, situation, object, or decision opportunity—is known as a *holistic hunch*. Intuition based on feelings—the involuntary emotional response to those same matters—is known as *automated experience*. It is important to try to develop your intuitive skills because they are as important as rational analysis in many decisions. Some suggestions appear in the table below. *(See Table 7.2.)*

table 7.2

GUIDELINES FOR DEVELOPING INTUITIVE AWARENESS

Recommendation	Description
1. Open up the closet.	To what extent do you experience intuition; trust your feelings; count on intuitive judgments; suppress hunches; covertly rely upon gut feel?
2. Don't mix up your I's.	Instinct, Insight, and Intuition are not synonymous; practice distinguishing between your instincts, your insights, and your intuitions.
3. Elicit good feedback.	Seek feedback on your intuitive judgments; build confidence in your gut feel; create a learning environment in which you can develop better intuitive awareness.
4. Get a feel for your batting average.	Benchmark your intuitions; get a sense of how reliable hunches are; ask yourself how your intuitive judgment might be improved.
5. Use imagery.	Use imagery rather than words; literally visualize potential future scenarios that take your gut feelings into account.
6. Play devil's advocate.	Test out intuitive judgments; raise objections to them; generate counterarguments; probe how robust gut feel is when challenged.
7. Capture and validate your intuitions.	Create the inner state to give your intuitive mind the freedom to roam; capture your creative intuitions; log them before they are censored by rational analysis.

Source: Republished with permission of Academy of Management, from E. Sadler-Smith and E. Shefy, "The Intuitive Executive: Understanding and Applying Gut Feeling in Decision Making," *Academy of Management Executive,* November 2004, p. 88.

   As a model for making decisions, intuition has at least two benefits. (1) It can speed up decision making, useful when deadlines are tight.[34] (2) It can be helpful to managers when resources are limited. A drawback, however, is that it can be difficult to convince others that your hunch makes sense. In addition, intuition is subject to the same biases as those that affect rational decision making, as we discuss in Section 7.5.[35] Still, we believe that intuition and rationality are complementary and that managers should develop the courage to use intuition when making decisions.[36] ●

How can I improve my decision making using evidence-based management and business analytics?

THE BIG PICTURE

Evidence-based decision making, which depends on an "attitude of wisdom," rests on three truths. This section describes seven principles for implementing evidence-based management. We also describe why it is hard to bring this approach to bear on one's decision making. Finally, we describe analytics and its three key attributes.

It was the jet that Boeing *didn't* build that avoided what could have been possibly the worst disaster in the company's history and gave the aircraft builder the opportunity to go in a new direction.

In late 2002, Boeing was desperately trying to figure out what kind of passenger airliner to build that would allow the company to effectively compete with its European rival Airbus. In October, Boeing executives met with several global airline representatives in Seattle. A Boeing manager drew a graph on a whiteboard, with axes representing cruising range and passenger numbers. Then he asked airline representatives to locate their ideal position on the graph. "The distribution of the data," reports *Time,* "favored efficiency over speed—the exact opposite of what Boeing was thinking. Two months later, Boeing ditched plans for a high-speed, high-cost jetliner to embark on a new program"—what became the massive attempt to build the 787 Dreamliner.[37]

Evidence-Based Decision Making

"Too many companies and too many leaders are more interested in just copying others, doing what they've always done, and making decisions based on beliefs in what ought to work rather than what actually works," say Stanford professors **Jeffrey Pfeffer** and **Robert Sutton.** "They fail to face the hard facts and use the best evidence to help navigate the competitive environment."[38] This is what Boeing narrowly averted in that Seattle conference, when it was getting ready to spend billions of dollars trying to outcompete Airbus by building a faster aircraft. Companies that use *evidence-based management*—the translation of principles based on best evidence into organizational practice, bringing rationality to the decision-making process, as we defined it in Chapter 2—routinely trump the competition, Pfeffer and Sutton suggest.[39]

Seven Implementation Principles Pfeffer and Sutton identify seven implementation principles to help companies that are committed to doing what it takes to profit from evidence-based management:[40]

- **Treat your organization as an unfinished prototype.** Leaders need to think and act as if their organization is an unfinished prototype that won't be ruined by dangerous new ideas or impossible to change because of employee or management resistance. Example: Some Internet startups that find their original plan not working have learned to master "the art of the pivot," to fail gracefully by cutting their losses and choosing a new direction—as did the founders of Fabulus, a review site and social network that attracted no users, and so they launched a high-end e-commerce site called Fab.com, which so far is doing well.[41]

- **No brag, just facts.** This slogan is an antidote for assertions made with complete disregard for whether they correspond to facts. Example: Former

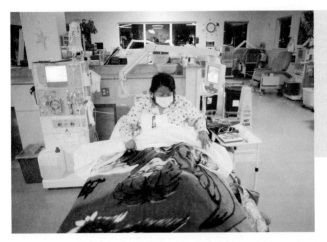

Hewlett-Packard CEO Carly Fiorina bragged to the press about HP's merger with Compaq but failed to consider facts about consumer dissatisfaction with Compaq products until after the merger. Other companies, such as DaVita, which operates dialysis centers, take pains to evaluate data before making decisions.

- **See yourself and your organization as outsiders do.** Most managers are afflicted with "rampant optimism," with inflated views of their own talents and prospects for success, which causes them to downplay risks and continue on a path despite evidence things are not working. "Having a blunt friend, mentor, or counselor," Pfeffer and Sutton suggest, "can help you see and act on better evidence."

- **Evidence-based management is not just for senior executives.** The best organizations are those in which everyone, not just the top managers, is guided by the responsibility to gather and act on quantitative and qualitative data and share results with others.

- **Like everything else, you still need to sell it.** "Unfortunately, new and exciting ideas grab attention even when they are vastly inferior to old ideas," the Stanford authors say. "Vivid, juicy stories and case studies sell better than detailed, rigorous, and admittedly dull data—no matter how wrong the stories or how right the data." To sell an evidence-based approach, you may have to identify a preferred practice based on solid if unexciting evidence, then use vivid stories to grab management attention.

- **If all else fails, slow the spread of bad practice.** Because many managers and employees face pressures to do things that are known to be ineffective, it may be necessary for you to practice "evidence-based misbehavior"—that is, ignore orders you know to be wrong or delay their implementation.

- **The best diagnostic question: What happens when people fail?** "Failure hurts, it is embarrassing, and we would rather live without it," the authors write. "Yet there is no learning without failure. . . . If you look at how the most effective systems in the world are managed, a hallmark is that when something goes wrong, people face the hard facts, learn what happened and why, and keep using those facts to make the system better." From the U.S. civil aviation system, which rigorously examines airplane accidents, near misses, and equipment problems, to Gap deciding to close a fifth of its North American stores and expand in China because of lackluster domestic sales, evidence-based management makes the point that failure is a great teacher.[42] This means, however, that the organization must "forgive and remember" people who make mistakes, not be trapped by preconceived notions, and confront the best evidence and hard facts.

What Makes It Hard to Be Evidence Based   Despite your best intentions, it's hard to bring the best evidence to bear on your decisions. Among the reasons:[43] (1) There's too much evidence. (2) There's not enough *good* evidence. (3) The evidence doesn't quite apply. (4) People are trying to mislead you. (5) *You* are trying to mislead you. (6) The side effects outweigh the cure. (Example: Despite the belief that social promotion in school is a bad idea—that is, that schools shouldn't advance children to the next grade when they haven't mastered the material—the side effect is skyrocketing costs because it crowds schools with older and angrier students, which demands more resources.) (7) Stories are more persuasive, anyway.

The proper approach for an evidence-based mindset is described in the Practical Action box "The Steps in Critical Thinking on p. 203."

EXAMPLE

Evidence-Based Decision Making: "If People Are Your Most Important Assets, Why Would You Get Rid of Them?"

It's an axiom of many managers that it's often necessary to cut back on workers during economic downturns—or even in good times—because it helps to increase profitability or drive the company's stock price higher. But Stanford professor Jeffrey Pfeffer, advocate for evidence-based management, takes issue with this assumption. "There is a growing body of academic research suggesting that firms incur big costs when they cut workers," he writes.[44]

What Are the Costs of Layoffs? While agreeing that there are circumstances in which layoffs are necessary for a firm to survive (as when an industry is shrinking or competitors are resorting to cheaper overseas labor), Pfeffer suggests companies incur big costs when they cut their labor forces. He cites the direct and indirect costs of layoffs listed by University of Colorado professor Wayne Cascio in his book *Responsible Restructuring*: "severance pay; paying out accrued vacation and sick pay; outplacement costs; higher unemployment-insurance taxes; the cost of rehiring employees when business improves; low morale and risk-averse survivors; potential lawsuits, sabotage, or even workplace violence from aggrieved employees or former employees; loss of institutional memory and knowledge; diminished trust in management; and reduced productivity."

Looking at the evidence, Pfeffer finds that firms that announce layoffs actually *do not* enjoy higher stock prices than their peers, either immediately or over time. Layoffs also don't increase individual company productivity and, in fact, don't even reliably cut costs (because companies often lose the best people first; there is lower morale among survivors, resulting in reduced customer service, innovation, and productivity; and remaining employees are spurred to look for other jobs once things improve).

The Most Successful Airline. Following the 9/11 tragedy in 2001, which coincided with the start of a recession, all U.S. airlines except one announced tens of thousands of layoffs. The exception was Southwest, which has never had an involuntary layoff in its 40-year history and which most Americans voted the most desirable brand in 2012.[45] "If people are your most important assets," Pfeffer quotes a former head of the airline's human resources department, "why would you get rid of them?"

YOUR CALL

Can you think of any instances of people being laid off unnecessarily? What is your evidence that it was not necessary?

In Praise of Analytics

Perhaps the purest application of evidence-based management is the use of *analytics,* or *business analytics,* **the term used for sophisticated forms of business data analysis.** One example of analytics is portfolio analysis, in which an investment adviser evaluates the risks of various stocks. Another example is the time-series forecast, which predicts future data based on patterns of historical data.

Some leaders and firms have become exceptional practitioners of analytics. Gary Loveman, CEO of the Harrah's gambling empire, wrote a famous paper "Diamonds in the Data Mine," in which he explained how data-mining software was used to analyze vast amounts of casino customer data to target profitable patrons.[46] Marriott International, through its Total Hotel Optimization program, has used quantitative data to establish the optimal price for hotel rooms, evaluate use of conference facilities and catering, and develop systems to optimize offerings to frequent customers.[47] To aid in recruitment, Microsoft studies correlations between its successful workers and the schools and companies they arrived from.[48]

EXAMPLE

Use of Analytics: The Oakland A's "Moneyball" Secret

The film *Moneyball*, which starred Brad Pitt and supporting actor Jonah Hill and which received six 2012 Academy Award nominations, was adapted from a book by Michael Lewis, *Moneyball: The Art of Winning an Unfair Game*. The book described how the Oakland Athletics, one of the poorest teams in Major League Baseball (2002 payroll $41 million, versus the New York Yankees' $126 million), managed to go to the playoffs five times in seven years against better-financed contenders. They accomplished this by avoiding the use of traditional baseball statistics and finding better indicators of player success in on-base percentage, slugging percentage, and the like. For a time, this creative use of analytics enabled managers of the California club to concentrate their limited payroll resources on draft picks who were primarily talented college players rather than veteran professionals.[49]

Analytics in the NBA. Since then the use of unusual analytics to find better ways to value players and strategies has found its way into other sports. In basketball, for instance, the Houston Rockets discovered they had allocated such a huge part of the payroll to superstars (Tracy McGrady, Yao Ming) that they couldn't afford more stars. "So we went looking for nonsuperstars that we thought were undervalued," says Daryl Morey, who was hired to rethink Rockets basketball.[50] Looking at midlevel NBA players, he finally settled on forward Shane Battier, who doesn't post many points, rebounds, assists, steals, or blocked shots but who applies a superior intelligence to an overview of the game that helps his teams produce winning records. (Battier is now with the Miami Heat.)

The *Moneyball* Effect. The effect of *Moneyball*, both book and film, was twofold. As Yankees general manager Brian Cashman pointed out, "It explored a certain method that has exploded in the game—and we're all utilizing [it] now. If you're not heavily invested in the statistical approach now, you've missed the boat."[51] The second result was equally predictable: *Moneyball*'s in-depth report provided too much of a blueprint for competitors for the A's to overcome. "It's like Coke and their secret formula—you don't let the secret out," says Cashman.

YOUR CALL

Executives and personnel people in other lines of work are often like the old sports traditionalists, relying on résumé, degree, years of experience, and even looks in evaluating job applicants. What other, more quantifiable measures might be used instead when hiring new college graduates?

Thomas H. Davenport and others at Babson College's Working Knowledge Research Center studied 32 organizations that made a commitment to quantitative, fact-based analysis and found three key attributes among analytics competitors.[52]

1. Use of Modeling: Going beyond Simple Descriptive Statistics Companies such as Capital One look well beyond basic statistics, using data mining and predictive modeling to identify potential and most profitable customers. *Predictive modeling* **is a data-mining technique used to predict future behavior and anticipate the consequences of change.** Thus, Capital One conducts more than 30,000 experiments a year, with different interest rates, incentives, direct-mail packaging, and other variables to evaluate which customers are most apt to sign up for credit cards and will pay back their debt.

2. Having Multiple Applications, Not Just One   UPS (formerly United Parcel Service) applies analytics not only to tracking the movement of packages but also to examining usage patterns to try to identify potential customer defections so that salespeople can make contact and solve problems. More recently, as the recession reduced package delivery demand, it began testing whether UPS could be in the business of delivering direct mail, to serve as an alternative to marketing mail delivered by the U.S. Postal Service.[53] Analytics competitors "don't gain advantage from one killer app [application], but rather from multiple applications supporting many parts of the business," says Davenport.

3. Support from the Top   "A companywide embrace of analytics impels changes in culture, processes, behavior, and skills for many employees," says Davenport. "And so, like any major transition, it requires leadership from executives at the very top who have a passion for the quantitative approach."

The Uses of "Big Data"

A recent study says the world's information is doubling every two years, with 1.8 zetta-bytes being created and replicated in 2011 alone.[54] That's an amount equal to more than 200 billion two-hour high-definition movies. This has led to a concept known as "big data" (often capitalized, Big Data), stores of data so vast that conventional database management systems cannot handle them and so very sophisticated analysis software and supercomputing-level hardware are required.[55] Attracting a lot of attention in science, business, medicine, and technology, the concept of big data has been dubbed "the next frontier for innovation, competition, and productivity."[56]

While big-data analysis, or data analytics, can be used to tackle large-scale problems such as how to make electricity grids and traffic flow more effective, it also has specific, practical uses in business. HP Labs researchers, for instance, used Twitter data to accurately predict box-office revenues of Hollywood movies.[57] Business is also interested in analyzing online behavior "to create ads, products, or experiences that are most appealing to consumers—and thus most lucrative to companies," says one technology journalist. "There's also great potential to more accurately predict market fluctuations or react faster to shifts in consumer sentiment or supply chain issues."[58] ●

Serving you. This server farm, or data center, contains thousands of computers storing terabytes of information on everyone and everything—"big data" that can be subjected to data analytics to work on large-scale projects. With data centers like this, you can see why everything you enter online, whether via e-mail, Facebook, texting, or twittering, no matter how innocuous, can be stored and used later to try to sell you things. Are you okay with this?

The Steps in Critical Thinking

Magical thinking is all around us. People believe in "crystal healing" and "color therapy" or think arthritis can be alleviated with copper bracelets. Fortunately, critical thinking can be learned, just as you can learn, say, how to study better.[59]

The four steps in critical thinking are these:

1. Get an understanding of the problem.
2. Gather information and interpret it.
3. Develop a solution plan and carry it out.
4. Evaluate the plan's effectiveness.

Let's consider these.

1. Get an Understanding of the Problem. Impulsiveness hurts. How many times have you been told, as for a test, to *carefully read the directions*? How often, when looking at a manual on how to operate a new machine, have you found yourself rereading the instructions? In both cases, you're taking the necessary first step: making sure you understand the problem. This is basic.

If you don't take time to comprehend the problem, you can waste hours trying to solve it and never do so. Getting an understanding might require you to read over the problem two or more times (as in math), ask someone for clarification (such as an instructor), or seek alternative explanations (as in going online). Often you can get a better understanding of a problem just by talking about it, as in a discussion in a study group with other students.

2. Gather Information and Interpret It. Sometimes just by making sure you understand a problem, you can see a solution to it. At other times, however, you might need to get additional information and interpret it. That is, you'll need to list resources that can give you help or identify areas that are preventing your solving the problem.

For instance, if your problem is that you are required to write a paper on better decision making for a management course, you'll need to search the Internet and/or get books and other information on the subject from the library. Then you'll need to interpret the information to make sure you know the difference between, say, the different decision-making styles (described in Section 7.3).

3. Develop a Solution Plan and Carry It Out. Developing a plan is sometimes the most difficult step because you might have to choose among several alternatives. For example, in writing about management decision making, you'll have to decide between several possible outlines and draw on a variety of examples.

Finally, you'll need to carry out the plan, which might or might not turn out to be workable. Maybe the direction of your paper can't be supported by the research you did, and you'll have to rethink your approach.

4. Evaluate the Plan's Effectiveness. So you completed the paper on management decision making. Maybe your experience was a disaster, in which case you'll want to know how to do it right next time. Maybe your plan worked out okay, but there were things that might have been handled better.

Drawing lessons from your experience is part and parcel of critical thinking, and it's a step that should not be neglected. If the experience was successful, can it be applied to other, similar problems? If it was only partly successful, can you see ways to change the information-gathering step or the solution-planning step to make it work better? If the experience was a disaster, is there a slogan you can draw from it that you can post over your desk? (Example: Look for recent articles when researching papers.)

YOUR CALL

No doubt there are some current big issues in your life that you would like to solve. Making a wise choice of major? Avoiding too much loan debt? Getting better at test taking? Increasing productivity by avoiding distractions? Relationship problems? Finding a mentor? Try applying the four steps of critical thinking and see if they improve your outlook.

THE BIG PICTURE
Your decision-making style reflects how you perceive and respond to information. It could be directive, analytical, conceptual, or behavioral.

Do men and women differ in the way they make decisions? Do they, for example, differ in risk propensity? ***Risk propensity* is the willingness to gamble or to undertake risk for the possibility of gaining an increased payoff.**

Perhaps another name for this is competitiveness. And research does seem to show that, as one scholar summarized it, "Even in tasks where they do well, women seem to shy away from competition, whereas men seem to enjoy it too much."[60] In an experiment involving winning small amounts of money in number-memorizing tournaments, men were avid competitors and were eager to continue, partly from overconfidence regardless of their success in earlier rounds, and they rated their abilities more highly than the women rated theirs. Most women declined to compete, even when they had done the best in earlier rounds.[61]

This brings us to the subject of decision-making style. **A *decision-making style* reflects the combination of how an individual perceives and responds to information.** A team of researchers developed a model of decision-making styles based on the idea that styles vary along two different dimensions: value orientation and tolerance for ambiguity.[62]

Value Orientation & Tolerance for Ambiguity

Value orientation reflects the extent to which a person focuses on either task and technical concerns or people and social concerns when making decisions. Some people, for instance, are very task focused at work and do not pay much attention to people issues, whereas others are just the opposite.

The second dimension pertains to a person's *tolerance for ambiguity*. This individual difference indicates the extent to which a person has a high need for structure or control in his or her life. Some people desire a lot of structure in their lives (a low tolerance for ambiguity) and find ambiguous situations stressful and psychologically uncomfortable. In contrast, others do not have a high need for structure and can thrive in uncertain situations (a high tolerance for ambiguity). Ambiguous situations can energize people with a high tolerance for ambiguity.

When the dimensions of value orientation and tolerance for ambiguity are combined, they form four styles of decision making: *directive, analytical, conceptual,* and *behavioral. (See Figure 7.3.)*

Success. Eli Manning, quarterback for the New York Giants, led his team to victory in the 2012 Super Bowl. As the leader of his team, a quarterback must make many decisions about what is the right way to success. If you were a quarterback, which of the four general decision-making styles do you think you would embody?

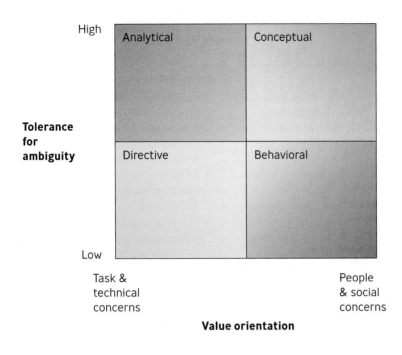

figure 7.3
DECISION-MAKING
STYLES

High

Tolerance for ambiguity

Low

| Analytical | Conceptual |
| Directive | Behavioral |

Task & technical concerns

People & social concerns

Value orientation

1. The Directive Style: Action-Oriented Decision Makers Who Focus on Facts

People with a *directive* style have a low tolerance for ambiguity and are oriented toward task and technical concerns in making decisions. They are efficient, logical, practical, and systematic in their approach to solving problems.

People with this style are action oriented and decisive and like to focus on facts. In their pursuit of speed and results, however, these individuals tend to be autocratic, to exercise power and control, and to focus on the short run.

2. The Analytical Style: Careful Decision Makers Who Like Lots of Information & Alternative Choices

Managers with an *analytical* style have a much higher tolerance for ambiguity and are characterized by the tendency to overanalyze a situation. People with this

Fortune 500 restaurant CEO. Clarence Otis Jr. is CEO of Darden Restaurants, Inc., a Fortune 500 company that is the world's largest publicly traded casual dining restaurant company, serving more than 350 million meals annually at such restaurants as Olive Garden and Red Lobster. Because of racial stereotyping, African American leaders operate at a disadvantage, according to a 2011 study by Andrew Carton and Shelby Rosette, with strong performance being attributed not to intellectual prowess but to market factors outside their control or to humor or public speaking skills. What kind of decision-making style would you expect Otis to have?

style like to consider more information and alternatives than those following the directive style.

Analytic individuals are careful decision makers who take longer to make decisions but who also respond well to new or uncertain situations.

3. The Conceptual Style: Decision Makers Who Rely on Intuition & Have a Long-Term Perspective

People with a *conceptual* style have a high tolerance for ambiguity and tend to focus on the people or social aspects of a work situation. They take a broad perspective to problem solving and like to consider many options and future possibilities.

Conceptual types adopt a long-term perspective and rely on intuition and discussions with others to acquire information. They also are willing to take risks and are good at finding creative solutions to problems. However, a conceptual style can foster an indecisive approach to decision making.

4. The Behavioral Style: The Most People-Oriented Decision Makers

The *behavioral* style is the most people oriented of the four styles. People with this style work well with others and enjoy social interactions in which opinions are openly exchanged. Behavioral types are supportive, receptive to suggestions, show warmth, and prefer verbal to written information.

Although they like to hold meetings, people with this style have a tendency to avoid conflict and to be concerned about others. This can lead behavioral types to adopt a wishy-washy approach to decision making and to have a hard time saying no.

Which Style Do You Have?

Research shows that very few people have only one dominant decision-making style. Rather, most managers have characteristics that fall into two or three styles. Studies also show that decision-making styles vary across occupations, job level, and countries.[63] There is not a best decision-making style that applies to all situations.

You can use knowledge of decision-making styles in three ways:

Know Thyself Knowledge of styles helps you to understand yourself. Awareness of your style assists you in identifying your strengths and weaknesses as a decision maker and facilitates the potential for self-improvement.

Influence Others You can increase your ability to influence others by being aware of styles. For example, if you are dealing with an analytical person, you should provide as much information as possible to support your ideas.

Deal with Conflict Knowledge of styles gives you an awareness of how people can take the same information and yet arrive at different decisions by using a variety of decision-making strategies. Different decision-making styles represent one likely source of interpersonal conflict at work.

To get a sense of your own decision-making style, see the Self-Assessment at the end of this chapter (p. 224). ●

What guidelines can I follow to be sure that decisions I make are not just lawful but ethical?

major question?

THE BIG PICTURE
A graph known as a decision tree can help one make ethical decisions.

The ethical behavior of businesspeople has become of increasing concern in recent years, brought about by a number of events.

The Dismal Record of Business Ethics

First were the business scandals of the early 2000s, from Enron to WorldCom, producing photos of handcuffed executives. "The supposedly 'independent' auditors, directors, accountants, and stock market advisers and accountants were all tarnished," wrote Mortimer Zuckerman, editor-in-chief of *U.S. News & World Report*, "the engine of the people's involvement, the mutual fund industry, was shown to be permeated by rip-off artists rigging the system for the benefit of insiders and the rich."[64] Then, as the Iraq war wore on, reports came back of sweetheart deals and gross abuses by civilian contractors working in Iraq war zones.

In 2007, it became apparent that banks and others in the financial industry had forsaken sound business judgment—including ethical judgments—by making mortgage loans (subprime loans) to essentially unqualified buyers, which led to a wave of housing foreclosures and helped push the country into a recession. Since then, the media have presented us with a display of Ponzi schemes (Bernard Madoff, Allen Stanford), insider trading (Sam Waksal, Raj Rajaratnam), and corporate sleaziness (work-stressed suicides at Apple's China supplier Foxconn, a fatal accident at a Kentucky coal mine evading safety regulations), and similar matters.

Through it all, voices were being raised that American capitalism was not doing enough to help the poorer nations in the world. Companies in wealthier countries, Microsoft's Bill Gates has urged, should focus on "a twin mission: making profits and also improving lives for those who don't fully benefit from market forces."[65]

All these concerns have forced the subject of right-minded decision making to the top of the agenda in many organizations. Indeed, many companies now have an *ethics officer,* **someone trained about matters of ethics in the workplace, particularly about resolving ethical dilemmas.** More and more companies are also creating values statements to guide employees as to what constitutes desirable business behavior.[66] As a result of this raised consciousness, managers now must try to make sure their decisions are not just lawful but also ethical.

For creative capitalism. Bill Gates, former chairman of Microsoft, has called for "creative capitalism" that uses market forces to address poor-country needs. Would you agree with him that the rate of improvement in technology, health care, and education for the bottom third of the world's people has been unsatisfactory?

Road Map to Ethical Decision Making: A Decision Tree

Undoubtedly the greatest pressure on top executives is to maximize shareholder value, to deliver the greatest return on investment to the owners of their company. But is a decision that is beneficial to shareholders yet harmful to employees—such as forcing them to contribute more to their health benefits, as IBM has done—unethical? Harvard Business School professor Constance Bagley suggests that what is needed is a decision tree to help with ethical decisions.[67] **A *decision tree* is a graph of decisions and their possible consequences; it is used to create a plan to reach a goal.** Decision trees are used to aid in making decisions. Bagley's ethical decision tree is shown on the next page. *(See Figure 7.4.)*

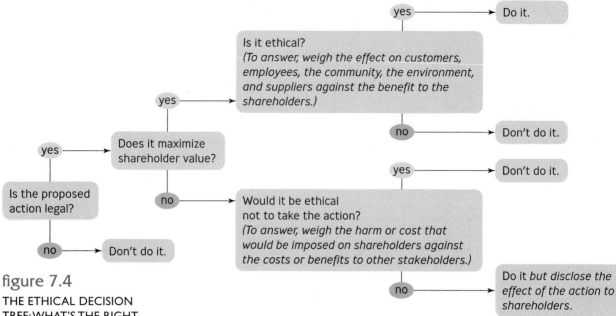

figure 7.4

THE ETHICAL DECISION TREE: WHAT'S THE RIGHT THING TO DO?

When confronted with any proposed action for which a decision is required, a manager should ask the following questions:

1. Is the Proposed Action Legal?   This may seem an obvious question. But, Bagley observes, "recent [2002–2003] corporate shenanigans suggest that some managers need to be reminded: If the action isn't legal, don't do it."

2. If "Yes," Does the Proposed Action Maximize Shareholder Value?   If the action is legal, one must next ask whether it will profit the shareholders. If the answer is "yes," should you do it? Not necessarily.

3. If "Yes," Is the Proposed Action Ethical?   As Bagley, points out, though directors and top managers may believe they are bound by corporate law to always maximize shareholder value, the courts and many state legislatures have held they are not. Rather, their main obligation is to manage "for the best interests of the corporation," which includes the interests of the larger community.

Thus, says Bagley, building a profitable-but-polluting plant in a country overseas may benefit the shareholders but be bad for that country—and for the corporation's relations with that nation. Ethically, then, managers should add pollution-control equipment.

4. If "No," Would It Be Ethical *Not* to Take the Proposed Action?   If the action would not directly benefit shareholders, might it still be ethical to go ahead with it?

Not building the overseas plant might be harmful to other stakeholders, such as employees or customers. Thus, the ethical conclusion might be to build the plant with pollution-control equipment but to disclose the effects of the decision to shareholders.

As a basic guideline to making good ethical decisions on behalf of a corporation, Bagley suggests that directors, managers, and employees need to follow their own individual ideas about right and wrong.[68] There is a lesson, she suggests, in the response of the pension fund manager who, when asked whether she would invest in a company doing business in a country that permits slavery, responded, "Do you mean me, personally, or as a fund manager?" When people feel entitled or compelled to compromise their own personal ethics to advance the interests of a business, "it is an invitation to mischief."[69]

To learn more about your own ethics, morality, and/or values (while also contributing to scientific research), go to **www.yourmorals.org**.[70] ●

Trying to be rational isn't always easy. What are the barriers?	major question?

THE BIG PICTURE
Responses to a decision situation may take the form of four ineffective reactions or three effective reactions. Managers should be aware of nine common decision-making biases.

Do your moods influence your decisions? Do you, for instance, spend more when you're sad and self-absorbed? That's what one experiment found: When researchers exposed student participants to a sadness-inducing video clip about the death of a boy's mentor, the students were inclined to offer more money for a product (a sporty-looking water bottle) than were other subjects who had watched a neutral clip.[71]

Decision Making & Expectations About Happiness

Not just the moods themselves but your expectations about how happy or unhappy you think future outcomes will make you perhaps also can influence your decisions. It seems that people expect certain life events to have a much greater emotional effect than in fact they do, according to Harvard University psychologist Daniel Gilbert, who has studied individual emotional barometers in decision making. College professors, for example, expect to be quite happy if they are given tenure and quite unhappy if they aren't. However, Gilbert found those who received tenure were happy but not as happy as they themselves had predicted, whereas those denied tenure did not become very unhappy.

The expectation about the level of euphoria or disappointment was also found to be true of big-jackpot lottery winners and of people being tested for HIV infection. That is, people are often right when they describe what outcome will make them feel good or bad, but they are often wrong when asked to predict how strongly they will feel that way and how long the feeling will last. Even severe life events have a negative impact on people's sense of well-being and satisfaction for no more than three months, after which their feelings at least go back to normal.[72]

Perhaps knowing that you have this "immune system" of the mind, which blunts bad feelings and smoothes out euphoric ones, can help make it easier for you to make difficult decisions.

How Do Individuals Respond to a Decision Situation? Ineffective & Effective Responses

What is your typical response when you're suddenly confronted with a challenge in the form of a problem or an opportunity? There are perhaps four ineffective reactions and three effective ones.[73]

Four Ineffective Reactions There are four defective problem-recognition and problem-solving approaches that act as barriers when you must make an important decision in a situation of conflict:

1. Relaxed Avoidance—"There's No Point in Doing Anything; Nothing Bad's Going to Happen" In *relaxed avoidance,* **a manager decides to take no action in the belief that there will be no great negative consequences.** This condition, then, is a form of complacency: You either don't see or you disregard the signs of danger (or of opportunity).

Example: Relaxed avoidance was vividly demonstrated in the months before the summer 2007 subprime mortgage meltdown, when banks made cheap housing loans to a lot of unqualified buyers, precipitating a huge financial crisis and drying up of credit. During that time, a lot of smart people in denial said not to worry, that the mortgage mess would be "contained." They included many bank presidents and even Ben Bernanke, chairman of the Federal Reserve.[74] One nationwide online survey has also found that investors' forecasts of future returns go up after the stock market has risen and go down after it has fallen—complacency indeed.[75]

2. Relaxed Change—"Why Not Just Take the Easiest Way Out?" In *relaxed change,* **a manager realizes that complete inaction will have negative consequences but opts for the first available alternative that involves low risk.** This is, of course, a form of "satisficing"; the manager avoids exploring a variety of alternatives in order to make the best decision.

Example: Perhaps people really don't like a lot of choices. In one experiment, 40% of customers stopped by a large assortment of jam jars (24) and only 30% by a small assortment (6)—but only 3% made a purchase in the first case versus 30% in the second.[76]

3. Defensive Avoidance—"There's No Reason for Me to Explore Other Solution Alternatives" In *defensive avoidance,* **a manager can't find a good solution and follows by (a) procrastinating, (b) passing the buck, or (c) denying the risk of any negative consequences.** This is a posture of resignation and a denial of responsibility for taking action. By procrastinating, you put off making a decision ("I'll get to this later").[77] In passing the buck, you let someone else take the consequences of making the decision ("Let George do it"). In denying the risk that there will be any negative consequences, you are engaging in rationalizing ("How bad could it be?"). As one article states, deliberating on the matter of why no one at Penn State did more to pursue allegations that an assistant football coach was abusing young boys, "companies overlook internal problems that at best impede performance and at worst could bring down the entire organization."[78]

Example: Defensive avoidance often occurs in firms with high turnover. Although some executives try to stop high performers from exiting by offering raises or promotions, others react defensively, telling themselves that the person leaving is not a big loss. "It's psychologically threatening to those who are staying to acknowledge there's a reason some people are leaving," says the CEO of a corporate-psychology consulting company, "so executives often dismiss them as untalented or even deny that an exodus is occurring."[79] He mentions one financial-services company whose executives insisted turnover was low when in fact 50% of hundreds of new employees quit within years.

4. Panic—"This Is So Stressful, I've Got to Do Something—Anything—to Get Rid of the Problem!" This reaction is especially apt to occur in crisis situations. **In *panic,* a manager is so frantic to get rid of the problem that he or she can't deal with the situation realistically.** This is the kind of situation in which the manager has completely forgotten the idea of behaving with "grace under pressure," of staying cool and calm. Troubled by anxiety, irritability, sleeplessness, and even physical illness, if you're experiencing this reaction, your judgment may be so clouded that you won't be able to accept help in dealing with the problem or to realistically evaluate the alternatives.

Example: Panic can even be life-threatening. When a jetliner skidded off the runway at Little Rock National Airport, passenger Clark Brewster and a flight attendant tried repeatedly to open an exit door that would not budge. "About that time I hear someone say the word 'Fire!'" Brewster said. "The flight attendant bends down and says, 'Please pray with me.'" Fortunately, cooler, quicker-thinking individuals were able to find another way out.[80]

Three Effective Reactions: Deciding to Decide In *deciding to decide,* **a manager agrees that he or she must decide what to do about a problem or opportunity and take effective decision-making steps.** Three ways to help you decide whether to decide are to evaluate the following:[81]

1. Importance—"How High Priority Is This Situation?" You need to determine how much priority to give the decision situation. If it's a threat, how extensive might prospective losses or damage be? If it's an opportunity, how beneficial might the possible gains be?

2. Credibility—"How Believable Is the Information About the Situation?" You need to evaluate how much is known about the possible threat or opportunity. Is the source of the information trustworthy? Is there credible evidence?

3. Urgency—"How Quickly Must I Act on the Information About the Situation?" Is the threat immediate? Will the window of opportunity stay open long? Can actions to address the situation be done gradually?

EXAMPLE

Deciding to Decide: How Should Netflix Reinvent Itself?

After Reed Hastings misplaced a rented videotape of *Apollo 13* and was charged a six-weeks-late fee of $40, he realized he had a better idea: allow video rental customers to pay a monthly subscription rate, with unlimited due dates and no late fees. Users would place their orders via the Internet and receive and return their videos by mail. The result was Netflix, created in 1997, now located in Los Gatos, California, with Hastings as CEO.

Then in the spring of 2011, Netflix and Hastings faced a turning point: Should the company devote fewer resources to DVD mail rentals and more to streaming movies over the Web? The evidence suggested that more people were watching programming online, in a gradual move away from TV networks and DVDs.[82] Hastings decided (1) to split off the DVD service and rename it Qwikster, keeping the name Netflix for the streaming service, and (2) to raise monthly prices from $9.99 for both services to $7.99 for each (a 60% hike). The uproar from customers, stockholders, and the public was immediate.

Is This High-Priority? The first decision about how to handle the response—*Should this be considered a high-priority matter?*—became apparent when the Netflix blog received 18,000 negative comments along the order of "This is a joke, right? Qwikster?" News spread quickly across the Internet, with most complaints centering on having to log in to two different sites and get two different credit card charges.[83] Clearly, this was a high-priority concern.

Is the Data Believable? The second decision—*How believable is the information?*—was reinforced when customers began deserting in droves, canceling their subscriptions in greater numbers than expected—"about a million in total," said *The New York Times,* "causing a projected quarterly loss in customers for only the second time in [Netflix's] history."[84] In addition, the price increases failed to offset the revenue loss from cancellations, which led investors to begin selling off their stock.[85]

How Fast Do We Need to Act? The answer to the final decision—*How quickly should this information be acted on?*—was evident in the speed of the preceding events. Although Hastings apologized ("I messed up," he wrote on the company blog and subscriber e-mails; "I owe everyone an apology") and rescinded the Qwikster name for the DVD service, the mishandled subscription price hike and failed rebranding of the DVD service wiped out about $12 billion in the company's market value.[86]

YOUR CALL

In the first quarter of 2012, it turned out that the DVD mail service *did* shrink, while more customers signed up for Netflix's streaming video. Although profits were down from a year previously, they still beat everyone's expectations.[87] With this knowledge in hindsight, how would you have handled Hasting's initial decisions about the rebranding and price hikes?

Nine Common Decision-Making Biases: Rules of Thumb, or "Heuristics"

If someone asked you to explain the basis on which you make decisions, could you even say? Perhaps, after some thought, you might come up with some "rules of thumb." Scholars call them *heuristics* (**pronounced "hyur-*ris*-tiks"**)—**strategies that simplify the process of making decisions.**

Despite the fact that people use such rules of thumb all the time, that doesn't mean they're reliable. Indeed, some are real barriers to high-quality decision making. Among those that tend to bias how decision makers process information are (1) *availability,* (2) *representativeness,* (3) *confirmation,* (4) *sunk cost,* (5) *anchoring and adjustment,* (6) *overconfidence,* (7) *hindsight,* (8) *framing,* and (9) *escalation of commitment.*[88]

1. The Availability Bias: Using Only the Information Available If you had a perfect on-time work attendance record for nine months but then were late for work four days during the last two months because of traffic, shouldn't your boss take into account your entire attendance history when considering you for a raise? Yet managers tend to give more weight to more recent behavior. This is because of the ***availability bias*—managers use information readily available from memory to make judgments.**

The bias, of course, is that readily available information may not present a complete picture of a situation. The availability bias may be stoked by the news media, which tends to favor news that is unusual or dramatic. Thus, for example, because of the efforts of interest groups or celebrities, more news coverage may be given to fighting AIDS or breast cancer than heart disease, leading people to think the former are the bigger killers when in fact the latter is.

2. The Representativeness Bias: Faulty Generalizing from a Small Sample or a Single Event As a form of financial planning, playing state lotteries leaves something to be desired. When, for instance, in one year the New York jackpot reached $70 million, a New Yorker's chance of winning was 1 in 12,913,588.[89] (A person has a greater chance of being struck by lightning.) Nevertheless, millions of people buy lottery tickets because they read or hear about a handful of fellow citizens who have been the fortunate recipients of enormous winnings. This is an example of the *representativeness bias,* **the tendency to generalize from a small sample or a single event.**

The bias here is that just because something happens once, that doesn't mean it is representative—that it will happen again or that it will happen to you. For example, just because you hired an extraordinary sales representative from a particular university, that doesn't mean that same university will provide an equally qualified candidate next time. Yet managers make this kind of hiring decision all the time.

3. The Confirmation Bias: Seeking Information to Support One's Point of View The *confirmation bias* **is when people seek information to support their point of view and discount data that do not.** Though this bias would seem obvious, people practice it all the time.

4. The Sunk-Cost Bias: Money Already Spent Seems to Justify Continuing The *sunk-cost bias,* **or** *sunk-cost fallacy,* **is when managers add up all the money already spent on a project and conclude it is too costly to simply abandon it.**

Most people have an aversion to "wasting" money. Especially if large sums have already been spent, they may continue to push on with an iffy-looking project to justify the money already sunk into it. The sunk-cost bias is sometimes called the "Concorde" effect, referring to the fact that the French and British governments continued to invest in the Concorde supersonic jetliner even when it was evident there was no economic justification for the aircraft.

5. The Anchoring & Adjustment Bias: Being Influenced by an Initial Figure

Managers will often give their employees a standard percentage raise in salary, basing the decision on whatever the workers made the preceding year. They may do this even though the raise may be completely out of alignment with what other companies are paying for the same skills. This is an instance of the *anchoring and adjustment bias,* **the tendency to make decisions based on an initial figure.**

The bias is that the initial figure may be irrelevant to market realities. This phenomenon is sometimes seen in real estate sales. Before the crash in the real estate markets, many homeowners might have been inclined at first to list their houses at an extremely high (but perhaps randomly chosen) selling price. These sellers were then unwilling later to come down substantially to match the kind of buying offers that reflected what the marketplace thought the house was really worth.

6. The Overconfidence Bias: Blind to One's Own Blindness

The *overconfidence bias* **is the bias in which people's subjective confidence in their decision making is greater than their objective accuracy.** "Overconfidence arises because people are often blind to their own blindness," says behavioral psychologist Daniel Kahneman. For instance, with experienced investment advisors whose financial outcomes simply depended on luck, he found "the illusion of skill is not only an individual aberration; it is deeply ingrained in the culture of the industry."[90] In general, he advises, we should not take assertive and confident people at their own evaluation unless we have independent reasons to believe they know what they're talking about.

7. The Hindsight Bias: The I-Knew-It-All-Along Effect

The *hindsight bias* **is the tendency of people to view events as being more predictable than they really are,** as when at the end of watching a game we decide the outcome was obvious and predictable, even though in fact it was not. Sometimes called the "I knew it all along" effect, this occurs when we look back on a decision and try to reconstruct why we decided to do something.

8. The Framing Bias: Shaping How a Problem Is Presented

The *framing bias* **is the tendency of decision makers to be influenced by the way a situation or problem is presented to them.** For instance, customers have been found to prefer meat that is framed as "85% lean meat" instead of "15% fat," although of course they are the same thing.[91] Framing is important because how a problem is presented may influence us to consider a certain solution simply because of the way it was framed. (Does an idea come from Democrats? Or Republicans?)

9. The Escalation of Commitment Bias: Feeling Overly Invested in a Decision

If you really hate to admit you're wrong, you need to be aware of the *escalation of commitment bias,* **whereby decision makers increase their commitment to a project despite negative information about it.** History is full of examples of heads of state (presidents Lyndon Johnson in Vietnam and George W. Bush in Iraq) who escalated their commitment to an original decision in the face of overwhelming evidence that it was producing detrimental consequences. A website called Swoopo .com capitalizes on this bias by offering a penny auction in which, say, a $1,500 laptop is offered for bidding starting at a penny and going up one cent at a time—but it costs bidders 60 cents to make a bid. "Once people are trapped into playing," suggests one account about this form of bias, "they have a hard time stopping."[92]

The bias is that what was originally made as perhaps a rational decision may continue to be supported for irrational reasons—pride, ego, the spending of enormous sums of money, and being "loss averse." Indeed, scholars have advanced what is known as the *prospect theory,* which suggests that decision makers find the notion of an actual loss more painful than giving up the possibility of a gain.[93] We see a variant of this in the tendency of investors to hold onto their losers but cash in their winners. ●

How do I work with others to make things happen?

THE BIG PICTURE
Group decision making has five potential advantages and four potential disadvantages. There are a number of characteristics of groups that a manager should be aware of, as well as participative management and group problem-solving techniques.

The movies celebrate the lone heroes who, like Clint Eastwood, make their own moves, call their own shots. Most managers, however, work with groups and teams (as we discuss in Chapter 13). Although groups don't make as high-quality decisions as the best individual acting alone, research suggests that groups make better decisions than *most* individuals acting alone.[94] Thus, to be an effective manager, you need to learn about decision making in groups.

Advantages & Disadvantages of Group Decision Making

Because you may often have a choice as to whether to make a decision by yourself or to consult with others, you need to understand the advantages and disadvantages of group-aided decision making.

Advantages   Using a group to make a decision offers five possible advantages.[95] For these benefits to happen, however, the group must be made up of diverse participants, not just people who all think the same way.

- **Greater pool of knowledge.** When several people are making the decision, there is a greater pool of information from which to draw. If one person doesn't have the pertinent knowledge and experience, someone else might.

- **Different perspectives.** Because different people have different perspectives—marketing, production, legal, and so on—they see the problem from different angles.

- **Intellectual stimulation.** A group of people can brainstorm or otherwise bring greater intellectual stimulation and creativity to the decision-making process than is usually possible with one person acting alone.

- **Better understanding of decision rationale.** If you participate in making a decision, you are more apt to understand the reasoning behind the decision, including the pros and cons leading up to the final step.

- **Deeper commitment to the decision.** If you've been part of the group that has bought into the final decision, you're more apt to be committed to seeing that the course of action is successfully implemented.

Disadvantages   The disadvantages of group-aided decision making spring from problems in how members interact.[96]

- **A few people dominate or intimidate.** Sometimes a handful of people will talk the longest and the loudest, and the rest of the group will simply give in.

Or one individual, such as a strong leader, will exert disproportional influence, sometimes by intimidation. This cuts down on the variety of ideas.

■ **Groupthink.** *Groupthink* **occurs when group members strive to agree for the sake of unanimity and thus avoid accurately assessing the decision situation.** Here the positive team spirit of the group actually works against sound judgment.[97]

Different perspectives or groupthink? A diversified team can offer differing points of view, as well as a greater pool of knowledge and intellectual stimulation. Or it can offer groupthink and satisficing. What has been your experience as to the value of decision making in the groups you've been in?

■ **Satisficing.** Because most people would just as soon cut short a meeting, the tendency is to seek a decision that is "good enough" rather than to push on in pursuit of other possible solutions. Satisficing can occur because groups have limited time, lack the right kind of information, or are unable to handle large amounts of information.[98]

■ **Goal displacement.** Although the primary task of the meeting may be to solve a particular problem, other considerations may rise to the fore, such as rivals trying to win an argument. *Goal displacement* **occurs when the primary goal is subsumed by a secondary goal.**

What Managers Need to Know About Groups & Decision Making

If you're a manager deliberating whether to call a meeting for group input, there are four characteristics of groups to be aware of:

1. They Are Less Efficient   Groups take longer to make decisions. Thus, if time is of the essence, you may want to make the decision by yourself. Faced with time pressures or the serious effect of a decision, groups use less information and fewer communication channels, which increases the probability of a bad decision.[99]

2. Their Size Affects Decision Quality   The larger the group, the lower the quality of the decision.[100]

3. They May Be Too Confident   Groups are more confident about their judgments and choices than individuals are. This, of course, can be a liability because it can lead to groupthink.

4. Knowledge Counts   Decision-making accuracy is higher when group members know a good deal about the relevant issues. It is also higher when a group leader has the ability to weight members' opinions.[101] Depending on whether group members know or don't know one another, the kind of knowledge also counts. For example, people who are familiar with one another tend to make better decisions when members have a lot of unique information. However, people who aren't familiar with one another tend to make better decisions when the members have common knowledge.[102]

Remember that individual decisions are not *necessarily* better than group decisions. As we said at the outset, although groups don't make as high-quality decisions as the *best* individual acting alone, groups generally make better decisions than *most* individuals acting alone. Some guidelines to using groups are presented on the next page. *(See Table 7.3.)*

table 7.3

WHEN A GROUP CAN HELP IN DECISION MAKING: THREE PRACTICAL GUIDELINES

The guidelines may help you as a manager decide whether to include people in a decision-making process and, if so, which people.

1. **When it can increase quality:** If additional information would increase the quality of the decision, managers should involve those people who can provide the needed information. Thus, if a type of decision occurs frequently, such as deciding on promotions or who qualifies for a loan, groups should be used because they tend to produce more consistent decisions than individuals do.

2. **When it can increase acceptance:** If acceptance within the organization is important, managers need to involve those individuals whose acceptance and commitment are important.

3. **When it can increase development:** If people can be developed through their participation, managers may want to involve those whose development is most important.

Source: Derived from George P. Huber, *Managerial Decision Making* (Glenview, IL: Scott Foresman, 1980), p. 149.

Participative Management: Involving Employees in Decision Making

"Only the most productive companies are going to win," says former General Electric CEO Jack Welch about competition in the world economy. "If you can't sell a top-quality product at the world's lowest price, you're going to be out of the game. In that environment, 6% annual improvement may not be good enough anymore; you may need 8% to 9%."[103]

What Is PM?   One technique that has been touted for meeting this productivity challenge is *participative management (PM),* **the process of involving employees in (a) setting goals, (b) making decisions, (c) solving problems, and (d) making changes in the organization.**[104] Employees themselves seem to want to participate more in management: In one nationwide survey of 2,408 workers, two-thirds expressed the desire for more influence or decision-making power in their jobs.[105] Thus, PM is predicted to increase motivation, innovation, and performance because it helps employees fulfill three basic needs: autonomy, meaningfulness of work, and interpersonal contact.[106]

Is PM Really Effective?   Does participative management really work? Certainly it can increase employee job involvement, organizational commitment, and creativity, and it can lower role conflict and ambiguity.[107] Yet it has been shown that, although participation has a significant effect on job performance and job satisfaction, that effect is small—a finding that calls into question the practicality of using PM at all.[108]

So what's a manager to do? In our opinion, PM is not a quick-fix solution for low productivity and motivation. Yet it can probably be effective in certain situations, assuming that managers and employees interact constructively—that is, have the kind of relationship that fosters cooperation and respect rather than competition and defensiveness.[109]

Although participative management doesn't work in all situations, it can be effective if certain factors are present, such as supportive managers and employee trust. *(See Table 7.4.)*

Group Problem-Solving Techniques: Reaching for Consensus

Using groups to make decisions generally requires that they reach a *consensus,* **which occurs when members are able to express their opinions and reach agreement to support the final decision.** More specifically, consensus is reached "when all members can say they either agree with the decision or have had their 'day in court' and were

table 7.4

FACTORS THAT CAN HELP MAKE PARTICIPATIVE MANAGEMENT WORK

- **Top management is continually involved:** Implementing PM must be monitored and managed by top management.

- **Middle and supervisory managers are supportive:** These managers tend to resist PM because it reduces their authority. Thus, it's important to gain the support and commitment of managers in these ranks.

- **Employees trust managers:** PM is unlikely to succeed when employees don't trust management.

- **Employees are ready:** PM is more effective when employees are properly trained, prepared, and interested in participating.

- **Employees don't work in interdependent jobs:** Interdependent employees generally don't have a broad understanding of the entire production process, so their PM contribution may actually be counterproductive.

- **PM is implemented with TQM:** A study of Fortune 1000 firms during three different years found employee involvement was more effective when it was implemented as part of a broader total quality management (TQM) program.

Sources: P. E. Tesluk, J. L. Farr, J. E. Matheieu, and R. J. Vance, "Generalization of Employee Involvement Training to the Job Setting: Individual and Situational Effects," *Personnel Psychology,* Autumn 1995, pp. 607–32; R. Rodgers, J. E. Hunter, and D. L. Rogers, "Influence of Top Management Commitment on Management Program Success," *Journal of Applied Psychology,* February 1993, pp. 151–55; and S. A. Mohrman, E. E. Lawler III, and G. E. Ledford Jr., "Organizational Effectiveness and the Impact of Employee Involvement and TQM Programs: Do Employee Involvement and TQM Programs Work?" *Journal for Quality and Participation,* January/February 1996, pp. 6–10.

unable to convince the others of their viewpoint," says one expert in decision making. "In the final analysis, everyone agrees to support the outcome."[110] This does not mean, however, that group members agree with the decision, only that they are willing to work toward its success.

One management expert offers the following dos and don'ts for achieving consensus.[111]

- **Dos.** Use active listening skills. Involve as many members as possible. Seek out the reasons behind arguments. Dig for the facts.

- **Don'ts.** Avoid log rolling and horse trading ("I'll support your pet project if you'll support mine"). Avoid making an agreement simply to keep relations amicable and not rock the boat. Finally, don't try to achieve consensus by putting questions to a vote; this will only split the group into winners and losers, perhaps creating bad feelings among the latter.

Toward consensus. Working to achieve cooperation in a group can tell you a lot about yourself. How well do you handle the negotiation process? What do you do when you're disappointed in a result achieved by consensus?

More Group Problem-Solving Techniques

Decision-making experts have developed several group problem-solving techniques to aid in problem solving. Three we will discuss here are (1) *brainstorming,* (2) the *Delphi technique,* and (3) *computer-aided decision making.*

1. Brainstorming: For Increasing Creativity *Brainstorming* **is a technique used to help groups generate multiple ideas and alternatives for solving problems.**[112] Developed by advertising executive A. F. Osborn, the technique consists in having members of a group meet and review a problem to be solved. Individual members are then asked to silently generate ideas or solutions, which are then collected (preferably without identifying their contributors) and written on a board or flip chart. A second session is then used to critique and evaluate the alternatives. A modern-day variation is *electronic brainstorming,* **sometimes called** *brainwriting,* **in which members of a group come together over a computer network to generate ideas and alternatives.**[113]

Some rules for brainstorming suggested by IDEO, a product design company, are shown below. *(See Table 7.5.)*

1. **Defer judgment.** Don't criticize during the initial stage of idea generation. Phrases such as "we've never done it that way," "it won't work," "it's too expensive," and "our manager will never agree" should not be used.
2. **Build on the ideas of others.** Encourage participants to extend others' ideas by avoiding "buts" and using "ands."
3. **Encourage wild ideas.** Encourage out-of-the-box thinking. The wilder and more outrageous the ideas, the better.
4. **Go for quantity over quality.** Participants should try to generate and write down as many new ideas as possible. Focusing on quantity encourages people to think beyond their favorite ideas.
5. **Be visual.** Use different colored pens (e.g., red, purple, blue) to write on big sheets of flip-chart paper, whiteboards, or poster boards that are put on the wall.
6. **Stay focused on the topic.** A facilitator should be used for keeping the discussion on target.
7. **One conversation at a time.** The ground rules are that no one interrupts another person, no dismissing of someone's ideas, no disrespect, and no rudeness.

Source: R. Kreitner and A. Kinicki, *Organizational Behavior,* 10th ed. (New York: McGraw-Hill/Irwin, 2012), p. 353. These recommendations and descriptions were derived from B. Nussbaum, "The Power of Design," *BusinessWeek,* May 17, 2004, pp. 86–94. Reprinted with permission of The McGraw-Hill Companies.

The benefit of brainstorming is that it is an effective technique for encouraging the expression of as many useful new ideas or alternatives as possible. For example, Mark Hurd, former CEO of Hewlett-Packard, used to engage in brainstorming with his top nine executives to generate ideas for how to increase sales in emerging markets.[114] That said, brainstorming also can waste time generating a lot of unproductive ideas, and it is not appropriate for evaluating alternatives or selecting solutions.

2. The Delphi Technique: For Consensus of Experts. The Delphi technique was originally designed for technological forecasting but now is used as a multipurpose planning tool. **The** *Delphi technique* **is a group process that uses physically dispersed experts who fill out questionnaires to anonymously generate ideas; the judgments are combined and in effect averaged to achieve a consensus of expert opinion.**

The Delphi technique is useful when face-to-face discussions are impractical. It's also practical when disagreement and conflicts are likely to impair communication, when certain individuals might try to dominate group discussions, and when there is a high risk of groupthink.[115]

3. Computer-Aided Decision Making As in nearly every other aspect of business life, computers have entered the area of decision making, where they are useful not only in collecting information more quickly but also in reducing roadblocks to group consensus.

The two types of computer-aided decision-making systems are *chauffeur driven* and *group driven,* as follows:[116]

- **Chauffeur-driven systems—for push-button consensus.** *Chauffeur-driven computer-aided decision-making systems* ask participants to answer predetermined questions on electronic keypads or dials. These have been used as polling devices, for instance, with audiences on live television shows such as *Who Wants to Be a Millionaire* allowing responses to be computer tabulated almost instantly.

- **Group-driven systems—for anonymous networking.** A *group-driven computer-aided decision system* involves a meeting within a room of participants who express their ideas anonymously on a computer network. Instead of talking with one another, participants type their comments, reactions, or evaluations on their individual computer keyboards. The input is projected on a large screen at the front of the room for all to see. Because participation is anonymous and no one person is able to dominate the meeting on the basis of status or personality, everyone feels free to participate, and the roadblocks to consensus are accordingly reduced.

Compared to traditional brainstorming, group-driven systems have been shown to produce greater quality and quantity of ideas for large groups of people, although there is no advantage with groups of four to six people.[117] The technique also produces more ideas as group size increases from 5 to 10 members.

Computer-aided decision making has been found to produce greater quality and quantity of ideas than traditional brainstorming for both small and large groups of people.[118] However, other research reveals that the use of online chat groups led to decreased group effectiveness and member satisfaction and increased time to complete tasks compared with face-to-face groups.[119] ●

Traditional group work. This photo shows the kind of traditional arrangement we expect of groups—colleagues are seated close together in clusters to better focus on their particular projects. Do you think you'd rather work in this type of arrangement than in one that is more individually based? Why or why not?

How Exceptional Managers Make Decisions

"Failure is a great teacher." That was one of the life lessons expressed by one CEO who has had to make thousands of decisions during his career.[120] Failure is always a possibility, but that possibility can't stop you from making decisions. And you can probably always learn from the result.

"When Should I Make a Decision & When Should I Delay?" Often you want to stay open-minded before making a decision. But sometimes that can just be a cover for procrastination. (After all, *not* making a decision is in itself a kind of decision.) How do you know when you're keeping an open mind or are procrastinating? Here are some questions to consider:[121]

Understanding: "Do I have a reasonable grasp of the problem?"

Comfort level about outcome: "Would I be satisfied if I chose one of the existing alternatives?"

Future possible alternatives: "Would it be unlikely that I could come up with a better alternative if I had more time?"

Seizing the opportunity: "Could the best alternatives disappear if I wait?"

If you can answer yes to those questions, you almost certainly should decide now, not wait.

"Are There Guidelines for Making Tough Choices?" "On a daily and weekly basis we can be faced with making hundreds of decisions," says management consultant Odette Pollar. "Most of them are small, but the larger ones where more is at stake can be truly painful." Here are some ways she suggests making decision making easier:[122]

Decide in a timely fashion: "Rarely does waiting significantly improve the quality of the decision," says Pollar. In fact, delay can result in greater unpleasantness in loss of money, time, and peace of mind.

Don't agonize over minor decisions: Postponing decisions about small problems can mean that they simply turn into large ones later.

Separate outcome from process: Does a bad outcome mean you made a bad decision? Not necessarily. The main thing is to go through a well-reasoned process of choosing among alternatives, which increases the chances of success. But even then you can't be sure there will always be a positive outcome.

Learn when to stop gathering facts: "Gather enough information to make a sound decision," suggests Pollar, "but not all the possible information." Taking extra time may mean you'll miss a window of opportunity.

When overwhelmed, narrow your choices: Sometimes there are many good alternatives, and you need to simplify decision making by eliminating some options.

YOUR CALL

Some experts suggest that to help make good decisions you should "Be visual," using more pictures and diagrams, and "Walk and point" to stimulate areas of the brain that control memory, emotion, and problem solving.[123] What have you found aids you in making decisions?

Key Terms Used in This Chapter

Summary

7.1 Two Kinds of Decision Making: Rational & Nonrational

A decision is a choice made from among available alternatives. Decision making is the process of identifying and choosing alternative courses of action.

Two models managers follow in making decisions are rational and nonrational.

In the rational model, there are four steps in making a decision: Stage 1 is identifying the problem or opportunity. A problem is a difficulty that inhibits the achievement of goals. An opportunity is a situation that presents possibilities for exceeding existing goals. This is a matter of diagnosis—analyzing the underlying causes. Stage 2 is thinking up alternative solutions. Stage 3 is evaluating the alternatives and selecting a solution. Alternatives should be evaluated according to cost, quality, ethics, feasibility, and effectiveness. Stage 4 is implementing and evaluating the solution chosen.

The rational model of decision making assumes managers will make logical decisions that will be the optimum in furthering the organization's best interests. The rational model is prescriptive, describing how managers ought to make decisions.

Nonrational models of decision making assume that decision making is nearly always uncertain and risky, making it difficult for managers to make optimum decisions. Three nonrational models are satisficing, incremental, and intuition. (1) Satisficing falls under the concept of bounded rationality—that is, that the ability of decision makers to be rational is limited by enormous constraints, such as time and money. These constraints force managers to make decisions according to the satisficing model—that is, managers seek alternatives until they find one that is satisfactory, not optimal. (2) In the incremental model, managers take small, short-term steps to alleviate a problem rather than steps that will accomplish a long-term solution. (3) Intuition is making choices without the use of conscious thought or logical inference. The sources of intuition are expertise and feelings.

7.2 Evidence-Based Decision Making & Analytics

Evidence-based management means translating principles based on best evidence into organizational practice. It is intended to bring rationality to the decision-making process.

Scholars Jeffrey Pfeffer and Robert Sutton identify seven implementation principles to help companies that are committed to doing what it takes to profit from evidence-based management: (1) treat your organization as an unfinished prototype; (2) "no brag, just facts"; (3) see yourself and your organization as outsiders do; (4) have everyone, not just top executives, be guided by the responsibility to gather and act on quantitative and qualitative data; (5) you may need to use vivid stories to sell unexciting evidence to others in the company; (6) at the very least, you should slow the spread of bad practices; and (7) you should learn from failure by using the facts to make things better.

Applying the best evidence to your decisions is difficult, for seven reasons: (1) There's too much evidence. (2) There's not enough *good* evidence. (3) The evidence doesn't quite apply. (4) People are trying to mislead you. (5) *You* are trying to mislead you. (6) The side effects outweigh the cure. (7) Stories are more persuasive, anyway.

Perhaps the purest application of evidence-based management is the use of analytics, or business analytics, the term used for sophisticated forms of business data analysis. Among organizations that have made a commitment to quantitative, fact-based analysis, scholars have found three key attributes: (1) They go beyond simple descriptive statistics and use data mining and predictive modeling to identify potential and most profitable customers. (2) Analytics competitors don't gain advantage from one principal application but rather from multiple applications supporting many parts of the business. (3) A companywide embrace of analytics impels changes in culture, processes, behavior, and skills for many employees, and so requires the support of top executives.

7.3 Four General Decision-Making Styles

A decision-making style reflects the combination of how an individual perceives and responds to information. Decision-making styles may tend to have a value orientation, which reflects the extent to which a person focuses on either task or technical concerns versus people and social concerns when making decisions. Decision-making styles may also reflect a person's tolerance for ambiguity, the extent to which a person has a high or low need for structure or control in his or her life. When the dimensions of value orientation and tolerance for ambiguity are combined, they form four styles of decision making: directive, analytical, conceptual, and behavioral.

7.4 Making Ethical Decisions

Corporate corruption has made ethics in decision making once again important. Many companies have an ethics officer to resolve ethical dilemmas, and more companies are creating values statements to guide employees as to desirable business behavior.

To help make ethical decisions, a decision tree—a graph of decisions and their possible consequences—may be helpful. Managers should ask whether a proposed action is legal and, if it is intended to maximize shareholder value, whether it is ethical—and whether it would be ethical *not* to take the proposed action.

7.5 How to Overcome Barriers to Decision Making

When confronted with a challenge in the form of a problem or an opportunity, individuals may respond in perhaps four ineffective ways and three effective ones.

The ineffective reactions are as follows: (1) In relaxed avoidance, a manager decides to take no action in the belief that there will be no great negative consequences. (2) In relaxed change, a manager realizes that complete inaction will have negative consequences but opts for the first available alternative that involves low risk. (3) In defensive avoidance, a manager can't find a good solution and follows by procrastinating, passing the buck, or denying the risk of any negative consequences. (4) In panic, a manager is so frantic to get rid of the problem that he or she can't deal with the situation realistically.

The effective reactions consist of deciding to decide—that is, a manager agrees that he or she must decide what to do about a problem or opportunity and take effective decision-making steps. Three ways to help a manager decide whether to decide are to evaluate (1) importance—how high priority the situation is; (2) credibility—how believable the information about the situation is; and (3) urgency—how quickly the manager must act on the information about the situation.

Heuristics are rules of thumb or strategies that simplify the process of making decisions. Some heuristics or barriers that tend to bias how decision makers process information are availability, confirmation representativeness, sunk-cost anchoring and adjustment, and escalation of commitment. (1) The availability bias means that managers use information readily available from memory to make judgments. (2) The confirmation bias means people seek information to support their own point of view and discount data that do not. (3) The representativeness bias is the tendency to generalize from a small sample or a single event. (4) The sunk-cost bias is when managers add up all the money already spent on a project and conclude that it is too costly to simply abandon it. (5) The anchoring and adjustment bias is the tendency to make decisions based on an initial figure or number. (6) The escalation of commitment bias describes when decision makers increase their commitment to a project despite negative information about it. An example is the prospect theory, which suggests that decision makers find the notion of an actual loss more painful than giving up the possibility of a gain.

7.6 Group Decision Making: How to Work with Others

Groups make better decisions than most individuals acting alone, though not as good as the best individual acting alone.

Using a group to make a decision offers five possible advantages: (1) a greater pool of knowledge; (2) different perspectives; (3) intellectual stimulation; (4) better understanding of the reasoning behind the decision; and (5) deeper commitment to the decision. It also has four disadvantages: (1) a few people may dominate or intimidate; (2) it will produce groupthink, when group members strive for agreement among themselves for the sake of unanimity and so avoid accurately assessing the decision situation; (3) satisficing; and (4) goal displacement, when the primary goal is subsumed to a secondary goal.

Some characteristics of groups to be aware of are (1) groups are less efficient, (2) their size affects decision quality, (3) they may be too confident, and (4) knowledge counts—decision-making accuracy is higher when group members know a lot about the issues.

Participative management (PM) is the process of involving employees in setting goals, making decisions, solving problems, and making changes in the organization. PM can increase employee job involvement, organizational commitment, and creativity and can lower role conflict and ambiguity.

Using groups to make decisions generally requires that they reach a consensus, which occurs when members are able to express their opinions and reach agreement to support the final decision.

Three problem-solving techniques aid in problem solving. (1) Brainstorming is a technique used to help groups generate multiple ideas and alternatives for solving problems. A variant is electronic brainstorming, in which group members use a computer network to generate ideas. (2) The Delphi technique is a group process that uses physically dispersed experts who fill out questionnaires to anonymously generate ideas; the judgments are combined and in effect averaged to achieve a consensus of expert opinion. (3) In computer-aided decision making, chauffeur-driven systems may be used, which ask participants to answer predetermined questions on electronic keypads or dials, or group-driven systems may be used, in which participants in a room express their ideas anonymously on a computer network.

Management in Action

Companies Recognize Mistakes in an Attempt to Increase Creativity & Innovation

To pitch a prospective client for her ad agency, Amanda Zolten knew she had to take a risk. But the client's product—kitty litter—posed a unique challenge.

Lucy Belle, Ms. Zolten's cat, furnished the answer.

Before she and her team met with six of the company's executives, Ms. Zolten buried Lucy Belle's mess in a box of the company's litter and pushed it under the conference-room table. No one noticed until Ms. Zolten pointed it out—and the fact that no one had smelled it.

Shocked, several executives pushed back from the table. Two left the room. After a pause, those who remained started laughing, says Ms. Zolten, a senior vice president with Grey New York. "We achieved what we hoped, which was creating a memorable experience," she says.

She won't know for a few weeks whether Grey won the business. But her boss, Tor Myhern, has already named Ms. Zolten the winner of his first quarterly "Heroic Failure" award—for taking a big, edgy risk.

Amid worries that we are becoming less innovative, some companies are rewarding employees for their mistakes or questionable risks. The tactic is rooted in research showing that innovations are often accompanied by a high rate of failure.

"Failure, and how companies deal with failure, is a very big part of innovation," says Judy Estrin of Menlo Park, California, a founder of seven high-tech companies and author of a book on innovation. . . .

Grey's Mr. Myhern recently started handing out the "Heroic Failure" award because he was worried that fast growth at the agency, a unit of WPP's Grey Group in New York, was making employees "a little more conservative, maybe a little slower," he says. Creator of E*Trade's talking-baby ads, Grey New York has more than doubled to 900 employees since 2008.

"I thought rewarding a little risk-taking was potentially the answer," Mr. Myhern says. The award is for ideas that are "edgier or riskier, or new and totally unproven," he says.

Mr. Myhern acknowledges that Ms. Zolten's prank could have gotten his eight-member team "kicked out of the room and told never to come back." He adds, "There was enough chaos in the room that we weren't sure whether it was a good or bad thing." Nevertheless, he calls the idea "absolutely brilliant" and deserving of the garish two-foot-tall "Heroic Failure" trophy. Regardless of how it turns out, he says, "we're proud that we had the idea.". . .

Extracting lessons from foul-ups is the focal point of Michael Alter's "Best New Mistake" awards at SurePayroll, a payroll-services company in Glenview, Illinois. Only people who are trying to do a good job, make a mistake, and learn from it are eligible for the $400 annual cash award. . . .

Employers use a variety of tactics to foster innovation. Grey New York blocks off a "no meeting zone" every Thursday morning, to allow employees sustained time to work on creative projects. Procter & Gamble Co. has set up a division for innovation, called FutureWorks.

Some add game or nap rooms, expansive art-filled atriums, hiking trails or private meditation rooms with music and adjustable lighting.

Intuitive Surgical, a Sunnyvale, California, maker of surgical robots, limits work teams to five members "like jazz bands," says Gary Guthart, president and chief executive. Team members tend to share ideas easily, respond quickly to problems, and hold each other accountable, he says.

However, all innovative companies tend to be alike in certain ways, Ms. Estrin says. They encourage coworkers to trust each other and take criticism in stride. Also, managers encourage intelligent risk-taking, tolerate failure, and insist that employees share information openly.

At the 150-employee Consumer Electronics Association, an Arlington, Virginia, trade group, Gary Shapiro, president and chief executive, tries to make it safe to fail by talking openly about screw-ups. In his eight-page manifesto called "Gary's Guidelines," writes Mr. Shapiro, co-author of a book on innovation: "Mistakes are OK—hiding them is not."

FOR DISCUSSION

1. Did Amanda Zolten use more of a rational or nonrational process when deciding to bring kitty litter to a meeting? Explain.

2. Which of the seven evidence-based decision-making implementation principles is consistent with the idea of recognizing failure to promote innovation? Provide examples to support your conclusions.

3. What type of decision-making styles were used by Amanda Zolten and Tor Myhren?

4. Which of the common decision-making biases is likely to be reduced by encouraging people to take risks and fail? Explain your rationale.

5. What are the pros and cons of encouraging people to take risks and fail in the pursuit of innovation? All told, do you think that it is a good idea to reward people for failure? Explain.

Source: Excerpted from Sue Shellenbarger, "Better Ideas Through Failure," *The Wall Street Journal,* September 27, 2011, pp. D1, D4. Copyright © 2011 by Dow Jones & Company, Inc. Reproduced with permission of Dow Jones & Company, Inc. via Copyright Clearance Center.

Self-Assessment

What Is Your Decision-Making Style?

OBJECTIVES

1. To assess your decision-making style.
2. To consider the implications of your decision-making style.

INTRODUCTION

This chapter discussed a model of decision-making styles. Decision-making styles are thought to vary according to a person's tolerance for ambiguity and value orientation. In turn, the combination of these two dimensions results in four different decision-making styles (see Figure 7.3). This exercise gives you the opportunity to assess your decision-making style.

INSTRUCTIONS

Following are nine items that pertain to decision making. Read each statement and select the option that best represents your feelings about the issue. Remember, there are no right or wrong answers.

1. I enjoy jobs that
   a. are technical and well defined.
   b. have considerable variety.
   c. allow independent action.
   d. involve people.

2. In my job, I look for
   a. practical results.
   b. the best solutions.
   c. new approaches or ideas.
   d. a good working environment.

3. When faced with solving a problem, I
   a. rely on proven approaches.
   b. apply careful analysis.
   c. look for creative approaches.
   d. rely on my feelings.

4. When using information, I prefer
   a. specific facts.
   b. accurate and complete data.
   c. broad coverage of many options.
   d. limited data that are easily understood.

5. I am especially good at
   a. remembering dates and facts.
   b. solving difficult problems.
   c. seeing many possibilities.
   d. interacting with others.

6. When time is important, I
   a. decide and act quickly.
   b. follow plans and priorities.
   c. refuse to be pressured.
   d. seek guidance and support.

7. I work well with those who are
   a. energetic and ambitious.
   b. self-confident.
   c. open-minded.
   d. polite and trusting.

8. Others consider me
   a. aggressive.
   b. disciplined.
   c. imaginative.
   d. supportive.

9. My decisions typically are
   a. realistic and direct.
   b. systematic or abstract.
   c. broad and flexible.
   d. sensitive to the needs of others.

SCORING & INTERPRETATION

Score the exercise by giving yourself one point for every time you selected an A, one point for every B, and so on. Add up your scores for each letter. Your highest score represents your dominant decision-making style. If your highest score was A, you have a directive style; B = analytical; C = conceptual; and D = behavioral. See the related material in this chapter for a thorough description of these four styles.

QUESTIONS

1. What are your highest- and lowest-rated styles?

2. Do the results accurately reflect your self-perceptions? Explain.

3. What are the advantages and disadvantages of your style? Discuss.

4. Which of the other decision-making styles is least consistent with your style? How might you work more effectively with someone who has this style? Discuss.

Adapted from A. J. Rowe, J. D. Boulgarides, and M. R. McGrath, *Managerial Decision Making* (Chicago: SRA, 1984).

Legal/Ethical Challenge

Should the Principal of Westwood High Allow an Exception to the Graduation Dress Code?

This dilemma involves a situation faced by Helen Riddle, the principal of Westwood High School in Mesa, Arizona. Westwood High has 225 Native American students, including 112 from the Salt River Pima-Maricopa Indian Community, most of which lies within the boundaries of the Mesa Unified School District. Districtwide there are 452 Native American high school students, 149 of whom are from the Salt River Reservation.

Here is the situation: Native American students asked the principal if they could be allowed to wear eagle feathers during their graduation ceremony. Although this may seem like a reasonable request given these students' customs and traditions, Westwood High had a rule stating that, according to a newspaper report, "students were only allowed to wear a traditional cap and gown for graduation, with no other adornments or clothing, including military uniforms. The rules were based on past practice and tradition at schools, not school board policy."

Advocates for the Native American students argued that students should be allowed to wear the eagle feathers because they represent a significant achievement in the lives of those individuals. In contrast, one school board member opposed the exception to the rule because "it would open the door for other students wanting to display symbols of their own culture or background."

SOLVING THE CHALLENGE

What would you do if you were the principal of Westwood High?

1. Allow the Native American students to wear the eagle feathers now and in the future. This shows an appreciation for diversity.

2. Do not allow the Native American students to wear the eagle feathers because it violates an existing rule. Allowing an exception opens the door for additional requests about changing the dress code. How will you defend one exception over another?

3. Allow the students to wear the eagle feathers only in this year's ceremony, then form a committee to review the dress code requirements.

4. Invent other options. Discuss.

Source: Excerpted from J. Kelley, "Westwood Students Get OK for Eagle Feathers," *The Mesa Republic*, May 25, 2006, p. 15.

chapter 8

Organizational Culture, Structure, & Design
Building Blocks of the Organization

Major Questions You Should Be Able to Answer

8.1 What Kind of Organizational Culture Will You Be Operating In?

Major Question: How do I find out about an organization's "social glue," its normal way of doing business?

8.2 Developing High-Performance Cultures

Major Question: What can be done to an organization's culture to increase its economic performance?

8.3 Organizational Structure

Major Question: How are for-profit, nonprofit, and mutual-benefit organizations structured?

8.4 The Major Elements of an Organization

Major Question: When I join an organization, what seven elements should I look for?

8.5 Basic Types of Organizational Design

Major Question: How would one describe the three types of organizational design?

8.6 Contingency Design: Factors in Creating the Best Structure

Major Question: What factors affect the design of an organization's structure?

When Should You Delegate & When Not? How Managers Get More Done

All managers must learn how to delegate—to assign management authority and responsibilities to people lower in the company hierarchy. But failure to delegate can happen even with high-powered executives, including those you might least suspect—such as the president of Harvard University. Dr. Neil L. Rudenstine, who became president of Harvard in 1991, initially became so exhausted from overwork that he had to stay home for 2 weeks to recover. The incident sent a message that his future survival would depend on his ability to set priorities and delegate responsibility.[1]

"To do more in a day, you must do less—not do everything faster," says Oakland, California, productivity expert Odette Pollar.[2] If as a manager you find yourself often behind, always taking work home, doing your subordinates' work for them, and constantly having employees seeking your approval before they can act, you're clearly not delegating well. How do you decide when to delegate and when not to? Here are some guidelines:[3]

Delegate Routine & Technical Matters

Always try to delegate routine tasks and routine paperwork. When there are technical matters, let the experts handle them.

Delegate Tasks That Help Your Subordinates Grow

Let your employees solve their own problems whenever possible. Let them try new things so they will grow in their jobs.

Don't Delegate Confidential & Personnel Matters

Any tasks that are confidential or that involve the evaluation, discipline, or counseling of subordinates should never be handed off to someone else.

Don't Delegate Emergencies

By definition, an emergency is a crisis for which there is little time for solution, and you should handle this yourself.

Don't Delegate Special Tasks That Your Boss Asked You to Do—Unless You Have His or Her Permission

If your supervisor entrusts you with a special assignment, such as attending a particular meeting, don't delegate it unless you have permission to do so.

Match the Tasks Delegated to Your Subordinates' Skills & Abilities

While recognizing that delegation involves some risk, make your assignments appropriate to the training, talent, skills, and motivation of your employees.

For Discussion Managers fail to delegate for many reasons.[4] An excessive need for perfection. A belief that only they should handle "special," "difficult," or "unusual" problems or clients. A wish to keep the parts of a job that are fun. A fear that others will think them lazy. A reluctance to let employees lower down in the hierarchy take risks. A worry that subordinates won't deliver. A concern that the subordinates will do a better job and show them up. Are any of these reasons why you might not be very good at delegating? What are some others?

forecast What's Ahead in This Chapter

We consider organizational cultures and organizational structures, and how they should be aligned to help coordinate employees in the pursuit of an organization's strategic goals. We then consider the three types of organizations and seven basic characteristics of an organization. We next discuss seven types of organizational structures. Finally, we look at five factors that should be considered when one is designing the structure of an organization.

How do I find out about an organization's "social glue," its normal way of doing business?

THE BIG PICTURE

The study of organizing, the second of the four functions in the management process, begins with a study of organizational culture, which exists on three levels. An organizational culture has four functions.

Want to get ahead in the workplace but hate the idea of "office politics"?

Probably you can't achieve the first without mastering the second. Although hard work and talent can take you a long way, "there is a point in everyone's career where politics becomes more important," says management professor Kathleen Kelley Reardon. You have to know the political climate of the company you work for, says Reardon, who is author of *The Secret Handshake* and *It's All Politics*.[5] "Don't be the last person to understand how people get promoted, how they get noticed, how certain projects come to attention. Don't be quick to trust. If you don't understand the political machinations, you're going to fail much more often."[6]

A great part of learning to negotiate the politics—that is, the different behavioral and psychological characteristics—of a particular office means learning to understand the organization's *culture*. The culture consists not only of the slightly quirky personalities you encounter but also all of an organization's normal way of doing business, as we'll explain.

How an Organization's Culture & Structure Are Used to Implement Strategy

Culture of risk. At Pfizer Inc., a Connecticut pharmaceutical company, drug discovery is a high-risk, costly endeavor in which hundreds of scientists screen thousands of chemicals against specific disease targets, but 96% of these compounds are ultimately found to be unworkable. The culture, then, is one of managing failure and disappointment, of helping drug researchers live for small victories.

Chapter 6 described strategy—the large-scale action plans that reflect the organization's vision and are used to set the direction for the organization. To implement a particular strategy, managers must determine the right kind of (1) *organizational culture* and (2) *organizational structure*. Let's consider these terms.

Organizational Culture: The System of Shared Beliefs & Values According to scholar **Edgar Schein, organizational culture, sometimes called corporate culture, is a system of shared beliefs and values that develops within an organization and guides the behavior of its members.**[7] This is the "social glue" that binds members of the organization together. Just as a human being has a personality—fun-loving, warm, uptight, competitive, or whatever—so an organization has a "personality," too, and that is its culture.

Culture can vary considerably, with different organizations having differing emphases on risk taking, treatment of employees, teamwork, rules and regulations, conflict and criticism, and rewards. And the sources of these characteristics also vary. They may represent the strong views of the founders, of the reward systems that have been instituted, of the effects of competitors, and so on.[8] We discuss organizational culture in this section and in Section 8.2.

Organizational Structure: Who Reports to Whom & Who Does What *Organizational structure* **is a formal system of task and reporting relationships that coordinates and motivate an organization's members so that they can work together to achieve**

the organization's goals. As we describe in Sections 8.3–8.5, organizational structure is concerned with who reports to whom and who specializes in what work.

Whether an organization is for-profit or nonprofit, the challenge for top managers is to create a culture and structure that will motivate its members to work together and coordinate their actions to achieve the organization's goals. *(See Figure 8.1.)* A major point is that there must be *consistency* among all these elements.

Vision
Strategy
Culture
Structure & internal practices
Collective attitudes & behaviors
Achievement of goals

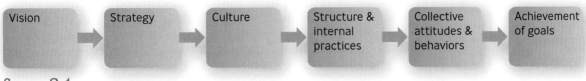

figure 8.1

CULTURE PLUS STRUCTURE

Once a strategy has been created that reflects an organization's vision, managers must design the kind of culture and structure that will motivate and coordinate employees in achieving the organization's goals.

Four Types of Organizational Culture: Clan, Adhocracy, Market, & Hierarchy

According to one common methodology known as the *competing values framework,* organizational cultures can be classified into four types: (1) *clan,* (2) *adhocracy,* (3) *market,* and (4) *hierarchy.*[9] *(See Figure 8.2.)*

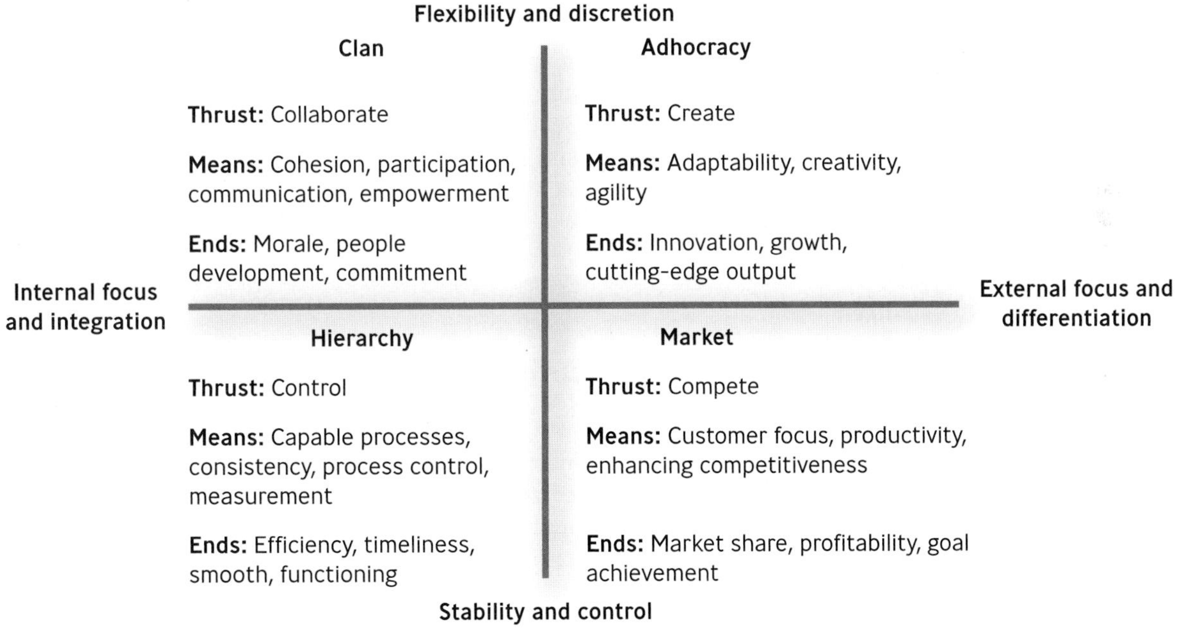

Flexibility and discretion
Clan
Thrust: Collaborate
Means: Cohesion, participation, communication, empowerment
Ends: Morale, people development, commitment
Adhocracy
Thrust: Create
Means: Adaptability, creativity, agility
Ends: Innovation, growth, cutting-edge output
Internal focus and integration
External focus and differentiation
Hierarchy
Thrust: Control
Means: Capable processes, consistency, process control, measurement
Ends: Efficiency, timeliness, smooth, functioning
Market
Thrust: Compete
Means: Customer focus, productivity, enhancing competitiveness
Ends: Market share, profitability, goal achievement
Stability and control

figure 8.2

COMPETING VALUES FRAMEWORK

Adapted from K. S. Cameron, R. E. Quinn, J. Degraff, and A. V. Thakor, *Competing Values Leadership* (Northampton, MA: Edward Elgar, 2006), p. 32.

1. Clan Culture: An Employee-Focused Culture Valuing Flexibility, Not Stability **A *clan culture* has an internal focus and values flexibility rather than stability and control.** Like a family-type organization, it encourages collaboration among employees, striving to encourage cohesion through consensus and job satisfaction

and to increase commitment through employee involvement. Clan organizations devote considerable resources to hiring and developing their employees, and they view customers as partners. Southwest Airlines is a good example of a company with a clan culture. So is online shoe seller Zappos, which encourages managers to spend 10%–20% of their off-work hours with employees.[10]

2. Adhocracy Culture: A Risk-Taking Culture Valuing Flexibility An *adhocracy culture* has an external focus and values flexibility. This type of culture attempts to create innovative products by being adaptable, creative, and quick to respond to changes in the marketplace. Employees are encouraged to take risks and experiment with new ways of getting things done. Adhocracy cultures are well suited for startup companies, those in industries undergoing constant change, and those in mature industries that are in need of innovation to enhance growth. W. L. Gore is an example of a company with an adhocracy culture. So is Google, which urges engineers to spend 20% of their time on personal projects.[11]

3. Market Culture: A Competitive Culture Valuing Profits Over Employee Satisfaction A *market culture* has a strong external focus and values stability and control. Because market cultures are focused on the external environment and driven by competition and a strong desire to deliver results, customers, productivity, and profits take precedence over employee development and satisfaction. Employees are expected to work hard, react fast, and deliver quality work on time; those who deliver results are rewarded. Kia Motors, which fires executives who don't meet their sales goals, is an example of a company with a very aggressive and competitive market culture.[12]

4. Hierarchy Culture: A Structured Culture Valuing Stability & Effectiveness A *hierarchy culture* has an internal focus and values stability and control over flexibility. Companies with this kind of culture are apt to have a formalized, structured work environment aimed at achieving effectiveness through a variety of control mechanisms that measure efficiency, timeliness, and reliability in the creation and delivery of products. General Motors has been an example of a company with a hierarchical structure. So also is UPS, the delivery company.[13]

EXAMPLE

The Corporate Cultures of Pfizer Pharmaceuticals: The Different "Personalities" Within an Organization

Organizational cultures are nearly as varied as human personalities. And often cultures may vary within the same company—or may vary over time—with, say, the cultural values of the sales and marketing department being quite different from those of the research and development department. Do you recognize the types of organizational cultures in the following?

$2.3 Billion in Fines. Connecticut-based Pfizer Inc. was fined $2.3 billion in 2009 for improperly marketing drugs to doctors. "The whole culture of Pfizer is driven by sales," said a former sales representative whose complaint helped the government's case, "and if you didn't sell drugs illegally, you were not seen as a team player."[14]

Almost every major drug company has in recent years been accused of giving kickbacks to doctors or short-changing federal programs.

Free Prescription Drugs to Unemployed. But also in that year, as unemployment hovered around 10% in the United States, Pfizer launched a program in which it offered to supply 70 of its name-brand drugs, such as Lipitor and Viagra, free of charge for up to a year to customers who had lost their jobs and lacked prescription coverage. "We did it because it was the right thing to do," said Pfizer CEO Jeffrey Kindler. "But it was motivational for our employees and got a great response from customers. In the long run, it will help our business."[15]

Ongoing Experimentation. At Pfizer, drug discovery is a high-risk, costly endeavor in which hundreds of scientists screen thousands of chemicals against specific disease targets, but 96% of these compounds are ultimately found to be unworkable. The culture, then, is one of managing failure and disappointment, of helping drug researchers live for the small victories. Thus, says one account, "when a researcher publishes a paper, or when a lab gets some positive results on a new therapy, it's trumpeted throughout the organization."[16] Another example of experimentation, aimed at helping remaining employees to be productive after heavy job cuts, is PfizerWorks, in which 4,000 employees pass off tedious and time-consuming parts of their jobs, such as creating PowerPoint slides and riffling through spreadsheets, to outsiders in India.[17]

The preceding are examples of market, clan, and adhocracy cultures, in that order.

YOUR CALL

Not all cultures work well. For instance, some Wall Street firms, such as Citigroup Inc., are reported to have such a strong perform-or-die culture—in which executives are pushed to maximize profits and are quickly fired if they fail to deliver—that it is difficult to find talent to promote from within when chief executives leave.[18] Sometimes a company will do a corporate overhaul in an attempt to improve its performance, but the actual results may turn out otherwise. This reportedly happened with Intel, the Santa Clara, California, computer chip giant, which cut its workforce in 2006, letting go many managers skilled at people development. In the aftermath, employees complained that Intel lost what made it such a celebrated place to work, including being "a place that prizes fresh ideas, frank talk, and employee engagement."[19] What kinds of cultures would these seem to be?

The Three Levels of Organizational Culture

Organizational culture appears as three layers: (1) *observable artifacts,* (2) *espoused values,* and (3) *basic assumptions.*[20] Each level varies in terms of outward visibility and resistance to change, and each level influences another level.

Level 1: Observable Artifacts—Physical Manifestations of Culture At the most visible level, organizational culture is expressed in *observable artifacts*— physical manifestations such as manner of dress, awards, myths and stories about the company, rituals and ceremonies, and decorations, as well as visible behavior exhibited by managers and employees. Department store retailer J. C. Penney Co. has tried to revamp itself from a traditional, hierarchical culture into one that is more informal and flexible by, for example, allowing such observable artifacts as business-casual dress on weekdays and jeans on Fridays.[21]

Level 2: Espoused Values—Explicitly Stated Values & Norms *Espoused values* **are the explicitly stated values and norms preferred by an organization,** as may be put forth by the firm's founder or top managers. For example, the founders of technology company Hewlett-Packard stressed the "HP Way," a collegial, egalitarian culture that gave as much authority and job security to employees as possible. Although managers may hope the values they espouse will directly influence employee behavior, employees don't always "walk the talk," frequently being more influenced by *enacted values,* **which represent the values and norms actually exhibited in the organization.** Thus, for example, an international corporation hung signs throughout the hallways of its headquarters proclaiming that "trust" was one of its driving principles (espoused value), yet had a policy of searching employees' belongings each time they entered or exited the building (enacted value).[22]

Level 3: Basic Assumptions—Core Values of the Organization *Basic assumptions,* which are not observable, represent the core beliefs that employees have about their organization—those that are taken for granted and, as a result, are difficult to change. Example: At insurance giant AIG, people worked so hard that the joke around the offices was "Thank heavens it's Friday, because that means there are only two more working days until Monday."[23] Another example: When Peter Swinburn took over in 2008 as CEO of Molson Coors, headquartered jointly in Denver and Montreal,

HP founders. David Packard, left, and William Hewlett created a close-knit organizational culture that gave a lot of responsibility to employees and fostered innovation within the company. What kind of culture is that?

the company had grown into one of the world's largest breweries through a process of 10 acquisitions and joint ventures during the preceding decade. "The challenge was getting a staff of 15,000 workers on three continents to think as one," says one account. "There were different languages and work practices."[24] Swinburn came up with an unofficial motto—"Challenge the expected"—that he hoped would motivate employees to think outside their roles. One survey found that 87% of employees said the company had a "clear vision for the future" in 2009, up from 73% in 2008.

How Employees Learn Culture: Symbols, Stories, Heroes, & Rites & Rituals

Culture is transmitted to employees in several ways, most often through such devices as (1) *symbols,* (2) *stories,* (3) *heroes,* and (4) *rites and rituals.*[25]

1. Symbols A *symbol* **is an object, act, quality, or event that conveys meaning to others.** In an organization, symbols convey its most important values. Example: One of the most iconic products of IKEA, maker of inexpensive home furnishings, whose vision is "to create a better life for the many," is the LACK table, a 22-inch by 22-inch side table that sells for only $9.99.[26]

2. Stories A *story* **is a narrative based on true events, which is repeated—and sometimes embellished upon—to emphasize a particular value.** Stories are oral histories that are told and retold by members about incidents in the organization's history.

Example: Marc Benioff is founder of cloud computing business Salesforce.com, a San Francisco company known for its great sense of social responsibility and generosity. Its spirit of philanthropy is embodied in a story called the 1-1-1 rule. "When we started the company," Benioff says, "we took 1% of our equity [stock value] and 1% of our profit and 1% of all our employees' time, and we put it into a . . . public charity. At the time, it was very easy because we had no profit, we had no time, we had no equity. But then, it turned out that our company is worth, you know, tens of billions of dollars."[27] Salesforce .com also runs 10,000 nonprofits for free, doesn't charge universities for its services, and, says Benioff, delivers "hundreds of thousands of hours of community service."

3. Heroes A *hero* **is a person whose accomplishments embody the values of the organization.** IKEA employees are expected to work hard, inspired by an anecdote from their Swedish founder, Invar Kamprad, in his 1976 "A Furniture Dealer's Testament," in which he recounts how he was berated by his father for failing repeatedly to get out of bed to milk the cows on his family's farm. Then one day he got an alarm clock. "'Now by jiminy, I'm going to start a new life,' he determined, setting the alarm for twenty to six and removing the 'off button.'"[28]

4. Rites & Rituals *Rites and rituals* **are the activities and ceremonies, planned and unplanned, that celebrate important occasions and accomplishments in the organization's life.** Military units and sports teams have long known the value of ceremonies handing out decorations and awards, but many companies have rites and rituals as well.

Example: Employees of New Belgium Brewery in Fort Collins, Colorado, which makes Fat Tire Ale, are given a cruiser bicycle during their first year. After five years, they get a free brewery-hopping trip to Belgium. Ten years of employment is acknowledged with a tree planted in their name in the campus orchard. (The company boasts a 97% employment retention rate.)[29]

The Importance of Culture

Culture can powerfully shape an organization's long-term success. For example, a recent study summarized 25 years of research on the relationship between organizational culture and various measures of organizational effectiveness. Results revealed that companies with clan, adhocracy, and market cultures had significantly higher levels of employee job satisfaction, innovation, and quality of products and services. Organizations with market cultures also reported higher profits and financial growth.[30]

Let us consider the four functions of organizational culture.[31] *(See Figure 8.3.)*

figure 8.3
FOUR FUNCTIONS
OF ORGANIZATIONAL
CULTURE

Source: Adapted from discussion in L. Smircich, "Concepts of Culture and Organizational Analysis," *Administrative Science Quarterly,* September 1983, pp. 339–58. Copyright © 1983 Johnson Graduate School of Management, Cornell University. Reprinted with permission.

1. It Gives Members an Organizational Identity   At Southwest Airlines, for instance, top executives constantly reinforce the company's message that workers should be treated like customers, and they continually celebrate employees whose contributions go beyond the call of duty.[32]

2. It Facilitates Collective Commitment   Consider 3M, one of whose corporate values is to be "a company that employees are proud to be part of." This collective commitment results in a turnover rate of less than 3% among salaried personnel. "I'm a 27-year 3Mer because, quite frankly, there's no reason to leave," says one manager. "I've had great opportunities to do different jobs and to grow a career. It's just a great company."[33]

3. It Promotes Social-System Stability   The more effectively conflict and change are managed within an organization and the more that employees perceive the work environment to be positive and reinforcing, the more stable the social system within the organization. At 3M, social stability is encouraged by promoting from within, by hiring capable college graduates in a timely manner, and by providing displaced workers 6 months to find new jobs.

4. It Shapes Behavior by Helping Employees Make Sense of Their Surroundings   The culture helps employees understand why the organization does what it does and how it intends to accomplish its long-term goals. 3M sets expectations for innovation, for example, by having an internship and co-op program, which provides 30% of the company's new college hires.

Sometimes culture can be strong enough to take the place of structure; that is, the expectations of the culture replace formal rules and regulations. In these cases, the sense of orderliness and predictability that employees look to for guidance are provided by the culture rather than by a rule book. ●

What can be done to an organization's culture to increase its economic performance?

THE BIG PICTURE

Three perspectives have been suggested to explain why an organization's culture can enhance the firm's economic performance: strength, fit, and adaptive. A particular culture can become embedded in an organization in many ways, 11 of which are described here.

What does a company do when it starts slowing down? This situation has confronted many companies, from Xerox to Kodak. But how successfully an organization reacts depends on its culture.

Cultures for Enhancing Economic Performance: Three Perspectives

What types of organizational culture can increase an organization's economic performance in terms of increasing competitiveness and profitability? Three perspectives have been proposed: (1) *strength,* (2) *fit,* and (3) *adaptive.*

1. The Strength Perspective: Success Results When a Firm Has a Strong Culture   The *strength perspective* assumes that the strength of a corporate culture is related to a firm's long-term financial performance. A culture is said to be "strong" when employees adhere to the organization's values because they believe in its purpose. A culture is said to be "weak" when employees are forced to adhere to the organization's values through extensive procedures and bureaucracies. The strength perspective embraces the point of view that strong cultures create goal alignment, employee motivation, and the appropriate structure and controls needed to improve organizational performance.[34]

The downside of a strong culture, critics believe, is that such financial success can so reinforce cultural norms that managers and employees become arrogant, inwardly focused, and resistant to change, with top managers becoming blinded to the need for new strategic plans. Example: A case could be made that the strong cultures of American automakers for many years made them resistant to the need to make radical adjustments.

2. The Fit Perspective: Success Results When Culture Fits with the Firm's Business Context   The *fit perspective* assumes that an organization's culture must align, or fit, with its business or strategic context. A "correct" fit is expected to foster higher financial performance.

Example: Prior to the arrival of Carleton Fiorina as CEO, Hewlett-Packard's "HP Way" culture from 1957 to the early 1990s pushed authority as far down as possible in the organization and created an environment that emphasized integrity, respect for individuals, teamwork, innovation, and an emphasis on customers and community improvement. This fit perspective was a key contributor to HP's success—until the high-technology industry began to change in the late 1990s.[35]

3. The Adaptive Perspective: Success Results When Culture Helps the Firm Adapt   The *adaptive perspective* assumes that the most effective cultures help organizations anticipate and adapt to environmental changes.

Which Perspective Is Accurate?   An investigation of 207 companies from 22 industries during the years 1977–1988 partly supported the strength and fit perspectives. However, findings were completely consistent with the adaptive perspective. Long-term financial performance was highest for organizations with an adaptive culture.[36]

EXAMPLE

The Grateful Dead Demonstrates an Adaptive Culture

You could understand that a successful rock band might be a subject for study by ethnomusicologists or sociologists, but as a topic of interest to business scholars and management theorists? Yet that's the point of view of Joshua Green, author of "Management Secrets of the Grateful Dead."[37]

Masters of Customer Value. Led by Jerry Garcia, the Grateful Dead became one of the most profitable bands of all time. "The Dead were masters of creating and delivering superior customer value," says Barry Barnes, a business professor at Nova Southeastern University in Florida.[38] How did this come about? "Without intending to—while intending, in fact, to do just the opposite—the band pioneered ideas and practices that were subsequently embraced by corporate America," writes Green.

The band lavished special attention on its most loyal fans, known as the Deadheads. It set up a telephone hotline to alert them to its tour dates ahead of any public announcement. It reserved some of the best seats for some of them, which it distributed through its own mail-order house. "Treating customers well may sound like common sense," says Green. "But it represented a break from the top-down ethos of many organizations of the 1960s and '70s." It was not until the 1980s that competition from Japan compelled American CEOs to adopt a customer-first orientation.

Solid Business Practices. The Dead also incorporated early on and established a board of directors consisting of members of the organization. It created a lucrative merchandising division and sued copyright

The adaptive Grateful Dead. The band featuring the late Jerry Garcia (left), shown here playing in Providence, Rhode Island, in 1979, demonstrated an adaptive culture of delivering "superior customer value" long before more conventional businesses did so.

violators, while at the same time permitting fans to record their shows, shrewdly recognizing that a ban would not only be unenforceable but tape sharing would widen their audience.

YOUR CALL

The kind of adaptability demonstrated by the Dead is what scholar Barnes thinks holds one of the greatest lessons for business—what he calls "strategic improvisation." Do you see evidence of this attribute among other bands you know? What does it take to implant a culture of adaptability within an organization?

The Process of Culture Change

Changing organizational culture is a teaching process in which organizational members teach each other about the organization's preferred values, beliefs, expectations, and behaviors. This process is accomplished by using one or more of the following mechanisms:[39]

1. Formal Statements   The first way to embed preferred culture is through the use of formal statements of organizational philosophy, mission, vision, and values, as well as materials used for recruiting, selecting, and socializing employees. Example: Walmart founder Sam Walton stated that three basic values represented the core of the retailer's culture: (1) respect for the individual, (2) service to customers, and (3) striving for excellence.[40]

2. Slogans & Sayings   The desirable corporate culture can be expressed in language, slogans, sayings, and acronyms. Example: Robert Mittelstaedt, Dean of the W. P. Carey School of Business at Arizona State University, promotes his goal of having a world-class university through the slogan "top-of-mind business school." This slogan encourages instructors to engage in activities that promote quality education and research.

3. Stories, Legends, & Myths   Until a decade ago, major drug companies treated third world countries as not worth the trouble of marketing to. But Andrew Witty, who in 2008 at age 43 became the youngest CEO of GlaxcoSmithKline, the world's second-largest pharmaceutical company, is making a name for himself by doing more for the poor people of the world than any other big drug company leader. While working in poor countries Witty found "just unbelievable energy to self-improve, to lift themselves up." He has promised to keep prices of drugs sold in poor countries to no more than 25% of what is charged in rich ones and to donate one-fifth of all profits made in such countries toward building their health systems. Now Glaxco is ranked No. 1 on the Access to Medicine index, which rates pharmaceutical companies on their stances toward the poor.[41]

4. Leader Reactions to Crises   How top managers respond to critical incidents and organizational crises sends a clear cultural message. Example: In 2001, Xerox Corporation was on the verge of bankruptcy, $19 billion in debt, and with only $100 million in cash. Anne Mulcahy, who had worked for the company for 25 years, assumed the post of CEO. Inspired by a history about adventurer Ernest Shackleton, who rescued his men after their ship was crushed by Antarctic ice in 1916, Mulcahy worked furiously for two years, not taking a single day off. She declined to file the company for bankruptcy and refused to cut research and development, believing that Xerox's long-term health depended on investment in new products. Five years later, the company reported a profit of more than $1 billion. And in 2008, she was named "CEO of the Year" by *Chief Executive* magazine.[42]

5. Role Modeling, Training, & Coaching   Triage Consulting Group, a health care financial consulting firm in California, places a high value on superior performance at achieving measurable goals. New employees are immediately prepared for this culture with a four-day orientation in Triage's culture and methods, followed by 15 training modules scheduled in six-week intervals. After less than a year, the best performers are ready to begin managing their own projects, furthering their career development. Performance evaluations take place four times a year, further reinforcing the drive for results.[43]

6. Physical Design   Intel originally had all its people work in uniform cubicles, consistent with the value it placed on equality. (Top managers don't have reserved parking spaces either.) However, the cubicle arrangement conflicted with the value Intel places on innovation, so the company is experimenting with open-seating arrangements combined with small conference rooms. Not only are open-seating arrangements thought to encourage collaboration, they also can reduce noise because employees can see when their activities are annoying to people nearby. Intel hopes that this environment will better support creative thinking.[44]

7. Rewards, Titles, Promotions, & Bonuses   At Triage Consulting Group, employees at the same level of their career earn the same pay, but employees are eligible for merit bonuses, again reinforcing the culture of achievement. The awarding of merit bonuses is partly based on coworkers' votes for who contributed most to the company's success, and the employees who received the most votes are recognized each year at the company's "State of Triage" meeting.[45]

8. Organizational Goals & Performance Criteria   Many organizations establish organizational goals and criteria for recruiting, selecting, developing, promoting, dismissing, and retiring people, all of which reinforce the desired organizational culture. Example: PepsiCo sets challenging goals that reinforce a culture aimed at high performance.

9. Measurable & Controllable Activities   An organization's leaders can pay attention to, measure, and control a number of activities, processes, or outcomes that can foster a certain culture. Example: ExxonMobil's credo is "efficiency in everything we do," so that managers make a concerted effort to measure, control, and reward cost efficiency. As a result, the company is famous for delivering consistent returns, regardless of whether the price of oil is up or down.[46]

10. Organizational Structure   The hierarchical structure found in most traditional organizations is more likely to reinforce a culture oriented toward control and authority compared with the flatter organization that eliminates management layers in favor of giving employees more power. Example: The hierarchical structure of a railroad provides a much different culture from that of the "spaghetti organization" formerly employed by Danish hearing-aid maker Oticon, in which employees worked at mobile desks on wheels and were always subject to reorganization.

11. Organizational Systems & Procedures   Companies are increasingly using electronic networks to increase collaboration among employees and to increase innovation, quality, and efficiency. For example, Molson Coors CEO Peter Swinburn, mentioned previously, in knitting together employees of several former companies made sure they had better tools to interact with each other. One technology he introduced was Yammer, a website for short messages similar to Twitter, on which some 2,000 employees now provide updates and collaborate on projects.[47] ●

major question? How are for-profit, nonprofit, and mutual-benefit organizations structured?

THE BIG PICTURE

The organizational structure of the three types of organizations—for-profit, non-profit, and mutual-benefit—may be expressed vertically or horizontally on an organization chart.

Once an organization's vision and strategy have been determined, as we stated at the beginning of this chapter, the challenge for top managers is to create, first, a culture that will motivate its members to work together and, second, a structure that will coordinate their actions to achieve the organization's strategic goals. Here let us begin to consider the second part—an organization's structure.

According to **Chester I. Barnard's** classic definition, an *organization* **is a system of consciously coordinated activities or forces of two or more people.**[48] By this definition, a crew of two coordinating their activities to operate a commercial tuna fishing boat is just as much an organization as the entire StarKist Tuna Co.

The Organization: Three Types

As we stated in Chapter 1, three types of organizations are classified according to the three different purposes for which they are formed:[49]

- **For-profit organizations.** These are formed to make money, or profits, by offering products or services.
- **Nonprofit organizations.** These are formed to offer services to some clients, not to make a profit (examples: hospitals, colleges).
- **Mutual-benefit organizations.** These are voluntary collectives whose purpose is to advance members' interests (examples: unions, trade associations).

Who sells the electricity? About 80% of U.S. drivers drive 40 miles or less a day—and 40 miles is what the hybrid Chevrolet Volt will drive on a single electric charge. (A small combustion engine cuts in to charge the battery, so the car is always running on the electric motor.) The Volt is made by General Motors, a for-profit organization. What kind of organizations might sell the electricity and the charging stations?

Clearly, you might have an occupation (such as auditor or police officer) that is equally employable in any one of these three sectors. As a manager, however, you would be principally required to focus on different goals—making profits, delivering public services, or satisfying member needs—depending on the type of organization.

The Organization Chart

Whatever the size or type of organization, it can be represented in an organization chart. **An *organization chart* is a box-and-lines illustration showing the formal lines of authority and the organization's official positions or work specializations.** This is the family tree–like pattern of boxes and lines posted in staff break rooms and given to new hires. *(See Figure 8.4.)*

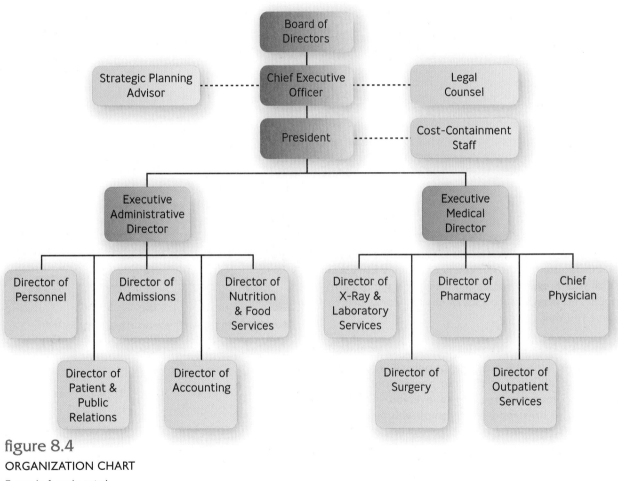

figure 8.4
ORGANIZATION CHART

Example for a hospital.

Two kinds of information that organization charts reveal about organizational structure are (1) the *vertical hierarchy of authority*—who reports to whom, and (2) the *horizontal specialization*—who specializes in what work.

The Vertical Hierarchy of Authority: Who Reports to Whom   A glance up and down an organization chart shows the *vertical hierarchy,* the chain of command. A formal vertical hierarchy also shows the official communication network—who talks to whom. In a simple two-person organization, the owner might communicate with just a secretary or an assistant. In a complex organization, the president talks principally to the vice presidents, who in turn talk to the assistant vice presidents, and so on.

The Horizontal Specialization: Who Specializes in What Work A glance to the left and right on the line of an organization chart shows the *horizontal specialization,* the different jobs or work specialization. The husband-and-wife partners in a two-person graphic arts firm might agree that one is the "outside person," handling sales, client relations, and finances, and the other is the "inside person," handling production and research. A large firm might have vice presidents for each task—marketing, finance, and so on. ●

PRACTICAL ACTION

Transition Problems on Your Way Up: How to Avoid the Pitfalls

Although you might expect training and support when you get a new job, that might not always happen, and you may be simply expected to know what to do. The same is true as you move up the management ladder. How can you avoid some pitfalls as you make your ascent? Some suggestions:[50]

Have Realistic Expectations & Think About the Kind of Manager You Want to Be. New managers often focus on the rights and privileges of their new jobs and underestimate the duties and obligations. Make a list of all your previous bosses and their good and bad attributes. This may produce a list of dos and don'ts that can serve you well.

Don't Forget to Manage Upward & Sideways as Well as Downward. You not only need to manage your subordinates but also the perceptions of your peers and your own managers above you. In addition, you need to have good relationships with managers in other departments—and be perceptive about their needs and priorities—since they have resources you need to get your job done. Don't make the mistake of thinking your own department is the center of the universe.

Get Guidance from Other Managers. You may not get advice on how to manage from your own manager, who may have promoted you to help reduce his or her workload, not add to it by expecting some coaching. If this is the case, don't be shy about consulting other managers as well as people in professional organizations.

Managing. Being a manager requires a lot of interaction with others—as in "town meetings" with staffers. Do you think you'll need to resist a tendency toward isolation?

Resist Isolation. If you're promoted beyond supervisor of a small team and you have to manage hundreds rather than dozens, or thousands rather than hundreds, you may find the biggest surprise is isolation. The way to stay in touch is to talk daily with your senior managers, perhaps have "town meetings" with staffers several times a year, and employ "management by walking around"—bringing teams together to talk.

YOUR CALL

How would you try to manage the perceptions not only of subordinates but of your peers?

When I join an organization, what seven elements should I look for?

major question?

THE BIG PICTURE
Seven basic elements or features of an organization are described in this section.

Whether for-profit, nonprofit, or mutual-benefit, organizations have a number of elements in common. We discuss four proposed by an organizational psychologist, and then describe three others that most authorities agree on.

Common Elements of Organizations: Four Proposed by Edgar Schein

Organizational psychologist **Edgar Schein** proposed the four common elements of (1) *common purpose,* (2) *coordinated effort,* (3) *division of labor,* and (4) *hierarchy of authority.*[51] Let's consider these.

1. Common Purpose: The Means for Unifying Members An organization without purpose soon begins to drift and become disorganized. **The *common purpose* unifies employees or members and gives everyone an understanding of the organization's reason for being.**

2. Coordinated Effort: Working Together for Common Purpose The common purpose is realized through *coordinated effort,* **the coordination of individual efforts into a group or organizationwide effort.** Although it's true that individuals can make a difference, they cannot do everything by themselves.

3. Division of Labor: Work Specialization for Greater Efficiency *Division of labor,* **also known as *work specialization,* is the arrangement of having discrete parts of a task done by different people.** Even a two-person crew operating a fishing boat probably has some work specialization—one steers the boat, the other works the nets. With division of labor, an organization can parcel out the entire complex work effort to be performed by specialists, resulting in greater efficiency.

4. Hierarchy of Authority: The Chain of Command The *hierarchy of authority,* or *chain of command,* **is a control mechanism for making sure the right people do the right things at the right time.** If coordinated effort is to be achieved, some people—namely, managers—need to have more authority, or the right to direct the work of others. Even in member-owned organizations, some people have more authority than others, although their peers may have granted it to them.

In addition, authority is most effective when arranged in a hierarchy. Without tiers or ranks of authority, a lone manager would have to confer with everyone in his or her domain, making it difficult to get things done. Even in newer organizations that flatten the hierarchy, there still exists more than one level of management.

Finally, a principle stressed by early management scholars was that of ***unity of command,* in which an employee should report to no more than one manager** in order to avoid conflicting priorities and demands. Today, however, with advances in computer technology and networks, there are circumstances in which it makes sense for a person to communicate with more than one manager (as is true, for instance, with the organizational structure known as the matrix structure, as we'll describe).

Common Elements of Organizations: Three More That Most Authorities Agree On

To Schein's four common elements we may add three others that most authorities agree on: (5) *span of control,* (6) *authority, responsibility, and delegation,* and (7) *centralization versus decentralization of authority.*

5. Span of Control: Narrow (or Tall) Versus Wide (or Flat) The *span of control,* **or** *span of management,* **refers to the number of people reporting directly to a given manager.**[52] There are two kinds of spans of control, narrow (or tall) and wide (or flat).

Narrow Span of Control This means a manager has a limited number of people reporting—three vice presidents reporting to a president, for example, instead of nine vice presidents. An organization is said to be *tall* when there are many levels with narrow spans of control.

Wide Span of Control This means a manager has several people reporting—a first-line supervisor may have 40 or more subordinates, if little hands-on supervision is required, as is the case in some assembly-line workplaces. An organization is said to be *flat* when there are only a few levels with wide spans of control.

Historically, spans of about 7 to 10 subordinates were considered best, but there is no consensus as to what is ideal. In general, when managers must be closely involved with their subordinates, as when the management duties are complex, they are advised to have a narrow span of control. This is why presidents tend to have only a handful of vice presidents reporting to them. By contrast, first-line supervisors directing subordinates with similar work tasks may have a wide span of control.

Today's emphasis on lean management staffs and more efficiency means that spans of control need to be as wide as possible while still providing adequate supervision. Wider spans also fit in with the trend toward allowing workers greater autonomy in decision making. Research suggests that, when aided by technology to communicate and monitor, a manager can oversee 30 employees or more.[53]

6. Authority, Responsibility, & Delegation: Line Versus Staff Positions
Male sea lions have to battle other males to attain authority over the herd. In human organizations, however, authority is related to the management authority in the organization; it has nothing to do with the manager's fighting ability or personal characteristics. With authority goes *accountability, responsibility,* and the ability to *delegate* one's authority.

Authority *Authority* **refers to the rights inherent in a managerial position to make decisions, give orders, and utilize resources.** (Authority is distinguished from *power,* which, as we discuss in Chapter 14, is the extent to which a person is able to influence others so they respond to orders.) In the military, of course, orders are given with the expectation that they will be obeyed, disobedience making one liable to a dishonorable discharge or imprisonment. In civilian organizations, disobeying orders may lead to less dire consequences (demotion or firing), but subordinates are still expected to accept that a higher level manager has a legitimate right to issue orders.

Accountability Authority means *accountability*—**managers must report and justify work results to the managers above them.** Being accountable means you have the responsibility for performing assigned tasks.

Responsibility With more authority comes more responsibility. *Responsibility* **is the obligation you have to perform the tasks assigned to you.** A car assembly-line worker has little authority but also little responsibility: just install those windshields over and over. A manager, however, has greater responsibilities.

It is a sign of faulty job design when managers are given too much authority and not enough responsibility, in which case they may become abusive to subordinates and capricious in exerting authority.[54] Conversely, managers may not be given enough authority, so the job becomes difficult.

Delegation *Delegation* **is the process of assigning managerial authority and responsibility to managers and employees lower in the hierarchy.** To be more efficient, most managers are expected to delegate as much of their work as possible. However, a business entrepreneur may fall into the common trap of perfection, believing, as one writer puts it, that "you are the only person who can handle a given situation, work with a special client, design a program."[55] But a surprising number of managers fail to realize that delegation is an important part of their job.

Regarding authority and responsibility, the organization chart distinguishes between two positions, *line* and *staff*. (*See Figure 8.5.*)

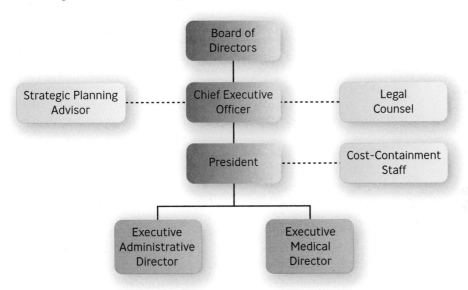

figure 8.5
LINE AND STAFF
Line responsibilities are indicated by solid lines, staff responsibilities by dotted lines.

Line Position *Line managers* **have authority to make decisions and usually have people reporting to them.** Examples: the president, the vice presidents, the director of personnel, and the head of accounting. Line positions are indicated on the organization chart by a *solid line* (usually a vertical line).

Staff Position *Staff personnel* **have authority functions; they provide advice, recommendations, and research to line managers.** Examples: specialists such as legal counsels and special advisers for mergers and acquisitions or strategic planning. Staff positions are indicated on the organization chart by a *dotted line* (usually a horizontal line).

7. Centralization Versus Decentralization of Authority Who makes the important decisions in an organization? That is what the question of centralization versus decentralization of authority is concerned with.

Centralized Authority **With** *centralized authority,* **important decisions are made by higher-level managers.** Very small companies tend to be the most centralized, although nearly all organizations have at least some authority concentrated at the top of the hierarchy. Sears and McDonald's are examples of companies using this kind of authority.

An advantage in using centralized authority is that there is less duplication of work, because fewer employees perform the same task; rather, the task is often performed by a department of specialists. Another advantage of centralization is that procedures are uniform and thus easier to control; all purchasing, for example, may have to be put out to competitive bids.

Decentralized Authority **With** *decentralized authority,* **important decisions are made by middle-level and supervisory-level managers.** Here, obviously, power has been delegated throughout the organization. Among the companies using decentralized authority are General Motors and Harley-Davidson.

With decentralized authority managers are encouraged to solve their own problems rather than buck decisions to a higher level. Decisions are also made more quickly, increasing the organization's flexibility and efficiency. ●

major question? How would one describe the three types of organizational design?

THE BIG PICTURE

Three types of organizational design are traditional design (including simple, functional, divisional, and matrix structures), horizontal designs, and boundaryless designs (hollow, modular, and virtual structures).

Small firm. What type of organizational structure is best suited to a local small business? Should the number of employees influence the decision?

Culture and structure are often intertwined. When Google cofounder (with Sergey Brin) and CEO Larry Page was asked in 2011 about the biggest threat to his company, Page answered in a single word: "Google."

Now 15 years old, Google started out as a freewheeling company in which engineers were given time to experiment on their own projects, producing the famed Google's culture of innovation. The problem, however, was that the company grew so quickly (to 31,000 people) that decision making had become molasses-like. For instance, the two cofounders, who had been trained as engineers, had hired a professional manager, Eric Schmidt, to be CEO, but the three of them "had to agree before anything could be done," says one report. "The unwieldy management and glacial pace of decision making were particularly noticeable in [Silicon Valley], where startups overtake behemoths in months."[56] Since then, Schmidt was promoted to chairman and Page took over as CEO, streamlining the company's structure and decision-making processes.

Organizational design **is concerned with designing the optimal structures of accountability and responsibility that an organization uses to execute its strategies.** We may categorize organizational designs as three types: (1) traditional designs, (2) horizontal designs, and (3) designs that open boundaries between organizations.[57]

1. Traditional Designs: Simple, Functional, Divisional, & Matrix Structures

Traditional organizational designs tend to favor structures that rely on a vertical management hierarchy, with clear departmental boundaries and reporting arrangements, as follows.

The Simple Structure: For the Small Firm The first organizational form is the simple structure. This is the form often found in a firm's very early, entrepreneurial stages, when the organization is apt to reflect the desires and personality of the owner or founder. **An organization with a *simple structure* has authority centralized in a single person, a flat hierarchy, few rules, and low work specialization.** *(See Figure 8.6.)*

Hundreds of thousands of organizations are arranged according to a simple structure—for instance, small mom-and-pop firms running landscaping, construction, insurance sales, and similar businesses. Examples: Both Hewlett-Packard and Apple Computer began as two-man garage startups that later became large.

The Functional Structure: Grouping by Similar Work Specialties The second organizational form is the functional structure. **In a *functional structure*, people with similar occupational specialties are put together in formal groups.** This is a quite commonplace structure, seen in all kinds of organizations, for-profit and non-profit. *(See Figure 8.7.)*

figure 8.6

SIMPLE STRUCTURE: AN EXAMPLE

There is only one hierarchical level of management beneath the owner.

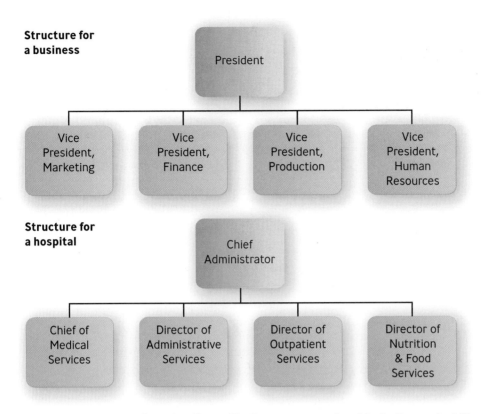

Structure for a business

President

- Vice President, Marketing
- Vice President, Finance
- Vice President, Production
- Vice President, Human Resources

Structure for a hospital

Chief Administrator

- Chief of Medical Services
- Director of Administrative Services
- Director of Outpatient Services
- Director of Nutrition & Food Services

figure 8.7

FUNCTIONAL STRUCTURE: TWO EXAMPLES

This shows the functional structure for a business and for a hospital.

Examples: A manufacturing firm will often group people with similar work skills in a marketing department, others in a production department, others in finance, and so on. A nonprofit educational institution might group employees according to work specialty under faculty, admissions, maintenance, and so forth.

The Divisional Structure: Grouping by Similarity of Purpose   The third organizational form is the *divisional structure*—**people with diverse occupational specialties are put together in formal groups by similar products or services, customers or clients, or geographic regions.** *(See Figure 8.8, next page.)*

Product Divisions: Grouping by Similar Products or Services   *Product divisions* **group activities around similar products or services.** Examples: The media giant Time Warner has different divisions for magazines, movies, recordings, cable television, and so on. The Warner Bros. part of the empire alone has divisions spanning movies and television, a broadcast network, retail stores, theaters, amusement parks, and music.

Customer Divisions: Grouping by Common Customers or Clients   *Customer divisions* **tend to group activities around common customers or clients.** Examples: Ford Motor Co. has separate divisions for passenger car dealers, for large trucking customers, and for farm products customers. A savings and loan might be structured with divisions for making consumer loans, mortgage loans, business loans, and agricultural loans.

Geographic Divisions: Grouping by Regional Location   *Geographic divisions* **group activities around defined regional locations.** Example: This arrangement is frequently used by government agencies. The Federal Reserve Bank, for instance, has 12 separate districts around the United States. The Internal Revenue Service also has several districts.

The Matrix Structure: A Grid of Functional & Divisional for Two Chains of Command   The fourth organizational form is the matrix structure. **In a *matrix structure,* an organization combines functional and divisional chains of command in a grid so that there are two command structures—vertical and horizontal.**

figure 8.8

DIVISIONAL STRUCTURE:
THREE EXAMPLES

This shows product,
customer, and geographic
divisions.

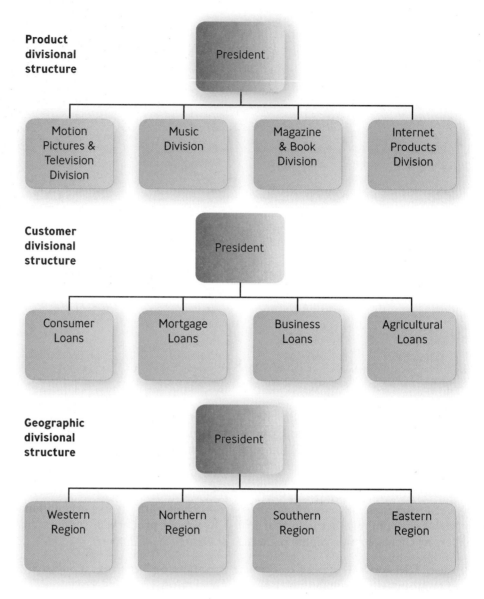

Product divisional structure

President

Motion Pictures & Television Division | Music Division | Magazine & Book Division | Internet Products Division

Customer divisional structure

President

Consumer Loans | Mortgage Loans | Business Loans | Agricultural Loans

Geographic divisional structure

President

Western Region | Northern Region | Southern Region | Eastern Region

The functional structure usually doesn't change—it is the organization's normal departments or divisions, such as Finance, Marketing, Production, and Research & Development. The divisional structure may vary—as by product, brand, customer, or geographic region. *(See Figure 8.9, opposite page.)*

A hypothetical example, using Ford Motor Co.: The functional structure might be the departments of Engineering, Finance, Production, and Marketing, each headed by a vice president. Thus, the reporting arrangement is vertical. The divisional structure might be by product (the new models of Taurus, Mustang, Explorer, and Expedition, for example), each headed by a project manager. This reporting arrangement is horizontal. Thus, a marketing person, say, would report to *both* the Vice President of Marketing *and* to the Project Manager for the Ford Mustang. Indeed, Ford Motor Co. used the matrix approach to create the Taurus and a newer version of the Mustang.

2. The Horizontal Design: Eliminating Functional Barriers to Solve Problems

The second organizational design is the horizontal design. **In a *horizontal design,* teams or workgroups, either temporary or permanent, are used to improve collaboration**

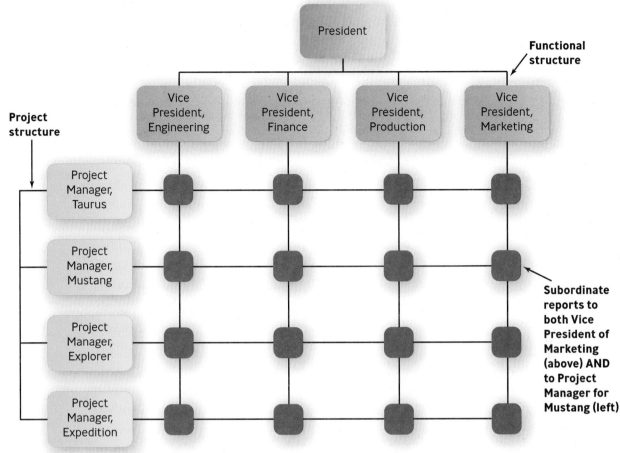

Functional structure

President

Vice President, Engineering

Vice President, Finance

Vice President, Production

Vice President, Marketing

Project structure

Project Manager, Taurus

Project Manager, Mustang

Project Manager, Explorer

Project Manager, Expedition

Subordinate reports to both Vice President of Marketing (above) AND to Project Manager for Mustang (left)

figure 8.9

MATRIX STRUCTURE

An example of an arrangement that Ford might use.

and work on shared tasks by breaking down internal boundaries. For instance, when managers from different functional divisions are brought together in teams—known as cross-functional teams—to solve particular problems, the barriers between the divisions break down. The focus on narrow divisional interests yields to a common interest in solving the problems that brought them together. Yet team members still have their full-time functional work responsibilities and often still formally report to their own managers above them in the functional-division hierarchy. *(See Figure 8.10, next page.)*

🔗 EXAMPLE

Use of a Horizontal Design: Whole Foods Market

Upscale natural and organic-food grocery Whole Foods Market started out in 1980 as one store in Austin, Texas, and today has revenues exceeding $10 billion and 310 stores in North America and the United Kingdom.[58] It was rated No. 28 in 2012 on *Fortune* magazine's annual "World's Most Admired Companies."[59] It has also been chosen as one of *Fortune's* "100 Best Companies to Work For" every year for 15 years (No. 32 in 2012).[60] But, as one writer observed, if its values are "soft-hearted," emphasizing Whole Food, Whole People, Whole Planet, "its

competitive logic is hard-headed."[61] That's because its management strategy is based not on hierarchy but on autonomous profit centers of self-managed teams.

"Radical Decentralizing": Empowering Small Teams. One of Whole Foods's core operating principles is that all work is teamwork. Thus, each store is organized into roughly eight self-managed teams, each with a designated team leader. The leaders in each store also operate as a team, as do the store leaders in each region.

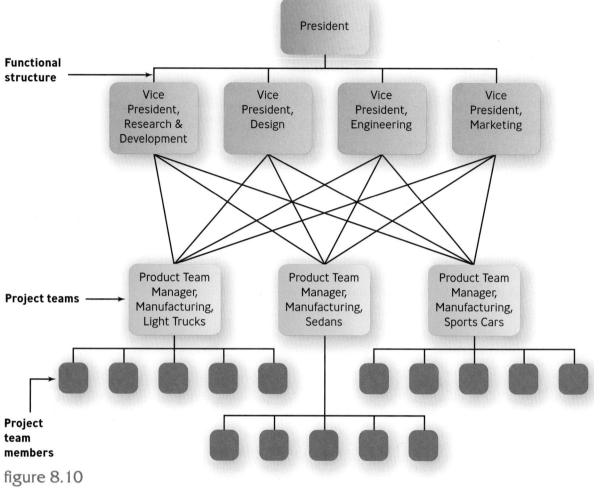

figure 8.10

HORIZONTAL DESIGN

This shows a mix of functional (vertical) and project-team (horizontal) arrangements.

Additionally, the directors of the company's 11 regions operate as a team.

At most retail companies, employees are hired by supervisors (not fellow employees), decisions about what products to order are made by someone high up at central headquarters, and the amounts of people's paychecks are kept secret. Whole Foods, however, believes in "radical decentralizing," in the words of influential management professor Gary Hamel.[62] At the individual-store level, compensation is tied to team rather than individual performance, and performance measurements and individual pay schedules are open to all. Each team has the mission of improving the food for which it is responsible; is given wide flexibility in how it manages its responsibilities, hires and fires its members, and stocks its shelves; and is given a lot of power in how it responds to the changing tastes of local consumers.

A Steady Diet of Growth. Whole Foods employees are given both the freedom to do the right thing for customers and the incentive to do the right thing for profits. The financial results of this business model are that Whole Foods is the most profitable food retailer in the United States, when measured by profit per square foot, and its stock price has risen about 37% year after year.[63]

YOUR CALL

In designing new products, such as cellphones, the horizontal design team approach, known as *concurrent engineering* or *integrated product development,* has been found to speed up design because all the specialists meet at once, instead of separately doing their own thing, then handing off the result to the next group of specialists. Why do you think a horizontal design would be better in a retail business such as groceries?

3. Designs That Open Boundaries Between Organizations: Hollow, Modular, & Virtual Structures

The opposite of a bureaucracy, with its numerous barriers and divisions, a ***boundaryless organization*** **is a fluid, highly adaptive organization whose members, linked by information technology, come together to collaborate on common tasks. The collaborators may include not only coworkers but also suppliers, customers, and even competitors.** This means that the form of the business is ever-changing, and business relationships are informal.[64]

Three types of structures in this class of organizational design are *hollow, modular,* and *virtual* structures.

The Hollow Structure: Operating with a Central Core to Outside Firms & Outsourcing Functions to Outside Vendors   In the ***hollow structure,*** **often called the *network structure,* the organization has a central core of key functions and outsources other functions to vendors who can do them cheaper or faster.** *(See Figure 8.11.)* A company with a hollow structure might retain such important core processes as design or marketing and outsource most other processes, such as human resources, warehousing, or distribution, thereby seeming to "hollow out" the organization.[65]

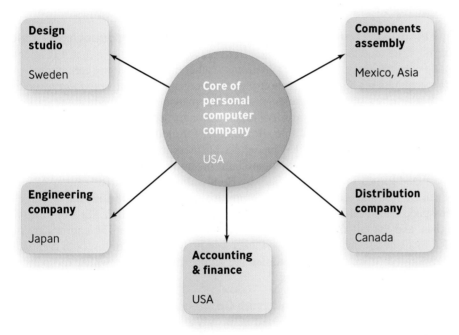

figure 8.11
HOLLOW STRUCTURE

This is an example of a personal computer company that outsources noncore processes to vendors.

A firm with a hollow structure might operate with extensive, even worldwide operations, yet its basic core could remain small, thus keeping payrolls and overhead down. The glue that holds everything together is information technology, along with strategic alliances and contractual arrangements with supplier companies.

EXAMPLE

EndoStim, a Medical Device Startup, Operates with a Hollow Structure

Nowadays a firm can be completely international. An example is the medical device startup EndoStim, nominally based in St. Louis but operating everywhere.

The Internationalists. Cuban immigrant Raul Perez, MD, came to St. Louis, where he met Dan Burkhardt, a local investor, with whom he began making medical investments.

Perez also suffered from acid reflux, reports *New York Times* columnist Thomas Friedman, and went to Arizona for treatment to an Indian-American physician, V. K. Sharma, who proposed an idea for a pacemaker-like device to control the muscle that would choke off acid reflux. Perez, Burkhardt, and Sharma joined South Africa–born Bevil Hogg, a founder of Trek Bicycle Corporation, who became the CEO of the company named EndoStim and helped to raise initial development funds. Two Israelis, a medical engineer and a gastroenterologist, joined a Seattle engineering team to help with the design, and a company in Uruguay specializing in pacemakers was lined up to build the prototype. The clinical trials for the device are being conducted in India and Chile.

Operating Differently. Continues Friedman, "This kind of very lean startup, where the principals are rarely in the same office at the same time, and which takes advantage of all the [technological communication tools]—teleconferencing, e-mail, the Internet, and faxes—to access the best expertise and low-cost, high-quality manufacturing anywhere, is the latest in venture investing."[66]

YOUR CALL

A hollow organization may well operate with just a few people in the home office—or even with no real office at all (everyone working from home with their laptops). Many people like the social interaction that comes with working in a physical office with other people. Others, however, are turned off by the "office politics" and time-wasting activities that seem to be a necessary concomitant and welcome the opportunity to do task-oriented work in a makeshift home office, occasionally having to cope with loneliness and restlessness. Which would you favor?

The Modular Structure: Outsourcing Pieces of a Product to Outside Firms   The modular structure differs from the hollow structure in that it is oriented around outsourcing certain *pieces of a product* rather than outsourcing certain *processes* (such as human resources or warehousing) of an organization. In a *modular structure,* **a firm assembles product chunks, or modules, provided by outside contractors.**

One article compares this form of organization to "a collection of Lego bricks that can snap together."[67] For example, Bombardier (pronounced "bom-*bar*-dee-ay"), of Wichita, Kansas, makes an eight-passenger business jet, the Continental, that is designed in a dozen large modules that are built in various places around the world. The cockpit and forward fuselage are built by Bombardier Montreal. The center section is built in Belfast, the wing by Mitsubishi in Japan, the stabilizers and rear fuselage by Aerospace Industrial Development in Taiwan, the landing gear by Messier-Dowty in Canada, and the tailcone by Hawker de Havilland in Australia. The engines are provided by General Electric and the avionics gear by Rockwell Collins, both companies in the United States. The 12 modules are shipped to Wichita, where the parts are snapped together in just four days.[68]

The Virtual Structure: An Internet-Connected Partner for a Temporary Project   "Strip away the highfalutin' talk," says one industry observer, "and at bottom the Internet is a tool that dramatically lowers the cost of communication. That means it can radically alter any industry or activity that depends heavily on the flow of information."[69] One consequence of this is the *virtual organization,* **an organization whose members are geographically apart, usually working with e-mail, collaborative computing, and other computer connections,** while often appearing to customers and others to be a single, unified organization with a real physical location.[70]

The virtual organization allows the form of boundaryless structure known as the *virtual structure,* **a company outside a company that is created "specifically to respond to an exceptional market opportunity that is often temporary,"** according to one definition.[71] The structure, in which members meet and communicate with each other by e-mail and videoconferencing instead of face to face, is valuable for organizations that want to grow through partnerships with other companies.[72] For instance, Finnish phone-maker Nokia, which had trouble gaining market share in the United States, changed its strategy to develop phones in partnership with U.S. carriers, as by assigning product developers to AT&T and Verizon. ●

8.6 CONTINGENCY DESIGN: FACTORS IN CREATING THE BEST STRUCTURE

What factors affect the design of an organization's structure?

major question?

THE BIG PICTURE
Four factors that should be considered when determining the best organizational structure involve whether an organization's environment is mechanistic or organic, whether its environment stresses differentiation or integration, where the organization is in its four-stage life cycle, and how its strategy can affect its structure.

What is the optimal size for an organization? How big is too big?

Medical records company gloStream, which sells software to doctors' offices, was founded in 2005 as a virtual organization, and for four years the approach worked well, with costs kept low and salespeople having no choice but to be out in the field. But in 2009, CEO Mike Sappington decided it was time to "take the company physical"—and move more people under the same roof. "We've gotten too big to be a virtual company," he told *Inc.* magazine. By the following year, gloStream planned to have 100 employees in the United States and another 100 in India. "Setting up a conference call or arranging everyone's schedules for a meeting," he said, "started to take an enormous amount of time."[73]

Four Factors to Be Considered in Designing an Organization's Structure

When managers are considering what organizational arrangements to choose from, stage of development is among the factors, or *contingencies,* they must consider. Recall from Chapter 2 that the *contingency approach* to management emphasizes that a manager's approach should vary according to—that is, be contingent on—the individual and environmental situation. Thus, the manager following the contingency approach simply asks, "What method is the best to use under these particular circumstances?" **The process of fitting the organization to its environment is called *contingency design.***

Managers taking a contingency approach must consider the following factors (among others) in designing the best kind of structure for their particular organization at that particular time:

1. *Environment—mechanistic versus organic*
2. *Environment—differentiation versus integration*
3. *Life cycle*
4. *Link between strategy and structure*

1. The Environment: Mechanistic Versus Organic Organizations—the Burns & Stalker Model

"Here every job is broken down into the smallest of steps, and the whole process is automated," wrote *BusinessWeek* correspondent Kathleen Deveny, reporting about a day she spent working in a McDonald's restaurant. "Anyone could do this, I think."[74]

Could anyone do this? McDonald's follows the model of a mechanistic organization.

Actually, Deveny found that she fell behind in, say, bagging french fries, but it was certainly the intention of McDonald's guiding genius Ray Kroc that, in fact, nearly anyone *should* be able to do this—and that a Big Mac should taste the same anywhere. Thus, for example, procedure dictates that a hamburger is always dressed the same way: first the mustard, then the ketchup, then two pickles.

McDonald's is a hugely successful example of what British behavioral scientists **Tom Burns** and **G. M. Stalker** call a *mechanistic organization,* as opposed to an *organic organization.*[75] *(See Table 8.1.)*

(See Table 8.1.)

table 8.1

MECHANISTIC VERSUS ORGANIC ORGANIZATIONS

Mechanistic Organizations	Organic Organizations
Centralized hierarchy of authority	Decentralized hierarchy of authority
Many rules and procedures	Few rules and procedures
Specialized tasks	Shared tasks
Formalized communication	Informal communication
Few teams or task forces	Many teams or task forces
Narrow span of control, taller structures	Wider span of control, flatter structures

Mechanistic Organizations: When Rigidity & Uniformity Work Best **In a *mechanistic organization,* authority is centralized, tasks and rules are clearly specified, and employees are closely supervised.** Mechanistic organizations, then, are bureaucratic, with rigid rules and top-down communication. This kind of structure is effective at McDonald's because the market demands uniform product quality, cleanliness, and fast service.

In general, mechanistic design works best when an organization is operating in a stable environment. Yet new companies that have gone through a rough-and-tumble startup period may decide to change their structures so that they are more mechanistic, with clear lines of authority.

Organic Organizations: When Looseness & Flexibility Work Best **In an *organic organization,* authority is decentralized, there are fewer rules and procedures, and networks of employees are encouraged to cooperate and respond quickly to unexpected tasks.** Tom Peters and Robert Waterman called this kind of organization a "loose" structure.[76]

Organic organizations are sometimes termed *adhocracies* because they operate on an ad hoc basis, improvising as they go along. As you might expect, information-technology companies such as Motorola favor the organic arrangement because they constantly have to adjust to technological change—yet so do companies that need to respond to fast-changing consumer tastes, such as clothing retailer The Worth Collection, which operates as a virtual company offering high-end women's clothing through direct selling in people's homes.[77]

2. The Environment: Differentiation Versus Integration—the Lawrence & Lorsch Model

Burns and Stalker's ideas were extended in the United States by Harvard University researchers **Paul R. Lawrence** and **Jay W. Lorsch.**[78] Instead of a *mechanistic-organic* *dimension,* however, they proposed a *differentiation-integration* dimension—forces that impelled the parts of an organization to move apart or to come together. The stability of the environment confronting the parts of the organization, according to Lawrence and Lorsch, determines the degree of differentiation or integration that is appropriate.

Differentiation: When Forces Push the Organization Apart   *Differentiation* **is the tendency of the parts of an organization to disperse and fragment.** The more subunits into which an organization breaks down, the more highly differentiated it is.

This impulse toward dispersal arises because of technical specialization and division of labor. As a result, specialists behave in specific, delimited ways, without coordinating with other parts of the organization. For example, a company producing dental floss, deodorants, and other personal care products might have different product divisions, each with its own production facility and sales staff—a quite differentiated organization.

Integration: When Forces Pull the Organization Together   *Integration* **is the tendency of the parts of an organization to draw together to achieve a common purpose.** In a highly integrated organization, the specialists work together to achieve a common goal. The means for achieving this are a formal chain of command, standardization of rules and procedures, and use of cross-functional teams and computer networks so that there is frequent communication and coordination of the parts.

3. Life Cycle: Four Stages in the Life of an Organization

Like living things, organizations go through a life cycle. **The four-stage** *organizational life cycle* **has a natural sequence of stages: birth, youth, midlife, and maturity.** In general, as an organization moves through these stages, it becomes not only larger but also more mechanistic, specialized, decentralized, and bureaucratic. Each stage offers different managerial challenges and different organizational design issues.[79]

Stage 1. The Birth Stage—Nonbureaucratic   The *birth stage* **is the nonbureaucratic stage, the stage in which the organization is created.** Here there are no written rules and little if any supporting staff beyond perhaps a secretary.

The founder may be a lone entrepreneur, such as Michael Dell, who began Dell Computers by selling microcomputers out of his University of Texas college dorm room. Or the founders may be pals who got together, as did Apple Computer founders Steve Jobs and Stephen Wozniak, who built the first computer in Wozniak's parents' Palo Alto, California, garage, using the proceeds from the sale of an old Volkswagen.

Stage 2. The Youth Stage—Prebureaucratic   In the *youth stage,* **the organization is in a prebureaucratic stage, a stage of growth and expansion.**

Now the company has a product that is making headway in the marketplace, people are being added to the payroll (more clerical than professional), and some division of labor and setting of rules are being instituted.

For Apple Computer, this stage occurred during the years 1978 to 1981, with the establishment of the Apple II product line.

Stage 3. The Midlife Stage—Bureaucratic   In the *midlife stage,* **the organization becomes bureaucratic, a period of growth evolving into stability.**

Now the organization has a formalized bureaucratic structure, staffs of specialists, decentralization of functional divisions, and many rules.

In the 1980s, Apple Computer became a large company with many of these attributes. In 1983, Pepsi-Cola marketer John Scully was hired as a professional top manager. Jobs became chairman. Wozniak left the company.

Stage 4. The Maturity Stage—Very Bureaucratic In the *maturity stage,* **the organization becomes very bureaucratic, large, and mechanistic.** The danger at this point is lack of flexibility and innovation.

After Jobs was fired in a boardroom struggle in 1985, Apple entered a period in which it seemed to lose its way, having trouble developing successful products and getting them to market. Scully, who emphasized the wrong technology (a "personal data assistant" called Newton, which failed to establish a following), was followed by two more CEOs who were unable to arrest the company's declining market share.

In 1997, Jobs was brought back as a "temporary" chairman, and Apple began an unprecedented era of innovation and profitability.

Employees who were present during birth and youth stages may long for the good old days of informality and fewer rules as the organization moves toward more formalized and bureaucratic structures. Whereas clearly some organizations jump the gun and institute such structures before they are appropriate, some expanding companies in effect never grow up, holding onto the prebureaucratic way of life for too long, hindering their ability to deliver goods or services efficiently in relation to their size.

4. The Link Between Strategy & Structure

It makes sense that a company's structure should help it achieve its goals, which represent an important part of its strategy. Thus, if the managers of an organization change its strategy, as gloStream did when it decided to add lots more people and put them under one roof instead of in a virtual network, they need to change the organization's structure to support that strategy. Indeed, companies often begin by offering a single product or product line that requires only a simple structure, but as they grow and their strategies become more ambitious and elaborate, so the structure changes to support those strategies.[80]

Most current strategy structures tend to reflect strategies of (1) cost minimization, (2) innovation, or (3) imitation. (Refer to Porter's competitive strategies in Chapter 6, Section 6.4.) For instance, cost minimizers, who tend to tightly control costs, opt for the stability and efficiency of the mechanistic structure. Innovative companies prefer the flexibility and free flow of information of the organic structure. Imitators, who minimize their risks by copying market leaders, might use a mechanistic structure to maintain cost controls and an organic structure to mimic the industry's innovative directions.[81]

Getting the Right Fit: What Form of Organizational Structure Works Best?[82]

All the organizational structures described in this chapter are used today because each structure has advantages that make it appropriate for some cases and disadvantages that make it not useful for others. For example, the clear roles and strict hierarchy of an extremely mechanistic organization are clearly suitable in a system valuing careful routines and checks and balances, such as a nuclear power plant. A fast-moving startup drawing on sources of expertise throughout the world may benefit from a more organic structure that lowers boundaries between functions and organizations.

As for the types of organizational structures described in Section 8.5, all have their uses. Functional structures save money by grouping together people who need similar materials and equipment. Divisional structures increase employees' focus on customers and products. A matrix structure tries to combine the advances of functional and divisional structures, but it can also slow decision making. Teams can arrive at creative solutions and develop new products faster than workers in more traditional structures. Finally, network and modular structures can tap people in particular specialties. ●

Key Terms Used in This Chapter

accountability 242
adaptive perspective 235
adhocracy culture 230
authority 242
birth stage 253
boundaryless organization 249
centralized authority 243
clan culture 229
common purpose 241
contingency design 251
coordinated effort 241
customer divisions 245
decentralized authority 243
delegation 243
differentiation 253
division of labor 241
divisional structure 245
enacted values 231
espoused values 231

fit perspective 234
functional structure 244
geographic divisions 245
hero 232
hierarchy culture 230
hierarchy of authority 241
hollow structure 249
horizontal design 246
integration 253
line managers 243
market culture 230
matrix structure 245
maturity stage 254
mechanistic organization 252
midlife stage 253
modular structure 250
network structure 249
organic organization 252
organization 238

organization chart 239
organizational culture 228
organizational design 244
organizational life cycle 253
organizational structure 228
product divisions 245
responsibility 242
rites and rituals 232
simple structure 244
span of control (management) 242
staff personnel 243
story 232
strength perspective 234
symbol 232
unity of command 241
virtual organization 250
virtual structure 250
youth stage 253

Summary

8.1 What Kind of Organizational Culture Will You Be Operating In?

Organizational culture is a system of shared beliefs and values that develops within an organization and guides the behavior of its members. Four types of culture are (1) clan, which has an internal focus and values flexibility; (2) adhocracy, which has an external focus and values flexibility; (3) market, which has a strong external focus and values stability and control; and (4) hierarchy, which has an internal focus and values stability and control.

Organizational culture appears as three layers. Level 1 is observable artifacts, the physical manifestations of culture. Level 2 is espoused values, explicitly stated values and norms preferred by an organization, although employees are frequently influenced by enacted values, which represent the values and norms actually exhibited in the organization. Level 3 consists of basic assumptions, the core values of the organization.

Culture is transmitted to employees in symbols, stories, heroes, and rites and rituals. A symbol is an object, act, quality, or event that conveys meaning to others. A story is a narrative based on true events, which is repeated—and sometimes embellished on—to emphasize a particular value. A hero is a person whose accomplishments embody the values of the organization. Rites and rituals are the activities

and ceremonies, planned and unplanned, that celebrate important occasions and accomplishments in the organization's life.

Culture, which can powerfully shape an organization's success over the long term, has four functions. (1) It gives members an organizational identity. (2) It facilitates collective commitment. (3) It promotes social-system stability. (4) It shapes behavior by helping employees make sense of their surroundings.

8.2 Developing High-Performance Cultures

What types of organizational culture can increase an organization's competitiveness and profitability? Three perspectives have been proposed: (1) The strength perspective assumes that the strength of a corporate culture is related to a firm's long-term financial performance; (2) the fit perspective assumes that an organization's culture must align, or fit, with its business or strategic context; and (3) the adaptive perspective assumes that the most effective cultures help organizations anticipate and adapt to environmental changes.

Among the mechanisms managers use to embed a culture in an organization are: (1) formal statements; (2) slogans and sayings; (3) stories, legends, and myths; (4) leader reactions to crises; (5) role modeling, training, and coaching; (6) physical design; (7) rewards, titles, promotions, and bonuses; (8) organizational goals and performance criteria; (9) measurable and controllable activities; (10) organizational structure; and (11) organizational systems and procedures.

8.3 Organizational Structure

An organization is a system of consciously coordinated activities or forces of two or more people. There are three types of organizations classified according to the three different purposes for which they are formed: for-profit, nonprofit, and mutual-benefit.

Whatever the size of organization, it can be represented in an organization chart, a boxes-and-lines illustration showing the formal lines of authority and the organization's official positions or division of labor. Two kinds of information that organizations reveal about organizational structure are (1) the vertical hierarchy of authority—who reports to whom, and (2) the horizontal specialization—who specializes in what work.

8.4 The Major Elements of an Organization

Organizations have seven elements: (1) common purpose, which unifies employees or members and gives everyone an understanding of the organization's reason for being; (2) coordinated effort, the coordination of individual efforts into a group or organizationwide effort; (3) division of labor, having discrete parts of a task done by different people; (4) hierarchy of authority, a control mechanism for making sure the right people do the right things at the right time; (5) span of control, which refers to the number of people reporting directly to a given manager; (6) authority and accountability, responsibility, and delegation. Authority refers to the rights inherent in a managerial position to make decisions, give orders, and utilize resources. Accountability means that managers must report and justify work results to the managers above them. Responsibility is the obligation you have to perform the tasks assigned to you. Delegation is the process of assigning managerial authority and responsibility to managers and employees lower in the hierarchy. Regarding authority and responsibility, the organization chart distinguishes between two positions, line and staff. Line managers have authority to make decisions and usually have people reporting to them. Staff personnel have advisory functions; they provide advice, recommendations, and research to line managers. (7) Centralization versus decentralization of authority. With centralized authority, important decisions are made by higher level managers. With decentralized authority, important decisions are made by middle-level and supervisory-level managers.

8.5 Basic Types of Organizational Design

Three types of organizational design are (1) traditional (including simple, functional, divisional, and matrix structures), (2) horizontal designs, and (3) boundary-less design (hollow, modular, and virtual structures).

(1) Traditional organizational designs tend to favor structures that rely on a vertical management hierarchy, with clear departmental boundaries and reporting arrangements. (a) In a simple structure, authority is centralized in a single person; this structure has a flat hierarchy, few rules, and low work specialization. (b) In a functional structure, people with similar occupational specialties are put together in formal groups. (c) In a divisional structure, people with diverse occupational specialties are put together in formal groups by similar products or services, customers or clients, or geographic regions. (d) In a matrix structure, an organization combines functional and divisional chains of command in grids so that there are two command structures—vertical and horizontal.

(2) In a horizontal design, teams or workgroups are used to improve collaboration and work on shared tasks by breaking down internal boundaries.

(3) A boundary-less organization is a fluid, highly adaptive organization whose members (which may include not only coworkers but also suppliers, customers, and even competitors), linked by information technology, come together to collaborate on common tasks. Among the three types of structures in this class of organizational design, (a) in the hollow structure, often called network structure, the organization has a central core of key functions and outsources other functions to vendors who can do them cheaper or faster. (b) In a modular structure, a firm assembles product chunks, or modules, provided by outside contractors. (c) In a virtual structure, a company outside a company is created specifically to respond to an exceptional market opportunity that is often temporary. (A virtual organization is one whose members are geographically apart, usually working with e-mail, collaborative computing, and other computer connections.)

8.6 Contingency Design: Factors in Creating the Best Structure

The process of fitting the organization to its environment is called contingency design. Managers taking a contingency approach must consider at least three factors in designing the best kind of structure for their organization at that particular time.

1. An organization may be either mechanistic or organic. In a mechanistic organization, authority is centralized, tasks and rules are clearly specified, and employees are closely supervised. In an organic organization, authority is decentralized, there are fewer rules and procedures, and networks of

employees are encouraged to cooperate and respond quickly to unexpected tasks.

2. An organization may also be characterized by differentiation or integration. Differentiation is the tendency of the parts of an organization to disperse and fragment. Integration is the tendency of the parts of an organization to draw together to achieve a common purpose.

3. The four-stage organizational life cycle has a natural sequence of stages: birth, youth, midlife, and maturity. The birth stage is the nonbureaucratic stage, the stage in which the organization is created. The youth stage is the prebureaucratic stage, a stage of growth and expansion. In the midlife stage, the organization becomes bureaucratic, a period of growth evolving into stability. In the maturity stage, the organization becomes very bureaucratic, large, and mechanistic. The danger at this point is lack of flexibility and innovation.

Management in Action

Verizon Is Creating a Culture That Focuses on Shareholder Value

One may be the loneliest number, but Verizon isn't complaining. After appearing five times in the Top 10 over the last six years, the telecommunications company captured the No. 1 spot on the Training Top 125 for the first time in 2012.

Despite a relatively flat training budget and a work stoppage that resulted from the expiration of union collective bargaining agreements, Verizon remained steadfast in its commitment to effective training tied to corporate strategic goals—and had the results to show for it.

"We focused on the major training initiatives that would advance our strategic business goals and business unit/functional-specific initiatives," says Al Torres, VP, Human Resources, Verizon Telecom and Business. "We remained relatively flat on full-time staff across Verizon, but we increased the number of internal subject matter experts (SMEs) significantly to help drive key initiatives deeply through the organization."

Verizon's three main business goals for 2011 were:

1. To build a business and workforce as good as its networks.
2. To lead in shareholder value creation.
3. To be recognized as an iconic technology company.

Verizon's strategic business units (BUs) align BU-specific priorities with the company's business goals and core values. "Our federated L&D organizations, supporting each BU, establish training priorities/initiatives that align with each BU's priorities and Verizon's business goals and values—top to bottom and across," says Magda Yrizarry, VP, Corporate Human Resources. . . .

Creating a leadership culture that leads for shareholder value was one of Verizon's significant goals in 2011, and the company's implementation of Leading for Shareholder Value (LSV) was a key lever for cultural change. . . .

Sponsored by a new president and CEO Lowell McAdam, LSV is a 1.5-day mandatory executive education program designed to help senior leaders understand how to drive long-term value creation. . . . Each LSV session is led by CEO McAdam and CFO Fran Shammo. . . .

As part of the program design, Yrizarry says, senior leaders are placed in cross-business units and cross-functional teams and given an assignment to identify obstacles preventing Verizon from creating more shareholder value. Each team recommends actions that will remove those obstacles. At the end of each session, each team reports to a panel of top executives. . . .

In addition, during the program, each senior leader submits an Individual Accountability Plan (IAP). These IAPs are aligned with "value drivers" or metrics by which shareholders, analysts, and potential investors assess company performance. . . . Each senior leader selects one to two action he or she will commit to as part of driving SHV. The IAPs then are digitized and provided to Lowell McAdam and business unit presidents for review and follow-up. More than 300 senior leaders now have SHV IAPs that will be incorporated into 2011 performance reviews and, where appropriate, into 2012 performance agreements, Yrizarry says. . . .

At the other end of Verizon's leadership development spectrum, "we are focused on attracting and retaining the best talent from colleges and universities as we see this as critical to building our leadership funnel for the future," Yrizarry says. In 2011, Verizon rolled out a new "Verizon Leadership Development Program" (VLDP) across the enterprise. . . .

"VLDP recruits the highest-performing college graduates at strategic partnership schools with 10- to 12-week Verizon internships and semester-long co-ops as a primary feeder pool for the full-time college hire VLDP," Yrizarry says. VLDP currently sponsors Finance, Network Operations, Engineering, IT, Human Resources, and Marketing. After graduation and upon hire, participants complete a minimum of two job rotations. The number and length of job rotations varies between functions over the course of two or three years in the program. All VLDP hires experience a 24-month customized leadership curriculum road map focused on cultural immersion and self-awareness, operational effectiveness, high performance, and leadership preparation. In addition, each function has a functional-specific curriculum road map and experiential development activities.

Innovation is at the core of who Verizon is, according to Verizon Wireless Human Resources VP Lou Tedrick, and "it's essential to be a leading innovator in order to achieve our goal of becoming an iconic technology company. Our 4G LTE network is key to our future ability to deliver innovative technology to our customers."

Prior to rolling out its 4G LTE network in December 2010, Verizon delivered 60,000-plus hours of 4G LTE technology and device training to its front-line Sales and Services reps between January and August. "We've maintained a one-stop online performance support 4G LTE Resource Center for employees to use at the moment of apply," Tedrick notes. . . .

With the volume of training taking place—particularly on new products and technology—just how does Verizon measure its effectiveness? At the onset of a training initiative, "we work with key stakeholders and business partners to define what success will look like in terms of employee knowledge, behaviors, and targeted business results," Tedrick says. "Then, we ideally get a pre-training 'snapshot' of knowledge, behaviors, and/or business results to compare with a post-training snapshot."

Verizon Wireless (VZW), for example, uses a CS New Hire Training (NHT) Scorecard to monitor new hire performance at 30, 60, 90, and 120 days post-training. "Working with our CS Operations Leaders, we measure new hire performance on a set of CS key performance indicators such as 'Entire Rep Performance,' 'Quality,' 'First Call Resolution,' and 'Average Handle Time.'" Tedrick says new hires consistently meet the expected key performance indicators (KPIs) by 120 days post-training and that VZW has used this scorecard to determine curriculum changes needed for a CS NHT redesign and for targeted reinforcement training. . . .

Tedrick says video/audio podcasts are fast becoming one of Verizon employees' favorite means for learning quickly. "We've built videos to demonstrate system processes for our B2B sales team-accessed from within their primary sales force automation tool. Videos demonstrating new devices provide a quick, effective,

on-demand learning approach." Viewership is viral, Tedrick says, with employees recommending to peers a video lesson they just watched in a matter of minutes. Indeed, Verizon's DROID Charge by Samsung video reached 1,240 views shortly after it launched.

"We distribute videos via VZTube, our internal YouTube site," Tedrick explains. Year-to-date total videos watched: 1,478,412; audio files played: 13,084; total VZTube members: 83,398. Viewership statistics on existing videos are used to make recommendations for future videos. Tedrick notes that low views on a particular video type are taken into consideration when planning future videos that are similar in style and message.

Verizon also expanded its My NetWork Social Networking platform for peer-to-peer collaboration to include My NetWork On-The-Go in 2011. Employees now can access my NetWork features using their mobile devices. . . .

"We've found that the keys to success for social media is to 'pilot' or 'trial' first, so you can work out any issues before expanding to a wider audience, *and* if you track the impact on KPIs, it can be a good case study to share with leaders who may be concerned about the net impact of social media," Tedrick says. "Additionally, we've found that taking a 'low-key' approach to social media for learning has let learners try things out for size, then recommend it to their peers. The result is organic versus forced utilization."

Verizon currently is exploring the use of tablets for delivering Online Performance Support System (InfoManager) content at "moment of apply," particularly for its Retail representatives, Tedrick says. "This way, our Retail representatives will have access to the information while interacting with our customers and not have to step out of their sales process flow." Verizon hopes to have it available by mid-year 2012.

FOR DISCUSSION

1. Using the competing values framework as a point of reference, how would you describe Verizon's current organizational culture? Provide examples to support your conclusions.

2. What type of culture is desired by CEO Lowell McAdam to meet his goals? Discuss.

3. Which of the 11 ways to change an organizational culture has Verizon used to create its current culture? Provide examples to support your conclusions.

4. Does Mr. Lowell want to create more of a mechanistic or organic organization? Explain.

5. What is the most important lesson from this case? Discuss.

Source: Excerpted from Lorri Freifeld, "Verizon's New #1," *Training*, January/February 2012, pp. 28–30, 32. Reprinted with permission of Training Magazine.

Is Your Organization a Learning Organization?

OBJECTIVES

1. To gain familiarity with the characteristics of learning organizations.
2. To identify whether your organization is a learning organization.

INTRODUCTION

As we learned in Chapter 2, a learning organization is one that actively creates, acquires, and transfers new knowledge. Learning organizations are places in which new ideas and patterns of thinking are nurtured and in which people are allowed to continually expand their abilities to achieve desired results. Most important, a learning organization is a place in which the organization and individuals in it are continually learning in order to achieve its goals. The purpose of this exercise is to identify whether the organization in which you work is a learning organization.

INSTRUCTIONS

The following survey was created to assess the extent to which an organization follows the principles of a learning organization. If you are currently working, you should answer the questions in regard to this organization. If you are not currently working but have worked in the past, use a past job in completing the survey. If you have never had a job, you can use your school as a reference or use an organization you might be familiar with. For example, you might interview your parents to determine the extent to which the organization they work for follows the principles of a learning organization. Read each statement and use the following scale to indicate which answer most closely matches your response: 1 = strongly disagree; 2 = disagree; 3 = neither agree nor disagree; 4 = agree; 5 = strongly agree.

1. Management uses rewards, praise, and recognition to get what they want done.	1	2	3	4	5
2. The company promotes teamwork.	1	2	3	4	5
3. People are recognized and rewarded on the basis of what they do rather than *who* they know.	1	2	3	4	5
4. I see more examples of optimistic attitudes/behaviors rather than negative and cynical ones.	1	2	3	4	5
5. I have a clear picture of the organization's vision and my role in helping to accomplish it.	1	2	3	4	5
6. This organization relies more on team-based solutions than individual ones.	1	2	3	4	5
7. This organization tends to look at the big picture rather than analyzing problems from a narrow perspective.	1	2	3	4	5
8. People have an open mind when working with others.	1	2	3	4	5
9. This company looks for the root cause of a problem rather than a "quick fix."	1	2	3	4	5
10. I have the skills and knowledge to continuously improve the way I do my job.	1	2	3	4	5

Total _____

SCORING

To get your score, add up the numbers that correspond to your responses. The range will be from 10 to 50. Comparative norms for learning organizations are as follows:

Total score of 10–23 = low learning organization
Total score of 24–36 = moderate learning organization
Total score of 37–50 = high learning organization

Legal/Ethical Challenge

What Type of Culture Is Being Created by the New Orleans Saints?

The New Orleans Saints are under investigation by the National Football League (NFL) for implementing "an institutional, management-sanctioned 'bounty' program—paying players fees to target opponents for injury." The bounty program was spearheaded by the Saints former defensive coordinator Gregg Williams, who was suspended from the NFL in March 2012. Williams used the bounty program when the Saints won the Super Bowl in 2009, and there is speculation that he may have used it while working for his previous employer, the Washington Redskins. Here is how the program works.

The Saints kept a pool of cash and offered payments "of up to $1,500 for knocking players out of the game." The goal of the program was to motivate players to purposely hurt or injure their opponents, thus providing competitive advantage on the field. Some players say that this type of thing happens all the time and it's just part of the game. Others think that this practice creates a negative culture that can undermine the integrity of the sport. How do you feel about the issue?

SOLVING THE CHALLENGE

Assume that you are the commissioner of the NFL and that you have the power to punish the Saints and Gregg Williams. What would you do?

1. I would take a stand against "bounty" programs and punish the wrongdoers. First, I would discipline Gregg Williams. This might entail a fine and a leave of absence with no pay. I also would fine the owners of the Saints for allowing this to happen. I then would continue to investigate whether or not Williams used this technique while working at other teams. If he did, these teams would be fined as well.

2. What's done is done, and there is no value in punishing people for something that happened in 2009. I would simply make a public statement calling for the end of "bounty" programs.

3. Bone-crushing contact is part of football. Players understand this reality and I see no reason to ask players to eliminate their aggression on the field. That said, I would create a new policy against such "bounty" programs. Violators would be fined.

4. Invent other options.

Source: This case was drawn from Jason Gay, "NFL's Mutiny on the Bounties," *The Wall Street Journal*, March 5, 2012, p. B10.

chapter 9

Human Resource Management

Getting the Right People for Managerial Success

How to Stand Out in a New Job: Fitting into an Organization in the First 60 Days

"Once you are in the real world—and it doesn't make any difference if you are 22 or 62, starting your first job or your fifth," say former *BusinessWeek* columnists Jack and Suzy Welch, "the way to look great and get ahead is to overdeliver."[1]

Overdelivering means doing more than what is asked of you—not just doing the report your boss requests, for example, but doing the extra research to provide him or her with something truly impressive.

Among things you should do in the first 60 days:[2]

Be Aware of the Power of First Impressions

Within three minutes of meeting someone new, people form an opinion about where the future of the relationship is headed, according to one study.[3] "When meeting someone for the first time, concentrate on one thing: your energy level," says Roger Ailes, CEO of Fox News, who thinks that seven seconds is all the time people need to start making up their minds about you. Amp it up, he advises. "If you don't demonstrate energetic attitude on your first day, you're already screwing up."[4] (Note: Don't be too upset if you feel you've blown it with someone on the first meeting. What's key, research shows, is to make sure you have other chances to meet that person again so that you can show different sides of yourself.)[5]

Come in 30 Minutes Early & Stay a Little Late to See How People Behave

"Many aspects of a company's culture can be subtle and easy to overlook," writes one expert. "Instead, observe everything."

Thus, try coming in early and staying a little late just to observe how people operate—where they take their lunches, for example.

Get to Know Some People & Listen to What They Have to Say

"You've got to realize that networking inside a company is just as important as when you were networking on the outside trying to get in," says one business consultant.[6] During the first two weeks, get to know a few people and try to have lunch with them. Find out how the organization works, how people interact with the boss, what the corporate culture encourages and discourages. Walk the halls and get to know receptionists, mail room clerks, and office managers, who can help you learn the ropes. Your role here is to listen, rather than to slather on the charm. Realize that you have a lot to learn.[7]

Make It Easy for Others to Give You Feedback

Ask your boss, coworkers, and subordinates to give you feedback about how you're doing. Be prepared to take unpleasant news gracefully.[8] At the end of 30 days, have a "How am I doing?" meeting with your boss.

Overdeliver

Because performance reviews for new hires generally take place at 60 to 90 days, you need to have accomplished enough—and preferably something big—to show your boss your potential. In other words, do as the Welches suggest: overdeliver.

For Discussion How does the foregoing advice square with your past experiences in starting a new job? Are there things you wish you could have done differently?

forecast | What's Ahead in This Chapter

This chapter considers human resource (HR) management—planning for, attracting, developing, and retaining an effective workforce. We consider how this subject fits in with the overall company strategy, the legal requirements of HR management, how to evaluate current and future employee needs, and how to recruit and select qualified people. We discuss orientation, training, and development and how to assess employee performance and give feedback. We consider how to manage compensation and benefits, promotions and discipline, and workplace performance problems. Finally, we consider the role of labor unions.

How do effective managers view the role of people in their organization's success?

THE BIG PICTURE

Human resource management consists of the activities managers perform to plan for, attract, develop, and retain an effective workforce. Planning the human resources needed consists of understanding current employee needs and predicting future employee needs.

How do you get hired by one of the companies on *Fortune* magazine's annual "100 Best Companies to Work For" list—companies such as Google, Boston Consulting Group, SAS Institute, and Wegmans Food Markets, which are on the 2012 list?[9] You try to get to know someone in the company, suggests one guide. You play up volunteer work on your résumé. You get ready to interview and interview and interview. And you do extensive research on the company (far more than just online research, as by talking to customers).[10]

And what kinds of things does an employee of a Fortune "Best" company get? At Google, the Mountain View, California, search engine company (ranked No. 1 in 2007, 2008, and 2012 and No. 4 in 2009, 2010, and 2011), you're entitled to eat in 1 of 11 free gourmet cafeterias, as well as to visit free snack rooms that contain various cereals, candy, nuts, fresh fruit, and other snacks. You can bring your dog to work, get haircuts on-site, work out at the gym, and attend subsidized exercise classes. You can study Mandarin or other languages, have your laundry done free, or consult five on-site doctors for a checkup, free of charge. The company has also launched numerous compensation incentives, special bonuses, and founders' awards that can run into millions of dollars.[11]

The reason for this exceptional treatment? "Happy people are more productive," says former CEO Eric Schmidt.[12] That productivity has made Google an earnings powerhouse; in 2011, for example, it reported a 29% growth in revenue and 31% profits.[13] Google has discovered, in other words, that its biggest competitive advantage lies in its human resources—its *people.*

Human Resource Management: Managing an Organization's Most Important Resource

***Human resource (HR) management* consists of the activities managers perform to plan for, attract, develop, and retain an effective workforce.** Whether it's McKenzie looking for entry-level business consultants, the U.S. Navy trying to fill its ranks, or churches trying to reverse the declining number of priests and ministers, all organizations must deal with staffing.

The fact that the old Personnel Department is now called the Human Resources Department is not just a cosmetic change. It is intended to suggest the importance of staffing to a company's success. Although talking about people as "resources" might seem to downgrade them to the same level as financial resources and material resources, in fact, people are an organization's most important resource. Indeed, companies ranked No. 1 on *Fortune* magazine's Best Companies list—which, besides Google, include software developer SAS (2011 and 2010), data storage company NetApp (2009), biotechnology firm Genentech (2006), supermarket chain Wegmans Food Markets (2005), jam maker J. M. Smucker (2004), stockbroker Edward Jones (2003 and 2002), and box retailer The Container Store (2001 and 2000)—have discovered that putting employees first has been the foundation for their success. "If you're not thinking all the time about making every person valuable, you don't have a chance," says former General Electric head Jack Welch. "What's the alternative? Wasted minds? Uninvolved people? A labor force that's angry or bored? That doesn't make sense!"[14]

Human Resources as Part of Strategic Planning   At many companies, human resources has become part of the strategic planning process. Thus, HR departments deal not only with employee paperwork and legal accountability—a very important area, as we describe in Section 9.2—but also with helping to support the organization's overall strategy.

For example, is it important, as Wegmans's owners think, to have loyal, innovative, smart, passionate employees who will give their best to promote customer satisfaction (the grocery chain's mission)? Who, then, should be recruited? How should they be trained? What's the best way to evaluate and reward their performance? The answers to these questions should be consistent with the firm's strategic mission. The purpose of the strategic human resource process, then—shown in the yellow-orange shaded boxes at right—is to get the optimal work performance that will help the company's mission and goals.[15] *(See Figure 9.1.)*

Three concepts important in this view of human resource management are *human capital, knowledge workers,* and *social capital.*

Human Capital: Potential of Employee Knowledge & Actions   "We are living in a time," says one team of human resource management authors, "when a new economic paradigm—characterized by speed, innovation, short cycle times, quality, and customer satisfaction—is highlighting the importance of intangible assets, such as brand recognition, knowledge, innovation, and particularly human capital."[16] **Human capital is the economic or productive potential of employee knowledge, experience, and actions.**[17]

Thinking about people as human capital has an obvious basis: "Attracting, retaining, and developing great people is sometimes the only way our organizations can keep up with the competition across the street or around the globe," says Susan Meisinger, president and CEO of the Society for Human Resource Management. "Research has shown that highly educated, knowledgeable workers—*the most in demand*—are the hardest to find and easiest to lose."[18]

Knowledge Workers: Potential of Brain Workers   A *knowledge worker* is **someone whose occupation is principally concerned with generating or interpreting information, as opposed to manual labor.** Knowledge workers add value to the organization by using their brains rather than the sweat of their brows, and as such they are the most common type of worker in 21st-century organizations. Because of globalization and information technology, the United States no longer has an advantage in knowledge workers. Indeed, because of the advancement of China, India, Russia, and Brazil; the offshoring of sophisticated jobs; the decrease in math and science skills among today's younger Americans; and other factors, the United States may be in danger of slipping behind.

Social Capital: Potential of Strong & Cooperative Relationships   *Social capital* is the economic or productive potential of strong, trusting, and cooperative relationships. Among aspects of social capital are goodwill, mutual respect, cooperation, trust, and teamwork. Relationships within a company are important: In one survey, 77% of the women and 63% of the men rated "good relationship with boss" extremely important, outranking such matters as good equipment, easy commute, and flexible hours.[19]

That relationships matter is shown by the brothers running family-owned J. M. Smucker, who follow a simple code of conduct set forth by their father: "Listen with your full attention, look for the good in others, have a sense of humor, and say thank you for a job well done."[20] (The company's voluntary employee turnover rate is a mere 3%.)

Planning the Human Resources Needed

When a building contractor, looking to hire someone for a few hours to dig ditches, drives by a group of idle day laborers standing on a street corner, is that a form of HR planning? Certainly it shows the contractor's awareness that a pool of laborers usually can be found

figure 9.1

THE STRATEGIC HUMAN RESOURCE MANAGEMENT PROCESS

Establish the mission & the vision

↓

Establish the grand strategy

↓

Formulate the strategic plans

↓

Plan human resources needed

↓

Recruit & select people

↓

Orient, train, & develop

↓

Perform appraisals of people

↓

Purpose: Get optimal work performance to help realize company's mission & vision

in that spot. But what if the builder needs a lot of people with specialized training—to give him or her the competitive advantage that the strategic planning process demands?

Here we are concerned with something more than simply hiring people on an "as needed" basis. ***Strategic human resource planning consists of developing a systematic, comprehensive strategy for (a) understanding current employee needs and (b) predicting future employee needs.*** Let's consider these two parts.

Understanding Current Employee Needs   To plan for the future, you must understand the present—what today's staffing picture looks like. This requires that you (or a trained specialist) first do a *job analysis* and from that write a *job description* and a *job specification.*[21]

- **Job analysis.** The purpose of ***job analysis* is to determine, by observation and analysis, the basic elements of a job.** Specialists who do this interview job occupants about what they do, observe the flow of work, and learn how results are accomplished. For example, package deliverer UPS has specialists who ride with the couriers and time how long it takes to deliver a load of packages and note problems encountered (traffic jams, vicious dogs, recipients not home, and so on).

- **Job description and job specification.** Once the fundamentals of a job are understood, then you can write a ***job description,* which summarizes what the holder of the job does and how and why he or she does it.** Next you can write a ***job specification,* which describes the minimum qualifications a person must have to perform the job successfully.**

This process can produce some surprises. Jobs that might seem to require a college degree, for example, might not after all. Thus, the process of writing job analyses, descriptions, and specifications can help you avoid hiring people who are overqualified (and presumably more expensive) or underqualified (and thus not as productive) for a particular job.

In addition, by entering a job description and specification with their attendant characteristics into a database, an organization can do computer searching for candidates by matching keywords (nouns) on their résumés with the keywords describing the job. A position in desktop publishing, for instance, might be described by the kinds

Big Brown. A UPS driver's problems of driving in a big city—traffic, double parking, addressees not at home—are different from those of driving in rural areas, where there may be long stretches of boredom. Specialists in job analysis can interview drivers about their problems in order to write job descriptions that allow for varying circumstances.

of software programs with which applicants should be familiar: Adobe FrameMaker, Adobe InDesign, Adobe PageMaker, Corel Ventura, QuarkXPress, and so on.

Predicting Future Employee Needs Job descriptions change, of course: auto mechanics, for instance, now have to know how computer chips work in cars. (A C-class Mercedes may have 153 processors on board.) And new jobs are created: Who could have visualized the position of "e-commerce accountant" 10 years ago, for example?

As you might expect, predicting future employee needs means you have to become knowledgeable about the *staffing the organization might need* and the *likely sources for that staffing:*

- **The staffing the organization might need.** You could assume your organization won't change much. In that case, you can fairly easily predict that jobs will periodically become unoccupied (because of retirement, resignations, and so on) and that you'll need to pay the same salaries and meet the same criteria about minority hiring to fill them.

    Better, however, to assume the organization will change. Thus, you need to understand the organization's vision and strategic plan so that the proper people can be hired to meet the future strategies and work. We discussed strategic plans in Chapter 6.

- **The likely sources for staffing.** You can recruit employees from either inside or outside the organization. In looking at those inside, you need to consider which employees are motivated, trainable, and promotable and what kind of training your organization might have to do. A device for organizing this kind of information is a ***human resource inventory,*** **a report listing your organization's employees by name, education, training, languages, and other important information.**

    In looking outside, you need to consider the availability of talent in your industry's and geographical area's labor pool, the training of people graduating from various schools, and such factors as what kind of people are moving into your area. The U.S. Bureau of Labor Statistics and the U.S. Census Bureau issue reports on such matters. ●

One way to attract potential employees. One of the first places companies—37%, in a 2012 CareerBuilder study—are apt to look for potential employees is online, such as the social networking sites Facebook and LinkedIn, as well as Twitter. (And sometimes they're looking for reasons *not* to hire a candidate.) Creative users also post unusual digital résumés featuring eye-catching graphics, YouTube videos, and PowerPoint slides on Pinterest, the popular online pin board for photos. As for job seekers, they can find useful job-hunting apps on Monster.com. Are you up to speed on these job-hunting advantages?

major question

To avoid exposure to legal liabilities, what areas of the law do I need to be aware of?

THE BIG PICTURE

Four areas of human resource law any manager needs to be aware of are labor relations, compensation and benefits, health and safety, and equal employment opportunity.

Whatever your organization's human resource strategy, in the United States (and in U.S. divisions overseas) it has to operate within the environment of American law. Four areas you need to be aware of are as follows. Some important laws are summarized in the table opposite. *(See Table 9.1.)*

1. Labor Relations

The earliest laws affecting employee welfare had to do with unions, and they can still have important effects. Legislation passed in 1935 (the Wagner Act) resulted in the ***National Labor Relations Board,* which enforces procedures whereby employees may vote to have a union and for collective bargaining. *Collective bargaining* consists of negotiations between management and employees about disputes over compensation, benefits, working conditions, and job security.**

A 1947 law (the Taft-Hartley Act) allows the president of the United States to prevent or end a strike that threatens national security. (We discuss labor-management issues further in Section 9.8.)

2. Compensation & Benefits

The Social Security Act in 1935 established the U.S. retirement system. The passage of the ***Fair Labor Standards Act* of 1938 established minimum living standards for workers engaged in interstate commerce, including provision of a federal minimum wage** (currently $7.25 an hour; several states have higher minimums) and a maximum workweek (now 40 hours, after which overtime must be paid), along with banning products from child labor.[22] Salaried executive, administrative, and professional employees are exempt from overtime rules.

3. Health & Safety

From miners risking tunnel cave-ins to cotton mill workers breathing lint, industry has always had dirty, dangerous jobs. Beginning with the Occupational Safety and Health Act (OSHA) of 1970, a body of law has grown that requires organizations to provide employees with nonhazardous working conditions. Later laws extended health coverage, including 2010 health care reform legislation, which requires employers with more than 50 employees to provide health insurance.[23]

4. Equal Employment Opportunity

The effort to reduce discrimination in employment based on racial, ethnic, and religious bigotry and gender stereotypes began with Title VII of the Civil Rights Act of

table 9.1

SOME IMPORTANT RECENT U.S. FEDERAL LAWS & REGULATIONS PROTECTING EMPLOYEES

Year	Law or Regulation	Provisions
Labor relations		
1974	Privacy Act	Gives employees legal right to examine letters of reference concerning them
1986	Immigration Reform & Control Act	Requires employers to verify the eligibility for employment of all their new hires (including U.S. citizens)
2003	Sarbanes-Oxley Act	Prohibits employers from demoting or firing employees who raise accusations of fraud to a federal agency
Compensation and benefits		
1974	Employee Retirement Income Security Act (ERISA)	Sets rules for managing pension plans; provides federal insurance to cover bankrupt plans
1993	Family & Medical Leave Act	Requires employers to provide 12 weeks of unpaid leave for medical and family reasons, including for childbirth, adoption, or family emergency
1996	Health Insurance Portability & Accountability Act (HIPAA)	Allows employees to switch health insurance plans when changing jobs and receive new coverage regardless of preexisting health conditions; prohibits group plans from dropping ill employees
2007	Fair Minimum Wage Act	Increased federal minimum wage to $7.25 per hour on July 24, 2009
Health and safety		
1970	Occupational Safety & Health Act (OSHA)	Establishes minimum health and safety standards in organizations
1985	Consolidated Omnibus Budget Reconciliation Act (COBRA)	Requires an extension of health insurance benefits after termination
2010	Patient Protection & Affordable Care Act	Employers with more than 50 employees must provide health insurance
Equal employment opportunity		
1963	Equal Pay Act	Requires men and women be paid equally for performing equal work
1964, amended 1972	Civil Rights Act, Title VII	Prohibits discrimination on basis of race, color, religion, national origin, or sex
1967, amended 1978 and 1986	Age Discrimination in Employment Act (ADEA)	Prohibits discrimination in employees over 40 years old; restricts mandatory retirement
1990	Americans with Disabilities Act (ADA)	Prohibits discrimination against essentially qualified employees with physical or mental disabilities or chronic illness; requires "reasonable accommodation" be provided so they can perform duties
1991	Civil Rights Act	Amends and clarifies Title VII, ADA, and other laws; permits suits against employers for punitive damages in cases of intentional discrimination

1964. This established the ***Equal Employment Opportunity (EEO) Commission, whose job it is to enforce antidiscrimination and other employment-related laws.*** Title VII applies to all organizations or their agents engaged in an industry affecting interstate commerce that employs 15 or more employees. Contractors who wish to do business with the U.S. government (such as most colleges and universities, which receive federal funds) must be in compliance with various executive orders issued by the president covering antidiscrimination. Later laws prevented discrimination against older workers and people with physical and mental disabilities.[24]

Three important concepts covered by EEO laws are *workplace discrimination, affirmative action,* and *sexual harassment.*

Workplace Discrimination   A large gap exists in perceptions between the sexes as to whether men or women have more opportunities for advancement. In a survey of 1,834 business professionals worldwide, 66% of men said opportunities to move to top management were gender neutral, compared with 30% of women.[25] (In actuality, only 3% of CEOs and 13.5% of executive-officer positions in Fortune 500 companies are occupied by women.)

***Workplace discrimination* occurs when people are hired or promoted—or denied hiring or promotion—for reasons not relevant to the job,** such as skin color or eye shape, gender, religion, national origin, and the like. (Recently, employment discrimination based on gender identity was also banned in federal jobs.)[26] Two fine points to be made here are that (1) although the law prohibits discrimination in all aspects of employment, it does not require an employer to extend *preferential treatment* because of race, color, religion, and so on; and (2) employment decisions must be made on the basis of job-related criteria.

There are two types of workplace discrimination:

- ***Adverse impact: Adverse impact* occurs when an organization uses an employment practice or procedure that results in unfavorable outcomes to a protected class (such as Hispanics) over another group of people (such as non-Hispanic whites).** For example, requiring workers to have a college degree can inadvertently create adverse impact against Hispanics because fewer Hispanics graduate from college than non-Hispanic whites. This example would not be a problem, however, if a college degree was required to perform the job.

- ***Disparate treatment: Disparate treatment* results when employees from protected groups (such as disabled individuals) are intentionally treated differently.** An example would be making a decision to give all international assignments to people with no disabilities because of the assumption that they won't need any special accommodations related to travel.

When an organization is found to have been practicing discrimination, the people discriminated against may sue for back pay and punitive damages. In 2011, such complaints rose to an all-time high, led by an increase in bias charges based on religion and national origin.[27] Charges to the Equal Employment Opportunity Commission (EEOC) of discrimination based on religion increased by 9.5% and those based on ancestry or national origin by 5%. Allegations of age discrimination were also up, by 1%, and claims of disability bias rose by 2%. Pregnancy bias complaints to the EEOC increased 35% in the last decade.[28]

The good news is that sexual discrimination claims fell by 2%. In recent years, pay discrepancies between women and men improved slightly, but as of 2010 women overall still earned only 77 cents to every $1 for a man.[29] (In some sectors, such as financial services, women earn as little as 65 cents to a man's dollar.)[30]

Affirmative Action *Affirmative action* **focuses on achieving equality of opportunity within an organization.** It tries to make up for past discrimination in employment by actively finding, hiring, and developing the talents of people from groups traditionally discriminated against. Steps include active recruitment, elimination of prejudicial questions in interviews, and establishment of minority hiring goals. It's important to note that EEO laws *do not* allow use of hiring quotas.[31]

Affirmative action has created tremendous opportunities for women and minorities, but it has been resisted more by some white males who see it as working against their interests.[32] Affirmative action plans are more successful when employees view them as being fair and equitable and when whites are not prejudiced against people of color.[33] In addition, research shows that women and minorities hired on the basis of affirmative action felt stigmatized as unqualified and incompetent and experienced lower job satisfaction and more stress than employees supposedly selected on the basis of merit.[34]

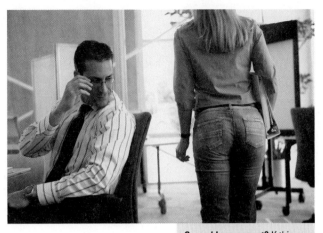

Sexual harassment? If this woman is unaware of the man men ogling her legs, does that make his behavior acceptable? Or does it still contribute to an offensive work environment?

Sexual Harassment *Sexual harassment* **consists of unwanted sexual attention that creates an adverse work environment.** This means obscene gestures, sex-stereotyped jokes, sexually oriented posters and graffiti, suggestive remarks, unwanted dating pressure, physical nonsexual contact, unwanted touching, sexual propositions, threatening punishment unless sexual favors are given, obscene phone calls, and similar verbal or physical actions of a sexual nature.[35] The harassment may be by a member of the opposite sex or a member of the same sex, by a manager, by a coworker, or by an outsider.[36] If the harasser is a manager or an agent of the organization, the organization itself can be sued, even if it had no knowledge of the situation.[37] According to the EEOC, the number of sexual harassment claims has decreased from 15,889 claims in 1997 to 11,364 in 2011.[38]

Two Types of Sexual Harassment. There are two types of sexual harassment, both of which violate Title VII of the 1964 Civil Rights Act. In the *quid pro quo harassment* type, the person to whom the unwanted sexual attention is directed is put in the position of jeopardizing being hired for a job or obtaining job benefits or opportunities unless he or she implicitly or explicitly acquiesces. More typical is the *hostile environment* type, in which the person being sexually harassed doesn't risk economic harm but experiences an offensive or intimidating work environment. According to one survey, 38% of women said they heard sexual innuendo, wisecracks, or taunts at the office.[39] Another growing problem is bullying on the job, experienced by 37% of workers, male as well as female.[40]

The table at right presents some guidelines for preventing sexual harassment. *(See Table 9.2.)*

What Managers Can Do. To help prevent harassment from occurring, managers can make sure their companies have an effective sexual harassment policy in place. All current and new employees should understand that sexual harassment will not be tolerated under any circumstances. A formal complaint procedure should establish how charges will be investigated and resolved. Supervisors should be trained in Title VII requirements and the proper procedures to follow when charges occur. Charges should be investigated promptly and objectively, and an offender should be disciplined at once—no matter what his or her rank in the company.[41] ●

table 9.2

GUIDELINES FOR PREVENTING SEXUAL HARASSMENT

- Don't suggest sexual favors for rewards related to work or promotion.

- Don't do uninvited touching, patting, or hugging of others' bodies—especially if they wince, frown, or pull away.

- Don't make sexually suggestive jokes, demeaning remarks, slurs, or obscene gestures or sounds.

- Don't display sexual pictures in your workplace or write notes of a sexual nature.

- Don't laugh at others' sexually harassing words or behaviors.

major question?

How can I reduce mistakes in hiring and find great people who might work for me?

THE BIG PICTURE

Qualified applicants for jobs may be recruited from inside or outside the organization. The task of choosing the best person is enhanced by such tools as reviewing candidates' application forms, résumés, and references; doing interviews, either structured or unstructured; and screening with ability, personality, performance, and other kinds of employment tests.

"Hiring great people is brutally hard," write Jack and Suzy Welch. "New managers are lucky to get it right half the time. And even executives with decades of experience will tell you that they make the right calls 75% of the time at best."[42]

However difficult it may be, it's important to try to get hiring right. "We're essentially in an innovation economy where good people come up with really good ideas," says one CEO. "Companies want to hit home runs with the next greatest product, and the imperative is making sure you have great people to do that."[43]

Recruitment: How to Attract Qualified Applicants

At some time nearly every organization has to think about how to find the right kind of people. **Recruiting is the process of locating and attracting qualified applicants for jobs open in the organization.** The word *qualified* is important: You want to find people whose skills, abilities, and characteristics are best suited to your organization. Recruiting is of two types: *internal* and *external*.

1. Internal Recruiting: Hiring from the Inside *Internal recruiting* means **making people already employed by the organization aware of job openings.** Indeed, most vacant positions in organizations are filled through internal recruitment, mainly through *job posting,* **placing information about job vacancies and qualifications on bulletin boards, in newsletters, and on the organization's intranet.** (Companies looking to make strategic changes do better hiring CEOs from within the ranks rather than from outside, according to a recent study.)[44]

2. External Recruiting: Hiring from the Outside *External recruiting* **means attracting job applicants from outside the organization.** In years past, notices of job vacancies were placed through newspapers, employment agencies, executive recruiting firms, union hiring halls, college job-placement offices, and word of mouth.

Today more and more companies are using social media as recruiting tools.[45] For example, experts estimate that 89% of U.S. organizations use social networks to recruit. LinkedIn, a social network with 135 million members, accounts for 73% of the people hired via social media.[46] In one survey of 3,500 U.S. college students, 80% said they use smartphones for job hunting or see themselves doing so in the future.[47]

Both internal and external methods have advantages and disadvantages, as indicated in the table on the next page. *(See Table 9.3.)*

table 9.3

INTERNAL AND EXTERNAL RECRUITING: ADVANTAGES & DISADVANTAGES

Internal Recruiting

Advantages	Disadvantages
1. Employees tend to be inspired to greater effort and loyalty. Morale is enhanced because they realize that working hard and staying put can result in more opportunities.	1. Internal recruitment restricts the competition for positions and limits the pool of fresh talent and fresh viewpoints.
2. The whole process of advertising, interviewing, and so on is cheaper.	2. It may encourage employees to assume that longevity and seniority will automatically result in promotion.
3. There are fewer risks. Internal candidates are already known and are familiar with the organization.	3. Whenever a job is filled, it creates a vacancy elsewhere in the organization.

External Recruiting

Advantages	Disadvantages
1. Applicants may have specialized knowledge and experience.	1. The recruitment process is more expensive and takes longer.
2. Applicants may have fresh viewpoints.	2. The risks are higher because the persons hired are less well known.

Which External Recruiting Methods Work Best? In general, the most effective sources are employee referrals, say human resource professionals, because, to protect their own reputations, employees are fairly careful about whom they recommend, and they know the qualifications of both the job and the prospective employee.[48] Other effective ways of finding good job candidates are e-recruitment tools, such as "dot-jobs" websites; membership directories for associations and trade groups; social networking sites; and industry-specific blogs, forums, and newsgroups.[49]

Realistic Job Previews A *realistic job preview (RJP)* **gives a candidate a picture of both positive and negative features of the job and the organization before he or she is hired.** This recruiting technique is very effective at reducing turnover within 30–90 days of employment. Many organizations, such as AT&T, Hilton, the Idaho State Police, and Assess Systems, reduced turnover and enhanced employee satisfaction by using RJPs.

Selection: How to Choose the Best Person for the Job

Whether the recruitment process turns up a handful of job applicants or thousands, now you turn to the *selection process,* **the screening of job applicants to hire the best candidate.** Essentially this becomes an exercise in *prediction:* How well will the candidate perform the job and how long will he or she stay?

Three types of selection tools are *background information, interviewing,* and *employment tests.*

I. Background Information: Application Forms, Résumés, & Reference Checks Application forms and résumés provide basic background information about job applicants, such as citizenship, education, work history, and certifications.

Unfortunately, a lot of résumé information consists of mild puffery and even outrageous fairy tales—as many as 35% of résumés, by one estimate.[50] InfoLink Screening Services, which does background checks, reported that 14% of the tens of thousands of applicants it had screened had lied about their education.[51] Vermont-based ResumeDoctor.com, a résumé-writing service, surveyed 1,133 résumés that had been uploaded to its site and found that nearly 42.7% had at least one inaccuracy and 12.6% had two or more factual errors.[52] And Background Information Services, a pre-employment screening company in Cleveland, found 56% of résumés contained falsehoods of some kind.[53] It is risky to lie about your background information because it can be used as a reason for terminating your employment.

PRACTICAL ACTION

Would You Lie Like This on Your Résumé?

What kind of lies do people put on their résumés? Consider the following examples.

Lying About Education. Lying about education is the most prevalent distortion (such as pretending to hold a degree or an advanced degree). A few years ago, RadioShack CEO David Edmondson achieved some notoriety and had to resign after a newspaper discovered he had falsely claimed on his résumé to hold degrees in psychology and theology.[54] In 2012, Yahoo CEO Scott Thompson was revealed to not have earned a college degree in computer science, as claimed on his résumé and on the company's website.[55] Automatic Data Processing of Roseland, New Jersey, which has studied employee background verification, reported that 41% of education records showed a difference between the information provided by an applicant and that provided by the educational institution.[56]

Lying About Employment Histories, Ages, Salaries, & Job Titles. Another common fabrication includes creative attempts to cover gaps in employment history (although there are straightforward ways an applicant can deal with this, such as highlighting length of service instead of employment dates).[57] People also lie about their ages for fear of seeming to be too experienced (hence

expensive) or too old.[58] As you might expect, people also embellish their salary histories, job titles, and achievements on projects.[59]

Lying About Criminal Background or Immigration Status. In 2007, it came out that the foundation that runs online encyclopedia Wikipedia had neglected to do a basic background check before hiring Carolyn Doran as its chief operating officer; she had been convicted of drunken driving and fleeing the scene of a car accident.[60] Now, more and more job seekers are seeking to legally clear their criminal records—to have their arrests or convictions expunged, when possible.[61]

In addition, as the numbers of illegal (undocumented) workers has risen, it has become incumbent on human resource officers to verify U.S. citizenship.[62] Use of E-Verify, the federal program that allows employers to quickly check the legal status of potential employees, has taken a big jump.[63] Still, perhaps half of illegal workers slip by the system.[64]

YOUR CALL

What past events are you most worried potential employers will find out about you? What can you do to put them in a better light?

Many companies are finding conventional résumés not all that useful (because they don't quantify an applicant's accomplishments or are too full of fluff descriptors such as "outstanding" or "energetic") and are increasingly relying on social networks such as LinkedIn, video profiles, or online quizzes to assess candidates.[65] Other firms are so inundated with résumés that they now have to use résumé-filtering software, causing applicants to learn to game the system by loading their résumés with keywords from the job description.[66]

References are also a problem. Many employers don't give honest assessments of former employees, for two reasons: (1) They fear that if they say anything negative, they can be sued by the former employee. (2) They fear if they say anything positive, and the job candidate doesn't pan out, they can be sued by the new employer.[67] Despite liability worries, HR recruiters know that if they get a former supervisor on the phone, they can find out a lot—such as the way he or she answers the question, "Can you enthusiastically recommend this person?" or "What were this person's strengths and weaknesses?"[68]

Many employers also like to check applicants' credit references, although there is no evidence that people with weak credit scores are apt to be unqualified or dishonest employees.[69] (Note: Prospective employers need to get written consent to run credit checks on job applicants.)[70]

PRACTICAL ACTION

Applying for a Job? Here Are Some Mistakes to Avoid

There are several mistakes that job candidates often make in initial interviews. Here are some tips.[71]

Be Prepared—Very Prepared. Can you pronounce the name of the company you're interviewing with? Of the people interviewing you? Do you understand the position you're interviewing for? The company and its competition? New products or services being offered? Your own job strengths? Your weaknesses? What do you need to improve on to move ahead?

Call the company and ask about pronunciation. Scrutinize the company's website. Read any news articles written about the firm. Determine how your strengths fit with what the prospective employer does. Prepare for when, asked about your weaknesses, how you recognized them, overcame a dilemma, and were improved by the experience. Take time to practice questions and answers so you'll sound confident.

Dress Right & Pay Attention to Your Attitude. Is the company dress code "business casual"? That doesn't mean you should dress that way (or the way you dress on campus) for the interview.

Dress professionally for the interview. Be aware of your attitude as soon as you enter the building. Be on time. (Time your commute by doing a test run a day or so before the interview, and make sure you know the exact location of the interview.) If unforeseeable circumstances arise and cause you to be late, call to inform your interviewer. Be polite to the receptionist, and greet everyone who greets you. Turn off your cellphone ringer.

Don't Get Too Personal with the Interviewer. Don't be overfriendly and share too much, especially in the initial interview. Although the interviewer will try to make you feel comfortable, you should focus on the position. Rehearse questions to ask the interviewer, such as the challenges for the position in the future. Don't make negative comments about your old company or boss. Rather, figure out the positives and convey what you learned and gained from your experience. If asked an inappropriate question (about age, marital status, whether you have children or plan to), politely state you don't believe the question is relevant to your qualifications. Be enthusiastic; enthusiasm is contagious. Incidentally, be sure to mention any organizational citizenship behavior, which scores well with interviewers.[72]

Be Aware That Your Background Will Be Checked—Including Your Social Networks. Because it seems to be getting harder to distinguish honest job applicants from dishonest ones, companies now routinely check résumés or hire companies that do so.[73] Ninety-six percent of employers conduct background checks, according to one study.[74]

And here's something to think about if you are a Facebook, YouTube, or Twitter user: employers now frequently use search engines to do continuous and stealthy background checks on prospective employees to see if they've posted any racy content. "Many job hunters," says one report, "are . . . continuing to overlook the dangers of posting provocative photos and other dubious content on social-media sites."[75] Checking your Facebook page is also a way employers can make an end run around discrimination laws.[76] Indeed, you may be asked in the interview for your Facebook user name and password so the interviewer can access your private settings—a practice whose legality is questionable but nevertheless being done by more companies.[77] (More and more people are getting savvy about privacy and pruning their friend lists and removing unwanted comments on their social networks.)[78]

2. Interviewing: Unstructured, Situational, & Behavioral-Description

The interview, which is the most commonly used employee-selection technique, may take place face to face, by videoconference, or—as is increasingly the case—via the Internet. (In-depth phone interviews of an hour or more may be on the rise, perhaps for cost reasons.[79] However, face-to-face interviews have been perceived as more fair and lead to higher job acceptance intentions than videoconferencing and telephone interviews.)[80] To help eliminate bias, interviews can be designed, conducted, and evaluated by a committee of three or more people. The most commonly used employee-selection technique, interviewing, takes three forms: unstructured interviews and two types of structured interviews.[81]

Unstructured Interview Like an ordinary conversation, an ***unstructured interview*** **involves asking probing questions to find out what the applicant is like.** There is no fixed set of questions asked of all applicants and no systematic scoring procedure. As a result, the unstructured interview has been criticized as being overly subjective and apt to be influenced by the biases of the interviewer. Equally important, it is susceptible to legal attack because some questions may infringe on non-job-related matters such as privacy, diversity, or disability.[82] However, compared with the structured interview method, the unstructured interview has been found to provide a more accurate assessment of an applicant's job-related personality traits.[83]

Structured Interview Type 1: The Situational Interview The ***structured interview*** **involves asking all applicants the same questions and comparing their responses to a standardized set of answers.**

In one type of structured interview, the ***situational interview,*** **the interviewer focuses on hypothetical situations.** Example: "What would you do if you saw two of your people arguing loudly in the work area?" The idea here is to find out if the applicant can handle difficult situations that may arise on the job.

Structured Interview Type 2: The Behavioral-Description Interview In the second type of structured interview, the ***behavioral-description interview,*** **the interviewer explores what applicants have actually done in the past.** Example: "What was the best idea you ever sold to a supervisor, teacher, peer, or subordinate?" This question (asked by the U.S. Army of college students applying for its officer training program) is designed to assess the applicant's ability to influence others.

PRACTICAL ACTION

The Right Way to Conduct an Interview

Because hiring people who later have to be let go is such an expensive proposition, companies are now putting a great deal of emphasis on effective interviewing. Although this is a subject worth exploring further, following are some minimal suggestions.[84]

Before the Interview: Define Your Needs & Review the Applicant's Résumé. Write out what skills, traits, and qualities the job requires. "Looking to hire somebody is like going to the supermarket," says one HR manager. "You need to have a list and know what you need."[85]

Look at the applicant's résumé or application form to determine relevant experience, gaps, and discrepancies.

Write Out Interview Questions. You should ask each candidate the same set of questions, so that you can compare their answers. (This helps keep you out of legal trouble, too.) In general, the questions should be designed to elicit the following types of information.

- **Does the applicant have the knowledge to do the job?** Examples: "Give an example where you came up with a creative solution." "How would you distinguish our product from competitors'?"

- **Can the applicant handle difficult situations?** Examples: "Tell me about a time when you dealt with an irate customer. How did you handle the situation and what was the outcome?"

- **Is the applicant willing to cope with the job's demands?** Examples: "How do you feel about making unpopular decisions?" "Are you willing to travel 30% of the time?"

- **Will the applicant fit in with the organization's culture?** Examples: "How would your last supervisor describe you?" "How much leeway did they give you in your previous job in charging travel expenses?"

Follow a Three-Scene Interview Scenario. The interview itself may follow a three-scene script.

- **Scene 1: The 3 minutes—small talk and "compatibility" test.** The first scene is really a "compatibility test." It takes about three minutes and consists of exchanging small talk, giving you a chance to establish rapport and judge how well the candidate makes a first impression.

   Note: As many as four out of five hiring decisions are made within the first 10 minutes of an interview, according to some research. Thus, be aware that if you are immediately impressed with a candidate, you may spend more time talking than listening—perhaps trying to sell the candidate on the job rather than screen his or her qualifications.[86]

- **Scene 2: The next 15–60 minutes—asking questions and listening to the applicant's "story."** In the next scene, you ask the questions you wrote out (and answer those the candidate directs to you). Allow the interviewee to do 70%–80% of the talking.

   Take notes to remember important points. Don't ignore your "gut feelings." Intuition plays a role in hiring decisions. (But be careful you don't react to people as stereotypes.)

- **Scene 3: The final 1 or 2 minutes—closing the interview and setting up the next steps.** In the final minute, you listen to see whether the candidate expresses interest in taking the job.

After the Interview. Write a short report making some sort of quantitative score of the candidate's qualifications. Indicate your reasons for your decision.

Check the applicant's references before inviting him or her to a second interview.

3. Employment Tests: Ability, Personality, Performance, Integrity, & Others It used to be that employment selection tests consisted of paper-and-pencil, performance, and physical-ability tests. Now, however, *employment tests* **are legally considered to consist of any procedure used in the employment selection decision process,** even application forms, interviews, and educational requirements.[87] Indeed, today applicants should expect just about anything, such as spending hours on simulated work tasks, performing role-playing exercises, or tackling a business case study.[88]

Probably the most common employment tests are the following.

Ability Tests *Ability tests* measure physical abilities, strength and stamina, mechanical ability, mental abilities, and clerical abilities. Telephone operators, for instance, need to be tested for hearing, and assembly-line workers for manual dexterity. Intelligence tests are also catching on as ways to predict future executive performance.[89] Corporate-event company Windy City Fieldhouse uses a test that measures attention to detail, asking takers to do such things as "do a count of the letter 'l' in a three-sentence paragraph to measure how carefully a respondent works," according to one account.[90]

Performance Tests   *Performance tests* or *skills tests* measure performance on actual job tasks, as when computer programmers take a test on a particular programming language such as C++ or middle managers work on a small project. Some companies have an ***assessment center*, in which management candidates participate in activities for a few days while being assessed by evaluators.**[91]

Personality Tests   *Personality tests* measure such personality traits as adjustment, energy, sociability, independence, and need for achievement. Career-assessment tests that help workers identify suitable jobs tend to be of this type.[92] One of the most famous personality tests, in existence for 65-plus years, is the 93-question Myers-Briggs Type Indicator, with about 2.5 million tests given each year throughout the world. Myers-Briggs endures, observers say, "because it does a good job of pointing up differences between people, offers individuals a revealing glimpse of themselves, and is a valuable asset in team-building, improving communication, and resolving personality-conflict."[93] However, this and other personality tests need to be interpreted with caution because of the difficulty of measuring personality characteristics and of making a legal defense if the results are challenged.[94]

EXAMPLE

Personality Tests: How a Sporting-Goods Chain Screens Job Applicants Online

More than 80% of midsize and large companies use personality and ability assessments for entry and mid-level jobs these days, according to one executive at a global human resources consulting firm.[95]

Southwest Airlines, for instance, has found the Myers-Briggs test helps build trust in developing teams.[96] Hewlett-Packard uses a personality test to see if employees are temperamentally suited to working alone at home—that is, telecommuting—and can handle limited supervision.[97] At Children's Healthcare of Atlanta, personality tests are used to find employees who will be "nice people"—those with "the qualities of being nurturing, kind, and warm-hearted," in the words of a human resources vice president.[98]

Online Personality Tests. At Finish Line, a nationwide chain of sporting-goods stores, store managers use the results of Web-based personality tests developed by Unicru, of Beaverton, Oregon, to screen applicants for jobs as retail sales clerks. Candidates may apply through Unicru's kiosks or computer phones, which are installed in the stores. One Finish Line store in Chicago screens as many as 70 applicants a week during the store's preholiday season.

Unicru's computer scores test takers according to how strongly they agree or disagree (on a four-point scale) with statements such as "You do not fake being polite" and "You love to listen to people talk about themselves." High scores on attributes such as sociability and initiative reward applicants with a "green" rating that allows them to move on to an interview with a human manager. Scores in the middle earn a "yellow," and a lesser chance of landing a job; low-scoring "reds" are out of luck.

Measurable Results. "The kinds of people who do well," says Unicru psychologist David Scarborough, "obviously have to have good self-control. They have to be patient. They have to enjoy helping people. All those characteristics are quite measurable."[99] Finish Line says that Unicru's system has reduced turnover by 24%.

YOUR CALL

There are, by some estimates, around 2,500 cognitive and personality employment tests on the market, and it's important that employers match the right test for the right purpose.[100] Moreover, tests aren't supposed to have a disparate impact on a protected class of people, such as certain racial or ethnic groups.[101] What questions would you want to ask about a personality test before you submitted yourself to it? (Note: Don't try to psych the test. You might wind up being miserable in a job that doesn't suit you.)

Integrity Tests   *Integrity tests* assess attitudes and experiences related to a person's honesty, dependability, trustworthiness, reliability, and prosocial behavior.[102] The tests are designed to identify people likely to engage in inappropriate, antisocial, or dishonest workplace behavior. Typically, integrity tests ask direct questions about past experiences related to ethics and integrity. You might be asked, for example, "What is the most you have ever stolen? (a) $0; (b) $1–$200; (c) $201–$500; (d) more than $500." Or interviewers may ask questions about preferences and interests from which inferences may be drawn about future behavior—so-called covert tests, where the answers give a sense of the person's conscientiousness, emotional maturity, and so on.[103]

Other Tests   The list of employment testing techniques has grown to include—in appropriate cases—drug testing, polygraph (lie detectors), genetic screening, and even (a questionable technique) handwriting analysis.[104] Human resource professionals need to be aware, incidentally, that there are a variety of products available on the Internet to help employees beat many kinds of drug tests.[105] Recently, however, the hair test (of hair follicles) has begun to find favor, since it's said to be able to detect a pattern of repetitive drug use over a period of up to 90 days.[106]

Reliability & Validity   Two important legal considerations about any test are its *reliability* and its *validity.*

- *Reliability—does it happen consistently? Reliability* **is the degree to which a test measures the same thing consistently**—so that an individual's score remains about the same over time, assuming the characteristics being measured also remain the same.

- *Validity—is it bias-free? Validity* **means the test measures what it purports to measure and is free of bias.** If a test is supposed to predict performance, then the individual's actual performance should reflect his or her score on the test. Using an invalid test to hire people can lead to poor selection decisions. It can also create legal problems if the test is ever challenged in a court of law. ●

Lie detectors. Defense contractors and other security-minded companies are apt to require polygraph testing. Would you object to taking such a test? What about drug tests? Tests for illegal substances may be requested of you after you've been offered a job, but failure can be grounds for dismissal. Some substances, such as marijuana and steroids, are detectable in the body even 30 days after last use.

major question? Once people are hired, what's the best way to see that they do what they're supposed to do?

THE BIG PICTURE

Three ways newcomers are helped to perform their jobs are through *orientation,* to fit them into the job and organization; *training,* to upgrade the skills of technical and operational employees; and *development,* to upgrade the skills of professionals and managers.

In muckraker Upton Sinclair's 1906 novel *The Jungle,* "employers barely paused when a worker swooned from overwork or fell into a rendering tank," writes columnist Sue Shellenbarger. "They just got another warm body to replace him."[107]

That's hardly the case anymore. Before the long recent economic downturn, when a hire was made, companies often resorted to what is known as "onboarding," rolling out a welcome by assigning "buddies," providing detailed orientations, even sending goody baskets, so as to bring rookies up to speed quickly and give them a fast introduction to company culture.[108]

Then and now, this is because, as we said, the emphasis is on "human capital." Only a third to half of most companies' stock-market value is accounted for by hard assets such as property, plant, and equipment, according to a Brookings Institution report. Most of a firm's value is in such attributes as patents, processes, and—important to this discussion—employee or customer satisfaction.[109] The means for helping employees perform their jobs are *orientation, training,* and *development.*

Orientation: Helping Newcomers Learn the Ropes

The finalist candidate is offered the job, has accepted it, and has started work. Now he or she must begin, in that old sailor's phrase, to "learn the ropes." This is the start of **_orientation,_ helping the newcomer fit smoothly into the job and the organization.**

Helping New Employees Get Comfortable: The First Six Months
"How well will I get along with other employees?" "What if I screw up on a project?" Coming into a new job can produce a lot of uncertainty and anxiety. In part this is because, depending on the job, a new hire can accomplish only 60% as much in the first three months as an experienced worker.[110]

The first six months on a job can be critical to how one performs over the long haul, because that's when the psychological patterns are established. Thus, employers have discovered that it's far better to give newcomers a helping hand than to let them learn possibly inappropriate behavior that will be hard to undo later.[111]

The Desirable Characteristics of Orientation
Like orientation week for new college students, the initial socialization period is designed to give new employees the information they need to be effective. In a large organization, orientation may be a formal, established process. In a small organization, it may be so informal that employees find themselves having to make most of the effort themselves.

Group training. In large companies, orientation and ongoing training are often conducted in group sessions led by a presenter while the employees follow along. Do you see any problems with this approach?

Following orientation, the employee should emerge with information about three matters (much of which he or she may have acquired during the job-application process):

- **The job routine.** At minimum, the new employee needs to have learned what is required in the job for which he or she was hired, how the work will be evaluated, and who the immediate coworkers and managers are. This is basic.

- **The organization's mission and operations.** Certainly all managers need to know what the organization is about—its purpose, products or services, operations, and history. And it's now understood that low-level employees perform better if they, too, have this knowledge.

- **The organization's work rules and employee benefits.** A public utility's HR department may have a brochure explaining formalized work rules, overtime requirements, grievance procedures, and elaborate employee benefits. A technology startup may be so fluid that many of these matters will have not been established yet. Even so, there are matters of law (such as those pertaining to sexual harassment) affecting work operations that every employee should be made aware of.

Training & Development: Helping People Perform Better

Which business strategy offers the highest returns: (1) downsizing; (2) total quality management, which focuses on work methods and process control; or (3) employee involvement, which focuses on upgrading workers' skills and knowledge? According to a study of 216 big firms, the winner is *employee involvement,* which had an average return on investment of 19.1% (versus 15.4% for downsizing and 15% for TQM).[112]

In hiring, you always try to get people whose qualifications match the requirements of the job. Quite often, however, there are gaps in what new employees need to know. These gaps are filled by training. The training process involves five steps, as shown below. *(See Figure 9.2.)*

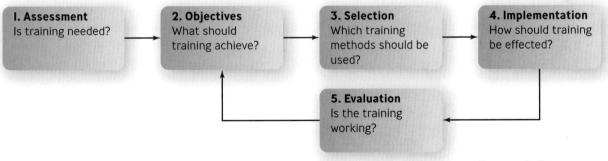

figure 9.2

FIVE STEPS IN THE TRAINING PROCESS

HR professionals distinguish between *training* and *development.*

- **Training—upgrading skills of technical and operational employees.** Electronics technicians, data processors, computer network administrators, and X-ray technicians, among many others, need to be schooled in new knowledge as the requirements of their fields change. *Training,* **then, refers to educating technical and operational employees in how to better do their current jobs.**

- **Development—upgrading skills of professionals and managers.** Accountants, nurses, lawyers, and managers of all levels need to be continually educated in how to do their jobs better not just today but also tomorrow. *Development* **refers to educating professionals and managers in the skills they need to do their jobs in the future.**

Typical areas for which employee training and development are given are customer service, safety, leadership, computer skills, quality initiatives, communications, human relations, ethics, diversity, and sexual harassment.[113]

The Different Types of Training or Development   There are all kinds of training and development methods, and their effectiveness depends on whether what is being taught are facts or skills. If people are to learn *facts*—such as work rules or legal matters—lectures, videotapes, and workbooks are effective. If people are to learn *skills*—such as improving interpersonal relations or using new tools—then techniques such as discussion, role-playing, and practice work better.

Another way to categorize training methods is to distinguish on-the-job from off-the-job methods.

- **On-the-job training.** This training takes place in the work setting while employees are performing job-related tasks. Four major training methods are coaching, training positions, job rotation, and planned work activities.

- **Off-the-job training.** This training consists of classroom programs, videotapes, workbooks, and the like. Lots of off-the-job training consists of **computer-assisted instruction (CAI), in which computers are used to provide additional help or to reduce instructional time.**

EXAMPLE

Off-the-Job Training: Getting Ahead Through E-Learning?

College students, of course, have already discovered e-learning (electronic learning). Several million other people are also taking short-term, practical courses related to their careers, mostly at business schools and continuing-education institutions around the country.

The Surge in Virtual Learning. Outside of education, in other U.S. organizations, e-learning has also become a well-established fact. Although instructor-led classrooms are still the dominant training method, at 65% of total student hours, online self-study e-learning and virtual classrooms made up 30%.[114] The benefits of e-learning, of course, are that no transportation is needed and you can follow a flexible schedule and often work at your own pace.[115]

However, there are some drawbacks. "The one thing e-learning boosters don't want to talk about is the simple fact that very few people ever actually finish an e-learning course when it involves a technically complex or lengthy subject such as software training or programming," says corporate trainer Roland Van Liew. "People perform the complex process of assimilating information best in socially interactive environments."[116]

What About Student-Teacher Interaction? Because of the lack of classroom interaction between students and teachers in online education, both must assume more responsibility. "If students do not receive adequate teacher feedback and reinforcement," points out one writer, "they will not always know whether they possess an accurate knowledge of the subject matter."[117]

Off-the-job training. How does receiving feedback from an instructor affect your retention of knowledge?

YOUR CALL

Neuroscientists are finding out that the human brain is a "social animal" that needs interaction with others.[118] How do you think this fact relates to e-learning? Do you think you learn better in a classroom rather than online?

What If No One Shows Up?   Many employers offer employee training, whether internal or external, or funding to attend seminars. But research has shown that a surprisingly high percentage of employees simply don't know about it. For instance, while 92% of employers in one survey offered funding to attend seminars and trade shows, only 28% of employees were aware the funding existed.[119] Clearly, then, employers need to find out whether the training offered fits with the majority of employee development goals.   ●

9.5 PERFORMANCE APPRAISAL

How can I assess employees' performance more accurately and give more effective feedback?

major question?

THE BIG PICTURE
Performance appraisal, assessing employee performance and providing them feedback, may be objective or subjective. Appraisals may be by peers, subordinates, customers, or oneself. Feedback may be formal or informal.

If you're a member of Gen Y or the Millennial Generation (born after 1980), you tend to want "frequent and candid performance feedback," according to one survey, and having your managers provide "detailed guidance in daily work" is very important to you.[120] Feedback about how you're doing at work is part of *performance appraisal,* **which consists of (1) assessing an employee's performance and (2) providing him or her with feedback.**

Many performance reviews are worthless, says UCLA management professor Samuel Culbert, coauthor of *Get Rid of the Performance Review!*[121] This is because evaluations are often dictated by a date on the calendar rather than need and are "one-sided, boss-dominated" assessments that come down to whether your superior "likes" you.[122] A recent worldwide survey of 1,300 workers also revealed that 7 in 10 people believed that their managers did not remain calm and constructive when discussing performance. This is why 20% of the respondents dreaded having difficult conversations with their boss.[123] It thus is no surprise that some firms (about 1%) have scrapped the practice altogether.[124]

Two Kinds of Performance Appraisal: Objective & Subjective

Clearly, performance appraisals need to be fair and accurate not just because it's right but also because it's essential to effective *performance management,* **the continuous cycle of improving job performance through goal setting, feedback and coaching, and rewards and positive reinforcement.** The purpose of performance management is to focus employees on attaining goals that are tied to the organization's strategic goals and vision, and to evaluate how successful they were in accomplishing those goals.

Appraisals are of two general types—objective and subjective.

1. Objective Appraisals *Objective appraisals,* **also called** *results appraisals,* **are based on facts and are often numerical.** In these kinds of appraisals, you would keep track of such matters as the numbers of products the employee sold in a month, customer complaints filed against an employee, miles of freight hauled, and the like.

There are two good reasons for having objective appraisals:

- **They measure results.** It doesn't matter if two appliance salespeople have completely different personal traits (one is formal, reserved, and patient; the other informal, gregarious, and impatient) if each sells the same number of washers and dryers. Human resource professionals point out that, just as in business we measure sales, profits, shareholder value, and other so-called metrics, it is likewise important to measure employee performance, benefit costs, and the like as an aid to strategy.[125]

"Here's the deal ..." One of the most important tasks of being a manager is giving employees accurate information about their work performance. Which would you be more comfortable giving—objective appraisals or subjective appraisals?

- **They are harder to challenge legally.** Not being as subject to personal bias, objective appraisals are harder for employees to challenge on legal grounds, such as for age, gender, or racial discrimination.

We discussed an objective approach in Chapter 5 under *management by objectives,* which can encourage employees to feel empowered to adopt behavior that will produce specific results. MBO, you'll recall, is a four-step process in which (1) managers and employees jointly set objectives for the employee, (2) managers develop action plans, (3) managers and employees periodically review the employee's performance, and (4) the manager makes a performance appraisal and rewards the employee according to results. For example, an objective for a copier service technician might be to increase the number of service calls 15% during the next three months.

2. Subjective Appraisals Few employees can be adequately measured just by objective appraisals—hence the need for ***subjective appraisals,* which are based on a manager's perceptions of an employee's (1) traits or (2) behaviors.**

- **Trait appraisals.** *Trait appraisals* are ratings of such subjective attributes as "attitude," "initiative," and "leadership." Trait evaluations may be easy to create and use, but their validity is questionable because the evaluator's personal bias can affect the ratings.

- **Behavioral appraisals.** Behavioral appraisals measure specific, observable aspects of performance—being on time for work, for instance—although making the evaluation is still somewhat subjective. An example is the ***behaviorally anchored rating scale (BARS),* which rates employee gradations in performance according to scales of specific behaviors.** For example, a five-point BARS rating scale about attendance might go from "Always early for work and has equipment ready to fully assume duties" to "Frequently late and often does not have equipment ready for going to work," with gradations in between.

Who Should Make Performance Appraisals?

If one of your employees was putting on a good show of solving problems that, it turned out, she had actually *created* herself so that she could be an "office hero" and look good, how would you know about it? (This phenomenon has been dubbed "Munchausen at work" because it resembles the rare psychological disorder in which sufferers seek attention by making up an illness.)[126] Most performance appraisals are done by managers; however, to add different perspectives, sometimes appraisal information is provided by other people knowledgeable about particular employees.

Peers, Subordinates, Customers, & Self Among additional sources of information are coworkers and subordinates, customers and clients, and the employees themselves.

- **Peers and subordinates.** Coworkers, colleagues, and subordinates may well see different aspects of your performance. Such information can be useful for development, although it probably shouldn't be used for evaluation. (Many managers will resist soliciting such information about themselves, of course, fearing negative appraisals.)

- **Customers and clients.** Some organizations, such as restaurants and hotels, ask customers and clients for their appraisals of employees. Publishers ask authors to judge how well they are doing in handling the editing, production, and marketing of their books. Automobile dealerships may send follow-up questionnaires to car buyers.

- **Self-appraisals.** How would you rate your own performance in a job, knowing that it would go into your personnel file? Probably the bias would be toward the favorable. Nevertheless, *self-appraisals* help employees become involved in the whole evaluation process and may make them more receptive to feedback about areas needing improvement.

360-Degree Assessment: Appraisal by Everybody   We said that performance appraisals may be done by peers, subordinates, customers, and oneself. Sometimes all these may be used in a technique called 360-degree assessment.

In a "theater in the round," the actors in a dramatic play are watched by an audience on all sides of them—360 degrees. Similarly, as a worker, you have many people watching you from all sides. Thus has arisen the idea of the ***360-degree assessment,* or *360-degree feedback appraisal,* in which employees are appraised not only by their managerial superiors but also by peers, subordinates, and sometimes clients,** thus providing several perspectives.

Typically, an employee chooses between 6 and 12 other people to make evaluations, who then fill out anonymous forms, the results of which are tabulated by computer. Or, using a Facebook-style program such as Performance Multiplier or Twitter-like software called Rypple, employees can solicit evaluations through social networking–style systems.[127] The employee then goes over the results with his or her manager and together they put into place a long-term plan for performance goals.

Incorporating 360-degree feedback into the performance appraisal process has advantages and disadvantages. Recent research found that "improvement is most likely to occur when feedback indicates that change is necessary, recipients have a positive feedback orientation, perceive a need to change their behavior, react positively to feedback, believe change is feasible, set appropriate goals to regulate their behavior, and take actions that lead to skill and performance improvement."[128] At the heart of the process is the matter of *trust.* "Trust determines how much an individual is willing to contribute for an employer," says one expert. "Using 360 confidentially, for developmental purposes, builds trust; using it to trigger pay and personnel decisions puts trust at risk."[129]

EXAMPLE

The 360-Degree Assessment: How Can It Be Compromised?

The 360-degree assessment can be very effective for performance improvement, career development, and even training. Texas computer maker Dell Inc., for instance, realized that it needed to nurture its talent in order to achieve better performance. Accordingly, it designed an in-house training program taught primarily by Dell's own top executives, chairman Michael Dell and then-CEO Kevin Rollins (no longer at the company), who submitted to 360-degree assessments in the hope of inspiring the executives beneath them to do the same. "Pay," says one report, "is now determined in part by how well a manager does at nurturing people."[130]

Differences in Perception. There are many ways, however, in which 360-degree assessments can become disasters. In one health care organization, the vice president of human resources was rated by his staff as being a strong, positive, effective leader, but his boss, the corporate senior vice president, did not rate him as being very effective. At a meeting to review the 360-degree assessment,

the HR manager asked to discuss the differences in perceptions, but his boss said, "Obviously, everyone else is right and I am wrong. So, we'll just go along with what others have said"—thereby destroying the opportunity to give constructive feedback or coaching to the HR VP.

Need for Accountability. In another case, a manager confronted specific employees about their 360 assessments, effectively compromising the integrity of the process. In a third case, a sales organization executed an effective assessment and feedback, but, as one writer says, "there was no accountability for development plans, there was no follow-up after the initial feedback meetings, and no training was offered or provided for clearly identified weaknesses in a majority of the sales people."[131]

YOUR CALL

If you were the recipient of a 360-degree assessment, what kind of steps would you like to see taken to ensure that you could trust the process?

table 9.4

HOW TO GIVE
PERFORMANCE FEEDBACK
TO EMPLOYEES

Think of yourself as a coach,
as though you were managing
a team of athletes.

- *Take a problem-solving
  approach, avoid criticism, and
  treat employees with respect.*
  Recall the worst boss you
  ever worked for. How did
  you react to his or her
  method of giving feedback?
  Avoid criticism that might
  be taken personally.
      Example: Don't say,
  "You're picking up that
  bag of cement wrong"
  (which criticizes by using
  the word *wrong*). Say,
  "Instead of bending at the
  waist, a good way to pick
  up something heavy is to
  bend your knees. That'll
  help save your back."

- *Be specific in describing
  the employee's present
  performance and in
  the improvement you
  desire.* Describe your
  subordinate's current
  performance in specific
  terms and concentrate on
  outcomes that are within
  his or her ability to
  improve.
      Example: Don't say,
  "You're always late turning
  in your sales reports." Say,
  "Instead of making calls on
  Thursday afternoon, why
  don't you take some of
  the time to do your sales
  reports so they'll be ready
  on Friday along with those
  of the other sales reps."

- *Get the employee's input.* In
  determining causes for a
  problem, listen to the
  employee and get his or
  her help in crafting a
  solution.
      Example: Don't say,
  "You've got to learn to get
  here by 9:00 a.m. every
  day." Say, "What changes
  do you think could be
  made so that your station
  is covered when people
  start calling at 9:00?"

Forced Ranking: Grading on a Curve   To increase performance, an estimated 60% of Fortune 500 companies (such as General Electric, Ford, Cisco, and Intel) have some variant of performance review systems known as forced ranking (or "rank and yank") systems.[132] **In *forced ranking performance review systems,* all employees within a business unit are ranked against one another and grades are distributed along some sort of bell curve**—just like students being graded in a college course. Top performers (such as the top 20%) are rewarded with bonuses and promotions, the worst performers (such as the bottom 20%) are rehabilitated or dismissed. For instance, every year 10% of GE's managers are assigned the bottom grade, and if they don't improve, they are asked to leave the company.

Proponents of forced ranking say it encourages managers to identify and remove poor performers and also structures a predetermined compensation curve, which enables them to reward top performers. If, however, the system is imposed on an organization overnight without preparation, by pitting employees against one another, it can produce shocks to morale, productivity, and loyalty. There may also be legal ramifications, as when employees file class-action lawsuits alleging that the forced ranking methods had a disparate effect on particular groups of employees.[133] One recent study found that 14% of all companies surveyed used a forced ranking system, down from 42% in 2009.[134]

Effective Performance Feedback

The whole point of performance appraisal, of course, is to stimulate better job performance. But, says Lawrence Bossidy, former CEO of AlliedSignal, the typical appraisal is often three pages long and filled with vague, uncommunicative language and is useless to ensure that improvement happens.[135] Bossidy recommends an appraisal take up half a page and cover just three topics: what the boss likes about your performance, what you can improve, and how you and your boss are going to make sure that improvement happens.

To help increase employee performance, a manager can use two kinds of appraisals—formal and informal.

1. Formal Appraisals   *Formal appraisals* **are conducted at specific times throughout the year and are based on performance measures that have been established in advance.** An emergency medical technician might be evaluated twice a year by his or her manager, using objective performance measures such as work attendance time sheets and more subjective measures such as a behaviorally anchored rating scales (BARS) to indicate the employee's willingness to follow emergency procedures and doctors' and nurses' orders.

As part of the appraisal, the manager should give the employee feedback, describing how he or she is performing well and not so well and giving examples. Managers are sometimes advised to keep diaries about specific incidents so they won't have to rely on their memories (and so that their evaluations will be more lawsuit-resistant). Facts should always be used rather than impressions.

2. Informal Appraisals   Formal appraisals are the equivalent of a student receiving a grade on a midterm test and a grade on a final test—weeks may go by in which you are unaware of how well you're doing in the course. Informal appraisals are the equivalent of occasional unscheduled pop quizzes and short papers or drop-in visits to the professor's office to talk about your work—you have more frequent feedback about your performance. *Informal appraisals* **are conducted on an unscheduled basis and consist of less rigorous indications of employee performance.**

You may not feel comfortable about critiquing your employees' performance, especially when you have to convey criticism rather than praise. Nevertheless, giving performance feedback is one of the most important parts of the manager's job.

Some suggestions for improvement appear in the table at left. *(See Table 9.4.)* ●

What are the various forms of compensation?

THE BIG PICTURE

Managers must manage for compensation—which includes wages or salaries, incentives, and benefits.

Do we work only for a paycheck? Many people do, of course. But money is only one form of compensation.

Compensation **has three parts: (1) wages or salaries, (2) incentives, and (3) benefits.** In different organizations one part may take on more importance than another. For instance, in some nonprofit organizations (education, government), salaries may not be large, but health and retirement benefits may outweigh that fact. In a high-technology startup, the salary and benefits may actually be somewhat humble, but the promise of a large payoff in incentives, such as stock options or bonuses, may be quite attractive. Let's consider these three parts briefly. (We expand on them in Chapter 12 when we discuss ways to motivate employees.)

Wages or Salaries

Base pay **consists of the basic wage or salary paid employees in exchange for doing their jobs.** The basic compensation is determined by all kinds of economic factors: the prevailing pay levels in a particular industry and location, what competitors are paying, whether the jobs are unionized, if the jobs are hazardous, what the individual's level is in the organization, and how much experience he or she has.

Incentives

To induce employees to be more productive or to attract and retain top performers, many organizations offer incentives, such as commissions, bonuses, profit-sharing plans, and stock options. We discuss these in detail in Chapter 12.

Stock options. Companies like to offer favored employees stock options rather than higher salaries as benefits. With stock options, employees have the right to buy stock in the future when it is (presumably) worth a higher price but buy it at today's lower price. The notion here is that employees will work harder and smarter to try to make the stock price go up. Not only do employees place a high value on options, but companies can issue as many as they want without hurting corporate profits because, under present accounting rules, they don't have to count the options' value as an expense.

How to Make Incentive Pay Plans Meet Company Goals: Communicate Them to Employees[136]

There are many incentive compensation plans, ranging from cash awards and gifts to profit sharing and stock ownership, as we discuss in detail in Chapter 12.

Here let's ask the question: Do they work?

A survey of 139 companies, more than a third of them in the Fortune 500, found that 72% had variable pay plans. But only 22% said their plans had helped them achieve all their business objectives, and 28% said their plans had achieved none of them.

What explains the difference? Good plan design is important, but so is good communication and oversight.

According to Ken Abosch, a consultant at Chicago-based Hewett Associates, which conducted the survey, often plans fail to deliver on their intended goals because employees aren't told enough about them and aren't kept up to date on the progress of the plans. Eighty-nine percent of companies that regularly communicated with their employees said their incentive plans met their goals, compared with only 57% of companies that did not discuss them with their employees.

Five keys to a successful incentive-pay plan are the following, according to Abosch:

1. **Simplicity.** Does the plan pass the simplicity test? As Abosch puts it, "Can you explain it on an elevator ride?"

2. **Clear goals.** Are the goals clear? Are the goals fully supported by management?

3. **Realistic goals.** Are the goals realistic—that is, neither too difficult nor too easy to achieve?

4. **Consistency with present goals.** Is the plan in line with the organization's present goals? Company goals change. "There are very few organizations that have the same business objective for five to seven years," points out Abosch.

5. **Regular communication.** Do managers regularly communicate with employees about the plan? "People want a scorecard," Abosch says.

Benefits

Benefits, or *fringe benefits,* **are additional nonmonetary forms of compensation** designed to enrich the lives of all employees in the organization, which are paid all or in part by the organization. Examples are many: health insurance, dental insurance, life insurance, disability protection, retirement plans, holidays off, accumulated sick days and vacation days, recreation options, country club or health club memberships, family leave, discounts on company merchandise, counseling, credit unions, legal advice, and education reimbursement. For top executives, there may be "golden parachutes," generous severance pay for those who might be let go in the event the company is taken over by another company.

Benefits are no small part of an organization's costs. In December 2011, private industry spent an average of $28.57 per hour worked in employment compensation, of which wages and salaries accounted for 70.5% and benefits for the remaining 29.5%.[137] ●

Communication is everything. The questions human resource managers need to keep in mind are: What good does it do a company to have attractive incentive plans if employees don't understand them? Will an employee exert the extra effort in pursuit of rewards if he or she doesn't know what the rewards are?

What are some guidelines for handling promotions, transfers, disciplining, and dismissals?

major
question ?

THE BIG PICTURE

As a manager, you'll have to manage employee replacement actions, as by promoting, transferring, demoting, laying off, or firing.

"The unemployment rate is an abstraction, an aggregation of bodiless data," writes journalist/novelist Walter Kirn, "but losing a job is a lived experience, written on the nerves. . . . Some blame themselves and some blame everybody. Still others, not knowing whom to blame, explode."[138]

Among the major—and most difficult—decisions you will make as a manager are those about employee movement within an organization: Whom should you let go (painful for all)? promote? transfer? discipline? All these matters go under the heading of *employee replacement*. And, incidentally, any time you need to deal with replacing an employee in a job, that's a time to reconsider the job description to see how it might be made more effective for the next person to occupy it.

You'll have to deal with replacement whenever an employee quits, retires, becomes seriously ill, or dies. Or you may initiate the replacement action by promoting, transferring, demoting, laying off, or firing.[139]

Promotion: Moving Upward

Promotion—moving an employee to a higher level position—is the most obvious way to recognize that person's superior performance (apart from giving raises and bonuses).

Three concerns are these:

Fairness   It's important that promotion be *fair*. The step upward must be deserved. It shouldn't be for reasons of nepotism (favoritism shown to relatives), cronyism (favoritism shown to close friends), or other kind of favoritism.

Nondiscrimination   The promotion cannot discriminate on the basis of race, ethnicity, gender, age, or physical ability.

Others' Resentments   If someone is promoted, someone else may be resentful about being passed over. As a manager, you may need to counsel the people left behind about their performance and their opportunities in the future. In fact, if you are passed over yourself, it is important not to let your anger build. Instead, you should gather your thoughts, then go in and talk to your boss and find out what qualities were lacking, suggests one report. You should also create a career action plan and look for ways to improve your knowledge, skills, and abilities.[140]

Transfer: Moving Sideways

Transfer is movement of an employee to a different job with *similar responsibility*. It may or may not mean a change in geographical location (which might be part of a promotion as well).

Employees might be transferred for four principal reasons: (1) to solve organizational problems by using their skills at another location; (2) to broaden their experience in being assigned to a different position; (3) to retain their interest and motivation by being presented with a new challenge; or (4) to solve some employee problems, such as personal differences with their bosses.

Disciplining & Demotion: The Threat of Moving Downward

Poorly performing employees may be given a warning or a reprimand and then *disciplined.* That is, they may be temporarily removed from their jobs, as when a police officer is placed on suspension or administrative leave—removed from his or her regular job in the field and perhaps given a paperwork job or told to stay away from work.

Alternatively, an employee may be *demoted*—that is, have his or her current responsibilities, pay, and perquisites taken away, as when a middle manager is demoted to a first-line manager. (Sometimes this may occur when a company is downsized, resulting in fewer higher-level management positions.)

Dismissal: Moving Out of the Organization

Dismissals are of three sorts:

Layoffs The phrase being *laid off* tends to suggest that a person has been dismissed *temporarily*—as when a carmaker doesn't have enough orders to justify keeping its production employees—and may be recalled later when economic conditions improve.

Downsizings A *downsizing* is a *permanent* dismissal; there is no rehiring later. An automaker discontinuing a line of cars or on the path to bankruptcy might permanently let go of its production employees.

Firings The phrase being *fired,* with all its euphemisms and synonyms—being "terminated," "separated," "let go," "canned"—tends to mean that a person was dismissed *permanently "for cause"*: absenteeism, sloppy work habits, failure to perform satisfactorily, breaking the law, and the like.

It used to be that managers could use their discretion about dismissals. Today, however, because of the changing legal climate, steps must be taken to avoid employees suing for "wrongful termination." That is, an employer has to carefully *document* the reasons for dismissals. You also need to take into account the fact that survivors in the company can suffer just as much as, if not more than, their colleagues who were let go.[141]

Incidentally, in terms of your own career, be aware that dismissals rarely come as a surprise. Most bosses are conflict-averse, and you may see the handwriting on the wall when your own manager begins to interact with you less.[142]

The Practical Action box on the next page offers some suggestions for handling dismissals. ●

The Right Way to Handle a Dismissal

"Employment at will" is the governing principle of employment in the great majority of states, which means that anyone can be dismissed at any time for any reason at all—or for no reason. Exceptions are whistle-blowers and people with employment contracts. Civil-rights laws also prohibit organizations' dismissing people for their gender, skin color, or physical or mental disability.[143]

Four suggestions for handling a dismissal are . . .

Give the Employee a Chance First. If you're dealing with someone who has a problem with absenteeism, alcohol/drug dependency, or the like, articulate to that employee what's wrong with his or her performance, then set up a plan for improvement (which might include counseling). Or if you're dealing with an employee who has a bad cultural or personality fit with the company—a buttoned-down, by-the-book style, say, that's at odds with your flexible, fast-moving organization—have a conversation and give the employee time to find a job elsewhere.[144]

Don't Delay the Dismissal, & Make Sure It's Completely Defensible. If improvements aren't forthcoming, don't carry the employee along because you feel sorry for him or her. Your first duty is to the performance of the organization. Make sure, however, that you've *documented* all the steps taken in advance of the dismissal. For instance, after you've verbally alerted the employee about what the problem is, the improvements you expect, and the consequences if they don't happen, you should send an e-mail to that person reiterating the same points, keeping a copy for yourself. Also be sure that the steps taken follow the law and all important organizational policies.[145]

Be Aware How Devastating a Dismissal Can Be—Both to the Individual & to Those Remaining. To the person being let go, the event can be as much of a blow as a divorce or a death in the family. Dismissals can also adversely affect those remaining with the company. This is what psychiatrist Manfred Kets de Vries calls *layoff survivor sickness,* which is characterized by anger, depression, fear, guilt, risk aversion, distrust, vulnerability, powerlessness, and loss of motivation. Indeed, a five-year study by Cigna and the American Management Association found an enormous increase in medical claims, particularly for stress-related illnesses, not only among those dismissed but among continuing employees as well.[146]

Offer Assistance in Finding Another Job. Dismissing a long-standing employee with only a few weeks of severance pay hurts not only the person let go but also the organization itself, as word gets back to the employees who remain, as well as to outsiders who might be prospective employees. Knowledgeable employers offer assistance in finding another job.

"The best demonstration that a company's values are real," says management scholar Rosabeth Moss Kanter, "is to act on them today even for people who will not be around tomorrow. A company, like a society, can be judged by how it treats its most vulnerable. . . . Bad treatment of departing employees can destroy the commitment of those who stay."[147]

YOUR CALL

If it hasn't happened to you already, at some point in your career you may find yourself let go from a job, perhaps for reasons that weren't your fault. (But if they are your fault, try to take it as a reality check and take the lesson forward into any future jobs.) You may take some consolation in the fact that many famous leaders have been fired from a job at some point in their lives (one of them was Apple's Steve Jobs—from the company he founded), only to bounce back and go on to do greater things. But you might also try to remember your experience when confronted with having to dismiss an employee and try to bring as much understanding and empathy to the task as you can. Have you ever been fired or dismissed? How did you react?

major question? What are the principal processes and issues involved in organizing labor unions?

THE BIG PICTURE

We describe the process by which workers get a labor union to represent them and how unions and management negotiate a contract. We also discuss the types of union and nonunion workplaces and right-to-work laws. We cover issues that unions and management negotiate, such as compensation, cost-of-living adjustments, two-tier wage systems, and givebacks. We conclude by describing mediation and arbitration.

table 9.5

SNAPSHOT OF TODAY'S U.S. UNION MOVEMENT

Who's in a union (2011)?

- 11.8% of full-time U.S. workers—down from 35.5% in 1945.

- 6.9% of private-sector workers (7.2 million).

- 37% of government workers (7.56 million).

- 51.4% of unionized workers are in government—they surpassed private-sector union membership in 2009.

- Most members: National Education Association; Service Employees International; State, County, & Municipal Employees; American Federation of Teachers; Food & Commercial Workers; Teamsters; Electrical Workers; Machinists & Aerospace Workers.

Source: Bureau of Labor Statistics, "Union Members Summary," *Economic News Release*, January 27, 2012; www.bls.gov/news.release/union2.nr0.htm (accessed June 1, 2012).

Starting in 1943, James Smith worked his way up from washing dishes in the galley of a passenger train's dining car to waiter, earning tips on top of his wages of 36 cents an hour. The union job with the Brotherhood of Sleeping Car Porters, the first African American union, enabled him to go to college, and when he left the railroad he was hired as a civil engineer for the city of Los Angeles. "His story," says one report, "is emblematic of the role the railroads and a railroad union played in building a foundation for America's black middle class."[148] Unions also helped to grow the American (and European) middle classes in general, bringing benefits to all, organized or not.

Labor unions are organizations of employees formed to protect and advance their members' interests by bargaining with management over job-related issues. Although the union movement is less the powerhouse than it was in the 1950s, it is still a force in many sectors of the economy.[149] *(See Table 9.5 at left.)*

How Workers Organize

When workers in a particular organization decide to form a union, they first must get each worker to sign an *authorization card,* which designates a certain union as the workers' bargaining agent. When at least 30% of workers have signed cards, the union may ask the employer for official recognition. Usually the employer refuses, at which point the union can petition the National Labor Relations Board (NLRB) to decide which union should become the *bargaining unit* that represents the workers, such as the Teamsters Union, United Auto Workers, the American Federation of Teachers, or the Service Employees International Union, as appropriate. (Some workers, however, are represented by unions you would never guess: Zookeepers, for instance, are represented by the Teamsters, which mainly organizes transportation workers. University of California, Berkeley, graduate student instructors are represented by the United Auto Workers.) An election is then held by the NLRB, and if 50% or more of the votes cast agree to unionization, the NLRB *certifies* the union as the workers' exclusive representative.

How Unions & Management Negotiate a Contract

Once a union is recognized as an official bargaining unit, its representatives can then meet with management's representatives to do *collective bargaining*—to negotiate pay and benefits and other work terms.

When agreement is reached with management, the union representatives take the collective bargaining results back to the members for *ratification*—they vote to accept or reject the contract negotiated by their leaders. If they vote yes, the union and management representatives sign a *negotiated labor-management contract,* which sets the general tone and terms under which labor and management agree to work together during the contract period.

The Issues Unions & Management Negotiate About

The key issues that labor and management negotiate are compensation, employee benefits, job security, work rules, hours, and safety matters. However, the first issue is usually union security and management rights.

Union Security & Types of Workplaces A key issue is: Who controls hiring policies and work assignments—labor or management? This involves the following matters:

- **The union security clause.** The basic underpinning of union security is the *union security clause,* **the part of the labor-management agreement that states that employees who receive union benefits must join the union, or at least pay dues to it.** In times past, a union would try to solidify the union security clause by getting management to agree to a *closed shop agreement*—which is illegal today—in which a company agreed it would hire only current union members for a given job.

- **Types of unionized and nonunionized workplaces.** The four basic kinds of workplaces are: *closed shop, union shop, agency shop,* and *open shop,* as shown below. *(See Table 9.6.)*

table 9.6 FOUR KINDS OF WORKPLACE LABOR AGREEMENTS

Workplace	Definition	Status
Closed shop	Employer may hire only workers for a job who are already in the union	Illegal
Union shop	Workers aren't required to be union members when hired for a job but must join the union within a specified time	Not allowed in 22 states (right-to-work states)
Agency shop	Workers must pay equivalent of union dues but aren't required to join the union	Applies to public-sector teachers in some states, prohibited in others
Open shop	Workers may choose to join or not join a union	Applies in 22 states (right-to-work states)

- **Right-to-work laws.** Individual states are allowed (under the 1947 Taft-Hartley Act) to pass legislation outlawing union and agency shops. As a result, 22 states have passed *right-to-work laws,* **statutes that prohibit employees from being required to join a union as a condition of employment.**

Business interests supporting such laws argue that forcing workers to join a union violates their rights and makes a state less attractive to businesses considering moving there. Union supporters say that states with such laws have overall lower wages and that all workers benefit from union gains, so everyone should be compelled to join.

The 22 work-to-right states are shown in the map on the next page. *(See Figure 9.3.)*

figure 9.3

STATES WITH RIGHT-TO-WORK LAWS

What kind of state do you live in? (Alaska and Hawaii are non–right-to-work states.)

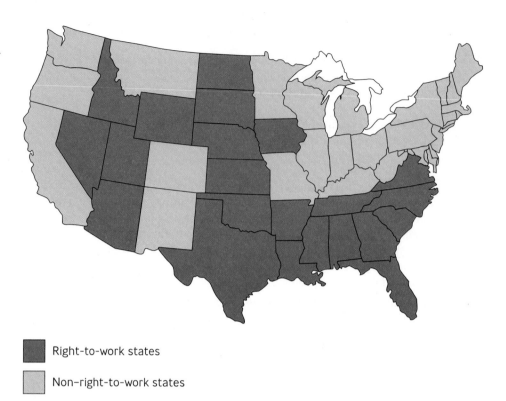

■ Right-to-work states

□ Non–right-to-work states

Compensation: Wage Rates, COLA Clauses, & Givebacks Unions strive to negotiate the highest wage rates possible, or to trade off higher wages for something else, such as better fringe benefits. Some issues involved with compensation are as follows:

- ■ **Wage rates—same pay or different rates?** Wage rates subject to negotiation include overtime pay, different wages for different shifts, and bonuses. In the past, unions tried to negotiate similar wage rates for unionized employees working in similar jobs for similar companies or similar industries. However, the pressure of competition abroad and deregulation at home has forced many unions to negotiate *two-tier wage contracts,* **in which new employees are paid less or receive lesser benefits than veteran employees have.**

  Example: Recently, as automakers began to create new jobs, new union hires were offered about half the pay ($14 an hour) that autoworkers were getting before ($28).[150] Such two-tier wage systems can be attractive to employers, who are able to hire new workers at reduced wages, but it also benefits veteran union members, who experience no wage reduction. However, some companies have been trying to make this wage concession permanent—a big setback for labor.[151]

- ■ **Cost-of-living adjustment.** Because the cost of living is always going up (at least so far), unions often try to negotiate a *cost-of-living adjustment (COLA) clause,* **which during the period of the contract ties future wage increases to increases in the cost of living,** as measured by the U.S. Bureau of Labor Statistics' consumer price index (CPI). (An alternative is the *wage reopener clause,* which allows wage rates to be renegotiated at certain stated times during the life of the contract. Thus, a 10-year contract might be subject to renegotiation every two years.)

- ■ **Givebacks.** During tough economic times, when a company (or, in the case of public employee unions, a municipality) is fighting for its very survival, management and labor may negotiate *givebacks,* **in which the union agrees to give up previous wage or benefit gains in return for something else.** Usually the union seeks job security, as in a no-layoff policy.

Settling Labor-Management Disputes

Even when a collective-bargaining agreement and contract has been accepted by both sides, there may likely be ongoing differences that must be resolved. Sometimes differences lead to walkouts and strikes, or management may lock out employees. However, conflicts can be resolved through *grievance procedures* and *mediation* or *arbitration*.

Grievance Procedures A *grievance* **is a complaint by an employee that management has violated the terms of the labor-management agreement.** Examples: An employee may feel he or she is being asked to work too much overtime, is not getting his or her fair share of overtime, or is being unfairly passed over for promotion. Grievance procedures are often handled initially by the union's *shop steward,* an official elected by the union membership who works at the company and represents the interests of unionized employees on a daily basis to the employees' immediate supervisors. If this process is not successful, the grievance may be carried to the union's chief shop steward and then to the union's grievance committee, which deals with its counterparts higher up in management.

If the grievance procedure is not successful, the two sides may decide to try to resolve their differences through mediation or arbitration.

Mediation *Mediation* **is the process in which a neutral third party, a *mediator,* listens to both sides in a dispute, makes suggestions, and encourages them to agree on a solution.** Mediators may be lawyers or retired judges or specialists in various fields, such as conflict resolution or labor matters.

Arbitration *Arbitration* **is the process in which a neutral third party, an *arbitrator,* listens to both parties in a dispute and makes a decision that the parties have agreed will be binding on them.** Arbitrators are often retired judges. ●

Key Terms Used in This Chapter

Summary

9.1 Strategic Human Resource Management

Human resource management consists of the activities managers perform to plan for, attract, develop, and retain an effective workforce. The purpose of the strategic human resource management process is to get the optimal work performance that will help realize the company's mission and vision.

Two concepts important to human resource management are (1) human capital, the economic or productive potential of employee knowledge, and (2) social capital, the economic or productive potential of strong, trusting, and cooperative relationships.

Strategic human resource planning consists of developing a systematic, comprehensive strategy for (a) understanding current employee needs and (b) predicting future employee needs.

Understanding current employee needs requires first doing a job analysis to determine, by observation and analysis, the basic elements of a job. Then a job description can be written, which summarizes what the holder of the job does and how and why he or she does it. Next comes the job specification, which describes the minimum qualifications a person must have to perform the job successfully.

Predicting employee needs means a manager needs to become knowledgeable about the staffing an organization might need and the likely sources of staffing, perhaps using a human resource inventory to organize this information.

9.2 The Legal Requirements of Human Resource Management

Four areas of human resource law that any manager needs to be aware of are as follows: (1) Labor relations are dictated in part by the National Labor Relations Board, which enforces procedures whereby employees may vote to have a union and for collective bargaining. Collective bargaining consists of negotiations between management and employees about disputes over compensation, benefits, working conditions, and job security. (2) Compensation and benefits are covered by the

Social Security Act of 1935 and the Fair Labor Standards Act, which established minimum wage and overtime pay regulations. (3) Health and safety are covered by the Occupational Safety and Health Act of 1970, among other laws. (4) Equal employment opportunity is covered by the Equal Employment Opportunity (EEO) Commission, whose job it is to enforce antidiscrimination and other employment-related laws. Three important concepts covered by EEO are (a) discrimination, which occurs when people are hired or promoted—or denied hiring or promotion—for reasons not relevant to the job, such as skin color or national origin; (b) affirmative action, which focuses on achieving equality of opportunity within an organization; and (c) sexual harassment, which consists of unwanted sexual attention that creates an adverse work environment and which may be of two types—the quid pro quo type, which may cause direct economic injury, and the hostile environment type, in which the person being harassed experiences an offensive work environment.

9.3 Recruitment & Selection: Putting the Right People into the Right Jobs

Recruiting is the process of locating and attracting qualified applicants for jobs open in the organization. (1) Internal recruiting means making people already employed by the organization aware of job openings. (2) External recruiting means attracting job applicants from outside the organization. A useful approach with external recruitment is the realistic job preview, which gives a candidate a picture of both positive and negative features of the job and organization before he or she is hired.

The selection process is the screening of job applicants to hire the best candidates. Three types of selection tools are background information, interviewing, and employment tests. (1) Background information is ascertained through application forms, résumés, and reference checks. (2) Interviewing takes three forms. (a) The unstructured interview involves asking probing questions to find out what the applicant is like. (b) The structured interview involves asking each applicant the same questions and comparing his or her responses to a standardized set of answers. The first type of structured interview is the situational interview, in which the interview focuses on hypothetical situations. (c) The second type of structured interview is the behavioral-description interview, in which the interviewer explores what applicants have actually done in the past. (3) Employment tests are legally considered to consist of any procedure used in the employment selection decision process, but the three most common tests are ability tests, personality tests, and performance tests. Some companies have assessment centers, in which management candidates participate in activities for a few days while being assessed in performance tests by evaluators. Other tests include drug testing, polygraphs, and genetic screening. With any kind of test, an important legal consideration is the test's reliability, the degree to which a test measures the same thing consistently, and validity, whether the test measures what it purports to measure and is free of bias.

9.4 Orientation, Training, & Development

Three ways in which newcomers are helped to perform their jobs are through orientation, training, and development. (1) Orientation consists of helping the newcomer fit smoothly into the job and organization. Following orientation, the employee should emerge with information about the job routine, the organization's mission and operations, and the organization's work rules and employee benefits. (2) Training must be distinguished from development. Training refers to educating technical and operational employees in how to do their current jobs better. (3) *Development* is the term describing educating professionals and managers in the skills they need to do their jobs in the future. Both training and development may be effected through on-the-job training methods and off-the-job training methods.

9.5 Performance Appraisal

Performance appraisal consists of assessing an employee's performance and providing him or her with feedback. Appraisals are of two general types—objective and subjective. Two good reasons for having objective appraisals are that they measure results and they are harder to challenge legally. (1) Objective appraisals are based on facts and are often numerical. An example is management by objectives. (2) Subjective appraisals are based on a manager's perceptions of an employee's traits or behaviors. Trait appraisals are ratings of subjective attributes such as attitude and leadership. Behavioral appraisals measure specific, observable aspects of performance. An example is the behaviorally anchored rating scale (BARS), which rates employee gradations in performance according to scales of specific behaviors.

Most performance appraisals are made by managers, but they may also be made by coworkers and subordinates, customers and clients, and employees themselves (self-appraisals). Sometimes all of these may be used, in a technique called the 360-degree assessment, in which employees are appraised not only by their managerial superiors but also by their peers, subordinates, and sometimes clients. In another evaluation technique, forced ranking performance review systems, all employees within a business unit are ranked against one another, and grades are distributed along some sort of bell curve.

Effective performance feedback can be effected in two ways: (1) Formal appraisals are conducted at specific times throughout the year and are based on performance measures that have been established in advance. (2) Informal appraisals are conducted on an unscheduled basis and consist of less rigorous indications of employee performance.

9.6 Managing an Effective Workforce: Compensation & Benefits

Compensation has three parts: wages or salaries, incentives, and benefits. (1) In the category of wages or salaries, the concept of base pay consists of the basic wage or salary paid employees in exchange for doing their jobs. (2) Incentives include commissions, bonuses, profit-sharing plans, and stock options. (3) Benefits are additional nonmonetary forms of compensation, such as health insurance, retirement plans, and family leave.

9.7 Managing Promotions, Transfers, Disciplining, & Dismissals

Managers must manage promotions, transfers, disciplining, and dismissals. (1) In considering promotions, managers must be concerned about fairness, nondiscrimination, and other employees' resentment. (2) Transfers, or moving employees to a different job with similar responsibility, may take place in order to solve organizational problems, broaden managers' experience, retain managers' interest and motivation, and solve some employee problems. (3) Poor-performing employees may need to be disciplined or demoted. (4) Dismissals may consist of layoffs, downsizings, or firings.

9.8 Labor-Management Issues

Labor unions are organizations of employees formed to protect and advance their members' interests by bargaining with management over job-related issues. Workers organize by signing authorization cards designating a certain union as their bargaining agent, and if enough cards are signed, the National Labor Relations Board will recognize the union as the bargaining unit. If 50% of workers agree, the NLRB certifies the union as the workers' exclusive representative. In negotiating a contract in collective bargaining, workers in the union must ratify the contract, after which union and management sign a negotiated labor-management contract.

Among the issues unions negotiate are the union security clause, which states that workers must join the union or at least pay benefits to it. The four types of workplaces are closed shop (now illegal), union shop, agency shop, and open shop. Twenty-two states have right-to-work laws that prohibit employees from being required to join a union as a condition of employment. Unions also negotiate wage rates, including two-tier wage contracts, with newer employees being paid less, and cost-of-living (COLA) adjustments giving wages that increase with the cost of living. Sometimes unions must negotiate givebacks, in which employees give up previous wage or benefit gains in return for something else. To avoid strikes, labor-management disputes may be resolved through grievance procedures or through mediation or arbitration.

Management in Action

Netflix's Human Resource Practices Enhance Employee Retention

[In the summer of 2009], an internal Netflix file found its way onto the Internet. The 128 PowerPoint slides set out the company's culture and talent management strategy. Observers speculated how leaders at the usually guarded Netflix had let such a document leak.

As the commentary—pro and con—continues to flow, Reed Hastings, Netflix's chief executive officer, concedes that corporate leaders leaked the document intentionally "to allow job candidates to self-select." Netflix has a controversial tough love approach to human capital management. It features a culture governed by few rules and zero tolerance for poor or average performers. Workers can earn top-of-market pay but no bonuses or long-term incentives, and they are responsible for their own development. "It's not the Bible, it's just our documentation of what's working for us," Patricia J. McCord, chief talent officer and one of the architects of the company, says of the approach. . . .

Today the company delivers movies by mail and video streaming. At the end of 2009, it had 12.2 million subscribers, and revenue for the year reached $1.67 billion, up 22% from the previous year. Netflix recruiters have added staff at a rate of more than 20% annually. The company has 1,644 employees, about 500 of whom are salaried professionals. . . .

At Netflix, HR professionals serve on the top management team, and McCord and Allison Hopkins, vice president for human resources set the tone. . . .

Software engineers, who make up the majority of the professional staff, are the creative lifeline of the organization, and McCord is obsessive about attracting and recruiting the best. Engineers, she observes, have little patience for bureaucracy. . . .

Hastings and McCord recognized that elite talent in the Silicon Valley could pick and choose where they worked; many other employers also pay top dollar. What else could Netflix do to recruit? The key to differentiation, they concluded, was to deliver a culture that attracted people who identified with and understood the business, who yearned for a flexible work environment with few constraints, and who—more than anything—wanted to be rubbing elbows with the best talent.

At Netflix's modern headquarters in Los Gatos, California, there are no badges or security checkpoints. There is also no dress code. People, most of whom are casually dressed, come and go continuously. . . .

The "creative employee we compete for thrives on freedom," Hastings says. "We're more focused on the absence of procedure—managing through talented people rather than a rule book." But the dearth of rules does not mean that it's a free-for-all environment: the few rules are reviewed by counsel and are "in compliance of federal laws," Hastings says. "We try to manage by strong ethics; we're strong on fairness and equity."

You won't see Netflix recruiters on college campuses or at entry-level career fairs. "We get a different kind of person than other software companies," McCord says. . . .

In contrast, new hires at Netflix typically have 7 to 15 years of experience. "They're accomplished deliverers," McCord says. "You need to know your craft so you can make a contribution when you walk in. You need to be mature, with enough experience to be able to make independent decisions."

And you need to be drawn to the business; Netflix's ranks overflow with film aficionados. People who are not interested in "the context" of the business need not apply. . . .

In other companies, Hopkins says, "policies are written for the lowest common denominator. Here, we don't have to do that. You don't have to write things down. When someone does something wrong, we tell them it was wrong. After that, either they get it or they're out." Hopkins contrasts Netflix with Hewlett-Packard, where, she says, "Everything was done by policy." . . .

"We are a performance culture based on intellectual prowess," Hastings says. "We try to be fair, but [the length of an employee's Netflix career] is not our primary concern. If someone is not extraordinary, we let them go." Based on personal observations, he says the payoff from an extraordinary performer vs. an average one in creative fields is tenfold.

Here then, is perhaps the characteristic that distinguishes Netflix from others recruiting top talent: Leaders are unwavering in their quest for quality and results. If even one person is assessed as mediocre or average during the annual review process but permitted to continue working for Netflix, the elite aura surrounding the workforce will be compromised. Loyalty to people not producing or facing minor setbacks or personal distractions is tolerated, but not for long.

"Keeping the house clean is essential to who we are," Hopkins says. "Too often, really good workers are frustrated at having to work with others who they perceive as average or worse performers. When we ask people why they chose us, they tell us it's not for the money. It's the other stuff. [It's] 'the places we worked didn't fire people they should have fired.'" . . .

Voluntary employee turnover at Netflix is low. The top six executives have been with the company from the beginning. When it comes to terminations, managers follow two rules:

No surprises. Employees must know where they stand. Annual 360-degree reviews provide "direct and honest feedback," employee Walter Stokes says. "It's tough to get used to doing them, but when they're done right, they're better than top-down evaluations." . . .

No-fault divorces. Wherever possible, an amicable departure is engineered. "We want them to keep their dignity," McCord says. "In many companies, once I want you to leave, my job is to prove you're incompetent. I have to give you all the documentation and fire you for poor performance. It can take months. Here, I write a check. We exchange severance for a release. To make Netflix a great company, people have to be able to leverage it when they leave" by subsequently getting good jobs.

The line manager delivers the news with coaching from HR professionals. "We don't coddle, it's not about asking how does someone feel," Hopkins says.

"Usually, people find new jobs quickly." To date, no one who has been terminated has sued. . . .

"There's no road map that plots out your career," Stokes adds. "I've been here three years, and so far my job and responsibilities have changed every six months."

Hastings says people should manage their own career paths and not rely on the company. "The way you develop yourself is to be surrounded by stunning colleagues. We surround people and let them develop themselves," he explains.

Formal training, except where mandated by law, is not offered. Hastings and HR leaders conclude that most training materials are not useful. "I used to worry that we didn't do training and developing, but then we previewed some training videos and supporting materials," McCord recalls. "It was awful. Reed said, 'This stuff is nauseating and a waste of time.'" . . .

Netflix salaries are based on market conditions but not on company performance—a practice shareholders could find vexing if the company experiences a downturn. For now, the rationale—comparing top talent to major-league pitchers who receive star-level pay whether the team wins or loses—prevails. To be promoted, a person has to be a superstar in his or her current role and often be willing to take a reduction in pay to take on the new assignment. Executives want people to move up for the challenge, with the expectation that they will earn more once they have proved themselves.

FOR DISCUSSION

1. How would you describe Netflix's organizational culture? Explain.

2. If you were hiring people at Netflix, what questions would you ask applicants to determine if they would fit into the corporate culture? Generate three to five questions.

3. What are the specific human resource practices that Netflix is using to recruit and retain high-quality employees? Explain why they are effective in this context.

4. What is your evaluation of Netflix's approach to training and performance appraisal? Discuss your rationale.

5. Do you like Netflix's approach to firing employees? Explain.

6. Would you like to work at Netflix? Provide your rationale.

Source: Excerpted from Robert J. Grossman, "Tough Love at Netflix," *HR Magazine,* April 2010, pp. 36–41. Copyright 2010, Society for Human Resource Management, Alexandria, VA. Used with permission. All rights reserved.

HR 101: An Overview

OBJECTIVES

1. To learn that there is more to HR than recruitment and hiring.
2. To assess your skills and determine if a career in HR is right for you.

INTRODUCTION

Your chosen career should optimally be based on your interests. The HR field, for example, offers many different career paths that require many different skills. The purpose of this exercise is to help you become familiar with the different career paths available to an HR professional and to see which path best fits your interests. This experience may help you decide if an HR career is right for you.

Among the professionals in the HR field are the following:

The HR generalist. HR generalists take on many different roles, whether negotiating a company's employee benefits package or interviewing a candidate for a director-level position. An HR generalist is supposed to be flexible and able to change gears at a moment's notice.

Compensation professional. Compensation professionals, who are very much in demand, design reward systems that attract, retain, and motivate employees. The job requires not only good technical skills but good people skills as well, a rare combination. It also requires a great amount of number crunching, creativity, and ingenuity, because a compensation package that might work for one employee might not work for another.

HRIS professional. HRIS stands for Human Resource Information Systems. With technology now such a key part of human resources, HRIS products help companies manage their personnel. Because the information systems are now so sophisticated, there is great demand for experienced HRIS professionals, who must be very detail oriented and, of course, enjoy working with computers. Such professionals are involved in product selection, systems customization, implementation, and ongoing administration.

Benefits professional. This individual is responsible for designing and implementing benefits plans. The job requires strong technical and communication skills.

Training and development professional. This individual is responsible for building environments that foster learning, management, and leadership development. People in this field may be involved in distance learning programs as well as on-site, computer-based training programs.

Organizational development professional. Organizational development (OD) professionals work with top management to make sure that the organizational design sticks to the company's mission, vision, and goals. Besides doing some training and development, an OD professional must be able to embrace change and work long hours.

INSTRUCTIONS

Ask yourself the following questions and circle whether the statement applies to you. Once you have answered all of the questions, use the interpretation guidelines to analyze your responses and determine if a career in HR is right for you.

1. Do I enjoy changing gears on a moment's notice?	Yes	No
2. Am I open to learning about areas in which I currently have no expertise?	Yes	No
3. Am I comfortable leaving a project unfinished to handle emergency situations?	Yes	No
4. Do I consider myself fairly flexible?	Yes	No
5. Am I good at creatively solving problems when resources and instructions are scarce?	Yes	No

6.	Do I have an aptitude for numbers?	Yes	No
7.	Am I comfortable seeing other people's salaries?	Yes	No
8.	Do I have strong communication skills?	Yes	No
9.	Do I have strong computer skills?	Yes	No
10.	Am I comfortable working at a computer all day?	Yes	No
11.	Am I well organized?	Yes	No
12.	Am I detail oriented?	Yes	No
13.	Am I comfortable constantly reworking projects I thought were already done?	Yes	No
14.	Am I willing to pay for and donate my free time to professional certifications?	Yes	No
15.	Am I good at taking complex ideas and making them understandable to the average person?	Yes	No
16.	Am I good at expressing my ideas and getting people to go along with them?	Yes	No
17.	Am I a creative person with strong computer skills?	Yes	No
18.	Am I comfortable in front of an audience?	Yes	No
19.	Am I comfortable working one very long project instead of lots of small projects?	Yes	No
20.	Am I passionate about learning and about teaching others?	Yes	No
21.	Can I handle change? Can I handle it well?	Yes	No
22.	Do I enjoy pulling together pieces of a puzzle?	Yes	No
23.	Do I perform well in times of stress?	Yes	No
24.	Am I a big-picture person?	Yes	No

INTERPRETATION

If you answered yes to three or more of questions 1–4 (which apply to the HR generalist), three or more of questions 5–8 (compensation professional), three or more of questions 9–12 (HRIS professional), three or more of questions 13–16 (benefits professional), three or more of questions 17–20 (training and development professional), and three or more of questions 21–24 (organizational development professional), then you are well suited for the field of HR.

If you answered no to most of the previous 24 questions, the field of HR may not be right for you. (However, since this is only a small sampling of the many aspects of this field, there may still be a place for you in HR.)

QUESTIONS FOR DISCUSSION

1. To what extent did the results fit your interests? Explain.

2. Look at the top two areas of HR for which you tested as being best suited. Look over the descriptions of these fields. What skills do you need to have to be successful? Describe.

3. Even if you do not pursue a career in HR, which skills do you feel you should continue to develop? Explain.

Adapted from R. C. Matuson, "HR 101: An Overview, Parts I and II," *Monster HR,* June 2002, www.monster.com.

You Have Been Offered a Promotion, but You're Pregnant: Should You Say Anything Before Receiving the Formal Offer?

This challenge is based on an actual case. Assume that you earned your MBA from a prestigious university five years ago. You have been working at the company since graduation and have been disappointed in promotion opportunities. Your mentors, however, told you to be patient and work hard and that ultimately you would be promoted. They appear to be right.

You had a meeting with your boss about the opportunity to work as the firm's director of overseas operations. The job would last 18 to 24 months, and then there was the potential to be promoted to a bigger and better international position. The job entails a lot of international travel, and your boss told you that it would take a lot of stamina to be successful. A number of qualified internal employees applied, but your boss told you last week that you were the leading candidate. This is a dream job for you and your husband, as you both want to live overseas and travel internationally.

Two days ago you learned that you are pregnant. It's early in the pregnancy and you are doing fine outside of feeling a bit more tired than usual. Yesterday, the director of HR saw you and asked whether you are still interested in the job. She also stated that this job is really important strategically and that your boss needs someone who is ready to work hard for an extended period of time. This made you wonder whether or not you would have the stamina to do the job and what would happen when you took the company's guaranteed four-month maternity leave. Your boss is traveling for a week and wants to meet upon his return.

Your husband is excited about the opportunity and wants you to take the promotion. His job is flexible, which will allow him to help out more than normal once you return to work. You also are worried about the pregnancy because your sister had two miscarriages.

SOLVING THE CHALLENGE

Would you tell your boss about your pregnancy? If yes, when would you tell him or her?

1. I would not tell him until after I relocate and feel comfortable making the pregnancy public news. Besides, the pregnancy is none of my boss's business and it won't affect my ability to do the job. I also want to make sure that I don't have a miscarriage.

2. I would not tell the boss before a formal offer is made, but would reveal the news before I relocated. I also would prepare a plan that outlines how I will manage both the new role and the pregnancy.

3. I would tell my boss before a formal offer is made. There are other great candidates, and the boss should have full disclosure to make the best decision. Further, failing to tell my boss might erode the trust and cooperation needed between us.

4. Invent other options. Explain.

Source: This case is based on T. Casciaro and V. W. Winston, "When to Make Private News Public," *Harvard Business Review,* March 2012, pp. 161–63.

chapter 10

Organizational Change & Innovation
Lifelong Challenges for the Exceptional Manager

Major Questions You Should Be Able to Answer

10.1 The Nature of Change in Organizations

Major Question: Since change is always with us, what should I understand about it?

10.2 The Threat of Change: Managing Employee Fear & Resistance

Major Question: How are employees threatened by change, and how can I help them adjust?

10.3 Organizational Development: What It Is, What It Can Do

Major Question: What are the uses of organizational development, and how effective is it?

10.4 Promoting Innovation within the Organization

Major Question: What do I need to know to encourage innovation?

Managing for Innovation & Change Takes a Careful Hand

We live in what Tom Peters calls Discontinuous Times, or "a brawl with no rules," where dealing with change is an ongoing challenge for every manager.[1] "The one constant factor in business today is we live in a perpetual hurricane season," says Mellon Bank Corp. vice chairman Martin McGuinn. "A leader's job is less about getting through the current storm and more about enabling people to navigate the ongoing series of storms."[2]

For instance, speed is emerging as the ultimate competitive weapon. "Some of the world's most successful companies," says one writer, "are proving to be expert at spotting new opportunities, marshaling their forces, and bringing to market new products or services in a flash. That goes for launching whole new ventures, too."[3] Speed is being driven by a new innovation imperative. "Competition is more intense than ever," he continues, "because of the rise of the Asian powerhouses and the spread of disruptive new Internet technologies and business models."

Managing for innovation and change takes a careful hand. "Even when their jobs depend on adopting and inventing new maneuvers," says columnist Carol Hymowitz, "most workers hold fast to old ones. The majority either are overwhelmed when asked to do things differently or become entrenched, clinging harder to the past."[4]

Some ways to deal with change and innovation include the following:[5]

Allow Room for Failure

"If somebody has an idea, don't stomp on it," says a psychologist and developer of ideas at Intuit, the software company famous for TurboTax and QuickBooks. "It's more important to get the stupidest idea out there and build on it than not to have it in the first place."[6] At Intuit, failure is very much an option as long as one learns from it.

Give One Consistent Explanation for the Change

When a company is undergoing change, myriad rumors will fly and employees will be uneasy; you and the managers who report to you need to give one consistent explanation. In McGuinn's case, the explanation for overhauling Mellon Bank's retail division was "We want to be the best retailer in financial services."

Look for Opportunities in Unconventional Ways

Most "new" products and services are really knockoffs or marginal variations of the things already on the market and hence are doomed to failure, says Robert Cooper, professor of marketing at Ontario's McMaster University. This doesn't mean, of course, that there isn't room for leveraging existing products with utterly unoriginal ideas. But most people are blinded by the limits of conventional wisdom and their own experience and fail to see huge potential markets in unconventional concepts. Try this advice from a Yale entrepreneurship instructor: Write down every hassle you encounter during the day. "At the end of the month, you will have 20 business ideas," he says, "and some of them will work."[7]

Have the Courage to Follow Your Ideas

This may be the hardest job of all—trying to convince others that your ideas for change are feasible, especially if the ideas are radical. This may mean working to gain allies within the organization, standing up to intimidating competitors inside and out, and perhaps being prepared to follow a lonely course for a long time.[8]

Allow Grieving, Then Move On

Managers overseeing change need to give long-term employees a chance to grieve over the loss of the old ways, says McGuinn, who found that staffers were more willing to change after they had a chance to vent their fears.

For Discussion If you were going to instill a culture of innovation in a company you worked for, what kinds of things would you do?

forecast | What's Ahead in This Chapter

In this chapter, we consider the nature of change in organizations, including the two types of change—reactive and proactive—and the forces for change originating outside and inside the organization. Next we explore the threat of change and how you can manage employee fear and resistance. We then describe the four areas in which change is often needed: people, technology, structure, and strategy. We then discuss organizational development, a set of techniques for implementing planned change. Finally, we discuss how to promote innovation within an organization.

major question?

Since change is always with us, what should I understand about it?

THE BIG PICTURE

Companies that do not adapt to change may go through five stages of institutional decline. Two types of change are reactive and proactive. Forces for change may consist of forces outside the organization—demographic characteristics, market changes, technological advancements, shareholder and customer demands, supplier practices, and social and political pressures. Or they may be forces inside the organization—employee problems and managers' behavior. Four areas in which change is often needed are people, technology, structure, and strategy.

People are generally uncomfortable about change, even change in apparently minor matters. Philosopher Eric Hoffer told how as a younger man he spent a good part of one year as an agricultural worker picking peas, starting in Southern California in January and working his way northward. He picked the last of the peas in June, then moved to another area where, for the first time, he was required to pick string beans. "I still remember," he wrote, "how hesitant I was that first morning as I was about to address myself to the string bean vines. Would I be able to pick string beans? Even the change from peas to string beans had in it elements of fear."[9]

If small changes can cause uneasiness, large changes can cause considerable stress—but they are often necessary for a company's survival.

Recognizing the Need for Change: Collins's Five Stages of Decline

Jim Collins, researcher of enduring great companies, has found that there are five stages of institutional decline.[10] The stages, which are largely self-inflicted, are as follows:

- **Stage 1, Hubris Born of Success.** This stage begins when a company develops arrogance (hubris) and its employees begin attributing the company's success to their own superior qualities, forgetting about the underlying factors that created that success.

- **Stage 2, Undisciplined Pursuit of More.** Growing out of the hubris of Stage 1, Stage 2 is the pursuit of more—more of whatever is defined as success, such as more growth—and companies begin overreaching, making undisciplined leaps into areas where they cannot be great, leading them to ignore their core business.

- **Stage 3, Denial of Risk and Peril.** In this stage, internal warning signs begin to increase, but managers explain them away, discounting negative data, amplifying positive data, and putting a positive spin on ambiguous data.

- **Stage 4, Grasping for Salvation.** At this stage, the difficulties of the previous stage reach the point of throwing the company into sharp decline, at which point managers begin making desperate leaps (Grasping for Salvation): trying bold but untested strategies, looking for a blockbuster product, trying to put together a game-changing acquisition, and similar attempts at silver-bulleted solutions.

- **Stage 5, Capitulation to Irrelevance or Death.** The longer an organization stays in Stage 4, the more apt it is to slip downward into Stage 5—at which point the company may be sold, allowed to go bankrupt, or left to shrivel into insignificance.

Fundamental Change: What Will You Be Called On to Deal With?

"It is hard to predict, especially the future," physicist Niels Bohr is supposed to have quipped.

But it is possible to identify and prepare for *the future that has already happened,* in the words of management theorist Peter Drucker, by looking at some of the fundamental changes that are happening now.[11] Declining population in developed countries. More diversity in the workforce. China becoming the second-largest economic power. The ascent of knowledge work. Increased globalization. Awareness of global warming and need for sustainability. The rise of business-to-business (B2B) technology. Digital long-distance networks. The increase in data storage. On-demand media. The capturing of customer-specific information. The customization of mass goods. Instant-gratification shopping. Sales in the form of auctions instead of fixed prices.[12]

Beyond these overarching trends are also some supertrends shaping the future of business:[13]

1. The Marketplace Is Becoming More Segmented & Moving Toward More Niche Products In the recent past, managers could think in terms of mass markets—mass communication, mass behavior, and mass values. Now we have "de-massification," with customer groups becoming segmented into smaller and more specialized groups responding to more narrowly targeted commercial messages. "Our culture and economy are increasingly shifting away from a focus on a relatively small number of hits (mainstream products and markets) . . . and moving toward a huge number of niches," says Chris Anderson in *The Long Tail.* "In an era without the constraints of physical shelf space and other bottlenecks of distribution, narrowly targeted goods and services can be as economically attractive as mainstream fare."[14] Or, as the book's subtitle states, "the future of business is selling less of more."

Example: In the Internet Age, retailers like Amazon and Apple are not constrained by physical shelf space and can offer consumers a much wider variety of products, yet small sales, one or two rather than millions of items at a time, can produce big profits.

2. More Competitors Are Offering Targeted Products, Requiring Faster Speed-to-Market Companies offering a broad range of products or services are now experiencing intense pressure from competitors offering specialized solutions—and beating them to the punch by devising novel speed-to-market strategies.

Example: Virgin Group Ltd., headed by Sir Richard Branson, is known mainly for its music and airline businesses, but it has entered several new businesses one after the other—mobile phones, credit cards, hotels, games, trains, even space travel—and very quickly. Virgin Comics, aimed at India's multibillion-dollar comics market, went from idea to public announcement in less than 11 months.

3. Some Traditional Companies May Not Survive Radically Innovative Change In *The Innovator's Dilemma: When New Technologies Cause Great Firms to Fail,* Clayton M. Christensen, a Harvard Business School professor, argues that when successful companies are confronted with a giant technological leap that transforms their markets, all choices are bad ones. Indeed, he thinks, it's very difficult for an existing successful company to take full advantage of a technological breakthrough such as digitalization—what he calls "disruptive innovation." Instead, he argues that such a company should set up an entirely separate organization that can operate much like a startup.[15]

Example: In 2009, Finnish phone maker Nokia held first place in world market share for cellphones. The following year, however, it fell to third place behind Apple and Samsung.[16] The company then began an accelerated program to switch its phones from its own Symbian software to Microsoft's Windows Phone 7 software to avoid being left behind in the fast-moving mobile phone industry. But as Nokia was shedding 10,000 employees to cut costs, Virtu, its independent, England-based luxury division, was

Rising to the challenge.
A technician checks a Vertu Constellation Quest mobile phone, whose diamond-encrusted design is intended for the luxury market. Do you think Nokia, which lost its first-place position in the world smartphone market, can reinvent itself using Windows Phone 7 and Virtu?

increasing its staff more than 50%. Virtu has become the dominant player in the luxury smartphone market (average price $6,800, with top-end, diamond-encrusted models more than twice that), mainly because of surging demand in status-conscious emerging markets such as China and the Persian Gulf.[17]

4. China, India, & Other Offshore Suppliers Are Changing the Way We Work As we said in Chapter 2, globalization and outsourcing are transforming whole industries and changing the way we work. China, India, Mexico, the Philippines, and other countries offer workers and even professionals who are willing to work twice as hard for half the pay, giving American businesses substantial labor savings. These developing nations also, says one writer, offer "enormous gains in efficiency, productivity, quality, and revenues that can be achieved by fully leveraging offshore talent."[18] While unquestionably some American jobs are lost, others become more productive, with some engineers and salespeople, for example, being liberated from routine tasks so they can spend more time innovating and dealing with customers.

Example: Querétaro is not a place you would probably go for spring break, but it is rapidly becoming known for something not normally associated with Mexico: aircraft construction. American aircraft makers from Bombardier to Cessna Aircraft to Hawker Beechcraft have various kinds of subassembly work here, where wages are lower but skill levels are not.[19] But if some manufacturing jobs have moved cross-border, so have many customers for American products. Houston-based SolArt, which offers energy management software and services to U.S. airlines, now has new clients such as Singapore Airlines.[20] IBM now makes two-thirds of its revenue abroad.[21] As often as not, however, overseas firms now look to the United States for talented workers, especially in technology and finance. As China, for instance, develops a high-tech economy, it is drawing on the United States for researchers.[22]

5. Knowledge, Not Information, Is Becoming the New Competitive Advantage "Information is rapidly becoming a profitless commodity, and knowledge is becoming the new competitive advantage," says San Diego management consultant Karl Albrecht.[23] That is, as information technology does more of the work formerly done by humans, even in high-tech areas (such as sorting data for relevance), many low-level employees previously thought of as knowledge workers are now being recognized as "data workers," who contribute very little added value to the processing of information. Unlike routine information handling, knowledge work is analytic and involves problem solving and abstract reasoning—exactly the kind of thing required of skillful managers, professionals, salespeople, and financial analysts. As futurists Alvin and Heidi Toffler suggest, knowledge work drives the future and creates wealth.[24]

Example: Many back-office systems and functions—those the customer does not see, such as inventory management and accounts payable—are now outsourced. Indeed, even some tasks of software engineers and other technical experts are sent overseas.

IBM's annual survey of 1,541 CEOs, general managers, and senior public-sector leaders from 60 countries and 33 industries concluded that "incremental changes are no longer sufficient in a world that is operating in fundamentally different ways."[25] Life in general, these executives agreed, is becoming more complex and the firms that are able to manage that complexity are the ones that will survive in the long term. Clearly, we are all in for an interesting ride.

Two Types of Change: Reactive Versus Proactive

As a manager, you will typically have to deal with two types of change: *reactive* and *proactive*.

1. Reactive Change: Responding to Unanticipated Problems & Opportunities When managers talk about "putting out fires," they are talking about *reactive change,* **making changes in response to problems or opportunities as they arise.** A good example is how grocers and government officials responded to 2012 social media's depiction of "pink slime," a beef additive. Although the product had been safely used for years as a way to make ground beef leaner, social media frenzy had caused people to fear its use in our food. This in turn led some grocers to stop using the product and a loss of jobs for people producing it. The U.S. Department of Agriculture and governors from five states responded by starting a public relations campaign to discredit the erroneous information being promoted to the public.[26]

EXAMPLE

Reactive Change: BP Takes a Chance—& Loses Big-Time[27]

Crises can happen quickly and without warning, and many companies have shown they don't deal with them well, as happened with Coca-Cola's reactions to the 1999 illness in Europe attributed to bottlers in Belgium and France, Bausch & Lomb's delay in 2006 in withdrawing a contaminated contact lens cleaner, and Toyota's slow reaction in 2010 to dealing with its cars' accelerator problems. (You can find out about these mishaps through an online search.)

Crisis in the Gulf of Mexico. For oil giant BP (formerly British Petroleum), the crisis was far bigger than any of these. In April 2010, an explosion on the BP drilling platform *Deepwater Horizon* in the Gulf of Mexico led to sinking of the rig, loss of 11 lives, and the largest oil spill ever to happen in U.S. waters. Oil wells have emergency shutoff valves called blowout preventers, which can be triggered from the rig. The *Deepwater Horizon,* which floated 5,000 feet above the ocean floor, was equipped with this device, which nearly always works when wells surge out of control. However, it failed to operate on the day of the Gulf accident.

And what the rig did not have was a *backup* shutoff switch, a remote-control device that carries an acoustic signal through the water that can be activated as a last resort. Such acoustic backup triggers, which cost about $500,000, are not mandated by U.S. regulators, but they also haven't been tested under real-world conditions, because major offshore oil-well blowouts are so rare. (Two other major oil-producing countries, Norway and Brazil, do require them, and some major oil companies, such as Royal Dutch Shell, use them even when regulators don't mandate them.)

BP Reacts. As 2.5 million gallons of oil a day leaked from the open wellhead, the question was asked: Why wasn't BP prepared for such an accident? "We will stop the leaks," said one consultant, "but it's not like the technology is just lying around."[28]

YOUR CALL

Twenty-four years after the *Exxon Valdez*'s famous 1989 oil spill in the Gulf of Alaska, the effects of which are still being felt, do you think oil companies have been shortsighted in planning for major accidents? What should BP have been doing?

2. Proactive Change: Managing Anticipated Problems & Opportunities In contrast to reactive change, *proactive change,* **or planned change, involves making carefully thought-out changes in anticipation of possible or expected problems or opportunities.**[29]

EXAMPLE

Proactive Change: Redbox's Parent, Coinstar, Gets Out Front on New Vending Machines

Burger King tests home delivery of burgers and fries, using special thermal packaging.[30] Toymakers convert classic games and toys such as Monopoly and Barbie for use on iPad screens to entertain technology-obsessed children.[31] Online bank ING Direct lures prospective customers by opening a café where staff members make lattes and answer questions about checking accounts and mortgages.[32] All are examples of companies trying to get out in front of trends rather than react to them.

The Coin-op Future. Headquartered in Bellevue, Washington, and known for its coin-counting kiosks in grocery and other retail chains, Coinstar was founded in 1991 by a Stanford University graduate student, Jens Molbak, who realized there wasn't an easy way to dispose of the change piling up in a jar on his dresser. The company's most recent success, responsible for 85% of Coinstar's revenue in 2011, has been its subsidiary Redbox, whose bright red DVD movie-rental machines are found in retail outlets everywhere. But as Coinstar anticipates that consumers will replace discs with online streaming for their movie watching, they are trying, says one writer, "to reinvent vending machines by applying them to new categories of retailing, as well as old ones like coffee."[33]

Kiosks for Coffee, Used Videogames, and Cellphone Trade-ins. Among the kiosks Coinstar is experimenting with are coffee kiosks (with which it is partnering with Starbucks); a concept called Gizmo, which sells used videogame consoles, iPads, and other electronics; and ecoATM, a kiosk that allows consumers to trade in old cellphones for cash (a camera evaluates their condition).

YOUR CALL

Most instances of proactive change involve technology companies, symbolized by Apple's willingness to make sharp turns in direction—to be a "cross-boundary disrupter," in one observer's phrase.[34] In 2007, Apple dropped "Computer" from its name, signaling a move beyond computers—the Apple I, Apple II, Macintosh, and so on—into products intended for what it calls "the digital lifestyle," as represented by the iPod, the iPhone, and the iPad. Can you think of other examples of proactive change?

The Forces for Change: Outside & Inside the Organization

How do managers know when their organizations need to change? The answers aren't clear-cut, but you can get clues by monitoring the forces for change—both outside and inside the organization. *(See Figure 10.1, next page.)*

Forces Originating Outside the Organization   External forces consist of six types, as follows.

1. Demographic Characteristics   Previously we discussed the demographic changes occurring in the U.S. workforce, with the workforce becoming more diverse. Example: So-called Millennials (those born after 1980) are vastly different from their parents in their views on everything from technology to politics to marriage to tattoos.[35]

2. Market Changes   Certainly the global economy has forced U.S. companies to change the way they do business, with Walmart, for example, stepping up its expansion into overseas markets.[36] The recent Great Recession has also drastically affected many organizations. Example: Second-hand shops have suffered from a recession-induced decline in thrift store donations, even as consumer demand for used goods has gone through the roof.[37] Beer makers have seen declining sales as consumers shift to wine and liquor.[38]

3. Technological Advancements   Technology may be one of the greatest forces for productivity in our lifetime, but it can also create real headaches for somebody. Example: Technology has made it easy for all kinds of illegal copycats in China and elsewhere to make pirated versions of American products—such as DVDs of U.S. movies still in theaters.[39] Another example: The invention of a machine to make plastic corks for wine bottles is severely affecting Portugal, which produces some 52% of the world's natural cork.[40]

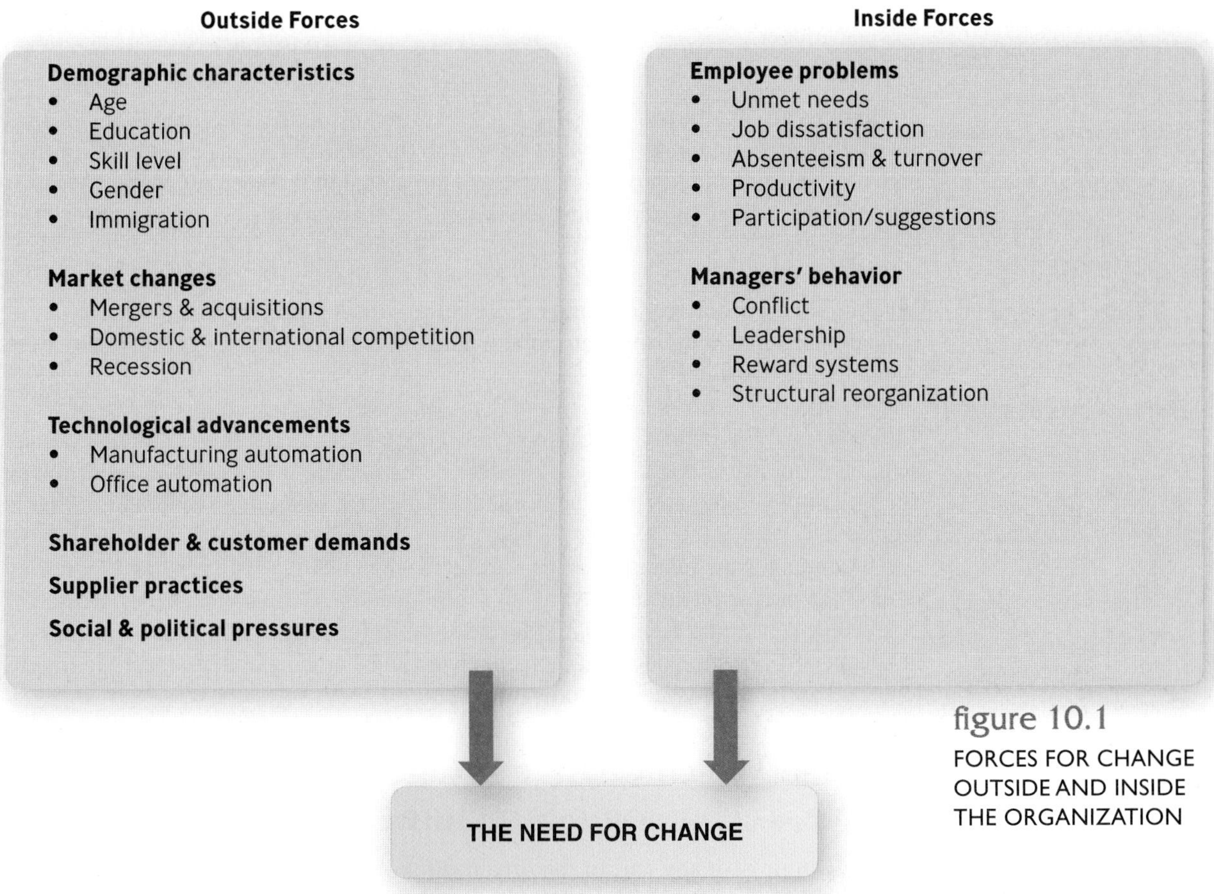

Outside Forces	Inside Forces
Demographic characteristics • Age • Education • Skill level • Gender • Immigration **Market changes** • Mergers & acquisitions • Domestic & international competition • Recession **Technological advancements** • Manufacturing automation • Office automation **Shareholder & customer demands** **Supplier practices** **Social & political pressures**	**Employee problems** • Unmet needs • Job dissatisfaction • Absenteeism & turnover • Productivity • Participation/suggestions **Managers' behavior** • Conflict • Leadership • Reward systems • Structural reorganization

THE NEED FOR CHANGE

figure 10.1

FORCES FOR CHANGE
OUTSIDE AND INSIDE
THE ORGANIZATION

4. Shareholder & Customer Demands   Shareholders have begun to be more active in pressing for organizational change. Insurance company Aflac, for example, has become the first U.S. company to allow shareholders to have a say on executive pay.[41] Customers are also becoming more demanding, being more inclined to take their business elsewhere if they do not get what they want from a given company. Thus, firms such as General Motors and McDonald's actively collect information about customer preferences and try to address them in their new products.[42]

5. Supplier Practices   In today's global economy, the actions of a company's suppliers can create the need for change. Example: An audit of Apple's suppliers in China created pressure for Apple to either change suppliers or force the suppliers to alter their human resource practices. A key supplier, Foxconn, agreed to change its policy on the number of hours worked per week and the maximum amount of overtime per month. The company also committed to creating a safer and more satisfying work environment.[43]

6. Social & Political Pressures   Social events can create great pressures. Example: Poor lifestyle choices have led to 68.8% of U.S. adults being overweight or obese, which in turn produced an increase in several types of cancer that are weight related. These health-related problems and their associated costs have prompted organizations to find ways of helping employees adopt more healthy lifestyles. Sprint Nextel, for example, started putting out a monthly employee wellness letter that provides tips for dealing with health issues.[44]

Forces Originating Inside the Organization   Internal forces affecting organizations may be subtle, such as low job satisfaction, or more dramatic, such as constant labor-management conflict. Internal forces may be of two types: employee problems or managers' behavior.

1. Employee Problems   Is there a gap between the employees' needs and desires and the organization's needs and desires? Job dissatisfaction—as expressed through high absenteeism and turnover—can be a major signal of the need for change. Organizations may respond by addressing job design, reducing employees' role conflicts, and dealing with work overload, to mention a few matters.

Example: As the recent recession lingered on, employees in many organizations became stressed out from months of dealing with layoff concerns, wage cuts, or scaled-back hours, requiring managers to hold meetings and change hiring practices to alleviate their worries.[45]

2. Managers' Behavior   Excessive conflict between managers and employees may be another indicator that change is needed. Perhaps there is a personality conflict, so that an employee transfer may be needed. Or perhaps some interpersonal training is required.

Example: "New managers tend to struggle when dealing with regular, day-to-day issues, like people on the team who don't meet deadlines," says Vicki Foley, a director of a career-consulting firm.[46] One solution is to become a "servant leader" (discussed in Chapter 14), seeing yourself as someone who helps others do their jobs, fixing problems and giving employees the tools they need.

Areas in Which Change Is Often Needed: People, Technology, Structure, & Strategy

Change can involve any part of the organization. Models of change, however, reveal four targeted areas in which change is most apt to be needed: *people, technology, structure,* and *strategy.*

1. Changing People   Even in a two-person organization, people changes may be required. The changes may take the following forms:

- **Perceptions.** Employees might feel they are underpaid for what they do. Managers might be able to show that pay and benefits are comparable or superior to those offered by competitors.
- **Attitudes.** In some companies, such as old-line manufacturing firms, employees may feel that it is the nature of things that managers don't listen to them (and they're often right).[47] It may be up to management to try to change the culture and the attitudes by using educational techniques to show why the old labor wars should become a thing of the past.
- **Performance.** Should an organization pay the people who contract to wash its windows by the hour? by the window? or by the total job? Will one method cause them to work fast and sloppily but cost less? Will one cause them to do pristine windows but cost too much? It's often a major challenge to find incentives to improve people's performance.
- **Skills.** Altering or improving skill levels is often an ongoing challenge, particularly these days, when new forms of technology can change an organization's way of doing business, as we describe next.

A world changer? Before it was rolled out in 2001, tech-world pundits predicted that the Segway, the battery-powered two-wheeled scooter, would revolutionize society. Although it has not lived up to such expectations, it has found success in law enforcement, private security, helping disabled vets—and transporting of tourists. Can you think of other forms of technology that did not realize the high hopes predicted for them?

2. Changing Technology Technology is a major area of change for many organizations. Of the top 30 innovations of the last 30 years, according to a Wharton School analysis, all involved technology. (The top five: the Internet and World Wide Web, PC/laptop computers, mobile phones, e-mail, and DNA testing and sequencing.)[48] ***Technology is not just computer technology; it is any machine or process that enables an organization to gain a competitive advantage in changing materials used to produce a finished product.***

EXAMPLE

Changing Technology: Web 2.0 Is Radically Altering How Business Is Done

Futurist Paul Saffo, director of the Institute for the Future in Menlo Park, California, says that new technologies lead to new products. The invention of television, for example, led to TV dinners and TV trays. The invention of the iPod led to the selling of music singles—something that hadn't happened since the 45 rpm record. "Each time it gets cheaper to do something," says Saffo, "you get more players. It's irreversibly more complex."[49]

Second-Generation Internet Services. Thus, the original World Wide Web has led to Web 2.0, a second generation of Internet-based services that lets people collaborate and share information online in a new way.[50] Among the results are social networking sites (MySpace, Facebook), photo-sharing sites (Flickr), and wikis (group-editable web pages, such as the reference source Wikipedia), which all demand active participation and social interaction.

Web 2.0 services have also come into the business world, with wikis, for example, being used by the Walt Disney Co. and other firms to enhance collaboration. Other companies are using social networking services such as LinkedIn Corp to gain sales leads and hiring prospects. The "mobile web," involving wireless communication and mobile gadgets (BlackBerrys, digital-music players), is changing commerce, allowing wireless shopping, for instance.[51] "In essence," says one article, "these services are coalescing into one giant computer that anyone with access to an Internet-connected [device] can use, from anywhere in the world."[52]

Flattened Lines of Authority. A significant structural result of Web 2.0 is further assault on conventional reporting arrangements, already being transformed by globalization and outsourcing. That is, the new free-form technologies help to further flatten clear lines of authority between managers and employees and to reduce organizational boundaries between the company and its partners and customers.

YOUR CALL

What possibilities do you see for applying social networking services, photo-sharing sites, blogs, and wikis to business uses? (Be aware that this area is still sort of the Wild West, with lots of consultants peddling such "measures" as blog mentions, YouTube hits, and number of Twitter followers as literal figures, when these catchphrases may not distinguish between what works and what doesn't.)[53]

3. Changing Structure Changes in strategy frequently require changes in structure. One of our clients, for example, changed from a product-based structure to a matrix structure in order to find new avenues for growing its business. Overall, recent trends are toward "flattening the hierarchy," eliminating several middle layers of management, and using work teams linked by electronic networks.

4. Changing Strategy Shifts in the marketplace often may lead organizations to have to change their strategy. Example: Surveys by the Pew Internet Project show that 75% of respondents ages 12–17 agree that music "file-sharing is so easy to do, it's unrealistic to expect people not to do it." "They are Generation Free," comments one writer, "and they just might kill the goose that lays the golden egg"—namely, the very record industry that makes music available.[54] But while illegal file sharing has had a negative effect on the CD sales of the largest "big four" record labels over the last decade, the broader music industry (independent music labels, live performances, merchandise) actually did extremely well, suggesting that old-line companies need to dramatically change their strategies.[55] ●

major question?

How are employees threatened by change, and how can I help them adjust?

THE BIG PICTURE

This section discusses the causes of resistance to change and the degree to which employees fear change, from least threatening to most threatening. It also describes Lewin's three-stage change model: unfreezing, changing, and refreezing. Finally, it describes Kotter's eight steps for leading organizational change, which can be linked to Lewin's three stages.

As a manager, particularly one working for an American organization, you may be pressured to provide short-term, quick-fix solutions. But when applied to organizational problems, this approach usually doesn't work: Quick-fix solutions have little staying power.

What, then, are effective ways to manage organizational change and employees' fear and resistance to it? In this section, we discuss the following:

- The causes of resistance to change.
- The extent to which employees fear change and reasons why employees resist change.
- Lewin's change model.
- Kotter's eight stages for leading organizational change.

The Causes of Resistance to Change[56]

***Resistance to change* is an emotional/behavioral response to real or imagined threats to an established work routine.** Resistance can be as subtle as passive resignation and as overt as deliberate sabotage.

Resistance can be considered to be the interaction of three causes: (1) employee characteristics, (2) change agent characteristics, and (3) the change agent–employee relationship. *(See Figure 10.2.)* For example, an employee's resistance is partly based on his or her perception of change, which is influenced by the attitudes and behaviors exhibited by the change agent and the level of trust between change agent and the employee.

Let us consider these three sources of resistance to change.

figure 10.2

A MODEL OF RESISTANCE TO CHANGE

Source: Adapted from R. Kreitner and A. Kinicki, *Organizational Behavior,* 9th ed. (Burr Ridge, IL: McGraw-Hill/ Irwin, 2010), p. 549. Reprinted with permission of The McGraw-Hill Companies.

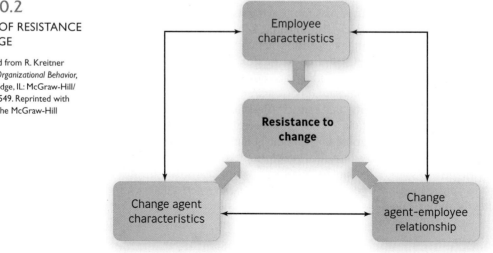

1. Employee Characteristics   The characteristics of a given employee consist of his or her individual differences (discussed in the next chapter), actions and inactions, and perceptions of change. We describe some of these characteristics in the upcoming subsection, "Ten Reasons Employees Resist Change."

2. Change-Agent Characteristics   The characteristics of the change agent—the individual who is a catalyst in helping organizations change—also consist of his or her individual differences, actions and inactions, and perceptions of change. Such characteristics that might contribute to employee resistance to change might include leadership style, personality, tactfulness, sense of timing, awareness of cultural traditions or group relationships, and ability to empathize with the employee's perspective.

3. Change Agent–Employee Relationship   As you might expect, resistance to change is reduced when change agents and employees have a trusting relationship—faith in each other's intentions. Mistrust, on the other hand, encourages secrecy, which begets deeper mistrust, and can doom an otherwise well-conceived change.

The Degree to Which Employees Fear Change: From Least Threatening to Most Threatening

Whether organizational change is administrative or technological, the degree to which employees feel threatened by it in general depends on whether the change is *adaptive, innovative,* or *radically innovative*.[57]

Least Threatening: Adaptive Change   *Adaptive change* **is reintroduction of a familiar practice**—the implementation of a kind of change that has already been experienced within the same organization. This form of change is lowest in complexity, cost, and uncertainty. Because it is familiar, it is the least threatening to employees and thus will create the least resistance.

For example, during annual inventory week, a department store may ask its employees to work 12 hours a day instead of the usual 8. During tax-preparation time, the store's accounting department may imitate this same change in work hours. Although accounting employees are in a different department from stockroom and sales employees, it's expected they wouldn't be terribly upset by the temporary change in hours since they've seen it in effect elsewhere in the store.

Somewhat Threatening: Innovative Change   *Innovative change* **is the introduction of a practice that is new to the organization.** This form of change involves moderate complexity, cost, and uncertainty. It is therefore apt to trigger some fear and resistance among employees.

For example, should a department store decide to adopt a new practice of its competitors by staying open 24 hours a day, requiring employees to work flexible schedules, the change may be felt as moderately threatening.

Very Threatening: Radically Innovative Change   *Radically innovative change* **involves introducing a practice that is new to the industry.** Because it is the most complex, costly, and uncertain of the levels of change, it will be felt as extremely threatening to managers' confidence and employees' job security and may well tear at the fabric of the organization.[58]

For example, a department store converting some of its operations to e-commerce—selling its goods on the Internet—may encounter anxiety among its staff, especially those fearing being left behind.

Ten Reasons Employees Resist Change   Whether changes are adaptive, innovative, or radically innovative, employees may resist them for all kinds of reasons. Ten of the leading ones are as follows.[59]

1. Individual's Predisposition Toward Change   How people react to change depends a lot on how they learned to handle change and ambiguity as children. One person's parents may have been patient, flexible, and understanding, and from the time the child was weaned she may have learned there were positive compensations for the loss of immediate gratification. Thus, she will associate making changes with love and approval. Another person's parents may have been unreasonable and unyielding, forcing him to do things (piano lessons, for example) that he didn't want to do. Thus, he will be distrustful of making changes because he will associate them with demands for compliance.[60]

2. Surprise and Fear of the Unknown   When radically different changes are introduced without warning—for example, without any official announcements—the office rumor mill will go into high gear, and affected employees will become fearful of the implications of the changes. Harvard business scholar Rosabeth Moss Kanter recommends that in such cases a transition manager should be appointed who is charged with keeping all relevant parties adequately informed.[61]

3. Climate of Mistrust   Trust involves reciprocal faith in others' intentions and behavior. Mistrust encourages secrecy, which causes deeper mistrust, putting even well-conceived changes at risk of failure. Managers who trust their employees make the change process an open, honest, and participative affair. Employees who trust their managers are more apt to expend extra effort and take chances with something different.

4. Fear of Failure   Intimidating changes on the job can cause employees to doubt their capabilities. Self-doubt erodes self-confidence and cripples personal growth and development.

5. Loss of Status or Job Security   Administrative and technological changes that threaten to alter power bases or eliminate jobs—as often happens during corporate restructurings that threaten middle-management jobs—generally trigger strong resistance.

6. Peer Pressure   Even people who are not themselves directly affected by impending changes may actively resist in order to protect the interests of their friends and coworkers.

7. Disruption of Cultural Traditions or Group Relationships   Whenever individuals are transferred, promoted, or reassigned, the change can disrupt existing cultural and group relationships. Example: Traditionally, Sony Corp. promoted insiders to new positions. When an outsider, Howard Stringer, was named as the next chairman and CEO and six corporate officers were asked to resign, creating a majority board of foreigners, the former CEO, Nobuyuki Idei, worried the moves might engender strong employee resistance.[62]

8. Personality Conflicts   Just as a friend can get away with telling us something we would resent hearing from an adversary, the personalities of change agents can breed resistance.

9. Lack of Tact or Poor Timing   Introducing changes in an insensitive manner or at an awkward time can create employee resistance. Employees are more apt to accept changes when managers effectively explain their value, as, for example, in demonstrating their strategic purpose to the organization.

10. Nonreinforcing Reward Systems   Employees are likely to resist when they can't see any positive rewards from proposed changes, as, for example, when one is asked to work longer hours without additional compensation.

To gauge how adaptable you're apt to be to organizational change, try the Self-Assessment at the end of this chapter (p. 333).

Lewin's Change Model: Unfreezing, Changing, & Refreezing

Most theories of organizational change originated with the landmark work of social psychologist **Kurt Lewin.** Lewin developed a model with three stages—*unfreezing, changing,* and *refreezing*—to explain how to initiate, manage, and stabilize planned change.[63]

1. "Unfreezing": Creating the Motivation to Change In the *unfreezing stage,* managers try to instill in employees the motivation to change, encouraging them to let go of attitudes and behaviors that are resistant to innovation. For this "unfreezing" to take place, employees need to become dissatisfied with the old way of doing things. Managers also need to reduce the barriers to change during this stage.

Example: Wireless handheld computers—personal digital assistants (PDAs)—are becoming established tools for health professionals, who use them to access patient records in hospital information systems. How well have they been accepted? Studies exploring nurses' perceptions about using PDAs in their daily patient practice found initial resistance, with some nurses concerned about the cost and short technological life cycle of these devices—the *unfreezing* stage.[64]

2. "Changing": Learning New Ways of Doing Things In the *changing stage,* employees need to be given the tools for change: new information, new perspectives, new models of behavior. Managers can help here by providing benchmarking results, role models, mentors, experts, and training. It's advisable, experts say, to convey the idea that change is a continuous learning process, not just a onetime event.[65]

Example: In the *changing* stage, nurses learning PDAs were allowed to continue their manual patient-charting systems while learning the PDA-accessible versions, but only for a limited time to avoid adding to their already heavy workloads. They were assisted with educational programs to help them learn and implement the new technology, programs that also stressed the need to protect confidential patient records.

3. "Refreezing": Making the New Ways Normal In the *refreezing stage,* employees need to be helped to integrate the changed attitudes and behavior into their normal ways of doing things. Managers can assist by encouraging employees to exhibit the new change and then, through additional coaching and modeling, by reinforcing the employees in the desired change. *(See Table 10.1, at right.)*

Example: In the *refreezing* stage, as hospitals eliminated barriers that precluded the use of wireless networks, nurses learned to appreciate the usefulness of having a widely pervasive and portable technology, with its easier access to drug and diagnostic/laboratory reference applications and improved communications.

One technique used in Stage 1 to help unfreeze organizations is **benchmarking, a process by which a company compares its performance with that of high-performing organizations.**[66] Professional sports teams do this all the time, but so do other kinds of organizations, including nonprofit ones.

For example, one company discovered that its costs to develop a computer system were twice those of competitors and that the time to get a new product to market was four times longer. These data were ultimately used to unfreeze employees' attitudes and motivate people to change the organization's internal processes in order to remain competitive.[67]

Kotter's Eight Steps for Leading Organizational Change

An expert in leadership and change management, **John Kotter** believes that, to be successful, organizational change needs to follow eight steps to avoid the eight common errors senior management usually commits.[68] *(See Table 10.2, next page.)* These correspond with Lewin's unfreezing-changing-refreezing steps.

table 10.1

SIX METHODS FOR MANAGING EMPLOYEE RESISTANCE TO CHANGE

1. Education and communication

2. Participation and involvement

3. Facilitation and support

4. Negotiation and rewards

5. Manipulation and co-optation

6. Explicit and implicit coercion

Source: Adapted from J. P. Kotter and L. A. Schlesinger, "Choosing Strategies for Change," *Harvard Business Review,* March–April 1979, pp. 106–14.

table 10.2

STEPS TO LEADING ORGANIZATIONAL CHANGE

Step	Description
1. Establish a sense of urgency.	Unfreeze the organization by creating a compelling reason for why change is needed.
2. Create the guiding coalition.	Create a cross-functional, cross-level group of people with enough power to lead the change.
3. Develop a vision and a strategy.	Create a vision and a strategic plan to guide the change process.
4. Communicate the change vision.	Create and implement a communication strategy that consistently communicates the new vision and strategic plan.
5. Empower broad-based action.	Eliminate barriers to change, and use target elements of change to transform the organization. Encourage risk taking and creative problem solving.
6. Generate short-term wins.	Plan for and create short-term "wins" or improvements. Recognize and reward people who contribute to the wins.
7. Consolidate gains and produce more change.	The guiding coalition uses credibility from short-term wins to create more change. Additional people are brought into the change process as change cascades throughout the organization. Attempts are made to reinvigorate the change process.
8. Anchor new approaches in the culture.	Reinforce the changes by highlighting connections between new behaviors and processes and organizational success. Develop methods to ensure leadership development and succession.

Source: Reprinted by permission of Harvard Business School Publishing. From *Leading Change* by J.P. Kotter, 1996. Copyright 1996 by the Harvard Business School Publishing Corporation; all rights reserved..

Steps 1–4 represent unfreezing: establish a sense of urgency, create the guiding coalition, develop a vision and strategy, and communicate the change vision.

Steps 5–7 represent the changing stage: empower broad-based action, generate short-term wins, and consolidate gains and produce more change.

Step 8, corresponding to refreezing, is to anchor new approaches in the organization's culture.

The value of Kotter's steps is that they provide specific recommendations about behaviors that managers need to exhibit to successfully lead organizational change. It is important to remember that Kotter's research reveals that it is ineffective to skip steps and that successful organizational change is 70%–90% leadership and only 10%–30% management. Senior managers are thus advised to focus on leading rather than on managing change.[69]   ●

EXAMPLE

Kotter's Steps in Organizational Change: Implementing an Electronic Health Record System

What if a health care manager is interested not in just getting nurses used to PDAs but getting an entire hospital staff changed over to an electronic health record (EHR) system? Robert James Campbell of East Carolina University proposes the following model, following Kotter's eight-step approach.[70]

1. **Establish a Sense of Urgency.** How do you energize your medical colleagues to realize there's a problem? One way, suggests Campbell, "is to create a video presentation showing an angry parent whose daughter has died at the hospital because of a medical error that could have been prevented if the patient's information was stored electronically rather than on paper."

2. **Create the Guiding Coalition.** Individuals who would guide the change management project would be selected from physicians and other hospital staff members with relevant knowledge about health care industry challenges (including EHR implementation), credibility with peers, knowledge of their department's operations, and the ability to communicate a vision and motivate others to achieve it (leadership).

3. **Develop a Vision & a Strategy.** The health care manager and team next need to frame a good vision statement with six or seven visions of the future, such as "What does it mean to be a paperless health care organization?" The vision and strategy should focus on how the change would improve service to patients and families and raise the urgency among staff members to motivate them to make the proposed changes a reality.

4. **Communicate the Change Vision.** A way to communicate the vision, says Campbell, is to create a "short, inexpensive video presentation showing an interview done with a patient injured by a medical error" to show how an EHR would reduce errors. Webcasts could also be used to demonstrate to staff members how the EHR would improve patient care.

5. **Empower Broad-Based Action.** Using Kotter's "see-feel-change" method of altering organizational behavior, the change team can show reluctant staffers how an EHR chart can beat a paper chart in providing a patient's history. Bonuses, raises, and promotions can also be given to individuals who embrace the change effort.

6. **Generate Short-Term Wins.** Empowered individuals need to clearly show that the change management project is succeeding by showing "short-term wins," as in showing how quickly an order is fulfilled.

7. **Consolidate Gains & Produce More Change.** Once the new system "goes live" (is fully implemented), it's up to the guiding coalition to resolve difficulties that arise among users through the creation of a special team called "red coats," who are immediately dispatched to solve problems (as when a belligerent physician claims that the system is too difficult to use or is "malfunctioning again").

8. **Anchor New Approaches in the Culture.** To make changes stick and embed the new technology within the organizational culture, the change team creates a practice called "Focused Rounds," in which an expert is sent on hospital rounds with a physician "to help physicians make more efficient use of the system."

YOUR CALL

Kotter's eight steps don't seem mysterious, though (depending on the size of the project or organization) they may require considerable effort. Could you apply them to something on your campus? For instance, in recent times, reducing concussions among athletes (such as football players) has been much in the news.[71] If you were to start a campaign to reduce them in a particular sport on your campus, how would you apply Kotter's methodology?

Lookalikes. One key to the success of Southwest Airlines is that all the planes in its fleet have been the same type, Boeing 737s, which saves on maintenance and training costs. In the wake of its merger with AirTran, as Southwest expands from being a short-haul, low-fare carrier to running long-haul flights as well, it has needed to add new-generation 737s, which can travel longer distances than the older planes did but with greater fuel savings. Southwest still offers no-frills service—no seat assignments and snacks instead of meals—and competes principally on fare price. In evolving from short routes to long ones, should the company expect to have to undergo any of the steps in Lewin's change model—unfreezing, changing, and refreezing?

major question What are the uses of organizational development, and how effective is it?

THE BIG PICTURE

Organizational development (OD) is a set of techniques for implementing change, such as managing conflict, revitalizing organizations, and adapting to mergers. OD has three steps: diagnosis, intervention, and evaluation. Four factors have been found to make OD programs effective.

Organizational development (OD) **is a set of techniques for implementing planned change to make people and organizations more effective.** Note the inclusion of people in this definition. OD focuses specifically on people in the change process. Often OD is put into practice by a person known as a *change agent,* **a consultant with a background in behavioral sciences who can be a catalyst in helping organizations deal with old problems in new ways.**

What Can OD Be Used For?

OD can be used to address the following three matters:

1. Managing Conflict Conflict is inherent in most organizations. Sometimes an OD expert in the guise of an executive coach will be brought in to help advise an executive on how to improve relationships with others in the organization. Example: The two cofounders of Network Appliance, a data-storage firm in Sunnyvale, California, were feuding with each other because one founder couldn't stick to his decisions, which drove the other founder crazy. An organizational behavior specialist began working with the warring executives in separate sessions to solve the problem.

2. Revitalizing Organizations Information technology is wreaking such change that nearly all organizations are now in the position of having to adopt new behaviors in order to resist decline. OD can help by opening communication, fostering innovation, and dealing with stress. Example: Family doctors are paid relatively modestly compared with other physicians and also do a lot of work outside office visits (making phone calls, writing prescriptions, reading lab reports) for which they are not compensated. They will be affected even more heavily by the preventive-medicine orientation of the 2010 health care legislation. By getting expert help in adopting electronic records and trying out pilot projects that compensate them for preventive and disease-management work (not just office visits), these physicians can reduce their costs and increase their revenue significantly.[72]

3. Adapting to Mergers Mergers and acquisitions are associated with increased anxiety, stress, absenteeism, turnover, and decreased productivity.[73] What is the organizational fit between two disparate organizations, such as United Airlines and Continental Airlines, which recently merged?[74] OD experts can help integrate two firms with varying cultures, products, and procedures.

How OD Works

Like physicians, OD managers and consultants follow a medical-like model. (Or, to use our more current formulation, they follow the rules of evidence-based management.) They approach the organization as if it were a sick patient, using *diagnosis, intervention,* and *evaluation*—"diagnosing" its ills, "prescribing" treatment or intervention, and "monitoring" or evaluating progress. If the evaluation shows that the procedure is not working effectively, the conclusions drawn are then applied (see feedback loop) to refining the diagnosis, and the process starts again. *(See Figure 10.3.)*

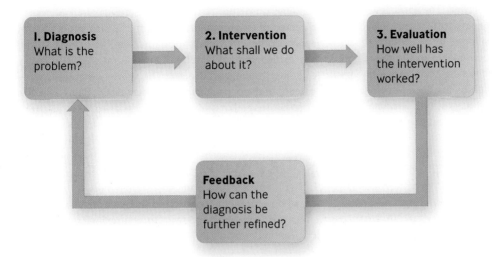

figure 10.3
THE OD PROCESS

Sources: Adapted from W. L. French and C. H. Bell Jr., *Organization Development: Behavioral Interventions for Organizational Improvement* (Englewood Cliffs, NJ: Prentice Hall, 1978); and E. G. Huse and T. G. Cummings, *Organizational Development and Change*, 3rd ed. (St. Paul: West, 1985).

1. Diagnosis: What Is the Problem? To carry out the diagnosis, OD consultants or managers use some combination of questionnaires, surveys, interviews, meetings, records, and direct observation to ascertain people's attitudes and to identify problem areas.

2. Intervention: What Shall We Do About It? "Treatment" or **intervention is the attempt to correct the diagnosed problems.** Often this is done using the services of an OD consultant who works in conjunction with management teams. Some OD activities for implementing planned change are communicating survey results to employees to engage them in constructive problem solving, observing employee communication patterns and teaching them skills to improve them, helping group members learn to function as a team, stimulating better cohesiveness among several work groups, and improving work technology or organizational design.

3. Evaluation: How Well Has the Intervention Worked? An OD program needs objective evaluation to see if it has done any good. Answers may lie in hard data about absenteeism, turnover, grievances, and profitability, which should be compared with earlier statistics. The change agent can use questionnaires, surveys, interviews, and the like to assess changes in employee attitudes.

EXAMPLE

Organizational Development: Patagonia Tries to Become Greener[75]

Founded by an environmentalist in 1979, apparel company Patagonia sells outdoor clothing and gear and has long been a strong supporter of the environmental movement. In fact, its mission statement is "Build the best product, cause no unnecessary harm, use business to inspire and implement solutions to the environmental crisis." However, as customers have become more eco-aware, the company has been getting more questions about how "green" the origins and handling of its products are. The approach Patagonia took resembles the steps in organizational development.

Diagnosis: "What Is the Problem?" Forced to examine how green it actually is, Patagonia sent employees in

May 2007 to track the "environmental footprint" of five products, from design studio to raw-materials stage to U.S. distribution center. The investigators visited yarn spinners in Thailand, a footwear factory in China, and a fiber manufacturer in North Carolina. The good news: they learned that transporting products took surprisingly little energy, because most were shipped by sea, which represented less than 1% of the total energy use in the supply chain. The bad news: manufacturing took more energy than was expected and sometimes produced ecologically unfriendly by-products, such as possibly toxic PFOA (perfluoro-octanoic acid), found in Patagonia parkas.

Intervention: "What Shall We Do About It?" The company believed that using PFOA-free materials might sacrifice performance, so it continued to use PFOA-containing water-repellant membranes and coatings while searching for alternatives. By fall 2008, it had replaced membranes with polyester and polyurethane. However, no satisfactory substitute was found for the existing coatings.

Evaluation: "How Well Has the Intervention Worked?" Not finding a PFOA substitute for the coatings is not ecologically satisfying, but the company insists on maintaining quality. "We don't want to sacrifice quality for environmental reasons," says Jill Dumain, Patagonia's director of environmental analysis. "If a garment is thrown away sooner due to a lack of durability, we haven't solved any environmental problem." In addition, the findings are of limited value, because only the primary materials were traced, and no packaging was evaluated. Patagonia has posted the results of its investigation of some of its products online under the heading "The Footprint Chronicles" at **www.patagonia.com/web/us/footprint/index.jsp.**

YOUR CALL

Do you think every company should take an organizational development approach to the environmental quality of its products and services? Do you believe putting production information in the public domain and available to competitors is risky? Or do the benefits of openness outweigh the costs, because it could spur others to action?

The Effectiveness of OD

Among organizations that have practiced organizational development are American Airlines, B. F. Goodrich, General Electric, Honeywell, ITT, Polaroid, Procter & Gamble, Prudential, Texas Instruments, and Westinghouse Canada—companies covering a variety of industries.

Research has found that OD is most apt to be successful under the following circumstances.

Team building. One technique for implementing change is team building. Teams are often diverse in gender, age, ethnicity, and educational background and experience. Would you prefer to work with a highly diverse team of people?

1. Multiple Interventions OD success stories tend to use multiple interventions. Goal setting, feedback, recognition and rewards, training, participation, and challenging job design have had good results in improving performance and satisfaction.[76] Combined interventions have been found to work better than single interventions.[77]

2. Management Support OD is more likely to succeed when top managers give the OD program their support and are truly committed to the change process and the desired goals of the change program.[78] Also, the expectations for change were not unrealistic.[79]

3. Goals Geared to Both Short- & Long-Term Results Change programs are more successful when they are oriented toward achieving both short-term and long-term results. Managers should not engage in organizational change for the sake of change. Change efforts should produce positive results.[80]

4. OD Is Affected by Culture OD effectiveness is affected by cross-cultural considerations. Thus, an OD intervention that worked in one country should not be blindly applied to a similar situation in another country.[81] ●

10.4 PROMOTING INNOVATION WITHIN THE ORGANIZATION

major question?

What do I need to know to encourage innovation?

THE BIG PICTURE

Innovation may be a product innovation or a process innovation, an incremental innovation or a radical innovation. Two myths about innovation are that it happens in a "Eureka!" moment and that it can be systematized. Ways to encourage innovation are by providing the organizational culture, the resources, and the reward system. To make innovation happen, you need to recognize problems and opportunities, gain allies, overcome employee resistance, and execute well.

Innovation, as we've said earlier in the book, is the activity of creating new ideas and converting them into useful applications—specifically new goods and services. Innovation is more likely to occur when organizations have the proper culture, resources, and reward systems to support it. We now take a closer look into innovation and how it can be encouraged within organizations.

Innovation is different from *invention,* which entails the creation of something new. It is also different from **creativity, which is the process of developing something new or unique.** "You need creativity and invention," says Procter & Gamble CEO A. G. Lafley, "but until you can connect the creativity to the customer in the form of a product or service that meaningfully changes their lives, I would argue you don't have innovation."[82] The spirit of innovation is essential to keeping an organization vital and in maintaining a competitive advantage. Otherwise, the innovation will come from your competitors, forcing you to scramble to catch up—if you can.

How Does Failure Impede Innovation?

"You learn more from failure than you do from success," says Lafley, "but the key is to fail early, fail cheaply, and don't make the same mistake twice."[83] Lafley, who doubled sales and quadrupled profits for P&G, admits to having had "my fair share of failure. But you have to get past the disappointment and blame and really understand what happened and why it happened."[84]

Lafley is comfortable with the idea of learning from failure, but many people are not. They're reluctant to experiment, they blame others, they refuse to recognize that not all failures are of equal seriousness. All of these can detract from an organization's ability to learn from its mistakes, as the table indicates. *(See Table 10.3, next page.)*

Two Myths About Innovation

Two myths about innovation that need to be dispelled are the following:

Myth No. 1: Innovation Happens in a "Eureka!" Moment Many people think that innovation often happens in a bolt-from-the-blue moment of discovery. In this view, innovation happens as a "Eureka!" or "Aha!" epiphany, like the instant revelation about the law of gravity supposedly experienced by Sir Isaac Newton under a tree when an apple fell on his head. Most of the time, however, innovation is the product of hard work and dedication, "forged by a mixed bag of coworkers from up, down, and across an organization, sitting and wrangling it out in the trenches," in the words of Jack and Suzy Welch.[85]

table 10.3

FACTORS THAT REDUCE AN ORGANIZATION'S ABILITY TO LEARN FROM FAILURE

Factor	Description
1. Employees play the "blame game."	Employees blame failures on a person when the causes are internal processes or external events. It's better to focus on short-term factors that lead to long-term success.
2. Employees suffer "self-serving bias."	Employees blame failures on others or on external events, when the fault may well lie with themselves.
3. Employees don't recognize that not all failures are created equal.	Failures may be preventable, as when employees don't follow acceptable procedures. Or they may be uncontrollable, as when suppliers can't deliver the right materials. Or the causes may be complex.
4. A company isn't a learning organization.	In a company without a culture of learning, employees are afraid to discuss failure and to take risks.
5. Employees are reluctant to experiment.	When the causes of failure are uncertain, employees are unwilling to try different solutions to problems or believe that failure is part of the improvement process.

Source: Reprinted by permission of *Harvard Business Review.* From "Strategies for Learning from Failure," by C. Edmonson, April 2011. Copyright 2011 by the Harvard Business School Publishing Corporation; all rights reserved.

Myth No. 2: Innovation Can Be Systematized   Lots of people also believe that innovation can be systematized—made a codified and standardized process that can be designed to always yield fruitful results. Obviously, if this could be done, many companies would be doing it. The problem with innovation, however, is that there are too many challenges associated with it, which makes success unpredictable, although it's possible to establish cultural and other conditions (as discussed next) that increase the likelihood of a payoff.

The Seeds of Innovation: Starting Point for Experimentation & Inventiveness

Former Microsoft employee Scott Berkun, author of *The Myths of Innovation,* has identified six *seeds of innovation,* **the starting point for organizational innovation.** They are as follows:[86]

1. Hard Work in a Specific Direction   Most innovations come from dedicated people diligently working to solve a well-defined problem, hard work that can span many years.

2. Hard Work with Direction Change   Innovations frequently occur when people change their approach to solving a problem. In other words, hard work closes some doors and opens others.

3. Curiosity   Innovations can begin when people are curious about something of interest to them, which leads to experimentation and inventiveness.

4. Wealth & Money   Innovations frequently occur because an organization or an individual simply wants to make money. Being near bankruptcy, for instance, drove Fiat, the Italian auto company, to look for innovative ways to cut costs and grow its market share in the United States. This is why Fiat took a stake in Chrysler in return for imparting its knowledge of small-car technology.[87]

5. Necessity   Many innovations grow from the desire to achieve something or to complete a task that is needed to accomplish a broader goal. For example, Xerox Corp. hired a pair of researchers as "innovation managers" to hunt for inventions and products from startups in India that Xerox might adapt for uses in North America.[88]

6. Combination of Seeds   Many innovations occur as a result of multiple factors.

Types of Innovation: Product or Process, Incremental or Radical

Innovations may be of the following two types.

Product Versus Process Innovations   As a manager, you may need to improve your organization's product or service itself; this is generally a technological innovation. Or you may need to improve the process by which the product or service is created, manufactured, or distributed; this is generally a managerial innovation.

More formally, a ***product innovation* is a change in the appearance or the performance of a product or a service or the creation of a new one. A *process innovation* is a change in the way a product or service is conceived, manufactured, or disseminated.**

Today, says an article about the world's most innovative companies, "innovation is about much more than new products. It is about reinventing business processes and building entirely new markets that meet untapped customer needs."[89]

Incremental Versus Radical Innovations   An innovation may be small or large. The difference is in modifying versus replacing existing products or services. That is, you might have ***incremental innovations*—the creation of products, services, or technologies that modify existing ones.** Or you might have ***radical innovations*—the creation of products, services, or technologies that replace existing ones.**

PRACTICAL ACTION

What Makes a Successful Startup?

According to the Ewing Marion Kauffman Foundation, which works to further understanding of entrepreneurship, the vast majority of entrepreneurs (called *replicative entrepreneurs*) are those with small businesses that replicate or duplicate products and services already in existence, such as restaurants and dry cleaners. Less common are those entrepreneurs (*innovative entrepreneurs*) who pioneer never-seen-before products and services or production methods, such as eBay.[90]

Entrepreneurship: Exploiting Niche Opportunities. Some replicative entrepreneurs, however, simply do things better and faster. Amar V. Bhidé, author of *The Origin and Evolution of New Businesses*, suggests that many successful entrepreneurs start out not by having radical ideas but by making "a small modification in what somebody else is doing."[91] Examples would be a

doctor offering a drive-through component for flu shots or a lawyer offering the same for legal services (a feature already available for banks and fast food, of course).

That is, they see a small niche opportunity—one in which the company they are currently working for is already involved, or a supplier or customer is involved. "And the person jumps in [to a new business] with very little preparation and analysis," says Bhidé, "but with direct firsthand knowledge of the profitability of that opportunity—and pretty much does what somebody else is already doing, but does it better and faster."

And "better and faster" seems to be the main difference. Usually, such entrepreneurs don't have anything in the way of technology or concept that differentiates them from other businesses. "They just work harder, hustle for customers, and know that the opportunity may not last for more than six or eight months," says Bhidé. "But they expect to make a reasonable return on those six to eight months. And along the way they'll figure out something else that will keep the business going."

Tolerance for Ambiguity.

Another quality of entrepreneurs is "a tolerance for ambiguity," Bhidé says. They are willing to jump into things when it's hard to even imagine what the possible outcomes will be, going ahead in the absence of information, very much capital— or even a very novel idea.

An example of a startup that fit these criteria was Build-a-Bear Workshop, which offers mall customers a make-your-own stuffed animal experience, choosing from models of teddy bears, bunnies, dogs, and the like, then adding "a unique personality" from hundreds of teddy bear–sized outfits and accessories. The idea came to Maxine Clark, a former department store executive, in 1997 when she was shopping with a friend who collected Ty Beanie Babies. When they couldn't find anything new, the friend said "we could make one." Says Clark, "Her words gave me the idea to create a company that would allow people to create their own customized stuffed animals. . . . Build-a-Bear Workshop would be like a theme park factory in a mall." There were no formal focus groups, but from the beginning she relied on children for advice. "Kids have insights and offer inspiration by looking at the world differently," says Clark.[92]

The Illusions of Entrepreneurship.

Think you'd like to create a startup yourself and make yourself rich? Before you do, you might want to read *The Illusions of Entrepreneurship* by Case Western professor Scott Shane.[93] Shane says that the average new venture will fail within 5 years and that even successful founders earn less than they would as employees—35% less over 10 years. The biggest myth, he says, is that entrepreneurs believe "the growth and performance of their startups depends more on their entrepreneurial talent than on the businesses they choose."

Over the past 20 years, he found, about 4% of all the startups in the computer and office equipment industry made *Inc.* magazine's list of 500 of America's fastest-growing companies. But only about 0.005% of startups in the hotel and motel industries made that list, and 0.007% of startups in eating and drinking establishments. "So that means the odds that you make the Inc. 500 are 840 times higher if you start a computer company than if you start a hotel or motel."[94] (Regarding information technology companies, despite the famous example of young entrepreneur Mark Zuckerberg, who created Facebook as a student, the average age of tech company founders is 38.)[95]

YOUR CALL

Suppose you want to be your own boss. What "better and faster" niche opportunity do you see? Assuming it's not a computer company that you're starting, what do you think your chances are of being successful?

Celebrating Failure: Cultural & Other Factors Encouraging Innovation

Innovation doesn't happen as a matter of course. Organizations have to develop ways to make it happen—over and over. Three ways to do so are by providing (1) the right organizational *culture,* (2) the appropriate *resources,* and (3) the correct *reward system.*

1. Culture: Is Innovation Viewed as a Benefit or a Boondoggle?

Unlike most Europeans, who abhor "precariousness," or the absence of security, Americans as a whole seem to be more comfortable with taking risks. As one writer puts it, "Risk, movement, and personal ambition are fundamental. . . . The United States is about the endless possibility of self-invention through hard work. It is inseparable from change."[96]

An organizational culture, as we said in Chapter 8, is the "social glue," or system of shared beliefs and values, that binds members together. An organizational culture that doesn't just allow but *celebrates* failure is vital toward fostering innovation. Most new ideas will fail. Only a few will be successful. But if an organization doesn't encourage this kind of risk taking—if people tend to view experimentation as a boondoggle—that organization won't become a superstar in innovation.

The top 15 companies in 2010 with cultures that strongly encourage innovation, according to *Bloomberg Businessweek,* are Apple, Google, Microsoft, IBM, Toyota Motor (Japan), Amazon.com, LG Electronics (South Korea), BYD (China), General Electric, Sony (Japan), Samsung Electronics (South Korea), Intel, Ford Motor, Research In Motion (Canada), and Volkswagen (Germany).[97]

2. Resources: Do Managers Put Money Where Their Mouths Are?　An organization's managers may say they encourage innovation, but if they balk at the expense, they aren't putting their money where their mouths are. Innovation doesn't come cheap. Its costs can be measured in all kinds of ways: dollars, time, energy, and focus. For instance, an organization's research and development (R&D) department may need to hire top scientists, whose salaries may be high.

Of course, because there is always competition within an organization for resources, innovation may simply be given short shrift because other concerns seem so urgent—even within a company with a culture encouraging experimentation. But the risk of downgrading innovation in favor of more immediate concerns is that a company may "miss the next wave"—the next big trend, whatever that is.

3. Rewards: Is Experimentation Reinforced in Ways That Matter? Top-performing salespeople are often rewarded with all kinds of incentives, such as commissions, bonuses, and perks. Are R&D people rewarded the same way? Every year Monsanto Corp., for instance, presents a $50,000 award to the scientist or scientists who developed the largest commercial breakthrough.

The converse is also important: People should not be punished when their attempts to innovate don't work out, or else they won't attempt new things in the future. By the nature of experimentation, the end result can't be foreseen. Top managers at 3M, for instance, recognize that three-fifths of the new ideas suggested each year fail in the marketplace. Only when people attempting an innovation are acting halfheartedly, sloppily, or otherwise incompetently should sanctions such as the withholding of raises and promotions be used.

Open source innovator. In 1991, computer programmer Linus Torvalds, then a graduate student in Finland, posted his free Linux operating system on the Internet. Linux is a free version of Unix, and its continual improvements result from the efforts of tens of thousands of volunteer programmers. Some companies have extended the "open source" idea by taking a Linux-style approach to innovation that taps thousands of people for inspiration. Indeed, because of the Internet, companies can test new ideas at speeds that were unimaginable even a decade ago. Can you think of any innovations that evolved from masses of people?

EXAMPLE

Achieving Success by Celebrating Failure: 3M's On-Again Off-Again On-Again Culture of Innovation

The year 2012 marked the 32nd anniversary of the Post-it Note, invented by 3M employee Art Fry when he found an experimental adhesive helped him hold bits of paper as bookmarks in his church Sunday services hymnbook.[98] 3M is famous for having a culture of innovation that celebrates taking chances—which means achieving success by celebrating failure.

No Failure, No Success. Only with 20-20 hindsight can people see that a policy of celebrating failure can lead to success. No one can know, when setting out on a new course, whether the effort will yield positive results, and usually, in fact, most such experiments *are* failures.

Courtesy of 3M Company.

But the *attempts* must be encouraged, or innovation will never happen.

For many years, 3M built innovation into its culture. Mistakes were allowed, destructive criticism was forbidden, experimentation was encouraged, and divisions and individuals were allowed to operate with a good deal of autonomy. 3M set goals decreeing that 25%–30% of annual sales must come from products that were only five years old or less. Investment in research and development was almost double the rate of that of the average American company.

In addition, 3M employees were permitted to spend 15% of their time pursuing personal research interests that were not related to current company projects, knowing that if their ideas weren't successful, they would be encouraged to pursue other paths. The result was a culture that produced a string of hit products: masking tape, Scotchgard, and optical films for coating liquid-crystal display screens.[99]

The Culture Change. That culture changed when a former General Electric executive, James McNerney, took over in 2001 as 3M's CEO and instituted a system known as Six Sigma (discussed in Chapter 16). "Efficiency programs such as Six Sigma are designed to identify problems in work processes—and then use rigorous measurement to reduce variation and eliminate defects," says one account. "When these types of initiatives become ingrained in a company's culture, as they did at 3M, creativity can easily get squelched. After all, a breakthrough innovation is something that challenges existing procedures and norms."[100]

Back to Innovating. By 2007, McNerney was gone, and his successor, George Buckley, was struggling to balance efficiency with innovation, which had declined. During the recent recession, Buckley asked employees to improve products with "tweaks and snips" rather than with a few grandiose inventions.[101] By 2010–2012, 3M was back to positions 17, 15, and 18 on *Fortune's* "Most Admired Companies" lists.[102]

YOUR CALL

Stanford University organizational behavior scholar Jerker Denrell believes there is too much study of successes and not enough of failures, although it's very likely that firms pursuing risky strategies tend to achieve either a very high or very low performance, whereas firms pursuing conservative strategies always achieve an average performance.[103]

But while risk taking can lead to either spectacular success or disastrous failure, looking only at successes will show a positive correlation between success and risk taking. Do you think this is true?

How You Can Foster Innovation: Four Steps

If you're going to not just survive but *prevail* as a manager, you need to know how to make innovation happen within an organization. Here we offer four steps for doing so. *(See Figure 10.4.)*

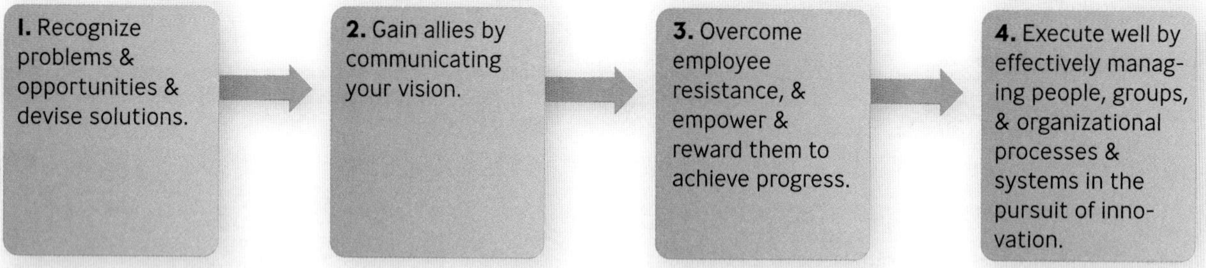

1. Recognize problems & opportunities & devise solutions. → **2.** Gain allies by communicating your vision. → **3.** Overcome employee resistance, & empower & reward them to achieve progress. → **4.** Execute well by effectively managing people, groups, & organizational processes & systems in the pursuit of innovation.

figure 10.4

FOUR STEPS FOR FOSTERING INNOVATION

Source: Adapted from eight steps in K. M. Bartol and D. C. Martin, *Management*, 3rd ed. (New York: McGraw-Hill/Irwin), 1998, pp. 360–63. Reprinted with permission of The McGraw-Hill Companies.

1. Recognize Problems & Opportunities & Devise Solutions Change may be needed because you recognize a *problem* or recognize an *opportunity*.

- **Recognizing a problem—find a "better way."** Problems, whether competitive threat, employee turnover, or whatever, tend to seize our attention—and sometimes these problems suggest solutions, such as new business ideas. Example: When Nevada real estate agents Barbara and Marshall Zucker watched the Las Vegas foreclosure rate skyrocket 169% from 2006 to 2007, they also noticed that 40% of all home sales were foreclosed properties. So in 2008 they bought a 24-seat Ford bus, named it the Vegas Foreclosure Express, and began offering prospective buyers tours of repossessed homes, offering 10-minute views of each property.[104]

- **Recognizing an opportunity.** Recognition of opportunities may come from long-term employees who regularly expose themselves to new ideas ("technological gate-keepers" in one phrase).[105] Ideas originating at the grassroots level of an organization may be a particularly fruitful source of innovation.

2. Gain Allies by Communicating Your Vision Once you've decided how you're going to handle the problem or opportunity, you need to start developing and communicating your vision. You need to create a picture of the future and paint in broad strokes how your innovation will be of benefit. That is, you need to start persuading others inside—and perhaps outside—the organization to support you. Having hard data helps. Others will be more persuaded, for example, if you can demonstrate that a similar idea has been successful in another industry. Or if you can take current trends (such as sales or demographics) and project them into the future.

Among the details you'll need to communicate to gain support are . . .

- **Showing how the product or service will be made.** You must figure out how to profitably make the new product or deliver the new service.

- **Showing how potential customers will be reached.** Innovations may fail because a company can't figure out how to get its new product or service into customers' hands. Thus, you might consider breaking down the task of what the customer wants into discrete steps (a task called *job mapping*), to determine the points at which customers might need help.[106]

- **Demonstrating how you'll beat your competitors.** Other companies may be pursuing the same breakthroughs. Thus, it's better to focus on a smaller number of innovations.

- **Explaining when the innovation will take place.** Timing is important. You'll need to think about when employees will be prepared to make the product and customers primed to buy it.

3. Overcome Employee Resistance, & Empower & Reward Them to Achieve Progress Once you've persuaded and gotten the blessing of your managerial superiors, then you need to do the same with the people reporting to you. It's possible, of course, that the idea for innovation came from them and that you already have their support.

Alternatively, you may have to overcome their resistance. Then you'll need to remove obstacles that limit them in executing the vision, such as having to get management to sign off on all aspects of a project. Finally, you'll need to hand out periodic rewards—recognition, celebrations, bonuses—for tasks accomplished. And the rewards should not be withheld until the end of the project, which may be many months away, but given out for the successful accomplishment of short-term phases in order to provide constant encouragement.

4. Execute Well What finally will make or break an organization's attempts at bringing new products and services to market is *execution*—the process, as we stated back in Chapter 6 (Section 6.5), of discussing hows and whats, of using questioning, analysis, and follow-through to achieve the results promised and ensure accountability.[107] Execution requires organizations to effectively manage people, groups, and organizational processes and systems in the pursuit of innovation.

In the end, then, the innovation process must be *managed*. This is precisely what is done at Apple, Google, Microsoft, IBM, Amazon.com, General Electric, Intel, Ford Motor, and other firms rated tops in the world's innovative companies.[108] ●

adaptive change 315
benchmarking 317
change agent 320
creativity 323
incremental innovations 325
innovative change 315

intervention 321
organizational development (OD) 320
proactive change 309
process innovation 325
product innovation 325

radical innovations 325
radically innovative change 315
reactive change 309
resistance to change 314
seeds of innovation 324
technology 313

Summary

10.1 The Nature of Change in Organizations

Among supertrends shaping the future of business: (1) The marketplace is becoming more segmented and moving toward more niche products. (2) There are more competitors offering targeted products, requiring faster speed-to-market. (3) Some traditional companies may not survive radically innovative change. (4) China, India, and other offshore suppliers are changing the way we work. (5) Knowledge, not information, is becoming the new competitive advantage.

Two types of change are reactive and proactive. Reactive change is making changes in response to problems or opportunities as they arise. Proactive change involves making carefully thought-out changes in anticipation of possible or expected problems or opportunities.

Forces for change may consist of forces outside the organization or inside it. (1) External forces consist of six types: demographic characteristics, market changes, technological advancements, shareholder and customer demands, supplier practices, and social and political pressures. (2) Internal forces may be of two types: employee problems and managers' behavior.

Four areas in which change is most apt to be needed are people, technology, structure, and strategy. (1) People changes may require changes in perceptions, attitudes, performance, or skills. (2) Technology is any machine or process that enables an organization to gain a competitive advantage in changing materials used to produce a finished product. (3) Changing structure may happen when one organization acquires another. (4) Changing strategy may occur because of changes in the marketplace.

10.2 The Threat of Change: Managing Employee Fear & Resistance

Resistance to change is an emotional/behavioral response to real or imagined threats to an established work routine. Resistance can be considered to be the interaction of three causes:

(1) employee characteristics, (2) change agent characteristics, and (3) the change agent–employee relationship.

The degree to which employees feel threatened by change depends on whether the change is adaptive, innovative, or radically innovative. Adaptive change, the least threatening, is reintroduction of a familiar practice. Innovative change is the introduction of a practice that is new to the organization. Radically innovative change, the most threatening, involves introducing a practice that is new to the industry.

Ten reasons employees resist change are as follows: (1) individuals' predisposition toward change; (2) surprise and fear of the unknown; (3) climate of mistrust; (4) fear of failure; (5) loss of status or job security; (6) peer pressure; (7) disruption of cultural traditions or group relationships; (8) personality conflicts; (9) lack of tact or poor timing; and (10) nonreinforcing reward systems.

Kurt Lewin's change model has three stages—unfreezing, changing, and refreezing—to explain how to initiate, manage, and stabilize planned change. (1) In the unfreezing stage, managers try to instill in employees the motivation to change. One technique used is benchmarking, a process by which a company compares its performance with that of high-performing organizations. (2) In the changing stage, employees need to be given the tools for change, such as new information. (3) In the refreezing stage, employees need to be helped to integrate the changed attitudes and behavior into their normal behavior.

In a model corresponding with Lewin's, John Kotter's suggests an organization needs to follow eight steps to avoid the eight common errors senior management usually commits. The first four represent unfreezing: establish a sense of urgency, create the guiding coalition, develop a vision and strategy, and communicate the change vision. The next three steps represent the changing stage: empower broad-based action, generate short-term wins, and consolidate gains and produce more change. The last step, corresponding to refreezing, is to anchor new approaches in the organization's culture.

10.3 Organizational Development: What It Is, What It Can Do

Organizational development (OD) is a set of techniques for implementing planned change to make people and organizations more effective. Often OD is put into practice by a change agent, a consultant with a background in behavioral sciences who can be a catalyst in helping organizations deal with old problems in new ways. OD can be used to manage conflict, revitalize organizations, and adapt to mergers.

The OD process follows a three-step process: (1) Diagnosis attempts to ascertain the problem. (2) Intervention is the attempt to correct the diagnosed problems. (3) Evaluation attempts to find out how well the intervention worked.

Four factors that make OD work successfully are (1) multiple interventions are used; (2) top managers give the OD program their support; (3) goals are geared to both short- and long-term results; and (4) OD is affected by culture.

10.4 Promoting Innovation within the Organization

Innovation is different from invention, which entails the creation of something new. It is also different from creativity, which is the process of developing something new or unique. Two myths about innovation are (1) innovation happens in a "eureka!" moment and (2) innovation can be systematized.

The starting point for organizational innovation involves the six seeds of innovation: (1) innovation comes from dedicated people working to solve a well-defined problem; (2) innovations often occur when people change their approach to solving a problem; (3) innovations can begin when people are curious about something of interest to them; (4) innovation happens because an organization wants to make money; (5) many innovations grow from the desire to achieve something; and (6) many innovations occur as a result of multiple factors.

Innovations may be a product innovation or a process innovation. A product innovation is a change in the appearance or performance of a product or service or the creation of a new one. A process innovation is a change in the way a product or service is conceived, manufactured, or disseminated. Innovations may also be an incremental innovation or a radical innovation. An incremental innovation is the creation of a product, service, or technology that modifies an existing one. A radical innovation is the creation of a product, service, or technology that replaces an existing one.

Innovation doesn't happen as a matter of course. Three ways to make it happen are to provide the right organizational culture, so that it is viewed as a benefit rather than as a boondoggle; to provide the resources; and to provide the rewards, so that experimentation is reinforced in ways that matter. Four steps for fostering innovation are as follows. (1) Recognize problems and opportunities and devise solutions. (2) Gain allies by communicating your vision. (3) Overcome employee resistance and empower and reward them to achieve progress. (4) Execute well by effectively managing people, groups, and organizational processes and systems in the pursuit of innovation.

Management in Action

SAP Is Counting on Organizational Change to Boost Revenue Growth

Potsdam, Germany–Hasso Plattner, who 20 years ago designed a computer program that supercharged SAP AG's growth, has been pursuing another breakthrough that could determine the software giant's fate.

Now SAP's chairman, the 68-year-old engineer is trying to take advantage of cheaper memory chips in servers to speed up complex business calculations and allow companies to do in seconds what can currently take hours or days. The aim is to allow executives to quickly access and analyze business data even on handheld devices.

If Mr. Plattner succeeds, he hopes to revolutionize business computing again and put his main competitor, Oracle Corp., on the defensive. But if he fails, SAP could end up stagnating in an industry full of bigger and richer tech adversaries.

Oracle chief executive Larry Ellison publicly derided Mr. Plattner's big bet as "whacko" in 2010 and said he wanted the name of SAP's "pharmacist." Counters Mr. Plattner: "If competitors are joking about you, they are vulnerable."

For his bet, Mr. Plattner decided to do an end run around SAP's corporate research-and-development department with thousands of engineers.

Instead, he recruited a bunch of university students in this small city outside Berlin. Working in a converted East German railway building dubbed "the villa," these T-shirt clad 20-somethings built the prototype of Mr. Plattner's new product.

"It's not so easy to break out as a large company and do something radically different," says Mr. Plattner. "At the university, you have the freedom."

What the students came up with—known initially as Hasso's New Architecture, and now called HANA—allows companies to store data in servers' main memory, instead of using the relational databases that Oracle dominates.

During its fourth-quarter news conference Wednesday, SAP co-chief executive officer Jim Hagemann Snabe called HANA "probably the biggest innovation in the business software industry in the last 20 years." He said it would allow HANA to grab leadership in the database business and in cloud computing—selling software as a metered service to customers over the Internet. SAP said HANA reached €160 million, or about $208 million, in sales in 2011, ahead of its earlier goal of €100 million. . . .

SAP already is the biggest player in software that businesses like retailers and manufacturers use to track sales and inventory. Its eventual goal with HANA is to sell software that tracks transactions and performs data analysis, and does it all in seconds. It expects to gradually evolve the software over the next two to three years, though some analysts think it could take longer.

There is a reason SAP is aiming high. The company's core business of selling business applications, which larger companies use to track everything from sales and inventory to customer contacts, is under attack by Oracle. SAP's share of the $58 billion business-application software fell to 14.8% in 2010 from 15.5% in 2007, while Oracle's jumped to 10.7% from 9.9% in the same period.

Mr. Plattner has pledged to rework all of SAP's software so it can run on HANA. "They're betting their business on it," says Yefim Natis, an analyst with Gartner, Inc. . . .

SAP started a HANA pilot program in 2010, offering the software as part of an integrated system to Procter & Gamble Co., Nestle SA and others, before selling it generally in June. . . .

Carrying out Mr. Plattner's grand plan won't be easy. For one, rewriting its software, which has roughly 400 million lines of code, will take years. SAP must convince companies to change technologies and practices they have held for a long time. Then there is Oracle, which in October launched a new in-memory analytics system aimed directly at SAP. . . .

In 1998, Mr. Plattner founded the Hasso Plattner Institute as a software-engineering affiliate of Potsdam University, and began teaching there. "I couldn't impress them," says Mr. Plattner of the young people in his class, who were besotted with Facebook Inc. and Google Inc. but saw SAP as stodgy.

So, in 2006, Mr. Plattner decided to shake things up. He took a bottle of red wine and sheet of paper into the garden behind his house. By the time he had reached the bottom of the bottle, he says, there wasn't much written on the paper. But, he says, he reached the conclusion that in-memory systems were the future.

Soon after, Mr. Plattner formed a group of three doctoral students and a handful of undergraduates at the institute to study in-memory technology. He sketched a diagram of a new database model on a white board and told them to start building. . . .

The students started experimenting with existing SAP database software as they worked to develop a new prototype. Mr. Plattner arranged for SAP software experts, including Vishal Sikka, now the company's chief technology officer, to teach them.

The students toiled away in the institute, their work space fitted out with red couches, a large screen TV, and a foosball table hooked up to an iPad that serves as a digital scoreboard. By June 2007, they were ready to unveil their first prototype. They traveled to SAP's headquarters in Walldorf to show it to Mr. Plattner.

In an auditorium at the company's sprawling glass-and-steel complex, the students found an audience of dozens of SAP's top engineers. As the students took turns nervously explaining aspects of the project, some of the SAP developers interrupted to point out problems with the prototype. One concern was what happens to the data stored in memory if the power goes out.

Mr. Plattner jumped up to defend their work. "Don't you get it? It's not about a product right now," he said. . . .

Mr. Plattner takes on a new group of six to eight undergraduate students a year to conduct research projects. By the summer of 2009, a new group of students had a working database prototype that could filter through 250 million customer records, find 380,000 unpaid invoices, and then single out the roughly 200,000 overdue bills in just 1.5 seconds. That compares with the roughly 20 minutes it would take standard software to do this, the students say.

Once again Mr. Plattner had the students demonstrate the prototype to a group of SAP executives in Walldorf. Some in the room were skeptical. But Mr. Plattner told them that such speed was necessary for SAP's survival.

Inside SAP, management allowed Mr. Plattner to create a new database group to turn the prototype into its next product. Mr. Plattner invited his students to join in and make suggestions for improvements.

SAP approached Erez Yarkoni, chief information officer of T-Mobile USA Inc., the U.S. unit of German operator Deutsche Telekom AG, last April, to pitch the new wares. . . .

SAP promised Mr. Yarkoni that if HANA didn't work, the company wouldn't have to pay.

T-Mobile wants to lure its customers to upgrade its data plans. To do that, the U.S. operator targets 33 million customers with almost countless variations of offers for different smartphones or data plans. . . .

Working with SAP, T-Mobile installed HANA in October. Instead of feeding the results into a disk-based data warehouse, it went into the memory of a HANA database machine. It spit out an answer in 15 minutes. "If it takes you a week to understand and refine the offer, you probably are missing the sweet spot with the customer," Mr. Yarkoni says.

FOR DISCUSSION

1. Which of the forces for change are causing SAP to undertake major organizational change? Explain.

2. Which of the four targeted areas of change is SAP focusing on? Provide examples.

3. To what extent has Hasso Plattner followed the four steps for fostering innovation? Do you think he could have done more to accomplish step 3? Explain.

4. Why are some SAP employees resisting change? Explain.

5. How might Plattner have used Lewin's and Kotter's models of change to increase the probability of achieving positive organizational change? Provide specific recommendations.

Self-Assessment

How Adaptable Are You?

OBJECTIVES

1. To assess your adaptability.
2. To examine how being adaptable can help you cope with organizational change.

INTRODUCTION

Ultimately all organizational change passes through an organization's people. People who adapt more easily are better suited to cope with organizational changes, and so they clearly are important assets to any organization. The purpose of this exercise is to determine your adaptability.

INSTRUCTIONS

Read the following statements. Using the scale provided, circle the number that indicates the extent to which you agree or disagree with each statement:

1 = strongly disagree
2 = disagree
3 = neither agree nor disagree
4 = agree
5 = strongly agree

1. In emergency situations, I react with clear, focused thinking and maintain emotional control in order to step up to the necessary actions.	1	2	3	4	5	
2. In stressful circumstances, I don't overreact to unexpected news. I keep calm, focused, and manage frustration well.	1	2	3	4	5	
3. I solve problems creatively by turning them inside out and upside down looking for new approaches to solving them that others may have missed.	1	2	3	4	5	
4. I easily change gears in response to uncertain or unexpected events, effectively adjusting my priorities, plans, goals, and actions.	1	2	3	4	5	

5. I enjoy learning new ways to do my work and I do what is necessary to keep my knowledge and skills current.	1	2	3	4	5	
6. I adjust easily to changes in my workplace by participating in assignments or training that prepare me for these changes.	1	2	3	4	5	
7. I am flexible and open-minded with others. I listen and consider others' viewpoints, adjusting my own when necessary.	1	2	3	4	5	
8. I am open to both negative and positive feedback. I work well in teams.	1	2	3	4	5	
9. I take action to learn and understand the values of other groups, organizations, or cultures. I adjust my own behavior to show respect for different customs.	1	2	3	4	5	
10. I adjust easily to differing environmental states such as extreme heat, humidity, cold, or dirtiness.	1	2	3	4	5	
11. I frequently push myself to complete strenuous or demanding tasks.	1	2	3	4	5	
Total					_____	

INTERPRETATION

When you are done, add up your responses to get your total score to see how adaptable you are. Arbitrary norms for adaptability:

11–24 = Low adaptability
25–39 = Moderate adaptability
40–55 = High adaptability

QUESTIONS FOR DISCUSSION

1. Were you surprised by your results? Why or why not?

2. Look at the areas where your score was the lowest. What are some skills you can work on or gain to increase your adaptability? Describe and explain.

3. What are some ways being adaptable can improve the way you handle change? Discuss.

Adapted from S. Arad, M. A. Donovan, K. E. Plamondon, and E. D. Pulakos, "Adaptability in the Workplace: Development of Taxonomy of Adaptive Performance," *Journal of Applied Psychology*, August 2000, pp. 612–24.

Legal/Ethical Challenge

Should People Be Allowed to Polish Their Nails in Flight?

This case occurred on a Southwest Airlines flight from Las Vegas to Houston. "A flight attendant asked a passenger not to polish her nails in flight, and the upset passenger began cursing." The woman has taken her story to a television station.

"The customer in question was taken into custody upon arrival in Houston," Southwest revealed. "The airport police became involved because of the passenger's behavior and a verbal altercation with a Southwest Airlines crew member. Southwest Airlines is responsible for the safety of all of our passengers and employees."

"Nail polish and polish remover are not prohibited from carry-on bags as long as they are travel size, according to the Transportation Security Administration, and Southwest says it has no policy on bringing either item on board. But as Beautylish.com noted, during the holiday travel season many passengers consider the smell offensive."

SOLVING THE CHALLENGE

What should Southwest Airlines do in response to the woman's complaint about how she was treated during the flight?

1. Nothing. This woman was inconsiderate to other passengers by not realizing that the smell of nail polish can be irritating to others. I'm glad that the airline stopped her from polishing her nails. Also, the woman was taken into custody by police because of her inappropriate behavior to a flight attendant.

2. Southwest should create a policy of banning nail polish remover and nail polish on flights. The airline should not reimburse the woman in any way because she acted rudely to one of its employees.

3. Southwest should apologize to the woman and give her a free flight to anywhere in the United States. After all, it is not against any rules to bring nail polish remover and nail polish on a plane. If you can bring them on a flight, then why shouldn't a person be allowed to use them?

4. Invent other options.

Source: Excerpted from "Nail Polish Leads to Altercation," *The Arizona Republic,* March 11, 2012, p. T2.

chapter 11

Managing Individual Differences & Behavior
Supervising People as People

Major Questions You Should Be Able to Answer

11.1 Personality & Individual Behavior
Major Question: In the hiring process, do employers care about one's personality and individual traits?

11.2 Values, Attitudes, & Behavior
Major Question: How do the hidden aspects of individuals—their values and attitudes—affect employee behavior?

11.3 Perception & Individual Behavior
Major Question: What are the distortions in perception that can cloud one's judgment?

11.4 Work-Related Attitudes & Behaviors Managers Need to Deal With
Major Question: Is it important for managers to pay attention to employee attitudes?

11.5 The New Diversified Workforce
Major Question: What trends in workplace diversity should managers be aware of?

11.6 Understanding Stress & Individual Behavior
Major Question: What causes workplace stress, and how can it be reduced?

Managing the Millennials: What's Different About Today's Generation of Younger Workers

Are the 75 million so-called Millennials, born between 1977 and 1994, really so different from earlier generations (the 78 million Baby Boomers, born 1946–1964, and 49 million Gen Xers, 1965–1976)? Does this new crop of twentysomethings—perhaps you're in this group—that is now the largest bloc of employees in the workforce (followed by Boomers) need to be managed in different ways? Experts say the answer to both questions is yes.[1]

Some major characteristics of Millennials are as follows: (1) They are extremely independent, because many were raised as day care or latchkey kids by two working parents or by a divorced, single parent, and so they have been left alone to make their own decisions. (2) They are tech-savvy, used to smartphones and the Internet as means of communication and accustomed to a faster pace of life. (3) They are racially and ethnically diverse. (4) They are probably the most educated in American history. (5) While in general they are confident, they are financially anxious and worry that they can't meet their educational, housing, and health care needs.

In the workplace, these characteristics translate into a skepticism about rules, policies, and procedures; a requirement for more autonomy; and a need for constant stimulation. What Millennials are looking for in the workplace is not only a good income and good relationships with their bosses and coworkers but also challenging daily work, the opportunity for growth, the chance to show off skills and be recognized for their accomplishments, casual dress environment, and flexible schedules for social and personal time.

What should leaders do in managing this group? Some suggestions:

Allow Them Independent Decision Making & Expression

Millennials are impatient, skeptical, and blunt and expressive, but they are used to adapting and making decisions. Show appreciation for their individuality and let them participate in decision making.

Train Them & Mentor Them

As the most education-oriented generation in history, Millennials are strongly attracted to education and training, the best kind not being classroom training but forms of independent learning. At the same time, they should be given the chance to create long-term bonds with mentors.

Give Them Constant Feedback & Recognition

Millennials need to know they are making an impact and need to be recognized for their workplace contributions. Thus, supervisors should show them how their work contributes to the bottom line. This generation revels in, even craves, constant praise, so managers should provide rewards in the form of praise, flextime, and extra responsibility.

Provide Them with Access to Technology

To attract and retain Millennial employees, companies need to provide the newest and best technology.

Create Customized Career Paths

Millennials would most like to be self-employed, but few are able to do it because of high startup costs. Employers can reinforce the sense of control that this generation desires by providing them with a realistic account of their progress and their future within the organization.

For Discussion As a worker, you might hope to be led by someone who would follow the preceding suggestions. But suppose your boss is of the old "tough guy" school and doesn't manage this way. In a difficult job market, would you stick it out? How would you try to let your supervisor know how you would prefer to be managed?

forecast | What's Ahead in This Chapter

This first of five chapters on leadership discusses how to manage for individual differences and behaviors. We describe personality and individual behavior; values, attitudes, and behavior; and specific work-related attitudes and behaviors managers need to be aware of. We next discuss distortions in perception, which can affect managerial judgment. Finally, we consider what stress does to individuals.

✓ 11.1 PERSONALITY & INDIVIDUAL BEHAVIOR

major question?

In the hiring process, do employers care about one's personality and individual traits?

THE BIG PICTURE

Personality consists of stable psychological and behavioral attributes that give you your identity. We describe five personality dimensions and five personality traits that managers need to be aware of to understand workplace behavior.

In this and the next four chapters we discuss the third management function (after planning and organizing)—namely, leading. *Leading,* as we said in Chapter 1, is defined as *motivating, directing, and otherwise influencing people to work hard to achieve the organization's goals.*

How would you describe yourself? Are you outgoing? aggressive? sociable? tense? passive? lazy? quiet? Whatever the combination of traits, which result from the interaction of your genes and your environment, they constitute your personality. More formally, ***personality* consists of the stable psychological traits and behavioral attributes that give a person his or her identity.**[2] As a manager, you need to understand personality attributes because they affect how people perceive and act within the organization.

Assertive and sociable. Does it take a certain kind of personality to be a good salesperson? Have you ever known people who were quiet, unassuming, even shy but who were nevertheless very persistent and persuasive—that is, good salespeople?

The Big Five Personality Dimensions

In recent years, the many personality dimensions have been distilled into a list of factors known as the Big Five.[3] **The *Big Five personality dimensions* are (1) extroversion, (2) agreeableness, (3) conscientiousness, (4) emotional stability, and (5) openness to experience.**

- **Extroversion.** How outgoing, talkative, sociable, and assertive a person is.

- **Agreeableness.** How trusting, good-natured, cooperative, and soft-hearted one is.

- **Conscientiousness.** How dependable, responsible, achievement-oriented, and persistent one is.

- **Emotional stability.** How relaxed, secure, and unworried one is.

- **Openness to experience.** How intellectual, imaginative, curious, and broad-minded one is.

Standardized personality tests are used to score people on each dimension to draw a person's personality profile that is supposedly as unique as his or her fingerprints. For example, if you scored low on the first trait, extroversion, you would presumably be prone to shy and withdrawn behavior. If you scored low on emotional stability, you supposedly would be nervous, tense, angry, and worried. (An example of a personality test is the Myer-Briggs, discussed in Chapter 9. To take a replica of this test for free, go to **www.personalitypathways.com/type_inventory.html**.)

Do Personality Tests Work for the Workplace?   As a manager, you would want to know if the Big Five model in particular and personality testing in general can help predict behavior in the workplace. Is a personality test helpful in predicting a match between personality and job performance? Two findings:

- **Extroversion—the outgoing personality.** As might be expected, extroversion (an outgoing personality) has been associated with success for managers and salespeople. Also, extroversion is a stronger predictor of job performance than agreeableness, across all professions, according to researchers. "It appears that being courteous, trusting, straightforward, and soft-hearted [that is, agreeableness] has a smaller impact on job performance," conclude the researchers, "than being talkative, active, and assertive [that is, extroversion]."[4]

- **Conscientiousness—the dependable personality.** Conscientiousness (strong work ethic) has been found to have the strongest positive correlation with job performance and training performance. According to researchers, "those individuals who exhibit traits associated with a strong sense of purpose, obligation, and persistence generally perform better than those who do not."[5]

The table below presents tips to help managers avoid abuses and discrimination lawsuits when using personality and psychological testing for employment decisions.[6] *(See Table 11.1.)*

table 11.1

CAUTIONS ABOUT USING PERSONALITY TESTS IN THE WORKPLACE

- *Use professionals.* Rely on reputable, licensed psychologists for selecting and overseeing the administration, scoring, and interpretation of personality and psychological tests. This is particularly important, since not every psychologist is expert at these kinds of tests.

- *Don't hire on the basis of personality test results alone.* Supplement any personality test data with information from reference checks, personal interviews, ability tests, and job performance records. Also avoid hiring people on the basis of specified personality profiles. As a case in point, there is no distinct "managerial personality."

- *Be alert for gender, racial, and ethnic bias.* Regularly assess any possible adverse impact of personality tests on the hiring of women and minorities. This is truly a matter of great importance, since you don't want to find your company (or yourself) embroiled in a lawsuit at some point downstream.

- *Graphology tests don't work, but integrity tests do.* Personality traits and aptitudes cannot be inferred from samples of people's penmanship, as proponents of graphology tests claim. However, dishonest job applicants can often be screened by integrity tests, since dishonest people are reportedly unable to fake conscientiousness, even on a paper-and-pencil test.

The Proactive Personality   A person who scores well on the Big Five dimension of conscientiousness is probably a good worker. He or she may also be a ***proactive personality,*** **someone who is more apt to take initiative and persevere to influence the environment.** Research reveals that proactive people tend to be more satisfied with their jobs, committed to their employer, and produce more work than nonproactive individuals.[7]

Five Traits Important in Organizations

Five of the most important personality traits that managers need to be aware of to understand workplace behavior are (1) *locus of control,* (2) *self-efficacy,* (3) *self-esteem,* (4) *self-monitoring,* and (5) *emotional intelligence.*

1. Locus of Control: "I Am/Am Not the Captain of My Fate" As we discussed briefly in Chapter 1, *locus of control* **indicates how much people believe they control their fate through their own efforts.** If you have an *internal locus of control,* you believe you control your own destiny. If you have an *external locus of control,* you believe external forces control you.

Research shows internals and externals have important workplace differences. Internals exhibit less anxiety, greater work motivation, and stronger expectations that effort leads to performance. They also obtain higher salaries.[8]

These findings have two important implications for managers:

- **Expect different degrees of structure and compliance for each type.** Employees with internal locus of control will probably resist close managerial supervision. Hence, they should probably be placed in jobs requiring high initiative and lower compliance. By contrast, employees with external locus of control might do better in highly structured jobs requiring greater compliance.

- **Employ different reward systems for each type.** Since internals seem to have a greater belief that their actions have a direct effect on the consequences of that action, internals likely would prefer and respond more productively to incentives such as merit pay or sales commissions. (We discuss incentive compensation systems in Chapter 12.)

2. Self-Efficacy: "I Can/Can't Do This Task" A related trait is *self-efficacy,* **belief in one's personal ability to do a task.** Unlike locus of control, this characteristic isn't about how much fate controls events (as in believing whether getting a high grade in a course is determined by you or by outside factors, such as the grade curve or trick questions). Rather, it's about your personal belief that you have what it takes to succeed.

Have you noticed that those who are confident about their ability tend to succeed, whereas those preoccupied with failure tend not to? Indeed, high expectations of self-efficacy have been linked with all kinds of positives: not only success in varied physical and mental tasks but also reduced anxiety and increased tolerance for pain.[9] One study found that the sales performance of life-insurance agents was much better among those with high self-efficacy.[10] A meta-analysis involving 21,616 people also found significant positive correlation between self-efficacy and job performance.[11] Low self-efficacy is associated with *learned helplessness,* **the debilitating lack of faith in one's ability to control one's environment.**[12]

Among the implications for managers:

- **Assign jobs accordingly.** Complex, challenging, and autonomous jobs tend to enhance people's perceptions of their self-efficacy. Boring, tedious jobs generally do the opposite.

- **Develop self-efficacy.** Self-efficacy is a quality that can be nurtured. Employees with low self-efficacy need lots of constructive pointers and positive feedback.[13] Goal difficulty needs to match individuals' perceived self-efficacy, but goals can be made more challenging as performance improves.[14] Small successes need to be rewarded. Employees' expectations can be improved through guided experiences, mentoring, and role modeling.[15]

3. Self-Esteem: "I Like/Dislike Myself" How worthwhile, capable, and acceptable do you think you are? The answer to this question is an indicator of your *self-esteem,* **the extent to which people like or dislike themselves, their overall self-evaluation.**[16] Research offers some interesting insights about how high or low self-esteem can affect people and organizations.

- **People with high self-esteem.** Compared with people with low self-esteem, people with high self-esteem are more apt to handle failure better, to emphasize the positive, to take more risks, and to choose more unconventional jobs.[17] However, when faced with pressure situations, high-self-esteem people have been found to become egotistical and boastful.[18] Some have even been associated with aggressive and violent behavior.

- **People with low self-esteem.** Conversely, low-self-esteem people confronted with failure have been found to have focused on their weaknesses and to have had primarily negative thoughts.[19] Moreover, they are more dependent on others and are more apt to be influenced by them and to be less likely to take independent positions.

Can self-esteem be improved? According to one study, "low self-esteem can be raised more by having the person think of *desirable* characteristics *possessed* rather than of undesirable characteristics from which he or she is free."[20] Some ways in which managers can build employee self-esteem are shown in the table at the top of the next page. *(See Table 11.2.)*

4. Self-Monitoring: "I'm Fairly Able/Unable to Adapt My Behavior to Others"   *Self-monitoring* **is the extent to which people are able to observe their own behavior and adapt it to external situations.** Of course, we would all like to think we are high in self-monitoring—able to regulate our "expressive self-presentation

Self-efficacy. Erik Weihenmayer (right), blind since age 13, is a self-described "unrealistic optimist." He became the first blind climber to scale Mt. Everest. Do you have a personal belief that you can succeed at great things?

table 11.2

SOME WAYS THAT MANAGERS CAN BOOST EMPLOYEE SELF-ESTEEM

- Reinforce employees' positive attributes and skills.

- Provide positive feedback whenever possible.

- Break larger projects into smaller tasks and projects.

- Express confidence in employees' abilities to complete their tasks.

- Provide coaching whenever employees are seen to be struggling to complete tasks.

for the sake of desired public appearances," as some experts write, "and thus be highly responsive to social and interpersonal cues" of others.[21] But whereas some high self-monitors are criticized for being chameleons, always able to adapt their self-presentation to their surroundings, low self-monitors are often criticized for being on their own planet and insensitive to others. Instead, their behavior may reflect their own inner states, including their attitudes and feelings.

EXAMPLE

Self-Monitoring Should Include "the Good, the Bad, & the Ugly"

Charlotte Beers is a former chairwoman and CEO of advertising agency Ogilvy & Mather Worldwide, but in her early 30s she was a management supervisor and "thought I was really doing well." Then she heard from a friend that a colleague described her management style as "menacing." That surprised her because Beers regarded herself as "a friendly, gentle Southern belle," and the criticism was the exact opposite of the way she thought of herself.[22]

She goes on: "I began to watch myself—something I think we all have to do—and I realized I did end meetings on a threatening note. I created urgency when there was none. I was taking on the persona of 'I really mean business' that I had learned from an earlier boss." After that she learned to watch herself more and to self-correct about talking too much and interrupting other people.

YOUR CALL

The comment about her coming off as menacing, though devastating, was important because "nothing is more helpful than finding out how others see you," says Beers. "[You need to learn to] keep your own scorecard, and it has to include the good, the bad, and the ugly." Do you agree? Could you conduct this kind of research about yourself in an impersonal way to find out how others see you?

It might be expected that people in top management are more apt to be high self-monitors able to play different roles—even contradictory roles—to suit different situations. Research shows a positive relationship between high self-monitoring and career success. Among 139 MBA graduates who were tracked for five years, high self-monitors enjoyed more internal and external promotions than did their low self-monitoring classmates.[23] Other research has found that managerial success (in terms of speed of promotions) was tied to political savvy (knowing how to socialize, network, and engage in organizational politics).[24]

5. Emotional Intelligence: "I'm Pretty Good/Not Good at Understanding My Emotions & the Emotions of Others" Emotional intelligence (EI) has been defined as "the ability to carry out accurate reasoning about emotions and the ability to use emotions and emotional knowledge to enhance thought."[25] Said another way, *emotional intelligence* is the ability to cope, to

empathize with others, and to be self-motivated. The trait of emotional intelligence was first introduced in 1909. Since that time much research has examined the components of EI and its consequences.

Why High EI Is Important   Recent research underscores the importance of developing higher EI. It was associated with (1) better social relations for children and adults, (2) better family and intimate relationships, (3) being perceived more positively by others, (4) better academic achievement, and (5) better psychological well-being. **Daniel Goleman,** a psychologist who popularized the trait of EI, concluded that EI is composed of four key components: self-awareness, self-management, social awareness, and relationship management.[26] *(See Table 11.3.)*

<table>
<tr><td>

1. *Self-awareness.* The most essential trait. This is the ability to read your own emotions and gauge your moods accurately, so you know how you're affecting others.

2. *Self-management.* This is the ability to control your emotions and act with honesty and integrity in reliable and adaptable ways. You can leave occasional bad moods outside the office.

3. *Social awareness.* This includes empathy, allowing you to show others that you care, and organizational intuition, so you keenly understand how your emotions and actions affect others.

4. *Relationship management.* This is the ability to communicate clearly and convincingly, disarm conflicts, and build strong personal bonds.

</td></tr>
</table>

table 11.3

THE TRAITS OF EMOTIONAL INTELLIGENCE

Sources: Adapted from D. Goleman, R. Boyatzis, and A. McKee, "Primal Leadership: The Hidden Driver of Great Performance," *Harvard Business Review,* December 2001, p. 49; and *Primal Leadership: Realizing the Power of Emotional Intelligence,* Harvard Business School Press, 2002, p. 39.

Can You Raise Your EI?   Is there any way to raise your own emotional intelligence, to sharpen your social skills? Although parts of EI represent stable traits that are not readily changed, other aspects, such as using empathy, can be developed.[27] Two suggestions for improvement are as follows:

- **Develop awareness of your EI level.** Becoming aware of your level of emotional intelligence is the first step. The Self-Assessment at the end of this chapter (p. 372) can be used for this purpose. (Some companies use the Personal Profile Analysis during the hiring process to provide insights into a person's EI.)[28]

- **Learn about areas needing improvement.** The next step is to learn more about those EI aspects in which improvement is needed. For example, to improve your skills at using empathy, find articles on the topic and try to implement their recommendations. One such article suggests that empathy in communications is enhanced by trying to (1) understand how others feel about what they are communicating and (2) gaining appreciation of what people want from an exchange.[29]

Preliminary evidence suggests that emotional intelligence can land you a job. A simulated interview process indicated that interviewers' assessments of an applicant's emotional intelligence were positively associated with their impression of the applicant.[30] However, given the difficulty of measuring emotional intelligence, further research is needed on this new leadership trait.[31] ●

major question?

How do the hidden aspects of individuals—their values and attitudes—affect employee behavior?

THE BIG PICTURE

Organizational behavior (OB) considers how to better understand and manage people at work. In this section, we discuss individual values and attitudes and how they affect people's actions and judgments.

Formal
Goals
Policies
Hierarchy
Structure

The Organization

Informal
Values
Attitudes
Personalities
Perceptions
Conflicts
Culture

figure 11.1

FORMAL AND INFORMAL ASPECTS OF AN ORGANIZATION

If you look at a company's annual report or at a brochure from its corporate communications department, you are apt to be given a picture of its *formal aspects:* Goals. Policies. Hierarchy. Structure.

Could you exert effective leadership if the formal aspects were all you knew about the company? What about the *informal aspects*? Values. Attitudes. Personalities. Perceptions. Conflicts. Culture. Clearly, you need to know about these hidden, "messy" characteristics as well. *(See Figure 11.1 at left.)*

Organizational Behavior: Trying to Explain & Predict Workplace Behavior

The informal aspects are the focus of the interdisciplinary field known as ***organizational behavior (OB), which is dedicated to better understanding and management of people at work.*** In particular, OB tries to help managers not only *explain* workplace behavior but also to *predict* it, so that they can better lead and motivate their employees to perform productively. OB looks at two areas:

1. **Individual behavior.** This is the subject of this chapter. We discuss such individual attributes as values, attitudes, personality, perception, and learning.

2. **Group behavior.** This is the subject of later chapters, particularly Chapter 13, where we discuss norms, roles, and teams.

Let us begin by considering individual values, attitudes, and behavior.

Values: What Are Your Consistent Beliefs & Feelings About *All* Things?

Values **are abstract ideals that guide one's thinking and behavior across all situations.**[32] Lifelong behavior patterns are dictated by values that are fairly well set by the time people are in their early teens. After that, however, one's values can be reshaped by significant life-altering events, such as having a child, undergoing a business failure, or surviving the death of a loved one, a war, or a serious health threat.

From a manager's point of view, it's helpful to know that values are those concepts, principles, things, people, or activities for which a person is willing to work hard—even make sacrifices for. Compensation, recognition, and status are common values in the workplace.[33] However, according to numerous surveys, employees are more interested in striking a balance between work and family life rather than just earning a paycheck.[34] For instance, 86% of 550 employees responding to one survey said flexibility to balance their work and personal life was an important aspect of job satisfaction.

Attitudes: What Are Your Consistent Beliefs & Feelings About *Specific* Things?

Values are abstract ideals—global beliefs and feelings—that are directed toward all objects, people, or events. Values tend to be consistent both over time and over related situations. By contrast, attitudes are beliefs and feelings that are directed toward *specific* objects, people, or events. More formally, an **attitude is defined as a learned predisposition toward a given object.**[35] It is important for you to understand the components of attitudes because attitudes directly influence our behavior.[36]

Example: If you dislike your present job, will you be happier if you change to a different job? Not necessarily. It depends on your attitude. In one study, researchers found that the attitudes of 5,000 middle-aged male employees toward their jobs were very stable over a five-year period. Men with positive attitudes tended to stay positive, those with negative attitudes tended to stay negative. More revealingly, even those who changed jobs or occupations generally expressed the same attitudes they had previously.[37]

The Three Components of Attitudes: Affective, Cognitive, & Behavioral

Attitudes have three components:[38]

1. **The affective component—"I feel." The *affective component of an attitude* consists of the feelings or emotions one has about a situation.** How do you *feel* about people who talk loudly on cellphones in restaurants? If you feel annoyed or angry, you're expressing negative emotions or affect. (If you're indifferent, your attitude is neutral.)

2. **The cognitive component—"I believe." The *cognitive component of an attitude* consists of the beliefs and knowledge one has about a situation.** What do you *think* about people in restaurants talking on cellphones? Is what they're doing inconsiderate, acceptable, even admirable (because it shows they're productive)? Your answer reflects your beliefs or ideas about the situation.

3. **The behavioral component—"I intend." The *behavioral component of an attitude,* also known as the *intentional component,* refers to how one intends or expects to behave toward a situation.** What would you *intend to do* if a person talked loudly on a cellphone at the table next to you? Your action may reflect your negative or positive feelings (affective), your negative or positive beliefs (cognitive), and your intention or lack of intention to do anything (behavioral).

All three components are often manifested at any given time. For example, if you call a corporation and get one of those telephone-tree menus ("For customer service, press 1 . . .") that never seems to connect you to a human being, you might be so irritated that you would say:

- "I hate being given the runaround." [*affective component—your feelings*]
- "That company doesn't know how to take care of customers." [*cognitive component—your perceptions*]
- "I'll never call them again." [*behavioral component—your intentions*]

When Attitudes & Reality Collide: Consistency & Cognitive Dissonance

One of the last things you want, probably, is to be accused of hypocrisy—to be criticized for saying one thing and doing another. Like most people, you no doubt want to maintain consistency between your attitudes and your behavior.

But what if a strongly held attitude bumps up against a harsh reality that contradicts it? Suppose you're extremely concerned about getting AIDS, which you believe you might get from contact with body fluids, including blood. Then you're in a life-threatening auto accident in a third-world country and require surgery and blood transfusions—including transfusions of blood from (possibly AIDS-infected) strangers in a blood bank. Do you reject the blood to remain consistent with your beliefs about getting AIDS?

In 1957, social psychologist **Leon Festinger** proposed the term *cognitive dissonance* **to describe the psychological discomfort a person experiences between his or her cognitive attitude and incompatible behavior.**[39] Because people are uncomfortable with inconsistency, Festinger theorized, they will seek to reduce the "dissonance" or tension of the inconsistency. How they deal with the discomfort, he suggested, depends on three factors:

Leon Festinger. In 1957, the psychologist and his associates penetrated a cult whose members predicted that most people on earth would perish in a cataclysmic event except for a handful that would be rescued by aliens in a flying saucer. Festinger found himself standing with cult members on a hilltop awaiting the event, which, of course, did not happen. Later he proposed the term *cognitive dissonance* to explain how they rationalized the failure of their prophecy. Have you observed people employing this mechanism when the surefire thing they predicted did not occur?

- **Importance.** How important are the elements creating the dissonance? Most people can put up with some ambiguities in life. For example, many drivers don't think obeying speed limits is very important, even though they profess to be law-abiding citizens. People eat greasy foods even though they know that ultimately they may contribute to heart disease.

- **Control.** How much control does one have over the matters that create dissonance? A juror may not like the idea of voting for the death penalty but believe that he or she has no choice but to follow the law in the case. A taxpayer may object to his taxes being spent on, say, special-interest corporate welfare for a particular company but not feel that he or she can withhold taxes.

- **Rewards.** What rewards are at stake in the dissonance? You're apt to cling to old ideas in the face of new evidence if you have a lot invested emotionally or financially in those ideas. If you're a police officer who worked 20 years to prove a particular suspect guilty of murder, you're not apt to be very accepting of contradictory evidence after all that time.

Among the main ways to reduce cognitive dissonance are the following. *(See Table 11.4.)*

table 11.4 EXAMPLES OF WAYS TO REDUCE COGNITIVE DISSONANCE

Technique	Examples
Change attitude and/or behavior	Gregory Withow once belonged to the White Aryan Resistance and other racist groups. He preached hatred and bashed Japanese tourists in San Francisco. Then he met Sylvia, who rejected his white-supremacist ideas. As he grew to love her, he found himself caught between his ideas and her disapproval. To decrease this cognitive dissonance, he renounced his old racist beliefs and changed his behavior, even becoming a spokesperson for the antiracist Anti-Defamation League.
Belittle importance of the inconsistent behavior	All cigarette smokers are repeatedly exposed to information that smoking is hazardous to health. But many belittle the habit as not being as risky as the antismoking messages suggest. ("My grandmother smokes, and she's in her 80s.")
Find consonant elements that outweigh dissonant ones	Ethics professor Sissela Bok says students may justify cheating on an exam by saying, "I don't usually do this, but here I really have to do it." As one MIT graduate student said, students see cheating take place and "feel they have to. People get used to it, even though they know it's not right."

Sources: R. Plotnik, *Introduction to Psychology,* 3rd ed. (Pacific Grove, CA: Brooks/Cole, 1993), p. 602; E. Aronson, R. D. Akert, and T. D. Wilson, *Social Psychology,* 6th ed. (Upper Saddle River, NJ: Pearson Prentice Hall, 2006); S. Bok, cited in E. Venant, "A Nation of Cheaters," *San Francisco Chronicle,* January 7, 1992, p. D3, reprinted from *Los Angeles Times;* A. Dobrzeniecki, quoted in D. Butler, "MIT Students Guilty of Cheating," *Boston Globe,* March 2, 1991, p. 25.

- **Change your attitude and/or behavior.** This would seem to be the most obvious, even rational, response to take when confronted with cognitive dissonance.

- **Belittle the importance of the inconsistent behavior.** This happens all the time.

The Five Levels of Needs In proposing this hierarchy of five needs, ranging from basic to highest level, Maslow suggested that needs are never completely satisfied. That is, our actions are aimed at fulfilling the "deprived" needs, the needs that remain unsatisfied at any point in time. Thus, for example, once you have achieved safety (security), which is the second most basic need, you will then seek to fulfill the third most basic need—love (belongingness).

In order of ascendance, from bottom to top, the five levels of needs are as follows. *(See Figure 12.3.)*

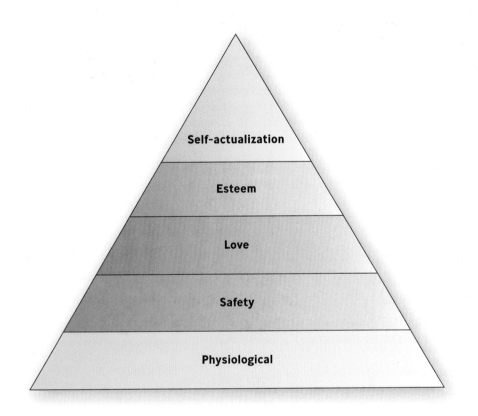

figure 12.3
MASLOW'S HIERARCHY
OF NEEDS

1. Physiological Needs These are the most basic human physical needs, in which one is concerned with having food, clothing, shelter, and comfort and with self-preservation.

2. Safety Needs These needs are concerned with physical safety and emotional security, so that a person is concerned with avoiding violence and threats.

3. Love Needs Once basic needs and security are taken care of, people look for love, friendship, and affection.

4. Esteem Needs After they meet their social needs, people focus on such matters as self-respect, status, reputation, recognition, and self-confidence.

5. Self-Actualization Needs The highest level of need, self-actualization is self-fulfillment—the need to develop one's fullest potential, to become the best one is capable of being.

Looking for Peak Performance: A Hotel CEO Applies Maslow's Hierarchy to Employees, Customers, & Investors

Chip Conley is CEO and founder of boutique hotel company Joie de Vivre (JDV), whose mission statement is "creating opportunities to celebrate the joy of life." In *Peak: How Great Companies Get Their Mojo from Maslow,* he describes how JDV used Maslow's theory to motivate the business's three key stakeholders—employees, customers, and investors—by tapping into the power of self-actualization to create peak performance.[13]

Motivating Employees. Applying the Maslow pyramid to employees, says Conley, "the basic need that a job satisfies is money. Toward the middle are needs like recognition for a job well done, and at the top are needs like meaning and creative expression."[14] Thus, housekeepers, who represent half of a hotel's workers, would be gathered in small groups and asked what the hotels would look like if they weren't there each day. Following their answers (unvacuumed carpets, piled-up trash, bathrooms filled with wet towels), they were then asked to come up with alternative names for housekeeping. Some responses: "serenity keepers," "clutter busters," "the peace-of-mind police." From this exercise, workers developed a sense of how the customer experience would not be the same without them.[15] And that, says Conley, "gets to a sense of

meaning in your work that satisfies that high-level human motivation." Addressing the highest-level need gives employees "a sense that the job helps them become the best people they can be."[16]

Motivating Customers. Many hotels offer clean, safe accommodations. JDV designs each of its 30 hotels to "flatter and vindicate a different category of customers' distinct self-image," says Conley. Thus, in San Francisco, the Hotel Rex's tweedy décor and Jack London touches appeal to urbane literary types. The Vitale's fitness-conscious services and minimalist design targets "the kind of bourgeois bohemian who might like *Dwell Magazine.*"[17]

Motivating Investors. Although most investors focus on a "returns-driven relationship" (bottom of the pyramid), some have higher motivations. They are driven not by the deal "but rather [by] an interesting, worthwhile deal," which JDV attempts to provide.[18]

YOUR CALL

What kind of higher-level needs do you think you could fulfill through your work?

Using the Hierarchy of Needs Theory to Motivate Employees Research does not clearly support Maslow's theory, although it remains popular among managers. Still, the importance of Maslow's contribution is that he showed that workers have needs beyond that of just earning a paycheck. To the extent the organization permits, managers should first try to meet employees' level 1 and level 2 needs, of course, so that employees won't be preoccupied with them. Then, however, they need to give employees a chance to fulfill their higher-level needs in ways that also advance the goals of the organization.[19]

Alderfer's ERG Theory: Existence, Relatedness, & Growth

Developed by **Clayton Alderfer** in the late 1960s, ***ERG theory* assumes that three basic needs influence behavior—existence, relatedness, and growth,** represented by the letters E, R, and G.

The Three Kinds of Needs Unlike Maslow's theory, ERG theory suggests that behavior is motivated by three needs, not five, and that more than one need may be activated at a time rather than activated in a stair-step hierarchy. From lowest to highest level, the three needs are as follows:

1. E—Existence Needs Existence needs are the desire for physiological and material well-being.

2. R—Relatedness Needs Relatedness needs are the desire to have meaningful relationships with people who are significant to us.

3. G—Growth Needs Growth needs are the desire to grow as human beings and to use our abilities to their fullest potential.

Alderfer also held that if our higher-level needs (such as growth needs) are frustrated, we will then seek more intensely to fulfill our lower-level needs (such as existence needs). This is called the *frustration-regression component.*[20]

Using the ERG Theory to Motivate Employees The frustration-regression component of ERG theory certainly has some applicability to the workplace. For example, if you work as a bill collector making difficult phone calls and having no contact with coworkers, you might lobby your boss for better pay and benefits. Also ERG theory is consistent with the finding that individual and cultural differences influence our need states. It's clear, for instance, that people are motivated by different needs at different times in their lives, which suggests that managers should customize their reward and recognition programs to meet employees' varying needs.

McClelland's Acquired Needs Theory: Achievement, Affiliation, & Power

David McClelland, a well-known psychologist, investigated the needs for affiliation and power and as a consequence proposed the ***acquired needs theory,* which states that three needs—achievement, affiliation, and power—are major motives determining people's behavior in the workplace.**[21] McClelland believes that we are not born with our needs; rather we learn them from the culture—from our life experiences.

The Three Needs Managers are encouraged to recognize three needs in themselves and others and to attempt to create work environments that are responsive to them. The three needs, one of which tends to be dominant in each of us, are as follows. *(See Figure 12.4.)*

- **Need for achievement—"I need to excel at tasks."** This is the desire to excel, to do something better or more efficiently, to solve problems, to achieve excellence in challenging tasks.

- **Need for affiliation—"I need close relationships."** This is the desire for friendly and warm relations with other people.

- **Need for power—"I need to control others."** This is the desire to be responsible for other people, to influence their behavior or to control them.[22]

McClelland identifies two forms of the need for power.

The negative kind is the need for *personal power,* as expressed in the desire to dominate others, and involves manipulating people for one's own gratification.

The positive kind, characteristic of top managers and leaders, is the desire for *institutional power,* as expressed in the need to solve problems that further organizational goals.

figure 12.4
McCLELLAND'S THREE NEEDS

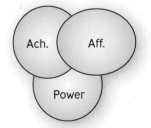

A "well-balanced" individual: achievement, affiliation, and power are of equal size.

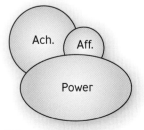

A "control freak" individual: achievement is normal, but affiliation is small and power is large.

Using Acquired Needs Theory to Motivate Employees McClelland associates the three needs with different sets of work preferences, as follows:[23]

Need for Achievement If you (or an employee) are happy with accomplishment of a task being its own reward, don't mind or even prefer working alone, and are willing to take moderate risks, then you probably have a *high need for achievement.* That being the case, you (or your employee) would probably prefer doing the kind of work that offers pay for performance, challenging but achievable goals, and individual responsibility for results. People high in need for achievement tend to advance in technical fields requiring creativity and individual skills.[24]

Need for Power If you, like most effective managers, have a *high need for power,* that means you enjoy being in control of people and events and being recognized for this responsibility. Accordingly, your preference would probably be for work that allows you to control or have an effect on people and be publicly recognized for your accomplishments.

Need for Affiliation If you tend to seek social approval and satisfying personal relationships, you may have a *high need for affiliation.* In that case, you may not be the most efficient manager because at times you will have to make decisions that will make people resent you. Instead, you will tend to prefer work, such as sales, that provides for personal relationships and social approval.

EXAMPLE

Acquired Needs Theory: What Motivates Facebook's COO Sheryl Sandberg?

A Harvard Business School graduate with a background in finance, advertising, and politics, Facebook chief operating officer (COO) Sheryl Sandberg, 42, was named the fifth most powerful woman in the world by *Forbes* and the 12th most powerful woman in business by *Fortune.*[25] But while representing the "business face" of Facebook, she's also "a passionate advocate for women to claim a far greater share of the top corporate leadership positions," says one writer.[26] Herself the mother of two young children, she told a 2011 commencement audience at Barnard College, "A world where men ran half our homes and women ran half our institutions would be just a much better world."[27]

"Hi, I'm Sheryl." After stints at the U.S. Treasury Department and Google and many discussions with founder Mark Zuckerberg, Sandberg joined Facebook in 2008 because, she told people, it was a company driven by instinct and human relationships.[28] She began work by asking questions and listening. "She walked up to hundreds of people's desks and interrupted them and said, 'Hi, I'm Sheryl Sandberg,'" recalled a Facebook vice president. "It was this overt gesture, like, 'O.K., let your guard down. I'm not going to hole up with [Zuckerberg]. I'm going to try and have a relationship with you guys.'"

The Perfect Fit. For his part, Zuckerberg considers Sandberg to be a perfect fit because "There are people who are really good managers, people who can manage a big organization. And then there are people who are very analytic or focused on strategy. Those two types don't usually tend to be in the same person." He's also grateful that Sandberg "handles things I don't want to," such as advertising strategy, hiring and firing, management, and dealing with political issues. "All that stuff that in other companies I might have to do. And she's much better at that."

YOUR CALL

How would you characterize where Sandberg fits according to acquired needs theory? Do you think people can have a mix of needs (power, achievement, affiliation)?

Herzberg's Two-Factor Theory: From Dissatisfying Factors to Satisfying Factors

Frederick Herzberg arrived at his needs-based theory as a result of a landmark study of 203 accountants and engineers, who were interviewed to determine the factors responsible for job satisfaction and dissatisfaction.[29] Job satisfaction was more frequently associated with achievement, recognition, characteristics of the work, responsibility, and advancement. Job dissatisfaction was more often associated with working conditions, pay and security, company policies, supervisors, and interpersonal relationships. The result was Herzberg's *two-factor theory,* **which proposed that work satisfaction and dissatisfaction arise from two different factors**—work satisfaction from *motivating factors* and work dissatisfaction from *hygiene factors.*

Hygiene Factors Versus Motivating Factors   In Herzberg's theory, the hygiene factors are the lower-level needs, the motivating factors are the higher-level needs. The two areas are separated by a zone in which employees are neither satisfied nor dissatisfied. *(See Figure 12.5.)*

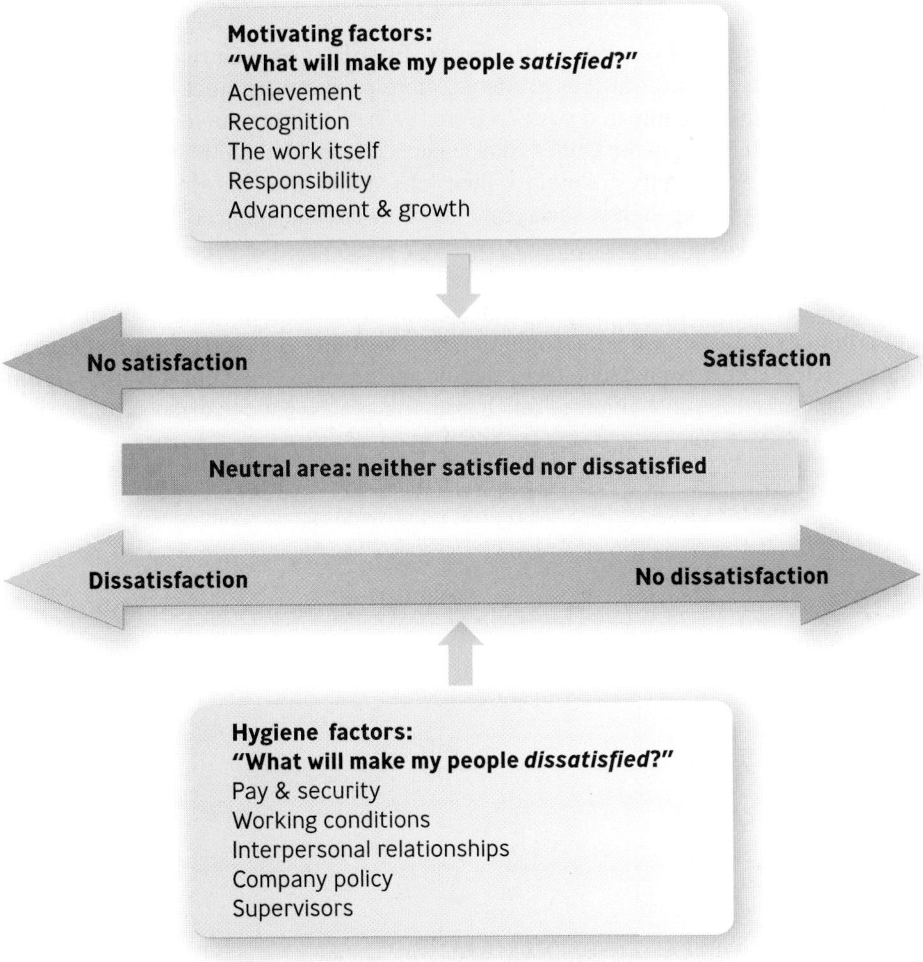

figure 12.5
HERZBERG'S TWO-FACTOR THEORY: SATISFACTION VERSUS DISSATISFACTION

- **Hygiene factors—"Why are my people dissatisfied?"** The lower-level needs, *hygiene factors,* are factors associated with job *dissatisfaction—*such as salary, working conditions, interpersonal relationships, and company policy—all of which affect the job *context* in which people work.

  An example of a hygiene factor is the temperature in a factory that's not air-conditioned during the summer. Installing air-conditioning will remove a cause of job dissatisfaction. It will not, however, spur factory workers' motivation and make them greatly satisfied in their work. Because motivating factors are absent, workers become, in Herzberg's view, merely neutral in their attitudes toward work—neither dissatisfied nor satisfied.

- **Motivating factors—"What will make my people satisfied?"** The higher-level needs, *motivating factors,* or simply *motivators,* are factors associated with job *satisfaction—*such as achievement, recognition, responsibility, and advancement—all of which affect the job content or the rewards of work performance. Motivating factors—challenges, opportunities, recognition—must be instituted, Herzberg believed, to spur superior work performance.

  An example of a motivating factor would be to give factory workers more control over their work. For example, instead of repeating a single task over and over, a worker might join with other workers on a team in which each one does several tasks. This is the approach that Swedish automaker Volvo took in building cars.

Using Two-Factor Theory to Motivate Employees   During the 2007–2009 Great Recession, with fewer jobs available, more people were stuck in jobs they disliked (61% in 2009, compared with 45% in 1987).[30] Another survey found that employee job satisfaction in the United States reached its peak in 2009, possibly because employees were especially grateful for their jobs at that time, but since then, satisfaction has been dropping slightly each year.[31] If you were managing such employees, the basic lesson of Herzberg's research is that you should first eliminate dissatisfaction (hygiene factors), making sure that working conditions, pay levels, and company policies are reasonable. You should then concentrate on spurring motivation by providing opportunities for achievement, recognition, responsibility, and personal growth (motivating factors). Positive hygiene factors could include allowing pets at work; offering videogame arcades, fitness classes, and intramural sports (volleyball, soccer); and providing a library of free movies, books, and magazines.[32]

The four needs theories are compared below. *(See Figure 12.6.)* ●

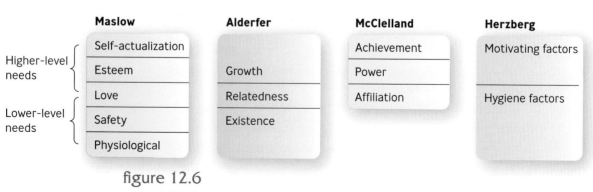

figure 12.6

A COMPARISON OF NEEDS THEORIES: MASLOW, ALDERFER, McCLELLAND, AND HERZBERG

McClelland has no classification for lower-level needs.

Is a good reward good enough? How do other factors affect motivation?

major
question?

THE BIG PICTURE

Process perspectives, which are concerned with the thought processes by which people decide how to act, have three viewpoints: equity theory, expectancy theory, and goal-setting theory.

Process perspectives **are concerned with the thought processes by which people decide how to act**—how employees choose behavior to meet their needs. Whereas need-based perspectives simply try to understand employee needs, process perspectives go further and try to understand why employees have different needs, what behaviors they select to satisfy them, and how they decide if their choices were successful.

In this section we discuss three process perspectives on motivation:

- Equity theory
- Expectancy theory
- Goal-setting theory

Equity Theory: How Fairly Do You Think You're Being Treated in Relation to Others?

Fairness—or, perhaps equally important, the *perception* of fairness—can be a big issue in organizations. For example, if, as a salesperson for Target, you received a 10% bonus for doubling your sales, would that be enough? What if other Target salespeople received 15%?

Equity theory **focuses on employee perceptions as to how fairly they think they are being treated compared with others.** Developed by psychologist **J. Stacey Adams,** equity theory is based on the idea that employees are motivated to see fairness in the rewards they expect for task performance.[33] Employees are motivated to resolve feelings of injustice. How, for example, might employees respond to knowing that the average pay for CEOs is 300 times the average worker's pay and that many workers are still struggling to find jobs?[34] (The average American with a bachelor's degree makes $2.3 million—over a lifetime. By contrast, Apple CEO Timothy Cook earns that amount in a shade over two days.)[35] How about the fact that in 2010 women made only 77% of men's earnings?[36] Some experts suggest that such imbalances are partly responsible for the more than $50 billion a year in employee theft.[37] (One time in France, workers about to be laid off at Caterpillar were so angry that they took their managers hostage.)[38]

The Elements of Equity Theory: Comparing Your Inputs & Outputs with Those of Others   The key elements in equity theory are *inputs, outputs (rewards),* and *comparisons. (See Figure 12.7, next page.)*

- **Inputs—"What do you think you're putting into the job?"** The inputs that people perceive they give to an organization are their time, effort, training, experience, intelligence, creativity, seniority, status, and so on.

- **Outputs or rewards—"What do you think you're getting out of the job?"** The outputs are the rewards that people receive from an organization: pay, benefits, praise, recognition, bonuses, promotions, status perquisites (corner office with a view, say, or private parking space), and so on.

figure 12.7

EQUITY THEORY

How people perceive they are being fairly or unfairly rewarded.

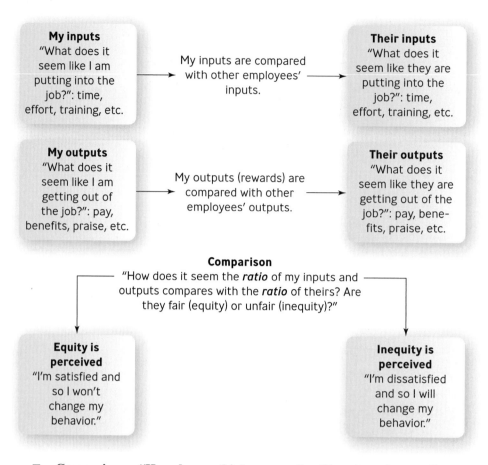

My inputs
"What does it seem like I am putting into the job?": time, effort, training, etc.

My inputs are compared with other employees' inputs.

Their inputs
"What does it seem like they are putting into the job?": time, effort, training, etc.

My outputs
"What does it seem like I am getting out of the job?": pay, benefits, praise, etc.

My outputs (rewards) are compared with other employees' outputs.

Their outputs
"What does it seem like they are getting out of the job?": pay, benefits, praise, etc.

Comparison
"How does it seem the *ratio* of my inputs and outputs compares with the *ratio* of theirs? Are they fair (equity) or unfair (inequity)?"

Equity is perceived
"I'm satisfied and so I won't change my behavior."

Inequity is perceived
"I'm dissatisfied and so I will change my behavior."

- **Comparison—"How do you think your ratio of inputs and rewards compares with those of others?"** Equity theory suggests that people compare the *ratio* of their own outcomes to inputs against the *ratio* of someone else's outcomes to inputs. When employees compare the ratio of their inputs and outputs (rewards) with those of others—whether coworkers within the organization or even other people in similar jobs outside it—they then make a judgment about fairness. Either they perceive there is *equity,* and so are satisfied with the ratio and so they don't change their behavior. Or they perceive there is *inequity,* and so they feel resentful and act to change the inequity.[39]

To get a sense of your own reaction to equity differences, see the Self-Assessment at the end of this chapter (p. 407).

Using Equity Theory to Motivate Employees   Adams suggests that employees who feel they are being underrewarded will respond to the perceived inequity in one or more negative ways, as by reducing their inputs, trying to change the outputs or rewards they receive, distorting the inequity, changing the object of comparison, or leaving the situation. *(See Table 12.1, opposite page.)*

By contrast, employees who think they are treated fairly are more likely to support organizational change, more apt to cooperate in group settings, and less apt to turn to arbitration and the courts to remedy real or imagined wrongs.

Three practical lessons that can be drawn from equity theory are as follows.

1. Employee Perceptions Are What Count   Probably the most important result of research on equity theory is this: no matter how fair managers think the organization's policies, procedures, and reward system are, each employee's *perception* of those factors is what counts. Thus, managers should provide positive recognition about employee behavior and performance and explain the reasons behind their decisions.

table 12.1
SOME WAYS EMPLOYEES
TRY TO REDUCE
INEQUITY

- **They will reduce their inputs:** They will do less work, take long breaks, call in "sick" on Mondays, leave early on Fridays, and so on.

- **They will try to change the outputs or rewards they receive:** They will lobby the boss for a raise, or they will pilfer company equipment.

- **They will distort the inequity:** They will exaggerate how hard they work so they can complain they're not paid what they're worth.

- **They will change the object of comparison:** They may compare themselves with another person instead of the original one.

- **They will leave the situation:** They will quit, transfer, or shift to another reference group.

2. Employee Participation Helps   Managers benefit by allowing employees to participate in important decisions. For example, a recent study showed that employees were more satisfied with changes to their jobs when they participated in creating the changes.[40]

3. Having an Appeal Process Helps   When employees are able to appeal decisions affecting their welfare, it promotes the belief that management treats them fairly. Perceptions of fair treatment promote job satisfaction, commitment, and citizenship behavior and reduce absenteeism and turnover.[41]

Expectancy Theory: How Much Do You Want & How Likely Are You to Get It?

Introduced by **Victor Vroom**, *expectancy theory* **suggests that people are motivated by two things: (1) how much they want something and (2) how likely they think they are to get it.**[42] In other words, assuming they have choices, people will make the choice that promises them the greatest reward if they think they can get it.

The Three Elements: Expectancy, Instrumentality, Valence   What determines how willing you (or an employee) are to work hard at tasks important to the success of the organization? The answer, says Vroom, is: You will do what you *can* do when you *want* to.

Your motivation, according to expectancy theory, involves the relationship between your *effort,* your *performance,* and the desirability of the *outcomes* (such as pay or recognition) of your performance. These relationships, which are shown in the following drawing, are affected by the three elements of *expectancy, instrumentality,* and *valence.* (See Figure 12.8.)

I. Expectancy—"Will I Be Able to Perform at the Desired Level on a Task?"   *Expectancy* **is the belief that a particular level of effort will lead to a particular level of performance.** This is called the *effort-to-performance expectancy.*

Example: If you believe that putting in more hours working at Target selling clothes will result in higher sales, then you have high effort-to-performance expectancy. That is, you believe that your efforts will matter. You think you have the ability, the product knowledge, and so on so that putting in extra hours of selling can probably raise your sales of clothes.

How much do you want? Would a well-appointed office represent the tangible realization of managerial success for you? How likely do you think you are to get it? The answers to these questions represent your important motivations, according to expectancy theory.

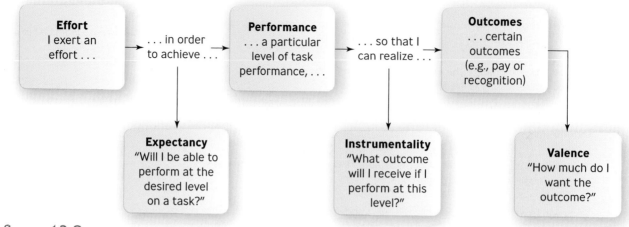

figure 12.8

EXPECTANCY THEORY:
THE MAJOR ELEMENTS

2. Instrumentality—"What Outcome Will I Receive If I Perform at This Level?" *Instrumentality* **is the expectation that successful performance of the task will lead to the outcome desired.** This is called the *performance-to-reward expectancy.*

Example: If you believe that making higher sales will cause Target to give you a bonus, then you have high performance-to-reward expectancy. You believe *if* you can achieve your goals, the outcome will be worthwhile. This element is independent of the previous one—you might decide you don't have the ability to make the extra sales, but if you did, you'll be rewarded. (Lately, because of the public's concern about the quality of the educational system in the United States, school boards and politicians are implementing programs that tie teachers' pay to performance.)[43]

3. Valence—"How Much Do I Want the Outcome?" *Valence* **is value, the importance a worker assigns to the possible outcome or reward.**

Example: If you assign a lot of importance or a high value to Target's prospective bonus or pay raise, then your valence is said to be high.

For your motivation to be high, you must be high on all three elements—expectancy, instrumentality, and valence. If any element is low, you will not be motivated. Your effort-to-performance expectancy might be low, for instance, because you doubt making an effort will make a difference (because retail clothing selling has too much competition). Or your performance-to-reward expectancy might be low because you don't think Target is going to give you a bonus for being a star at selling. Or your valence might be low because you don't think the bonus or raise is going to be high enough to justify working evenings and weekends.

Using Expectancy Theory to Motivate Employees   The principal problem with the expectancy theory is that it is complex. Even so, the underlying logic is understandable, and research seems to show that managers are not following its principles.[44]

When attempting to motivate employees, managers should ask the following questions:

- **What rewards do your employees value?** As a manager, you need to get to know your employees and determine what rewards (outcomes) they value, such as pay raises or recognition.

- **What are the job objectives and the performance level you desire?** You need to clearly define the performance objectives and determine what performance level or behavior you want so that you can tell your employees what they need to do to attain the rewards.

Champions. For athletes, such as these Baylor University women's basketball team members, winners of the 2012 Women's NCAA playoffs, performance seems easily measured by a simple outcome—whether you win or not. Do you think performance can be as clearly measured in the business world?

■ **Are the rewards linked to performance?** You want to reward high performance, of course. Thus, employees must be aware that *X* level of performance within *Y* period of time will result in *Z* kinds of rewards. In a team context, however, research shows that it is best to use a combination of individual and team-based rewards.[45]

■ **Do employees believe you will deliver the right rewards for the right performance?** Your credibility is on the line here. Your employees must believe that you have the power, the ability, and the will to give them the rewards you promise for the performance you are requesting.

EXAMPLE

Use of Expectancy Theory: A Drug Company Ties CEO Pay to Performance

Would it surprise you to learn that bankers would not pay for a study on their industry concerning how bonuses affect performance—probably because they were being richly rewarded regardless of results?[46]

While most ordinary workers are paid well if they perform well (and shown the door if they do poorly), this has frequently not been true in the top ranks of management, where bonuses and grants of stock are given outright even when achievement is lacking.[47] Thus, critics applauded a new system of compensation devised for CEO J. Michael Pearson of midsize drug maker Valeant Pharmaceuticals International.

Bigger Bang for the Buck? Arranged by the board of directors' compensation committee, the deal requires Pearson to buy lots of stock with his own money (not given to him by the company) and to hold many shares for years without selling them. It also ties annual equity grants (giving him ownership of additional stock in the company) to how well the company performs for investors.

"Pay experts say the deal gives Mr. Pearson incentives to boost long-term value for investors," says a *Wall Street Journal* story. "For example, the 49-year-old CEO only gets to keep certain restricted shares if Valeant's share price increased at least 15% a year" through the next two years.

Other Shareholder-Friendly Pay Ideas. G. Mason Morfit, head of Valeant's compensation committee, who devised the plan, also has some other suggestions for shareholder-friendly pay packages for top managers: Be generous on the upside, but tough on the downside—meaning pay executives well at the start, but don't pay them more if they fail. "Don't backslide," he says; "No bonuses if executives miss targets." Another recommendation: "Scrap 'entitlement' perks like car allowances and club dues."[48]

YOUR CALL

Pearson's compensation, including salary, bonuses, and stock, was $24 million in 2009 and $4.8 million in 2010; the values reflecting the rising price of Valeant's stock, rewarding both investors and himself. But the total shares of stock he owned were worth over $320 million as of early 2012.[49] Clearly, a pay-for-performance plan may work for CEOs. Why do you suppose, then, that a New York City pilot project that gave parents of poor children payments for things like going to the dentist ($100), holding down a full-time job ($150 per month), and getting children to school regularly ($25–$50 per month) produced no educational or attendance gains, at least for elementary and middle-school students?[50]

Goal-Setting Theory: Objectives Should Be Specific & Challenging but Achievable

***Goal-setting theory* suggests that employees can be motivated by goals that are specific and challenging but achievable.** According to psychologists **Edwin Locke** and **Gary Latham,** who developed the theory, goal setting has four motivational mechanisms.[51] *(See Table 12.2.)* It is natural for people to set and strive for goals; however, the goal-setting process is useful only if people *understand* and *accept* the goals.

Some Practical Results of Goal-Setting Theory   A *goal* is defined as an objective that a person is trying to accomplish through his or her efforts. To result in high motivation and performance, according to recent research, goals must have a number of characteristics, as follows:

1. Goals Should Be Specific   Goals such as "Sell as many cars as you can" or "Be nicer to customers" are too vague. Instead, goals need to be specific—usually meaning *quantitative,* as in "Boost your revenues 25%" and "Cut absenteeism by 10%."[52]

2. Goals Should Be Challenging but Achievable   Goals should be tailored to fit individual abilities and training, not set so low that lots of people can achieve them nor set so high that most people will give up. Difficult goals will lead to higher performance only when employees are committed to them; if they are not, difficult goals may simply lead to low performance.[53]

3. Goals Should Be Linked to Action Plans   An action plan outlines the activities or tasks that need to be accomplished in order to obtain a goal and reminds us of what we should be working on. Both individuals (such as college students) and organizations are more likely to achieve their goals when they develop detailed action plans.[54]

4. Goals Need Not Be Set Jointly to Be Effective   It doesn't seem to matter whether goals are set by managers, by employees, or by both together to be effective.[55] Thus, managers should probably do whatever suits the individual and the situation (a contingency approach). On the other hand, employees should be encouraged to develop their own action plans, which will foster stronger goal commitment.[56]

5. Feedback Enhances Goal Attainment   Feedback lets employees know if they are on or off course, provides them with performance standards, and gives them the information they need to adjust their efforts.

Some of the preceding recommendations are embodied in the advice we presented in Chapter 5—namely, that goals should be SMART: Specific, Measurable, Attainable, Results-oriented, and have Target dates.   ●

Small business. Do employees in small businesses, such as these two men high-fivin' each other after closing an important sale, need the same kind of motivational goals as employees in large corporations? Is setting goals in small businesses, where there's apt to be less specialization, more or less difficult than in large organizations?

12.4 JOB DESIGN PERSPECTIVES ON MOTIVATION

THE BIG PICTURE

Job design, the division of an organization's work among employees, applies motivational theories to jobs to increase performance and satisfaction. The traditional approach to job design is to fit people to the jobs; the modern way is to fit the jobs to the people, using job enrichment and approaches that are based on Herzberg's landmark two-factor theory, discussed earlier in this chapter. The job characteristics model offers five job attributes for better work outcomes.

About half of workers reported in a recent year that their current job was stagnant.[57] Is there anything that can be done about this?

Job design **is (1) the division of an organization's work among its employees and (2) the application of motivational theories to jobs to increase satisfaction and performance.** There are two different approaches to job design, one traditional, one modern, that can be taken in deciding how to design jobs. The traditional way is *fitting people to jobs;* the modern way is *fitting jobs to people.*[58]

Fitting people to jobs is based on the assumption that people will gradually adapt to any work situation. Even so, jobs must still be tailored so that nearly anyone can do them. This is the approach often taken with assembly-line jobs and jobs involving routine tasks. For managers the main challenge becomes "How can we make the worker most compatible with the work?"

One technique is *job simplification,* **the process of reducing the number of tasks a worker performs.** When a job is stripped down to its simplest elements, it enables a worker to focus on doing more of the same task, thus increasing employee efficiency and productivity. This may be especially useful, for instance, in designing jobs for mentally disadvantaged workers, such as those run by Goodwill Industries. However, research shows that simplified, repetitive jobs lead to job dissatisfaction, poor mental health, and a low sense of accomplishment and personal growth.[59]

Fitting Jobs to People

Fitting jobs to people is based on the assumption that people are underutilized at work and that they want more variety, challenges, and responsibility. This philosophy, an outgrowth of Herzberg's theory, is one of the reasons for the popularity of work teams in the United States. The main challenge for managers is "How can we make the work most compatible with the worker so as to produce both high performance and high job satisfaction?" Two techniques for this type of job design include (1) *job enlargement* and (2) *job enrichment.*

Job Enlargement: Putting More Variety into a Job   The opposite of job simplification, *job enlargement* **consists of increasing the number of tasks in a job to increase variety and motivation.** For instance, the job of installing flat screens in television sets could be enlarged to include installation of the circuit boards as well.

Although proponents claim job enlargement can improve employee satisfaction, motivation, and quality of production, research suggests job enlargement by itself won't have a significant and lasting positive effect on job performance. After all, working at two boring tasks instead of one doesn't add up to a challenging job. Instead, job enlargement is just one tool of many that should be considered in job design.[60]

Job Enrichment: Putting More Responsibility & Other Motivating Factors into a Job Job enrichment is the practical application of Frederick Herzberg's two-factor motivator-hygiene theory of job satisfaction.[61] Specifically, *job enrichment* **consists of building into a job such motivating factors as responsibility, achievement, recognition, stimulating work, and advancement.**

However, instead of the job-enlargement technique of simply giving employees additional tasks of similar difficulty (known as *horizontal loading*), with job enrichment employees are given more responsibility (known as *vertical loading*). Thus, employees take on chores that would normally be performed by their supervisors. For example, one department store authorized thousands of its sales clerks to handle functions normally reserved for store managers, such as handling merchandise-return problems and approving customers' checks.

The Job Characteristics Model: Five Job Attributes for Better Work Outcomes

Developed by researchers **J. Richard Hackman** and **Greg Oldham,** the job characteristics model of design is an outgrowth of job enrichment.[62] **The *job characteristics model* consists of (a) five core job characteristics that affect (b) three critical psychological states of an employee that in turn affect (c) work outcomes—the employee's motivation, performance, and satisfaction.** The model is illustrated below. *(See Figure 12.9.)*

figure 12.9

THE JOB CHARACTERISTICS MODEL

Source: From J. Richard Hackman and Greg R. Oldham, *Work Redesign,* 1e © 1980. Reproduced by permission of Pearson Education, Inc., Upper Saddle River, New Jersey.

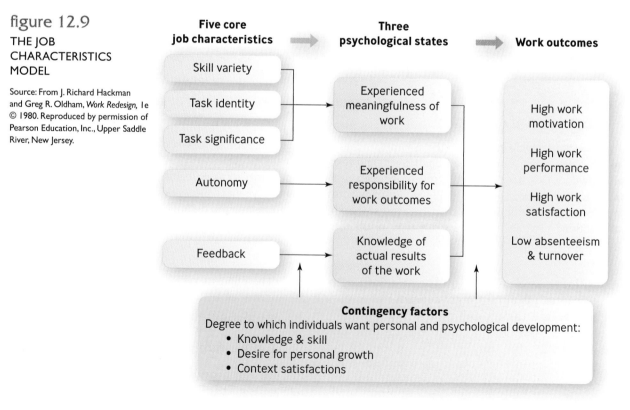

Five Job Characteristics The five core job characteristics are as follows.

1. Skill Variety—"How Many Different Skills Does Your Job Require?"

Skill variety describes the extent to which a job requires a person to use a wide range of different skills and abilities.

Example: The skill variety required by a rocket scientist is higher than that for a short-order cook.

2. Task Identity—"How Many Different Tasks Are Required to Complete the Work?"

Task identity describes the extent to which a job requires a worker to perform all the tasks needed to complete the job from beginning to end.

Example: The task identity for a craftsperson who goes through all the steps to build a handmade acoustic guitar is higher than it is for an assembly-line worker who just installs windshields on cars.

3. Task Significance—"How Many Other People Are Affected by Your Job?"

Task significance describes the extent to which a job affects the lives of other people, whether inside or outside the organization.

Example: A technician who is responsible for keeping a hospital's electronic equipment in working order has higher task significance than a person wiping down cars in a carwash.

4. Autonomy—"How Much Discretion Does Your Job Give You?"

Autonomy describes the extent to which a job allows an employee to make choices about scheduling different tasks and deciding how to perform them.

Skill variety. Being an airline pilot—or a jewelry designer, a building contractor, a physician, or an orchestra conductor—requires a greater number of skills than, say, driving a truck. Do highly skilled employees typically make good managers? What skills do airline pilots have that would make them effective managers in other kinds of work?

Example: College-textbook salespeople have lots of leeway in planning which campuses and professors to call on. Thus, they have higher autonomy than do toll-takers on a bridge, whose actions are determined by the flow of vehicles.

5. Feedback—"How Much Do You Find Out How Well You're Doing?"

Feedback describes the extent to which workers receive clear, direct information about how well they are performing the job.

Example: Professional basketball players receive immediate feedback on how many of their shots are going into the basket. Engineers working on new weapons systems may go years before learning how effective their performance has been.

How the Model Works According to the job characteristics model, these five core characteristics affect a worker's motivation because they affect three critical psychological states: *meaningfulness of work, responsibility for results,* and *knowledge of results.* (Refer to Figure 12.9 on p. 392 again.) In turn, these positive psychological states fuel *high motivation, high performance, high satisfaction,* and *low absenteeism and turnover.*

One other element—shown at the bottom of Figure 12.9—needs to be discussed: *contingency factors.* This refers to the degree to which a person wants personal and psychological development. Job design works when employees are motivated; to be so, they must have three attributes: (1) necessary knowledge and skill, (2) desire for personal growth, and (3) context satisfactions—that is, the right physical working conditions, pay, and supervision.

Job design works. A meta-analysis of 259 studies involving 219,625 people showed that job design was positively associated with employee performance, job satisfaction, organizational commitment, and physical and psychological well-being. Job design also was associated with lower absenteeism and intentions to quit.[63] Similar results were found in another meta-analysis involving studies of over 75,000 people.[64]

Applying the Job Characteristics Model There are three major steps to follow when applying the model.

- **Diagnose the work environment to see whether a problem exists.** Hackman and Oldham developed a self-report instrument for managers to use called the *job diagnostic survey.* This will indicate whether an individual's so-called motivating potential score (MPS)—the amount of internal work motivation associated with a specific job—is high or low.

- **Determine whether job redesign is appropriate.** If a person's MPS score is low, an attempt should be made to determine which of the core job characteristics is causing the problem. You should next decide whether job redesign is appropriate for a given group of employees. Job design is most likely to work in a participative environment in which employees have the necessary knowledge and skills.

- **Consider how to redesign the job.** Here you try to increase those core job characteristics that are lower than national norms.

Example: Employers want to save on health costs by helping employees with diabetes, heart disease, and similar chronic conditions avoid emergency room visits and hospital admissions.[65] However, since primary care doctors, who could help patients manage their conditions (as by reminding diabetics to monitor their blood-glucose levels daily), are paid less than physicians in other specialties, the system has turned such doctors "into little chipmunks on a wheel, pumping out patients every five minutes," as one observer described it.[66] The solution? Redesign the job by rewarding primary care doctors for spending more time with patients.[67] ●

What are the types of incentives I might use to influence employee behavior?

THE BIG PICTURE

Reinforcement theory suggests behavior will be repeated if it has positive consequences and won't be if it has negative consequences. There are four types of reinforcement: positive reinforcement, negative reinforcement, extinction, and punishment. This section also describes how to use some reinforcement techniques to modify employee behavior.

Reinforcement evades the issue of people's needs and thinking processes in relation to motivation, as we described under the need-based and process perspectives. Instead, the reinforcement perspective, which was pioneered by **Edward L. Thorndike** and **B. F. Skinner,** is concerned with how the consequences of a certain behavior affect that behavior in the future.[68]

Skinner was the father of *operant conditioning,* the process of controlling behavior by manipulating its consequences. Operant conditioning rests on Thorndike's *law of effect,* which states that behavior that results in a pleasant outcome is likely to be repeated and behavior that results in unpleasant outcomes is not likely to be repeated.

From these underpinnings has come **reinforcement theory, which attempts to explain behavior change by suggesting that behavior with positive consequences tends to be repeated, whereas behavior with negative consequences tends not to be repeated.** The use of reinforcement theory to change human behavior is called *behavior modification.*

The Four Types of Reinforcement: Positive, Negative, Extinction, & Punishment

Reinforcement is anything that causes a given behavior to be repeated or inhibited, whether praising a child for cleaning his or her room or scolding a child for leaving a tricycle in the driveway. There are four types of reinforcement: (1) *positive reinforcement,* (2) *negative reinforcement,* (3) *extinction,* and (4) *punishment. (See Figure 12.10, next page.)*

Positive Reinforcement: Strengthens Behavior   *Positive reinforcement* is the use of positive consequences to strengthen a particular behavior.

Example: A supervisor who's asked an insurance salesperson to sell more policies might reward successful performance by saying, "It's great that you exceeded your quota, and you'll get a bonus for it. Maybe next time you'll sell even more and will become a member of the Circle of 100 Top Sellers and win a trip to Paris as well." Note the rewards: praise, more money, recognition, awards. Presumably this will *strengthen* the behavior and the sales rep will work even harder in the coming months.

Negative Reinforcement: Also Strengthens Behavior   *Negative reinforcement* is the process of strengthening a behavior by withdrawing something negative.

Example: A supervisor who has been nagging a salesperson might say, "Well, so you exceeded your quota" and stop the nagging. Note the neutral statement; there is no praise but also no longer any negative statements. This could cause the sales rep to *maintain* his or her existing behavior.

Extinction: Weakens Behavior   *Extinction* is the weakening of behavior by ignoring it or making sure it is not reinforced.

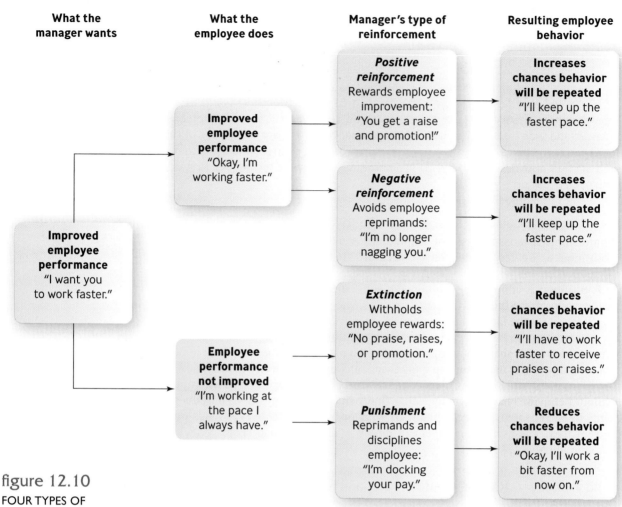

What the manager wants	What the employee does	Manager's type of reinforcement	Resulting employee behavior
Improved employee performance "I want you to work faster."	**Improved employee performance** "Okay, I'm working faster."	***Positive reinforcement*** Rewards employee improvement: "You get a raise and promotion!"	**Increases chances behavior will be repeated** "I'll keep up the faster pace."
		Negative reinforcement Avoids employee reprimands: "I'm no longer nagging you."	**Increases chances behavior will be repeated** "I'll keep up the faster pace."
	Employee performance not improved "I'm working at the pace I always have."	***Extinction*** Withholds employee rewards: "No praise, raises, or promotion."	**Reduces chances behavior will be repeated** "I'll have to work faster to receive praises or raises."
		Punishment Reprimands and disciplines employee: "I'm docking your pay."	**Reduces chances behavior will be repeated** "Okay, I'll work a bit faster from now on."

figure 12.10

FOUR TYPES OF REINFORCEMENT

These are different ways of changing employee behavior.

Example: A supervisor might tell a successful salesperson, "I know you exceeded your quota, but now that our company has been taken over by another firm, we're not giving out bonuses anymore." Presumably this will *weaken* the salesperson's efforts to perform better in the future.

Punishment: Also Weakens Behavior *Punishment* is the process of weakening behavior by presenting something negative or withdrawing something positive.

Example: A supervisor might tell an unsuccessful salesperson who's been lazy about making calls to clients and so didn't make quota, "Well, if this keeps up, you'll probably be let go." This could *inhibit* the salesperson from being so lackadaisical about making calls to clients. (Incidentally, criticism has a stronger impact than praise, suggests one social psychologist, and is longer lasting in its effects.)[69]

Using Reinforcement to Motivate Employees

The following are some guidelines for using two types of reinforcement—positive reinforcement and punishment.

Positive Reinforcement There are several aspects of positive reinforcement, which should definitely be part of your toolkit of managerial skills:

■ **Reward only desirable behavior.** You should give rewards to your employees only when they show *desirable* behavior. Thus, for example, you should give praise to employees not for showing up for work on time (an expected part of any job) but for showing up early.

- **Give rewards as soon as possible.** You should give a reward as soon as possible after the desirable behavior appears. Thus, you should give praise to an early-arriving employee as soon as he or she arrives, not later in the week.

- **Be clear about what behavior is desired.** Clear communication is everything. You should tell employees exactly what kinds of work behaviors are desirable and you should tell everyone exactly what they must do to earn rewards.

- **Have different rewards and recognize individual differences.** Recognizing that different people respond to different kinds of rewards, you should have different rewards available. Thus, you might give a word of praise verbally to one person, shoot a line or two by e-mail to another person, or send a hand-scrawled note to another.

Punishment Unquestionably there will be times when you'll need to threaten or administer an unpleasant consequence to stop an employee's undesirable behavior. Sometimes it's best to address a problem by combining punishment with positive reinforcement. Some suggestions for using punishment are as follows.

- **Punish only undesirable behavior.** You should give punishment only when employees show frequent *undesirable* behavior. Otherwise, employees may come to view you negatively as a tyrannical boss. Thus, for example, you should reprimand employees who show up, say, a half hour late for work but not 5 or 10 minutes late.

- **Give reprimands or disciplinary actions as soon as possible.** You should mete out punishment as soon as possible after the undesirable behavior occurs. Thus, you should give a reprimand to a late-arriving employee as soon as he or she arrives.

- **Be clear about what behavior is undesirable.** Tell employees exactly what kinds of work behaviors are undesirable and make any disciplinary action or reprimand match the behavior. A manager should not, for example, dock an hourly employee's pay if he or she is only 5 or 10 minutes late for work.

- **Administer punishment in private.** You would hate to have your boss chew you out in front of your subordinates, and the people who report to you also shouldn't be reprimanded in public, which would lead only to resentments that may have nothing to do with an employee's infractions.

- **Combine punishment and positive reinforcement.** If you're reprimanding an employee, be sure to also say what he or she is doing right and state what rewards the employee might be eligible for. For example, while reprimanding someone for being late, say that a perfect attendance record over the next few months will put that employee in line for a raise or promotion. ●

Punishment. Does getting a wallet-busting speeding ticket change your behavior? What if it happens several times? Yet consider also other, presumably stronger forms of governmental punishment that are supposed to act as deterrents to bad behavior. Does the possibility of the death punishment really deter homicides? Why or why not?

How can I use compensation and other rewards to motivate people?

THE BIG PICTURE
Compensation, the main motivator of performance, includes pay for performance, bonuses, profit sharing, gainsharing, stock options, and pay for knowledge. Other non-monetary incentives address needs that aren't being met, such as work–life balance, growth in skills, and commitment.

"In the past, people could see the fruits of their labor immediately: a chair made or a ball bearing produced," writes *Wall Street Journal* columnist Jared Sandberg. However, in the information age, when so much of a person's time is spent looking into a smartphone display or computer screen and working on partial tasks seemingly unconnected to something whole, "it can be hard to find gratification from work that is largely invisible."[70] As work becomes more invisible and intangible, more team based rather than individual based, it also becomes harder to measure, harder to define its successful accomplishment—and harder to motivate employees to perform well at it.

Is Money the Best Motivator?

Perhaps the first thing that comes to mind when you think about motivating performance is compensation—how much money you or your employees can make. But consider how motivation worked for Mary Morse, a software engineer, who turned down several offers from other San Francisco–area tech firms, at least one of which would have made her wealthy, in order to stay with the computer-aided design firm Autodesk. The reason? She liked her bosses.[71]

Morse demonstrates the truth of several surveys that found that most workers rate having a caring boss higher than they value monetary benefits.[72] The Great Place to Work Institute has determined that great employers have three traits in common: employee trust in management, pride in the company, and camaraderie with colleagues.[73] Clearly, then, motivating doesn't just involve dollars.

Motivation & Compensation

Most people are paid an hourly wage or a weekly or monthly salary. Both of these are easy for organizations to administer, of course. But by itself a wage or a salary gives an employee little incentive to work hard. Incentive compensation plans try to do so, although no single plan will boost the performance of all employees.

Characteristics of the Best Incentive Compensation Plans In accordance with most of the theories of motivation we described earlier, for incentive plans to work, certain criteria are advisable, as follows. (1) Rewards must be linked to performance and be measurable. (2) The rewards must satisfy individual needs. (3) The rewards must be agreed on by manager and employees. (4) The rewards must be believable and achievable by employees.

Popular Incentive Compensation Plans How would you like to be rewarded for your efforts? Some of the most well-known incentive compensation plans are *pay*

Motivation as a small business owner. Susan Brown of Golden, Colorado, had dreamed of opening her own business since she was a child. However, she invented the Boppy, a simple pillow stuffed with foam, almost accidentally, when her daughter's day care center asked parents to bring in pillows to prop up infants who couldn't sit up on their own. Today the Boppy Co. has annual sales of $15–$25 million. For some people, like Brown, the only way to merge motivation and compensation is to own and manage their own business. What factors or incentives motivate you to work hard?

for performance, bonuses, profit sharing, gainsharing, stock options, and *pay for knowledge.*

- **Pay for performance.** Also known as *merit pay, **pay for performance** bases pay on one's results.* Thus, different salaried employees might get different pay raises and other rewards (such as promotions) depending on their overall job performance.[74]

  Examples: One standard pay-for-performance plan, already mentioned, is payment according to a ***piece rate,** in which employees are paid according to how much output they produce,* as is often used with farmworkers picking fruit and vegetables. Another is the ***sales commission,** in which sales representatives are paid a percentage of the earnings the company made from their sales,* so that the more they sell, the more they are paid. A good deal of the criticism of excessive executive pay is that it has not been tied to company performance.[75]

- **Bonuses.** *Bonuses* **are cash awards given to employees who achieve specific performance objectives.**

  Example: Nieman Marcus, the department store, pays its salespeople a percentage of the earnings from the goods they sell.

  Unfortunately, the documents that most companies file (proxy documents to the Securities and Exchange Commission) to explain what specific targets executives had to meet to earn their bonuses are not very clear, being couched mainly in legalese.[76] (Bonuses for bankers in particular became a hot-button political issue after banks received a $700 billion rescue from taxpayers in 2008, then surging financial markets caused a rebound that allowed such companies to set aside billions of dollars for year-end bonuses.)[77]

- **Profit sharing.** *Profit sharing* **is the distribution to employees of a percentage of the company's profits.**

  Example: In one T-shirt and sweatshirt manufacturing company, 10% of pretax profits are distributed to employees every month, and more is given out at the end of the year. Distributions are apportioned according to such criteria as performance, attendance, and lateness for individual employees.

- **Gainsharing.** *Gainsharing* **is the distribution of savings or "gains" to groups of employees who reduced costs and increased measurable**

productivity. Perhaps a quarter of Fortune 1000 companies have adopted gainsharing.[78] In one version (the so-called *Scanlon plan),* a portion of any cost savings, usually 75%, are distributed to employees. Example: Indianapolis-based Mike's Carwash, which was named one of 2009's top small workplaces by *The Wall Street Journal,* paid out $569,000 in gainsharing the previous year to 437 employees in 37 locations who had been challenged to beat targets set at the corporate level.

- **Stock options.** With *stock options,* **certain employees are given the right to buy stock at a future date for a discounted price.** The motivator here is that employees holding stock options will supposedly work hard to make the company's stock rise so that they can obtain it at a cheaper price. By giving stock options to all employees who work 20 or more hours a week, Starbucks Corp. was able, prior to the recession, to hold its annual turnover rate to 60%—in an industry (fast food and restaurants) in which 300% is not unheard of.[79] (The use of stock options has been criticized recently because many companies allowed "backdating"—permitting their executives to buy company stock at low purchase prices from previous days or weeks. As one writer points out, this is sort of like being able to make a fortune by betting on a Kentucky Derby whose outcome you've known for some time.)[80]

- **Pay for knowledge.** Also known as *skill-based pay,* *pay for knowledge* **ties employee pay to the number of job-relevant skills or academic degrees they earn.**

  Example: The teaching profession is a time-honored instance of this incentive, in which elementary and secondary teachers are encouraged to increase their salaries by earning further college credit. However, firms such as FedEx also have pay-for-knowledge plans.

Nonmonetary Ways of Motivating Employees

Employees who can behave autonomously, solve problems, and take the initiative are apt to be the very ones who will leave if they find their own needs aren't being met—namely:

- **The need for work–life balance.** A PricewaterhouseCoopers survey of 2,500 university students in 11 countries found that 57% named as their primary career goal "attaining a balance between personal life and career."[81] A 25-year study of values in the United States found that "employees have become less convinced that work should be an important part of one's life or that working hard makes me a better person."[82] Millennials in particular are apt to say the most important things in life are "being a good parent" (52%) and "having a successful marriage" (30%) rather than "having a high-paying career" (15%).[83]

- **The need to expand skills.** Having watched their parents undergo downsizing, younger workers in particular are apt to view a job as a way of gaining skills that will enable them to earn a decent living in the future.

- **The need to matter.** Workers now want to be with an organization that allows them to feel they matter. They want to commit to their profession or fellow team members rather than have to profess a blind loyalty to the corporation.[84]

There is a whole class of nonmonetary incentives to attract, retain, and motivate employees. The foremost example is the *flexible workplace*—including part-time work, flextime, compressed workweek, job sharing, and telecommuting, as described in the Practical Action box.

The Flexible Workplace[85]

With so many two-paycheck families, single parents, and other diverse kinds of employees in the workforce, many employers now recognize the idea of a *flexible workplace* as a way of recruiting, retaining, and motivating employees. For example, a 2011 survey of 637 employees revealed that 33% planned to look for another job that allowed greater flexibility.[86] Among the types of alternative work schedules available are the following.

Part-Time Work—Less Than 40 Hours. Part-time work is any work done on a schedule less than the standard 40-hour workweek. Some part-time workers—so-called temporary workers or contingency workers—actually want to work 40 hours or more, but can't find full-time jobs.[87] Others, however, work part time by choice. Today an organization can hire not only part-time clerical help, for instance, but also part-time programmers, market researchers, lawyers, even part-time top executives.

Flextime—Flexible Working Hours. Flextime, or flexible time, consists of flexible working hours, or any schedule that gives one some choices in working hours. If, for example, an organization's normal working hours are 9 a.m. to 5 p.m., a flextime worker might be allowed to start and finish an hour earlier or an hour later—for instance, to work from 8 a.m. to 4 p.m. The main requirement is that the employee be at work during certain core hours, to be available for meetings, consultations, and so on. By offering flextime hours, organizations can attract and keep employees with special requirements such as the need to take care of children or elderly parents. It also benefits employees who wish to avoid commuting during rush hour.

Compressed Workweek—40 Hours in Four Days. In a compressed workweek, employees perform a full-time job in less than 5 days of standard 8- (or 9-) hour shifts. The most common variation is a 40-hour week performed in 4 days of 10 hours each, which gives employees three (instead of two) consecutive days off. The benefits are that organizations can offer employees more leisure time and reduced wear and tear and expense from commuting. The disadvantages are possible scheduling problems, unavailability of an employee to co-workers and customers, and fatigue from long workdays.

Job Sharing—Two People Split the Same Job. In job sharing, two people divide one full-time job. Usually, each person works a half day, although there can be other arrangements (working alternate days or alternate weeks, for example). As with a compressed workweek, job sharing provides employees with more personal or leisure time. The disadvantage is that it can result in communication problems with coworkers or customers.

Telecommuting & Other Work-at-Home Schedules. There have always been some employees who have had special full-time or part-time arrangements whereby they are allowed to work at home, keeping in touch with their employers and coworkers by e-mail and phone. The fax machine, the personal computer, smartphones, the Internet, and overnight-delivery services have made work-at-home arrangements much more feasible.

Working at home with telecommunications between office and home is called telecommuting. The advantages to employers are increased productivity because telecommuters experience less distraction at home and can work flexible hours.[88]

YOUR CALL

For what you're doing right now at this point in your life, which of these possibilities would suit you best, and why? Would it be workable for your employer if all your co-workers did it as well?

Other incentives can be expressed simply as *treat employees well,* some examples of which follow.

Thoughtfulness: The Value of Being Nice   A study by Walker Information, an Indianapolis-based research firm, found that employers spend too little time showing workers they matter, as manifested in lack of communication and lack of interest in new ideas and contributions.[89] A majority of employees feel underappreciated, according to one survey. Forty percent of employees who rated their boss's performance as poor said they were likely to look for a new job; only 11% of those who rated it excellent said they would.[90] "Being nice" to employees means, for example, reducing criticism, becoming more effusive in your praise, and writing thank-you notes to employees for exceptional performance.[91]

The number one reason people quit their jobs, it's believed, is their dissatisfaction with their supervisors, not their paychecks. Thus, industrial psychologist B. Lynn Ware suggests that if you learn valued employees are disgruntled, you should discuss it with them.[92] Employers can promote personal relationships, which most employees are concerned about on the job, by offering breaks or other opportunities in which people can mix and socialize.

Work–Life Benefits   Work–life benefits, according to Kathie Lingle, are programs "used by employers to increase productivity and commitment by removing certain barriers that make it hard for people to strike a balance between their work and personal lives."[93]

Lingle, who is national work–life director for KPMG, an accounting and consulting firm, emphasizes that work–life benefits "are not a reward, but a way of getting work done." After all, some employees are low performers simply because of a lack of life–work balance, with great demands at home. "If you only give these 'rewards' to existing high performers," says Lingle, "you're cutting people off who could, with some support, be high performers." Nevertheless, handing out extra time off can be used to reward performance and prevent burnout.[94]

Besides alternative scheduling, work–life benefits include helping employees with day care costs or even establishing on-site centers; domestic-partner benefits; job-protected leave for new parents; and provision of technology such as mobile phones and laptops to enable parents to work at home.[95]

Surroundings   The cubicle, according to new research, is stifling the creativity and morale of many workers, and the bias of modern-day office designers for open spaces and neutral colors is leading to employee complaints that their workplaces are too noisy or too bland. Some businesses, such as advertising giant Grey Group in New York, have even moved beyond cubicles to completely open offices, which has required a business psychologist to hold "space therapy" sessions to ease employee concerns.[96]

"There is no such thing as something that works for everybody," says Alan Hedge, a professor of environmental analysis at Cornell University.[97] An 8-foot-by-8-foot cubicle may not be a good visual trigger for human brains, and companies wanting to improve creativity and productivity may need to think about giving office employees better things to look at.[98]

Skill-Building & Educational Opportunities   Learning opportunities can take two forms. Managers can see that workers are matched with coworkers from whom

Cubicle culture. It might be too difficult to design a setup in which everyone has an office with a view. But would it be possible to design a layout in which everyone has a private office? Do you think it would better motivate employees?

they can learn, allowing them, for instance, to "shadow" (watch and imitate) workers in other jobs or be in interdepartmental task forces. There can also be tuition reimbursement for part-time study at a college or university.[99]

Sabbaticals   Intel and Apple understand that in a climate of 80-hour weeks people need to recharge themselves. But even McDonald's offers sabbaticals to longtime employees, giving a month to a year of paid time off in which to travel, learn, and pursue personal projects. The aim, of course, is to enable employees to recharge themselves but also, it is hoped, to cement their loyalty to the organization.[100]   ●

Key Terms Used in This Chapter

Summary

12.1 Motivating for Performance

Motivation is defined as the psychological processes that arouse and direct goal-directed behavior. In a simple model of motivation, people have certain needs that motivate them to perform specific behaviors for which they receive rewards that feed back and satisfy the original need. Rewards are of two types: (1) An extrinsic reward is the payoff, such as money, a person receives from others for performing a particular task. (2) An intrinsic reward is the satisfaction, such as a feeling of accomplishment, that a person receives from performing the particular task itself.

As a manager, you want to motivate people to do things that will benefit your organization—join it, stay with it, show up for work at it, perform better for it, and do extra for it.

Four major perspectives on motivation are (1) content, (2) process, (3) job design, and (4) reinforcement.

12.2 Content Perspectives on Employee Motivation

Content perspectives or need-based perspectives emphasize the needs that motivate people. Needs are defined as physiological or psychological deficiencies that arouse behavior. Besides the McGregor Theory X/Theory Y (Chapter 1), need-based perspectives include (1) the hierarchy of needs theory, (2) the ERG theory, (3) the acquired needs theory, and (4) the two-factor theory.

The hierarchy of needs theory proposes that people are motivated by five levels of need: physiological, safety, love, esteem, and self-actualization needs.

ERG theory assumes that three basic needs influence behavior; existence, relatedness, and growth.

The acquired needs theory states that three needs—achievement, affiliation, and power—are major motives determining people's behavior in the workplace.

The two-factor theory proposes that work satisfaction and dissatisfaction arise from two different factors: work satisfaction from so-called motivating factors, and work dissatisfaction from so-called hygiene factors. Hygiene factors, the lower-level needs, are factors associated with job dissatisfaction—such as salary and working conditions—which affect the environment in which people work. Motivating factors, the higher-level needs, are factors associated with job satisfaction—such as achievement and advancement—which affect the rewards of work performance.

12.3 Process Perspectives on Employee Motivation

Process perspectives are concerned with the thought processes by which people decide how to act. Three process perspectives on motivation are (1) equity theory, (2) expectancy theory, and (3) goal-setting theory.

Equity theory focuses on employee perceptions as to how fairly they think they are being treated compared with others. The key elements in equity theory are inputs, outputs (rewards), and comparisons. (1) With inputs, employees consider what they are putting into the job in time, effort, and so on. (2) With outputs or rewards, employees consider what they think they're getting out of the job in terms of pay, praise, and so on. (3) With comparison, employees compare the ratio of their own outcomes to inputs against the ratio of someone else's outcomes to inputs. Three practical lessons of equity theory are that employee perceptions are what count, employee participation helps, and having an appeal process helps.

Expectancy theory suggests that people are motivated by how much they want something and how likely they think they are to get it. The three elements affecting motivation are expectancy, instrumentality, and valence. (1) Expectancy is the belief that a particular level of effort will lead to a particular level of performance. (2) Instrumentality is the expectation that successful performance of the task will lead to the outcome desired. (3) Valence is the value, the importance a worker assigns to the possible outcome or reward. When attempting to motivate employees, according to the logic of expectancy theory, managers should ascertain what rewards employees value, what job objectives and performance level they desire, whether there are rewards linked to performance, and whether employees believe managers will deliver the right rewards for the right performance.

Goal-setting theory suggests that employees can be motivated by goals that are specific and challenging but achievable and linked to action plans. In addition, the theory suggests that goals should be set jointly with the employee, be measurable, and have a target date for accomplishment and that employees should receive feedback and rewards.

12.4 Job Design Perspectives on Motivation

Job design is, first, the division of an organization's work among its employees and, second, the application of motivational theories to jobs to increase satisfaction and performance. Two approaches to job design are fitting people to jobs (the traditional approach) and fitting jobs to people.

Fitting jobs to people assumes people are underutilized and want more variety. Two techniques for this type of job design include (1) job enlargement, increasing the number of tasks in a job to increase variety and motivation, and (2) job enrichment, building into a job such motivating factors as responsibility, achievement, recognition, stimulating work, and advancement.

An outgrowth of job enrichment is the job characteristics model, which consists of (a) five core job characteristics that affect (b) three critical psychological states of an employee that in turn affect (c) work outcomes—the employee's motivation, performance, and satisfaction. The five core job characteristics are (1) skill variety—how many different skills a job requires; (2) task identity—how many different tasks are required to complete the work; (3) task significance—how many other people are affected by the job; (4) autonomy—how much discretion the job allows the worker; and (5) feedback—how much employees find out how well they're doing. These five characteristics affect three critical psychological states: meaningfulness of work, responsibility for results, and knowledge of results. Three major steps to follow when applying the job characteristics model are (1) diagnose the work environment to see if a problem exists, (2) determine whether job redesign is appropriate, and (3) consider how to redesign the job.

12.5 Reinforcement Perspectives on Motivation

Reinforcement theory attempts to explain behavior change by suggesting that behavior with positive consequences tends to be repeated whereas behavior with negative consequences tends not to be repeated. Reinforcement is anything that causes a given behavior to be repeated or inhibited.

There are four types of reinforcement. (1) Positive reinforcement is the use of positive consequences to strengthen a particular behavior. (2) Negative reinforcement is the process of strengthening a behavior by withdrawing something negative. (3) Extinction is the weakening of behavior by ignoring it or making sure it is not reinforced. (4) Punishment is the process of weakening behavior by presenting something negative or withdrawing something positive.

In using positive reinforcement to motivate employees, managers should reward only desirable behavior, give rewards as soon as possible, be clear about what behavior is desired, and have different

rewards and recognize individual differences. In using punishment, managers should punish only undesirable behavior, give reprimands or disciplinary actions as soon as possible, be clear about what behavior is undesirable, administer punishment in private, and combine punishment and positive reinforcement.

12.6 Using Compensation & Other Rewards to Motivate

Compensation is only one form of motivator. For incentive compensation plans for work, rewards must be linked to performance and be measurable; they must satisfy individual needs; they must be agreed on by manager and employee; and they must be perceived as being equitable, believable, and achievable by employees.

Popular incentive compensation plans are the following. (1) Pay for performance bases pay on one's results. One kind is payment according to piece rate, in which employees are paid according to how much output they produce. Another is the sales commission, in which sales representatives are paid a percentage of the earnings the company made from their sales. (2) Bonuses are cash awards given to employees who achieve specific performance objectives. (3) Profit sharing is the distribution to employees of a percentage of the company's profits. (4) Gainsharing is the distribution of savings or "gains" to groups of employees who reduced costs and increased measurable productivity. (5) Stock options allow certain employees to buy stock at a future date for a discounted price. (6) Pay for knowledge ties employee pay to the number of job-relevant skills or academic degrees they earn.

There are also nonmonetary ways of compensating employees. Some employees will leave because they feel the need for work–life balance, the need to expand their skills, and the need to matter. To retain such employees, nonmonetary incentives have been introduced, such as the flexible workplace. Other incentives that keep employees from leaving are thoughtfulness by employees' managers, work–life benefits such as day care, attractive surroundings, skill-building and educational opportunities, and work sabbaticals.

Management in Action

School Officials from Marshall Metro High School Attempt to Motivate Students & Teachers to Achieve Higher Performance

At 7:15 on a chilly May morning, Marshall Metro High School attendance clerk Karin Henry punched numbers into a telephone, her red nails clacking as she dialed.

"Good morning, Miss MeMe," she said to Barbara "MeMe' Diamond, a 17-year-old junior with a habit of oversleeping. "This is Ms. Henry, your stalker."

The timing of the call was key. Earlier in the year, Ms. Henry and a coworker were spending nearly two hours a day calling every student who hadn't checked into school by 9:30 a.m. But weekly data tracked by their office found that only about 9% of those students ever arrived. So they changed tactics, zeroing in on habitual latecomers like MeMe, and delivering wake-up calls starting at 6:30. On that May morning, 19 of the 26 students called showed up. "I just stay in bed if no one calls me," MeMe said. "That 6:30 call be bugging me, but it gets me here."

District officials are betting that data—the relentless collection, evaluation, and application of them—can serve as a wake-up call for Marshall as well.

Chicago won $20 million in federal money over three years to help improve its worst-performing schools, part of a $3.5 billion program that targeted 1,247 failing schools nationwide. The district is kicking in another $7 million in local money, and officials were determined to invest in programs that would help them measure progress, use the information to fine-tune tactics on the fly, and hold staff and students accountable for the results.

"We want to move investments to things that work," said Don Fraynd, the district official overseeing Marshall's turnaround.

One year in results from Marshall are far from conclusive, but district officials see promising trends. Average attendance rose 22 points to 75% for the year, and 79% of freshmen were on track to advance to 10th grade, up from 34%. At each grade level, scores on standardized tests improved from fall to spring in English, math, reading, and science. Other Chicago schools that have been in the program longer have reported similar gains. . . .

Data collection and analysis aren't new to public education; Houston's district was an early proponent and judged it a success. But few districts have embraced them to manage student and staff performance the way Chicago has. Mr. Fraynd said the data he tracks have played a role in disciplinary actions and job losses for employees of his office and the schools he oversees. The data haven't been used against teachers, as their union contract bars it. But by 2013, such benchmarks as student academic growth will become part of broader teacher performance evaluations.

Chicago's program was partly modeled on Comp-Stat, a New York City police system that required precinct commanders to analyze and answer for weekly crime statistics. Proponents said CompStat sharply reduced crime, though critics said the pressure led precincts to manipulate results. Similar concerns have been voiced about data-driven reform in schools.

An informal 2009 study by the Chicago Teachers Union found that a third of teachers felt pressured to alter student grades, in part because of the district's focus on data. The union said it doesn't object to data analysis to manage teacher performance, but worries that it will be used to punish teachers rather than help them. CTU spokeswoman Liz Brown said the union opposes the district's proposed method for incorporating student test data into teacher evaluations, calling it "unreliable and erratic." . . .

At Marshall, many staffers grumbled about the data-collection and entry requirements. Teachers, for example, had to log every incidence of student misconduct, from texting in class to fighting. Deans and department chairs input scores from every classroom teacher observation.

For Didi Afaneh, the year ended in frustration. As lead freshman teacher, she was responsible for keeping students on track to pass to 10th grade. She missed her goal by one percentage point, despite a series of steps teachers tried, from before- and after-school tutoring to visiting students at home to assigning mentors and counselors.

"For people who bust their butt every day to reach kids, and still we don't make our goals, it gets really depressing," she said at a May staff meeting. . . .

District officials targeted Marshall—a basketball powerhouse spotlighted in the documentary *Hoop Dreams*—based on some grim statistics. It had the city's lowest percentage of freshmen on track to become 10th-graders, and the lowest attendance rate among Chicago's conventional high schools: 53%. Half of its students were dropouts; only 3% passed state proficiency exams. . . .

The school used its turn-around funds to replace 80% of its faculty, revamp curriculum, and enhance antitruancy efforts, among other steps; it adopted the CompStat-style system to measure progress on all those fronts.

Two number crunchers at Marshall digested tens of thousands of data points, from the frequency of fights to cheerleaders' GPAs. Charts lining the hallways listed attendance rates of individual students. Staff members gathered regularly for "performance management" meetings to review data and outline solutions. . . .

Principal Kenyatta Stansberry, who's ultimately responsible for the stats, proposed more training for teachers in data analysis so they can better track students, and a requirement that teachers complete detailed reports on student progress every five weeks. She also pledged to be more selective in picking teachers for the online program.

Kyle Birch, a first-year special-education teacher, adopted Marshall's data mining to scrutinize his own teaching methods. He picked apart every answer on one 40-question exam and found only 17% of his students could graph a sloped line, despite his spending days teaching the skill.

So Mr. Birch summoned his students outside and had them plot points with chalk on a grid drawn on the sidewalk. He made them walk a path connecting the dots, hoping the movement would aid their comprehension. In retesting later, he found that most of them understood. . . .

Marshall's most aggressive turnaround efforts focused on its most persistent challenge: attendance. Two years ago, barely half the students showed up on an average day.

Such absenteeism can doom broader reform efforts. Research shows that dropouts follow a process of gradual disengagement, where students miss more and more school until they find it impossible to catch up. Sporadic attendance makes it difficult for teachers to stay on pace with their lessons.

Ayesha El-Amin Calhoun, head of the attendance office, tried a number of tactics to boost attendance, from calling kids at home before school to dangling common attendance rewards such as bus passes and MP3 players. She also hired "student advocates," to cruise neighborhoods searching for students. Each of these efforts was measured, evaluated and, when warranted, adjusted or dropped.

At a January 27 meeting, Ms. Calhoun reported that her office was most effective with the most chronic absentees: 88% of students who showed up just a third of the time during the first quarter boosted their attendance the second quarter after some contact with her office.

She and her coworkers decided to focus more effort on students who were chronically late or absent, calling them before school and sending advocates out to find them. By the end of the year, attendance had risen to 75%.

What made the biggest difference, Ms. Calhoun concluded, was not the calls, but the quantity and

quality of interactions between students and her staffers. "The kids who make a connection to Ms. Henry or other adults in this office are the ones who keep coming back," she said. She wants her staff to spend more time cultivating relationships with students like MeMe.

The most successful attendance program—the Calhoun Challenge—evolved over time. At the beginning of the year, Ms. Calhoun asked 74 chronically truant students to sign in every day for six weeks.

During the first few weeks, their attendance improved to 50% from 45%, but eventually trailed off to about 40%.

"I realized a short-term goal of 10 days was [more] attainable," she said.

From there, Ms. Calhoun kept tweaking the challenges to boost response rates and test variables. In late October, she asked 43 frequent absentees to sign a contract promising to attend school for 10 straight days. In that span, they nearly closed the 20-point gap between their attendance rates and Marshall's average. Once the challenge ended, the students lapsed.

Next year, Ms. Calhoun plans to open the challenges to more students, with competitions pitting siblings or groups against each other and follow-up contracts for students who slough off. She also plans to devote more effort to students who have the intellectual ability to do well in school but who fall behind because of absenteeism.

FOR DISCUSSION

1. To what extent are Marshall Metro's attempts to motivate students consistent with recommendations derived from need theories? Discuss.

2. Which needs contained in Maslow, Alderfer, and McClelland's theories are likely to motivate teachers to higher levels of performance? Explain your rationale.

3. To what extent is Marshall's attempts to motivate students and teachers consistent with both equity and expectancy theory? Explain.

4. What type of reinforcement is Marshall using to motivate students to attend classes and study?

5.. What are the key lessons learned from this case? Discuss.

Source: Excerpted from Stephanie Banchero, "School Reform, Chicago Style," *The Wall Street Journal,* June 25–26, 2011, pp. A1, A12. Copyright © 2011 by Dow Jones & Company, Inc. Reproduced with permission of Dow Jones & Company, Inc. via Copyright Clearance Center.

Self-Assessment

What Is Your Reaction to Equity Differences?

OBJECTIVES

1. Assess your reaction to equity differences.
2. Gain more insight into yourself.

INTRODUCTION

Have you ever noticed that certain people scream "No fair!" whenever they perceive something as unequal? Have you also noticed that other people don't seem bothered by inequity at all? According to researchers, when given the same amount of inequity, people respond differently depending on their individual equity sensitivity. There are varying degrees of equity sensitivity:

Benevolents are individuals who prefer their outcome-input ratios to be less than the others being compared. These are people who don't mind being underrewarded.

Equity Sensitives are individuals who prefer outcome-input ratios to be equal. These people are concerned with obtaining the rewards they perceive to be fair in relation to what others are receiving.

Entitleds are individuals who prefer that their outcome-input ratios go above those of the others being compared. These people aren't worried by inequities and actually prefer situations in which they see themselves as overrewarded.

The purpose of this exercise is to assess your equity sensitivity.

INSTRUCTIONS

The five statements below ask what you would like your relationship to be within any organization. For each question, *divide* 10 points between the two answers (A and B) *by giving the most points to the answer that is most like you and the fewest points to the answer least like you.* You can give an equal number of points to A and B. You can make use of zeros if you like. Just be sure to use all 10 points on each question. (For instance, if statement A is completely appropriate and B is not at all appropriate, give A ten points and B zero points. If A is somewhat appropriate and B is not completely appropriate, give A seven points and B three points.) Place your points next to each letter.

In any organization where I might work . . .

1. It would be more important for me to:
   A. Get from the organization.   _____
   B. Give to the organization.   _____

2. It would be more important for me to:
   A. Help others.   _____
   B. Watch out for my own good.   _____

3. I would be more concerned about:
   A. What I received from the organization.   _____
   B. What I contributed to the organization.   _____

4. The hard work I would do should:
   A. Benefit the organization.   _____
   B. Benefit me.   _____

5. My personal philosophy in dealing with the organization would be:
   A. If you don't look out for yourself, nobody else will.   _____
   B. It's better to give than to receive.   _____

Calculate your total score by adding the points you allocated to the following items: 1B, 2A, 3B, 4A, and 5B. Total score = _____

ANALYSIS & INTERPRETATION

Your total will be between 0 and 50. If you scored less than 29, you are an Entitled; if your score was between 29 and 32, you are an Equity Sensitive; and if your score was above 32, you are a Benevolent.

QUESTIONS FOR DISCUSSION

1. To what extent are the results consistent with your self-perception? Explain.

2. Using the survey items as a foundation, how should managers try to motivate Benevolents, Equity Sensitives, and Entitleds? Discuss in detail.

Source: Reproduced with permission of authors and publisher from: Huseman, R.C., Hatfield, J.D., & Miles, E.W. Test for Individual Perceptions of Job Equity: Some Preliminary Findings. *Perceptual and Motor Skills,* 1985, vol. 61, 1055–1064. © Perceptual and Motor Skills 1985.

Legal/Ethical Challenge

Should Senior Executives Receive Bonuses for Navigating a Company Through Bankruptcy?

"On the way to bankruptcy court, Lear Corporation, a car-parts supplier, closed 28 factories, cut more than 20,000 jobs, and wiped out shareholders. Still, Lear sought $20.6 million in bonuses for key executives and other employees, including an eventual payout of more than $5.4 million for then-chief executive Robert Rossiter."

The U.S. Justice Department objected to these bonuses, arguing that they violated a federal law established in 2005. The goal of the law was to restrict companies from paying bonuses to executives before and during a bankruptcy process. However, a judge ruled that the bonuses were legal because they were tied to the individuals meeting specific earnings milestones. A company spokesperson further commented that the bonuses were "customary" and "fully market competitive." Lear has subsequently rebounded, adding 23,000 jobs since completing the bankruptcy process.

The practice of giving bonuses to senior executives who navigate a company through bankruptcy is quite common. A study of 21 of the 100 biggest corporate bankruptcies by *The Wall Street Journal* revealed that CEOs from these firms were paid more than $350 million in various forms of compensation.

"Over the past few years, fights have erupted during a handful of Chapter 11 bankruptcy cases. The central argument has been over whether companies are adhering to federal laws when giving their executives the extra pay." While judicial decisions regarding this issue have been mixed, we want you to consider the ethics of paying executives large bonuses when "gutting" a company by laying off workers, closing plants, and eliminating health care and retirement benefits to retirees.

SOLVING THE CHALLENGE

Is it ethical to pay bonuses?

1. Yes. Navigating a company through bankruptcy is hard work and involves making hard decisions. Executives at Lear, for example, earned those bonuses by helping to turn around the company. The company is now healthy and employs 23,000 more people than it did at the start of the bankruptcy process.

2. Yes, if all employees receive some sort of bonus for staying through a bankruptcy process. In other words, executives should be paid the same as other surviving employees. If everyone took a 10% pay cut or gets a 10% bonus, so should executives. What's fair for one is fair for all.

3. Absolutely not. It just is not right to close plants, displace employees, and eliminate retiree benefits while simultaneously giving executives hefty bonuses.

4. Invent other options.

Source: This case was drawn from M. Spector and T. McGinty, "The CEO Bankruptcy Bonus," *The Wall Street Journal,* January 27, 2012, pp. A1, A12.

chapter 13

Groups & Teams
Increasing Cooperation, Reducing Conflict

Major Questions You Should Be Able to Answer

 13.1 Groups Versus Teams
Major Question: How is one collection of workers different from any other?

 **13.2 Stages of Group & Team Development**
Major Question: How does a group evolve into a team?

13.3 Building Effective Teams
Major Question: How can I as a manager build an effective team?

13.4 Managing Conflict
Major Question: Since conflict is a part of life, what should a manager know about it in order to deal successfully with it?

Reaching Across Time & Space: The Challenge of Managing Virtual Teams

Once upon a time, managers subscribed to the so-called Fifty-Foot Rule—namely, "If people are more than 50 feet apart, they are not likely to collaborate." That is no longer true in today's era of virtual teams. Virtual teams (also known as geographically dispersed teams) are groups of people who use information technology—computers and telecommunications—to collaborate across space, time, and organizational boundaries.[1]

As technology has made it easier for workers to function from remote places, it has posed challenges for managers. Following are some suggestions for managing virtual workers, whether close by or on the other side of the world:[2]

Take Baby Steps & Manage by Results

When trying out virtual arrangements with new employees, take it slow. Let them show they can handle the challenge. Focus on what's accomplished. Set interim deadlines on projects and stick to them.

State Expectations

Nip problems in the bud by letting virtual workers know what you expect from them. With home-based workers, for example, go over the terms of your virtual arrangement—whether, for example, you want them to carry an office cellphone—and tell them if there are specific ways you want the job done.

Write It Down

Record directions, project changes, and updates in writing, by sending an e-mail or fax or by using web-based services that allow for sharing calendars and tracking projects. Keep all communications in a shared database, so that a historical document of the group's work is available for new team members to study.

Communicate, but Be Considerate

Team members should know what times are appropriate to call one another (think time zones here) and what days (considering cultural, family, or work schedules) are off-limits. Make sure everyone is reachable during normal business hours, as via phone, e-mail, fax, or chat.

Be Aware of Cultural Differences

Even if everyone on a global team speaks English, be aware that others may not understand slang, culturally narrow expressions, and American humor. Encourage everyone to slow down their speech. Realize that team members from China and India, say, may have difficulty saying no or may fall silent in order to save face. Building global and virtual teams is all about building trust—being respectful and doing what you say you're going to do. Handle serious conflicts face-to-face whenever possible.

Meet Regularly

Human contact still matters. If possible, launch the team with a face-to-face meeting. When possible, schedule periodic and regular meetings where all team members can discuss current projects and telecommuters can catch up on office gossip. Fly out-of-towners in at least quarterly, so they can develop working friendships with your in-office staff.

For Discussion What do you think are the greatest difficulties of working online with numerous people you never see? How would you try to handle these difficulties?

forecast | What's Ahead in This Chapter

In this chapter, we consider groups versus teams and discuss different kinds of teams. We describe how groups evolve into teams and discuss how managers can build effective teams. We also consider the nature of conflict, both good and bad.

How is one collection of workers different from any other?

THE BIG PICTURE

Teamwork promises to be a cornerstone of future management. A team is different from a group. A group typically is management-directed, a team self-directed. Groups may be formal, created to do productive work, or informal, created for friendship. Work teams, which engage in collective work requiring coordinated effort, may be organized according to four basic purposes: advice, production, project, and action. Two types of teams are continuous improvement and self-managed teams.

Twenty-five years ago, management philosopher Peter Drucker predicted that future organizations would not only be flatter and information-based but also organized around teamwork—and that has certainly come to pass.[3]

"You lead today by building teams and placing others first," says General Electric CEO Jeffrey Immelt. "It's not about you."[4] "We have this mythology in America about the lone genius," says Tom Kelley, general manager of Ideo, a Palo Alto, California, multidisciplinary industrial design company that helped create the Apple mouse, first laptop computer, and soft-handled Gripper toothbrush for Oral-B. "We love to personify things. But Michelangelo didn't paint the Sistine Chapel alone, and Edison didn't invent the light bulb alone."[5]

The argument for promoting diversity suggested by scholar Scott E. Page (see Chapter 3)—namely, that different kinds of people "bring to organizations more and different ways of seeing a problem and, thus, faster/better ways of solving it"—is also a principal strength of teams.[6] However, teamwork is now the cornerstone of progressive management for many other reasons, as the table below shows. *(See Table 13.1.)* Regardless, when you take a job in an organization, the chances are you won't be working as a lone genius or even as a lone wolf. You'll be working with others in situations demanding teamwork.

table 13.1

WHY TEAMWORK IS IMPORTANT

The Improvements	Example
Increased productivity	At one GE factory, teamwork resulted in a workforce that was 20% more productive than comparable GE workforces elsewhere.
Increased speed	Guidant Corp., maker of lifesaving medical devices, halved the time it took to get products to market.
Reduced costs	Boeing used teamwork to develop the 777 at costs far less than normal.
Improved quality	Westinghouse used teamwork to improve quality performance in its truck and trailer division and within its electronic components division.
Reduced destructive internal competition	Men's Wearhouse fired a salesman who wasn't sharing walk-in customer traffic, and total clothing sales volume among all salespeople increased significantly.
Improved workplace cohesiveness	Cisco Systems told executives they would gain or lose 30% of their bonuses based on how well they worked with peers and in three years had record profits.

Groups & Teams: How Do They Differ?

Aren't a group of people and a team of people the same thing? By and large, no. One is a collection of people, the other a powerful unit of collective performance. One is typically management-directed, the other self-directed.

Consider the differences.

What a Group Is: A Collection of People Performing as Individuals A *group* **is defined as two or more freely interacting individuals who share collective norms, share collective goals, and have a common identity.**[7] A group is different from a crowd, a transitory collection of people who don't interact with one another, such as a crowd gathering on a sidewalk to watch a fire. And it is different from an organization, such as a labor union, which is so large that members also mostly don't interact.[8]

An example of a work group would be a collection of, say, 10 employees meeting to exchange information about various companies' policies on wages and hours.

What a Team Is: A Collection of People with Common Commitment McKinsey & Company management consultants Jon R. Katzenbach and Douglas K. Smith say it is a mistake to use the terms *group* and *team* interchangeably. Successful teams, they say, tend to take on a life of their own. Thus, a *team* **is defined as a small group of people with complementary skills who are committed to a common purpose, performance goals, and approach for which they hold themselves mutually accountable.**[9] "The essence of a team is common commitment," say Katzenbach and Smith. "Without it, groups perform as individuals; with it, they become a powerful unit of collective performance."[10]

An example of a team would be a collection of 2–10 employees who are studying industry pay scales, with the goal of making recommendations for adjusting pay grades within their own company.

Formal Versus Informal Groups

Groups may be either formal or informal.

- **Formal groups—created to do productive work. A** *formal group* **is a group established to do something productive for the organization and is headed by a leader.** A formal group may be a division, a department, a work group, or a committee. It may be permanent or temporary. In general, people are assigned to them according to their skills and the organization's requirements.

- **Informal groups—created for friendship. An** *informal group* **is a group formed by people seeking friendship and has no officially appointed leader, although a leader may emerge from the membership.** An informal group may be simply a collection of friends who hang out with one another, such as those who take coffee breaks together, or it may be as organized as a prayer breakfast, a bowling team, a service club, or other voluntary organization.

What's important for you as a manager to know is that informal groups can advance or undercut the plans of formal groups. The formal organization may make efforts, say, to speed up the plant assembly line or to institute workplace reforms. But these attempts may be sabotaged through the informal networks of workers who meet and gossip over lunch pails and after-work beers.[11]

However, interestingly, informal groups can also be highly productive—even more so than formal groups.

Informal Groups & Informal Learning: Sharing Knowledge in the Lunchroom & on Social Media

As a manager, what would you think if you saw employees making brief conversation near the lunchroom coffeepot? "The assumption was made that this was chitchat, talking about their golf game," said a training director at the Siemens Power Transmission and Distribution plant in Wendell, North Carolina, where managers worried about workers gathering so often in the cafeteria. "But there was a whole lot of work activity."[12]

Workplace Learning: Mostly Informal. And indeed research has found that 70% of workplace learning is informal.[13] With this knowledge, Siemens managers alerted supervisors about the informal meetings and even placed overhead projectors and empty pads of paper in the lunchroom to facilitate the exchange of information. Technology firm Qualcomm uses employees' storytelling tendencies as a way to communicate information, as well as to reinforce the company's culture and values.[14]

The Peer-to-Peer Web. What about when employees are in far-flung places? "Sales reps are out in the field and they're kind of on islands," pointed out an Indianapolis software firm executive. "It's a challenge to keep everyone connected."[15] So when the 75 reps started overwhelming the sales-support staff with questions about product details and client information, the company created a website on which the reps could post and answer questions in an informal peer-to-peer learning setting. (Incidentally, to do parts of their jobs, 47% of business technology users at

Talking it out. Ever worked in a job in which you got a lot of informal training through conversations over coffee? Could this be done with social networking?

North American and European companies use websites that are not sanctioned by their corporate information technology department, according to one study.)[16]

YOUR CALL

Can games (such as the online multiplayer game Second Life) or other social media (Facebook, Twitter, discussed in Chapter 15) be used to foster informal workplace collaboration? How about allowing employees to BYOD— "bring your own device" to work, such as their own smartphone or tablet computer?[17]

Work Teams for Four Purposes: Advice, Production, Project, & Action

The names given to different kinds of teams can be bewildering. We have identified some important ones in the table opposite. *(See Table 13.2.)*

You will probably benefit most by understanding the various types of work teams distinguished according to their purpose. Work teams, which engage in collective work requiring coordinated effort, are of four types, which may be identified according to their basic purpose: *advice, production, project,* or *action.*[18]

1. Advice Teams *Advice teams* are created to broaden the information base for managerial decisions. Examples are committees, review panels, advisory councils, employee involvement groups, and continuous improvement teams (as we'll discuss).

2. Production Teams *Production teams* are responsible for performing day-to-day operations. Examples are mining teams, flight-attendant crews, maintenance crews, assembly teams, data processing groups, and manufacturing crews.

table 13.2

VARIOUS TYPES OF TEAMS

These teams are not mutually exclusive. Work teams, for instance, may also be self-managed, cross-functional, or virtual.

Continuous improvement team	Volunteers of workers and supervisors who meet intermittently to discuss workplace and quality-related problems; formerly called quality circle
Cross-functional team	Members composed of people from different departments, such as sales and production, pursuing a common objective
Problem-solving team	Knowledgeable workers who meet as a temporary team to solve a specific problem and then disband
Self-managed team	Workers are trained to do all or most of the jobs in a work unit, have no direct supervisor, and do their own day-to-day supervision
Top-management team	Members consist of the CEO, president, and top department heads and work to help the organization achieve its mission and goals
Virtual team	Members interact by computer network to collaborate on projects
Work team	Members engage in collective work requiring coordinated effort; purpose of team is advice, production, project, or action *(see text discussion)*

3. Project Teams   *Project teams* work to do creative problem solving, often by applying the specialized knowledge of members of a **cross-functional team, which is staffed with specialists pursuing a common objective.** Examples are task forces, research groups, planning teams, architect teams, engineering teams, and development teams.

4. Action Teams   *Action teams* work to accomplish tasks that require people with (1) specialized training and (2) a high degree of coordination, as on a baseball team, with specialized athletes acting in coordination. Examples are hospital surgery teams, airline cockpit crews, mountain-climbing expeditions, police SWAT teams, and labor contract negotiating teams. (A unique challenge for action teams is to exhibit peak performance on demand.)[19]

Self-Managed Teams: Workers with Own Administrative Oversight

To give you an idea of how teams work, consider self-managed teams. These kinds of teams have emerged out of what were called quality circles, now known as *continuous improvement teams,* **which consist of small groups of volunteers or workers and supervisors who meet intermittently to discuss workplace- and quality-related problems.** Typically a group of 10–12 people will meet for 60–90 minutes once or twice a month, with management listening to presentations and the important payoff for members usually being the chance for meaningful participation and skills training.[20]

From Continuous Improvement Teams to Self-Managed Teams   In many places, such as the Texas Instruments electronics factory in Malaysia, the continuous improvement teams have evolved into a system made up almost entirely of self-managed teams, with routine activities formerly performed by supervisors now performed by team members. "Self-managed" does not, however, mean simply turning workers

Team building. The team ethic at Hong Kong–based Cathay Pacific has helped the multinational airline provide excellent service that pleases both passengers and shareholders. Here Cathay trainees get practice handling unruly passengers and putting on their best face. Do you think there are better ways to get this training?

loose to do their own thing. *Self-managed teams* **are defined as groups of workers who are given administrative oversight for their task domains.** Administrative oversight involves delegated activities such as planning, scheduling, monitoring, and staffing. More than 75% of the top 1,000 U.S. companies currently use some form of self-managed work teams.[21]

Self-managed teams are an outgrowth of a blend of behavioral science and management practice.[22] The goal has been to increase productivity and employee quality of work life. The traditional clear-cut distinction between manager and managed is being blurred as nonmanagerial employees are delegated greater authority and granted increased autonomy.

Are Self-Management Teams Effective?   The most common chores of today's self-managed teams are work scheduling and customer interaction, and the least common are hiring and firing. Most self-managed teams are also found at the shop-floor level in factory settings, although some experts predict growth of the practice in service operations and even management ranks.[23] Self-managed teams have been found to have a positive effect on productivity and attitudes of self-responsibility and control, although there is no significant effect on job satisfaction and organizational commitment.[24] Although these conclusions don't qualify as a sweeping endorsement of self-managed teams, experts expect a trend toward such teams in North America because of a strong cultural bias in favor of direct participation. The following table shows some ways to empower self-managed teams. *(See Table 13.3.)* ●

table 13.3

SOME WAYS TO EMPOWER SELF-MANAGED TEAMS

1. Managers should make team members accountable for their work, allow them to set their own team goals, and let them solve their own work-related problems.
2. The team should work with a whole product or service (not just a part), assign jobs and tasks to its members, develop its own quality standards and measurement techniques, and handle its own problems with internal and external customers.
3. Team members are cross-trained on jobs within their (and other) teams; do their own hiring, training, and firing; do their own evaluations of each other; and are paid (at least in part) as a team.
4. The team has access to important information and resources inside and outside the organization, is allowed to communicate with and draw support from other teams and departments, and sets its own rules and policies.

Source: Adapted from B. L. Kirkman and B. Rosen, "Powering Up Teams," *Organizational Dynamics,* Winter 2000, p. 56. Reprinted with permission of Elsevier.

13.2 STAGES OF GROUP & TEAM DEVELOPMENT

THE BIG PICTURE
Groups may evolve into teams by going through five stages of development: forming, storming, norming, performing, and adjourning.

Managers often talk of products and organizations going through stages of development, from birth to maturity to decline. Groups and teams go through the same thing. One theory proposes five stages of development: *forming, storming, norming, performing, adjourning.*[25] *(See Figure 13.1.)* Let us consider these stages in which groups may evolve into teams—bearing in mind that the stages often aren't of the same duration or intensity or even necessarily always in this sequence.

figure 13.1

FIVE STAGES OF
GROUP AND TEAM
DEVELOPMENT

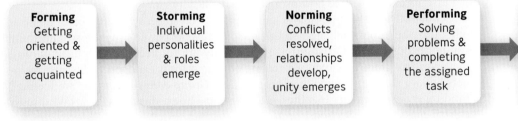

Stage 1: Forming—"Why Are We Here?"

The first stage, *forming,* **is the process of getting oriented and getting acquainted.** This stage is characterized by a high degree of uncertainty as members try to break the ice and figure out who is in charge and what the group's goals are. For example, if you were to become part of a team that is to work on a class project, the question for you as an individual would be "How do I fit in here?" For the group, the question is "Why are we here?"[26]

At this point, mutual trust is low, and there is a good deal of holding back to see who takes charge and how. If the formal leader (such as the class instructor or a supervisor) does not assert his or her authority, an emergent leader will eventually step in to fill the group's need for leadership and direction.

What the Leader Should Do Leaders typically mistake this honeymoon period as a mandate for permanent control, but later problems may force a leadership change. During this stage, leaders should allow time for people to become acquainted and to socialize.

Stage 2: Storming—"Why Are We Fighting Over Who Does What & Who's in Charge?"

The second stage, *storming,* **is characterized by the emergence of individual personalities and roles and conflicts within the group.** For you as an individual, the question is "What's my role here?" For the group, the issue is "Why are we fighting over who does what and who's in charge?" This stage may be of short duration or painfully long, depending on the goal clarity and the commitment and maturity of the members.

This is a time of testing. Individuals test the leader's policies and assumptions as they try to determine how they fit into the power structure.[27] Subgroups take shape, and subtle forms of rebellion, such as procrastination, occur. Many groups stall in stage 2 because power politics may erupt into open rebellion.

What the Leader Should Do   In this stage, the leader should encourage members to suggest ideas, voice disagreements, and work through their conflicts about tasks and goals.

Stage 3: Norming—"Can We Agree on Roles & Work as a Team?"

In the third stage, *norming*, **conflicts are resolved, close relationships develop, and unity and harmony emerge.** For individuals, the main issue is "What do the others expect me to do?" For the group, the issue is "Can we agree on roles and work as a team?" Note, then, that the *group* may now evolve into a *team.*

Teams set guidelines related to what members will do together and how they will do it. The teams consider such matters as attendance at meetings, being late, and missing assignments as well as how members treat one another.

Groups that make it through stage 2 generally do so because a respected member other than the leader challenges the group to resolve its power struggles so something can be accomplished. Questions about authority are resolved through unemotional, matter-of-fact group discussion. A feeling of team spirit is experienced because members believe they have found their proper roles. **Group cohesiveness, a "we feeling" binding group members together,** is the principal by-product of stage 3. (We discuss cohesiveness next, in Section 13.3.)

What the Leader Should Do   This stage generally does not last long. Here the leader should emphasize unity and help identify team goals and values.

Stage 4: Performing—"Can We Do the Job Properly?"

In *performing*, **members concentrate on solving problems and completing the assigned task.** For individuals, the question here is "How can I best perform my role?" For the group/team, the issue is "Can we do the job properly?"

What the Leader Should Do   During this stage, the leader should allow members the empowerment they need to work on tasks.

Stage 5: Adjourning—"Can We Help Members Transition Out?"

In the final stage, *adjourning*, **members prepare for disbandment.** Having worked so hard to get along and get something done, many members feel a compelling sense of loss. For the individual, the question now is "What's next?" For the team, the issue is "Can we help members transition out?"

What the Leader Should Do   The leader can help ease the transition by rituals celebrating "the end" and "new beginnings." Parties, award ceremonies, graduations, or mock funerals can provide the needed punctuation at the end of a significant teamwork project. The leader can emphasize valuable lessons learned in group dynamics to prepare everyone for future group and team efforts.   ●

13.3 BUILDING EFFECTIVE TEAMS

THE BIG PICTURE

To build a group into a high-performance team, managers must consider matters of cooperation, trust, and cohesiveness, followed by performance goals and feedback, motivation through mutual accountability, team size, roles, norms, and awareness of groupthink.

"What is a high-performance team?" Answers to that question in a nationwide survey of team members from many organizations revealed several attributes: participative leadership, shared responsibility, sense of common purpose, trust and open communication, application of creative talents, seeing change as an opportunity for growth, task focus, and rapid acting on opportunities.[28] Thus, as a future manager, the first thing you have to realize is that building a high-performance team is going to require some work. But the payoff will be a stronger, better-performing work unit.[29]

The most essential considerations in building a group into an effective team are (1) *cooperation*, (2) *trust*, and (3) *cohesiveness*. These are followed by (4) *performance goals and feedback*, (5) *motivation through mutual accountability*, (6) *size*, (7) *roles*, (8) *norms*, and (9) *awareness of groupthink*.

1. Cooperation: "We Need to Systematically Integrate Our Efforts"

Human cooperation has a long history, with some hunter-gatherers in Tanzania—who live much as humans did about 10,000 years ago—living in social networks very much like ours—without the cellphones and other connections, of course.[30] Indeed, unlike other animals (such as chimpanzees and monkeys), humans are able to build bigger and better tools by sharing knowledge and learning from one another—in short, by cooperating.[31] Individuals are said to be **cooperating when their efforts are systematically integrated to achieve a collective objective.**[32] One meta-analysis of 122 studies suggests that cooperation is superior to competition and individualistic efforts in promoting achievement and productivity.[33]

2. Trust: "We Need to Have Reciprocal Faith in Each Other"

Trust is defined as reciprocal faith in others' intentions and behaviors.[34] The word *reciprocal* emphasizes the give-and-take aspect of trust—that is, we tend to give what we get: trust begets trust, distrust begets distrust. Trust is based on *credibility*—how believable you are based on your past acts of integrity and follow-through on your promises. Besides enhancing your credibility by showing professionalism, technical ability, and good business sense, you can build trust in your team members by the methods shown at right. *(See Table 13.4.)*

3. Cohesiveness: The Importance of Togetherness

Another important characteristic of teams is **cohesiveness, the tendency of a group or team to stick together.** This is the familiar sense of togetherness or "we-ness" you feel, for example, when you're a member of a volleyball team, a fraternity or a sorority, or a company's sales force.[35] Managers can stimulate cohesiveness by encouraging people to have face-to-face exchanges at work. A recent study found that patterns of communication

table 13.4

HOW TO BUILD & MAINTAIN TRUST WITH TEAM MEMBERS

1. *Communicate truthfully.* Be candid about problems and limitations (including your own), explain decisions, provide accurate feedback.

2. *Offer support—by being available.* Be approachable, provide help, coaching, and support members' ideas.

3. *Show respect—by delegating and listening.* Respect members' decision making by delegating authority and actively listening.

4. *Show fairness—by giving credit and being impartial.* Give recognition when deserved, be objective when evaluating performance.

5. *Show predictability—by keeping promises,* both expressed and implied.

Source: Reprinted by permission of *Harvard Business Review.* Adapted from "Nobody Trusts the Boss Completely—Now What?" by F. Bartolome, March–April 1989. Copyright 1989 by the Harvard Business School Publishing Corporation; all rights reserved.

among team members were the most important predictor of team success.[36] Cohesiveness is also achieved by following the tips in the following table. *(See Table 13.5.)*

table 13.5

HOW TO ENHANCE
COHESIVENESS IN TEAMS:
TEN FACTORS THAT LEAD
TO SUCCESS

1. Keep the team small.
2. Encourage members' interaction and cooperation.
3. Emphasize members' common characteristics.
4. Strive for a favorable public image to enhance the team's prestige.
5. Give each member a stake in the team's success—a "piece of the action."
6. Point out threats from competitors to enhance team togetherness.
7. Ensure performance standards are clear, and regularly update members on team goals.
8. Frequently remind members they need each other to get the job done.
9. Direct each member's special talents toward the common goals.
10. Recognize each member's contributions.

Source: Adapted and modified from R. Kreitner and A. Kinicki, *Organizational Behavior,* 10th ed. (New York: McGraw-Hill/Irwin, 2013), p. 315.

4. Performance Goals & Feedback

As an individual, you no doubt prefer to have measurable goals and to have feedback about your performance. The same is true with teams. Teams are not just collections of individuals. They are individuals organized for a collective purpose. That purpose needs to be defined in terms of specific, measurable performance goals with continual feedback to tell team members how well they are doing.

An obvious example are the teams you see on television at Indianapolis or Daytona Beach during automobile racing. When the driver guides the race car off the track to make a pit stop, a team of people quickly jack up the car to change tires, refuel the tank, and clean the windshield—all operating in a matter of seconds. The performance goals are to have the car back on the track as quickly as possible. The number of seconds of elapsed time—and the driver's place among competitors once back in the race—tells them how well they are doing.

Cooperation and collaboration. A crew swarms over a car driven by A. J. Allmendinger during a pit stop in the NASCAR 2012 Sprint Cup All-Star Race in Concord, North Carolina. Cereal maker General Mills was able to cut the time workers changed a production line for a Betty Crocker product from 4.5 hours to just 12 minutes by adapting ideas in efficiency and high performance from a NASCAR pit crew working at blinding speed.

5. Motivation Through Mutual Accountability

Do you work harder when you're alone or when you're in a group? When clear performance goals exist, when the work is considered meaningful, when members believe their efforts matter, and when they don't feel they are being exploited by others—this kind of culture supports teamwork.[37] Being mutually accountable to other members of the team rather than to a supervisor makes members feel mutual trust and commitment—a key part in motivating members for team effort. To bring about this team culture, managers often allow teams to do the hiring of new members.

6. Size: Small Teams or Large Teams?

Size, which is often determined by the team's purpose, can be important in affecting members' commitment and performance. Whereas in some flat-organization structures groups may consist of 30 or more employees, teams seem to range in size from 2 to 16 people, with those of 5–12 generally being the most workable and 5–6 considered optimal.[38] A survey of 400 workplace team members in the United States found that the average team consisted of 10 members, with 8 being the most common size.[39]

Small and large teams have different characteristics, although the number of members is, to be sure, somewhat arbitrary.[40]

Small Teams: 2–9 Members for Better Interaction & Morale   Teams with 9 or fewer members have two advantages:

- **Better interaction.** Members are better able to interact, share information, ask questions of one another, and coordinate activities than are those in larger teams. In particular, teams with five or fewer offer more opportunity for personal discussion and participation.

- **Better morale.** They are better able to see the worth of their individual contributions and thus are more highly committed and satisfied. Members are less apt to feel inhibited in participating. Team leaders are subject to fewer demands and are able to be more informal.[41]

However, small teams also have some disadvantages:

- **Fewer resources.** With fewer hands, there will be fewer resources—less knowledge, experience, skills, and abilities to apply to the team's tasks.

- **Possibly less innovation.** A group that's too small may show less creativity and boldness because of the effect of peer pressure.

- **Unfair work distribution.** Because of fewer resources and less specialization, there may be an uneven distribution of the work among members.

Large Teams: 10–16 Members for More Resources & Division of Labor
Teams with 10–16 members have different advantages over small teams. (Again, the numbers are somewhat arbitrary.)

- **More resources.** Larger teams have more resources to draw on: more knowledge, experience, skills, abilities, and perhaps time. These will give them more leverage to help them realize the team's goals.

- **Division of labor.** In addition, a large team can take advantage of *division of labor,* **in which the work is divided into particular tasks that are assigned to particular workers.**

Yet bigness has its disadvantages:

- **Less interaction.** With more members, there is less interaction, sharing of information, and coordinating of activities. Leaders may be more formal and autocratic, since members in teams this size are apt to be more tolerant of autocratic leadership. The larger size may also lead to the formation of cliques.

- **Lower morale.** Because people are less able to see the worth of their individual contributions, they show less commitment and satisfaction and more turnover and absenteeism. They also express more disagreements and turf struggles and make more demands on leaders.

- **Social loafing.** The larger the size, the more likely performance is to drop, owing to the phenomenon known as *social loafing,* **the tendency of people to exert less effort when working in groups than when working alone.**[42]

(Today social loafers are more apt to be known as *sliders*—high achievers who have "checked out," in the words of columnists Jack and Suzy Welch, and who have to be dealt with "before they begin to suck the team into their negative energy field and drag it down.")[43]

7. Roles: How Team Members Are Expected to Behave

Roles **are socially determined expectations of how individuals should behave in a specific position.** As a team member, your role is to play a part in helping the team reach its goals. Members develop their roles based on the expectations of the team, of the organization, and of themselves, and they may do different things. You, for instance, might be a team leader. Others might do some of the work tasks. Still others might communicate with other teams.

Two types of team roles are task and maintenance.[50]

Task Roles: Getting the Work Done A *task role,* or *task-oriented role,* **consists of behavior that concentrates on getting the team's tasks done.** Task roles keep the team on track and get the work done. If you stand up in a team meeting and say, "What is the real issue here? We don't seem to be getting anywhere," you are performing a task role.

Examples: Coordinators, who pull together ideas and suggestions; orienters, who keep teams headed toward their stated goals; initiators, who suggest new goals or ideas; and energizers, who prod people to move along or accomplish more are all playing task roles.

Maintenance Roles: Keeping the Team Together A *maintenance role,* or *relationship-oriented role,* **consists of behavior that fosters constructive relationships among team members.** Maintenance roles focus on keeping team members. If someone at a team meeting says, "Let's hear from those who oppose this plan," he or she is playing a maintenance role.

Examples: Encouragers, who foster group solidarity by praising various viewpoints; standard setters, who evaluate the quality of group processes; harmonizers, who mediate conflict through reconciliation or humor; and compromisers, who help resolve conflict by meeting others "halfway."

8. Norms: Unwritten Rules for Team Members

Norms are more encompassing than roles. *Norms* **are general guidelines or rules of behavior that most group or team members follow.** Norms point up the boundaries between acceptable and unacceptable behavior.[51] Although some norms can be made explicit (as the example below shows), typically they are unwritten and seldom discussed openly; nevertheless, they have a powerful influence on group and organizational behavior.

EXAMPLE

How to Develop Team Norms: Creating a "Fear-Free Zone" of Trust

Trust is everything. The CEO of Siemens, the German electronics and electrical engineering powerhouse, says that a climate of trust is required to make teams work.[52] So does the lead scientist of the IBM team that built Watson, the computer smart enough to beat the grand champions of the game of *Jeopardy*.[53] And so does Pamela Fields, CEO of Stetson, the hat and apparel company.[54]

"You're Not Telling Us What You Want." In her first management job, which was at cosmetics giant Avon, Fields was "just a bull in a china shop," she said, failing to direct the three people reporting to her. Finally, they sat her down and told her "You're not telling us what you want and you're not telling us how you think we should get there." From this and other frank discussion, Fields learned the necessity for creating a workplace where honesty is valued. Thus, she says, "I vowed to create an environment in which truth is important. It takes a lot of spine to tell the truth, especially in a large organization, where obfuscation is a political skill that I don't have."

Fields's way of establishing the norms for a "truth-telling" climate, she said in an interview, is to tell her team members that everyone matters, that she has their back, that if something goes wrong, it's her problem and that if something goes right, it's their success. "And people know that they can come to me and let me have it. . . . There's a complete fear-free zone."

YOUR CALL

Creating a fear-free zone starts with establishing the norms in a public forum, as when Fields tells audiences about an employee coming to her and saying that an idea is dumb, that it isn't going to work, and they should talk about it. Such public acknowledgments by the boss encourage a spirit of openness and candor among team members. As a manager of a team, do you think you could adopt a climate of trust in which your team members understand that if something goes wrong it's your problem, not theirs?

Why Norms Are Enforced: Four Reasons   Norms tend to be enforced by group or team members for four reasons:[55]

- **To help the group survive—"Don't do anything that will hurt us."** Norms are enforced to help the group, team, or organization survive.

    Example: The manager of your team or group might compliment you because you've made sure it has the right emergency equipment.

- **To clarify role expectations—"You have to go along to get along."** Norms are also enforced to help clarify or simplify role expectations.

    Example: At one time, new members of Congress wanting to buck the system by which important committee appointments were given to those with the most seniority were advised to "go along to get along"—go along with the rules in order to get along in their congressional careers.

- **To help individuals avoid embarrassing situations—"Don't call attention to yourself."** Norms are enforced to help group or team members avoid embarrassing themselves.

    Examples: You might be ridiculed by fellow team members for dominating the discussion during a report to top management ("Be a team player, not a show-off"). Or you might be told not to discuss religion or politics with customers, whose views might differ from yours.

- **To emphasize the group's important values and identity—"We're known for being special."** Finally, norms are enforced to emphasize the group, team, or organization's central values or to enhance its unique identity.

    Examples: Nordstrom's department store chain emphasizes the great lengths to which it goes in customer service. Every year a college gives an award to the instructor whom students vote best teacher.

9. Groupthink: When Peer Pressure Discourages "Thinking Outside the Box"

On a hot day, as the family is comfortably playing dominoes on a porch in Coleman, Texas, the father-in-law suggests taking a 53-mile trip to Abilene for dinner. Though the rest of the family—wife, husband, and mother-in-law—would rather not make the long, hot drive, they keep their preferences to themselves and agree to the trip. Later, back home after suffering a good deal of discomfort (including bad food), the mother-in-law says she would rather have stayed home. The husband and wife chime in that they agreed only to keep the others happy; the father-in-law then announces he only suggested it because he thought the others might be bored. This, says scholar James Harvey, is what he calls the *Abilene paradox*—the tendency of people to go along with others for the sake of avoiding conflict.[56]

The Abilene paradox shows that cohesiveness isn't always good. An undesirable by-product that may occur, according to psychologist **Irvin Janis,** is *groupthink*—**a cohesive group's blind unwillingness to consider alternatives.** In this phenomenon, group or team members are friendly and tight-knit, but they are unable to think "outside the box." Their "strivings for unanimity override their motivation to realistically appraise alternative courses of action," said Janis.[57]

Examples: The Senate Intelligence Committee said groupthink was a major factor in the U.S. invasion of Iraq because too many people in the government had tended to think alike and therefore failed to challenge basic assumptions about Iraq's weapons capability.[58] Investors in Silicon Valley often show a herd mentality to be part of "the next big thing."[59]

It cannot be said, however, that group opinion is always risky. Indeed, financial writer James Surowiecki, author of *The Wisdom of Crowds,* argues, "Under the right circumstances, groups are remarkably intelligent, and are often smarter than the smartest people in them."[60] As evidence, he cites how groups have been used to predict the election of the president of the United States, find lost submarines, and correct the spread on a sporting event.[61]

Symptoms of Groupthink   How do you know that you're in a group or team that is suffering from groupthink? Some symptoms include the following:[62]

- **Invulnerability, inherent morality, and stereotyping of opposition.** Because of feelings of invulnerability, group members have the illusion that nothing can go wrong, breeding excessive optimism and risk taking. Members may also be so assured of the rightness of their actions that they ignore the ethical implications of their decisions. These beliefs are helped along by stereotyped views of the opposition, which leads the group to underestimate its opponents.

- **Rationalization and self-censorship.** Rationalizing protects the pet assumptions underlying the group's decisions from critical questions. Self-censorship also stifles critical debate. It is especially hard to argue with success, of course. But if enough key people, such as outside analysts, had challenged Lehman Brothers, the fourth-largest U.S. investment bank, when it seemed to be flying high, it might not have led to the largest bankruptcy filing in corporate history.

- **Illusion of unanimity, peer pressure, and mindguards.** The illusion of unanimity is another way of saying that silence by a member is interpreted to mean consent. But if people do disagree, peer pressure leads other members to question the loyalty of the dissenters. In addition, in a groupthink situation there may exist people who might be called *mindguards*—self-appointed protectors against adverse information.

- **Groupthink versus "the wisdom of crowds."** Groupthink is characterized by a pressure to conform that often leads members with different ideas to censor themselves—the opposite of collective wisdom, says James Surowiecki, in which "each person in the group is offering his or her best independent forecast. It's not at all about compromise or consensus."[63]

The Results of Groupthink: Decision-Making Defects   Groups with a moderate amount of cohesiveness tend to produce better decisions than groups with low or high cohesiveness. Members of highly cohesive groups victimized by groupthink make the poorest decisions—even though they show they express great confidence in those decisions.[64]

Among the decision-making defects that can arise from groupthink are the following:

- **Reduction in alternative ideas.** The principal casualty of groupthink is a shrinking universe of ideas. Decisions are made based on few alternatives. Once preferred alternatives are decided on, they are not reexamined, and, of course, rejected alternatives are not reexamined.

- **Limiting of other information.** When a groupthink group has made its decision, others' opinions, even those of experts, are rejected. If new information is considered at all, it is biased toward ideas that fit the group's preconceptions. Thus, no contingency plans are made in case the decision turns out to be faulty.

Groupthink: An Enthusiasm for Brainstorming, a Technique That Often Doesn't Work

Promoted as an idea-generation machine, brainstorming has become "practically a religion" at design firm Ideo (developer of the first Apple mouse) and other companies.[65] As we described in Chapter 7, p. 217, brainstorming consists of employees getting together and pouring forth as many ideas as possible ("go for quantity") while withholding criticism and negative feedback ("defer judgment"). In an era of open work environments and team-based collaboration, brainstorming would seem to be a perfect fit.

Groupthink About Group Thinking. Unfortunately, the enthusiasm for this group-thinking technique may itself be a form of groupthink—a belief that brainstorming is more productive than in fact it is. According to Washington University psychologist Keith Sawyer, "Decades of research have consistently shown that brainstorming groups think of far fewer ideas than the same number of people who work alone and pool their ideas."[66] Three characteristics of brainstorming have been called into question:

1. **Free Association.** A problem with free association is that it doesn't produce much creativity because for most people the first thoughts that come to mind are entirely predictable (if you say "blue," most people will say "green," "sky," or "ocean").[67] To develop original ideas, one must first get past the layer of predictability.

2. **No Criticism.** Brainstorming orthodoxy dictates that there should be no criticism during idea generation. However, research comparing three groups—no criticism allowed, debate and criticism encouraged, and no guidelines given—found that the debaters produced more ideas than the brainstormers and no-guidelines groups.[68] Although staying positive and not hurting people's feelings is all well and good, debate seems to spur more creativity.

3. **Groups Versus Individuals.** "Research strongly suggests that people are more creative when they enjoy privacy and freedom from interruption," says Susan Cain.[69] The author of *Quiet: The Power of Introverts in a World That Can't Stop Talking*, Cain cites evidence that the most spectacularly creative people in many fields (such as Steve Wozniak, who invented the user-friendly personal computer and cofounded Apple with Steve Jobs) are often introverted and need solitude as a catalyst to innovation.

YOUR CALL

Do you agree that brainstorming has endured too long because of admirers' groupthink? An important exception to its dismal record, says Cain, is Internet "electronic brainstorming, where large groups outperform individuals." Why do you suppose that is?

Fighting groupthink. For a long time, the Coca-Cola Co. had a culture of politeness and consensus that kept it from developing new products, at a time when consumers were flocking to a new breed of coffees, juices, and teas. Now the company boasts 500 different products, including Full Throttle, an energy drink. Do you believe this kind of thinking is enough to stave off a stronger challenge from PepsiCo, which is pouring millions into marketing to boost its soda and other businesses?

Preventing Groupthink: Making Criticism & Other Perspectives Permissible Janis believes it is easier to prevent groupthink than to cure it. As preventive measures, he suggests the following:

- **Allow criticism.** Each member of a team or group should be told to be a critical evaluator, able to actively voice objections and doubts. Subgroups within the group should be allowed to discuss and debate ideas. Once a consensus has been reached, everyone should be encouraged to rethink his or her position to check for flaws.

- **Allow other perspectives.** Outside experts should be used to introduce fresh perspectives. Different groups with different leaders should explore the same policy questions. Top-level executives should not use policy committees to rubber-stamp decisions that have already been made. When major alternatives are discussed, someone should be made devil's advocate to try to uncover all negative factors. ●

Since conflict is a part of life, what should a manager know about it in order to deal successfully with it?

major
question

THE BIG PICTURE

Conflict, an enduring feature of the workplace, is a process in which one party perceives that its interests are being opposed or negatively affected by another party. Conflict can be dysfunctional (bad) or functional (good). Indeed, either too much or too little conflict can affect performance. This section identifies three sources of conflict in organizations and also describes four ways to stimulate constructive conflict.

Mistakes, pressure-cooker deadlines, increased workloads, demands for higher productivity, and other kinds of stress—all contribute to on-the-job conflict.[70] Most people envision *conflict* as meaning shouting and fighting, but as a manager you will encounter more subtle, nonviolent forms: opposition, criticism, arguments. Thus, a definition of conflict seems fairly mild: **Conflict is a process in which one party perceives that its interests are being opposed or negatively affected by another party.**[71]

The Nature of Conflict: Disagreement Is Normal

Conflict is simply disagreement, a perfectly normal state of affairs. Conflicts may take many forms: between individuals, between an individual and a group, between groups, within a group, and between an organization and its environment. (To see what your own conflict-management style is, see the Self-Assessment at the end of this chapter.)

Although all of us might wish to live lives free of conflict, it is now recognized that certain kinds of conflict can actually be beneficial.[72] Let us therefore distinguish between *dysfunctional conflict* (bad) and *functional conflict* (good).

- **Dysfunctional conflict—bad for organizations.** From the standpoint of the organization, *dysfunctional conflict* **is conflict that hinders the organization's performance or threatens its interests.** As a manager, you need to do what you can to remove dysfunctional conflict, sometimes called *negative conflict.*

- **Functional conflict—good for organizations.** The good kind of conflict is *functional conflict,* **which benefits the main purposes of the organization and serves its interests.**[73] There are some situations in which this kind of conflict—also called *constructive conflict* or *cooperative conflict*—is considered advantageous.

EXAMPLE

Dysfunctional & Functional Conflict: Do Nasty Bosses Get Better Performance?

In the film *The Devil Wears Prada,* Meryl Streep stars as a fear-inspiring fashion-magazine editor who keeps her new assistant quivering with dread. Is the portrait real? Says Liz Lange, a maternity-clothes designer, who was herself an editorial assistant, "If you happen to be working for the wrong editor, you could find yourself doing their kid's homework or being yelled at, or crying in the bathroom."[74]

Unfortunately, this kind of tyranny is very common, with 35% of American workers in a 2010 survey reporting they had been bullied at work (62% of bullies are men,

58% of targets are women, but the majority of bullying is same-gender).[75]

Abuse Flows Downhill. Does such negative conflict get results? Surprisingly, often it does. One study of 373 randomly chosen employees found that, although some reacted to abusive bosses by doing little or nothing, others performed better—in part, it's speculated, to make themselves look good and others look worse.[76]

Yet other research shows that abuse flows downhill, and when supervisors feel they have been unjustly treated, they may vent their resentment by abusing those who report to them. Subordinates generally cope either through avoidance or, less commonly, through confrontation and are in any case less inclined to feel committed to their organizations, and more inclined to speak unfavorably about their companies to outsiders and to seek jobs elsewhere.[77]

The "No-Jerk Rule." When Stanford organizational psychologist Robert Sutton published a short essay in which he urged more civility in organizations by steady application of what he calls "the no-jerk rule" (although he used a far stronger word than "jerk"), he elicited more e-mails than he had received on any other subject, showing the topic had touched a nerve.[78]

Jerks may be everywhere, he says, but "the key is to make explicit to everyone involved in hiring decisions that candidates who have strong skills but who show signs they will belittle and disrespect others cannot be hired under any circumstances." In addition, "Insults, put-downs, nasty teasing, and rude interruptions [should be] dealt with as soon as possible, preferably by the most respected and powerful members" of the company.[79]

YOUR CALL

Have you ever worked for jerks (otherwise known, as Sutton puts it, as "tyrants, bullies, boors, destructive narcissists, and psychologically abusive people")? How did you respond to them?

Can Too Little or Too Much Conflict Affect Performance?

It's tempting to think that a conflict-free work group is a happy work group, as indeed it may be. But is it a productive group? In the 1970s, social scientists specializing in organizational behavior introduced the revolutionary idea that organizations could suffer from *too little* conflict.

The jerk. Ever worked for an angry boss? How did you deal with the situation? Have there been circumstances in which people working for you might have called *you* a jerk? What should you have done differently?

428   PART 5 ✳ Leading

- **Too little conflict—indolence.** Work groups, departments, or organizations that experience too little conflict tend to be plagued by apathy, lack of creativity, indecision, and missed deadlines. The result is that organizational performance suffers.

- **Too much conflict—warfare.** Excessive conflict, on the other hand, can erode organizational performance because of political infighting, dissatisfaction, lack of teamwork, and turnover. Workplace aggression and violence are manifestations of excessive conflict.[80]

Thus, it seems that a moderate level of conflict can induce creativity and initiative, thereby raising performance, as shown in the diagram below. *(See Figure 13.2.)* As might be expected, however, the idea as to what constitutes "moderate" will vary among managers.

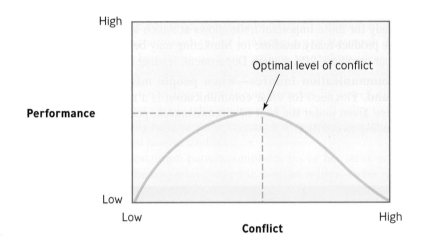

figure 13.2

THE RELATIONSHIP BETWEEN LEVEL OF CONFLICT AND LEVEL OF PERFORMANCE

Too little conflict or too much conflict causes performance to suffer.

Three Kinds of Conflict: Personality, Intergroup, & Cross-Cultural

There are a variety of sources of conflict—so-called *conflict triggers*. Three of the principal ones are (1) between personalities, (2) between groups, and (3) between cultures. By understanding these, you'll be better able to take charge and manage the conflicts rather than letting the conflicts take you by surprise and manage you.

1. Personality Conflicts: Clashes Because of Personal Dislikes or Disagreements We've all had confrontations, weak or strong, with people because we disagreed with them or disliked their personalities, such as their opinions, their behavior, their looks, whatever. *Personality conflict* **is defined as interpersonal opposition based on personal dislike, disagreement, or differing styles.** Such conflicts often begin with instances of *workplace incivility,* or employees' lack of regard for each other, which, if not curtailed, can diminish job satisfaction and organizational loyalty.[81]

Some particular kinds of personality conflicts are the following:

- **Personality clashes—when individual differences can't be resolved.** Personality, values, attitudes, and experience can be so disparate that sometimes the only way to resolve individual differences—personality clashes—is to separate two people.

    Example: Are you easygoing, but she's tense and driven? Does he always shade the facts, while you're a stickler for the truth? If you're basically

Dealing with Disagreements: Five Conflict-Handling Styles

Even if you're at the top of your game as a manager, working with groups and teams of people will now and then put you in the middle of disagreements, sometimes even destructive conflict. How can you deal with it?

There are five conflict-handling styles, or techniques, a manager can use for handling disagreements with individuals, as follows.[88]

Avoiding—"Maybe the Problem Will Go Away"

Avoiding involves ignoring or suppressing a conflict. Avoidance is appropriate for trivial issues, when emotions are high and a cooling-off period is needed, or when the cost of confrontation outweighs the benefits of resolving the conflict. It is not appropriate for difficult or worsening problems.

The benefit of this approach is that it buys time in unfolding and ambiguous situations. The weakness is that it provides only a temporary fix and sidesteps the underlying problem.

Accommodating—"Let's Do It Your Way"

An accommodating manager is also known as a "smoothing" or "obliging" manager. *Accommodating* is allowing the desires of the other party to prevail. As one writer describes it, "An obliging [accommodating] person neglects his or her own concern to satisfy the concern of the other party."[89] Accommodating may be an appropriate conflict-handling strategy when it's possible to eventually get something in return or when the issue isn't important to you. It's not appropriate for complex or worsening problems.

The advantage of accommodating is that it encourages cooperation. The weakness is that once again it's only a temporary fix that fails to confront the underlying problem.

Forcing—"You Have to Do It My Way"

Also known as "dominating," *forcing* is simply ordering an outcome, when a manager relies on his or her formal authority and power to resolve a conflict. Forcing is appropriate when an unpopular solution must be implemented and when it's not important that others be committed to your viewpoint.

The advantage of forcing is speed: It can get results quickly. The disadvantage is that in the end it doesn't resolve personal conflict—if anything, it aggravates it by breeding hurt feelings and resentment.

Compromising—"Let's Split the Difference"

In *compromising,* both parties give up something in order to gain something. Compromise is appropriate when both sides have opposite goals or possess equal power. But compromise isn't workable when it is used so often that it doesn't achieve results—for example, continual failure to meet production deadlines.

The benefit of compromise is that it is a democratic process that seems to have no losers. However, since so many people approach compromise situations with a win-lose attitude, they may be disappointed and feel cheated.

Collaborating—"Let's Cooperate to Reach a Win-Win Solution That Benefits Both of Us"

Collaborating strives to devise solutions that benefit both parties. Collaboration is appropriate for complex issues plagued by misunderstanding. It is inappropriate for resolving conflicts rooted in opposing value systems.

The strength of collaborating is its longer-lasting impact because it deals with the underlying problem, not just its symptoms. Its weakness is that it's very time-consuming. Nevertheless, collaboration is usually the best approach for dealing with groups and teams of people.

YOUR CALL

Which style are you most likely to use, based on your experience?

How to Stimulate Constructive Conflict

As a manager you are being paid not just to manage conflict but even to create some, where it's constructive and appropriate, in order to stimulate performance. Constructive conflict, if carefully monitored, can be very productive under a number of circumstances: when your work group seems afflicted with inertia and apathy, resulting in low performance; when there's a lack of new ideas and resistance to change; when there seem to be a lot of yes-men and yes-women (expressing groupthink) in the work unit; when there's high employee turnover; or when managers seem unduly concerned with peace, cooperation, compromise, consensus, and their own popularity rather than in achieving work objectives.

Some ways in which intergroup conflicts are expressed are as follows:

- **Inconsistent goals or reward systems—when people pursue different objectives.** It's natural for people in functional organizations to be pursuing different objectives and to be rewarded accordingly, but this means that conflict is practically built into the system.

  Example: The sales manager for a college textbook publisher may be rewarded for achieving exceptional sales of newly introduced titles. But individual salespeople are rewarded for how many books they sell overall, which means they may promote the old tried-and-true books they know.

- **Ambiguous jurisdictions—when job boundaries are unclear.** "That's not my job and those aren't my responsibilities." "Those resources belong to me because I need them as part of my job." When task responsibilities are unclear, that can often lead to conflict.

  Examples: Is the bartender or the waiter supposed to put the lime in the gin and tonic and the celery in the Bloody Mary? Is management or the union in charge of certain work rules? Is Marketing or Research & Development supposed to be setting up focus groups to explore ideas for new products?

- **Status differences—when there are inconsistencies in power and influence.** It can happen that people who are lower in status according to the organizational chart actually have disproportionate power over those theoretically above them, which can lead to conflicts.

  Examples: If a restaurant patron complains his or her steak is not rare enough, the chef is the one who cooked it, but the waiter—who is usually lower in status—is the one who gave the chef the order. Airlines could not hold their schedules without flight crews and ground crews working a certain amount of overtime. But during labor disputes, pilots, flight attendants, and mechanics may simply refuse managers' requests to work the extra hours.

3. Multicultural Conflicts: Clashes Between Cultures
With cross-border mergers, joint ventures, and international alliances common features of the global economy, there are frequent opportunities for clashes between cultures. Often success or failure, when business is being conducted across cultures, arises from dealing with differing assumptions about how to think and act.

Example: When in early 2010, drivers of Toyota automobiles were losing control because of sudden acceleration problems, resulting in the manufacturer recalling thousands of vehicles, Toyota failed to recognize differences in the way that Japanese and Americans perceive recalls and safety. For the Japanese, conflicts are all about personal honor. "Japanese consumers are horrified by recalls," says one account, "while Japanese companies avoid them at all costs in order to protect their image. But for U.S. consumers, knowing that any flaw will trigger a recall gives them greater confidence in their cars." By delaying recall, Toyota erred in making a "typically Japanese judgment" for an American market.[86]

Dealing with cross-cultural conflict begins with having an understanding of the GLOBE project's nine cultural dimensions, as discussed in Chapter 4 (p. 117). In that chapter, we also described other cultural variations in language, interpersonal space, communication, time orientation, and religion (pp. 118–122). One study of 409 expatriates (14% of them female) from U.S. and Canadian multinational firms working in 51 different countries identified nine specific ways to facilitate interaction with host-country nationals, the results of which are shown at right. *(See Table 13.6.)* Note that "Be a good listener" tops the list—the very thing lacking in so many American managers, who are criticized for being blunt to the point of insensitivity.[87]

table 13.6

WAYS TO BUILD CROSS-CULTURAL RELATIONSHIPS

"Be sensitive to others' needs" and "Be cooperative" are tied for second place.

1. Be a good listener.

2. Be sensitive to others' needs.

3. Be cooperative, not overly competitive.

4. Advocate inclusive (participative) leadership.

5. Compromise rather than dominate.

6. Build rapport through conversations.

7. Be compassionate and understanding.

8. Avoid conflict by emphasizing harmony.

9. Nurture others (develop and mentor).

Source: Adapted from R. L. Tung, "American Expatriates Abroad: From Neophytes to Cosmopolitans," *Journal of World Business,* Summer 1998, table 6, p. 136. Reprinted with permission of Elsevier.

Dealing with Disagreements: Five Conflict-Handling Styles

Even if you're at the top of your game as a manager, working with groups and teams of people will now and then put you in the middle of disagreements, sometimes even destructive conflict. How can you deal with it?

There are five conflict-handling styles, or techniques, a manager can use for handling disagreements with individuals, as follows.[88]

Avoiding—"Maybe the Problem Will Go Away"

Avoiding involves ignoring or suppressing a conflict. Avoidance is appropriate for trivial issues, when emotions are high and a cooling-off period is needed, or when the cost of confrontation outweighs the benefits of resolving the conflict. It is not appropriate for difficult or worsening problems.

The benefit of this approach is that it buys time in unfolding and ambiguous situations. The weakness is that it provides only a temporary fix and sidesteps the underlying problem.

Accommodating—"Let's Do It Your Way"

An accommodating manager is also known as a "smoothing" or "obliging" manager. *Accommodating* is allowing the desires of the other party to prevail. As one writer describes it, "An obliging [accommodating] person neglects his or her own concern to satisfy the concern of the other party."[89] Accommodating may be an appropriate conflict-handling strategy when it's possible to eventually get something in return or when the issue isn't important to you. It's not appropriate for complex or worsening problems.

The advantage of accommodating is that it encourages cooperation. The weakness is that once again it's only a temporary fix that fails to confront the underlying problem.

Forcing—"You Have to Do It My Way"

Also known as "dominating," *forcing* is simply ordering an outcome, when a manager relies on his or her formal authority and power to resolve a conflict. Forcing is appropriate when an unpopular solution must be implemented and when it's not important that others be committed to your viewpoint.

The advantage of forcing is speed: It can get results quickly. The disadvantage is that in the end it doesn't resolve personal conflict—if anything, it aggravates it by breeding hurt feelings and resentment.

Compromising—"Let's Split the Difference"

In *compromising,* both parties give up something in order to gain something. Compromise is appropriate when both sides have opposite goals or possess equal power. But compromise isn't workable when it is used so often that it doesn't achieve results—for example, continual failure to meet production deadlines.

The benefit of compromise is that it is a democratic process that seems to have no losers. However, since so many people approach compromise situations with a win-lose attitude, they may be disappointed and feel cheated.

Collaborating—"Let's Cooperate to Reach a Win-Win Solution That Benefits Both of Us"

Collaborating strives to devise solutions that benefit both parties. Collaboration is appropriate for complex issues plagued by misunderstanding. It is inappropriate for resolving conflicts rooted in opposing value systems.

The strength of collaborating is its longer-lasting impact because it deals with the underlying problem, not just its symptoms. Its weakness is that it's very time-consuming. Nevertheless, collaboration is usually the best approach for dealing with groups and teams of people.

YOUR CALL

Which style are you most likely to use, based on your experience?

How to Stimulate Constructive Conflict

As a manager you are being paid not just to manage conflict but even to create some, where it's constructive and appropriate, in order to stimulate performance. Constructive conflict, if carefully monitored, can be very productive under a number of circumstances: when your work group seems afflicted with inertia and apathy, resulting in low performance; when there's a lack of new ideas and resistance to change; when there seem to be a lot of yes-men and yes-women (expressing groupthink) in the work unit; when there's high employee turnover; or when managers seem unduly concerned with peace, cooperation, compromise, consensus, and their own popularity rather than in achieving work objectives.

- **Too little conflict—indolence.** Work groups, departments, or organizations that experience too little conflict tend to be plagued by apathy, lack of creativity, indecision, and missed deadlines. The result is that organizational performance suffers.

- **Too much conflict—warfare.** Excessive conflict, on the other hand, can erode organizational performance because of political infighting, dissatisfaction, lack of teamwork, and turnover. Workplace aggression and violence are manifestations of excessive conflict.[80]

Thus, it seems that a moderate level of conflict can induce creativity and initiative, thereby raising performance, as shown in the diagram below. *(See Figure 13.2.)* As might be expected, however, the idea as to what constitutes "moderate" will vary among managers.

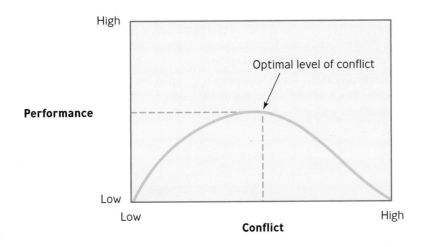

figure 13.2

THE RELATIONSHIP BETWEEN LEVEL OF CONFLICT AND LEVEL OF PERFORMANCE

Too little conflict or too much conflict causes performance to suffer.

Three Kinds of Conflict: Personality, Intergroup, & Cross-Cultural

There are a variety of sources of conflict—so-called *conflict triggers*. Three of the principal ones are (1) between personalities, (2) between groups, and (3) between cultures. By understanding these, you'll be better able to take charge and manage the conflicts rather than letting the conflicts take you by surprise and manage you.

1. Personality Conflicts: Clashes Because of Personal Dislikes or Disagreements
We've all had confrontations, weak or strong, with people because we disagreed with them or disliked their personalities, such as their opinions, their behavior, their looks, whatever. *Personality conflict is defined as interpersonal opposition based on personal dislike, disagreement, or differing styles.* Such conflicts often begin with instances of *workplace incivility,* or employees' lack of regard for each other, which, if not curtailed, can diminish job satisfaction and organizational loyalty.[81]

Some particular kinds of personality conflicts are the following:

- **Personality clashes—when individual differences can't be resolved.** Personality, values, attitudes, and experience can be so disparate that sometimes the only way to resolve individual differences—personality clashes—is to separate two people.

    Example: Are you easygoing, but she's tense and driven? Does he always shade the facts, while you're a stickler for the truth? If you're basically

Ms. Straight Arrow and he's Mr. Slippery, do you think you could adapt your personality to fit his? Maybe you should ask for a transfer.

- **Competition for scarce resources—when two parties need the same things.** Within organizations there is often a scarcity of needed resources—for example, funds, office space, equipment, employees, and money for raises. When resources are scarce, being a manager becomes more difficult and conflict more likely.[82]

  Example: There are lots of computer glitches but not enough on-site technicians to fix them.

- **Time pressure—when people believe there aren't enough hours to do the work.** Setting a deadline is a useful way of inducing people to perform. Or it can be a source of resentment, rage, and conflict if employees think their manager has unrealistic expectations.

  Example: If you're in the business of marketing Christmas items to department stores and gift shops, it's imperative that you have your product ready for those important trade shows at which store buyers will appear. But the product-ready deadline for Marketing may be completely unworkable for your company's Production Department, leading to angry conflict.

- **Communication failures—when people misperceive and misunderstand.** The need for clear communication is a never-ending, ongoing process. Even under the best of circumstances, people misunderstand others, leading to conflict.

EXAMPLE

"What We Have Here Is a Failure to Communicate": The Plight of the Tongue-Tied

Miscommunication happens for all kinds of reasons—sometimes because there is no communication at all.

Clamming Up in Small Groups. Some people simply clam up in small-group settings, often because they think others are smarter or of higher status. Becoming tongue-tied this way seems to be more common in women and in people with higher IQs, according to a Virginia Tech study.[83] The researchers speculate they are "more attuned to group social dynamics, subconsciously worrying about their performance and evaluating themselves in relation to others," says one report.[84]

Ways to Cope. If speaking up is hard for you to do in small groups, you can take comfort that the people who froze the most in the study were actually the smartest.

Otherwise, you can cope by preparing before the meeting (practice your delivery and bring notes), telling the person running the meeting beforehand that you have some points and would like the opportunity to be called upon, or joining with a more outgoing or higher-status member in the group who can bring up your points and then toss you an opening.[85]

YOUR CALL

Do you tend to go silent during some small-group settings or social situations? Perhaps it's not that you're shy but rather an introvert and want to collect your thoughts before speaking—hard to do in the company of extroverts who "think out loud." Could any of the advice above work for you?

2. Intergroup Conflicts: Clashes Between Work Groups, Teams, & Departments The downside of cohesiveness, the "we" feeling discussed earlier, is that it can translate into "we versus them." This produces conflict among work groups, teams, and departments within an organization.

The following four devices are used to stimulate constructive conflict:

1. Spur Competition Among Employees

Competition is, of course, a form of conflict, but competition is often healthy in spurring people to produce higher results. Thus, a company will often put its salespeople in competition with one another by offering bonuses and awards for achievement—a trip to a Caribbean resort, say, for the top performer of the year.

2. Change the Organization's Culture & Procedures

Competition may also be established by making deliberate and highly publicized moves to change the corporate culture—by announcing to employees that the organization is now going to be more innovative and reward original thinking and unorthodox ideas. Procedures, such as paperwork sign-off processes, can also be revamped. Results can be reinforced in visible ways through announcements of bonuses, raises, and promotions.

Top employee. Companies frequently stimulate constructive competition among employees to produce better performance. Top salespeople, for instance, may be rewarded with a plaque or even a trip to a Mexican resort. Do you think you would do well in a company that makes you compete with others to produce higher results?

3. Bring in Outsiders for New Perspectives

Without "new blood," organizations can become inbred and resistant to change. This is why managers often bring in outsiders—people from a different unit of the organization, new hires from competing companies, or consultants. With their different backgrounds, attitudes, or management styles, these outsiders can bring a new perspective and can shake things up.

4. Use Programmed Conflict: Devil's Advocacy & the Dialectic Method

Programmed conflict **is designed to elicit different opinions without inciting people's personal feelings.**[90]

Sometimes decision-making groups become so bogged down in details and procedures that nothing of substance gets done. The idea here is to get people, through role-playing, to defend or criticize ideas based on relevant facts rather than on personal feelings and preferences.

The method for getting people to engage in this debate of ideas is to do disciplined role-playing, for which two proven methods are available: *devil's advocacy* and the *dialectic method.*

These two methods work as follows:

- **Devil's advocacy—role-playing criticism to test whether a proposal is workable.** *Devil's advocacy* **is the process of assigning someone to play the role of critic** to voice possible objections to a proposal and thereby generate critical thinking and reality testing.[91]

  Periodically role-playing devil's advocate has a beneficial side effect in that it is good training for developing analytical and communicative skills. However, it's a good idea to rotate the job so no one person develops a negative reputation.

- **The dialectic method—role-playing two sides of a proposal to test whether it is workable.** Requiring a bit more skill than devil's advocacy, the *dialectic method* **is the process of having two people or groups play opposing roles in a debate in order to better understand a proposal.** After the structured debate, managers are better able to make a decision.[92]

Whatever kind of organization you work for, you'll always benefit from knowing how to manage conflict. ●

adjourning 418

cohesiveness 419

conflict 427

continuous improvement teams 415

cooperating 419

cross-functional team 415

devil's advocacy 433

dialectic method 433

division of labor 421

dysfunctional conflict 427

formal group 413

forming 417

functional conflict 427

group 413

group cohesiveness 418

groupthink 424

informal group 413

maintenance role 422

norming 418

norms 423

performing 418

personality conflict 429

programmed conflict 433

roles 422

self-managed teams 416

social loafing 421

storming 417

task role 422

team 413

trust 419

Summary

13.1 Groups Versus Teams

Groups and teams are different—a group is typically management-directed, a team self-directed. A group is defined as two or more freely interacting individuals who share collective norms, share collective goals, and have a common identity. A team is defined as a small group of people with complementary skills who are committed to a common purpose, performance goals, and approach for which they hold themselves mutually accountable.

Groups may be either formal, established to do something productive for the organization and headed by a leader, or informal, formed by people seeking friendship with no officially appointed leader.

Teams are of various types, but one of the most important is the work team, which engages in collective work requiring coordinated effort. Work teams may be of four types, identified according to their basic purpose: advice, production, project, and action. A project team may also be a cross-functional team, staffed with specialists pursuing a common objective.

Two types of teams worth knowing about are continuous improvement teams, consisting of small groups of volunteers or workers and supervisors who meet intermittently to discuss workplace and quality-related problems, and self-managed teams, defined as groups of workers given administrative oversight for their task domains.

13.2 Stages of Group & Team Development

A group may evolve into a team through five stages. (1) Forming is the process of getting oriented and getting acquainted. (2) Storming is characterized by the emergence of individual personalities and roles and conflicts within the group. (3) In norming,

conflicts are resolved, close relationships develop, and unity and harmony emerge. (4) In performing, members concentrate on solving problems and completing the assigned task. (5) In adjourning, members prepare for disbandment.

13.3 Building Effective Teams

There are nine considerations managers must take into account in building a group into an effective team. (1) They must ensure individuals are cooperating, or systematically integrating their efforts to achieve a collective objective. (2) They must establish a climate of trust, or reciprocal faith in others' intentions and behaviors. (3) They must consider the team's cohesiveness, the tendency of a group or team to stick together. (4) They must establish measurable goals and have feedback about members' performance. (5) They must motivate members by making them mutually accountable to one another. (6) They must consider what size is optimal. Teams with nine or fewer members have better interaction and morale, yet they also have fewer resources, are possibly less innovative, and may have work unevenly distributed among members. Teams of 10–16 members have more resources and can take advantage of division of labor, yet they may be characterized by less interaction, lower morale, and social loafing. (7) They must consider the role each team member must play. A role is defined as the socially determined expectation of how an individual should behave in a specific position. Two types of team roles are task and maintenance. A task role consists of behavior that concentrates on getting the team's tasks done. A maintenance role consists of behavior that fosters constructive relationships among team members. (8) They must consider team norms, the general guidelines or rules of behavior that most group or team members follow. Norms tend to be enforced by group or team members for four reasons: to help the group survive, to clarify role expectations, to help individuals avoid embarrassing situations, and to emphasize the group's important values and identity. (9) They must be aware of groupthink, a cohesive group's blind unwillingness to consider alternatives. Symptoms of groupthink are feelings of invulnerability, certainty of the rightness of their actions, and stereotyped views of the opposition; rationalization and self-censorship; and illusion of unanimity, peer pressure, and the appearance of self-appointed protectors against adverse information. The results of groupthink can be reduction in alternative ideas and limiting of other information. Two ways to prevent groupthink are to allow criticism and to allow other perspectives.

13.4 Managing Conflict

Conflict is a process in which one party perceives that its interests are being opposed or negatively affected by another party. Conflict can be dysfunctional, or negative. However, functional, or constructive, conflict benefits the main purposes of the organization and serves its interests. Too little conflict can lead to indolence; too much conflict can lead to warfare.

Three types of conflict are clashes between personalities, intergroup conflict, and cross-cultural conflict.

Four devices for stimulating constructive conflict are (1) spurring competition among employees, (2) changing the organization's culture and procedures, (3) bringing in outsiders for new perspectives, and (4) using programmed conflict to elicit different opinions without inciting people's personal feelings. Two methods used in programmed conflict are (1) devil's advocacy, in which someone is assigned to play the role of critic to voice possible objections to a proposal, and (2) the dialectic method, in which two people or groups play opposing roles in a debate in order to better understand a proposal.

Management in Action

Hiring Decisions Influence Teamwork & Performance

Superstars get a lot of attention from bosses. But bad apples deserve even more.

A growing body of research suggests that having just a few nasty, lazy, or incompetent characters around can ruin the performance of a team or an entire organization—no matter how stellar the other employees.

Bad apples distract and drag down everyone, and their destructive behaviors, such as anger, laziness, and incompetence, are remarkably contagious. Leaders who let a few bad apples in the door—perhaps in exchange for political favors—or look the other way when employees are rude or incompetent are setting the stage for even their most skilled people to fail.

It's crucial for leader to screen out bad apples before they're hired—and if they do slip through the cracks, bosses must make every effort to reform or (if necessary) oust them.

How can organizations squash those negative influences? The easiest way, obviously, is to avoid hiring bad apples in the first place—and that means taking a different approach to assessing candidates for jobs.

The usual means of screening are often weak when it comes to determining if a job candidate is a bad apple. Candidates may have gone to the best schools or may come across as charming and brilliant in interviews—thus disguising laziness, incompetence, or nastiness.

That's why one of the best ways to screen employees is to see how they actually do the job under realistic conditions. Akshay Kothari and Ankit Gupta favor that approach. When they're hiring new people for their Palo Alto, California, company, Pulse, which makes a news-reading app for mobile devices, they consider evaluations from peers and superiors and do multiple rounds of interviews. But they say the most effective thing is to bring candidates in for a day or two and give them a short job to accomplish. (The candidates are paid for their time.)

Not only do they learn a lot about the candidates' technical skills, Messrs. Kothari and Gupta say, but they also learn about their personality. How do they deal with setbacks? Do they know when to ask for help and to give others help? Is the candidate the type of person they want to work with? The partners say there have been several candidates who looked great on paper and came highly recommended but weren't offered jobs—because technical and interpersonal weaknesses surfaced during the selection process.

Beyond smarter screening, it's important to develop a culture that doesn't tolerate jerks. The best organizations make explicit their intolerance for bad apples; they spell out which behaviors are unacceptable in the workplace and act decisively to prevent and halt them.

Consider Robert W. Baird & Co., a financial-services firm that has won praise as a great place to work. The company is serious about creating a culture where disrespect and selfishness are unacceptable. They call this the "no jerk rule" (though they also use a more colorful word than "jerk").

The company starts sending the message during the hiring process, says CEO Paul Purcell. "During the interview, I look them in the eye and tell them, 'if I discover that you are a jerk, I am going to fire you,'" he says. "Most candidates aren't fazed by this, but every now and then, one turns pale, and we never see them again—they find some reason to back out of the search."

When the company makes a hiring error and brings aboard an employee who persistently demeans colleagues or puts personal needs ahead of others, Baird acts quickly to deal with or expel the bad apple.

Mr. Purcell's crusty approach won't work in every company culture. . . .

There are times, of course, when an organization can't—or won't—remove a destructive personality. Maybe the person is a star as well as a bad apple, for instance, or is otherwise crucial to the organization. In such cases, leaders might try to use coaching, warnings, and incentives to curb the toxic employee's behavior. Another tactic is to physically isolate the bad apple.

In one organization, there was a deeply skilled and incredibly nasty engineer whom leaders could not bring themselves to fire. So, they rented a beautiful private office for him several blocks from the building where his colleagues worked. His coworkers were a lot happier—and so was he, since he preferred working alone.

But beware: Leaders who believe the destructive superstars are "too important" to fire often underestimate the damage they can do.

FOR DISCUSSION

1. Using Table 13.2 as a guide, which type of team do you think is most likely to be affected by "bad apples"? Discuss your rationale.

2. How would "bad apples" affect each stage of the group and team development process? Explain.

3. Which of the characteristics of high-performing teams would be negatively influenced by hiring "bad apples"?

4. What are the pros and cons of the hiring process used at Pulse? Why does this process potentially reduce the number of "bad apples" that are hired?

5. Do you like the approach used to handle the deeply skilled and incredibly nasty engineer described in the case? Explain your rationale, and describe what you might have done differently.

Source: Excerpted from Robert Sutton, "How a Few Bad Apples Ruin Everything," *The Wall Street Journal*, October 24, 2011, p. R5. Copyright © 2011 by Dow Jones & Company, Inc. Reproduced with permission of Dow Jones & Company, Inc. via Copyright Clearance Center.

Self-Assessment

What Is Your Conflict-Management Style?

OBJECTIVES

1. To assess your conflict-management style.
2. To gain insight on how you manage conflict.

INTRODUCTION

Have you ever had a professor whose viewpoints were in conflict with your own? Have you worked in a group with someone who seems to disagree just to cause conflict? How did you react in that situation? In this chapter, you learned that there are five different ways of handling conflict: (1) *avoiding*—this approach is seen in people who wish to suppress conflict or back down from it altogether; (2) *accommodating*—this approach is seen in people who place the other party's interests above their own; (3) *forcing*—this approach is seen when people rely on their authority to solve conflict; (4) *compromising*—this approach is seen in people who are willing to give up something in order to reach a solution; and (5) *collaborating*—this approach is seen in people who desire a win-win situation, striving to address concerns and desires of all the parties involved in the conflict. The purpose of this exercise is to determine your conflict-handling style.

INSTRUCTIONS

Read each of the statements below and use the following scale to indicate how often you rely on each tactic.

1 = very rarely
2 = rarely
3 = sometimes
4 = fairly often
5 = very often

1. I work to come out victorious no matter what.   1 2 3 4 5

2. I try to put the needs of others above my own.   1 2 3 4 5

3. I look for a mutually satisfactory solution.   1 2 3 4 5

4. I try to get involved in conflicts.   1 2 3 4 5

5. I strive to investigate and understand the issues involved in the conflict.   1 2 3 4 5

6. I never back away from a good argument.   1 2 3 4 5

7. I strive to foster harmony.   1 2 3 4 5

8. I negotiate to get a portion of what I propose.   1 2 3 4 5

9. I avoid open discussion of controversial subjects.   1 2 3 4 5

10. When I am trying to resolve disagreements, I openly share information.   1 2 3 4 5

11. I would rather win than compromise.   1 2 3 4 5

12. I work through conflict by accepting suggestions of others.   1 2 3 4 5

13. I look for a middle ground to resolve disagreements.   1 2 3 4 5

14. I keep my true opinions to myself to avoid hard feelings.   1 2 3 4 5

15. I encourage the open sharing of concerns and issues.   1 2 3 4 5

16. I am reluctant to admit I am wrong.   1 2 3 4 5

17. I try to save others from embarrassment in a disagreement.   1 2 3 4 5

18. I stress the advantages of give and take.   1 2 3 4 5

19. I give in early on rather than argue about a point.   1 2 3 4 5

20. I state my position and stress that it is the only correct point of view.   1 2 3 4 5

SCORING & INTERPRETATION

Enter your responses, item by item, in the five categories below. Add your responses to get your total for each of the five conflict-handling styles. Your primary conflict-handling style will be the area where you scored the highest. Your backup conflict-handling style will be your second-highest score.

Avoiding		Accommodating		Forcing		Compromising		Collaborating	
Item	Score	Item	Score	Item	Score	Item	Score	Item	Score
4.	____	2.	____	1.	____	3.	____	5.	____
9.	____	7.	____	6.	____	8.	____	10.	____
14.	____	12.	____	11.	____	13.	____	15.	____
19.	____	17.	____	16.	____	18.	____	20.	____
Total = ____		Total = ____		Total = ____		Total = ____		Total = ____	

QUESTIONS FOR DISCUSSION

1. Were you surprised by the results? Why or why not? Explain.

2. Were the scores for your primary and backup conflict-handling styles relatively similar, or was there a large gap? What does this imply? Discuss.

3. Is your conflict-handling style one that can be used in many different conflict scenarios? Explain.

4. What are some skills you can work on to become more effective at handling conflict? Describe and explain.

The survey was developed using conflict-handling styles defined by K. W. Thomas, "Conflict and Conflict Management," in M. Dunnette, ed., *Handbook of Industrial and Organizational Psychology* (Chicago: Rand McNally, 1976), pp. 889–935.

Legal/Ethical Challenge

When Employees Smoke Marijuana Socially: A Manager's Quandary

You are a supervisor at a telephone call center and have very positive relationships with members of your work team and your manager. A friend of yours, Christina, is also a supervisor, and her younger brother, Blake, is a member of her work team.

Christina invites you to her birthday party at her home, and you happily agree to attend. During the party, you walk out to the backyard to get some fresh air and notice that Blake and several other employees of your company are smoking marijuana. You have been told on several occasions by members of your own work team that these same individuals have used marijuana at other social events.

Blake and his friends are not part of your work team, and you never noticed any of them being impaired at work.

SOLVING THE CHALLENGE

As a supervisor, what would you do?

1. Report the drug users and the incident to the company's human resources department.

2. Mind your own business. The employees are not on your team and don't appear to be impaired at work.

3. Talk to your boss and get her opinion about what should be done.

4. Invent other options. Discuss.

chapter 14

Power, Influence, & Leadership
From Becoming a Manager to Becoming a Leader

Major Questions You Should Be Able to Answer

14.1 The Nature of Leadership: Wielding Influence

Major Question: I don't want to be just a manager; I want to be a leader. What's the difference between the two?

14.2 Trait Approaches: Do Leaders Have Distinctive Personality Characteristics?

Major Question: What does it take to be a successful leader?

14.3 Behavioral Approaches: Do Leaders Show Distinctive Patterns of Behavior?

Major Question: Do effective leaders behave in similar ways?

14.4 Contingency Approaches: Does Leadership Vary with the Situation?

Major Question: How might effective leadership vary according to the situation at hand?

14.5 The Full-Range Model: Uses of Transactional & Transformational Leadership

Major Question: What does it take to truly inspire people to perform beyond their normal levels?

14.6 Four Additional Perspectives

Major Question: If there are many ways to be a leader, which one would describe me best?

Advancing Your Career: Staying Ahead in the Workplace of Tomorrow

Someday maybe you can afford to have a *personal career coach*—the kind long used by sports and entertainment figures and now adopted in the upper ranks of business. These individuals "combine executive coaching and career consulting with marketing and negotiations," says one account. "They plot career strategy, help build networks of business contacts, . . . and shape their clients' images."[1]

One such career coach is Richard L. Knowdell, president of Career Research and Testing in San Jose, California. He offers the following strategies for staying ahead in the workplace of tomorrow.[2]

Take Charge of Your Career, & Avoid Misconceptions

Because you, not others, are in charge of your career, and it's an ongoing process, you should develop a career plan and base your choices on that plan. When considering a new job or industry, find out how that world *really* works, not what it's reputed to be. When considering a company you might want to work for, find out its corporate "style" or culture by talking to its employees.

Develop New Capacities

"Being good at several things will be more advantageous in the long run than being excellent at one narrow specialty," says Knowdell. "A complex world will not only demand *specialized knowledge* but also *general and flexible skills.*"

Anticipate & Adapt to, Even Embrace, Changes

Learn to analyze, anticipate, and adapt to new circumstances in the world and in your own life. For instance, as technology changes the rules, *embrace* the new rules.

Keep Learning

"You can take a one- or two-day course in a new subject," says Knowdell, "just to get an idea of whether you want to use those specific skills and to see if you would be good at it. Then, if there is a match, you could seek out an extended course."

Develop Your People & Communications Skills

No matter how much communication technology takes over the workplace, there will always be a strong need for effectiveness in interpersonal relationships. In particular, learn to listen well. Incidentally, one poll found that "appearance"—meaning clothes, accessories, and shoes—ranked second only to "communication skills" as the quality most associated with professionalism.[3] (You might try imitating your bosses' clothing styles.)

For Discussion Which of these five rules do you think is most important—and why?

forecast What's Ahead in This Chapter

Are there differences between managers and leaders? This chapter considers this question. We discuss the sources of a leader's power and how leaders use persuasion to influence people. We then consider the following approaches to leadership: trait, behavioral, contingency, full-range, and four additional perspectives.

I don't want to be just a manager; I want to be a leader. What's the difference between the two?

THE BIG PICTURE

Being a manager and being a leader are not the same. That said, they both are necessary in the pursuit of organizational goals. For example, leadership skills are needed to create and communicate a company's vision, strategies, and goals, while management skills are needed to execute on these plans and goals. This section highlights how management and leadership skills are complementary and describes five sources of power leaders draw on to influence others. Leaders use the power of persuasion to get others to follow them. Five approaches to leadership are described in the next five sections.

Leadership. What is it? Is it a skill anyone can develop?

Leadership is the ability to influence employees to voluntarily pursue organizational goals.[4] In an effective organization, leadership is present at all levels, say Tom Peters and Nancy Austin in *A Passion for Excellence,* and it represents the sum of many things. Leadership, they say, "means vision, cheerleading, enthusiasm, love, trust, verve, passion, obsession, consistency, the use of symbols, paying attention as illustrated by the content of one's calendar, out-and-out drama (and the management thereof), creating heroes at all levels, coaching, effectively wandering around, and numerous other things."[5]

Managers & Leaders: Not Always the Same

You see the words *manager* and *leader* used interchangeably all the time. However, as one pair of leadership experts has said, "Leaders manage and managers lead, but the two activities are not synonymous."[6]

"Management," says Tim Bucher, CEO of TastingRoom.com, a wine site, "is about doing things right—dotting the I's, crossing the T's. . . . But leadership is about doing the right thing. . . . You have to make a call, and in some ways it might be against company policy."[7]

Managers do planning, organizing, directing, and control. Leaders inspire, encourage, and rally others to achieve great goals. Managers implement a company's vision and strategic plan. Leaders create and articulate that vision and plan. The table opposite summarizes key characteristics of each. *(See Table 14.1.)*

Managerial Leadership: Can You Be *Both* a Manager & a Leader?

Absolutely. The latest thinking is that individuals are able to exhibit a broad array of contrasting behaviors, as shown in Table 14.1 (a concept called *behavioral complexity*).[8] Thus, in the workplace, many people are capable of exhibiting *managerial leadership,* **defined as "the process of influencing others to understand and agree about what needs to be done and the process of facilitating individual and collective efforts to accomplish shared objectives."**[9] Here the "influencing" part is leadership and the "facilitating" part is management.

table 14.1

CHARACTERISTICS OF
BEING A MANAGER & A
LEADER

Being a Manager Means ...	Being a Leader Means ...
Planning, organizing, directing, controlling	Being visionary
Executing plans and delivering goods and services	Being inspiring, setting the tone, and articulating the vision
Managing resources	Managing people
Being conscientious	Being inspirational (charismatic)
Acting responsibly	Acting decisively
Putting customers first—responding to and acting for customers	Putting people first—responding to and acting for followers
Mistakes can happen when managers don't appreciate people are the key resource, underlead by treating people like other resources, or fail to be held accountable	Mistakes can happen when leaders choose the wrong goal, direction, or inspiration; overlead; or fail to implement the vision

Source: Adapted from P. Lorenzi, "Managing for the Common Good: Prosocial Leadership," *Organizational Dynamics* 33, no. 3 (2004), p. 286. Copyright © 2004 with permission of Elsevier.

Managerial leadership may be demonstrated not only by managers appointed to their positions but also by those who exercise leadership on a daily basis but don't carry formal management titles (such as certain coworkers on a team).

Coping with Complexity Versus Coping with Change: The Thoughts of John Kotter

In considering management versus leadership, retired Harvard Business School professor **John Kotter** suggests that one is not better than the other, that in fact they are *complementary* systems of action. The difference is that . . .

- *Management* is about coping with *complexity*,
- *Leadership* is about coping with *change*.[10]

Let's consider these differences.

Being a Manager: Coping with Complexity Management is necessary because complex organizations, especially the large ones that so much dominate the economic landscape, tend to become chaotic unless there is good management.[11] (For a good description of a manager's busy day, review Chapter 1, as analyzed by Henry Mintzberg.)

According to Kotter, companies manage complexity in three ways:

- **Determining what needs to be done—planning and budgeting.** Companies manage complexity first by *planning and budgeting*—setting targets or goals for the future, establishing steps for achieving them, and allocating resources to accomplish them.

- **Creating arrangements of people to accomplish an agenda—organizing and staffing.** Management achieves its plan by *organizing and staffing,* Kotter says—creating the organizational structure and hiring qualified individuals to fill the necessary jobs, then devising systems of implementation.

- **Ensuring people do their jobs—controlling and problem solving.** Management ensures the plan is accomplished by *controlling and problem solving,* says Kotter. That is, managers monitor results versus the plan in some detail by means of reports, meetings, and other tools. They then plan and organize to solve problems as they arise.

Being a Leader: Coping with Change   As the business world has become more competitive and volatile, doing things the same way as last year (or doing it 5% better) is no longer a formula for success. More changes are required for survival—hence the need for leadership.

Leadership copes with change in three ways:

- **Determining what needs to be done—setting a direction.** Instead of dealing with complexity through planning and budgeting, leaders strive for constructive change by *setting a direction.* That is, they develop a vision for the future, along with strategies for realizing the changes.

- **Creating arrangements of people to accomplish an agenda—aligning people.** Instead of organizing and staffing, leaders are concerned with *aligning people,* Kotter says. That is, they communicate the new direction to people in the company who can understand the vision and build coalitions that will realize it.

- **Ensuring people do their jobs—motivating and inspiring.** Instead of controlling and problem solving, leaders try to achieve their vision by *motivating and inspiring.* That is, they appeal to "basic but often untapped human needs, values, and emotions," says Kotter, to keep people moving in the right direction, despite obstacles to change.

Do Kotter's ideas describe real leaders in the real business world? Certainly many participants in a seminar convened by *Harvard Business Review* appeared to agree. "The primary task of leadership is to communicate the vision and the values of an organization," Frederick Smith, chairman and CEO of FedEx, told the group. "Second, leaders must win support for the vision and values they articulate. And third, leaders have to reinforce the vision and the values."[12]

Do You Have What It Takes to Be a Leader?   Managers have legitimate power (as we'll describe) that derives from the formal authority of the positions to which they have been appointed. This power allows managers to hire and fire, reward and punish. Managers plan, organize, and control, but they don't necessarily have the characteristics to be leaders.

Whereas management is a process that lots of people are able to learn, leadership is more visionary. As we've said, leaders inspire others, provide emotional support, and try to get employees to rally around a common goal. Leaders also play a role in creating a vision and strategic plan for an organization, which managers are then charged with implementing.

Five Sources of Power

To really understand leadership, we need to understand the concept of power and authority. *Authority* is the right to perform or command; it comes with the job. In

Amazing Amazon. Jeffrey Bezos, founder and CEO of online retailer Amazon.com, has done nearly everything Kotter suggests. For instance, Bezos's "culture of divine discontent" permits employees to plunge ahead with new ideas even though they know that most will probably fail.

contrast, *power* is the extent to which a person is able to influence others so they respond to orders.

People who pursue *personalized power*—**power directed at helping oneself**—as a way of enhancing their own selfish ends may give the word *power* a bad name. However, there is another kind of power, *socialized power*—**power directed at helping others.**[13] This is the kind of power you hear in expressions such as "My goal is to have a powerful impact on my community."

Within organizations there are typically five sources of power leaders may draw on: *legitimate, reward, coercive, expert,* and *referent.*

1. Legitimate Power: Influencing Behavior Because of One's Formal Position *Legitimate power,* **which all managers have, is power that results from managers' formal positions within the organization.** All managers have legitimate power over their employees, deriving from their position, whether it's a construction supervisor, ad account supervisor, sales manager, or CEO. This power may be exerted both positively or negatively—as praise or as criticism, for example.

2. Reward Power: Influencing Behavior by Promising or Giving Rewards *Reward power,* **which all managers have, is power that results from managers' authority to reward their subordinates.** Rewards can range from praise to pay raises, from recognition to promotions.

Example: "Talking to people effectively is all about being encouraging," says Andrea Wong, president and CEO of Lifetime Network and Entertainment Services. She tries to use praise to reward positive behavior. "When I have something bad to say to someone, it's always hard because I'm always thinking of the best way to say it."[14]

3. Coercive Power: Influencing Behavior by Threatening or Giving Punishment *Coercive power,* **which all managers have, results from managers' authority to punish their subordinates.** Punishment can range from verbal or written reprimands to demotions to terminations. In some lines of work, fines and suspensions may be used. Coercive power has to be used judiciously, of course, since a manager who is seen as being constantly negative will produce a lot of resentment among employees. But there have been many leaders who have risen to the top of major corporations—such as Disney's Michael Eisner, Miramax's Harvey Weinstein, and Apple's Steve Jobs—who have been abrasive and intimidating.[15]

4. Expert Power: Influencing Behavior Because of One's Expertise *Expert power* **is power resulting from one's specialized information or expertise.** Expertise, or special knowledge, can be mundane, such as knowing the work schedules and assignments of the people who report to you. Or it can be sophisticated, such as having computer or medical knowledge. Secretaries may have expert power because, for example, they have been in a job a long time and know all the necessary contacts. CEOs may have expert power because they have strategic knowledge not shared by many others.

5. Referent Power: Influencing Behavior Because of One's Personal Attraction *Referent power* **is power deriving from one's personal attraction.** As we will see later in this chapter (under the discussion of transformational leadership, Section 14.5), this kind of power characterizes strong, visionary leaders who are able to persuade their followers by dint of their personality, attitudes, or background. Referent power may be associated with managers, but it is more likely to be characteristic of leaders.

Set a Goal, Maintain Intensity: The Man Who Built Zynga, a Tightly Wired Machine

"He has built a machine," says venture capitalist Marc Andreessen. "Google is a tightly wired business machine. Microsoft is a tightly wired business machine. Apple is too. Zynga is very much in the mold of those other companies."[16]

The "he" Andreessen is talking about is Mark Pincus, CEO of San Francisco–based Zynga, the social-gaming company that offers the online hit titles *Farmville*, *CityVille*, and *Draw Something*. Zynga makes money by offering games for free and then charging for virtual items, such as a puppy, horse, or barn in *Farmville*, that are "avidly hoarded by collectors, competitive players, and obsessives," in one description.[17] (Interestingly, perhaps only 1% of Zynga's 232 million active users are responsible for a quarter to a half of the firm's revenues.) Zynga, which went public in 2011 in the biggest initial public offering since Google in 2004, was valued at $6.65 billion in April 2012.

The Fearsome Negotiator.[18]
With a degree in economics (University of Pennsylvania), jobs in banking, and an MBA from Harvard, Pincus moved to San Francisco in 1995 during the dot-com boom. After starting five companies and investing in many more—experience that helped him "hone his negotiating skills and attention to analytical detail," in one account—he started Zynga in 2007 at age 41.

In August 2010, while trying to negotiate a five-year partnership with Facebook, Pincus demanded a face-to-face meeting with Mark Zuckerberg. During the course of three marathon meetings, Pincus convinced the Facebook CEO that adding Zynga's games would help Facebook gain users and revenue. "He is a we're-going-to-make-this-happen-or-else type of person," says former Google CEO Eric Schmidt, who negotiated with Pincus earlier about Google's taking a small stake in Zynga. "He is a fearsome, strong negotiator."[19]

Powering Through.
Pincus, says Zuckerberg, "can deal with the pain of any short-term hit, to power through and get to where he wants to go." One result is that Pincus has frequently clashed with board members and employees at companies he founded. He reportedly alienated some Zynga staffers by pushing them to work long hours and in a few cases even asking some founding team members to return equity (stakes in the company) because their potential rewards didn't match what they were contributing. "Mark didn't get where he is by being a softie," says one former employee.[20]

Leadership. Zynga CEO Mark Pincus.

Looking for Internet Treasure.
What explains this kind of intensity? Perhaps it came about because "I reached the point when I was 28 or 29 and . . . I literally thought my career was washed up. I just thought I had made a series of wrong decisions," Pincus says. "A lot of times, I think, you become an entrepreneur when you feel like you have nothing else to lose." The period of uncertainty began to crystallize for him that "my passion was creating consumer services that would change people's lives. . . . [by developing] Internet treasure—products that people can't remember life before, or they can't imagine life without. . . . That's the cellphone. That's Google. I hope it's Zynga."[21]

Set a Goal First.
From his early experience, Pincus learned that the most important thing is to "know what your goal is, because if you don't . . . , you will definitely never achieve it." At Zynga, the goal is to not only provide users with entertainment but also to enhance the relationships in their lives. "I challenge our product teams that our games should let you meet one new person a day. We are getting there. People are getting married through it. It's a whole new way to date. What I hope is that we create one of those forever brands and experiences like Google, that people look for in their lives."[22]

YOUR CALL

Which of the five sources of leadership power do you think Pincus represents? Do you think you could follow his example?

Leadership & Influence: Using Persuasion to Get Your Way at Work

Steve Harrison, CEO of a career management firm, was escorting Ray, his newly hired chief operating officer, to meet people at a branch office. After greeting the receptionist and starting to lead Ray past her into the interior offices, Harrison felt himself being pulled back. He watched as Ray stuck out his hand, smiled, and said, "Good morning, Melissa, I'm Ray. I'm new here. It's so great to meet you!" He then launched into a dialogue with Melissa, to her obvious delight.

Afterward, Harrison asked Ray, "What was that all about?" "It's called the two-minute schmooze," Ray replied. "Our receptionists meet or talk by phone to more people critical to our company in one day than you or I will ever meet in the course of a year."[23]

Ray would probably be considered a leader because of his ability to *influence* others—to get them to follow his wishes. There are nine tactics for trying to influence others, but some work better than others. In one pair of studies, employees were asked in effect, "How do you get your boss, coworker, or subordinate to do something you want?" The nine answers—ranked from most used to least used tactics—were as follows.[24]

I. Rational Persuasion   Trying to convince someone by using reason, logic, or facts.
　　Example: "You know, all the cutting-edge companies use this approach."

2. Inspirational Appeals   Trying to build enthusiasm or confidence by appealing to others' emotions, ideals, or values.
　　Example: "If we do this as a goodwill gesture, customers will love us."

3. Consultation   Getting others to participate in a decision or change.
　　Example: "Wonder if I could get your thoughts about this matter."

4. Ingratiating Tactics   Acting humble or friendly or making someone feel good or feel important before making a request.
　　Example: "I hate to impose on your time, knowing how busy you are, but you're the only one who can help me."

5. Personal Appeals   Referring to friendship and loyalty when making a request.
　　Example: "We've known each other a long time, and I'm sure I can count on you."

6. Exchange Tactics   Reminding someone of past favors or offering to trade favors.
　　Example: "Since I backed you at last month's meeting, maybe you could help me this time around."

7. Coalition Tactics   Getting others to support your effort to persuade someone.
　　Example: "Everyone in the department thinks this is a great idea."

8. Pressure Tactics   Using demands, threats, or intimidation to gain compliance.
　　Example: "If this doesn't happen, you'd better think about cleaning out your desk."

9. Legitimating Tactics   Basing a request on one's authority or right, organizational rules or policies, or express or implied support from superiors.
　　Example: "This has been green-lighted at the highest levels."

These influence tactics are considered *generic* because they are applied in all directions—up, down, and sideways within the organization. The first five influence tactics are considered "soft" tactics because they are considered friendlier than the last four "hard," or pressure, tactics. As it happens, research shows that of the three possible responses to an influence tactic—enthusiastic commitment, grudging compliance, and outright resistance—commitment is most apt to result when the tactics used are consultation, strong rational persuasion, and inspirational appeals.[25]

Knowing this, do you think you have what it takes to be a leader? To answer this, you need to understand what factors produce people of leadership character. We consider these in the rest of the chapter.

Five Approaches to Leadership

The next five sections describe five principal approaches or perspectives on leadership, which have been refined by research. They are (1) *trait,* (2) *behavioral,* (3) *contingency,* (4) *full-range,* and (5) *three additional. (See Table 14.2.)* ●

table 14.2

FIVE APPROACHES TO LEADERSHIP

1. **Trait approaches**
   - *Kouzes & Posner's five traits*—honest, competent, forward-looking, inspiring, intelligent
   - *Gender studies*—motivating others, fostering communication, producing high-quality work, and so on
   - *Leadership lessons from the GLOBE project*—visionary and inspirational charismatic leaders who are good team builders are best worldwide

2. **Behavioral approaches**
   - *Michigan model*—two leadership styles: job-centered and employee-centered
   - *Ohio State model*—two dimensions: initiating-structure behavior and consideration behavior

3. **Contingency approaches**
   - *Fiedler's contingency model*—task-oriented style and relationship-oriented style—*and three dimensions of control:* leader-member, task structure, position power
   - *House's path–goal revised leadership model*—clarifying paths for subordinates' goals, and employee characteristics and environmental factors that affect leadership behaviors

4. **Full-range approach**
   - *Transactional leadership*—clarify employee roles and tasks, and provide rewards and punishments
   - *Transformational leadership*—transform employees to pursue organizational goals over self-interests, using inspirational motivation, idealized influence, individualized consideration, intellectual stimulation

5. **Three additional perspectives**
   - *Leader–member exchange (LMX) model*—leaders have different sorts of relationships with different subordinates
   - *Greenleaf's servant leadership model*—providing service to others, not oneself
   - *E-Leadership*—using information technology for one-to-one, one-to-many, and between group and collective interactions

Followers—we also describe the role of followers in the leadership process.

14.2 TRAIT APPROACHES: DO LEADERS HAVE DISTINCTIVE PERSONALITY CHARACTERISTICS?

What does it take to be a successful leader?

major question?

THE BIG PICTURE

Trait approaches attempt to identify distinctive characteristics that account for the effectiveness of leaders. We describe (1) the trait perspective expressed by Kouzes and Posner, (2) some results of gender studies, and (3) leadership lessons from the GLOBE project.

Consider a leader dubbed "CEO of the Decade" in 2009 by *Fortune* magazine for 10 years of achievements in the fields of music, movies, and mobile phones, not to mention computing. "Remaking any one business is a career-defining achievement," wrote *Fortune* editor Adam Lashinsky; "four is unheard of."[26]

That leader was, of course, the late Steve Jobs of Apple. Did he have distinctive personality traits that might teach us something about leadership? Perhaps he did. He seemed to embody the traits of (1) dominance, (2) intelligence, (3) self-confidence, (4) high energy, and (5) task-relevant knowledge.

These are the five traits that researcher **Ralph Stogdill** in 1948 concluded were typical of successful leaders.[27] Stogdill is one of many contributors to *trait approaches to leadership,* **which attempt to identify distinctive characteristics that account for the effectiveness of leaders.**[28]

Is Trait Theory Useful?

Traits play a central role in how we perceive leaders, and they ultimately affect leadership effectiveness.[29] On the basis of past studies, we can suggest a list of positive traits that are important for leaders to have, as shown below.[30] *(See Table 14.3.)* If assuming a leadership role interests you, you might wish to cultivate these traits for your future success, using personality tests to evaluate your strengths and weaknesses in preparing (perhaps with the aid of an executive coach) a personal development plan.[31]

General Trait	Specific Characteristics
Task competence	Intelligence, knowledge, problem-solving skills
Interpersonal competence	Ability to communicate and ability to demonstrate caring and empathy
Intuition	
Traits of character	Conscientiousness, discipline, moral reasoning, integrity, honesty
Biophysical traits	Physical fitness, hardiness, energy level
Personal traits	Self-confidence, sociability, self-monitoring, extraversion, self-regulating, self-efficacy

table 14.3

KEY POSITIVE LEADERSHIP TRAITS

Source: Adapted from R. Kreitner and A. Kinicki, *Organizational Behavior,* 10th ed. (New York: McGraw-Hill/Irwin, 2013), p. 469. These traits were identified in B. M. Bass and R. Bass, *The Bass Handbook of Leadership* (New York: The Free Press, 2008), p. 135.

Two ways in which organizations may apply trait theory are as follows:

Use Personality & Trait Assessments Organizations may incorporate personality and trait assessments into their selection and promotion processes (being careful to use valid measures of leadership traits).

Use Management Development Programs To enhance employee leadership traits, organizations such as General Electric and Verizon send targeted employees to management development programs that include management classes, coaching sessions, trait assessments, and the like.[32]

Kouzes & Posner's Research: Is Honesty the Top Leadership Trait?

During the 1980s, **James Kouzes** and **Barry Posner** surveyed more than 20,000 people around the world as to what personal traits they looked for and admired in their superiors.[33] The respondents suggested that a credible leader should have four traits. He or she should be (1) honest, (2) forward looking, (3) inspiring, and (4) competent. These four traits, researchers concluded, constitute a leader's credibility, and the research suggests people want their leaders to be credible and to have a sense of direction.

Although this research does reveal the traits preferred by employees, it has not, however, been able to predict which people might be successful leaders.

Gender Studies: Do Women Have Traits That Make Them Better Leaders?

"High-Paying Careers Top More Young Women's Lists," declared the *USA Today* headline. A 2012 study by Pew Research Center found that 66% of 18- to 34-year-old women say being successful in a high-paying career is "one of the most important things" or "very important" in their lives—surpassing the percentage of young men, 59%, with the same stance.[34] A major reason for this reversal from 1997 (then 56% young women, 58% young men with this attitude) may be that today's generation of females "are more highly skilled and educated, so they can compete in a different way," suggested one of the researchers.[35]

In addition, a New York research firm found that 55% of women and 57% of men aspire to be CEO, challenging the notion that more women aren't at the top because they don't want to be there.[36] Indeed, women have been found to be as equally assertive as men.[37] In fact, it's possible that women may have traits that make them better managers—indeed, better leaders—than men.

The Evidence on Women Executives A number of management studies conducted in the United States for companies ranging from high-tech to manufacturing to consumer services were reviewed by *BusinessWeek*.[38] By and large, the magazine reports, the studies showed that "women executives, when rated by their peers, underlings, and bosses, score higher than their male counterparts on a wide variety of measures—from producing high-quality work to goal-setting to mentoring employees." Researchers accidentally stumbled on these findings about gender differences while compiling hundreds of routine performance evaluations and analyzing the results. In one study of 425 high-level executives, women won higher ratings on 42 of the 52 skills measured.[39]

What are the desirable traits in which women excel?

- Women were found to be better at teamwork and partnering, being more collaborative, seeking less personal glory, being motivated less by self-interest than in what they can do for the company, being more stable, and being less turf conscious. Women were also found to be better at producing quality work, recognizing trends, and generating new ideas and acting on them. Women used a more democratic or participative style than men, who were apt to use a more autocratic and directive style than women.[40]

- Women have been found to display more social leadership, whereas men have been found to display more task leadership.[41]

- Women executives, when rated by their peers, managers, and direct reports, scored higher than their male counterparts on a variety of effectiveness criteria.[42]

The Lack of Women at the Top We mentioned (in Chapter 11) that 56% of 357 global senior executives reported their companies have one or no women among their top executives.[43] At Fortune 500 companies in 2011, females accounted for only 16.4% of corporate-officer positions.[44] Interestingly, companies with the top 10 highest paid female CEOs produce significantly higher dividends than firms with the top 10 highest paid male CEOs—2.98% versus 2.45%, according to one study.[45] So why, then, aren't more women in positions of leadership? Among the possible explanations:

- **Unwillingness to compete or sacrifice.** Though hardworking, many women simply aren't willing to compete as hard as most men are or are not willing to make the required personal sacrifices.[46] As Jamie Gorelick, former vice chair of Fannie Mae but also mother of two children ages 10 and 15, said when declining to be considered for CEO: "I just don't want that pace in my life."[47]

- **Modesty.** Women have a tendency to be overly modest and to give credit to others rather than taking it for themselves, which can undermine opportunities for promotions and raises.[48]

- **Lack of mentor.** Women are less likely than their male counterparts to have access to a supportive mentor.[49]

- **Starting out lower, and more likely to quit.** Perhaps most important, early-career success is pivotal; women MBAs start out at lower levels than men do in their first jobs, putting them at a disadvantage that is hard to overcome. Further, findings from a study of over 475,000 people from 20 corporations revealed that women quit their jobs more than men.[50] Higher quit rates can deprive women from obtaining promotions and experiences needed for career advancement.

Things may be gradually changing, though not as fast as they should. In 2012, there were 17 female CEOs (3.4%) heading the Fortune 500 largest companies and 19 more (3.6%) heading the next largest 500 firms.[51] Females heading firms in the Standard & Poor's 500 index averaged earnings of $14.2 million in their latest fiscal years, 43% more than the male average.[52] Moreover, with more than half of college students being women and with women making up half the workforce, it's possible that the new group rising through middle management could well lead to more than 100 Fortune 500 CEOs in the next 10 years, some believe, up from 36 today.[53]

Leadership Lessons from the GLOBE Project

Project GLOBE (Global Leadership and Organizational Behavior Effectiveness), you'll recall from Chapter 4, is a massive and ongoing attempt to develop an empirically based theory to "describe, understand, and predict the impact of specific cultural variables on leadership and organizational processes and the effectiveness of these processes."[54] Surveying 17,000 middle managers working for 951 organizations across 62 countries, the researchers determined that certain attributes of leadership were universally liked or disliked. *(See Table 14.4.)* Visionary and inspirational *charismatic leaders* (described on p. 462) who are good team builders generally do the best. *Self-centered leaders* seen as loners or face-savers generally receive a poor reception worldwide. ●

table 14.4

LESSONS FROM GLOBE: LEADERSHIP ATTRIBUTES UNIVERSALLY LIKED AND DISLIKED ACROSS 62 NATIONS

Universally Positive Leader Attributes
Trustworthy
Just
Honest
Foresight
Plans ahead
Encouraging
Positive
Dynamic
Motive arouser
Confidence builder
Motivational
Dependable
Intelligent
Decisive
Effective bargainer
Win-win problem solver
Administrative skilled
Communicative
Informed
Coordinator
Team builder
Excellence oriented

Universally Negative Leader Attributes
Loner
Asocial
Noncooperative
Irritable
Nonexplicit
Egocentric
Ruthless
Dictatorial

Source: Excerpted and adapted from P. W. Dorfman, P. J. Hanges, and F. C. Brodbeck, "Leadership and Cultural Variation: The Identification of Culturally Endorsed Leadership Profiles," in R. J. House, P. J. Hanges, M. Javidan, P. W. Dorfman, and V. Gupta eds., *Culture, Leadership and Organizations: The GLOBE Study of 62 Societies* (Thousand Oaks, CA: Sage, 2004), Tables 21.2 and 21.3 , pp. 677–78.

major question? Do effective leaders behave in similar ways?

THE BIG PICTURE
Behavioral leadership approaches try to determine the distinctive styles used by effective leaders. Two models we describe are the University of Michigan model and the Ohio State model.

Maybe what's important to know about leaders is not their *personality traits* but rather their *patterns of behavior* or *leadership styles*. This is the line of thought pursued by those interested in **behavioral leadership approaches, which attempt to determine the distinctive styles used by effective leaders.** By *leadership styles,* we mean the combination of traits, skills, and behaviors that leaders use when interacting with others.

What all models of leadership behavior have in common is the consideration of *task orientation versus people orientation.* Two classic studies came out of the universities of Michigan and Ohio State.

The University of Michigan Leadership Model

In the late 1940s, researchers at the University of Michigan came up with what came to be known as the **University of Michigan Leadership Model.** A team led by **Rensis Likert** began studying the effects of leader behavior on job performance, interviewing numerous managers and subordinates.[55] The investigators identified two forms of leadership styles: *job-centered* and *employee-centered.*

Working on the railroad. What kind of leadership behavior is appropriate for directing these kinds of workers?

Job-Centered Behavior—"I'm Concerned More with the Needs of the Job" In *job-centered behavior,* managers paid more attention to the job and work procedures. Thus, their principal concerns were with achieving production efficiency, keeping costs down, and meeting schedules.

Employee-Centered Behavior—"I'm Concerned More with the Needs of Employees" In *employee-centered behavior,* managers paid more attention to employee satisfaction and making work groups cohesive. By concentrating on subordinates' needs they hoped to build effective work groups with high-performance goals.

The Ohio State Leadership Model

A second approach to leadership research was begun in 1945 at Ohio State University under **Ralph Stogdill** (mentioned in the last section). Hundreds of dimensions of leadership behavior were studied, resulting in what came to be known as the **Ohio State Leadership Model.**[56] From surveys of leadership behavior, two major dimensions of leader behavior were identified, as follows.

Initiating Structure—"What Do I Do to Get the Job Done?" *Initiating structure* is leadership behavior that organizes and defines what group members should be doing. It consists of the efforts the leader makes to get things organized and get the job done. This is much the same as Likert's "job-centered behavior."

Consideration—"What Do I Do to Show Consideration for My Employees?" *Consideration* is leadership behavior that expresses concern for employees by establishing a warm, friendly, supportive climate. This behavior, which resembles Likert's "employee-centered behavior," is sensitive to subordinates' ideas and feelings and establishes mutual trust.

What Is More Important, Leadership Traits or Behaviors? A team of researchers studied this question by analyzing all published studies between 1887 and 2008. Results demonstrated that both leadership traits and behaviors predicted leadership effectiveness criteria, but leader behaviors were more important. These results suggest that it is very important for organizations to train managers in how to effectively exhibit key leadership behaviors.[57]

The late Peter Drucker, the famed management expert, recommended a set of nine behaviors that managers can focus on to improve their leadership behaviors. These are shown below. *(See Table 14.5.)* ●

table 14.5

PETER DRUCKER'S TIPS FOR IMPROVING LEADERSHIP EFFECTIVENESS

Drucker believed practices 1 and 2 provide the knowledge leaders need, 3–6 help leaders convert knowledge into effective action, 7–8 ensure that the whole organization feels responsible and accountable, and 9 should be a managerial rule.

1. Determine what needs to be done.

2. Determine the right thing to do for the welfare of the entire enterprise or organization.

3. Develop action plans that specify desired results, probable restraints, future revisions, check-in points, and implications for how one should spend his or her time.

4. Take responsibility for decisions.

5. Take responsibility for communication action plans and give people the information they need to get the job done.

6. Focus on opportunities rather than problems. Do not sweep problems under the rug, and treat change as an opportunity rather than as a threat.

7. Run productive meetings. Different types of meetings require different forms of preparation and different results. Prepare accordingly.

8. Think and say "we" rather than "I." Consider the needs and opportunities of the organization before thinking of your own opportunities and needs.

9. Listen first, speak last.

Source: Reprinted by permission of *Harvard Business Review.* Recommendations derived from "What Makes an Effective Executive," by P. F. Drucker, June 2004, pp. 58–63. Copyright 2004 by the Harvard Business School Publishing Corporation; all rights reserved.

How might effective leadership vary according to the situation at hand?

THE BIG PICTURE

Effective leadership behavior depends on the situation at hand, say believers in two contingency approaches: Fiedler's contingency leadership model and House's path–goal leadership model.

Perhaps leadership is not characterized by universally important traits or behaviors. Perhaps there is no one best style that will work in all situations. This is the point of view of proponents of the ***contingency approach* to leadership, who believe that effective leadership behavior depends on the situation at hand.** That is, as situations change, different styles become appropriate.

Let's consider two contingency approaches: (1) the *contingency leadership model* by Fiedler and (2) the *path–goal leadership model* by House.

1. The Contingency Leadership Model: Fiedler's Approach

The oldest model of the contingency approach to leadership was developed by **Fred Fiedler** and his associates in 1951.[58] **The *contingency leadership model* determines if a leader's style is (1) task oriented or (2) relationship oriented and if that style is effective for the situation at hand.** Fiedler's work was based on 80 studies conducted over 30 years.

Two Leadership Orientations: Tasks Versus Relationships Are you task oriented or relationship oriented? That is, are you more concerned with task accomplishment or with people?

To find out, you or your employees would fill out a questionnaire (known as the least preferred coworker, or LPC, scale), in which you think of the coworker you least enjoyed working with and rate him or her according to an eight-point scale of 16 pairs of opposite characteristics (such as friendly/unfriendly, tense/relaxed, efficient/inefficient). The higher the score, the more the relationship oriented the respondent; the lower the score, the more task oriented.

Cone head. Do successful entrepreneurs or small-business managers need to be task oriented, relationship oriented, or both? What style of leadership model would best suit a small ice cream store in which employees work without the owner always being present?

The Three Dimensions of Situational Control
Once the leadership orientation is known, then you determine *situational control*—how much control and influence a leader has in the immediate work environment.

There are three dimensions of situational control: *leader-member relations, task structure,* and *position power.*

1. **Leader-member relations—"Do my subordinates accept me as a leader?"** This dimension, the most important component of situational control, reflects the extent to which a leader has or doesn't have the support, loyalty, and trust of the work group.

2. **Task structure—"Do my subordinates perform unambiguous, easily understood tasks?"** This dimension refers to the extent to which tasks are routine, unambiguous, and easily understood. The more structured the jobs, the more influence a leader has.

3. **Position power—"Do I have power to reward and punish?"** This dimension refers to how much power a leader has to make work assignments and reward and punish. More power equals more control and influence.

For each dimension, the amount of control can be *high*—the leader's decisions will produce predictable results because he or she has the ability to influence work outcomes. Or it can be *low*—he or she doesn't have that kind of predictability or influence. By combining the three different dimensions with different high/low ratings, we have eight different leadership situations. These are represented in the diagram below. *(See Figure 14.1.)*

figure 14.1

REPRESENTATION
OF FIEDLER'S
CONTINGENCY MODEL

Situational Control	High-Control Situations			Moderate-Control Situations				Low-Control Situations
Leader-member relations	Good	Good	Good	Good	Poor	Poor	Poor	Poor
Task structure	High	High	Low	Low	High	High	Low	Low
Position power	Strong	Weak	Strong	Weak	Strong	Weak	Strong	Weak
Situation	I	II	III	IV	V	VI	VII	VIII

Optimal Leadership Style	Task-Motivated Leadership	Relationship-Motivated Leadership	Task-Motivated Leadership

Source: Adapted from F.E. Fiedler, "Situational Control and a Dynamic Theory of Leadership," in *Managerial Control and Organizational Democracy*, ed B. King, S. Streufert and F. E. Fiedler, John Wiley & Sons, Inc., p. 114. Reprinted from R. Kreitner and A. Kinciki, *Organizational Behavior* 9E, 2010, p. 478.

Which Style Is Most Effective?   Neither leadership style is effective all the time, Fiedler's research concludes, although each is right in certain situations.

■ **When task-oriented style is best.** The task-oriented style works best in either *high-control* or *low-control* situations.

Example of *high-control* situation (leader decisions produce predictable results because he or she can influence work outcomes): Suppose you were supervising parking-control officers ticketing cars parked illegally in expired meter zones, bus zones, and the like. You have (1) high leader-member relations because your subordinates are highly supportive of you and (2) high task structure because their jobs are clearly defined. (3) You have high position control because you have complete authority to evaluate their performance and dole out punishment and rewards. Thus, a task-oriented style would be best.

Example of *low-control* situation (leader decisions can't produce predictable results because he or she can't really influence outcomes): Suppose you were a high school principal trying to clean up graffiti on your private-school campus, helped only by students you can find after school. You might have

(1) low leader-member relations because many people might not see the need for the goal. (2) The task structure might also be low because people might see many different ways to achieve the goal. And (3) your position power would be low because the committee is voluntary and people are free to leave. In this low-control situation, a task-oriented style would also be best.

■ **When relationship-oriented style is best.** The relationship-oriented style works best in situations of *moderate control.*

Example: Suppose you were working in a government job supervising a group of firefighters fighting wildfires. You might have (1) low leader-member relations if you were promoted over others in the group but (2) high task structure, because the job is fairly well defined. (3) You might have low position power, because the rigidity of the civil-service job prohibits you from doing much in the way of rewarding and punishing. Thus, in this moderate-control situation, relationship-oriented leadership would be most effective.

What do you do if your leadership orientation does not match the situation? Then, says Fiedler, it's better to try to move leaders into suitable situations rather than try to alter their personalities to fit the situations.[59]

2. The Path–Goal Leadership Model: House's Approach

A second contingency approach, advanced by **Robert House** in the 1970s and revised by him in 1996, is the ***path–goal leadership model,* which holds that the effective leader makes available to followers desirable rewards in the workplace and increases their motivation by clarifying the *paths,* or behavior, that will help them achieve those *goals* and providing them with support.** A successful leader thus helps followers by tying meaningful rewards to goal accomplishment, reducing barriers, and providing support, so as to increase "the number and kinds of personal payoffs to subordinates for work-goal attainment."[60]

Numerous studies testing various predictions from House's original path–goal theory provided mixed results.[61] As a consequence, he proposed a new model, a graphical version of which is, shown below. *(See Figure 14.2.)*

figure 14.2

GENERAL
REPRESENTATION
OF HOUSE'S REVISED
PATH–GOAL THEORY

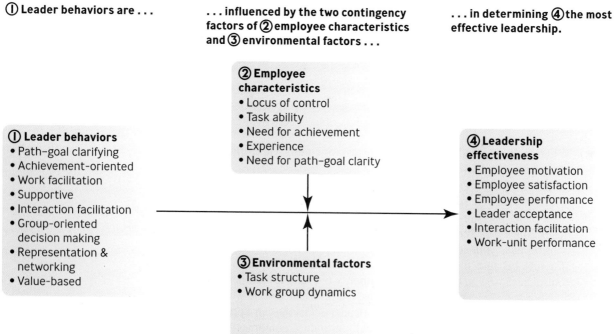

① **Leader behaviors are . . .**

. . . influenced by the two contingency factors of ② employee characteristics and ③ environmental factors . . .

. . . in determining ④ the most effective leadership.

② **Employee characteristics**
• Locus of control
• Task ability
• Need for achievement
• Experience
• Need for path–goal clarity

① **Leader behaviors**
• Path–goal clarifying
• Achievement-oriented
• Work facilitation
• Supportive
• Interaction facilitation
• Group-oriented decision making
• Representation & networking
• Value-based

④ **Leadership effectiveness**
• Employee motivation
• Employee satisfaction
• Employee performance
• Leader acceptance
• Interaction facilitation
• Work-unit performance

③ **Environmental factors**
• Task structure
• Work group dynamics

What Determines Leadership Effectiveness: Employee Characteristics & Environmental Factors Affect Leader Behavior

As the drawing indicates, two contingency factors, or variables—*employee characteristics* and *environmental factors*—cause some *leadership behaviors* to be more effective than others.

- **Employee characteristics.** Five employee characteristics are locus of control (described in Chapter 11), task ability, need for achievement, experience, and need for path–goal clarity.

- **Environmental factors.** Two environmental factors are task structure (independent versus interdependent tasks) and work group dynamics.

- **Leader behaviors.** Originally House proposed that there were four leader behaviors, or leadership styles—*directive* ("Here's what's expected of you and here's how to do it"), *supportive* ("I want things to be pleasant, since everyone's about equal here"), *participative* ("I want your suggestions in order to help me make decisions"), and *achievement-oriented* ("I'm confident you can accomplish the following great things"). The revised theory expands the number of leader behaviors from four to eight. *(See Table 14.6.)*

table 14.6

EIGHT LEADERSHIP STYLES OF THE REVISED PATH–GOAL THEORY

Style of Leader Behaviors	Description of Behavior Toward Employees
1. Path–goal clarifying ("Here's what's expected of you and here's how to do it.")	Clarify performance goals. Provide guidance on how employees can complete tasks. Clarify performance standards and expectations. Use positive and negative rewards contingent on performance.
2. Achievement oriented ("I'm confident you can accomplish the following great things.")	Set challenging goals. Emphasize excellence. Demonstrate confidence in employee abilities.
3. Work facilitation ("Here's the goal, and here's what I can do to help you achieve it.")	Plan, schedule, organize, and coordinate work. Provide mentoring, coaching, counseling, and feedback to assist employees in developing their skills. Eliminate roadblocks. Provide resources. Empower employees to take actions and make decisions.
4. Supportive ("I want things to be pleasant, since everyone's about equal here.")	Treat as equals. Show concern for well-being and needs. Be friendly and approachable.
5. Interaction facilitation ("Let's see how we can all work together to accomplish our goals.")	Emphasize collaboration and teamwork. Encourage close employee relationships and sharing of minority opinions. Facilitate communication, resolve disputes.
6. Group-oriented decision making ("I want your suggestions in order to help me make decisions.")	Pose problems rather than solutions to work group. Encourage members to participate in decision making. Provide necessary information to the group for analysis. Involve knowledgeable employees in decision making.
7. Representation & networking ("I've got a great bunch of people working for me whom you'll probably want to meet.")	Present work group in positive light to others. Maintain positive relationships with influential others. Participate in organization-wide social functions and ceremonies. Do unconditional favors for others.
8. Value-based ("We're destined to accomplish great things.")	Establish a vision, display passion for it, and support its accomplishment. Communicate high performance expectations and confidence in others' abilities to meet their goals. Give frequent positive feedback. Demonstrate self-confidence.

Source: Adapted from R. J. House, "Path–Goal Theory of Leadership: Lessons, Legacy, and a Reformulated Theory," *Leadership Quarterly,* Autumn 1996, pp. 323–52.

Thus, for example, employees with an internal locus of control are more likely to prefer achievement-oriented leadership or group-oriented decision-making (formerly participative) leadership because they believe they have control over the work environment. The same is true for employees with high task ability and experience.

Employees with an external locus of control, however, tend to view the environment as uncontrollable, so they prefer the structure provided by supportive or path–goal clarifying (formerly directive) leadership. The same is probably true of inexperienced employees.

Besides expanding the styles of leader behavior from four to eight, House's revision of his theory also puts more emphasis on the need for leaders to foster intrinsic motivation through empowerment. Finally, his revised theory stresses the concept of shared leadership, the idea that employees do not have to be supervisors or managers to engage in leader behavior but rather may share leadership among all employees of the organization.

Does the Revised Path–Goal Theory Work?

There have not been enough direct tests of House's revised path–goal theory using appropriate research methods and statistical procedures to draw overall conclusions. Research on transformational leadership, however, which is discussed in Section 14.5, is supportive of the revised model.[62]

Although further research is needed on the new model, it offers three important implications for managers:[63]

1. *Use more than one leadership style.* Effective leaders possess and use more than one style of leadership. Thus, you are encouraged to study the eight styles offered in path–goal theory so that you can try new leader behaviors when a situation calls for them.

Co-leaders. Seth Goldstein (left) is chair and Billy Chasen is CEO of Turntable. fm, a social media website they co-founded in early 2011 that allows users to interactively share music. Which of the eight path–goal leadership styles would you expect to find dominating this organization?

2. ***Help employees achieve their goals.*** Leaders should guide and coach employees in achieving their goals by clarifying the path and removing obstacles to accomplishing them.

3. ***Modify leadership style to fit employee and task characteristics.*** A small set of employee characteristics (ability, experience, and need for independence) and environmental factors (task characteristics of autonomy, variety, and significance) are relevant contingency factors, and managers should modify their leadership style to fit them.

Applying Situational Theories: Five Steps

Is there a general strategy that managers can use to apply situational theories across many situations? One team of researchers thinks so. Their approach contains five steps, as follows.[64]

Step 1: Identify Important Outcomes: "What Goals Am I Trying to Achieve?" First, the manager must determine the goals he or she is trying to achieve for a specific point in time.

Examples: For a coach, the goals might be "To win" or "Avoid injury to key players." For a sales manager, they might be "Increase sales 10%" or "Decrease customer complaints."

Step 2: Identify Relevant Employee Leadership Behaviors: "What Management Characteristics Are Best?" Next managers need to identify which specific behaviors may be appropriate for the situation.

Examples: Relying on the list in Table 14.6 on p. 457, a coach might prefer to stress achievement-oriented behaviors, which emphasize challenging goals and excellence. A sales manager might consider which work-facilitation and supportive behaviors from that list are best for his or her sales team.

Step 3: Identify Situational Conditions: "What Particular Events Are Altering the Situation?" Fiedler and House both identify potential contingency factors to be considered, but there may also be other practical considerations.

Examples: An injured star quarterback may force a coach to alter the strategy for a game. A virtual sales force spread around the world may affect the kind of leadership required of a sales manager.

Step 4: Match Leadership to the Conditions at Hand: "How Should I Manage When There Are Multiple Conditions?" If there are too many possible situational conditions, the research may not be able to provide conclusive recommendations. Thus, managers will need to rely on their knowledge of organizational behavior to determine which leadership behavior is best for the situation at hand.

Examples: Referring to Table 14.6, a coach with an injured star quarterback might decide to boost team confidence by drawing on supportive and values-based behavior. A sales manager in charge of a virtual sales force might decide to avoid directive leadership and use empowering leadership plus work-facilitation behaviors.

Step 5: Determine How to Make the Match: "Change the Manager or Change the Manager's Behavior?" Implementing the decisions reached in Step 4, a manager can take either a contingency theory approach or a House path–goal theory approach. That is, the person in the leadership role can be changed or the manager can change his or her behavior.

Examples: It is not possible for the coach to be changed for a championship game, so the coach will have to change his or her behavior. If the sales manager is considered too directive and doesn't like to empower others, he or she might be replaced or, alternatively, change his or her behavior. ●

major question ?   What does it take to truly inspire people to perform beyond their normal levels?

THE BIG PICTURE

Full-range leadership describes leadership along a range of styles, with the most effective being transactional/transformational leaders. Four key behaviors of transformational leaders in affecting employees are they inspire motivation, inspire trust, encourage excellence, and stimulate them intellectually.

We have considered the major traditional approaches to understanding leadership—the trait, behavioral, and contingency approaches. But newer approaches seem to offer something more by trying to determine what factors inspire and motivate people to perform beyond their normal levels.

One recent approach proposed by **Bernard Bass and Bruce Avolio,** known as *full-range leadership,* **suggests that leadership behavior varies along a full range of leadership styles, from take-no-responsibility (*laissez-faire*) "leadership" at one extreme, through transactional leadership, to transformational leadership at the other extreme.**[65] Not taking responsibility can hardly be considered leadership (although it often seems to be manifested by CEOs whose companies got in trouble, as when they say "I had no idea about the criminal behavior of my subordinates"). Transactional and transformational leadership behaviors, however, are both positive aspects of being a good leader.[66]

Transactional Versus Transformational Leaders

Some people are able to be both a transactional and a transformational leader. Let us consider the differences.

Transactional Leadership   As a manager, your power stems from your ability to provide rewards (and threaten reprimands) in exchange for your subordinates' doing the work. When you do this, you are performing *transactional leadership,* **focusing on clarifying employees' roles and task requirements and providing rewards and punishments contingent on performance.** Transactional leadership also encompasses the fundamental managerial activities of setting goals and monitoring progress toward their achievement.[67]

Transactional leader? Apple's successor as CEO to the late Steve Jobs is Tim Cook, who does not have Jobs's dynamism and charisma but is considered good on problem solving and follow-through.

When Apple's Steve Jobs resigned as CEO in August 2011 shortly before his death, the world mourned the loss of a visionary leader.[68] His successor, Tim Cook, on the other hand, was celebrated as "a logistics whiz who had adroitly shepherded the company during Jobs' medical leaves."[69] Other writers described him as "the former chief operating officer known as an operations genius" and lauded his success at helping lock down precious electronic components that let Apple escape unscathed during the supply-chain disruptions created by the 2011 tsunami in Japan.[70] So, is Cook simply a competent caretaker of the machine Jobs created, or will he become the inspirational, visionary leader some observers think Apple needs?[71]

We shouldn't think of a transactional leader as being a mediocre leader—indeed, competent transactional leaders are badly needed. But transactional leaders are best in stable situations. What's needed in rapidly changing situations, as is often the case in many organizations today, is a transformational leader.

Transformational Leadership *Transformational leadership* **transforms employees to pursue organizational goals over self-interests.** Transformational leaders, in one description, "engender trust, seek to develop leadership in others, exhibit self-sacrifice, and serve as moral agents, focusing themselves and followers on objectives that transcend the more immediate needs of the work group."[72] Whereas transactional leaders try to get people to do *ordinary* things, transformational leaders encourage their people to do *exceptional* things—significantly higher levels of intrinsic motivation, trust, commitment, and loyalty—that can produce significant organizational change and results.

Transformational leaders are influenced by two factors:

1. **Individual characteristics.** The personalities of such leaders tend to be more extroverted, agreeable, proactive, and open to change than nontransformational leaders. (Female leaders tend to use transformational leadership more than male leaders do.)[73]

2. **Organizational culture.** Adaptive, flexible organizational cultures are more likely than are rigid, bureaucratic cultures to foster transformational leadership.

The Best Leaders Are Both Transactional & Transformational

It's important to note that transactional leadership is an essential *prerequisite* to effective leadership, and the best leaders learn to display both transactional and transformational styles of leadership to some degree. Indeed, research suggests that transformational leadership leads to superior performance when it "augments" or adds to transactional leadership.[74]

EXAMPLE

The Superior Performance of Both a Transactional & Transformational Leader: PepsiCo's CEO Indra Nooyi

For PepsiCo CEO Nooyi, one of her "most stunning talents is the art of suasian," says one writer. "She can rouse an audience and rally them around something as mind-numbing as a new companywide software installation. Her new motto, 'Performance With Purpose,' is both a means of 'herding the organization' and of presenting PepsiCo globally."[75]

The Nooyi Vision. Most important is her vision for moving the company beyond what it calls "fun for you foods" (soda pop and salty snacks) and into "better for you" foods, and into tackling issues like obesity and sustainability.[76]

Long Term: Healthier Food. Nooyi, says Howard Schultz, CEO of Starbucks, which has a joint-venture partnership with PepsiCo, was "way ahead of her competitors in moving the company toward healthier products. She pushed for PepsiCo to buy Quaker Oats and Tropicana,

and . . . PepsiCo removed trans fats from its products well before most other companies did."[77]

Short Term: Stay Profitable. However, in remaking PepsiCo over the long term so that it sells less fat and sugar, Nooyi has also has run up against the other goal for a public company—short-term results, or "maximizing shareholder value," where the company fell behind in 2011 and early 2012. Even so, Nooyi must be careful not to stray too far back to being driven by short-term results, especially at a time when soft drink sales have been in a long-term slide.[78]

YOUR CALL

Do you think you might have what it takes to be both a transactional and transformational leader? What's the evidence?

Four Key Behaviors of Transformational Leaders

Whereas transactional leaders are dispassionate, transformational leaders excite passion, inspiring and empowering people to look beyond their own interests to the interests of the organization. They appeal to their followers' self-concepts—their values and personal identity—to create changes in their goals, values, needs, beliefs, and aspirations.

Transformational leaders have four key kinds of behavior that affect followers.[79]

1. Inspirational Motivation: "Let Me Share a Vision That Transcends Us All"
Transformational leaders have *charisma* ("kar-*riz*-muh"), a form of interpersonal attraction that inspires acceptance and support. At one time, *charismatic leadership*—which was assumed to be an individual inspirational and motivational characteristic of particular leaders,* much like other trait-theory characteristics—was viewed as a category of its own, but now it is considered part of transformational leadership.[80] Someone with charisma, then, is presumed to be more able to persuade and influence people than someone without charisma.[81]

A transformational leader inspires motivation by offering an agenda, a grand design, an ultimate goal—in short, a *vision,* "a realistic, credible, attractive future" for the organization, as leadership expert Burt Nanus calls it. The right vision unleashes human potential, says Nanus, because it serves as a beacon of hope and common purpose. It does so by attracting commitment, energizing workers, creating meaning in their lives, establishing a standard of excellence, promoting high ideals, and bridging the divide between the organization's problems and its goals and aspirations.[82]

Examples: Civil rights leader Martin Luther King Jr. had a vision—a "dream," as he put it—of racial equality. Candy Lightner, founder of Mothers Against Drunk Driving, had a vision of getting rid of alcohol-related car crashes. Apple Computer's Steve Jobs had a vision of developing an "insanely great" desktop computer. Indra Nooyi wants to develop healthier foods, while still making a profit. "Companies today are bigger than many economies," she says. "If companies don't do [responsible] things, who is going to?"[83]

2. Idealized Influence: "We Are Here to Do the Right Thing"
Transformational leaders are able to inspire trust in their followers because they express their integrity by being consistent, single-minded, and persistent in pursuit of their goal. Not only do they display high ethical standards and act as models of desirable values, but they are also able to make sacrifices for the good of the group.[84]

Example: Nooyi's goal of reinventing PepsiCo's product line to concentrate on more nutritional drinks and snacks (and double revenue to $30 billion by 2020) is ambitious, but it actually is in accord with the times. Americans are paying more attention to healthy eating, especially because of the U.S. obesity problem, and more consumers—and companies—are focusing on corporate responsibility and issues of greenness and sustainability.[85]

3. Individualized Consideration: "You Have the Opportunity Here to Grow & Excel"
Transformational leaders don't just express concern for subordinates' well-being. They actively encourage them to grow and to excel by giving them challenging work, more responsibility, empowerment, and one-on-one mentoring.

Example: When Indra Nooyi was chosen over her friend Mike White to lead PepsiCo, she went to great lengths to try to keep him on. "I treat Mike as my partner," she said. "He could easily have been CEO." At

Sir Branson. One of today's most flamboyant businessmen, Britain's Richard Branson is shown here announcing new service for his Virgin Atlantic airline. Branson left school at 16 to start a 1960s counterculture magazine. By 2006, he was heading a $5 billion-plus empire—the Virgin Group—that includes airlines, entertainment companies, car dealerships, railroads, bridal gowns, soft drinks, financial services, and a space tourism company. Knighted in 2000—which entitles him to be called "Sir"—Branson, who is dyslexic, says he is not for scrutinizing spreadsheets and plotting strategies based on estimates of market share. "In the end," he says, "it is your own gut and your own experience of running businesses." Do you think charismatic business leaders like Sir Branson are able to be more successful than more conventional and conservative managers?

meetings, she always made sure he was seated at her right.[86] (Even so, in 2010 he left to become CEO of DirectTV.)[87]

4. Intellectual Stimulation: "Let Me Describe the Great Challenges We Can Conquer Together"   These leaders are gifted at communicating the organization's strengths, weaknesses, opportunities, and threats so that subordinates develop a new sense of purpose. Employees become less apt to view problems as insurmountable or "that's not my department." Instead they learn to view them as personal challenges that they are responsible for overcoming, to question the status quo, and to seek creative solutions.

Example: Nooyi seeks to have "a positive impact on the world," as she puts it. However, in 2012, with shareholders complaining about PepsiCo's slipping share price, she had to pull back somewhat from emphasizing nutritious products to boosting the old Pepsi brand. She compared the change to a racecar taking a pit stop as the company sought to regain momentum in its soft drink business. Still, as one commentator pointed out, "She needs to soothe investors, but she shouldn't surrender to them." He endorsed Nooyi's moves to achieve long-term gains—"that is, if Nooyi can fend off those looking for the financial equivalent of a sugar rush."[88]

Implications of Transformational Leadership for Managers

The research shows that transformational leadership yields several positive results. For example, it is positively associated with (1) measures of organizational effectiveness;[89] (2) measures of leadership effectiveness and employee job satisfaction;[90] (3) more employee identification with their leaders and with their immediate work groups;[91] (4) commitment to organizational change;[92] and (5) higher levels of intrinsic motivation, group cohesion, work engagement, setting of goals consistent with those of the leader, and proactive behavior.[93]

Besides the fact that, as we mentioned, the best leaders are *both* transactional and transformational, there are three important implications of transformational leadership for managers, as follows.

1. It Can Improve Results for Both Individuals & Groups   You can use the four types of transformational behavior just described to improve results for individuals—such as job satisfaction, organizational commitment, and performance. You can also use them to improve outcomes for groups—an important matter in today's organization, where people tend not to work in isolation but in collaboration with others.

2. It Can Be Used to Train Employees at Any Level   Not just top managers but employees at any level can be trained to be more transactional and transformational.[94] This kind of leadership training among employees should be based on an overall corporate philosophy that constitutes the foundation of leadership development.

3. It Requires Ethical Leaders   For a long time, top managers were assumed to be ethical. But in recent years, that notion has been disabused by news stories about scurrilous leaders ranging from the CEOs of Enron to pyramid schemer Bernard Madoff to failed commercial bankers paying themselves huge bonuses even as they accepted taxpayer bailouts and resisted regulation.[95] With such high-profile revelations, the need for ethical leadership has become more apparent. Without honesty and trust, even transformational leaders lose credibility—not only with employees but also with investors, customers, and the public.[96]

To better ensure positive results from transformational leadership, top managers should follow the practices shown at right. *(See Table 14.7.)* ●

table 14.7

THE ETHICAL THINGS TOP MANAGERS SHOULD DO TO BE EFFECTIVE TRANSFORMATIONAL LEADERS

- **Employ a code of ethics.** The company should create and enforce a clearly stated code of ethics.

- **Choose the right people.** Recruit, select, and promote people who display ethical behavior.

- **Make performance expectations reflect employee treatment.** Develop performance expectations around the treatment of employees; these expectations can be assessed in the performance-appraisal process.

- **Emphasize value of diversity.** Train employees to value diversity.

- **Reward high moral conduct.** Identify, reward, and publicly praise employees who exemplify high moral conduct.

Source: These recommendations were derived from J. M. Howell and B. J. Avolio, "The Ethics of Charismatic Leadership: Submission or Liberation?" *The Executive,* May 1992, pp. 43–54.

If there are many ways to be a leader, which one would describe me best?

THE BIG PICTURE

Three other kinds of leadership are the *leader–member exchange model*, which emphasizes that leaders have different sorts of relationships with different subordinates; *servant leadership*, in which leaders provide service to employees and the organization; and *e-leadership*, which involves leader interactions with others via information technology. A fourth perspective is the role of followers in the leadership process.

Three additional kinds of leadership deserve discussion: (1) *leader–member exchange (LMX) model of leadership*, (2) *servant leadership*, and (3) *e-leadership*. We also consider (4) the role of *followers*.

Leader–Member Exchange (LMX) Leadership: Having Different Relationships with Different Subordinates

Proposed by **George Graen and Fred Dansereau, the *leader–member exchange (LMX) model of leadership* emphasizes that leaders have different sorts of relationships with different subordinates.**[97] Unlike other models we've described, which focus on the behaviors or traits of leaders or followers, the LMX model looks at the quality of relationships between managers and subordinates. Also, unlike other models, which presuppose stable relationships between leaders and followers, the LMX model assumes each manager–subordinate relationship is unique (what behavioral scientists call a "vertical dyad").

In-Group Exchange Versus Out-Group Exchange The unique relationship, which supposedly results from the leader's attempt to delegate and assign work roles, can produce two types of leader–member exchange interactions.[98]

- **In-group exchange: trust and respect.** In the *in-group exchange,* the relationship between leader and follower becomes a partnership characterized by mutual trust, respect and liking, and a sense of common fates. Subordinates may receive special assignments and may also receive special privileges.

- **Out-group exchange: lack of trust and respect.** In the *out-group exchange,* leaders are characterized as overseers who fail to create a sense of mutual trust, respect, or common fate. Subordinates receive less of the manager's time and attention than those in in-group exchange relationships.

Is the LMX Model Useful? It is not clear why a leader selects particular subordinates to be part of the in-group, but presumably the choice is made for reasons of compatibility and competence. Certainly, however, a positive (that is, in-group) leader–member exchange is positively associated with goal commitment, trust between managers and employees, work climate, satisfaction with leadership, and—important to any employer—job performance and job satisfaction.[99] There is also a moderately strong positive relationship between LMX and organizational citizenship behaviors.[100]

Servant Leadership: Meeting the Goals of Followers & the Organization, Not of Oneself

The term *servant leadership,* coined in 1970 by **Robert Greenleaf,** reflects not only his onetime background as a management researcher for AT&T but also his views as a lifelong philosopher and devout Quaker.[101] ***Servant leadership* focuses on providing increased service to others—meeting the goals of both followers and the organization—rather than to oneself.**

Servant leadership is not a quick-fix approach to leadership. Rather, it is a long-term, transformational approach to life and work. Ten characteristics of the servant leader are shown below. *(See Table 14.8.)* One can hardly go wrong by trying to adopt these characteristics.

1. Focus on listening.
2. Ability to empathize with others' feelings.
3. Focus on healing suffering.
4. Self-awareness of strengths and weaknesses.
5. Use of persuasion rather than positional authority to influence others.
6. Broad-based conceptual thinking.
7. Ability to foresee future outcomes.
8. Belief they are stewards of their employees and resources.
9. Commitment to the growth of people.
10. Drive to build community within and outside the organization.

table 14.8

TEN CHARACTERISTICS OF THE SERVANT LEADER

Source: From L. C. Spears, "Introduction: Servant-Leadership and the Greenleaf Legacy," in L. C. Spears, ed., *Reflections on Leadership: How Robert K. Greenleaf's Theory of Servant-Leadership Influenced Today's Top Management,* 1994, pp. 1–14. Reprinted with permission of John Wiley & Sons, Inc.

EXAMPLE

Servant Leadership: Leaders Who Work for the Led

Who are some famous servant leaders?

A Covenant with Customers. John Donahoe, CEO of eBay, thinks of customers first, and employees second. He tries his best to deliver what customers want. For example, reports one article, "on trips around the world he takes along a Flip video camera and films interviews with eBay sellers to share their opinions with his staff. He has even tied managers' compensation to customer loyalty, measured through regular surveys."[102]

A Covenant with Employees. Starbucks CEO Howard Schultz is also cited as being one of the foremost practitioners of servant-style leadership. Schultz has made sure his employees have health insurance and work in a positive environment, and as a result Starbucks has a strong brand following.[103] Max De Pree, former chairman of furniture maker Herman Miller Inc., promoted a "covenant" with his employees. Leaders, he wrote, should give employees "space so that we can both give and receive such beautiful things as ideas, openness, dignity, joy, healing, and inclusion."[104]

YOUR CALL

Understandably, servant leadership is popular with employees. Can you think of situations in which this kind of leadership role would *not* be appropriate?

E-Leadership: Managing for Global Networks

The Internet and other forms of advanced information technology have led to new possible ways for interacting within and between organizations (e-business) and with customers and suppliers (e-commerce). Leadership within the context of this electronic technology, called *e-leadership,* **can involve one-to-one, one-to-many, within-group and between-group, and collective interactions via information technology.**[105] E-leadership means having to deal with quite a number of responsibilities, such as developing business opportunities through cooperative relationships, restructuring a company into global networks, decentralizing the company's organization, and energizing the staff.[106]

E-leaders, says one writer, "have a global mind-set that recognizes that the Internet is opening new markets and recharging existing ones. They don't bother fighting mere battles with competitors because they're too busy creating businesses that will surround and destroy them."[107] Harvard Business School professor D. Quinn Mills, author of *E-Leadership,* suggests that individual companies will be replaced by much broader global networks that a single CEO will not be able to manage. Thus, while 20th-century management emphasized competition, he says, future organizations will run on knowledge sharing and open exchange.[108]

Followers: What Do They Want, How Can They Help?

Is the quality of leadership dependent on the qualities of the followers being led? So it seems. Leaders and followers need each other, and the quality of the relationship determines how we behave as followers.[109]

What Do Followers Want in Their Leaders?   Research shows that followers seek and admire leaders who create feelings of . . .

- **Significance.** Such leaders make followers feel that what they do at work is important and meaningful.
- **Community.** These leaders create a sense of unity that encourages followers to treat others with respect and to work together in pursuit of organizational goals.
- **Excitement.** The leaders make people feel energetic and engaged at work.[110]

What Do Leaders Want in Their Followers?   Followers vary, of course, in their level of compliance with a leader, with *helpers* (most compliant), showing deference to their leaders, *independents* (less compliant) distancing themselves, and *rebels* (least compliant) showing divergence.[111]

Leaders clearly benefit from having helpers (and, to some extent, independents). They want followers who are productive, reliable, honest, cooperative, proactive, and flexible. They do not want followers who are reluctant to take the lead on projects, fail to generate ideas, are unwilling to collaborate, withhold information, provide inaccurate feedback, or hide the truth.[112]

We give some suggestions on how to be a better follower—and enhance your own career prospects—in the Practical Action box on the opposite page. ●

How to Be a Great Follower: Benefiting Your Boss—& Yourself

"We degrade the very idea of followers—lemmings!—yet the world needs people who can follow intelligently," says Dress for Success founder Nancy Lublin. "The key word is 'intelligently.' Good followers ask good questions. They probe their leaders. They crunch the numbers to ensure that their visionary boss's gorgeous plans actually work."[113]

How do you become an intelligent follower? Here are four suggested steps:[114]

1. Learn About Your Boss

It's critical you understand your boss—interpersonal style, leadership style, pressures, goals, expectations. and strengths and weaknesses. To discover these, you might try asking him or her some of the following questions.[115]

1. How can I help you?
2. How do you want me to communicate with you— e-mail, phone, in person?
3. When do you like to be approached with questions, and are some situations (such as social occasions) off-limits?
4. What is your approach toward giving feedback?
5. Are there attitudes or behaviors you won't tolerate?
6. What is your most effective way of working?

2. Learn About Yourself

Do some self-analysis. Make an attempt to understand your own needs, expectations, goals, style, and strengths and weaknesses.

3. Analyze Your Differences

Does your boss expect you to read his or her mind, run crisply organized meetings, perform marvelously at small talk, and work late hours—whereas none of these characteristics apply to you? Do a "gap analysis" to see where the two of you differ.

4. Try to Adjust to the Boss's Style, While Building on Your Mutual Strengths

Naturally you will have to adapt your work style to the boss's style rather than the other way around (after all, he or she *is* the boss). But, based on your analysis in step 3, you're in a position to see how your strengths can help cover your boss's weaknesses. For instance, if your manager is pushed for time, as most managers are, and so tends to be a bit scattered, then if you're an organized type you can help by preparing well-thought-out agendas for meetings. You can also be respectful of the boss's time when you drop in to have a question answered.

Although it's always in your and the leader's best interest if you become an "intelligent follower," we recognize that sometimes the two of you may differ so completely in habits, dislikes, and so on that you may simply have to look for opportunities outside your present work situation.

Key Terms Used in This Chapter

behavioral leadership approaches 452

charisma 462

charismatic leadership 462

coercive power 445

contingency approach 454

contingency leadership model 454

e-leadership 466

expert power 445

full-range leadership 460

leader–member exchange (LMX) model of leadership 464

leadership 442

legitimate power 445

managerial leadership 442

path–goal leadership model 456

personalized power 445

referent power 445

reward power 445

servant leaders 465

socialized power 445

trait approaches to leadership 449

transactional leadership 460

transformational leadership 461

14.1 The Nature of Leadership: Wielding Influence

Leadership is the ability to influence employees to voluntarily pursue organizational goals. Being a manager and being a leader are not the same. Management is about coping with complexity, whereas leadership is about coping with change. Companies manage complexity by planning and budgeting, organizing and staffing, and controlling and problem solving. Leadership copes with change by setting a direction, aligning people to accomplish an agenda, and motivating and inspiring people.

To understand leadership, we must understand authority and power. Authority is the right to perform or command; it comes with the manager's job. Power is the extent to which a person is able to influence others so they respond to orders. People may pursue personalized power, power directed at helping oneself, or, better, they may pursue socialized power, power directed at helping others.

Within an organization there are typically five sources of power leaders may draw on; all managers have the first three. (1) Legitimate power is power that results from managers' formal positions within the organization. (2) Reward power is power that results from managers' authority to reward their subordinates. (3) Coercive power results from managers' authority to punish their subordinates. (4) Expert power is power resulting from one's specialized information or expertise. (5) Referent power is power deriving from one's personal attraction.

There are nine influence tactics for trying to get others to do something you want, ranging from most used to least used tactics as follows: rational persuasion, inspirational appeals, consultation, ingratiating tactics, personal appeals, exchange tactics, coalition tactics, pressure tactics, and legitimating tactics.

Four principal approaches or perspectives on leadership, as discussed in the rest of the chapter, are (1) trait, (2) behavioral, (3) contingency, and (4) emerging.

14.2 Trait Approaches: Do Leaders Have Distinctive Personality Characteristics?

Trait approaches to leadership attempt to identify distinctive characteristics that account for the effectiveness of leaders. Representatives of this approach are Kouzes and Posner, gender studies, and leadership lessons from the GLOBE project. (1) Kouzes and Posner identified five traits of leaders. A leader should be honest, competent, forward-looking, inspiring, and intelligent. (2) Women may rate higher than men do on producing high-quality work, goal setting, mentoring employees, and other measures. Women excel in such traits as

teamwork and partnering, being more collaborative, seeking less personal glory, being motivated less by self-interest than company interest, being more stable, and being less turf-conscious. (3) Project GLOBE surveyed 17,000 middle managers in 62 countries and determined that visionary and inspirational charismatic leaders who are good team builders do best.

14.3 Behavioral Approaches: Do Leaders Show Distinctive Patterns of Behavior?

Behavioral leadership approaches try to determine the distinctive styles used by effective leaders. Leadership style means the combination of traits, skills, and behaviors that leaders use when interacting with others. We described some important models of leadership behavior.

In the University of Michigan Leadership Model, researchers identified two forms of leadership styles. In job-centered behavior, managers paid more attention to the job and work procedures. In employee-centered behavior, managers paid more attention to employee satisfaction and making work groups cohesive.

In the Ohio State Leadership Model, researchers identified two major dimensions of leader behavior: Initiating structure organizes and defines what group members should be doing. Consideration is leadership behavior that expresses concern for employees by establishing a supportive climate.

14.4 Contingency Approaches: Does Leadership Vary with the Situation?

Proponents of the contingency approach to leadership believe that effective leadership behavior depends on the situation at hand—that as situations change, different styles become effective. Two contingency approaches are described.

The Fiedler contingency leadership model determines if a leader's style is task-oriented or relationship-oriented and if that style is effective for the situation at hand. Once it is determined whether a leader is more oriented toward tasks or toward people, then it's necessary to determine how much control and influence a leader has in the immediate work environment. The three dimensions of situational control are leader–member relations, which reflect the extent to which a leader has the support of the work group; the task structure, which reflects the extent to which tasks are routine and easily understood; and position power, which reflects how much power a leader has to reward and punish and make work assignments. For each dimension, the leader's control may be high or low. A task-oriented style has been found to work best in either high-control or low-control situations; the relationship-oriented style is best in situations of moderate control.

The House path–goal leadership model, in its revised form, holds that the effective leader clarifies paths through which subordinates can achieve goals and provides them with support. Two variables, employee characteristics and environmental factors, cause one or more leadership behaviors—which House expanded to eight from his original four—to be more effective than others.

14.5 The Full-Range Model: Uses of Transactional & Transformational Leadership

Full-range leadership describes leadership along a range of styles, with the most effective being transactional/transformational leaders. Transactional leadership focuses on clarifying employees' roles and task requirements and providing rewards and punishments contingent on performance. Transformational leadership transforms employees to pursue goals over self-interests. Transformational leaders are influenced by two factors: (1) Their personalities tend to be more extroverted, agreeable, and proactive. (2) Organizational cultures are more apt to be adaptive and flexible.

The best leaders are both transactional and transformational. Four key behaviors of transformational leaders in affecting employees are they inspire motivation, inspire trust, encourage excellence, and stimulate them intellectually.

Transformational leadership has three implications. (1) It can improve results for both individuals and groups. (2) It can be used to train employees at any level. (3) It can be used by both ethical or unethical leaders.

14.6 Four Additional Perspectives

Three additional kinds of leadership are (1) leader–membership exchange model, (2) servant leadership, and (3) e-leadership. We also cover (4) followers.

The leader–member exchange (LMX) model of leadership emphasizes that leaders have different sorts of relationships with different subordinates.

Servant leaders focus on providing increased service to others—meeting the goals of both followers and the organization—rather than to themselves.

E-leadership involves leader interactions with others via the Internet and other forms of advanced information technology, which have made possible new ways for interacting within and between organizations (e-business) and with customers and suppliers (e-commerce). E-leadership can involve one-to-one, one-to-many, within-group and between-group, and collective interactions via information technology.

Whatever their type, leaders need followers, who vary in compliance from helpers to independents to rebels. Leaders want followers who are productive, reliable, honest, cooperative, proactive, and flexible. They do not want followers who are reluctant to take the lead on projects, fail to generate ideas, are unwilling to collaborate, withhold information, provide inaccurate feedback, or hide the truth.

Management in Action

Lynn Tilton's Leadership Helps Turn Around Failing Companies

Earlier this year [2011], private-equity chief Lynn Tilton flew to Detroit to try to improve sales at one of her auto-parts companies. She got a cool reception from Ford Motor Co.'s purchasing chief, Tony Brown, who asked if she was like other private-equity chiefs that "strip and flip" their companies.

"You must be mistaken," she shot back. "It's only men that I strip and flip. My companies I hold long and close to my heart."

With her platinum blonde hair, tight leather skirts, and penchant for racy remarks, Ms. Tilton has a talent for getting people's attention. Yet behind the glam facade is a sophisticated distressed-debt investor and manufacturing tycoon who has quickly become one of the richest self-made women in America.

Through her New York–based holding company, Patriarch Partners, Ms. Tilton owns all or parts of 74 companies, with revenues of more than $8 billion and 120,000 employees. By most measures, Patriarch is now the largest woman-owned business in America.

Ms. Tilton, 52 years old, built her fortune from an unlikely corner of the economy: down-and-out industrial firms. Her strategy is to buy manufacturers headed for the scrap heap and bring them back to life with new management teams and products. In the process, she's become an unlikely crusader for America's rust-belt.

"The key to America's future is manufacturing," she says. "We simply have to become a country that can make things again." . . .

Ms. Tilton also has had her share of mistakes. After buying American LaFrance, the firetruck maker, she drove down revenue by more than 50% in an effort to improve profits. Four years later, she still is trying to turn the company around.

"That was a purchase I made more with my heart than my head," she said.

Ms. Tilton has the added distraction of her personality. Her office uniform usually includes five-inch stilettos, an eight-carat diamond necklace and the occasional black leather jumpsuit. Her office walls are filled with whips and handcuffs sent to her by friends, Hashemite daggers given to her by Middle Eastern royals, New Age paintings, and a portrait of her stretched across the hood of a black Mercedes. Ms. Tilton makes no apologies for her unconventional look.

"I am all woman," she says. "Sometimes it makes men uncomfortable, sure. But in business and in life, I have to remain faithful to my inner truth. In the end, I'd hope people judge me on my accomplishments and intelligence."

Ms. Tilton started on Wall Street as a single mother, working 15-hour days and putting herself through Columbia's business school. She had graduated from Yale as a nationally ranked college tennis player and aspiring poet and married her college sweetheart. Soon after starting work on Wall Street, she got divorced and plunged into her work. . . .

In 2000, she founded Patriarch, named after her late father. Her plan was to trade debt with her own money. Yet after buying two giant portfolios of distressed debt, she realized the only way to succeed was to take control of the companies in the portfolio. Suddenly, Ms. Tilton had gone from a debt investor to the accidental chief executive of dozens of failed companies. Her turnarounds were so profitable that she went on to buy more companies. . . .

She sleeps only a few hours a night and sips a homemade concoction of clay, salt, and chlorophyll. She often stays up late reading science fiction on her Kindle.

Walking down the manufacturing line at her MD Helicopter plant in Arizona on a recent afternoon, Ms. Tilton looked out of place in her shimmering dress and heels. Yet she quickly bonded with workers with her earthy jokes and detailed knowledge of metal alloys and machine-tools.

"Workers really take to Lynn," said Duane Lugdon, a United Steelworkers union staffer who led tense negotiations with Ms. Tilton at the Maine paper plant. "She's just human and honest with people. I don't say that about many CEOs."

Her personal involvement in each company—she's still CEO of MD—is a blessing and a curse, former employees say. They say employee churn at Patriarch is high because of Ms. Tilton's tough personality.

"I'm a benevolent dictator," Ms. Tilton says. "I like to control things. What we do, the distressed area, is not for the faint of heart."

FOR DISCUSSION

1. Use Table 14.3 to evaluate the extent to which Lynn Tilton displays the characteristics associated with being a good leader and good manager.

2. Which different positive and negative leadership traits and styles are displayed by Tilton? Cite examples.

3. To what extent does Tilton display situational approaches toward leadership? Explain.

4. Which of the four types of transformational leadership behavior are displayed by Tilton? Provide examples.

5. Would you like to work for Lynn Tilton? Explain why or why not.

6. What did you learn about leadership from this case?

Source: Excerpted from R. Frank, "Tilton Flaunts Her Style at Patriarch," *The Wall Street Journal*, January 8–9, 2011, pp. B1, B17.

Self-Assessment

Assessing Your Leader–Member Exchange

OBJECTIVES

1. To assess the quality of your relationship with a current or former boss—your LMX.

2. To consider how your LMX affects your satisfaction.

INTRODUCTION

The quality of the relationship between you and your manager affects a host of important outcomes such as job satisfaction, performance, and turnover. The purpose of this exercise is for you to assess the LMX with a current or former manager and then consider its impact on your job satisfaction.

INSTRUCTIONS

For each of the items shown below, circle the number that best represents your self-perceptions, where 1 = strongly disagree, 2 = disagree, 3 = neither agree nor disagree, 4 = agree, 5 = strongly agree. There is no right or wrong answer. After circling a response for each of the 12 items, use the scoring key to compute scores for the subdimensions within your leader–member exchange.

1. I like my supervisor very much as a person.	1 2 3 4 5
2. My supervisor is the kind of person one would like to have as a friend.	1 2 3 4 5
3. My supervisor is a lot of fun to work with.	1 2 3 4 5
4. My supervisor defends my work actions to a superior, even without complete knowledge of the issue in question.	1 2 3 4 5
5. My supervisor would come to my defense if I were "attacked" by others.	1 2 3 4 5
6. My supervisor would defend me to others in the organization if I made an honest mistake.	1 2 3 4 5
7. I do work for my supervisor that goes beyond what is specified in my job description.	1 2 3 4 5
8. I am willing to apply extra effort, beyond that normally required, to meet my supervisor's work goals.	1 2 3 4 5
9. I do not mind working my hardest for my supervisor.	1 2 3 4 5
10. I am impressed with my supervisor's knowledge of his or her job.	1 2 3 4 5
11. I respect my supervisor's knowledge of and competence on the job.	1 2 3 4 5
12. I admire my supervisor's professional skills.	1 2 3 4 5

SCORING KEY

Mutual affection (add items 1–3)

Loyalty (add items 4–6)

Contribution to work activities (add items 7–9)

Professional respect (add items 10–12)

Overall score (add all 12 items)

Arbitrary Norms

Low mutual affection = 3–9

High mutual affection = 10–15

Low loyalty = 3–9

High loyalty = 10–15

Low contribution to work activities = 3–9

High contribution to work activities = 10–15

Low professional respect = 3–9

High professional respect = 10–15

Low overall leader–member exchange = 12–38

High overall leader–member exchange = 39–60

QUESTIONS FOR DISCUSSION

1. Were you surprised by your results? Why or why not?

2. Look at the dimension of LMX in which you scored lowest. What can you do to improve scores on this dimension? Explain.

3. Do you have low or high job satisfaction? Does this assessment correlate with the quality of your leader–member exchange? Explain.

4. Who owns the quality of your leader–member exchange? Discuss your rationale.

Source: From R. C. Liden and J. M. Maslyn, "Multidimensionality of Leader-Member Exchange: An Empirical Assessment Through Scale Development," *Journal of Management* 24, no. 1 (1998), p. 56.

Legal/Ethical Challenge

Is It Ethical to Use Subversive Approaches to Influence Others?

"Last week, National Public Radio's chief executive [Vivian Schiller] and senior fundraiser [Ron Schiller] resigned after off-the-cuff remarks were made to conservative activists posing as potential donors."[116] The Schillers are unrelated. The potential donors, headed by James O'Keefe, met with Ron Schiller at a posh restaurant for lunch under the guise that they wanted to donate $5 million as representatives from a Muslim organization. O'Keefe secretly recorded the interview and later released a doctored video clip that portrayed NPR in a very bad light. Schiller made negative and damaging comments about the Republican Party in general and the tea party in particular. You can imagine how this video was received by politicians, particularly those that vote on funding for National Public Radio (NPR).

A reporter from the *Washington Post* described the video as "selective and deceptive." He stated that "O'Keefe's final product excludes explanatory context, exaggerates [Ron] Schiller's tolerance for Islamist radicalism, and attributes sentiments to Schiller that are actually quotes by others—all the hallmarks of a hit piece." The reporter concluded that "O'Keefe did not merely leave a false impression; he manufactured an elaborate lie. . . . The stingers bought access with fake money. There is no ethical canon or tradition that would excuse such deception on the part of a professional journalist."[117]

The video led some government officials to call for major, if not total funding cuts to NPR, which would threaten the organization's very existence. The end result is that the U.S. Senate voted in March 2011 to block public radio stations from spending federal money on programming. It appears that O'Keefe's influence attempts had some success.[118]

Not everyone agrees that O'Keefe did anything wrong. Some think that subversive techniques are a good way to keep people accountable. After all, TV programs like *20/20* have used hidden cameras for years to catch people doing bad things. The subversive trend is growing. For example, "The subversive approach has become so popular that the Yes Men, anticorporate jokers who have made two critically acclaimed movies, recently opened the Yes Lab, which trains others in the art of dirty work." Mike Bonanno, who cofounded Yes Men, concluded that "with mainstream media being defunded, there is less real reporting out there and more people are resorting to these kind of tactics to get the work out on stuff that should be obvious."[119] Further, "O'Keefe defenders contend he is not really a journalist but a new breed of 'citizen journalist.' This can be defined as the simultaneous demands for journalistic respect and for release from journalistic standards, including a commitment to honesty."[120]

SOLVING THE CHALLENGE

What do you think should be done about James O'Keefe?

1. Although O'Keefe did not violate any laws, he should be punished. His behavior was unethical. He lied about his identity to Ron Schiller and edited the video to present false impressions about NPR. His subversive actions also led to a negative vote about funding for public radio.

2. O'Keefe didn't break any laws, so he should be left alone. He actually is providing a service to the public.

What should be done about citizen journalism?

1. Given today's technology, we need regulations to govern this aspect of modern life. If people like James O'Keefe want to do journalistic work on their own, then they should be held to the same standards as professionals.

2. Wake up and smell the coffee. The only way to expose people like Ron Schiller is to use subversive techniques. I have no problem with what O'Keefe did. Besides, others are doing the same thing.

chapter 15

Interpersonal & Organizational Communication
Mastering the Exchange of Information

Major Questions You Should Be Able to Answer

15.1 The Communication Process: What It Is, How It Works

Major Question: What do I need to know about the communication process to be an effective communicator?

15.2 Barriers to Communication

Major Question: What are the important barriers I need to be aware of, so I can improve my communication skills?

15.3 How Managers Fit into the Communication Process

Major Question: How can I use the different channels and patterns of communication to my advantage?

15.4 Communication in the Information Age

Major Question: How do contemporary managers use information technology to communicate more effectively?

15.5 Improving Communication Effectiveness

Major Question: How can I be a better listener, reader, writer, and speaker?

Acing the Interview: Communicating Counts in Landing a Job

In an interview situation, you need to prove you're the one best candidate for the available position. Thus, you need to think out your strategy, deal with your nervousness, and perform well—as follows:[1]

Think Out Your Strategy: "I Know What This Company Is About"

You need to do your homework, anticipate the questions, and rehearse your selling points.

Use the web and other resources to learn about the company—past, present, and future events and initiatives, which you can use when discussing the firm. Anticipate the questions you'll be asked—such as "What do you consider your greatest weakness?"—that you can respond to briefly and turn to your advantage. ("I tend to be too impatient and want to get things done quickly.")

Identify your top three selling points—such as, if you have little experience, your personal qualities ("I'm results oriented, a good listener, and will work all hours") or, if you have lots of experience, your significant achievements. Have evidence (stories or data) to substantiate your claims.

Deal with Your Nervousness: "I'll Just Take My Time"

Preparation will help you stay calm during the interview. So will the use of visualization and positive self-talk to keep your confidence up ("I can handle this!"). Don't admit you're nervous. Breathe slowly. Don't rush to answer. Take a one-second pause before responding to a question.

Give a Strong Performance: "I Can Help This Company"

Your focus is *to show the company what's in it for them* by hiring you. To give your best impression, dress as people in the company do. Smile—it's one of the easiest ways to win people over. Make eye contact. Above all, express your enthusiasm and show your willingness "to do anything," not just the interesting stuff. Close with a thank you, a firm handshake, and ask the interviewer when he or she would like you to follow up. Drop the interviewer a note of thanks.

For Discussion How good are you at preparing for and rehearsing for an event (the job interview) that is as important as the application you did to get into college? How good are you at listening? How do you think you appear to other people in an important interaction?

forecast   What's Ahead in This Chapter

This chapter describes the process of transferring information and understanding from one person to another. It also describes three communication barriers—physical, semantic, and personal. It shows how you can use different channels and patterns of communication, both formal and informal, to your advantage. It discusses how star managers use information technology to communicate more effectively. Finally, we talk about how to be a better listener, reader, writer, and speaker.

major question

What do I need to know about the communication process to be an effective communicator?

THE BIG PICTURE

Communication is the transfer of information and understanding from one person to another. The process involves sender, message, and receiver; encoding and decoding; the medium; feedback; and dealing with "noise," or interference. Managers need to tailor their communication to the appropriate medium (rich or lean) for the appropriate situation.

Do you have difficulty accepting compliments, especially from close friends and loved ones? When you're ridiculed, as online, do you respond with over-the-top rage? Do you know how to apologize to someone—and do it in person, not by e-mail or text message, the coward's way? Are you so used to using profanity that you assume others are comfortable with it as well?[2]

All these matters show how difficult it is to communicate well.

Problems with communicating are a fact of human existence. That said, it is essential to develop your communication skills, which 636 human resource professionals rated as the most important factor in advancing their careers.[3]

No wonder faulty communication has become such a problem in the workplace. According to one survey, executives say 14% of each 40-hour workweek is wasted because of poor communication between staff and managers.[4] That's the equivalent of seven workweeks of lost productivity a year. Thus, there's a hardheaded argument for better communication: It can save money.

Communication Defined: The Transfer of Information & Understanding

Communication—**the transfer of information and understanding from one person to another**—is an activity that you as a manager will have to do a lot of. Indeed, one study found that 81% of a manager's time in a typical workday is spent communicating.[5]

Everything's clicking. Today some people can work almost anywhere, even more so as laptops, tablets, and cellphones have become such versatile instruments permitting Internet and e-mail access, text messaging, and access to huge databases. Do you think our ability to work outside traditional offices because of today's technology will negatively affect the communication process and employee camaraderie?

The fact that managers do a lot of communicating doesn't mean they're necessarily good at it—that is, that they are efficient or effective. You are an *efficient communicator* when you can transmit your message accurately in the least time. You are an *effective communicator* when your intended message is accurately understood by the other person. Thus, you may well be efficient in sending a group of people a reprimand by e-mail. But it may not be effective if it makes them angry so that they can't absorb its meaning.

From this, you can see why it's important to have an understanding of the communication process.

How the Communication Process Works

Communication has been said to be a process consisting of "a sender transmitting a message through media to a receiver who responds."[6] Let's look at these and other parts of the process.

Sender, Message, & Receiver   The *sender* **is the person wanting to share information—called a** *message***—and the** *receiver* **is the person for whom the message is intended,** as follows.

Sender → Message → Receiver

Encoding & Decoding   Of course, the process isn't as simple as just sender/ message/receiver. If you were an old-fashioned telegraph operator using Morse code to send a message over a telegraph line, you would first have to encode the message, and the receiver would have to decode it. But the same is true if you are sending the message by voice to another person in the same room, when you have to decide what language to speak in and what terms to use.

Encoding **is translating a message into understandable symbols or language.** *Decoding* **is interpreting and trying to make sense of the message.** Thus, the communication process is now

Sender **[Encoding]** → Message → **[Decoding]** Receiver

The Medium   The means by which you as a communicator send a message is important, whether it is by typing an e-mail traveling over the Internet, by voice over a telephone line, or by hand-scrawled note. This is the *medium,* **the pathway by which a message travels:**

Sender [Encoding] → Message **[Medium]** Message → [Decoding] Receiver

Feedback   "Flight 123, do you copy?" In the movies, that's what you hear the flight controller say when radioing the pilot of a troubled aircraft to see if he or she received ("copied") the previous message. And the pilot may radio back, "Roger, Houston, I copy." This is an example of *feedback,* **whereby the receiver expresses his or her reaction to the sender's message.**

Sender [Encoding] → Message [Medium]   Message → [Decoding] Receiver

[Feedback]   Message

Noise   Unfortunately, the entire communication process can be disrupted at several different points by what is called *noise*—**any disturbance that interferes with the transmission of a message.** The noise can occur in the medium, of course, as when you have static in a radio transmission or fadeout on a cellphone or when there's loud music when you're trying to talk in a noisy restaurant. Or it can occur in the encoding or decoding, as when a pharmacist can't read a prescription because of a doctor's poor handwriting.[7]

Noise also occurs in *nonverbal communication* (discussed later in this chapter), as when our physical movements send a message that is different from the one we are speaking, or in *cross-cultural communication* (discussed in Chapter 4), as when we make assumptions about other people's messages based on our own culture instead of theirs. We discuss noise further in the next section.

The communication process is shown below. *(See Figure 15.1.)*

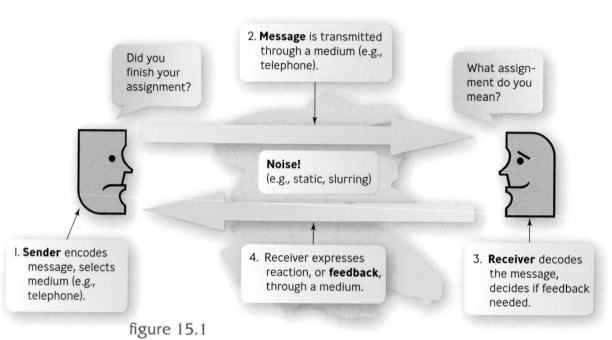

2. **Message** is transmitted through a medium (e.g., telephone).

Did you finish your assignment?

What assignment do you mean?

Noise!
(e.g., static, slurring)

I. **Sender** encodes message, selects medium (e.g., telephone).

4. Receiver expresses reaction, or **feedback**, through a medium.

3. **Receiver** decodes the message, decides if feedback needed.

figure 15.1

THE COMMUNICATION PROCESS

"Noise" is not just noise or loud background sounds but any disturbance that interferes with transmission—static, fadeout, distracting facial expressions, uncomfortable meeting site, competing voices, and so on.

Selecting the Right Medium for Effective Communication

All kinds of communications tools are available to managers, ranging from one-to-one face-to-face conversation all the way to use of the mass media. However, managers need to know how to use the right tool for the right condition—when to use e-mail or when to meet face-to-face, for example. Should you praise an employee by voicing a compliment, sending an e-mail, posting an announcement near the office coffee machine—or all three? How about when carrying out a reprimand?

Is a Medium Rich or Lean in Information? As a manager, you will have many media to choose from: conversations, meetings, speeches, the telephone, e-mail, memos, letters, bulletin boards, PowerPoint presentations, videoconferencing, printed publications, videos, and so on. Beyond these are the sophisticated communications possibilities of the mass media: public relations; advertising; news reports via print, radio, TV, the Internet.

Media richness **indicates how well a particular medium conveys information and promotes learning.** That is, the "richer" a medium is, the better it is at conveying information. The term *media richness* was proposed by respected organizational theorists Richard Daft and Robert Lengel as part of their contingency model for media selection.[8]

Ranging from high media richness to low media richness, types of media may be positioned along a continuum as follows:

High media richness
(Best for nonroutine,
ambiguous situations)

Low media richness
(Best for routine,
clear situations)

| Face-to-face presence | Video-conferencing | Telephone | Personal written media (e-mail, text messages, memos, letters) | Impersonal written media (newsletters, fliers, general reports) |

Face-to-face communication, also the most personal form of communication, is the richest. It allows the receiver of the message to observe multiple cues, such as body language and tone of voice. It allows the sender to get immediate feedback, to see how well the receiver comprehended the message. At the other end of the media richness scale, impersonal written media is just the reverse—only one cue and no feedback—making it low in richness.

Matching the Appropriate Medium to the Appropriate Situation   In general, follow these guidelines:[9]

Rich Medium: Best for Nonroutine Situations & to Avoid Oversimplification
A *rich* medium is more effective with nonroutine situations. Examples: In what way would you like to learn the facts from your boss of a nonroutine situation such as a major company reorganization, which might affect your job? Via a memo tacked on the bulletin board (a lean medium)? Or via face-to-face meeting or phone call (rich medium)?

The danger of using a rich medium for routine matters (such as monthly sales reports) is that it results in information *overloading*—more information than necessary.

Lean Medium: Best for Routine Situations & to Avoid Overloading   A *lean* medium is more effective with routine situations. Examples: In what manner would you as a sales manager like to get routine monthly sales reports from your 50 sales reps? Via time-consuming phone calls (somewhat rich medium)? Or via e-mails or text messages (somewhat lean medium)? The danger of using a lean medium for nonroutine matters (such as an announcement of a company reorganization) is that it results in information *oversimplification*—it doesn't provide enough of the information the receiver needs and wants.

E-mail and Facebook and Twitter messages (social media, discussed in Section 15.4) vary in media richness, being leaner if they impersonally blanket a large audience and richer if they mix personal textual and video information that prompts quick conversational feedback.[10] ●

major question ? What are the important barriers I need to be aware of, so I can improve my communication skills?

THE BIG PICTURE

We describe three barriers to communication. Physical barriers include sound, time, and space. Semantic barriers include unclear use of words and jargon. Personal barriers include variations in communication skills, trustworthiness and credibility, stereotypes and prejudices, and faulty listening skills. We also describe how misunderstandings can arise from nonverbal communication and gender-related communication differences.

How hard is it to place an order in a fast-food drive-through lane? Maybe not always so easy.

A Georgia fast-food worker urges customers to "please have a general idea of what you want *before* you reach the speaker" (because the company has employees on a timer). She also asks that you "speak clearly (but don't yell!) into the speaker. Also, although it may seem cute to you, I can barely understand your 4-year-old when she asks me for her kiddie meal." Further, "if you can't hear yourself over your car radio, I can't either."[11]

Customers have their own complaints. "How are we supposed to have any idea of what to order when we don't see the menu until we pull up to the window?" asks one.[12] Says another, "Those of us at the other end of the speaker often cannot understand a word being said, either because the speaker isn't working properly, because the order-taker has a thick accent, or the person is speaking too fast."[13]

All these are examples of communication *barriers*—a barrier being anything interfering with accurate communication between two people. Some barriers may be thought of as happening within the communication process itself, as the table on the opposite page shows. *(See Table 15.1.)* It's more practical, however, to think of barriers as being of three types: (1) *physical barriers,* (2) *semantic barriers,* and (3) *personal barriers.*

Without walls. Supposedly businesses that have open floor plans with cubicles instead of private offices function better because people can more easily talk across the shoulder-high partitions. But do you think the absence of floor-to-ceiling physical barriers might, in fact, lead to other kinds of barriers—such as others' talking making it hard to hear while you're on the phone?

table 15.1 SOME BARRIERS THAT HAPPEN WITHIN THE COMMUNICATION PROCESS

All it takes is one blocked step in the communication process described in the text for communication to fail. Consider the following.

- **Sender barrier—no message gets sent.** Example: If a manager has an idea but is afraid to voice it because he or she fears criticism, then obviously no message gets sent.

- **Encoding barrier—the message is not expressed correctly.** Example: If your vocabulary is lacking or English is not your first language, you may have difficulty expressing to a supervisor, coworker, or subordinate what it is you mean to say.

- **Medium barrier—the communication channel is blocked.** Example: When someone's phone always has a busy signal or a computer network is down, these are instances of the communication medium being blocked.

- **Decoding barrier—the recipient doesn't understand the message.** Example: Perhaps you're afraid to show your ignorance when someone is throwing computer terms at you and says that your computer connection has "a bandwidth problem."

- **Receiver barrier—no message gets received.** Example: Because you were talking to a coworker, you weren't listening when your supervisor announced today's work assignments.

- **Feedback barrier—the recipient doesn't respond enough.** Example: You give some people street directions, but since they only nod their heads and don't repeat the directions back to you, you don't really know whether you were understood.

1. Physical Barriers: Sound, Time, Space, & So On

Try shouting at someone on the far side of a construction site—at a distance of several yards over the roar of earth-moving machinery—and you know what physical barriers are. Other such barriers are time-zone differences, telephone-line static, and crashed computers. Office walls can be physical barriers, too, which is one reason for the trend toward open-floor plans with cubicles instead of offices in many workplace settings.[14]

2. Semantic Barriers: When Words Matter

When a supervisor tells you, "We need to get this done right away," what does it mean? Does "We" mean just you? You and your coworkers? Or you, your coworkers, and the boss? Does "right away" mean today, tomorrow, or next week? These are examples of semantic barriers. **Semantics is the study of the meaning of words.**

As global communications have become so important, so have semantic difficulties, which we may often encounter when dealing with other cultures (as we discussed in Chapter 4). When talking on the phone with Indians working in call centers in India, for example, we may find their pronunciation unusual. Perhaps that is because, according to one Indian speech-voice consultant, whereas "Americans think in English, we think in our mother tongue and translate it while speaking."[15]

In addition, as our society becomes more technically oriented, semantic meaning becomes a problem because jargon develops. **Jargon is terminology specific to a particular profession or group.** (Example: "The HR VP wants the RFP to go out ASAP." Translation: "The vice president of human resources wants the request for proposal to go out as soon as possible.") Another problem is the use of *buzzwords*, such as "leverage," "interface," or "circle back"—annoying words primarily designed to impress rather than inform. (Example: "Could you interface with that team on its ad campaign that's gone viral, and then circle back with me? If we can leverage similar assets, we'll have a game changer.")[16] As a manager in a specialized field, you need to remember that what are ordinary terms for you may be mysteries to outsiders.

3. Personal Barriers: Individual Attributes That Hinder Communication

"Is it them or is it me?"

How often have you wondered, when someone has shown a surprising response to something you said, how the miscommunication happened? Let's examine nine personal barriers that contribute to miscommunication.

Variable Skills in Communicating Effectively As we all know, some people are simply better communicators than others. They have the vocabulary, the writing ability, the speaking skills, the facial expressions, the eye contact, the dramatic ability, the "gift of gab," the social skills to express themselves in a superior way. Conversely, other people don't have these qualities. But better communication skills can be learned.[17]

Variations in How Information Is Processed & Interpreted Zheng Yu, a young woman from China teaching her native language to students in Lawton, Oklahoma, was explaining a vocabulary quiz when a student interrupted: "Sorry, I was zoning out. What are we supposed to be doing?" Zheng repeated the instructions, but she was taken aback. "In China," she said afterward, "if you teach the students and they don't get it, that's their problem. Here if you don't get it, you teach it again."[18]

Are you from a working-class or privileged background? Are you from a particular ethnic group? Are you better at math or at language? Are you from a chaotic household filled with alcoholism and fighting, which distracts you at work? Because people use different frames of reference and experiences to interpret the world around them, they are selective about what things have meaning to them and what don't. All told, these differences affect what we say and what we think we hear.

Variations in Trustworthiness & Credibility Without trust between you and the other person, communication is apt to be flawed. Instead of communicating, both of you will be concentrating on defensive tactics, not the meaning of the message being exchanged. How will subordinates react to you as a manager if your predecessors in your job lied to them? They may give you the benefit of a doubt, but they may be waiting for the first opportunity to be confirmed in the belief that you will break their trust.[19]

Oversized Egos Our egos—our pride, our self-esteem, even arrogance—are a fifth barrier. Egos can cause political battles, turf wars, and the passionate pursuit of power, credit, and resources. Egos influence how we treat each other as well as how receptive we are to being influenced by others. Ever had someone take credit for an idea that was yours? Then you know how powerful ego feelings can be.

Big egos are certainly a factor when managers tune out workers' ideas, a frequent employee complaint—and often they're right, according to some research.[20] "People in powerful positions, such as managers, tend to dismiss others' advice when making decisions," says one summary.[21] Indeed, people with high levels of power—motivated by feelings of competitiveness—tend to discount advice from experts and novices equally. (Individuals with neutral and low levels of power weigh advice from experts and experienced advisors more heavily than advice from novices.) Researchers found that women were more likely than men to take others' advice.

Faulty Listening Skills When you go to a party, do people ever ask questions of you and about who you are and what you're doing? Or are they too ready to talk about themselves? And do they seem to be waiting for you to finish talking so that they can then resume saying what they want to say? (But here's a test: Do you actually *listen* when they're talking?)

Tendency to Judge Others' Messages Suppose another student in this class sees you reading this text and says, "I like the book we're reading." You might say, "I agree." Or you might say, "I disagree—it's boring." The point is that we all have a natural tendency, according to psychologist Carl Rogers, to judge others' statements from our own point of view (especially if we have strong feelings about the issue).[22]

Inability to Listen with Understanding To really listen with understanding, you have to imagine yourself in the other person's shoes. Or, as Rogers and his coauthor put it, you have to "see the expressed idea and attitude from the other person's point of view, to sense how it feels to him, to achieve his frame of reference in regard to the thing he is talking about."[23] When you listen with understanding, it makes you feel less defensive (even if the message is criticism) and improves your accuracy in perceiving the message.

Stereotypes & Prejudices We discussed stereotyping in Chapter 11. **A *stereotype* consists of oversimplified beliefs about a certain group of people.** There are, for instance, common stereotypes about old people, young people, males, and females. Wouldn't you hate to be categorized according to just a couple of exaggerated attributes—by your age and gender, for example? ("Young men are reckless." "Old women are scolds." Yes, *some* young men and *some* old women are this way, but it's unrealistic and unfair to tar every individual in these groups with the same brush.)

We consider matters of gender communication later in this chapter.

Nonverbal Communication Do your gestures and facial expressions contradict your words? This is the sort of nonverbal communication of which you may not even be aware. We discuss this subject in more detail next.

Nonverbal Communication: How Unwritten & Unspoken Messages May Mislead

"The best waiters know what type of service you prefer before you tell them," says one report. It's called "having eyes" for a table or "feeling" or "reading" the table—noting diners' nonverbal communication: body language, eye contact, expressions, moods.[24] ***Nonverbal communication* consists of messages sent outside of the written or spoken word.** Says one writer, it includes such factors as "use of time and space, distance between persons when conversing, use of color, dress, walking behavior, standing, positioning, seating arrangement, office locations, and furnishings."[25]

Perhaps 65% of every conversation is partially interpreted through nonverbal communication, according to some experts.[26] Others estimate nonverbal communication is responsible for as much as 93–95% of a message.[27] Given the prevalence of nonverbal communication and its impact on organizational behavior (such as hiring decisions, perceptions of others, and getting one's ideas accepted by others), it is important that you become familiar with the various sources of nonverbal communication.[28] Indeed, this is particularly so when you are dealing with people of other cultures around the world, as we saw back in Chapter 4 (Section 4.5) in our discussion of cultural differences.[29]

Bored or tired? People's behavior doesn't always reflect what's going on around them. It may reflect what's going on *inside* of them. Perhaps this man was up late the night before with a sick child or working to meet a project deadline. Even so, when speaking, you need to watch your audience for their reactions.

Six ways in which nonverbal communication is expressed are through (1) *eye contact,* (2) *facial expressions,* (3) *body movements and gestures,* (4) *touch,* (5) *setting,* and (6) *time.* (Some lists add interpersonal space, which we discussed in Chapter 4.)

1. Eye Contact Eye contact serves four functions in communication: (1) It signals the beginning and end of a conversation; there is a tendency to look *away* from others when beginning to speak and to look *at* them when done. (2) It expresses emotion; for instance, most people tend to avoid eye contact when conveying bad news or negative feedback. (3) Gazing monitors feedback because it reflects interest and attention. (4) Depending on the culture, gazing also expresses the type of relationship between the people communicating. For instance, Westerners are taught at an early age to look at their parents when spoken to. However, Asians are taught to avoid eye contact with a parent or superior in order to show obedience and subservience.[30]

2. Facial Expressions Probably you're accustomed to thinking that smiling represents warmth, happiness, or friendship whereas frowning represents dissatisfaction or anger. But these interpretations of facial expressions don't apply across all cultures.[31] A smile, for example, doesn't convey the same emotions in different countries.

3. Body Movements & Gestures An example of a body movement is leaning forward; an example of a gesture is pointing. Open body positions, such as leaning backward, express openness, warmth, closeness, and availability for communication. Closed body positions, such as folding one's arms or crossing one's legs, represent defensiveness. Body movements can be extremely subtle; for instance, when we say, "I'm looking forward to . . . ," guess which direction we tend to lean (if only very slightly)?[32]

Some body movements and gestures are associated more with one sex than the other, according to communication researcher Judith Hall. For instance, women nod their heads and move their hands more than men do. Men exhibit large body shifts and foot and leg movements more than women do.[33]

We need to point out, however, that interpretations of body language are subjective, hence easily misinterpreted, and highly dependent on the context and cross-cultural differences.[34] You'll need to be careful when trying to interpret body movements, especially when you're operating in a different culture.

4. Touch Norms for touching vary significantly around the world. For example, as we noted in Chapter 4, in the Middle East it is normal for two males who are friends to walk together holding hands—not commonplace behavior in the United States. In Latin America, there may be effusive hugging and kissing during a business deal.[35]

Men and women interpret touching differently, with women tending to do more touching during conversations than men do.[36] If women touch men, it is viewed as sexual; the same interpretation is made when men touch other men.[37] Yet even handshakes and embracing seem to be changing, with the male handshake now evolving into a range of more intimate gestures—"the one-armed hug, the manly shoulder bump, the A-frame clasp with handshake in the middle, the mutual back-slap," as one article puts it.[38] Good teams tend to use touch more than bad teams do, according to some research.[39]

5. Setting How do you feel when you visit someone who sits behind a big desk and is backlit by a window so her face is obscured? What does it say when someone comes out from behind his desk and invites you to sit with him on his office couch? The location of an office (such as corner office with window versus interior office with no window), its size, and the choice of furniture often expresses the accessibility of the person in it.

6. Time When your boss keeps you waiting 45 minutes for an appointment with him, how do you feel? When she simply grunts or makes one-syllable responses to your comments, what does this say about her interest in your concerns? As a manager yourself, you should always give the people who work for you adequate time. You should also talk with them frequently during your meetings with them so they will understand your interest.

The table below gives some suggestions for better nonverbal communication skills. *(See Table 15.2.)*

Do ...	Don't ...
Maintain eye contact	Look away from the speaker
Lean toward the speaker	Turn away from the speaker
Speak at a moderate rate	Speak too quickly or slowly
Speak in a quiet, reassuring tone	Speak in an unpleasant tone
Smile and show animation	Yawn excessively
Occasionally nod head in agreement	Close your eyes
Be aware of your facial expressions	Lick lips, bite nails, play with your hair

table 15.2

TOWARD BETTER NONVERBAL COMMUNICATION SKILLS

You can practice these skills by watching TV with the sound off and interpreting people's emotions and interactions.

Source: Adapted from P. Preston, "Nonverbal Communication: Do You Really Say What You Mean?" *Journal of Healthcare Management,* March–April 2005, pp. 83–86.

Communication Differences Between Men & Women

Do men dominate the top rungs of business in part because they exaggerate more? Men are said to be "overconfident" when recalling their past accomplishments—and are able to convince their peers to make them leaders—whereas women recall their accomplishments more accurately, putting them at a competitive disadvantage. At least that's what one study suggests.[40]

Men are also eight times as likely as women to bargain over starting pay. Indeed, says one account, "Women often are less adroit at winning better salaries, assignments, and jobs—either because they don't ask or because they cave in when they do."[41] In other words, women need to hone their negotiation skills, or else they will fall behind.

Some possible general differences in communication between genders are summarized below. *(See Table 15.3.)* Note, however, that these don't apply in all cases, which would constitute stereotyping.

table 15.3 COMMUNICATION DIFFERENCES

How do men and women differ?

Linguistic Characteristic	Men	Women
Taking credit	Greater use of "I" statements (e.g., "I did this" and "I did that"); more likely to boast about their achievements	Greater use of "We" statements (e.g., "We did this" and "We did that"); less likely to boast about their achievements
Displaying confidence	Less likely to indicate that they are uncertain about an issue	More likely to indicate a lack of certainty about an issue
Asking questions	Less likely to ask questions (e.g., asking for directions)	More likely to ask questions
Conversation rituals	Avoid making apologies because it puts them in a one-down position	More frequently say "I'm sorry"
Giving feedback	More direct and blunt	More tactful; tend to temper criticism with praise
Giving compliments	Stingy with praise	Pay more compliments than men do
Indirectness	Indirect when it comes to admitting fault or when they don't know something	Indirect when telling others what to do

Source: Derived from D. Tannen, "The Power of Talk: Who Gets Heard and Why," *Harvard Business Review,* September–October 1995; and D. Tannen, *You Just Don't Understand: Women and Men in Conversation* (New York: Ballantine Books, 1990).

How useful do you think these specific styles are in a managerial context? (Recall the discussion of men and women with reference to leadership in Chapter 14.)

Author Judith Tingley suggests that women and men should learn to "genderflex"— temporarily use communication behaviors typical of the other gender to increase the potential for influence.[42] For example, a female manager might use sports analogies to motivate a group of males.

Deborah Tannen, by contrast, recommends that everyone become aware of how differing linguistic styles affect our perceptions and judgments. A **linguistic style is a person's characteristic speaking patterns**—pacing, pausing, directness, word choice, and use of questions, jokes, stories, apologies, and similar devices. For example, in a meeting, regardless of gender, "those who are comfortable speaking up in groups, who need little or no silence before raising their hands, or who speak out easily without waiting to be recognized are more apt to be heard," she says. "Those who refrain from talking until it's clear that the previous speaker is finished, who wait to be recognized, and who are inclined to link their comments to those of others will do fine at a meeting where everyone else is following the same rules but will have a hard time getting heard in a meeting with people whose styles are more like the first pattern."[43]

Do Female Executives Have an Edge in Business? Women & Communication

Women in business have the edge in two ways, says Chris Clarke, head of an executive search firm with offices in more than 40 countries. "There is increasing evidence," he says, "that women are superior at multitasking, which is needed to handle business complexities, and that they are better at relationships, which is important in developing effective teams."[44] For instance, the social-media style of young women (and increasingly women over 40, too) is use of highly expressive language, showing a greater emphasis on relationships and connecting with others.[45]

Overcommunicating. There is another way that women also have an edge, suggests a *BusinessWeek* article: Instead of tightly controlling information, they are more willing to share it.[46] For instance, one study found that management teams with a high proportion of women monitored feedback more closely and also promoted more interpersonal communication and employee involvement in decision making.[47]

A representative of this viewpoint is Anu Shukla, who sold her Internet marketing company for $390 million and made 65 of her 85 employees millionaires. "It's better to overcommunicate," she says. As an example, she made it her policy to share information with all her employees rather than to impart it to selected employees on a need-to-know basis.

His and Her Styles? Anne Cummings, professor of business administration at the University of Minnesota at Duluth, suggests there are "masculine" and "feminine" styles in business, in which men tend to be more task oriented and assertive and to take greater intellectual risks whereas women tend to be more relationship oriented and "democratic" and to be more efficient at solving problems.[48] (Of course, all this behavior operates on a continuum, and most people have a multitude of styles.)

YOUR CALL

Do you think a woman can be successful by taking on the "masculine" style? Can a man be successful taking on the "feminine" style?

Learning "Soft Skills"   Today there are executive-training programs designed to teach men the value of emotion in relationships—the use of "soft skills" to communicate, build teams, and develop flexibility. "The nature of modern business requires what's more typical to the female mold of building consensus as opposed to the top-down male military model," says Millington F. McCoy, managing director of a New York executive search firm

Interestingly, although men hold most of the top corporate jobs, when they want the advice of an executive coach—a trained listener to help them with their goals and personal problems—they usually turn to a woman. And, in fact, females always want another female as a coach. As a result, 7 out of 10 graduates of Coach U, the largest training school for executive coaches, are women. Because good coaches, says Coach U's CEO Sandy Vilas (who is male), are intuitive communicators and have done a lot of personal development work, "that profile tends to fit women better." Says Susan Bloch, who heads an executive coaching practice, "When a man is asked to coach another, they have a tendency to compete. Man to man, they have to show each other how great they are."[49]   ●

Exchange of views? Men and women have different communication styles. How effective do you think you are at communicating with the opposite sex?

major question

How can I use the different channels and patterns of communication to my advantage?

THE BIG PICTURE

Formal communication channels follow the chain of command, which is of three types—vertical, horizontal, and external. Informal communication channels develop outside the organization's formal structure. One type is gossip and rumor. Another is management by wandering around, in which a manager talks to people across all lines of authority.

If you've ever had a low-level job in nearly any kind of organization, you know that there is generally a hierarchy of management between you and the organization's president, director, or CEO. If you had a suggestion that you wanted him or her to hear, you doubtless had to go up through management channels. That's formal communication. However, you may have run into that top manager in the elevator. Or in the restroom. Or in a line at the bank. You could have voiced your suggestion casually then. That's informal communication.

Formal Communication Channels: Up, Down, Sideways, & Outward

***Formal communication channels* follow the chain of command and are recognized as official.** The organizational chart we described in Chapter 8 (page 239) indicates how official communications—memos, letters, reports, announcements—are supposed to be routed.

Formal communication is of three types: (1) *vertical*—meaning upward and downward, (2) *horizontal*—meaning laterally (sideways), and (3) *external*—meaning outside the organization.

1. Vertical Communication: Up & Down the Chain of Command Vertical communication is the flow of messages up and down the hierarchy within the organization: bosses communicating with subordinates, subordinates communicating with bosses. As you might expect, the more management levels through which a message passes, the more it is prone to some distortion.

Upward bound. How do you communicate with a manager two or three levels above you in the organization's hierarchy? You can send a memo through channels. Or you can watch for when that manager goes to the watercooler or the coffeepot.

- **Downward communication—from top to bottom.** *Downward communication flows from a higher level to a lower level (or levels).* In small organizations, top-down communication may be delivered face-to-face. In larger organizations, it's delivered via meetings, e-mail, official memos, and company publications.

- **Upward communication—from bottom to top.** *Upward communication flows from a lower level to a higher level(s).* Often this type of communication is from a subordinate to his or her immediate manager, who in turn will relay it up to the next level, if necessary. Effective upward communication depends on an atmosphere of trust. No subordinate is going to want to be the bearer of bad news to a manager who is always negative and bad-tempered.

Types of downward and upward communication are shown below. *(See Table 15.4.)*

table 15.4 TYPES OF DOWNWARD & UPWARD COMMUNICATION

Downward Communication

Most downward communication involves one of the following kinds of information:

- Instructions related to particular job tasks. Example (supervisor to subordinate): "The store will close Monday for inventory. All employees are expected to participate."

- Explanations about the relationship between two or more tasks. Example: "While taking inventory, employees need to see what things are missing. Most of that might be attributable to shoplifting."

- Explanations of the organization's procedures and practices. Example: "Start counting things on the high shelves and work your way down."

- A manager's feedback about a subordinate's performance. Example: "It's best not to try to count too fast."

- Attempts to encourage a sense of mission and dedication to the organization's goals. Example: "By keeping tabs on our inventory, we can keep our prices down and maintain our reputation of giving good value."

Upward Communication

Most upward communication involves the following kinds of information:

- Reports of progress on current projects. Example: "We shut down the store yesterday to take inventory."

- Reports of unsolved problems requiring help from people higher up. Example: "We can't make our merchandise count jibe with the stock reports."

- New developments affecting the work unit. Example: "Getting help from the other stores really speeded things up this year."

- Suggestions for improvements. Example: "The stores should loan each other staff every time they take inventory."

- Reports on employee attitudes and efficiency. Example: "The staff likes it when they go to another store and sometimes they pick up some new ways of doing things."

Sources: D. Katz and R. Kahn, *The Social Psychology of Organizations* (New York: Wiley, 1966); and E. Planty and W. Machaver, "Upward Communications: A Project in Executive Development," *Personnel* 28 (1952), pp. 304–18.

2. Horizontal Communication: Within & Between Work Units

Horizontal communication flows within and between work units; its main purpose is coordination. As a manager, you will spend perhaps as much as a third of your time in this form of communication—consulting with colleagues and coworkers at the same level as you within the organization. In this kind of sideways communication, you will be sharing information, coordinating tasks, solving problems, resolving conflicts, and getting the support of your peers. Horizontal communication is encouraged through the use of committees, task forces, and matrix structures.

Horizontal communication can be impeded in three ways: (1) by specialization that makes people focus just on their jobs alone; (2) by rivalry between workers or work units, which prevents sharing of information; and (3) by lack of encouragement from management.

3. External Communication: Outside the Organization *External communication* **flows between people inside and outside the organization.** These are other stakeholders: customers, suppliers, shareholders or other owners, and so on. Companies have given this kind of communication heightened importance, especially with customers or clients, who are the lifeblood of any company.

Informal Communication Channels

Informal communication channels **develop outside the formal structure and do not follow the chain of command**—they skip management levels and cut across lines of authority.

Two types of informal channels are (1) the *grapevine* and (2) *management by wandering around.*

The Grapevine The *grapevine* **is the unofficial communication system of the informal organization,** a network of gossip and rumor of what is called "employee language." Research shows that the grapevine (1) is faster than formal channels, (2) is about 75% accurate, and (3) is used by employees when they are insecure, threatened, or faced with organizational change.[50] Of course, employee language—otherwise known as "gossip"—can be notoriously misleading and a great reducer of morale in a dysfunctional company.[51]

Management by Wandering Around *Management by wandering around (MBWA)*—**also known as** *management by walking around*—**is the term used to describe a manager's literally wandering around his or her organization and talking with people across all lines of authority.**[52] Management by wandering around helps to reduce the problems of distortion that inevitably occur with formal communication flowing up a hierarchy. MBWA allows managers to listen to employees and learn about their problems as well as to express to employees what values and goals are important. ●

MBWA. Management by wandering around is sort of the reverse of employees exchanging informal views with top managers at the watercooler. That is, by wandering around the organization, top managers can stop and talk to nearly anyone—and thus perhaps learn things that might be screened out by the formal up-the-organization reporting process. If top managers can do MBWA, do you think midlevel managers can as well?

PRACTICAL ACTION

How to Streamline Meetings

When Steve Jobs was CEO of Apple, he used to hold marathon Monday meetings. The reason, he said, was "I want [Apple employees] making good or better decisions than I would. So the way to do that is have them know everything, not just in their part of the business but in every part of the business. So . . . we review the whole business."[53]

By contrast when Larry Page took over as CEO of Google, he announced that meetings should be run more efficiently—like those in a hungry startup instead of a 31,000-person company. Thus, meetings can be only 50 minutes long, to allow for a 10-minute bathroom break. No more than 10 people should attend, and every person should give input. Every meeting must have one clear decision maker, otherwise the meeting shouldn't happen. If a decision can't be made without a meeting, then the meeting should be scheduled immediately.[54]

Which form do you prefer, Apple's or Google's?

What to Do as a Meeting Participant

It is frustrating to be a victim of a poorly run meeting. In fact, workers reportedly judge nearly 50% of their meetings to be a waste of time.[55] In one survey, 50% of workers at big companies (and 26% at smaller ones) said they had attended a meeting where at least one participant fell asleep.[56] Problem meetings can result from a lack of focus, nobody watching the clock, and no leader to keep the meeting on track.[57] Or managers may discourage conflict, which ignores crucial issues and makes meetings boring.[58]

What can you do as a participant to make meetings run better?

- **Pull discussions back on point:** As a participant, you can always pull an off-track conversation back by saying, for example, "We were discussing next year's budget, but now we seem to be discussing the shortfalls of last year." Or you can try making a summary of a series of comments to prevent others from covering the same ground again.

- **Help the leader create the agenda:** If you're constantly exposed to ineffective meetings, you can also offer your assistance to the meeting leader in creating an agenda, with time frames attached for each item.

What to Do as a Meeting Leader

If you're leading meetings, here are some good ways to streamline them:[59]

- **Eliminate unnecessary meetings and meeting attendance:** Don't call a meeting if the same result can be accomplished in some other way: text message, e-mail, phone call, memo, or one-on-one visit. Invite only people who need to attend, and tell them they need stay for only those parts that concern them. Hold the meeting in a place where distractions will be minimal.

- **Distribute meeting agenda in advance:** Do your homework and prepare a list of meeting objectives, topics to be covered (the most important ones first), and the number of minutes allowed for discussion. Distribute the agenda a day or more in advance, and tell participants what information they should bring. Even for informal meetings, phone conversations, and one-on-one appointments, you should make a list of items to cover.

- **Stay in control of the meeting:** Start on time and stay within the time frame of the agenda items. (Coffee breaks, lunchtime, or quitting time provide built-in limits.) Announce politely at the start of the meeting that you value everyone's time and so you will intervene if discussion becomes off-point. Reserve judgments and conclusions until after discussion so that everyone will feel free to give their input.

  Don't allow a few members to monopolize the discussion. Encourage silent members to participate. Try to reach a decision or make an assignment for every item. Use two pieces of paper, one for general notes, the other for tasks and assignments. Summarize the highlights at the end of the meeting. Map out a timetable for actions to be taken.

- **Do follow-up:** After the meeting, type up tasks and assignments for distribution. Set a date for a follow-up meeting to assess progress.

YOUR CALL

What can you add to these suggestions to make meetings run better? (For more about running meetings, go to EffectiveMeetings.com, **www.effectivemeetings.com**.)

major question? How do contemporary managers use information technology to communicate more effectively?

THE BIG PICTURE

We discuss digital communication technology and workplace behavior, including the characteristics of the "Always On" (Millennial or Internet) generation. We also describe three technologies that are altering the communication process: videoconferencing, telecommuting, and teleworking. Finally, we discuss some difficulties of the digital age: security problems, privacy concerns, e-mail overload, and cellphone abuse.

The use of computers and information technology, which has so dramatically affected many aspects of the workplace, has taken us beyond communicating into multicommunicating. **Multicommunicating represents "the use of technology to participate in several interactions at the same time,"** in one explanation.[60] Examples would be answering e-mail messages during a lecture, and texting during a dinner conversation or while participating in a group conference call. Although multicommunicating sometimes enables us to get more things done in a shorter amount of time, there are times and places when it also can create *miscommunication* and lead to stress and hurt feelings.[61] For example, texting and checking your-email while working with colleagues can be seen as not only annoying but insulting.[62]

Digital Communication Technology & Workplace Behavior[63]

Multicommunicating is an example of how the worldwide digital communication revolution affects how we act and interact in workplace settings—both positively and negatively. The universal digital language of 1s and 0s gives us immediate access to unprecedented amounts of information and globe-spanning opportunities.

However, the very act of using technologies such as e-mail, texting, Facebook, and Twitter may influence the content of our communications. For example, researchers found that peers rate each other differently depending on the medium they use, with people being "far more likely to trash their colleagues via e-mail than when filling out a paper form," according to a *Fortune* writer.[64] Moreover, faster, far-flung digital communication doesn't necessarily mean better communication. In one organization, for example, employees with the most extensive personal digital networks were found to be 7% more productive than their colleagues, but those with the most cohesive face-to-face networks were even more productive—30% more, in fact. Research on high-performing teams similarly found that effective teams had more face-to-face than digital encounters.[65]

The "Always On" Generation

With the rise of the Internet has also come the rise of the "Always On" generation—or the Net Generation, Gen Y, the Millennials—88 million people born 1977–1997, the largest such cohort in U.S. history. The Always On generation is accustomed to spending 8 hours a day or more looking at various screens—on cellphones, on computers, on TVs—constantly busy with text messaging, e-mail, and the Internet.[66] This generation is much more likely (83%) to sleep with their cellphone next to their bed compared with Gen X (born 1965–1980) at 68% and Baby Boomers (born 1945–1964) at 50%.[67]

Hard on the heels of the Millennials is today's young "iGeneration," for whom technology is "simply a part of their DNA," as one child psychologist observed.[68] Indeed, if you are an 18- to 24-year-old, you generally watch the smallest amount of live TV (3½ hours a day) compared with any other age group, but you spend the most time text messaging (19 minutes a day) and watch the most online video (5½ minutes a day).[69] The average teenager now sends a median of 60 texts a day (up from 50 in 2009).[70]

In a few years, Millennials (Net Gen, Gen Y) will account for nearly half the employees in the world, and in some companies they already constitute a majority.[71] Their outlook, therefore, is having a profound impact on the workplace, "bringing new approaches to collaboration, knowledge sharing, and innovation in businesses and governments," says University of Toronto professor Don Tapscott, author of *Grown Up Digital*.[72] Tapscott and his fellow researchers have identified eight norms for this generation. *(See Table 15.5.)*

table 15.5

EIGHT NORMS OF THE MILLENNIAL OR INTERNET GENERATION

1. **Freedom—the desire to experience new and different things.** This norm, which takes precedence over long-term commitments, is expressed in a desire for flexible work hours and locations, to have a say in how things are done, and for freedom of choice.

2. **Customization—the desire to have personalized products and choices.** Customization covers everything from ring tone choices to Facebook layouts to lifestyle choices.

3. **Scrutiny—not taking "facts" and authority figures at face value.** Knowing that there is both treasure and trash on the Internet, this generation has learned to be skeptical, to check things out, to ask probing questions. Candor and straight talk are favored.

4. **Integrity—trust in people, products, and employers is important.** This generation cares about honesty, transparency, and keeping commitments—although they are elastic when it comes to pirating music and plagiarism.

5. **Collaboration—relationships are of key importance.** Members of this generation value volunteering, know how to work and play with others, and are eager to offer opinions and suggestions.

6. **Entertainment—keep things moving and interesting.** A job should be both challenging and fun, not a life sentence. For this multitasking generation, the Internet is not only a productivity tool and information source but also a personal communication device and "fun tool of choice."

7. **Speed—instant feedback is expected.** Used to instant-feedback video games and nanosecond answers from Google, Millennials prefer rapid-fire texting, instant messaging, and Tweeting to the slower e-mail. This leads them to urge faster decision making and feedback on job performance.

8. **Innovation—impatience for new and different user experiences.** In the workplace, the traditional hierarchy is rejected in favor of work processes that encourage collaboration and creativity.

Source: Adapted from discussion in D. Tapscott, *Grown Up Digital: How the Net Generation Is Changing Your World* (New York: McGraw-Hill, 2009), pp. 73–96, and from A. Kreitner and A. Kinicki, *Organizational Behavior,* 10th ed. (New York: McGraw-Hill/Irwin, 2013), p. 421.

What kind of attitudes, preferences, and expectations do Millennials have that employers have to take into account in managing them? Millennials exhibit a thirst for instant gratification and quick fixes and problems with focus and diminished attention spans, says one study.[73] They also "place a strong emphasis on finding work that's personally fulfilling," says one article. "They want work to afford them the opportunity to make new friends, learn new skills, and connect to a larger purpose."[74] At least as important as compensation are six types of rewards, expressed in order as high-quality colleagues, flexible work arrangements, prospects for advancement, recognition from one's company or boss, a steady rate of advancement and promotion, and access to new experiences and challenges.[75] To deal with this cohort of employees, IBM advises managers giving feedback to be clear, keep it loose, promote a dialogue, and keep notes to make feedback sessions more constructive.[76]

Digital Communication & the New Workplace: Videoconferencing, Telecommuting, & Teleworking

Digital communication has significantly altered the traditional linkages between work, place, and time. Let's consider videoconferencing, telecommuting, and telework.

Videoconferencing. In this arrangement, people in different locations can interact while viewing each other on a large screen. Videoconferencing offers considerable savings in time and money over the cost of travel. Do you think you would feel inhibited working with people in this way?

Videoconferencing Fueled by recession-induced cutbacks in travel budgets, many corporations turned to *videoconferencing,* also known as *teleconferencing,* using video and audio links along with computers to allow people in different locations to see, hear, and talk with one another.[77]

Videoconferencing does not beat face-to-face meetings for opening a relationship with a prospective client or closing a decision. Indeed, one study found that when a company reduces its travel budget for personal meetings, it loses both revenue and profits. In fact, if a company completely eliminated business travel, corporate profits could drop 17% in the first year, the study found, and it would take more than 3 years for profits to reach the same level as before.[78] Still, meetings via videoconferencing certainly are better than no meetings at all.

Many organizations set up special videoconferencing rooms or booths with specially equipped television cameras. Some of the more sophisticated equipment is known as *telepresence technology,* **high-definition videoconference systems that simulate face-to-face meetings between users.** Whereas traditional videoconferencing systems can be set up in a conventional conference room, telepresence systems require a specially designed room with multiple cameras and high-definition video screens, simulating "the sensation of two groups of people at identical tables facing each other through windows," according to one report.[79]

Clearly, telepresence technology can be quite expensive. Other equipment enables people to attach small cameras and microphones to their desks or computer monitors. This enables employees to conduct long-distance meetings and training classes without leaving their office or cubicle.[80]

Telecommuting *Telecommuting* involves doing work that is generally performed in the office away from the office, using a variety of information technologies. Employees typically receive and send work from home via phone and fax or by using a modem to link a home computer to an office computer. Among the benefits are (1) reduction of capital costs, because employees work at home; (2) increased flexibility and autonomy for workers; (3) competitive edge in recruiting hard-to-get employees; (4) increased job satisfaction and lower turnover; (5) increased productivity; and (6) ability to tap nontraditional labor pools (such as prison inmates and homebound disabled people).[81]

About 24% of rural businesses and 35% of nonrural businesses in the United States currently allow employees to telecommute or telework.[82] Telecommuting is more common for jobs that involve computer work, writing, and phone or brain work that requires concentration and limited interruptions. Although telecommuting represents an attempt to accommodate employee needs and desires, it requires adjustments and is not for everybody.[83] People who enjoy the social camaraderie of the office setting, for instance, probably won't like it. Others lack the self-motivation needed to work at home.[84] However, people like Sylvia Marino of Mill Valley, California, who for many years has been telecommuting 350 miles away with Santa Monica–based Edmunds.com, which provides information to car buyers, find it a great way to sustain a career and still be with their children. [85]

Teleworking   Recently, the term *telework* (or *virtual office*) has been adopted to replace the term "telecommuting" because it encompasses not just working from home but working from anywhere: "a client's office, a coffee shop, an airport lounge, a commuter train," in one description. "With cellphones, broadband at home, Wi-Fi, virtual private networks, and instant messaging becoming ubiquitous, telework has become easier than ever."[86] Some of those who lack a conventional office may sign up for shared, or "coworking," spaces, where they socialize around a coffeepot.[87] Whatever the arrangement, employees in different locations and time zones can work simultaneously (called synchronous communication) and team members can work on the same project at different times (asynchronous communication).

The Downside of the Digital Age

It's fair to say that the digital age has introduced almost as many difficulties as efficiencies into people's lives. Describing them all would fill a book in itself, but here let us concentrate on just a few that managers have to struggle with. Some difficulties are those we mentioned earlier, such as the lack of focus brought on by the constant distraction of available electronic gadgets. Other problems are with security, privacy, e-mail overkill, and cellphone abuse.

Security: Guarding Against Cyberthreats   *Security* **is defined as a system of safeguards for protecting information technology against disasters, system failures, and unauthorized access that result in damage or loss.** Security is a continuing challenge, with computer and cellphone users constantly having to deal with threats ranging from malicious software (malware) that tries to trick people into yielding passwords, Social Security numbers, and financial information to deviant programs (viruses) that can destroy or corrupt data. According to the Norton *Cyber Crime Report for 2011,* 431 million adults worldwide were victims of cyber crime the preceding year, with the total cost of those crimes amounting to $114 billion.[88]

The key to protecting digital communication systems against fraud, hackers, identity theft, and other threats is prevention. The table below presents some ways to protect yourself. *(See Table 15.6.)*

table 15.6

PROTECTING AGAINST SECURITY & PRIVACY BREACHES ON THE INTERNET

- **Don't use passwords that can be easily guessed.** Use weird combinations of letters, numbers, and punctuation, and mix uppercase and lowercase, along with special characters such as !, #, and %.

- **Don't use the same password for multiple sites.** Avoid using the same password at different sites, since if hackers or scammers obtain one account, they potentially have your entire online life.

- **Don't reveal sensitive information on social networking sites.** Even people who set their profiles to Facebook's strictest privacy settings may find sensitive information leaked all over the web.

- **Be careful about free and illegal downloads.** File-sharing programs often contain spyware, as do sites containing free and illegal songs, movies, and TV shows.

- **Be mindful of liability issues.** Employers routinely monitor employee email for offensive messages or risky material that may expose them to lawsuits.

- **Keep antivirus software updated.** The antivirus software on your computer won't protect you forever. Visit the antivirus software maker's website and enable the automatic update features.

Source: Derived from B.K. Williams and S.C. Sawyer, *Using Information Technology: A Practical Introduction,* 10th ed. (New York: McGraw-Hill/Irwin, 2013), pp. 100, 107, 356, 364, 481.

Privacy: Keeping Things to Yourself *Privacy* **is the right of people not to reveal information about themselves.** Threats to privacy can range from name migration, as when a company sells its customer list to another company, to online snooping, to government prying and spying. A particularly aggravating violation of privacy is *identity theft,* **in which thieves hijack your name and identity and use your good credit rating to get cash or buy things.**

In some cases, Internet users are their own worst enemies, posting compromising information about themselves on social networking sites that may be available to, say, potential employers. Supposedly such websites have various options whereby users can choose who is and is not allowed access to their personal information, but Facebook, for one, came in for a good deal of criticism because it altered its privacy controls in such a way as to expose many of its members' personal information online.[89]

Interestingly, however, 18- to 29-year-olds have been found to be more likely than older users of social networks to keep a keen eye on their online profiles and who can access them—just the opposite of what many people expected.[90]

E-Mail: Productivity Enhancer or Time Waster? People tend to have a love-hate relationship with e-mail. We love that we can send and receive e-mail 24/7 from practically anywhere. But we hate the fact that the average worker receives 200 e-mails a day, according to some research.[91] (But most people say they can't keep up with more than 50.)[92] Some other disadvantages of e-mail are that (1) there has been a decrease in all other forms of communication among coworkers—including greetings and informal conversations; (2) emotions often are poorly communicated or miscommunicated via e-mail messages; and (3) the greater the use of e-mail, the less connected coworkers reportedly feel.[93]

The table below provides some practical tips for handling e-mail. *(See Table 15.7.)*

table 15.7

TIPS FOR BETTER E-MAIL HANDLING

- **Treat all e-mail as confidential.** Pretend every message is a postcard that can be read by anyone. (Supervisors may legally read employee e-mail.)

- **Be careful with jokes and informality.** Nonverbal language and other subtleties are lost, so jokes may be taken as insults or criticism.

- **Avoid sloppiness, but avoid criticizing others' sloppiness.** Avoid spelling and grammatical errors, but don't criticize errors in others' messages.

- **When replying, quote only the relevant portion.** Edit long e-mail messages you've received down to the relevant paragraph and put your response immediately following.

- **Not every topic belongs on e-mail.** Complicated topics may be better discussed on the phone or in person to avoid misunderstandings.

Sources: D. Halpern, "Dr. Manners on E-Mail Dos and Don'ts," *Monitor of Psychology,* April 2004, p. 5; P. R. Brown, "Same Office, Different Planets," *The New York Times,* January, 26, 2008, p. 135; D. Newlund, "E-Mail's High Cost," *The Arizona Republic,* July 20, 2011, p. CL1; and B. K. Williams and S. C. Sawyer, *Using Information Technology,* 10th ed. (New York: McGraw-Hill, 2013), p. 90.

Smartphones: Use & Abuse

Cellphones are now mostly smartphones that can text, access e-mail and web pages, view TV programs, and so on. They are so widespread that the majority of respondents in one survey said they would sooner give up their landline phones, TVs, the Internet, and e-mail than surrender their mobile phones.[94] And as smartphones develop more features and make available more applications ("apps"), their importance will only increase.

Smartphone problems range from merely annoying (loud ring tones and loud conversations in public places) to unethical and illegal (sending pornographic photos and photographing restricted areas of materials) to deadly (distracting drivers from the road). One survey found that 78% of those interviewed said that people are less polite, courteous, and respectful in smartphone manners than they were 5 years earlier.[95] Phone use by car drivers makes even young people drive erratically, moving and reacting more slowly and increasing their risk of accidents.[96]

Some tips for handling smartphones are shown in the table below. *(See Table 15.8.)*

1. Keep the volume of your voice down while on the phone; no need to SHOUT.
2. Don't force defenseless others on buses, in restaurants, and so on to have to listen to your phone conversations.
3. Shut off your ringer during meetings and public performances; set the phone on "vibrate," and return calls at a discreet distance.
4. Don't text during meetings or other conversations.
5. Don't dial/text while driving.

table 15.8

FIVE RULES FOR USING SMARTPHONES

Social Media: Pros & Cons

Social media are Internet-based and mobile technologies used to generate interactive dialogue with members of a network. Two-thirds of online adults in the United States use social media platforms such as Facebook, Twitter, MySpace, or LinkedIn—mainly, they say, to stay in touch with current friends (67%) and family members (62%) and to connect with old friends with whom they've lost touch (50%).[97] Social media also is being used in business.

Some Business Benefits of Social Media   The essence of these technologies is *connectivity,* and social media enable businesses to connect in real time and over distances with many customers, suppliers, employees, potential talent, and other key stakeholders. We've seen such connectivity demonstrated in virtual teams and other attempts to redefine conventional organizational boundaries. Social media have also become contributors to what is known as *crowdsourcing,* the practice of obtaining needed services, ideas, or content by soliciting contributions from a large group of people and especially from the online community, such as Facebook and Twitter users.

EXAMPLE

Crowdsourcing: Using Facebook & Twitter to Develop New Ideas

Crowdsourcing is being applied in many fields, and not just Wikipedia. Owngig.com uses it to connect musicians and their fans to help organize private concerts. Innocentive .com uses it to solve scientific and technological problems; companies can put a problem up on the site and offer a cash prize for the solution, which is solved by an outsider about 30% of the time.[98]

Using Facebook to Design a Beer. Boston-based brewer Sam Adams joined with social media enthusiast

Guy Kawasaki for a Facebook crowdsourcing campaign that asked fans what a good beer should taste like. By voting on yeast, hops, malt, color, and the like, fans essentially helped create a new recipe that Sam Adams brought out as B'Austin in March 2012.[99]

Using Twitter to Improve Weapons Systems. The Pentagon is setting aside $32 million to develop "fun-to-play" computer games based on Twitter crowdsourcing that can refine the way weapons systems are tested to ensure they are free from software errors and security bugs.[100]

YOUR CALL
What are the pros and cons of using crowdsourcing to develop a product?

The Downside of Social Media We already alluded to problems of privacy and security associated with information technology in general, and these certainly apply to social media. Some other drawbacks:

- **Distraction.** "How have e-mail, social media, and other tools designed to organize information morphed into their own kind of relentless taskmasters?" asks one business journalist.[101] Productivity guru David Allen, however, argues that technology isn't the problem; it's just that people *let* themselves be distracted because they're not clear about their own goals.

- **Leaving wrong impression.** Ill-advised tweets can lead to unpleasant consequences, as happened to musician Courtney Love, who was sued for defamation as a result of making derogatory statements about a designer in her Twitter feed. Twitter users need to think twice before spontaneously making an announcement or spontaneously responding.[102]

- **Replacing real conversation.** "Human relationships are rich; they're messy and demanding," says psychologist Sherry Turkle. "We have learned the habit of cleaning them up with technology." But the little "sips" of online connection do not substitute for face-to-face conversation. "We think constant connection will make us feel less lonely," she says. "The opposite is true."[103]

Some recommendations for using Facebook are shown below. *(See Table 15.9.)* ●

table 15.9

USING FACEBOOK IN YOUR PROFESSIONAL LIFE

- Brand the product or organizational profile, but go light on sales messages. Follow the service standards of your organization.

- Use language relevant to your particular audience members and communicate with, not at, them. Show appreciation for them.

- Remember all wall posts are public. Don't write anything not intended for public consumption.

- All updates should be relevant.

- Take customer-sensitive issues off Facebook, into a private sphere, online or offline.

- Ask questions on the wall posts, but follow up and respond to any feedback received.

Sources: Excerpted and adapted from M. Ramsay, "Social Media Etiquette: A Guide and Checklist to the Benefits and Perils of Social Marketing," *Database Marketing & Customer Strategy Management* 16, no. 4 (2010), pp. 257–61; and A. Kinicki and M. Fugate, *Organizational Behavior: Key Concepts, Skills & Best Practices,* 5th ed. (New York: McGraw-Hill/Irwin, 2012), p. 334.

How can I be a better listener, reader, writer, and speaker? **major question?**

THE BIG PICTURE

We describe how you can be a more effective listener, as in learning to concentrate on the content of a message. We also describe how to be an effective reader. We offer four tips for becoming a more effective writer. Finally, we discuss how to be an effective speaker, through three steps.

The principal activities the typical manager performs have to do with communication—listening, 40%; talking, 35%; reading, 16%; and writing, 9%.[104] Listening and speaking often take place in meetings (see the Practical Action box "How to Streamline Meetings" on p. 491 in this chapter), although they are not the only occasions. Human resource managers consider interpersonal communication skills the most important factor in advancing their careers, according to one survey.[105] Let's see how you can be more effective at the essential communication skills.

Being an Effective Listener

Is listening something you're good at? Then you're the exception. Generally, people comprehend only about 35% of a typical verbal message, experts say.[106] Two-thirds of all employees feel management isn't listening to them.[107] Interestingly, the average speaker communicates 125 words per minute, while we can process 500 words per minute.

Poor listeners use this information-processing gap to daydream. They think about other things, thus missing the important parts of what's being communicated. Good listeners know how to use these gaps effectively, mentally summarizing the speaker's remarks, weighing the evidence, and listening between the lines. Listening skills, incidentally, are particularly important when you're communicating in the global culture.

Actively listening, truly listening, involves more than hearing, which is merely the physical component. **Active listening is the process of actively decoding and interpreting verbal messages.** Active listening requires full attention and processing of information, which hearing does not.

What's Your Listening Style—or Styles?   To begin to improve your active listening skills, you should first try to determine your two or three dominant listening styles, of the following five styles:[108]

Understand me. What's the recipe for effective listening—for really finding out what someone has to say? Probably it is *listen, watch, write, think, question.* What do you do to fight flagging concentration if you're tired or bored? You suppress negative thoughts, ignore distractions about the speaker's style of delivery or body language, and encourage the speaker with eye contact, an interested expression, and an attentive posture. This will make you more involved and interested in the subject matter.

1. **Appreciative style—listening to be amused.** An *appreciative listener* tends to listen for pleasure, doing easy listening and tending to tune out when there's no amusement or humor in what he or she is listening to.

2. **Empathic style—tuning into the speaker's emotions.** An *empathic listener* focuses on the speaker's feelings, concentrating on what he or she sees as well as says and reading people's body language and reactions.

3. **Comprehensive style—focusing on the speaker's logic.** A *comprehensive listener* tries to determine the rationale of the speaker's

argument, preferring logical presentations without interruptions, focusing on relationships among ideas, relating messages to his or her own experiences, waiting until all the information is available before expressing opinions.

4. **Discerning style—focusing on the main message.** A *discerning listener* tries to determine the speaker's main message and important points, often taking copious notes and concentrating hard on what the speaker says. Discerning listeners are good listeners and like information that flows evenly.

5. **Evaluative style—challenging the speaker.** An *evaluative listener* listens analytically, all the while formulating challenges to the speaker's points, asking lots of questions (perhaps to the point of being interruptive), and sometimes tuning out the speaker and missing data. If evaluative listeners receive too much illogical information, they often leave.

Which of these listening styles seems to apply to you?

Concentrate on the Content of the Message   Effective listening is a learned skill, but it takes energy and desire to develop it. Basically, however, it comes down to *pay attention to the content of the message.* Following are some suggestions for increasing your listening skills, which you can practice in your college lectures and seminars. *(See Table 15.10.)*

table 15.10

SIX KEYS TO EFFECTIVE LISTENING

1. **Don't rush to respond.** Don't think about what you're going to say until the other person has finished talking.
2. **Judge content, not delivery.** Don't tune out someone because of his or her accent, clothing, mannerisms, personality, or speaking style.
3. **Ask questions, summarize remarks.** Good listening is hard work. Ask questions to make sure you understand. Recap what the speaker said.
4. **Listen for ideas.** Don't get diverted by the details; try to concentrate on the main ideas.
5. **Resist distractions, show interest.** Don't get distracted by things other people are doing, paperwork on your desk, things happening outside the window, television or radio, and the like. Show the speaker you're listening, periodically restating in your own words what you've heard.
6. **Give a fair hearing.** Don't shut out unfavorable information just because you hear a term—"Republican," "Democrat," "union," "big business," "affirmative action," "corporate welfare"—that suggests ideas you're not comfortable with. Try to correct for your biases.

Sources: Derived from N. Skinner, "Communication Skills," *Selling Power,* July–August 1999, pp. 32–34; G. Manning, K. Curtis, and S. McMillen, *Building the Human Side of Work Community* (Cincinnati, OH: Thomson Executive Press, 1996), pp. 127–54; and J. Sandberg, "What Exactly Was It That the Boss Said? You Can Only Imagine," *The Wall Street Journal,* September 19, 2006, p. B1.

Being an Effective Reader

Reading shares many of the same skills as listening. You need to concentrate on the content of the message, judge the content and not the delivery, and concentrate on the main ideas. But because managers usually have to do so much reading, you also need to learn to apply some other strategies.

Realize That Speed Reading Doesn't Work   Perhaps you've thought that somewhere along the line you could take a course on speed reading. By and large, however, speed reading isn't effective. Psychologists have found that speed reading or skimming may work well with easy or familiar reading material, but it can lead to problems with dense or unfamiliar material. For instance, in one study, when questioned about their reading of difficult material, average readers got half the questions right, while speed readers got only one in three.[109]

Learn to Streamline Reading Management consultant and UCLA professor Kathryn Alesandrini offers a number of suggestions for how managers can streamline their reading.[110]

- **Be savvy about periodicals and books.** As a manager, you should review your magazine and newspaper subscriptions and eliminate as many as possible. You can subscribe to just a few industry publications, scan and mark interesting material, later read what's marked, and pitch the rest. Read summaries and reviews that condense business books and articles.

- **Transfer your reading load.** With some material you can ask some of your employees to screen or scan it first, then post an action note on each item that needs additional reading by you. You can also ask your staff to read important books and summarize them in four or five pages.

- **Make internal memos and e-mail more efficient.** Ask others to tell you up front in their e-mails, memos, and reports what they want you to do. Instruct them to include a one-page executive summary of a long report. When you communicate with them, give them specific questions you want answered.

Speed-read this? Maybe you could—if it's easy or familiar material. But lots of things managers are required to read take patient study. How are you going to manage such reading day after day?

Do Top-Down Reading—SQ3R "The key to better reading is to be a productive rather than a passive reader," writes Alesandrini. "You'll get more out of what you read if you literally produce meaningful connections between what you already know and what you're reading."[111] This leads to what she calls a "top-down" strategy for reading, a variant on the SQ3R (Survey, Question, Read, Recite, Review) method we discussed in the box at the end of Chapter 1. The top-down system is shown below. *(See Table 15.11.)*

table 15.11

FIVE STEPS TO BETTER READING

1. **Rate reasons to read.** Rate your reasons for reading ("Why should I read this? Will reading it contribute to my goals?").

2. **Question and predict answers.** Formulate specific questions you want the reading to answer. This will give you reasons for reading—to get answers to your questions.

3. **Survey the big picture.** Survey the material to be read so you can get a sense of the whole. Take a few minutes to get an overview so that you'll be better able to read with purpose.

4. **Skim for main ideas.** Skimming the material is similar to surveying, except it's on a smaller scale. You look for the essence of each subsection or paragraph.

5. **Summarize.** Summarize as you skim. Verbally restate or write notes of the main points, using your own words. Visualize or sketch the main points. Answer your initial questions as you skim the material.

Source: Derived from K. Alesandrini, *Survive Information Overload* (Homewood, IL: Irwin, 1992), pp. 191–202.

table 15.12

FIVE RULES FOR BUSINESS WRITING, BOTH ONLINE & OFFLINE

Don't ...
1. begin an e-mail with "Hey."
2. use abbreviations.
Do ...
3. spell words correctly.
4. use complete sentences.
5. use proper capitalization and punctuation.

Source: Derived from J. R. Fine, "Enhancing Gen Y Communication Skills," *Society for Human Resource Management,* March 13, 2009.

Being an Effective Writer

Writing is an essential management skill, all the more so because e-mail and texting have replaced the telephone in so much of business communication. In addition, downsizing has eliminated the administrative assistants who used to edit and correct business correspondence, so even upper-level executives often do their own correspondence now.[112] A lot of students, however, don't get enough practice in writing, which puts them at a career disadvantage. Most will have to be able to write standout job-seeking cover letters to accompany their résumés and later to write winning business proposals.[113] Taking a business writing class can be a real advantage. (Indeed, as a manager, you may have to identify employees who need writing training.)

Following are some tips for writing more effectively. These apply particularly to memos and reports but are also applicable to e-mail messages.

Don't Show Your Ignorance   E-mail correspondence and texting have made people more relaxed about spelling and grammar rules. Although this is fine among friends, as a manager you'll need to create a more favorable impression in your writing. Besides using the spelling checkers and grammar checkers built in to your word processing program, you should reread, indeed proofread, your writing before sending it on.

Some other tips are shown at left. *(See Table 15.12.)*

Understand Your Strategy Before You Write   Following are three strategies for laying out your ideas in writing.

1. **Most important to least important.** This is a good strategy when the action you want your reader to take is logical and not highly political.
2. **Least controversial to most controversial.** This builds support gradually and is best used when the decision is controversial or your reader is attached to a particular solution other than the one you're proposing.
3. **Negative to positive.** This strategy establishes a common ground with your reader and puts the positive argument last, which makes it stronger.[114]

Start with Your Purpose   Often people organize their messages backward, putting their real purpose last, points out Alesandrini. You should *start* your writing by telling your purpose and what you expect of the reader.

Write Simply, Concisely, & Directly   Keep your words simple and use short words, sentences, and phrases. Be direct instead of vague, and use the active voice rather than the passive. (Directness, active voice: "Please call a meeting for Wednesday." Vagueness, passive voice: "It is suggested that a meeting be called for Wednesday.")

Telegraph Your Writing with a Powerful Layout   Make your writing as easy to read as possible, using the tools of highlighting and white space.

- **Highlighting.** Highlighting consists of using **boldface** and *italics* to emphasize key concepts and introduce new concepts, and bullets—small circles or squares like the ones in the list you're reading—to emphasize list items. (Don't overuse any of these devices, or they'll lose their effect. And particularly don't use ALL CAPITAL LETTERS for emphasis, except rarely.)
- **White space.** White space, which consists of wide margins and a break between paragraphs, produces a page that is clean and attractive.[115]

Being an Effective Speaker

Speaking or talking covers a range of activities, from one-on-one conversations, to participating in meetings, to giving formal presentations. In terms of personal oral communication, most of the best advice comes under the heading of listening, since effective listening will dictate the appropriate talking you need to do.

However, the ability to talk to a room full of people—to make an oral presentation— is one of the greatest skills you can have. A study conducted by AT&T and Stanford University found that the top predictor of success and professional upward mobility is how much you enjoy public speaking and how effective you are at it.[116]

The biggest problem most people have with public speaking is controlling their nerves, since 46% of adults say the activity they dread most—exceeding housecleaning, 43%, and visiting the dentist, 41%—is public speaking (called glossophobia).[117] Author and lecturer Gael Lindenfield suggests that you can prepare your nerves by practicing your speech until it's near perfect, visualizing yourself performing with brilliance, getting reassurance from a friend, and getting to the speaking site early and releasing physical tension by doing deep breathing. (And staying away from alcohol and caffeine pick-me-ups before your speech.)[118] Some people find they do better if they stay away from their notes and just speak from the heart.[119]

As for the content of the speech, some brief and valuable advice is offered by speechwriter Phil Theibert, who says a speech comprises just three simple rules: (1) Tell them what you're going to say. (2) Say it. (3) Tell them what you said.[120]

1. Tell Them What You're Going to Say   The introduction should take 5–15% of your speaking time, and it should prepare the audience for the rest of the speech. Avoid jokes and such tired phrases as "I'm honored to be with you here today . . ." Because everything in your speech should be relevant, try to go right to the point. For example:

> *"Good afternoon. The subject of identity theft may seem far removed from the concerns of most employees. But I intend to describe how our supposedly private credit, health, employment, and other records are vulnerable to theft by so-called identity thieves and how you can protect yourself."*

2. Say It   The main body of the speech takes up 75–90% of your time. The most important thing to realize is that your audience won't remember more than a few points anyway. Thus, you need to decide which three or four points must be remembered.[121] Then cover them as succinctly as possible.

Be particularly attentive to transitions during the main body of the speech. Listening differs from reading in that the listener has only one chance to get your meaning. Thus, be sure you constantly provide your listeners with guidelines and transitional phrases so they can see where you're going. Example:

> *"There are five ways the security of your supposedly private files can be compromised. The first way is . . ."*

3. Tell Them What You Said   The end might take 5–10% of your time. Many professional speakers consider the conclusion to be as important as the introduction, so don't drop the ball here. You need a solid, strong, persuasive wrap-up.

Use some sort of signal phrase that cues your listeners that you are heading into your wind-up. Examples:

> *"Let's review the main points . . ."*
> *"In conclusion, what CAN you do to protect against unauthorized invasion of your private files? I point out five main steps. One . . ."*

Predictor for success. Enjoying public speaking and being good at it are the top predictors of success and upward mobility. Do you think you could develop these skills?

Give some thought to the last thing you will say. It should be strongly upbeat, a call to action, a thought for the day, a little story, a quotation. Examples:

"I want to leave you with one last thought . . ."
"Finally, let me close by sharing something that happened to me . . . "
"As Albert Einstein said, 'Imagination is more important than knowledge.'"

Then say "Thank you" and stop talking.   ●

Key Terms Used in This Chapter

active listening 499

communication 476

crowdsourcing 497

decoding 477

downward communication 489

encoding 477

external communication 490

feedback 477

formal communication channels 488

grapevine 490

horizontal communication 489

identity theft 496

informal communication channels 490

jargon 481

linguistic style 486

management by wandering around (MBWA) 490

media richness 479

medium 477

message 477

multicommunicating 492

noise 477

nonverbal communication 483

privacy 496

receiver 477

security 495

semantics 481

sender 477

social media 497

stereotype 483

telepresence technology 494

upward communication 489

Summary

15.1 The Communication Process: What It Is, How It Works

Communication is the transfer of information and understanding from one person to another. The process involves sender, message, and receiver; encoding and decoding; the medium; feedback; and dealing with "noise." The sender is the person wanting to share information. The information is called a message. The receiver is the person for whom the message is intended. Encoding is translating a message into understandable symbols or language. Decoding is interpreting and trying to make sense of the message. The medium is the pathway by which a message travels. Feedback is the process in which a receiver expresses his or her reaction to the sender's message. The entire communication process can be disrupted at any point by noise, defined as any disturbance that interferes with the transmission of a message.

For effective communication, a manager must select the right medium. Media richness indicates how well a particular medium conveys information and promotes learning. The richer a medium is,

the better it is at conveying information. Face-to-face presence is the richest; an advertising flyer would be one of the lowest. A rich medium is best for nonroutine situations and to avoid oversimplification. A lean medium is best for routine situations and to avoid overloading.

15.2 Barriers to Communication

Barriers to communication are of three types:
(1) Physical barriers are exemplified by walls, background noise, and time-zone differences.
(2) Semantics is the study of the meaning of words. Jargon, terminology specific to a particular profession or group, can be a semantic barrier.
(3) Personal barriers are individual attributes that hinder communication. Nine such barriers are
(a) variable skills in communicating effectively,
(b) variations in frames of reference and experiences that affect how information is interpreted,
(c) variations in trustworthiness and credibility,
(d) oversized egos, (e) faulty listening skills,
(f) tendency to judge others' messages, (g) inability to listen with understanding, (h) stereotypes

(oversimplified beliefs about a certain group of people) and prejudices, and (i) nonverbal communication (messages sent outside of the written or spoken word, including body language).

Six ways in which nonverbal communication is expressed are through (1) eye contact, (2) facial expressions, (3) body movements and gestures, (4) touch, (5) setting, and (6) time.

15.3 How Managers Fit into the Communication Process

Communication channels may be formal or informal.

Formal communication channels follow the chain of command and are recognized as official. Formal communication is of three types: (1) Vertical communication is the flow of messages up and down the organizational hierarchy. (2) Horizontal communication flows within and between work units; its main purpose is coordination. (3) External communication flows between people inside and outside the organization.

Informal communication channels develop outside the formal structure and do not follow the chain of command. Two aspects of informal channels are the grapevine and management by wandering around. (1) The grapevine is the unofficial communication system of the informal organization. The grapevine is faster than formal channels, is about 75% accurate, and is used by employees to acquire most on-the-job information. (2) In management by wandering around (MBWA), a manager literally wanders around his or her organization and talks with people across all lines of authority; this reduces distortion caused by formal communication.

15.4 Communication in the Information Age

A modern-day trend is multicommunicating, the use of technology to participate in several interactions at the same time. The universal language of 1s and 0s gives us immediate access to unprecedented amounts of information; however, faster, far-flung digital communication does not necessarily mean better communication.

With the rise of the Internet has come the rise of the "Always On" generation (Net Generation, Gen Y, the Millennials), 88 million people born 1977–1997, who are accustomed to digital communication and who in a few years will account for nearly half the employees in the world. Their outlook is having a profound impact on the workplace, bringing new approaches to collaboration, knowledge sharing, and innovation. This generation puts a strong emphasis on finding work that's personally fulfilling, craves stimulation, and seeks high-quality colleagues and flexible work arrangements.

Digital communication has altered traditional links between work, place, and time, as seen in videoconferencing (teleconferencing) and telepresence technology (high-definition videoconferencing systems that simulate face-to-face meetings between users); telecommuting, involving performing office work at home; and teleworking, involving performing office work nearly anywhere.

The downside of the digital age involves problems with security, safeguards for protecting information technology against disasters, system failures, and unauthorized access; privacy, the right of people not to reveal information about themselves, particularly identify theft, in which thieves highjack a person's name and identity and use his or her good credit rating to get cash or buy things; e-mail productivity problems; and cellphone use and abuse.

Social media—Internet-based and mobile technologies (Facebook, Twitter) used to generate interactive dialogue with members of a network— enable businesses to connect in real time and over distances with many customers, suppliers, and employees. Social media are also used in crowdsourcing—obtaining needed services, ideas, or content by soliciting contributions from a large group of people.

15.5 Improving Communication Effectiveness

People tend to favor only a few of five listening styles—appreciative, empathic, comprehensive, discerning, and evaluative. Active listening, the process of actively decoding and interpreting verbal messages, requires full attention and processing of information. To become a good listener, you should concentrate on the content of the message, not delivery; ask questions and summarize the speaker's remarks; listen for ideas; resist distractions and show interest; and give the speaker a fair hearing.

To become a good reader, you need to first realize that speed reading usually doesn't work. You should also be savvy about how you handle periodicals and books, transfer your reading load to some of your employees, and ask others to use e-mails and reports to tell you what they want you to do. A top-down reading system that's a variant on the SQ3R system (survey, question, read, recite, review) is also helpful.

To become an effective writer, you can follow several suggestions. Use spelling and grammar checkers in word processing software. Use three strategies for laying out your ideas in writing: go from most important topic to least important; go from least controversial topic to most controversial; and go from negative to positive. When organizing your message, start with your purpose. Write simply, concisely, and directly. Telegraph your writing through use of highlighting and white space.

To become an effective speaker, follow three simple rules. Tell people what you're going to say. Say it. Tell them what you said.

Management in Action

Procter & Gamble Company Restricts Use of Internet Sites

At Procter & Gamble Co., P&G employees used to need approval from senior executives to use the Internet. Recently, though, web access got so loose that the company is now blocking some sites altogether.

The consumer-products giant sent an internal memo to its 129,000 employees limiting their use of Pandora Media Inc.'s P streaming music service and Netflix Inc.'s NFLX-streaming movies.

The move, announced to employees Tuesday, came after information-technology staffers looking into an Internet slowdown at P&G found that on an average day employees were viewing 50,000 five-minute YouTube videos and listening to 4,000 hours of music on Pandora.

Since P&G uses YouTube for business, it decided to block Netflix instead, as well as Pandora. Both heavily stream media and contributed to the bandwidth slowdown, said P&G Spokesman Paul Fox.

"They're both great sites," he added. "But if you want to download movies, do it on your own time. If you want to download music, do it on your own time."

P&G severely restricted Internet access when it first made the web available to employees around 1995, said Manjit Singh, a former P&G employee who worked in technology and helped launch P&G's first website. Approval by a senior vice president was necessary to get extensive access, and some sites, including the precursor to ESPN.com, were banned, said Mr. Singh, who is now a chief information officer in the entertainment and hospitality industry.

A number of businesses are struggling with bandwidth problems as extensive downloading soaks up network capacity and risks slowing connections.

For instance, if a company has 500 employees and three are watching Netflix movies, they could use most of a company's bandwidth if it doesn't have a lot.

Indeed, 300 employees surfing the web could use the same amount as the movie watchers, said Art Reisman, chief technology officer of NetEqualizer, which is part of traffic-management firm APconnections Inc. . . .

P&G looked at other companies in the area and found that its policies were much more lenient than theirs, Mr. Fox said. The company also found the manufacturing and financial sectors restrict almost all Internet access, especially sites like Facebook, Twitter and YouTube.

Cincinnati-based uniform maker Cintas Corp. (CTAS) enforced a social-media policy in January 2011, blocking sites like Facebook, Twitter, Pandora, and Netflix that it deemed inappropriate for business use, spokeswoman Heather Maley said.

Mr. Fox said P&G has no plans to block social-networking sites because they have become important platforms for its digital marketing campaigns and staffers need them for work.

FOR DISCUSSION

1. Which of the downsides to social media are occurring at P&G? Explain.
2. Will P&G's decision result in the loss of any of the benefits associated with social media? Discuss your rationale.
3. What is your overall opinion about P&G's decision to restrict the use of various Internet sites?
4. Do you agree with Cintas Corp.'s decision to block access to Facebook, Twitter, Pandora, and Netflix during work hours? Why?
5. What does this case teach you about effective communication? Explain.

Source: Excerpted from Emily Glazer, "P&G Curbs Employees' Internet Use," *The Wall Street Journal,* April 4, 2012, p. B5. Copyright © 2012 by Dow Jones & Company, Inc. Reproduced with permission of Dow Jones & Company, Inc. via Copyright Clearance Center.

Self-Assessment

What Is Your Most Comfortable Learning Style?

OBJECTIVES

1. To learn about your visual, auditory, and kinesthetic learning/communication style.
2. To consider how knowledge about learning/communication styles can be used to enhance your communication effectiveness.

INTRODUCTION

The purpose of this exercise is to find out what your most prominent learning style is—that is, what forms of communication can you best learn from. You should find the information of value for understanding not only your own style but those of others. Knowing your own style should also allow you to be a much more effective learner.

INSTRUCTIONS

Read the following 36 statements and indicate the extent to which each statement is consistent with your behavior by using the following rating scale: 1 = almost never applies; 2 = applies once in a while; 3 = sometimes applies; 4 = often applies; 5 = almost always applies.

1. I take lots of notes.	1	2	3	4	5
2. When talking to others, I have the hardest time handling those who do not maintain good eye contact with me.	1	2	3	4	5
3. I make lists and notes because I remember things better when I write them down.	1	2	3	4	5
4. When reading a novel, I pay a lot of attention to passages picturing the clothing, scenery, setting, etc.	1	2	3	4	5
5. I need to write down directions so that I can remember them.	1	2	3	4	5
6. I need to see the person I am talking to in order to keep my attention focused on the subject.	1	2	3	4	5
7. When meeting a person for the first time, I initially notice the style of dress, visual characteristics, and neatness.	1	2	3	4	5
8. When I am at a party, one of the things I love to do is stand back and "people watch."	1	2	3	4	5
9. When recalling information, I can see it in my mind and remember where I saw it.	1	2	3	4	5
10. If I had to explain a new procedure or technique, I would prefer to write it out.	1	2	3	4	5
11. With free time I am most likely to watch television or read.	1	2	3	4	5
12. If my boss has a message for me, I am most comfortable when he or she sends a memo.	1	2	3	4	5
Total A (the minimum is 12 and the maximum is 60)				_____	

1. When I read, I read out loud or move my lips to hear the words in my head.	1	2	3	4	5
2. When talking to someone else, I have the hardest time handling those who do not talk back with me.	1	2	3	4	5
3. I do not take a lot of notes, but I still remember what was said. Taking notes distracts me from the speaker.	1	2	3	4	5
4. When reading a novel, I pay a lot of attention to passages involving conversations.	1	2	3	4	5

5. I like to talk to myself when solving a problem or writing.	1	2	3	4	5
6. I can understand what a speaker says, even if I am not focused on the speaker.	1	2	3	4	5
7. I remember things easier by repeating them again and again.	1	2	3	4	5
8. When I am at a party, one of the things I love to do is have in-depth conversations about a subject that is important to me.	1	2	3	4	5
9. I would rather receive information from the radio than a newspaper.	1	2	3	4	5
10. If I had to explain a new procedure or technique, I would prefer telling about it.	1	2	3	4	5
11. With free time I am most likely to listen to music.	1	2	3	4	5
12. If my boss has a message for me, I am most comfortable when he or she calls on the phone.	1	2	3	4	5

Total B (the minimum is 12 and the maximum is 60) _____

1. I am not good at reading or listening to directions.	1	2	3	4	5
2. When talking to someone else, I have the hardest time handling those who do not show any kind of emotional support.	1	2	3	4	5
3. I take notes and doodle, but I rarely go back and look at them.	1	2	3	4	5
4. When reading a novel, I pay a lot of attention to passages revealing feelings, moods, action, drama, etc.	1	2	3	4	5
5. When I am reading, I move my lips.	1	2	3	4	5
6. I will exchange words and places and use my hands a lot when I can't remember the right thing to say.	1	2	3	4	5
7. My desk appears disorganized.	1	2	3	4	5
8. When I am at a party, one of the things I love to do is enjoy activities, such as dancing, games, and totally losing myself.	1	2	3	4	5
9. I like to move around. I feel trapped when seated at a meeting or desk.	1	2	3	4	5
10. If I had to explain a new procedure or technique, I would prefer actually demonstrating it.	1	2	3	4	5
11. With free time, I am most likely to exercise.	1	2	3	4	5
12. If my boss has a message for me, I am most comfortable when he or she talks to me in person.	1	2	3	4	5

Total C (the minimum is 12 and the maximum is 60) _____

SCORING & INTERPRETATION

Total A is your Visual Score _____; Total B is your Auditory Score _____; and Total C is your Kinesthetic Score _____. The area in which you have your highest score represents your "dominant" learning style. You can learn from all three, but typically you learn best using one style. Communication effectiveness is increased when your dominant style is consistent with the communication style used by others. For example, if you are primarily kinesthetic and your boss gives you directions orally, you may have trouble communicating because you do not learn or process communication well by just being told something. You must consider not only how you communicate but also how the people you work with communicate.

QUESTIONS FOR DISCUSSION

1. Do you agree with the assessment? Why or why not? Explain.

2. How valuable is it to know your learning style? Does it help explain why you did well in some learning situations and poorly in others? Describe and explain.

3. How important is it to know the learning style of those you work with? Explain.

Source: From www.nwlink.com/~donclark/hrd/vak.html. Reprinted with permission.

Legal/Ethical Challenge

Should Companies Be Allowed to Check Personal E-Mail Accounts?

This case involves actions taken by the Food and Drug Administration (FDA) against a group of six of its scientists and doctors. The employees had warned Congress about some medical devices that the agency was planning to approve because they thought the devices were unsafe. The FDA ultimately "secretly monitored the personal e-mail" of this group of employees.

The surveillance spanned a two-year period of time, and the employees have filed a lawsuit against the FDA claiming that information obtained via the e-mails led to harassment or termination.

Said a newspaper story, "Copies of the e-mails show that, starting in January 2009, the FDA intercepted communications with congressional staffers and draft versions of whistle-blower complaints complete with editing notes in the margins. The agency also took electronic snapshots of the computer desktops of the FDA employees and reviewed documents they saved on the hard drives of their government computers.

"FDA computers post a warning, visible when users log on, that they should have 'no reasonable expectation of privacy' in any data passing through or stored on the system, and that the government may intercept any such data at any time for any lawful government purpose.

"But in the suit, the doctors and scientists say the government violated their constitutional privacy rights by gazing into personal e-mail accounts for the purpose of monitoring activity that they say was lawful."

SOLVING THE CHALLENGE

What is your opinion about companies monitoring personal e-mail accounts?

1. These doctors and scientists used computer equipment owned by the FDA to complain to Congress and they were warned to have no expectations about privacy. It thus seems reasonable that the FDA should be allowed to check someone's personal e-mail accounts.

2. I agree that companies should be allowed to check e-mails made on equipment owned by the company. That said, these employees were complaining about legitimate concerns involving medical devices. It thus seems unfair that complaints like this on personal e-mail accounts should be used to harass or dismiss an employee.

3. Personal e-mail accounts are personal, and companies or governmental agencies should not be allowed to monitor contents on these accounts. It does not matter who owns the equipment.

4. Invent other options.

Source: Excerpted from "FDA Staffers Sue Agency Over Monitoring of Personal E-Mail," *The Arizona Republic,* January 31, 2012, p. A11. A11; reprinted from *The Washington Post.*

chapter 16

Control Systems & Quality Management
Techniques for Enhancing Organizational Effectiveness

Improving Productivity: Going Beyond Control Techniques to Get the Best Results

How, as a manager, can you increase productivity—get better results with what you have to work with?

In this chapter we discuss control techniques for achieving better results. What are other ways for improving productivity? Following are some suggestions:[1]

Establish Base Points, Set Goals, & Measure Results

To be able to tell whether your work unit is becoming more productive, you need to establish systems of measurement. You can start by establishing the base point, such as the number of customers served per day, quantity of products produced per hour, and the like. You can then set goals to establish new levels that you wish to attain, and institute systems of measurement with which to ascertain progress. Finally, you can measure the results and modify the goals or work processes as necessary.

Use New Technology

Clearly, this is a favorite way to enhance productivity. With a computerized database, you can store and manipulate information better than you can using a box of file cards. Still, computerization is not a panacea; information technology also offers plenty of opportunities for simply wasting time.

Improve Match Between Employees & Jobs

You can take steps to ensure the best fit between employees and their jobs: improve employee selection, training, job redesign, and incentives.

Encourage Employee Involvement & Innovation

Companies improve productivity by funding research and development (R&D) departments. As a manager, you can encourage your employees, who are closest to the work process, to come up with suggestions for improving their own operations. And, of course, you can give workers a bigger say, provide flextime, and reward people for learning new skills and taking on more responsibility.

Encourage Employee Diversity

By hiring people who are diverse in gender, age, race, and ethnicity, you're more likely to have a workforce with different experience, outlooks, values, and skills. By melding their differences, a team can achieve results that exceed the previous standards.

Redesign the Work Process

Some managers think productivity can be enhanced through cost cutting, but this is not always the case. Sometimes the work process can be redesigned to eliminate inessential steps.

For Discussion Some observers think the pressure on managers to perform will be even more intense than before, because the world is undergoing a transformation on the scale of the industrial revolution 200 years ago as we move further into an information-based economy.[2] In what ways do you think you'll have to become a champion of adaptation?

forecast | What's Ahead in This Chapter

This final chapter explores the final management function—control. Controlling is monitoring performance, comparing it with goals, and taking corrective action as needed. We discuss managing for *productivity,* explaining why it's important. We then discuss *controlling,* identify six reasons it's needed, explain the steps in the control process, and describe three types of control managers use. Next we discuss levels and areas of control. In the fifth section, we discuss financial tools for control—budgets, financial statements, ratio analysis, and audits. We then discuss total quality management (TQM), identifying its core philosophies and showing some TQM techniques. We conclude by describing the four keys to successful control and five barriers to successful control.

16.1 MANAGING FOR PRODUCTIVITY

major question

How do managers influence productivity?

THE BIG PICTURE
The purpose of a manager is to make decisions about the four management functions—planning, organizing, leading, and controlling—to get people to achieve productivity and realize results. Productivity is defined by the formula of outputs divided by inputs for a specified period of time. Productivity is important because it determines whether the organization will make a profit or even survive.

In Chapter 1, we pointed out that as a manager in the 21st century you will operate in a complex environment in which you will need to deal with seven challenges—managing for (1) competitive advantage, (2) diversity, (3) globalization, (4) information technology, (5) ethical standards, (6) sustainability, and (7) your own happiness and life goals.

Within this dynamic world, you will draw on the practical and theoretical knowledge described in this book to make decisions about the four management functions of planning, organizing, leading, and controlling.

The purpose is to get the people reporting to you *to achieve productivity and realize results.*

This process is diagrammed below, pulling together the main topics of this book. *(See Figure 16.1.)*

figure 16.1
MANAGING FOR PRODUCTIVITY & RESULTS

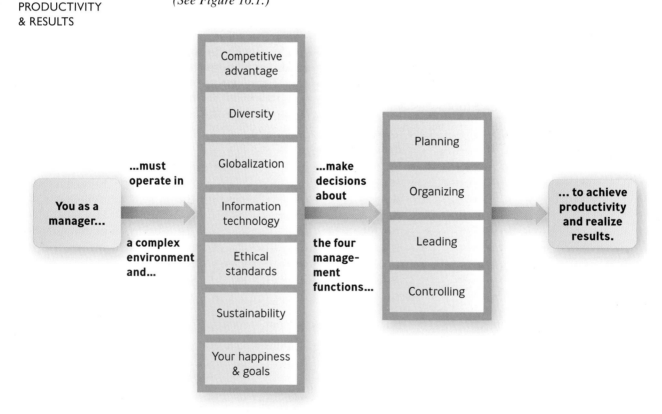

What Is Productivity?

Productivity can be applied at any level, whether for you as an individual, for the work unit you're managing, or for the organization you work for. Productivity is defined by the formula of *outputs divided by inputs* for a specified period of time. Outputs are all the goods and services produced. Inputs are not only labor but also capital, materials, and energy. That is,

$$\text{productivity} = \frac{\text{outputs}}{\text{inputs}} \quad \text{or} \quad \frac{\text{goods} + \text{services}}{\text{labor} + \text{capital} + \text{materials} + \text{energy}}$$

What does this mean to you as a manager? It means that you can increase overall productivity by making substitutions or increasing the efficiency of any one element: labor, capital, materials, energy. For instance, you can increase the efficiency of labor by substituting capital in the form of equipment or machinery, as in employing a backhoe instead of laborers with shovels to dig a hole.[3] Or you can increase the efficiency of materials inputs by expanding their uses, as when lumber mills discovered they could sell not only boards but also sawdust and wood chips for use in gardens. Or you can increase the efficiency of energy by putting solar panels on a factory roof so the organization won't have to buy so much electrical power from utility companies.

Why Increasing Productivity Is Important

"Productivity growth is the elixir that makes an economy flourish," says one business article.[4] "Our society is wealthy," says another, "precisely because it can churn out products like automobiles, flush toilets, and Google search algorithms at relatively low cost."[5] That is, the more goods and services that are produced and made easily available to us and for export, the higher our standard of living. Increasing the gross domestic product—the total dollar value of all the goods and services produced in the United States—depends on raising productivity, as well as on a growing workforce.

The U.S. Productivity Track Record   During the 1960s, productivity in the United States averaged a hefty 2.9% a year, then sank to a disappointing 1.5% right up until 1995. Because the decline in productivity no longer allowed the improvement in wages and living standards that had benefited so many Americans in the 1960s, millions of people took second jobs or worked longer hours to keep from falling behind. From 1995 to 2000, however, during the longest economic boom in American history, the productivity rate jumped to 2.5% annually, as the total output of goods and services rose faster than the total hours needed to produce them. From the business cycle peak in the first quarter of 2001 to the end of 2007, productivity grew at an annual rate of 2.7%.[6] Then came the recession year 2008, when it fell to 2%. Then, from the fourth quarter of 2008 to the fourth quarter of 2009, productivity rose 5.4%—"a turnaround unprecedented in modern history," says *Newsweek*—and it also rose an impressive 4.1% in 2010.[7] From the first quarter of 2011 to the first quarter of 2012, however, the rate was only 0.5%, as companies began to approach the limit of how much they could squeeze from the workforce.[8]

The Role of Information Technology   Most economists seem to think the recent productivity growth is the result of organizations' huge investment in information technology—computers, the Internet, other telecommunications advances, and computer-guided production line improvements.[9] From 1995 to 2001, for example, labor productivity in services grew at a 2.6% rate (outpacing the 2.3% for goods-producing sectors), the result, economists think, of information technology.[10] (Since 2001, productivity has continued to advance in the service sectors in relation to the goods-producing sectors.)[11] In particular, many companies have implemented *enterprise resource planning (ERP)* **software systems, information systems for integrating virtually all aspects of a business,** helping managers stay on top of the latest developments.

Maintaining productivity depends on *control.* Let's look at this. ●

Competing internationally for productivity. This oil tanker represents the continual competition among companies and among nations to achieve productivity—"a matter of survival" for the United States, some leaders believe. Is our nation doing everything it could to be more productive? What about taking measures to reduce dependence on foreign oil?

major question

Why is control such an important managerial function?

THE BIG PICTURE

Controlling is monitoring performance, comparing it with goals, and taking corrective action. This section describes six reasons why control is needed and four steps in the control process.

Control is making something happen the way it was planned to happen. **Controlling is defined as monitoring performance, comparing it with goals, and taking corrective action as needed.** Controlling is the fourth management function, along with planning, organizing, and leading, and its purpose is plain: to make sure that performance meets objectives.

figure 16.2

CONTROLLING FOR PRODUCTIVITY

What you as a manager do to get things done, with controlling shown in relation to the three other management functions. (These are not lockstep; all four functions happen concurrently.)

- **Planning** is setting goals and deciding how to achieve them.
- **Organizing** is arranging tasks, people, and other resources to accomplish the work.
- **Leading** is motivating people to work hard to achieve the organization's goals.
- **Controlling** is concerned with seeing that the right things happen at the right time in the right way.

All these functions affect one another and in turn affect an organization's productivity. *(See Figure 16.2.)*

| **Planning** You set goals & decide how to achieve them. | **Organizing** You arrange tasks, people, & other resources to accomplish the work. | **Leading** You motivate people to work hard to achieve the organization's goals. | **Controlling** You monitor performance, compare it with goals, & take corrective action as needed. | For productivity |

Why Is Control Needed?

Lack of control mechanisms can lead to problems for both managers and companies. For example, the CEO of Yahoo, Scott Thompson, is discovered to have falsified his résumé by claiming to have a computer science degree—and 11 days later he is out, bringing turmoil to an already troubled company.[12] The senior banker of J. P. Morgan Chase, Ina Drew, contracts Lyme disease and is frequently out of the office when traders begin taking more and more risky bets, culminating in a loss of at least $3 billion and public demands for greater bank regulation.[13] California-based Pacific Gas & Electric Co. accidentally overpressurizes pipelines on its gas system more than 120 times since its 2010 San Bruno explosion that killed eight people, raising risks of another disaster.[14] Could greater control have helped avoid or reduce the consequences of these situations? Of course.

There are six reasons why control is needed.

1. To Adapt to Change & Uncertainty Markets shift. Consumer tastes change. New competitors appear. Technologies are reborn. New materials are invented. Government regulations are altered. All organizations must deal with these kinds of environmental changes and uncertainties. Control systems can help managers anticipate, monitor, and react to these changes.[15]

Example: As is certainly apparent by now, the issue of climate change or global warming has created a lot of change and uncertainty for many industries. The restaurant industry in particular is feeling the pressure to become "greener," since restaurants are the retail world's largest energy user, with a restaurant using five times more energy per square foot than any other type of commercial building, according to Pacific Gas & Electric's Food Service Technology Center.[16] Nearly 80% that commercial food service spends annually for energy use is lost in inefficient food cooking, holding, and storage. In addition, a typical restaurant generates 100,000 pounds of garbage per location per year. Thus, restaurants are being asked to reduce their "carbon footprints" by instituting tighter controls on energy use.[17]

2. To Discover Irregularities & Errors Small problems can mushroom into big ones. Cost overruns, manufacturing defects, employee turnover, bookkeeping errors, and customer dissatisfaction are all matters that may be tolerable in the short run. But in the long run, they can bring about even the downfall of an organization.

Example: You might not even miss a dollar a month looted from your credit card account. But an Internet hacker who does this with thousands of customers can undermine the confidence of consumers using their credit cards to charge online purchases at Amazon.com, Priceline.com, and other web retailers. Thus, a computer program that monitors Internet charge accounts for small, unexplained deductions can be a valuable control strategy.

3. To Reduce Costs, Increase Productivity, or Add Value Control systems can reduce labor costs, eliminate waste, increase output, and increase product delivery cycles. In addition, controls can help add value to a product so that customers will be more inclined to choose it over rival products.

Example: As we have discussed early in the book (and will again in this chapter), the use of quality controls among Japanese car manufacturers resulted in cars being produced that were perceived as being better built than American cars. Another example: 3M Co.'s system for creating plastic picture-hanging hooks used to be split among four states and take 100 days; after reworking the system to get rid of "hairballs," as the former CEO called them, now all production takes place at one hub and takes a third as much time.[18]

4. To Detect Opportunities Hot-selling products. Competitive prices on materials. Changing population trends. New overseas markets. Controls can help alert managers to opportunities that might have otherwise gone unnoticed.

Example: A markdown on certain grocery-store items may result in a rush of customer demand for those products, signaling store management that similar items might also sell faster if they were reduced in price.

5. To Deal with Complexity Does the right hand know what the left hand is doing? When a company becomes larger or when it merges with another company, it may find it has several product lines, materials-purchasing policies, customer bases, even workers from different cultures. Controls help managers coordinate these various elements.

Example: In recent years, Macy's Inc. has twice had to deal with complexity. In 2006, it pulled together several chains with different names—Marshall Field's, Robinsons-May, Kaufmann's, and other local stores—into one chain with one name, Macy's, and a much-promoted national strategy. But after losing money in 2007, CEO Terry Lundgren began altering course from a one-size-fits-all nationwide approach to a strategy that tailors the merchandise in local stores to cater to local tastes.[19]

6. To Decentralize Decision Making & Facilitate Teamwork Controls allow top management to decentralize decision making at lower levels within the organization and to encourage employees to work together in teams.

Example: At General Motors, former chairman Alfred Sloan set the level of return on investment he expected his divisions to achieve, enabling him to push decision-making authority down to lower levels while still maintaining authority over the sprawling GM organization.[20] Later GM used controls to facilitate the team approach in its joint venture with Toyota at its California plant.

The six reasons are summarized below. *(See Figure 16.3.)*

figure 16.3

SIX REASONS WHY CONTROL IS NEEDED

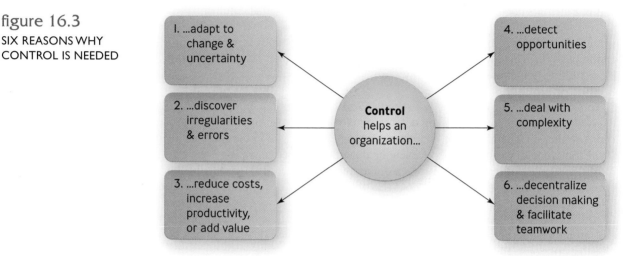

Steps in the Control Process

Control systems may be altered to fit specific situations, but generally they follow the same steps. The four *control process steps* **are (1) establish standards; (2) measure performance; (3) compare performance to standards; and (4) take corrective action, if necessary.** *(See Figure 16.4.)*

figure 16.4

STEPS IN THE CONTROL PROCESS

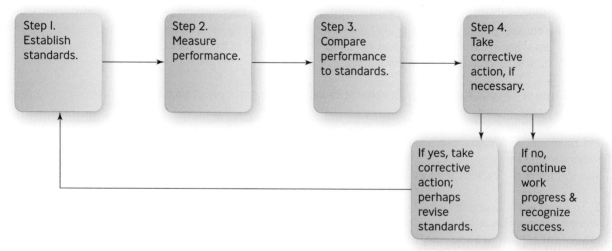

Let's consider these four steps.

1. Establish Standards: "What Is the Outcome We Want?" A *control standard,* **or** *performance standard* **or simply** *standard,* **is the desired performance level for a given goal.** Standards may be narrow or broad, and they can be set for almost anything, although they are best measured when they can be made quantifiable.

Nonprofit institutions might have standards for level of charitable contributions, number of students retained, or degree of legal compliance. For-profit organizations might have standards of financial performance, employee hiring, manufacturing defects, percentage increase in market share, percentage reduction in costs, number of customer complaints, and return on investment. More subjective standards, such as level of employee morale, can also be set, although they may have to be expressed more quantifiably as reduced absenteeism and sick days and increased job applications.

One technique for establishing standards is to use *the balanced scorecard,* as we explain later in this chapter.

2. Measure Performance: "What Is the Actual Outcome We Got?"
The second step in the control process is to measure performance, such as by number of products sold, units produced, or cost per item sold. For example, Hyundai has a quality goal signified by GQ 3-3-5-5. The goal represents the company's desire, expressed in 2010, to finish in the top three in quality ratings provided by J. D. Power's dependability survey within three years, and to be among the top five quality automakers within five years.[21] (In 2012, the Hyundai Genesis was named the most dependable midsize premium car by J. D. Power.)[22]

Performance measures are usually obtained from three sources: (1) written reports, including computerized printouts; (2) oral reports, as in a salesperson's weekly recitation of accomplishments to the sales manager; and (3) personal observation, as when a manager takes a stroll of the factory floor to see what employees are doing.

As we've hinted, measurement techniques can vary for different industries, as for manufacturing industries versus service industries. We discuss this further later in the chapter.

3. Compare Performance to Standards: "How Do the Desired & Actual Outcomes Differ?"
The third step in the control process is to compare measured performance against the standards established. Most managers are delighted with performance that exceeds standards, which becomes an occasion for handing out bonuses, promotions, and perhaps offices with a view. For performance that is below standards, they need to ask: Is the deviation from performance significant? The greater the difference between desired and actual performance, the greater the need for action.

How much deviation is acceptable? That depends on *the range of variation* built in to the standards in step 1. In voting for political candidates, for instance, there is supposed to be no range of variation; as the expression goes, "every vote counts" (although the 2000 U.S. presidential election was an eye-opener for many people in this regard). In political polling, however, a range of 3%–4% error is considered an acceptable range of variation. In machining parts for the spacecraft *Orion* (NASA's scheduled 2015 successor to the space shuttle), the range of variation may be a good deal less tolerant than when machining parts for a power lawnmower.

The range of variation is often incorporated in computer systems into a principle called management by exception. **Management by exception is a control principle that states that managers should be informed of a situation only if data show a significant deviation from standards.**

4. Take Corrective Action, If Necessary: "What Changes Should We Make to Obtain Desirable Outcomes?"
There are three possibilities here: (1) Make no changes. (2) Recognize and reinforce positive performance. (3) Take action to correct negative performance.

When performance meets or exceeds the standards set, managers should give rewards, ranging from giving a verbal "Job well done" to more substantial payoffs such as raises, bonuses, and promotions to reinforce good behavior.

When performance falls significantly short of the standard, managers should carefully examine the reasons why and take the appropriate action. Sometimes it may turn out the standards themselves were unrealistic, owing to changing conditions, in which case the standards need to be altered. Sometimes it may become apparent that employees haven't been given the resources for achieving the standards. And sometimes the employees may need more attention from management as a way of signaling that they have been insufficient in fulfilling their part of the job bargain. ●

Steps in the Control Process: What's Expected of UPS Drivers?

UPS, which employs 99,000 U.S. drivers, has established Integrad, an 11,500-square-foot training center 10 miles outside Washington, D.C. There trainees practice UPS-prescribed "340 Methods" shown to save seconds and improve safety. Graduates of the training, who are generally former package sorters, are eligible to do a job that pays an average of $74,000 annually.[23] (Because about 30% of driver candidates flunk training based on books and lectures, UPS now uses videogames, a contraption that simulates walking on ice, and an obstacle course around an artificial village.)

Establishing Standards. UPS establishes certain standards for its drivers that set projections for the number of miles driven, deliveries, and pickups. For instance, drivers are taught to walk at a "brisk pace" of 2.5 paces per second, except under icy or other unsafe conditions. However, because conditions vary depending on whether routes are urban, suburban, or rural, standards vary for different routes.[24]

Measuring Performance. Every day, UPS managers look at a computer printout showing the miles, deliveries, and pickups a driver attained during his or her shift the previous day. In general, drivers are expected to make five deliveries in 19 minutes.

Comparing Performance to Standards. UPS managers compare the printout of a driver's performance (miles driven and number of pickups and deliveries) with the standards that were set for his or her particular route. For instance, the printout will show whether drivers took longer than the 15.5 seconds allowed to park a truck and retrieve one package from the cargo. A range of variation may be allowed to take into account such matters as winter or summer driving or traffic conditions that slow productivity.

Taking Corrective Action. When a UPS driver fails to perform according to the standards set for him or her, a supervisor then rides along and gives suggestions for improvement. If drivers are unable to improve, they are warned, then suspended, and then dismissed.

YOUR CALL

The UPS controls were devised by industrial engineers based on experience. Do you think the same kinds of controls could be established for, say, filling out tax forms for H&R Block?

Small business. How important is it for small businesses to implement all four steps of the control process? Do you think that employees in small companies—such as a bicycle shop, restaurant, or landscaping firm—typically have more or less independence from managerial control than those in large companies do?

THE BIG PICTURE

This section describes three levels of control—strategic, tactical, and operational—and six areas of control: physical, human, informational, financial, structural (bureaucratic and decentralized), and cultural.

How are you going to apply the steps of control to your own management area? Let's look at this in three ways: First, you need to consider the *level* of management at which you operate—top, middle, or first level. Second, you need to consider the *areas* that you draw on for resources—physical, human, information, and/or financial. Finally, you need to consider the *style* or control philosophy—bureaucratic, market, or clan, as we will explain.

Levels of Control: Strategic, Tactical, & Operational

There are three levels of control, which correspond to the three principal managerial levels: *strategic* planning by top managers, *tactical* planning by middle managers, and *operational* planning by first-line (supervisory) managers.

1. Strategic Control by Top Managers *Strategic control* **is monitoring performance to ensure that strategic plans are being implemented and taking corrective action as needed.** Strategic control is mainly performed by top managers, those at the CEO and VP levels, who have an organization-wide perspective. For example, Ford Motor Company CEO Alan Mulally and his senior managers meet every Thursday to review performance across the company's global operations. They specifically review the performance of its suppliers because these companies have a significant effect on Ford's profitability and quality. They ultimately determine which suppliers to keep and which ones to let go. [25]

2. Tactical Control by Middle Managers *Tactical control* **is monitoring performance to ensure that tactical plans—those at the divisional or departmental level—are being implemented and taking corrective action as needed.** Tactical control is done mainly by middle managers, those with such titles as "division head," "plant manager," and "branch sales manager." Reporting is done on a weekly or monthly basis.

3. Operational Control by First-Level Managers *Operational control* **is monitoring performance to ensure that operational plans—day-to-day goals—are being implemented and taking corrective action as needed.** Operational control is done mainly by first-level managers, those with titles such as "department head," "team leader," or "supervisor." Reporting is done on a daily basis.

Considerable interaction occurs among the three levels, with lower-level managers providing information upward and upper-level managers checking on some of the more critical aspects of plan implementation below them.

Six Areas of Control

The six areas of organizational control are *physical, human, informational, financial, structural,* and *cultural.*

1. Physical Area The physical area includes buildings, equipment, and tangible products. Examples: There are equipment controls to monitor the use of computers, cars, and other machinery. There are inventory-management controls to keep track of how many products are in stock, how many will be needed, and what their delivery dates are from suppliers. There are quality controls to make sure that products are being built according to certain acceptable standards.

2. Human Resources Area   The controls used to monitor employees include personality tests and drug testing for hiring, performance tests during training, performance evaluations to measure work productivity, and employee surveys to assess job satisfaction and leadership.

3. Informational Area   Production schedules. Sales forecasts. Environmental impact statements. Analyses of competition. Public relations briefings. All these are controls on an organization's various information resources.

4. Financial Area   Are bills being paid on time? How much money is owed by customers? How much money is owed to suppliers? Is there enough cash on hand to meet payroll obligations? What are the debt-repayment schedules? What is the advertising budget? Clearly, the organization's financial controls are important because they can affect the preceding three areas.

5. Structural Area   How is the organization arranged from a hierarchical or structural standpoint?[26] Two examples are *bureaucratic control* and *decentralized control*.

- ■ **Bureaucratic control. *Bureaucratic control* is an approach to organizational control that is characterized by use of rules, regulations, and formal authority to guide performance.** This form of control attempts to elicit employee compliance, using strict rules, a rigid hierarchy, well-defined job descriptions, and administrative mechanisms such as budgets, performance appraisals, and compensation schemes (external rewards to get results). The foremost example of use of bureaucratic control is perhaps the traditional military organization.

   Bureaucratic control works well in organizations in which the tasks are explicit and certain. While rigid, it can be an effective means of ensuring that performance standards are being met. However, it may not be effective if people are looking for ways to stay out of trouble by simply following the rules, or if they try to beat the system by manipulating performance reports, or if they try to actively resist bureaucratic constraints.

- ■ **Decentralized control. *Decentralized control* is an approach to organizational control that is characterized by informal and organic structural arrangements,** the opposite of bureaucratic control. This form of control aims to get increased employee commitment, using the corporate culture, group norms, and workers taking responsibility for their performance. Decentralized control is found in companies with a relatively flat organization.

6. Cultural Area   The cultural area is an informal method of control. It influences the work process and levels of performance through the set of norms that develop as a result of the values and beliefs that constitute an organization's culture. If an organization's culture values innovation and collaboration, then employees are likely to be evaluated on the basis of how much they engage in collaborative activities and enhance or create new products.

Bureaucratic control. In businesses such as large railroads, tasks are explicit and certain, and employees are expected to perform them the same way each time. However, a small railroad, such as one line serving tourists, need not be bureaucratic.

Example: Earlier (Chapter 12), we mentioned that Google, the search-engine company, which appeared as No. 1 on *Fortune*'s 2012 list of "100 Best Companies to Work For," is a good example of an organization that promotes, measures, and rewards employee motivation. For instance, in a program called Innovation Time Off, engineers are encouraged to spend 20% of their workweek on pet projects, which has led to such new products as Gmail and Google News. Google's tremendous revenue growth over the last decade is clearly driven by a set of cultural values, norms, and internal processes that reinforce creativity.[27] ●

How can three techniques—balanced scorecard, strategy maps, and measurement management—help me establish standards and measure performance?

major question?

THE BIG PICTURE

To establish standards, managers often use the balanced scorecard, which provides four indicators for progress. A visual representation of the balanced scorecard is the strategy map. Measurement management techniques help managers make evidence-based judgments about performance.

Wouldn't you, as a top manager, like to have displayed in easy-to-read graphics all the information on sales, orders, and the like assembled from data pulled in real time from corporate software? The technology exists and it has a name: a *dashboard*, like the instrument panel in a car.

"The dashboard puts me and more and more of our executives in real-time touch with the business," says Ivan Seidenberg, former CEO at Verizon Communications. "The more eyes that see the results we're obtaining every day, the higher the quality of the decisions we can make."[28]

Throughout this book we have stressed the importance of *evidence-based management*—the use of real-world data rather than fads and hunches in making management decisions. When properly done, the dashboard is an example of the important tools that make this kind of management possible. Others are the *balanced scorecard, strategy maps,* and *measurement management*, techniques that even new managers will find useful.

The Balanced Scorecard: A Dashboard-like View of the Organization

Robert Kaplan is a professor of accounting at the Harvard Business School. David Norton is founder and president of Renaissance Strategy Group, a Massachusetts consulting firm. Kaplan and Norton developed what they call the **balanced scorecard, which gives top managers a fast but comprehensive view of the organization via four indicators: (1) customer satisfaction, (2) internal processes, (3) innovation and improvement activities, and (4) financial measures.**

"Think of the balanced scorecard as the dials and indicators in an airplane cockpit," write Kaplan and Norton. For a pilot, "reliance on one instrument can be fatal. Similarly, the complexity of managing an organization today requires that managers be able to view performance in several areas simultaneously."[29] It is not enough, say Kaplan and Norton, to simply measure financial performance, such as sales figures and return on investment. Operational matters, such as customer satisfaction, are equally important.[30]

The Balanced Scorecard: Four "Perspectives" The balanced scorecard establishes (a) *goals* and (b) *performance measures* according to four "perspectives" or areas—*financial, customer, internal business,* and *innovation and learning. (See Figure 16.5, next page.)*

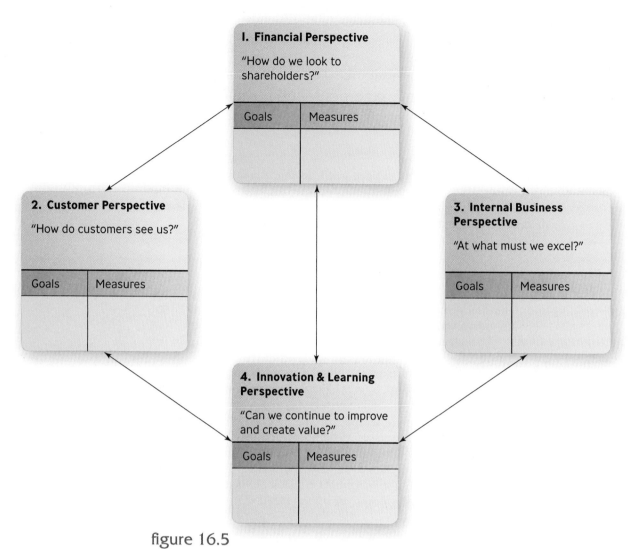

figure 16.5

THE BALANCED SCORECARD: FOUR PERSPECTIVES

1. Financial Perspective: "How Do We Look to Shareholders?"   Typical financial goals have to do with profitability, growth, and shareholder values. Financial measures such as quarterly sales have been criticized as being shortsighted and not reflecting contemporary value-creating activities. Moreover, critics say that traditional financial measures don't improve customer satisfaction, quality, or employee motivation.

However, making improvements in just the other three operational "perspectives" we will discuss won't *necessarily* translate into financial success. Kaplan and Norton mention the case of an electronics company that made considerable improvements in manufacturing capabilities that did not result in increased profitability.

The hard truth is that "if improved [operational] performance fails to be reflected in the bottom line, executives should reexamine the basic assumptions of their strategy and mission," say Kaplan and Norton. "Not all long-term strategies are profitable strategies. . . . A failure to convert improved operational performance, as measured in the scorecard, into improved financial performance should send executives back to their drawing boards to rethink the company's strategy or its implementation plans."[31]

2. Customer Perspective: "How Do Customers See Us?" Many organizations make taking care of the customer a high priority. The balanced scorecard translates the mission of customer service into specific measures of concerns that really matter to customers—time between placing an order and taking delivery, quality in terms of defect level, satisfaction with products and service, and cost.

Quiznos is a good example. The company uses a speed-dining approach to develop new products and test out different pricing strategies. The company invites groups of 25 people to a location in which they move from station to station and try out new menu options. This technique has reduced the time from test kitchen to market to six months, as opposed to the one year needed by a key competitor.[32]

3. Internal Business Perspective: "What Must We Excel At?" This part translates what the company must do internally to meet its customers' expectations. These are business processes such as quality, employee skills, and productivity.[33]

Top management's judgment about key internal processes must be linked to measures of employee actions at the lower levels, such as time to process customer orders, get materials from suppliers, produce products, and deliver them to customers. Computer information systems can help, for example, in identifying late deliveries, tracing the problem to a particular plant. (ERP systems, mentioned earlier, can aid this technological boost.)

4. Innovation & Learning Perspective: "Can We Continue to Improve & Create Value?" Learning and growth of employees is the foundation for innovation and creativity. Thus, the organization must create a culture that encourages rank-and-file employees to make suggestions and question the status quo and it must provide employees with the environment and resources needed to do their jobs. The company can use employee surveys and analysis of training data to measure the degree of learning and growth.

Strategy Map: Visual Representation of a Balanced Scorecard

Since they devised the balanced scorecard, Kaplan and Norton have come up with an improvement called the strategy map.[34] **A *strategy map* is a visual representation of the four perspectives of the balanced scorecard that enables managers to communicate their goals so that everyone in the company can understand how their jobs are linked to the overall objectives of the organization.** As Kaplan and Norton state, "Strategy maps show the cause-and-effect links by which specific improvements create desired outcomes," such as objectives for revenue growth, targeted customer markets, the role of excellence and innovation in products, and so on.

An example of a strategy map for a company such as Target is shown on the next page, with the goal of creating long-term value for the firm by increasing productivity growth and revenue growth. *(See Figure 16.6, next page.)* Measures and standards can be developed in each of the four operational areas—financial goals, customer goals, internal goals, and learning and growth goals—for the strategy.

Measurement Management: "Forget Magic"

"You simply can't manage anything you can't measure," said Richard Quinn, then–vice president of quality at the Sears Merchandising Group.[35]

Is this really true? Concepts such as the balanced scorecard seem like good ideas, but how well do they actually work? John Lingle and William Schiemann, principals in a New Jersey consulting firm specializing in strategic assessment, decided to find out.[36]

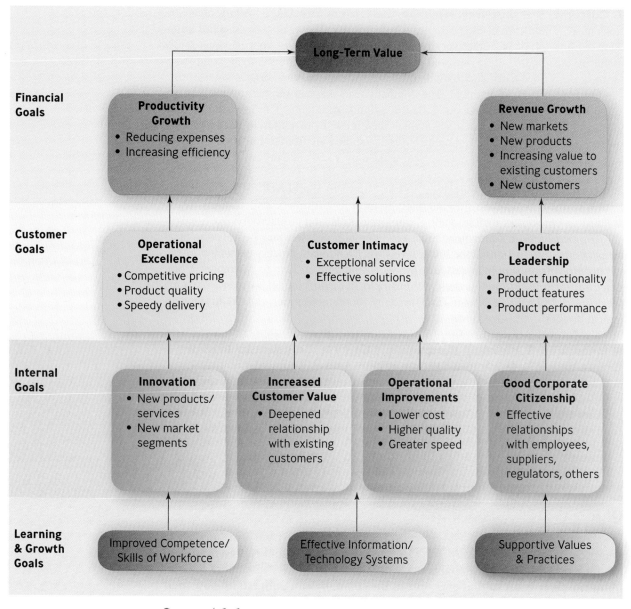

Financial Goals

Customer Goals

Internal Goals

Learning & Growth Goals

figure 16.6

THE STRATEGY MAP

This example might be used for a retail chain such as Target or Walmart.

Source: From T.S. Bateman and S.A. Snell, *Management: Leading & Collaborating in a Competitive World* 7E, 2007, p. 124. Reprinted with permission of The McGraw-Hill Companies, Inc.

In a survey of 203 executives in companies of varying size they identified the organizations as being of two types: *measurement-managed* and *non-measurement-managed*. The measurement-managed companies were those in which senior management reportedly agreed on measurable criteria for determining strategic success, and management updated and reviewed semiannual performance measures in three or more of six primary performance areas. The six areas were financial performance, operating efficiency, customer satisfaction, employee performance, innovation/change, and community/environment.

The results: "A higher percentage of measurement-managed companies were identified as industry leaders," concluded Lingle and Schiemann, "as being financially in the top third of their industry, and as successfully managing their change effort." (The last indicator suggests that measurement-managed companies tend to anticipate the future and are likely to remain in a leadership position in a rapidly changing environment.) "Forget magic," they say. "Industry leaders we surveyed simply have a greater handle on the world around them."

Why Measurement-Managed Firms Succeed: Four Mechanisms of Success
Why do measurement-managed companies outperform those that are less disciplined? The study's data point to four mechanisms that contribute to these companies' success:[37]

- **Top executives agree on strategy.** Most top executives in measurement-managed companies agreed on business strategy, whereas most of those in non-measurement-managed companies reported disagreement. Translating strategy into measurable objectives helps make them specific.

- **Communication is clear.** The clear message in turn is translated into good communication, which was characteristic of managed-measurement organizations and not of non-measurement-managed ones.

- **There is better focus and alignments.** Measurement-managed companies reported more frequently that unit (division or department) performance measures were linked to strategic company measures and that individual performance measures were linked to unit measures.

- **The organizational culture emphasizes teamwork and allows risk taking.** Managers in measurement-managed companies more frequently reported strong teamwork and cooperation among the management team and more willingness to take risks.

Four Barriers to Effective Measurement
The four most frequent barriers to effective measurement, according to Lingle and Schiemann, are as follows:

- **Objectives are fuzzy.** Company objectives are often precise in the financial and operational areas but not in areas of customer satisfaction, employee performance, and rate of change. Managers need to work at making "soft" objectives measurable.

- **Managers put too much trust in informal feedback systems.** Managers tend to overrate feedback mechanisms such as customer complaints or sales-force criticisms about products. But these mechanisms aren't necessarily accurate.

- **Employees resist new measurement systems.** Employees want to see how well measures work before they are willing to tie their financial futures to them. Measurement-managed companies tend to involve the workforce in developing measures.

- **Companies focus too much on measuring activities instead of results.** Too much concern with measurement that is not tied to fine-tuning the organization or spurring it on to achieve results is wasted effort.

Are There Areas That Can't Be Measured?
It's clear that some areas are easier to measure than others—manufacturing, for example, as opposed to services. We can understand how it is easier to measure the output of, say, a worker in a steel mill than that of a bellhop in a hotel or a professor in a classroom. Nevertheless, human resource professionals are trying to have a greater focus on employee productivity "metrics."[38] In establishing quantifiable goals for "hard to measure" jobs, managers should seek input from the employees involved, who are usually more familiar with the details of the jobs.[39] ●

major question

Financial performance is important to most organizations. What are the financial tools I need to know about?

THE BIG PICTURE

Financial controls are especially important. These include budgets, financial statements, ratio analysis, and audits.

Do you check your credit card statement line by line when it comes in? Or do you just look at the bottom-line amount owed and write a check?

Just as you should monitor your personal finances to ensure your survival and avoid catastrophe, so managers need to do likewise with an organization's finances. Whether your organization is for-profit or nonprofit, you need to be sure that revenues are covering costs.

There are a great many kinds of financial controls, but here let us look at the following: *budgets, financial statements, ratio analysis,* and *audits.* (Necessarily this is merely an overview of this topic. Financial controls are covered in detail in other business courses.)

Budgets: Formal Financial Projections

A *budget* is a formal financial projection. It states an organization's planned activities for a given period of time in quantitative terms, such as dollars, hours, or number of products. Budgets are prepared not only for the organization as a whole but also for the divisions and departments within it. The point of a budget is to provide a yardstick against which managers can measure performance and make comparisons (as with other departments or previous years).

Incremental Budgeting   Managers can take essentially two budget-planning approaches. One of them, *zero-based budgeting (ZBB),* which forces each department to start from zero in projecting funding needs, is no longer favored. The other approach, the traditional form of a budget, which is mainly used now, is incremental budgeting.

***Incremental budgeting* allocates increased or decreased funds to a department by using the last budget period as a reference point; only incremental changes in**

Passing fancy. The truck fleet represents a huge part of a beer distributor's capital expenditures budget. What types of data would be needed to justify expansion of this delivery system?

the budget request are reviewed. One difficulty is that incremental budgets tend to lock departments into stable spending arrangements; they are not flexible in meeting environmental demands. Another difficulty is that a department may engage in many activities—some more important than others—but it's not easy to sort out how well managers performed at the various activities. Thus, the department activities and the yearly budget increases take on lives of their own.

Fixed Versus Variable Budgets   There are numerous kinds of budgets, and some examples are listed below. *(See Table 16.1.)* In general, however, budgets may be categorized as two types: *fixed* and *variable.*

table 16.1

EXAMPLES OF TYPES OF BUDGETS

Type of Budget	Description
Cash or cashflow budget	Forecasts all sources of cash income and cash expenditures for daily, weekly, or monthly period
Capital expenditures budget	Anticipates investments in major assets such as land, buildings, and major equipment
Sales or revenue budget	Projects future sales, often by month, sales area, or product
Expense budget	Projects expenses (costs) for given activity for given period
Financial budget	Projects organization's source of cash and how it plans to spend it in the forthcoming period
Operating budget	Projects what an organization will create in goods or services, what financial resources are needed, and what income is expected
Nonmonetary budget	Deals with units other than dollars, such as hours of labor or office square footage

- **Fixed budgets—where resources are allocated on a single estimate of costs.** Also known as a *static budget,* a *fixed budget* **allocates resources on the basis of a single estimate of costs.** That is, there is only one set of expenses; the budget does not allow for adjustment over time. For example, you might have a budget of $50,000 for buying equipment in a given year—no matter how much you may need equipment exceeding that amount.

- **Variable budgets—where resources are varied in proportion with various levels of activity.** Also known as a *flexible budget,* a *variable budget* **allows the allocation of resources to vary in proportion with various levels of activity.** That is, the budget can be adjusted over time to accommodate pertinent changes in the environment. For example, you might have a budget that allows you to hire temporary workers or lease temporary equipment if production exceeds certain levels.

Financial Statements: Summarizing the Organization's Financial Status

A *financial statement* is a summary of some aspect of an organization's financial status. The information contained in such a statement is essential in helping managers maintain financial control over the organization.

There are two basic types of financial statements: the *balance sheet* and the *income statement.*

The Balance Sheet: Picture of an Organization's Financial Worth for a Specific Point in Time
A *balance sheet* summarizes an organization's overall financial worth—that is, assets and liabilities—at a specific point in time.

Assets are the resources that an organization controls; they consist of current assets and fixed assets. *Current assets* are cash and other assets that are readily convertible to cash within 1 year's time. Examples are inventory, sales for which payment has not been received (accounts receivable), and U.S. Treasury bills or money market mutual funds. *Fixed assets* are property, buildings, equipment, and the like that have a useful life that exceeds 1 year but are usually harder to convert to cash. *Liabilities* are claims, or debts, by suppliers, lenders, and other nonowners of the organization against a company's assets.

The Income Statement: Picture of an Organization's Financial Results for a Specified Period of Time
The balance sheet depicts the organization's overall financial worth at a specific point in time. By contrast, the ***income statement* summarizes an organization's financial results—revenues and expenses—over a specified period of time,** such as a quarter or a year.

Revenues are assets resulting from the sale of goods and services. *Expenses* are the costs required to produce those goods and services. The difference between revenues and expenses, called the *bottom line,* represents the profits or losses incurred over the specified period of time.

Ratio Analysis: Indicators of an Organization's Financial Health

The bottom line may be the most important indicator of an organization's financial health, but it isn't the only one. Managers often use ***ratio analysis*—the practice of evaluating financial ratios**—to determine an organization's financial health.

Among the types of financial ratios are those used to calculate liquidity, debt management, asset management, and return. *Liquidity ratios* indicate how easily an organization's assets can be converted into cash (made liquid). *Debt management* ratios indicate the degree to which an organization can meet its long-term financial obligations.

Asset management ratios indicate how effectively an organization is managing its assets, such as whether it has obsolete or excess inventory on hand. *Return ratios*—often called return on investment (ROI) or return on assets (ROA)—indicate how effective management is in generating a return, or profits, on its assets.

Audits: External Versus Internal

When you think of auditors, do you think of grim-faced accountants looking through a company's books to catch embezzlers and other cheats? That's one function of auditing,

Accountants at the Academy Awards? No, these are the 2012 Oscar winners. Meryl Streep was voted Best Actress for her role as prime minister Margaret Thatcher in *The Iron Lady,* and Jean Dujardin was voted Best Actor for his role in *The Artist.* But every year since 1929 the secret ballots for Oscar nominees voted on by members of the Academy of Motion Picture Arts and Sciences have been tabulated by accountants from the firm now known as PricewaterhouseCoopers. The accounting firm takes this event very seriously; secrecy is tight, and there is no loose gossip around the office watercooler. Two accountants tally the votes, stuff the winners' names in the envelopes—the ones that will be handed to award presenters during the Academy Awards—and then memorize the winners' names, just in case the envelopes don't make it to the show. Accounting is an important business because investors depend on independent auditors to verify that a company's finances are what they are purported to be.

but besides verifying the accuracy and fairness of financial statements it also is intended to be a tool for management decision making. *Audits* **are formal verifications of an organization's financial and operational systems.**

Audits are of two types—*external* and *internal.*

External Audits—Financial Appraisals by Outside Financial Experts   An *external audit* **is a formal verification of an organization's financial accounts and statements by outside experts.** The auditors are certified public accountants (CPAs) who work for an accounting firm (such as PricewaterhouseCoopers) that is independent of the organization being audited. Their task is to verify that the organization, in preparing its financial statements and in determining its assets and liabilities, followed generally accepted accounting principles.

Internal Audits—Financial Appraisals by Inside Financial Experts   An *internal audit* **is a verification of an organization's financial accounts and statements by the organization's own professional staff.** Their jobs are the same as those of outside experts—to verify the accuracy of the organization's records and operating activities. Internal audits also help uncover inefficiencies and thus help managers evaluate the performance of their control systems. ●

How do top companies improve the quality of their products or services?

THE BIG PICTURE

Total quality management (TQM) is dedicated to continuous quality improvement, training, and customer satisfaction. Two core principles are people orientation and improvement orientation. Some techniques for improving quality are employee involvement, benchmarking, outsourcing, reduced cycle time, and statistical process control.

The Ritz-Carlton Hotel Co., LLC, a luxury chain of 77 hotels worldwide in 25 countries that is an independently operated division of Marriott International, puts a premium on doing things right. First-year managers and employees receive 250–310 hours of training. The president meets each employee at a new hotel to ensure he or she understands the Ritz-Carlton standards for service. The chain has also developed a database that records the preferences of more than 1 million customers, so that each hotel can anticipate guests' needs.[40]

Because of this diligence, the Ritz-Carlton has twice been the recipient (in 1992 and in 1999) of the Malcolm Baldrige National Quality Award. This award was created by Congress in 1987 to be the most prestigious recognition of quality—the total ability of a product or service to meet customer needs—in the United States. It is given annually to U.S. organizations in manufacturing, service, small business, health care, education, and nonprofit fields.[41] (That the award actually means something is shown by a study that found that hospitals that received the honor significantly outperformed other hospitals on nearly every count.)[42]

The Baldrige award is an outgrowth of the realization among U.S. managers in the early 1980s that three-fourths of Americans were telling survey takers that the label "Made in America" no longer represented excellence—that they considered products made overseas, especially in Japan, to be equal or superior in quality to U.S.-made products. As we saw in Chapter 2, much of the impetus for quality improvements in Japanese products came from American consultants W. Edwards Deming and Joseph M. Juran. As we mentioned, two strategies for ensuring quality are *quality control,* the strategy for minimizing errors by managing each stage of production, and *quality assurance,* focusing on the performance of workers and urging them to strive for "zero defects."

Deming Management: The Contributions of W. Edwards Deming to Improved Quality

Previously, Frederick Taylor's scientific management philosophy, designed to maximize worker productivity, had been widely instituted. But by the 1950s, scientific management had led to organizations that were rigid and unresponsive to both employees and customers. **W. Edwards Deming's** challenge, known as ***Deming management,* proposed ideas for making organizations more responsive, more democratic, and less wasteful.** These included the following principles:

1. Quality Should Be Aimed at the Needs of the Consumer   "The consumer is the most important part of the production line," Deming wrote.[43] Thus, the efforts of individual workers in providing the product or service should be directed toward meeting the needs and expectations of the ultimate user.

2. Companies Should Aim at Improving the System, Not Blaming Workers   Deming suggested that U.S. managers were more concerned with blaming problems on individual workers rather than on the organization's structure, culture, technology, work rules, and management—that is, "the system." By treating employees well, listening to their views and suggestions, Deming felt, managers could bring about improvements in products and services.

3. Improved Quality Leads to Increased Market Share, Increased Company Prospects, & Increased Employment   When companies work to improve the quality of goods and services, they produce less waste, fewer delays, and are more efficient. Lower prices and superior quality lead to greater market share, which in turn leads to improved business prospects and consequently increased employment.

4. Quality Can Be Improved on the Basis of Hard Data, Using the PDCA Cycle   Deming suggested that quality could be improved by acting on the basis of hard data. The process for doing this came to be known as the ***PDCA cycle,*** **a plan-do-check-act cycle using observed data for continuous improvement of operations.** *(See Figure 16.7.)*

figure 16.7

THE PDCA CYCLE: PLAN-DO-CHECK-ACT

The four steps continuously follow each other, resulting in continuous improvement.

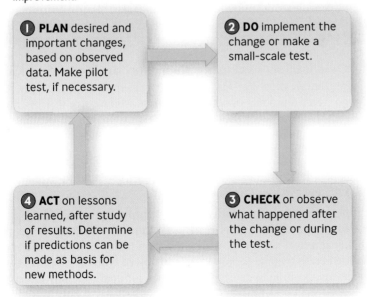

① **PLAN** desired and important changes, based on observed data. Make pilot test, if necessary.

② **DO** implement the change or make a small-scale test.

③ **CHECK** or observe what happened after the change or during the test.

④ **ACT** on lessons learned, after study of results. Determine if predictions can be made as basis for new methods.

Source: From W. Edwards Deming, *Out of the Crisis.* Copyright © 2000 Massachusetts Institute of Technology, by permission of MIT Press.

Continuous improvement. In the 1980s, building contractor Fred Carl found restaurant-style commercial stoves impractical for his own home kitchen, so he designed his own. He then opened a manufacturing plant in Greenwood, Mississippi, under the name Viking Range Corporation. From Toyota, Viking borrowed Japanese manufacturing techniques grouped under the word *kaizen,* which translates into *continuous improvement.* Production is set up so that if there is a problem everyone on the line is instantly aware of it, and the problem is solved right on the plant floor—so that customers are continuously supplied with elegant yet dependable stoves like the one shown here.

Core TQM Principles: Deliver Customer Value & Strive for Continuous Improvement

Total quality management (TQM) **is defined as a comprehensive approach—led by top management and supported throughout the organization—dedicated to continuous quality improvement, training, and customer satisfaction.**

In Chapter 2 we said there are four components to TQM:

1. Make continuous improvement a priority.
2. Get every employee involved.
3. Listen to and learn from customers and employees.
4. Use accurate standards to identify and eliminate problems.

These may be summarized as *two core principles of TQM*—namely, **(1)** *people orientation*—**everyone involved with the organization should focus on delivering value to customers**—and **(2)** *improvement orientation*—**everyone should work on continuously improving the work processes.**[44] Let's look at these further.

I. People Orientation—Focusing Everyone on Delivering Customer Value Organizations adopting TQM value people as their most important resource—both those who create a product or service and those who receive it. Thus, not only are employees given more decision-making power, so are suppliers and customers.

This people orientation operates under the following assumptions.

- **Delivering customer value is most important.** The purpose of TQM is to focus people, resources, and work processes to deliver products or services that create value for customers.

- **People will focus on quality if given empowerment.** TQM assumes that employees (and often suppliers and customers) will concentrate on making quality improvements if given the decision-making power to do so. The reasoning here is that the people actually involved with the product or service are in the best position to detect opportunities for quality improvements.

- **TQM requires training, teamwork, and cross-functional efforts.** Employees and suppliers need to be well trained, and they must work in teams.

Teamwork is considered important because many quality problems are spread across functional areas. For example, if cellphone design specialists conferred with marketing specialists (as well as customers and suppliers), they would find the real challenge of using a cellphone for older people is pushing 11 tiny buttons to call a phone number.

Teams may be *self-managed teams,* as described in Chapter 13, with groups of workers given administrative oversight of activities such as planning, scheduling, monitoring, and staffing for their task domains. Sometimes, however, an organization needs a ***special-purpose team* to meet to solve a special or onetime problem.** The team then disbands after the problem is solved. These teams are often cross-functional, drawing on members from different departments. American medicine, for instance, is moving toward a team-based approach for certain applications, involving multiple doctors as well as nurse practitioners and physician assistants.[45]

2. Improvement Orientation—Focusing Everyone on Continuously Improving Work Processes

Americans seem to like big schemes, grand designs, and crash programs. Although these approaches certainly have their place, the lesson of the quality movement from overseas is that the way to success is through continuous small improvements. ***Continuous improvement* is defined as ongoing small, incremental improvements in all parts of an organization**—all products, services, functional areas, and work processes.[46]

This improvement orientation has the following assumptions.

- **It's less expensive to do it right the first time.** TQM assumes that it's better to do things right the first time than to do costly reworking. To be sure, there are many costs involved in creating quality products and services—training, equipment, and tools, for example. But they are less than the costs of dealing with poor quality—those stemming from lost customers, junked materials, time spent reworking, and frequent inspection, for example.[47]

- **It's better to do small improvements all the time.** This is the assumption that continuous improvement must be an everyday matter, that no improvement is too small, that there must be an ongoing effort to make things better a little bit at a time all the time.

- **Accurate standards must be followed to eliminate small variations.** TQM emphasizes the collection of accurate data throughout every stage of the work process. It also stresses the use of accurate standards (such as benchmarking, as we discuss) to evaluate progress and eliminate small variations, which are the source of many quality defects.

- **There must be strong commitment from top management.** Employees and suppliers won't focus on making small incremental improvements unless managers go beyond lip service to support high-quality work, as do the top managers at Ritz-Carlton, Amazon.com, and Ace Hardware.

EXAMPLE

Chrysler Does a Makeover: Initiating a New Quality Strategy

When in 2009 Italian carmaker Fiat SpA took control of the Chrysler Group, the third of the Big Three U.S. auto companies, it gave quality control chief Doug Betts far-reaching authority. "Betts can shut the whole company down and nobody is going to overrule him, including me," CEO Sergio Marchionne is reported to have said.[48]

Looking for One-Millimeter Defects. Chrysler is working hard to achieve what Ford and General Motors (following trailblazers Toyota and Honda) have already been doing—namely, raise quality and leave behind a reputation for lousy craftsmanship.[49] This covers everything from safety to interior materials to how parts fit together. For instance, in 2011, the company spent $50,000 modifying a part involving a barely noticeable (one-millimeter) projection on a taillight of a Chrysler 300 prototype, enough to "catch a rag if someone was hand-washing" the car, Betts said.

Assembly plants are being outfitted with special clean zones, where workers use devices (called Meisterbock gauges) that laser-scan the surface of a vehicle for defects as small as a few millimeters, which trigger adjustments at the plant or with suppliers.

Moving Up. In 2008, when Chrysler was controlled by private-equity firm Cerberus Capital Management LP, the company's reputation was so bad that a review of the now-discontinued Sebring called it "almost certainly the worst car in the entire world." Three years later, *Consumer Reports* gave Chrysler's brands the highest reliability ratings in years, moving them from the bottom to the middle of the list.[50] Still, there have been setbacks, with Chrysler recalling late model Dodge Charger and Chrysler 300 sedans because of stability control and brake-system problems.

YOUR CALL

It's easy for a company to lose its reputation. How long do you think it takes to get it back? Is Chrysler there yet, in your opinion?

Applying TQM to Services

Manufacturing industries provide tangible products (think jars of baby food); service industries provide intangible products (think child care services). Manufactured products can be stored (such as dental floss in a warehouse); services generally need to be consumed immediately (such as dental hygiene services). Services tend to involve a good deal of people effort (although there is some automation, as with bank automated teller machines). Finally, services are generally provided at locations and times convenient for customers; that is, customers are much more involved in the delivery of services than they are in the delivery of manufactured products.

Customer Satisfaction: A Matter of Perception? Perhaps you're beginning to see how judging the quality of services is a different animal from judging the quality of manufactured goods, because it comes down to meeting the customer's *satisfaction,* which may be a matter of *perception.* (After all, some hotel guests, restaurant diners, and supermarket patrons, for example, are more easily satisfied than others.)

The RATER Scale How, then, can we measure the quality of a delivered service? For one, we can use the ***RATER scale,* which enables customers to rate the quality of a service along five dimensions—*reliability, assurance, tangibles, empathy,* and *responsiveness* (abbreviated *RATER*)—each on a scale from 1 (for very poor) to 10 (for very good).**[51] The meanings of the RATER dimensions are as follows:

- *Reliability*—ability to perform the desired service dependably, accurately, and consistently.
- *Assurance*—employees' knowledge, courtesy, and ability to convey trust and confidence.
- *Tangibles*—physical facilities, equipment, appearance of personnel.
- *Empathy*—provision of caring, individualized attention to customers.
- *Responsiveness*—willingness to provide prompt service and help customers.

What Makes a Service Company Successful? Four Core Elements

With services now employing more than 75% of American workers, universities are bringing more research attention to what is being called "services science." This is a field that uses management, technology, mathematics, and engineering expertise to improve the performance of service businesses, such as retailing and health care.[52]

Harvard Business School scholar Frances X. Frei has determined that a successful service business must make the right decisions about four core elements and balance them effectively:[53]

The Offering: Which Features Are Given Top-Quality Treatment?

Which service attributes, as informed by the needs of customers, does the company target for excellence and which does it target for inferior performance? Does a bank, for example, offer more convenient hours and friendlier tellers (excellence) but pay less attractive interest rates (inferior performance)?

The Funding Mechanism: Who Pays for the Service?

How should the company fund its services? Should it have the customer pay for them? This can be done in a palatable way, as when Starbucks funds its stuffed-chair ambience by charging more for coffee. Or it can be done by making savings in service features, as when Progressive Casualty Insurance cuts down on frauds and lawsuits by deploying its own representatives to the scene of an auto accident.

Or should the company cover the cost of excellence with operational savings, as by spending now to save later or having the customer do the work? Call centers usually charge for customer support, but Intuit offers free support and has product-development people, as well as customer-service people, field calls so that subsequent developments in Intuit software are informed by direct knowledge of customer problems. Other companies, such as gas stations, save money by having customers pump their own gas.

The Employee Management System: How Are Workers Trained & Motivated?

Service companies need to think about what makes their employees *able* to achieve excellence and what makes them reasonably *motivated* to achieve excellence. For instance, bank customers may expect employees to meet a lot of complex needs, but the employees aren't *able* to meet these needs because they haven't been trained. Or they aren't *motivated* to achieve excellence because the bank hasn't figured out how to screen in its hiring, as in hiring people for attitude first and training them later versus paying more to attract highly motivated people.

The Customer Management System: How Are Customers "Trained"?

Like employees, customers in a service business must also be "trained" as well, as the airlines have done with check-in. At Zipcar, the popular car-sharing service, the company keeps its costs low by depending on customers to clean, refuel, and return cars in time for the next user. In training customers, service companies need to determine which customers they're focusing on, what behaviors they want, and which techniques will most effectively influence customer behavior.

YOUR CALL

Pick a services company you're familiar with, such as Domino's Pizza, Starbucks, or the college bookstore. In integrating the four core features just discussed, a service company needs to determine the following: Are the decisions it makes in one area supported by those it makes in the other areas? Does the service model create long-term value for customers, employees, and shareholders? Is the company trying to be all things to all people or specific things to specific people? How do you think the company you picked rates?

Some TQM Tools & Techniques

Several tools and techniques are available for improving quality. Here we describe *benchmarking, outsourcing, reduced cycle time, ISO 9000 and ISO 14000, statistical process control,* and *Six Sigma.*

Benchmarking: Learning from the Best Performers   We discussed benchmarking briefly in Chapter 10. As we stated there, *benchmarking* is a process by which a company compares its performance with the best practices of high-performing organizations. For example, at Xerox Corp., generally thought to be the first American company to use benchmarking, it is defined as, in one description, "the continuous process of measuring products, services, and practices against the toughest competitors or those companies recognized as industry leaders."[54]

EXAMPLE

Do Social Media Ads Work? The Need for Benchmarking

Benchmarking is a search for "best practices" that can be applied to one's own business. Southwest Airlines, for instance, studied auto-racing pit crews to learn how to reduce the turnaround time of its aircraft at each scheduled stop. Toyota managers got the idea for just-in-time inventory deliveries by looking at how U.S. supermarkets replenish their shelves. AutoNation, a conglomeration of car dealers, tested what combination of factors made for more effective newspaper ads by using multivariable testing, a statistical technique originated during World War II to better shoot down German bombers.

The Trouble with Facebook. Sometimes, however, benchmarking is difficult. In May 2012, General Motors made headlines when it announced that it would no longer run paid ads on Facebook because they had little impact on car buyers.[55] "Proving that social-media advertising works is incredibly difficult to do," says a *USA Today* report, citing an analyst at media research firm BIA/Kelsey. "The big problem Facebook and many social-media sites have . . . is that they don't have consistent, clear-cut metrics that prove advertising on their sites works."[56] Even by traditional measures, such as how many people click on an ad, Facebook doesn't look particularly effective: 57% of Facebook users in one poll said they never click on the site's ads.[57] (Other research disagrees.)

YOUR CALL

Do you think that GM abandoned Facebook too soon, that social-media marketing and metrics are still maturing? (Ford, by contrast, increased its expenditures on social media, including Later, in July 2012, Facebook and GM began discussions about possibly re-engaging.)

Outsourcing: Let Outsiders Handle It   *Outsourcing* (discussed in detail in Chapter 4) is the subcontracting of services and operations to an outside vendor. Usually this is done because the subcontractor vendor can do the job better or cheaper. Or, stated another way, when the services and operations are done in-house, they are not done as efficiently or are keeping personnel from doing more important things.

For example, despite its former (2004–2009) well-known advertising campaign, "An American Revolution," Chevrolet outsources the engine for its Chevrolet Equinox to China, where it found it could get high-quality engines built at less cost.[58] And when IBM and other companies outsource components inexpensively for new integrated software systems, says one researcher, offshore programmers make information technology affordable to small and medium-size businesses and others who haven't yet joined the productivity boom.[59]

Outsourcing is also being done by many state and local governments, which, under the banner known as privatization, have subcontracted traditional government services such as fire protection, correctional services, and medical services.

Reduced Cycle Time: Increasing the Speed of Work Processes   Another TQM technique is the emphasis on increasing the speed with which an organization's operations and processes can be performed. This is known as *reduced cycle time,* **or reduction in steps in a work process,** such as fewer authorization steps required to grant a contract to a supplier. The point is to improve the organization's performance by eliminating wasteful motions, barriers between departments, unnecessary procedural steps, and the like.

ISO 9000 & ISO 14000: Meeting Standards of Independent Auditors   If you're a sales representative for Du Pont, the American chemical company, how will your overseas clients know that your products have the quality they are expecting? If you're a purchasing agent for an Ohio-based tire company, how can you tell if the synthetic rubber you're buying overseas is adequate?

At one time, buyers and sellers simply had to rely on a supplier's past reputation or personal assurances. In 1979, the International Organization for Standardization (ISO), based in Geneva, Switzerland, created a set of quality standards known as the 9000 series—"a kind of Good Housekeeping seal of approval for global business," in one description.[60] There are two such standards:

- **ISO 9000. The *ISO 9000 series* consists of quality-control procedures companies must install—from purchasing to manufacturing to inventory to shipping—that can be audited by independent quality-control experts, or "registrars."** The goal is to reduce flaws in manufacturing and improve productivity. Companies must document the procedures and train their employees to use them. For instance, DocBase Direct is a web-delivered document and forms-management system that helps companies comply with key ISO management standards, such as traceable changes and easy reporting.

    The ISO 9000 designation is now recognized by more than 100 countries around the world, and a quarter of the corporations around the globe insist that suppliers have ISO 9000 certification. "You close some expensive doors if you're not certified," says Bill Ekeler, general manager of Overland Products, a Nebraska tool-and-die-stamping firm.[61] In addition, because the ISO process forced him to analyze his company from the top down, Ekeler found ways to streamline manufacturing processes that improved his bottom line.

- **ISO 14000. The *ISO 14000 series* extends the concept, identifying standards for environmental performance.** ISO 14000 dictates standards for documenting a company's management of pollution, efficient use of raw materials, and reduction of the firm's impact on the environment.

Statistical Process Control: Taking Periodic Random Samples   As the pages of this book were being printed, every now and then a press person would pull a few pages out of the press run and inspect them (under a bright light) to see that the consistency of the color and quality of the ink were holding up. This is an ongoing human visual check for quality control.

All kinds of products require periodic inspection during their manufacture: hamburger meat, breakfast cereal, flashlight batteries, wine, and so on. The tool often used for this is *statistical process control,* **a statistical technique that uses periodic random samples from production runs to see if quality is being maintained within a standard range of acceptability.** If quality is not acceptable, production is stopped to allow corrective measures.

Statistical process control is the technique that McDonald's uses, for example, to make sure that the quality of its burgers is always the same, no matter where in the world they are served. Companies such as Intel and Motorola use statistical process control to ensure the reliability and quality of their products.

Six Sigma & Lean Six Sigma: Data-Driven Ways to Eliminate Defects

"The biggest problem with the management technique known as Six Sigma is this: It sounds too good to be true," says a *Fortune* writer. "How would your company like a 20% increase in profit margins within one year, followed by profitability over the long-term that is *ten times* what you're seeing now? How about a 4% (or greater) annual gain in market share?"[62]

What is this name, Six Sigma (which is probably Greek to you), and is it a path to management paradise? The name comes from *sigma,* the Greek letter that statisticians use to define a standard deviation. The higher the sigma, the fewer the deviations from the norm—that is, the fewer the defects. Developed by Motorola in 1985, Six Sigma has since been embraced by General Electric, Allied Signal, American Express, and other companies. There are two variations, *Six Sigma* and *lean Six Sigma.*

- **Six Sigma. *Six Sigma* is a rigorous statistical analysis process that reduces defects in manufacturing and service-related processes.** By testing thousands of variables and eliminating guesswork, a company using the technique attempts to improve quality and reduce waste to the point where errors nearly vanish. In everything from product design to manufacturing to billing, the attainment of Six Sigma means there are no more than 3.4 defects per million products or procedures.

  "Six Sigma gets people away from thinking that 96% is good, to thinking that 40,000 failures per million is bad," says a vice president of consulting firm A. T. Kearney.[63] Six Sigma means being 99.9997% perfect. By contrast, Three Sigma or Four Sigma means settling for 99% perfect—the equivalent of no electricity for 7 hours each month, two short or long landings per day at each major airport, or 5,000 incorrect surgical operations per week.[64]

  Six Sigma may also be thought of as a philosophy—to reduce variation in your company's business and make customer-focused, data-driven decisions. The method preaches the use of Define, Measure, Analyze, Improve, and Control (DMAIC). Team leaders may be awarded a Six Sigma "black belt" for applying DMAIC.

- **Lean Six Sigma.** More recently, companies are using an approach known as *lean Six Sigma,* **which focuses on problem solving and performance improvement—speed with excellence—of a well-defined project.**[65]

  Xerox Corp., for example, has focused on getting new products to customers faster, which has meant taking steps out of the design process without loss of quality. A high-end, $200,000 machine that can print 100 pages a minute traditionally has taken three to five cycles of design; removing just one of those cycles can shave up to a year off time to market.[66] The grocery chain Albertsons Inc. announced in 2004 that it was going to launch Six Sigma training to reduce customer dissatisfaction and waste to the lowest level possible.[67]

Six Sigma and lean Six Sigma may not be perfect, since they cannot compensate for human error or control events outside a company. Still, they let managers approach problems with the assumption that there's a data-oriented, tangible way to approach problem solving.[68] ●

What are the keys to successful control, and what are the barriers to control success?

major question?

THE BIG PICTURE

This section describes four keys to successful control and five barriers to successful control.

How do you as a manager make a control system successful, and how do you identify and deal with barriers to control? We consider these topics next.[69]

The Keys to Successful Control Systems

Successful control systems have a number of common characteristics: (1) They are strategic and results oriented. (2) They are timely, accurate, and objective. (3) They are realistic, positive, and understandable and they encourage self-control. (4) They are flexible.[70]

1. They Are Strategic & Results Oriented   Control systems support strategic plans and are concentrated on significant activities that will make a real difference to the organization. Thus, when managers are developing strategic plans for achieving strategic goals, that is the point at which they should pay attention to developing control standards that will measure how well the plans are being achieved.

Example: Global warming is now shifting the climate on a continental scale, changing the life cycle of animals and plants, scientists say, and surveys show more Americans feel guilty for not living greener.[71] A growing number of companies are discovering that embracing environmental safe practices is paying off in savings of hundreds of millions of dollars, as we saw with Subaru of Indiana in Chapter 3.[72]

Doing good. Created by Microsoft founder Bill Gates and his wife, the Bill & Melinda Gates Foundation of Seattle is the largest private foundation in the world. It aims to reduce poverty and enhance health care throughout the world and to expand educational opportunities in the United States. The way it seeks to apply business techniques to giving makes it a leader in global philanthropy.

2. They Are Timely, Accurate, & Objective   Good control systems—like good information of any kind—should . . .

- **Be timely—meaning when needed.** The information should not necessarily be delivered quickly, but it should be delivered at an appropriate or specific time, such as every week or every month. And it certainly should be often enough to allow employees and managers to take corrective action for any deviations.

- **Be accurate—meaning correct.** Accuracy is paramount, if decision mistakes are to be avoided. Inaccurate sales figures may lead managers to mistakenly cut or increase sales promotion budgets. Inaccurate production costs may lead to faulty pricing of a product.

- **Be objective—meaning impartial.** Objectivity means control systems are impartial and fair. Although information can be inaccurate for all kinds of reasons (faulty communication, unknown data, and so on), information that is not objective is inaccurate for a special reason: It is biased or prejudiced. Control systems need to be considered unbiased for everyone involved so that they will be respected for their fundamental purpose—enhancing performance.

3. They Are Realistic, Positive, & Understandable & Encourage Self-Control   Control systems have to focus on working for the people who will have to live with them. Thus, they operate best when they are made acceptable to the organization's members who are guided by them. Thus, they should . . .

- **Be realistic.** They should incorporate realistic expectations. If employees feel performance results are too difficult, they are apt to ignore or sabotage the performance system.

- **Be positive.** They should emphasize development and improvement. They should avoid emphasizing punishment and reprimand.

- **Be understandable.** They should fit the people involved, be kept as simple as possible, and present data in understandable terms. They should avoid complicated computer printouts and statistics.

- **Encourage self-control.** They should encourage good communication and mutual participation. They should not be the basis for creating distrust between employees and managers.

4. They Are Flexible   Control systems must leave room for individual judgment, so that they can be modified when necessary to meet new requirements.

Barriers to Control Success

Among the several barriers to a successful control system are the following:[73]

1. Too Much Control   Some organizations, particularly bureaucratic ones, try to exert too much control. They may try to regulate employee behavior in everything from dress code to timing of coffee breaks. Allowing employees too little discretion for analysis and interpretation may lead to employee frustration—particularly among professionals, such as college professors and medical doctors. Their frustration may lead them to ignore or try to sabotage the control process.

2. Too Little Employee Participation   As highlighted by W. Edwards Deming, discussed elsewhere in the book (Chapter 2), employee participation can enhance productivity. Involving employees in both the planning and execution of control systems can bring legitimacy to the process and heighten employee morale.

3. Overemphasis on Means Instead of Ends

We said that control activities should be strategic and results oriented. They are not ends in themselves but the means to eliminating problems. Too much emphasis on accountability for weekly production quotas, for example, can lead production supervisors to push their workers and equipment too hard, resulting in absenteeism and machine breakdowns. Or it can lead to game playing—"beating the system"—as managers and employees manipulate data to seem to fulfill short-run goals instead of the organization's strategic plan.

4. Overemphasis on Paperwork

A specific kind of misdirection of effort is management emphasis on getting reports done, to the exclusion of other performance activity. Reports are not the be-all and end-all. Undue emphasis on reports can lead to too much focus on quantification of results and even to falsification of data.

Example: A research laboratory decided to use the number of patents the lab obtained as a measure of its effectiveness. The result was an increase in patents filed but a decrease in the number of successful research projects.[74]

5. Overemphasis on One Instead of Multiple Approaches

One control may not be enough. By having multiple control activities and information systems, an organization can have multiple performance indicators, thereby increasing accuracy and objectivity.

Example: An obvious strategic goal for gambling casinos is to prevent employee theft of the cash flowing through their hands. Thus, casinos control card dealers by three means. First, they require prospective hires to have a dealer's license before they are hired. Second, they put them under constant scrutiny, using direct supervision by on-site pit bosses as well as observation by closed-circuit TV cameras and through overhead one-way mirrors. Third, they require detailed reports at the end of each shift so that transfer of cash and cash equivalents (such as gambling chips) can be audited.[75] ●

Temptation. Because legal gambling is a heavy cash business, casinos need to institute special controls against employee theft. One of them is the "eye in the sky" over card and craps tables.

THE BIG PICTURE

As we end the book, this section describes some life lessons to take away.

We have come to the end of the book, our last chance to offer some suggestions to take with you that we hope will benefit you in the coming years. Following are some life lessons pulled from various sources that can make you a "keeper" in an organization and help you be successful.

- **Find your passion and follow it.** "The mission matters," writes Gary Hamel, cofounder of the Management Innovation Lab. "People change for what they care about." Employees aren't motivated much by the notion of "increasing shareholder value" (or if they are, the result may be an environment in which greed overwhelms higher-minded goals). Says Hamel, "A company must forever be on the way to *becoming* something more than it is right now."[76] And the same should apply to you. Find something you love to do, and do it vigorously.

- **Encourage self-discovery, and be realistic.** To stay ahead of the pack, you need to develop self-awareness, have an active mind, and be willing to grow and change. Here's a life lesson: "Be brutally honest with yourself about what you know, and ask what skills you need to take the next step." This includes not just the tools of your trade—finance, technology, and so on—but most importantly people skills.

- **Every situation is different, so be flexible.** No principle, no theory will apply under all circumstances. Industries, cultures, supervisors, customers will vary. If you're the new kid in a new job, for instance, you should know that "culture is critical," suggests Angeli R. Rasbury in *Black Enterprise*. A life lesson: "Before you can begin to set goals, know the organization in which you're working. Learn how employees conduct business and view success, and how the company rewards achievement. An organization's culture defines its management and business guidelines."[77] Another life lesson: "Remove 'It's not my job' from your vocabulary."

- **Fine-tune your people skills.** The workplace is not an area where lone individuals make their silent contributions. Today we live and work in a team universe. If, as is the case with Whole Foods Market, getting and keeping a job depends on the reviews of your peers, with teammates voting on your fate, you can see that communication skills become ever more important. Recommendation: Get feedback on your interpersonal skills and develop a plan for improvement.

- **Learn how to develop leadership skills.** Every company should invest in the leadership development of its managers if it is to improve the quality of its future leaders. But you can also work to develop your own leadership skills. An example and a life lesson: "Leaders who wait for bad news to come to them are taking a major risk, so learn to seek it out—as by encouraging employees to bring you news of potential problems and thanking them for it, not punishing them for their candor."[78] You can also pick up news about problems, potential and actual, by practicing "management by wandering around." Another life lesson: "If you set the bar high, even if you don't reach it, you end up in a pretty good place—that is, achieving a pretty high mark."

- **Treat people as if they matter, because they do.** If you treat employees and customers with dignity, they respond accordingly. The highly successful online shoe retailer Zappos, for instance, "is fanatical about great service," says the writer of a *Harvard Business Publishing* online blog, "not just satisfying customers, but amazing them," as in promising delivery in four days and delivering in one. How? It's all in the hiring, which Zappos does with great intensity. After four weeks' training, new call-center employees are offered $1,000 on top of what they have earned to that point if they want to quit—the theory being that people who take the money "obviously don't have the commitment" that Zappos requires of its employees. (About 10% of the trainees take the offer.)[79] The life lesson: "Companies don't engage emotionally with their customers—people do. If you want to create a memorable company, you have to fill your company with memorable people."

- **Draw employees and peers into your management process.** The old top-down, command-and-control model of organization is moving toward a flattened, networked kind of structure. Managers now work more often with peers, where lines of authority aren't always clear or don't exist, so that one's persuasive powers become key. Power has devolved to front-line employees who are closest to the customer and to small, focused, self-managed teams that have latitude to pursue new ideas. The life lesson: "The best organizations will be those whose employees have the power to innovate, not just follow orders from on high."

- **Be flexible, keep your cool, and take yourself lightly.** Things aren't always going to work out your way, so flexibility is important. In addition, the more unflappable you appear in difficult circumstances, the more you'll be admired by your bosses and coworkers. Having a sense of humor helps, since there are enough people spreading gloom and doom in the workplace. Life lesson: "When you're less emotional, you're better able to assess a crisis and develop a workable solution."

We wish you the very best of luck. And we mean it!

Angelo Kinicki
Brian K. Williams

Key Terms Used in This Chapter

audits 529
balance sheet 528
balanced scorecard 521
budget 526
bureaucratic control 520
continuous improvement 533
control process steps 516
control standard 516
controlling 514
decentralized control 520
Deming management 530
enterprise resource planning (ERP) 513

external audit 529
financial statement 528
fixed budget 527
income statement 528
incremental budgeting 526
internal audit 529
ISO 9000 series 537
ISO 14000 series 537
lean Six Sigma 538
management by exception 517
operational control 519
PDCA cycle 531

RATER scale 534
ratio analysis 528
reduced cycle time 537
Six Sigma 538
special-purpose team 533
statistical process control 537
strategic control 519
strategy map 523
tactical control 519
total quality management (TQM) 532
two core principles of TQM 532
variable budget 527

Summary

16.1 Managing for Productivity

A manager has to deal with six challenges—managing for competitive advantage, diversity, globalization, information technology, ethical standards, sustainability, and his or her own happiness and life goals. The manager must make decisions about the four management functions—planning, organizing, leading, and controlling—to get people to achieve productivity and realize results.

Productivity is defined by the formula of outputs divided by inputs for a specified period of time. Productivity is important because it determines whether the organization will make a profit or even survive. Much of productivity growth is thought to result from the implementation of information technology, including enterprise resource planning (ERP) systems. Productivity depends on control.

16.2 Control: When Managers Monitor Performance

Controlling is defined as monitoring performance, comparing it with goals, and taking corrective action as needed. There are six reasons why control is needed: (1) to adapt to change and uncertainty; (2) to discover irregularities and errors; (3) to reduce costs, increase productivity, or add value; (4) to detect opportunities; (5) to deal with complexity; and (6) to decentralize decision making and facilitate teamwork.

There are four control process steps. (1) The first step is to set standards. A control standard is the desired performance level for a given goal. (2) The second step is to measure performance, based on written reports, oral reports, and personal observation. (3) The third step is to compare measured performance against the standards established. (4) The fourth step is to take corrective action, if necessary, if there is negative performance.

16.3 Levels & Areas of Control

In applying the steps and types of control, managers need to consider (1) the level of management at which they operate, (2) the areas they can draw on for resources, and (3) the style of control philosophy.

There are three levels of control, corresponding to the three principal managerial levels. (1) Strategic control, done by top managers, is monitoring performance to ensure that strategic plans are being implemented. (2) Tactical control, done by middle managers, is monitoring performance to ensure that tactical plans are being implemented. (3) Operational control, done by first-level or supervisory managers, is monitoring performance to ensure that day-to-day goals are being implemented.

Most organizations have six areas that they can draw on for resources. (1) The physical area includes buildings, equipment, and tangible products; these use equipment control, inventory-management control,

and quality controls. (2) The human resources area uses personality tests, drug tests, performance tests, employee surveys, and the like as controls to monitor people. (3) The informational area uses production schedules, sales forecasts, environmental impact statements, and the like to monitor the organization's various resources. (4) The financial area uses various kinds of financial controls, as we discuss in Section 16.5. (5) The structural area uses hierarchical or other arrangements such as bureaucratic control, which is characterized by use of rules, regulations, and formal authority to guide performance, or decentralized control, which is characterized by informal and organic structural arrangements. (6) The cultural area influences the work process and levels of performance through the set of norms that develop as a result of the values and beliefs that constitute an organization's culture.

16.4 The Balanced Scorecard, Strategy Maps, & Measurement Management

To establish standards, managers often use the balanced scorecard, which provides a fast but comprehensive view of the organization via four indicators: (1) financial measures, (2) customer satisfaction, (3) internal processes, and (4) innovation and improvement activities.

The strategy map, a visual representation of the four perspectives of the balanced scorecard—financial, customer, internal business, and innovation and learning—enables managers to communicate their goals so that everyone in the company can understand how their jobs are linked to the overall objectives of the organization.

Measurement-managed companies use measurable criteria for determining strategic success, and management updates and reviews three or more of six primary performance areas: financial performance, operating efficiency, customer satisfaction, employee performance, innovation/change, and community/environment. Four mechanisms that contribute to the success of such companies are top executives agree on strategy, communication is clear, there is better focus and alignments, and the organizational culture emphasizes teamwork and allows risk taking. Four barriers to effective measurement are objectives are fuzzy, managers put too much trust in informal feedback systems, employees resist new management systems, and companies focus too much on measuring activities instead of results.

Some areas are difficult to measure, such as those in service industries.

16.5 Some Financial Tools for Control

Financial controls include (1) budgets, (2) financial statements, (3) ratio analysis, and (4) audits.

A budget is a formal financial projection. The most important budget-planning approach is incremental budgeting, which allocates increased or decreased funds to a department by using the last budget period as a reference point; only incremental changes in the budget request are reviewed. Budgets are either fixed, which allocate resources on the basis of a single estimate of costs, or variable, which allow resource allocation to vary in proportion with various levels of activity.

A financial statement is a summary of some aspect of an organization's financial status. One type, the balance sheet, summarizes an organization's overall financial worth—assets and liabilities—at a specific point in time. The other type, the income statement, summarizes an organization's financial results—revenues and expenses—over a specified period of time.

Ratio analysis is the practice of evaluating financial ratios. Managers may use this tool to determine an organization's financial health, such as liquidity ratios, debt management ratios, or return ratios.

Audits are formal verifications of an organization's financial and operational systems. Audits are of two types. An external audit is formal verification of an organization's financial accounts and statements by outside experts. An internal audit is a verification of an organization's financial accounts and statements by the organization's own professional staff.

16.6 Total Quality Management

Much of the impetus for quality improvement came from W. Edwards Deming, whose philosophy, known as Deming management, proposed ideas for making organizations more responsive, more democratic, and less wasteful. Among the principles of Deming management are (1) quality should be aimed at the needs of the consumer; (2) companies should aim at improving the system, not blaming workers; (3) improved quality leads to increased market share, increased company prospects, and increased employment; and (4) quality can be improved on the basis of hard data, using the PDCA, or plan-do-check-act, cycle.

Total quality management (TQM) is defined as a comprehensive approach—led by top management and supported throughout the organization—dedicated to continuous quality improvement, training, and customer satisfaction. The two core principles of TQM are people orientation and improvement orientation.

In the people orientation, everyone involved with the organization is asked to focus on delivering value to customers, focusing on quality. TQM requires training, teamwork, and cross-functional efforts.

In the improvement orientation, everyone involved with the organization is supposed to make ongoing small, incremental improvements in all parts of the organization. This orientation assumes that it's less expensive to do things right the first time, to do small improvements all the time, and to follow accurate standards to eliminate small variations.

TQM can be applied to services using the RATER scale, which stands for reliability, assurance, tangibles, empathy, and responsiveness.

Several techniques are available for improving quality. (1) Employee involvement can be implemented through quality circles, self-managed teams, and special-purpose teams—teams that meet to solve a special or one-time problem. (2) Benchmarking is a process by which a company compares its performance with that of high-performing organizations. (3) Outsourcing is the subcontracting of services and operations to an outside vendor. (4) Reduced cycle time consists of reducing the number of steps in a work process. (5) Statistical process control is a statistical technique that uses periodic random samples from production runs to see if quality is being maintained within a standard range of acceptability.

16.7 Managing Control Effectively

Successful control systems have four common characteristics: (1) They are strategic and results oriented. (2) They are timely, accurate, and objective. (3) They are realistic, positive, and understandable and they encourage self-control. (4) They are flexible.

Among the barriers to a successful control system are the following: (1) Organizations may exert too much control. (2) There may be too little employee participation. (3) The organization may overemphasize means instead of ends. (4) There may be an overemphasis on paperwork. (5) There may be an overemphasis on one approach instead of multiple approaches.

Management in Action

Control Mechanisms & Quality Processes Save a Steel Mill Plant in Burns Harbor, Indiana

Some steel mills are destroyed by globalization, others reborn.

Left for dead a decade ago, this 50-year-old facility on the shores of Lake Michigan has been rejuve-nated thanks to an unusual experiment by its owner, Luxembourg-based ArcelorMittal.

In 2008, Burns Harbor was "twinned" with a hyper-modern mill in Gent, Belgium. Over 100 U.S. engineers and managers, who were flown across the Atlantic, were told: Do as the Belgians do.

Burns Harbor now enjoys record output. Its furnaces, where steel is made out of iron ore, coal, and limestone, are run with software developed in Belgium. Robots are in. Pencils are out. Workers are learning to make the same amount of steel with nearly half the people it employed three decades ago. Productivity is nearing Belgium levels.

The transition hasn't been seamless. As a collective bargaining session looms this summer, union leaders say a tough battle is expected over wages, safety risks, and the next wave of automation. But there is also an acknowledgement that increased productivity has saved the mill from oblivion. . . .

Globalization often is blamed for the travails of American manufacturing—from the relentless pressure of imports from lower-wage countries to outsourcing and overseas production by U.S.-based manufacturers. But globalization has its upsides as well. Not only does it often mean cheaper goods for American manufacturers, but it puts pressure on U.S. factories to become more efficient to keep up with global competition, making it possible for them to survive. . . .

A wave of globalization in the 1980s created a true international street market, straining less profitable mills, especially in the U.S., and leading many to bankruptcy. The U.S. steel industry produced 95.6 million tons in 2011, about three-quarters of what it made 30 years ago. It employed about 95,000 people in its core mills and plants, one fifth as many as in 1981, according to the American Iron and Steel Institute.

That laid the groundwork for Lakshmi Mittal, the billionaire Indian who began assembling what is now the world's first successful international steel conglomerate of its size, and the largest by production, with 263,000 employees in 20 countries and 112 steelmaking facilities.

Mr. Mittal perfected a simple business model: Buy rundown, often state-owned, mills, cut costs, lay off workers, improve productivity, turn a profit. It worked from Slovakia to South Africa, from Ukraine to Trinidad.

Twinning—benchmarking two mills against each other—represents the next evolution. "The process doesn't change: melt iron, cast, roll. But there are always incremental improvements you can make," Mr. Mittal said in an interview.

Modern benchmarking was pioneered by Xerox in the 1980s and has become a common tool for multinationals. But industrial historians say that what Mr. Mittal is actually doing is taking a page out of the productivity obsessed playbook of 19th-century steel pioneer Andrew Carnegie and applying it globally. . . .

In a similar fashion, ArcelorMittal twins pairs of mills—usually of similar size, age, product mix, and output—against each other. In addition to Indiana and Belgium, mills in Germany and Poland, and France and Romania, have been twinned. The weaker mill is ordered to copy the practices of the better mill, while the stronger is told to keep its edge. Managers are summoned to regular meetings and ordered to divulge and compare their performances. Although there is no explicit policy on the consequences of poor performance, ArcelorMittal has been quick to idle or shut down unprofitable mills, as it did in Liège, Belgium, last year.

Many in the industry thought high wages would permanently sink the U.S. steel industry. Workers at Burns Harbor averaged about $80,000 in wages and benefits in 2011, up about 14% from 2007. . . .

"Gent really is one of the best mills in the world," says Peter Marcus, president of World Steel Dynamics, an Englewood Cliffs, N.J.-based consultancy. The measure his company favors, man-hours per ton, shows Gent at 1.25 and Burns Harbor behind at 1.32. "Those are both currently among the better numbers in the world," he says. The average in the U.S. is 2.0.

Mr. Mittal said Gent was a star. "We wanted Burns Harbor to be more like Gent." Thus the development of the twinning program, which began in late 2007, and accelerated after the U.S. recession put a premium on productivity.

That year, Larry Fabina, a hulking 56-year-old engineer from Johnstown, Pa., who had worked at the mill since 1973, traveled to Belgium, where he toured the medieval town and spent six weeks taking careful notes at the mill.

When Burns Harbor engineers returned, they made the quick and easy fixes first. They changed hose nozzles and moved the nozzle on 2,500 horse-power hoses used to scrub flakes off the steel closer, thus reducing the amount of power needed to propel the water. Those two changes saved the Indiana plant $1.4 million in energy costs, the company said.

Workers were directed to trim less rough steel off the sides of coil, saving the equivalent of 725 coils a year. "That's 17,000 cars," says Mr. Fabina, the mill's manager for continuous improvement.

Adopting the Coordi computer model took longer. Workers used to gathering information on their own and relying on experience and intuition had to attend classes on computer modeling.

Last year, Burns Harbor implemented Coordi at a cost of under $1 million. Since then, the mill has increased the average number of 298-ton caldrons of molten steel it produces daily, known as "heats," to 50 from 42. . . .

"Steel working used to be 80% back and 20% brain, now it's the other way around," says Mr. Trinidad, the union rep, who started when the plant employed 6,700 workers in 1974. Now it has 3,700. . . .

Burns Harbor achieved a record slab production of 4.8 million tons in 2011, says Bill Steers, the company spokesman, compared with 5 million at Gent. Productivity is almost at 900 tons per employee per year, while Gent has improved to around 950. "Much of this can be attributed to twinning," says Mr. Steers.

ArcelorMittal executives say they are focused on pushing even harder. At a recent meeting, Gent managers boasted they would soon reach 1,100 tons per employee. Burns Harbor managers declined to comment on whether that is feasible.

FOR DISCUSSION

1. What are the pros and cons of ArcelorMittal's twinning program? Explain.

2. To what extent do the changes at the Burns Harbor plant follow the control process shown in Figure 16.4? Discuss.

3. If you were charged with creating a balanced scorecard for the Burns Harbor plant, what SMART goals (see Chapter 5) would you use as standards to assess performance in the four categories in your scorecard? Develop one SMART goal for each scorecard category.

4. To what extent does the control program being used in the plant follow the keys to successful control systems? Discuss.

5. Why would the union be opposed to the changes taking place in the plant? Explain.

6. What are the most important takeaways from this case? Explain your rationale.

Source: Excerpted from John W. Miller, "Indiana Steel Mill Revived with Lessons from Abroad," *The Wall Street Journal*, May 21, 2012, pp. A1, A12. Copyright © 2012 by Dow Jones & Company, Inc. Reproduced with permission of Dow Jones & Company, Inc. via Copyright Clearance Center.

Self-Assessment

Do You Have Good Time-Management Skills?

OBJECTIVES

1. To determine how productive you are.

2. To discuss what time-management skills need developing.

INTRODUCTION

As we learned in this chapter, productivity is important to companies because it determines their profitability. For managers, productivity depends on effective time management, a skill involving planning and self-discipline that should be perfected in college. The purpose of this exercise is to evaluate your time-management skills.

INSTRUCTIONS

Read each question, and answer each one "Yes" or "No." Answer not as you feel you *should* but rather as you feel you *would* if you were being completely truthful.

1. I have a hard time saying "no."

2. I sometimes postpone a task so long that I'm embarrassed to do it.

3. I feel like I'm always in a hurry.

4. I feel guilty when I play or goof off instead of studying.

5. I tend to make excuses when I don't finish my work.

6. I often feel like I have too much to do.

7. I work better under pressure.

8. I feel resentful when someone reminds me I haven't finished my work.

9. I have difficulty deciding how to use my time.

10. I generally put off semester projects until the week before they're due.

INTERPRETATION

Count the number of "No" responses. Your time-management skills may be characterized as follows:

9–10: Excellent

8–9: Good, but they could be improved in minor ways

6–8: Somewhat inadequate; you could benefit from training

4–6: Poor; you definitely need training.

4 or less: Emergency! You know little about time management and need to pay immediate attention here.

QUESTIONS FOR DISCUSSION

1. Were you surprised by the results? Why or why not?

2. Many statements in the assessment represent procrastination, with good intentions being eclipsed by excuses and bad time management. Do you frequently procrastinate?

3. What are some ways you could improve your time-management skills? Discuss.

Source: Thomas Harriot College of Arts & Sciences, Advising Center, East Carolina University, Greenville, NC, www.ecu.edu/aretsci/cas/advising/TimeManagement.com.

Legal/Ethical Challenge

Is Corporate Monitoring of Employee Behavior Going Too Far?

Companies are increasingly using a new set of tools called auto-analytics to track how employees spend their time at work.

As one newspaper article states, "These devices—from computer software and smartphone apps to gadgets that you wear—let users gather data about what they do at work, analyze that information, and use it do their job better. They give workers a fascinating window into the unseen, unconscious little things that can make such a big difference in their daily work lives. . . .

"Software like RescueTime measures things like how long you spend on an open window, how long you're idle, and how often you switch from one window to another. The software turns all those measurements into charts so you can see where you're spending your time. From there, you can set up automatic alerts to keep yourself away from distractions."

Companies purchase auto-analytics because of the potential to increase employee productivity and potentially their well-being. The question to consider is whether companies should mandate or encourage employees to use these tools. Would you like to have your boss watching over you by looking at reports generated from auto-analytics? Do these tools invade our privacy, or do they amount to a legitimate way for employers to increase employee productivity? For example, a tool called emWave2 can track your pulse during the workday. This data could be used to determine when you are experiencing stress, and the program will spit out recommendations for reducing stress based on your pulse rate. It also is possible that such data might be used against you in some way. Does an employer need to know your pulse rate?

What is your view about the use of auto-analytics at work?

SOLVING THE CHALLENGE

1. I think auto-analytics are a great idea, and employers should force employees to use these tools. Why? Because these tools can increase employee productivity, which ultimately leads to greater profits and shareholder value. Results from the tools, however, should not be linked to any incentives.

2. I think auto-analytics are a great idea, and employers should force employees to use these tools. I also recommend that management use the output or metrics generated by these tools as incentives. I would reward employees for demonstrating increased productivity or efficiency in the reports generated by the tools.

3. I think that auto-analytics are a great idea, but employers should not force employees to use these tools. I would explain the tools to employees and gently encourage them to use them. I also would ensure that management cannot see the data or reports generated by the tools.

4. It is not possible to make a blanket conclusion about these tools. For example, while some tools may be useful (for example, tracking how employees use their computers), others may be a violation of our privacy (for example, tracking one's pulse). The application of these tools needs to be considered on a case-by-case basis and their use should be voluntary.

5. Invent other options.

Source: Excerpted from H. J. Wilson, "Employees, Measure Yourselves," *The Wall Street Journal,* April 2, 2012, pp. R1, R2. Copyright © 2012 by Dow Jones & Company, Inc. Reproduced with permission of Dow Jones & Company, Inc. via Copyright Clearance Center.

The Project Planner's Toolkit
Flowcharts, Gantt Charts, & Break-Even Analysis

MAJOR QUESTIONS YOU SHOULD BE ABLE TO ANSWER

How can you use planning tools to enhance your performance and achieve utmost success?

major question?

THE BIG PICTURE
Three tools used in project planning, which was covered in Chapter 5, are flowcharts, Gantt charts, and break-even analysis.

Project planning may begin (in the definition stage) as a back-of-the-envelope kind of process, but the client will expect a good deal more for the time and money being invested. Fortunately, there are various planning and monitoring tools that give the planning and execution of projects more precision. Three tools in the planner's toolkit are (1) flowcharts, (2) Gantt charts, and (3) break-even analysis.

Tool #1: Flowcharts—for Showing Event Sequences & Alternate Decision Scenarios

A *flowchart* is a useful graphical tool for representing the sequence of events required to complete a project and for laying out "what-if" scenarios. Flowcharts have been used for decades by computer programmers and systems analysts to make a graphical "road map," as it were, of the flow of tasks required. These professionals use their own special symbols (indicating "input/output," "magnetic disk," and the like), but there is no need for you to make the process complicated. Generally, only three symbols are needed: (1) an oval for the beginning and end, (2) a box for a major activity, and (3) a diamond for a yes or no decision. *(See Figure A.1, next page.)*

Computer programs such as Micrographix's ABC Flow Charter are available for constructing flowcharts. You can also use the drawing program in word processing programs such as Microsoft Word.

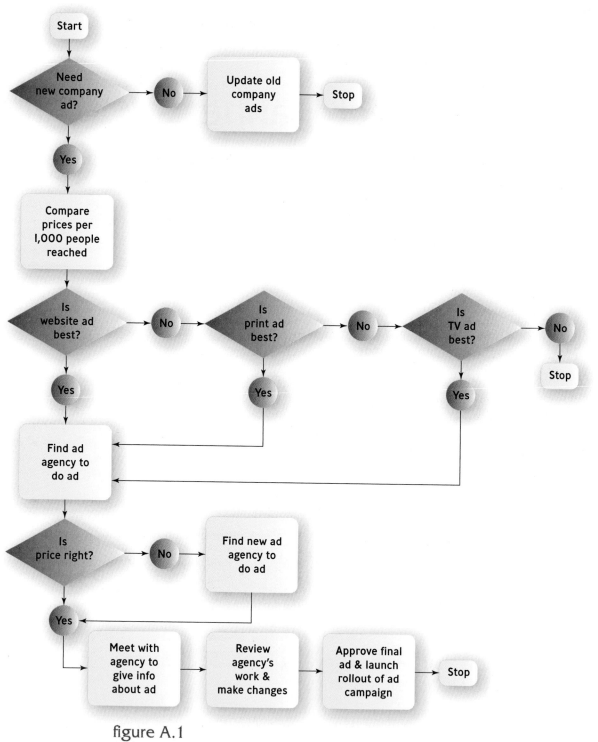

figure A.1

FLOWCHART: WEBSITE, PRINT, OR TELEVISION?

Example of a flowchart for improving a company's advertising

Benefits   Flowcharts have two benefits:

- **Planning straightforward activities.** A flowchart can be quite helpful for planning ordinary activities—figuring out the best way to buy textbooks or a car, for example. It is also a straightforward way of indicating the sequence of events in, say, thinking out a new enterprise that you would then turn into a business plan.

- **Depicting alternate scenarios.** A flowchart is also useful for laying out "what-if" scenarios—as in if you answer "yes" to a decision question you should follow Plan A, or if you answer "no" you should follow Plan B.

Limitations   Flowcharts have two limitations:

- **No time indication.** They don't show the amounts of time required to accomplish the various activities in a project. If you're building a house, the foundation might take only a couple of days, but the rough carpentry might take weeks. These time differences can't be represented graphically on a flowchart (although you could make a notation).

- **Not good for complex projects.** They aren't useful for showing projects consisting of several activities that must all be worked on at the same time. An example would be getting ready for football season's opening game, by which time the players have to be trained, the field readied, the programs printed, the band rehearsed, the ticket sellers recruited, and so on. These separate activities might each be represented on their own flowcharts, of course. But trying to express them all together all at once would produce a flowchart that would be unwieldy, even unworkable.

Tool #2: Gantt Charts—Visual Time Schedules for Work Tasks

We have mentioned how important deadlines are to making a project happen. Unlike a flowchart, a Gantt chart can graphically indicate deadlines.

The Gantt chart was developed by **Henry L. Gantt,** a member of the school of scientific management (discussed in Chapter 2). **A *Gantt chart* is a kind of time schedule—a specialized bar chart that shows the relationship between the kind of work tasks planned and their scheduled completion dates.** *(See Figure A.2, below.)*

A number of software packages can help you create and modify Gantt charts on your computer. Examples are CA-SuperProject, Microsoft Project Manager, SureTrak Project Manager, and TurboProject Professional.

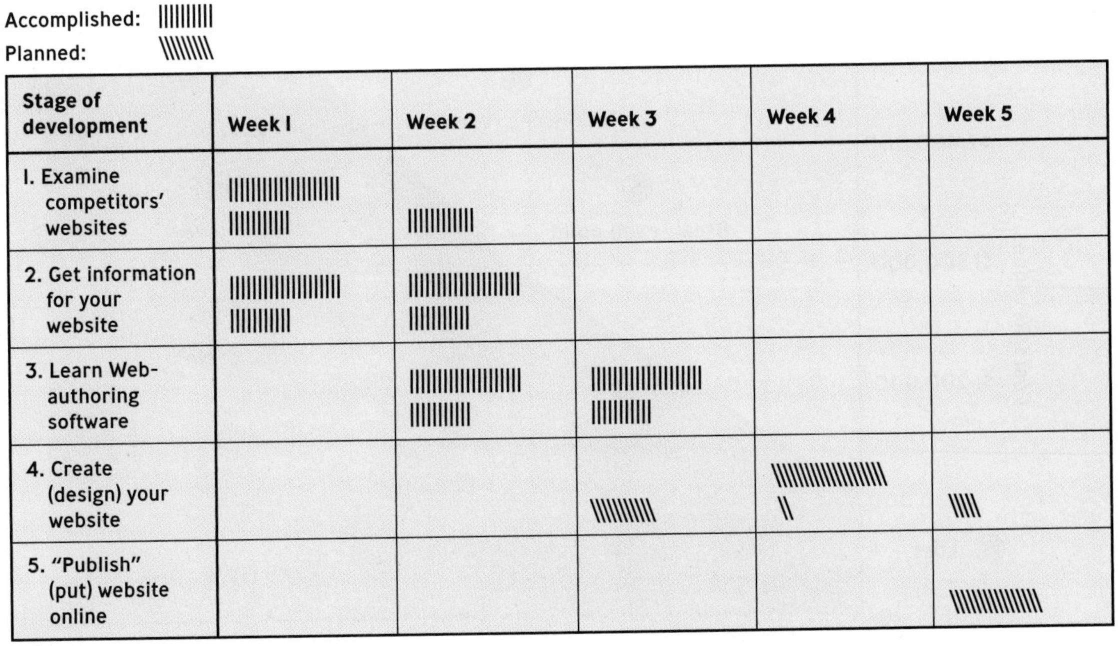

Accomplished: ||||||||||
Planned: \\\\\\\\\

Stage of development	Week 1	Week 2	Week 3	Week 4	Week 5
1. Examine competitors' websites	||||||||||||||||||||||	||||||||||			
2. Get information for your website	||||||||||||||||||||||	||||||||||||||||||			
3. Learn Web-authoring software		||||||||||||||||||||	||||||||||||||||||		
4. Create (design) your website			\\\\\\\\\	\\\\\\\\\\\\\\\ \\	\\\\\\
5. "Publish" (put) website online					\\\\\\\\\\\\\

figure A.2

GANTT CHART FOR DESIGNING A WEBSITE

This shows the tasks accomplished and the time planned for remaining tasks to build a company website.

Benefits   There are three benefits to using a Gantt chart:

- **Express time lines visually.** Unlike flowcharts, Gantt charts allow you to indicate visually the time to be spent on each activity.

- **Compare proposed and actual progress.** A Gantt chart may be used to compare planned time to complete a task with actual time taken to complete it, so that you can see how far ahead or behind schedule you are for the entire project. This enables you to make adjustments so as to hold to the final target dates.

- **Simplicity.** There is nothing difficult about creating a Gantt chart. You express the time across the top and the tasks down along the left side. As Figure A.2 shows, you can make use of this device while still in college to help schedule and monitor the work you need to do to meet course requirements and deadlines (for papers, projects, tests).

Limitations   Gantt charts have two limitations:

- **Not useful for large, complex projects.** Although a Gantt chart can express the interrelations among the activities of relatively small projects, it becomes cumbersome and unwieldy when used for large, complex projects. More sophisticated management planning tools may be needed, such as PERT networks.

- **Time assumptions are subjective.** The time assumptions expressed may be purely subjective; there is no range between "optimistic" and "pessimistic" of the time needed to accomplish a given task.

Tool #3: Break-Even Analysis—How Many Items Must You Sell to Turn a Profit?

***Break-even analysis* is a way of identifying how much revenue is needed to cover the total costs of developing and selling a product.** Let's walk through the computation of a break-even analysis, referring to the illustration. *(See Figure A.3.)* We assume

figure A.3
BREAK-EVEN ANALYSIS

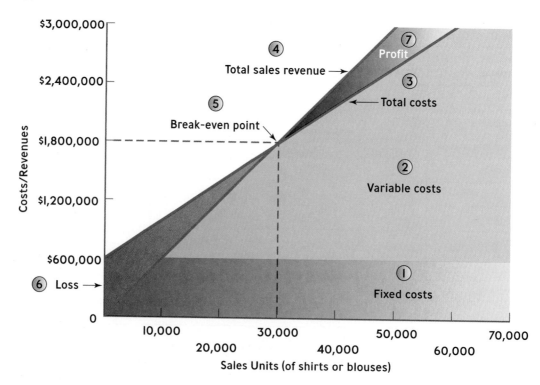

APPENDIX ✳ The Project Planner's Toolkit

① *Fixed costs (green area):* Once you start up a business, whether you sell anything or not, you'll have expenses that won't vary much, such as rent, insurance, taxes, and perhaps salaries. These are called *fixed costs,* **expenses that don't change regardless of your sales or output.** Fixed costs are a function of time—they are expenses you have to pay out on a regular basis, such as weekly, monthly, or yearly. Here the chart shows the fixed costs (green area) are $600,000 per year no matter how many sales units (of shirts or blouses) you sell.

② *Variable costs (blue area):* Now suppose you start producing and selling a product, such as blouses or shirts. At this point you'll be paying for materials, supplies, labor, sales commissions, and delivery expenses. These are called *variable costs,* **expenses that vary directly depending on the numbers of the product that you produce and sell.** (After all, making more shirts will cost you more in cloth, for example.) Variable costs, then, are a function of volume—they go up and down depending on the number of products you make or sell. Here the variable costs (blue area) are relatively small if you sell only a few thousand shirts but they go up tremendously if you sell, say, 70,000 shirts.

③ *Total costs (first right upward-sloping line—green plus blue area added together):* The sum of the fixed costs and the variable costs equals the total costs (the green and blue areas together). This is indicated by the line that slopes upward to the right from $600,000 to $3,000,000.

④ *Total sales revenue (second right upward-sloping line):* This is the total dollars received from the sale of however many units you sell. The sales revenue varies depending on the number of units you sell. Thus, for example, if you sell 30,000 shirts, you'll receive $1,800,000 in revenue. If you sell 40,000 shirts, you'll receive somewhat more than $2,400,000 in revenue.

⑤ *Break-even point (intersection of dashed lines):* Finding this point is the purpose of this whole exercise. **The *break-even point* is the amount of sales revenue at which there is no profit but also no loss to your company.** On the graph, this occurs where the "Total sales revenues" line crosses the "Total costs" line, as we've indicated here where the dashed lines meet. This means that you must sell 30,000 shirts and receive $1,800,000 in revenue in order to recoup your total costs (fixed plus variable). Important note: Here is where pricing the shirts becomes important. If you raise the price per shirt, you may be able to make the same amount of money (hit your break-even point) by selling fewer of them—but that may be harder to do because customers may resist buying at the higher price.

⑥ *Loss (red area):* If you fail to sell enough shirts at the right price (the break-even point), you will suffer a loss. *Loss* **means your total costs exceed your total sales revenue.** As the chart shows, here you are literally "in the red"—you've lost money.

⑦ *Profit (black area):* Here you are literally "in the black"—you've made money. All the shirts you sell beyond the break-even point constitute a profit. *Profit* **is the amount by which total revenue exceeds total costs.** The more shirts you sell, of course, the greater the profit.

　　The kind of break-even analysis demonstrated here is known as the *graphic method.* The same thing can also be done algebraically.

you are an apparel manufacturer making shirts or blouses. Start in the lower-right corner of the diagram on the previous page and follow the circled numbers as you read the descriptions above.

Benefits　Break-even analysis has two benefits:

■　**For doing future "what-if" alternate scenarios of costs, prices, and sales.** This tool allows you to vary the different possible costs, prices, and sales

Break-Even Analysis: Why Do Airfares Vary So Much?

Why do some airlines charge four times more than others for a flight of the same distance?

There are several reasons, but break-even analysis enters into it.

United Airlines' average cost for flying a passenger 1 mile in a recent year was 11.7 cents, whereas Southwest's was 7.7 cents. Those are the break-even costs. What they charged beyond that was their profit.

Why the difference? One reason, according to a study by the U.S. Department of Transportation, is that Southwest's expenses are lower. United flies more long routes than short ones, so its costs are stretched out over more miles, making its costs for flying shorter routes higher than Southwest's.

Another factor affecting airfares is the type of passengers flying a particular route—whether they are high-fare-paying business travelers or more price-conscious leisure travelers. Business travelers often don't mind paying a lot (they are reimbursed by their companies), and those routes (such as Chicago to Cincinnati) tend to have more first-class seats, which drives up the average price. Flights to vacation spots (such as Las Vegas) usually have more low-price seats because people aren't willing to pay a lot for pleasure travel. Also, nonstop flight fares often cost more than flights with connections.

quantities to do rough "what-if" scenarios to determine possible pricing and sales goals. Since the numbers are interrelated, if you change one, the others will change also.

- **For analyzing the profitability of past projects.** While break-even analysis is usually used as a tool for future projects, it can also be used retroactively to find out whether the goal of profitability was really achieved, since costs may well have changed during the course of the project. In addition, you can use it to determine the impact of cutting costs once profits flow.

Limitations   Break-even analysis is not a cure-all.

- **It oversimplifies.** In the real world, things don't happen as neatly as this model implies. For instance, fixed and variable costs are not always so readily distinguishable. Or fixed costs may change as the number of sales units goes up. And not all customers may pay the same price (some may get discounts).

- **The assumptions may be faulty.** On paper, the formula may work perfectly for identifying a product's profitability. But what if customers find the prices too high? Or what if sales figures are outrageously optimistic? In the marketplace, your price and sales forecasts may really be only good guesses. ●

CHAPTER 1

1. Descriptions of Rometty by Fred Amoroso, reported in C. Hymowitz and S. Frier, "IBM's Rometty Breaks Ground as the Company's First Female Leader," *Bloomberg Businessweek*, October 26, 2011, http://news.businessweek.com/article.asp?documentKey=1376-LRUA8R1A74E901-6HJ5G2BD8B-8KV67V79BOHGBTKF; and Judith Hurwitz and Chris Ambrose, reported in C. Metz, "IBM Names Virginia Rometty as First Female CEO," *Wired*, October 25, 2011, www.wired.com/wiredenterprise/2011/10/virginia-rometty (both accessed January 7, 2012).

2. Rometty, quoted in C. C. Miller, "For Incoming I.B.M. Chief, Self-Confidence Rewarded," *The New York Times*, October 28, 2011, pp. B1, B10; and in J. B. Stewart, "Top Aide to a C.E.O.: Her Husband," *The New York Times*, November 5, 2011, pp. B1, B2.

3. Rometty, quoted in Hymowitz and Frier, "IBM's Rometty Breaks Ground as the Company's First Female Leader," 2011.

4. R. Barker, "No, Management Is *Not* a Profession," *Harvard Business Review*, July–August 2010, pp. 52–60.

5. M. P. Follett, quoted in J. F. Stoner and R. E. Freeman, *Management*, 5th ed. (Englewood Cliffs, NJ: Prentice Hall, 1992), p. 6.

6. B. A. Carpenter, "Customer Service Automated Phone Answerer Irksome," *Reno Gazette-Journal*, September 23, 2009, p. 11A.

7. Harris Interactive for IMShopping, June 12–16, 2009, in "Ability to Get Human Help Clicks with Online Shoppers," *USA Today*, August 25, 2009, p. 1A.

8. Associated Press, "'Survey Fatigue' Hits Consumers," *Reno Gazette-Journal*, January 8, 2012, p. 1B.

9. Emily Yellin, author of *Your Call Is (Not That) Important to Us*, quoted in B. D. Phillips, "Please, Stay on the Line," *The Wall Street Journal*, March 24, 2009, p. A15.

10. Scott Broetzmann of CustomerCare Measurement Consulting, quoted in D. Oldenburg, Associated Press, "Tired of Automated Phone Menus? Press 1," *Reno Gazette-Journal*, March 15, 2004, p. 3E.

11. Richard Shapiro, quoted in W. C. Taylor, "Your Call Should Be Important to Us, but It's Not," *The New York Times*, February 26, 2006, sec. 3, p. 3; and G. J. Carter, "How to Get a Human to Answer the Phone," *USA Weekend*, April 14–16, 2006, p. 4. See also the Get Human website at www.gethuman.com.

12. Taylor, 2006.

13. G. Colvin, "Catch a Rising Star," *Fortune*, February 6, 2006, pp. 46–50.

14. "Usual Weekly Earnings of Wage and Salary Workers, Third Quarter 2011," *Economic News Release*, Bureau of Labor Statistics, October 20, 2011, www.bls.gov/news.release/wkyeng.nr0.htm (accessed April 7, 2012).

15. A. Sherter, "Highest-Paid CEOs: Top Earner Takes Home $145 Million," *CBSNews.com*, December 15, 2011, www.cbsnews.com/8301-505123_162-57343611/highest-paid-ceos-top-earner-takes-home-$145-million (accessed January 7, 2012).

16. M. Krantz and B. Hansen, "CEO Pay Soars While Workers' Pay Stalls," *USA Today*, April 4, 2011, www.usatoday.com/money/companies/management/story/CEO-pay-2010/45634384/1 (accessed January 7, 2012).

17. E. Marzec, "What Is the Beginning Salary for a Chief Executive?" *eHow*, July 3, 2011, www.ehow.com/info_8680671_beginning-salary-chief-executive.html (accessed January 11, 2011).

18. "Salary.com Survey Reveals Salary Differentials for CEOs at Small, Medium, and Large Companies," *HR.com*, November 29, 2007, www.hr.com/en/communities/salarycom%E2%84%A2-survey-reveals-salary-differentials-fo_f9rdbd5a.html (accessed January 11, 2012).

19. O. Pollar, "Are You Sure You Want to Be a Manager?" *San Francisco Examiner*, October 4, 1998, p. J-3.

20. M. Csikszentmihalyi, *Flow: The Psychology of Optimal Experience* (New York: HarperCollins, 1990), and *Beyond Boredom and Anxiety* (San Francisco: Jossey-Bass, 1975), *Creativity: Flow and the Psychology of Discovery and Invention* (New York: Harper Perennial, 1996), *Finding Flow: The Psychology of Engagement with Everyday Life* (New York: Basic Books, 1998); and *Good Business: Leadership, Flow, and the Making of Meaning* (New York: Penguin Books, 2003).

21. "NAA President and CEO John Sturm Comments on ABC FAS-FAX Report," *Editor & Publisher*, May 4, 2011, www.editorandpublisher.com/AdCirc/Article/NAA-President-and-CEO-John-Sturm-Comments-on-ABC-FAS-FAX-Report (accessed January 11, 2012).

22. J. Temple, "Journalism Struggles for Digital Niche," *San Francisco Chronicle*, October 21, 2011, pp. D1, D4.

23. P. R. Kann, "Quality Reporting Doesn't Come Cheap," *The Wall Street Journal*, September 25, 2009, p. A15.

24. D. Carr, "After a Year of Ruin, Some Hope," *The New York Times*, December 21, 2009, pp. B1, B6.

25. P. Coy, M. Conlin, and M. Herbst, "The Disposable Worker," *Bloomberg Businessweek*, January 18, 2010, pp. 32–39.

26. U.S. Census Bureau analysis, reported in S. Roberts, "Census Finds Increase in Foreign-Born Workers," *The New York Times*, December 8, 2009, p. A21.

27. U.S. Census Bureau, "An Older and More Diverse Nation by Midcentury," *U.S. Census Bureau News*, August 14, 2008, www.census.gov/Press-Release/www/releases/archives/population/012496.html (accessed January 11, 2012); and U.S. Census Bureau, "2010 Census Shows 65 and Older Population Growing Faster Than Total U.S. Population," Newsroom release, November 30, 2011, www.census.gov/newsroom/releases/archives/2010_census/cb11-cn192.html (accessed January 12, 2012).

28. See, for instance, S. E. Page, *The Difference: How the Power of Diversity Creates Better Groups, Firms, Schools and Societies* (Princeton, NJ: Princeton University Press, 2007); C. Dreifus, "In Professor's Model, Diversity = Productivity," *The New York Times*, January 8, 2008, p. D2; and M. J. Pearsall, A. Ellis, and J. Evans, "Unlocking the Effects of Gender Faultlines on Team Creativity: Is Activation Key?" *Journal of Applied Psychology*, January 2008, pp. 225–234.

29. S. McCartney, "Teaching Americans How to Behave Abroad," *The Wall Street Journal*, April 11, 2006, pp. D1, D4. See also J. Clark, "That 'Ugly American' Image Is Getting a Makeover Guide," *USA Today*, April 28, 2006, p. 9D.

30. T. L. Friedman, *The World Is Flat: A Brief History of the Twenty-first Century* (New York: Farrar, Straus and Giroux, 2005).

31. Projection by Cisco System's Economics & Research Practice, reported in A. Enright, "Global Commerce to Reach $1.4 Trillion in 2015," *Internet Retailer*, June 7, 2011, www.internetretailer.com/2011/06/07/global-e-commerce-reach-14-trillion-2015 (accessed January 14, 2012).

32. M. J. Mandel and R. D. Hof, "Rethinking the Internet," *BusinessWeek*, March 26, 2001, p. 118. See also B. Powell, "The New World Order," *Fortune*, May 14, 2001, pp. 134, 136.

33. See C. Graham, "In-Box Overload," *The Arizona Republic*, April 16, 2007, p. A14; J. Vascellaro, "What's a Cellphone For?" *The Wall Street Journal*, March 26, 2007, p. R5; and F. Bruni, "Sorry, Wrong In-Box," *The New York Times*, September 1, 2011, p. A23.

34. A. L. Penenberg, "They Have Hacked Your Brain," *Fast Company*, September 2011, pp. 85–113, 124–125; J. Temple, "Data Explosion Revolutionizing Online World," *San Francisco Chronicle*, October 19, 2011, pp. D1, D4; N. Singer, "Just Give Me the Right to Be Forgotten," *The New York Times*, August 21, 2011, Business section, p. 3; and N. Bilton, "Privacy Fades in Facebook Era," *The New York Times*, December 12, 2011, p. B8.

35. B. Levisohn, "How to Make a Madoff," *BusinessWeek*, December 16, 2008, www.businessweek.com/investor/content/dec2008/

pi20081215_232943.htm?chan=investing_investing+index+page_top+stories (accessed January 14, 2012). See also D. Gross, "Membership Has Its Penalties," *Newsweek,* January 12, 2009, p. 18; and M. Hosenball, "Made Money with Madoff? Don't Count on Keeping It," *Newsweek,* January 12, 2009, p. 9.

36. D. R. Henriques, "Madoff, Apologizing, Is Given 150 Years," *The New York Times,* June 30, 2009, pp. A1, B4.

37. M. Elias, "Study: Today's Youth Think Quite Highly of Themselves," *USA Today,* November 19, 2008, p. 7D. The study is J. M. Twenge and W. K. Campbell, "Increases in Positive Self-Views among High School Students: Birth-Cohort Changes in Anticipated Performance, Self-Satisfaction, Self-Liking, and Self-Competence," *Psychological Science,* November 2008, pp. 1082–86.

38. L. Powers, "Study Finds Teens Believe Lying, Cheating Required to Succeed," *Reno Gazette-Journal,* November 24, 2009, pp. 1A, 4A.

39. *A Study of Values and Behavior Concerning Integrity: The Impact of Age, Cynicism, and High School Character* (Los Angeles: Josephson Institute of Ethics, 2009).

40. D. Seidman, "Building Trust by Trusting," *BusinessWeek,* September 7, 2009, p. 76. See also R. Hurley, "Trust Me," *The Wall Street Journal,* October 24, 2011, p. R4. Hurley is the author of *The Decision to Trust: How Leaders Can Create High Trust Companies* (New York: Wiley, 2011).

41. A. Gore, *An Inconvenient Truth* (Emmaus, PA: Rodale, 2006). See also A. Gore and D. Blood, "For People and Planet," *The Wall Street Journal,* March 28, 2006, p. A20.

42. This definition of *sustainability* was developed in 1987 by the World Commission on Environment and Development.

43. J. Saseen, "Who Speaks for Business?" *BusinessWeek,* October 19, 2009, pp. 22–24.

44. A. S. Ross, "Apple Heats Up Climate Battle," *San Francisco Chronicle,* October 6, 2009, pp. D1, D3; and D. R. Baker, "Shifting Alliances in Debate," *San Francisco Chronicle,* October 9, 2009, pp. C1, C2.

45. S. Lohr, "The Cost of an Overheated Planet," *The New York Times,* December 12, 2006, pp. C1, C5; B. Walsh, "How Business Saw the Light," *Time,* January 15, 2007, pp. 56–57; and J. Ball, "In Climate Controversy, Industry Cedes Ground," *The Wall Street Journal,* January 23, 2007, pp. A1, A17.

46. J. Sandberg, "Down Over Moving Up: Some Bosses Find They Hate Their Jobs," *The Wall Street Journal,* July 27, 2005, p. B1. See also D. Jones, "Besides Being Lonely at the Top, It Can Be 'Disengaging' as Well," *USA Today,* June 21, 2005, pp. 1B, 2B.

47. J. Flanigan, "Managing Your Career as a Business," *The New York Times,* October 15, 2009, p. B4.

48. S. Armour, "Who Wants to Be a Middle Manager?" *USA Today,* August 13, 2007, pp. 1B, 2B; A. Bryant, "I Never Wanted to Be a Manager, But I've Learned," *The New York Times,* October 23, 2011, Business section, p. 2; and "Boss's Job Safe: Most Workers Don't Want It," *HR Magazine,* December 2011, p. 14.

49. Associated Press–Viacom poll, reported in Associated Press, "Economy Crushes Youthful Dreams," *USA Today,* April 19, 2011, p. 2B.

50. Pollar, "Are You Sure You Want to Be a Manager?" 1998.

51. For an instructive account of employee happiness and culture, see the example set by the founder of Nick's Pizza & Pub, described in B. Burlingham, "Lessons from a Blue-Collar Millionaire," *Inc.,* February 2010, pp. 56–63.

52. P. Drucker, reported in R. L. Knowdell, "A Model for Managers in the Future Workplace: Symphony Conductor," *The Futurist,* June–July 1998, p. 22.

53. The role of middle managers is discussed by C. R. Ren and C. Guo, "Middle Managers' Strategic Role in the Corporate Entrepreneurial Process: Attention-Based Effects," *Journal of Management,* November 2011, pp. 1586–1610.

54. A. Thompson, "The Hardest Management Job," *The Costco Connection,* August 2005, pp. 30–33.

55. "5-Year Winners," *Fast Company,* December 2007–January 2008, p. 115.

56. P. M. Blau and W. R. Scott, *Formal Organizations* (San Francisco: Chandler, 1962).

57. H. Mintzberg, *The Nature of Managerial Work* (New York: Harper & Row, 1973).

58. Mintzberg, 1973.

59. Ed Reilly, quoted in W. J. Holstein, "Attention-Juggling in the High-Tech Office," *The New York Times,* June 4, 2006, sec. 3, p. 9.

60. J. P. Kotter, "What Effective General Managers Really Do," *Harvard Business Review,* March–April 1999, pp. 145–59.

61. L. Stroh, quoted in A. Muoio, "Balancing Acts," *Fast Company,* February–March 1999, pp. 83–90.

62. S. MacDermid, Purdue University, and M. D. Lee, McGill University, two-year study cited in R. W. Huppke, Associated Press, "Take This Job, and Love It," *San Francisco Chronicle,* January 28, 1999, p. B2.

63. A. Deutschman, "The CEO's Secret of Managing Time," *Fortune,* June 1, 1992, pp. 135–46.

64. D. G. Lepore, quoted in Muoio, "Balancing Acts," 1999.

65. J. Cooper-Kahn and L. Dietzel, "What Is Executive Functioning?" *LD Online,* 2008, www.ldonline.org/article/What_Is_Executive_Functioning%3F (accessed January 21, 2010).

66. R. Hannaman, "Understanding Generation Z: The Workforce of the Future," *Nevada Appeal,* December 25, 2011, p. C6.

67. *Generation M²: Media in the Lives of 8- to 18-Year-olds* (Menlo Park, CA: Kaiser Family Foundation, 2010).

68. L. Rosen, cited in B. Stone, "Old Fogies by Their Twenties," *The New York Times,* January 10, 2010, Week in Review section, p. 5. Rosen is the author of *Rewired: Understanding the iGeneration and the Way They Learn* (New York: Palgrave Macmillan, 2010).

69. R. E. Bohn and J. E. Short, *How Much Information? 2009 Report on American Consumers* (San Diego: Global Information Industry Center, University of California, San Diego, 2009).

70. W. Gallagher, quoted in book review, D. G. Myers, "Please Pay Attention," *The Wall Street Journal,* April 20, 2009, p. A13. Gallagher is author of *Rapt* (New York: Penguin Press, 2009).

71. J. Tierney, "Ear Plugs to Lasers: The Science of Concentration," *The New York Times,* May 5, 2009, p. D2.

72. Psychiatrist E. M. Hallowell, quoted in A. Tugend, "Multitasking Can Make You Lose . . . Um . . . Focus," *The New York Times,* October 25, 2008, p. B7. Hollowell is the author of *CrazyBusy: Overstretched, Overbooked, and About to Snap!* (New York: Ballantine, 2006).

73. P. Steel, "The Nature of Procrastination: A Meta-Analytic and Theoretical Review of Quintessential Self-Regulatory Failure," *Psychological Bulletin,* January 2007, pp. 65–94. See also S. Borenstein, "Study: More Americans Doing Less," *San Francisco Chronicle,* January 12, 2007, p. A2.

74. M. Chafkin, "You've Been Yelped," *Inc.,* February 2010, pp. 48–55.

75. "Yelp Announces First Quarter 2012 Financial Results," Reuters, May 2, 2012, http://www.reuters.com/article/2012/05/02/idUS238956+02-May-2012+PRN20120502 (accessed May 29, 2012).

76. S. Perman, "The Entrepreneurial Melting Pot," *BusinessWeek Online,* June 6, 2005; www.businessweek.com/smallbiz/content/jun2006/sb20060606_980_521.htm?chan=smallbiz_smallbiz+index+page_getting+started (accessed January 14, 2012). See also J. Mehring, "The Real Job Engines," *BusinessWeek SmallBiz,* Spring 2006, p. 42; and A. Weintraub, "Hot Growth," *BusinessWeek,* June 5, 2006, pp. 48–52.

77. S. A. Shane, "How Start-Ups Really Create Jobs—and What This Means for Employment Growth," *The New York Times,*

October 19, 2009, http://boss.blogs.nytimes.com/2009/10/19/how-start-ups-really-create-jobs-and-what-this-means-for-employment-growth (accessed January 14, 2012).

78. Study by The Guardian Life Small Business Research Institute, reported in M. D. Wolf, "Women-Owned Businesses: America's New Job Creation Engine," *Forbes.com,* January 12, 2010, www.forbes.com/2010/01/12/smallbusiness-job-market-forbes-women-entrepreneurs-economic-growth.html (accessed January 14, 2012).

79. M. Mayer, quoted in "Leading the Way," *Newsweek,* September 25, 2006, pp. 51–52.

80. P. F. Drucker, *Innovation and Entrepreneurship* (New York: Harper & Row, 1986), pp. 27–28.

81. M. Webber, "Danger: Toxic Company," *Fast Company,* November 1998, pp. 152–61.

82. D. C. McClelland, *The Achieving Society* (New York: Van Nostrand, 1961); D. C. McClelland, *Human Motivation* (Glenview, IL: Scott, Foresman, 1985); D. L. Sexton and N. Bowman, "The Entrepreneur: A Capable Executive and More," *Journal of Business Venturing* 1 (1985), pp. 129–40; D. Hisrich, "Entrepreneurship/Intrapreneurship," *American Psychologist,* February 1990, p. 218; T. Begley and D. P. Boyd, "Psychological Characteristics Associated with Performance in Entrepreneurial Firms and Smaller Businesses," *Journal of Business Venturing* 2 (1987), pp. 79–93; and C. R. Kuehl and P. A. Lambing, *Small Business: Planning and Management* (Fort Worth, TX: Dryden Press, 1990).

83. Global Entrepreneurship Monitor, 2011 National Entrepreneurial Assessment for the United States, study by London Business School and Babson College, reported in C. Rubin, "Report: Necessity Driving Entrepreneurship," *Inc.,* November 15, 2011, www.inc.com/news/articles/201111/necessity-driving-entrepreneurship.html (accessed January 14, 2012).

84. R. L. Zweigenhaft and G. W. Domhoff, *The New CEOs: Women, African American, Latino, and Asian American Leaders of Fortune 500 Companies* (Lanham, MD: Rowman & Littlefield, 2011).

85. Stewart, "Top Aide to a CEO: Her Husband," 2011.

86. R. L. Katz, "Skills of an Effective Administrator," *Harvard Business Review,* September–October, 1974, p. 94. Also see M. K. De Vries, "The Eight Roles Executives Play," *Organizational Dynamics,* 2007, pp. 28–44.

87. S. Martin, "30-Year IBM Veteran Named as New CEO," *USA Today,* October 26, 2011, p. 3B.

88. Martin Feldstein, quoted in Hymowitz and Frier, "IBM's Rometty Breaks Ground as Company's First Female Leader," 2011; and Judith Hurwitz, quoted in Metz, "IBM Names Virginia Rometty as First Female CEO," 2011.

89. Rometty, quoted in Hymowitz and Frier, 2011.

90. S. E. Ante and J. S. Lublin, "Rometty Replacing IBM's Palmisano," *The Wall Street Journal,* October 26, 2011, pp. B1, B5.

91. Fred Amoroso, quoted in Hymowitz and Frier, "IBM's Rometty Breaks Ground as Company's First Female Leader," 2011.

92. George F. Colony, chairman of Forester Research, quoted in S. Lohr, "IBM Names a New Chief," *The New York Times,* October 26, 2011, pp. B1, B8.

93. CEO recruiter, quoted in Colvin, "Catch a Rising Star," 2006.

94. Colvin, 2006.

95. This box is adapted from B. K. Williams and S. C. Sawyer, *Using Information Technology: A Practical Introduction,* 10th ed. (New York: McGraw-Hill, 2013), pp. 41–42.

96. T. Schwartz, "The Personal Energy Crisis," *The New York Times,* July 24, 2011, p. BU-8.

97. W. Gallagher, cited in blog by J. Tierney, "Attention Must Be Paid—but How?" *The New York Times–Tierney Lab,* May 4, 2009, http://tierneylab.blogs.nytimes.com (accessed January 14, 2012). Gallagher is author of *Rapt* (New York: The Penguin Press, 2009).

98. W. Gallagher, quoted in Tierney, 2009.

99. F. P. Robinson, *Effective Study,* 4th ed. (New York: Harper & Row, 1970).

100. H. C. Lindgren, *The Psychology of College Success: A Dynamic Approach* (New York: Wiley, 1969).

101. R. J. Palkovitz and R. K. Lore, "Note Taking and Note Review: Why Students Fail Questions Based on Lecture Material," *Teaching of Psychology* 7(1980), pp. 159–61.

CHAPTER 2

1. C. Hymowitz, "Executives Must Stop Jumping Fad to Fad and Learn to Manage," *The Wall Street Journal,* May 15, 2006, p. B1. See also M. Miller, *The Tyranny of Dead Ideas: Letting Go of the Old Ways of Thinking to Unleash a New Prosperity* (New York: Times Books, 2009).

2. S. Cummings and T. Bridgman, "The Relevant Past: Why the History of Management Should Be Critical for Our Future," *Academy of Management Learning & Education* 10, no. 1 (2011), pp. 77–93.

3. D. M. Rosseau, "Is There Such a Thing as 'Evidence-Based Management'?" *Academy of Management Review,* April 2006, pp. 256–69. Other debates about evidence-based management may be found in T. Reay, W. Berta, and M. Kazman Kohn, "Where's the Evidence on Evidence-Based Management?" *Academy of Management Perspectives,* November 2009, pp. 5–18; R. Briner, D. Denyer, and D. M. Rousseau, "Evidence-Based Management: Concept Cleanup Time?" *Academy of Management Perspectives,* November 2009, pp. 19–32; and S. D. Charlier, K. G. Brown, and S. L. Rynes, "Teaching Evidence-Based Management in MBA Programs: What Evidence Is There?" *Academy of Management Learning & Education* 10, no. 2 (2011), pp. 222–36.

4. J. Pfeffer and R. I. Sutton, "Profiting from Evidence-Based Management," *Strategy & Leadership* 34, no. 2 (2006), pp. 35–42; J. Pfeffer and R. I. Sutton, "Evidence-Based Management," *Harvard Business Review,* January 2006, pp. 63–74; and J. Pfeffer and R. Sutton, "Trust the Evidence, Not Your Instincts," *The New York Times,* September 4, 2011, Business section, p. 8. Pfeffer and Sutton are authors of *Hard Facts, Dangerous Half-Truths, and Total Nonsense* (Boston: Harvard Business School Press, 2006). For a discussion of this book, see Hymowitz, "Executives Must Stop Jumping Fad to Fad and Learn to Manage," 2006.

5. R. I. Sutton, interviewed in "Asked & Answered: Prove It," *Stanford Magazine,* May–June 2006, www.stanfordalumni.org/news/magazine/2006/mayjun/dept/management.html (accessed January 14, 2012). Discussions about the need for an evidence-based process in medicine may be found in D. Sanghavi, "Plenty of Guidelines, but Where's the Evidence?" *The New York Times,* December 9, 2008, p. D6; and R. Winslow, "Study Questions Evidence behind Heart Therapies," *The Wall Street Journal,* February 25, 2009, p. D1.

6. Tom Peters, quoted in J. A. Byrne, "The Man Who Invented Management," *BusinessWeek,* November 28, 2005, www.businessweek.com/magazine/content/05_48/b3961001.htm (accessed January 14, 2012).

7. Byrne, 2005. See also R. Karlgaard, "Peter Drucker on Leadership," *Forbes.com,* November 19, 2004, www.forbes.com/2004/11/19/cz_rk_1119drucker.html; B. J. Feder, "Peter F. Drucker, a Pioneer in Social and Management Theory, Is Dead at 95," *The New York Times,* November 12, 2005, www.nytimes.com/2005/11/12/business/12drucker.html; and P. Sullivan, "Management Visionary Peter Drucker Dies," *The Washington Post,* November 12, 2005, www.washingtonpost.com/wp-dyn/content/article/2005/11/11/AR2005111101938.html (all accessed January 14, 2012).

8. Pfeffer and Sutton, "Profiting from Evidence-Based Management," 2006.

9. C. M. Christensen and M. E. Raynor, "Why Hard-Nosed Executives Should Care about Management Theory," *Harvard Business Review,* September 2003, pp. 67–74.

10. Christensen and Raynor, 2003, p. 68.

11. G. Hamel, *The Future of Management* (Boston: Harvard Business School Press, 2007).

12. John Chambers, quoted in B. Worthen, "Cisco CEO John Chamber's Big Management Experiment," *The Wall Street Journal,* August 5, 2009, http//blogs.wsj.com/digits/2009/08/05/cisco-ceo-jophn-chamberss-big-management-experiment (accessed January 14, 2012).

13. P. Burrows, "Cisco's Extreme Ambitions," *BusinessWeek,* November 30, 2009, pp. 26–27.

14. P. Burrows and J. Galante, "Cisco Reins in Management System That Spurred Exodus at the Top," *Bloomberg Businessweek,* May 5, 2011, www.bloomberg.com/news/2011-05-05/cisco-departures-reflect-frustration-over-management-structure.html (accessed January 15, 2012).

15. B. Rice, "The Hawthorne Defect: Persistence of a Flawed Theory," *Psychology Today,* February 1982, pp. 70–74. See also S. Highhouse, "Applications of Organizational Psychology: Learning through Failure or Failure to Learn?" pp. 331–48 in L. L. Koppes, *Historical Perspectives in Industrial and Organizational Psychology* (Hillsdale, NJ: Lawrence Erlbaum, 2007).

16. A. Maslow, "A Theory of Human Motivation," *Psychological Review,* July 1943, pp. 370–96.

17. D. McGregor, *The Human Side of Enterprise* (New York: McGraw-Hill, 1960).

18. See K. G. Smith, S. J. Carroll, and S. J. Ashford, "Intra- and Interorganizational Cooperation: Toward a Research Agenda," *Academy of Management Journal,* February 1995, pp. 7–23; R. Crow, "Institutionalized Competition and Its Effects on Teamwork," *Journal for Quality and Participation,* June 1995, pp. 46–54; J. T. Delaney, "Workplace Cooperation: Current Problems, New Approaches," *Journal of Labor Research,* Winter 1996, pp. 45–61; H. Mintzberg, D. Dougherty, J. Jorgensen, and F. Westley, "Some Surprising Things About Collaboration—Knowing How People Connect Makes It Work Better," *Organizational Dynamics,* Spring 1996, pp. 60–71; M. E. Haskins, J. Liedtka, and J. Rosenblum, "Beyond Teams: Toward an Ethic of Collaboration," *Organizational Dynamics,* Spring 1998, pp. 34–50; and C. C. Chen, X. P. Chen, and J. R. Meindl, "How Can Cooperation Be Fostered? The Cultural Effects of Individualism-Collectivism," *Academy of Management Review,* April 1998, pp. 285–304.

19. A. Kohn, "How to Succeed without Even Vying," *Psychology Today,* September 1986, pp. 27–28. Sports psychologists discuss "cooperative competition" in S. Sleek, "Competition: Who's the Real Opponent?" *APA Monitor,* July 1996, p. 8.

20. D. W. Johnson, G. Maruyama, R. Johnson, D. Nelson, and L. Skon, "Effects of Cooperative, Competitive, and Individualistic Goal Structures on Achievement: A Meta-Analysis," *Psychological Bulletin,* January 1981, pp. 56–57. An alternative interpretation of the foregoing study that emphasizes the influence of situational factors can be found in J. L. Cotton and M. S. Cook, "Meta-Analysis and the Effects of Various Reward Systems: Some Different Conclusions from Johnson et al.," *Psychological Bulletin,* July 1982, pp. 176–83. Also see A. E. Ortiz, D. W. Johnson, and R. T. Johnson, "The Effect of Positive Goal and Resource Interdependence on Individual Performance," *The Journal of Social Psychology,* April 1996, pp. 243–49; and S. L. Gaertner, J. F. Dovidio, M. C. Rust, J. A. Nier, B. S. Banker, C. M. Ward, G. R. Mottola, and M. Houlette, "Reducing Intergroup Bias: Elements of Intergroup Cooperation," *Journal of Personality and Social Psychology,* March 1999, pp. 388–402.

21. B. Elbel, R. Kersh, V. L. Brescoll, and L. B. Dixon, "Calorie Labeling and Food Choices: A First Look at the Effects on Low-Income People in New York City," *Health Affairs,* published online October 6, 2009, http://content.healthaffairs.org/cgi/content/abstract/hlthaff.28.6.w1110 (accessed January 14, 2012).

22. A. Hartocollis, "Study Finds Calorie Postings in Restaurants Do Not Change Habits," *The New York Times,* October 6, 2009, p. A25.

23. S. F. Brown, "Wresting New Wealth from the Supply Chain," *Fortune,* November 9, 1998, pp. 204[C]–204[Z]. See also M. Maynard, "Toyota Shows Big Three How It's Done," *The New York Times,* January 13, 2006, pp. C1, C4.

24. See P. Davidson, "Lean Manufacturing Helps Companies Survive," *USA Today,* November 2, 2009, pp. 1B, 2B.

25. Y. Takahashi, "Toyota Accelerates Its Cost-Cutting Efforts," *The Wall Street Journal,* December 23, 2009, p. B4; C. Woodyard, "Toyota's Reputation Needs Some TLC," *USA Today,* December 31, 2009, pp. 1B, 2B; M. Maynard and H. Tabuchi, "Rapid Growth Has Its Perils, Toyota Learns," *The New York Times,* January 28, 2010, pp. A1, A8; pp. A1, B4 ; K. Linebaugh and N. Shirouzu, "Toyota Heir Faces Crisis at the Wheel," *The Wall Street Journal,* January 28, 2010, pp. A1, A8; and M. Dolan, "Supplier Perplexed by Toyota's Action," *The Wall Street Journal,* January 28, 2010, p. A9.

26. J. Bennett and K. Linebaugh, "Acceleration Mishaps Worry Vehicle Owners," *The Wall Street Journal,* January 28, 2010, p. A8.

27. Statistics by Safety Research and Strategies, reported in Dolan, "Supplier Perplexed by Toyota's Action," 2010.

28. M. Ramsey, "Toyota Fixes Five Million Recalled Cars," *The Wall Street Journal,* October 5, 2010, p. B4; and M. Ramsey, "Toyota Comeback Hinges on Camry," *The Wall Street Journal,* August 24, 2011, pp. B1, B2.

29. M. Liedtke, "Netflix Price Boost Provides Chance for Redbox to Glow," *San Francisco Chronicle,* September 1, 2011, p. S3; and B. Stelter, "Customers Angry Over Revamped Pricing Are Deserting Netflix," *The New York Times,* September 16, 2011, p. B3.

30. B. Evangelista, "After Apology, Netflix Makes Many Angrier," *San Francisco Chronicle,* September 20, 2011, pp. A1, A10; J. Wortham and B. Stelter, "Latest Move Gets Netflix More Wrath," *The New York Times,* September 20, 2011, pp. B1, B2; E. Smith, "Netflix CEO Unbowed," *The Wall Street Journal,* September 20, 2011, pp. B1, B7; and T. Loftus, "'Confusing Mess,' Say Customers," *The Wall Street Journal,* September 20, 2011, p. B7.

31. C. Edwards and R. Grover, "Companies & Industries: Netflix," *Bloomberg Businessweek,* October 24–30, 2011, pp. 21–22; B. Stelter, "Netflix Reverses Course on Breakup Plan," *The New York Times,* October 11, 2011, pp. B1, B6; M. Snider, "Netflix Ditches Qwikster Plan," *USA Today,* October 11, 2011, p. 1B; M. Liedtke, "Netflix Plummets Amid Note, Stock Sale," *San Francisco Chronicle,* November 23, 2011, pp. D1, D5; and N. Winfield and B. Stelter, "A Juggernaut Stumbles," *The New York Times,* October 25, 2011, pp. B1, B4.

32. B. Evangelista, "Despite Struggles, Netflix Profit Beats Expectations," *San Francisco Chronicle,* January 26, 2012, pp. D1, D3; and B. Stelter, "A Turnaround at Netflix as Its Mail Sector Shrinks," *The New York Times,* January 26, 2012, p. B4.

33. J. Surowiecki, "The Next Level," *The New Yorker,* October 18, 2010, p. 28.

34. *Stress in the Workplace* survey by Harris Interactive for the American Psychological Association, described in "APA Survey Finds Many U.S. Workers Feel Stressed Out and Undervalued," American Psychological Association, press release, March 8, 2011, www.apa.org/news/press/releases/2011/03/workers-stressed.aspx (accessed January 15, 2012).

35. Survey of 5,000 U.S. households conducted for The Conference Board by L. Barrington, L. Franco, and J. Gibbons, *I Can't Get No . . . Job Satisfaction, That Is: America's Unhappy Workers,* January 2010, www.conference-board-org/utilities/pressDetail.cfm?press_ID=3820 (accessed January 16, 2012).

36. L. Petrecca, "Quirky Perks for Workers: Pet Insurance, Massages," *USA Today*, December 30, 2011, p. 1A.

37. D. Mattioli, "Rewards for Extra Work Come Cheap in Lean Times," *The Wall Street Journal*, January 4, 2010, p. B7.

38. "The Top Gurus," *The Wall Street Journal*, May 5, 2008, p. B6.

39. G. Hamel, with B. Breen, *The Future of Management* (Boston: Harvard Business School Press, 2007), p. 6.

40. G. Hamel, "Break Free!" *Fortune*, September 19, 2007, http://money.cnn.com/magazines/fortune/fortune_archive/2007/10/01/100352608/index.htm (accessed January 14, 2012).

41. E. J. Langer, *Mindfulness* (Reading, MA: Addison-Wesley, 1989). See also D. J. Siegel, *The Mindful Brain: Reflection and Attunement in the Cultivation of Well-Being* (New York: W.W. Norton, 2007); and M. Landau, "When Doctors Negotiate Uncertainty," *Focus Online: News from Harvard Medical, Dental, and Public Health Schools*, May 4, 2007, http://focus.hms.harvard.edu/2007/050407/education.shtml (accessed January 16, 2012). See also E. Dane, "Paying Attention to Mindfulness and Its Effects on Task Performance in the Workplace," *Journal of Management*, July 2011, pp. 997–1018.

42. E. J. Langer, *The Power of Mindful Learning* (Reading, MA: Addison-Wesley, 1997), p. 4.

43. Langer, *Mindfulness*, 1989, pp. 12–13.

44. Langer, 1989, p. 69.

45. C. Walton, "Comparison Test: 2011 Cadillac CTS-V Coupe vs. 2011 BMW M3 Coupe," *Edmunds Inside Line*, August 16, 2010, www.insideline.com/cadillac/cts-v/2011/comparison-test-2011-cadillac-cts-v-coupe-vs-2011-bmw-m3-coupe.html (accessed January 16, 2012).

46. A. Garvin, "Building a Learning Organization," *Harvard Business Review*, July–August 1993, pp. 78–91; and R. Hodgetts, F. Luthans, and S. Lee, "New Paradigm Organizations: From Total Quality to Learning to World-Class," *Organizational Dynamics*, Winter 1994, pp. 5–19D. See also T. Kelly, "Measuring Informal Learning: Encourage a Learning Culture and Track It!" *Trainingindustry.com*, March 31, 2009, www.trainingindustry.com/articles/measuring-informal-learning.aspx (accessed January 16, 2012).

47. A. S. Miner and S. J. Mezias, "Ugly Duckling No More: Pasts and Futures of Organizational Learning Research," *Organization Science*, January–February 1996, pp. 88–99; and R. P. Mai, *Learning Partnerships: How Leading American Companies Implement Organizational Learning* (Chicago: Irwin, 1996).

48. B. Breen, "How EDS Got Its Groove Back," *Fast Company*, September 2001, p. 106.

49. D. Ulrich, T. Jick, and M. Von Glinow, "High-Impact Learning: Building and Diffusing Learning Capability," *Organizational Dynamics*, Autumn 1993, pp. 52–66; S. F. Slater, "Learning to Change," *Business Horizons*, November–December 1995, pp. 13–20; and D. M. Noer, *Breaking Free: A Prescription for Personal and Organizational Change* (San Francisco: Jossey-Bass, 1996).

50. Pfeffer and Sutton, "Profiting from Evidence-Based Management," 2006.

51. M. Arndtent, *Strategy & Leadership* 34, no. 2 (2006), pp. 35–42.

CHAPTER 3

1. Marianne Jennings, professor of legal and ethical studies, W. P. Carey School of Business, Arizona State University, quoted in "College Cheating Is Bad for Business," *Knowledge@W.P. Carey*, September 24, 2008, http://knowledge.wpcarey.asu.edu/article.cfm?articleid=1679 (accessed January 23, 2012).

2. B. Carey, "Stumbling Blocks on the Path of Righteousness," *The New York Times*, May 5, 2009, p. D5.

3. M. H. Bazerman and A. E. Tenbrunsel, "Stumbling into Bad Behavior," *The New York Times*, April 20, 2011, p. A2. The two are authors of *Blind Spots: Why We Fail to Do What's Right and What to Do about It* (Princeton, NJ: Princeton University Press, 2011).

4. Poll by Beneson Strategy Group for Common Sense Media, reported in "35% of Teenagers Reports Using Cell Phones to Cheat," *Common Sense Media*, June 18, 2009, www.commonsensemedia.org/about-us/press-room/hi-tech-cheating-poll (accessed January 20, 2012); J. Tucker, "Tech-Savvy Students Invent New Ways to Cheat," *San Francisco Chronicle*, June 19, 2009, pp. A1, A16; J. D. Glater, "Colleges Chase as Cheats Shift to High Tech," *The New York Times*, May 18, 2006, pp. A1, A20; and D. L. McCabe, K. D. Butterfield, and L. K. Trevino, "Academic Dishonesty in Graduate Business Programs: Prevalence, Causes, and Proposed Action," *Academy of Management Learning & Education*, September 2006, pp. 294–305.

5. B. Staples, "Cutting and Pasting: A Senior Thesis by (Insert Name)," *The New York Times*, July 12, 2010, www.nytimes.com/2010/07/13/opinion/13tue4.html (accessed January 20, 2012).

6. D. J. Palazzo, Y.-J. Lee, R. Warnakulasooriya, and D. E. Pritchard, "Patterns, Correlates, and Reduction of Homework Copying," *Physical Review Special Topics*, March 2010, http://prst-per.aps.org/abstract/PRSTPER/v6/i1/e010104 (accessed January 20, 2012).

7. "PG&E's Shame," editorial, *San Francisco Chronicle*, January 16, 2012, p. A9.

8. J. Van Derbeken, "PG&E Incentive System Blamed for Leak Oversights," *San Francisco Chronicle*, December 25, 2011, p. A1; and E. Nalder, "PG&E Diverted Safety Money for Profit, Bonuses," *San Francisco Chronicle*, January 13, 2012, p. A1.

9. Audit by Overland Consulting, reported in Nalder, 2012.

10. Nalder, 2012.

11. J. Goodnight, quoted in D. A. Kaplan, "The Best Company to Work For," *Fortune*, February 8, 2010, pp. 56–64.

12. "The Employee Ownership 100: America's Largest Majority Employee-Owned Companies," The National Center for Employee Ownership, May 2011, www.nceo.org/main/article.php/id/11 (accessed January 20, 2012).

13. Forester Research reported in P. Korkki, "When Industries Care about Their Customers," *The New York Times*, December 20, 2009, Business section, p. 2. See also M. Burns, H. Manning, and J. Peterson, *The Customer Experience Index, 2011*, Forrester Research, January 11, 2011, updated April 12, 2011, www.forrester.com/rb/Research/customer_experience_index%2C_2011/q/id/58251/t/2?src=58592pdf (accessed January 20, 2012).

14. J. Nocera, "Put Buyers First? What a Concept," *The New York Times*, January 5, 2008, pp. B1, B9.

15. Jeff Bezos, quoted in Nocera, 2008, p. B9.

16. UTest review by 600 software professionals, reported in B. Acohido, "Study: Amazon Most User Friendly," *USA Today*, December 7, 2009, p. 2B. See also UTest, "Software Testing Leader Holds Competition to Compare E-Tailers Based on Pricing, Usability, Product Search and Other Feature Sets," December 7, 2009, www.utest.com/press/utest-%E2%80%9Cbattle-e-tailers%E2%80%9D-uncovers-more-500-bugs-amazoncom-walmartcom-and-targetcom (accessed January 20, 2012).

17. J. Yap, ""Amazon's Q4 Profits Dip 58%," *ZDNet*, February 1, 2012, www.zdnetasia.com/amazons-q4-profits-dip-58-percent-62303670.htm (accessed January 20, 2012).

18. B. De Lollis and R. Yu, "Indie Hotels Cater to Elite Travelers," *USA Today*, January 29, 2008, p. 4B.

19. Bureau of Labor Statistics, U.S. Department of Labor, "Union Members Summary," *Economic News Release*, January 27, 2012, www.bls.gov/news.release/union2.nr0.htm (accessed January 20, 2012).

20. Bureau of Labor Statistics, reported in S. Greenhouse, "Most U.S. Union Members Are Working for the Government, New Data Shows," *The New York Times*, January 23, 2010, pp. B1, B5.

21. J. Schmitt and K. Warner, *The Changing Face of Labor, 1983–2008*, Center for Economic Policy Research, November 12, 2009, www.cepr.net/index.php/press-releases/press-releases/

demographics-of-labor-movement (accessed January 20, 2012). See also S. Greenhouse, "Survey Finds Deep Shift in the Makeup of Unions," *The New York Times*, November 11, 2009, p. B5.

22. A. G. Sulzberger, "Boeing Departure Shakes Wichita's Identity as Airplane Capital," *The New York Times*, January 19, 2012, pp. A1, A13.

23. D. Barry, "In a Company's Hometown, the Emptiness Echoes," *The New York Times*, January 25, 2010, p. A9.

24. D. Babwin, "Cities Holding Firms to the Deals They Have," *San Francisco Chronicle*, January 3, 2010, p. A13.

25. S. Medintz, "Getting the Loan Officer on Your Side," *The New York Times*, May 28, 2009, p. B8; and S. Brown, as told to M. Zouhali-Worrall, "Tend to Your Lender," *FSB*, September 2009, p. 53. See also P. Davidson, "This Recession Isn't Being Kind to Entrepreneurs," *USA Today*, June 8, 2009, p. 1B; K. Chu and S. Block, "As Lenders Clamp Down, Credit Scores Take a Hit," *USA Today*, September 22, 2009, pp. 1A, 2A; and P. S. Goodman, "Clamps on Credit Tighten," *The New York Times*, October 13, 2009, pp. B1, B4.

26. F. Ma, quoted in M. Lagos, "Faux Fur May Not Be—State Labeling Law in the Works," *San Francisco Chronicle*, January 21, 2010, p. C2.

27. R. Lieber, "Punishing BP Is Harder Than Boycotting Stations," *The New York Times*, June 11, 2010, www.nytimes.com/2010/06/12/your-money/12money.html (accessed January 20, 2012). For a discussion of how politically passionate consumers take aim at certain businesses, see R. S. Dunham, "Companies in the Crossfire," *BusinessWeek*, April 17, 2006, pp. 30–33.

28. N. Singer, "In Recall, Role Model Stumbles," *The New York Times*, January 18, 2010, pp. B1, B2.

29. S. Todd, "For Johnson & Johnson, Rebound from Recall Is Slow-Going as Brand Names Remain Damaged," *The Star-Ledger*, November 22, 2011, www.nj.com/business/index.ssf/2011/11/for_johnson_johnson_rebound_fr.html (accessed January 20, 2012); and P. Loftus, "J&J Net Slumps on Charges," *The Wall Street Journal*, January 25, 2012, http://online.wsj.com/article/SB20001424052970203806504577180620348232662.html (accessed February 1, 2012).

30. Interview with Gene Grabowski by M. Philips, "Toyota's 'Tylenol Moment,'" *Newsweek*, February 15, 2010, p. 12.

31. S. Tavernise, "Poverty Reaches a 52-Year Peak, Government Says," *The New York Times*, September 14, 2011, pp. A1, A19; J. Deparle and S. Tavernise, "Poor Are Still Getting Poorer, but Downturn's Punch Varies, Census Data Show," *The New York Times*, September 15, 2011, p. A24; U.S. Census Bureau, reported in M. Bello, "The New Faces of Poverty," *USA Today*, September 29, 2011, pp. 1C, 2C. See also H. El Nasser and P. Overberg, "Recession Reshapes Life in USA," *USA Today*, September 22, 2011, p. 3A; M. Cooper and A. Kopicki, "Facing Hardship, Jobless Still Say They Have Hope," *The New York Times*, October 27, 2011, pp. A1, A16; J. Medina and S. Tavernise, "Economy Alters How Many Americans Are Moving," *The New York Times*, October 28, 2011, pp. A12, A14; "Following Recession, Workers in Middle Class Get Squeezed Out," *Reno Gazette-Journal*, October 30, 2011, p. 2E; S. Tavernise, "Survey Finds Rising Strain between Rich and the Poor," *The New York Times*, January 12, 2012, pp. A11, A13; and K. Greene and A. Tergesen, "More Elderly Find They Can't Afford Not to Work," *The Wall Street Journal*, January 21, 2012, pp. A1, A10.

32. Bureau of Labor Statistics, *International Comparisons of Manufacturing Productivity and Unit Labor Cost Trends 2008*, October 22, 2009, www.bls.gov/news.release/prod4.nr0.htm (accessed January 20, 2012). Bureau of Labor Statistics, reported in P. Wiseman, "Productivity Leaps at 6.2% Rate as Firms Wait to Hire," *USA Today*, February 5, 2010, p. 3B; and Bureau of Labor Statistics, "Productivity and Costs, Fourth Quarter and An-

nual Averages 2011, Preliminary," *Economic News Release*, February 2, 2012, www.bls.gov/news.release/prod2.nr0.htm (accessed February 15, 2012).

33. D. Wessel, "The Factory Floor Has a Ceiling on Job Creation," *The Wall Street Journal*, January 12, 2012, p. A6; and T. Aeppel, "Man vs. Machine, a Jobless Recovery," *The Wall Street Journal*, January 17, 2012, pp. B1, B6. See also T. L. Friedman, "Average Is Over," *The New York Times*, January 28, 2012, p. A25, on the extension of technology into service jobs and possible further increased unemployment.

34. D. St. George, "More Teens Are Choosing to Wait to Get Driver's Licenses," *The Washington Post*, January 25, 2010, p. A1. The article reports on data from the U.S. Department of Transportation, Federal Highway Administration, "Distribution of Licensed Drivers—2008 by Sex and Percentage in Each Age Group and Relation to Population," *Policy Information*, January 2010, Table DL20, www.fhwa.dot.gov/policyinformation/statistics/2008/dl20.cfm (accessed January 20, 2012).

35. M. Kabel, "Diet Trends Affect U.S. Meat Glut," *Reno Gazette-Journal*, May 16, 2006, p. 4D.

36. Centers for Disease Control and Prevention, cited in C. Lochhead, "First Lady Leads Fight over Youths' Obesity," *San Francisco Chronicle*, February 3, 2010, pp. A1, A14.

37. R. Rubin, "Drop in Births Attributed to Economy," *USA Today*, April 7, 2010, p. 5D; H. Yen, "Rural America Disappears," *Reno Gazette-Journal*, July 28, 2011, p. 2C; H. El Nasser, "Black-White Marriages Increasing," *USA Today*, September 20, 2011, p. 3A; and H. El Nasser and P. Overberg, "Census Tracks 20 Years of Sweeping Change," *USA Today*, October 10, 2011.

38. M. Mather, "Four Scenarios for U.S. Population Growth," Population Reference Bureau, December 2009, www.prb.org/Articles/2009/uspopulationgrowth.aspx (accessed January 20, 2012).

39. M. Galanter, reported in W. Glaberson, "When the Verdict Is Just a Fantasy," *The New York Times*, June 6, 1999, sec. 4, pp. 1, 6.

40. D. Bass, "Microsoft Makes Changes to Ease EU Competition," Bloomberg.com, February 21, 2008, www.bloomberg.com/apps/news?pid=20601087&sid=azE39eAmWCLU&refer=home (accessed January 20, 2012).

41. American Council on Education, reported by P. Wingert, "'F' in Global Competence," *Newsweek*, May 20, 2002, p. 11. See also D. J. Lynch, "U.S. Firms Becoming Tongue-Tied," *USA Today*, February 9, 2006, p. 6B; and "Execs Learning to Speak Second Language," *Reno Gazette-Journal*, May 5, 2006, p. 6D.

42. G. Allred, quoted in S. Armour, "Facing a Tough Choice: Your Ethics or Your Job," *USA Today*, September 21, 1998, p. B1.

43. L. T. Hosmer, *The Ethics of Management* (Homewood, IL: Irwin, 1987). See also S. Welch, "The Uh-Oh Feeling," *O Magazine*, November 2007, pp. 117–20. For more on money-and-ethics matters, see J. Fleming and L. Schwartz, *Isn't It Their Turn to Pick Up the Check?* (New York: Free Press, 2008).

44. Study by LRN, consultant on corporate ethics, cited in "Corporate Ethics Affect Employee Productivity," *HR Magazine*, July 2007, p. 16.

45. S. Saul, "Unease on Industry's Role in Hypertension Debate," *The New York Times*, May 20, 2006, pp. A1, B9; and C. Arnst, "Hey, You Don't Look So Good," *BusinessWeek*, May 8, 2006, pp. 30–32. For the results of a survey concerning doctors' ethics, see E. G. Campbell, S. Regan, R. L. Gruen, T. G. Ferris, S. R. Rao, P. D. Cleary, and D. Blumenthal, "Professionalism in Medicine: Results of a National Survey of Physicians," *Annals of Internal Medicine*, December 4, 2007, pp. 795–802.

46. B. Kabanoff, "Equity, Equality, Power, and Conflict," *Academy of Management Review*, April 1991, pp. 416–41. See also S. T. Hannah, B. J. Avolio, and D. R. May, "Moral Maturation and Moral Conation: A Capacity Approach to Explaining Moral Thought and Action," *Academy of Management Review* 36 (2011), pp. 633–85.

47. D. Fritzsche and H. Baker, "Linking Management Behavior to Ethical Philosophy: An Empirical Investigation," *Academy of Management Journal,* March 1984, pp. 166–75.

48. "Chemicals in Our Water Are Affecting Humans and Aquatic Life in Unanticipated Ways," *Science Daily,* February 21, 2008, www.sciencedaily.com/-releases/2008/02/080216095740.htm (accessed January 20, 2012).

49. J. Sandberg, "Monitoring of Workers Is Boss's Right but Why Not Include Top Brass?" *The Wall Street Journal,* May 18, 2005, p. B1.

50. G. Morgenson, "The Big Winner, Again, Is 'Scandalot,'" *The New York Times,* January 1, 2006, sec. 3, pp. 1, 7; C. Said, "From White Collars to Prison Blues," *San Francisco Chronicle,* May 26, 2006, pp. D1, D6; G. Morgenson, "Are Enrons Bustin' Out All Over?" *The New York Times,* May 28, 2006, sec. 3, pp. 1, 8; K. Clark and M. Lavelle, "Guilty as Charged!" *U.S. News & World Report,* June 5, 2006; A. Sloan, "Laying Enron to Rest," *Newsweek,* June 5, 2006, pp. 25–30, pp. 44–45; M. Gimein, "The Skilling Trap," *BusinessWeek,* June 12, 2006, pp. 31–32. See also S. Labaton, "Four Years Later, Enron's Shadow Lingers as Change Comes Slowly," *The New York Times,* January 5, 2006, pp. C1, C4; J. H. Zamansky, "At the Least, Former Enron Chiefs Are Guilty of Moral Bankruptcy," *USA Today,* February 1, 2006, p. 11A; A. Shell, "Enron Verdicts Good for Investors," *USA Today,* May 30, 2006, p. 1B; K. Eichenwald and A. Barrionuevo, "Enron Shows Businesses Face Tough Tactics," *The New York Times,* May 27, 2006, pp. A1, B4; and D. Glovin, "Refco Ex-Finance Chief Trosten Pleads Guilty to Fraud," *Bloomberg.com,* February 20, 2008, www.bloomberg.com/apps/news?pid=206 01087&sid=aBl5wsezRDT4&refer=home# (accessed January 20, 2012).

51. "Wall Street's Dirty Little Secret," *The Week,* November 13, 2009, p. 13; and P. Hurtado, B. V. Voris, and D. Glovin, "Galleon Co-founder Gets 11-Year Term for Insider Trading," *San Francisco Chronicle,* October 14, 2011, pp. D1, D6.

52. B. Levisohn, "How to Make a Madoff," *BusinessWeek,* December 16, 2008, http://www.businessweek.com/investor/content/dec2008/pi20081215_232943.htm?chan=investing_investing+index+page_top+stories (accessed January 20, 2012). See also D. Gross, "Membership Has Its Penalties," *Newsweek,* January 12, 2009, p. 18; and M. Hosenball, "Made Money with Madoff? Don't Count on Keeping It," *Newsweek,* January 12, 2009, p. 9.

53. D. R. Henriques, "Madoff, Apologizing, Is Given 150 Years," *The New York Times,* June 30, 2009, pp. A1, B4.

54. S. Stecklow, "Hard Sell Drove Stanford's Rise and Fall," *The Wall Street Journal,* April 3, 2009, pp. A1, A12; E. Perez and J. A. Favole, "Stanford, 5 Others Face Ponzi Charges," *The Wall Street Journal,* June 20, 2009, pp. B1, B3; and C. Krauss, "Stanford Convicted by Jury in $7 Billion Ponzi Scheme," *The New York Times,* March 6, 2012, www.nytimes.com/2012/03/07/business/jury-convicts-stanford-in-7-billion-ponzi-fraud.html?_r=1&pagewanted=all (accessed June 2, 2012).

55. F. Norris, "Goodbye to Reforms of 2002," *The New York Times,* November 6, 2009, pp. B1, B6.

56. See D. R. Dalton and C. M. Dalton, "Sarbanes-Oxley Legislation and the Private Company: If Not a Marriage, Then Certainly an Engagement," *Journal of Business Strategy,* February 2005, pp. 7–8; "SOX: No One-Size-Fits-All Solution to Dishonest Accounting," Knowledge@W.P.Carey, June 7, 2006, http://knowledge.wpcarey.asu.edu/index.cfm?fa=viewArticle&id=1259; "Research Supports Value of IT Consults in Post-SOX Age," Knowledge@W.P. Carey, June 7, 2006, http://knowledge.wpcarey.asu.edu/index.cfm?fa=view Article&id=1261; and W. Cienke, "Small Companies Also Can Benefit from Sarbanes-Oxley," *Small Business Times,* February 22, 2008, www.biztimes.com/news/2008/2/22/small-companies-also-can-benefit-from-sarbanes-oxley (all accessed January 20, 2012).

57. J. Van Derbeken, "Ex-bank Employee Accused of Swindling Elderly Woman," *San Francisco Chronicle,* February 5, 2010, p. C6.

58. F. J. Evans, quoted in C. S. Stewart, "A Question of Ethics: How to Teach Them?" *The New York Times,* March 21, 2004, sec. 3, p. 11.

59. D. A. Kaplan, "MBAs Get Schooled in Ethics," *Fortune,* October 26, 2009, p. 27.

60. Research by the Center for Academic Integrity, Kenan Institute for Ethics, Duke University, cited in H. Oh, "Biz Majors Get an F for Honesty," *BusinessWeek,* February 6, 2006, p. 14.

61. L. Kohlberg, "Moral Stages and Moralization: The Cognitive Developmental Approach," in T. Lickona, ed., *Moral Development and Behavior: Theory, Research, and Social Issues* (New York: Holt, Rinehart and Winston, 1976), pp. 31–53; and J. W. Graham, "Leadership, Moral Development and Citizenship Behavior," *Business Ethics Quarterly,* January 1995, pp. 43–54. See also S. J. Reynolds and T. L. Ceranic, "The Effects of Moral Judgment and Moral Identity on Moral Behavior: An Empirical Examination of the Moral Individual," *Journal of Applied Psychology,* November 2007, pp. 1610–24.

62. Adapted in part from W. E. Stead, D. L. Worrell, and J. Garner Stead, "An Integrative Model for Understanding and Managing Ethical Behavior in Business Organizations," *Journal of Business Ethics,* March 1990, pp. 233–42. Also see D. Lange, "A Multidimensional Conceptualization of Organizational Corruption Control," *Academy of Management Review,* July 2008, pp. 710–29; J. DesJardins, *An Introduction to Business Ethics,* 3rd ed. (New York: McGraw-Hill, 2009); and M. J. Pearsall and A. P. J. Ellis, "Thick as Thieves: The Effects of Ethical Orientation and Psychological Safety on Unethical Team Behavior," *Journal of Applied Psychology* 96 (2011), pp. 401–11.

63. W. M. Welch, "Employee Screenings See Growth," *USA Today,* June 24, 2009, p. 3A.

64. A. Bennett, "Ethics Codes Spread Despite Criticism," *The Wall Street Journal,* July 15, 1988, p. 13.

65. Society for Human Resource Management Weekly Survey, 2005, cited in J. Thilmany, *HR Magazine,* September 2007, pp. 105–12.

66. T. R. Mitchell, D. Daniels, H. Hopper, J. George-Falvy, and G. R. Ferris, "Perceived Correlates of Illegal Behavior in Organizations," *Journal of Business Ethics,* April 1996, pp. 439–55. See also M. W., "Ethics Training Works," *Training,* November 2005, p. 15; L. Paine, R. Deshpandé, J. D. Margolis, and K. E. Bettcher, "Up to Code: Does Your Company's Conduct Meet World-Class Standards?" *Harvard Business Review,* December 1, 2005, pp. 122–35; and J. Brockner, "Why It's So Hard to Be Fair," *Harvard Business Review,* March 1, 2006, p. 122–32.

67. R. Pear, "Whistleblowers Likely to Get Stronger Federal Protections," *The New York Times,* March 15, 1999, pp. A1, A17.

68. T. Herman, "Tipster Rewards Require Patience," *The Wall Street Journal,* December 26, 2007, p. D3.

69. Associated Press, "Whistle-blowers Help U.S. Recoup Billions," *Reno Gazette-Journal,* September 2, 2008, p. 2B.

70. J. H. Pryor, L. DeAngelo, L. P. Blake, S. Hurtado, and S. Tran, *The American Freshman: National Norms, Fall 2011* (Los Angeles: Higher Education Research Institute, University of California, Los Angeles, 2011).

71. Jed Emerson, quoted in C. Dahle, "60 Seconds with Jed Emerson," *Fast Company,* March 2004, p. 42.

72. This definition of *sustainability* was developed in 1987 by the World Commission on Environment and Development.

73. Brian Walker, interviewed by J. Akresh-Gonzales, "Herman Miller CEO Brian Walker on Meeting Sustainability Goals—with Customers' Help," *Harvard Business Review,* December 2009, p. 26.

74. M. Friedman, *Capitalism and Freedom* (Chicago: University of Chicago Press, 1962). See also S. Gallagher, "A Strategic

Response to Freidman's Critique of Business Ethics," *Journal of Business Strategy*, January 2005, pp. 55–60.

75. P. Samuelson, "Love That Corporation," *Mountain Bell Magazine*, Spring 1971.

76. A. B. Carroll, "Managing Ethically with Global Stakeholders: A Present and Future Challenge," *Academy of Management Executive*, May 2004, p. 118. Also see B. W. Husted and D. B. Allen, "Corporate Social Responsibility in the Multinational Enterprise: Strategic and Institutional Approaches," *Journal of International Business Studies*, November 2006, pp. 838–49.

77. T. L. Friedman, "Yes, They Could. So They Did," *The New York Times*, February 14, 2009, www.nytimes.com/2009/02/15/opinion/15friedman.html.

78 A. G. Robinson and D. M. Schroeder, "Greener and Cheaper," *The Wall Street Journal*, March 23, 2009, p. R4.

79. N. B. Kurland and D. Zell, "Green Management: Principles and Examples," *Organizational Dynamics* 40 (2011), pp. 49–56.

80. J. Mincer and S. Banjo, "Insurers Offer Rewards for Going Green," *The Wall Street Journal*, April 22, 2009, p. D5.

81. C. Palmeri, "The Dividends from Green Offices," *BusinessWeek*, December 7, 2009, p. 15.

82. C. Batchelor, "Hotels: Relax with a Clear Conscience," *Financial Times*, January 25, 2010, www.ft.com/cms/s/0/68c23a26-0953-11df-ba88-00144feabdc0,dwp_uuid=68347df0-11df-ba88-00144feabdc0.html (accessed January 20, 2012); and S. Nassauer, "Less Housekeeping, More Perks," *The Wall Street Journal*, February 4, 2010, p. D3.

83. United Nations Intergovernmental Panel on Climate Change, *Fourth Assessment Report, Climate Change 2007: Synthesis Report, Summary for Policy Makers*, November 2007, www1.ipcc.ch/ipccreports/assessments-reports.htm (accessed January 20, 2012). See also F. Guterl, "Iceberg Ahead," *Newsweek*, March 1, 2010, pp. 34–37.

84. B. J. Creyts, A. Derkach, S. Nyquist, K. Ostrowski, and J. Stephenson, *Reducing U.S. Greenhouse Gas Emissions: How Much at What Cost?* U.S. Greenhouse Gas Abatement Mapping Initiative, Executive Report, December 2007, McKinsey & Company, www.mckinsey.com/clientservice/ccsi/pdf/US_ghg_-final_-report.pdf (accessed January 20, 2012). See also M. L. Wald, "Study Details How U.S. Could Cut 28% of Greenhouse Gases," *The New York Times*, November 30, 2007, p. C5.

85. Center for Small Business and the Environment, reported in E. Iwata, "Small Businesses Take Big Steps into Green Practices," *USA Today*, December 3, 2007, p. 4B.

86. See R. J. Samuelson, "Greenhouse Simplicities," *Newsweek*, August 27, 2007, p. 47. Also see R. Abrams, "Going Green Makes Good Business Sense," *Reno Gazette-Journal*, March 13, 2007, p. 6D; C. H. Deutsch, "For Suppliers, the Pressure Is On," *The New York Times*, November 7, 2007, pp. H1, H11; B. Feder, "Aiding the Environment, a Nanostep at a Time," *The New York Times*, November 7, 2007, p. H6; A. Martin, "If It's Fresh and Local, Is It Always Greener?" *The New York Times*, December 9, 2007, p. BU11; J. Carlton, "Tech Aims to Green Up Its Act," *The Wall Street Journal*, January 7, 2008, p. B6; M. Judkis, "10 Ways to Save by Going Green," *U.S. News & World Report*, March 2010, pp. 34–36; C. Lochhead, "Farming Method Gaining Ground in Nation," *San Francisco Chronicle*, May 26, 2011, pp. A1, A7; and M. L. Wald, "Storehouses for Solar Energy Can Step in When the Sun Goes Down," *The New York Times*, January 3, 2012, pp. B1, B4.

87. J. Ramirez, "How to Live a Greener Life," *Newsweek*, April 16, 2007, p. 82; W. Koch, "More States Ban Disposal of Electronics in Landfills," *USA Today*, December 19, 2011, p. 1B.

88. D. Gross, "Edison's Dimming Bulbs," *Newsweek*, October 15, 2007, p. E22.

89. Ramirez, "How to Live a Greener Life," 2007.

90. D. Ransom, "Consider the Source," *The Wall Street Journal*, November 12, 2007, p. R4.

91. American Wind Energy Association, reported in P. Davidson, "Wind Power Growth Gusts Strongly in U.S.A. in 2007," *USA Today*, January 18, 2008, p. 3B.

92. Iwata, "Small Businesses Take Big Steps into Green Practices," 2007.

93. J. Markoff and S. Lohr, "Gates to Reduce Microsoft Role as Era Changes," *The New York Times*, June 16, 2008, pp. A1, C8; and J. Guynn, "He's Opening Windows to Philanthropy," *San Francisco Chronicle*, June 18, 2006, pp. F1, F5.

94. T. L. O'Brien and S. Saul, "Buffet to Give Bulk of Fortune to Gates Charity," *The New York Times*, June 26, 2006, pp. A1, A15; and D. G. McNeil Jr. and R. Lyman, "Buffet's Billions Will Aid Fight Against Disease," *The New York Times*, June 27, 2006, pp. A1, C4.

95. H. Rubin, "Google's Searches Now Include Ways to Make a Better World," *The New York Times*, January 18, 2008, pp. C1, C5; and K. J. Delaney, "Google: From 'Don't Be Evil' to How to Do Good," *The Wall Street Journal*, January 18, 2008, pp. B1, B2.

96. A.-A. Jarvis, "Pulling Off an Impressive Feet," *Newsweek*, July 3–10, 2006, p. 64.

97. A. Fox, "Corporate Social Responsibility Pays Off," *HR Magazine*, August 2007, pp. 43–47. For an example of an advertising agency that profits from developing social-responsibility campaigns, see S. Kang, "Agency's Social Responsibility Focus," *The Wall Street Journal*, August 17, 2007, p. B3.

98. R. Gildea, "Consumer Survey Confirms Corporate Social Action Affects Buying Decisions," *Public Relations Quarterly*, Winter 1994, pp. 20–21.

99. Caravan survey from Opinion Research developed by LRN of 2,037 adults, reported in "Ethics vs. Price," *USA Today*, June 14, 2006, p. 1B.

100. D. H. Pink, *Drive: The Surprising Truth about What Motivates Us* (New York: Riverhead, 2010).

101. N. T. Washburn, "Why Profit Shouldn't Be Your Top Goal," *Harvard Business Review*, December 2009, p. 23.

102. Results can be found in "Tarnished Employment Brands Affect Recruiting," *HR Magazine*, November 2004, pp. 16, 20.

103. 2003 National Business Ethics Survey, cited in *The Hidden Costs of Unethical Behavior* (Los Angeles: Josephson Institute of Ethics, 2004), p. 3, www.josephsoninstitute.org/pdf/workplace-flier_0604.pdf (accessed January 20, 2012). See also D. Turban and G. Greening, "Corporate Social Performance and Organizational Attractiveness to Prospective Employees," *Academy of Management Journal* 40 (1997), pp. 658–72.

104. M. Baucus and D. Baucus, "Paying the Piper: An Empirical Examination of Longer-Term Financial Consequences of Illegal Corporate Behavior," *Academy of Management Journal* 40 (1997), pp. 129–51.

105. 2003 survey by Wirthlin Worldwide, cited in *The Hidden Costs of Unethical Behavior*, p. 2.

106. 2000 National Business Ethics Survey, cited in *The Hidden Costs of Unethical Behavior*, p. 3.

107. "ACFE's Highly-Anticipated Report to the Nation to Be Published in June," preview of *2006 ACFE Report to the Nation on Occupational Fraud & Abuse*, Association of Certified Fraud Examiners www.acfe.com/announcement-rttn-preview.asp (accessed January 20, 2012).

108. Ernst & Young survey 2002 and KPMG Fraud Survey 2003, both cited in *The Hidden Costs of Unethical Behavior*, p. 2.

109. 2003 survey by Wirthlin Worldwide, cited in *The Hidden Costs of Unethical Behavior*, p. 2.

110. D. M. Long and S. Rao, "The Wealth Effects of Unethical Business Behavior," *Journal of Economics and Finance*, Summer 1995, pp. 65–73.

111. A discussion of ethics and financial performance is provided by R. M. Fulmer, "The Challenge of Ethical Leadership," *Organizational Dynamics,* August 2004, pp. 307–17.

112. C. M. Daily, D. R. Dalton, and A. A. Cannella Jr., "Corporate Governance: Decades of Dialogue and Data," *Academy of Management Review* 28 (2003), pp. 371–83; D. R. Dalton, M. A. Hitt, S. T. Certo, and C. M. Dalton, "The Fundamental Agency Problem and Its Mitigation," *Academy of Management Annals* 1 (2007), pp. 1–64; and M. L. McDonald, P. Khanna, and J. D. Westphal, "Getting Them to Think Outside the Circle: Corporate Governance, CEOs' External Advice Network, and Firm Performance," *Academy of Management Journal,* 51 (2009), pp. 453–75.

113. C. Helman, "The Two Sides of Aubrey," *Forbes.com,* October 24, 2011, www.forbes.com/forbes/2011/1024/feature-aubrey-mcclendon-hero-energy-chesapeake-risk-christopher-helman.html (accessed January 20, 2012).

114. M. Leder, "For Chesapeake's Chief, Some Big Money in Maps," *New York Times DealBook,* May 1, 2009, http://dealbook.nytimes.com/2009/05/01/for-chesapeakes-chief-some-big-money-in-maps; and M. Leder, "Chesapeake's McClendon Buys Back the Maps," *Footnoted.org,* November 3, 2011, www.footnoted.com/buried-treasure/chesapeakes-mcclendon-buys-back-the-maps (both accessed January 20, 2012).

115. Chesapeake Energy proxy filing notes, reported in Leder, 2011.

116. C. Hilman, "In Legal Settlement, Chesapeake's McClendon to Buy Back Antique Maps," *Forbes.com,* November 3, 2011, www.okctalk.com/showthread.php?t=28160&page=1 (accessed January 20, 2012).

117. Helman, "In Legal Settlement, Chesapeake's McClendon to Buy Back Antique Maps," 2011; and J. Polson, "Chesapeake CEO McClendon to Buy Back Maps, Ending Pay Suit," *Bloomberg,* November 3, 2011, www.bloomberg.com/news/2011-11-03/chesapeake-ceo-mcclendon-to-buy-back-maps-ending-pay-dispute.html (accessed January 20, 2012).

118. R. Dezember and D. Gilbert, "Gas Titan's Blueprint Rests on More Deals," *The Wall Street Journal,* January 26, 2012, pp. B1, B2.

119. R. Hurley, "Trust Me," *The Wall Street Journal,* October 24, 2011, p. R4. Hurley is author of *The Decision to Trust: How Leaders Can Create High-Trust Companies* (San Francisco: Jossey-Bass, 2011).

CHAPTER 4

1. K. Reinhard, quoted in S. McCartney, "Teaching Americans How to Behave Abroad," *The Wall Street Journal,* April 11, 2006, pp. D1, D4. See also R. Yu, "Cultural Training Has Global Appeal," *USA Today,* December 22, 2009, p. 3B.

2. DDB Worldwide survey, cited in J. Clark, "That 'Ugly American' Image Is Getting a Makeover Guide," *USA Today,* April 28, 2006, p. 9D.

3. *World Citizens Guide,* Business for Diplomatic Action, May 2006, www.worldcitizensguide.org/index2.html (accessed February 14, 2012).

4. T. Lowry and F. Balfour, "It's All about the Face-to-Face," *BusinessWeek,* January 28, 2008, pp. 48, 50.

5. E. Schmitt, "A Man Does Not Ask a Man about His Wife," *The New York Times,* January 8, 2006, sec. 4, p. 7.

6. T. Rivas, "Name Game Hits a Global Roadblock," *The Wall Street Journal,* May 30, 2006, p. B5.

7. B. Morris, "The Pepsi Challenge: Can This Snack and Soda Giant Go Healthy?" *Fortune,* March 3, 2008, pp. 55–66.

8. L. Nardon and R. M. Steers, "The New Global Manager: Learning Cultures on the Fly," *Organizational Dynamics,* January–March 2008, pp. 47–59.

9. R. Simmermaker, *How Americans Can Buy American: The Power of Consumer Patriotism,* 3rd ed. (Orlando, FL: Rivercross Publications, 2010).

10. Roger Simmermaker, quoted in W. T. Price, "Exploring Financial Viability of Buying American Products," *Reno Gazette-Journal,* September 10, 2011, pp. 6A, 8A.

11. G. Hale and B. Hobijn, "The U.S. Content of 'Made in China,'" *FRBSF Economic Letter,* August 8, 2011, Federal Reserve Bank of San Francisco, www.frbsf.org/publications/economics/letter/2011/el2011-25.html (accessed February 14, 2012).

12. See the related discussion in J. McGregor and S. Hamm, "Managing the Global Workforce," *BusinessWeek,* January 28, 2008, p. 34; C. Boles, "Last Call? Gates Pushes Globalism in Remarks," *The Wall Street Journal,* March 13, 2008, p. B3; and M. Herbst, "Guess Who's Getting the Most Work Visas," *BusinessWeek,* March 17, 2008, pp. 62, 64.

13. Cellular Telecommunications Industry Association, cited in A. Dunkin, "Smart, Useful—and They Won't Put a Sag in Your Suit," *BusinessWeek,* May 30, 1994, p. 141.

14. *The World in 2011: ICT Facts and Figures,* International Telecommunications Union, Geneva, www.itu.int/ITU-D/ict/facts/2011/material/ICTFactsFigures2011.pdf (accessed February 14, 2012).

15. *The World in 2011.*

16. See J. Quittner, "Tim Berners-Lee," *Time,* March 29, 1999, pp. 193–94.

17. "Quarterly Retail E-Commerce Sales 3rd Quarter 2011," *U.S. Census Bureau News,* November 17, 2011, www.census.gov/retail/mrts/www/data/pdf/ec_current.pdf (accessed February 14, 2012).

18. Needleman, "When the Shoe Fits, but Needs a Fix," *The Wall Street Journal,* February 11, 2010, p. D2.

19. R. M. Kantor, quoted in K. Maney, "Economy Embraces Truly Global Workplace," *USA Today,* December 31, 1998, pp. 1B, 2B.

20. Maney, 1998.

21. Kris Gopalakrishnan, interviewed in R. M. Smith, "A Titan of Globalism," *Newsweek,* November 19, 2007, p. E26.

22. M. Srivastava and M. Herbst, "The Return of the Outsourced Job," *Bloomberg BusinessWeek,* January 11, 2010, pp. 16–17.

23. J. Rosen, "Foreign Influence Needn't Be a Bad Thing," *USA Today,* November 23, 2009, p. 8B. See also M. Maynard, *The Selling of the American Economy: How Foreign Companies Are Remaking the American Dream* (New York: Broadway Business, 2009).

24. G. Easterbrook, "The Boom Is Nigh," *Newsweek,* February 22, 2010, pp. 48–49. Easterbrook is the author of *Sonic Boom: Globalization at Mach Speed* (New York: Random House, 2009). See also P. Ghemawat, *World 3.0: Global Prosperity and How to Achieve It* (Boston: Harvard Business Press, 2011), who argues that globalization, when finally realized, will offer more benefits than threats.

25. "Is Global Finance Sector a Force for Good or Ill?" *The Wall Street Journal,* November 28, 2007, p. B9; and P. Krugman, "Don't Cry for Me, America," *The New York Times,* January 18, 2008, p. A23.

26. L. Uchitelle, "Another Shifting Industry," *The New York Times,* January 19, 2010, pp. B1, B5.

27. P. Izzo, "Many Jobs Gone Forever, Economists Say," *The Wall Street Journal,* February 12, 2010, p. A4; and D. Peck, "How a New Jobless Era Will Transform America," *The Atlantic,* March 2010, pp. 42–56. See also M. Whitehouse, "Radical Shifts Take Hold in U.S. Manufacturing," *The Wall Street Journal,* February 3, 2010, pp. B1, B4.

28. Easterbrook, "The Boom Is Nigh," 2010.

29. N. Negroponte, quoted in Maney, "Economy Embraces Truly Global Workplace," 1998.

30. A. Troianvski, "AT&T Hangs Up on T-Mobile," *The Wall Street Journal,* December 20, 2011, pp. A1, A2; and C. Rauwald, "Volkswagen Calls Off Porsche Merger," *The Wall Street Journal,* January 10, 2012, http://online.wsj.com/article/SB1000142405

297020412420457715056097135 1488.html (accessed February 14, 2012).

31. J. Mouawad, "More Deals Expected in Energy," *The New York Times,* February 17, 2010, pp. B1, B6; and A. Aston, "Utilities Turn to Mergers as Demand for Power Slows," *New York Times Dealbook,* June 16, 2011, http://dealbook.nytimes.com/2011/06/16/utilities-turn-to-mergers-as-demand-for-power-wanes (accessed February 14, 2012).

32. S. Weimer, "Mannequin Madness," *California Materials— Exchange,* Integrated Waste Management Board, April 23, 2004, www.ciwmb.ca.gov/CalMAX/Creative/2003/Winter.htm (accessed February 14, 2012).; I. DeBare, "New Lease on Life for Mannequins," *San Francisco Chronicle,* July 29, 2006, p. J2; S. L. Thomas, "Warehouse Visit Spawns Mannequin Madness," *East Bay Business Times,* February 24, 2006, http://eastbay.bizjournals.com/eastbay/stories/ 2006/02/27/smallb1.html (accessed February 14, 2012).

33. P. McDonald, quoted in M. L. Levin, "Global Experience Makes Candidates More Marketable," *The Wall Street Journal,* September 11, 2007, p. B6.

34. D. Mattioli, "With Fewer U.S. Opportunities, Home Looks Appealing to Expats," *The Wall Street Journal,* December 15, 2009, p. D7. See also P. Engardio, "China's Reverse Brain Drain," *BusinessWeek,* November 30, 2009, p. 58; and T. Abate, "U.S. May Be Set for Brain Drain," *San Francisco Chronicle,* February 27, 2010, pp. D1, D2.

35. P. Davidson, "U.S. Job Hunters Eye Other Nations' Help Wanted Ads," *USA Today,* November 16, 2009, p. 1B.

36. J. Androshick, quoted in H. Chura, "A Year Abroad (or 3) as a Career Move," *The New York Times,* February 25, 2006, p. B5.

37. T. Chea, "Americans Seek Opportunity in Bangalore," *Reno Gazette-Journal,* April 3, 2006, p. 3E.

38. S. Stapleton, quoted in R. Erlich, "Going Far in the East," *San Francisco Chronicle,* June 24, 2006, pp. C1, C2.

39. J. Schickler, quoted in K. Chu, "Americans Turn to Asia to Find Work," *USA Today,* September 14, 2011, pp. 1B, 2B.

40. R. C. Carter, senior vice president for human resources at A&E Television Networks, quoted in Chura, "A Year Abroad (or 3) as a Career Move," 2006. For more about Americans working overseas, see N. Lakshman, "Subcontinental Drift," *BusinessWeek,* January 16, 2006, pp. 42–43; R. J. Newman, "Coming and Going," *U.S. News & World Report,* January 23, 2006, pp. 50–52; Fishman, "Why the Jobs Are Going Over There," 2011; and Schickler, 2011.

41. "The World's Biggest Public Companies," Forbes.com, www.forbes.com/global2000 (accessed February 14, 2012).

42. T. C. Fishman, "Why the Jobs Are Going Over There," *USA Today,* May 18, 2011, p. 9A.

43. Survey by the Zimmerman Agency for Residence Inn by Marriott, in "Things You Love to Miss," *USA Today,* March 1, 1999, p. 1B.

44. Lowry and Balfour, "It's All about the Face-to-Face," 2008.

45. Paul Calello of Credit Suisse, quoted in Lowry and Balfour, 2008.

46. Don G. Lents, chairman of international law firm Bryan Cave, quoted in J. Sharkey, "E-Mail Saves Time, but Being There Says More," *The New York Times,* January 26, 2010, p. B7.

47. Ty Morse, interviewed by J. Raymond, "To Asia and Back, Sleep Not an Option," *The New York Times,* January 3, 2012, p. B6.

48. L. Bergson, "A Road Scholar's Bag of Tricks," *BusinessWeek,* September 29, 2003, www.businessweek.com/smallbiz/content/sep2003/sb20030929_6259_sb002.htm?chan=search (accessed February 14, 2012).

49. Yu, "Cultural Training Has Global Appeal," 2009.

50. Bergson, "A Road Scholar's Bag of Tricks," 2003.

51. C. Jones, "Little Things Make Life on the Go Much Better," *USA Today,* January 31, 2012, p. 6B.

52. G. Stoller, "Doing Business Abroad? Simple Faux Pas Can Sink You," *USA Today,* August 24, 2007, pp. 1B, 2B.

53. J. R. Hagerty, "U.S. Loses High-Tech Jobs as R&D Shifts Toward Asia," *The Wall Street Journal,* January 18, 2012, pp. B1, B2.

54. D. A. Heenan and H. V. Perlmutter, *Multinational Organization Development* (Reading, MA: Addison-Wesley, 1979).

55. D. Jones, "Do Foreign Executives Balk at Sports Jargon?" *USA Today,* March 30, 2007, pp. 1B, 2B.

56. R. Kopp, "International Human Resource Policies and Practices in Japanese, European, and United States Multinationals," *Human Resource Management,* Winter 1994, pp. 581–99.

57. C. Duhigg and K. Bradsher, "How U.S. Lost Out on iPhone Work," *The New York Times,* January 22, 2012, News section, pp. 1, 22, 23.

58. W. J. Holstein, "Colonial Roots Have Spread Worldwide," *The New York Times,* June 16, 2007, p. B3.

59. Associated Press, "P&G Targets Developing Markets as U.S. Slows," *CourierJournal.com,* January 27, 2012, www.courier-journal.com/article/20120127/BUSINESS/301270094/P-G-targets-developing-markets-U-S-slows (accessed February 14, 2012).

60. E. Byron, "P&G's Global Target: Shelves of Tiny Stores," *The Wall Street Journal,* July 16, 2007, pp. A1, A10. See also L. Wayne, "P. & G. Sees the World as Its Client," *The New York Times,* December 12, 2009, pp. B1, B2.

61. W. M. Cox, "An Order of Prosperity, to Go," *The New York Times,* February 17, 2010, p. A23.

62. D. Gross, "China Leaves Its Wallet at Home," *Newsweek,* December 21, 2009, p. 10; and F. Norris, "Making More Things in the U.S.A.," *The New York Times,* January 6, 2012, pp. B1, B7.

63. N. Kulish and M. Cieply, "Around World in One Movie: Film Financing's Global Future," *The New York Times,* December 6, 2011, pp. A1, A3.

64. S. McCartney, "Who's Inspecting Your Airplane?" *The Wall Street Journal,* March 3, 2004, pp. D1, D12.

65. J. R. Hagerty and K. Linebaugh, "U.S.: A Cheaper Labor Pool," *The Wall Street Journal,* January 6, 2012, pp. B1, B2.

66. H. L. Sirkin, M. Zinser, and D. Hohner, *Made in America, Again: Why Manufacturing Will Return to the U.S.* (Boston: Boston Consulting Group, 2011), www.bcg.com/documents/file84471.pdf (accessed February 14, 2012).

67. Study of government data by Economic Policy Institute, Washington, DC, cited in R. Keil and L. Arnold, "New Jobs Created at Low End," *San Francisco Chronicle,* April 13, 2004, p. C5; and J. Hernandez, "Manufacturing Shows Signs of Strengthening," *The New York Times,* February 2, 2010, p. B8. See also A. S. Ross, "Growth Doesn't Always Mean Jobs," *San Francisco Chronicle,* August 7, 2011, pp. D1, D2; L. Uchitelle, "Is Manufacturing Falling Off the Radar?" *The New York Times,* September 11, 2011, Business section, pp. 1, 6; and L. Uchitelle, "The U.S. Gains Factory Jobs, but Workers Give Ground on Wages," *The New York Times,* December 30, 2011, pp. B1, B2.

68. Forrester Research, cited in G. Epstein, "Static Disrupts the Bangalore Connection," *Barron's Online,* September 10, 2007, http://online.barrons.com/article/SB118921200748221265.html (accessed February 14, 2012).

69. Forrester Research, "Losing Our Edge? Estimated Number of High-Skilled U.S. Jobs Moving Offshore," reported in K. Madigan, "Yes: This Is No Longer About a Few Low-Wage or Manufacturing Jobs. Now One Out of Three Jobs Is at Risk," *BusinessWeek,* August 25, 2003, pp. 37–38.

70. B. Schlender, "Peter Drucker Sets Us Straight," *Fortune,* January 12, 2004, pp. 115–18. See also P. Engardio, "The Future of Outsourcing," *BusinessWeek,* January 30, 2006, pp. 50–58; E. White, "Smaller Companies Join the Outsourcing Trend," *The Wall Street Journal,* May 8, 2006, p. B3; and L. Buchanan,

"The Thinking Man's Outsourcing," *Inc. Magazine,* May 2006, pp. 31–33.

71. J. Thottam, "Is Your Job Going Abroad?" *Time,* March 1, 2004, pp. 26–34.

72. F. Levy, quoted in D. Wessel, "The Future of Jobs: New Ones Arise, Wage Gap Widens," *The Wall Street Journal,* April 2, 2004, pp. A1, A5.

73. For some caveats about offshoring, see M. Bolch, "Going Global," *Training,* January 2008, pp. 28–29; M. Weinstein, "On Target Offshore," *Training,* January 2008, pp. 34–36; and M. Bandyk, "Now Even Small Firms Can Go Global," *U.S. News & World Report,* March 10, 2008, p. 52.

74. E. A. Spiegel, "America Can 'Insource' Jobs through Innovation," *USA Today,* January 25, 2012, p. 11A.

75. A. M. Chaker, "Where the Jobs Are," *The Wall Street Journal,* March 18, 2004, pp. D1, D3; J. Shinal, "Which Types of Jobs Will Be in Demand?" *San Francisco Chronicle,* March 25, 2004, pp. C1, C4; and D. Wessel, "The Future of Jobs: New Ones Arise, Wage Gap Widens," *The Wall Street Journal,* April 2, 2004, pp. A1, A5.

76. J. Spohrer, quoted in Shinal, 2004.

77. P. Drucker, quoted in Schlender, "Peter Drucker Sets Us Straight," 2004.

78. L. Uchitelle, "College Degree Still Pays, but It's Leveling Off," *The New York Times,* January 17, 2005, pp. C1, C2.

79. M. Bartiromo, "Toys R Us Makes Play for Global Sales," *USA Today,* December 19, 2011, p. 4B; R. Ahmed, "Starbucks Looks to India," *The Wall Street Journal,* October 11, 2011, p. B9; S. Finz, "Gap Turning to Foreign Market," *San Francisco Chronicle,* October 14, 2011, pp. D1, D6; C. H. Shinn, "Wendy's Marks Return to Japan with High-End Foie Gras Burger," *San Francisco Chronicle,* December 29, 2011, p. D3; and M. Bahree, "Starbucks Will Open Cafés in India," *The Wall Street Journal,* January 31, 2012, p. B10.

80. M. Thorneman, B. Lannes, and N. Palmer, "Resurrecting the China Joint-Venture," *Far Eastern Economic Review,* October 2008, www.feer.com/economics/2008/october/Resurrecting-the-China-Joint-Venture; and J. Gopwani and M. Szczepanski, "Buick Remains Popular with China's Upper-Middle Class," *Detroit Free Press,* August 30, 2009, www.allbusiness.com/automotive/motor-vehicle-models-new-car/12783271-1.html(both accessed February 14, 2012).

81. K. Bradsher, "7 U.S. Solar Panel Makers File Case Accusing China of Violating Trade Rules," *The New York Times,* October 20, 2011, pp. B1, B10.

82. M. L. Wald and K. Bradsher, "4 U.S. Makers of Towers for Wind Turbines File Complaint over China's Steel Subsidies," *The New York Times,* December 30, 2011, p. B2.

83. S. Terlep, "Auto Makers Face Changes in China," *The Wall Street Journal,* January 6, 2012, p. B4.

84. "China to Cancel Car Import Quota in 2005," *China Daily,* February 13, 2004, www.chinadaily.com.cn/english/doc/2004-02/13/ content_305954.htm (accessed February 14, 2012).

85. Terlep, "Auto Makers Face Changes in China," 2012. See also A. Back, "U.S. Raps 'Damaging' China Policies," *The Wall Street Journal,* January 29–29, 2012, p. A9; and T. Barkley, "China Loses Trade Appeal over Its Curbs on Exports," *The Wall Street Journal,* January 31, 2012, p. A9.

86. K. Maher and H. J. Pulizzi, "Chinese Slapped in Steel Dispute," *The Wall Street Journal,* December 31, 2009, p. A3.

87. J. Borger, "The Iranian Oil Embargo: Does This Mean War?" *The Guardian,* January 23, 2012, www.guardian.co.uk/world/2012/jan/23/iran-oil-embargo-mean-war (accessed February 14, 2012).

88. J. Bhagwati, *Protectionism* (Cambridge, MA: MIT Press, 1988).

89. "WTO Telecoms Deal Will Ring in the Changes on 5 February 1998," *World Trade Organization,* January 26, 1998.

90. M. Landler, "Britain Overtakes U.S. as Top World Bank Donor," *The New York Times,* December 15, 2007, www.nytimes.com/2007/12/15/world/15worldbank.html (accessed February 14, 2012).

91. A. Lowrey, "International Monetary Fund Offers Short-Term Credit as Insurance for Nations," *The New York Times,* November 23, 2011, p. B4.

92. R. E. Scott, "Trade Deficit with Mexico Has Resulted in 682,900 Jobs Lost or Displaced," Economic Policy Institute, October 12, 2011, http://useconomy.about.com/gi/o.htm?zi=1/XJ&zTi=1&sdn=useconomy&cdn=newsissues&tm=85&gps=680_553_1276_627&f=00&su=p284.13.342.ip_&tt=11&bt=0&bts=0&zu=http%3A//www.epi.org/publication/heading_south_u-s-mexico_trade_and_job_displacement_after_nafta1 (accessed February 14, 2012).

93. U.S. Census Bureau, "Trade in Goods with Mexico," *Foreign Trade,* January 13, 2012, www.census.gov/foreign-trade/balance/c2010.html (accessed February 14, 2012).; and U.S. Census Bureau, "Trade in Goods with Canada," *Foreign Trade,* January 13, 2012, www.census.gov/foreign-trade/balance/c1220.html (accessed February 14, 2012).

94. S. Erlanger, "Euro, Meant to Unite Europe, Seems to Be Rending It," *The New York Times,* October 20, 2011, p. A9.

95. See, for example, E. Papaioannou, R. Portes, and G. Siourounis, "Optimal Currency Shares in International Reserves: The Impact of the Euro and the Prospects for the Dollar," *NBER Working Paper* No. 12333, June 2006, National Bureau of Economic Research, http://papers.nber.org/papers/wl2333 (accessed February 14, 2012).; and Associated Press, "Report: Greenspan Says Euro Could Replace U.S. Dollar as Reserve Currency of Choice," *International Herald Tribune,* September 17, 2007, www.iht.com/articles/ap/2007/09/17/business/EU-FIN-MKT-Germany-Greenspan-Euro.php (accessed February 14, 2012).

96. S. Erlanger, "Euro, Meant to Unite Europe, Seems to Be Rending It," *The New York Times,* October 20, 2011, p. A9; P. Krugman, "The Hole in Europe's Bucket," *The New York Times,* October 24, 2011, p. A19; P Krugman, "Killing the Euro," *The New York Times,* December 2, 2011, p. A27; N. Kulish, "Euro, Introduced with Flourish, Gets Little Celebration at Its 10-Year Mark," *The New York Times,* January 1, 2012, News section, p. 1; T. Lauricella, "Euro's Resilience Is Tested," *The Wall Street Journal,* January 6, 2012, pp. C1, C2; and L. Di Leo and A. Zibel, "Fed Survey: Euro Crisis Has Hurt U.S. Loans," *The Wall Street Journal,* January 31, 2012, p. A2.

97. D. Roberts and P. Engardio, "China's End Run around the U.S.," *BusinessWeek,* November 23, 2009, pp. 22–24; T. Wright, "Obama Aims to Regain U.S. Heft in Southeast Asia," *The Wall Street Journal,* November 12, 2009, p. A16; and L. Gooch, "Asia Free-Trade Zone Raises Hopes, and Some Fears about China," *The New York Times,* January 1, 2010, p. B3.

98. See M. A. O'Grady, "One Year After CAFTA," *The Wall Street Journal,* February 26, 2007, p. A18.

99. Dean Foster, president of Dean Foster Associates, an intercultural consulting firm, quoted in T. Mohn, "Going Global, Going Stateside," *The New York Times,* March 9, 2010, p. B8.

100. G. A. Fowler, "In China's Offices, Foreign Colleagues Might Get an Earful," *The Wall Street Journal,* February 13, 2007, p. D1.

101. "How Cultures Collide," *Psychology Today,* July 1976, p. 69.

102. See P. R. Harris and R. T. Moran, *Managing Cultural Differences,* 4th ed. (Houston: Gulf Publishing, 1996), pp. 223–28; and M. Hilling, "Avoid Expatriate Culture Shock," *HR Magazine,* July 1993, pp. 58–63.

103. M. Javidan and R. J. House, "Cultural Acumen for the Global Manager: Lessons from Project GLOBE," *Organizational Dynamics,* Spring 2001, pp. 289–305; R. J. House, P. J. Hanges, M. Javidan, P. W. Dorfman, and V. Gupta, eds., *Culture, Leadership, and Organizations: The GLOBE Study of 62 Societies* (Thousand Oaks, CA: Sage, 2004); and M. Javidan, P. W. Dorfman, M. S. de Luque, and R. J. House, "In the Eye of the Beholder: Cross Cultural Lessons in Leadership from Project GLOBE," *Academy of Management Perspectives,* February 2006, pp. 67–90.

104. A discussion of Japanese stereotypes in America can be found in L. Smith, "Fear and Loathing of Japan," *Fortune,* February 26, 1990, pp. 50–57. See also V. Taras, P. Steel, and B. L. Kirkman, "Three Decades of Research on National Culture in the Workplace: Do the Differences Still Make a Difference?" *Organizational Dynamics,* vol. 40 (2001), pp. 189–98.

105. G. A. Michaelson, "Global Gold," *Success,* March 1996, p. 16. English is increasingly becoming the language of business and more and more is being taught in foreign business universities. See D. Carvajal, "English as Language of Global Education," *The New York Times,* April 11, 2007, p. A21. In U.S. institutions, enrollments in Arabic-language classes are skyrocketing, but there is a great shortage of teachers. See T. Yahalom, "Surge in Students Studying Arabic Outstrips Supply of Teachers," *USA Today,* September 5, 2007, p. 7D.

106. Harris Poll, National Foreign Language Center, reported in "Lingua Franca?" *USA Today,* February 23, 1999, p. 1A.

107. D. Einstein, "Free Translation Apps Can Turn Smart Phone into Interpreter," *San Francisco Chronicle,* August 8, 2011, p. D1.

108. D. J. Lynch, "U.S. Firms Becoming Tongue-Tied," *USA Today,* February 9, 2006, p. 6B.

109. Center for Applied Linguistics 2008 survey, released November 2009, reported in "What Are the Most Common Foreign Languages Taught in U.S. Schools," *USA Today,* February 16, 2010, p. A1.

110. Samir Khalaf, quoted in H.M. Fattah, "Why Arab Men Hold Hands," *The New York Times,* May 1, 2005, sec. 34, p. 2.

111. "How Cultures Collide," 1976.

112. Kari Heistad, CEO of Culture Coach International, quoted in E. Maltby, "Expanding Abroad? Avoid Cultural Gaffes," *The Wall Street Journal,* January 19, 2010, p. B5. See also L. Nardon, R. M. Steers, and C. J. Sanchez-Runde, "Seeking Common Ground: Strategies for Enhancing Multicultural Communication, *Organizational Dynamics,* vol. 40 (2011), pp. 85–95.

113. Neil Currie, quoted in K. Tyler, "Global Ease," *HR Magazine,* May 2011, pp. 41–48.

114. B. Stone, "What's in a Name? For Apple, iPad Said More Than Intended," *The New York Times,* January 29, 2010, pp. A1, A3.

115. Michael Norman, senior vice president at Sibson Consulting, quoted in H. Seligson, "For American Workers in China, a Culture Clash," *The New York Times,* December 24, 2009, pp. B1, B2.

116. K. Seong-Kon, writing in *The Korea Herald,* summarized in "A Society That Needs No Appointment," *The Week,* May 29, 2009, p. 14.

117. E. T. Hall, *The Hidden Dimension* (New York: Doubleday, 1966).

118. C. Salazar, "Time Is of the Essence in Peru's Punctuality Effort," *San Francisco Chronicle,* March 2, 2007, p. A16.

119. Robert Levine, quoted in R. Vecchio, "Global Psyche: On Their Own Time," *Psychology Today,* July-August 2007, http://psychologytoday.com/articles/pto-20070723-000007.html (accessed February 14, 2012).

120. C. Woodward, "AP Poll Paints Portrait of Impatient American," *Reno Gazette-Journal,* May 29, 2006, pp. 1C, 7C.

121. A. R. Sorkin, "A Financial Mirage in the Desert," *The New York Times,* December 1, 2009, pp. B1, B5.

122. Results adapted from and value definitions quoted from S. R. Safranski and I.-W. Kwon, "Religious Groups and Management Value Systems," in R. N. Farner and E. G. McGoun, eds., *Advances in International Comparative Management,* vol. 3 (Greenwich, CT: JAI Press, 1988), pp. 171–83.

123. U.S. State Department, cited in W. McGurn, "Washington's Assault on American Expats," *The Wall Street Journal,* January 3, 2012, p. A13.

124. Jacqui Hauser, vice president of consulting services for Cendant Mobility, a relocation-services firm, cited in P. Capell, "Employers Seek to Trim Pay for U.S. Expatriates," *The Wall Street Journal,* April 16, 2005, www.careerjournal.com (accessed February 14, 2012).

125. J. S. Black and H. B. Gregersen, "The Way to Manage Expats," *Harvard Business Review,* March-April 1999, p. 53.

126. See A. Maingault, L. Albright, and V. Neal, "Policy Tips, Repatriation, Safe Harbor Rules," *HR Magazine,* March 2008, pp. 34–35.

127. S. Dallas, "Rule No. 1: Don't Diss the Locals," *BusinessWeek,* May 15, 1995, p. 8. Also see M. A. Shaffer, D. A. Harrison, H. Gregersen, J. S. Black, and L. A. Ferzandi, "You Can Take It with You: Individual Differences and Expatriate Effectiveness," *Journal of Applied Psychology,* January 2006, pp. 109–25.

CHAPTER 5

1. D. Middleton, "Landing a Job of the Future Takes a Two-Track Mind," *The Wall Street Journal,* December 29, 2009, p. D4. See also J. A. Challenger, "Finding a Job in the 21st Century," *The Futurist,* September–October 2009, pp. 29–33; and E. Gordon, "The Global Talent Crisis," *The Futurist,* September–October 2009, pp. 34–39.

2. M. J. Driver, "Careers: A Review of Personnel and Organizational Research," in C. L. Cooper and I. Robertson, eds., *International Review of Industrial and Organizational Psychology* (New York: Wiley, 1988).

3. T. Gutner, "Doubling Up on Careers Suits More Workers," *The Wall Street Journal,* February 5, 2008, p. B4. See also M. Alboher, *One Person/Multiple Careers: A New Model for Work/Life Success* (New York: Warner Books, 2007).

4. E. White, "Profession Changes Take Time but May Be Worth Wait," *The Wall Street Journal,* November 27, 2007, p. B6; and P. Korkki, "The Big Switch, One Step at a Time," *The New York Times,* June 19, 2011, Business section, p. 8.

5. R. Kreitner, *Management,* 7th ed. (Boston: Houghton Mifflin, 1998), p. 160.

6. B. Vlasic, "Ford's Bet: It's a Small World After All," *The New York Times,* January 10, 2010, Business section, pp. 1, 6.

7. M. Ramsey, "Ford Aims to Shake Up Family Car Market," *The Wall Street Journal,* January 6, 2012, p. B4.

8. J. O'Donnell, "Ford's Touch Software to Be Upgraded," *USA Today,* February 9, 2012, p. 2B; and C. Woodyard, "Apps Behind the Wheel," *USA Today,* January 6, 2012, pp. 1B, 2B.

9. R. E. Miles and C. C. Snow, *Organizational Strategy, Structure, and Process* (New York: McGraw-Hill, 1978).

10. "What's Wrong with This Picture: Kodak's 30-Year Slide into Bankruptcy," *Knowledge@Wharton,* February 1, 2012, http://knowledge.wharton.upenn.edu/article.cfm?articleid=2935 (accessed February 14, 2012); and Associated Press, "Picture This: Kodak to Leave the Digital Camera Business," *Reno Gazette-Journal,* February 10, 2012, p. 10A.

11. R. Newman, "The Great Retail Revolution," *U.S. News & World Report,* March 2010, pp. 19–20; and P. Moeller, "Tough Times Are Molding Tough Customers," *U.S. News & World Report,* March 2010, pp. 22–25.

12. A. D'Innocenzio, "It'll Be All Sales All the Time at J.C. Penney," *USA Today*, January 26, 2012, p. 1B; and S. Clifford, "J.C. Penney to Revise Pricing Methods and Limit Promotions," *The New York Times*, January 26, 2012, pp. B1, B4.

13. E. Holmes, "Gap Looks Abroad for New Sales, Profit Gains," *The Wall Street Journal*, February 26, 2010, p. B5. See also A. Cordeiro, "Goods Makers Look Abroad," *The Wall Street Journal*, February 24, 2010, p. B7; and D. Mattioli and K. Hudson, "Gap to Slash Its Store Count," *The Wall Street Journal*, October 14, 2011, pp. B1, B2.

14. See, for example, D. Brass, "Microsoft's Creative Destruction," *The New York Times*, February 4, 2010, p. A25.

15. See M. Olson, D. van Bever, and S. Verry, "When Growth Stalls," *Harvard Business Review*, March 2008, pp. 51–61.

16. M. Bustillo and G. Fowler, "Sears Scrambles Online for Lifeline," *The Wall Street Journal*, January 15, 2010, pp. A1, A16.

17. D. C. Hambrick, "On the Staying Power of Defenders, Analyzers, and Prospectors," *Academy of Management Executive*, November 2003, pp. 115–18. For more about the four basic strategy types, see also D. J. Ketchen Jr., "Introduction: Raymond E. Miles and Charles C. Snow's *Organizational Strategy, Structure, and Process*," *Academy of Management Executive*, November 2003, pp. 95–96; D. J. Ketchen Jr., "An Interview with Raymond E. Miles and Charles C. Snow," *Academy of Management Executive*, November 2003, pp. 97–104; S. E. Brunk, "From Theory to Practice: Applying Miles and Snow's Ideas to Understand and Improve Firm Performance," *Academy of Management Executive*, November 2003, pp. 105–8; and S. Ghoshal, "Miles and Snow: Enduring Insights for Managers," *Academy of Management Executive*, November 2003, pp. 109–14.

18. D. Leider, "Purposeful Work," *Utne Reader*, July-August 1988, p. 52; excerpted from *On Purpose: A Journal about New Lifestyles & Workstyles*, Winter 1986.

19. P. F. Drucker, *The Practice of Management* (New York: Harper & Row, 1954), p. 122.

20. T. A. Stewart, "A Refreshing Change: Vision Statements That Make Sense," *Fortune*, September 30, 1996, pp. 195–96.

21. For application of vision to nonprofits, see A. Kilpatrick and L. Silverman, "The Power of Vision," *Strategy & Leadership*, February 2005, pp. 24–26.

22. Survey conducted by the Society for Human Resource Management and the Balance Scorecard Collaborative, reported in J. Mullich, "Get in Line," *Workforce Management*, December 2003, pp. 43–44.

23. P. J. Below, G. L. Morrisey, and B. L. Acomb, *The Executive Guide to Strategic Planning* (San Francisco: Jossey-Bass, 1987), p. 2.

24. R. L. Brandt, "Birth of a Salesman," *The Wall Street Journal*, October 15–16, 2011, pp. C1, C2.

25. Ownership data from "Amazon.com Inc.," *AOL Money & Finance*, February 9, 2012, www.thomsoninvestortools.com/component/firm/aol/view.asp?uid=stocks/ownership&country=US&tier=default&symbol=AMZN (accessed February 14, 2012).

26. Bezos, quoted in J. B. Stewart, "At Amazon, Talking Long Term," *The New York Times*, December 17, 2011, pp. B1, B7.

27. S. Woo and J. Letzing, "Amazon's Spending Habit Hurts Profit," *The Wall Street Journal*, February 1, 2012, pp. B1, B2. In a study of 280 CEOs by research firm Oxford Economics, 7 in 10 CEOs investors' emphasis on short-term rewards present an obstacle to long-term planning; see L. Kwoh, "More Revealing CEOs," *The Wall Street Journal*, January 31, 2012, p. B6.

28. J. Bosman, "The Bookstore's Last Stand," *The New York Times*, January 29, 2012, Business section, pp. 1, 4, 5.

29. Stewart, "At Amazon, Talking Long Term," 2011.

30. "Southwest Records Profit," *Reno Gazette-Journal*, January 20, 2012.

31. M. Esterl, "Southwest Airlines Results Signal Clearer Skies," *The Wall Street Journal*, October 16, 2009, p. B3; D. Reed, "Reshuffled Deck Leaves Low-Cost Carriers King," *USA Today*, November 10, 2009, pp. 1B, 2B; S. Carey and M. Esterl, "Airlines Appear Headed for Recovery," *The Wall Street Journal*, December 8, 2009, p. B2; "Southwest Airlines Fact Sheet," Southwest.com, revised December 31, 2009, www.southwest.com/about_swa/press/factsheet.html#About%20the%20Company (accessed February 14, 2012); A. Keeton, "Southwest Airlines Hedges Its Bets," *The Wall Street Journal*, January 22, 2010, p. B3; and Hoover's, "Southwest Airlines Company Description," Hoovers.com, www.hoovers.com/company/Southwest_Airlines_Co/rrykki-1.html (accessed February 9, 2012).

32. James Parker, quoted in W. J. Holstein, "At Southwest, the Culture Drives Success," *BusinessWeek.com*, February 21, 2008, www.businessweek.com/managing/content/feb2008/ca20080221_179423.htm (accessed February 14, 2012). Parker is author of *Do the Right Thing: How Dedicated Employees Create Loyal Customers and Large Profits* (Philadelphia: Wharton School Publishing, 2008).

33. S. Stellin, "Now Boarding Business Class," *The New York Times*, February 26, 2008, p. C6.

34. Willie Wilson, quoted in J. Bailey, "On Some Flights, Millionaires Serve the Drinks," *The New York Times*, May 15, 2006, pp. A1, A16.

35. "Best and Worst Airlines," *Consumer Reports Magazine*, June 2011, www.consumerreports.org/cro/magazine-archive/2011/june/money/airlines/overview/index.htm (accessed February 14, 2012).

36. "Smiles and Free Peanuts," *The Economist*, June 2, 2011, www.economist.com/node/18774997?story_id=18774997 (accessed February 14, 2012).

37. T. Steinmetz, "Tough Times Call for Tough Measures: Southwest Airlines Strategy Gets Pragmatic about Fees," *eTurboNews*, June 2, 2009, www.eturbonews.com/9578/tough-times-call-tough-measures-southwest-airlines-strategy-gets (accessed February 14, 2012).

38. Herb Kelleher, quoted in "How Herb Keeps Southwest Hopping," *Money*, June 1999, pp. 61–62.

39. Reed, "Reshuffled Deck Leaves Low-Cost Carriers King," 2009.

40. S. Carey and D. Cameron, "Southwest Takes a Breather," *The Wall Street Journal*, February 27, 2012, p. B3.

41. See E. A. Locke and G. P. Latham, "Building a Practically Useful Theory of Goal Setting and Task Motivation," *American Psychologist*, September 2002, pp. 705–17.

42. Drucker, *The Practice of Management*, 1954.

43. Lock and Latham, "Building a Practically Useful Theory of Goal Setting and Task Motivation," 2002.

44. The performance management process is discussed by H. Aguinis and C. Pierce, "Enhancing the Relevance of Organizational Behavior by Embracing Performance Management Research," *Journal of Organizational Behavior*, January 2008, pp. 139–45.

45. R. Rodgers and J. E. Hunter, "Impact of Management by Objectives on Organizational Productivity," *Journal of Applied Psychology*, April 1991, pp. 322–36.

46. M. Barbaro, "Wal-Mart Sets Agenda of Change," *The New York Times*, January 24, 2008, p. C3; and K. Ohannessian, "CEO Lee Scott Speaks About Wal-Mart's New Strategies," *FastCompany.com*, January 24, 2008, http://blog.fastcompany.com/archives/2008/01/24/ceo_lee_scott_speaks_about_walmarts_new_strategies.html (accessed February 14, 2012).

47. A. S. Ross, "Wal-Mart's Grand Green Alternative," *San Francisco Chronicle*, February 28, 2010, pp. D1, D2.

48. "Walmart Rockets from 15th to Third in EPA Green Power Rankings," *Environmental Leader*, February 1, 2012, www.environmentalleader.com/2012/02/01/walmart-rockets-from-15th-to-third-on-epa-green-power-rankings (accessed February 14, 2012).

49. S. Strom, "To Promote Healthier Food Choices, Walmart Adds Labels," *The New York Times*, February 8, 2012, p. B2; and A. Lomax, "Walmart's New Health Food Push: Is It Too Hard to Swallow?" *DailyFinance*, February 10, 2012, www.dailyfinance.com/2012/02/10/walmarts-new-health-food-push-is-it-too-hard-to-swallow (accessed February 14, 2012).

50. J. Tierney, "The Advantages of Closing a Few Doors," *The New York Times*, February 26, 2008, pp. D1, D6.

51. D. Ariely, *Predictably Irrational: The Hidden Forces That Shape Our Decisions* (New York: HarperCollins, 2008).

52. Adapted from N. Wingfield, "At Apple, Secrecy Complicates Life but Maintains Buzz," *The Wall Street Journal*, June 28, 2006, pp. A1, A11. See also A. L. Peneberg, "All Eyes on Apple," *Fast Company*, December 2007/January 2008, pp. 83–87, 133–36; "The World's 50 Most Innovative Companies," *Fast Company*, March 2008, p. 92; B. Morris, "What Makes Apple Golden," *Fortune*, March 17, 2008, pp. 68–74; P. Ekind, "The Trouble with Steve," *Fortune*, March 17, 2008, pp. 88–98, 156–60; "The World's 50 Most Innovative Companies," *Fast Company*, March 2009, p. 52; "The World's 50 Most Innovative Companies," *Fast Company*, March 2010, p. 53; and A. Lashinsky, "The Secrets Apple Keeps," *Fortune*, February 6, 2012, pp. 84–94. The last article is adapted from Lashinsky's *Inside Apple: How America's Most Admired—and Secretive—Company Really Works* (New York: Business Plus, 2012).

53. N. Wingfield, "Apple Sets April 3 iPad Debut," *The Wall Street Journal*, March 6–7, 2010, p. B5.

CHAPTER 6

1. G. Hamel, "What Is Management's Moonshot?" *Management 2.0*, December 7, 2007, http://discussionleader.hbsp.com/hamel/2007/12/what_is_managements_moonshot.html. See also G. Hamel, "Moon Shots for Management," *Harvard Business Review*, February 2009, pp. 91–98.

2. J. Best, *Flavor of the Month: Why Smart People Fall for Fads* (Berkeley: University of California Press, 2006).

3. J. Best, interviewed by A. Manser, "Flavor of the Month," UDaily, University of Delaware website, May 22, 2006, www.udel.edu/PR/UDaily/2006/may/jbest052206.html.

4. D. Rigby and B. Bilodeau, "Management Tools and Trends 2011," May 11, 2011, www.bain.com/publications/business-insights/management-tools-and-trends-2011.aspx (accessed March 9, 2012).

5. G. Colvin, "The Most Valuable Quality in a Manager," *Fortune*, December 29, 1997, pp. 279–80.

6. J. Pfeffer and R. I. Sutton, "Profiting from Evidence-Based Management," *Strategy & Leadership* 34, no. 2 (2006), pp. 35–42.

7. J. Kellner, "17-Year-Old Entrepreneur Writes Own Business Plan," *Reno Gazette-Journal*, January 29, 2007, p. 8E.

8. Study by Amar Bhide, cited in K. K. Spors, "Do Start-Ups Really Need Formal Business Plans?" *The Wall Street Journal*, January 9, 2007, p. B9.

9. F. Delmar and S. Shane, "Does Business Planning Facilitate the Development of New Ventures?" *Strategic Management Journal*, December 2003, pp. 1165–85.

10. C. McNamara, "Strategic Planning (in Nonprofit or For-Profit Organizations)," Free Management Library, www.managementhelp.org/plan_dec/str_plan/str_plan.htm (accessed March 9, 2012).

11. A. A. Thompson Jr. and A. J. Strickland III, *Strategic Management: Concepts and Cases*, 6th ed. (Homewood, IL: BPI/Irwin, 1992).

12. D. J. Collis and M. G. Rukstad, "Can You Say What Your Strategy Is?" *Harvard Business Review*, April 2008, pp. 82–90.

13. See G. Hamel, with B. Breen, *The Future of Management* (Boston: Harvard Business School Press, 2007), p. 191; and C. Rampell, "How Industries Survive Change, If They Do," *The New York Times*, November 16, 2008, Week in Review section, p. 3. For a discussion of the effect of the World Wide Web on newspapers, see E. Alterman, "Out of Print," *The New Yorker*, March 31, 2008, pp. 48–59; P. R. Kann, "Quality Reporting Doesn't Come Cheap," *The Wall Street Journal*, September 26, 2009, p. A15; R. Pérez-Peña, "Newspaper Circulation Falls by More Than 10%," *The New York Times*, October 27, 2009, p. B3; B. Wyman, "What Newspapers Can Learn from Craigslist," *The Wall Street Journal*, February 13, 2010, p. A13; and B. Evangelista, "Internet Seen as Shaping Delivery, Sharing of News," *San Francisco Chronicle*, March 1, 2010, pp. D1, D2.

14. A. Busch III, quoted in interview with G. Hamel, "Turning Your Business Upside Down," *Fortune*, June 23, 1997, pp. 87–88. See also D. Kesmodel, "Beer Distributors Want More Than One Best Bud," *The Wall Street Journal*, February 6, 2006, pp. B1, B2.

15. L. G. Hrebiniak, "Obstacles to Effective Strategy Implementation," *Organizational Dynamics*, February 2006, pp. 12–31.

16. H. Mintzberg, "The Strategy Concept II: Another Look at Why Organizations Need Strategies," *California Management Review*, 30, no. 1 (1987), pp. 25–32.

17. Hamel and Breen, 2007, p. 33.

18. B. Horovitz, "Starbucks Perks Up with First Dividend," *USA Today*, March 25, 2010, p. 1B.

19. P. Hochman, "Ford's Big Revival," *Fast Company*, April 2010, pp. 90–95, 105.

20. C. Woodyard, "Apps behind the Wheel," *USA Today*, January 6, 2012, pp. 1B, 2B; and M. Ramsey, "Don't Look Now: A Car That Tweets," *The Wall Street Journal*, February 10, 2012, pp. B1, B2.

21. For more on apps, see M. R. della Cava, "It's an App World," *USA Today*, March 31, 2010, pp. 1A, 2A.

22. Thilo Koslowski, lead automotive analyst for Gartner, quoted in Hochman, "Ford's Big Revival," 2010.

23. Ramsey, "Don't Look Now: A Car That Tweets," 2012.

24. F. Manjoo, "Killer Apps," *Fast Company*, February 2010, p. 38.

25. M. Richtel, "Carmakers Urged to Limit Dashboard Distractions," *The New York Times*, February 17, 2012, p. A18.

26. J. Surowiecki, "The Return of Michael Porter," *Fortune*, February 1, 1999, pp. 135–38.

27. M. E. Porter, "What Is Strategy?" *Harvard Business Review*, November–December 1996, pp. 61–78. Porter has updated his 1979 paper on competitive forces in M. E. Porter, "The Five Competitive Forces That Shape Strategy," *Harvard Business Review*, January 2008, pp. 79–93.

28. Porter, 1996.

29. J. A. Byrne, "Going Where the Money Is," *BusinessWeek*, January 26, 1998, p. 14, review of A. J. Slywotzky and D. J. Morrison, with B. Andelman, *The Profit Zone* (New York: Times Business, 1998).

30. D. Streitfeld, "Seeking the Captive Consumer," *The New York Times*, February 13, 2012, pp. B1, B7.

31. Michael Gartenberg, Gartner analyst, quoted in Streitfeld, 2012.

32. Harold Pollack, quoted in S. Clifford and C. C. Miller, "Rooting for the Little Guy," *The New York Times*, January 16, 2012, pp. B1, B2.

33. D. Darlin, "A New Weapon for Electronics Shoppers," *The New York Times*, December 7, 2011, p. F5.

34. N. Shirouzu, "Toyoda Rues Excessive Profit Focus," *The Wall Street Journal*, March 2, 2010, p. B3. Also see K. Linebaugh, D. Searcey, and N. Shirouzu, "Secretive Culture Led Toyota Astray," *The Wall Street Journal*, February 10, 2010, pp. A1, A6; N. Bunkley, "1.1 Million Toyotas Recalled to Correct Engine Problems," *The New York Times*, August 27, 2010, p. B2; M. Ramsey, "Toyota Fixes Five Million Recalled Cars," *The Wall Street Journal*, October 5, 2010, p. B4; D. Leinwand and C. Woodyard, "No Flaws Found in Toyota Electronics," *USA Today*, February 9,

2011, p. 1B; and M. Ramsey, J. Mitchell, and C. Dawson, "U.S. Absolves Toyota Electronics," *The Wall Street Journal,* February 9, 2011, pp. B1, B2.

35. R. Farzad and M. Arndt, "Stuck with Sears," *Bloomberg Business-Week,* April 5, 2010, pp. 41–48; and A. Ahmed, "Sales Down, Sears to Shut 120 Stores," *The New York Times,* December 28, 2011, pp. B1, B5.

36. S. Carey and P. Prada, "Course Change: Why JetBlue Shuffled Top Rank," *The Wall Street Journal,* May 11, 2007, pp. B1, B2.

37. Carey and Prada, 2007.

38. J. Hanna, "HBS Cases: JetBlue's Valentine's Day Crisis," *Harvard Business School Working Knowledge,* March 31, 2008, http://hbswk.hbs.edu/item/5880.html (accessed March 9, 2012).

39. "Winter Storm Rattles JetBlue," *BusinessWeek,* February 20, 2007, www.businessweek.com/investor/content/feb2007/pi20070220_742628.htm?chan=search.

40. Hanna, "HBS Cases: JetBlue's Valentine's Day Crisis," 2008.

41. Walt Disney, quoted in B. Nanus, *Visionary Leadership: Creating a Compelling Sense of Direction for Your Organization* (San Francisco: Jossey-Bass, 1992), p. 28; reprinted from B. Thomas, *Walt Disney: An American Tradition* (New York: Simon & Schuster, 1976), p. 247.

42. B. Iyer and T. Davenport, "Reverse Engineering Google's Innovation Machine," *Harvard Business Review,* April 2008, pp. 59–68.

43. Nanus, *Visionary Leadership,* 1992, pp. 28–29.

44. R. Kreitner, *Management,* 7th ed. (Boston: Houghton Mifflin, 1998), p. 206. Also see S. Kapner, "How Fashion's VF Supercharges Its Brands," *Fortune,* April 14, 2008, pp. 108–10.

45. M. Krantz and J. Swartz, "IBM Shows Secret to Corporate Longevity," *USA Today,* June 16, 2011, pp. 1B, 3B; and S. Lohr, "Even a Giant Can Learn to Run," *The New York Times,* January 1, 2012, p. BU-3.

46. M. Kaminski, "An Airline That Makes Money. Really," *The Wall Street Journal,* February 4–5, 2012, p. A13.

47. B. Acohido, S. Sink, and M. Daneman, "Kodak Focuses on Fresh Start with Printers," *USA Today,* January 20, 2012, pp. 1B, 2B.

48. See A Kinicki, K Jacobson, B Galvin, and G Prussia, "A Multilevel Systems Model of Leadership," *Journal of Leadership & Organizational* Studies, May 2011, pp. 133–49.

49. B. W. Barry, "A Beginner's Guide to Strategic Planning," *The Futurist,* April 1998, pp. 33–36 from B. W. Barry, *Strategic Planning Workbook for Nonprofit Organizations,* revised and updated (St. Paul, MN: Amherst H. Wilder Foundation, 1997).

50. N. Wingfield, "A Tech Show Loses Clout as Industry Shifts," *The New York Times,* January 8, 2012, www.nytimes.com/2012/01/09/technology/consumer-electronics-show-loses-clout-as-industry-shifts.html?_r=1&pagewanted=all (accessed March 9, 2012).

51. Toyota Motor president Akio Toyoda, quoted in A. Ohnsman, J. Green, and K. Inoue, "The Humbling of Toyota," *Bloomberg BusinessWeek,* March 22, 29, 2010, pp. 32–36.

52. M. Ramsey and C. Dawson, "Toyota, Honda Lose U.S. Edge," *The Wall Street Journal,* November 15, 2010, pp. B1, B2.

53. A. Taylor III, "Toyota's Comeback Kid," *Fortune,* February 27, 2012, pp. 72–79.

54. D. Wakabayashi, "'Toyota Way' Retains Management Followers," *The Wall Street Journal,* February 26, 2010, p. B4.

55. Ohnsman, Green, and Inoue, "The Humbling of Toyota," 2010.

56. Toyota top engineer Takeshi Uchiyamada, quoted in Taylor, "Toyota's Comeback Kid," 2012, p. 77.

57. Y. Takahashi, "Toyota Accelerates Its Cost-Cutting Efforts," *The Wall Street Journal,* December 23, 2009, p. B4; C. Woodyard, "Toyota's Reputation Needs Some TLC," *USA Today,* December 31, 2009, pp. 1B, 2B; M. Maynard and H. Tabuchi, "Rapid Growth Has Its Perils, Toyota Learns," *The New York Times,* January 28, 2010, pp. A1, B4 ; K. Linebaugh and N. Shirouzu, "Toyota Heir Faces Crisis at the Wheel," *The Wall Street Journal,* January

28, 2010, pp. A1, A8; and M. Dolan, "Supplier Perplexed by Toyota's Action," *The Wall Street Journal,* January 28, 2010, p. A9.

58. J. R. Healey and A. DeBarros, "Toyota Tops Speed Control Complaints," *USA Today,* March 26, 2010, pp. 1B, 2B.

59. N. Bunkley, "Toyota Halts Production of 8 Models," *The New York Times,* January 27, 2010, pp. B1, B2; J. R. Healey, "Toyota Halts U.S. Sales of 8 Models," *USA Today,* January 27, 2010, p. 1A; and C. Said, "Reports on Priuses Add to Toyota's Woes," *San Francisco Chronicle,* February 4, 2010, pp. D1, D2.

60. Leinwand and Woodyard, "No Flaws Found in Toyota Electronics," 2011; and Ramsey, Mitchell, and Dawson, "U.S. Absolves Toyota Electronics," 2011.

61. James P. Womack, quoted in Maynard and Tabuchi, "Rapid Growth Has Its Perils, Toyota Learns," 2010.

62. Taylor, "Toyota's Comeback Kid," 2012, p. 75.

63. C. Woodyard, "Toyota PR Blitz Plays Catch-Up," *USA Today,* February 10, 2010, p. 2B; K. Linebaugh and D. Searcey, "Cause of Sudden Acceleration Proves Hard to Pinpoint," *The Wall Street Journal,* February 25, 2010, p. A7; and D. Searcey and K. Linebaugh, "Toyota Moves to Discredit Its Critics," *The Wall Street Journal,* March 6–7, 2010, pp. B1, B5.

64. N. Bunkley, "Ford and Toyota to Work Together on Hybrid System for Trucks," *The New York Times,* August 23, 2011, p. B3; and J. Bennett and M. Ramsey, "Putting Egos Aside, Ford, Toyota Pair Up for Hybrids," *The Wall Street Journal,* August 23, 2011, pp. B1, B2.

65. C. Woodyard and B. Snavely, "Lexus Tops Auto Reliability Survey," *USA Today,* February 16, 2012, p. 2B.

66. Y. Kageyama, "Toyota Lifts Profit Forecast as Disaster Woes Fade," Yahoo Finance, February 7, 2012, http://finance.yahoo.com/news/Toyota-lifts-profit-forecast-apf-2011760126.html (accessed March 9, 2012); and C. Dawson and Y. Takahashi, "Toyota Boosts Forecast," *The Wall Street Journal,* February 8, 2012, p. B7.

67. D. Welch, K. Naughton, and B. Helm, "Detroit's Big Chance," *Bloomberg BusinessWeek,* February 22, 2010, pp. 38–44.

68. Taylor, "Toyota's Comeback Kid," 2012, p. 74.

69. Kageyama, "Toyota Lifts Profit Forecast as Disaster Woes Fade," 2012.

70. M. DeBord, "Toyota's Blind Spot," *The New York Times,* February 6, 2010, p. A17.

71. "'Commercial Jet Fuel Supply: Impact & Cost on the U.S. Airline Industry' Hearing Scheduled for Wednesday Morning," press release, U.S. House Committee on Transportation and Infrastructure, Washington, DC, February 14, 2006, www.house.gov/transportation/press/press2006/release5.html.

72. J. C. Ogg, "Fuel Hedges Aren't Helping Southwest Shares," 14/7 Wall St., February 5, 2008, www.247wallst.com/2008/02/fuel-hedges-are.html (accessed March 9, 2012).

73. D. Levin, "Hedging Helps Low-Cost Airlines Hold Down Price of Aviation Fuel," *Detroit News,* March 18, 2004, www.detnews.com/2004/business/0403/18/c01-95805.htm.

74. S. Carey, "Airline Profits Slip as Fuel Costs Rise," *The Wall Street Journal,* July 22, 2011, p. B3; and T. W. Martin, "Southwest Preps for Turbulence," *The Wall Street Journal,* August 5, 2011, p. B3.

75. T. Stynes, "Southwest Air Net Up 16%, Helped by Hedging," *MarketWatch.com,* January 19, 2012, www.marketwatch.com/story/southwest-air-net-up-16-helped-by-hedging-2012-01-19 (accessed March 9, 2012).

76. T. Romo, quoted in E. Roston, "Hedging Their Costs," *Time,* June 20, 2005, www.time.com/time/globalbusiness/article/0.9171,1074147,00.html (accessed March 9, 2012).

77. D. Grossman, "Oil Prices Put Business Travelers Over a Barrel," *USA Today,* March 31, 2008, www.usatoday.com/travel/columnist/grossman/2008-03-28-oil-prices-rising_N.htm (accessed March 9, 2012).

78. M. E. Porter, *Competitive Strategy* (New York: The Free Press, 1980). See also Porter, 2008.

79. Example from Michael J. Silverstein, *Treasure Hunt*, cited in M. Archer, "Author Finds 'Value Calculus' at Work," *USA Today*, June 12, 2006, p. 7B.

80. P. L. Brown, "Surfers in Turmoil with the Loss of a Major Supplier," *The New York Times*, December 30, 2006, p. A12; and M. Overfelt, "Rough Surf," *USA Today*, February 17, 2006, http://money.cnn.com/magazines/fsb/fsb_archive/2006/02/01/8368201/index.htm (accessed March 9, 2012).

81. L. Rohter, "With Big Boost from Sugar Cane, Brazil Is Satisfying Its Fuel Needs," *The New York Times*, April 10, 2006, p. A1. See also R. Cohen, "Is Ethanol for Everybody?" *The New York Times*, January 10, 2008, www.nytimes.com/2008/01/10/opinion/10cohen.html (accessed March 9, 2012).

82. J. Greenberg, quoted in B. Horovitz, "Restoring the Golden Arch Shine," *USA Today*, June 16, 1999, p. 3B.

83. D. Gannon, "Green Toys," *Inc.*, April 11, 2011, www.inc.com/best-industries-2011/green-toys.html (accessed March 9, 2012).

84. K. Zezima, "A Push to Eat Local Food Is Hampered by a Shortage," *The New York Times*, March 28, 2010, News section, p. 12.

85. G. Drevenstedt, "2012 Indian Motorcycle—First Look," *Rider Magazine*, November 29, 2011, www.ridermagazine.com/latest-news/2012-indian-motorcycle-first-look.htm (accessed March 9, 2012).

86. L. Aguilar, "Auto Suppliers Branch Out to Other Sectors to Survive," *San Francisco Chronicle*, February 16, 2010, p. D2; reprinted from the *Detroit News*.

87. L. Bossidy and Ram Charan, with C. Burck, *Execution: The Discipline of Getting Things Done* (New York: Crown Business, 2002).

88. Results can be found in "Wanted: Employees Who Get Things Done," *HR Magazine*, January 2008, p. 10.

89. Also see R. Kaplan and D. Norton, "Mastering the Management System," *Harvard Business Review*, January 2008, pp. 66–77.

90. Execution is also discussed by C. Montgomery, "Putting Leadership Back into Strategy," *Harvard Business Review*, January 2008, pp. 54–60; and J. Lorsch and R. Clark, "Leading from the Boardroom," *Harvard Business Review*, April 2008, pp. 105–11.

91. Bossidy and Charan, *Execution: The Discipline of Getting Things Done*, 2002, pp. 27–28.

92. Development Dimension International (DDI) Global Leadership Forecast of 4,561 respondents from 42 countries, reported in "Mentoring Impact," *USA Today*, March 22, 2006, p. 1B.

93. M. Cottle, "Minding Your Mentors," *The New York Times*, March 7, 1999, sec. 3, p. 8; C. Dahle, "HP's Mentor Connection," *Fast Company*, November 1998, pp. 78–80; and I. Abbott, "If You Want to Be an Effective Mentor, Consider These Tips," *San Francisco Examiner*, October 18, 1998, p. J-3; D. A. Thomas, "The Truth about Mentoring Minorities—Race Matters," *Harvard Business Review*, April 2001, pp. 366–91; S. A. Mehta, "Best Companies for Minorities: Why Mentoring Works," *Fortune*, July 9, 2001, www.fortune.com/fortune/-diversity/articles/0,15114,370475,00.html (accessed March 9, 2012); F. Warner, "Inside Intel's Mentoring Movement," *Fast Company*, April 2002, p. 116; B. Raabe and T. A. Beehr, "Formal Mentoring versus Supervisor and Coworker Relationships: Differences in Perceptions and Impact," *Journal of Organizational Behavior* 24(2003), pp. 271–93; A. Fisher, "A New Kind of Mentor," *Fortune*, July 2004, www.fortune.com/fortune/annie/0,15704,368863,00.html; T. Kreiner, "Social Entrepreneurship: Why Mentors Matter," *BusinessWeek.com*, March 9, 2012, www.businessweek.com/articles/2012-03-09/social-entrepreneurship-why-mentors-matter (accessed March 9, 2012); and L. Bradshaw, "Dina Kaplan on Mentoring the Next Generation," *Forbes*, March 9, 2012, www.forbes.com/sites/lesliebradshaw/2012/03/09/dina-kaplan-on-mentoring-the-next-generation (accessed March 9, 2012).

94. Anne Hayden, quoted in Cottle, 1999.

CHAPTER 7

1. M. H. Bazerman, *Judgment in Managerial Decision Making*, 7th ed. (New York: Wiley, 2008). See also D. E. Bell, H. Raiffa, and A. Tversky, eds., *Decision Making: Descriptive, Normative, and Prescriptive Interactions* (Cambridge: Cambridge University Press, 1988).

2. M. Easterby-Smith and M. A. Lyles, *The Blackwell Handbook of Organizational Learning and Knowledge Management* (Oxford: Blackwell Publishing, 2003).

3. B. Fischoff, "Hindsight ± Foresight: The Effect of Outcome Knowledge on Judgment under Uncertainty," *Journal of Experimental Psychology: Human Perception and Performance* 1 (1975), pp. 288–99.

4. E. Rosenthal, "Slow and Steady Across the Sea Aids Profit and the Environment," *The New York Times*, February 17, 2010, pp. A1, A3.

5. J. B. White, "Why 70 Miles Per Hour Is the New 55," *The Wall Street Journal*, March 17, 2010, p. D3.

6. "Fuel Economy: Save Money on Gas," *ConsumerReports.org*, April 2011, www.consumerreports.org/cro/cars/tires-auto-parts/car-maintenance/fuel-economy-save-money-on-gas/overview/index.htm (accessed February 24, 2012).

7. C. F. Chabris, "Old Habits Die Hard," *The Wall Street Journal*, February 19, 2010, p. A13. The article is a book review of C. Heath and D. Heath, *Switch: How to Change Things When Change Is Hard* (New York: Broadway, 2010). See also D. Kahneman, *Thinking, Fast and Slow* (New York: Farrar, Straus and Giroux, 2011).

8. "Wean Wall Street Off Its Gambling Addictions," editorial, *USA Today*, March 1, 2010, p. 15A.

9. Chip Heath, quoted in J. Rae-Dupree, "Innovative Minds Don't Think Alike," *The New York Times*, December 30, 2007, business section, p. 3. C. Heath and D. Heath are coauthors of *Made to Stick: Why Some Ideas Survive and Others Die* (New York: Random House, 2007). For other writings pertaining to the curse of knowledge, see J. Fox, "Herd on the Street," *Time*, September 17, 2007, p. 59; D. Jones, "Even Good CEOs Pick the Wrong Direction," *USA Today*, November 7, 2007, pp. 1B, 2B; F. Norris, "Bank Profits Had Whiff of Suspicion," *The New York Times*, November 16, 2007, pp. C1, C2; and P. L. Bernstein, "To Botch a Forecast, Rely on Past Experience," *The New York Times*, December 30, 2007, business section, p. 4.

10. L. DiCosmo, "Warren Buffett Invests Like a Girl," *The Motley Fool*, March 20, 2008, www.fool.com/investing/value/2008/03/20/warren-buffett-invests-like-a-girl.aspx (accessed February 24, 2012).

11. A. Markels, "Built to Make Billions?" *U.S. News & World Report*, August 6, 2007, pp. 51–52. See also A. Markels, "How to Make Money the Buffett Way," *U.S. News & World Report*, August 6, 2007, pp. 46–51.

12. D. Mitchell, "At Last, Buffett's Key to Success," *The New York Times*, April 5, 2008, p. B5. See also J. Clements, "He Invests, She Invests: Who Gets the Better Returns?" *The Wall Street Journal*, February 6, 2008, p. D1.

13. B. M. Barber and T. Odean, "Boys Will Be Boys: Gender, Overconfidence, and Common Stock Investment," *The Quarterly Journal of Economics*, February 2001, pp. 261–92, faulty.haas.berkeley.edu/odean/papers/gender/BoysWillBeBoys.pdf (accessed February 24, 2012). See also J. H. Dobrzynski, "Maybe the Meltdown's a Guy Thing," *The New York Times*, November 16, 2008, p. WR-5.

14. Markels, "Built to Make Billions?" 2007.

15. "The World's Billionaires: #3 Warren Buffett," *Forbes.com*, March 10, 2010, www.forbes.com/lists/2010/10/billionaires-2010_Warren-Buffett_C0R3.html (accessed February 24, 2012).

16. A. Farnham, "Teaching Creativity Tricks to Buttoned-Down Executives," *Fortune*, January 10, 1994, pp. 94–100.

17. I. DeBare, "The Business May Change, but the Values Are the Same," *San Francisco Chronicle*, April 2, 2006, p. G5.

18. C. Hymowitz, "Everyone Likes to Laud Service to the Customer; Doing It Is the Problem," *The Wall Street Journal*, February 27, 2006, p. B1.

19. The Retail Customer Dissatisfaction Study 2006, conducted by the Jay H. Baker Retailing Initiative, Wharton, University of Pennsylvania, and the Verde Group, Toronto, reported in "Beware of Dissatisfied Customers: They Like to Blab," Knowledge@Wharton, April 5, 2006, http://knowledge.wharton.upenn.edu/index (accessed February 24, 2012).

20. Hymowitz, "Everyone Likes to Laud Service," 2006.

21. B. Kiviat, "The End of Customer Service," *Time*, March 24, 2008, p. 42.

22. S. Holmes, "The 787 Encounters Turbulence," *BusinessWeek*, June 19, 2006, pp. 38–40. See also S. Holmes, "Cleaning Up Boeing," *BusinessWeek*, March 13, 2006, pp. 63–68; and S. Holmes, "Boeing Straightens Up and Flies Right," *BusinessWeek*, May 8, 2006, pp. 69–70.

23. For a discussion of the strategy behind the Dreamliner, see C. Masters, "How Boeing Got Going," *Time*, September 10, 2007, pp. Global 1–Global 6.

24. J. L. Lunsford, "Boeing, in Embarrassing Setback, Says 787 Dreamliner Will Be Delayed," *The Wall Street Journal*, October 11, 2007, pp. A1, A16.

25. R. Yu, "Boeing Again Delays Dreamliner's Debut," *USA Today*, January 17, 2008, p. 3B.

26. J. L. Lunsford, "Boeing Delays Dreamliner Delivery Again," *The Wall Street Journal*, April 10, 2008, p. B3.

27. C. Drew, "Another Flight Delay for Troubled Dreamliner," *The New York Times*, June 24, 2009, p. B3; P. Sanders, D. Michaels, and A. Cole, "Boeing Delays New Jet Again," *The Wall Street Journal*, June 24, 2009, pp. A1, A6; D. Reed, "Problems Pile Up on Boeing," *USA Today*, August 6, 2009, pp. 1B, 2B; P. Sanders, "Boeing Settles in for a Bumpy Ride," *The Wall Street Journal*, October 7, 2009, p. B1; D. Michaels and P. Sanders, "Dreamliner Production Gets Closer Monitoring," *The Wall Street Journal*, October 7, 2009, pp. B1, B2; and P. Sanders, "At Boeing, Dreamliner Fix Turns Up New Issue," *The Wall Street Journal*, November 13, 2009, pp. B1, B2.

28. P. Sanders and D. Michaels, "Boeing Looks Beyond Dreamliner's First Flight," *The Wall Street Journal*, December 16, 2009, pp. B1, B2.

29. C. Jones, "New Era in Aircraft Arrives," *USA Today*, October 21, 2011, pp. 1B, 3B; and B. Mutzabaugh, "First Dreamliner Fliers Sing Its Praises," *USA Today*, October 28, 2011, pp. 1B, 2B.

30. N. Shirouzu, "Boeing's 787 on 'World Tour,'" *The Wall Street Journal*, December 15, 2011, p. B4; and D. Michaels and S. Carey, "Boeing's Orders Trail Airbus," *The Wall Street Journal*, January 6, 2012, p. B5.

31. H. A. Simon, *Administrative Behavior*, 3rd ed. (New York: Free Press, 1996); and H. A. Simon, "Making Management Decisions: The Role of Intuition and Emotion," *The Academy of Management Executive*, February 1987, pp. 57–63.

32. J. Jargon, "Can M'm, M'm Good Translate?" *The Wall Street Journal*, July 9, 2007, p. A16; and N. Groom, "Campbell to Start Russia, China Soup Sales," Reuters, July 9, 2007, www.reuters.com/article/2007/07/09/campbellsoup-idUSN0928240820070709 (accessed February 24, 2012).

33. J. Wortham, "Once Just a Site with Funny Cat Pictures, and Now a Web Empire," *The New York Times*, June 14, 2010, pp. B1, B8.

34. See E. Dane and M. G. Pratt, "Exploring Intuition and Its Role in Managerial Decision Making," *Academy of Management Review*, January 2007, pp. 33–54.

35. See D. Begley, "You Might Help a Teen Avoid Dumb Behavior by Nurturing Intuition," *The Wall Street Journal*, November 3, 2006, p. B1.

36. Courage and intuition are discussed by K. K. Reardon, "Courage as a Skill," *Harvard Business Review*, March 2007, pp. 51–56.

37. Masters, "How Boeing Got Going," 2007.

38. J. Pfeffer and R. I. Sutton, "Profiting from Evidence-Based Management," *Strategy & Leadership* 34, no. 2 (2006), pp. 35–42; and J. Pfeffer and R. I. Sutton, "Evidence-Based Management," *Harvard Business Review*, January 2006, pp. 63–74. Pfeffer and Sutton have also produced a book, *Hard Facts, Dangerous Half-Truths, and Total Nonsense: Profiting from Evidence-Based Management* (Cambridge, MA: Harvard Business School Press, 2006). For a discussion of the book, see C. Hymowitz, "Executives Must Stop Jumping Fad to Fad and Learn to Manage," *The Wall Street Journal*, May 15, 2006, p. B1.

39. Additional discussion of this topic may be found in T. Reay, W. Berta, and M. Kazman Kohn, "What's the Evidence on Evidence-Based Management?" *Academy of Management Perspectives*, November 2009, pp. 5–18; and R. B. Briner, D. Denyer, and D. M. Rousseau, "'Evidence-Based Management'" Concept Cleanup Time?" *Academy of Management Perspectives*, November 2009, pp. 19–32.

40. Pfeffer and Sutton, "Profiting from Evidence-Based Management," 2006.

41. J. Wortham, "In Tech, Starting Up by Failing," *The New York Times*, January 18, 2012, pp. B1, B6.

42. D. Mattioli and Kris Hudson, "Gap to Slash Its Store Count," *The Wall Street Journal*, October 14, 2011, pp. B1, B2.

43. Pfeffer and Sutton, "Evidence-Based Management," 2006, pp. 66–67.

44. J. Pfeffer, "Lay Off the Layoffs," *Newsweek*, February 15, 2010, pp. 32–37.

45. "U.S. Men & Women Agree Southwest Airlines, Google and Dove Are Most Desired Brands in 2012," *PR Newswire*, February 17, 2012, www.prnewswire.com/news-releases/us-men--women-agree-southwest-airlines-google-and-dove-are-most-desired-brands-in-2012-139506748.html (accessed February 24, 2012).

46. G. Loveman, "Diamonds in the Data Mine," *Harvard Business Review*, May 2003, pp. 109–13. See also T. Davenport, L. Prusak, and B. Strong, "Putting Ideas to Work," *The Wall Street Journal*, March 10, 2008, p. R11.

47. T. H. Davenport, "Competing on Analytics," *Harvard Business Review*, January 2006, pp. 99–107.

48. S. Baker, "How Much Is That Worker Worth?" *BusinessWeek*, March 23 & 30, 2009, pp. 46–48.

49. M. Lewis, *Moneyball: The Art of Winning an Unfair Game* (New York: W.W. Norton, 2004). For comment on the Oakland A's and *Moneyball*, see J. Manuel, "Majoring in Moneyball," Baseball America Features, December 23, 2003, www.baseballamerica.com/today/features/031223collegemoneyball.html; J. Zasky, "Pay for Performance, Stupid," *Failure Magazine*, June 2003, http://failuremag.com/archives_business_sports_money-ball.html; R. Van Zandt, "Billy Beane's Perfect Draft: A Baseball Revolution?" BaseballEvolution.com, April 13, 2006, http://baseballevolution.com/guest/richard/rvzbeanel.html; and "Moneyball: The Art of Winning an Unfair Game," Wikipedia, July 12, 2006, http://en.wikipedia.org/wiki/Moneyball (all accessed February 24, 2012). For more on the use of technology and software in baseball, see A. Schwarz, "Digital Eyes Will Chart Baseball's Unseen Skills," *The New York Times*, July 10, 2009, pp. A1, A3; and R. Sandomir, "Bloomberg Technology Embraces Baseball," *The New York Times*, December 6, 2009, Sports section, pp. 1, 6. For a discussion of the analytics of the Super Bowl–winning NFL team the New England Patriots, see

C. Price, *The Blueprint: How the New England Patriots Beat the System to Create the Last Great NFL Superpower* (New York: Thomas Dunne/St. Martin's Press, 2007).

50. Daryl Morley, quoted in M. Lewis, "The No-Stats All-Star," *The New York Times Magazine,* February 15, 2009, pp. 26–33, 56, 63–64.

51. Brian Cashman, quoted in S. Slusser, "Price of a Best-Seller," *San Francisco Chronicle,* September 18, 2011, pp. B1, B13.

52. Davenport, "Competing on Analytics," 2006.

53. S. Elliott, "Delivering Something Extra," *The New York Times,* September 29, 2009, p. B3.

54. Study by IDC for EMC Corp., reported in J. Lloren, "Our Ever-Expanding Digital Cosmos," *SFGate, The Tech Chronicles,* June 27, 2011, http://blog.sfgate.com/techchron/2011/06/27/our-ever-expanding-digital-cosmos (accessed March 2, 2012).

55. A. Brust, "Big Data: Defining Its Definition," *ZDNet,* March 1, 2012, www.zdnet.com/blog/big-data/big-data-defining-its-definition/109 (accessed March 1, 2012).

56. McKinsey Global Institute report, May 2011, quoted in J. Temple, "Big Data Can Lead to Big Breakthroughs in Research," *San Francisco Chronicle,* December 9, 2011, www.sfgate.com/cgi-bin/article.cgi?f=/c/a/2011/12/08/BUDC1M9I8A.DTL (accessed March 1, 2012).

57. J. Markoff, "Government Aims to Build a 'Data Eye in the Sky,'" *The New York Times,* October 10, 2011, www.nytimes.com/2011/10/11/science/11predict.html?_r=1&pagewanted=all (accessed March 1, 2012). See also A. Vance, "Data Analytics: Crunching the Future," *Bloomberg Businessweek,* September 8, 2011 www.businessweek.com/magazine/data-analytics-crunching-the-future-09082011.html (accessed March 1, 2012); Q. Hardy, "Bigger Patterns in Big Data," *The New York Times,* February 20, 2012, p. B4.

58. Temple, "Big Data Can Lead to Big Breakthroughs in Research," 2011.

59. Adapted from B. K. Williams, S. C. Sawyer, and C. M. Wahlstrom, *Marriages, Families, & Intimate Relationships,* 2nd ed. (Boston: Allyn & Bacon, 2009), pp. 54–55. For more on critical reflection, see L. Carson and K. Fisher, "Raising the Bar on Criticality: Students' Critical Reflection in an Internship Program," *Journal of Management Education,* October 2006, pp. 700–23.

60. Muriel Niederle, quoted in J. Tierney, "What Women Want," *The New York Times,* May 24, 2005, p. A25.

61. M. Niederle and L. Vesterlund, "Do Women Shy Away from Competition? Do Men Compete Too Much?" *Quarterly Journal of Economics,* August 2007, pp. 1067–1101.

62. The discussion of styles was based on material contained in A. J. Rowe and R. O. Mason, *Managing with Style: A Guide to Understanding, Assessing and Improving Decision Making* (San Francisco: Jossey-Bass, 1987), pp. 1–17.

63. See Rowe and Mason, 1987; and M. J. Dollinger and W. Danis, "Preferred Decision-Making Styles: A Cross-Cultural Comparison," *Psychological Reports,* 1998, pp. 755–61; and K. R. Brousseau, M. J. Driver, G. Hourihan, and R. Larsson, "The Seasoned Executive's Decision-Making Style," *Harvard Business Review,* February 2006, p. 111, http://custom.hbsp.com/custom/KORNFR0602F2006012769.pdf;jsessionid=BBCU302NQJFKOAKRGWCB5VQBKE0YIIPS (accessed February 29, 2012).

64. M. B. Zuckerman, "Policing the Corporate Suites," *U.S. News & World Report,* January 19, 2004, p. 72.

65. Bill Gates, quoted in R. A. Guth, "Bill Gates Issues Call for Kinder Capitalism," *The Wall Street Journal,* January 24, 2008, pp. A1, A15. See also C. Boles, "Last Call? Gates Pushes Globalism in Remarks," *The Wall Street Journal,* March 13, 2008, p. B3; and M. J. Sandel, "What Isn't for Sale?" *The Atlantic,* April 2012, pp. 62–66. Sandel is author of *What Money Can't Buy: The Moral Limits of Markets* (London: Penguin Books, 2012).

66. C. McNamara, "Complete Guide to Ethics Management: An Ethics Toolkit for Managers," www.mapnp.org/library/ethics/ethxgde.htm (accessed February 24, 2012).

67. C. E. Bagley, "The Ethical Leader's Decision Tree," *Harvard Business Review,* February 2003, pp. 18–19.

68. Bagley, 2003, p. 19.

69. Bagley, 2003.

70. The website YourMorals.org studies morality and values, offering questionnaires for readers to fill out. Some of the results are described in J. Haidt, *The Righteous Mind: Why Good People Are Divided by Politics and Religion* (New York: Random House, 2012).

71. C. E. Cryder, J. S. Lerner, J. J. Gross, and R. E. Dahl, "Misery Is Not Miserly: Sad and Self-Focused Individuals Spend More," *Psychological Science,* June 1, 2008, pp. 525–30. See also S. Finkelstein, J. Whitehead, and A. Campbell, "How Inappropriate Attachments Can Drive Good Leaders to Make Bad Decisions," *Organizational Dynamics,* 38 (2009), pp. 83–92.

72. D. Gilbert, *Stumbling on Happiness* (New York: Vintage, 2007).

73. D. D. Wheeler and I. L. Janis, *A Practical Guide for Making Decisions* (New York: Free Press, 1980), pp. 34–35; and I. L. Janis and L. Mann, *Decision Making: A Psychological Analysis of Conflict, Choice, and Commitment* (New York: The Free Press, 1977).

74. R. Beck, "The Difference a Year Made in Mortgage Mess," *San Francisco Chronicle,* December 26, 2007, p. D2. See also S. Lohr, "Wall Street's Math Wizards Forgot a Few Variables," *The New York Times,* September 13, 2009, business section, p. 3; D. Leonhardt, "If Fed Missed Bubble, How Will It See the Next One?" *The New York Times,* January 6, 2010, pp. A1, A4; and J. Pressley, "They Did the Math—and Lost Billions," *Bloomberg Businessweek,* March 1, 2010, p. 70.

75. Decision Research study, reported in J. Zweig, "This Is Your Brain on a Hot Streak," *The Wall Street Journal,* February 11, 2012, pp. B1, B2.

76. S. S. Iyengar and M. Lepper, "When Choice Is Demotivating: Can One Desire Too Much of a Good Thing?" *Journal of Personality and Social Psychology* 79 (2000), pp. 995–1006. Sheena Iyengar is author of *The Art of Choosing* (New York: Hachette Book Group, 2010).

77. P. Steel, "The Nature of Procrastination: A Meta-Analytic and Theoretical Review of Quintessential Self-Regulatory Failure," *Psychological Bulletin* 133 (2007), pp. 65–94.

78. "Don't Mention It: How 'Undiscussables' Can Undermine an Organization," *Knowledge@Wharton,* December 20, 2011, http://knowledge.wharton.upenn.edu/article.cfm?articleid=2921 (accessed March 1, 2012).

79. Gurnek Bains, CEO of YSC, London, quoted in C. Hymowitz, "Best Way to Save: Analyze Why Talent Is Going Out the Door," *The Wall Street Journal,* September 24, 2007, p. B1.

80. A. Levin and L. Parker, "Human, Mechanical Flaws Cut Off Path to Survival," *USA Today,* July 12, 1999, pp. 1A, 8A, 9A. Sometimes observers speak of a "fog of war," in which too much information or scattered information overwhelms decision-making abilities. See, for example, E. Lipson, "Hurricane Investigators See 'Fog of War' at White House," *The New York Times,* January 28, 2006, p. A8. Decision makers may also often be unable to discriminate between relevant and irrelevant alternatives, including extraneous considerations in their probability judgments. See M. R. Dougherty and A. Sprenger, "The Influence of Improper Sets of Information on Judgment: How Irrelevant Information Can Bias Judged Probability," *Journal of Experimental Psychology: General,* May 2006, pp. 262–81.

81. Wheeler and Janis, *A Practical Guide for Making Decisions,* 1980.

82. S. Woo and M. Kung, "Netflix, Amazon Add to Movies," *The Wall Street Journal,* September 27, 2011, p. B10; and C. Edwards and R. Grover, "Companies & Industries: Netflix," *Bloomberg Businessweek,* October 24–October 31, 2011, pp. 21–22.

83. B. Evangelista, "After Apology, Netflix Makes Many Angrier," *San Francisco Chronicle,* September 20, 2011, pp. A1, A10; and S. Martin and M. Snider, "Netflix CEO Apologizes to Customers," *USA Today,* September 20, 2011, p. 1B.

84. B. Stelter, "Customers Angry over Revamped Pricing Are Deserting Netflix," *The New York Times,* September 16, 2011, p. B3.

85. M. Liedtke, "Netflix Plummets Amid Note, Stock Sale," *San Francisco Chronicle,* November 23, 2011, pp. D1, D5.

86. B. Evangelista, "Stumbles Don't Topple Netflix CEO Hastings," *San Francisco Chronicle,* November 3, 2011, pp. D1, D5.

87. B. Evangelista, "Despite Struggles, Netflix Profit Beats Expectations," *San Francisco Chronicle,* January 26, 2012, pp. D1, D3; and B. Stelter, "A Turnaround at Netflix, as Its Mail Sector Shrinks," *The New York Times,* January 26, 2012, p. B4.

88. D. Kahnemann and A. Tversky, "Judgment under Uncertainty: Heuristics and Biases," *Science* 185 (1974), pp. 1124–31; A. Tversky and D. Kahneman, "Availability: A Heuristic for Judging Frequency and Probability," *Cognitive Psychology* 5 (1975), pp. 207–32; A. Tversky and D. Kahneman, "The Belief in the Law of Numbers," *Psychological Bulletin* 76 (1971), pp. 105–10; C. R. Schwenk, "Cognitive Simplification Processes in Strategic Decision Making," *Strategic Management Journal* 5 (1984), pp. 111–28; K. McKean, "Decisions," *Discover,* June 1985, pp. 22–31; J. Rockner, "The Escalation of Commitment to a Failing Course of Action: Toward Theoretical Progress," *Academy of Management Review* 17 (1980), pp. 39–61; D. R. Bobocel and J. P. Meyer, "Escalating Commitment to a Failing Course of Action: Separating the Roles of Choice and Justification," *Journal of Applied Psychology,* June 1994, pp. 360–63; B. M. Shaw, "The Escalation of Commitment to a Course of Action," *Academy of Management Review,* October 1981, pp. 577–87; and M. Useem and J. Useem, "Great Escapes," *Fortune,* June 27, 2005, pp. 97–102; K. Sengupta, T. Abdel-Hamid, and L. Van Wassenhove, "The Experience Trap," *Harvard Business Review,* February 2008, pp. 94–101; and M. Heilman and T. Okimoto, "Motherhood: A Potential Source of Bias in Employment Decisions," *Journal of Applied Psychology,* January 2008, pp. 189–98; and R. Kreitner and A. Kinicki, *Organizational Behavior,* 10th ed. (New York: McGraw-Hill/Irwin, 2012), pp. 337–38.

89. W. Goodman, "How Gambling Makes Strange Bedfellows," *The New York Times,* June 10, 1997, p. B3.

90. D. Kahneman, "The Surety of Fools," *The New York Times Magazine,* October 19, 2011, pp. 30–33, 62.

91. S. Li, Y. Sun, and Y. Wang, "50% Off or Buy One, Get One Free? Frame Preference as a Function of Consumable Nature in Dairy Products," *Journal of Social Psychology* 147 (2007), pp. 413–21.

92. R. H. Thaler, "Paying a Price for the Thrill of the Hunt," *The New York Times,* November 15, 2009, Business section, p. 5.

93. P. Slovic, "The Construction of a Preference," *American Psychologist* 50 (1995), pp. 364–71; K. J. Dunegan, "Framing, Cognitive Roles, and Image Theory: Toward an Understanding of a Glass Half Full," *Journal of Applied Psychology* 78 (1993), pp. 491–503; and K. F. E. Wong, M. Yik, and J. Y.Y. Kwong, "Understanding the Emotional Aspects of Escalation of Commitment: The Role of Negative Affect," *Journal of Applied Psychology,* March 2006, pp. 282–97.

94. G. W. Hill, "Group versus Individual Performance: Are *n* + 1 Heads Better Than 1?" *Psychological Bulletin,* May 1982, pp. 517–39. Also see W. T. H. Koh, "Heterogeneous Expertise and Collective Decision-Making," *Social Choice and Welfare,* April 2008, pp. 457–73.

95. N. F. R. Maier, "Assets and Liabilities in Group Problem Solving: The Need for Integrative Function," *Psychological Review* 74 (1967), pp. 239–49.

96. Maier, 1967.

97. For more about groupthink, see R. J. Shiller, "Challenging the Crowd in Whispers, Not Shouts," *The New York Times,* November 2, 2008, Business section, p. 5; J. Zweig, "How Group Decisions End Up Wrong-Footed," *The Wall Street Journal,* April 25 & 26, 2009, p. B1; S. Cain, "The Rise of the New Groupthink," *The New York Times,* January 15, 2012, pp. WR1, WR6; and J. Lehrer, "Groupthink," *The New Yorker,* January 30, 2012, pp. 22–27.

98. Methods for increasing group consensus were investigated by R. L. Priem, D. A. Harrison, and N. K. Muir, "Structured Conflict and Consensus Outcomes in Group Decision Making," *Journal of Management,* December 22, 1995, pp. 691–710.

99. See D. L. Gladstein and N. P. Reilly, "Group Decision Making under Threat: The Tycoon Game," *Academy of Management Journal,* September 1985, pp. 613–27.

100. These conclusions were based on the following studies: J. H. Davis, "Some Compelling Intuitions about Group Consensus Decisions, Theoretical and Empirical Research, and Interpersonal Aggregation Phenomena: Selected Examples, 1950–1990," *Organizational Behavior and Human Decision Processes,* June 1992, pp. 3–38; and J. A. Sniezek, "Groups Under Uncertainty: An Examination of Confidence in Group Decision Making," *Organizational Behavior and Human Decision Processes,* June 1992, pp. 124–55.

101. Supporting results can be found in J. R. Hollenbeck, D. R. Ilgen, D. J. Sego, J. Hedlund, D. A. Major, and J. Phillips, "Multilevel Theory of Team Decision Making: Decision Performance in Teams Incorporating Distributed Expertise," *Journal of Applied Psychology,* April 1995, pp. 292–316.

102. See D. H. Gruenfeld, E. A. Mannix, K. Y. Williams, and M. A. Neale, "Group Composition and Decision Making: How Member Familiarity and Information Distribution Affect Process and Performance," *Organizational Behavior and Human Decision Processes,* July 1996, pp. 1–15.

103. "Jack Welch's Lessons for Success," *Fortune,* January 25, 1993, p. 86.

104. See D. Pojidaeff, "Human Productivity and Pride in Work: The Core Principles of Participative Management," *Journal for Quality and Participation,* December 1995, pp. 44–47; and N. A. Holland, "A Pathway to Global Competitiveness and Total Quality: Participative Management," *Journal for Quality and Participation,* September 1995, pp. 58–62.

105. Results are presented in J. T. Delaney, "Workplace Cooperation: Current Problems, New Approaches," *Journal of Labor Research,* Winter 1996, pp. 45–61.

106. For an extended discussion, see M. Sashkin, "Participative Management Is an Ethical Imperative," *Organizational Dynamics,* Spring 1984, pp. 4–22. Also see S. Meisinger, "Management Holds Key to Employee Engagement," *HR Magazine,* February 2008, p. 8.

107. Supporting results can be found in C. R. Leana, R. S. Ahlbrandt, and A. J. Murrell, "The Effects of Employee Involvement Programs on Unionized Workers' Attitudes, Perceptions, and Preferences in Decision Making," *Academy of Management Journal,* October 1992, pp. 861–73; and D. Plunkett, "The Creative Organization: An Empirical Investigation of the Importance of Participation in Decision Making," *Journal of Creative Behavior,* Second Quarter 1990, pp. 140–48. Results pertaining to role conflict and ambiguity can be found in C. S. Smith and M. T. Brannick, "A Role Replication and Theoretical Extension," *Journal of Organizational Behavior,* March 1990, pp. 91–104.

108. See J. A. Wagner III, "Participation's Effects on Performance and Satisfaction: A Reconsideration of Research Evidence," *Academy of Management Review*, April 1994, pp. 312–30.

109. A thorough discussion of this issue is provided by W. A. Randolph, "Navigating the Journey to Empowerment," *Organizational Dynamics*, Spring 1995, pp. 19–32.

110. G. M. Parker, *Team Players and Teamwork: The New Competitive Business Strategy* (San Francisco: Jossey-Bass, 1990).

111. These recommendations were obtained from G. M. Parker, *Team Players and Teamwork*.

112. A. F. Osborn, *Applied Imagination: Principles and Procedures of Creative Thinking*, 3rd ed. (New York: Scribner's, 1979). For an example of how brainstorming works, see P. Croce, "Think Brighter," *FSB*, January 2006, p. 35.

113. W. H. Cooper, R. Brent Gallupe, S. Pallard, and J. Cadsby, "Some Liberating Effects of Anonymous Electronic Brainstorming," *Small Group Research*, April 1998, pp. 147–78.

114. These recommendations and descriptions were derived from B. Nussbaum, "The Power of Design," *BusinessWeek*, May 17, 2004, pp. 86–94.

115. See N. C. Dalkey, D. L. Rourke, R. Lewis, and D. Snyder, *Studies in the Quality of Life: Delphi and Decision Making* (Lexington, MA: Lexington Books, 1972). An application of the Delphi technique can be found in T. Grisham, "The Delphi Technique: A Method for Testing Complex and Multifaceted Topics," *International Journal of Managing Projects in Business*, 2009, pp. 112–30.

116. A thorough description of computer-aided decision-making systems is provided by M. C. Er and A. C. Ng, "The Anonymity and Proximity Factors in Group Decision Support Systems," *Decision Support Systems*, May 1995, pp. 75–83; and A. LaPlante, "Brainstorming," *Forbes*, October 25, 1993, pp. 45–61.

117. Results can be found in J. S. Valacich and C. Schwenk, "Devils' Advocacy and Dialectical Inquiry Effects on Face-to-Face and Computer-Mediated Group Decision Making," *Organizational Behavior and Human Decision Processes*, August 1995, pp. 158–73; R. B. Gallupe, W. H. Cooper, M. Grise, and L. M. Bastianutti, "Blocking Electronic Brain-storms," *Journal of Applied Psychology*, February 1994, pp. 77–86; and A. R. Dennis and J. S. Valacich, "Computer Brainstorms: More Heads Are Better Than One," *Journal of Applied Psychology*, August 1993, pp. 531–37.

118. Supportive results can be found in S. S. Lam and J. Schaubroeck, "Improving Group Decisions by Better Polling Information: A Comparative Advantage of Group Decision Support Systems," *Journal of Applied Psychology*, August 2000, pp. 565–73; and I. Benbasat and J. Lim, "Information Technology Support for Debiasing Group Judgments: An Empirical Evaluation," *Organizational Behavior and Human Decision Processes*, September 2000, pp. 167–83.

119. B. B. Baltes, M. W. Dickson, M. P. Sherman, C. C. Bauer, and J. S. LaGanke, "Computer-Mediated Communication and Group Decision Making: A Meta-Analysis," *Organizational Behavior and Human Decision Processes*, January 2002, pp. 156–79.

120. David Dorfman, quoted in H. Lancaster, "How Life Lessons Have Helped a Successful Manager," *San Francisco Sunday Examiner & Chronicle*, August 15, 1999, p. CL-33; reprinted from *The Wall Street Journal*.

121. J. S. Hammond, R. L. Keeney, and H. Raiffa, *Smart Choices: A Practical Guide to Making Better Decisions* (Boston: Harvard Business School Press, 1999).

122. O. Pollar, "Six Steps for Making Tough Choices," *San Francisco Examiner & Chronicle*, April 4, 1999, p. J-3.

123. Lorien Pratt and Mark Zangari, reported in "Making Good Decisions," *The Straits Times*, August 6, 2009, p. C26.

CHAPTER 8

1. S. Stecklow, "Management 101," *The Wall Street Journal*, December 9, 1994, p. B1.

2. O. Pollar, "Don't Overlook the Importance of Delegating," *San Francisco Examiner*, August 8, 1999, p. J-3.

3. C. M. Avery, M. A. Walker, and E. O'Toole, *Teamwork Is an Individual Skill: Getting Your Work Done When Sharing Responsibility* (San Francisco: Berrett-Koehler, 2001); S. Gazda, "The Art of Delegating: Effective Delegation Enhances Employee Morale, Manager Productivity, and Organizational Success," *HR Magazine*, January 2002, pp. 75–79; R. Burns, *Making Delegation Happen: A Simple and Effective Guide to Implementing Successful Delegation* (St. Leonards, Australia: Allen & Unwin, 2002); D. M. Genett, *If You Want It Done Right, You Don't Have to Do It Yourself! The Power of Effective Delegation* (Sanger, CA: Quill Driver Books, 2003); R. Charan, "People Acumen," *Fast Company*, December 2007, www.fastcompany.com/articles/2007/12/ram-charan-acumen.html (accessed March 10, 2012).

4. Pollar, "Don't Overlook the Importance of Delegating," 1999; Avery, et al., 2001; Burns, 2002; and Genett, 2003.

5. K. K. Reardon, *The Secret Handshake: Mastering the Politics of the Business Inner Circle* (New York: Doubleday, 2002) and *It's All Politics: Winning in a World Where Hard Work and Talent Aren't Enough* (New York: Currency/Random House, 2005).

6. K. K. Reardon, interviewed by J. Vishnevsky, "Ask the Expert: Kathleen Kelley Reardon," *U.S. News & World Report*, July 25, 2005, p. EE10. See also C. Bush, "Learn How to Work with Others," *The Arizona Republic*, August 21, 2005, p. EC1.

7. E. H. Schein, "The Role of the Founder in Creating Organizational Culture," *Organizational Dynamics*, Summer 1983, pp. 13–28; E. H. Schein, *Organizational Culture and Leadership* (San Francisco: Jossey-Bass, 1985); and E. H. Schein, "Organizational Culture," *American Psychologist* 45 (1990), pp. 109–19.

8. Reward systems are discussed in J. Kerr and J. W. Slocum, "Managing Corporate Culture through Reward Systems," *Academy of Management Executive*, November 2005, pp. 83–94.

9. A thorough description of the competing values framework is provided in K. S. Cameron, R. E. Quinn, J. Degraff, and A. V. Thakor, *Creating Values Leadership* (Northhampton, MA: Edward Elgar, 2006); and K. S. Cameron and R. E. Quinn, *Diagnosing and Changing Organizational Culture* (New York: Addison-Wesley, 1999).

10. J. M. O'Brien, "Zappos Knows How to Kick It," *Fortune*, February 2, 2009, pp. 55–60; and C. Palmeri, "Now for Sale, the Zappos Culture," *Bloomberg Businessweek*, January 11, 2010, p. 57.

11. K. Auletta, *Googled: The End of the World as We Know It* (New York: Penguin Press, 2009).

12. D. Welch, D. Kiley, and M. Ihlwan, "My Way or the Highway at Hyundai," *BusinessWeek*, March 17, 2008, pp. 48–51.

13. L. Robbins, "For Delivery Companies, Welcome Stress," *The New York Times*, December 13, 2009, news section, p. 3.

14. G. Harris, "Pfizer Pays $2.3 Billion to Settle Marketing Case," *The New York Times*, September 3, 2009, www.nytimes.com/2009/09/03/business/03health.html?_r=1&scp=1&sq=Pfizer%20Fraud%20September%202009&st=cse (accessed March 10, 2012).

15. J. Kindler, quoted in R. M. Murphy, "Why Doing Good Is Good for Business," *Fortune*, February 8, 2010, pp. 90–95.

16. B. Breen, "The Thrill of Defeat," *Fast Company*, June 2004, pp. 76–81. A comprehensive article about companies that cultivate cultures that embrace failure and learn from it is J. McGregor, "How Failure Breeds Success," *BusinessWeek*, July 10, 2006, pp. 42–52.

17. J. McGregor, "The Chore Goes Offshore," *BusinessWeek*, March 23 and 30, 2009, pp. 50–51.

18. A. Lucchetti and M. Langley, "Amid Turmoil, a Shake-up at Citi: Perform-or-Die Culture Leaves Thin Talent Pool for Top Wall Street Jobs," *The Wall Street Journal,* November 5, 2007, pp. A1, A16.

19. E. Frauenheim, "Lost in the Shuffle," *Workforce Management,* January 14, 2008, pp. 1, 12–17.

20. E. H. Schein, *Organizational Culture and Leadership,* 2nd ed. (San Francisco: Jossey-Bass, 1992).

21. E. Byron, "Call Me Mike!" *The Wall Street Journal,* March 27, 2006, p. B1.

22. P. Babcock, "Is Your Company Two-Faced?" *HR Magazine,* January 2004, p. 43.

23. Anastasia Kelly, former chief lawyer for AIG, quoted in interview with C. Loomis, "Inside the Crisis at AIG," *Fortune,* March 1, 2010, pp. 47–54.

24. D. MacMillan, "Survivor: CEO Edition," *Bloomberg Businessweek,* March 1, 2010, pp. 33–38.

25. T. E. Deal and A. A. Kennedy, *Corporate Cultures: The Rites and Rituals of Corporate Life* (Reading, MA: Addison-Wesley, 1982), p. 22. See also T. E. Deal and A.A. Kennedy, *The New Corporate Cultures: Revitalizing the Workplace After Downsizing, Mergers, and Reengineering* (Cambridge, MA: Perseus, 2000).

26. L. Collins, "House Perfect," *The New Yorker,* October 3, 2011, pp. 54–65.

27. Marc Benioff, interviewed by C. Rose, "Charlie Rose Talks to Marc Benioff," *Bloomberg Businessweek,* December 5–December 11, 2011, p. 52.

28. Ingvar Kamprad, quoted in Collins, "House Perfect," 2011, p. 60.

29. S. Bailey, "Benefits on Tap," *Bloomberg Businessweek,* March 21–March 27, 2011, pp. 96–97.

30. See C. Hartnell, A. Ou, and A. Kinicki, "Organizational Culture and Organizational Effectiveness: A Meta-Analytic Investigation of the Competing Values Framework's Theoretical Suppositions," *Journal of Applied Psychology* 96 (2011), pp. 677–94.

31. Adapted from L. Smircich, "Concepts of Culture and Organizational Analysis," *Administrative Science Quarterly,* September 1983, pp. 339–58.

32. S. McCarney, "Airline Industry's Top-Rated Woman Keeps Southwest's Small-Fry Spirit Alive," *The Wall Street Journal,* November 30, 1996, pp. B1, B11.

33. D. Anfuso, "3M's Staffing Strategy Promotes Productivity and Pride," *Personnel Journal,* February 1995, pp. 28–34.

34. The strength perspective was promoted by Deal and Kennedy, *Corporate Cultures: The Rites and Rituals of Corporate Life,* 1982.

35. The HP Way is thoroughly discussed in J. Dong, "The Rise and Fall of the HP Way," *Palo Alto Weekly Online Edition,* April 10, 2002; www.paloaltoonline.com/weekly/morgue/2002/2002_04_10.hpway10.html (accessed March 10, 2012).

36. J. P. Kotter and J. L. Heskett, *Corporate Culture and Performance* (New York: Free Press, 1992).

37. J. Green, "Management Secrets of the Grateful Dead," *The Atlantic,* March 2010, pp. 64–67. See also "What a Long, Strange Business Plan It's Been," *Bloomberg Businessweek,* March 8, 2010, p. 8.

38. B. Barnes, quoted in Green, 2010.

39. The mechanisms are based on material contained in E. H. Schein, "The Role of the Founder in Creating Organizational Culture," *Organizational Dynamics,* Summer 1983, pp. 13–28.

40. Walmart's values are stated on its corporate website, "About Walmart," www.walmart.com/catalog/cata-log.gsp?cat=131473#null (accessed March 10, 2012).

41. D. G. McNeil Jr., "Ally for the Poor in an Unlikely Corner," *The New York Times,* February 9, 2010, pp. D1, D6.

42. J. Collins, "How the Mighty Fall," *BusinessWeek,* May 24, 2009, pp. 26–38.

43. D. Moss, "Triage: Methodically Developing Its Employees," *HR Magazine,* July 2007, p. 45.

44. D. Clark, "Why Silicon Valley Is Rethinking the Cubicle Office," *The Wall Street Journal,* October 15, 2007, http://online.wsj.com/article/SB119240097861658633.html?mod=hps_us_mostpop_viewed (accessed March 10, 2012).

45. Moss, "Triage: Methodically Developing Its Employees," 2007.

46. J. Ball, "Might Profit Maker," *The Wall Street Journal,* April 8, 2005, p. B1.

47. MacMillan, "Survivor: CEO Edition," 2010.

48. C. I. Barnard, *The Functions of the Executive* (Cambridge, MA: Harvard University Press, 1938), p. 73.

49. P. M. Blau and W. R. Scott, *Formal Organizations* (San Francisco: Chandler, 1962).

50. M. Stettner, *Skills for New Managers* (New York: McGraw-Hill, 2000); J. H. Grossman and J. R. Parkinson, *Becoming a Successful Manager: How to Make a Smooth Transition from Managing Yourself to Managing Others* (New York: McGraw-Hill, 2001); and L. A. Hill, *Becoming a Manager: How New Managers Master the Challenges of Leadership,* 2nd ed. (Boston: Harvard Business School Press, 2003). For more on becoming a leader, also see B. Kellerman, "What Every Leader Needs to Know About Followers," *Harvard Business Review,* December 2007, pp. 84–91; M. Gottfredson, S. Schaubert, and H. Saenz, "The New Leader's Guide to Diagnosing the Business," *Harvard Business Review,* February 2008, pp. 63–73; "Timeless Leadership: A Conversation with David McCullough," *Harvard Business Review,* March 2008, pp. 45–49; S. D. Friedman, "Be a Better Leader, Have a Richer Life," *Harvard Business Review,* April 2008, pp. 112–18; and B. Reeves, T. W. Malone, and T. O'Driscoll, "Leadership's Online Labs," *Harvard Business Review,* May 2008, pp. 58–66.

51. E. H. Schein, *Organizational Psychology,* 3rd ed. (Englewood Cliffs, NJ: Prentice Hall, 1980).

52. For an overview of the span of control concept, see D. D. Van Fleet and A. G. Bedeian, "A History of the Span of Management," *Academy of Management Review,* July 1977, pp. 356–72.

53. Research by V. Smeets and F. Warzynski, "Too Many Theories, Too Few Facts? What the Data Tell Us about the Link between Span of Control, Compensation, and Career Dynamics," *Labour Economics, Special Issue on Firms and Employees* 15 (2008). Reported in G. Anders, "Overseeing More Employees—With Fewer Managers," *The Wall Street Journal,* March 24, 2008, p. B6.

54. T. A. Stewart, "CEOs See Clout Shifting," *Fortune,* November 6, 1989, p. 66.

55. Pollar, "Don't Overlook the Importance of Delegating," 1999.

56. C. C. Miller, "Google's Chief Works to Trim a Bloated Ship," *The New York Times,* November 10, 2011, pp. A1, A3.

57. This section was adapted from R. Kreitner and A. Kinicki, *Organizational Behavior,* 10th ed. (New York: McGraw-Hill/Irwin, 2013), pp. 503–8.

58. "About Whole Foods Market," company website, www.wholefoodsmarket.com/company (accessed March 10, 2012).

59. "The World's Most Admired Companies: The 50 All-Stars," *Fortune,* March 19, 2012, p. 140.

60. M. Moskowitz and R. Levering, "The 100 Best Companies to Work For," *Fortune,* February 6, 2012, pp. 117–27.

61. C. Fishman, "Whole Foods Is All Teams," *Fast Company, Greatest Hits,* 1 (1997), pp. 103–13. See also C. Fishman, "The Whole Foods Recipe for Teamwork," *FastCompany.com,* December 18, 2007, www.fastcompany.com/magazine/02/team2.html (accessed March 12, 2012).

62. G. Hamel, "Break Free," *Fortune,* September 19, 2007, http://money.cnn.com/magazines/fortune/fortune_archive/2007/10/01/100352608/index.htm (accessed March 12, 2012).

63. A. Alix, "Whole Foods Market: A Steady Diet of Growth and Profit," *The Motley Fool,* February 21, 2012, www.fool.com/investing/general/2012/02/21/whole-foods-market-a-steady-diet-of-growth-and-pro.aspx (accessed March 10, 2012).

64. Adapted from "Boundaryless," *Encyclopedia of Small Business*, ed. K. Hillstrom and L. C. Hillstrom (Farmington Hills, MI: Thomson Gale, 2002, and Seattle, WA: eNotes. com, 2006), http://business.enotes.com/small-business-encyclopedia/boundaryless (accessed March 10, 2012). Regarding the impact of web services on organizational boundaries, see R. D. Hof, "Web 2.0: The New Guy at Work," *BusinessWeek*, June 19, 2006, pp. 58–59.

65. N. Anand and R. L. Daft, "What Is the Right Organization Design?" *Organizational Dynamics* 36 (2007), pp. 329–44.

66. T. L. Friedman, "Just Doing It," *The New York Times*, April 18, 2010, Week in Review section, p. 10.

67. Anand and Daft, "What Is the Right Organization Design?" 2007, p. 336.

68. S. Siekman, "The Snap-Together Business Jet," *Fortune*, January 21, 2002, http://money.cnn.com/magazines/fortune/fortune_archive/2002/01/21/316585/index.htm (accessed March 10, 2012); and Anand and Daft, "What Is the Right Organization Design?" 2007, p. 336.

69. M. J. Mandel and R. D. Hof, "Rethinking the Internet," *BusinessWeek*, March 26, 2001, p. 118.

70. Adapted from "Virtual Organization," *Whatis.com;* http://whatis.techtarget.com/definition/0,,sid9_gci213301,00.html (accessed March 10, 2012).

71. Anand and Daft, "What Is the Right Organizational Design?" 2007, p. 332.

72. See "Successfully Transitioning to a Virtual Organization," *SHRM Research Quarterly*, First Quarter 2010, pp. 1–9.

73. M. Sappington, "When to Go Unvirtual," *Inc.*, April 2010, p. 73.

74. K. Deveny, "Bag Those Fries, Squirt That Ketchup, Fry That Fish," *BusinessWeek*, October 13, 1986, p. 86.

75. T. Burns and G. M. Stalker, *The Management of Innovation* (London: Tavistock, 1961). See also W. D. Sine, H. Mitsuhashi, and D. A. Kirsch, "Revisiting Burns and Stalker: Formal Structure and New Venture Performance in Emerging Economic Sectors," *Academy of Management Journal*, February 2006, pp. 121–32.

76. T. J. Peters and R. H. Waterman, *In Search of Excellence* (New York: Harper & Row, 1982).

77. Inc.com, "Virtual Company Advice," *101 Great Ideas for Managing People from America's Most Innovative SmallCompanies*, October 1999, www.inc.com/articles/1999/10/19238.html (accessed March 10, 2012); and M. Puente, "Direct Selling Brings It All Home," *USA Today*, October 27, 2003, www.usatoday.com/life/2003-10-27-home-shopping_x.htm (accessed March 10, 2012).

78. P. R. Lawrence and J. W. Lorsch, *Organization and Environment* (Homewood, IL: Irwin, 1967).

79. J. R. Kimberly, R. H. Miles, et al., *The Organizational Life Cycle* (San Francisco: Jossey-Bass, 1980).

80. A. D. Chandler Jr., *Strategy and Structure: Chapters in the History of the Industrial Enterprise* (Cambridge, MA: MIT Press, 1962).

81. See H. L. Boschken, "Strategy and Structure: Reconceiving the Relationship," *Journal of Management*, March 1990, pp. 135–50.

82. This section was adapted from Kreitner and Kinicki, *Organizational Behavior*, 2013, pp. 511–13.

CHAPTER 9

1. J. Welch and S. Welch, "Dear Graduate . . . ," *BusinessWeek*, June 19, 2006, p. 100.

2. E. Holton, S. Naquin, and E. Holton, *So You're New Again: How to Succeed When You Change Jobs* (San Francisco: Berrett-Koehler Publishers, 2001); M. Watkins, *The First 90 Days: Critical Success Strategies for New Leaders at All Levels* (Boston: Harvard Business School Press, 2003); J. S. Lublin, "How to Win Support from Colleagues at Your New Job," *The Wall Street Journal*, November 25, 2003, p. B1; J. Burke, "Dip, Before Diving, into That New Job," *BusinessWeek Online*, June 28, 2004, http://www.businessweek.com/bschools/content/jun2004/bs20040628_9967_bs001.htm (accessed April 19, 2010); L. Wolgemuth, "Breaking Out of the First-Job Trap," *U.S. News & World Report*, March 24/March 31, 2008, pp. 56, 58; and L. Buhl, "7 Deadly Sins for New Hires," *San Francisco Chronicle*, April 4, 2010, p. E14.

3. M. Sunnafrank and A. Ramirez Jr., "At First Sight: Persistent Relational Effects of Get-Acquainted Conversations," *Journal of Social and Personal Relationships*, June 1, 2004, pp. 361–79. See also J. Zaslow, "First Impressions Get Faster," *The Wall Street Journal*, February 16, 2006, p. D4.

4. R. Ailes, in "Your First Seven Seconds," *Fast Company*, June–July 1998, p. 184.

5. J. Denrell, "Why Most People Disapprove of Me: Experience Sampling in Impression Formation," *Psychological Review*, October 2005, pp. 951–78. See also M. Krakovsky, "Researcher Disputes Notion You Have Only One Chance to Make a Good Impression," *Stanford Report*, August 18, 2004, http://news-service.stanford.edu/news/2004/august18/impressions-818.html (accessed March 15, 2012).

6. Thom Singer, quoted in A. Bruzzese, "You Must Keep Networking Even After You Get in the Door," *Reno Gazette-Journal*, February 25, 2010, p. 5A.

7. K. Madden, "Start New Job on the Right Foot," *Reno Gazette-Journal*, March 18, 2012, p. 1-J.

8. L. P. Frankel, in "Your First Impression," *Fast Company*, June–July 1998, p. 188.

9. M. Moskowitz and R. Levering, "The 100 Best Companies to Work For," *Fortune*, February 6, 2012, pp. 117–27.

10. A. Fisher, "How to Get Hired by a 'Best' Company," *Fortune*, February 4, 2008, p. 96.

11. A. Lashinsky, "The Perks of Being a Googler," *Fortune*, January 8, 2007, http://money.cnn.com/galeries/2007/fortune/0701/gallery.Google_perks (accessed April 19, 2010).

12. E. Schmidt, quoted in interview by A. Lashinsky, "Back2Back Champs," *Fortune*, February 4, 2008, p. 70.

13. "2011 Financial Tables," Google Investor Relations, http://investor.google.com/financial/tables.html (accessed March 15, 2012).

14. J. Welch, quoted in N. M. Tichy and S. Herman, *Control Your Destiny or Someone Else Will: How Jack Welch Is Making General Electric the World's Most Competitive Corporation* (New York: Doubleday, 1993), p. 251.

15. P. Capelli and A. Crocker-Hefter, "Distinctive Human Resources Are Firms' Core Competencies," *Organizational Dynamics*, Winter 1996, pp. 7–22.

16. B. E. Becker, M. A. Huselid, and D. Ulrich, *The HR Scorecard: Linking People, Strategy, and Performance* (Boston: Harvard Business School Press, 2001), p. 4.

17. B. E. Becker, M. A. Huselid, and D. Ulrich, *The HR Scorecard: Linking People, Strategy, and Performance* (Boston: Harvard Business School Press, 2001), p. 4. See also D. Stamps, "Measuring Minds," *Training*, May 2000, pp. 76–85; C. A. Bartlett and S. Ghoshal, "Building Competitive Advantage through People," *MIT Sloan Management Review*, Winter 2002, pp. 34–41; G. Gohlander, S. Snell, and A. Sherman, *Managing Human Resources*, 13th ed. (Mason, OH: South-Western Publishing, 2004); and R. Rodriguez, "Meet the New Learning Executive," *HR Magazine*, April 2005, pp. 64–69.

18. S. Meisinger, "Taking the Measure of Human Capital," *HR Magazine*, January 2003, p. 10. See also R. J. Grossman, "Blind Investment," *HR Magazine*, January 2005, pp. 40–47; and *Unlocking the DNA of the Adaptable Workforce: The Global Human Capital Study 2008*, IBM Global Services, www.935.ibm.com/

services/us/gbs/bus/html/2008ghcs.html (accessed March 15, 2012).

19. P. S. Adler and S. Kwon, "Social Capital: Prospects for New Concept," *Academy of Management Review,* January 2002, pp. 17–40. See also R. A. Baaron and G. D. Markman, "Beyond Social Capital: How Social Skills Can Enhance Entrepreneurs' Success," *Academy of Management Executive,* February 2000, pp. 106–16; D. Lidsky, "Winning the Relationship Game," *Fast Company,* October 2004, pp. 113–15; J. Steinberg, "One Heart at a Time," *Fast Company,* November 2004, p. 49; K. H. Hammonds, "A Lever Long Enough to Move the World," *Fast Company,* January 2005, pp. 60–63; and A. C. Inkpen and E. W. K. Tsang, "Social Capital, Networks, and Knowledge Transfer," *Academy of Management Review,* January 2005, pp. 146–65; and L. Prusak and D. Cohen, "How to Invest in Social Capital," *BusinessWeek Online,* October 23, 2007, www.businessweek.com/-managing/content/oct2007/ca20071023_070114.htm?chan=search (accessed March 15, 2012).

20. R. Levering and M. Moskowitz, "The 100 Best Companies to Work For," *Fortune,* January 12, 2004, p. 68.

21. R. J. Mirabile, "The Power of Job Analysis," *Training,* April 1990, pp. 70–74; and S. F. Mona, "The Job Description," *Association Management,* February 1991, pp. 33–37.

22. P. Davidson, "Minimum Wage Rates May Climb This Year," *USA Today,* February 2, 2012, www.usatoday.com/money/economy/income/story/2012-02-02/raising-minimum-wage/52940286/1 (accessed March 15, 2012).

23. S. G. Stolberg and R. Pear, "Obama Signs Health Care Overhaul Bill, with a Flourish," *The New York Times,* March 23, 2010, www.nytimes.com/2010/03/24/health/policy/24health.html (accessed March 15, 2012).

24. See S. E. Needleman, "More Programs to Halt Bias Against Gays," *The Wall Street Journal,* November 26, 2007, p. B3. A countertrend to age discrimination may be the result of baby boomers retiring, bringing an overall shortfall in workers. See E. White, "The New Recruits: Older Workers," *The Wall Street Journal,* January 14, 2008, p. B3.

25. J. Coffman, O. Gadiesh, and W. Miller, *The Great Disappearing Act: Gender Parity Up the Corporate Ladder,* World Economic Forum White Paper, survey by Bain & Co. and Harvard Business Review, January 30, 2010, www.bain.com/bainweb/publications/publications_detail.asp?id=27564&menu_url=publications%5Fresults%2Easp (accessed March 15, 2012).

26. B. Knowlton, "U.S. Job Site Bans Bias over Gender Identity," *The New York Times,* January 6, 2010, p. A15.

27. Equal Employment Opportunity Commission, reported in Associated Press, "Job Bias Claims at Record Level," *The Daily Record,* January 24, 2012, http://thedailyrecord.com/2012/01/24/job-bias-claims-in-u-s-at-record-level (accessed March 15, 2012).

28. P. Rochman, "Pregnant at Work? Why Your Job Could Be at Risk," *Time Healthland,* February 16, 2012, http://healthland.time.com/2012/02/16/pregnant-at-work-why-your-job-could-be-at-risk/?iid=hl-main-lede (accessed March 15, 2012).

29. F. Bass, "Women Make 77 Cents to Every $1 for a Man," *San Francisco Chronicle,* March 17, 2012, p. D2. See also U.S. Bureau of Labor Statistics, Department of Labor, *Highlights of Women's Earnings in 2010,* Report 1031, July 2011, www.bls.gov/cps/cpswom2010.pdf (accessed March 15, 2012).

30. U.S. Census Bureau, 2010, reported in J. Malveaux, "More Female Grads, but What about Pay?" *USA Today,* May 13, 2011, p. 11A.

31. For a thorough discussion of affirmative action, see F. J. Crosby, A. Iyer, S. Clayton, and R. A. Downing, "Affirmative Action," *American Psychologist,* February 2003, pp. 93–115.

32. See H. J. Walker, H. S. Feild, W. F. Giles, J. B. Bernerth, and L. A. Jones-Farmer, "An Assessment of Attraction Toward Affirmative Action Organizations: Investigating the Role of Individual Differences," *Journal of Organizational Behavior,* May 2007, pp. 455–507.

33. E. H. James, A. P. Brief, J. Dietz, and R. R. Cohen, "Prejudice Matters: Understanding the Reactions of Whites to Affirmative Action Programs Targeted to Benefit Blacks," *Journal of Applied Psychology,* December 2001, pp. 1120–28.

34. For a thorough review of relevant research, see M. E. Heilman, "Affirmative Action: Some Unintended Consequences for Working Women," in B. M. Staw and L. L. Cummings, eds., *Research in Organizational Behavior,* vol. 16 (Greenwich, CT: JAI Press, 1994), pp. 125–69.

35. M. Rotundo, D.-H. Nguyen, and P. R. Sackett, "A Meta-Analytic Review of Gender Differences in Perceptions of Sexual Harassment," *Journal of Applied Psychology,* October 2001, pp. 914–22.

36. Most research on sexual harassment has focused on harassment inside organizations. For a discussion of harassment beyond the boundaries of the organization, see H. J. Gettman and J. J. Gelfand, "When the Customer Shouldn't Be King: Antecedents and Consequences of Sexual Harassment by Clients and Customers," *Journal of Applied Psychology,* May 2007, pp. 757–70.

37. S. Armour, "More Men Say They Are Sexually Harassed at Work," *USA Today,* September 17, 2004, p. 1B; C. A. Pierce and H. Aguinis, "Legal Standards, Ethical Standards, and Responses to Social–Sexual Conduct at Work," *Journal of Organizational Behavior* 26 (2005), pp. 727–32; L. A. Baar, "Harassment Case Proceeds Despite Failure to Report," *HR Magazine,* June 2005, p. 159; and S. Shellenbarger, "Supreme Court Takes on How Employers Handle Worker Harassment Complaints," *The Wall Street Journal,* April 13, 2006, p. D1.

38. See Equal Employment Opportunity Commission, "Sexual Harassment Charges EEOC & FEPAs Combined: FY 1997-2011, www.eeoc.gov/eeoc/statistics/enforcement/sexual_harassment.cfm (accessed March 26, 2012).

39. Survey in 2007 by Novations Group, Boston, reported in D. Stead, "Is the Workplace Getting Raunchier?" *BusinessWeek,* March 17, 2008, p. 19.

40. Survey in 2007 by Zogby International, reported in T. Parker-Pope, "When the Bully Sits in the Next Cubicle," *The New York Times,* March 25, 2008, p. D5. See also J. A. Segal, "'I Did It, But . . . ,'" *HR Magazine,* March 2008, pp. 91–93.

41. G. Bohlander, S. Snell, and A. Sherman, *Managing Human Resources,* 12th ed. (Mason, OH: South-Western, 2001).

42. J. Welch and S. Welch, "Hiring Wrong—and Right," *BusinessWeek,* January 29, 2007, p. 102.

43. Dave Lefkow, CEO of TalentSpark, quoted in C. Winkler, "Quality Check," *HR Magazine,* May 2007, pp. 93–98.

44. R. Zeidner, "People Promoted to the Top Jobs Measure Up," *HR Magazine,* April 2010, p. 20. The article reports on a study by Y. Zhang and N. Rajagopalan, "Once an Outsider, Always an Outsider? CEO Origin, Strategic Change, and Firm Performance," *Strategic Management Journal* 31 (2010), pp. 969–89. See also M. Bidwell, "Paying More to Get Less: The Effects of External Hiring versus Internal Mobility," *Administrative Science Quarterly,* December 27, 2011, http://asq.sagepub.com/content/56/3/369.abstract (accessed March 23, 2012); "Why External Hires Get Paid More, and Perform Worse, Than Internal Staff," *Knowledge@Wharton,* March 28, 2012, http://knowledge.wharton.upenn.edu/article.cfm?articleid=2961 (accessed March 28, 2012).

45. B. Tedeschi, "Searching for a Job? Try Looking at Your Hand-Held First," *The New York Times,* May 19, 2011, p. B8; and B. Evangelista, "More Job Seekers Turning to Online Social Networks," *San Francisco Chronicle,* November 17, 2011, p. D5.

46. A. D. Wright, "Your Social Media Is Showing: A Candidate's Online Presence May Say More Than a Résumé," *HR Magazine,* March 2012, p. 16.

47. Survey conducted by Potential Park Communications, Stockholm, reported in J. Walker, "Young Job Seekers Turn to Smartphones," *The Wall Street Journal,* March 7, 2012, p. B9. Also see B. Tedeschi, "Searching for a Job? Try Looking at Your Hand-Held First," *The New York Times,* Mahy 19, 2011, p. B8.

48. G. McWilliams, "The Best Way to Find a Job," *The Wall Street Journal,* December 6, 1999, pp. R16, R22. Respondents to the Society for Human Resource Management's *2007 E-Recruiting Survey* also reported that employee referrals generated the highest quality of job candidates and best return on investment for their organization. See T. Minton-Eversole, "E-Recruitment Comes of Age, Survey Says," *HR Magazine,* August 2007, p. 34. Also see D. G. Allen and R. V. Mahto, "Web-Based Recruitment: Effects of Information, Organizational Brand, and Attitudes Toward a Web Site on Applicant Attraction," *Journal of Applied Psychology,* November 2007, pp. 1696–1708.

49. Minton-Eversole, 2007. Also see D. Kirkpatrick, "Web 2.0 Gets Over Its Goofing-Off Phase," *Fortune,* March 31, 2008, pp. 32–34; J. De Avila, "Beyond Job Boards: Targeting the Source," *The Wall Street Journal,* July 2, 2009, pp D1, D5; M. Weinstein, "Virtual Handshake," *Training,* September 2009, pp. 18–22; D. Koeppel, "HR by Twitter," *FSB,* September 23, 2009, p. 57; J. Greer, "The Art of Self-Marketing Online," *U.S. News & World Report,* May 2010, p. 30; Tedeschi, "Searching for a Job? Try Looking at Your Hand-Held First," 2011; Evangelista, "More Job Seekers Turning to Online Social Networks," 2011; Walker, "Young Job Seekers Turn to Smartphones," 2012; and Wright, "Your Social Media Is Showing: A Candidate's Online Presence May Say More Than a Résumé," 2012. See M. A. Tucker, "Show and Tell," *HR Magazine,* January 2012, pp. 51–53.

50. A. Bruzzese, "Lying on Résumé Is Treading on Dangerous Ground," *Reno Gazette-Journal,* March 8, 2012, p. 5A.

51. Survey by InfoLink Screen Services, reported in H. B. Herring, "On Our Résumés, Couldn't We All Have Gone to Yale?" *The New York Times,* March 12, 2006, sec. 3, p. 2.

52. Survey by ResumeDoctor.com, reported in C. Soltis, "Eagle-Eyed Employers Scour Résumés for Little White Lies," *The Wall Street Journal,* March 21, 2006, p. B7.

53. Survey by Background Information Services, reported in M. Villano, "Served as King of England, Said the Résumé," *The New York Times,* March 19, 2006, sec. 3, p. 9.

54. C. W. Nevius, "If You Like Fiction, Read the Job Resumes," *San Francisco Chronicle,* February 28, 2006, pp. B1, B2. See also D. Koeppel, "That Padded Résumé Won't Help Break Your Fall," *San Francisco Chronicle,* April 23, 2006, p. F5; reprinted from *The New York Times.*

55. A. Efrati and J. S. Lublin, "Résumé Trips Up Yahoo Chief," *The Wall Street Journal,* May 5–6 , 2012, pp. A1, A12.

56. Report by Automatic Data Processing, Roseland, NJ, cited in J. L. Seglin, "Lies Can Have a (Long) Life of Their Own," *The New York Times,* June 16, 2002, sec. 3, p. 4. See also S. Armour, "Security Checks Worry Workers," *USA Today,* June 19, 2004, p. 1B.

57. J. S. Lublin, "Job Hunters with Gaps in Their Résumés Need to Write Around Them," *The Wall Street Journal,* May 6, 2003, p. B1.

58. M. Conlin, "Don't Hedge Your Age," *BusinessWeek,* October 6, 2003, p. 14. See also C. Dahle, "A Nip and Tuck for the Résumé," *The New York Times,* April 17, 2005, sec. 3, p. 10.

59. S. McManis, "Little White-Collar Lies," *San Francisco Chronicle,* October 1, 1999, pp. B1, B3.

60. B. Bergstein, "Ex-Wiki Exec's Criminal History," *San Francisco Chronicle,* December 27, 2007, pp. C1, C2.

61. D. Belkin, "More Job Seekers Scramble to Erase Their Criminal Past," *The Wall Street Journal,* November 11, 2009, pp. A1, A16.

62. See E. Krell, "Unmasking Illegal Workers," *HR Magazine,* December 2007, pp. 49–52; and S. Berfield, "Illegals and Business: A Glimpse of the Future?" *BusinessWeek,* January 14, 2008, pp. 52–54.

63. W. M. Welch, "Employee Screenings See Growth," *USA Today,* June 24, 2009, p. 3A. The adverse effect of E-Verify on agricultural hiring is described in N. Leiber, "A Verification System for New Hires Backfires," *Bloomberg Businessweek,* October 24–October 30, 2011, p. 60.

64. L. Radnofsky and M. Jordan, "Illegal Workers Slip by System," *The Wall Street Journal,* February 25, 2010, p. A6.

65. B. Braccio Hering, "Words to Use, Lose on Résumé," *Reno Gazette-Journal,* June 26, 2011, p. 1F; K. Madden, "Increase Job Search Success," *Reno Gazette-Journal,* August 14, 2011, p. 1F; D. Auerbach, "Error-Free Résumés, Cover Letters a Must," *Reno Gazette-Journal,* October 23, 2011, p. 1F; R. E. Silverman, "No More Résumés, Say Some Firms," *The Wall Street Journal,* January 24, 2012, p. B6; D. Auerbach, "Employers Checking Social Sites," *Reno Gazette-Journal,* May 6, 2006, p. 1G.

66. L. Weber, "Your Résumé vs. Oblivion," *The Wall Street Journal,* January 24, 2012, pp. B1, B6.

67. References are even a problem in faculty hiring in universities. See D. M. Barden, "The Unreliability of References," *The Chronicle of Higher Education,* January 11, 2008, pp. C1, C4.

68. A. Bruzzese, "Don't Let References Torpedo Your Job Chances," *Reno Gazette-Journal,* January 26, 2012, pp. 5A, 6A.

69. A. Martin, "As a Hiring Filter, Credit Checks Draw Questions," *The New York Times,* April 10, 2010, pp. B1, B4.

70. C. Choi, "Credit Reports: Who's Looking at Yours, and Why?" *Reno Gazette-Journal,* April 12, 2010, p. 8A.

71. Based on P. Bathurst, "How to Avoid Those Fatal Interview Mistakes," *The Arizona Republic,* March 9, 2008, p. EC1; "Preparation Key to Snaring Job," *The Arizona Republic,* April 15, 2009, p. EC1; T. Musbach, "Common Interview Surprise: Inappropriate Questions," *San Francisco Chronicle,* January 3, 2010, p. D1; J. S. Lublin, "The New Job Is in the Details," *The Wall Street Journal,* January 5, 2010, p. D5; "4 Keys to Interview Success," *The Arizona Republic,* April 4, 2010, p. EC1; A. Bruzzese, "Market Yourself Like a Product to Get Employers' Attention," *USA Today,* December 2, 2011, www.usatoday.com/money/jobcenter/workplace/bruzzese/story/2011-11-30/learn-to-market-yourself-to-get-job/51482754/1 (accessed March 15, 2012); and K. Madden, "Proper Preparation Enhances Job Interviews," *Reno Gazette-Journal,* February 25, 2012, p. 1F. For a discussion of standard interview questions, see survey by jobs website Glassdoor.com, reported in "Job Interviews Touch on Weak Economy," *The Wall Street Journal,* January 3, 2012, p. B7.

72. N. P. Podsakoff, S. W. Whiting, P. M. Podsakoff, and P. Mishra, "Effects of Organizational Citizenship Behaviors on Selection Decisions in Employment Interviews," *Journal of Applied Psychology* 96 (2011), pp. 310–26.

73. See "Carefully Chosen References Can Give You an Edge," *Arizona Republic,* October 26, 2011, p. CL1.

74. Survey by Society for Human Resource Management, reported in J. Schramm, "Background Checking," *HR Magazine,* January 2005, p. 128.

75. A. Finder, "When a Risqué Online Persona Undermines a Chance for a Job," *The New York Times,* June 11, 2006, pp. A1, A24; and S. E. Needleman, "Job Hunters, Beware," *The Wall Street Journal,* February 2, 2010, p. D4.

76. M. Conlin, "You Are What You Post," *BusinessWeek,* March 27, 2006, pp. 52–53; and L. Nicita, "Fired Before You're Hired," *The Arizona Republic,* July 28, 2007, pp. E1, E5.

77. Associated Press, "Job Seekers Asked for Facebook Keys," *San Francisco Chronicle,* March 21, 2012, pp. D1, D2. For more

about the effects of social media on hiring, see S. Hananel, "Facebook Tricky for Employers, Workers," *Reno Gazette-Journal*, October 2, 2011, p. 5E; K. Weise, "Who Does Google Think You Are?" *Bloomberg Businessweek*, February 6–February 12, 2012, pp. 39–40; A. Townsend, "This Is Your Life," *Time*, February 13, 2012, pp. 34–39; L. Kwoh, "Workplace Crystal Ball, Courtesy of Facebook," *The Wall Street Journal*, February 21, 2012, p. B8; K. Pender, "Behavior on Social Networks Could Cost Students," *San Francisco Chronicle*, March 6, 2012, pp. D1, D5; K. Trinko, "Keep Your Hands Off of My Facebook Password," *USA Today*, March 14, 2012, p. 9A; and L. Andrews, *I Know Who You Are and I Saw What You Did: Social Networks and the Death of Privacy* (New York: Free Press, 2012).

78. M. Madden, *Privacy Management on Social Media Sites*, Pew Research Center, Pew Internet & American Life Project, February 24, 2012, www.pewinternet.org/~/media/Files/Reports/2012/PIP_Privacy_management_on_social_media_sites_022412.pdf (accessed March 19, 2012). See also J. Angwin, "Sites Are Accused of Privacy Failings," *The Wall Street Journal*, February 13, 2012, pp. B1, B8: B. Evangelista, "Is It Time to Unfriend?" *San Francisco Chronicle*, February 25, 2012, pp. D1, D3; and B. Ortutay, "Profile Pruning," *Reno Gazette-Journal*, February 28, 2012, p. 6A.

79. S. E. Needleman, "The New Trouble on the Line," *The Wall Street Journal*, June 2, 2009, pp. B7, B10.

80. D. S. Chapman, K. L. Uggerslev, and J. Webster, "Applicant Reactions Face-to-Face and Technology-Mediated Interviews: A Field Investigation," *Journal of Applied Psychology* 88 (2003), pp. 944–53.

81. See J. Levashina and M. A. Campion, "Measuring Faking in the Employment Interview: Development and Validation of an Interview Faking Behavior Scale," *Journal of Applied Psychology*, November 2007, pp. 1638–56.

82. E. D. Pursell, M. A. Campion, and S. R. Gaylord, "Structured Interviewing: Avoiding Selection Problems," *Personnel Journal*, November 1980.

83. M. C. Blackman, "Personality Judgment and the Utility of the Unstructured Employment Interview," *Basic and Applied Social Psychology* 24 (2002), pp. 241–50. See also B. W. Swider, M. R. Barrick, T. B. Harris, and A. C. Stoverink, " Managing and Creating an Image in the Interview: The Role of Interviewee Initial Impressions," *Journal of Applied Psychology* 96 (2011), pp. 1275–88.

84. A. Arredondo, "Prepare Yourself for the Behavioral Interview," *The Arizona Republic*, March 2, 2008, p. EC1; K. Weirick, "The Perfect Interview," *HR Magazine*, April 2008, pp. 85–88; and AllBusiness.com, "Interviewing Skills Will Help Land the Right Employee for Your Firm," *San Francisco Chronicle*, April 9, 2008, p. C4. Some other articles useful for interviewees are C. Cadwell, C. Binkley, "Tassels, Pantsuits, and Other Interview Don'ts," *The Wall Street Journal*, January 17, 2008, p. D8; J. S. Lublin, "Notes to Interviewers Should Go Beyond a Simple Thank You," *The Wall Street Journal*, February 15, 2008, p. B1; M. Weinstein, "You're Hired!" *Training*, July/August 2011, pp. 34–37; A. Bryant, "A Deal-Breaker Question for Job Interviews," *The New York Times*, August 28, 2011, p. BU-2; Y. Gonzalez, "Prepare for the Tough Questions," *The Arizona Republic*, November 13, 2011, p. EC1; V. Kaskey, "5 Tips to Make a Great First Impression," *The Arizona Republic*, November 6, 2011, p. EC1; A. Bruzzese, "Your First 'Hello' Can Make or Break a Job Search," *Reno Gazette-Journal*, February 23, 2012, p. 6A.

85. H. Lancaster, "Making a Good Hire Takes a Little Instinct and a Lot of Research," *The Wall Street Journal*, March 3, 1998, p. B1.

86. L. G. Otting, "Don't Rush to Judgment," *HR Magazine*, January 2004, pp. 95–98.

87. M. P. Cronin, "This Is a Test," *Inc.*, August 1993, pp. 64–68.

88. J. S. Lublin, "What Won't You Do for a Job?" *The Wall Street Journal*, June 2, 2009, pp. B7, B11.

89. M. J. Frase, "Smart Selections," *HR Magazine*, December 2007, pp. 63–67.

90. T. Gutner, "Applicants' Personalities Put to the Test," *The Wall Street Journal*, August 26, 2008, p. D4.

91. For more about skills testing, see J. T. Arnold, "Getting Facts Fast," *HR Magazine*, February 2008, pp. 57–62.

92. J. Hodges, "a) Doctor b) Builder c) Cop d) HELP!" *The Wall Street Journal*, April 22, 2010, p. D2.

93. D. P. Shuit, "At 60, Myers-Briggs Is Still Sorting Out and Identifying People's Types," *Workforce Management*, December 2003, pp. 72–74.

94. S. Adler, "Personality Tests for Salesforce Selection: Worth a Fresh Look," *Review of Business*, Summer/Fall 1994, pp. 27–31.

95. Scott Erker, Development Dimensions International, reported in Gutner, "Applicants' Personalities Put to the Test," 2008.

96. "Personality Assessment Soars at Southwest," *Training*, January 2008, p. 14.

97. "Out of Sight, Yes. Out of Mind, No," *BusinessWeek*, February 18, 2008, p. 60.

98. Senior vice president of human resources Linda Matzigkeit, quoted in M. Bolch, "Nice Work," *HR Magazine*, February 2008, pp. 78–81.

99. B. Rose, "Critics Wary as More Jobs Hinge on Personality Tests," *Chicago Tribune*, October 31, 2004, p. 15.

100. S. Clifford, "The Science of Hiring," *Inc.*, August 2006, pp. 90–98.

101. V. Knight, "More Employers Are Using Personality Tests as Hiring Tools," *CareerJournal.com*, March 21, 2006; www.career-journal.com/jobhunting/interviewing/20060321-knight.html (accessed March 15, 2012).

102. Society for Industrial & Organizational Psychology, website, www.siop.org/workplace/employment%20testing/testtypes.aspx (accessed March 15, 2012).

103. B. Roberts, "Your Cheating Heart," *HR Magazine*, June 2011, pp. 55–60.

104. For a discussion of some of these tests, see P. Bathurst, "Pre-Job Tests Weed Out Imperfect Fits," *The Arizona Republic*, January 28, 2007, p. EC1.

105. D. Cadrain, "Are Your Employee Drug Tests *Accurate?*" *HR Magazine*, January 2003, pp. 41–45.

106. P. Korkki, "Workers May Lie about Drug Use, but Hair Doesn't," *The New York Times*, December 13, 2009, Business section, p. 2.

107. S. Shellenbarger, "Companies Are Finding It Really Pays to Be Nice to Employees," *The Wall Street Journal*, July 22, 1998, p. B1. For more about *The Jungle*, see C. Phelps, "How Should We Teach 'The Jungle'?" *The Chronicle of Higher Education*, March 3, 2006, pp. B10–B11.

108. R. Rigby, "Balloons and Buddies That Help New Recruits Fit In," *Financial Times*, March 17, 2008, http://us.ft.com/ftgateway/superpage.ft?news_id=fto031720081550034310 (accessed March 15, 2012).

109. Brookings Institution, cited in Shellenbarger, "Companies Are Finding It Really Pays to Be Nice to Employees," 1998.

110. MCI Communications surveys, reported in Shellenbarger, 1998.

111. G. R. Jones, "Organizational Socialization as Information Processing Activity: A Life History Analysis," *Human Organization* 42, no. 4 (1983), pp. 314–20.

112. The *Global Workforce Study*, by consultancy Towers Perrin, found that only 21% of employees surveyed around the world are engaged in their work, meaning they are willing to go the extra mile to help their companies succeed. See Towers Perrin, *2007 Global Workforce Study: Key Facts and Figures*, www.towersperrin.com/tp/getwebcachedoc?webc=HRS/USA/2007/200710/GWS_Fact_Sheet_draft_10_9_07_v5.pdf

(accessed March 15, 2012). Also see S. Meisinger, "Management Holds Key to Employee Engagement," *HR Magazine,* February 2008, p. 8.

113. C. McNamara, "Employee Training and Development: Reasons and Benefits," Free Management Library, 1999; www.managementhelp.org/trng_dev/basics/reasons.htm (accessed March 15, 2012). See also "Training Top 125 2008," *Training,* February 2008, pp. 76–111.

114. See "Training: 2007 Industry Report," *Training,* November/December 2007, pp. 8–24; and I. Bakir and S. Carliner, "Training Spending Stuck in Neutral," *Training,* February 2010, pp. 16–20.

115. For more about the coming revolution in online learning, see D. Brooks, "The Campus Tsunami," *The New York Times,* May 4, 2012, p. A23.

116. R. Van Liew, quoted in "E-Learning's Dirty Little Secret," *Training,* February 2006, p. 6. See also J. Gordon, "Seven Revelations about E-Learning," *Training,* April 2006, pp. 28–31.

117. B. Muirhead, "Looking at Net Colleges" [letter], *USA Today,* November 12, 1999, p. 14A.

118. For a discussion from a training standpoint of how the brain learns, see A. Fox, "The Brain at Work," *HR Magazine,* March 2008, pp. 37–42.

119. "What If You Held a Training Session and No One Showed Up?" *Training,* January 2006, p. 10.

120. Survey of workers at Ernst & Young, reported in B. Hite, "Employers Rethink How They Give Feedback," *The Wall Street Journal,* October 13, 2008, p. B5.

121. S. A. Culbert and L. Rout, *Get Rid of Performance Reviews! How Companies Can Stop Intimidating, Start Managing—and Focus on What Really Matters* (New York: Business Plus, 2010).

122. S. A. Culbert, "Yes, Everyone Really Does Hate Performance Reviews," *The Wall Street Journal,* April 19, 2010, http://finance.yahoo.com/career-work/article/109343/yes-everyone-really-does-hate-performance-reviews (accessed March 15, 2012).

123. See L. Kwoh, "Difficult Bosses Hurt Workers' Motivation," *The Wall Street Journal,* February 29, 2012, p. B8.

124. R. E. Silverman, "Work Reviews Losing Steam," *The Wall Street Journal,* December 19, 2011, p. B7.

125. D. J. Cohen, "HR Metrics: A Must," *HR Magazine,* February 2003, p. 136. On the subject of quantifying performance appraisals, see also K. Tyler, "Evaluating Values," *HR Magazine,* April 2011, pp. 57–61.

126. The term "Munchausen at work" was created by Georgia Institute of Technology business professor Nathan Bennett. See N. Bennett, "Munchausen at Work," *Harvard Business Review,* November 16, 2007, pp. 24–25

127. J. McGregor, "Job Review in 140 Keystrokes," *BusinessWeek,* March 23 & 30, 2009, p. 58.

128. A meta-analysis of 24 360-degree feedback studies appears in J. W. Smither, M. London, and R. R. Reilly, "Does Performance Improve Following Multisource Feedback? A Theoretical Model, Meta-Analysis, and Review of Empirical Findings," *Personnel Psychology,* Spring 2005, p. 33.

129. D. E. Coates, "Don't Tie 360 Feedback to Pay," *Training,* September 1998, pp. 68–78. See also A. S. Wellner, "Everyone's a Critic," *Inc.,* July 2004, pp. 38, 41; and W. C. Byham, "Fixing the Instrument," *Training,* July 2004, p. 50.

130. "Dell: Home Schooled by the Brass," *BusinessWeek Online,* October 10, 2005; www.businessweek.com/magazine/content/05_41/b3954007.htm (accessed March 15, 2012).

131. C. S. Peck, "360-Degree Feedback: How to Avoid a Disaster," Workinfo.com, www.workinfo.com/free/downloads/71.htm (accessed March 15, 2012).

132. L. Kwoh, "'Rank and Yank' Retains Vocal Fans," *The Wall Street Journal,* January 31, 2012, p. B6.

133. S. Scherreik, "Your Performance Review: Make It Perform," *BusinessWeek Online,* December 17, 2001, www.businessweek.com/magazine/content/01_51/b3762136.htm?chan=search (accessed March 15, 2012); and J. McGregor, "The Struggle to Measure Performance," *BusinessWeek Online,* January 9, 2006, www.businessweek.com/magazine/content/06_02/b3966060.htm?chan=search (accessed March 15, 2012). See also criticism of forced ranking in J. Pfeffer and R. I. Sutton, *Hard Facts, Dangerous Half-Truths & Total Nonsense: Profiting from Evidence-Based Management* (Boston: Harvard Business School Press, 2006).

134. Study by the Institute for Corporate Productivity, reported in Kwoh, "'Rank and Yank' Retains Vocal Fans," 2012.

135. L. A. Bossidy, "What Your Leader Expects of You," *Harvard Business Review,* April 3, 2007, pp. 58–65.

136. Adapted from D. L. McClain, "Tricks for Motivating the Pay to Motivate the Ranks," *The New York Times,* November 15, 1998, sec. 3, p. 5.

137. Bureau of Labor Statistics, "Employer Costs for Employee Compensation—December 2011," *Economic News Release,* March 14, 2012, www.bls.gov/news.release/ecec.nr0.htm (accessed March 15, 2012).

138. W. Kirn, "More Than a Numbers Game," *The New York Times Magazine,* May 10, 2009, pp. 13–14.

139. For a discussion of workplace discipline, see L. E. Atwater, J. F. Brett, and A. C. Charles, "The Delivery of Workplace Discipline: Lessons Learned," *Organizational Dynamics* 36 (2007), pp. 392–403.

140. A. Sherman, "Do You Feel Like You've Hit a Brick Wall at Work?" *The Arizona Republic,* March 21, 2010, p. C1.

141. M. Conlin, "When the Laid-Off Are Better Off," *BusinessWeek,* November 2, 2009, p. 65.

142. D. Mattioli, "Layoff Sign: Boss's Cold Shoulder," *The Wall Street Journal,* October 23, 2008, p. D6.

143. A. Fisher, "Dumping Troublemakers, and Exiting Gracefully," *Fortune,* February 15, 1999, p. 174.

144. C. Hymowitz, "Why Managers Take Too Long to Fire Employees," *San Francisco Examiner,* February 21, 1999, p. J-2; reprinted from *The Wall Street Journal.*

145. For a discussion of the threat of litigation attending dismissals, see M. Orey, "Fear of Firing," *BusinessWeek,* April 23, 2007, pp. 52–62.

146. R. Moss Kanter, "Show Humanity When You Show Employees the Door," *The Wall Street Journal,* September 21, 1997, p. A22.

147. Moss Kanter, 1997.

148. H. Benson, "Porters Found Road to Success Aboard Nation's 'Rolling Hotels,'" *San Francisco Chronicle,* February 11, 2009, pp. A1, A12.

149. S. Greenhouse, "Union Membership Rate Fell Again in 2011," *The New York Times,* January 28, 2012, p. B3.

150. R. Reich, "Jobs Growing Slowly, Wages Falling Fast," *San Francisco Chronicle,* March 13, 2011, p. F8.

151. L. Uchitelle, "Unions Yield on Wage Scales to Preserve Jobs," *New York Times,* November 19, 2010, www.nytimes.com/2010/11/20/business/20/wages.html (accessed March 15, 2012).

CHAPTER 10

1. T. Peters, "A Brawl with No Rules," *Forbes ASAP,* February 21, 2000, p. 155.

2. M. McGuinn, quoted in C. Hymowitz, "Task of Managing in Workplace Takes a Careful Hand," *The Wall Street Journal,* July 1, 1997, p. B1.

3. S. Hamm, "Speed Demons," *BusinessWeek,* March 27, 2006, pp. 68–75. See also J. McGregor, "The World's Most Innovative Companies," *BusinessWeek,* April 24, 2006, pp. 63–74.

4. Hymowitz, "Task of Managing in Workplace Takes a Careful Hand," 1997.

5. M. Weinstein, "Innovate or Die Trying," *Training Magazine,* May 2006, pp. 38–44; D. Hall, "The Customer Is Clueless," *BusinessWeek SmallBiz,* Spring 2006, p. 20; D. Brady, "Ideas That Bloom," *BusinessWeek SmallBiz,* Spring 2006, pp. 46–53; and P. Loewe and J. Dominiquini, "Overcoming the Barriers to Effective Innovation," *Strategy & Leadership* 34, no. 1 (2006), pp. 24–31.

6. Anthony Creed, quoted in D. Kirkpatrick, "Throw It at the Wall and See If It Sticks," *Fortune,* December 12, 2005, pp. 142–50.

7. Bruce Judson, quoted in J. M. Pethokoukis, "Bootstrapping Your Way into Business," *U.S. News & World Report,* March 27, 2006, p. 58. See also M. Bandyk, "Launching a Start-Up? Here's What Really Works," *U.S. News & World Report,* February 18, 2008, p. 58.

8. K. Stebbins, "Take a Risk," *Northern Nevada Healthy Living,* February 2008, p. 1.

9. E. Hoffer, *Ordeal of Change* (New York: Harper & Row, 1963).

10. J. Collins, "How the Mighty Fall," *BusinessWeek,* May 24, 2009, pp. 26–38. Collins is the author of *How the Mighty Fall: And Why Some Companies Never Give In* (New York: HarperCollins, 2009).

11. P. Drucker, "The Future That Has Already Happened," *The Futurist,* November 1998, pp. 16–18.

12. Drucker, 1998; J. C. Glenn, "Scanning the Global Situation and Prospects for the Future," *The Futurist,* January–February 2008, pp. 41–46; M. J. Cetron and O. Davies, "Trends Shaping Tomorrow's World: Forecasts and Implications for Business, Government, and Consumers (Part One), *The Futurist,* March–April 2008, pp. 35–52; M. J. Cetron and O. Davies, "Trends Shaping Tomorrow's World: Forecasts and Implications for Business, Government, and Consumers (Part Two), *The Futurist,* May–June 2008, pp. 35–50; M. Richarme, "Ten Forces Driving Business Futures," *The Futurist,* July–August 2009, pp. 40–43; and N. Easton, "*Fortune*'s Guide to the Future," *Fortune,* January 16, 2012, pp. 45–57.

13. Some of these trends are based on K. Albrecht, "Eight Supertrends Shaping the Future of Business," *The Futurist,* September–October 2006, pp. 25–29.

14. C. Anderson, quoted in A. T. Saracevic, "Economic Theories in 'The Long Tail' Don't Deserve Short Shrift," *San Francisco Chronicle,* July 16, 2006, pp. F1, F5. See also C. Anderson, *The Long Tail: Why the Future of Business Is Selling Less of More* (New York: Hyperion, 2006).

15. C. M. Christensen, *The Innovator's Dilemma: When New Technologies Cause Great Firms to Fail* (Boston, MA: Harvard Business School Press, 1997). See also F. Arner and R. Tiplady, "'No Excuse Not to Succeed,'" *BusinessWeek,* May 10, 2004, pp. 96–98.

16. L. Whitney, "Apple, Android Surge in 2010; Nokia, RIM Slip," *CNET News,* February 7, 2011, http://news.cnet.com/8301-13579_3-20030831-37.html (accessed March 23, 2012); and C. Lawton and Y.-H. Kim, "Nokia Updates Smartphones," *The Wall Street Journal,* August 25, 2011, p. B5.

17. D. ben-Aaron and M. Campbell, "There's No Camera, but Plenty of Rubles," *Bloomberg Businessweek,* October 3–October 9, 2011, pp. 42–43. See also "Nokia to Reduce Product Line-Up Further in Transition, Elop Says," *Bloomberg Businessweek,* February 28, 2012, http://news.businessweek.com/article.asp?documentKey=1376-M03WJU6JIK0Y01-7PG10DKNKIRFV9BUK6JGHS6A7C (accessed March 23, 2012).

18. P. Engardio, "The Future of Outsourcing," *BusinessWeek,* January 30, 2006, pp. 50–58.

19. C. Hawley, "Mexico Takes on More Aircraft Construction," *USA Today,* April 7, 2008, p. 11A.

20. M. Bandyk, "Now Even Small Firms Can Go Global," *U.S. News & World Report,* March 10, 2008, p. 52.

21. S. Lohr, "Global Strategy Stabilized I.B.M. During Downturn," *The New York Times,* April 20, 2010, p. B2.

22. K. Bradsher, "China Drawing High-Tech Research from U.S.," *The New York Times,* March 18, 2010, pp. A1, A14.

23. Albrecht, "Eight Supertrends Shaping the Future of Business," 2006. See also T. O'Driscoll, "Join the Webvolution," *Training,* February 2008, p. 24.

24. A. Toffler and H. Toffler, *Revolutionary Wealth* (New York: Alfred A. Knopf, 2006). Also see T. H. Davenport, L. Prusak, and B. Strong, "Putting Ideas to Work," *The Wall Street Journal,* March 10, 2008, p. R11.

25. *Capitalizing on Complexity: Insights from the Global Chief Executive Officer Survey,* International Business Machines, Somers, New York, 2010, http://public.dhe.ibm.com/common/ssi/ecm/en/gbe03297usen/GBE03297USEN.PDF (accessed March 23, 2012).

26. B. Tomson and M. Peters, "'Pink Slime' Defenders Line Up," *The Wall Street Journal,* March 29, 2012, pp. B1, B2.

27. R. Gold, B. Casselman, and G. Chazan, "Oil Well Lacked Safeguard Device," *The Wall Street Journal,* April 29, 2010, pp. A1, A8; S. Power and J. R. Emshwiller, "Investigators Focus on Failed Device," *The Wall Street Journal,* May 6, 2010, p. A5; and D. Vergano, "New Equipment Headed to Battle Oil Spill," *USA Today,* May 6, 2010, p. 5A.

28. Kenneth Arnold of K Arnold Consulting, quoted in Vergano, "New Equipment Headed to Battle Oil Spill," 2010.

29. P. Robertson, D. Roberts, and J. Porras, "Dynamics of Planned Organizational Change: Assessing Empirical Support for a Theoretical Model," *Academy of Management Journal* 36, no. 3 (1993), p. 619.

30. B. Horovitz, "Burger King Tests Home Delivery," *USA Today,* January 17, 2012, p. 3B.

31. S. Clifford, "Go Directly, Digitally to Jail? Classic Toys Learn New Clicks," *The New York Times,* February 26, 2012, News section, pp. 1, 4.

32. K. Pender, "Online Bank's 1st S.F. Branch a Café," *San Francisco Chronicle,* December 29, 2011, pp. D1, D6.

33. N. Wingfield, "Thinking Outside the Redbox," *The New York Times,* February 18, 2012, pp. B1, B2.

34. Andy Grove of Intel, quoted in L. Berlin, "A Look at Apple through the Years: Never Afraid to Change Its Direction," *San Francisco Chronicle,* January 15, 2008, pp. C1, C2.

35. "Millennials: Portrait of Generation Next," Pew Research Center, February 24, 2010, http://pewresearch.org/millennials (accessed March 23, 2012); K. K. Myers and K. Sadaghiani, "Millennials in the Workplace: A Communication Perspective on Millennials' Organizational Relationships and Performance," *Journal of Business Psychology,* June 2010, pp. 225–38; L. S. Rikleen, "Creating Tomorrow's Leaders: The Expanding Roles of Millennials in the Workplace," *Executive Briefing Series,* Boston College Center for Work & Family, www.bc.edu/content/dam/files/centers/cwf/pdf/BCCWF%20EBS-Millennials%20FINAL.pdf (accessed March 23, 2012); and J. Mandese, "MTV Studies Millennials in the Workplace: Uses It to Transform Its Own, Maybe Even Yours," *Media Daily News,* March 15, 2012, www.mediapost.com/publications/article/169980/mtv-studies-millennials-in-the-workplace-uses-it.html (accessed March 23, 2012).

36. K. Talley, "Wal-Mart Ramps Up Online Efforts Globally," *The Wall Street Journal,* April 7, 2010, p. B6; Mike Duke, interviewed by M. Bartiromo, "Wal-Mart CEO Has Global View," *USA Today,* September 19, 2011, p. 3B; and O. Schell, "How Walmart Is Changing China, and Vice Versa," *The Atlantic,* December 2011, pp. 80–98.

37. W. M. Welch, "Secondhand Shops at Forefront of Economic Pinch," *USA Today,* April 22, 2010, p. 3A.

38. M. Esterl, "MillerCoors Lite Brew Brings Big Challenge to New Chief," *The Wall Street Journal,* December 19, 2011, p. B6;

and M. Esterl, "Introducing Iced-Tea Beer," *The Wall Street Journal*, March 7, 2012, p. B1.

39. J. Brinkley, "West Needs to Stand Up to China, End Counterfeiting," *San Francisco Chronicle*, April 25, 2010, p. E8; A. Jacobs, "Rampant Fraud Threat to China's Brisk Ascent," *The New York Times*, October 6, 2010, www.nytimes.com/2010/10/07/world/asia/07fraud.html?pagewanted=all (accessed March 23, 2012); and L. Lim, "Plagiarism Plague Hinders China's Scientific Ambition," *npr.org*, August 3, 2011, www.npr.org/2011/08/03/138937778/plagiarism-plague-hinders-chinas-scientific-ambition (accessed March 23, 2012).

40. T. Aeppel, "Show Stopper: How Plastic Cork Popped the Cork Monopoly," *The Wall Street Journal*, May 1–2, 2010, pp. A1, A10.

41. P. Dvorak, "Companies Seek Shareholder Input on Pay Practices," *The Wall Street Journal*, April 6, 2009, p. B4.

42. D. Welch, "For Dan Akerson, a Magic Moment to Remake GM," *Bloomberg Businessweek*, January 24–January 30, 2011, pp. 21–22; and J. Shambora, A. Lashinsky, B. Gimbel, and J. Schlosser, "A View from the Top," *Fortune*, March 16, 2009, p. 110.

43. J. E. Vascellaro, "Audit Faults Apple Supplier," *The Wall Street Journal*, March 30, 2012, pp. B1, B2.

44. B. McKay, "Obesity-Linked Cancers Increase," *The Wall Street Journal*, March 29, 2012, p. A3; and S. Price, "Ante Up for Wellness," *HR Magazine*, February 2012, pp. 40–42.

45. S. E. Needleman, "Business Owners Try to Motivate Employees," *The Wall Street Journal*, January 14, 2010, p. B5.

46. V. Foley, director of Lee Hecht Harrison, quoted in E. Zimmerman, "As a New Manager, Get to Know Your Team," *The New York Times*, December 20, 2009, Business section, p. 9. See also "APA Survey Finds Feeling Valued Linked to Well-Being and Performance," press release, American Psychological Association, March 8, 2012, www.apa.org/news/press/releases/2012/03/well-being.aspx (accessed March 23, 2012).

47. A recent study reports that people in powerful positions, such as managers, tend to dismiss others' advice when making decisions. See K. E. See, E. W. Morrison, N. B. Rothman and J. B. Soll, "The Detrimental Effects of Power on Confidence, Advice Taking, and Accuracy," *Organizational Behavior and Human Decision Processes*, November 2011, pp. 272–85.

48. "A World Transformed: What Are the Top 30 Innovations of the Last 30 Years?" *Knowledge@Wharton*, February 19, 2009, http://knowledge.wharton.upenn.edu/article.cfm?articleid=2163 (accessed March 23, 2012).

49. R. D. Hof, "Online Extra: Trading in a Cloud of Electrons," *BusinessWeek Online*, May 20, 2004, www.businessweek.com/@@TUSaZYUQTmOUSw0A/magazine/content/04_19/b3882621.htm (accessed March 23, 2012).

50. The term *Web 2* was popularized by Tim O'Reilly, CEO of O'Reilly Media Inc. See T. O'Reilly, "What Is Web 2.0?" O'Reilly, September 30, 2005; www.oreillynet.com/pub/a/oreilly/tim/news/2005/09/30/what-is-web-20.html (accessed March 23, 2012).

51. See W. E. Halal, "Technology's Promise: Highlights from the TechCast Project," *The Futurist*, November–December 2007, pp. 41–50; B. Charney, "Technological Gadgets Smarten Up," *The Wall Street Journal*, December 31, 2007, p. B3; L. Cauley, "Race Is On for Mobile Web's Pot of Gold," *USA Today*, January 10, 2008, pp. 1B, 2B; M. Mangalindan, "How We Shop," *The Wall Street Journal*, January 28, 2008, p. R3; E. Steel, "Target-Marketing Becomes More Communal," *The Wall Street Journal*, November 5, 2009, p. B10; B. Evangelista, "Retailers Use Social Media to Dangle Deals," *San Francisco Chronicle*, November 25, 2009, pp. D1, D3; S. Rosenbloom and K. A. Cullotta, "Buying, Selling, and Twittering All the Way," *The New York Times*, November 28, 2009, pp. B1, B4; K. Hannon, "How Viral Business Takes Off," *USA Today*, November 30, 2009, p. 4B; A. P. McAfee, interviewed by A. P. Raman, "How a Connected Workforce Innovates," *The Harvard Business Review*, December 2009, p. 80; S. E. Needleman, "Services Combine Social Media, Marketing," *The Wall Street Journal*, February 23, 2010, p. B7; and A. Levy and J. Galante, "Who Wants to Buy a Digital Elephant?" *Bloomberg Businessweek*, March 8, 2010, pp. 64–65.

52. R. D. Hof, "Web 2.0: The New Guy at Work," *BusinessWeek*, June 19, 2006, pp. 58–59.

53. See S. Baker, "Beware Social Media Snake Oil," *Bloomberg Businessweek*, December 15, 2009, pp. 49–51.

54. M. McArdle, "The Freeloaders," *The Atlantic*, May 2010, pp. 34–36.

55. M. Masnick and M. Ho, *The Sky Is Rising: A Detailed Look at the State of the Entertainment Industry*, January 12, 2012, www.techdirt.com/skyisrising (accessed March 23, 2012).

56. Adapted from R. Kreitner and A. Kinicki, *Organizational Behavior*, 10th ed. (New York: McGraw-Hill/Irwin, 2013), pp. 546–48.

57. This three-way typology of change was adapted from discussion in P. C. Nutt, "Tactics of Implementation," *Academy of Management Journal*, June 1986, pp. 230–61.

58. Radical organizational change is discussed by T. E. Vollmann, *The Transformational Imperative* (Boston: Harvard Business School Press, 1996); and J. A. Neal and C. L. Tromley, "From Incremental Change to Retrofit: Creating High-Performance Work Systems," *Academy of Management Executive*, February 1995, pp. 42–53.

59. Adapted in part from J. D. Ford, L. W. Ford, and A. D'Amelio, "Resistance to Change: The Rest of the Story," *Academy of Management Review*, April 2008, pp. 362–77.

60. See "Vulnerability and Resilience," *American Psychologist*, January 1996, pp. 22–28. See also T. Kiefer, "Feeling Bad: Antecedents and Consequences of Negative Emotions in Ongoing Change," *Journal of Organizational Behavior*, December 2005, pp. 875–97.

61. See R. Moss Kanter, "Managing Traumatic Change: Avoiding the 'Unlucky 13,'" *Management Review*, May 1987, pp. 23–24.

62. Details of this example are provided by B. Schlender, "Inside the Shakeup at Sony," *Fortune*, April 4, 2005, pp. 94–104.

63. K. Lewin, *Field Theory in Social Science* (New York: Harper & Row, 1951).

64. T. T. Lee, "Adopting a Personal Digital Assistant System: Application of Lewin's Change Theory," *Journal of Advanced Nursing*, August 2006, pp. 487–96; B. Garrett and G. Klein, "Value of Wireless Personal Digital Assistants for Practice: Perceptions of Advanced Practice Nurses," *Journal of Clinical Nursing*, August 2008, pp. 2146–54; and S. Bassendowski, P. Petrucka, L. Breitkreuz, J. Partyka, L. MacDougall, B. Hanson, and K. Ayers, "Integration of Technology to Support Nursing Practice: A Saskatchewan Initiative," *Online Journal of Nursing Informatics*, June 2011, http://ojni.org/issues/?p=635 (accessed March 23, 2012).

65. The role of learning within organizational change is discussed by C. Hendry, "Understanding and Creating Whole Organizational Change through Learning Theory," *Human Relations*, May 1996, pp. 621–41; and D. Ready, "Mastering Leverage, Leading Change," *Executive Excellence*, March 1995, pp. 18–19.

66. C. Goldwasser, "Benchmarking: People Make the Process," *Management Review*, June 1995, p. 40; and *Cambridge Advanced Learner's Dictionary* (Cambridge: Cambridge University Press, 2004), http://dictionary.cambridge.org/define.asp?key=94109&dict=CALD (accessed March 23, 2012).

67. Kreitner and Kinicki, *Organizational Behavior*, 2013, p. 536.

68. These errors are discussed by J. P. Kotter, "Leading Change: The Eight Steps to Transformation," in J. A. Conger, G. M. Spreitzer, and E. E. Lawler III, eds., *The Leader's Change Handbook* (San Francisco: Jossey-Bass, 1999), pp. 87–99.

69. The type of leadership needed during organizational change is discussed by S. Furst and D. M. Cable, "Employee Resistance to Organizational Change: Managerial Influence Tactics and Leader-Member Exchange," *Journal of Applied Psychology,* March 2008, pp. 453–62; and D. M. Herold, D. B. Fedor, S. Caldwell, and Y. Liu, "The Effects of Transformational and Change Leadership on Employees' Commitment to a Change: A Multilevel Study," *Journal of Applied Psychology,* March 2008, pp. 346–57.

70. Adapted from R. J. Campbell, "Change Management in Health Care," *The Health Care Manager* 27, 1 (2008), pp. 23–39.

71. See, for example, K. Belson, "NFL Concussion Suits May Be Test for Sport Itself," *The New York Times,* December 30, 2011, pp. A1, B10.

72. R. J. Baron, "What's Keeping Us So Busy in Primary Care? A Snapshot from One Practice," *New England Journal of Medicine,* April 29, 2010, pp. 1632–36. See also S. Lohr, "Study Shows Extent of 'Invisible Work' by Family Doctors, *The New York Times,* April 29, 2010, p. B3.

73. M. Fugate, A. Kinicki, and C. L. Scheck, "Coping with an Organizational Merger over Four Stages," *Personnel Psychology,* Winter 2002, pp. 905–28.

74. D. Reed, "United, Continental Plan Merger," *USA Today,* May 3, 2010, p. 1B.

75. Based on A. Walker, "Measuring Footprints," *Fast Company,* April 2008, pp. 59–60.

76. See "Change Management: The HR Strategic Imperative as a Business Partner," *Research Quarterly,* Fourth Quarter 2007, pp. 1–9; and D. A. Garvin, A. C. Edmondson, and F. Gino, "Is Yours a Learning Organization?" *Harvard Business Review,* March 2008, pp. 109–16.

77. W. G. Dyer, *Team Building: Current Issues and New Alternatives,* 3rd ed. (Reading, MA: Addison-Wesley, 1995).

78. See R. Rodgers, J. E. Hunter, and D. L. Rogers, "Influence of Top Management Commitment on Management Program Success," *Journal of Applied Psychology,* February 1993, pp. 151–55.

79. R. J. Schaffer and H. A. Thomson, "Successful Change Programs Begin with Results," *Harvard Business Review,* January–February 1992, pp. 80–89.

80. P. J. Robertson, D. R. Roberts, and J. I. Porras, "Dynamics of Planned Organizational Change: Assess Empirical Support for a Theoretical Model," *Academy of Management Journal,* June 1993, pp. 619–34.

81. C.-M. Lau and H.-Y. Ngo, "Organization Development and Firm Performance: A Comparison of Multinational and Local Firms," *Journal of International Business Studies,* First Quarter 2001, pp. 95–114.

82. A. G. Lafley, interviewed by R. O. Crockett in "How P&G Plans to Clean Up," *BusinessWeek,* April 13, 2009, p. 44.

83. Lafley, quoted in Crockett, 2009.

84. A. G. Lafley, interviewed by K. Dillon, "'I Think of My Failures as a Gift,'" *Harvard Business Review,* April 2011, pp. 68–74.

85. J. Welch and S. Welch, "Finding Innovation Where It Lives," *BusinessWeek,* April 21, 2008, p. 84.

86. This discussion was adapted from Kreitner and Kinicki, *Organizational Behavior,* 2013, p. 526, which is based on S. Berkun, *The Myths of Innovation* (Sebastapol, CA: O'Reilly Media, 2007).

87. See D. Kiley and C. Matlack, "Fiat: On the Road Back to America," *BusinessWeek,* April 20, 2009, p. 28.

88. R. Jana, "Inspiration from Emerging Economies," *BusinessWeek,* May 12, 2008, pp. 54–55.

89. J. McGregor, "The World's Most Innovative Companies," *BusinessWeek,* April 24, 2006, pp. 63–74.

90. Analysis by Kauffman Foundation, reported by D. Archer, "Learn to Innovate by Thinking Like an Entrepreneur," *Reno Gazette-Journal,* November 8, 2009, p. 13A.

91. A. V. Bhidé, quoted in G. Gendron, "The Origin of the Entrepreneurial Species," *Inc.,* February 2000, pp. 105–14.

92. Maxine Clark, quoted in D. Eng, "Who Built Build-a-Bear?" *Fortune,* March 19, 2012, pp. 49–52.

93. S. A. Shane, *The Illusions of Entrepreneurship: The Costly Myths That Entrepreneurs, Investors, and Policy Makers Live By* (New Haven, CT: Yale University Press, 2008).

94. Scott Shane, interviewed by J. Tozzi, "The Entrepreneurship Myth," *BusinessWeek,* January 23, 2008, www.businessweek.com/smallbiz/content/jan2008/sb20080123_809271.htm?chan=search (accessed March 23, 2012).

95. V. Wadhwa, R. Freeman, and B. Rissing, *Education and Tech Entrepreneurship,* May 2008, Ewing Marion Kauffman Foundation, www.kauffman.org/research-and-policy/education-and-tech-entrepreneurship.aspx (accessed March 23, 2012). See also S. Berfield, "The Truth about Tech Startups," *BusinessWeek,* May 19, 2008, p. 16.

96. R. Cohen, "Vive La Dolce Vita," *The New York Times,* April 16, 2006, sec. 4, pp. 1, 4.

97. "The 50 Most Innovative Companies 2010," *Bloomberg Businessweek,* April 26, 2010, http://bwnt.businessweek.com/interactive_reports/innovative_companies_2010/?chan=magazine+channel_special+report (accessed March 23, 2012).

98. C. Wilson, "Post-it Notes Have Stuck Around for a Reason," *USA Today,* April 21, 2010, p. 1D.

99. J. C. Collins and J. I. Porris, *Built to Last: Successful Habits of Visionary Companies* (New York: HarperBusiness, 1994). See also T. J. Martin, "Ten Commandments for Managing Creative People," *Fortune,* January 16, 1995, pp. 135–36.

100. B. Hindo, "At 3M, a Struggle between Efficiency and Creativity," *BusinessWeek,* June 2007, pp. 8IN–14IN.

101. D. Mattioli and K. Maher, "At 3M, Innovation Comes in Tweaks and Snips," *The Wall Street Journal,* March 1, 2010, pp. B1, B4.

102. "America's Most Admired Companies: The 50 All-Stars," *Fortune,* March 22, 2010, pp. 121–26 and March 19, 2012, p. 140. See also D. Weil, "Innovation Leader 3M Sees Growth Abroad," *MoneyNews,* April 28, 2011, www.moneynews.com/StreetTalk/3M-Post-ItNotes-Scotchtape-Minnesota/2011/04/28/id/394448 (accessed March 23, 2012).

103. J. Denrell, "Vicarious Learning, Undersampling of Failure, and the Myths of Management," *Organizational Science,* May–June 2003, pp. 227–43.

104. J. Freese, "Magical Misery Tour," *Fortune Small Business,* May 2008, p. 29.

105. T. J. Allen and S. I. Cohen, "Information Flow in Research and Development Laboratories," *Administrative Science Quarterly,* March 1969, pp. 12–19.

106. L. A. Bettencourt, "The Customer-Centered Innovation Map," *Harvard Business Review,* May 2008, p. 109.

107. L. Bossidy and R. Charan, with C. Burck, *Execution: The Discipline of Getting Things Done* (New York: Crown Business, 2002).

108. "The 50 Most Innovative Companies 2010," *Bloomberg Businessweek,* April 26, 2010, http://bwnt.businessweek.com/interactive_reports/innovative_companies_2010/?chan=magazine+channel_special+report (accessed March 23, 2012).

CHAPTER 11

1. *The Millennials: Confident. Connected. Open to Change,* Pew Research Center Publications, February 2010, www.pewresearch.org/millennials (accessed March 28, 2012); A. Lenhart, K. Purcell, A. Smith, and K. Zickuhr, *Social Media & Mobile Internet Use among Teens and Young Adults,* Pew Internet & American Life Project, February 3, 2010, www.pewinternet.org/Reports/2010/Social-Media-and-Young-Adults.aspx?r=1 (accessed March 28, 2012); S. Jayson, "'iGeneration' Has No

Off Switch," *USA Today,* February 10, 2010, pp. 1D, 2D; K. Palmer, "Talking to Gen Y about the New Culture of Thrift," *U.S. News & World Report,* March 2010, pp. 29–32; *Survey of Young Americans' Attitudes Toward Politics and Public Service,* 17th ed., March 9, 2010, Institute of Politics, Harvard University, www.iop.harvard.edu/Research-Publications/Polling/Spring-2010-Survey (accessed March 28, 2012); and C. Dugas, "'Generation Y' Faces Some Steep Financial Hurdles," *USA Today,* April 23–25, 2010, pp. 1A, 2A; T. Abate, "Survey Reveals Attitudes of Millennials Toward Work," *San Francisco Chronicle,* May 30, 2010, p. D3; B. Kowske and R. Rasche, *Attitude? What Attitude? The Evidence Behind the Work Attitudes of Millennials,* Kenexa High Performance Institute, August 11, 2011, www.kenexa.com/getattachment/9aafa3e9-ae99-4db1-8376-76449e41293e/Millennials.aspx (accessed March 28, 2012); and J. Mandese, "MTV Studies Millennials in the Workplace: Uses It to Transform Its Own, Maybe Even Yours," *MediaDailyNews,* March 12, 2012, www.mediapost.com/publications/article/169980/mtv-studies-millennials-in-the-workplace-uses-it.html (accessed March 28, 2012)

2. For a thorough discussion of personality psychology, see D. P. McAdams and J. L. Pals, "A New Big Five: Fundamental Principles for an Integrative Science of Personality," *American Psychologist,* April 2006, pp. 204–17.

3. The landmark report is J. M. Digman, "Personality Structure: Emergence of the Five-Factor Model," *Annual Review of Psychology* 41 (1990), pp. 417–40. Also see M. R. Barrick and M. K. Mount, "Autonomy as a Moderator of the Relationships between the Big Five Personality Dimensions and Job Performance," *Journal of Applied Psychology,* February 1993, pp. 111–18; C. Viswesvaran and D. S. Ones, "Measurement Error in 'Big Five Factors' Personality Assessment: Reliability Generalization across Studies and Measures," *Education and Psychological Measurement,* April 2000, pp. 224–35; and P. Sackett and F. Lievens, "Personnel Selection," *Annual Review of Psychology,* 2008, pp. 419–50.

4. M. R. Barrick and M. K. Mount, "The Big Five Personality Dimensions and Job Performance: A Meta-Analysis," *Personnel Psychology,* Spring 1991, pp. 1–26.

5. Barrick and Mount, 1991, p. 18; also see H. Moon, "The Two Faces of Conscientiousness: Duty and Achievement Striving in Escalation of Commitment Dilemmas," *Journal of Applied Psychology,* June 2001, pp. 533–40; and M. R. Barrick, G. L. Stewart, and M. Piotrowski, "Personality and Job Performance: Test of the Mediating Effects of Motivation among Sales Representatives," *Journal of Applied Psychology,* February 2002, pp. 43–51.

6. See F. P. Morgeson, M. A. Campion, R. L. Dipboye, J. R. Hollenbeck, K. Murphy, and N. Schmitt, "Reconsidering the Use of Personality Tests in Personnel Selection," *Personnel Psychology,* Autumn 2007, pp. 683–729; and D. Armstrong, "Malingerer Test Roils Personal-Injury Law," *The Wall Street Journal,* March 5, 2008, pp. A1, A13.

7. J. P. Thomas, D. S. Whitman, and V. Chockalingam, "Employee Proactivity in Organizations: A Comparative Meta-Analysis of Emergent Proactive Constructs," *Journal of Occupational & Organizational Psychology,* June 2010, pp. 275–300.

8. For an overall view of research on locus of control, see P. E. Spector, "Behavior in Organizations as a Function of Employee's Locus of Control," *Psychological Bulletin,* May 1982, pp. 482–97. The relationship between locus of control and other dimensions of personality is examined by R. E. Johnson, C. C. Rosen, and P. E. Levy, "Getting to the Core of Core Self-Evaluation: A Review and Recommendations," *Journal of Organizational Behavior,* April 2008, pp. 391–413.

9. See, for example, V. Gecas, "The Social Psychology of Self-Efficacy," in W. R. Scott and J. Blake, eds., *Annual Review of Sociology,* vol. 15 (Palo Alto, CA: Annual Reviews, 1989), pp. 291–316; and C. K. Stevens, A. G. Bavetta, and M. E. Gist, "Gender Differences in the Acquisition of Salary Negotiation Skills: The Role of Goals, Self-Efficacy, and Perceived Control," *Journal of Applied Psychology,* October 1993, pp. 723–35; and D. Eden and Y. Zuk, "Seasickness as a Self-Fulfilling Prophecy: Raising Self-Efficacy to Boost Performance at Sea," *Journal of Applied Psychology,* October 1995, pp. 628–35.

10. J. Barling and R. Beattie, "Self-Efficacy Beliefs and Sales Performance," *Journal of Organizational Behavior Management,* Spring 1983, pp. 41–51.

11. A. D. Stajkovic and F. Luthans, "Self-Efficacy and Work-Related Performance: A Meta-Analysis," *Psychological Bulletin,* September 1998, pp. 240–61.

12. For more on learned helplessness, see M. J. Martinko and W. L. Gardner, "Learned Helplessness: An Alternative Explanation for Performance Deficits," *Academy of Management Review,* April 1982, pp. 195–204; and C. R. Campbell and M. J. Martinko, "An Integrative Attributional Perspective of Employment and Learned Helplessness: A Multimethod Field Study," *Journal of Management* 24, no. 2 (998), pp. 173–200.

13. W. S. Silver, T. R. Mitchell, and M. E. Gist, "Response to Successful and Unsuccessful Performance: The Moderating Effect of Self-Efficacy on the Relationship between Training and Newcomer Adjustment," *Journal of Applied Psychology,* April 1995, pp. 211–25.

14. See J. V. Vancouver, K. M. More, and R. J. Yoder, "Self-Efficacy and Resource Allocation: Support for a Nonmonotonic, Discontinuous Model," *Journal of Applied Psychology,* January 2008, pp. 35–47.

15. The positive relationship between self-efficacy and readiness for retraining is documented in L. A. Hill and J. Elias, "Retraining Midcareer Managers: Career History and Self-Efficacy Beliefs," *Human Resource Management,* Summer 1990, pp. 197–217.

16. V. Gecas, "The Self-Concept," in R. H. Turner and J. F. Short Jr., eds., *Annual Review of Sociology,* vol. 8 (Palo Alto, CA: Annual Reviews, 1982); also see N. Branden, *Self-Esteem at Work: How Confident People Make Powerful Companies* (San Francisco: Jossey-Bass, 1998).

17. P. G. Dodgson and J. V. Wood, "Self-Esteem and the Cognitive Accessibility of Strengths and Weaknesses after Failure," *Journal of Personality and Social Psychology,* July 1998, pp. 178–97; and D. B. Fedor, J. M. Maslyn, W. D. Davis, and K. Mathieson, "Performance Improvement Efforts in Response to Negative Feedback: The Roles of Source Power and Recipient Self-Esteem," *Journal of Management,* January–February 2001, pp. 79–97.

18. B. R. Schlenker, M. F. Weigold, and J. R. Hallam, "Self-Serving Attributions in Social Context: Effects of Self-Esteem and Social Pressure," *Journal of Personality and Social Psychology,* May 1990, pp. 855–63; and P. Sellers, "Get Over Yourself," *Fortune,* April 2001, pp. 76–88.

19. D. A. Stinson, C. Logel, M. P. Zanna, J. G. Holmes, J. V. Wood, and S. J. Spencer, "The Cost of Lower Self-Esteem: Testing a Self- and Social-Bonds Model of Health," *Journal of Personality and Social Psychology,* March 2008, pp. 412–28.

20. J. W. McGuire and C. V. McGuire, "Enhancing Self-Esteem by Directed-Thinking Tasks: Cognitive and Affective Positivity Asymmetries," *Journal of Personality and Social Psychology,* June 1996, p. 1124.

21. M. Snyder and S. Gangestad, "On the Nature of Self-Monitoring: Matters of Assessment, Matters of Validity," *Journal of Personality and Social Psychology,* July 1986, p. 125.

22. Charlotte Beers, interviewed by A. Bryant, "The Best Scorecard Is the One That You Keep for Yourself," *The New York Times,* April 1, 2012, p. BU-2.

23. Data from M. Kilduff and D. V. Day, "Do Chameleons Get Ahead? The Effects of Self-Monitoring on Managerial Careers," *Academy of Management Journal*, August 1994, pp. 1047–60.

24. See F. Luthans, "Successful vs. Effective Managers," *Academy of Management Executive*, May 1988, pp. 127–32; also see W. H. Turnley and M. C. Bolino, "Achieving Desired Images While Avoiding Undesired Images: Exploring the Role of Self-Monitoring in Impression Management," *Journal of Applied Psychology*, April 2001, pp. 351–60.

25. J. D. Mayer, R. D. Roberts, and S. G. Barsade, "Human Abilities: Emotional Intelligence," *Annual Review of Psychology*, January 2008, http://ssrn.com/abstract=1082096 (accessed April 1, 2012).

26. D. Goleman, "What Makes a Leader," *Harvard Business Review*, November–December 1998, pp. 93–102.

27. See J. E. Stellar, V. M. Manzo, "M. W. Kraus, and D. Keltner, "Class and Compassion: Socioeconomic Factors Predict Responses to Suffering," *Emotion*, December 12, 2011, www.ncbi.nlm.nih .gov/pubmed/22148992 (accessed March 28, 2012).

28. The Personal Profile Analysis (PPA), by Thomas International, is described in M. Weinstein, "Emotional Evaluation," *Training*, July–August 2009, pp. 20–23.

29. See A. Chapman, "Empathy, Trust, Diffusing Conflict and Handling Complaints," *Businessballs.com*, www.businessballs.com/ empathy.htm (accessed March 28, 2012).

30. S. Fox and P. E. Spector, "Relations of Emotional Intelligence, Practical Intelligence, General Intelligence, and Trait Affectivity with Interview Outcomes: It's Not All Just 'G,'" *Journal of Organizational Behavior*, March 2000, pp. 203–20.

31. See B. Kidwell, D. M. Hardesty, B. R. Murtha, and S. Sheng, "Emotional Intelligence in Marketing Exchanges," *Journal of Marketing*, January 2011, pp 78–95.

32. See M. Rokeach, *Beliefs, Attitudes, and Values* (San Francisco: Jossey-Bass, 1968), p. 168.

33. M. Rokeach, *The Nature of Human Values* (New York: Free Press, 1973).

34. See "Survey: Work/Life Balance Off-Kilter in U.S.," *HR News*, September 15, 2010, Society for Human Resource Management, www.shrm.org/Publications/HRNews/Pages/ WorkLifeOffKilter.aspx; D. Meinert, "The Gift of Time," *HR Magazine*, November 2011, p. 37; and "Men, Too, Desire Work/Life Balance," *HR Disciplines*, December 6, 2011, Society for Human Resource Management, www.shrm.org/ hrdisciplines/benefits/Articles/Pages/WorkLifeMen.aspx (both accessed March 28, 2012).

35. M. Fishbein and I. Ajzen, *Belief, Attitude, Intention and Behavior: An Introduction to Theory and Research* (Reading, MA: Addison-Wesley Publishing, 1975), p. 6.

36. See M. Reid and A. Wood, "An Investigation into Blood Donation Intentions Among Non-Donors," *International Journal of Nonprofit and Voluntary Sector Marketing*, February 2008, pp. 31–43; and J. Ramsey, B. J. Punnett, and D. Greenidge, "A Social Psychological Account of Absenteeism in Barbados," *Human Resource Management Journal*, April 2008, pp. 97–117.

37. B. M. Shaw and J. Ross, "Stability in the Midst of Change: A Dispositional Approach to Job Attitudes," *Journal of Applied Psychology*, August 1985, pp. 469–80; see also J. Schaubroeck, D. C. Ganster, and B. Kemmerer, "Does Trait Affect Promote Job Attitude Stability?" *Journal of Organizational Behavior*, March 1996, pp. 191–96.

38. J. S. Becker, "Empirical Validation of Affect, Behavior, and Cognition as Distinct Components of Attitude," *Journal of Personality and Social Psychology*, May 1984, pp. 1191–205; the components or structure of attitudes is thoroughly discussed by A. P. Brief, *Attitudes in and around Organizations* (Thousand Oaks, CA: Sage, 1998), pp. 49–84.

39. L. Festinger, *A Theory of Cognitive Dissonance* (Stanford, CA: Stanford University Press, 1957).

40. R. Moss Kanter, "How Great Companies Think Differently," *Harvard Business Review*, November 2011, pp. 66–78.

41. A. H. Tangari, J. Kees, J. C. Andrews, and S. Burton, "Can Corrective Ad Statements Based on U.S. v. Philip Morris USA Inc. Impact Consumer Beliefs about Smoking?" *Journal of Public Policy & Marketing* 29, no. 2 (2010), pp. 153–169.

42. Adapted from R. Kreitner and A. Kinicki, *Organizational Behavior*, 10th ed. (New York: McGraw-Hill/Irwin, 2013), Figure 7-1, p. 181.

43. Definition adapted from C. M. Judd and B. Park, "Definition and Assessment of Accuracy in Social Stereotypes," *Psychological Review*, January 1993, p. 110. See also D. T. Wegener, J. K. Clark, and R. E. Petty, "Not All Stereotyping Is Created Equal: Differential Consequences of Thoughtful Versus Nonthoughtful Stereotyping," *Journal of Personality and Social Psychology*, January 2006, pp. 42–59.

44. B. P. Allen, "Gender Stereotypes Are Not Accurate: A Replication of Martin (1987) Using Diagnostic vs. Self-Report and Behavioral Criteria," *Sex Roles*, May 1995, pp. 583–600.

45. Work & Power Survey conducted by Elle and MSNBC.com, reported in E. Tahmincioglu, "Men Rule—At Least in Workplace Attitudes," *MSNBC*, March 8, 2007, www.msnbc.msn .com/id/17345308/ns/business-careers/t/men-rule-least-workplace-attitudes (accessed April 1, 2012); J. V. Sanchez-Hucles and D. D. Davis, "Women and Women of Color in Leadership," *American Psychologist*, April 2010, pp. 171–81; and S. Bruckmuller and N. R. Brandscombe, "How Women End Up on the 'Glass Cliff,'" *Harvard Business Review*, January–February 2011, p. 26.

46. J. D. Olian, D. P. Schwab, and Y. Haberfeld, "The Impact of Applicant Gender Compared to Qualifications on Hiring Recommendations: A Meta-Analysis of Experimental Studies," *Organizational Behavior and Human Decision Processes*, April 1988, pp. 180–95; and K. P. Carson, C. L. Sutton, and P. D. Corner, "Gender Bias in Performance Appraisals: A Meta-Analysis," paper presented at the 49th Annual Academy of Management Meeting, Washington, DC: 1989.

47. J. Landau, "The Relationship of Race and Gender to Managers' Ratings of Promotion Potential," *Journal of Organizational Behavior*, July 1995, pp. 391–400. See also I. H. Lang, "Have Women Shattered Corporate Glass Ceiling? No," *USA Today*, April 15, 2010, p. 11A.

48. R. A. Posthuma and M. A. Campion, "Age Stereotypes in the Workplace: Common Stereotypes, Moderators, and Future Research Directions" *Journal of Management*, February 2009, pp. 158–88.

49. J. Levitz and P. Shishkin, "More Workers Cite Age Bias after Layoffs," *The Wall Street Journal*, March 11, 2009, pp. D1, D2; and L. Wolgemuth, "When Age Bias Hinders the Job Hunt," *U.S. News & World Report*, October 2009, p. 72.

50. S. R. Rhodes, "Age-Related Differences in Work Attitudes and Behavior: A Review and Conceptual Analysis," *Psychological Bulletin*, March 1983, p. 38.

51. See T. W. H. Ng and D. C. Feldman, "The Relationship of Age to Ten Dimensions of Job Performance," *Journal of Applied Psychology*, March 2008, pp. 392–423; and R. J. Grossman, "Keep Pace with Older Workers," *HR Magazine*, May 2008, pp. 39–46.

52. J. J. Martocchio, "Age-Related Differences in Employee Absenteeism: A Meta-Analysis," *Psychology and Aging*, December 1989, pp. 409–14; and M. C. Healy, M. Lehman, and M. A. McDaniel, "Age and Voluntary Turnover: A Quantitative Review," *Personnel Psychology*, Summer 1995, pp. 335–45.

53. Central Intelligence Agency, *The World Factbook, 2010*, https:// www.cia.gov/library/publications/the-world-factbook/geos/us .html (accessed April 1, 2012).

54. L. A. Jacobsen, M. Kent, and M. Mather, "America's Aging Population," *Population Bulletin,* February 2011, Population Reference Bureau, www.prb.org/pdf11/aging-in-america.pdf (accessed April 1, 2012).

55. K. Helliker, "The Doctor Is Still In: Secrets of Health from a Famed 96-Year-Old Physician," *The Wall Street Journal,* March 8, 2005, p. D1.

56. Statistics are reported in Table A-20, "Employed Persons by Occupation, Race, Hispanic or Latino Ethnicity, and Sex," February 2012, in *Employment and Earnings,* U.S. Department of Labor, Bureau of Labor Statistics, www.bls.gov/web/empsit/cpseea20.pdf (accessed April 1, 2012).

57. Data analysis by D. D. Kallick, Fiscal Policy Institute, reported in J. Preston, "Immigrants in Work Force: Study Belies Image," *The New York Times,* April 16, 2010, pp. A1, A3.

58. J. C. Brigham, "Limiting Conditions of the 'Physical Attractiveness Stereotype': Attributions about Divorce," *Journal of Research and Personality* 14 (1980), pp. 365–75; H. Hatfield and S. Sprecher, *Mirror, Mirror ... The Importance of Looks in Everyday Life* (Albany, NY: State University of New York Press, 1986).

59. I. Waismel-Manor and Y. Tsfati, "Do Attractive Congresspersons Get More Media Coverage?" *Political Communication* 28 (2011), pp. 440–63. See also S. Roberts, "Study Says Looks Matter as TV Covers Congress," *The New York Times,* January 6, 2012, p. A15.

60. M. M. Clifford and E. H. Walster, "The Effect of Physical Attractiveness on Teacher Expectation," *Sociology of Education* 46 (1973), pp. 248–58.

61. Varian, "Beauty and the Fattened Wallet," *The New York Times,* April 6, 2006, www.nytimes.com/2006/04/06/business/06scene.html?ref=halrvarian (accessed April 1, 2012).

62. D. S. Hamermesh and J. Abrevaya, "Beauty Is the Promise of Happiness?" March 1, 2011. IZA Discussion Paper No. 5600, Institute for the Study of Labor, Bonn, Germany, http://ssrn.com/abstract=1801666 (accessed April 1, 2012).

63. D. S. Hamermesh, "Ugly? You May Have a Case," *The New York Times,* August 27, 2011, www.nytimes.com/2011/08/28/opinion/sunday/ugly-you-may-have-a-case.html (accessed April 1, 2012).

64. D. S. Hamermesh, *Beauty Pays: Why Attractive People Are More Successful* (Princeton, NJ: Princeton University Press, 2011).

65. Hamermesh, quoted in S. Jayson, "The Ugly Truth: Good Looks Make You Richer, Happier," *USA Today,* March 30, 2011, p. 2B.

66. M. M. Mobius and T. S. Rosenblat, "Why Beauty Matters," *American Economic Review,* March 2006, pp. 222–35.

67. H. R. Varian, "Beauty and the Fattened Wallet," 2006.

68. M. W. Howard and M. J. Kahana, "A Distributed Representation of Temporal Context," *Journal of Mathematical Psychology* 46 (2002), pp. 269–99.

69. T. Odean and B. M. Barber, "All That Glitters: The Effect of Attention and News on the Buying Behavior of Individual and Institutional Investors," *The Review of Financial Studies* 21, no. 2 (2008), pp. 785–818. See also P. Sullivan, "Want an Active Investment Manager? Here's What to Look For," *The New York Times,* March 30, 2012, p. B8.

70. Business manager Gopal Sharma, quoted in R. Subramanian, "Get Noticed by Your Bosses in Second Half for a Good Bonus," *The Economic Times* (India), March 30, 2012, http://articles.economictimes.indiatimes.com/2012-03-30/news/31260832_1_bonuses-hr-manager-quantum (accessed April 2, 2012).

71. D. Sengupta, "Adobe Systems Set to Scrap Annual Appraisals, to Rely on Regular Feedback to Reward Staff," *The Economic Times* (India), March 27, 2012, http://articles.economictimes.indiatimes.com/2012-03-27/news/31245058_1_adobe-systems-appraisal-feedback (accessed April 2, 2012).

72. S. J. Linton and L. E. Warg, "Attributions (Beliefs) and Job Satisfaction Associated with Back Pain in an Industrial Setting," *Perceptual and Motor Skills,* February 1993, pp. 51–62.

73. W. S. Silver, T. R. Mitchell, and M. E. Gist, "Responses to Successful and Unsuccessful Performance: The Moderating Effect of Self-Efficacy on the Relationship between Performance and Attributions," *Organizational Behavior and Human Decision Processes,* June 1995, pp. 286–99; and D. Dunning, A. Leuenberger, and D. A. Sherman, "A New Look at Motivated Inference: Are Self-Serving Theories of Success a Product of Motivational Forces?" *Journal of Personality and Social Psychology,* July 1995, pp. 58–68.

74. C. Forelle and S. Fidler, "Europe's Original Sin," *The Wall Street Journal,* March 3, 2010, p. A1.

75. See D. Eden and Y. Zuk, "Seasickness as a Self-Fulfilling Prophecy: Raising Self-Efficacy to Boost Performance at Sea," *Journal of Applied Psychology,* October 1995, pp. 628–35. For a thorough review of research on the Pygmalion effect, see D. Eden, *Pygmalion in Management: Productivity as a Self-Fulfilling Prophecy* (Lexington, MA: Lexington Books, 1990), ch. 2.

76. L. Iorio, quoted in Dutton, "Yes! It's Monday," 2009, p. 32.

77. D. B. McNatt, "Ancient Pygmalion Joins Contemporary Management: A Meta-Analysis of the Result," *Journal of Applied Psychology,* April 2000, pp. 314–22. See also T. Inamori and F. Analoui, "Beyond Pygmalion Effect: The Role of Managerial Perception," *Journal of Management Development* 29 (2010), pp. 306–21.

78. These recommendations were adapted from J. Keller, "Have Faith—in You," *Selling Power,* June 1996, pp. 84, 86; and R. W. Goddard, "The Pygmalion Effect," *Personnel Journal,* June 1985, p. 10.

79. See J. K. Harter, F. L. Schmidt, and T. L. Hayes, "Business-Unit-Level Relationship between Employee Satisfaction, Employee Engagement, and Business Outcomes: A Meta-Analysis," *Journal of Applied Psychology,* April 2002, pp. 268–79. For another definition, see W. A. Kahn, "Psychological Conditions of Personal Engagement and Disengagement at Work," *Academy of Management Journal,* December 1990, p. 75.

80. W. H. Macey, B. Schneider, K. M. Barbera, and S. A. Young, *Employee Engagement: Tools for Analysis, Practice, and Competitive Advantage* (West Sussex, United Kingdom: Wiley-Blackwell, 2009), p. 20.

81. See W. H. Macey and B. Schneider, "The Nature of Employee Engagement," *Industrial and Organizational Psychology: Perspectives on Science and Practice,* 2008, pp. 3–30; and A. J. Wefald and R. G. Downey, "Job Engagement in Organizations: Fad, Fashion, or Folderol?" *Journal of Organizational Behavior,* January 2009, pp. 141–45. A proprietary measure of employee engagement is provided by Development Dimensions International, Inc.; see M. Phelps, "Is It Time to Rethink Employee Engagement?" *DDI White Paper,* www.ddiworld.com/products_services/e3.asp (accessed April 2, 2012).

82. See *5 Rules for Talent Management in the New Economy,* Watson Wyatt Worldwide, 2009, www.towerswatson.com/research/1354 (accessed April 2, 2012).

83. Results based on survey sent by the Hay Group and Bloomberg BusinessWeek.com to 1,863 global respondents in 1,109 organizations, reported in R. Lash and C. Huber, "2009 Best Companies for Leadership," Hay Group Webinar, February 18, 2010, www.rb.ru/dop_upload/file_2010-02-26_17.49.48_presentation_final.pdf (accessed April 2, 2012).

84. See W. H. Macy and B. Schneider, "The Meaning of Employee Engagement," *Industrial and Organizational Psychology,* March 2008, pp. 3–30.

85. C. A. Hartnell, A. Y. Lou, and A. Kinicki, "Organizational Culture and Organizational Effectiveness: A Meta-Analytic Investigation

of the Competing Values Framework's Theoretical Suppositions," *Journal of Applied Psychology* 96 (2011), pp. 677–95; and C. D'Angela, "In Post-Recession World, Recognition Boosts Recovery," *The Power of Incentives: Special Advertising Supplement in HR Magazine,* September 2010, pp. 93–97.

86. See Kahn, "Psychological Conditions of Personal Engagement and Disengagement at Work," 1990.

87. These five job dimensions are developed by researchers at Cornell University as part of the Job Descriptive Index. For a review of the development of the JDI, see P. C. Smith, L. M. Kendall, and C. L. Hulin, *The Measurement of Satisfaction in Work and Retirement* (Skokie, IL: Rand McNally, 1969).

88. See A. J. Kinicki, F. M. McKee-Ryan, C. A. Schriesheim, and K. P. Carson, "Assessing the Construct Validity of the Job Descriptive Index: A Review and Meta-Analysis," *Journal of Applied Psychology,* February 2002, pp. 14–32.

89. These figures come from the annual employee satisfaction survey by the Conference Board, reported in S. Shellenbarger, "Thinking Happy Thoughts at Work," *The Wall Street Journal,* January 27, 2010, p. D2.

90. Society for Human Resource Management, "Employee Job Satisfaction: The External Forces Influencing Employee Attitudes," *Workplace Visions,* Issue 4 (2011), pp. 1–4, www .shrm.org/Research/FutureWorkplaceTrends/Documents/ 11-0697%20Workplace_Visions_Issue4%20FINAL. pdf; and *2011 Employee Job Satisfaction and Engagement: Gratification and Commitment at Work in a Sluggish Economy,* a research report by the Society for Human Resource Management, www .shrm.org/Research/SurveyFindings/Articles/Documents/ 11-0618%20Job_Satisfaction_FNL.pdf (both accessed April 2, 2012).

91. P. Davidson, "Overworked and Underpaid?" *USA Today,* April 16, 2012, pp. 1A, 2A.

92. The various models are discussed in T. A. Judge, C. J. Thoresen, J. E. Bono, and G. K. Patton, "The Job Satisfaction–Job Performance Relationship: A Qualitative and Quantitative Review," *Psychological Bulletin,* May 2001, pp. 376–407. See also Kreitner and Kinicki, *Organizational Behavior,* 2013, pp. 168–70.

93. Ibid. Also see M. Riketta, "The Causal Relation between Job Attitudes and Performance: A Meta-Analysis of Panel Studies," *Journal of Applied Psychology,* March 2008, pp. 472–81.

94. Survey of adults conducted for Adecco Staffing North America, reported in K. Gurchiek, "Good News for Moms Reconsidering Work," *HR Magazine,* July 2006, p. 30.

95. See N. Podsakoff, J. A. LePine, and M. A. LePine, "Differential Challenge Stressor-Hindrance Stressor Relationships with Job Attitudes, Turnover Intentions, Turnover, and Withdrawal Behavior: A Meta-Analysis," *Journal of Applied Psychology,* March 2007, pp. 438–54; and M. Riketta, "Attitudinal Organizational Commitment and Job Performance: A Meta-Analysis," *Journal of Organizational Behavior,* March 2002, pp. 257–66.

96. See M. Riketta, "Attitudinal Organizational Commitment and Job Performance: A Meta-Analysis," *Journal of Organizational Behavior,* March 2002, pp. 257–66.

97. Meta-analysis across results summarizing 27,500 people can be found in R. W. Griffeth, P. W. Hom, and S. Gaertner: A Meta-Analysis of Antecedents and Correlates of Employee Turnover: Update, Moderator Tests, and Research Implications for the Next Millennium," *Journal of Management* 26 (2000), pp. 463–88.

98. See R. D. Hackett, "Work Attitudes and Employee Absenteeism: A Synthesis of the Literature," *Journal of Occupational Psychology,* 1989, pp. 235–48.

99. Results can be found in M. R. Barrick and R. D. Zimmerman, "Reducing Voluntary Turnover through Selection," *Journal of Applied Psychology,* January 2005, pp. 159–66.

100. Costs of turnover are discussed by R. W. Griffeth and P. W. Hom, *Retaining Valued Employees* (Thousand Oaks, CA: Sage, 2001).

101. Y. Lermusiaux, "Calculating the High Cost of Employee Turnover," www.ilogos.com/en/expertviews/articles/strategic/ 2003320007_YL.htm (accessed April 2, 2012). An automated program for calculating the cost of turnover can be found at "Calculate Your Turnover Costs," www.keepemployees.com/ turnovercalc.htm (accessed April 2, 2012).

102. Onboarding is discussed by T. Arnold, "Ramping Up Onboarding," *HR Magazine,* May 2010, pp. 75–76.

103. Techniques for reducing turnover are discussed by M. A. Tucker, "Show and Tell," *HR Magazine,* January 2012, pp. 51–53; E. Krell, "5 Ways to Manage High Turnover," *HR Magazine,* April 2012, pp. 63–65; and A. Quirk, "The Business Case for Flex," *HR Magazine,* April 2012, pp. 44–46.

104. D. W. Organ, "The Motivational Basis of Organizational Citizenship Behavior," in B. M. Staw and L. L. Cummings, eds., *Research in Organizational Behavior* (Greenwich, CT: JAI Press, 1990), p. 46.

105. See N. P. Podsakoff, S. W. Whiting, P. M. Podsakoff, and B. D. Blume, "Individual-and Organizational-Level Consequences of Organizational Citizenship Behaviors: A Meta-Analysis," *Journal of Applied Psychology,* January 2009, pp. 122–41; and D. S. Whitman, D. L. Van Rooy, and C. Viswesvaran, "Satisfaction, Citizenship Behaviors, and Performance in Work Units: A Meta-Analysis of Collective Relations," *Personnel Psychology,* Spring 2010, pp. 41–81.

106. D. S. Ones, "Introduction to the Special Issue on Counterproductive Behaviors at Work," *International Journal of Selection and Assessment* 10, no. 1–2 (2002), pp. 1–4. See also P. E. Spector and S. Fox, "Theorizing about the Deviant Citizen: An Attributional Explanation of the Interplay of Organizational Citizenship and Counterproductive Work Behavior," *Human Resource Management Review,* June 2010, pp. 132–43; K. Tyler, "Helping Employees Cool It," *HR Magazine,* April 2010, pp. 53–55; M. S. Hershcovis, "'Incivility, Social Undermining, Bullying . . . Oh My!': A Call to Reconcile Constructs within Workplace Aggression Research," *Journal of Organizational Behavior,* 32 (2010), pp. 499–519; and J. Wu and J. M. Lebreton, "Reconsidering the Dispositional Basis of Counterproductive Work Behavior: The Role of Aberrant Personality," *Personnel Psychology* 64 (2011), pp. 593–626.

107. J. Janove, "Jerks at Work," *HR Magazine,* May 2007, pp. 111–17.

108. S. Dilchert, D. S. Ones, R. D. Davis, and C. D. Rostow, "Cognitive Ability Predicts Objectively Measured Counterproductive Work Behaviors," *Journal of Applied Psychology,* May 2007, pp. 616–27.

109. J. R. Detert, L. K. Treviño, E. R. Burris, and M. Andiappan, "Managerial Modes of Influence and Counterproductivity in Organizations: A Longitudinal Business-Unit-Level Investigation," *Journal of Applied Psychology,* July 2007, pp. 993–1005.

110. B. Leonard, "Study: Bully Bosses Prevalent in U.S.," *HR Magazine,* May 2007, pp. 22, 28.

111. See M. Sandy Hershcovis and J. Barling, "Toward a Multi-Foci Approach to Workplace Aggression: A Meta-Analytic Review of Outcomes from Different Perpetrators," *Journal of Organizational Behavior,* January 2010, pp. 24–44; and J. Chamberlin, A. Novotney, E. Packard, and M. Price, "Enhancing Worker Well-Being," *Monitor on Psychology,* May 2008, pp. 26–29.

112. C. Kavanaugh, "'Murder by Proxy,'" *Royal Oak (Michigan) Daily Tribune,* April 19, 2010, www.dailytribune.com/articles/2010/ 04/19/news/doc4bc8dc24905c3220900250.txt (accessed April 2, 2012).

113. R. Brunswick, quoted in C. Hymowitz, "Bosses Have to Learn How to Confront Troubled Employees," *The Wall Street Journal,* April 23, 2007, p. B1.

114. Hymowitz, 2007.

115. Study by the Migration Policy Institute, Washington, DC, reported in L. Burton, "Illegal Immigration Impact on Economy Small, Group Says," *San Francisco Chronicle,* December 3, 2009, p. A24.

116. Study by David R. Hekman, *The Academy of Management Journal,* reported in "A Customer Bias in Favor of White Men," *The New York Times,* June 23, 2009, p. D6.

117. Data from Economic Policy Institute, reported in J. R. Hagerty, "Young Adults See Their Pay Decline," *The Wall Street Journal,* March 7, 2012, p. A3.

118. S. E. Page, *The Difference: How the Power of Diversity Creates Better Groups, Firms, Schools and Societies* (Princeton, NJ: Princeton University Press, 2007).

119. S. E. Page, quoted in C. Dreifus, "In Professor's Model, Diversity = Productivity," *The New York Times,* January 8, 2008, p. D2. See also G. A. Van Kleef and C. KI. W. De Dreu, "Bridging Faultlines by Valuing Diversity: Diversity Beliefs, Information, Elaboration, and Performance in Diverse Work Groups," *Journal of Applied Psychology,* September 2007, pp. 1189–99.

120. M. Loden, *Implementing Diversity* (Chicago: Irwin, 1996), pp. 14–15.

121. H. Collingwood, "Who Handles a Diverse Work Force Best?" *Working Woman,* February 1996, p. 25.

122. See A. Karr, "Work Week: A Special News Report about Life on the Job—and Trends Taking Shape There," *The Wall Street Journal,* June 1, 1999, p. A1. See also E. Bazar, "Prayer Leads to Disputes in Workplace," *USA Today,* October 16, 2008, p. 3A.

123. B. Schlender, "Peter Drucker Takes the Long View," *Fortune,* September 28, 1998, pp. 162–73.

124. M. McArdle, "Europe's Real Crisis," *The Atlantic,* April 2012, www.theatlantic.com/magazine/archive/2012/04/europe-8217-s-real-crisis/8915 (accessed April 2, 2012).

125. S. Theil, "The Incredible Shrinking Continent," *Newsweek,* March 1, 2010, pp. 38–39.

126. K. Bradsher, "Defying Global Slump, China Has Labor Shortage," *The New York Times,* February 26, 2010, p. A1; and K. Bradsher, "Two Sides to Labor in China," *The New York Times,* March 30, 2012, www.nytimes.com/2012/03/31/business/global/labor-shortage-complicates-changes-in-chinas-factories.html?pagewanted=all (accessed April 2, 2012).

127. M. Toossi, "Labor Force Projections to 2022: A More Slowly Growing Workforce," *Monthly Labor Review,* January 2012, www.bls.gov/opub/mlr/2012/01/art3full.pdf (accessed April 2, 2012).

128. E. Porter, "Stretched to Limit, Women Stall March to Work," *The New York Times,* March 2, 2006, pp. A1, C2.

129. M. Meece, "One in Four Businesses Calls the Owner 'Ma'am,'" *The New York Times,* November 5, 2009, p. B4.

130. L. Petracca, "Number of Female 'Fortune' 500 CEOs at Record High," *USA Today,* October 26, 2011, www.usatoday.com/money/companies/management/story/2011-10-26/women-ceos-fortune-500-companies/50933224/1 (accessed April 2, 2012).

131. F. Bass, "Women Make 77 Cents to Every $1 for a Man," *San Francisco Chronicle,* March 17, 2012, p. D2. See also U.S. Bureau of Labor Statistics, Department of Labor, *Highlights of Women's Earnings in 2010,* Report 1031, July 2011, www.bls.gov/cps/cpswom2010.pdf (accessed March 15, 2012).

132. Study by Hilary Lips, Radford University, reported in B. Morris, "How Corporate America Is Betraying Women," *Fortune,* January 10, 2005, pp. 64–74. See also C. Buck, "Author's Theory on Why Women Earn Less," *San Francisco Chronicle,* September 27, 2009, pp. D1, D4, reprinted from *Sacramento Bee.*

133. U.S. Census Bureau, 2010, reported in J. Malveaux, "More Female Grads, but What about Pay?" *USA Today,* May 13, 2011, p. 11A.

134. Association of Executive Search Consultants, *BlueSteps 2007 Diversity Report,* cited in J. D. McCool, "Diversity Pledges Ring Hollow," *BusinessWeek.com,* February 5, 2008, www.businessweek.com/managing/content/feb2008/ca2008025_080192.htm?chan=search (accessed April 2, 2012).

135. D. Brady, K. Isaacs, M. Reeves, R. Burroway, and M. Reynolds, "Sector, Size, Stability, and Scandal: Explaining the Presence of Female Executives in Fortune 500 Firms," *Gender in Management: An International Journal* 26, no. 1 (2011), pp. 84–105.

136. For further discussion of various aspects of the glass ceiling, see also R. Morris, "To Get Ahead, Own the Store," *The New York Times,* November 18, 2004, p. C10; R. E. Herzlinger, "A Corporate Push—Against Women," *USA Today,* December 7, 2004, p. 13A; C. H. Deutsch, "Are Women Responsible for Their Own Low Pay?" *The New York Times,* February 27, 2005, sec. 3, p. 7; T. L. O'Brien, "Up the Down Staircase," *The New York Times,* March 19, 2006, sec. 3, pp. 1, 4; E. White, "Why Few Women Run Plants," *The Wall Street Journal,* May 1, 2006, pp. B1, B5; and R. Parloff, "The War Over Unconscious Bias," *Fortune,* October 1, 2007, http://money.cnn.com/magazines/fortune/fortune_archive/2007/10/15/100537276/-index.htm (accessed February 2, 2010). See also K. Miner-Rubino and L. M. Cortina, "Beyond Targets: Consequences of Vicarious Exposure to Misogyny at Work," *Journal of Applied Psychology,* September 2007, pp. 1254–69.

137. B. R. Ragins, B. Townsend, and M. Mattis, "Gender Gap in the Executive Suite: CEOs and Female Executives Report on Breaking the Glass Ceiling," *Academy of Management Review,* February 1998, pp. 28–42.

138. R. Sharpe, "As Leaders, Women Rule," *BusinessWeek,* November 20, 2000, pp. 75–84.

139. K. Wisul, "The Bottom Line on Women at the Top," *BusinessWeek,* January 26, 2004; www.businessweek.com/bwdaily/dnflash/jan2004/nf20040126_3378_db035.htm (accessed April 2, 2012).

140. U.S. Census Bureau, reported in "Census: More Diversity, Slower Growth in U.S.A. 2050," *IMdiversity.com,* 2011, www.imdiversity.com/villages/asian/reference/census_2050_asian_projections.asp (accessed April 2, 2012).

141. "Table 691. Money Income of Households—Median Income by Race and Hispanic Origin, in Current and Constant (2009) Dollars: 1980 to 2009," U.S. Census Bureau, September 2010, www.census.gov/compendia/statab/2012/tables/12s0690.pdf (accessed April 2, 2012).

142. See Equal Employment Opportunity Commission, "Race-Based Charges FY 1997–FY 2009," www.eeoc.gov/eeoc/statistics/enforcement/race.cfm (accessed April 2, 2012); B. Leonard, "Web, Call Center Fuel Rise in EEOC Claims," *HR Magazine,* June 2008, p. 30; and M. Luo, "In Job Hunt, Even a College Degree Can't Close the Racial Gap," *The New York Times,* December 1, 2009, pp. A1, A4.

143. B. E. Whitley, Jr., and M. E. Kite, "Sex Differences in Attitudes toward Homosexuality: A Comment on Oliver and Hyde (1993)," *Psychological Bulletin,* January 1995, pp. 146–54.

144. October 1, 2003, study by Harris Interactive Inc. and Witeck Combs Communications Inc., reported in C. Edwards, "Coming Out in Corporate America," *BusinessWeek,* December 15, 2003; www.businessweek.com/print/magazine/content/03_50/b3862080.htm?bw (accessed February 2, 2010).

145. J. M. Croteau, "Research on the Work Experiences of Lesbian, Gay, and Bisexual People: An Integrative Review of Methodology and Findings," *Journal of Vocational Behavior,* April 1996, pp. 195–209; and L. Badgett, "The Wage-Effects of Sexual Orientation Discrimination," *Industrial and Labor Relations Review,* July 1995, pp. 726–39. See also B. R. Ragins, R. Singh, and J. M. Cornwell, "Making the Invisible Visible: Fear and Disclosure

of Sexual Orientation at Work," *Journal of Applied Psychology,* July 2007, pp. 1103–18; and "The Rights of Gay Employees," editorial, *The New York Times,* September 13, 2009, Week in Review section, p. 15.

146. Human Rights Campaign survey, reported in I. DeBare, "Gay, Lesbian Workers Gradually Gain Benefits," *San Francisco Chronicle,* June 30, 2006, pp. D1, D2.

147. K. Springen, "A Boost for Braille," *Newsweek,* May 20, 2002, p. 13.

148. "High School Dropout Rates on Decline Since 1972; Disparities Exist Across Race and Foreign-Born Status," High School Dropout Rates, Child Trends Databank, February 2011, www.childtrendsdatabank.org/sites/default/files/01_Dropout_Rates_0.pdf (accessed April 2, 2012).

149. The latest assessment is reported in M. Schneider, "2003 National Assessment of Adult Literacy Results," National Center for Education Statistics, December 15, 2005, http://nces.ed.gov/whatsnew/commissioner/remarks2005/12_15_2005.asp (accessed April 2, 2012). See also M. Kutner, E. Greenberg, Y. Jin, B. Boyle, Y.-c. Hsu, and E. Dunleavy, *Literacy in Everyday Life: Results from the 2003 National Assessment of Adult Literacy* (Washington, DC: National Center for Education Statistics, 2007).

150. T. L. Smith, "The Resource Center: Finding Solutions for Literacy," *HR Focus,* February 1995, p. 7. See also A. Bernstein, "The Time Bomb in the Workforce: Illiteracy," *BusinessWeek,* February 25, 2002, p. 122.

151. M. Loden, 1996; E. E. Spragins, "Benchmark: The Diverse Work Force," *Inc.,* January 1993, p. 33; and A. M. Morrison, *The New Leaders: Guidelines on Leadership Diversity in America* (San Francisco: Jossey-Bass, 1992).

152. N. Silver, "Jeremy Lin Is No Fluke," *The New York Times,* February 11, 2012, http://fivethirtyeight.blogs.nytimes.com/2012/02/11/jeremy-lin-is-no-fluke (accessed April 2, 2012).

153. G. Dell'Orto, "Special Classes Help 3M Workers Learn How to Get Along," *San Francisco Chronicle,* June 2, 2000, p. B4.

154. Bureau of Labor Statistics, Table 4. Families with Own Children: Employment Status of Parents by Age of Youngest Child and Family Type, 2009–10 Annual Averages, *Economic News Release,* March 24, 2011, www.bls.gov/news.release/famee.t04.htm (accessed April 2, 2012).

155. S. Shellenbarger, "Please Send Chocolate: Moms Now Face Stress Moving In and Out of Work Force," *The Wall Street Journal,* May 9, 2002, p. D1. See also A. Bernstein, "Too Many Workers? Not for Long," *BusinessWeek,* May 20, 2002, pp. 126–30; C. Benko, "Up the Ladder? How Dated, How Linear," *The New York Times,* November 9, 2008, Business section, p. 2; K. Evans, "In Downturn's Wake, Women Hold Half of U.S. Jobs," *The Wall Street Journal,* November 12, 2009, http://online.wsj.com/article/SB125797318108844061.html (accessed April 2, 2012); and McQueen, "Better Education Shields Women from Worst Job Cuts," 2010.

156. R. S. Lazarus, *Psychological Stress and Coping Processes* (New York: McGraw-Hill, 1966); and R. S. Schuler, "Definition and Conceptualization of Stress in Organizations," *Organizational Behavior and Human Performance,* April 1980, p. 1980.

157. "APA Survey Finds Feeling Valued at Work Linked to Well-Being and Performance," American Psychological Association, March 8, 2012.

158. American Institute of Stress, cited in J. W. Upson, D. J. Ketchen Jr., and R. D. Ireland, "Managing Employee Stress: A Key to the Effectiveness of Strategic Supply Chain Management," *Organizational Dynamics* 36 (2007), pp. 78–92.

159. See E. Zimmerman, "When Stress Flirts with Burnout," *The New York Times,* January 17, 2010, Business section, p. 7.

160. S. Shellenbarger, "'Desk Rage': To Vent or Not to Vent," *The Wall Street Journal,* January 26, 2010, p. D3.

161. Supportive results can be found in F. M. McKee-Ryan, Z. Song, C. R. Wanberg, and A. J. Kinicki, "Psychological and Physical Well-Being during Unemployment: A Meta-Analytic Study," *Journal of Applied Psychology,* January 2005, pp. 53–76; and F. M. McKee-Ryan, M. Virick, G. E. Prussia, J. Harvey, and J. D. Lilly, "Life after the Layoff: Getting a Job Worth Keeping," *Journal of Organizational Behavior,* May 2009, pp. 561–80.

162. M. Luo, "For Workers at Closing Plant, Ordeal Included Heart Attacks," *The New York Times,* February 25, 2010, pp. A1, A17.

163. See M. A. Cavanaugh, W. R. Boswell, M. V. Roehling, and J. W. Boudreau, "An Empirical Examination of Self-Reported Work Stress among U.S. Managers," *Journal of Applied Psychology,* February 2000, pp. 65–74; A. J. Kinicki, F. M. McKee-Ryan, C. A. Schriesheim, and K. P. Carson, "Assessing the Construct Validity of the Job Descriptive Index: A Review and Meta-Analysis," *Journal of Applied Psychology,* February 2002, pp. 14–32; A. Weintraub, "Inside Drugmakers' War on Fat," *BusinessWeek,* March 17, 2008, pp. 41–46; and M. R. Frone, "Are Work Stressors Related to Employee Substance Use? The Importance of Temporal Context in Assessments of Alcohol and Illicit Drug Use," *Journal of Applied Psychology,* January 2008, pp. 199–206.

164. H. Selye, *Stress without Distress* (New York: Lippincott, 1974), p. 27.

165. R. S. Lazarus and S. Folkman, "Coping and Adaptation," in W. D. Gentry, ed., *Handbook of Behavioral Medicine* (New York: Guilford, 1982).

166. Selye, *Stress without Distress,* 1974, pp. 28–29.

167. M. Beck, "When Fretting Is in Your DNA: Overcoming the Worry Gene," *The Wall Street Journal,* January 15, 2008, p. D1. See also L. M. Hilt, L. C. Sander, S. Nolen-Hoeksema, and A. A. Simen, "The BDNF Val66Met Polymorphism Predicts Rumination and Depression Differently in Young Adolescent Girls and Their Mothers," *Neuroscience Letters,* December 2007, pp. 12–16.

168. M. Friedman and R. H. Rosenman, *Type A Behavior and Your Heart* (Greenwich, CT: Fawcett Publications, 1974), p. 84.

169. See M. S. Taylor, E. A. Locke, C. Lee, and M. E. Gist, "Type A Behavior and Faculty Research Productivity: What Are the Mechanisms?" *Organizational Behavior and Human Performance,* December 1984, pp. 402–18; S. D. Bluen, J. Barling, and W. Burns, "Predicting Sales Performance, Job Satisfaction, and Depression by Using the Achievement Strivings and Impatience–Irritability Dimensions of Type A Behavior," *Journal of Applied Psychology,* April 1990, pp. 212–16.

170. S. Booth-Kewley and H. S. Friedman, "Psychological Predictors of Heart Disease: A Quantitative Review," *Psychological Bulletin,* May 1987, pp. 343–62; S. A. Lyness, "Predictors of Differences between Type A and B Individuals in Heart Rate and Blood Pressure Reactivity," *Psychological Bulletin,* September 1993, pp. 266–95; and T. Q. Miller, T. W. Smith, C. W. Turner, M. L. Guijarro, and A. J. Hallet, "A Meta-Analytic Review of Research on Hostility and Physical Health," *Psychological Bulletin,* March 1996, pp. 322–48.

171. J. O'Donnell, "Wanted: Retail Managers," *USA Today,* December 24, 2007, pp. 1B, 3B.

172. M. Richtel, "In Web World of 24/7 Stress, Writers Blog Till They Drop," *The New York Times,* April 6, 2008, News section, pp. 1, 23.

173. M. Culp, "Coping When Co-Worker Is Under Stress," *The Hartford Courant,* February 25, 2008, courant.com/business/hc-midred0225.artfeb25,0,4210457.story.com (accessed February 25, 2008).

174. "Lousiest Bosses," *The Wall Street Journal,* April 4, 1995, p. A1. For more about bad managers, see J. Sandberg, "Had It Up to

HERE? Despite Risk, Some Say Quitting Is Way to Go," *The Wall Street Journal*, August 14, 2007, p. B1; G. G. Scott, *A Survival Guide for Working with Bad Bosses: Dealing with Bullies, Idiots, Back-Stabbers, and Other Managers from Hell* (New York: AMACOM, 2005); and A. Dobson, "Working It Out: Fixing a Strained Relationship with Your Boss," *San Francisco Chronicle*, March 2, 2008, p. H1.

175. J. Schaubroeck and D. C. Ganster, "Chronic Demands and Responsivity to Challenge," *Journal of Applied Psychology*, February 1993, pp. 73–85; E. Demerouti, A. B. Bakker, F. Nachreiner, and W. B. Schaufeli, "The Job Demands Resources Model of Burnout," *Journal of Applied Psychology*, June 2001, pp. 499–512.

176. J. M. Plas, *Person-Centered Leadership: An American Approach to Participatory Management* (Thousand Oaks, CA: Sage, 1996).

177. M. Patsalos-Fox, quoted in W. J. Holstein, "Tension Headaches in the Corner Office," *The New York Times*, March 12, 2006, sec. 3, p. 1.

178. M. Staver, quoted in C. H. Deutsch, "Winning the Battle Against Burnout," *The New York Times*, August 27, 2006, sec. 3, p. 5.

179. See Deutsch, 2006.

180. M. Ferri, L. Amato, and M. Davoli, "Alcoholics Anonymous and Other 12-Step Programmes for Alcohol Dependence (Review)," *Cochrane Database of Scientific Reviews*, 2006, issue 3. See also report in N. Bakalar, "Review Sees No Advantage in 12-Step Programs," *The New York Times*, July 25, 2006, p. D6.

181. See S. Price, "Ante Up for Wellness," *HR Magazine*, February 2012, pp. 40–42; and S. J. Wells, "Wellness Rewards," *HR Magazine*, February 2012, pp. 67–69.

182. R. Kreitner, "Personal Wellness: It's Just Good Business," *Business Horizons*, May–June 1982, p. 28.

CHAPTER 12

1. Kleiman, "Work-Life Rewards Grow," *San Francisco Examiner*, January 16, 2000, p. J-2; reprinted from *Chicago Tribune*.

2. M. Buckingham and C. Coffman, *First, Break All the Rules: What the World's Greatest Managers Do Differently* (New York: Simon & Schuster, 1999).

3. Kimberly Scott, project leader for Hewitt Associates, which helps compile the *Fortune* list, reported in D. Murphy, "Can Morale Contribute to Safer Skies?" *San Francisco Examiner*, February 11, 2000, p. J-1.

4. S. Shellenbarger, "Work & Family Mailbox," *The Wall Street Journal*, August 5, 2009, p. D3; and C. Tkaczyk, "Offer Affordable (Awesome) Day Care," *Fortune*, August 17, 2009, p. 26.

5. Adapted from definition in T. R. Mitchell, "Motivation: New Directions for Theory, Research, and Practice," *Academy of Management Review*, January 1982, p. 81.

6. See R. M. Ryan and E. L. Deci, "Intrinsic and Extrinsic Motivations: Classic Definitions and New Directions," *Contemporary Educational Psychology*, January 2000, pp. 54–67.

7. K. G. Volpp, A. B. Troxel, M. V. Pauly, H. A. Glick, et al., "A Randomized, Controlled Trial of Financial Incentives for Smoking Cessation," *New England Journal of Medicine*, February 12, 2009, pp. 699–709. Other research finds that such extrinsic rewards have little lasting effect on making workers healthier. See A. Kohn, "Cash Incentives Won't Make Us Healthier," *USA Today*, May 21, 2009, p. 11A.

8. *2011 Employer Survey on Purchasing Value in Health Care Report*, Towers Watson/National Business Group on Health, www.towerswatson.com/assets/pdf/3946/TowersWatson-NBGH-2011-NA-2010-18560.pdf (accessed April 7, 2012). See also S. J. Wells, "Wellness Rewards," *HR Magazine*, February 2012, pp. 67–69; and S. Price, "Ante Up for Wellness," *HR Magazine*, February 2012, pp. 40–42.

9. S. E. Needleman, "The Latest Office Perk: Getting Paid to Volunteer," *The Wall Street Journal*, April 29, 2008, p. D1.

10. See P. W. Hom, L. Roberson, and A. D. Ellis, "Challenging Conventional Wisdom about Who Quits: Revelations from Corporate America," *Journal of Applied Psychology*, January 2008, pp. 1–34; J. B. Olson-Buchanan and W. R. Boswell, "An Integrative Model of Experiencing and Responding to Mistreatment at Work," *Academy of Management Review*, January 2008, pp. 76–96; and M. Riketta, "The Causal Relation Between Job Attitudes and Performance: A Meta-Analysis of Panel Studies," *Journal of Applied Psychology*, March 2008, pp. 472–81.

11. K. Down and L. Liedtka, "What Corporations Seek in MBA Hires: A Survey," *Selections*, Winter 1994, pp. 34–39; see also S. Armour, "Companies Get Tough on Absent Employees," *The Arizona Republic*, February 7, 2003, p. A2; reprinted from *USA Today*.

12. A. Maslow, "A Theory of Human Motivation," *Psychological Review*, July 1943, pp. 370–96.

13 C. Conley, *Peak: How Great Companies Get Their Mojo from Maslow* (San Francisco: Jossey-Bass, 2007).

14. Chip Conley, interview by M. Hofman, "The Idea That Saved My Company," *Inc.*, October 11, 2007, www.inc.com/magazine/20071001/the-idea-that-saved-my-company.html (accessed April 7, 2012).

15. C. Conley, interviewed in K. Pattison, "Chip Conley Took the Maslow Pyramid, Made It an Employee Pyramid, and Saved His Company," *Fast Company*, August 26, 2010, www.fastcompany.com/1685009/chip-conley-wants-your-employees-to-hit-their-peak (accessed April 7, 2012).

16. C. Conley, interviewed in E. Schurenberg, "Chip Conley: The 5 Things Everyone Wants from You," *Inc.*, December 12, 2011, www.inc.com/eric-schurenberg/Chip-Conley-5-Things-Everyone-Wants.html (accessed April 7, 2012).

17. Conley, in Schurenberg, 2011.

18. Hofman, "The Idea That Saved My Company," 2007.

19. See W. B. Swann Jr., C. Chang-Schneider, and K. I. McClarty, "Do People's Self-Views Matter?" *American Psychologist*, February–March 2007, pp. 84–94.

20. For a complete review of ERG theory, see C. P. Alderfer, *Existence, Relatedness, and Growth: Human Needs in Organizational Settings* (New York: Free Press, 1972).

21. D. C. McClelland, *Human Motivation* (Glenview, IL: Scott, Foresman, 1985).

22. D. McClelland and H. Burnham, "Power Is the Great Motivator," *Harvard Business Review*, March–April 1976, pp. 100–10.

23. S. W. Spreier, M. H. Fontaine, and R. L. Malloy, "Leadership Run Amok," *Harvard Business Review*, June 2006, pp. 72–82.

24. Some studies of achievement motivation can be found in H. Grant and C. S. Dweck, "A Goal Analysis of Personality and Personality Coherence," in D. Cervone and Y. Shoda, eds., *The Coherence of Personality* (New York: Guilford Press, 1999), pp. 345–71. See also D. B. Turban and T. L. Keon, "Organizational Attractiveness: An Interactionist Perspective," *Journal of Applied Psychology*, April 1993, pp. 184–93.

25. "The World's 100 Most Powerful Women," *Forbes*, August 24, 2011, www.forbes.com/wealth/power-women; and "50 Most Powerful Women in Business," *Fortune*, October 17, 2011, http://money.cnn.com/magazines/fortune/most-powerful-women/2011/full_list (both accessed April 7, 2012).

26. B. Evangelista, "Chief Operating Officer Emerges as Facebook's Public Power Broker," *San Francisco Chronicle*, January 22, 2012, pp. A1, A10.

27. S. Sandberg, in "Transcript and Video of Speech by Sheryl Sandberg, Chief Operating Officer, Facebook," commencement

speech, Barnard College, May 17, 2012, http://barnard.edu/headlines/transcript-and-video-speech-sheryl-sandberg-chief-operating-officer-facebook (accessed April 7, 2012).

28. K. Auletta, "A Woman's Place," *The New Yorker*, July 11 and 18, 2011, pp. 55–63.

29. F. Herzberg, B. Mausner, and B. B. Snyderman, *The Motivation to Work* (New York: Wiley, 1959); and F. Herzberg, "One More Time: How Do You Motivate Employees?" *Harvard Business Review*, January–February 1968, pp. 53–62.

30. Survey by the Conference Board, reported in P. Korkki, "With Jobs Few, Most Workers Aren't Satisfied," *The New York Times*, January 10, 2009, Business section, p. 2. See also P. Coy, "Are Your Employees Just Biding Their Time?" *BusinessWeek*, November 16, 2009, p. 27.

31. Society for Human Resource Management, *2011 Employee Job Satisfaction and Engagement: Gratification and Commitment at Work in a Sluggish Economy*, December 2011, www.shrm.org/Research/SurveyFindings/Articles/Documents/11-0618%20Job_Satisfaction_FNL.pdf (accessed April 7, 2012). See also J. M. Gibbons, *I Can't Get No . . . Job Satisfaction, That Is*, The Conference Board, 2010, www.conference-board.org/publications/publicationdetail.cfm?publicationid=1727 (accessed April 7, 2012). See also F. Norris, "In a Sign of Labor Recovery, More Workers Are Quitting," *The New York Times*, December 17, 2011, p. B3. On the subject of employees filing more wage-and-hour lawsuits following the recession, see P. Davidson, "Overworked and Underpaid?" *USA Today*, April 16, 2012, pp. 1A, 2A.

32. See J. Flint, "How to Be a Player," *Bloomberg Businessweek*, January 24–January 30, 2011, pp. 108–9.

33. J. S. Adams, "Toward an Understanding of Inequity," *Journal of Abnormal and Social Psychology*, November 1963, pp. 422–36; and J. S. Adams, "Injustice in Social Exchange," in L. Berkowitz, ed., *Advances in Experimental Social Psychology*, 2nd ed. (New York: Academic Press, 1965), pp. 267–300.

34. M. Spector and T. McGinty, "The CEO Bankruptcy Bonus," *The Wall Street Journal*, January 27, 2012, pp A1, A2; and B. Hanson, "Most Workers Still Struggle to Find Jobs," *Reno Gazette-Journal*, March 29, 2012, p. 8A.

35. N. Singer, "CEO Pay Gains May Have Slowed, but the Numbers Are Still Numbing," *The New York Times*, April 8, 2012, pp. BU-1, BU-4.

36. U.S. Bureau of Labor Statistics, Department of Labor, *Highlights of Women's Earnings in 2010*, Report 1031, July 2011, www.bls.gov/cps/cpswom2010.pdf (accessed April 7, 2012).

37. U.S. Department of Commerce, cited in A. Salkever, "An Easy Antidote to Employee Theft," *BusinessWeek online*, May 20, 2003, www.businessweek.com/smallbiz/content/may2003/sb20030520_9328_sb018.htm (accessed April 7, 2012). See also J. Greenberg, "Employee Theft as a Reaction to Underpayment Inequity: The Hidden Cost of Pay Cuts," *Journal of Applied Psychology* 75 (1990), pp. 561–68.

38. L. Abboud and M. Colchester, "French Bosses Come Under Siege as Worker Anger Rises," *The Wall Street Journal*, April 1, 2009, p. B1; and D. Gauthier-Villars and L. Abboud, "In France, CEOs Can Become Hostages," *The Wall Street Journal*, April 3, 2009, pp. B1, B5.

39. The comparison process was discussed by S. T. Fiske, "Envy Up, Scorn Down: How Comparison Divides Us," *American Psychologist*, November 2010, pp. 698–706.

40. See D. J. Holman, C. M. Axtell, C. A Sprigg, P. Totterdell, and T. D. Wall, "The Mediating Role of Job Characteristics in Job Redesign Interventions: A Serendipitous Quasi-Experiment," *Journal of Organizational Behavior*, January 2010, pp. 84–105. Also see S. W. Whiting, P. M. Podsakoff, and J. R. Pierce, "Effects of Task Performance, Helping, Voice, and Organizational Loyalty

on Performance Appraisal Ratings," *Journal of Applied Psychology*, January 2008, pp. 125–39.

41. See R. A. Posthuma, C. P. Maertz Jr., and J. B. Dworkin, "Procedural Justice's Relationship with Turnover: Explaining Past Inconsistent Findings," *Journal of Organizational Behavior*, May 2007, pp. 381–98; Y. Cohen-Charash and J. S. Mueller, "Does Perceived Unfairness Exacerbate or Mitigate Interpersonal Counterproductive Work Behaviors Related to Envy?" *Journal of Applied Psychology*, May 2007, pp. 666–80; and H. Moon, D. Kamdar, D. M. Mayer, and R. Takeuchi, "Me or We? The Role of Personality and Justice as Other-Centered Antecedents to Innovative Citizenship Behaviors within Organizations," *Journal of Applied Psychology*, January 2008, pp. 84–94.

42. V. H. Vroom, *Work and Motivation* (New York: Wiley, 1964).

43. C. Wallis, "How to Make Great Teachers," *Time*, February 25, 2008, pp. 28–34; "Teacher Bonus Systems Tested," *Reno Gazette-Journal*, October 22, 2008, p. 1D: S. Dillon, "Incentives for Advanced Work Let Pupils and Teachers Cash In," *The New York Times*, October 3, 2011, pp. A1, A13; S. Dillon, "In Washington, Large Rewards in Teacher Pay," *The New York Times*, January 1, 2012, News section, pp. 1, 18; and W. Kopp, "The Trouble with Humiliating Teachers," *The Wall Street Journal*, March 7, 2012, p. A15.

44. A Hudson survey of 10,000 employees March 20–26, 2006, found that 48% of managers but only 31% of nonmanagers agreed with the statement "Employees who do a better job get paid more"; 46% of managers but only 29% of nonmanagers agreed with the statement "My last raise was based on performance." Information cited in "Reasons for Raises," *BusinessWeek*, May 29, 2006, p. 11.

45. See M. J. Pearsall, M. S. Christian, and A. P. J. Ellis, "Motivating Interdependent Teams: Individual Rewards, Shared Rewards, or Something in Between?" *Journal of Applied Psychology*, January 2010, pp. 183–91.

46. See D. Ariely, "What's the Value of a Big Bonus?" *The New York Times*, November 20, 2008, www.nytimes.com/2008/11/20/opinion/20ariely.html (accessed April 4, 2012). Also see letters to the editor, "Getting the Bonus You Deserve," *The New York Times*, November 28, 2008, p. A30.

47. See E. Dash, "The Lucrative Fall from Grace," *The New York Times*, September 30, 2011, pp. B1, B4; and J. B. Stewart, "Rewarding CEOs Who Fail," *The New York Times*, October 1, 2011, pp. B1, B2.

48. J. S. Lublin, "Valeant CEO's Pay Package Draws Praise as a Model," *The Wall Street Journal*, August 24, 2009, p. B4.

49. "J. Michael Pearson," Pass/Fail, April 11, 2012, www.passfail.com/vrx/executive/j-michael-pearson/j-michael-pearson.htm (accessed April 11, 2012).

50. J. Bosman, "New York to End Program Giving Cash to the Poor for Desired Behavior," *The New York Times*, March 31, 2010, p. A18.

51. For a thorough discussion of goal-setting theory and application, see E. A. Locke and G. P. Latham, "Building a Practically Useful Theory of Goal Setting and Task Motivation," *American Psychologist*, September 2002, pp. 705–17.

52. See G. P. Latham and E. A. Locke, "Enhancing the Benefits and Overcoming the Pitfalls of Goal Setting," *Organizational Dynamics*, November 2006, pp. 332–40.

53. See J. J. Donovan and D. J. Radosevich, "The Moderating Role of Goal Commitment on the Goal-Difficulty Performance Relationship: A Meta-Analytic Summary and Critical Reanalysis," *Journal of Applied Psychology*, April 1998, pp. 308–15.

54. See D. Morisano, J. B. Hirsh, J. B. Peterson, R. O. Phil, and B. M. Shore, "Setting, Elaborating, and Reflecting on Personal Goals Improves Academic Performance," *Journal of Applied Psychology*, March 2010, pp. 255–64.

55. See E. A. Locke and G. P. Latham, *A Theory of Goal Setting and Task Performance* (Englewood Cliffs, NJ: Prentice Hall, 1990).

56. Supportive results can be found in S. E. Humphrey, J. D. Nahrgang, and F. P. Morgeson, "Integrating Motivational, Social, and Contextual Work Design Features: A Meta-Analytic Summary and Theoretical Extension of the Work Design Literature," *Journal of Applied Psychology,* September 2007, pp. 1332–56.

57. DDI Pulse of the Workforce Survey of 1,000 employees, reported in "Stagnating on the Job," *USA Today,* September 21, 2009, p. 1B.

58. See G. R. Oldham and J. R. Hackman, "Not What It Was and Not What It Will Be: The Future of Job Design," *Journal of Organizational Behavior,* February 2010, pp. 463–79.

59. S. Melamed, I. Ben-Avi, J. Luz, and M. S. Green, "Objective and Subjective Work Monotony: Effects on Job Satisfaction, Psychological Distress, and Absenteeism in Blue-Collar Workers," *Journal of Applied Psychology,* February 1995, pp. 29–42; and B. Melin, U. Lundberg, J. Söderlund, and M. Granqvist, "Psychological and Physiological Stress Reactions of Male and Female Assembly Workers: A Comparison between Two Different Forms of Work Organization," *Journal of Organizational Behavior,* January 1999, pp. 47–61.

60. M. A. Campion and C. L. McClelland, "Follow-Up and Extension of the Interdisciplinary Costs and Benefits of Enlarged Jobs," *Journal of Applied Psychology,* June 1993, pp. 339–51.

61. Herzberg et al., *The Motivation to Work,* 1959.

62. J. R. Hackman and G. R. Oldham, *Work Redesign* (Reading, MA: Addison-Wesley, 1980).

63. See S. E. Humphrey, J. D. Nahrgang, and F. P. Morgeson, "Integrating Motivational, Social, and Contextual Work Design Features: A Meta-Analytic Summary and Theoretical Extension of the Work Design Literature," *Journal of Applied Psychology,* September 2007, pp. 1332–56. Also see A. M. Grant, "The Significance of Task Significance: Job Performance Effects, Relational Mechanisms, and Boundary Conditions," *Journal of Applied Psychology,* January 2008, pp. 108–24; and F. W. Bond, P. E. Flaxman, and D. Bunce, "The Influence of Psychological Flexibility on Work Redesign: Mediated Moderation of a Work Reorganization Intervention," *Journal of Applied Psychology,* May 2008, pp. 645–54.

64. See D. J. Holman, C. M. Axtell, C. A. Sprigg, P. Totterdell, and T. D. Wall, "The Mediating Role of Job Characteristics in Job Redesign Interventions,: A Serendipitous Quasi-Experiment," *Journal of Organizational Behavior,* January 2010, pp. 84–105.

65. See B. Reagan, "Perks with a Payoff," *The Wall Street Journal,* October 24, 2011, p. R3. Some employees have resisted such employer efforts, as when PepsiCo tried to charge its employees $50 a month if they smoke or have obesity-related medical problems. H. Rosenkrantz and D. Stanford, "PepsiCo Workers Balk at 'Sin Tax,'" *San Francisco Chronicle,* March 18, 2012, p. D5.

66. Dr. Paul H. Grundy, I.B.M.'s director of Health Care Technology and Strategic Initiatives, quoted in M. Freudenheim, "A Model for Health Care That Pays for Quality," *The New York Times,* November 7, 2007, p. C3. See also C. Lochhead, "Lessons on Health Care from Europe," *San Francisco Chronicle,* January 29, 2009, pp. A1, A18.

67. S. Frier, "Wellpoint to Tie Payouts to Quality," *San Francisco Chronicle,* January 28, 2012, p. D3.

68. See E. L. Thorndike, *Educational Psychology: The Psychology of Learning,* Vol. II (New York: Columbia University Teachers College, 1913); B. F. Skinner, *Walden Two* (New York: Macmillan, 1948); *Science and Human Behavior* (New York: Macmillan, 1953); and *Contingencies of Reinforcement* (New York: Appleton-Century-Crofts, 1969).

69. Roy F. Baumeister, reported in A. Tugend, "Praise Is Fleeting, but Brickbats We Recall," *The New York Times,* March 24, 2012, p. B5. See also R. F. Baumeister, E. Bratslavsky, C. Finkenauer, and K. D. Vohs, "Bad Is Stronger Than Good," *Review of General Psychology* 5, no. 4 (2001), pp. 323–70.

70. J. Sandberg, "A Modern Conundrum: When Work's Invisible, So Are Its Satisfactions," *The Wall Street Journal,* February 19, 2008, p. B1.

71. A. Zipkin, "The Wisdom of Thoughtfulness," *The New York Times,* May 31, 2000, pp. C1, C10. For an article about the importance of congeniality, see D. Brady, "Charm Offensive," *BusinessWeek,* June 26, 2006, pp. 76–80.

72. Gallup Organization study, reported in Zipkin, "The Wisdom of Thoughtfulness," 2000. See also J. Yang and A. Gonzalez, "Most Preferred Forms of Recognition at Workplace," *USA Today,* May 4, 2009, p. 1B; and N. Lublin, "Two Little Words," *Fast Company,* November 2010, p. 56. A McKinsey global survey also found that employees view praise and commendation from their immediate manager as more effective than cash. See L. Freifeld, "Why Cash *Doesn't* Motivate," *Training,* July–August 2011, pp. 17–22. These results are also in line with a survey by the Society for Human Resource Management, *2011 Job Satisfaction Survey Report,* in which employees said the top five "very important" aspects of job satisfaction were job security, opportunity to use skills and abilities, organization's financial stability, compensation pay, and benefits. See Society for Human Resource Management, "Employee Job Satisfaction: The External Forces Influencing Employee Attitudes," *Workplace Visions,* issue 4, 2011, www.shrm.org/Research/FutureWorkplaceTrends/Documents/11-0697%20Workplace_Visions_Issue4%20FINAL.pdf (accessed April 7, 2012).

73. Great Place to Work Institute, Trust Index Employee Survey, described in L. Petrecca, "Tech Companies Top List of 'Great Workplaces,'" *USA Today,* October 31, 2011, p. 7B.

74. E. White, "The Best vs. the Rest," *The Wall Street Journal,* January 30, 2006, pp. B1, B3; and J. Pfeffer, "Stopping the Talent Drain," *Business 2.0,* July 2006, p. 80.

75. See, for example, J. Anderson, "Tying One's Pay to Performance: What a Concept," *The New York Times,* July 15, 2005, p. C7; and G. Farrell and B. Hansen, "Stocks May Fall, but Pay Doesn't," *USA Today,* April 10, 2008, pp. 1B, 2B. See also M. J. Canyon, "Executive Compensation and Incentives," *Academy of Management Perspectives,* February 2006, pp. 25–44.

76. P. Hodson, *2008 Proxy Season Foresights #2—Performance Targets Targeted,* February 15, 2008, Corporate Library, www.thecorporatelibrary.com/info.php?id=88 (accessed April 4, 2012). This study by Corporate Library, an independent governance research organization for the Securities and Exchange Commission, is reported in E. Simon, "How Execs Get Bonus Not Clear," *San Francisco Chronicle,* February 21, 2008, p. C3.

77. See S. Bernard, "No Bonuses for Top Goldman Execs," *San Francisco Chronicle,* December 11, 2009, p. A12.

78. "Percentage of Business That Have Gainsharing," *Zunaif.net,* May 12, 2011, http://zunaif.net/2011/05/percentage-business-gain-sharing (accessed April 7, 2012).

79. "Take Stock of Stock Options," *Human Resource Executive Magazine,* June 3, 2004, workindex.com; www.workindex.com/editorial/hre/hre0406-03.asp (accessed April 4, 2012).

80. K. Clark, "Too Safe a Bet?" *U.S. News & World Report,* June 19, 2006, pp. 37–38. For more on backdating of stock options, see J. Ledbetter, "Backdating: It Ain't Over," *Fortune,* March 20, 2008, http://dailybriefing.blogs.fortune.cnn.com/2008/03/20/backdating-it-aint-over (accessed April 4, 2012); and H. W. Jenkins Jr., "One Last Backdating Whipping Boy?" *The Wall*

Street Journal, April 30, 2008, http://online.wsj.com/article/SB120951511131354625.html (accessed April 4, 2012).

81. PricewaterhouseCoopers survey, reported in S. Shellenbarger, "What Job Candidates Really Want to Know: Will I Have a Life?" *The Wall Street Journal,* November 17, 1999, p. B1. See also S. F. Premeaux, C. L. Adkins, and K. W. Mossholder, "Balancing Work and Family: A Field Study of Multi-Dimensional, Multi-Role Work-Family Conflict," *Journal of Organizational Behavior,* August 2007, pp. 705–27; S. Cummins, "Life, Liberty, and the Pursuit of Balance," *BusinessWeek,* October 23, 2007, www.businessweek.com/managing/content/oct2007/ca20071023_799034.htm?campaign_id=rss_daily (accessed April 4, 2012); J. Herzlich, "Work/Life Balance Tops List," *The Arizona Republic,* January 6, 2008, p. EC1.

82. K. W. Smola and C. D. Sutton, "Generational Differences: Revisiting Generational Work Values for the New Millennium," *Journal of Organizational Behavior,* June 2002, p. 379.

83. *The Millennials: Confident. Connected. Open to Change,* Pew Research Center Publications, February 2010, www.pewresearch.org/millennials (accessed April 4, 2012).

84. See D. H. Pink, "*Drive: The Surprising Truth about What Motivates Us* (New York: Riverhead, 2010). The book proposes that workers are more efficient, loyal, and creative when they feel that their work has meaning.

85. See J. Turano, "Two Workers, Wearing One Hat," *The New York Times,* October 4, 2009, Business section, p. 8; "Half a Job's Better Than One," *The Week,* November 6, 2009, p. 42; T. Pugh, "'Work Sharing' Helps Limit Layoffs' Impact," *San Francisco Chronicle,* November 15, 2009, p. D3; S. A. Hewlett, "Making Flex Time a Win-Win," *The New York Times,* December 13, 2009, Business section, p. 13; and S. Brown, "Line between Home, Work Will Blur More," *USA Today,* February 8, 2010, p. 11B.

86. A. Quirk, "The Business Case for Flex," *HR Magazine,* April 2012, pp. 44–46.

87. See I. J. Dugan, "Working Two Jobs and Still Underemployed," *The Wall Street Journal,* December 1, 2009, p. A15; and S. Shellenbarger, "Recession Tactic: The Mini-Shift," *The Wall Street Journal,* February 24, 2010, p. D4.

88. D. Meinert, "Make Telecommuting Pay Off," *HR Magazine,* June 2011, pp. 33–7; A. Tugend, "How to Make Working at Home Work for You," *The New York Times,* October 8, 2011, p. B5; and B. A. Lautsch and E. E. Kossek, "Managing a Blended Workforce: Telecommuters and Non-commuters," *Organizational Dynamics* 40 (2011), pp. 10–17.

89. Walker Information Global Network and Hudson Institute, *2000 Global Employee Relationship Report,* in "Global Workforce Study Highlights Alarming Trends," September 19, 2000, www.hudson.org/index.cfm?fuseaction=public-ation_details&id=697 (accessed April 4, 2012).

90. Spherion and Louis Harris Associates 1999 survey, reported in Zipkin, "The Wisdom of Thoughtfulness," 2000.

91. See P. Falcone, "Doing More with Less: How to Motivate and Reward Your Overworked Staff During Lean Times," *HR Magazine,* February 2003, pp. 101–3; D. Kehrer, "Here Are Some Keys to Keeping Good Employees," *Reno Gazette Journal,* March 30, 2004, p. 4D; J. Noveck, "Do Bosses Need to Be Mean to Get Work Done?" *Nevada Appeal,* July 9, 2006, pp. D1, D2" and D. Volz, "How to Keep Workers When Raises Not Option," *Arizona Republic,* December 11, 2011, p. EC1.

92. B. L. Ware, quoted in Zipkin, "The Wisdom of Thoughtfulness," 2000.

93. K. Lingle, quoted in C. Kleiman, "Work-Life Rewards Grow," *San Francisco Examiner,* January 16, 2000, p. J-2; reprinted from *Chicago Tribune.*

94. S. Shellenberger, "Companies Retool Time-Off Policies to Prevent Burnout, Reward Performance," *The Wall Street Journal,* January 5, 2006, p. D1.

95. See A. Fisher, "The Rebalancing Act," *Fortune,* October 6, 2003, pp. 110–13; D. Cadrain, "Cash vs. Non-cash Rewards," *HR Magazine,* April 2003, pp. 81–87; C. Hymowitz, "While Some Women Choose to Stay Home, Others Gain Flexibility," *The Wall Street Journal,* March 30, 2004, p. B1; J. Shramm, "Fuel Economy," *HR Magazine,* December 2005, p. 120; S. Armour, "Cost-Effective 'Homesourcing' Grows," *USA Today,* March 13, 2006, p. 1B; S. E. Needleman, "Pick Worker Rewards Carefully," *The Wall Street Journal,* March 28, 2006, p. B8; M. P. McQueen, "Employers Expand Elder-Care Benefits," *The Wall Street Journal,* July 27, 2006, pp. D1, D6; A. Pomeroy, "The Future Is Now," *HR Magazine,* September 2007, pp. 46–51; S. Shellenbarger, "Good News for Professionals Who Want to Work at Home," *The Wall Street Journal,* November 15, 2007, p. D1; S. Armour, "As Dads Push for Family Time, Tensions Rise in Workplace," *USA Today,* December 11, 2007, pp. 1A, 2A; K. R. Lewis, "Getting Time Off and Getting Work Done a Balancing Act," *San Francisco Chronicle,* December 16, 2007, p. E6; and D. Hudepohl, "Working from Home: Mapping Out Your First 90 Days," *The Wall Street Journal,* February 19, 2008, p. B8.

96. J. Vatner, "Changing a Culture by Removing Walls," *The New York Times,* February 10, 2010, p. B7.

97. A. Hedge, quoted in P. Wen, "Drab Cubicles Can Block Workers' Creativity, Productivity," *San Francisco Chronicle,* March 10, 2000, pp. B1, B3; reprinted from *Boston Globe.*

98. See A. Johnson, "It's True: A Nicer Office Can Boost Morale," *The Arizona Republic,* September 3, 2007, www.azcentral.com/arizonarepublic/business/articles/0903biz-workenvironment0903.html (accessed April 4, 2012), which describes a study by Harvard Medical School psychologist Nancy Etcoff that reinforces the idea that a person's physical environment has a big impact on his or her mood at work. Also see I. DeBare, "Shared Work Spaces a Sign of the Times," *San Francisco Chronicle,* February 19, 2008, pp. A1, A7.

99. J. Sturges, N. Conway, D. Guest, and A. Liefooghe, "Managing the Career Deal: The Psychological Contract as a Framework for Understanding Career Management, Organizational Commitment, and Work Behavior," *Journal of Organizational Behavior,* November 2005, pp. 821–38; and J. Badal, "'Career Path' Programs Help Retain Workers," *The Wall Street Journal,* July 24, 2006, pp. B1, B4.

100. J. P. Smith, "Sabbaticals Pervade Business Sector," *Reno Gazette-Journal,* February 22, 2004, p. H1; M. Arndt, "Nice Work If You Can Get It," *BusinessWeek,* January 9, 2006, pp. 56–57; and L. Chao, "Sabbaticals Can Offer Dividends for Employers," *The Wall Street Journal,* July 17, 2006, p. B5.

CHAPTER 13

1. D. L. Duarte and N. T. Snyder, *Mastering Virtual Teams: Strategies, Tools, and Techniques That Succeed,* 3rd ed. (San Francisco: Jossey-Bass, 2006).

2. M. K. Brown, B. Huettner, and C. James-Tanny, *Managing Virtual Teams: Getting the Most from Wikis, Blogs, and Other Collaborative Tools* (Plano, TX: Wordware Publishing, 2007); M. Goldsmith, "Crossing the Cultural Chasm," *BusinessWeek,* May 30, 2007, www.businessweek.com/careers/content/may2007/ca20070530_521679.htm?chan=search (accessed May 12, 2012); and L. Noeth, "Supervising a Virtual Team Is Still All about Basics," *Rochester Democrat & Chronicle,* April 27, 2008, www.democratandchronicle.com/apps/pbcs.dll/article?AID=/20080427/BUSINESS01/804270332/-1/COLUMNS (accessed May 12, 2012).

3. P. F. Drucker, "The Coming of the New Organization," *Harvard Business Review,* January–February 1988, pp. 45–53.

4. "Top 10 Leadership Tips from Jeff Immelt," *Fast Company,* April 2004, p. 96.

5. T. Kelley, quoted in P. Sinton, "Teamwork the Name of the Game for Ideo," *San Francisco Chronicle,* February 23, 2000, pp. D1, D3. Kelley is coauthor, with J. Littman, of *The Art of Innovation: Lessons in Creativity from IDEO, America's Leading Design Firm* (New York: Random House, 2001) and of *The Ten Faces of Innovation: IDEO's Strategies for Defeating the Devil's Advocate and Driving Creativity Throughout Your Organization* (New York: Currency/Doubleday, 2005).

6. S. E. Page, quoted in C. Dreifus, "In Professor's Model, Diversity = Productivity," *The New York Times,* January 8, 2008, p. D2.

7. This definition is based in part on one found in D. Horton Smith, "A Parsimonious Definition of 'Group': Toward Conceptual Clarity and Scientific Utility," *Sociological Inquiry,* Spring 1967, pp. 141–67.

8. E. H. Schein, *Organizational Psychology,* 3rd ed. (Englewood Cliffs, NJ: Prentice-Hall, 1980), p. 145.

9. J. R. Katzenbach and D. K. Smith, *The Wisdom of Teams: Creating the High-Performance Organization* (Boston: Harvard Business School Press, 1993), p. 45.

10. J. R. Katzenbach and D. K. Smith, "The Discipline of Teams," *Harvard Business Review,* March–April 1995, p. 112.

11. D. Krackhardt and J. R. Hanson, "Informal Networks: The Company Behind the Chart," *Harvard Business Review,* July–August 1993, p. 104.

12. Study by Center for Workforce Development, Newton, MA, reported in M. Jackson, "It's Not Chitchat, It's Training," *San Francisco Chronicle,* January 7, 1998, p. D2.

13. K. Kim, H.M. Collins, J. Williamson, and J. Chapman, *Participation in Adult Education and Lifetime Learning: 2000–01,* NCES 2004-050, U.S. Department of Education, National Center for Education Statistics (Washington, DC: U.S. Government Printing Office, 2008). For more on informal learning, see L. Dublin, "Formalizing Informal Learning," *Chief Learning Officer,* March 2010, www.clomedia.com/features/2010/March/2870/index.php (accessed April 16, 2012).

14. T. Elkeles, "In Practice: Storytelling Drives Knowledge and Information Sharing Across Qualcomm," *HBSCO Host Connection,* March 2010, http://connection.ebscohost.com/c/articles/48417152/practice-storytelling-drives-knowledge-information-sharing-across-qualcomm; and A. Lewis, "Innovative Learning and Development Practices," *HCI Blogs,* March 23, 2010, www.hci.org/node/551943 (both accessed April 16, 2012).

15. K. K. Spors, "Getting Workers to Share Their Know-How with Peers," *The Wall Street Journal,* April 3, 2008, p. B6. For more on virtual knowledge sharing, see B. Rosen, S. Furst, and R. Blackburn, "Overcoming Barriers to Knowledge Sharing in Virtual Teams," *Organizational Dynamics* 36 (2007), pp. 259–73.

16. Forrester Research, reported in R. Reitsma, "The Data Digest: How Democratization of Technology Empowers Employees," *Forrester Blogs,* February 11, 2011, http://blogs.forrester.com/reineke_reitsma/11-02-11-the_data_digest_how_democratization_of_technology_empowers_employees (accessed April 16, 2012).

17. For more on social networks and employee collaboration, see S. Ahmed, "Catching the Wave; IBM CIO Talks about Social Media at Big Blue," *PC Advisor,* April 18, 2012, www.pcadvisor.co.uk/news/internet/3352201/catching-wave-ibm-cio-talks-about-social-media-at-big-blue; R. Shah, "A New Organizational Learning Goal: The Accrual of Awareness," *Forbes,* May 1, 2012, www.forbes.com/sites/rawnshah/2012/05/01/a-new-organizational-learning-goal-the-accrual-of-awareness; and

M. Benioff, "Welcome to the Social Media Revolution," *BBC News,* May 10, 2012, www.bbc.co.uk/news/business-18013662. Also see Cisco study that found that allowing employees to bring their own handheld device to work could help encourage workplace collaboration, reported in "Cisco Study: IT Saying Yes to BYOD," *Market Watch,* May 16, 2012, www.marketwatch.com/story/cisco-study-it-saying-yes-to-byod-2012-05-16 (all accessed May 16, 2012).

18. E. Sundstrom, K. P. DeMeuse, and D. Futrell, "Work Teams," *American Psychologist,* February 1990, pp. 120–33.

19. For example, see A. Zimmerman, "Wal-Mart's Emergency-Relief Team Girds for Hurricane Gustav," *The Wall Street Journal,* August 30, 2008, p. A3; and S. Sternberg, "Saved by 96 Minutes of CPR," *USA Today,* March 3, 2011, pp. 1D, 2D.

20. See M. Roberts, *Performance Hubs: Engaging Teams in Focused Continuous Improvement* (London: CRC Press, 2011); and R. R. Bassett, "How to Create and Sustain Successful Continuous Improvement Teams," *Automation World,* November 30, 2011, www.automationworld.com/operations/how-create-and-sustain-successful-continuous-improvement-teams (accessed May 16, 2012).

21. Data from J. P. Millikin, P. W. Hom, and C. C. Manz, "Self-Management Competencies in Self-Managing Teams: Their Impact on Multi-Team System Productivity," *The Leadership Quarterly,* October 2010, pp. 687–702.

22. See R. Rico, M. Sánchez-Manzanares, F. Gil, and C. Gibson, "Team Implicit Coordination Processes: A Team Knowledge-Based Approach," *Academy of Management Review,* January 2008, pp. 163–84.

23. For a preview of the future workplace, see L. C. Lancaster and D. Stillman, *The M-Factor: How the Millennial Generation Is Rocking the Workplace* (New York: HarperCollins, 2010).

24. Based on three meta-analyses covering 70 studies. See P. S. Goodman, R. Devadas, and T. L. Griffith Hughson, "Groups and Productivity: Analyzing the Effectiveness of Self-Managed Teams," in *Productivity in Organizations,* ed. J. P. Campbell, R. J. Campbell, and Associates (San Francisco: Jossey-Bass, 1998), pp. 295–327. Also see S. Kauffeld, "Self-Directed Work Groups and Team Competence," *Journal of Occupational and Organizational Psychology,* March 2006, pp. 1–21; and K. A. Smith-Jentsch, J. A. Cannon-Bowers, S. L. Tannenbaum, and E. Salas, "Guided Team Self-Correction: Impacts on Team Mental Models, Processes, and Effectiveness," *Small Group Research,* June 2008, pp. 303–27.

25. See B. W. Tuckman, "Developmental Sequence in Small Groups," *Psychological Bulletin,* June 1965, pp. 384–99; and B. W. Tuckman and M. A. C. Jensen, "Stages of Small-Group Development Revisited," *Group & Organization Studies,* December 1977, pp. 419–27. An instructive adaptation of the Tuckman model can be found in L. Holpp, "If Empowerment Is So Good, Why Does It Hurt?" *Training,* March 1995, p. 56. See also C. Gersick, "Marking Time: Predictable Transitions in Task Groups," *Academy of Management Journal,* June 1989, pp. 274–309; and S. Wait, "Team Building Is Critical for Successful Growth," *Reno Gazette-Journal,* August 5, 2006, p. 5E.

26. See F. P. Morgeson, M. H. Reider, and M. A. Campion, "Selecting Individuals in Team Settings: The Importance of Social Skills, Personality Characteristics, and Teamwork Knowledge," *Personnel Psychology,* Autumn 2005, pp. 583–611.

27. Practical advice on handling a dominating group member can be found in M. Finley, "Belling the Bully," *HR Magazine,* March 1992, pp. 82–86; see also B. Carey, "Fear in the Workplace: The Bullying Boss," *The New York Times,* June 22, 2004, pp. D1, D6. A description of three unhelpful coworkers you should try to sidestep (the chronic complainer, the shoulder rubber, and the chatterbox) are described in C. Potter, "Steer Clear: Three Coworkers to Avoid," *San Francisco Chronicle,* January 10, 2010,

p. D1. The problem of overcommunication among coworkers appears in J. Spolsky, "A Little Less Conversation," *Inc.*, February 2010, pp. 28–29.

28. S. Bucholz and T. Roth, *Creating the High-Performance Team* (New York: John Wiley & Sons, 1987), p. xi.

29. F. P. Morgeson, D. S. DeRue, and E. P. Karam, "Leadership in Teams: A Functional Approach to Understanding Leadership Structures and Processes," *Journal of Management*, January 2010, pp. 5–39.

30. "Human Cooperation Has Long History," *San Francisco Chronicle*, January 26, 2012, p. A9; reprinted from *Los Angeles Times*. See study by J. Henrich, "Social Science: Hunter-Gatherer Cooperation," *Nature*, January 26, 2012, pp. 449–50.

31. "With Teamwork, Humans Best Other Primates," *The New York Times*, March 6, 2012, p. D3. See study by L. G. Dean, R. Kendal, S. Schapiro, B. Thierry, and K. N. Laland, "Identification of the Social and Cognitive Processes Underlying Human Cumulative Culture," *Science* 335 (2012), pp. 1114–18.

32. See C. M. Christensen, M. Marx, and H. H. Stevenson, "The Tools of Cooperation and Change," *Harvard Business Review*, October 2006, pp. 73–80.

33. D. W. Johnson, G. Maruyama, R. Johnson, D. Nelson, and L. Skon, "Effects of Cooperative, Competitive, and Individualistic Goal Structures in Achievement: A Meta-Analysis," *Psychological Bulletin*, January 1981, pp. 56–57.

34. See J. O'Toole and W. Bennis, "What's Needed Next: A Culture of Candor," *Harvard Business Review*, June 2009, pp. 54–61; M. Yakovleva, R. R. Reilly, and R. Werko, "Why Do We Trust? Moving Beyond Individual to Dyadic Perceptions," *Journal of Applied Psychology*, January 2010, pp. 79–91; and J. P. MacDuffie, "Inter-Organizational Trust and the Dynamics of Distrust," *Journal of International Business Studies*, January 2011, pp. 35–47.

35. A big part of cohesiveness is building trust. See D. De Cremer and T. R. Tyler, "The Effects of Trust in Authority and Procedural Fairness on Cooperation," *Journal of Applied Psychology*, May 2007, pp. 639–49; J. A. Colquitt, B. A. Scott, and J. A. Lepine, "Trust, Trustworthiness, and Trust Propensity: A Meta-Analytic Test of Their Unique Relationships with Risk Taking and Job Performance," *Journal of Applied Psychology*, July 2007, pp. 909–27; and R. Ilies, D. T. Wagner, and F. P. Morgeson, "Explaining Affective Linkages in Teams: Individual Differences in Susceptibility to Contagion and Individualism–Collectivism," *Journal of Applied Psychology*, July 2007, pp. 1140–48.

36. A. Pentland, "The New Science of Building Great Teams," *Harvard Business Review*, April 2012, pp. 61–70.

37. J. Schaubroeck, S. S. K. Lam, and S. E. Cha, "Embracing Transformational Leadership: Team Values and the Impact of Leader Behavior on Team Performance," *Journal of Applied Psychology*, July 2007, pp. 1020–30.

38. "Is Your Team Too Big? Too Small? What's the Right Number?" *Knowledge@Wharton*, June 14, 2006, Wharton School, University of Pennsylvania, http://knowledge.wharton.upenn.edu/article.cfm?articleid-1501&CFID-1653072&CFTOKEN-14318984 (accessed April 16, 2012).

39. "A Team's-Eye View of Teams," *Training*, November 1995, p. 16. For more discussion of team size, see V. Hazrati, "Is Five the Optimal Team Size?" *InfoQ*, April 14, 2009, http://www.infoq.com/news/2009/04/agile-optimal-team-size (accessed April 16, 2012).

40. M. E. Shaw, *Group Dynamics*, 3rd ed. (New York: McGraw-Hill, 1981); G. Manners, "Another Look at Group Size, Group Problem-Solving and Member Consensus," *Academy of Management Journal* 18 (1975), pp. 715–24.

41. H.-S. Hwang and J. Guynes, "The Effect of Group Size on Group Performance in Computer-Supported Decision Making," *Information & Management*, April 1994, pp. 189–98.

42. S. J. Karau and K. D. Williams, "Social Loafing: Research Findings, Implications, and Future Directions," *Current Directions in Psychological Science*, October 1995, pp. 134–40; S. J. Zacarro, "Social Loafing: The Role of Task Attractiveness," *Personality and Social Psychology Bulletin* 10 (1984), pp. 99–106; P. W. Mulvey, L. Bowes-Sperry, and K. J. Klein, "The Effects of Perceived Loafing and Defensive Impression Management on Group Effectiveness," *Small Group Research*, June 1998, pp. 394–415; and L. Karakowsky and K. McBey, "Do My Contributions Matter? The Influence of Imputed Expertise on Member Involvement and Self-Evaluations in the Work Group," *Group & Organization Management*, March 2001, pp. 70–92.

43. J. Welch and S. Welch, "When a Star Slacks Off," *BusinessWeek*, March 17, 2008, p. 88.

44. B.-C. Lim and K. J. Klein, "Team Mental Models and Team Performance: A Field Study of the Effects of Team Mental Model Similarity and Accuracy," *Journal of Organizational Behavior*, January 2006, pp. 403–18.

45. J. L. Yang, "The Power of Number 4.6," *Fortune*, June 12, 2006, p. 122.

46. Deutschman, "The Managing Wisdom of High-Tech Superstars," *Fortune*, October 17, 1994, pp. 197–206.

47. J. R. Hackman, *Leading Teams: Setting the Stage for Great Performances* (Boston: Harvard Business School Press, 2002).

48. J. R. Hackman and N. J. Vidmar, "Effects of Size and Task Type on Group Performance and Member Reactions," *Sociometry* 33 (1970), pp. 37–54.

49. K. J. Klein, cited in "Is Your Team Too Big? Too Small? What's the Right Number?" 2006.

50. K. D. Benne and P. Sheats, "Functional Roles of Group Members," *Journal of Social Issues*, Spring 1948, pp. 41–49. See also E. C. Dierdorff and F. P. Morgeson, "Consensus in Work Role Requirements: The Influence of Discrete Occupational Contest on Role Expectations," *Journal of Applied Psychology*, September 2007, pp. 1228–41; and D. J. McAllister, D. Kamdar, E. W. Morrison, and D. B. Turban, "Disentangling Role Perceptions: How Perceived Role Breadth, Discretion, Instrumentality, and Efficacy Relate to Helping and Taking Charge," *Journal of Applied Psychology*, September 2007, pp. 1200–11.

51. D. C. Feldman, "The Development and Enforcement of Group Norms," *Academy of Management Review*, January 1984, pp. 47–53.

52. Siemens President and CEO Peter Löscher, interviewed by A. Bryant, "The Trust That Makes a Team Click," *The New York Times*, July 31, 2011, p. BU-1.

53. David A. Ferrucci, interviewed by P. R. Olsen, "Building the Team That Built Watson," *The New York Times*, January 8, 2012, p. BU-7.

54. Pamela Fields, CEO of Stetson, interviewed by A. Bryant, "Valuing Those Who Tell You the Bitter Truth," *The New York Times*, October 2, 2011, p. BU-2.

55. Feldman, "The Development and Enforcement of Group Norms," 1984.

56. J. B. Harvey, "The Abilene Paradox: The Management of Agreement," *Organizational Dynamics*, Summer 1988, pp. 17–43.

57. I. Janis, *Groupthink*, 2nd ed. (Boston: Houghton Mifflin, 1982), p. 9. See also K. D. Lassila, "A Brief History of Groupthink," *Yale Alumni Magazine*, January–February 2008, pp. 59–61, www.philosophy-religion.org/handouts/pdfs/BRIEF-HISTORY_GROUPTHINK.pdf (accessed April 16, 2012).

58. V. Kemper, "Senate Intelligence Report: Groupthink Viewed as Culprit in Move to War," *Los Angeles Times*, July 10, 2004, p. A.17.

59. See N. Bilton, "Tech Valuations Defy Restraints of Reality," *The New York Times*, January 23, 2012, p. B4.

60. J. Surowiecki, quoted in J. Freeman, "Books," *The Christian Science Monitor*, May 25, 2004; www.csmonitor.com/2004/0525/p15s01-bogn.html (accessed April 16, 2012). Also see

J. Surowiecki, *The Wisdom of Crowds: Why the Many Are Smarter Than the Few and How Collective Wisdom Shapes Business, Economies, Societies, and Nations* (New York: Doubleday, 2004).

61. See K. Weise, "Humans Plus Computers Equals Better Crowdsourcing," *Bloomberg Businessweek*, November 14–20, 2011, p. 49; and A. Vance, "MassMotion's Algorithms Bring Wisdom to the Virtual Crowds," *Bloomberg Businessweek*, November 21–27, 2011, p. 50.

62. V. H. Palmieri, quoted in L. Baum, "The Job Nobody Wants," *Business Week*, September 8, 1986, p. 60.

63. Surowiecki, quoted in Kemper, "Senate Intelligence Report: Groupthink Viewed as Culprit in Move to War," 2004. See also J. A. LePine, "Adaptation of Teams in Response to Unforeseen Change: Effects of Goal Difficulty and Team Composition in Terms of Cognitive Ability and Goal Orientation," *Journal of Applied Psychology* 90 (2005), pp. 1153–67.

64. M. R. Callway and J. K. Desser, "Groupthink: Effects of Cohesiveness and Problem-Solving Procedures on Group Decision Making," *Social Behavior and Personality*, no. 2, 1984, pp. 157–64.

65. See J. Lehrer, "Groupthink," *The New Yorker*, January 30, 2012, pp. 22–27. Jonah Lehrer is author of *Imagine: How Creativity Works* (Boston: Houghton-Mifflin, 2012).

66. K. Sawyer, quoted in Lehrer, "Groupthink," 2012, p. 23.

67. See D. Palermo and J. Jenkins, *Word Association Norms: Grade School Through College* (Minneapolis: University of Minnesota Press, 1964).

68. C. J. Nemeth, M. Personnaz, B. Personnaz, and J. A. Goncalo, "The Liberating Role of Conflict in Group Creativity: A Cross-Cultural Study," Institute of Industrial Relations Working Paper No. iirwps-090-03, October 13, 2003, http://ssrn.com/abstract=440663 (accessed April 16, 2012).

69. S. Cain, "The Rise of the New Groupthink," *The New York Times*, January 15, 2012, pp. SR-1, SR-6. Cain is also author of *Quiet: The Power of Introverts in a World That Can't Stop Talking* (New York: Crown Publishing Group, 2012).

70. Some discussions of sources of conflict appear in E. Bernstein, "When a Co-Worker Is Stressed Out," *The Wall Street Journal*, August 26, 2008, pp. D1, D2; M. Steen, "Apologizing on the Job," *San Francisco Chronicle*, February 28, 2010, p. D1; E. Zimmerman, "The Office Skirmish: How to Avoid Round 2," *The New York Times*, March 14, 2010, Business section, p. 9; and D. Nishi, "What to Do If Your Boss Is the Problem," *The Wall Street Journal*, April 20, 2010, p. D4.

71. J. A. Wall Jr. and R. Robert Callister, "Conflict and Its Management," *Journal of Management*, no. 3 (1995), p. 517.

72. C. Alter, "An Exploratory Study of Conflict and Coordination in Interorganizational Service Delivery Systems," *Academy of Management Journal*, September 1990, pp. 478–502; S. P. Robbins, "'Conflict Management' and 'Conflict Resolution' Are Not Synonymous Terms," *California Management Review*, Winter 1978, p. 70.

73. Cooperative conflict is discussed in D. Tjosvold, *Learning to Manage Conflict: Getting People to Work Together Productively* (New York: Lexington, 1993); and D. Tjosvold and D. W. Johnson, *Productive Conflict Management Perspectives for Organizations* (New York: Irvington, 1983). See also A. C. Amason, K. R. Thompson, W. A. Hochwarter, and A. W. Harrison, "Conflict: An Important Dimension in Successful Management Teams," *Organizational Dynamics*, Autumn 1995, pp. 20–35; and A. C. Amason, "Distinguishing the Effects of Functional and Dysfunctional Conflict on Strategic Decision Making: Resolving a Paradox for Top Management Teams," *Academy of Management Journal*, February 1996, pp. 123–48.

74. L. Lange, quoted in J. Noveck, "Do Bosses Need to Be Mean to Get Work Done?" *Nevada Appeal*, July 9, 2006, pp. D1, D2. See also D. Brady, "Charm Offensive," *BusinessWeek*, June 26, 2006,

pp. 76–80; and A. Dobson and R. Berman, "Building a Better Boss," *San Francisco Chronicle*, September 23, 2007, p. H-1.

75. G. Namie, *The WBI U.S. Workplace Bullying Survey*, 2010, conducted by Workplace Bullying Institute and Zogby International, http://workplacebullying.org/multi/pdf/WBI_2010_Natl_Survey.pdf (accessed April 16, 2012).

76. K. L. Zellars, B. J. Tepper, and M. K. Duffy, "Abusive Supervision and Subordinates' Organizational Citizenship Behavior," *Journal of Applied Psychology*, December 2002, pp. 1068–76.

77. B. J. Tepper and E. C. Taylor, "Relationships Among Supervisors' and Subordinates' Procedural Justice Perceptions and Organizational Citizenship Behaviors," *Academy of Management Journal*, February 2003, pp. 97–105; B. J. Tepper, M. K. Duffy, J. Hoobler, and M. D. Ensley, "Moderators of the Relationship between Coworkers' Organizational Citizenship Behavior and Fellow Employees' Attitudes," *Journal of Applied Psychology*, June 2005, pp. 455–65; B. J. Tepper, M. Uhl-Bien, G. F. Kohut, S. G. Rogelberg, D. E. Lockhart, and M. D. Ensley, "Subordinates' Resistance and Managers' Evaluations of Subordinates' Performance," *Journal of Management*, April 1, 2006, pp. 185–209; B. J. Tepper, M. K. Duffy, C. A. Henle, and L. S. Lambert, "Procedural Injustice, Victim Precipitation, and Abusive Supervision," *Personnel Psychology*, March 2006, pp. 101–23; B. J. Tepper, S. E. Moss, D. E. Lockhart, and J. C. Carr, "Abusive Supervision, Upward Maintenance Supervision, and Subordinates' Psychological Distress," *Academy of Management Journal* 50 (2007), pp. 1169–80; and B. J. Tepper, "Abusive Supervision in Formal Organizations: Review, Synthesis, and Research Agenda," *Journal of Management*, June 1, 2007, pp. 261–89.

78. R. I. Sutton in "Breakthrough Ideas for 2004: The HBR List," *Harvard Business Review*, February 2004, pp. 13–24, 32–37. Sutton's topic was headed "More Trouble Than They Are Worth." His book based on these ideas is *The No Asshole Rule: Building a Civilized Workplace and Surviving One That Isn't* (New York: Warner, 2007).

79. R. I. Sutton, "R. I. Sutton: Nasty People," *CIO Insight*, May 1, 2004, www.cioinsight.com/c/a/Past-Opinions/Robert-I-Sutton-Nasty-People (accessed April 16, 2012).

80. A. M. O'Leary-Kelly, R. W. Griffin, and D. J. Glew, "Organization-Motivated Aggression: A Research Framework," *Academy of Management Review*, January 1996, pp. 225–53. See also G. A. Van Kleef and S. Côté, "Expressing Anger in Conflict: When It Helps and When It Hurts," *Journal of Applied Psychology*, November 2007, pp. 1557–69.

81. C. M. Pearson and C. L. Porath, "On the Nature, Consequences, and Remedies of Workplace Incivility: No Time for 'Nice'? Think Again," *Academy of Management Executive*, February 2005, p. 7. See also C. L. Porath and C. M. Pearson, "The Cost of Bad Behavior," *Organizational Dynamics*, January–March 2010, pp. 64–71.

82. L. R. Pondy, "Organizational Conflict: Concepts and Models," *Administrative Science Quarterly* 2 (1967), pp. 296–320.

83. K. T. Kishida, D. Yang, K. H. Quartz, S. R. Quartz, and P. R. Montague, "Implicit Signals in Small Group Settings and Their Impact on the Expression of Cognitive Capacity and Associated Brain Responses," *Philosophical Transactions of the Royal Society B*, March 5, 2012, pp. 704–16.

84. E. Bernstein, "Speaking Up Is Hard to Do: Researchers Explain Why," *The Wall Street Journal*, February 7, 2012, pp. D1, D4.

85. "Help for the Tongue-Tied," sidebar to Bernstein, 2012, p. D4.

86. "Japan: Toyota Falls Victim to a Clash of Cultures," *The Week*, March 12, 2010, p. 18.

87. See K. A. Crowne, "What Leads to Cultural Intelligence?" *Business Horizons*, September–October 2008, pp. 391–99; and N. Goodman, "Cultivating Cultural Intelligence," *Training*, March–April 2011, p. 38.

88. K. W. Thomas, "Conflict and Conflict Management," in *Handbook of Industrial and Organizational Psychology*, M. Dunnette, ed. (Chicago: Rand McNally, 1976), pp. 889–935; K. W. Thomas "Toward Multiple Dimensional Values in Teaching: The Example of Conflict Behaviors," *Academy of Management Review*, July 1977, pp. 484–90; and M.A Rahim, "A Strategy for Managing Conflict in Complex Organizations," *Human Relations*, January 1985, p. 84.

89. Rahim, "A Strategy for Managing Conflict in Complex Organizations," 1985.

90. R. A. Cosier and C. R. Schwenk, "Agreement and Thinking Alike: Ingredients for Poor Decisions," *Academy of Management Executive*, February 1990, p. 71. Also see J. P. Kotter, "Kill Complacency," *Fortune*, August 5, 1996, pp. 168–70.

91. See "Facilitators as Devil's Advocates," *Training*, September 1993, p. 10; and C. R. Schwenk, "Devil's Advocacy in Managerial Decision Making," *Journal of Management Studies*, April 1984, pp. 153–68.

92. S. G. Katzenstein, "The Debate on Structured Debate: Toward a Unified Theory," *Organizational Behavior and Human Decision Processes*, June 1996, pp. 316–32.

CHAPTER 14

1. H. Lancaster, "If Your Career Needs More Attention, Maybe You Should Get an Agent," *The Wall Street Journal*, October 20, 1998, p. B1.

2. R. L. Knowdell, "The 10 New Rules for Strategizing Your Career," *The Futurist*, June–July 1998, pp. 19–24. See also K. Madden, "Plan a Successful Career Change," *Reno Gazette-Journal*, March 11, 2012, p. 1F.

3. Center for Professional Excellence, York College, 2010 national poll, reported in "Outfits Key to How You Are Perceived," *Arizona Republic*, September 21, 2011, p. CL1.

4. C. A. Schriesheim, J. M. Tolliver, and O. C. Behling, "Leadership Theory: Some Implications for Managers," *MSU Business Topics*, Summer 1978, p. 35. See also G. Yukl, "Managerial Leadership: A Review of Theory and Research," *Journal of Management* 15 (1989), pp. 251–89.

5. T. Peters and N. Austin, *A Passion for Excellence* (New York: Random House, 1985), pp. 5–6; but see also B. Kellerman, "Leadership—Warts and All," *Harvard Business Review*, January 1, 2004, pp. 40–45.

6. B. M. Bass and R. Bass, The *Bass Handbook of Leadership: Theory, Research, and Managerial Applications*, 4th ed. (New York: Free Press, 2008), p. 654.

7. Tim Bucher, interviewed by A. Bryant, "Monday-Night Strategizing with the Team," *The New York Times*, February 12, 2012, p. BU-2.

8. See R. Hooijberg and R. E. Quinn, "Behavioral Complexity and the Development of Effective Managers." In R. L. Phillips and J. G. Hunt, eds., *Strategic Management: A Multiorganizational-Level Perspective* (New York: Quorum, 1992); and K. A. Lawrence, P. Lenk, and R. E. Quinn, "Behavioral Complexity in Leadership: The Psychometric Properties of a New Instrument to Measure Behavioral Repertoire," *The Leadership Quarterly* 20 (2009), pp. 87–102.

9. G. A. Yuki, *Leadership in Organizations*, 7th ed. (Upper Saddle River, NJ: Prentice Hall, 2008), p. 8.

10. J. P. Kotter, "What Leaders Really Do," *Harvard Business Review*, December 2001, pp. 85–96; the role of leadership within organizational change is discussed in J. P. Kotter, *Leading Change* (Boston: Harvard Business School Press, 1996).

11. Managing in the world of complexity is discussed in G. Sargut and R. G. McGrath, "Learning to Live with Complexity," *Harvard Business Review*, September 2011, pp. 68–76; and M. J. Mauboussin, "Embracing Complexity," *Harvard Business Review*, September 2011, pp. 88–92.

12. F. Smith, quoted in "All in a Day's Work," *Harvard Business Review*, December 2001, pp. 54–66.

13. L. H. Chusmir, "Personalized versus Socialized Power Needs among Working Women and Men," *Human Relations*, February 1986, p. 149.

14. A. Wong, quoted in "My Journey to the Top," *Newsweek*, October 15, 2007, pp. 49–65.

15. R. M. Kramer, "The Great Intimidators," *Harvard Business Review*, February 2006, pp. 88–96.

16. Marc Andreessen, quoted in D. MacMillan, "Maintaining Intensity," *San Francisco Chronicle*, December 12, 2011, pp. 1D, 2D, from Bloomberg News.

17. D. MacMillan and B. Stone, "Zynga's Quest for Big-Spending Whales," *Bloomberg Businessweek*, July 6, 2011, www.businessweek.com/magazine/zyngas-quest-for-bigspending-whales-07072011.html (accessed April 24, 2012).

18. MacMillan, "Maintaining Intensity," 2011.

19. Eric Schmidt, quoted in MacMillan, 2011.

20. Former Zynga employee Roger Dickie, quoted in MacMillan, 2011.

21. M. Pincus, in interview by J. Swartz, "Feeling Washed Up, Then Finding 'Treasure,'" *USA Today*, April 23, 2012, p. 2B.

22. M. Pincus, in interview by J. Swartz, "Set a Goal First, Says CEO of Zynga," *USA Today*, April 23, 2012, pp. 1B, 2B. See also I. Sherr, "Zynga Sees World Beyond Facebook," *The Wall Street Journal*, April 27, 2012, p. B4.

23. S. Harrison, "Deliberate Acts of Decency," *HR Magazine*, July 2007, pp. 97–99.

24. Based on Table 1 in G. Yukl, C. M. Falbe, and J. Y. Youn, "Patterns of Influence Behavior for Managers," *Group & Organization Management*, March 1993, pp. 5–28.

25. G. Yukl, H. Kim, and C. M. Falbe, "Antecedents of Influence Outcomes," *Journal of Applied Psychology*, June 1996, pp. 309–317.

26. A. Lashinsky, "The Decade of Steve," *Fortune*, November 5, 2009, http://tech.fortune.cnn.com/2009/11/05/the-decade-of-steve (accessed April 25, 2012).

27. R. M. Stogdill, "Personal Factors Associated with Leadership: A Survey of the Literature," *Journal of Psychology* 25 (1948), pp. 35–71; and R. M. Stogdill, *Handbook of Leadership* (New York: Free Press, 1974).

28. B. Bass, *Stogdill's Handbook of Leadership*, rev. ed. (New York: Free Press, 1981).

29. But see D. S. DeRue, J. D. Nahrgang, N. Wellman, S. E. Humphrey, "Trait and Behavioral Theories of Leadership: An Integration and Meta-Analytic Test of Their Relative Validity," *Personnel Psychology* 64 (2011), pp. 7–52.

30. See J. Hogan, R. Hogan, and R. B. Kaiswer, "Management Derailment: Personality Assessment and Mitigation," in S. Zedeck, ed., *Handbook of Industrial and Organizational Psychology*, 2011, pp 555–75; and S. J. Zaccaro, "Trait-Based Perspectives of Leadership," *American Psychologist*, January 2007, pp. 6–16.

31. Executive coaching is discussed in S. Labadessa, "Now Go Out and Lead!" *BusinessWeek*, January 8, 2007, pp. 72–73.

32. Leadership development programs are discussed in L. Freifeld, "Verizon's New # Is 1," *Training*, January–February 2012, pp. 28–32; and K. Linebaugh, "The New GE Way: Go Deep, Not Wide," *The Wall Street Journal*, March 7, 2012, pp. B1, B9.

33. J. M. Kouzes and B. Z. Posner, *The Leadership Challenge: How to Get Extraordinary Things Done in Organizations* (San Francisco: Jossey-Bass, 1995).

34. E. Patten and K. Parker, *A Gender Reversal on Key Aspirations*, Pew Research Center, April 19, 2012, www.pewsocialtrends.org/2012/04/19/a-gender-reversal-on-career-aspirations (accessed April 25, 2012).

35. Kim Parker, quoted in L. Petrecca, "High-Paying Careers Top More Young Women's Lists," *USA Today*, April 20, 2012, p. 1A.

36. Study by Catalyst, New York, reported in J. S. Lublin, "Women Aspire to Be Chief as Much as Men Do," *The Wall Street Journal,* June 28, 2004, p. D2.

37. Supportive findings are contained in J. M. Twenge, "Changes in Women's Assertiveness in Response to Status and Roles: A Cross-Temporal Meta-Analysis, 1931–93," *Journal of Personality and Social Psychology,* July 2001, pp. 133–45.

38. R. Sharpe, "As Leaders, Women Rule," *BusinessWeek,* November 20, 2000, pp. 75–84.

39. Study by Hagberg Consulting Group, Foster City, California, reported in Sharpe, 2000, p. 75.

40. See A. H. Eagly, S. J. Karau, and B. T. Johnson, "Gender and Leadership Style among School Principals: A Meta-Analysis," *Educational Administration Quarterly,* February 1992, pp. 76–102.

41. Gender and the emergence of leaders was examined by A. H. Eagly and S. J. Karau, "Gender and the Emergence of Leaders: A Meta-Analysis," *Journal of Personality and Social Psychology,* May 1991, pp. 685–710; J. L. Prime, N. M. Carter, and T. M. Welbourne, "Women 'Take Care,' Men 'Take Charge': Managers' Stereotypic Perceptions of Women and Men Leaders," *The Psychologist-Manager Journal,* January 2009, pp. 25–49; and R. Ayman and K. Korabik, "Leadership: Why Gender and Culture Matter," *Harvard Business Review,* May 2010, pp. 117–21.

42. For a summary of this research, see H. Ibarra and O. Obodaru, "Women and Vision Thing," *Harvard Business Review,* January 2009, pp. 62–70.

43. Association of Executive Search Consultants, *BlueSteps 2007 Diversity Report,* cited in J. D. McCool, "Diversity Pledges Ring Hollow," *BusinessWeek.com,* February 5, 2008, www.businessweek.com/managing/content/feb2008/ca2008025_080192.htm?chan=search (accessed April 2, 2012).

44. D. Brady, K. Isaacs, M. Reeves, R. Burroway, and M. Reynolds, "Sector, Size, Stability, and Scandal: Explaining the Presence of Female Executives in Fortune 500 Firms," *Gender in Management: An International Journal* 26, no. 1 (2011), pp. 84–105.

45. E. McBride, "Companies with Female CEOs Pay Out Significantly Higher Dividends," *Business Insider,* March 17, 2012, http://financialfeeder.net/2012/03/companies-with-female-ceos-pay-out-significantly-higher-dividends (accessed April 30, 2012).

46. L. Tischler, "Where Are the Women?" *Fast Company,* February 2004, pp. 52–60.

47. P. Sellers, "Power: Do Women Really Want It?" *Fortune,* October 13, 2003, p. 88.

48. See M. Conlin, "Self-Deprecating Women," *BusinessWeek,* June 14, 2004, p. 26. For more on this subject, see also "The 'Masculine' and 'Feminine' Sides of Leadership and Culture: Perception vs. Reality," *Knowledge@Wharton,* October 5, 2005, http://knowledge.wharton.upenn.edu/index.cfm?fa=printArticle & ID (accessed April 26, 2012); "Guiding Aspiring Female Execs Up the Ladder," *HR Magazine,* January 2006, p. 14; Q. M. Roberson and C. K. Stevens, "Making Sense of Diversity in the Workplace: Organizational Justice and Language Abstraction in Employees' Accounts of Diversity-Related Incidents," *Journal of Applied Psychology,* March 2006, pp. 379–91; E. Porter, "Women in Workplace—Trend Is Reversing," *San Francisco Chronicle,* March 2, 2006, p. A2, reprinted from *The New York Times;* J. Zaslow, "A New Generation Gap: Differences Emerge Among Women in the Workplace," *The Wall Street Journal,* May 4, 2006, p. D1; W. A. Holsetin, "Glass Ceiling? Get a Hammer," *The New York Times,* June 18, 2006, sec. 3, p. 12; C. Hymowitz, "Women Swell Ranks as Middle Managers, but Are Scarce at Top," *The Wall Street Journal,* July 24, 2006, p. B1; S. Vedantam, "Glass Ceiling Breaks When Women Are in Charge, Study Says," *San Francisco Chronicle,* August 13, 2006, p. A17, reprinted from *Washington Post.*

49. B. Groysberg, "How Star Women Build Portable Skills," *Harvard Business Review,* February 2008, pp. 74–81. See also R. D. Arvey, Z. Zhang, B. J. Avolio, and R. F. Krueger, "Developmental and Genetic Determinants of Leadership Role Occupancy among Women," *Journal of Applied Psychology,* May 2007, pp. 693–706. Some popular treatments on the subject of woman and leadership are C. V. Flett, *What Men Don't Tell Women about Business: Opening Up the Heavily Guarded Alpha Male Playbook* (New York: Wiley, 2008) and N. DiSesa, *Seducing the Boys Club: Uncensored Tactics from a Woman at the Top* (New York: Ballantine Books, 2008).

50. See research by N. M. Carter and C. Silva, "Women in Management: Delusions of Progress," *Harvard Business Review,* March 2010, pp. 19–21. Quit rates were studied by P. W. Hom, L. Roberson, and A. Ellis, "Challenging Conventional Wisdom About Who Quits: Revelations from Corporate America," *Journal of Applied Psychology,* January 2008, pp. 1–34.

51. "Women CEOs of the Fortune 1000," Catalyst, April 23, 2012, www.catalyst.org/publication/271/women-ceos-of-the-fortune-1000 (accessed April 30, 2012).

52. Data compiled by Bloomberg News from proxy filings, reported in A. Leondis, "CEOs Crack Glass Ceiling," *San Francisco Chronicle,* May 14, 2010, pp. D1, D4.

53. R. Foroohar and S. H. Breenberg, "Working Women Are Poised to Become the Biggest Economic Engine the World Has Ever Known," *Newsweek,* November 2, 2009, pp. B3–B5. See also L. Mundy, *The Richer Sex: How the New Majority of Female Breadwinners Is Transforming Sex, Love, and Family* (New York: Simon & Schuster, 2012).

54. R. House, M. Javidan, P. Hanges, and P. Dorfman, "Understanding Cultures and Implicit Leadership Theories Across the Globe: An Introduction to Project GLOBE," *Journal of World Business,* Spring 2004, p. 4.

55. R. Likert, *New Patterns of Management* (New York: McGraw-Hill, 1961); and R. Likert, *The Human Organization* (New York: McGraw-Hill, 1967).

56. C. A. Schriesman and B. J. Bird, "Contributions of the Ohio State Studies to the Field of Leadership," *Journal of Management Studies* 5 (1979), pp. 135–45; and C. L. Shartle, "Early Years of the Ohio State University Leadership Studies," *Journal of Management* 5 (1979), pp. 126–34.

57. The steps were developed by H. P. Sims Jr., S. Faraj, and S. Yun, "When Should a Leader Be Directive or Empowering? How to Develop Your Own Situational Theory of Leadership," *Business Horizons,* March–April 2009, pp. 149–58.

58. F. E. Fiedler, "Assumed Similarity Measures as Predictors of Team Effectiveness," *Journal of Abnormal and Social Psychology* 49 (1954), pp. 381–88; F. E. Fiedler, *Leader Attitudes and Group Effectiveness* (Urbana, IL: University of Illinois Press, 1958); and F. E. Fiedler, *A Theory of Leadership Effectiveness* (New York: McGraw-Hill, 1967).

59. See M. V. Vugt, R. Hogan, and R. B. Kaiser, "Leadership, Followership, and Evolution," *American Psychologist,* April 2008, pp. 182–96.

60. R. J. House, "A Path-Goal Theory of Leader Effectiveness," *Administrative Science Quarterly,* September 1971, pp. 321–38. The most recent version of the theory is found in R. J. House, "Path–Goal Theory of Leadership: Lessons, Legacy, and a Reformulated Theory," *Leadership Quarterly,* Autumn 1996, pp. 323–52.

61. These studies are summarized in House, "Path–Goal Theory of Leadership: Lessons, Legacy, and a Reformulated Theory," 1996.

62. See G. Wang, I-S. Oh, S. H. Courtright, and A. E. Colbert, "Transformational Leadership and Performance Across

Criteria and Levels: A Meta-Analytic Review of 25 Years of Research," *Group & Organization Management,* 2011, pp 223–70.

63. Results can be found in P. M. Podsakoff, S. B. MacKenzie, M. Ahearne, and W. H. Bommer, "Searching for a Needle in a Haystack: Trying to Identify the Illusive Moderators of Leadership Behaviors," *Journal of Management,* 1995, pp. 422–70.

64. Sims, Faraj, and Yun, "When Should a Leader Be Directive or Empowering?" 2009.

65. For a complete description of the full-range leadership theory, see B. J. Bass and B. J. Avolio, *Revised Manual for the Multi-Factor Leadership Questionnaire* (Palo Alto, CA: Mindgarden, 1997).

66. See Wang, Oh, Courtright, and Colbert, "Transformational Leadership and Performance Across Criteria and Levels: A Meta-Analytic Review of 25 Years of Research," 2011.

67. A definition and description of transactional leadership is provided by J. Antonakis and R. J. House, "The Full-Range Leadership Theory: The Way Forward," in B. J. Avolio and F. J. Yammarino, eds., *Transformational and Charismatic Leadership: The Road Ahead* (New York: JAI Press, 2002), pp. 3–34. See also L. Y. C. Leong and R. Fischer, "Is Transformational Leadership Universal? A Meta-Analytical Investigation of Multi-factor Leadership Questionnaire Means Across Cultures," *Journal of Leadership & Organizational Studies* 18, no. 2 (2011), pp. 164–74.

68. See K. Pender, "Companies Can Thrive Even After Exit of Star CEO," *San Francisco Chronicle,* August 26, 2011, pp. D1, D5.

69. J. Swartz, "Silicon Valley Ruminates over Loss of Leader," *USA Today,* August 26, 2011, p. 3B.

70. S. Martin, "Apple CEO Tim Cook as Pitchman No. 1," *USA Today,* August 26, 2011, p. 3B.

71. For more about Tim Cook see P. Svensson, Associated Press, "Out of the Shadows," *Reno Gazette-Journal,* April 28, 2012, pp. 7A, 8A.

72. U. R. Dundum, K. B. Lowe, and B. J. Avolio, "A Meta-Analysis of Transformational and Transactional Leadership Correlates of Effectiveness and Satisfaction: An Update and Extension," in Avolio and Yammarino, eds., *Transformational and Charismatic Leadership: The Road Ahead,* 2002, p. 38.

73. Supportive results can be found in T. A. Judge and J. E. Bono, "Five-Factor Model of Personality and Transformational Leadership," *Journal of Applied Psychology,* October 2000, pp. 751–65; and S. Oreg and Y. Berson, "Leadership and Employees' Reactions to Change: The Role of Leaders' Personal Attributes and Transformational Leadership," *Personnel Psychology* 64 (2011), pp. 627–59.

74. Supportive research is summarized by Antonakis and House, "The Full-Range Leadership Theory: The Way Forward," 2002. See also W. Zhu, R. E. Riggio, B. J. Avolio, and J. J. Sosik, "The Effect of Leadership on Follower Moral Identity: Does Transformational/Transactional Style Make a Difference?" *Journal of Leadership & Organizational Studies* 18 (2011), pp. 150–63.

75. B. Morris, "What Makes Pepsi Great?" *Fortune,* March 3, 2008, pp. 54–66.

76. J. P. Mangalindan, "PepsiCo CEO: 'If All Consumers Exercised … Obesity Wouldn't Exist,'" *Fortune,* April 27, 2010, http://money .cnn.com/2010/04/27/news/companies/indra_nooyi_pepsico .fortune/index.htm (accessed April 26, 2012).

77. H. Schultz, "Indra Nooyi," *Time,* April 30, 2008, www.time .com/time/specials/2007/article/0,28804,1733748_ 1733758,00.html (accessed April 26, 2012). See also D. Brady, "Keeping Cool in Hot Water," *BusinessWeek,* June 11, 2007, p. 49.

78. "R. Wartzman, "The Pepsi Challenge," *Forbes,* April 9, 2012, www.forbes.com/sites/drucker;2012/04/09/the-pepsi-challenge.

See also "Pop Quiz: Can Indra Nooyi Revive PepsiCo," *Knowledge@Wharton,* March 28, 2012, http://knowledge.wharton. upenn.edu/article.cfm?articleid=2966; S. Strom, "PepsiCo's Profit Beats Estimates," *The New York Times,* April 26, 2012, www.nytimes.com/2012/04/27/business/pepsicos-profit- beats-estimates.html?_r=1 (all accessed April 26, 2012); and M. Esterl, "PepsiCo Slips Despite New Ads," *The Wall Street Journal,* April 27, 2012, p. B5.

79. These definitions are derived from R. Kark, B. Shamir, and C. Chen, "The Two Faces of Transformational Leadership: Empowerment and Dependency," *Journal of Applied Psychology,* April 2003, pp. 246–55. See A. E. Colbert, A. L. Kristof-Brown, B. H. Bradley, and M. R. Barrick, "CEO Transformational Leadership: The Role of Goal Importance Congruence in Top Management Teams," *Academy of Management Journal,* February 2008, pp. 81–96.

80. See A. Erez, V. F. Misangyi, D. E. Johnson, M. A. LePine, and K. C. Halverson, "Stirring the Hearts of Followers: Charismatic Leadership as the Transferal of Affect," *Journal of Applied Psychology* 93 (2008), pp. 602–15.

81. See J. Antonakis, M. Fenley, and S. Liechti, "Can Charisma Be Taught? Tests of Two Interventions," *Academy of Management Learning & Education* 10, no. 3 (2011), pp. 374–96; and J. P. Balkundi, M. Kilduff, and D. A. Harrison, "Centrality and Charisma: Comparing How Leader Networks and Attributions Affect Team Performance," *Journal of Applied Psychology,* November 2011, pp. 1209–22.

82. B. Nanus, *Visionary Leadership* (San Francisco: Jossey-Bass, 1992), p. 8. See also J. Murphy, "Ghosn Hedges Bets on Emissions," *The Wall Street Journal,* May 15, 2008, p. B2: and D. Enrich, "Citigroup Pandit Faces Test as Pressure on Bank Grows," *The Wall Street Journal,* May 6, 2008, pp. A1, A20.

83. Morris, "What Makes Pepsi Great?" 2008.

84. See R. E. Quinn, "Moments of Greatness: Entering the Fundamental State of Leadership," *Harvard Business Review,* July–August 2005, pp. 75–83.

85. "Pop Quiz: Can Indra Nooyi Revive PepsiCo?" 2012.

86. Morris, "What Makes Pepsi Great?" 2008.

87. D. Brady, "PepsiCo's Nooyi Is Focused on Retention, Not Succession," *Bloomberg Businessweek,* March 12, 2012, www .businessweek.com/articles/2012-03-12/pepsicos-nooyi-is-fo- cused-on-retention-not-succession (accessed April 12, 2012).

88. Wartzman, "The Pepsi Challenge," 2012.

89. See H. Lui, and A. Chuang, "Transforming Service Employees and Climate: A Multilevel, Multisource Examination of Transformational Leadership in Building Long-Term Service Relationships," *Journal of Applied Psychology,* July 2007, pp. 2006–19.

90. Results can be found in Dundum, Lowe, and Avolio, 2002; and Erez, Misangyi, Johnson, LePine, and Halverson, "Stirring the Hearts of Followers: Charismatic Leadership as the Transferal of Affect," 2008, pp. 602–15.

91. See Kark, Shamir, and Chen, "The Two Faces of Transformational Leadership: Empowerment and Dependency," 2003.

92. D. N. Den Hartog and F. D. Belschak, "When Does Transformational Leadership Enhance Employee Proactive Behavior? The Role of Autonomy and Role Breadth Self-Efficacy," *Journal of Applied Psychology,* January 2012, pp. 194–202.

93. Supportive results can be found in B. M. Bass, B. J. Avolio, D. I. Jung, and Y. Berson, "Predicting Unit Performance by Assessing Transformational and Transactional Leadership," *Journal of Applied Psychology,* April 2003, pp. 207–18; and D. N. Den Hartog and F. D. Belschak, "When Does Transformational Leadership Enhance Employee Proactive Behavior? The Role of Autonomy and Role Breadth Self-Efficacy," *Journal of Applied Psychology,* January 2012, pp. 194–202.

94. B. J. Avolio, R. J. Reichard, S. T. Hannah, F. O Walumbwa, and A. Chan, "A Meta-Analytic Review of Leadership Impact Research: Experimental and Quasi-Experimental Studies," *Leadership Quarterly* 20 (2009), pp. 764–84; J. Kanengieter and A. Rajagopal-Durbin, "Wilderness Leadership—On the Job," *Harvard Business Review,* April 2012, pp. 127–31.

95. See J. E. Stiglitz, "Who Do These Bankers Think They Are?" *Harvard Business Review,* March 2010, p. 36.

96. See K. K. Mihelic, B. Lipicnik, and M. Tekavcic, "Ethical Leadership," *International Journal of Management and Information Systems,* Fourth Quarter 2010, pp. 31–41; and F. O. Walumbwa, A. L. Christensen, and F. Hailey, "Authentic Leadership and the Knowledge Economy: Sustaining Motivation and Trust among Knowledge Workers," *Organizational Dynamics* 40 (2011), pp. 110–18.

97. G. Graen and J. F. Cashman, "A Role-Making Model of Leadership in Formal Organizations: A Developmental Approach," in J. G. Hunt and L. L. Larson, eds., *Leadership Frontiers* (Kent, OH: Kent State University Press, 1975), pp. 143–65; F. Dansereau Jr., G. Graen, and W. J. Haga, "A Vertical Dyad Linkage Approach to Leadership Within Formal Organizations: A Longitudinal Investigation of the Role-Making Process," *Organizational Behavior and Human Performance,* February 1975, pp. 46–78; and K. S. Wilson, H.-P. Sin, and D. E. Conlon, "What About the Leader in Leader–Member Exchange? The Impact of Resource Exchanges and Substitutability in the Leader," *Academy of Management Review,* July 2010, pp. 358–72.

98. See D. Duchon, S. G. Green, and T. D. Taber, "Vertical Dyad Linkage: A Longitudinal Assessment of Antecedents, Measures, and Consequences," *Journal of Applied Psychology,* February 1986, pp. 56–60.

99. See B. Erdogan and T. N. Bauer, "Differentiated Leader-Member Exchanges: The Buffering Role of Justice Climate," *Journal of Applied Psychology,* November 2010, pp. 1104–20; F. O. Walumbwa, R. Cropanzano, and B. M. Goldman, "How Leader–Member Exchange Influences Effective Work Behaviors: Social Exchange and Internal External Efficacy Perspectives," *Personnel Psychology* 64 (2011), pp. 739–70; and E. Xu, X. Huang, C. K. Lam, and Q. Miao, "Abusive Supervision and Work Behaviors: The Mediating Role of LMX," *Journal of Organizational Behavior,* May 2012, pp. 531–43.

100. See Walumbwa, Cropanzano, and Goldman, 2011.

101. An overall summary of servant leadership is provided by L. C. Spears, *Reflections on Leadership: How Robert K. Greenleaf's Theory of Servant-Leadership Influenced Today's Top Management Thinkers* (New York: Wiley, 1995). See also D. Van Dierendonck, "Servant Management: A Review and Synthesis," *Journal of Management* 37 (2011), pp. 1228–61.

102. D. MacMillan, "Survivor: CEO Edition," *Bloomberg Businessweek,* March 1, 2010, p. 35.

103. D. Gergen, "Bad News for Bullies," *U.S. News & World Report,* June 19, 2006, p. 54.

104. M. De Pree, quoted in Gergen, "Bad News for Bullies," 2006. The quote is from M. De Pree, *Leadership Is an Art* (New York: Dell, 1989).

105. See B. J. Avolio, J. J. Sosik, D. I. Jung, and Yair Berson, "Leadership Models, Methods, and Applications," in *Handbook of Psychology* (New York: John Wiley, 2003), pp. 295–98.

106. L. Capotosto, "Millennial Management," *Darwin,* www2 .darwinmag.com/connect/books/book.cfm?ID-188 (accessed April 26, 2012).

107. D. MacRae, "Six Secrets of Successful E-Leaders," *Business Week online,* September 6, 2001; www.businessweek.com/ technology/content/sep2001/tc2001096_619.htm (accessed April 26, 2012).

108. D. Q. Mills, *E-Leadership: Guiding Your Business to Success in the New Economy* (Paramus, NJ: Prentice Hall, 2001). See also R. Hargrove, *E-Leader: Reinventing Leadership in a Connected Economy* (Boulder, CO: Perseus Books, 2001); T. M. Siebel, *Taking Care of eBusiness: How Today's Market Leaders Are Increasing Revenue, Productivity, and Customer Satisfaction* (New York: Doubleday, 2001); S. Annunzio, *eLeadership: Bold Solutions for the New Economy* (New York: Free Press, 2002); and B. J. Avolio and S. S. Kahai, "Adding the 'E' to E-leadership: How It May Impact Your Leadership," *Organizational Dynamics* 31 (2003), pp. 325–38.

109. The role of followers is discussed by D. S. DeRue and S. J. Ashford, "Who Will Lead and Who Will Follow? A Social Process of Leadership Identity Construction in Organizations," *Academy of Management Review,* October 2010, pp. 627–47.

110. See R. Goffee and G. Jones, "Followership: It's Personal, Too," *Harvard Business Review,* December 2001, p. 148.

111. Bass and Bass, *The Bass Handbook of Leadership,* 2008, p. 408.

112. See L. Bossidy, "What Your Leader Expects of You and What You Should Expect in Return," *Harvard Business Review,* April 2007, pp. 58–65.

113. N. Lublin, "Let's Hear It for the Little Guys," *FastCompany,* April 2010, p. 33.

114. This checklist was proposed by J. J. Gabarro and J. P. Kotter, "Managing Your Boss," *Harvard Business Review,* January 2005, pp. 92–99.

115. Ideas partly based on P. Drucker, "Managing Oneself," *Harvard Business Review,* January 2005, pp. 2–11; and B. Dattner, "Forewarned Is Forearmed," *BusinessWeek,* September 1, 2008, p. 50.

116. N. Justin, "Political Pranksters Keep Getting Savvier," *The Arizona Republic,* March 17, 2011, p. A10.

117. M. Gerson, "No Journalism Ethic Justifies NPR Video Attack," *The Arizona Republic,* March 17, 2011, p. B5.

118. J. Hook and D. Yadron, "Spending Bill Passes, NPR Targeted," *The Wall Street Journal,* March 18, 2011, p. A4.

119. Justin, "Political Pranksters Keep Getting Savvier," 2011.

120. Gerson, "No Journalism Ethic Justifies NPR Video Attack," 2011.

CHAPTER 15

1. Adapted from M. Civello, "Communication Counts in Landing a Job," *Training & Development,* February 2009, pp. 82–83; and from A. Kinicki and M. Fugate," *Organizational Behavior: Key Concepts, Skills & Best Practices,* 5th ed. (New York: McGraw-Hill/ Irwin, 2012), p. 313.

2. For more on these matters, see E. Bernstein, "Why Do Compliments Cause So Much Grief?" *The Wall Street Journal,* May 4, 2010, pp. D1, D6; J. Zaslow, "Surviving the Age of Humiliation," *The Wall Street Journal,* May 5, 2010, pp. D1, D3; A. Tugend, "An Attempt to Revive the Lost Art of Apology," *The New York Times,* January 30, 2010, p. B5; L. Garcia, "Curses, Roiled Again," *The Arizona Republic,* June 21, 2009, p. EC1, reprinted from *The Washington Post;* and S. Elliott, "Bleep or No Bleep, Bolder Words Blow In," *The New York Times,* May 14, 2010, pp. B1, B4.

3. See K. Gurchiek, "Survey: 'Key Skills Advance HR Career,'" *HR Magazine,* April 2008, p. 38.

4. September 1998 survey by Office Team, reported in S. Armour, "Failure to Communicate Costly for Companies," *USA Today,* September 30, 1998, p. B1.

5. J. R. Hinrichs, "Communications Activity of Industrial Research Personnel," *Personnel Psychology,* Summer 1964, pp. 193–204.

6. J. Kotter, "Power, Dependence, and Effective Management," *Harvard Business Review* 55 (1977), pp. 125–36.

7. J. Sandberg, "From Crib to Cubicle, a Familiar Voice—Our Own—Reassures," *The Wall Street Journal*, March 25, 2008, p. B1.

8. R. L. Daft and R. H. Lengel, "Information Richness: A New Approach to Managerial Behavior and Organizational Design," in B. M. Staw and L. L. Cummings, eds., *Research in Organizational Behavior* (Greenwich, CT: JAI Press, 1984), p. 196; and R. H. Lengel and R. L. Daft, "The Selection of Communication Media as an Executive Skill," *Academy of Management Executive*, August 1988, pp. 225–32.

9. See B. Barry and I. S. Fulmer, "The Medium and the Message: The Adaptive Use of Communication Media in Dyadic Influence," *Academy of Management Review*, April 2004, pp. 272–92; and A. F. Simon, "Computer-Mediated Communication: Task Performance and Satisfaction," *The Journal of Social Psychology*, June 2006, pp. 349–79.

10. For discussion of uses of social media, see A. M. Kaplan and M. Haenlein, "Users of the World, Unite! The Challenges and Opportunities of Social Media," *Business Horizons*, January–February 2010, pp. 59–68; G. A. Fowler, "Are You Talking to Me?" *The Wall Street Journal*, April 25, 2011, p. R5; T. L. Griffith, "Tapping into Social Media Smarts," *The Wall Street Journal*, April 25, 2011, p. R6; and A. Samuel, "Better Leadership Through Social Media," *The Wall Street Journal*, April 2, 2012, p. R4.

11. Letter by "Working the Window in Georgia" to J. Phillips ("Dear Abby"), in "Server Gives Tips on Drive-Through Etiquette," *San Francisco Chronicle*, January 22, 2012, www.sfgate.com/cgi-bin/article.cgi?f=/c/a/2012/01/19/PKPH1MLC2S.DTL (accessed May 1, 2012).

12. Libby in Little Rock, Arkansas, in letter to J. Phillips, "Fast-Food Windows Drive Readers Mad," *Reno Gazette-Journal*, May 1, 2012, p. 3C.

13. Peggy in Thornton, Colorado, in letter to Phillips, 2012.

14. R. Cross, P. Gray, S. Cunningham, M. Showers, and R. J. Thomas, "The Collaborative Organization: How to Make Employee Networks Work," *MIT Sloan Management Review*, Fall 2010, pp. 83–91.

15. S. Merchant, quoted in S. Srivastava, "Why India Worries about Outsourcing," *San Francisco Chronicle*, March 21, 2004, p. E3.

16. T. Musbach, "The Most Annoying, Overused Words in the Workplace," *San Francisco Chronicle*, October 11, 2009, p. A1.

17. See A. Stein, "Straight Talk," *FSB*, December 2009/January 2010, p. 23.

18. S. Dillon, "Guest-Teaching Chinese, and Learning America," *The New York Times*, May 10, 2010, pp. A1, A14. For more about what a difference culture makes, see S. Begley, "West Brain, East Brain," *Newsweek*, March 1, 2010, p. 22.

19. For some interesting ideas about possible biochemical bases of trust, see P. J. Zak, "The Trust Molecule," *The Wall Street Journal*, April 28–29, 2012, pp. C1, C2.

20. L. P. Tost, F. Gino, and R. P. Larrick, "Power, Competitiveness, and Advice Taking: Why the Powerful Don't Listen," *Organizational Behavior and Human Decision Processes*, January 2012, pp. 63–65. See also N. J. Fast, N. Sivanathan, N. D. Mayer, and A. D. Galinsky, "Power and Overconfident Decision Making," *Organizational Behavior and Human Decision Processes*, March 2012, pp. 249–60; and M. Baer and G. Brown, "Blind in One Eye: How Psychological Ownership of Ideas Affects the Types of Suggestions People Adopt," *Organizational Behavior and Human Decision Processes*, May 2012, pp. 60–71.

21. R. E. Silverman, "Some Managers Just Won't Take Advice," *The Wall Street Journal*, September 19, 2011, p. B8.

22. C. R. Rogers and F. J. Roethlisberger, "Barriers and Gateways to Communication," *Harvard Business Review*, July–August 1952, pp. 46–52.

23. Rogers and Roethlisberger, p. 47.

24. S. Nassauer, "How Waiters Read Your Table," *The Wall Street Journal*, February 22, 2012, pp. D1, D2.

25. W. D. St. John, "You Are What You Communicate," *Personnel Journal*, October 1985, p. 40. Also see S. Baker, "Reading the Body Language of Leadership," *BusinessWeek*, March 23–30, 2009, p. 48.

26. Statistic reported in R. O. Crockett, "The 21st Century Meeting," *BusinessWeek*, February 26, 2007, pp. 72–79.

27. D. B. Rane, "Effective Body Language for Organizational Success," *The IUP Journal of Soft Skills*, December 2010, pp. 17–26; and I. Talley "Body Language: Read It or Weep," *HR Magazine*, July 1, 2010, www.highbeam.com/doc/1G1-232814994.html (accessed May 2, 2012).

28. See N. Morgan, "The Kinesthetic Speaker: Putting Action into Words," *Harvard Business Review*, April 2001, pp. 113–20. Also see A. Bruzzese, "Communication Is Critical to Coping with Workplace Stress," *Reno Gazette-Journal*, September 4, 2008, p. 6A; and Alex Pentland, interviewed by M. E. Mangelsdorf, "The Power of Nonverbal Communication," *The Wall Street Journal*, October 20, 2008, p. R2.

29. See L. Nardon, R. M. Steers, C. J. Sanchez-Runde, "Seeking Common Ground: Strategies for Enhancing Multicultural Communication," *Organizational Dynamics* 40 (2011), pp. 85–95.

30. Norms for cross-cultural eye contact are discussed by C. Engholm, *When Business East Meets Business West: The Guide to Practice and Protocol in the Pacific Rim* (New York: John Wiley, 1991). Also see G. Ward and Y. Al Bayyari, "American and Arab Perceptions of an Arabic Turn-Taking Cue," *Journal of Cross-Cultural Psychology*, March 2010, pp. 270–75.

31. See J. A. Russell, "Facial Expressions of Emotion: What Lies Beyond Minimal Universality?" *Psychological Bulletin*, November 1995, pp. 379–91; and Rane, "Effective Body Language for Organizational Success," 2010. Also see B. Azar, "A Case for Angry Men and Happy Women," *Monitor on Psychology*, April 2007, pp. 18–19.

32. See N. Angier, "Abstract Thoughts? The Body Takes Them Literally," *The New York Times*, February 2, 2010, p. D2.

33. Related research is summarized by J. A. Hall, "Male and Female Nonverbal Behavior," in A. W. Siegman and S. Feldstein, eds., *Multichannel Integrations of Nonverbal Behavior* (Hillsdale, NJ: Lawrence Erlbaum, 1985), pp. 195–226.

34. A thorough discussion of cross-cultural differences is provided by R. E. Axtell, *Gestures: The Do's and Taboos of Body Language Around the World* (New York: John Wiley, 1998). Problems with body language analysis also are discussed by C. L. Karrass, "Body Language: Beware the Hype," *Traffic Management*, January 1992, p. 27; and M. Everett and B. Wiesendanger, "What Does Body Language Really Say?" *Sales & Marketing Management*, April 1992, p. 40.

35. P. Korkki, "More Courses Get You Ready to Face the World," *The New York Times*, March 1, 2012, p. F7.

36. Results can be found in Hall, "Male and Female Nonverbal Behavior," 1985.

37. J. N. Cleveland, M. Stockdale, and K. R. Murphy, *Women and Men in Organizations: Sex and Gender Issues at Work* (Mahwah, NJ: Lawrence Erlbaum, 2002), p. 108.

38. P. Leo, "Thorny Etiquette Problem for Men: Hug, Kiss, or Handshake?" *Pittsburgh Post-Gazette*, March 23, 2006, www.post-gazette.com/pg/06082/675002-294.stm (accessed May 2, 2012). See also D. Brown, "Men Are Hugging Men More, but Rules Aren't Always Clearly Defined," *Seattle Post-Intelligencer*, July 11, 2005, http://seattlepi.nwsource.com/lifestyle/231855_guyhugs.html (accessed May 2, 2012).

39. See B. Carey, "Evidence That Little Touches Do Mean So Much," *The New York Times*, February 23, 2010, p. D5.

40. E. Reuben, P. Rey-Biel, P. Sapienza, and L. Zingales, "The Emergence of Male Leadership in Competitive Environments," *Journal of Economic Behavior & Organization,* available online June 23, 2011, www.sciencedirect.com/science/article/pii/S0167268111001612 (accessed May 4, 2012).

41. See J. S. Lublin, "Women Fall Behind When They Don't Hone Negotiation Skills," *The Wall Street Journal,* November 4, 2003, p. B1. See also "Do Women Shy Away from Competition, Even When They Can Win?" *Knowledge@Wharton,* November 16, 2005, http://knowledge.whart.upenn.edu/article.cfm?articleid=1308 (accessed May 2, 2012); and J. R. Curhan and A. Pentland, "Thin Slices of Negotiation: Predicting Outcomes from Conversational Dynamics within the First 5 Minutes," *Journal of Applied Psychology,* May 2007, pp. 802–11.

42. J. C. Tingley, *Genderflex: Men & Women Speaking Each Other's Language at Work* (New York: American Management Association, 1994), p. 16.

43. D. Tannen, "The Power of Talk: Who Gets Heard and Why," in *Negotiation: Readings, Exercises, and Cases,* 3rd ed., R. J. Lewicki and D. M. Saunders, eds. (Burr Ridge, IL: Irwin/McGraw-Hill, 1999), pp. 147–48. Research on gender differences in communication can be found in V. N. Giri and H. O. Sharma, "Brain Wiring and Communication Style," *Psychological Studies* 48 (2003), pp. 59–64; and E. L. MacGeorge, A. R. Graves, B. Feng, S. J. Gillihan, and B. R. Burleson, "The Myth of Gender Cultures: Similarities Outweigh Differences in Men's and Women's Provision of Responses to Supportive Communication," *Sex Roles* 50 (2004), pp. 143–75.

44. C. Clarke, quoted in A. Pomeroy, "Female Executives May Have a Business Edge," *HR Magazine,* August 2005, p. 16. See also C. Clarke, "A (Necessary) End to Male Dominance," *Pittsburgh Post-Gazette,* March 17, 2012, www.post-gazette.com/pg/06080/673640-334.stm (accessed May 2, 2012).

45. Study by R. E. Page, reported in H. C. Bristol, "Women Set Casual Tone on Social Media (v. Eexxcciiittting!)," *USA Today,* December 8, 2011, p. 3D. Her research appears in R. E. Page, *Stories and Social Media: Identities and Interaction* (Oxford: Routledge, 2012).

46. R. Sharpe, "As Leaders, Women Rule," *BusinessWeek,* November 20, 2000, pp. 75–84.

47. E. Melero, "Are Workplaces with Many Women in Management Run Differently?" *Journal of Business Research* 64 (2011), pp. 385–93.

48. A. Cummings, reported in "The 'Masculine' and 'Feminine' Sides of Leadership and Culture: Perception vs. Reality," *Knowledge@Wharton,* October 5, 2005, knowledge.wharton.upenn.edu/article.cfm?articleide=1287 (accessed May 2, 2012).

49. D. Jones, "Male Execs Like Female Coaches," *USA Today,* October 24, 2001, p. 3B.

50. Drawn from S. M. Crampton, J. W. Hodge, and J. M. Mishra, "The Informal Communication Network: Factors Influencing Grapevine Activity," *Public Personnel Management,* Winter 1998, pp. 569–84.

84; J. Yang and V. Salazar, "What Is the Most Taboo Topic to Discuss at Work?" *USA Today,* June 17, 2008, p. 1B; and C. Mills, "Experiencing Gossip: The Foundations for a Theory of Embedded Organizational Gossips," *Group and Organization Management,* April 2010, pp. 213–40.

51. See S. McKnight, "Workplace Gossip? Keep It to Yourself," *The New York Times,* November 15, 2009, Business section, p. 9.

52. T. J. Peters and R. H. Waterman Jr., *In Search of Excellence* (New York: Harper & Row, 1982); and T. Peters and N. Austin, *A Passion for Excellence: The Leadership Difference* (New York: Random House, 1985).

53. Steve Jobs, interviewed by B. Morris, "What Makes Apple Golden," *Fortune,* March 17, 2008, pp. 72, 74.

54. C. C. Miller, "Google's Chief Works to Trim a Bloated Ship," *The New York Times,* November 9, 2011, www.nytimes.com/2011/11/10/technology/googles-chief-works-to-trim-a-bloated-ship.html?_r=2&pagewanted=1; and M. Rosoff, "How Larry Page Changed Meetings at Google After Taking Over Last Spring," *Business Insider,* January 10, 2012, www.businessinsider.com/this-is-how-larry-page-changed-meetings-at-google-after-taking-over-last-spring-2012-1?nr_email_referer=1&amp (both accessed May 4, 2012).

55. A. Bruzzese, "Tame the Meeting Beast with These 8 Tips," *Reno Gazette-Journal,* March 1, 2012, p. 8A.

56. K. Maher, "Running Meetings," *The Wall Street Journal,* January 13, 2004, p. B6.

57. C. L. Romero, "Tedious Meetings Top Time-Wasters," *The Arizona Republic,* April 22, 2003, p. D2.

58. P. Lencioni, reported in D. Murphy, "Making Sense of Meetings," *San Francisco Chronicle,* April 3, 2004, p. 1C. See also P. M. Lencioni, *Death by Meeting: A Leadership Fable . . . About Solving the Most Painful Problem in Business* (San Francisco: Jossey-Bass, 2004).

59. D. Batstone, "Right Reality: Most Meetings Stink . . . 5 Tips for Making Yours Useful," *The Wag,* December 21, 2005, www.rightreality.com/wag_items/issues/051221wag.html (accessed May 2, 2012); S. G. Rogelberg, D. J. Leach, P. B. Warr, and J. L. Burnfield, "'Not Another Meeting!' Are Meeting Time Demands Related to Employee Well-Being?" *Journal of Applied Psychology,* January 2006, pp. 86–96; M. Linksky, "The Morning Meeting Ritual," *Harvard Management Communication Letter,* June 19, 2006, http://hbswk.hbs.edu/archive/5388.html (accessed May 2, 2012); D. Robinson, "Keep Meetings on Schedule," *San Francisco Chronicle,* March 15, 2009, p. D5; and Bruzzese, "Tame the Meeting Beast with These 8 Tips," 2012.

60. N. L. Reinsch Jr., J. W. Turner, and C. H. Tinsley, "Multicommunicating: A Practice Whose Time Has Come?" *Academy of Management Review,* April 2008, p. 391.

61. See Reinsch et al., pp. 391–403, for a complete discussion of multicommunicating.

62. C. Pearson, "Sending a Message That You Don't Care," *The New York Times,* May 16, 2010, Business section, p. 9.

63. Portions of the material that follows were adapted from R. Kreitner and A. Kinicki, *Organizational Behavior,* 10th ed. (New York: McGraw-Hill/Irwin, 2013), pp. 418–26.

64. A. Fisher, "E-Mail Is for Liars," *Fortune,* November 24, 2008, p. 57.

65. Studies at Massachusetts Institute of Technology, reported in A. Pentland, "How Social Networks Network Best," *Harvard Business Review,* February 2009, p. 37. Also see A. Pentland, "The New Science of Building Great Teams," *Harvard Business Review,* April 2012, pp. 61–70.

66. Study by Council for Research Excellence, reported in B. Stelter, "8 Hours a Day Spent on Screens, Study Finds," *The New York Times,* March 27, 2009, p. B6. See also J. Wortham, "Everyone Is Using Cellphones, but Not So Many Are Talking," *The New York Times,* May 14, 2010, pp. A1, B4.

67. Pew Research Center, "The Millennials: Confident. Connected. Open to Change," reported in S. Jayson, "A Detailed Look at Millennials," *USA Today,* February 24, 2010, p. 10B.

68. David Verhaagen, quoted in S. Jayson, "'iGeneration' Has No Off Switch," *USA Today,* February 10, 2010, pp. 1D, 2D.

69. "Ground-Breaking Study of Video Viewing Finds Younger Boomers Consume More Video Media Than Any Other Group," press release, March 27, 2009, on study conducted on behalf of Council for Research Excellence by Ball State University's Center for Media Design, www.researchexcellence.com/news/032609_vcm.php (accessed May 2, 2012). See also Stelter, "8 Hours a Day Spent on Screens, Study Finds," 2009.

70. A. Lenhart, *Teens, Smartphones, & Texting,* March 15, 2012, Pew Research Center Internet and American Life Project report, http://pewresearch.org/pubs/2223/teens-cellphones-texting-phone-calls (accessed May 5, 2012).

71. J. C. Meister and K. Willyerd, "Mentoring Millennials," *Harvard Business Review,* May 2010, pp. 68–72.

72. D. Tapscott, *Grown Up Digital: How the Net Generation Is Changing Your World* (New York: McGraw-Hill, 2009), p. 36.

73. J. Q. Anderson and L. Rainie, *Millennials Will Benefit and Suffer Due to Their Hyperconnected Lives,* February 29, 2012, Pew Research Center Internet and American Life Project report, www.pewinternet.org/~/media//Files/Reports/2012/PIP_Future_of_Internet_2012_Young_brains_PDF.pdf (accessed May 5, 2012).

74. Meister and Willyerd, "Mentoring Millennials," 2010, p. 69.

75. S. A. Hewlett, L. Sherbin, and K. Sumberg, "How Gen Y & Boomers Will Reshape Your Agenda," *Harvard Business Review,* July–August 2009, pp. 71–76.

76. B. Yite, "Employers Rethink How They Give Feedback," *The Wall Street Journal,* October 13, 2008, p. B5. See also T. J. Erickson, "Gen Y in the Workforce," *Harvard Business Review,* February 2009, pp. 43–49.

77. M. Esterl, "More Lucrative Business Travelers Now Teleconference, Fly Coach," *The Wall Street Journal,* February 18, 2010, pp. B1, B2; C. Jones, "What Helps You Decide When to Travel?" *USA Today,* April 15, 2010, 1B, 2B; J. Sharkey, "Turning to Teleconferencing as Air Travel Stalls," *The New York Times,* April 20, 2010, p. B6; and J. S. Lublin, "Video Comes to Board Meetings," *The Wall Street Journal,* April 25, 2011, p. B6.

78. *The Return on Investment on U.S. Business Travel,* study by Oxford Economics USA, reported in J. Mullich, "The New Face of Face-to-Face Meetings," *The Wall Street Journal,* September 22, 2009, pp. A17, A18.

79. J. Scheck and B. White, "'Telepresence' Is Taking Hold," *The Wall Street Journal,* May 6, 2008, http://online.wsj.com/article/SB121003318054369255.html (accessed May 2, 2012).

80. J. S. Lublin, "Some Dos and Don'ts to Help You Hone Videoconference Skills," *The Wall Street Journal,* February 7, 2006, p. B1.

81. D. E. Baily and N. B. Kurland, "A Review of Telework Research: Findings, New Directions, and Lessons for the Study of Modern Work," *Journal of Organizational Behavior,* June 2002, pp. 383–400.

82. *The 2012 Jobs and Broadband Report, National Projections on How American Businesses Use Computers and Broadband to Grow, Hire, and Thrive,* reported in "Report: Broadband an Economic Driver Vital to Continuing Recovery," *The Lane Report,* May 3, 2012, www.lanereport.com/5235/2012/05/report-broadband-an-economic-driver-vital-to-continuing-recovery (accessed May 5, 2012).

83. See E. Garone, "How to Make Working at Home Work for You," *The Wall Street Journal,* April 29, 2008, p. D4; R. S. Gajendran and D. A. Harrison, "The Good, the Bad, and the Unknown about Telecommuting: Meta-Analysis of Psychological Mediators and Individual Consequences," *Journal of Applied Psychology,* November 2007, pp. 1524–41; S. Brown, "Line Between Home, Work Will Blur More," *USA Today,* February 8, 2010, p. 11B; and C. L. Tan, "Working in Style: The Accidental Home Office," *The Wall Street Journal,* March 8, 2012, p. D3.

84. See S. Shellenbarger, "Some Companies Rethink the Telecommuting Trend," *The Wall Street Journal,* February 28, 2008, p. D1.

85. S. Marino, "Debunking the Myths of the Telecommute," *The New York Times,* April 18, 2010, Business section, p. 9.

86. C. Said, "Work Is Where You Hang Your Coat," *San Francisco Chronicle,* July 18, 2005, p. E5.

87. J. Hodges, "Office (and Beanbag) Sharing among Strangers," *The Wall Street Journal,* December 31, 2009, p. D3.

88. Norton *Cyber Crime Report for 2011,* reported in F.-S. Gady, "Statistics and the 'Cyber Crime Epidemic,'" *Huffington Post,* September 22, 2011, www.huffingtonpost.com/franzstefan-gady/cybercrime-statistics_b_974005.html (accessed May 5, 2012).

89. B. Worthen, "Facebook Alters Privacy Controls, but Critics Say It's Not Enough," *The Wall Street Journal,* May 27, 2010, pp. B1, B2. See also A. Bruzzese, "Nurture Your Reputation to Avoid Career Trouble Now, in the Future," *Reno Gazette-Journal,* March 4, 2010, p. 5A; J. Temple, "It's Tough to Keep Online Rep Intact," *San Francisco Chronicle,* May 30, 2010, pp. D1, D6; B. Acohido, "Member or Not, Visit Facebook, and It Tracks You," *USA Today,* November 16, 2011, pp. 1A, 2A; N. Bilton, "Privacy Fades in Facebook Era," *The New York Times,* December 12, 2011, p. B8; H. Alford, "Watching Every Click You Make," *The New York Times,* April 22, 2012, p. ST-2; and J. Temple, "Social App Really Not Your Friend," *San Francisco Chronicle,* April 20, 2012, pp. D1, D6.

90. Study by Pew Internet & American Life Project, reported in L. M. Holson, "The Tell-All Generation Learns to Keep Some Things Offline," *The New York Times,* May 9, 2010, News section, pp. 1, 4. See also D. MacMillan, "Younger Adults Vigilant about Online Identities," *San Francisco Chronicle,* May 27, 2010, p. D2; and M. Bond, "Your Facebook Past on Display?" *USA Today,* November 3, 2011, p. 3B.

91. Research firm Basex, reported in R. Scoble, "Reengineering Your Inbox," *Fast Company,* February 2009, p. 50.

92. Harris Interactive survey, reported in K. M. Huessner, "Tech Stress: How Many Emails Can You Handle a Day?" *ABC News,* July 20, 2010, http://abcnews.go.com/Technology/tech-stress-emails-handle-day/story?id=11201183 (accessed May 5, 2012).

93. Based on K. Byron, "Carrying Too Heavy a Load? The Communication and Miscommunication of Emotion by Email," *Academy of Management Review,* April 2008, pp. 309–27.

94. Pew survey, reported in "Americans More Dependent on Cellphones Than Landlines," *The Arizona Republic,* March 8, 2008, p. D3; J. Kornblum, "Text Messaging Taps Out a Family-Friendly Result," *USA Today,* October 20, 2008, p. 7D; and A. R. Carey and J. Snider," Replacing Land-Line Phones with Cellphones," *USA Today,* April 7, 2009, p. 1A.

95. 2004 Sprint Wireless Courtesy Report, cited in S. Winn, "The Cell Phone Warning Has a Familiar Ring. Who's Listening?" *San Francisco Chronicle,* December 16, 2004, pp. E1, E4.

96. "Phone Use Slows Driver Reaction," *The Wall Street Journal,* February 3, 2005, p. D5.

97. A. Smith, *Why Americans Use Social Media,* Pew Research Center Internet and American Life Project report, November 14, 2011, www.pewinternet.org/~/media//Files/Reports/2011/Why%20Americans%20Use%20Social%20Media.pdf (accessed May 5, 2012).

98. T. Rosenberg, "Crowdsourcing a Better World," *The New York Times,* March 28, 2011, http://opinionator.blogs.nytimes.com/2011/03/28/crowdsourcing-a-better-world (accessed May 5, 2011).

99. E. Janzen, "Samuel Adams Crowd-Sourced Beer Debuts During SXSW," *Liquid,* March 11, 2012, www.austin360.com/blogs/content/shared-gen/blogs/austin/bws/entries/2012/03/11/samuel_adams_crowd_sourced_bre.html (accessed May 5, 2012).

100. D. Lim, "Pentagon-Funded Games Would Crowdsource Weapons Testing," *Netguv,* January 19, 2012, www.nextgov.com/defense/2012/01/pentagon-funded-games-would-crowdsource-weapons-testing/50479 (accessed May 5, 2012).

101. J. Temple, "How Trivial Distractions Divert Us from Our Goals," *San Francisco Chronicle,* April 22, 2012, pp. D1, D7.

102. G. Mosier, "Tweeting Can Leave the Wrong Impression," *Reno Gazette-Journal*, May 9, 2012, p. 7A.

103. S. Turkel, "The Flight from Conversation," *The New York Times*, April 22, 2012, pp. SR-1, SR-6, SR-7. See also J. O'C. Hamilton, "Separation Anxiety," *Stanford Magazine*, January/February 2011, pp. 55–59; and E. Keller and B. Fay, "Facebook Can't Replace Face-to-Face Conversation," *USA Today*, April 30, 2012, p. 9A.

104. See M. Burley-Allen, "Listen Up," *HR Magazine*, November 2001, pp. 115–20.

105. Online Survey conducted July 2007 by Society for Human Resource Management, reported in Gurchiek, "Survey: 'Key Skills Advance HR Career,'" 2008.

106. Burley-Allen, 2001; see also C. G. Pearce, "How Effective Are We as Listeners?" *Training & Development*, April 1993, pp. 79–80; and R.A. Luke Jr., "Improving Your Listening Ability," *Supervisory Management*, June 1992, p. 7.

107. Research by The Discovery Group, reported in "Hey, I'm Talking Here," *Training*, December 2005, p. 9.

108. Five listening styles proposed by Edward Dvorak, president of ECD Associates, discussed in "Listening and Thinking: What's Your Style?" Pediatric Services, November 25, 2011, www.pediatricservices.com/prof/prof-10.htm (accessed May 5, 2012).

109. M. Just, P. A. Carpenter, and M. Masson, reported in J. Meer, "Reading More, Understanding Less," *Psychology Today*, March 1987, p. 12.

110. K. Alesandrini, *Survive Information Overload* (Homewood, IL: Irwin, 1992), pp. 191–202.

111. Alesandrini, p. 197.

112. K. Tyler, "Toning Up Communications," *HR Magazine*, March 2003, pp. 87–89.

113. See S. E. Needleman, "Standout Letters to Cover Your Bases," *The Wall Street Journal*, March 9, 2010, p. D4; and R. Abrams, "Writing Winning Business Proposals Is Critical to Your Success," *Reno Gazette-Journal*, September 9, 2008, p. 6A.

114. T. Alessandra and P. Hunsaker, *Communicating at Work* (New York: Fireside, 1993), p. 231.

115. Alessandra and Hunsaker, p. 241.

116. Cited in Alessandra and Hunsaker, p. 169.

117. TNS for LG Spring Cleaning Survey of 1,000 adults, March 2010, reported in "Activities Adults Say They Dread," *USA Today*, May 14, 2010, p. A1. See also E. Garone, "Improving Your, Um, You Know, Public Speaking," *The Wall Street Journal*, November 3, 2011, p. D6.

118. G. Lindenfield, "Don't Be Nervous," *Management Today*, June 2003, p. 81. Also see A. Bruzzese, "Put Yourself in Your Listener's Place When Communicating," *Reno Gazette-Journal*, June 9, 2011, p. 5A; and "Speaking Publicly Is a Big Help," *Arizona Republic*, October 12, 2011, p. CL1.

119. See D. Molina, "Conquering My Fear of Speaking in Public," *The New York Times*, October 2, 2011, p. BU-8.

120. P. Theibert, "Speechwriters of the World, Get Lost!" *The Wall Street Journal*, August 2, 1993, p. A16. This section adapted from C. Wahlstrom and B. Williams, *Learning Success: Being Your Best at College & Life*, 3rd ed. (Belmont, CA: Wadsworth, 2002), pp. 243–45.

121. L. Waters, *Secrets of Successful Speakers: How You Can Motivate, Captivate, and Persuade* (New York: McGraw-Hill, 1993), p. 203.

CHAPTER 16

1. Some new ideas are found in J. Quittner, "How Jeff Bezos Rules the Retail Space," *Fortune*, May 5, 2008, pp. 127–34; A. Taylor III, "Can This Car Save Ford?" *Fortune*, May 5, 2008, pp. 170–78; M. V. Copeland, "Boeing's Big Dream," *Fortune*, May 5, 2008, pp. 180–91; and R. J. Grossman, "Keep Pace with Older Workers," *HR Magazine*, May 2008, pp. 39–46.

2. See, for example, G. Colvin, "Who Wants to Be the Boss?" *Fortune*, February 20, 2006, pp. 76–78.

3. When labor costs rise, productivity slows down, unless other variables are changed. When companies are able to get more output from fewer workers, productivity rises. See C. Dougherty, "Workforce Productivity Falls," *The Wall Street Journal*, May 4, 2012, p. A5.

4. A. Kowalski and I. Kolet, "Productivity Is Not the Savior You Think It Is," *Bloomberg Businessweek*, October 24–October 30, 2011, pp. 13–14.

5. T. Cowen, "The Sad Statistic That Trumps the Others," *The New York Times*, August 21, 2011, p. BU-6.

6. Office of Macroeconomic Analysis, U.S. Treasury, "Profile of the Economy," February 16, 2012, www.docstoc.com/docs/117787321/Profile-of-the-Economy (accessed May 18, 2012).

7. D. Gross, "Listen, the U.S. Is Better, Stronger, and Faster Than Anywhere Else in the World," *Newsweek*, May 7, 2012, pp. 22–30.

8. "Productivity and Costs, First Quarter 2012, Preliminary," Economic News Release, May 3, 2012, Bureau of Labor Statistics, www.bls.gov/news.release/prod2.nr0.htm (accessed May 18, 2012); and Dougherty, "Workforce Productivity Falls," 2012.

9. L. Uchitelle, "Productivity Finally Shows the Impact of Computers," *The New York Times*, March 12, 2000, sec. 3, p. 4; J. Reingold, M. Stepanek, and D. Brady, "Why the Productivity Revolution Will Spread," *BusinessWeek*, February 14, 2000, p. 112–18; G. S. Becker, "How the Skeptics Missed the Power of Productivity," *BusinessWeek*, January 1, 2004, p. 26; and J. Aversa, "Bernanke Bullish on Productivity Gains," *BusinessWeek Online*, August 31, 2006, www.businessweek.com/ap/financialnews/D8JRJTJO0.htm?chan=search (accessed May 18, 2012).

10. See study by B. P. Bosworth and J. E. Triplett, "Productivity Measurement Issues in Services Industries: 'Baumol's Disease' Has Been Cured," *The Brookings Institution*, September 1, 2003, www.brookings.org/views/articles/bosworth/200309.htm (accessed May 18, 2012). Also see H. R. Varian, "Information Technology May Have Been What Cured Low Service-Sector Productivity," *The New York Times*, February 12, 2004, p. C2; S. Lohr, "More Jobs Predicted for Machines, Not People," *The New York Times*, October 23, 2011, www.nytimes.com/2011/10/24/technology/economists-see-more-jobs-for-machines-not-people.html?ref=productivity (accessed May 18, 2012); and Associated Press, "Growth in Service Sector Is Slow but Steady, Suggesting Modest Economic Gains," *The New York Times*, November 3, 2011. www.nytimes.com/2011/11/04/business/service-sector-growth-is-slow-but-steady.html?ref=productivity (accessed May 18, 2012). See also interview of venture capitalist Ben Horowitz by M. Bartiromo, "Technology Soars Again as Economic Driver," *USA Today*, February 20, 2012, p. 3B.

11. C. Holman, B. Joyeux, and C. Kask, "Labor Productivity Since 2000, by Sector and Industry," *Monthly Labor Review*, February 2008, Bureau of Labor Statistics, www.bls.gov/opub/mlr/2008/02/art4full.pdf (accessed May 18, 2012). See also A. Hirsch and C. E. Weller, *The State of American Productivity Growth*, Center for American Progress, August 18, 2011, www.americanprogress.org/issues/2011/08/productivity_growth.html (accessed May 18, 2012).

12. J. B. Stewart, "In the Undoing of a CEO, a Puzzle," *The New York Times*, May 19, 2012, pp. B1, B7.

13. J. Silver-Greenberg and N. D. Schwartz, "Discord at Key J.P. Morgan Unit Is Blamed in Bank's Huge Loss," *The New York Times*, May 20, 2012, news section, pp. 1, 4.

14. J. Van Derbeken, "PG&E Alarmed at Rate of Surges," *San Francisco Chronicle*, May 20, 2012, pp. A1, A14.

15. W. Taylor, "Control in an Age of Chaos," *Harvard Business Review,* November–December 1994, pp. 64–70.

16. B. Horovitz, "Can Eateries Go Green, Earn Green?" *USA Today,* May 16, 2008, pp. 1B, 2B.

17. Also see A. Kelso, "Restaurant Chains Going Green in Response to Consumer Demand," *PizzaMarketplace.com,* March 26, 2012, www.pizzamarketplace.com/article/192243/Restaurant-chains-going-green-in-response-to-consumer-demand; and M. B. McNatt, "The Rewards for Restaurants Going Green," *Eco-GreenOffice,* April 25, 2012, www.ecogreenoffice.com/rewards-for-restaurants-going-green.html (both accessed May 18, 2012).

18. J. R. Hagerty, "3M Begins Untangling Its 'Hairballs,'" *The Wall Street Journal,* May 17, 2012, pp. B1, B2.

19. V. O'Connell, "Reversing Field, Macy's Goes Local," *The Wall Street Journal,* March 6, 2008, pp. B1, B8; and M. D. Beller, "Moody's Upgrade Validates Macy's Strategy: CEO," *CNBC.com,* January 10, 2012, www.cnbc.com/id/45943122/Moody_s_Upgrade_Validates_Macy_s_Strategy_CEO (accessed May 18, 2012).

20. A. P. Sloan Jr., *My Years with General Motors* (New York: Doubleday, 1964).

21. A. Taylor III, "Hyundai Smokes the Competition," *Fortune,* January 5, 2010, http://money.cnn.com/2010/01/04/autos/hyundai_competition.fortune/index.htm (accessed May 18, 2012).

22. "Hyundai Genesis Named Most Dependable Midsize Premium Car by J. D. Power and Associates," *PR Newswire,* February 15, 2012, www.prnewswire.com/news-releases/hyundai-genesis-named-most-dependable-midsize-premium-car-by-jd-power-and-associates-139358268.html (accessed May 18, 2012). See also Z. Bowman, "Hyundai Tops J. D. Power's Customer Retention Survey," *AutoBlog.com,* January 15, 2012, www.autoblog.com/2012/01/15/hyundai-tops-j-d-powers-customer-retention-study (accessed May 19, 2012).

23. J. Levitz, "UPS Thinks Outside the Box on Driver Training," *The Wall Street Journal,* April 6, 2010, http://online.wsj.com/article/SB20001424052702303912104575164573823418844.html (accessed May 18, 2012).

24. D. Foust, "Big Brown's New Bag," *BusinessWeek,* July 19, 2004, pp. 54–56. See also M. Brewster and F. Dalzell, *Driving Change: The UPS Approach to Business* (New York: Hyperion, 2007).

25. B. G. Hoffman, "Inside Ford's Fight to Avoid Disaster," *The Wall Street Journal,* March 9, 2012, pp. B1, B7.

26. R. E. Walton, "From Control to Commitment in the Workplace," *Harvard Business Review,* March–April 1985, pp. 76–84.

27. A description of Google's culture is provided in an interview of cofounder Larry Page by A. Lashinsky, "The *Fortune* Interview: Larry Page," *Fortune,* February 6, 2012, pp. 98–99.

28. I. G. Seidenberg, quoted in S. E. Ante, "Giving the Boss the Big Picture," *BusinessWeek,* February 13, 2006, pp. 48–51.

29. R. S. Kaplan and D. P. Norton, "The Balanced Scorecard—Measures That Drive Performance," *Harvard Business Review,* January–February 1992, pp. 71–79.

30. For more on the uses of the balanced scorecard, see K. R. Thompson and N. J. Mathys, "The Aligned Balanced Scorecard: An Improved Tool for Building High Performance Organizations," *Organizational Dynamics,* October–December 2008, pp. 378–93; S. C. Voelpel and C. K. Streb, "A Balanced Scorecard for Managing the Aging Workforce," *Organizational Dynamics* 39 (2009), pp. 84–90; and R. S. Kaplan, D. P. Norton, and B. Rugelsjoen, "Managing Alliances with the Balanced Scorecard," *Harvard Business Review,* January–February 2010, pp. 114–20.

31. Kaplan and Norton, "The Balanced Scorecard—Measures That Drive Performance," 1992.

32. See M. Arndt, "Damn! Torpedoes Get Quiznos Back on Track," *Bloomberg Businessweek,* January 25, 2010, pp. 54–55.

33. See S. Thomke and D. Reinertsen, "Six Myths of Product Development," *Harvard Business Review,* May 2012, pp. 84–94.

34. R. S. Kaplan and D. P. Norton, "Having Trouble with Your Strategy? Then Map It," *Harvard Business Review,* September–October 2000, pp. 167–76. See also R. Kaplan and D. Norton, "Plotting Success with 'Strategy Maps,'" *InformationWeek,* February 1, 2004, www.informationweek.com/news/18200733 (accessed May 18. 2012).

35. R. Quinn, quoted in J. H. Lingle and W. A. Schiemann, "From Balanced Scorecard to Strategic Gauges: Is Measurement Worth It?" *American Management Association,* March 1996, pp. 56–61.

36. Lingle and Schiemann, 1996.

37. See G. L. Neilson, K. L. Martin, and E. Powers, "The Secrets to Successful Strategy Execution," *Harvard Business Review,* June 2008, pp. 61–70.

38. For discussions of how to measure services and intangible assets, see R. S. Kaplan and D. P. Norton, "Measuring the Strategic Readiness of Intangible Assets," *Harvard Business Review,* February 2004, pp. 52–63; Y. Lee, "How Do I Determine the HR Metrics That Are Most Helpful for My Company?" *HR Magazine,* September 2011, p. 26; D. Grote, "The Myth of Performance Metrics," *HBR Blog Network,* September 12, 2011, http://blogs.hbr.org/cs/2011/09/the_myth_of_performance_metric.html (accessed May 18, 2012); and D. Robb, "Creating Metrics for Senior Management," *HR Magazine,* December 2011, pp. 109–11.

39. See H. C. Ott, "Are Scorecards and Metrics Killing Employee Engagement?" *HBR Blog Network,* July 12, 2011, http://blogs.hbr.org/cs/2011/07/are_scorecards_and_metrics_kil.html (accessed May 18, 2012).

40. For more about Ritz-Carlton, see C. Gallo, "How Ritz-Carlton Maintains Its Mystique," *BusinessWeek,* February 13, 2007, www.businessweek.com/smallbiz/content/feb2007/sb20070213_171606.htm?chan=search; and C. Gallo, "Employee Motivation the Ritz-Carlton Way," *BusinessWeek,* February 29, 2008, www.businessweek.com/smallbiz/content/feb2008/sb20080229_347490.htm?chan=search; and "Beyond Satisfaction: J. D. Power 2012 Customer Service Champions," March 13, 2012, www.jdpower.com/content/special-report/12TU3X9/beyond-satisfaction-j-d-power-2012-customer-service-champions.htm (all accessed May 18, 2012).

41. D. Jones, "Baldrige Winners Named," *USA Today,* November 24, 1999, p. 3B. See also D. Jones, "Baldrige Award Honors Record 7 Quality Winners," *USA Today,* November 26, 2003, p. B6; and R. O. Crockett, "Keeping Ritz-Carlton at the Top of Its Game," *BusinessWeek Online,* May 29, 2006, www.businessweek.com/magazine/content/06_22/b3986130.htm?chan=search (accessed May 18, 2012). For more about the Baldrige awards, go to the Baldrige National Quality Program website at www.quality.nist.gov.

42. D. A. Foster and J. Chenoweth, *Comparison of Baldrige Award Applicants and Recipients with Peer Hospitals on a National Balanced Scorecard,* October 2011, Thomson Reuters, www.nist.gov/baldrige/upload/baldrige-hospital-research-paper.pdf (accessed May 20, 2012).

43. W. E. Deming, *Out of the Crisis* (Cambridge, MA: MIT Press, 1986), p. 5.

44. R. N. Lussier, *Management: Concepts, Applications, Skill Development* (Cincinnati, OH: South-Western College Publishing, 1997), p. 260.

45. J. Goldstein, "As Doctors Get a Life, Strains Show," *The Wall Street Journal,* April 29, 2008, pp. A1, A14.

46. The Japanese have taken efficiency to a high level. See the example of Matsushita Electric Industrial Co., described in K. Hall, "No One Does Lean Like the Japanese," *BusinessWeek,* July 10, 2006, pp. 40–41.

47. O. Port, "The Push for Quality," *BusinessWeek,* June 8, 1987, pp. 130–36.

48. J. Bennett, "New Chrysler Battling Old Defects," *The Wall Street Journal*, May 10, 2012, pp. B1, B2.

49. Planning Perspectives, Inc., "Chrysler and GM Continue Strong Improvement, Ford Stalled in 3rd, Toyota and Honda Continue Their Slide in Annual Study of Automaker Buyer-Supplier Relations Share," *Sacramento Bee*, May 14, 2012, www.sacbee.com/2012/05/14/4487887/chrysler-and-gm-continue-strong.html#storylink=cpy (accessed May 18, 2012).

50. See, for example, S. S. Carty, "Consumer Reports Raves about New Chrysler 300," *AOL Autos*, September 29, 2011, http://autos.aol.com/article/consumer-reports-raves-about-new-chrysler-300 (accessed May 18, 2012).

51. See H. Liao and M. Subramony, "Employee Customer Orientation in Manufacturing Organizations: Joint Influences of Customer Proximity and the Senior Leadership Team," *Journal of Applied Psychology*, March 2008, pp. 317–28. Also see P. Hellman, "Rating Your Dentist," *Management Review*, July–August 1998, p. 64.

52. S. Lohr, "Academia Dissects the Service Sector, but Is It a Science?" *The New York Times*, April 18, 2008, www.nytimes.com/2006/04/18/business/18services.html (accessed May 18, 2012).

53. F. X. Frei, "The Four Things a Service Business Must Get Right," *Harvard Business Review*, April 2008, pp. 70–80.

54. H. Rothman, "You Need Not Be Big to Benchmark," *Nation's Business*, December 1992, pp. 64–65.

55. S. Terlep, S. Vranica, and S. Raice, "GM Says Facebook Ads Don't Pay Off," *The Wall Street Journal*, May 16, 2012, pp. A1, A2; and T. Vega, "After Study, G.M. to Quit Advertising on Facebook," *The New York Times*, May 16, 2012, pp. B1, B4. See also S. Terlep and S. Raice, "Facebook, GM Talk New Friendship," *The Wall Street Journal*, July 3, 2012, p. B5.

56. Jed Williams, BIA/Kelsey, cited in L. Petrecca, G. Strauss, and H. Malcolm, "Facebook Ad Impact in Spotlight," *USA Today*, May 17, 2012, p. 3B.

57. Associated Press-CNBC Poll, May 3–7, 2012, "Poll Shows Low Opinion of Facebook; Lack of Trust May Hold Back Ad Sales," *The Washington Post*, May 15, 2012, www.washingtonpost.com/national/poll-shows-low-opinion-of-facebook-lack-of-trust-may-hold-back-ad-sales/2012/05/15/gIQA7psWSU_story.html (accessed May 18, 2012). However, also see A. Couts, "Actually, Facebook Ads Work Great, Says comScore," *Digital Trends*, June 8, 2012, www.digitaltrends.com/social-media/actually-facebook-ads-work-great-says-comscore (accessed June 14, 2012).

58. I. Austen, "In a Chevy, Engine from China and Transmission from Japan," *The New York Times*, March 26, 2008, pp. C1, C8.

59. C. L. Mann, "Globalization of I.T. Services and White-Collar Jobs: The Next Wave of Productivity Growth," December 2003, *International Economics Policy Briefs*, no. PB03-11, www.iie.com/publications/pb/pb03-11.pdf (accessed May 18, 2012). See also V. Postrel, "A Researcher Sees an Upside in the Outsourcing of Programming Jobs," *The New York Times*, January 29, 2004, p. C2.

60. H. Menzies, "Quality Counts When Wooing Overseas Clients," *Fortune*, June 1, 1997, www.fortune.com/fortune/subs/article/0,15114,378797,00.html (accessed May 18, 2012).

61. B. Ekeler, quoted in Menzies, 1997. See also M. V. Uzumeri, "ISO 9000 and Other Metastandards: Principles for Management Practice?" *Academy of Management Executive* 11, no 1. (1997), pp. 21–28; and T. B. Schoenrock, "ISO 9000: 2000 Gives Competitive Edge," *Quality Progress*, May 2002, p. 107.

62. A. Fisher, "Rules for Joining the Cult of Perfectability," *Fortune*, February 7, 2000, p. 206.

63. J. E. Morehouse, quoted in C. H. Deutsch, "Six Sigma Enlightenment," *The New York Times*, December 7, 1998, pp. C1, C7. For more on Six Sigma, see M. S. Sodhi and N. S. Sodhi, "Six Sigma Pricing," *Harvard Business Review*, May 2005, pp. 135–42; and J. Gordon, "Take *That* to the Bank," *Training*, June 2006, p. 41.

64. D. Jones, "Firms Aim for Six Sigma Efficiency," *USA Today*, July 21, 1998, pp. 1B, 2B.

65. See M. Poppendieck, "Why the Lean in Lean Six Sigma?" *The Project Management Best Practices Report*, June 2004, www.poppendieck.com/pdfs/Lean_Six_Sigma.pdf (accessed May 18, 2012).

66. Arner and Aston, 2004; and A. Aston, J. Carey, and O. Kharif, "Online Extra: The New Factory Floor, and Tomorrow's," *BusinessWeek Online*, May 3, 2004; www.businessweek.com/=@@vr3DfocQkImUSw0A/magazine/content/04_18/b3881601.htm (accessed May 18, 2012).

67. K. Day and J. Howard, "Albertsons Officials to Implement New Efficiency Program," *Reno Gazette-Journal*, February 25, 2004, pp. 1D, 3D.

68. Six Sigma has come under fire for hurting creativity, yet it was adopted as a major initiative by the conglomerate Textron in 2002, and since then the stock has soared. See B. Hindo and B. Grow, "Six Sigma: So Yesterday?" *BusinessWeek*, June 11, 2007, www.businessweek.com/-magazine/content/07_24/b4038409.htm (accessed May 18, 2012); and D. Jones, "CEO Expects Good Things as Textron Does Six Sigma Right," *USA Today*, January 21, 2008, p. 3B.

69. See R. J. Aldag and T. M. Stearns, Management (Cincinnati, OH: South-Western Publishing, 1987), pp. 653–54; D. Robertson and E. Anderson, "Control System and Task Environment Effects on Ethical Judgment: An Exploratory Study of Industrial Salespeople," *Organizational Science*, November 1993, pp. 617–29.

70. K. A. Merchant, *Control in Business Organizations* (Boston: Pitman, 1985), pp. 10–11; K. M. Bartol and D. C. Martin, *Management*, 3rd ed. (Burr Ridge, IL: Irwin/McGraw-Hill, 1998), pp. 533–34; and J. R. Schermerhorn Jr., *Management for Productivity*, 3rd ed. (New York: John Wiley, 1993), p. 592.

71. See D. Rice, "Climate Now Shifting on a Continental Scale," *USA Today*, May 15, 2008, p. 4D; and annual Rechargeable Recycling Corporation green guilt survey, reported in J. Kornblum, "Survey: More Americans Feel Guilty for Not Living Greener," *USA Today*, May 8, 2008, p. 5D.

72. Subaru of Indiana's environmental cost-saving practices are described in A. G. Robinson and D. M. Schroeder, "Greener and Cheaper," *The Wall Street Journal*, March 23, 2009, p. 4; and R. Farzad, "The Scrappiest Car Manufacturer in America," *Bloomberg Businessweek*, June 6, 2011, pp. 68–74.

73. Bartol and Martin, *Management*, 1998, pp. 532–33; and S. C. Certo, *Modern Management*, 8th ed. (Upper Saddle River, NJ: Prentice Hall, 2000), pp. 435–36.

74. J. P. Kotter, L. A. Schlesinger, and V. Sathe, *Organization: Text, Cases, and Readings on the Management of Organizational Design and Change* (Homewood, IL: Irwin, 1979).

75. Merchant, *Control in Business Organizations*, 1985.

76. G. Hamel, with B. Breen, *The Future of Management* (Boston: Harvard Business School Press, 2007), p. 6.

77. A. R. Rasbury, "New Kid on the Job: How to Get Off to a Good Start," *Black Enterprise*, May 1, 2008, www.thefreelibrary.com/New+kid+on+the+job:+{how+to+get+off+to+a+good+start.-a0178674810 (accessed May 18, 2012).

78. K. Holland, "For the Chief, a Little Skepticism Can Go a Long Way," *The New York Times*, May 25, 2008, business section, p. 14.

79. B. Taylor, "Why Zappos Pays New Employees to Quit—and You Should Too," *Harvard Business Review*, May 18, 2008, http://discussionleader.hbsp.com/taylor/2008/05/wy_zappos_pays_new_employees_t.html (accessed May 18, 2012).

CHAPTER 1

Photos: p. 4: Dima Gavrysh/AP Images; p. 5: © Dynamic Graphics/PictureQuest; p. 6: David Maxwell/Bloomberg via Getty Images; p. 8: Eric Audras/PhotoAlto/PictureQuest; p. 10: Spencer Platt/Getty Images; p. 11: Imaginechina via AP Images; p. 13: JUSTIN LANE/epa/Corbis; p. 16: Christophe Ena/AP Images; p. 18: Mark Lennihan/AP Images; p. 19: Mark Sakuma/AP Images; p. 20: © Mark Leet Photography; p. 21: Ingram Publishing; p. 22: Christopher Farina/Corbis; p. 25: Eric Risberg/AP Images; p. 27: James Leynse/Corbis; p. 28: Manish Swarup/AP Images; p. 30: Louis Lanzano/AP Images

CHAPTER 2

Photos: p. 43: © Bettmann/Corbis; p. 44: © Underwood & Underwood/Corbis; p. 45: Paul Sancya/AP Images; p. 46: Public Domain; p. 47: Courtesy of AT&T Archives and History Center, Warren, NJ; p. 49: Sadie Dayton/Anyone/amanaimages/Corbis; p. 50: Justin Sullivan/Getty Images; p. 56: Ryan McVay/Getty Images; p. 59: Bettmann/Corbis; p. 60: © Hill Street Studios/Blend Images LLC

CHAPTER 3

Photos: p. 68: © Paul Sakuma/AP/Corbis; p. 70: © The McGraw-Hill Companies, Inc./John Flournoy; p. 71: George Doyle/Getty Images; p. 74 (top): Kent Knudson/PhotoLink/Getty Images; p. 74 (bottom): Scott Olson/Getty Images; p. 76: © age fotostock/SuperStock; p. 78: © Jose Luis Pelaez Inc/Blend Images LLC; p. 80: SHANNON STAPLETON/Reuters/Corbis; p. 85: Royalty-Free/Corbis; p. 89: F. Carter Smith/Bloomberg via Getty Images

CHAPTER 4

Photos: p. 100: Joseph Van Os/Getty Images; p. 101: Stephen Yang/Bloomberg/Getty Images; p. 103: Digital Vision/Getty Images; p. 105: © arabianEye/PunchStock; p. 106: © Universal Pictures/Courtesy Everett Collection; p. 110: Steven Senne/AP Images; p. 112: © Imaginechina/Corbis; p. 116: Steve Mason/Getty Images; p. 123: PRNewsFoto/American Honda Motor Co., Inc./AP Images

CHAPTER 5

Photos: p. 133: Royalty-Free/Corbis; p. 134: Courtesy of Ford Motor Company; p. 135: Iain Cooper/Alamy; p. 143: Comstock Images/Getty Images; p. 145: Courtesy of Walmart; p. 148: Courtesy of Apple

CHAPTER 6

Photos: p. 157: Courtesy of P&G; p. 158: David Martin; p. 161: Frank Franklin II/AP Images; p. 163: Chuck Savage/Corbis; p. 166: Darren McCollester/Getty Images; p. 167: © Chris Farina/Corbis; p. 171: Craig Trudell/Bloomberg via Getty Images; p. 172: Courtesy of Southwest Airlines; p. 175: South Florida Sun-Sentinel, Joe Cavaretta/AP Images; p. 178: Courtesy of SAS; p. 181: Jose Luis Pelaez, Inc/Getty Images

CHAPTER 7

Photos: p. 193: Jupiterimages/Getty Images; p. 194: Boeing/AP Images; p. 196: Courtesy of North Star Moving Company; p. 199: Yakima Herald-Republic, Kris Holland/AP Images; p. 202: Courtesy of IBM; p. 204: Larry French/Getty Images; p. 205: © JOHN GRESS/Reuters/Corbis; p. 207: Marcus R. Donner/AP Images; p. 215: Comstock/PunchStock; p. 217: Photodisc/PunchStock; p. 219: Photodisc/PunchStock

CHAPTER 8

Photos: p. 228: Adam Gault/Getty Images; p. 231: Courtesy of HP; p. 235: Clayton Call/Redferns/Getty Images; p. 238: Courtesy of General Motors; p. 240: © Emmanuel Faure/Corbis; p. 244: Ariel Skelley/Blend Images LLC; p. 251: © Najlah Feanny/CORBIS

CHAPTER 9

Photos: p. 266: Andrew Resek/The McGraw-Hill Companies, Inc.; p. 267: Ian Shaw/Alamy; p. 271: © Jon Feingersh/Blend Images LLC; p. 279: © Bob Daemmrich/The Image Works; p. 280: BananaStock/PictureQuest; p. 282: Digital Vision/Getty Images; p. 283: Asia Images Group/Getty Images; p. 287: Comstock Images; p. 288: Alistair Berg/Getty Images

CHAPTER 10

Photos: p. 308: Matthew Lloyd/Bloomberg via Getty Images; p. 312: © Krasilnikov Stanislav/ITAR-TASS Photo/Corbis; p. 319: Charles Rex Arbogast/AP Images; p. 322: BananaStock/PictureQuest; p. 327: Paul Sakuma/AP Images

CHAPTER 11

Photos: p. 338: Purestock/SuperStock; p. 341: © Didrik Johnck/Corbis; p. 346: Courtesy of New School University; p. 347: Courtesy of IBM; p. 350: E.Audras/PhotoAlto; p. 354: Courtesy of Zingerman's; p. 359: John A Rizzo/Pixtal/SuperStock; p. 361: Scott T. Baxter/Getty Images; p. 362: Mina Chapman/Corbis; p. 364: © Royalty-Free/Corbis; p. 366: © ColorBlind Images/Blend Images LLC

CHAPTER 12

Photos: p. 378: BananaStock/PunchStock; p. 387: © Ocean/Corbis; p. 389: Julie Jacobson/AP Images; p. 390: Somos Photography/Veer; p. 393: © Digital Vision/Getty Images; p. 397: © Jose Luis Pelaez Inc/Blend Images LLC; p. 399: Photo by Howard Sokol/Courtesy of The Boppy Pillow; p. 402: Comstock/PunchStock

CHAPTER 13

Photos: p. 414: PhotoAlto/Sigrid Olsson/Getty Images; p. 416: © Gerhard Joren/OnAsia Images; p. 420: Davie Hinshaw/Charlotte Observer/MCT via Getty Images; p. 424 (left): Seth Wenig/AP Images; p. 424 (right): Suzanne DeChillo/The New York Times/Redux Pictures; p. 426: Courtesy of Coca-Cola Company; p. 428: Frederic Cirou/PhotoAlto/Getty Images; p. 433: © Digital Vision

CHAPTER 14

Photos: p. 444: David Brabyn/Corbis; p. 446: © Karsten Lemm/dpa/Corbis; p. 452: PhotoLink/Getty Images; p. 454: © Lew Robertson/Brand X/Getty Images; p. 458: Sean Mathis/WireImage/Getty Images; p. 460: Jeff Chiu/AP Images; p. 462: © Ringo Chiu/ZUMA Press/Corbis

CHAPTER 15

Photos: p. 476: Tom Pennington/Getty Images; p. 480: Photodisc/Getty Images; p. 484: Christopher Robbins/Getty Images; p. 487: Brand X Pictures/PunchStock; p. 488: Keith Brofsky/Getty Images; p. 490: Image Source/PunchStock; p. 494: B Busco/Getty Images; p. 499: Image Source/PunchStock; p. 501: © Comstock/CORBIS; p. 503: Hill Street Studios/Getty Images

CHAPTER 16

Photos: p. 513: Getty Images; p. 518: © Moxie Productions/Blend Images LLC; p. 520: Getty Images; p. 526: Bloomberg via Getty Images; p. 529: Joel Ryan/AP Images; p. 532: Courtesy of Viking Corporation; p. 539: LAURENT GILLIERON/epa/Corbis; p. 541: Brand X Pictures

TMZ, 10
Torrenzano Group, 92
Toyota Motor Corp., 51, 75, 150, 151, 157, 161, 169–171, 309, 327, 431, 516, 532, 534, 536
Toys R Us, 110
Trader Joe's, 158
Trek Bicycle Corporation, 250
Triage Consulting Group, 236–237
Tropicana, 461
TRPA (Tahoe Regional Planning Authority), 74
TurboProject, A3
TurboTax, 305
Turnbull & Asser, 175
Turntable.fm, 458
Twitter, 21, 76, 92, 135, 158, 159, 202, 237, 275, 285, 313, 414, 479, 492, 497–498, 506
Ty, 326
Tyco International, 13, 80, 88

U

Unicru, 278
Union Pacific, 100
United Airlines, 140, 172, 320, A6
United Auto Workers, 73, 292
United Parcel Service (UPS), 102, 202, 230, 266, 518
U.S. Chamber of Commerce, 14
United Steelworkers Union, 470
United Way, 73
University of California, 20
University of California, Berkeley, 292
University of California, Los Angeles, 283, 501
University of Colorado, 200
University of Delaware, 155
University of Georgia, 84
University of Michigan, 357, 448t, 452
University of Minnesota at Duluth, 487
University of Pennsylvania, 446

University of Southern California, 163
University of Texas, 253, 350
University of Toronto, 493
University of Wisconsin, 77
Unix, 327
UPS (United Parcel Service), 102, 202, 230, 266, 518
US Airways, 140
US Grant hotel, 72

V

Valeant Pharmaceuticals International, 389
Vanguard Group, 160
Vaupell Holdings, Inc., 63
Vauxhall Motor Cars Ltd., 110
Verizon, 250, 257–258, 450
Verizon Communications, 521
Viking Range Corporation, 532
Virgin America, 140
Virgin Atlantic Airways Ltd., 63, 462
Virgin Comics, 307
Virgin Group Ltd., 307, 462
Virginia Tech, 356, 430
Virtu, 307–308
Visa, 156
The Vitale, 380
Volkswagen, 101, 151, 170, 327
Volvo, 384, 422

W

Walker Information, 401
Walmart, 35, 70, 103, 134, 135, 139, 145, 156, 157, 158, 173, 236, 310
Walmart.com, 72
Walt Disney Company (Disney), 100, 163, 176, 313, 371, 445
Warner Bros., 245
Washington Redskins, 260
Washington University, 426
Wegmans Food Markets, 264, 265
Wells Fargo, 103

Wendy's, 110
Western Electric, 47
Westinghouse, 412t
Westinghouse Canada, 322
Westwood High School (Arizona), 225
Wharton School, 313, 422
Whirlpool, 107
White Aryan Resistance, 346
White Castle, 141
Whole Foods Market, 100, 145, 247–248, 542
Wikipedia, 41, 274, 313, 497
Wild Oats, 100
Windy City Fieldhouse, 277–278
W. L. Gore & Associates, 70, 230
WorldCom, 13, 80, 88, 207
World Steel Dynamics, 546
The Worth Collection, 252
W. P. Carey School of Business, 236
WPP Grey Group, 223

X

Xerox Corp., 4, 234, 236, 325, 371, 536, 538, 546

Y

Yahoo, 274, 514
Yale University, 363, 364, 470
Yammer, 237
Yelp, 25–26
Yes Men, 472
YouTube, 41, 258, 275, 313, 506

Z

Zachary's Chicago Pizza, 70
Zagat, 20
Zappos, 230, 543
Zenith, 20
Zingerman's, 354
Zipcar, 535
Zynga, 376, 446

A page number with an *f* indicates a figure; an *n* a note; a *t*, a table.

A

Abilene paradox, 424

Ability tests, 277–278

Absenteeism *When an employee doesn't show up for work,* 349

Accommodating, 432

Accountability *Describes expectation that managers must report and justify work results to the managers above them,* 17, 242

Achievement needs, 381, 382

Acquired needs theory *Theory that states that there are three needs—achievement, affiliation, and power—that are the major motives determining people's behavior in the workplace,* 381–382

Acquisitions and mergers, 320

Action plan *Course of action needed to achieve a stated goal,* 139–140, 144

Action teams, 415

Active listening *The process of actively decoding and interpreting verbal messages,* 499

ADA; *see* Americans with Disabilities Act

Adaptive change *Reintroduction of a familiar practice, the kind of change that has already been experienced within the same organization,* 315

Adaptive cycle, 135

Adaptive perspective *Perspective of organizational culture that assumes that the most effective cultures help organizations anticipate and adapt to environmental change,* 235

ADEA (Age Discrimination in Employment Act), 269t

Adhocracy culture *Type of organizational culture that has an external focus and values flexibility,* 230, 252

Adjourning *One of five stages of forming a team; the stage in which members of an organization prepare for disbandment,* 418

Administrative decisions, 135

Administrative management *Management concerned with managing the total organization,* 44–45

Adverse impact *Effect an organization has when it uses an employment practice or procedure that results in unfavorable outcomes to a protected class (such as Hispanics) over another group of people (such as non-Hispanic whites),* 270

Advice teams, 414

Affective component of an attitude *The feelings or emotions one has about a situation,* 345

Affiliation needs, 381, 382

Affirmative action *The focus on achieving equality of opportunity,* 271

Age Discrimination in Employment Act (ADEA), 269t

Age in workforce, 23, 349, 359

Agency shop, 293

Agreeableness, 338

Alcoholism and drug abuse, 279, 366

"Always on" generation, 492–493; *see also* Millennial Generation (Gen Y)

American Institute of Stress, 363

American Management Association, 21, 291

American Psychological Association, 363

Americans with Disabilities Act (ADA) *Passed by the U.S. in 1992, act that prohibits discrimination against the disabled,* 269t, 361

Analytical style, 205–206

Analytics (business analytics) *Term used for sophisticated forms of business data analysis, such as portfolio analysis or time-series forecast,* 200–202

Analyzers *Organizations that allow other organizations to take the risks of product development and marketing and then imitate (or perhaps slightly improve on) what seems to work best,* 135

Anchoring and adjustment bias *The tendency to make decisions based on an initial figure,* 213

APEC; *see* Asia-Pacific Economic Cooperation

Appreciative listening style, 499

Arab culture, 104, 116–117, 120, 121, 122, 484

Arbitration *The process in which a neutral third party, an arbitrator, listens to both parties in a dispute and makes a decision that the parties have agreed will be binding on them,* 295

ASEAN; *see* Association of Southeast Asian Nations

Asia-Pacific Economic Cooperation (APEC) *A group of 21 Pacific Rim countries whose purpose is to improve economic and political ties,* 114–115

Assertiveness, 118

Assessment center *Company department where management candidates participate in activities for a few days while being assessed by evaluators,* 278

Asset management ratios, 528

Assets, 528

Associated Press, 122

Association of Executive Search Consultants, 360

Association of Southeast Asian Nations (ASEAN) *A trading bloc consisting of 11 countries in Asia,* 115

Assurance, 534

Attainable goals, 142, 165, 390

Attitude *A learned predisposition toward a given object; a mental position with regard to a fact, state, or person,* 345–347

Audits *Formal verifications of an organization's financial and operational systems,* 528–529

Authority *The right to perform or command; also, the rights inherent in a managerial position to make decisions, give orders, and utilize resources,* 242, 444–445

Authorization cards, 292

Automated experience, 197

Autonomy, 393–394

Availability bias *Tendency of managers to use information readily available from memory to make judgments; they tend to give more weight to recent events,* 212

Avoiding, 432

B

Baby Boomers, 492

Background information, 273–275

Balance sheet *A summary of an organization's overall financial worth—assets and liabilities—at a specific point in time,* 528

Balanced scorecard *Gives top managers a fast but comprehensive view of the organization via four indicators: (1) customer satisfaction, (2) internal processes, (3) the organization's innovation and improvement activities, and (4) financial measures,* 517, 521–523

Bargaining unit, 292

BARS; *see* Behaviorally anchored rating scale

Base pay *Consists of the basic wage or salary paid employees in exchange for doing their jobs,* 287

Basic assumptions, 231–232

BCG matrix *A means of evaluating strategic business units on the basis of (1) their business growth rates and (2) their share of the market,* 177

Beauty Pays (Hamermesh), 350

Behavior *Actions and judgments,* 347, 355–356

Behavior modification, 395

Behavioral approach, 448t

Behavioral component of an attitude *Also known as intentional component, this refers to how one intends or expects to behave toward a situation,* 345, 346

Behavioral leadership approaches *Attempts to determine the distinctive styles used by effective leaders,* 452–453

Behavioral science approach *Relies on scientific research for developing theories about human behavior that can be used to provide practical tools for managers,* 49

Behavioral style, 206

Behavioral viewpoint *Emphasizes the importance of understanding human behavior and of motivating employees toward achievement,* 46–49

Behavioral-description interview *Type of structured interview in which the interviewer explores what applicants have done in the past,* 276

Behaviorally anchored rating scale (BARS) *Employee gradations in performance rated according to scales of specific behaviors,* 284

Benchmarking *A process by which a company compares its performance* with that of high-performing organizations, 155, 317, 536, 546

Benefits *Additional nonmonetary forms of compensation,* 288

Bias, 189, 212–213, 351–352

Big Data, 202

Big Five personality dimensions *They are (1) extroversion, (2) agreeableness, (3) conscientiousness, (4) emotional stability, and (5) openness to experience,* 338–339

Birth stage *The nonbureaucratic stage, the stage in which the organization is created,* 253

Black Enterprise magazine, 542

Bloomberg Businessweek magazine, 19, 327

Board of directors, 70, 88–89, 186–187

Board of regents, 70

Board of trustees, 70

Bonuses *Cash awards given to employees who achieve specific performance objectives,* 399

Bottom line, 528

Boundaryless organization *A fluid, highly adaptive organization whose members, linked by information technology, come together to collaborate on common tasks; the collaborators may include competitors, suppliers, and customers,* 249–250

Bounded rationality *One type of nonrational decision making; the ability of decision makers to be rational is limited by numerous constraints,* 195–196

Boycotts, 74

Brainstorming *Technique used to help groups generate multiple ideas and alternatives for solving problems; individuals in a group meet and review a problem to be solved, then silently generate ideas, which are collected and later analyzed,* 217–218, 426

Brainwriting; *see* Electronic brainstorming

Brand, 175

Brazil, 120–121

Break-even analysis *A way of identifying how much revenue is needed to cover the total costs of developing and selling a product,* A4–A6

Break-even point, A5

Budget *A formal financial projection,* 443–444, 526–527

Buffers *Administrative changes that managers can make to reduce the stressors that lead to employee burnout,* 366–367

Bullying at work, 271, 356, 427–428

Bureaucracy, 44

Bureaucratic control *The use of rules, regulations, and formal authority to guide performance,* 520

Burnout *State of emotional, mental, and even physical exhaustion,* 366

Business analytics, 200–202

Business plan *A document that outlines a proposed firm's goals, the strategy for achieving them, and the standards for measuring success,* 156

BusinessWeek magazine, 103, 251, 263, 450, 487

Buzzwords, 481–482

C

CAFTA-DR; *see* Central America Free Trade Agreement

CAI; *see* Computer-assisted instruction

Canada, 111, 114

Careers in management, 131

Cascading *Objectives are structured in a unified hierarchy, becoming more specific at lower levels of the organization,* 145

Causal attribution *The activity of inferring causes for observed behavior,* 351

Central America Free Trade Agreement (CAFTA-DR) *Trade agreement involving the United States and Costa Rica, the Dominican Republic, El Salvador, Guatemala, Honduras, and Nicaragua and which is intended to reduce tariffs and other barriers to free trade,* 115

Centralized authority *Organizational structure in which important decisions are made by upper managers—power is concentrated at the top,* 243

Chain of command, 239, 241

Change; *see* Organizational change

Change agent *A person inside or outside the organization who can be a catalyst in helping deal with old problems in new ways,* 314–315, 320

Changing stage, 317, 318

Charisma *Form of personal attraction that inspires acceptance and support,* 462

Charismatic leadership *Once assumed to be an individual inspirational and motivational characteristic of particular leaders, now considered part of transformational leadership,* 451, 462

Chauffeur-driven computer-aided decision-making systems, 219

Cheaper by the Dozen (Gilbreth), 44

Cheating, 67

Chief Executive magazine, 236

China, 104, 112, 116, 117, 121, 128, 359

Church of Latter Day Saints, 103

Civil Rights Act, 268–270, 271

Clan culture *Type of organizational culture that has an internal focus and values flexibility rather than stability and control,* 229–230

Classical model of decision making; *see* Rational model of decision making

Classical viewpoint *In the historical perspective, the viewpoint that emphasizes finding ways to manage work more efficiently; it has two branches—scientific and administrative,* 42–45

Clawbacks *Rescinding the tax breaks when firms don't deliver promised jobs,* 73

Closed shop, 293

Closed system *A system that has little interaction with its environment,* 54

Cloud Atlas (movie), 107

Coaching, 236–237

Coalition tactics, 447

COBRA (Consolidated Omnibus Budget Reconciliation Act), 269t

Code of ethics *A formal, written set of ethical standards that guide an organization's actions,* 82

Coercive power *One of five sources of a leader's power that results from the authority to punish subordinates,* 445

Cognitive component of an attitude *The beliefs and knowledge one has about a situation,* 345, 346

Cognitive dissonance *Term coined by social psychologist Leon Festinger to describe the psychological discomfort a person experiences between what he or she already knows and new information or contradictory behavior, or by inconsistency among a person's beliefs, attitudes, and/or actions,* 345–347

Cohesiveness *The tendency of a group or team to stick together,* 419–420

COLA; *see* Cost-of-living adjustment clause

Collaborating, 432

Collaborative computing *Using state-of-the-art computer software and hardware, to help people work better together,* 12

Collective bargaining *Negotiations between management and employees regarding disputes over compensation, benefits, working conditions, and job security,* 268

Collective commitment, 233

Collins's five stages of institutional decline, 306

Commitment bias; *see* Escalation of commitment bias

Common purpose *A goal that unifies employees or members and gives everyone an understanding of the organization's reason for being,* 241

Commonweal organization, 20

Communication *The transfer of information and understanding from one person to another,* 476–477

"always on" generation, 492–493

barriers
    gender, 484–487
    nonverbal, 478, 483–485
    personal, 482–483
    physical, 481
    semantic, 481–482

case study, 506

cultural differences, 117, 120–121, 478, 481, 484

digital, 492–496

ethical dilemma, 509

global management, 97, 98–99, 120–121

listening skills, 32, 499–500

manager roles and, 21, 23, 75, 488–491

medium for, 477, 478–479

meetings effectiveness, 491

process of, 477–478

reading skills, 32, 500–501

smartphones, 496–497

social media, 497–498

speaking skills, 502–504

Downsizing, 290

Downward communication
Communication that flows from a higher level to a lower level, 489

Drug abuse and alcoholism, 279, 366

Dumping *The practice of a foreign company's exporting products abroad at a lower price than the price in the home market—or even below the costs of production—in order to drive down the price of the domestic product,* 112

Dwell magazine, 380

Dysfunctional conflict *Conflict that hinders the organization's performance or threatens its interests,* 427–428

E

EAPs; *see* Employee assistance programs

E-business *Using the Internet to facilitate every aspect of running a business,* 12

E-commerce *Electronic commerce—the buying and selling of goods or services over computer networks,* 12, 99

Economic communities, 113–115

Economic forces *General economic conditions and trends—unemployment, inflation, interest rates, economic growth—that may affect an organization's performance,* 75–76

Economic performance, 78

Education and workforce needs, 361

Educational opportunities, 402–403

EEO; *see* Equal Employment Opportunity Commission

Effectiveness *To achieve results, to make the right decisions, and to successfully carry them out so that they achieve the organization's goals,* 5, 192

Efficiency *To use resources—people, money, raw materials, and the like—wisely and cost effectively,* 5, 10–11

Effort-to-performance expectancy, 387

E-Leadership (Mills), 466

E-leadership *Leadership that involves one-to-one, one-to-many, and within and between-group and collective interactions via information technology,* 448t, 466

E-learning, 282

Electronic brainstorming (brainwriting) *Technique in which members of a group come together over a computer network to generate ideas and alternatives,* 218

E-mail *Text messages and documents transmitted over a computer network,* 12, 496, 509

Embargo *A complete ban on the import or export of certain products,* 112

Emotional intelligence *The ability to cope, to empathize with others, and to be self-motivated,* 342–343

Emotional stability, 338

Empathic listening style, 499

Empathy, 534

Employee assistance programs (EAPs) *Host of programs aimed at helping employees to cope with stress, burnout, substance abuse, health-related problems, family and marital issues, and any general problems that negatively influence job performance,* 367

Employee characteristics, 457

Employee engagement *An individual's involvement, satisfaction, and enthusiasm for work,* 353

Employee organizations, 73

Employee replacement, 289

Employee Retirement Income Security Act (ERISA), 269t

Employee Stock Ownership Plan (ESOP), 70

Employee-centered behavior, 452

Employees; *see also* Human resource management; Motivation; individual behavior
  as assets, 200, 264
  decision-making involvement, 216, 217t
  foreign, 104
  fostering innovation, 329
  involvement of, 281
  organizational change and, 312, 314–319
  social responsibility of, 87
  as stakeholders, 70

Employment tests *Tests legally considered to consist of any procedure used in the employment selection process,* 277–279

Enacted values *Values and norms actually exhibited in the organization,* 231

Encoding *Translating a message into understandable symbols or language,* 477, 481t

Engineering decisions, 135

Enterprise resource planning (ERP) *Software information systems for integrating virtually all aspects of a business,* 513

Entrepreneur *Someone who sees a new opportunity for a product or service and launches a business to try to realize it,* 25–28, 156, 325–326

Entrepreneurial decisions, 135

Entrepreneurship *The process of taking risks to try to create a new enterprise,* 25–28, 325–326

Environment of management; *see* Ethical responsibilities; Global management; Work environment

Environmental Defense Fund, 145

Environmental Protection Agency, 145

Environmental scanning *Careful monitoring of an organization's internal and external environments to detect early signs of opportunities and threats that may influence the firm's plans,* 168

Equal Employment Opportunity (EEO) Commission *U.S. panel whose job it is to enforce antidiscrimination and other employment related laws,* 270, 271, 359

Equal Pay Act, 269t

Equity theory *In the area of employee motivation, the focus on how employees perceive how fairly they think they are being treated compared with others,* 385–387

ERG theory *Theory proposed by Clayton Alderfer that assumes that three basic needs influence behavior—existence, relatedness, and growth—represented by the letters E, R, and G,* 380–381

ERISA (Employee Retirement Income Security Act), 269t

ERP; *see* Enterprise resource planning

Escalation of commitment bias *When decision makers increase their commitment to a project despite negative information about it,* 213

ESOP (Employee Stock Ownership Plan), 70

Espoused values *Explicitly stated values and norms preferred by an organization,* 231

Esteem needs, 379

Ethical behavior *Behavior that is accepted as "right" as opposed to "wrong" according to those standards,* 78–79

Ethical climate *A term that refers to employees' perceptions about the extent to which work environments support ethical behavior,* 82

Ethical dilemma *A situation in which you have to decide whether to pursue a course of action that may benefit you or your organization but that is unethical or even illegal,* 78
  approaches to, 79–80
  bonuses, 408–409
  children and the Internet, 94
  dress codes, 225
  employee monitoring, 509, 548
  global management, 128–129
  government intervention, 65
  human resources management, 302
  influence tactics, 472
  management decisions, 36
  marijuana usage, 438
  nail polish dispute, 334–335
  organizational culture, 260
  strategic management, 186–187
  tobacco-free hiring, 373
  whistle-blowers, 153

Ethical responsibilities
  approaches to, 79–80
  case study, 91–92
  corporate governance, 88–89
  ethics and values definitions, 78–79
  Kohlberg's theories, 81
  Sarbanes-Oxley, 81
  social responsibility and, 83–87
  white-collar crime, 80–81
  within an organization, 82

Ethics officer *A person trained about matters of ethics in the workplace, particularly about resolving ethical dilemmas,* 207

Ethics *Standards of right and wrong that influence behavior,* 78–79
  in decision making, 192, 207–208
  leadership and, 12–13, 463

Ethnicity and race in workforce, 349, 360

Ethnocentric managers *Managers who believe that their native country, culture, language, and behavior are superior to all others,* 105

Ethnocentrism *The belief that one's native country, culture, language, abilities, and/or behavior are superior to those of another culture,* 361–362

European Union (EU) *Union of 27 trading partners in Europe,* 114, 359

Evaluation
  decision making and, 194
  financial, 528
  in hiring, 278
  of individual behavior, 355–356
  in OD process, 321
  performance, 283–285

Evaluative listening style, 500

Evidence-based management *Translating principles based on best evidence into organizational practice, bringing rationality to the decision-making process,* 39, 40, 189, 198–203, 521

Exchange rate *The rate at which the currency of one area or country can be exchanged for the currency of another's,* 114

Exchange tactics, 447

Execution *As proposed by Larry Bossidy and Ram Charan, execution is not simply tactics, it is a central part of any company's strategy. It consists of using questioning, analysis, and follow-through in order to mesh strategy with reality, align people with goals, and achieve the results promised,* 178–180, 329

Execution: The Discipline of Getting Things Done (Bossidy and Charan), 178

Executive functioning, 23

Existence needs, 381

Expatriates *People living or working in a foreign country,* 123

Expectancy *The belief that a particular level of effort will lead to a particular level of performance,* 387

Expectancy theory *Theory that suggests that people are motivated by two things: (1) how much they want something and (2) how likely they think they are to get it,* 387–389

Expenses, 528

Expert power *One of five sources of a leader's power, resulting from specialized information or expertise,* 445

Expertise, 197

Exporting *Producing goods domestically and selling them outside the country,* 109

External audit *Formal verification by outside experts of an organization's financial accounts and statements,* 529

External communication *Communication between people inside and outside an organization,* 490

External dimensions of diversity *Human differences that have an element of choice; they consist of the personal characteristics that people acquire, discard, or modify throughout their lives,* 359

External locus of control, 340

External recruiting *Attracting job applicants from outside the organization,* 272–273

External stakeholders *People or groups in the organization's external environment that are affected by it,* 69f, 71
  general environment, 75–77
  task environment, 71–75

Extinction *The withholding or withdrawal of positive rewards for desirable behavior, so that the behavior is less likely to occur in the future,* 395–396

Extrinsic reward *The payoff, such as money, that a person receives from others for performing a particular task,* 377

Extroversion, 338, 339

Eye contact, 484

F

FAA (Federal Aviation Agency), 74

Face-to-face contact, 103, 108

Facial expressions, 484

Fads in management, 155

Failure and mistakes
  decison-making and, 199, 220
  innovation and, 223–224, 323, 324t, 326–328
  root-cause analysis, 51

Fair Labor Standards Act *Legislation passed in 1938 that established minimum living standards for workers engaged in interstate commerce, including provision of a federal minimum wage,* 268

Fair Minimum Wage Act, 269t

Fairness, 80

Family & Medical Leave Act, 269t

Family demands, 344, 362, 365

Fast Company magazine, 19, 20, 27

Feasibility, 192

Federal Aviation Agency (FAA), 74

Federal Reserve, 210

Federal Trade Commission, 94

Feedback *The receiver's expression of his or her reaction to the sender's message. Also, the information about the reaction of the environment to the outputs that affect the inputs; one of four parts of a system, along with inputs, outputs, and transformational processes,* 53, 390, 394, 477, 481t

Financial institutions as stakeholders, 74

Financial management
  control systems, 81, 269t, 520, 522
  Greek crisis, 351–352
  tools for, 526–529

Financial statement *Summary of some aspect of an organization's financial status,* 528

Finding Nemo (movie), 27

Firing, 290–291

First-line managers *One of three managerial levels; they make short-term operating decisions, directing the daily tasks of nonmanagerial personnel,* 19, 138–139

Fit perspective *Perspective of organizational culture that assumes that an organization's culture must align, or fit, with its business or strategic context,* 234, 254

Fitting jobs to people, 391–392

Fixed assets, 528

Fixed budget *Allocation of resources on the basis of a single estimate of costs,* 527

Fixed costs, A5

Flavor of the Month (Best), 155

Flexible workplace, 400–401

Flowchart *A useful graphical tool for representing the sequence of events required to complete a project and for laying out "what-if" scenarios,* A1–A3

Flow of work, 51

Focused-differentiation strategy *One of Porter's four competitive strategies; offering products or services that are of unique and superior value compared to those of competitors and to target a narrow market,* 175

Followers, 466–467

Forbes magazine, 19, 88, 382

Forced ranking performance review systems *Performance review systems whereby all employees within a business unit are ranked against one another, and grades are distributed along some sort of bell curve, like students being graded in a college course,* 286

Forcing, 432

Forecast *A vision or projection of the future,* 171–172

Foreign firms, 105

Formal appraisals *Appraisals conducted at specific times throughout the year and based on performance measures that have been established in advance,* 286

Formal communication channels *Communications that follow the chain of command and are recognized as official,* 488–490

Formal group *A group, headed by a leader, that is established to do something productive for the organization,* 413

Forming *The first of the five stages of forming a team, in which people get oriented and get acquainted,* 417

For-profit organizations, 20, 238

Fortune 500 companies, 4, 29, 148, 156, 205, 270, 286, 288, 360, 451

Fortune 1000 companies, 186, 217t, 360, 400

Fortune magazine, 4, 17, 19, 148, 192, 375, 382, 449

Fortune's "100 Best Companies to Work For," 70, 178, 247, 264, 375, 520

Fortune's Most Admired Companies, 140, 148, 158, 247, 328

Four generic strategies; *see* Porter's four competitive strategies

Four management functions *The management process that "gets things done": planning, organizing, leading, and controlling,* 15–16, 514

Framing bias *The tendency of decision makers to be influenced by the way a situation or problem is presented to them,* 213

Influence and persuasion, 447–448
Informal appraisals *Appraisals conducted on an unscheduled basis and consisting of less rigorous indications of employee performance than those used in formal appraisals,* 286
Informal communication channels *Communication that develops outside the formal structure and does not follow the chain of command,* 490
Informal group *A group formed by people seeking friendship that has no officially appointed leader, although a leader may emerge from the membership,* 413–414
Information technology; *see* Technology
Informational area of control, 520
Informational roles *One of the three types of managerial roles; managers receive and communicate information with other people inside and outside the organization as monitors, disseminators, and spokespersons,* 23–24
Ingratiating tactics, 447
In-group collectivism, 118
In-group exchange, 464
Initiating structure, 452–453
Innovation *Introduction of something new or better, as in goods or services,* 10
    balanced scorecard perspective, 523
    case study, 331–333
    culture and, 326–327
    decision making and, 192, 202, 216, 223–224
    ethical dilemma, 334–335
    failure lessons, 223–224, 323, 324t, 326–328
    fostering, 328–329
    managing for, 305
    myths about, 323–324
    organizational structure and, 254
    resources and, 327
    rewards and, 327
    seeds of, 324–325
    types of, 325–326
Innovative change *The introduction of a practice that is new to the organization,* 315
Innovative entrepreneurs, 325
The Innovator's Dilemma (Christensen), 307
Inputs *The people, money, information, equipment, and materials required to produce an organization's goods or services,* 53, 385–387, 513
Inside directors, 88
Insider trading *The illegal trading of a company's stock by people using confidential company information,* 80–81
Inspirational appeals, 447
Institutional collectivism, 117
Institutional power, 381
Instrumentality *The expectation that successful performance of the task will lead to the outcome desired,* 388
Integrated product development, 248
Integration *The tendency of the parts of an organization to draw together to achieve a common purpose,* 47, 253
Integrity tests, 279
Intergroup conflicts, 430–431
Internal audit *A verification of an organization's financial accounts and statements by the organization's own professional staff,* 529
Internal business perspective, 523
Internal dimensions of diversity *The human differences that exert a powerful, sustained effect throughout every stage of people's lives (gender, age, ethnicity, race, sexual orientation, physical abilities),* 358–359
Internal locus of control *The belief that you control your own destiny,* 28, 340
Internal recruiting *Hiring from the inside, or making people already employed by the organization aware of job openings,* 272, 273t
Internal Revenue Service (IRS), 82
Internal stakeholders *Employees, owners, and the board of directors, if any,* 68–70
International Consumer Electronics Show (CES), 167, 168
International forces *Changes in the economic, political, legal, and technological global system that may affect an organization,* 77
International management, 102–105; *see also* Global management
International Monetary Fund (IMF) *One of three principal organizations designed to facilitate international trade: its purpose is to assist in smoothing the flow of money between nations,* 113
International Organization for Standardization (ISO), 537
International Red Cross, 103
Internet *The global network of independently operating but interconnected computers, linking hundreds of thousands of smaller networks around the world,* 12, 99, 101, 202
Interpersonal roles *Of the three types of managerial roles, the roles in which managers interact with people inside and outside their work units. The three interpersonal roles include figurehead, leader, and liaison activities,* 23–24
Interpersonal space, 120
Intervention *Interference in an attempt to correct a problem,* 321, 322
Interviews, 276–277, 475
Intrapreneur *Someone who works inside an existing organization who sees an opportunity for a product or service and mobilizes the organization's resources to try to realize it,* 26–27
Intrinsic reward *The satisfaction, such as a feeling of accomplishment, a person receives from performing a task,* 377
Intuition *Making a choice without the use of conscious thought or logical inference,* 197
Invention, 323
Investment decisions, 192
IRS (Internal Revenue Service), 82
ISO 9000 series *Set of company quality-control procedures, developed by the International Organization for Standardization in Geneva, Switzerland, that deals with all activities—from purchasing to manufacturing to inventory to shipping—that can be audited by independent quality-control experts, or "registrars,"* 537
ISO 14000 series *Set of quality-control procedure that extends the concept of the ISO 9000 series, identifying standards for environmental performance,* 537
It's All Politics (Reardon), 228

J

Japan, 58–59, 170–171, 431
Jargon *Terminology specific to a particular profession or group,* 481
Job analysis *The determination of the basic elements of a job,* 266
Job characteristics model *The job design model that consists of five core job characteristics that affect three critical psychological states of an employee that in turn affect work outcomes—the employee's motivation, performance, and satisfaction,* 392–394
Job description *A summary of what the holder of the job does and how and why he or she does it,* 266
Job design *The division of an organization's work among its employees and the application of motivational theories to jobs to increase satisfaction and performance,* 391–394
Job diagnostic survey, 394
Job enlargement *Increasing the number of tasks in a job to increase variety and motivation,* 391–392
Job enrichment *Building into a job such motivating factors as responsibility, achievement, recognition, stimulating work, and advancement,* 392
Job posting *Placing information about job vacancies and qualifications on bulletin boards, in newsletters, and on the organization's intranet,* 272
Job satisfaction *The extent to which one feels positive or negative about various aspects of one's work,* 353–354
Job simplification *The process of reducing the number of tasks a worker performs,* 391
Job specification *Description of the minimum qualifications a person must have to perform the job successfully,* 266
Job-centered behavior, 452

Joint venture *Also known as a strategic alliance, a U.S firm may form a joint venture with a foreign company to share the risks and rewards of starting a new enterprise together in a foreign country,* 110

The Jungle (Sinclair), 280

Justice approach *One of four approaches to solving ethical dilemmas; ethical behavior is guided by respect for impartial standards of fairness and equity,* 80

Just-in-time approach, 51

K

Kaizen, 170, 532

Knowledge management *Implementation of systems and practices to increase the sharing of knowledge and information throughout an organization,* 12

Knowledge of results, 394

Knowledge work, 308

Knowledge worker *Someone whose occupation is principally concerned with generating or interpreting information, as opposed to manual labor,* 265

Kotter's model for leading change, 317–319

L

Labor Statistics Bureau, 6, 108, 267, 294

Labor unions *Organizations of employees formed to protect and advance their members' interests by bargaining with management over job-related issues,* 73, 292–295

Language differences, 119

Latin America, 121

Law of effect, 395

Layoff survivor sickness, 291

Layoffs, 290–291

Leader-member exchange (LMX) model of leadership *Model proposed by George Graen and Fred Dansereau that emphasizes that leaders have different sorts of relationships with different subordinates,* 448t, 464

Leader-member relations, 454, 455f

Leadership *The ability to influence employees to voluntarily pursue organizational goals,* 442

behavioral approaches, 448t, 452–453

case study, 469–470

contingency approaches, 448t, 454–459

e-leadership, 448t, 466

ethical dilemma, 472

follower roles, 466–467

as foundation of execution, 179–180

full-range approaches, 448t, 460–463

influence and persuasion, 447–448

keys to success, 542–543

leader-member exchange, 448t, 464

management contrasted with, 442–443

nature of, 442–448

power sources, 444–445

servant, 448t, 465

styles, 457–458

trait approaches, 448t, 449–451, 453

Leading *Motivating, directing, and otherwise influencing people to work hard to achieve the organization's goals,* 16, 338, 514; *see also* Communication; Group; Leadership; Motivation; Individual behavior

Lean management, 51

Lean Six Sigma *Quality-control approach that focuses on problem solving and performance improvement—speed with excellence—of a well-defined project,* 538; *see also* Six Sigma

Learned helplessness *The debilitating lack of faith in one's ability to control one's environment,* 341

Learning organization *An organization that actively creates, acquires, and transfers knowledge within itself and is able to modify its behavior to reflect new knowledge,* 60–61, 523

Legal issues; *see also* Ethics

human resource management, 268–271

white-collar crime, 13, 80–81, 207

Legitimate power *One of five sources of a leader's power that results from formal positions with the organization,* 445

Legitimating tactics, 447

Lewin's change model, 317

Liabilities, 528

Licensing *Company X allows a foreign company to pay it a fee to make or distribute X's product or service,* 110

Life goals, 14

Line managers *Managers who have the authority to make decisions and usually have people reporting to them,* 243; *see also* First-line managers

Linear careers, 131

Linguistic style *A person's characteristic speaking patterns—pacing, pausing, directness, word choice, and use of questions, jokes, stories, apologies, and similar devices,* 486

Liquidity ratios, 528

Listening skills, 32, 499–500

Literacy skills, 32, 361, 500–501

LMX model; *see* Leader-member exchange model of leadership

Local communities as stakeholders, 73

Locus of control *Measure of how much people believe they control their fate through their own efforts,* 340

The Long Tail (Anderson), 307

Loss, A5

Love needs, 379

Low-context culture *Culture in which shared meanings are primarily derived from written and spoken words,* 117

Low-control situations, 455–456

M

Macroenvironment *Also called general environment, in contrast to the task environment, it includes six forces: economic, technological, sociocultural, demographic, political-legal, and international,* 75–77

Maintenance role *Relationship-related role consisting of behavior that fosters constructive relationships among team members,* 422–423

Malcolm Baldrige National Quality Award, 530

Management Secrets of the Grateful Dead (Green), 235

Management *The pursuit of organizational goals efficiently and effectively by integrating the work of people through planning, organizing, leading, and controlling the organization's resources,* 4–5; *see also* Leadership; Management theory; Managers

complexity, 443–444

evidence-based, 39, 40, 189, 198–203

fads in, 155

keys to success, 542–543

levels and areas of, 17–20, 138–139

planning types and, 138–139

positive/negative attributes, 30, 118, 120t

rewards, 6–8

Management by exception *Control principle that states that managers should be informed of a situation only if data show a significant deviation from standards,* 517

Management by objectives (MBO) *Four-step process in which (1) managers and employees jointly set objectives for the employee, (2) managers develop action plans, (3) managers and employees periodically review the employee's performance, and (4) the manager makes a performance appraisal and rewards the employee according to results,* 143–145, 284

Management by wandering around (MBWA) *Style of management whereby a manager literally wanders around the organization and talks with people across all lines of authority,* 490

Management process *Performing the planning, organizing, leading, and controlling necessary to get things done,* 15–16

Management science *Sometimes called operations research; branch of quantitative management; focuses on using mathematics to aid in problem solving and decision making,* 50–51

Management theory

behavioral viewpoint, 46–49

case study, 63–64, 65

classical viewpoint, 42–45

contingency viewpoint, 55–57

evolving viewpoints, 40–41

learning organizations and, 60–61

quality-management viewpoint, 58–59

quantitative viewpoints, 50–51

systems viewpoint, 52–54

Managerial leadership *The process of influencing others to understand and agree about what needs to be done and the process of facilitating individual and* collective efforts to accomplish shared objectives, 442–443

Managers; *see also* Human resource management
    challenges of, 9–14
    entrepreneurs contrasted with, 27–28
    foundation of execution by, 180
    functions, 15–16
    as internal forces for change, 312
    international, 105
    leaders contrasted with, 442–443
    multiplier effect, 6
    rewards of, 4–8
    roles, 21–24, 443–444
    skill requirements, 29–30
    successful, 155
    transition problems, 240

Maquiladoras *Manufacturing plants allowed to operate in Mexico with special privileges in return for employing Mexican citizens,* 107

Market changes, 311

Market culture *Type of organizational culture that has a strong external focus and values stability and control,* 230

Mass media, 75

Matrix structure *Fourth type of organizational structure, which combines functional and divisional chains of command in a grid so that there are two command structures—vertical and horizontal,* 245–246, 247f

Maturity stage *A stage when the organization becomes very bureaucratic, large, and mechanistic. Also the third stage in the product life cycle; period in which the product starts to fall out of favor, and sales and profits fall off,* 254

MBO; *see* Management by objectives

MBWA; *see* Management by wandering around

Meaningfulness of work, 394

Means-end chain *A hierarchy of goals; in the chain of management (operational, tactical, strategic), the accomplishment of low-level goals are the means leading to the accomplishment of high-level goals or ends,* 139

Measurable and controllable activities, 237

Measurable goals, 142, 165

Measurement management, 523–525

Mechanistic organization *Organization in which authority is centralized, tasks and rules are clearly specified, and employees are closely supervised,* 252, 254

Media, 75

Media richness *Indication of how well a particular medium conveys information and promotes learning,* 479

Mediation *The process in which a neutral third party, a mediator, listens to both sides in a dispute, makes suggestions, and encourages them to agree on a solution,* 295

Medium *The pathway by which a message travels,* 477, 478–479, 481t

Meetings effectiveness, 491

Megamergers, 100–101

Memory skills, 31–32

Mentoring, 181

Mercosur *The largest trade bloc in Latin America with four core members—Argentina, Brazil, Paraguay, and Uruguay,* 115

Mergers and acquisitions, 320

Message *The information to be shared,* 477

Mexico, 107, 111, 114, 308

Middle managers *One of three managerial levels; they implement the policies and plans of the top managers above them and supervise and coordinate the activities of the first-line managers below them,* 18, 138–139

Midlife stage *A period of growth evolving into stability when the organization becomes bureaucratic,* 253

Millennial Generation (Gen Y), 283, 310, 337, 492–493

Mindfulness versus mindlessness, 57

Mindguards, 425

Minifirms, 101

Mission *An organization's purpose or reason for being,* 136–137

Mission statement *Statement that expresses the purpose of the organization,* 136–137, 155, 162, 164t, 236

Mistakes; *see* Failure and mistakes

Moderate-control situations, 456

Modular structure *Seventh type of organizational structure, in which a firm assembles product chunks, or modules, provided by outside contractors,* 250

Money; *see* Compensation

Moneyball (Lewis), 201

Monochronic time *The standard kind of time orientation in U.S. business; a preference for doing one thing at a time,* 121

Moral-rights approach *One of four approaches to solving ethical dilemmas; ethical behavior is guided by respect for the fundamental rights of human beings,* 79–80

Most favored nation *This trading status describes a condition in which a country grants other countries favorable trading treatment such as the reduction of import duties,* 115

Motion studies, 43

Motivated blindness, 67

Motivating factors *Factors associated with job satisfaction—such as achievement, recognition, responsibility, and advancement—all of which affect the job content or the rewards of work performance,* 383–384

Motivation *Psychological processes that arouse and direct goal-directed behavior,* 376–377
    case study, 405–407
    compensation, 398–400
    content perspectives
        Alderfer's ERG Theory, 380–381

Herzberg's two-factor theory, 383–384
        Maslow's hierarchy of needs, 378–380
        McClelland's acquired needs theory, 381–382
        McGregor's Theory X/Theory Y, 48, 378
    ethical dilemma, 408–409
    job design perspectives, 391–394
    leadership roles, 444, 462
    management by objectives and, 143–145
    managing for, 375
    mutual accountability and, 420
    nonmonetary rewards, 400–403
    process perspectives
        equity theory, 385–387
        expectancy theory, 387–389
        goal-setting theory, 390
    reinforcement perspectives, 395–397

Muda, 170

Multicommunicating *The use of technology to participate in several interactions at the same time,* 492

Multicultural conflicts, 431

Multinational corporation *A business firm with operations in several countries,* 103

Multinational organization *A nonprofit organization with operations in several countries,* 103

Multiplier effect, 6

"Munchausen at work," 284

Murder by Proxy (film), 356

Mutual-benefit organizations, 20, 238

Myers-Briggs Type Indicator, 278, 338

Myths, 236, 323–324

The Myths of Innovation (Berkun), 324

N

NAFTA; *see* North American Free Trade Agreement

NASA, 517

National Business Ethics Survey, 87

National Highway Traffic and Safety Administration, 170

National Labor Relations Board (NLRB) *Legislated in 1935, U.S. commission that enforces procedures whereby employees may vote to have a union and for collective bargaining,* 268, 292

National Workrights Institute, 373

Necessity entrepreneurs, 28

Need-based perspectives; *see* Content perspectives

Needs *Physiological or psychological deficiencies that arouse behavior,* 378, 381, 382, 400–403

Negative conflict, 427

Negative reinforcement *Removal of unpleasant consequences following a desired behavior,* 395

Negative stressors, 364

Negotiated labor-management contract, 292

Net Generation, 23, 492–493

Network structure, 249–250

New York Stock Exchange, 70

The New York Times, 10, 11, 73, 85, 190, 211, 250

Newspaper industry, 9–10

Newsweek magazine, 148, 513

NLRB; *see* National Labor Relations Board

Relationship orientation, 452, 454, 455f, 456

Relaxed avoidance *The situation in which a manager decides to take no action in the belief that there will be no great negative consequences,* 209–210

Relaxed change *The situation in which a manager realizes that complete inaction will have negative consequences but opts for the first available alternative that involves low risk,* 210

Reliability *Degree to which a test measures the same thing consistently, so that an individual's score remains about the same over time, assuming the characteristics being measured also remain the same,* 279, 534

Religious values, 122

Replicative entrepreneurs, 325

Representative bias *The tendency to generalize from a small sample or a single event,* 212

Resistance to change *An emotional/behavioral response to real or imagined threats to an established work routine,* 314–315

Resources for innovation, 327

Responsibility for results, 394

Responsibility *The obligation one has to perform the assigned tasks,* 242

Responsible Restructuring (Cascio), 200

Responsiveness, 534

Results appraisals, 283–284

Results-oriented goals, 142, 165, 390

Résumés, 273–274

Retrenchment strategy; *see* Defensive strategy

Return ratios, 528

Revenues, 528

Reverse discrimination, 362

Reward power *One of five sources of a leader's power that results from the authority to reward subordinates,* 445

Rewards
for innovation, 223–224, 327
of managers, 4–8
as motivation, 377, 385–389, 400–403

Right-to-work laws *Statutes that prohibit employees from being required to join a union as a condition of employment,* 293, 294f

Risk propensity *Willingness to gamble or to undertake risk for the possibility of gaining an increased payoff,* 204

Rites and rituals *The activities and ceremonies, planned and unplanned, that celebrate important occasions and accomplishments in an organization's life,* 232

Role modeling, 236–237

Roles *Socially determined expectations of how an individual should behave in a specific position; sets of behaviors that people expect of occupants of a position,* 365, 422–423

Root-cause analysis, 51

Rule *A standing plan that designates specific required action,* 141

S

Sabbaticals, 403

Safety needs, 379

Salaries or wages, 287, 294

Sales commission *The percentage of a company's earnings as the result of a salesperson's sales that is paid to that salesperson,* 399

San Francisco Chronicle, 68, 69

Sarbanes-Oxley Act of 2002 *Often shortened to SarbOx or SOX, established requirements for proper financial record keeping for public companies and penalties for noncompliance,* 81, 269t

Satisficing model *One type of nonrational decision-making model; managers seek alternatives until they find one that is satisfactory, not optimal,* 196, 215

Scanlon plan, 400

Scenario analysis *Also known as scenario planning and contingency planning; the creation of alternative hypothetical but equally likely future conditions,* 171–172

Scenario planning; *see* Scenario analysis

Scientific management *Management approach that emphasizes the scientific study of work methods to improve the productivity of individual workers,* 42–44, 45

Secondary dimensions of diversity, 358–359

The Secret Handshake (Reardon), 228

Securities and Exchange Commission (SEC), 81, 168, 399

Security *A system of safeguards for protecting information technology against disasters, system failures, and unauthorized access that result in damage or loss,* 495

Seeds of innovation *The starting point for organizational innovation,* 324–325

Selection process *The screening of job applicants to hire the best candidate,* 273
background information, 273–275
employment tests, 277–279
interviews, 276–277, 475

Self-actualization needs, 378, 379

Self-appraisals, 284–285

Self-centered leaders, 451

Self-efficacy *Belief in one's personal ability to do a task,* 341

Self-esteem *Self-respect; the extent to which people like or dislike themselves,* 341, 342t

Self-fulfilling prophecy *Also known as the Pygmalion effect; the phenomenon in which people's expectations of themselves or others leads them to behave in ways that make those expectations come true,* 352

Self-managed teams *Groups of workers who are given administrative oversight for their task domains,* 415–416, 533

Self-monitoring *Observing one's own behavior and adapting it to external situations,* 341–342

Self-serving bias *The attributional tendency to take more personal responsibility for success than for failure,* 351–352

Semantics *The study of the meaning of words,* 481–482

Sender *The person wanting to share information,* 477, 481t

Sense of surroundings, 233

Servant leadership *Providing increased service to others—meeting the goals of both followers and the organization—rather than to oneself,* 312, 448t, 465

Services, 20, 534–535

Setting and communication, 485

Sex-role stereotypes, 349

Sexual harassment *Unwanted sexual attention that creates an adverse work environment,* 271

Sexual orientation, 360–361

Shareholders, 69, 70, 311, 522

Shop steward, 295

Simple structure *The first type of organizational structure, whereby an organization has authority centralized in a single person, as well as a flat hierarchy, few rules, and low work specialization,* 244, 254

Single-product strategy *Strategy by which a company makes and sells only one product within its market,* 175–176

Single-use plans *Plans developed for activities that are not likely to be repeated in the future; such plans can be either programs or projects,* 141

Situational analysis, 168

Situational control, 454–455

Situational interview *A structured interview in which the interviewer focuses on hypothetical situations,* 276

Six Sigma *A rigorous statistical analysis process that reduces defects in manufacturing and service-related industries,* 328, 538

Skill building, 402–403

Skill variety, 393

Skill-based pay, 400

Skills tests, 278

Sliders, 422

Slogans and sayings, 236

Small Business Administration, 26

SMART goal *A goal that is Specific, Measurable, Attainable, Results oriented, and has Target dates,* 142–143, 146, 165, 390

Smartphones, 496–497

Social and political pressures, 311

Social capital *Economic or productive potential of strong, trusting, and cooperative relationships,* 265

Social loafing *The tendency of people to exert less effort when working in groups than when working alone,* 421–422

Social media *Internet-based and mobile technologies used to generate interactive dialogue with members of a network,* 497–498, 536

System *A set of interrelated parts that operate together to achieve a common purpose,* 53

Systems viewpoint *Perspective that regards the organization as a system of interrelated parts,* 52–54

T

Tactical control *Monitoring performance to ensure that tactical plans—those at the divisional or departmental level—are being implemented and taking corrective action as needed,* 519

Tactical goals *Goals that are set by and for middle managers and focus on the actions needed to achieve strategic goals,* 139, 140

Tactical planning *Determining what contributions departments or similar work units can make with their given resources during the next 6 months to 2 years; done by middle management,* 138

Taft-Hartley Act, 268, 293

Tangibles, 534

Target dates, 142, 146, 165, 390

Tariffs *A trade barrier in the form of a customs duty, or tax, levied mainly on imports,* 107, 112

Task environment *Eleven groups that present you with daily tasks to handle: customers, competitors, suppliers, distributors, strategic allies, employee organizations, local communities, financial institutions, government regulators, special-interest groups, and mass media,* 71–75

Task identity, 393

Task management, 22

Task orientation, 452, 454

Task role *Behavior that concentrates on getting the team's task done,* 422

Task significance, 393

Task structure, 455–456

Team *A small group of people with complementary skills who are committed to a common purpose, performance goals, and approach to which they hold themselves mutually accountable,* 413

  development stages, 417–418

  group versus, 412–416, 418

  success characteristics

    cohesiveness, 419–420

    cooperation, 419

    goals and feedback, 420

    groupthink, 424–426

    motivation, 420

    norms, 423–424

    role types, 422–423

    size, 421–422

    trust, 419

  types

    continuous improvement, 415–416

    self-managed, 415–416, 533

    special-purpose, 533

    virtual, 411, 415t

    work, 414–415

Technical skills *Skills that consist of the job-specific knowledge needed to perform well in a specialized field,* 29

Technological forces *New developments in methods for transforming resources into goods or services,* 76

Technology *All the tools and ideas for transforming material, data, or labor (inputs) into goods or services (outputs). It applies not just to computers but any machine or process that enables an organization to gain a competitive advantage in changing materials used to produce a finished product*

  big data, 202

  changing, 310, 313

  digital communication, 492–496

  knowledge versus, 308

  managing for, 12

  role of, 513

  telepresence, 494

Telecommute *To work from home or remote locations using a variety of information technologies,* 12, 401, 494

Teleconferencing, 494

Telepresence technology *High-definition videoconference systems that simulate face-to-face meeting among users,* 494

Telework, 495

Thailand, 104

Theory X, 48, 378

Theory Y, 48, 378

Thoughtfulness, 401–402

360-degree assessment *A performance appraisal in which employees are appraised not only by their managerial superiors but also by peers, subordinates, and sometimes clients,* 285

Time magazine, 148, 198

Time management, 22, 121–122, 485

Tolerance for ambiguity, 204–206

Top managers *One of three managerial levels; they make long-term decisions about the overall direction of the organization and establish the objectives, policies, and strategies for it,* 17–18, 138–139

Top-management teams, 415t

Total costs, A5

Total quality management (TQM) *A comprehensive approach—led by top management and supported throughout the organization—dedicated to continuous quality improvement, training, and customer satisfaction. It has four components: (1) Make continuous improvement a priority. (2) Get every employee involved. (3) Listen to and learn from customers and employees. (4) Use accurate standards to identify and eliminate problems,* 58–59, 532

  core principles, 532–534

  Deming management, 530–531

  as participative management factor, 217t

  services applications of, 534–535

  tools and techniques, 535–538

Total sales revenue, A5

Touch and communication, 484–485

Toy Story (movie), 27

TQM; *see* Total quality management

Trade protectionism *The use of government regulations to limit the import of goods and services,* 111–112

Trading bloc *Also known as an economic community, it is a group of nations within a geographical region that have agreed to remove trade barriers with one another,* 113–115

Training *Educating technical and operational employees in how to better do their current jobs,* 236–237, 281–282

Trait appraisals, 284, 450

Trait approaches to leadership *Attempts to identify distinctive characteristics that account for the effectiveness of leaders,* 448t, 449–451, 453

Transactional leadership *Leadership style that focuses on clarifying employees' roles and task requirements and providing rewards and punishments contingent on performance,* 448t, 460–461

Transfer, 290

Transformation processes *An organization's capabilities in management, internal processes, and technology that are applied to converting inputs into outputs,* 53

Transformational leadership *Leadership style that transforms employees to pursue organizational goals over self-interests,* 448t, 461–463

Transitory careers, 131

Transportation Security Administration, 335

Trend analysis *A hypothetical extension of a past series of events into the future,* 171

Trust *Reciprocal faith in others' intentions and behaviors,* 285, 419, 423

Turnover *The movement of employees in and out of an organization when they obtain and then leave their jobs,* 355

20/20 (TV series), 472

Two core principles of TQM *(1) People orientation—everyone involved with the organization should focus on delivering value to customers; and (2) improvement orientation—everyone should work on continuously improving the work processes,* 532

Two-factor theory *Herzberg's theory that proposes that work satisfaction and dissatisfaction arise from two different work factors—work satisfaction from so-called motivating factors and work dissatisfaction from so-called hygiene factors,* 383–384

Two-tier wage contracts *Contracts in which new employees are paid less or receive lesser benefits than veteran employees have,* 294

Type A behavior pattern *Behavior describing people involved in a chronic, determined struggle to accomplish more in less time,* 364